Hydrology in Mountainous Regions I

Hydrological Measurements

The Water Cycle

TITLES RECENTLY PUBLISHED BY IAHS

Drainage Basin Sediment Delivery. Proceedings of the Albuquerque Symposium, August 1986
Publ.no.159 (1986), price $45

Hydrologic Applications of Space Technology. Proceedings of the Cocoa Beach Workshop, August 1985
Publ.no.160 (1986), price $45

Karst Water Resources. Proceedings of the Ankara Symposium, July 1985
Publ.no.161 (1986), price $45

Avalanche Formation, Movement and Effects. Proceedings of the Davos Symposium, September 1986
Publ.no.162 (1987), price $50

Developments in the Analysis of Groundwater Flow Systems. Report prepared by a Working Group of the IAHS International Commission on Groundwater
Publ.no.163 (1986), price $35

Water for the Future: Hydrology in Perspective
Proceedings of the Rome Symposium, April 1987
Publ.no.164 (1987), price $50

Erosion and Sedimentation in the Pacific Rim. Proceedings of the Corvallis Symposium, August 1987
Publ.no.165 (1987), price $55

Proceedings of the symposia held during the IUGG Assembly, Vancouver, August 1987:

- **Large Scale Effects of Seasonal Snow Cover**
  Publ.no.166 (1987), price $42
- **Forest Hydrology and Watershed Management**
  Publ.no.167 (1987), price $55
- **The Influence of Climate Change and Climatic Variability on the Hydrologic Regime and Water Resources**
  Publ.no.168 (1987), price $55
- **Irrigation and Water Allocation**
  Publ.no.169 (1987), price $32
- **The Physical Basis of Ice Sheet Modelling**
  Publ.no.170 (1987), price $40

Hydrology 2000. Report of the IAHS Hydrology 2000 Working Group
Publ.no.171 (1987), price $22

Side Effects of Water Resources Management. Report prepared by an IHP-III Working Group
Publ.no.172 (1988), price $40

Groundwater Monitoring and Management. Proceedings of the Dresden Symposium, March 1987
Publ.no.173 (1990), price $55

Sediment Budgets. Proceedings of the Porto Alegre Symposium, December 1988
Publ.no.174 (1988), price $60

Consequences of Spatial Variability in Aquifer Properties and Data Limitations for Groundwater Modelling Practice. Report prepared by a Working Group of the International Commission on Groundwater
Publ.no.175 (1988), price $45

Karst Hydrogeology and Karst Environment Protection. Proceedings of the IAH/IAHS Guilin Symposium, October 1988
Publ.no.176 (1988), price $55

Estimation of Areal Evapotranspiration. Proceedings of a workshop held during the IUGG Assembly, Vancouver, August 1987
Publ.no.177 (1989), price $45

Remote Data Transmission. Proceedings of a workshop held during the IUGG Assembly, Vancouver, August 1987
Publ.no.178 (1989), price $30

Proceedings of symposia held during the Third IAHS Scientific Assembly, Baltimore, Maryland, May 1989:

- **Atmospheric Deposition**
  Publ.no.179 (1989), price $45
- **Systems Analysis for Water Resources Management: Closing the Gap Between Theory and Practice**
  Publ.no.180 (1989), price $45
- **Surface Water Modeling: New Directions for Hydrologic Prediction**
  Publ.no.181 (1989), price $50
- **Regional Characterization of Water Quality**
  Publ.no.182 (1989), price $45
- **Snow Cover and Glacier Variations**
  Publ.no.183 (1989), price $30
- **Sediment and the Environment**
  Publ.no.184 (1989), price $40
- **Groundwater Contamination**
  Publ.no.185 (1989), price $40
- **Remote Sensing and Large-Scale Global Processes**
  Publ.no.186 (1989), price $40

FRIENDS in Hydrology. Proceedings of the Bolkesjø Symposium, April 1989
Publ.no.187 (1989), price $50

Groundwater Management: Quantity and Quality
Proceedings of the Benidorm Symposium, October 1989
Publ.no.188 (1989), price $60

Erosion, Transport and Deposition Processes. Proceedings of the Jerusalem Workshop, March-April 1987
Publ.no.189 (1990), price $40

Hydrology of Mountainous Areas. Proceedings of the Strbske Pleso Workshop, Czechoslovakia, June 1988
Publ.no.190 (1990), price $45

Regionalization in Hydrology. Proceedings of the Ljubljana Symposium, April 1990
Publ.no.191 (1990), price $45

Research Needs and Applications to Reduce Erosion and Sedimentation in Tropical Steeplands. Proceedings of the Suva, Fiji, Symposium, June 1990
Publ.no.192 (1990), price $50

Hydrology in Mountainous Regions. I - Hydrological Measurements; the Water Cycle. Proceedings of two Lausanne Symposia, August 1990
Publ.no.193 (1990)

Hydrology in Mountainous Regions. II - Artificial Reservoirs; Water and Slopes. Proceedings of two Lausanne Symposia, August 1990
Publ.no.194 (1990)

First of New Series!

Hydrological Phenomena in Geosphere-Biosphere Interactions: Outlooks to Past, Present and Future
by Mälin Falkenmark
Monograph no.1 (1989), price $15

*Available **only** from IAHS Press, Wallingford*

PLEASE SEND ORDERS AND/OR ENQUIRIES TO:

Office of the Treasurer IAHS, 2000 Florida Avenue NW, Washington, DC 20009, USA
[telephone: +1 202 462 6900; telex: 7108229300; fax: +1 202 328 0566]

IAHS Press, Institute of Hydrology, Wallingford, Oxfordshire OX10 8BB, UK
[telephone: +44 (0)491 38800; telex: 849365 hydrol g; fax: +44 (0)491 32256]

Please send credit card orders (VISA, ACCESS, MASTERCARD, EUROCARD) and IAHS Membership orders to the Wallingford address only. A catalogue of publications may be obtained free of charge from either address.

Hydrology in Mountainous Regions I

HYDROLOGICAL MEASUREMENTS

THE WATER CYCLE

Edited by

H. LANG

Geographisches Institut ETH, Abteilung Hydrologie, Winterthurerstrasse 190, CH-8057 Zürich, Switzerland

A. MUSY

Institut d'Aménagement des Terres et des Eaux, Ecole Polytechnique Fédérale de Lausanne, GR Ecublens, CH-1015 Lausanne, Switzerland

Proceedings of two international symposia, the Symposium on Improved Methods of Hydrological Measurements in Mountain Areas (S1) and the Symposium on Quantitative and Qualitative Water Cycle Aspects in Heterogeneous Basins (S2), held at Lausanne, Switzerland, 27 August–1 September 1990. The symposia were part of the International Conference on Water Resources in Mountainous Regions jointly convened by the International Association of Hydrological Sciences (IAHS) and the International Association of Hydrogeologists (IAH).

IAHS Publication No. 193

Published by the International Association of Hydrological Sciences 1990.

IAHS Press, Institute of Hydrology, Wallingford, Oxfordshire OX10 8BB, UK.

IAHS Publication No. 193.

ISBN 0-947571-57-4.

The camera-ready copy for the papers was prepared by the authors and assembled/finished at IAHS Press.

Printed in The Netherlands by Krips Repro Meppel.

PREFACE

Most of our sound knowledge and modeling of the hydrological cycle and of the water resources in river basins is primarily based on measurements of the variations of water fluxes in space and in time. And many often any further advance is only achieved on basis of improved measurements i.e.improved techniques of signal receivers, or extension resp. optimization of the networks. There is the sequence of measurements - analysis of data - improved understanding of processes - feedback on observation techniques and network design - improved information from observations - advanced level of modeling, knowledge and understanding, including accuracy: a sequence in which we include techniques of mathematical analysis, geostatistics, regionalisation. If we are successful in some cases even a reduction of the networks may be the result. In many other cases more observation sites, the measurement of more parameters, or a higher resolution in time is needed. Probably a title "Improved methods of assessment of hydrological processes" would have taken better account of the scientific overall aspect of this symposium. In this context the term measurement is to be taken in its broader meaning. This is fully reflected in the papers which were contributed to this part of the Lausanne Conference.

The variation of water processes together with the wide spectrum of catchment characteristics and severe operational conditions make investigations in mountain areas a fascination, where at the same time the level of challenge increases with the levels of altitude. The convener would like to point out here on this particular aspect: Our present knowledge in mountain hydrology needed many strong efforts of hard fieldwork and still does, to maintain the networks and collect all the measurement data. Therefore a particular appreciation of all those involved in this part of our science is to be expressed here.

Herbert Lang

PREFACE

L'importance que revêt l'eau pour nos sociétés et le rôle primordial qu'elle joue ne sont plus à démontrer. Les questions inhérentes à la disponibilité en eau et à son utilisation ont depuis toujours préoccupé l'homme et ont engendré de nombreux problèmes. Ces derniers se sont encore compliqués en raison de la dégradation qualitative de cette substance, due essentiellement à des activités anthropiques.

Jusqu'à ce jour, les zones de montagne ont été relativement épargnées par les développements socio-économiques, ce qui conférait à l'eau de ces régions une très grande potentialité tant au point de vue quantitatif que qualitatif. Cette situation se modifie toutefois rapidement en raison d'un changement dans nos comportements (augmentation des zones secondaires d'habitation, développement de nouvelles zones de loisirs, etc.) et de quelques variations climatiques observées (déficit pluviométrique, acidification, réchauffement, etc.).

Il est donc nécessaire et urgent de s'inquiéter de cette évolution et d'entreprendre des actions efficaces pour tenter de résoudre les nouveaux problèmes qui se posent dans ce contexte.

La compréhension des phénomènes liés au cycle de l'eau n'est pas simple. En région de montagne, celle-ci prend encore des allures plus complexes en raison de l'hétérogénéité des bassins versants qui induit de nombreuses interactions entre les composantes hydrologiques

Cerner ces multiples relations pour mieux les connaître, voire les simuler, c'est saisir toute la problématique de la mesure, de sa variation spatio-temporelle et des interactions des paramètres du bilan hydrologique avec les diverses caractéristiques physiques, chimiques et géomorphologiques du milieu. Ces connaissances serviront, par le biais de la modélisation, à l'appréciation de la réaction des bassins versants lorsque soumis à diverses sollicitations d'une part et à évaluer, utiliser et gérer les potentialités hydrauliques de ces régions d'autre part.

L'objectif du Symposium no 2 de la conférence internationale sur les ressources en eau en régions montagneuses a précisément pour but de confronter des idées, de faire connaître et d'échanger toutes informations d'ordre scientifique et technique dans ce domaine. Les très nombreuses communications présentées sous ce thème illustrent bien l'acuité de ces problèmes, mais aussi la difficulté à les résoudre. Gageons que leur excellente qualité servira aux développements de la science hydrologique ainsi qu'à la mise en oeuvre de méthodes adéquates, utiles à l'exploitation rationnelle des eaux dans des régions à relief accidenté.

Je tiens à remercier tous les auteurs des communications figurant dans cet ouvrage pour la qualité de leur travail et ne peux que les encourager à poursuivre leurs actions dans cette direction, tant il est nécessaire de mieux satisfaire nos divers besoins en eau tout en préservant notre environnement.

A. Musy

Contents

TOPIC D: IMPROVED METHODS OF MEASURING DISCHARGE IN MOUNTAIN RIVERS, INCLUDING PROBLEMS OF BED LOAD

Symposium on Quantitative and Qualitative Water Cycle Aspects in Heterogeneous Basins

TOPIC A: QUANTITATIVE SPACE-TIME WATER VARIABILITY

TOPIC B: QUALITATIVE SPACE-TIME WATER VARIABILITY

TOPIC C: HYDROLOGICAL MODELLING IN REGIONS OF RUGGED RELIEF

TOPIC E: ASSESSMENT OF THE UTILIZATION POTENTIAL OF SURFACE WATER RESOURCES

TOPIC F: GENERAL PAPER

Symposium on Improved Methods of Hydrological Measurements in Mountain Areas

Topic A:

Reliability of Precipitation Measurements

Hydrology in Mountainous Regions. I - Hydrological Measurements; the Water Cycle
(Proceedings of two Lausanne Symposia, August 1990). IAHS Publ. no. 193, 1990.

Evaluation of precipitation gauges for measuring precipitation on mountainous watersheds

C. L. HANSON
US Department of Agriculture, Agricultural Research Service, Northwest Watershed Research Center, 270 South Orchard, Boise, Idaho 83705, USA

ABSTRACT The dual-gauge system, which consists of a shielded and an unshielded universal recording gauge, successfully measures rain and snowfall at remote mountain sites on the Reynolds Creek Watershed in southwestern Idaho. Precipitation amount is calculated from the ratio of shielded to unshielded precipitation catch. Results indicate that Wyoming shielded gauge and the dual-gauge system catch was the same when air temperatures were higher than -2.2°C, but dual-gage system catch was slightly more for snowfall ($T \leq -2.2$°C) especially under windy conditions. Heated tipping-bucket gauge catch was about 30% less than universal recording gauges at two Idaho sites and 50% less at three Oregon sites. The Wyoming shielded gauge and the dual-gauge system had the greatest snowfall catch and the Tretyakov gauge the least during a two-year World Meteorological Organization (WMO) study. In the WMO study, all seven gauge and shield configurations' total snowfall catch amounts were within 16%.

INTRODUCTION

The Reynolds Creek Watershed in southwestern Idaho was established in 1960 as an outdoor hydrology laboratory that represents rangeland areas of the inland Pacific Northwest, USA. (Robins et al., 1965). The watershed is located near the north end of the Owyhee Mountains in southwestern Idaho. The average precipitation varies from 230 mm on the lowest elevations (about 1180 m) of the watershed to 1130 mm at the highest elevations (about 2160 m). The major portion of the annual precipitation occurs as snow at the higher elevations, which led to the investigation of several methods for measuring precipitation with special emphasis on measuring snowfall. This paper presents precipitation gauge catch and operation based on results from studies that have been conducted on the watershed to determine which gauges consistently give reliable results with a minimum of servicing. The paper also discusses recording gauge modifications and maintenance that have been required to obtain a consistent record when gauges are operated in harsh conditions.

DUAL-GAUGE SYSTEM

The dual-gauge network was installed on the watershed as the standard system to measure precipitation under windy conditions. One shielded and one unshielded universal recording gauge are located at each site (Hamon, 1971, 1973). The gauges are 6.1 m apart with orifices at 3.05 m above ground to prevent being covered by snow. The shields are the Alter type, 1.17 m in diameter, with the baffles individually constrained at an angle of 30° from the vertical. All gauges are charged with an oil-antifreeze solution to melt the snow, prevent the solution from freezing, and retard evaporation.

Universal recording gauges are used in the network because both the time and amount of precipitation for each event is required from remote sites. Also very small events occur quite frequently at all sites on the watershed and at the higher elevations, winter storms can last several days and produce upwards of 100 mm of precipitation.

Several modifications have been made to the gauges to improve their accuracy and reliability. In the major modification, different springs are used in the weighing mechanism to double the accuracy of the catch which, in turn, reduces gauge capacity by half. This modification was done because of the frequency of small, low intensity rain and snow events. Other modifications such as using an antifreeze solution in the dash pots are given by Morris and Hanson (1983), and Winter and Sturges (1989).

Computed precipitation from the dual-gauge system is obtained from the following equation:

$$\ln\left(\frac{U}{A}\right) = B \ln\left(\frac{U}{S}\right) \tag{1}$$

where A is the computed precipitation, U is unshielded precipitation, S is shielded precipitation, and B is a coefficient. Hamon (1973) found that B remained reasonably constant at 1.70 for wind speeds up to 13.4 m/sec for both rain and snow.

WYOMING SHIELD

Rain and snow catch by universal recording gauges protected by Wyoming shields (Rechard and Wei, 1980) was compared to the catch computed from dual-gauge systems located at different elevations on Reynolds Creek Watershed (Hanson, 1989). The Wyoming shield gauge system consisted of two concentric shields mounted around a universal recording gauge. The gauge orifice was 2.29 m above ground, which was the same height as the top of the inner shield. The top of the outer shield was 2.90 m above ground. The diameter of the top of the inner shield was 3.05 m, and the diameter of the top of the outer shield was 6.10 m. The inner shield was 45° and the outer shield was 30° from the vertical. The shielding was constructed from 1.22 m, 50% density snow fence. The Wyoming shielded gauge and the dual gauges were about 50 m apart at each study site.

Results from this study show that for rainfall (T > 1.7°C), Wyoming shielded gauge catch was 1 to 5% greater than the catch computed from the dual-gauge systems for all sites except the site with the highest wind speeds, where the computed catch was 2% greater. When all site information was combined, Wyoming shielded gauge rainfall catch was 2% greater than computed catch from the dual-gauge systems. For mixed precipitation (1.7°C ≥ T > -2.2°C), Wyoming shielded gauge catch and computed catch were about the same for all sites except the site with the highest wind speeds where the computed catch was 9% greater. When the mixed precipitation data for all sites was combined, the catch was the same for the two measuring systems. For snowfall (T ≤ -2.2°C), Wyoming shielded gauge catch was 4 to 24% less than computed catch depending upon wind speed at the site. Wyoming shielded gauge undercatch of snowfall was greatest at sites with the highest average wind speeds per event. When considering the catch of all precipitation types at all sites, Wyoming shielded gauge catch was not significantly different from computed catch from the dual-gauge system. Wind speed had little or no effect on the catch by Wyoming shielded gauges for the mixed category, but there was a small but significant decrease in the Wyoming shielded gauge catch as wind speeds increased during snowfall (T ≤ -2.2°C).

HEATED TIPPING-BUCKET GAUGES

A study of heated tipping-bucket gauges was conducted during two winters on five sites at two locations in the intermountain region of the Pacific Northwest, USA (Hanson *et al.*, 1983). Two of the sites were on the Reynolds Creek Watershed and three sites were near Pendleton, Oregon. Four gauges were heated with open flame and constant heat input, and one was heated by electricity. The electric heater turned on at 3°C and off at 16°C which resulted in an average funnel temperature of 10°C. Universal recording gauges with funnels removed and an antifreeze solution in the buckets were used as control gauges. All of the gauges were shielded by fixed Alter shields at the Reynolds Creek Watershed sites and none of the gauges were shielded at the Pendleton, Oregon sites.

For events with precipitation amounts of 1.3 mm and greater, the tipping-bucket gauges recorded 25% less precipitation at the sites on the Reynolds Creek Watershed. At the Pendelton, Oregon sites, the undercatch by the heated gauges was 19% for the electrically heated gauge and 45% and 78% for the two gauges heated by propane gas. The average tipping-bucket gauge deficiency for the five sites was 28% for precipitation events of 1.3 mm and greater.

Data from events with less than 1.3 mm of precipitation at the two Reynolds Creek Watershed sites and the electrically heated site at Pendleton show that precipitation was not measured 75% of the time by the heated gauges when universal recording gauges recorded small precipitation events. The tipping-bucket gauges measured only 16% of the precipitation measured by the universal recording gauges. In general, the heated tipping-bucket gauges measured 30 to 80% less winter precipitation than universal recording gauges, depending on site location and gauge type (controlled or uncontrolled heating of the collector).

WORLD METEOROLOGICAL ORGANIZATION (WMO) SOLID (SNOW) PRECIPITATION STUDY

One of three World Meteorological Organization (WMO) solid precipitation study sites in the United States is located at the Reynolds Creek Watershed. Gauges at this site include the Double Fence Intercomparison Reference (DFIR), Tretyakov gauge and shield, universal recording gauge with Alter shield, universal recording gauge with Wyoming shield, Canadian Nipher shield snow gauge, US Weather Bureau standard nonrecording gauge, and the dual-gauge system. Analyses of the data from the first two seasons of a five-year study showed that all gauges measured snowfall within 16% of each other. The dual-gauge system and the Wyoming shielded gauge recorded the greatest amount and the Tretyakov gauge the least. For rainfall, all gauges caught within 8% of each other, with the DFIR and Wyoming shielded gauges having the greatest catch and the Canadian Nipher shielded gauge the least.

REFERENCES

Hamon, W. R. (1971) Reynolds Creek, Idaho. Chapter 4 in: Agricultural Research Service Precipitation Facilities and Related Studies (D. M. Hershfield, ed.), 25-35. USDA-Agricultural Research Service, ARS 41-176.

Hamon, W. R. (1973) Computing actual precipitation. In: Distribution of Precipitation in Mountainous Areas (Geilo Symp. Norway, August 1972), vol. 1, 159-174. World Meteorological Organization, Geneva, WMO/OMM no. 326.

Hanson, C. L. (1989) Precipitation catch measured by the Wyoming shield and the dual-gage system. Wat. Resour. Bull. 25 (1), 159-164.

Hanson, C. L., Zuzel, J. F. & Morris, R. P. (1983) Winter precipitation catch by heated tipping-bucket gages. Trans. Am. Soc. Agric. Engrs. 26 (5), 1479-1480.

Morris, R. P & Hanson, C. L. (1983) Weighing and recording precipitation gage modification. Trans. Am. Soc. Agric. Engrs. 26 (1), 167-168.

Rechard, P. A. & Wei, T. C. (1980) Performance Assessments of Precipitation Gages for Snow Measurement. Wat. Resour. Ser. no. 76, Wat. Resour. Res. Inst., University of Wyoming, Laramie, WY.

Robins, J. S., Kelly, L. L. & Hamon, W. R. (1965) Reynolds Creek in southwest Idaho: An outdoor hydrologic laboratory. Wat. Resour. Res. 1 (3), 407-413.

Winter, C. J. & Sturges, D. L. (1989) Improved procedures for installing and operating precipitation gages and Alter shields on windswept lands. USDA, Forest Service, Rocky Mountain Forest & Range Exp. Sta., Res. Note Rm-489.

Hydrology in Mountainous Regions. I - Hydrological Measurements; the Water Cycle
(Proceedings of two Lausanne Symposia, August 1990). IAHS Publ. no. 193, 1990.

Methods of estimating precipitation inputs to the Balquhidder experimental basins, Scotland

R.C.JOHNSON
Institute of Hydrology, Balquhidder,
Lochearnhead, Perthshire, Scotland, UK
J.R.BLACKIE & J.A.HUDSON
Institute of Hydrology, Wallingford,
Oxon OX10 8BB, UK

ABSTRACT The Balquhidder experiment in highland Scotland is concerned with the effects of forestry on water use, streamflow and water quality. Precipitation input measurements form an important part of the experiment and therefore need to be as accurate as possible. The ground level gauge is used for rainfall measurements and standard gauges, in forest clearings, used for snowfall. The problems with snow measurement are identified and suggestions for overcoming them are given. Precipitation gauge distribution was based on domain theory, where precipitation is assumed to be controlled by altitude, aspect and slope. Rainfall relationships are developed between sites for the quality control of the data, the methods of deriving the basin mean precipitation are illustrated and an example is given of monthly results in 1986.

INTRODUCTION

The Balquhidder experiment in Highland Scotland was started in 1981, to look at the effects of forestry on water use, streamflow and water quality. Two small basins, at different stages of the forest cycle, are being studied: one which has been changed from moorland to a juvenile forest and the other which is gradually being clear felled.

In the experiment, measurements of precipitation and streamflow form the basis for all studies in the basins. Precipitation data are used in the water use analysis, evaporation studies from the main vegetation types, chemical load analysis and erosion studies. It is therefore very important to measure precipitation systematically and as accurately as possible.

Measuring precipitation in mountain environments can

be very difficult because of the topography and climate affecting the gauges. The rugged topography at Balquhidder has a large effect on the wind patterns producing turbulence and giving problems in siting precipitation gauges. In addition the harsh climate includes snow, which is very difficult to measure, and freezing conditions which affect automatic gauges.

DESCRIPTION OF THE EXPERIMENTAL BASINS

The Balquhidder experimental basins (fig.1) are located in the central Scottish highlands, 60 km north of Glasgow. The two basins, the Kirkton (6.85 km²) and the Monachyle (7.70 km²) form part of the headwaters of the River Forth. Their orientation is north-south across the prevailing westerly winds, and both have similar altitude ranges of around 600 metres and mean slopes angles of 20° At the start of the study the Kirkton supported a mature coniferous forest covering 42% of the lower basin, with the vegetation at higher altitudes being mainly coarse grass and heather. In the Monachyle the vegetation was heather and coarse grass with many rock outcrops at high altitudes. A full description of the basins and of the initial stages of the study is given in Blackie (1987).

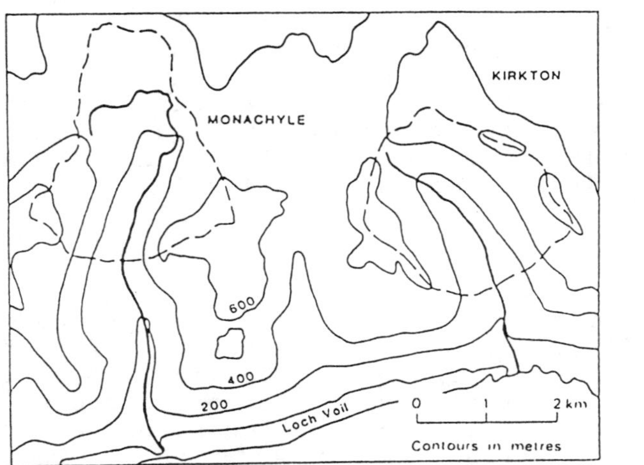

FIG. 1 Location of the Balquhidder basins.

Weather patterns in the region are dominated by westerly airflows bringing frequent depressions with associated frontal systems. Precipitation totals are very variable, with the lowest annual amounts, around 2000 mm, in the valley bottoms and the highest amounts near the ridge crests, 3500 mm. Snow in the winter months is frequent, especially at the higher altitudes, and contributes an estimated 10-20% of the annual precipitation.

Measurements of precipitation started in 1981 and have continued as the land-uses in both basins changed. The clear felling of the Kirkton forest was started in 1986 and by the end of 1989, 45% of the forest had been felled. In the Monachyle, also in 1986, the lower part of the basin was planted with coniferous saplings.

PRECIPITATION GAUGES USED IN THE BASINS

The best design of rain gauge for use in exposed, mountainous basins is the ground level gauge installed with its rim parallel to the slope and surrounded by an anti-splash grid, Rodda (1967). Much work has been done on the comparison between this gauge, the UK standard (Mk.2) gauge, Rodda (1970) and other standard gauges, Sevruk & Hamon (1984) all showing the ground level gauge to be the most efficient collector. The ground level gauge was, therefore, selected as the main rain gauge in the Balquhidder basins.

In snow conditions the ground level gauge becomes inaccurate because of its exposure to drifting snow, snow melt and possibly flooding. At the start of the experiment in 1981 there was no gauge available which could accurately measure snow or mixed precipitation. Recent results from the WMO intercomparison of all types of snow gauges with the double fence intercomparison reference (DFIR) indicate that the DFIR is now by far the best snow gauge available (Goodison et al., 1989).

The measurement of snow at Balquhidder has relied on a method of using standard rain gauges in sheltered forest clearings to give estimates of snow in the lower Kirkton. In the more exposed areas, inter-site relationships have been derived in rain conditions to estimate the snow input to these areas. The assumptions that gauges behave similarly in rain and snow and the spatial distribution of falling snow is the same as rain are likely to be a significant source of error. There is therefore a great need for a reliable reference gauge, such as the DFIR, to investigate these assumptions and make the necessary corrections.

TIME DISTRIBUTION AND CORRECTION OF GAUGE READINGS

The remoteness of many of the gauge sites means that it is very rare for all of the storage gauges to be read exactly at the end of each month. In rainfall conditions the gauge readings are time distributed into daily and hourly values using the automatic gauge nearest to each storage gauge site. In snowfall a low altitude gauge is read manually each day and used to distribute gauge readings into daily totals.

The readings of the ground level gauges are adjusted for angle of the gauge rims. Errors in the standard gauge catches due to their exposure are corrected by deriving relationships, at each site and in rainfall, between the ground level and standard gauges. These corrections are re-calculated each year as site exposures change due to forest clearfelling etc.

Two further corrections which were considered, are wetting and evaporation losses. The wetting losses, from the inner walls of the collecting funnel, have previously been shown to be quite large (Sevruk, 1985) depending on which type of standard gauge is being used. The octapent gauge funnel has an internal maximum storage measured at 0.6 mm, but because of the shape of the collector and as the gauge is installed at ground level specifically to reduce turbulence, then the wetting loss is minimised.

Evaporation losses are also considered to be small as the octapent gauge has a covered inner container and the ground level installation minimises radiant heating.

DESIGN AND ASSESSMENT OF THE PRECIPITATION GAUGE NETWORKS

A method of raingauge distribution, developed at Plynlimon in mid-Wales, uses the assumption that precipitation distribution in mountainous areas is controlled by altitude, aspect and slope (Clarke et al.,1973). The basins were divided into blocks of 1 hectare and by linking blocks with similar altitude, aspect and slope ranges, homogeneous domains were identified. Three blocks in each domain were then selected by random, to represent the first, second and third choices of sites where the gauge would be installed.

The number of domains sampled in each basin was determined by the practical number which the field operator could maintain, and by choosing a number of domains whose total area formed a significant proportion of the basin area. By choosing the 11 largest domains in each basin the percentage of the total areas gauged are: Kirkton 57% and Monachyle 59%.

To check the domain homogeneity, one domain in each basin was selected for a second gauge to be installed, as far from the original gauge as possible. Results from a two year comparison period, excluding the winter months when snow might have been an influencing factor, are shown in fig. 2. The comparison in the two domains show quite large monthly variations in the ratios of the check gauge to the first gauge site. The mean ratios are: Kirkton 0.976 and Monachyle 1.005 with the standard error for both 0.017, i.e. there is not a significant difference between the gauge catches in either domain at the 95% confidence level.

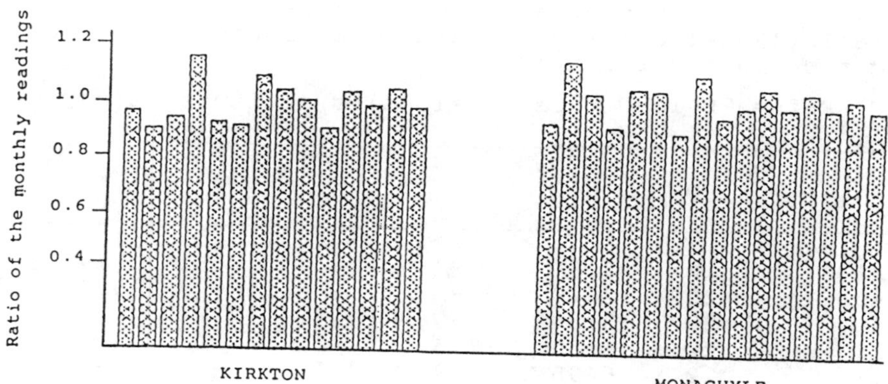

FIG. 2 Ratios of the monthly readings from a check gauge and the first gauge in two domains.

INTER-SITE RELATIONSHIPS FOR QUALITY CONTROL OF DATA

Comparisons between the gauge totals at each site are carried out to quality control the data, mainly to identify snow affected readings. Two methods are used: a regression analysis using altitude, aspect, slope and longitude as the independent variables and a stationarity analysis of each gauge against the mean for the whole basin.

Simple and multiple regression analyses of annual precipitation totals from all 22 gauges against the gauge site parameters are shown in table 1. Using a single variable, longitude gives the best correlation coefficient (0.658). The best fit using two variables is when longitude and altitude are used (0.829), and increasing the number to four makes a further slight improvement (0.879).

The stationarity analysis checks the data from each site by comparing the cumulative total of each gauge to the cumulative basin total. A sudden departure from the ratio of the two totals indicates a possible error in the data, as illustrated in Fig. 3.

DERIVATION OF THE BASIN MEAN PRECIPITATION

With the gauge networks having been designed using topographic variations and a systematic spatial distribution, an arithmetic mean and domain weighted mean are both considered suitable methods for estimating the basin means. The domain method can be extended by using the inter-site relationships but this introduces smoothing errors, especially when extrapolating to the highest, most exposed, domains. The other method which is used, is the isohyetal method, although this is often criticised

TABLE 1 Regression analyses of mean annual point rainfall (1982-1988) against altitude, aspect, slope and longitude in the format:

Rain=a+b(longitude)+c(slope)+d(altitude)+e(aspect)

	n	a	b	c	d	e	r
Al	22	2284	-	-	0.5	-	0.100
As	22	2648	-	-	-	-0.1	0.027
S	22	2734	-	-14.1	-	-	0.111
L	22	6350	-7.5	-	-	-	0.658
L+S	22	6495	-7.9	3.4	-	-	0.663
L+Al	22	6198	-8.0	-	0.7	-	0.829
L+S+Al	22	6228	-8.0	0.7	0.7	-	0.829
L+S+Al+As	22	6172	-7.8	0	0.8	-0.6	0.879

where: Al=Altitude (metres), As=Aspect (degrees), S=Slope (degrees), L=Longitude (degree and minute) r=correlation coefficient, n=Number of samples

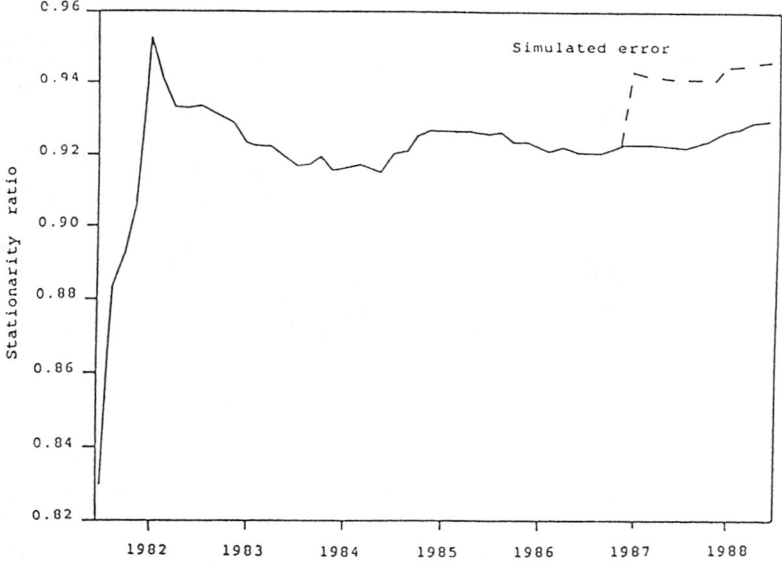

FIG. 3 Stationarity analysis for one Kirkton gauge. Ratio is that of the cumulative totals of precipitation for the gauge site and the basin mean. The simulated error shows how errors are identified.

for being very subjective and time consuming.

Table 2 shows the calculations of the monthly totals for the Kirkton basin in 1986 using three of these methods. For monthly data the domain weighting mean shows a difference of less than 2% compared to the arithmetic mean and less than 1% for the annual data. The isohyetal method shows more variability between months although the annual total is again within 1% of the arithmetic mean. The three methods are always used in the calculation of the basin mean to give a final check on the data, with the isohyetal method being particularly useful because it gives a visual indication of the areal distribution.

TABLE 2 Monthly mean precipitation (mm) for the Kirkton basin, 1986, calculated by the arithmetic, domain weighted means and isohyetal method, with percentage difference to the arithmetic mean in brackets.

	Arithmetic	Domain weighted		Isohyetal	
January	304.6	308.1	(1.1)	309.0	(1.4)
February	17.8	17.6	(-1.1)	18.1	(1.7)
March	315.7	319.3	(1.1)	302.6	(-4.1)
April	108.9	109.2	(0.3)	107.3	(-1.5)
May	378.1	384.6	(1.7)	393.4	(4.0)
June	89.0	90.6	(1.8)	90.4	(1.6)
July	110.2	111.6	(1.3)	108.4	(-1.6)
August	184.0	185.9	(1.0)	183.8	(-0.1)
September	51.5	52.2	(1.4)	52.8	(2.5)
October	278.5	282.5	(1.4)	280.8	(0.8)
November	402.3	396.2	(-1.5)	400.2	(-0.5)
December	460.0	459.3	(0.2)	458.3	(-0.4)
Total	2700.5	2717.2	(0.6)	2705.1	(0.2)

CONCLUSIONS

Precipitation measurements have been made in the Balquhidder experimental basins since 1981, and form one of the most important data sets in the study. Conditions at Balquhidder are harsh, with a very rugged topography and significant snowfall in winter months.

The ground level gauge was selected as the main rain gauge with snow measured by standard gauges in forest clearings or estimated by developing intersite relationships. The distribution of the gauges in the basins was based on domain theory using altitude, aspect and slope as the three variables. Gauges were installed in 11 domains in each basin covering 57% of the Kirkton basin and 59% of the Monachyle. Check gauges in two of the domains showed that there were insignificant differences between the first and check gauges.

Relationships between sites have been developed to check the data for snow affected readings. The mean precipitation for the basins is calculated by three methods: arithmetic and domain weighted means and the isohyetal method. There is a difference of less than 1% for annual values calculated by these methods.

ACKNOWLEDGMENTS The authors would like to thank the Balquhidder funding consortium for their support over the years, and the Director of the Institute of Hydrology, Professor B. Wilkinson for permission to submit this paper.

REFERENCES

Blackie, J.R. (1987) The Balquhidder catchments, Scotland: the first four years. Trans. R. Soc. Edinburgh, 78, 227-239.

Clarke, R.T., Leese, M.N. & Newson, A.J. (1973) Analysis of data from Plynlimon raingauge networks. Institute of Hydrology Report No. 27, Wallingford.

Goodison, B.E., Sevruk, B. & Klemm, S. (1989) WMO solid precipitation measurement intercomparison: objectives, methodology, analysis. In: Atmospheric Deposition (Proc. Symp., Baltimore, May 1989) 57-64, IAHS Publ. No. 179.

Rodda, J.C. (1967) The systematic error in rainfall measurement. J. Inst Water Engrs., 21, 173-177.

Rodda, J.C. (1970) On the questions of rainfall measurement and representativeness. In: World Water Balance (Proc. IAHS Symp. Reading, July 1970), 174-186.

Sevruk, B. & Hamon, W.R. (1984) International comparison of national precipitation gauges with a reference pit gauge. WMO Instruments and Observing Methods Report No. 17, Geneva.

Sevruk, B. (1985) Correction of monthly precipitation for wetting losses. WMO Instruments and Observing Methods Report No.22, 7-12.

Hydrology in Mountainous Regions. I - Hydrological Measurements; the Water Cycle
(Proceedings of two Lausanne Symposia, August 1990). IAHS Publ. no. 193, 1990.

Simulation of weather radar ground clutters in a mountainous area using a digitized elevation model

T. LEBEL
ORSTOM, Laboratoire d'Hydrologie,
BP 5045, 34032 MONTPELLIER CEDEX, FRANCE

ABSTRACT Beam interception by ground obstacles is a major problem for radar-based precipitation measurements in mountainous regions. The error introduced may however be minimized by choosing an appropriate radar installation site. A method has therefore been developed to simulate ground clutter zones for various sites based on topographic information provided by a Digital Elevation Model. Both the interception of the main radar beam and the backscattering energy coming from the side lobes are assessed, producing an interception map and an echo index map respectively. The simulated maps obtained from a Digital Elevation Model of the French Cevennes region are compared with the ground clutter zones observed during the Cevennes radar experiment carried out in south-eastern France by the Laboratoire Associé de Météorologie Physique de Clermont-Ferrand and the Institut de Mécanique de Grenoble.

RESUME La possibilité de simuler des cartes d'écho de sol, qui font obstacle à la mesure de la pluie par un radar météorologique, est étudiée en s'appuyant sur l'information topographique fournie par un Modèle Numérique de Terrain. Une carte de visibilité du relief par le faisceau radar pour un site de tir donné est tout d'abord calculée. Cette carte est ensuite convertie en une carte d'indice d'echo, par le biais d'une intégration simplifiée de l'équation fournissant la puissance rétrodiffusée du signal en fonction des caractéristiques de l'antenne émettrice d'une part et de la cible rétrodiffusante d'autre part. La validité des cartes obtenues est analysée à travers une étude de cas ayant pour cadre la campagne de qualification d'un radar hydrométéorologique menée conjointement par le Laboratoire Associé de Météorologie Physique de Clermont-Ferrand et l'Institut de Mécanique de Grenoble sur la région des Cévennes (Sud-Est de la France).

1. RELIEF - A PROBLEM FOR RADAR-BASED PRECIPITATION MEASUREMENTS

Due to its large coverage and high spatial resolution, weather radar is used increasingly to measure precipitation. Such measurements are possible because hydrometeors reflect electromagnetic waves of an appropriate length (generally between 3 and 10 cm). Aside from the problems related to the system electronics and the calibration of the backscatter intensity (i.e. its transformation into rainfall intensity), one of the major difficulties encountered in implementing radar precipitation measurements is the presence of obstacles that intercept part of the incident beam.

When interception occurs for distances over which precipitation is measured (5 to 200 km), undesirable echo zones referred to as ground clutter zones appear on the backscatter display screen. These ground echoes create shadowed zones within which precipitation cannot be detected.

Weather radar is a remote sensing technique, a major advantage in regions of difficult access, in particular in mountainous areas where an accurate real time estimate of areal precipitation is essential for effective flood forecasting. It is therefore important to select the radar site in such a way that the precipitation echoes are affected as little as possible by ground clutter.

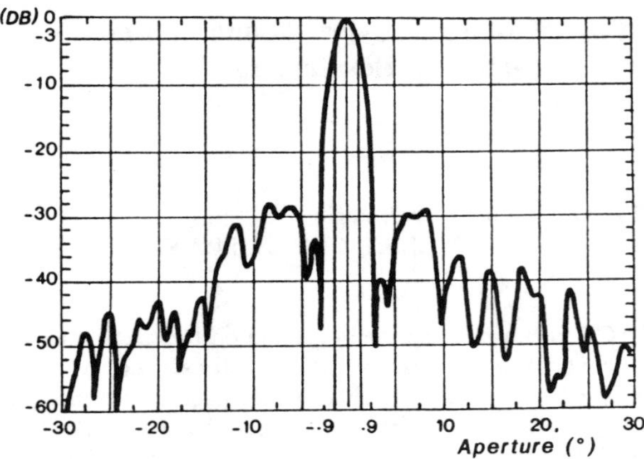

FIG.1 Example of an antenna radiation diagram.

Site assessment involves two steps : a) Determination of the obstacles "seen" by the radar beam, forming the intervisibility map and providing the boundaries of the obstructed zones; b) Calculation of the intensity of the backscatter produced by these obstacles in order to determine whether it is significant compared to that produced by the precipitation.

What could have been a relatively simple geometry problem is complicated by the unequal distribution of the energy within the incident beam. This beam is produced by a parabolic antenna that focuses an isotropic electromagnetic radiation source. The resulting beam is thus characterized by the antenna radiation diagram (fig. 1) which can be divided into several parts. First of all there is the main beam centred around the antenna axis, the useful part being defined as the zone over which the energy is greater than half the maximum value along the axis. We refer to an "aperture of 3 db" since the ratio of the radiated power fluxes (i.e. the gain) is measured in decibels. A gain of -3 db is equivalent to a power flux ratio of 1:2. Apart from the main beam, there are also local radiated energy peaks called side lobes, however the gain within them is low (maximum -30 db, i.e. 1/1000 of the intensity of the radiated power on the antenna). It is nevertheless these side lobes that complicate the determination of significant ground clutter zones since, as shown in figure 1, they can intercept obstacles located several kilometers away, well under the lower limit of the useful beam. If these obstacles fill the side lobes completely, the backscattered power can be of the same order of magnitude as that of the precipitation clouds.

A Digital Elevation Model (DEM) will be used here to simulate the masked zones of the main beam (intervisibility) and the ground clutter zones that can be confused with precipitation clouds. The DEM makes it possible to simulate the location of these zones for a given radar site and angle, an approach already employed in Great Britain within the framework of the North West Weather Radar Project (Crowther and Ryder, 1985).

2. GENERAL DISCUSSION OF DIGITAL ELEVATION MODELS

2.1 What is a DEM ?

DEMs are data files containing the determined, measured or interpolated elevations of a region at the nodes of a regular grid. Topographic information coded in this way can be easily processed by computers. The DEM data may be obtained from aerial or satellite photographs, but the most widely used method is based on the interpolation of digitized contour lines.

The creation of the DEM is a critical step in any study using digitized elevations. The resolution of the digitization, both in terms of horizontal and vertical distances, tends to smooth the relief, and a threshold exists below which it is no longer of any use to look for a link between the studied processes (e.g. hydrology, intervisibility) and the local topography.

2.2 Creation of a DEM by interpolation

Another equally important aspect is the interpolation method used. Interpolation is used to create information at locations where none is directly available, i.e. at the nodes of a regular grid which are not intersected by contour lines. This process inevitably produces artifacts that can lead to errors in subsequent calculations.

The methods most widely used are of two types. The first type considers the digitized points corresponding to the contour lines as point fields and the second type considers them as point chains forming polygons.

Three main point field methods exist : i) interpolation based on neighbouring points; several interpolation procedures have already been developed along these lines, for example a polynomial approximation with a least squares solution, barymetric interpolation , Kriging and surface sums (e.g.Schut, 1976; Chiles et Delfiner, 1975); ii) superposition of a square mesh network; iii) interpolation based on point field triangulation. The digitizing of contour lines supposes a discretization of the topographic information. When the objective is to produce DEMs with a fine mesh size (in the order of 150 metres), the method used must provide a reasonably accurate reconstitution of the convex/concave catchment area shape. Now, when a chain of points representing a contour line is considered as a point field, the available information is considerably downgraded since the constancy of the elevation between the points is not taken into account. Thus point field models do not appear to be suitable for the processing of digitized elevation contours. To avoid this shortcoming, the contours may be considered as a chain of points defining a polygon.

The interpolation methods using such discretized contours are either based on the line of greatest slope (eg Leberl and Olson, 1980), or on a system of axes. Those based solely on the line of greatest slope do not integrate the transversal structure of the catchment area. Interpolation based on a system of axis would seem to be the method best suited to our needs as long as the number of axes is high enough to take into account the main orientations of the topography making it difficult to obtain a good shape definition. The method the most widely used involves two orthogonal axes, but Yoeli (1986) used four axes forming angles of 45° between them. Furthermore, various interpolation methods may be used depending on the axes, e.g. linear, cubic, spline, polynomial. For a linear interpolation, the DEM exhibits a step structure that must subsequently be smoothed as for instance in the so-called "elastic grid" method used by the I.G.N. (Masson d'Autume, 1979). The method proposed by Yoeli(1986) best satisfies our needs since the elevations are interpolated using cubic spline curves calculated on the basis of four axes and weighted as a function of the criterion taking into account the distance from the contours. However, it does not sufficiently account for the line of greatest slope criteria for certain topographic sites with very curved contour lines.

2.3 Correction of the Yoeli's Method by additional weighting

In Yoeli's method each point of the DEM is located at the intersection of four directions belonging to the axis systems (fig. 2):

- East-West axes, i.e. the X1 profiles,
- North-South axes, i.e. the Y1 profiles,
- Southeast-Northwest axes, i.e. the X2 profiles,
- Southwest-Northeast axes, i.e. the Y2 profiles.

The intersections between the contour lines and the four axis systems are first stored and then sorted in ascending order by profile number and by coordinates within the profiles. For each

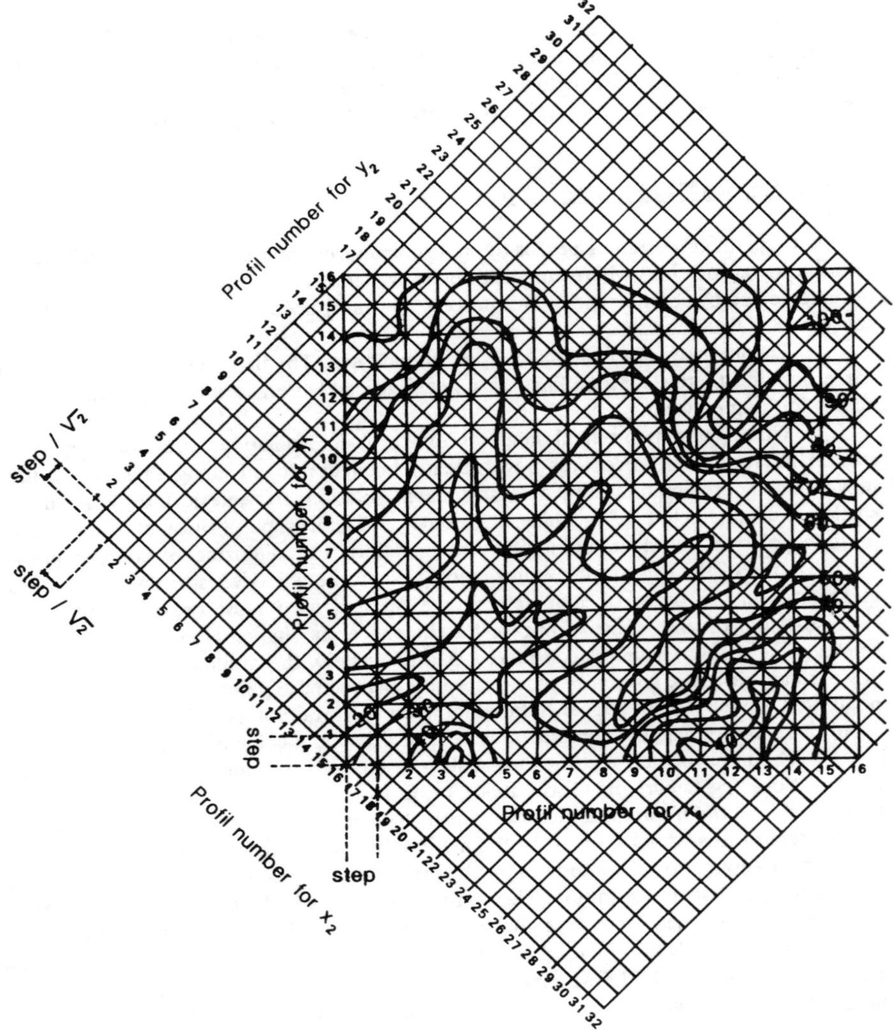

FIG.2 Axis systems associated with DEM points.

profile, a cubic spline curve is fitted passing through all the points corresponding to the intersections with the contour lines. The elevations of the DEM points are interpolated by a set of points regularly spaced according to a user-defined step length.

Assuming that the elevation of the intersections between the profiles and the contour lines is exact, the accuracy of the interpolated points depends mainly on:

- the slope of the profile at this point, as well as on the distance and the elevation difference between the two contour lines surrounding the point. The steeper the slope, the nearer are the curves and the more accurate are the interpolated values.

- the proximity of the DEM point with respect to one of the two intersections of the surrounding contour lines. The closer the DEM point is to a profile point, the closer their values will be and the better will be the accuracy of the interpolation.

To quantify these two effects, each elevation of a DEM point relative to an axis will be attributed a weight equal to the sum of two sub-weights. These are inversely proportional to the distances between the DEM point and the profile points : $P = 1/D1 + 1/D2$

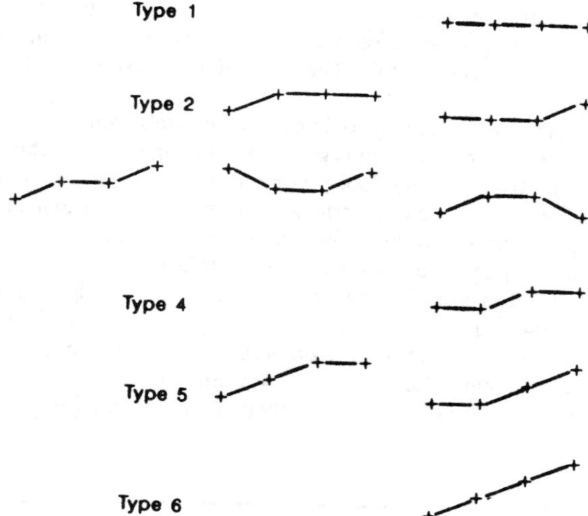

FIG. 3 Typology of the altitudinal structure of the contour lines (ASC).

The most probable value of the elevation is given by the weighted average of the axial values:

$$E = \Sigma E_i P_i / \Sigma P_i$$

Yoeli's weighting criterion proves insufficient for sites with highly curved contour lines, i.e. for valley bottoms and ridges. In such locations, the distance to the contour lines is not the only criterion to be considered. It is important to also take into account the altitudinal structure of the contour lines (ASC) along the axes. For instance consider a ridge. The axis corresponding to the orientation of the ridge must carry more information than the three other axes that are only transversal profiles of the ridge. This axis is characterized morphologically by a drift of the four contour lines. On the other hand, on the other axes, the interpolated elevation is obtained with a spline curve passing through two contour lines of the same elevation. The general principle would therefore be to add further weight to the elevations obtained on the axes presenting the greatest ASC.

The computer program (OROLOG) used in our study for the creation of a DEM was developped by C. Depraetere (1990). It is based on a simple typology of the ASC and runs on a basic microcomputer. This typology is based on the relative elevations of the four contour lines surrounding a DEM point (figure 3). Six cases are distinguished, extending from minimum ASC (the four contours having the same elevation) up to maximum ASC (the four contours increasing in elevation in a given direction).

The additional weighting is obtained by attributing a weight proportional to ASC, e.g. 1 for sites with minimum ASC and 6 for sites with maximum ASC. The value E of the calculated elevation as a function of the average weighted by the Yoeli criterion Pi associated with the ASC criterion S_i is:

$$E = \Sigma E_i P_i S_i / \Sigma P_i S_i,$$ S_i having a value between 1 and 6.

3. THE GROUND CLUTTER MAP

Mean elevations, orientations, slopes and curvatures corresponding to each mesh of the DEM may be extracted from the files. In the LAMONT computer Program (Depraetere, 1989) used here, the mean elevation on a pixel is calculated using the arithmetic mean of the elevations of the four nodes that bound it. The slopes, directions and curvatures are calculated by exploring a 3 x 3 window centred on the concerned mesh. The elevation is first used alone to compute the intervisibility.

The DEM is explored systematically to detect all the pixels which are visible from the radar and those which are masked. This exploration is performed taking into account the beam width, and distinguishing the main lobe from the side lobes. For a given beam elevation (1° for instance), the pixels interfering with the main lobe are those who are viewed from the radar at an angle comprised between $-\theta_m$ and $+\theta_m$, where θ_m is the main lobe width (generally around 1° for C band radar systems). Those pixels are displayed in colour number 1 (black in figure 4) on the screen, while those intercepting the side lobes are displayed with another colour (light grey in figure 4). This ground clutter map is relatively easy to compute and thus gives a first and quick appraisal of the main areas interfering with the radar beam (in figure 4 the elevation beam is 1°).

The DEM used to obtain the ground clutter map of figure 4 was digitized using a topographic contour map with isocontours every fourty meters. The resulting isometric view is given in figure 5.

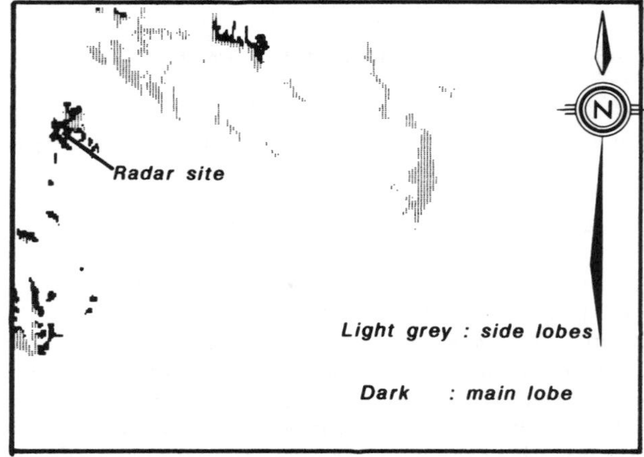

FIG. 4 Simulated ground clutter map for the Radar-Cevennes experiment.

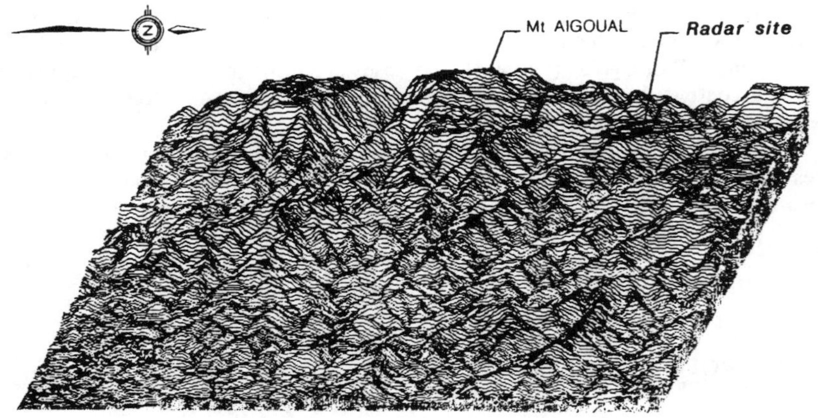

FIG. 5 Isometric view of the DEM area in the Cevennes region.

4. THE ECHO INDEX MAP

By projecting the ground clutter map onto the radar polar grid (fig.6), it is possible to compute the backscattering energy for each radar pixel which includes at least one DEM pixel interferring with the radar beam. This computation requires to take into account the main factors influencing the backscattering mechanism. Those factors are those related to the beam geometry and the energy repartition within this beam. Given a few assumptions, Roux et al.(1989) have shown that the theoretical reflectivity factor associated to ground clutters Z^* (in m^6/m^3)may be computed as :

$$Z^* = 3.85\ 10^{-11} .\sigma_0 \frac{r^2}{K^2} . \frac{\lambda^4}{\tau} . F(f,r,n) \quad (1)$$

and

$$F(f,r,n) = \sum_{ir=1}^{n} \frac{f^4(\theta_{ir})}{r_{ir}^4} . \delta S_{ir} \quad (2)$$

$f^2(\theta)$: antenna function,
θ : beam width in polar coordinates,
λ : wavelength (cm),
σ_0 : backscattering section of the target (cm^2),
r : distance between the target and the radar (m),
K^2: water dielectric factor,
τ : pulse duration (s).
ir : DEM pixels belonging to the radar pixel and interfering with the radar beam.
δS : projection of the target surface onto the plane perpendicular to the line joining the radar to the target (m^2).

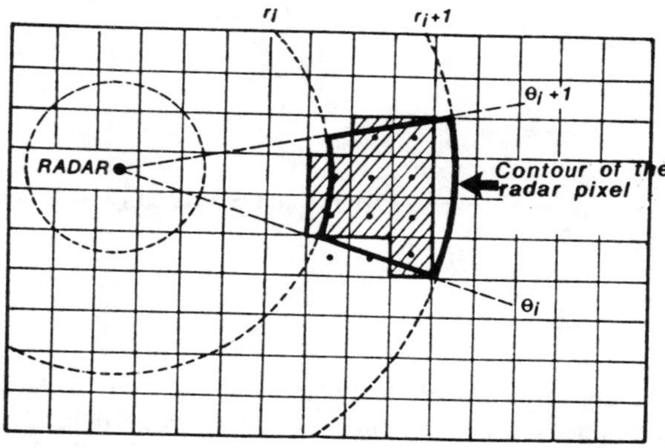

FIG.6 Projection of the radar grid onto the DEM grid.

F(f,r,n) is a function of : i)the DEM pixel position within the radar beam; ii) the antenna function(f); iii) the distance from the centre of the radar pixel to the radar(r) and; iv) the number of DEM pixels intercepted by the radar beam(n). At this point the accuracy of the orientation and slope extracted from the DEM strongly influences the overall computation accuracy of F(f,r,n), hence the importance of creating a precise model of the areas where the contour lines are highly curved.

It is then possible to compare Z^*, used as an echo index, with Z, the reflectivity factor measured by operating the radar in cloudless skies. In expression (1), λ , τ and $\theta_0{}^2$ are characteristics of the radar, while σ_0 characterizes the backscattering properties of the ground.

The validity of expression (1) was thus tested during the Radar-Cevennes experiment (Andrieu et al.), with the Anatol radar (λ = 10 cm; τ = 0.5 s; $\theta_0{}^2$ = 1.8°). The quantity 10 log σ_0 was taken equal to -20 db , which seems to be a resonnable first guess for a mountainous area.

Thus with K^2 = .93, expression(1) becomes :

$$Z^* = 8.38\ 10^{12}\ .\sigma_0\ .\ r^2\ .\ F(f,r,n) \quad (Z^* \text{ in } mm^6/m^3) \qquad (3)$$

or, in dbZ, for a reference value Z_o = 1 mm^6/m^3 :

$$Z^*(dbZ) = 109 + 10 \log(F(f,r,n)\ .\ r^2) \qquad (4)$$

The results of the comparison between the observed echoes Z and the simulated echoes Z^* (computed with the DEM of figure 6) are given in figure 7 for a beam elevation of 1°. The colour table of the echo index maps is as follows : light grey : IE < 47 dB; dark grey : 47< IE < 63dB; black : IE > 63dB), and the observed ground clutter maps are isocontour maps with 6 levels : 39, 47, 55, 63, 71, 79 db. The overall similitude between the two maps is striking. Similarly good results were obtained for four other beam elevations (2,3,4,5°) as shown in the paper by Roux et al.(1989).

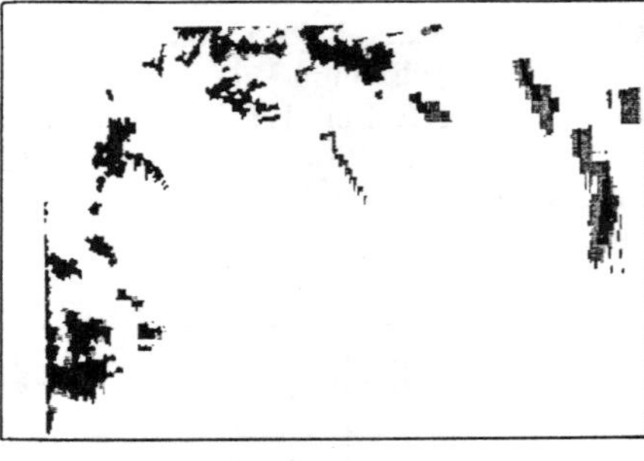

FIG. 7 Comparison of observed (right) and simulated (left) ground echos for an elevation beam of 1°.

5. CONCLUSION

In regions of high spatial variability of rainfall, the radar could make up for the shortcomings of raingauge networks, especially when it comes to estimating reliable areal rainfall. It has nevertheless its own array of impediments, the main one in mountainous areas being the interception of the radar beam by ground obstacles. This study has shown that DEMs provide a simple approach in dealing with such ground clutter problems. Geometric factors alone can give a relatively accurate simulation of the ground clutter zones with however certain limits concerning the low intensity echoes due to the side lobes. In its present highly simplified form, the method may already be used to select radar sites that minimize ground clutter problems and the associated masking effects.

Another important point is the possibility for any user of creating its own DEM, with the sole help of a topographic map and a basic microcomputer. However special care has to be taken in deriving the interpolation algorithm used for this purpose. Errors of order zero will affect the computation of the intervisibility map, while errors of order one (i.e. affecting the first derivatives of the topographical surface) are of importance if an attempt is made at taking into account the orientation of the DEM pixel with respect to the incident radar beam. As a matter of fact, once the geometric aspects of the problem are satisfactorily treated, any improvement of the proposed method relies on a better assessment of the backscattering properties of the ground obstacles. These properties are presumably themselves strongly dependent on the angle between the radar beam and the normal to the surface of the elementary target.

As a first practical application of the technique presented here, a study is presently underway concerning an installation of the the French radar network in the Nimes region. Although the site has already been selected on the basis of logistic considerations, the objective is to study the measurement and acquisition protocol taking into account the ground clutter phenomena produced by the Cevennes mountain range.

Acknowledgements: This study was made possible by the work of research teams at the Laboratoire Associé de Météorologie Physique (Clermont-Ferrand), the Observatoire de Physique du Globe de Clermont and the Institut de Mécanique de Grenoble. We would like to extend special thanks to Mr. Pointin (LAMP), Mr. Fournet-Fayard (OPGC), Mr. Creutin (IMG) and all those involved in implementing and running the 1986-88 Cévennes radar campaigns.

REFERENCES

ANDRIEU H., CREUTIN J.D., LEOUSSOF J., POINTIN Y. (1988), Cévennes 86-88 : a french hydrometeorological experiment to evaluate weather radar capabilities for medium elevation mountain hydrology. In : Hydrology of Mountainous Areas, Czecholovakia, 22 p. (to be published in IAHS publications.)

CHILES J.P., DELFINER P. (1975), Reconstitution par krigeage de la surface topographique à partir de divers schémas d'échantillonnage photogrammétrique. Bulletin de la Société Française de Photogramétrie, 35, 42-50.

CROWTHER L., RYDER P. (1985), North West Weather Radar Project, Report of the Steering Group, North West Water Authorithy - Meteorological Office. 73 p.

DEPRAETERE C. (1989), Logiciel d'Application pour Modèle Numérique de Terrain (LAMONT). Note Technique OVNIH n°4, Laboratoire d'hydrologie, ORSTOM, Montpellier,128 p.

DEPRAETERE C. (1990), OROLOG : Logiciel de fabrication de Modèles Numériques de Terrain. Notice interne du laboratoire d'hydrologie, ORSTOM, Montpellier.

LEBERL F. and OLSON D. (1982), Raster scanning for operationnal digitizing. Photometric Engineering and Remote Sensing, 48(4), 615-627.

MASSON D'AUTUME M. (1979), Surface Modelling by Means of an Elastic Grid. Photogrammetria, 35, 65-74.

ROUX C., T. LEBEL, C. DEPRAETERE, H. ANDRIEU (1989), Simulation à l'aide d'un modèle numérique de terrain des échos de sol détectés par un radar météorologique. Hydrologie Continentale, 4(2).

SHUT G. (1976), Review of Interpolation Methods for Digital Terrain Models. XIII ISP Congress, Helsinki, 21 p.

YOELI P. (1986), Computer executed production of a regular grid of height points from digital contours. The American Cartographer. Vol. 13, N° 3, 219-229.

Hydrology in Mountainous Regions. I - Hydrological Measurements; the Water Cycle (Proceedings of two Lausanne Symposia, August 1990). IAHS Publ. no. 193, 1990.

Amount and variability of cloud moisture input in a tropical cloud forest

T. STADTMULLER
Tropical Agricultural Research and Training Center (CATIE), Turrialba, Costa Rica
N. AGUDELO
Escuela Agrícola Panamericana, El Zamorano, Honduras

ABSTRACT To assess the amount and variability of cloud moisture input in a tropical cloud forest, daily throughfall measurements were conducted over one year in three topographical units (concave slope, convex slope, ridge). Comparison with rainfall measurements in an open area indicates high additional water input by cloud moisture depending on topography, cloud occurrence and windspeed. High daily and monthly variation of throughfall are attributed to presence and amount, or absence of cloud moisture input. On days without rainfall, considerable water input was frequently measured in the cloud forest. The increase and variation of net precipitation affected by cloud moisture input should be taken into account in assessing the hydrological importance of tropical cloud forests. Lack of consideration of cloud moisture input may constitute a serious error in the determination of the water balance of tropical watersheds incorporating cloud forests.

INTRODUCTION

Outside the humid tropics cloud moisture input (horizontal precipitation, occult precipitation) in forests has been a research subject studied in many different places (Kerfoot, 1968). On the other hand, very little research has been carried out on hydrological processes in cloud forests in the humid tropics, although several authors have drawn attention to their wider hydrological importance (Grubb & Whitmore, 1966; Kerfoot, 1968; Budowski, 1976; Hamilton & King, 1983).

Tropical cloud forests, one of the most fragile forest ecosystems, cover approximately 500,000 km^2 of tropical mountain ranges, mainly at altitudes between 1200 and 2400 masl (Bockor, 1979; Stadtmüller, 1987). It has been suggested that tropical cloud forests increase net precipitation due to additional water input from cloud moisture, regulate the flow regime, especially during dry periods, and reduce evapotranspiration rates (Zadroga, 1981).

Only few studies have been carried out to measure net precipitation in tropical cloud forests. (Baynton, 1969; Weaver, 1972; Steinhardt, 1978; Cáceres, 1981). Results of these studies which have been conducted on small plots show net precipitation values between approximately 80% and 100% of rainfall. Stemflow did not amount to even 1% of precipitation. To date no data have been published on spatial variation of net precipitation in cloud forest belts of tropical mountain ranges.

STUDY SITE AND PERIOD

The present research was conducted at the upper part of the Uyuca mountain in Honduras from june 1987 to may 1988. The study area comprises 26 ha of cloud forest between 1720 and 1870 masl which forms part of the Cerro Uyuca Biological Reserve. The study area shows slope angles between 40% and 130% and is exposed to the cloud bearing NE-trade winds. Extrapolating from Holdridge's life zone system (Holdridge, 1982), annual rainfall is estimated to vary between 2000 and 4000 mm. Soils have been classified as Vertic Ustorthents and Andeptic Troporthents (Agudelo, 1988). The vegetation is lush and heavily covered by epiphytes. Treeferns (Cyatheaceae) are frequent while climbers are rather rare. The upper storey is composed by many different tree species among which dominate those belonging to the families Fagaceae, Lauraceae, Aquifoliaceae and Podocarpaceae (Agudelo, 1988).

METHODS

The area was stratified according to its topographical characteristics into concave slopes (unit A), convex slopes (unit B), and ridge (unit C). To measure throughfall, four troughs were randomly distributed in each topographical unit. Each trough had a orifice of a quarter of square meter. Stemflow was not measured, since all relevant studies carried out in tropical rain and cloud forests show that stemflow rarely surpasses 1% of rainfall (Steinhardt, 1978, Caceres, 1981, Clarke 1986). Rainfall was measured by three standard raingauges in a 2 ha open and rather flat area within the cloud forest. Unfortunately, no recording raingauge was available.

Daily measurements were taken from the raingauges in the open area and from the throughfall troughs within the three topographical units of the cloud forest. Cloudiness and windspeed were observed and estimated four times per day (at 6.00, 10.00, 14.00 and 18.00 o'clock). Windspeed was classified according to the Beaufort scale and cloudiness was graded into four different classes (0,1,2,3) according to visibility, being 3 the value for very low visibility due to thick cloud cover. Temperature and relative humidity were recorded by a thermohygrograph installed in a shelter on the open area.

Throughfall was calculated for each topographical unit and for the whole study area . Cloud moisture input could be estimated by assuming interception losses according to critical literature reviews on the subject (Jackson, 1975; Clarke, 1986), while taking into account the climatic and weather conditions of the study site.

RESULTS

Rainfall over the year of measurements amounted 1468.5 mm. Throughfall values showed 1372.8 mm (94% of rainfall) on unit A, 1892.3 mm (129%) on unit B, and 2629.4 mm (179%) on unit C. The average for the whole study area was 1922.1 mm (131%). The relation A < B < C appeared on 8 out of 12 months. During all months unit C received more water input than unit B. These throughfall values (net precipitation) correspond much better to the estimates for water input at the study site by the Holdridge Life Zone System (Holdridge, 1982) than the value for rainfall. Monthly variation of net precipitation in the different topographic units is shown in Table 1.

TABLE 1 Monthly variation of net precipitation in different topographical units of a tropical cloud forest in Honduras.

Month	Rainfall	Net Precipitation							
		Unit A Concave slope		Unit B Convex slope		Unit C Ridge		Average over the whole study area	
	mm	mm	% of rainfall	mm	% of rainfall	mm	% of rainfall	mm	% of rainfall
6/87	251.9	219.9	(87%)	219.7	(87%)	326.2	(130%)	249.6	(99%)
7/87	270.0	312.0	(116%)	431.2	(160%)	571.1	(212%)	429.8	(159%)
8/87	219.6	209.5	(95%)	311.8	(142%)	465.0	(212%)	319.9	(146%)
9/87	226.8	197.0	(87%)	177.2	(78%)	313.0	(138%)	222.0	(98%)
10/87	64.7	40.5	(63%)	42.0	(65%)	71.7	(111%)	49.8	(77%)
11/87	22.0	18.9	(86%)	62.2	(283%)	101.2	(460%)	58.4	(265%)
12/87	66.1	69.0	(104%)	149.1	(226%)	179.3	(271%)	130.3	(197%)
1/88	30.0	48.6	(162%)	190.0	(633%)	210.4	(701%)	147.6	(492%)
2/88	28.4	31.7	(112%)	102.1	(396%)	120.7	(425%)	83.4	(294%)
3/88	45.7	35.1	(77%)	60.8	(133%)	85.8	(188%)	59.1	(129%)
4/88	101.9	88.3	(87%)	63.5	(62%)	71.2	(70%)	74.1	(73%)
5/88	141.4	102.3	(72%)	82.7	(59%)	113.8	(81%)	98.1	(69%)
year	1468.5	1372.8	(94%)	1892.3	(129%)	2629.4	(179%)	1922.1	(131%)

Out of the four rainy months (with rainfall > 200 mm) July and August showed high cloud moisture input, while June and September showed low cloud moisture input. During April and May which represent months with clear weather conditions and moderate rainfall, throughfall values do not indicate cloud moisture input (except on a few days). Out of the six rather dry months (October to March, with rainfall values lower than 70 mm), five months (November to March) showed high cloud moisture input. Net precipitation values for the whole study area during these months showed values considerably higher than rainfall (265%, 197%, 492%, 294% and 129% of rainfall).

High daily variation of net precipitation over the whole study area indicating occurrence and amount of cloud moisture input is shown in Figs 1 to 5. In most cases, this variation corresponds well to the observations taken on cloudiness and windspeed, as can be seen in Fig. 3.

Figs 1 and 2 show two rather rainy months, while Figs 3 and 4 represent two rather dry months. During these four months net precipitation values indicate high cloud moisture input on most days. Net precipitation values lower than rainfall occur only on a few days, particularly on those with high rainfall. In contrast, a month with almost no cloud moisture input is shown in Fig. 5, where moderate rainfall and relatively clear weather conditions prevailed. In this case, the relation rainfall/net precipitation follows a rather common pattern, well known from forests without cloud incidence.

Particular attention must be paid to cloud moisture input on days without rainfall as shown for instance in Fig. 2 (september 10-15). During the whole year of study 117 days occurred without rainfall. Out of these 117 days, water input was measured within the forest on 37 days at

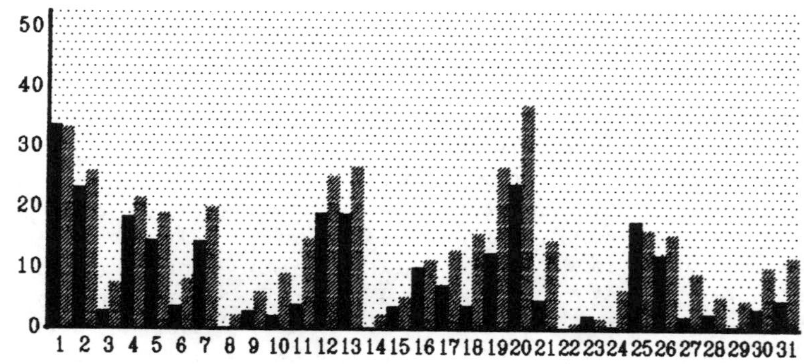

FIG. 1 Daily amounts of rainfall and net precipitation in mm over the whole study area for July, 1987.

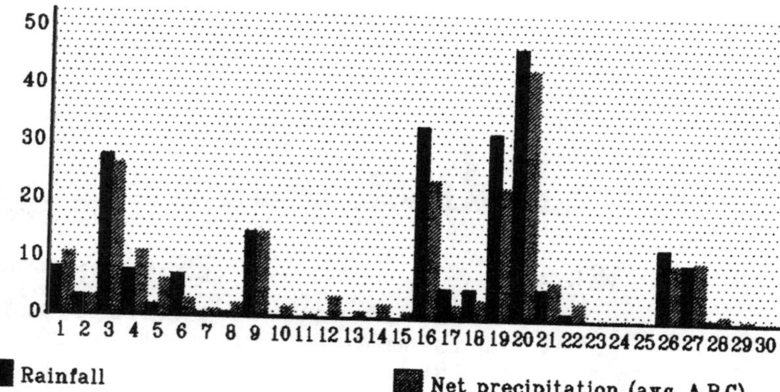

FIG. 2 Daily amounts of rainfall and net precipitation in mm over the whole study area for September, 1987.

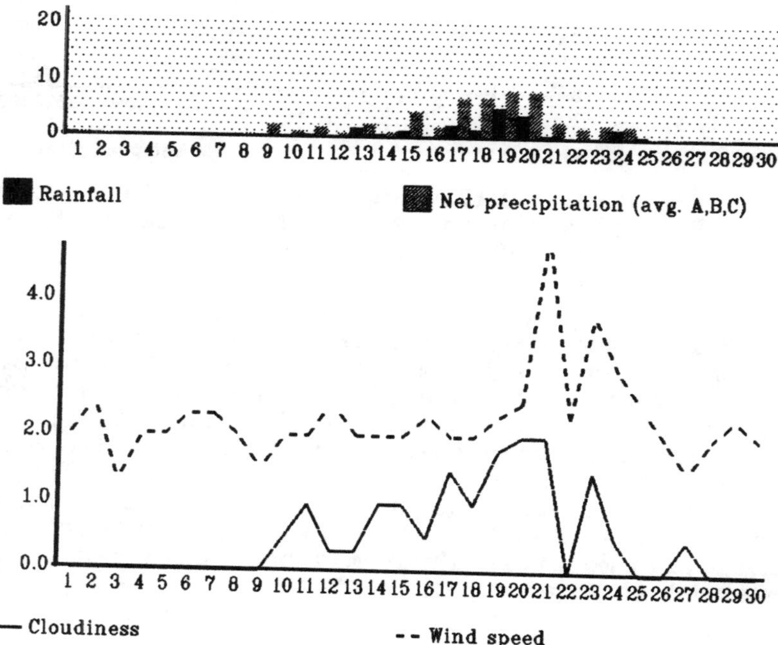

FIG. 3 Daily amounts of rainfall and net precipitation, in mm over the whole study area, and daily average cloudiness (graded from 0 to 3) and windspeed (Beaufort scale) for November, 1987.

unit A, on 77 days on unit B, and on 96 days on unit C. The total water input during these periods was 9.6 mm, 56.1 mm, and 124.9 mm respectively and the average for the whole study area was 59.6 mm. During the longest period without

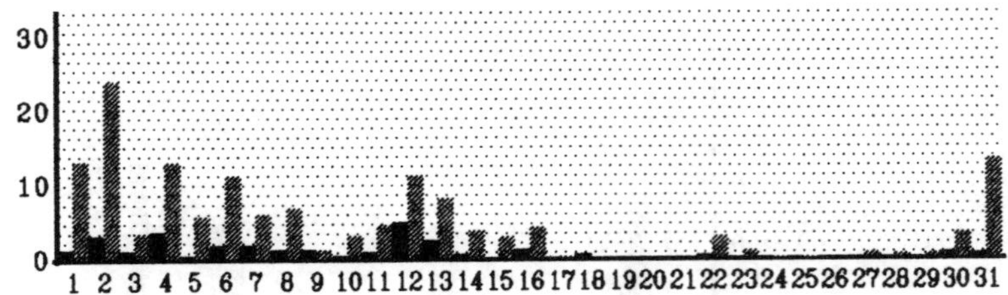

FIG. 4 Daily amounts of rainfall and net precipitation in mm over the whole study area for January, 1987.

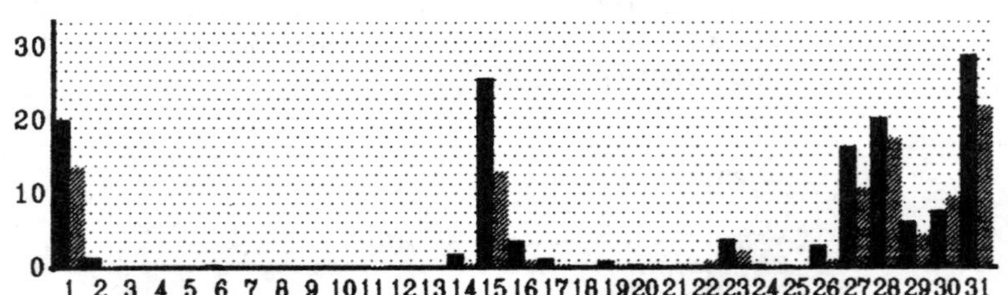

FIG. 5 Daily amounts of rainfall and net precipitation in mm over the whole study area for May, 1987.

rainfall (14 days), water input measured at unit A was 0.0 mm, at unit B 9.2 mm, and at unit C 17.5 mm.

The continuous water input, even during days without rainfall should be considered particularly important in assessing the hydrological importance of cloud forests. During days with low rainfall, net precipitation affected by cloud moisture input can exceed rainfall more than eleven times (See Fig. 4). Even on days with heavy rainfall cloud moisture input may be considerable, as can be observed in Fig. 1.

CONCLUSIONS

Even though spatial and temporal variation of throughfall in tropical rain forests is generally more pronounced than in temperate forests (Jackson, 1975; Lloyd & Marquez, 1988), the results of the present study show a markedly higher variation. This variation and the high net precipitation values (frequently much higher than rainfall) is attributed to cloud moisture input which varies strongly according to orographic and slope properties, as well as to cloud occurrence and wind speed.

The general increase of net precipitation, and particularly the frequent and considerable water input during days without rainfall should be taken into account in assessing the hydrological importance of cloud forests. Future studies on the subject should be encouraged since the lack of consideration of the contribution and variation of cloud moisture input in tropical watersheds incorporating cloud forests, may constitute a serious error in the determination of the water balance.

A better knowledge of the subject would allow an improved assessment of the hydrological importance of tropical mountain forests within the cloud belt. Lack of knowledge in this field and the need for more research has already been pointed out during the International Symposium on Tropical Forest Hydrology and Application held in Chiang Mai, Thailand (Stadtmüller, 1986). The symposium's final recommendations included the cloud forest topic as one of five major future research subjects in tropical forest hydrology. The present study is meant to be a first step. Treatment oriented experimental research as proposed by Adams & Hamilton (1987) should be the next logical step.

REFERENCES

Adams, P.W & Hamilton L.S. (1987) Future Directions for Watershed Research in the Asia-Pacific Region. East-West Center, Environment & Policy Inst., Hawaii.

Agudelo, N. (1988) Plan de manejo para el bosque del Uyuca de la Escuela Agricola Panamericana, El Zamorano, Honduras. M.Sc. Thesis, CATIE, Turrialba. Costa Rica.

Baynton, H.W. (1969) The ecology of an elfin forest in Puerto Rico. 3. Hilltop and forest influences on the microclimate of Pico del Oeste. Journal of the Arnold Arboretum 49:419-430.

Bockor, I. (1979) Analyse von Baumartenzusammensetzung und Bestandesstrukturen eines andinen Wolkenwaldes in Westvenezuela als Grundlage zur Waldtypengliederung. Dissertation, Universität Göttingen, FRG.

Budowski, G. (1976) Why save tropical rain forests? Some arguments for campaigning conservationists. In: Jordan C.F. (Ed.) Tropical Ecology. Hutchinson Ross Publishing Company, London, pp. 324-333.

Cáceres, G. (1981) Importancia hidrológica de la intercepción horizontal en un bosque muy húmedo premontano en Balalaica, Turrialba, Costa Rica. M.Sc. Thesis, CATIE, Costa Rica.

Clarke, R.T. (1986) The interception process in tropical rain forests: a literature review and critique. Acta Amazonica 16/17:225-237.

Grubb, P.J. & Whitmore, T.C. (1966) A comparison of montane and lowland rain forest in Ecuador. II. The climate and its effect on the distribution and physiognomy of forests. Journal of Ecology 55:313-333.

Hamilton, L.S. & King, P.N. (1983) Tropical Forested Watersheds. Westview Press, Boulder, Colorado.

Holdridge, L. (1982) Ecología Basada en Zonas de Vida. Tropical Science Center, San José, Costa Rica.

Jackson, I.J. (1975) Relationships between rainfall parameters and interception by tropical forests. J. Hydrol. 24:215-238.

Kerfoot, O. (1968) Mist precipitation on vegetation. Leading review article, Forestry Abstracts 29:8-20.

Lloyd, C.R. & de Marquez, O. (1988) Spatial variability of throughfall and stemflow measurements in Amazonian rainforest. Agricultural & Forest Meteorology 42:63-73.

Stadtmüller, T. (1986) Cloud forests in the humid tropics: distribution and hydrological characteristics. Proceedings of the International Symposium on Tropical Forest Hydrology and Application. Chiang Mai, Thailand.

Stadtmüller, T. (1987) Cloud Forests in the Humid Tropics. United Nations University, Tokyo, Natural Resources Technical Series, No. 33.

Steinhardt, U. (1978) Untersuchungen über den Wasser- und Nährstoffhaushalt eines andinen Wolkenwaldes in Venezuela. Dissertation, Universität Göttingen, FRG.

Weaver, P.L. (1972) Cloud moisture interception in the Luquillo Mountains of Puerto Rico. Caribbean Journal of Science 12(3-4):129 -144.

Zadroga, F. (1981) The hydrological importance of a montane cloud forest area of Costa Rica. In: Lal R. and Russel E.W. (Eds.) Tropical Agricultural Hydrology. John Wiley & Sons Ltd., New York, pp. 59-73.

Hydrology in Mountainous Regions. I - Hydrological Measurements; the Water Cycle (Proceedings of two Lausanne Symposia, August 1990). IAHS Publ. no. 193, 1990.

Rainfall variations in mountainous regions

G. DU T. DE VILLIERS
Department of Geography, University of Durban-Westville,
Private Bag X54001, Durban, 4000, South Africa

ABSTRACT Daily rainfall data obtained from 6 rain gauges set up in 5 different ways are analysed. The effect of wind on rainfall measurements are illustrated and the need for the correction of vertical gauge values when measuring rain on slopes is illustrated. Regional rainfall variations are discussed.

INTRODUCTION

Records of man's first attempt to measure rainfall are lost in antiquity. Biswas (1967) notes that rainfall records were collected as early as 400 B.C. and their use indicated knowledge of rainfall amounts, crop requirements and forecasting techniques. Apparently rainfall records in some or other form have been kept for thousands of years with surprisingly little difference between measurement techniques. Ward (1975) notes that since its inception, both the principles and the purpose of precipitation measurement have remained unchanged, the aim being to intercept precipitation over a known, carefully defined area bounded by the raingauge rim, to measure the amount of water so collected, and to express this measurement in units of depth. It is then assumed that this depth of water caught by the raingauge is the same as the depth of rain falling on a large area surrounding the gauge.

ACCURACY OF RAINFALL MEASUREMENT

The measurements produced by well-exposed and well-maintained standard raingauges in areas of minor relief are, for many purposes, sufficiently near the true rainfall. An objective estimate of the volume of water which passes the lowest part of the atmosphere during a given time period is obtained. The result of such measurement is objective in the sense that it is independent of the geometric position of the ground surface or the angle of incidence of raindrops. It is well to recognise however, that the catch of a standard gauge is not the true ground rainfall, namely the amount of rain which would have reached the ground if the gauge had not been there.

The errors that may arise in obtaining a representative sample at a gauge location are referred to as 'local' errors. These include splash in or out, evaporation losses, losses in wetting of the gauge surfaces and inaccuracies due to improper exposure of the gauge orifice. These errors are mostly of such a small nature that they can be ignored but the effect of wind, the major error source, should be considered in measurements where small differences in readings between certain parameters are significant. Wind consequences are not avoided by the usual method of rain installation, particularly at windy sites. The gauge forms an obstacle in the path of the wind thus the wind speed is increased over the gauge orifice and a turbulent eddying effect is produced. Drop trajectories are distorted and drops are carried over the gauge resulting in an underestimate of the fall. At a wind velocity of 3,5 ms^{-1}, air speed over the gauge is increased by up to 37% (Ward, 1975). Hence, all rainfall measurements are relative, a fact not generally recognised. Loss of catch is greatest in storms with small drops and high wind speeds, while tall gauges are more susceptible to loss from wind action than short ones because of higher wind speeds around elevated gauges where the surface friction effect is lower (Court, 1960; Sharon et al., 1976; Rodda et al., 1976).

In an effort to reduce the rainfall distribution effects caused by the gauge in the wind, various forms of shields have been devised. The most popular of these are the Nipher shields, consisting of an inverted cone, and Alter or Tretyakov shields, which consist of a ring of slats around the gauge. The effect of wind shields on rain gauges is to divert the airflow down and around the gauge, thus minimizing updrafts, downdrafts, and turbulent eddies over the gauge orifice. These measuring problems, linked to differences in exposed heights and gauge diameters, result in uncertainties about the accuracy of rainfall data. The W.M.O. Interim Reference Precipitation Gauge was thus introduced in an attempt to provide a basis for comparison, and differences between readings from this and the various national gauges range from 5 to 15 per cent (Ward, 1975).

MEASUREMENT OF RAINFALL IN UNDULATING TERRAIN

A different approach should be adopted in quantifying rainfall in undulating terrain or in mountainous catchments. Here an additional element comes in, namely, the position of the rain receiving surface in relation to the paths of the falling drops. Rain falls obliquely as a result of wind action, and inclinations of 40° have been reported by Hamilton (1954) and Court (1960). Under these circumstances the windward facing slope will be more thoroughly wetted than a slope facing the opposite direction. Sharon et al. (1976) calculated percentage differences in catch between windward and leeward facing slopes for various inclinations of the ground and of the rain vector. These differences vary between 34% and 85%, but a difference of a factor as high as two is possible. On a macro-spatial scale it is possible for these differences to be cancelled out in the sense that what is lost on the one slope is gained on the other and the horizontal catch therefore would give a measure of the mean over the area. In many instances this does however not apply, and it thus necessitates the use of inclined gauges or gauges with the orifices lying in a plane parallel to the sloping surface concerned. Several types of stationary and rotating directional rain gauges are in use of which the installation and functioning are, amongst others, discussed by Hamilton (1954); van Heerden (1961); and Sharon et al. (1976). The rain vector is the basis on which the design of the directional rain gauges rests. Van Heerden (1961) states that the direction and magnitude of showers may be represented by vectors. The direction of the vectors is the same as that of the showers and their magnitude is determined by the quantity of water precipitated per unit area - the area being measured perpendicular to the direction of the rain.

THEORETICAL ASPECTS OF INCLINED RAIN MEASUREMENTS

Obviously the catch volume in an inclined gauge is determined by the relation between the gauge aperture and the storm vector. In practice this angle (T) varies continuously with fluctuations in wind speed, wind direction and drop size.

Sharon et al. (1976) demonstrates that the catch volume in a gauge is determined by T and the area R and diameter S of the orifice,

$$R = \frac{\pi}{4} S^2$$

When the resultant direction of drop trajectories is perpendicular to the aperture, the gauge collects a sample with diameter S (Fig. 1), identical to the gauge aperture. Any deviation from this situation results in a distortion of the rain column into an elliptical sample where the area R_1 is given by

$$R_1 = \frac{\pi}{4} d_o d_i = R \cos T$$

where

$d_o d_i$ = the change in axis of the sample column expressed as

$$d_i = d_o \cos T$$

From the above it becomes clear that inclined rainfall measurements are affected by variations in the rainfall intercepted on slopes with different gradients and aspects in relation to the falling rain. The general meso-scale wind systems as well as local wind flow patterns induced by local topography are further complicating factors.

EXPERIMENTAL PROCEDURE

A rainfall measurement experiment was set up in the meteorological station of the University of Durban-Westville to quantify the variability of the catch in the various types of gauges discussed in the previous sections. The experimental site's environment is particularly suitable for this purpose because of relatively windy conditions and steep gradients. A total of six gauges were used to collect data during the 1988/89 rain season. Two of the gauges were set up in the normal vertical fashion with the orifices 1,2m above ground level. A third was set up in the same way, but with the orifice 2,4m above ground level. The fourth gauge was similar to the first two, but it was protected against wind effects by a Nipher screen. A pit gauge and an inclined rotating gauge completed the set-up. This gauge, with its orifice 1,2m above ground level was tilted at a 20° angle to simulate a slope effect, and thus making an assessment of slope rainfall from any given wind direction possible.

DATA COLLECTION

Thirty-seven storms were selected for analysis. The values of these storms are given in Table 1. No meaningful differences could be traced between the data sets of the pit and shielded gauges and the catch average per storm was therefore accepted as the true values for the two gauges. The fact that no meaningful differences existed

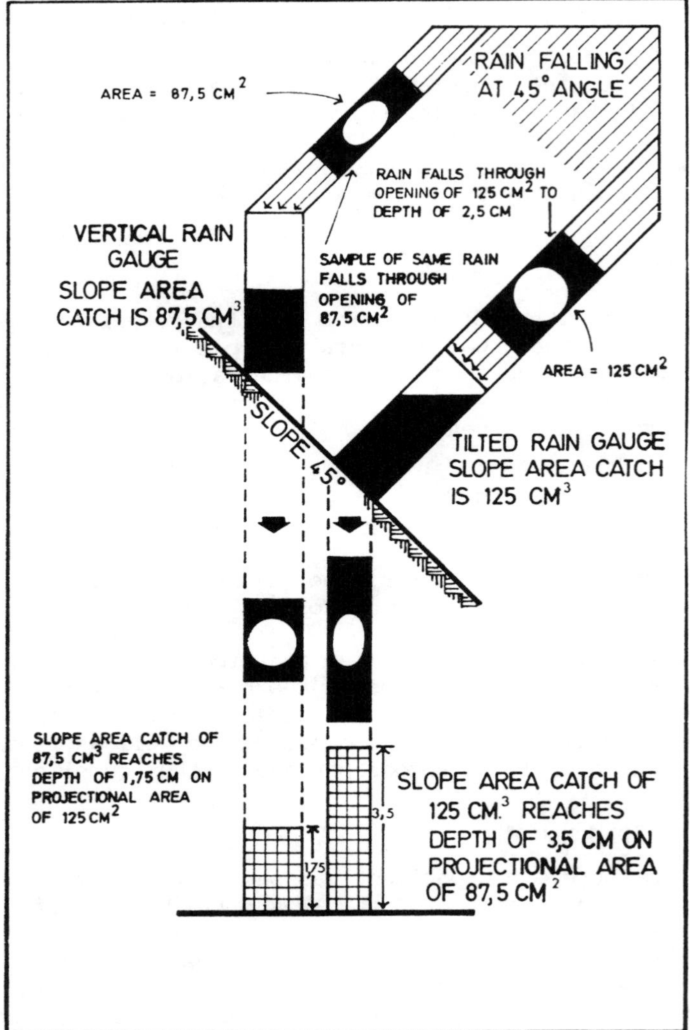

FIG. 1 The correct sampling of inclined rainfall on a slope.

substantiated that the two gauges functioned properly and that no splash in or losses occurred. The catch average per storm was also used for the two standard height gauges.

Initially both the screened gauge and the inclined gauge presented problems. The Nipher screen gauge consistently showed lower readings than the perpendicular control gauges which is contrary to the theory discussed in the first part of the paper. This was seemingly caused by a turbulent eddying effect around the gauge which was placed deep down in the Nipher cone. The differences in level between the horizontal top side of the Nipher screen and the gauge orifice was apparently just large enough to cause slight eddying around the orifice, which resulted in a lower catch.

TABLE 1 Daily Rainfall in mm at Six Rain Gauges.

Storms	Exposed gauges	Elevated gauge	Protected gauges	Inclined gauge
1	50,4	48,0	56,4	66,9
2	9,0	8,5	10,4	14,4
3	26,2	24,7	30,8	40,0
4	30,1	29,6	32,0	35,5
5	15,0	14,0	16,5	19,0
6	9,6	9,3	11,0	13,7
7	12,3	11,9	14,0	16,0
8	7,4	7,3	9,0	14,6
9	23,4	22,3	26,3	42,0
10	15,0	14,6	16,8	20,9
11	7,2	7,1	8,1	15,7
12	15,2	15,0	16,5	28,0
13	25,5	24,3	25,7	35,5
14	9,7	9,3	10,5	20,0
15	9,4	9,0	10,5	16,5
16	7,8	7,2	8,0	16,0
17	16,0	15,0	16,2	20,6
18	27,5	27,0	29,0	32,0
19	10,5	10,3	11,9	18,5
20	5,0	4,4	5,8	7,8
21	3,1	2,8	3,3	5,1
22	7,0	6,8	7,2	9,6
23	7,4	7,0	8,0	11,8
24	33,6	32,1	36,4	50,3
25	4,8	4,5	5,2	8,0
26	5,1	4,5	5,6	8,4
27	17,2	16,8	18,5	25,8
28	9,2	9,0	10,4	17,0
29	12,9	12,7	13,6	16,9
30	11,5	11,1	12,8	17,0
31	21,6	21,0	23,4	28,8
32	4,8	4,7	5,0	7,0
33	15,9	15,4	17,4	21,9
34	6,2	6,0	6,8	9,0
35	13,5	13,0	15,1	21,1
36	3,9	3,6	4,2	5,5
37	4,9	4,4	5,7	8,0
T	594,8	548,0	656,0	873,8
A	16,1	14,8	17,7	23,6

This was corrected by bringing the orifice and the screen top to the same level which excluded the turbulent eddying. Inspection of the inclined gauge during and after the first few storms suggested possible losses. Modifications were made to the catch container and it functioned well for the rest of the period. The rain gauges were read on a daily basis.

DATA ANALYSIS

The daily rainfall data presented in Table 1 was tested to establish whether a meaningful difference existed between the values for the different gauges. An analysis of variance was carried out on the 37 showers registered and it indicated that the daily differences between the gauges were significant at a 5% level.

In comparing the total values for the 37 showers in Table 1 it becomes apparent that relatively large discrepancies are present. The total catch for the inclined gauge is, for example, significantly higher than any of the other totals. This pattern was consistent from shower to shower, but inconsistent in the sense that storms of approximately the same catch in the exposed gauges did not register the same values in the inclined gauge. This is explained by variations in the relation between the gauge aperture and the storm vector for the given storms.

A comparison between the inclined gauge values and the wind protected gauges, which is often accepted as control gauges or gauges with a higher degree of accuracy, reveals an average difference of 24,9%. Evidently the protection obtained in using shielded or pit gauges is just against turbulant eddies, updrafts and downdrafts in the micro-environment of the gauge orifice. If the rain in the meso-environment falls obliquely, shielded or pit gauges contribute little towards higher accuracy. Under these circumstances the effect of the aperture setting of the inclined rain gauge is more important.

In comparing the inclined gauge with the exposed gauge the differences are more striking, the average for the 37 showers being 31,9%. The effect of protection discussed in the previous paragraphs is obvious. The same pattern is obvious, however more intense, when the inclined gauge and the elevated gauge is compared. Further illustration of the effect of wind protection lies in a comparison between the data of protected and exposed gauges. The protected gauges yielded on average a 9,3% higher catch with relatively small deviations from the average.

The relation between the gauges was then analysed using linear least squared regressions and coefficients of determination. In three cases the exposed rain gauges set up at the standard height of 1,2m was accepted as the independent variable with the elevated,

TABLE 2 Linear Regression in mm per Storm:
Standard Gauge against Elevated Gauge;
Standard Gauge against Protected Gauge:
Standard Gauge against Inclined Gauge;
Protected Gauge against Inclined Gauge.

Equation	R^2
Eg = 0,96 Sg - 0,04	0,99
Pg = 1,09 Sg + 0,02	0,99
Ig = 1,29 Sg + 2,66	0,95
Ig = 1,18 Pg + 2,53	0,95

protected and inclined gauges respectively the dependent variables. In a further calculation the protected gauge values as independent variables were analysed against the inclined gauge values as the dependent variables. The results are shown in Table 2.

From Table 2 it is obvious that the correlation coefficients of the data sets are high, indicating that a large percentage of variance in the dependent variable is explained by the independent variable. From this it follows that the dependent variable values could be assessed with relative accuracy from a knowledge of the independent variable alone. This is of particular interest in the third equation in Table 2 depicting the relation between the exposed and inclined gauges. Exposed gauge values are commonly used erroneously instead of inclined gauge values. The limitations of a fixed tilt inherent in this particular model must however be conceded.

REGIONAL RAINFALL VARIATIONS

The data from 25 rain gauges in the coastal foot hills of Natal, in the Durban region, were subsequently analysed. The Kolmogorov-Smirnov goodness of fit test was employed to determine whether the amount of rainfall differed significantly among stations and multiple correlation and regression analysis to examine the factors causing spatial variations.

The study area is well dissected by rivers and has an undulating topography with overland slopes that often exceeds 20%. Figure 2 depicts the topography of the region, and figure 3 the mean annual

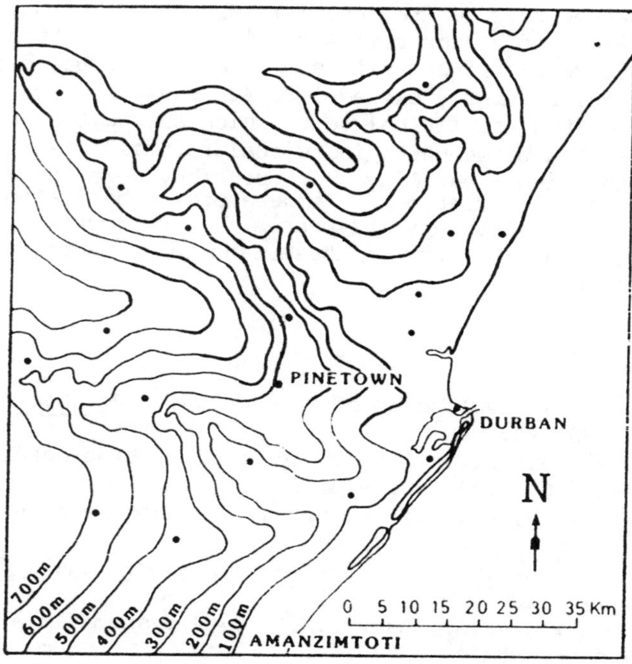

FIG. 2 Topography.

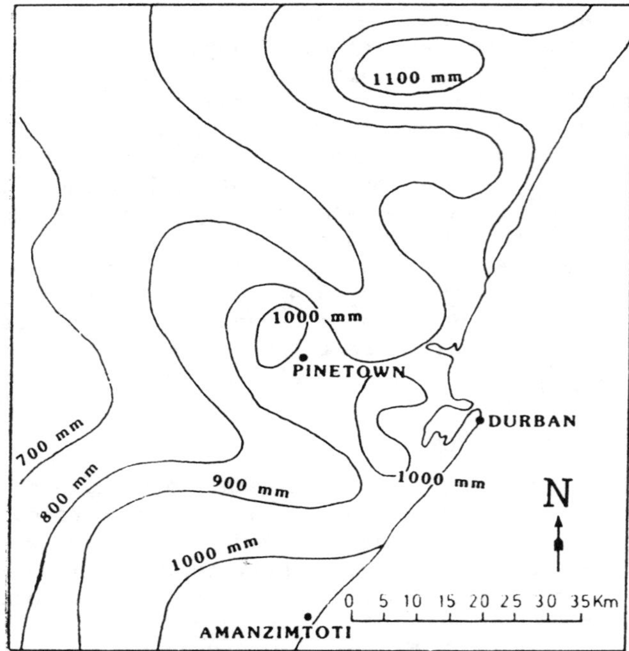

FIG. 3 Mean annual rainfall.

rainfall. The dependence of mean annual rainfall on continentality is evident with the decrease of rainfall from the coast to the interior. However this general trend is disturbed by the undulating topography. Areas of higher relief receive more rain than areas of lower relief, like the river valleys. On an individual storm basis these differences regularly exceeded 200%. These observations were substantiated by the statistical tests which showed that meaningful differences existed between the individual rainfall stations, and furthermore, that continentality and topography were the main factors causing the rainfall variations. Temperature, urbanization and vegetation had only secondary influences. No corrections were made for inclined rainfall effects as these tend to be cancelled out over time in a large area.

REFERENCES

Biswas, A.K. (1967) Development of rain gauges. Am. Soc. Civ. Eng. 93 (IR 3), 99-124.

Court, A. (1960) Reliability of hourly precipitation data. J. geophys. Res. 65 (12), 4017-4023.

Hamilton, E.L. (1954) Rainfall sampling on rugged terrain. U.S. Dep. Agric. Tech. Bull. 1096. 41 pp.

Neff, E.L. (1977) How much rain does a rain gauge gage? J. Hydrol. 35 (3/4), 213-220.

Rodda, J.C., Downing, R.A., Law, F.M. (1976) Systematic Hydrology, London: Butterworth's, 25-83.

Sharon, D., Yisraeli, A. and Lavee, H. (1986) A model for the distribution of the effective rainfall incident on slopes and it's application at the Sdeh Boqer experimental watershed. Hebrew University of Jerusalem, technical paper no. 26, 30 pp.

Van Heerden, W.M. (1961) The direction of rain and its measurement S. Afr. J. Agric. Sci. 4 (1), 51-61.

Ward, R.C. (1975) Principles of Hydrology, 2nd Ed., London: McGraw Hill, 16-49.

Symposium on Improved Methods of Hydrological Measurements in Mountain Areas

Topic B:

Methods of Direct Estimation of Evaporation

Hydrology in Mountainous Regions. I - Hydrological Measurements; the Water Cycle
(Proceedings of two Lausanne Symposia, August 1990). IAHS Publ. no. 193, 1990.

Atmosphere and surface control on evaporation from alpine tundra in the Canadian Cordillera

W. G. BAILEY, I. R. SAUNDERS & J. D. BOWERS
Department of Geography, Simon Fraser University, Burnaby, British Columbia, Canada V5A 1S6

ABSTRACT The mountain environments of western Canada are dominated by high solar irradiance and persistent wind during the spring and summer months. This leads to high potential evaporation values but these are rarely met by the surface energy and water balance regimes. Micrometeorological investigations of alpine tundra found that potential rates of evaporation only occurred immediately after precipitation. When the bare rock surfaces dried, it was usual for latent and sensible heat flux densities to be similar in magnitude. If surface drying continued, sensible heat flux density usually exceeded latent heat flux density on a daily basis. As a consequence of the absence of efficient physical or physiological mechanisms to transport subsurface water to the atmosphere, atmospheric demands were not met even though subsurface soil moisture remained abundant. These characteristics have significant implications for the concept of potential evaporation in mountain environments as well as for operational evaporation modelling procedures.

INTRODUCTION

In North America, the dearth of energy and water balance studies in mountain environments has been noted by several authors (Barry, 1981; Price, 1981). This paper acknowledges these concerns and presents some of the results of energy balance studies conducted at two alpine sites in the Canadian Cordillera during the spring and summer seasons. Emphasis is placed on understanding atmospheric and surface control of evaporation from alpine tundra. These controls have implications for the concept of potential evaporation in mountain environments as well as for operational evaporation modelling procedures.

THEORETICAL BACKGROUND

In the absence of advection, the dissipation of the net radiation Q^* at the surface can be described by

$$Q^* = Q_H + Q_E + Q_G \qquad (1)$$

where Q_H is the sensible heat flux density, Q_E the latent heat flux density and Q_G the ground heat flux density. With measurements or model estimates of Q^* and Q_G, principal attention is directed towards the partitioning of available energy between Q_H and Q_E. This necessitates quality measurement and/or modelling procedures.

Following Monteith (1965), the combination model is written as

$$Q_E = \frac{S(Q^* - Q_G) + \rho Cp[e_s(T_z) - e_z]/ r_a}{S + \gamma + \gamma r_s/r_a} \tag{2}$$

where S is the slope of the saturation vapour pressure curve evaluated at air temperature, ρ the density of air, Cp the specific heat of air at constant pressure, $e_s(T_z)$ the saturation vapour pressure at air temperature T_z, e_z the vapour pressure at height z, γ the psychrometer constant, r_a the aerodynamic resistance to heat and vapour transfer and r_s the surface resistance. The utility of this approach has been illustrated for a host of surfaces and it provides a superior tool for examining atmospheric and surface control on the evaporative process. As a consequence of its derivation for complete canopy agricultural crops, its application to alpine tundra must be done with care. The limitation of this approach has been the need to explicitly specify r_a and r_s.

Special cases can be defined where r_a and/or r_s need not be specified in the combination model. When vapour pressure deficits at the surface and in the air are equal, equation 2 reduces to

$$Q_{ES} = \frac{S}{S + \gamma} (Q^* - Q_G) \tag{3}$$

where Q_{ES} is the latent heat flux density equivalent to equilbrium evaporation (Slatyer & McIlroy, 1961). This rate can occur in two very different environments: in a saturated environment when both deficits are equal and in a drier environment when they are greater than zero but equal.

Priestley & Taylor (1972) presented a modified version of equation 3 to calculate potential latent heat flux density Q_{PE}

$$Q_{PE} = \alpha_p \frac{S}{S + \gamma} (Q^* - Q_G) \tag{4}$$

From a review of empirical studies, they showed that values of α_p in non-advective, potential conditions have an overall daily average of 1.26. Similar results have been found for surfaces worldwide with the notable exceptions found for forests (Spittlehouse and Black, 1981).

To accommodate reduced evaporation when surface moisture availability became limiting, Davies & Allen (1973) replaced α_p with a variable α which was a statistical function of available moisture in the surface layer. This provided for the calculation of actual latent heat flux density

$$Q_E = \alpha \frac{S}{S + \gamma} (Q^* - Q_G) \tag{5}$$

Although developed for usage in other environments, the approaches presented can have considerable utility in mountain environments for the understanding, modelling and estimation of evaporation.

EXPERIMENTAL PROCEDURE

Field research was undertaken at two locations in the Canadian Cordillera (Fig. 1). The first site was on Plateau Mountain in the Livingstone Range of the Rocky Mountains of southwestern Alberta. The second site was on Scout Mountain in the Okanagan Range of the Cascade Mountains.

The Plateau Mountain experiment was conducted during June and July 1985. Plateau Mountain's summit is characterized by extensive areas of flat to gently rolling terrain and the surface consisted primarily of frost hummocks. In the area of the instrumentation, there were several hundred meters of homogeneous fetch in all directions and this translated to a turbulent boundary layer depth exceeding 1.0 m. Weather during the experiment was mostly clear and warm, and only two significant precipitation events occurred.

The Scout Mountain experiment was conducted from November 1986 to July 1987 and during April and May 1988. Consideration for this

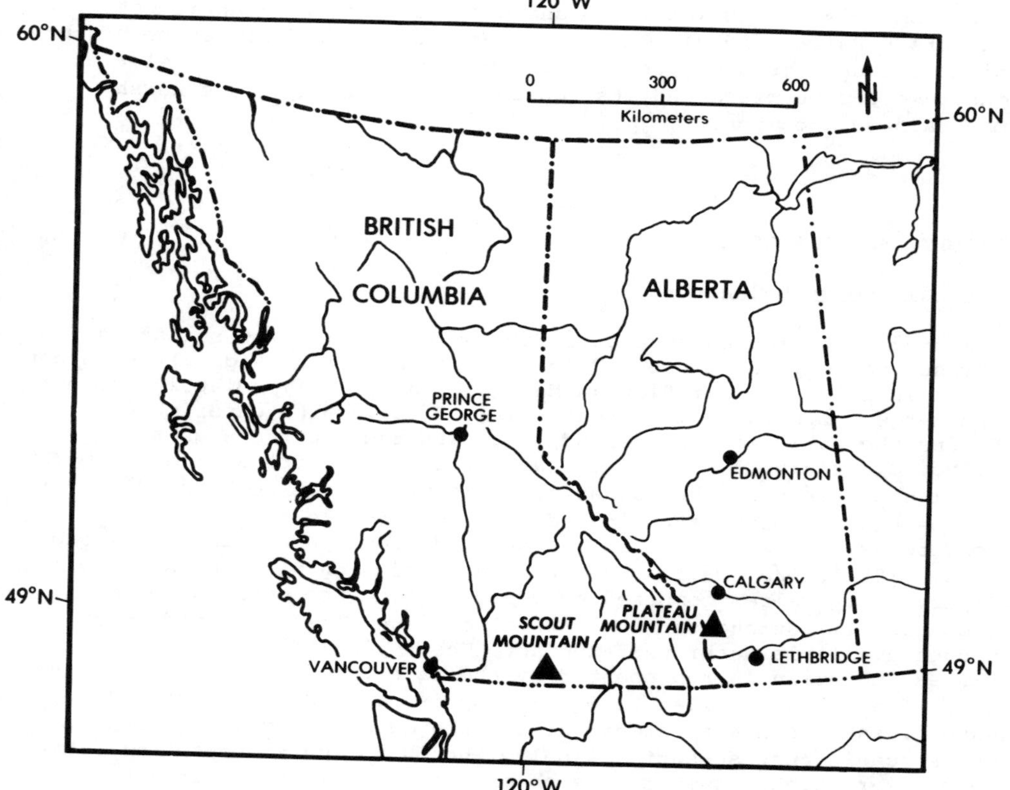

FIG. 1 Map of Alberta and British Columbia, Canada showing the the location of Plateau Mountain and Scout Mountain.

present paper will be restricted to conditions when the surface was snowfree. The site area was smaller than that on Plateau Mountain but the fetch was sufficient for a turbulent boundary layer of 1.0 m. When compared with Plateau Mountain, both the soil and vegetation were more developed on Scout Mountain. When comparing the observation periods, 1988 was wetter than 1987.

The instrumentation used during both experiments was of a similar high quality. Net radiation was measured with a net pyrradiometer (Middleton). Ground heat was monitored with a series of heat flux transducers (Thornthwaite) buried at a depth of 50 mm. Temperature measurements permitted the correction for heat flux divergence in the surface layers of the ground. Vertical profiles of temperature and vapour pressure using a differential psychrometer system permitted the evaluation of latent and sensible heat flux densities using the Bowen ratio - energy balance approach. In addition, eddy correlation measurements of sensible heat flux density were undertaken. For this, a fast response thermocouple and sonic anemometer (Campbell Scientific) were interrogated at a rate of 10 Hz. All data recording was done with Campbell Scientific data systems.

For both Plateau Mountain and Scout Mountain, the daily soil heat flux density during snowfree conditions was approximately 10% of daily net radiation (Bowers & Bailey, 1989). Independent confirmation of the utility of the energy balance equation and quality of the sensible heat flux density measurements was provided by the intercomparison of Bowen ratio and eddy correlation measurements (Bowers & Bailey, 1989). Quality comparisons were found at both study sites but unfortunately the fragile nature of the eddy correlation instrumentation precluded its continuous operation in the harsh mountain environment.

RESULTS AND DISCUSSION

Diurnal energy balance regimes

The diurnal energy balance data for representative wet surface and dry surface days is presented for Plateau Mountain (Fig. 2) and Scout Mountain (Fig. 3). For Plateau Mountain, July 18 immediately followed the largest precipitation event measured during the experiment. During the early morning period, the bare rock surfaces quickly dried. Q_E tracks Q^* throughout the day and was quite similar to Q_H in magnitude. Although the subsurface moisture was quite high, Q_E never approached the rates anticipated for these apparent potential conditions. It is clear that r_a, derived from wind profile analysis (Thom, 1975), was small as a consequence of high windspeeds. Employing r_s values computed by residual from the combination model (equation 2), strong surface control on water loss is noted even though available water was abundant. The typical drying regime for Plateau Mountain is represented by the data for July 6. Q_E values are low, often quite similar to Q_G, and Q_H is high. Surface control on water loss is quite apparent through the daily trend in r_s. During these conditions, subsurface (below the 50 to 100 mm depth) moisture levels were high. However, the absence of efficient physical and physiological mechanisms to transfer this moisture to accomodate atmospheric demands is apparent. When comparison is made with results that would be found for similar radiation and windspeed conditions in

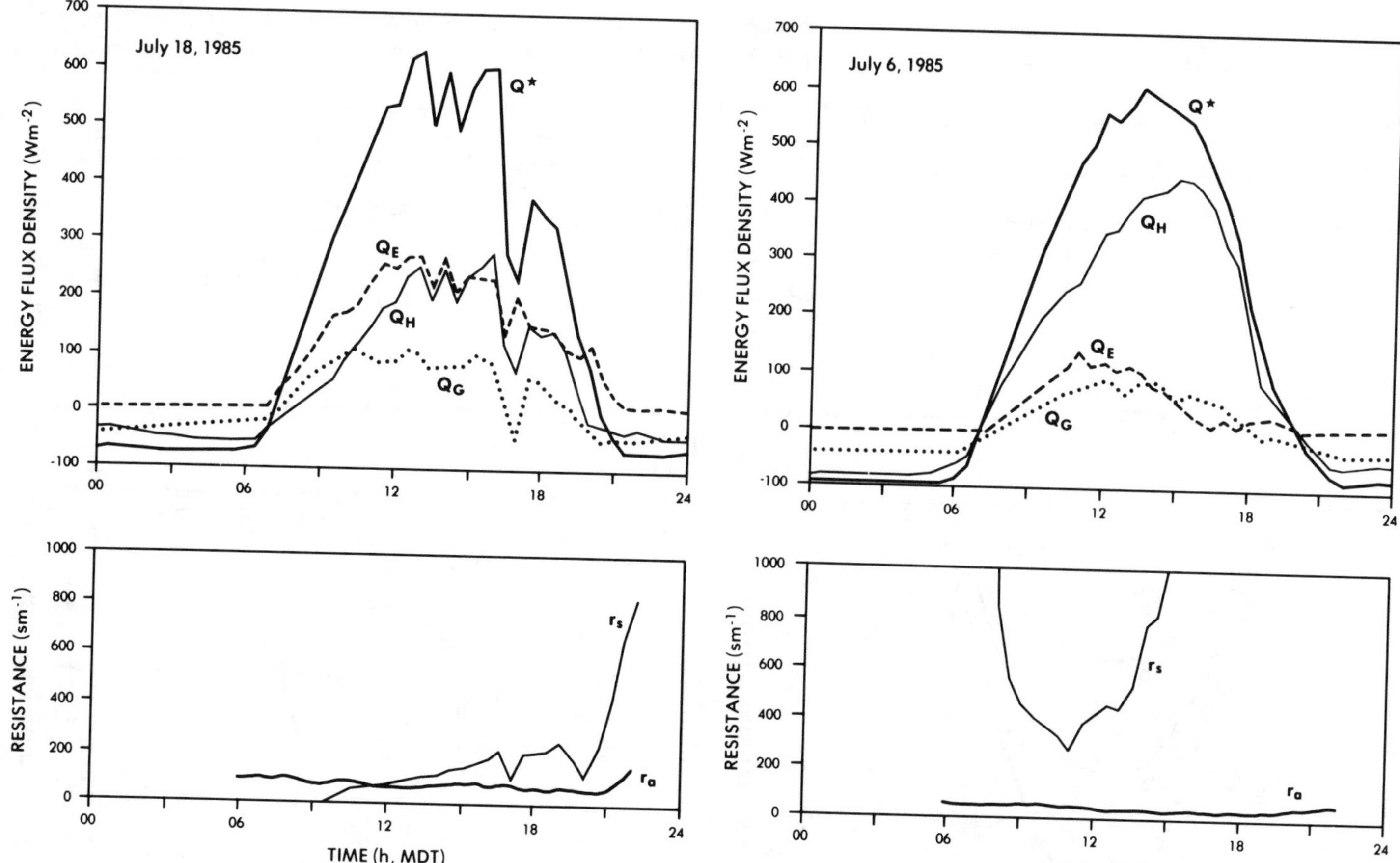

FIG. 2 The diurnal trend of energy balance components, r_a and r_s for a wet surface day (July 18, 1985) and a dry surface day (July 6, 1985) for Plateau Mountain alpine tundra.

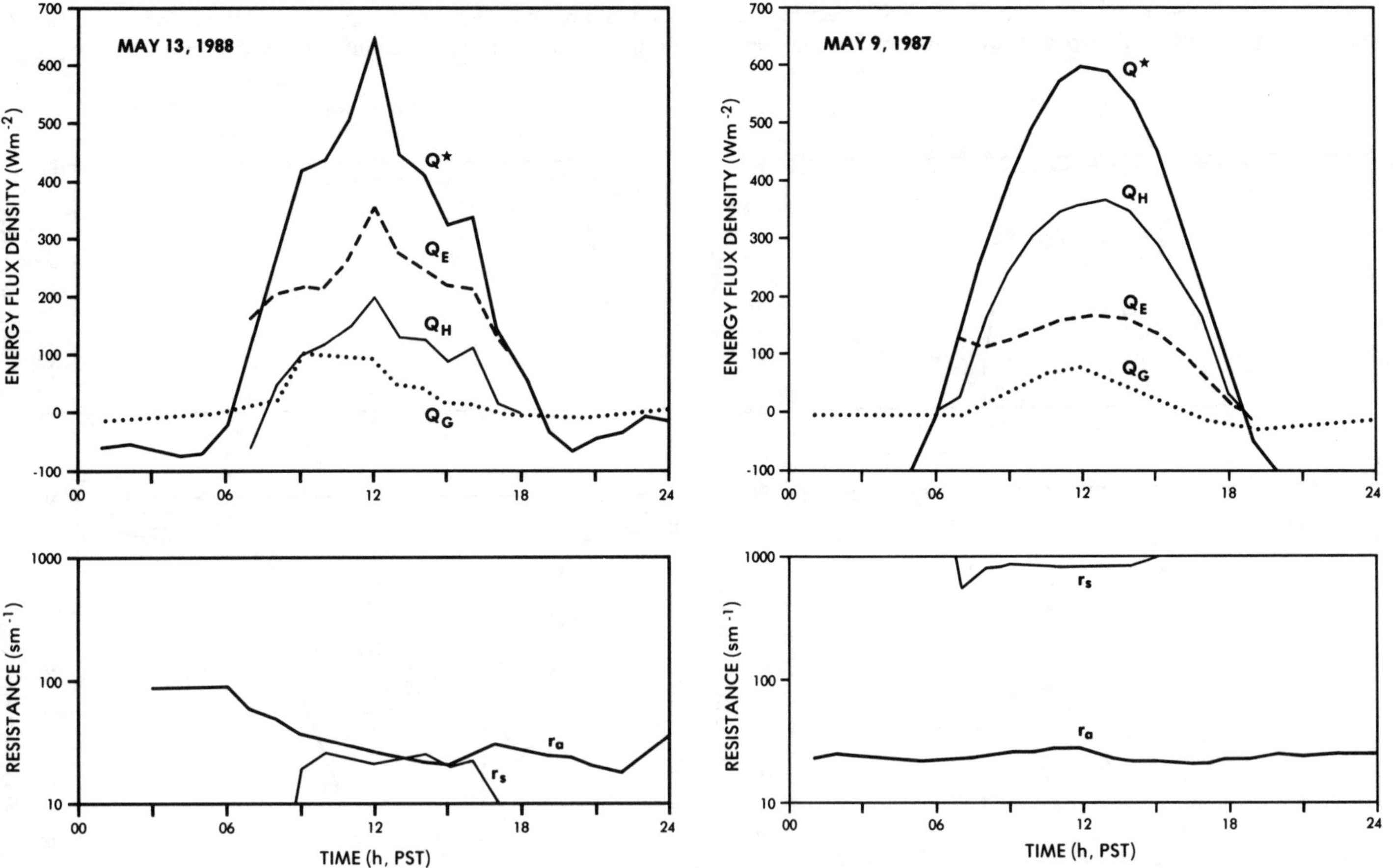

FIG. 3 The diurnal trend of energy balance components, r_a and r_s for a wet surface day (May 13, 1988) and a dry surface day (May 9, 1987) for Scout Mountain alpine tundra. Note that the scale for resistance is logarithmic.

an agricultural environment, the absence of a plant canopy with a well developed root system is obvious.

The data for Scout Mountain (Fig. 3) is complimentary to the general regimes found at Plateau Mountain. However, differences in the nature of the Scout Mountain surface plays an important role in the trend of the diurnal energy balance regimes. The data for May 13 illustrates a wet surface day in which Q_E tracks Q^* and exceeds Q_H during the daylight hours. This arises as a consequence of a more developed soil and plant community on Scout Mountain. The bare rock at Scout Mountain accounted for about 25% of the surface area whereas at Plateau Mountain, it was approximately 40%. During the dry conditions present on May 9, Q_H is dominant throughout the daylight hours. The diurnal trend is similar to that which characterized most of the data collected at Plateau Mountain.

Application of a generalized Priestley & Taylor model

With daily measurements of Q_E, equations 4 and 5 can be solved to evaluate α_p and α. When the surface at Plateau Mountain was wet, it was rare that α_p exceeded unity. This is attributed to the role played by the bare rock surfaces. As bare rock was a smaller component of the surface area at Scout Mountain, α_p values were higher but nevertheless less than for agricultural surfaces that had similar surface roughness and moisture availability characteristics. When comparing the variation of α with volumetric surface moisture, a trend relating the two is found. As anticipated, when moisture levels are low, α values are low. As moisture values increase, α values increase. Without exception, the values for Scout Mountain are the highest as a consequence of the more developed soil, more flourishing vegetation and the smaller amount of bare rock when compared to the Plateau Mountain site. A large amount of scatter exists in the relationship between α and volumetric soil moisture. This large scatter is a consequence of errors in Q_E measurement but it particularly reflects the problems faced in the sampling and measurement of surface moisture in mountain environments.

CONCLUSIONS

Examination of the diurnal energy balance data for both Plateau Mountain and Scout Mountain illustrate that high rates of evaporation only occur when the surface is completely wet. When the bare rock surfaces dry, even though subsurface moisture levels remain high and for most surfaces evaporation would proceed at potential rates, the magnitudes of Q_E and Q_H are usually similar. With any continued drying, Q_H dominates the energy balance at both hourly and daily timescales.

The modelling of short-term evaporation is difficult as a consequence of the inability to easily specify surface moisture availability. In fact, more progress may be achieved in evaluating the partitioning of available energy into Q_E and Q_H by modelling Q_H. The potential for using an Ohm's law approach has been suggested by Bowers & Bailey (1989) in which aerodynamic resistance, surface temperature and air temperature can be easily specified.

The application of the Priestley & Taylor (1972) approach for evaluating daily potential evaporation requires careful site calibration as a consequence of the need to account for the impact of bare rock on the assigned value of α_p. Although the generalized form of the model (equation 5) has merit, the measurement of surface moisture in mountain environments remains a challenge. Further, large errors in moisture specification are likely and may account for large uncertainties in the estimates derived.

With the demands on the water resources of mountain environments increasing, future research is merited. The utilization of potential evaporation models that do not account for the role of dry bare rock, even though subsurface soil moisture is abundant, are limited. Approaches that overcome this limitation are required. Techniques for improved specification of available surface moisture are needed. Short-term evaporation modelling using the combination model necessitates the development of procedures for assembling the microscale variations in surface types into representative surface resistances. Application of procedures similar to that proposed by Shuttleworth & Wallace (1985) may have utility. Development of physically based energy balance models for realistic sloping surfaces is needed. These approaches must be able to fully acknowledge the role of advection. The development of regional modelling procedures which link the atmospheric boundary layer and the surface (McNaughton & Spriggs, 1986) will play a key role in future operational evaporation estimation and prediction procedures.

ACKNOWLEDGEMENTS This research was funded by the Natural Sciences and Engineering Research Council of Canada (Operating Grant A2614).

REFERENCES

Barry, R. G. (1981) Mountain Weather and Climate. Methuen, New York.

Bowers, J. D. & Bailey, W. G. (1989) Summer energy balance regimes for alpine tundra, Plateau Mountain, Alberta, Canada. Arctic and Alpine Res. 21, 135-143.

Davies, J. A. & Allen, C. D. (1973) Equilibrium, potential and actual evaporation from cropped surfaces in southern Ontario. J. Appl. Meteor. 12, 649-657.

McNaughton, K. G. & Spriggs, T. W. (1986) A mixed layer model for regional evaporation. Boundary-Layer Meteorol. 34, 243-262.

Monteith, J. L. (1965) Evaporation and the environment. In: The State and Movement of Water in Living Organisms, G. F. Fogg, ed., Academic Press, New York, 205-234.

Price, L. W. (1981) Mountains and Man. University of California Press, Berkeley.

Priestley, C. H. B. & Taylor, R. J. (1972) On the assessment of surface heat flux and evaporation using large scale parameters. Mon. Weath. Rev. 100, 81-92.

Shuttleworth, W. J. & Wallace, J. (1985) Evaporation from sparse crops - an energy combination theory. Quart. J. Roy. Met. Soc. 111, 839-855.

Slatyer, R. O. & McIlroy, I. C. (1961) Practical Micrometeorology. UNESCO Press, Paris.

Spittlehouse, D. L. & Black, T. A. (1981) Measuring and modelling forest evapotranspiration. Can. J. Chem. Eng. 59, 173-180.

Thom, A. S. (1975) Momentum, mass and heat exchange of plant communities. In: Vegetation and the Atmosphere, Principles, Vol.1, J. L. Monteith, ed., Academic Press, New York, 57-109.

Hydrology in Mountainous Regions. I - Hydrological Measurements; the Water Cycle (Proceedings of two Lausanne Symposia, August 1990). IAHS Publ. no. 193, 1990.

Evaporation measurements in the Alpine basin Gletsch during the ALPEX/RHONEX project

A. BERNATH
Geographisches Institut ETH, Winterthurerstr.190, CH-8057 Zürich, Switzerland

ABSTRACT During the summer months of 1981 to 83 and in early spring 1982 energy balance and evaporation measurements were made at Gletsch [1765 m.a.s.l.] and at Oberwald [1370 m.a.s.l.]. For profile data acquisition a 2-meter-tower with a mobile instrument package moving between five levels was used. Latent and sensible heat fluxes were calculated with the Bowen-ratio, profile and bulk transfer methods. While the Bowen-ratio showed plausible results, profile method suffered from problems of the wind conditions which were affected by the surrounding topographic irregularities. The classical Monin-Obukhov-functions failed.

INTRODUCTION

Until a few years ago evaporation, the smallest component in the alpine water balance, did not obtain as much experimental attention as precipitation, runoff and glacier mass balance. Often evaporation was calculated from water balance equation resulting in accumulating the errors of the other terms. Despite strong efforts in the latest past, few information is available for alpine regions. Important results were reported from Staudinger (1983) and Kaser (1983). Lang (1978, 1981) summarizes the knowledge of various works. The lack of information is due to the difficult environmental conditions in the mountains and the extensive instrumentation needed for direct determination of the evaporation. In the context of the ALPEX/RHONEX-project (Alpine Experiment/Rhone Experiment as a part of the GARP (Global Atmospheric Reserach Program) of WMO and ICSU), the Department of Climatology at the Institute of Geography of the Federal Institute of Technology, Zürich (ETHZ), among other reserach work, carried out direct measurements of evaporation in the alpine catchment of Gletsch (Central Swiss Alps) using profile and energy balance method. The base camp Gletsch, where most of the measurements took place was situated at 46°33'52'' N / 8°21'59" E at the height of 1765 m.a.s.l. in the uppermost Rhone Valley. Extensive investigations were made from 1980 to 1983 in the months from June till October. The winter situation was studied in March/April 82 at Oberwald (46°32'01" N / 8°21'05'' E, 1368 m.a.s.l.) because of danger of avalanches at Gletsch. Oberwald is located about 3 kilometers southeast from Gletsch also in Rhone Valley.

METHODS AND INSTRUMENTATION

One of the classic and well known methods to determine evaporation is the Bowen-ratio/energy balance method postulated by Bowen (1926). Assuming the similarity of the processes of sensible and latent heat flux the formulation is

$$\beta = \frac{H}{LE} = a\frac{c_p\,\delta\Theta}{L\,\delta q} \quad \text{with} \quad a = \frac{K_h}{K_w} \qquad (1)$$

where β is the Bowen-ratio, H the sensible heat flux, LE the latent heat flux, cp the specific heat of air under constant pressure, $\delta\Theta$ and δq the differences of potential temperature and specific humidity between two levels respectively, L the latent heat of evaporation and K_h, K_w the eddy diffusivities for heat and water vapour. By using the energy balance at the surface R + LE + H + B = 0 and measuring the potential temperature and specific humidity at two levels the sensible and latent heat fluxes can be calculated. R is the net radiation and B the heat flux into the soil or into a snow cover. In spite of its age and with much discussions about the ratio K_h/K_w the Bowen-ratio still seems a valuable approach to evaporation as pointed out among others by Denmead and Bradley (1985). Nevertheless there are some severe restrictions to this method. Firstly, we have to assume the steady state condition and the constant flux values between the measurement level and the surface. Secondly, we are forced to exclude β-values near -1 because of their unrealistic flux results and situations where - gradients and fluxes show the same direction. The needed relations were formulated by Ohmura (1981). The third problem is the accumulation of errors made in measurements of radiation balace, soil heat flux, temperature and humidity.

The profile method is based on the existence of known relationships between the surface fluxes and the profiles of relevant mean parameters, temperature, humidity and horizontal wind speed in the surface layer using the Monin-Obukhov- similarity theory and the eddy diffusivity concept. A detailed overview is given by Brutsaert (1982). The resulting relations for calculating sensible and latent heat fluxes used in the present work are

$$H = \left(\frac{-\rho c_p k^2}{\Phi_m \Phi_h}\right)\left(\frac{\delta u\, \delta\Theta}{\left(\ln\left(\frac{z_2 - d}{z - d}\right)\right)^2}\right) \tag{2}$$

and

$$LE = \left(\frac{-\rho L k^2}{\Phi_m \Phi_w}\right)\left(\frac{\delta u\, \delta q}{\left(\ln\left(\frac{z_2 - d}{z - d}\right)\right)^2}\right) \tag{3}$$

where ρ is the density of the air, k the von-Karman-constant = 0.4, $\Phi_{h,m,w}$ the - Monin- Obukhov-functions for heat, momentum and water vapour, δu the difference of the wind speed between two levels, d the zero plane displacement and $z_{1,2}$ the used profile levels. Zero plane displacement was calculated from linear regression at neutral conditions with

$$u = (u_*/k)\ \ln\left(\frac{z - d}{z_0}\right) \tag{4}$$

where u_* is the friction velocity and z_0 is the roughness lenght. As stability criterion the gradient-Richardson-number Ri was used with

$$Ri = \left(\frac{g}{\Theta_m}\right)\left(\frac{\delta\Theta\ \delta z^2}{2}\right) \tag{5}$$

with g the acceleration due to gravity and Θ_m the mean level potential temperature. The advantage of gradient-Richardson-number over the Obukhov-length and the flux-Richardson-number is the possibility of direct calculation from profiles.

There are some problems connected with profile method. One is the most popular expression of the Monin-Obukhov-functions $\Phi_{h,m,w}$ as a function of stability criterion, mostly z/L. An excellent overview of present knowledge is given in Högström (1988). Most of the well known functions are determined over more or less ideal i.e. flat, homogenous surfaces with constant roughness at a few to a few tenth of meters over the surface. The formulation of the influence of roughness changes normally is available only for well defined obstacles. In the mountains changes of roughness even with wind direction are normal. Further changes of surface conditions are caused by clouds, precipitation and diurnal change of solar radiation. Changes in surface conditions result in a layer commonly described as internal sublayer. This leads to violation of the postulate of constant flux layer and changes of the scaling functions reported among others by Garratt (1980) and Beljaars et al. (1983).

In the present work profiles of temperature, humidity and wind speed were measured simultaneously with two identical specially constructed towers with moving instrument platform using stops at 200, 120, 80, 50 and 30 cm above the ground. By using only one set of probes calibration problems between the 5 distinct levels were avoided. To compensate for the loss of time resolution one hour i.e. 3 profiles was the smallest time intervall used. An additional tower with fixed level probes at 2, 6 and 10 m operated during field seasons 1982 and 83 delivering continous data. Measuring time at each level was set to 3 min resulting in a 20 min intervall for a whole profile the running time included. The registration frequency was set to 30 s for tower 1 respectively 30 s or 2 s for tower 2 as a compromise between registration performance and measuring resolution. Temperature was measured with a ventillated and shadowed platinum thermometer (PT100). Humidity, i.e. dew point temperature was measured with a dew point mirror hygrometer (General Eastern) mounted together with the thermometer. Wind speed was measured with a cup anemometer (Thornthwaite).

Due to severe data problems at Oberwald, bulk-transfer-method was used as an alternative with the bulk transfer coefficients $C_H = 0.002$ and $C_E = 0.0021$ following Kondo and Yamazawa (1985),

$$H = C_H \rho u_1 (\Theta_s - \Theta_1) c_p \quad \text{and} \quad LE = C_E \rho u_1 (q_s - q_1) L \tag{7}$$

where the subscript s means temperature respectively humidity at the surface. The level 1 was selected at a height of 120 cm.

Radiation balance formulated by (8) was measured with a four component "Davos-type" pyrano/pyrradiometer (PD4) and a pyranometer with shadow-ring:

$$R = G - r + L_i - L_o \tag{8}$$

G is the global radiation, r the reflected shortwave radiation and L_i means the incoming and L_o the outgoing longwave radiation.

Soil heat flux was determinated using temperature values in the depth of one and four centimeters and the results of a "Thornthwaite" heat-flux-plate combined with (9). The c_B-values were determinated by a temperature-profile measured by thermistors and platinum thermometers (PT100).

$$B = \int c_B \frac{\delta T}{\delta t} dz + B_{HFP} \tag{9}$$

where c_B is the heat capacity of the soil, δT the temperature difference, δt the time difference and B_{HFP} the soil heat flux measured with the heat flux plate.

During the winter in addition to soil heat flux the heat flux in the snow cover has to be included in the calculations. The energy balance of a snow cover is formulated after Ohmura (1981)

$$\rho_S c_P \int \frac{dT}{dt} dz = B_0 - B_h + (S_i - S_o) + \int L \frac{dm}{dt} dz, \quad \text{with } B_0 = -\lambda_S \frac{dT}{dz} \text{ and } B_h = -\lambda_B \frac{dT}{dz} \tag{10}$$

$B_{0,h}$ is the heat flux at the top and at the bottom of snow cover, $S_{i,o}$ is the incoming respectively the outgoing shortwave radiation at the inner side of upper boundary of snow cover, $\lambda_{S,B}$ is the heat conductivity for snow and soil and m is the mass of melted snow. The melting energy was measured with a calorimeter (Ohmura, 1981), the heat flux in snow and ground with temperature profiles using platinum thermometers (PT100) and thermistors (UUB31J).

MEASURING SITES

The selection of measuring sites in mountain regions is somewhat difficult. The main problems apart from the rough climate are optimizing the site against large and small topography and natural or artificial obstacles and finding a horizontal, easy accessible place with a representative, homogenous surface cover out of the zone of avalanches. The base station for summer campaigns was situated in the valley floor of the Gletschboden between the Rhone Glacier moraines from 1818 and 1856 stages. This place was free of obstacles within a radius of 80 to 100 m. The ratio between the height of the nearest obstacles to their distance in direction of the valley, which was identical to the main wind direction, was between 1/20 to 1/30. The vegetation was classified as a Poa alpina-, Salix retusa community (alpine tundra). The vegetation height changed from 5 to 15 cm during the observed periods. Below a small layer of about 5 cm of soil we found the sandy gravel of Rhone Glacier ground moraine. The winter measuring site, Oberwald was also situated in the Rhone Valley floor. The broader even valley floor and the larger distance of more than 200 m to the next obstacles offered better conditions for the profile measurements. During the whole measuring period the surroundings were covered with 110 to 253 cm of snow cover. Cold temperatures, snowfall and snowdrift gave severe difficulties to instruments and registration causing often loss of data. The small gradients of temperature and humidity required a high resolution of the measurements.

RESULTS AND DISCUSSION

During the summer 83 an extensive comparison of the two towers with mobile platform were made to check quantitative differences between continous measurements and the 3 min average samples at the 2 m level. The horizontal distance between the two gradient towers was 5 m. Standard deviation σ of temperature changes from standard registration frequency/rate (3 * 3 min/h, 30 s) for both towers with 0.436 °C to 0.529 °C with high registration frequency (3 * 20 min/h, 2s (fixed probe) at tower 2, i.e. 0.093 °C or 21.3 %. For dew point measurements the values are similar with σ = 0.41 respectively 0.48 °C, i.e. a difference of 0.07 °C or 17.1 %. The results for wind speed are σ = 25.3 respectively 29.8 cm s^{-1}, i.e. the difference is 4.5 cm s^{-1} or 17.8 %. Essential seems the large deviation between the two towers, both using identical sampling rates, compared with vertical gradients, which are in the same magnitude or even smaller.

The exclusion of unrealistic Bowen-ratio values specially takes place in principal in the hours around sunset and sunrise and between the measuring levels 200 and 120 respectively 80 cm where gradients often are very small and changing. The differences of the resulting fluxes calculated with different levels are small though basic parameters are strongly different as shown in Table 1.

TABLE 1 Normalized parameters and results of Bowen-ratio calculations with different levels (Average of 15.7.-25.7.83, 11.8.-22.8. and 28.8.-8.9.83).

Levels	$\delta\Theta$	σ	δq	σ	β	σ	H	σ	LE	σ
200- 30	1		1		1		1		1	
200-120	0.03	2.11	0.115	2.21	0.7	2.3	0.6	1.6	0.8	1.0
120- 80	1.76	2.08	0.824	2.01	1.2	2.0	0.8	1.4	0.9	0.9
80- 50	1.73	2.82	1.659	2.41	0.6	1.8	0.6	1.4	0.9	0.9
50- 30	2.20	4.00	1.732	3.34	1.0	3.4	1.0	1.6	1.0	1.2

For the profile method, which includes wind measurements, simple test calculations using (2),(3) and several of the well known formulas for the Φ-functions showed large differences between the levels and in general a strong underestimation for the measurements at Gletsch. The differences in the temperature, humidity and wind speed values were only partly compensated by the scaling functions. Assuming the identity of Φ_h and Φ_w it is possible to extract the function $F = 1/(\Phi_m \Phi_h)$ from (1) and (2). Using the energy balance equation for the surface, we can calculate F from the measured data. Averaging these results gives the following relation between F and Ri:

$$\begin{array}{ll} Ri > 0 & F = -0.8\ Ri + 0.5 \\ 0 < Ri < 0.03 & F = 277.44\ Ri^2 - 21.03\ Ri + 0.85 \\ Ri < 0 & F = -36.8\ Ri + 1.14 \end{array} \tag{11}$$

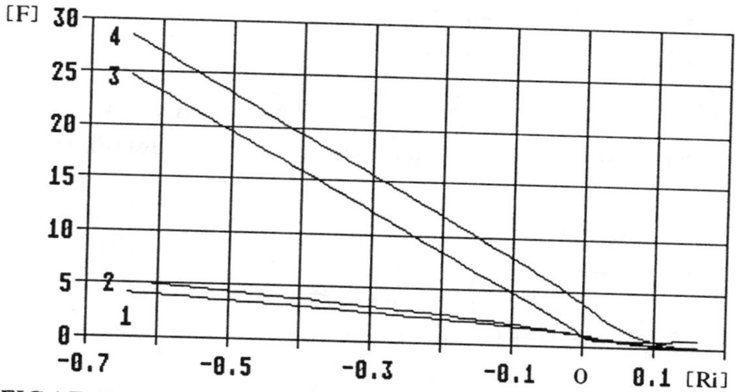

FIG.1 F-Functions from Webb (1), Wieringa(2), Bernath (3) and Garratt(4).

Fig. 1 shows beside the mentioned function, the relations calculated using results from Webb(1970) and Wieringa(1980) over ideal surfaces and from Garratt (1980) over wood i.e. a very rough surface. Using (11) with the present data leads to acceptable results for latent and sensible heat fluxes. Detailed explanations and further information is given in Bernath (1989).

Average z_0 for Gletsch (Alpine tundra) is 1.2 cm with d = 13.2 cm. The values for Oberwald (Snow cover) are z_0 = 1.6 cm and d = 16.5 cm. The results from Gletsch are realistic. The values for Oberwald show large standard deviations and seem to be too large. Reasons may be the disturbed surface near the instruments and the lack of the lowest level.

An example for diurnal change of main parameters of the energy balance and climate is shown for Gletsch in Fig.2 and 3 for a typical radiation day in July 83 in true solar time. The unsymmetrical course of net radiation is due to topograpy. Wind speed typically is high during the day and small at night. At night wind blows down the valley, turns in the early morning to the SE slope and in the afternoon the main wind direction is up the valley. Temperature follows the radiation except in the evening. The minimum occurs at about 5 a.m. true solar time, the maximum at 3 p.m.. The diurnal change of specific humidity shows a double wave. After reaching the minimum in the early morning, humidity increases until 10 a.m.. About noon we notice a slight recession and then an increase to the maximum at 19 p.m.. Net radiation reaches its maximum at noon, soil heat flux is shifted about three hours. During the morning a major part of net radiation is used for latent heat flux. From 11 a.m. to 15 p.m. sensible heat flux increases. In the later afternoon evaporation increases again. Temperature gradients are small and so is sensible heat flux. Dispite increasing wind speed around noon which could increase transport of humidity, evaporation and specific humidity decrease during this period. Possible reasons are the closing of plant stomata and a diurnal change of advection with the change of wind direction. The gradients of specific humidity decrease with increasing wind speed. About 18 p.m. wind direction turns again to the SE slope.

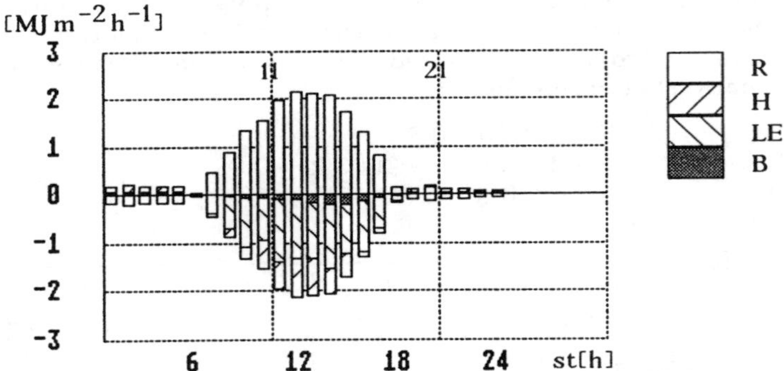

FIG.2 Diurnal change of energy balance at Gletsch (16.7.1983).

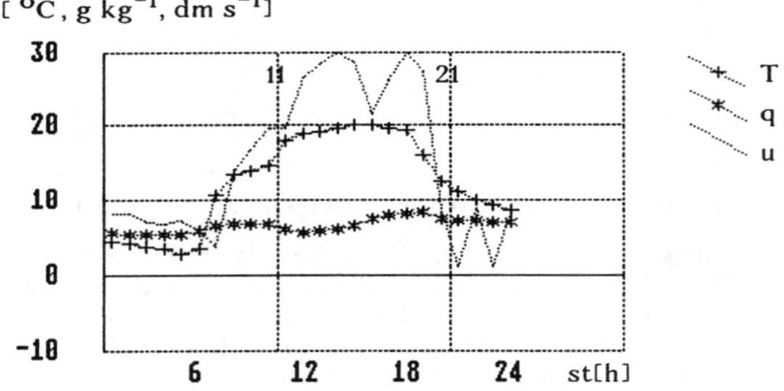

FIG. 3 Diurnal change of temperature, specific humidity and wind speed at Gletsch (16.7.83).

Fig.4 and 5 show the average diurnal change of energy balance, temperature, specific humidity and wind speed at Oberwald averaged over 11 days between 29.3.82 and 9.4.82. The main part, about 96 %, of available energy at the surface is used for snow melt M. Besides net radiation an important contribution is made by sensible heat flux in the afternoon with about 30 %. The latent heat flux takes 4 % or 0.2 MJ m^{-2} d^{-1} i.e. evaporation amounts to 0.1 mm d^{-1}. During the night slight condensation occurs while evaporation shows its maximum about noon. The differences between the Bowen-ratio, the bulk transfer- and the profile method are small. For profile method standard Monin-Obukov-functions were used. The maximum evaporation measured with this methods amounts to 0.22 mm d^{-1}, the maximum condensation to 0.07 mm d^{-1}. Measurements with a snow lysimeter of 15 cm diameter showed values beween 1.93 mm d^{-1} evaporation and 0.09 mm d^{-1} condensation. The average values were about 30 % larger than the profile calculations, mainly due to the internal heating of the lysimeter.

The mean values of energy balance and climatological measurements at Gletsch and Oberwald are presented in Table 2. The main differences between Gletsch and Oberwald appart the season are due to the snow cover. Due to its large albedo about 60 % of global radiation was reflected at Oberwald. The values

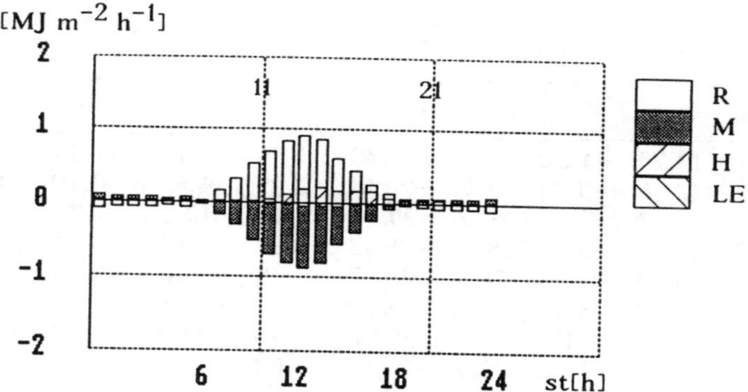

FIG. 4 Mean diurnal change of energy balance at Oberwald (11 days).

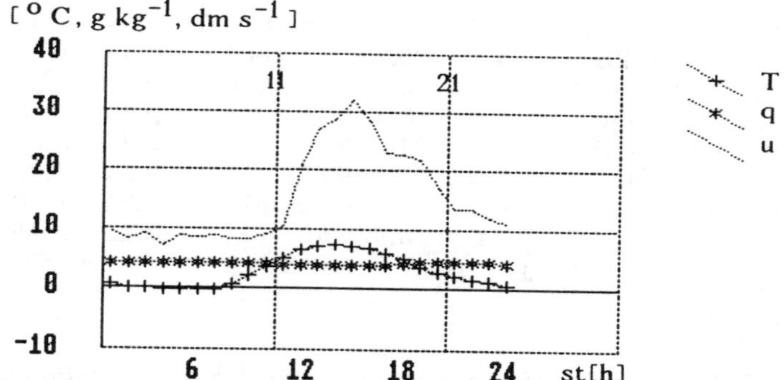

FIG. 5 Mean diurnal change of temperature, specific humidity and wind speed at Oberwald (11 days).

and gradients and the diurnal change of temperature and mainly specific humidity were smaller at Oberwald. At Gletsch between 53 and 79 % of available energy at the surface were used for evaporation, at Oberwald only 4 %. There the main part of the energy was used for the melt. At Gletsch sensible heat flux was a heat sink, while at Oberwald it delivered one third of available energy for the surface.

CONCLUSIONS

The evaporation values found at Gletsch and Oberwald are comparable and in good agreement with the results published by Staudinger (1983) and Kaser (1983). By using profile measurements for the determination of the evaporation under alpine conditions the Bowen-ratio showed less problems than the profile method. Further research is needed to determine more exactly the influence of roughness changes. The instrumentation and registration need further refinement, e.g. combination of fixed level and mobile measurements and higher resolution. More work is also needed to reveal the height dependency of the evaporation in higher regions over different surfaces, specially over rock and rock debris.

ACKNOWLEDGEMENTS This manuscript is an extract of the authors thesis (Bernath,1989) which was realized between 1980 and 1989 with financial support of Swiss National Foundation and the ETHZ. Special thanks are due to my teachers Prof. Dr. A. Ohmura and Prof. Dr. H. Lang and to my colleagues K. Schroff, Dr. M.Funk and Dr. M. Woywod.

TABLE 2 Mean values of energy-balance and climatological measurements at Gletsch and at Oberwald.*

Period	G	r	L_i	L_o	R	B(M+B)	LE	H [MJ $m^{-2}d^{-1}$]
28.7. - 14.8.81	18.20	-4.30	25.41	-30.70	12.16	-0.52	-6.19	-5.45
28.3. - 17.4.82*	17.56	-9.99	21.90	-26.18	3.29	-4.61	-0.20	1.45
14.7. - 31.7.82	14.07	-3.20	26.24	-29.58	9.58	0.52	-7.97	-2.13
1.8. - 31.8.82	14.10	-3.51	25.98	-29.13	8.22	0.49	-6.51	-2.22
1.9. -10.9.82	16.10	-3.88	24.28	-28.67	7.98	0.48	-6.65	-1.92
15.7. -25.7.83	24.63	-5.98	25.18	-31.40	12.52	-0.61	-8.21	-3.70
11.8. -22.8.83	17.81	-4.16	25.18	-29.57	9.34	0.09	-6.82	-2.61
28.8. - 8.9.83	13.78	-2.88	25.91	-29.16	8.63	0.18	-6.21	-2.56

Period	T [°C]	u [cm s^{-1}]	s [g kg^{-1}]	RH [%]	DD [mb]	P [mb]	Alb	E [mm d^{-1}]	LE/R+B [%]	N [mm]
28.7 - 14.8.81	12.2	161.9	5.7	48.4	7.08	829.0	0.24	2.15	53	26.2
28.3. - 17.4.82*	2.9	153.0	4.2	75.7	5.67	860.4	0.58	0.79	4	54.2
14.7. - 31.7.82	10.2	207.1	7.0	78.0	9.65	826.6	0.23	3.15	79	102.5
1.8. - 31.8.82	9.6	146.5	7.0	78.4	9.74	826.5	0.28	2.58	75	182.8
1.9. -10.9.82	8.8	160.5	6.4	74.6	8.76	830.4	0.26	2.63	77	60.7
15.7. -25.7.83	14.3	185.5	7.0	57.1	9.81	829.6	0.25	3.25	69	4.4
11.8. -22.8.83	10.5	158.5	6.9	72.1	9.50	827.2	0.23	2.70	72	13.0
28.8. - 8.9.83	9.6	214.6	7.0	76.9	9.68	827.3	0.22	2.46	70	71.1

REFERENCES

Beljaars, A., Schotanus, P. and Nieuwstadt, F. (1983) Surface layer similarity under nonuniform fetch conditions. J. Climatol. Appl. Meteorol., 22, p.1800-1810.

Bernath, A. (1989) Beiträge zum Wasserhaushalt im Einzugsgebiet der Rhone bis Gletsch. Diss., Geogr. Institut ETH Zürich.

Bowen, I.S. (1926) The ratio of heat losses by conduction and by evaporation from any water surface. Phys. Rev., 27, p.779-787.

Brutsaert, W. (1982) Evaporation into the Atmosphere, Reidel, Dordrecht.

Denmead, O. and Bradley, E. (1985) Flux-Gradient relationships in a forest canopy. The Forest-Atmosphere Interaction, Reidel, Dordrecht, p. 421-442.

Garratt, J.R. (1980) Surface influence upon vertical profiles in the atmospheric near-surface layer. Quart. J.R. Meteorol. Soc., 106, p.803-819.

Högström, U. (1988) Non-dimensionalwind and temperature profiles in the atmospheric surface layer, a re-evaluation. Boundary Layer Meteorol., 42, p.55-78.

Kaser, G. (1983) Verdunstung von Schnee und Eis. Diss., Univ. Innsbruck.

Kondo, J. and Yamazawa, H. (1985) Bulk transfer coeffizient over a snow surface. Boundary Layer Meteorol., 34, p.123-135.

Lang, H. (Ed) (1978) Die Verdunstung in der Schweiz. Beiträge zur Geologie der Schweiz - Hydrologie, 25, SNG, Kümmerly u. Frey, Bern.

Lang, H. (1981) Is evaporation an important component in high alpine hydrology? Nordic Hydrology, 12, p.217-224.

Ohmura, A. (1981) Climate and Energy Balance on Arctic Tundra. ZGS, 3.

Staudinger, M. (1983) Der Wärmehaushalt zweier hochalpiner Stationen während der Vegetationsperiode. Dissertation, Univ. Innsbruck.

Webb, E.K. (1970) Profile relationship: the log-linear range, and extension to strong stability. Quart.J.R. Meteorol. Soc., 96, p.67-90.

Wieringa, J. (1980) A revaluation of the Kansas mast influence of stress and cup anemometer overspeeding. Boundary Layer Meteorol., 18, p. 411-430.

Hydrology in Mountainous Regions. I - Hydrological Measurements; the Water Cycle (Proceedings of two Lausanne Symposia, August 1990). IAHS Publ. no. 193, 1990.

On the spatial variability of hydrologic processes in a small mountainous basin

G. PESCHKE, K. MIEGEL, CH. ETZENBERG & H. HEBENTANZ
Department of Water Sciences, Dresden
University of Technology, GDR
8027 Dresden, Mommsenstraße 13

ABSTRACT The high spatial variability of hydrologic processes caused by geological, pedological, geomorphological heterogeneity and differences of land utilization becomes evident especially in the mountainous basin of the Wernersbach. Both the discussion of the soil water dynamics on various sites and the quick flow analysis of floods show, that quite different processes dominate in single parts of the basin.

INTRODUCTION

Hydrologic basins are characterized by a large spatial variability, especially in mountainous regions. An input distribution on the area (rain, snow melt, radiation), different land utilization and management by man and the heterogeneity of the watershed features (geology, soils, morphology, microrelief, river network) form a spatially variable state of the system (soil moisture, water levels in surface and subsurface storage systems) and very different area-specific system outputs (runoff components, evapotranspiration) composing a complex total system output.

The knowledge of this spatial variability of hydrologic processes is necessary for

- the identification of runoff components and their place of origin,
- the estimation of the danger potential of various subareas concerning flood and erosion,
- the quantification of the possible pollutant input into rivers, lakes and groundwater,
- the effective utilization of partial areas by building industries, agriculture and forestry,
- establishment of subareas as protection field within the environmental protection.

Since the sixties there has been enormous international efforts to solve this problem. They reach from the investigation of heterogeneity of basin features and state variables (Beckett et al., 1971; Nielsen et al., 1973; Peck et al., 1977; Reynolds, 1974; Sharma et al., 1980; Tricker, 1981) to the derivation of representative parameters (Bruch et al., 1974; Mc Cuen et al., 1981), from the experimental investigation of subareas (Ragan, 1968; Dunne & Black, 1970) to the concept of the effectively contributing area (Bernier, 1980; Kölla, 1986) and to very different principles of modelling (Crawford & Linsley, 1966; England & Holtan, 1969; Gupta & Solomon, 1977; Abbot et al., 1978; Becker & Gurtz, 1981; Carvey & Croley, 1984; Hensel et al., 1985; Bauer et al., 1985; Schwarze, 1985; Richter, 1987).

Many of the still unanswered questions can be solved only, if theoretical and experimental investigations are regarded as equally important methods of research. Intensly observed representative and test areas are especially suited to such investigations.

DEPENDENCE OF RUNOFF FORMATION ON SITE FACTORS

Where in a catchment area the water suffered by precipitation is stored, runs off as surface flow or interflow, or whrere it percolates into the groundwater, that depends on pedological and plant site factors of the considered subareas together with parameters of the precipitation process (Peschke, 1987). Therefore the temporal and spatial variability of precipitation fields is essential for the spatial variability of the runoff formation (Schilling & Harms, 1983).

Partial areas with rocky, loose top-soils can infiltrate high rain intensities. This tendency is strengthened especially by well rooted humus horizons in forests. If these macropores penetrate the soil into greater depths, then the percolation and the formation of delayed runoff components dominate. If top-soils with small thickness are underlaid by compressed clay, then at the layer boundary interflow is formed (Peschke, 1979, 1987b). The slope of such subareas has a modifying effect, it stops or strengthens these processes. Unpermeable partial areas with low slope are quickly saturated, independent on their soil physical storage properties, and form variable saturation areas, delivering surface flow as a consequence of rainfall.

This qualitative discussion can be precised by results of the infiltration theory (Dyck & Peschke, 1982), according to which subareas with a well permeable (feature of the area) and dry soil (proceding soil moisture as state of the system) and with low rain intensity (system input) never or temporarily form runoff. In the opposite case runoff components (surface flow and interflow) are found on such subareas, for which the relation of precipitation intensity to hydraulic conductivity is much greater than 1.

THE WERNERSBACH WATERSHED

The mountainous basin of the Wernersbach (Fig. 1) is situated in the northwesterly part of the Tharandter Wald. Its area amounts to 4.6 km^2. The altitude has a range from 322 to 424 m over sea level. The climate of the Tharandter Wald in the continental-maritime transition zone is characterized by the following annual average values: temperature: 7.4 °C; precipitation: 800 mm; wind speed: 1.9 m s^{-1}.

The basin of the Wernersbach has a heterogeneous geological structure. Besides the predominant parts of the porphyry there are also areas with formations of Cretaceus. The soil cover consists of mainly cohesive weathering products of porphyry (loamy grit, stoany loam) and of loamy-silty Pleistocene depositions (only in flood plains with crushed rock). Sandy permeable soils are inferior.

The Wernersbach basin is completely used by forestry. The tree

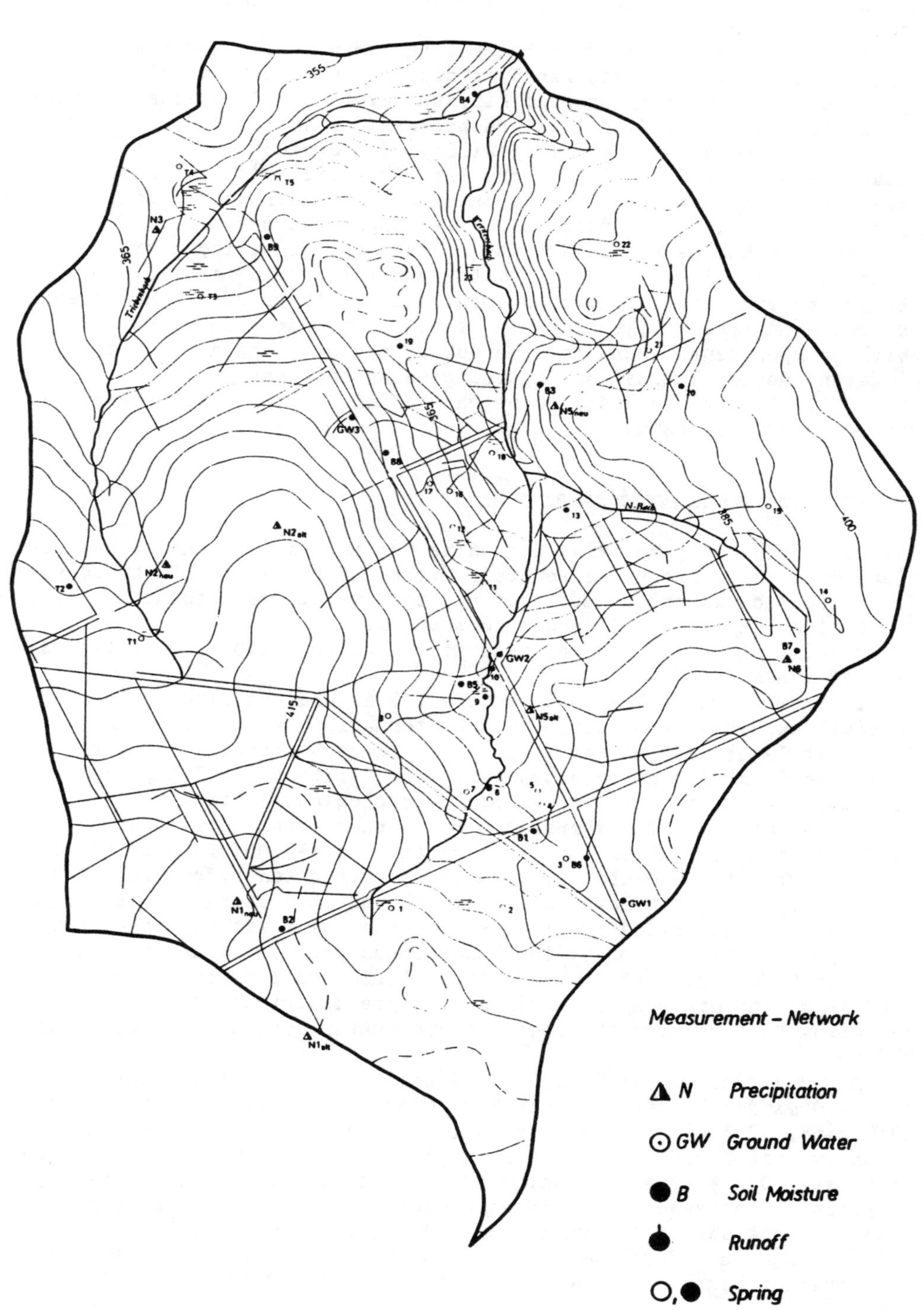

FIG. 1 The Wernersbach basin.

stock is composed mainly by spruce with different ages and locally by deciduous trees.

In the basin are two main brooks, the Wernersbach and the Triebenbach. Additionally the watershed is drained by an artificial dense system of ditches. The observed minimum, average and maximum of runoff amount to 0.4 l s^{-1}, 37.4 l s^{-1} respectively 6540 l s^{-1}.

In order to observe the variability of hydrologic processes a measuring network (Fig. 1) was created. The soil moisture measuring points (9 stations) are situated on sites with characteristical behavior, reflecting very different conditions in the basin . They are discussed in the next chapter. The measurement of spring outflow and discharge (17 points) as well as the runoff recording at the gauge station provide the information about the runoff process. The network is completed by six raingauges and three groundwater level stations. Further experimental work is done during periods, characterized by different meteorological and hydrological conditions, in form of a special field work in order to watch the various temporal and spatial reactions of the basin.

THE SOIL WATER DYNAMICS OF PARTIAL AREAS

The soil physical properties determine the relation of the main functions of soil to store and to drain water. If the slope of the considered location is taken into account, then we obtain information about kind and amount of runoff components.

We will discuss these relationships with the help of four typical partial areas.

B 2 - no runoff: The soil profile B 2 is characterized by only vertical exchange of moisture without formation of flow components. The first layer (150 mm thickness) is a humus horizon. The second layer consists of a homogeneous compressed silty soil (5 % gravel, 18 % sand, 69 % silt, 8 % clay) of the geological initial material sandstone (Fig. 2). The comparison of storage parameters (porosity 44 % per volume, moisture by field capacity 34 %, moisture by wilting point 20 %) with conductivity parameters (saturated hydraulic conductivity 9 10^{-7} m s^{-1}) shows poor dynamics and good storage properties which are characterized by slow percolation and moisture extraction by evapotranspiration only. The homogeneous profile structure and the slope of 0.06 % prevent the formation of flow components. Both the profile of the minimum and maximum moisture distribution measured till now allow to recognize the begin of back-water horizon in a depth of 850 mm.

B 8 - interflow: The profile B 8 shows a well rooted A-horizon (0 - 100 mm depth) over an extremly compressed loamy silt (8 % gravel, 23 % sand, 57 % silt, 12 % clay) which is followed by a consolidated porphyry grit-horizon from 800 mm depth on. The low storage parameters (porosity 38 %; field capacity 32 %; wilting point 14 %) caused by compression decrease the storaged amount of moisture. The extreme change of the saturated hydraulic conductivity from 5 10^{-4} m s^{-1} to 6 10^{-7} m s^{-1} in a depth of 150 mm in connection with great slope of 16 % characterizes this location as typical for formation of interflow.

B 4 - surface flow: The locatio B 4 (Fig. 3) is situated in a variable saturation area. A great part of skeleton (72 % skeleton, 19 %

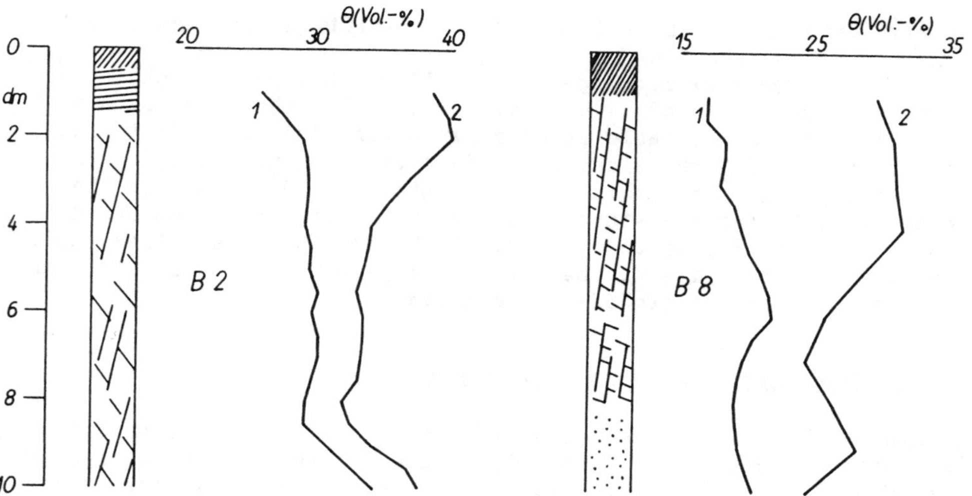

FIG. 2 Soil profile and soil moisture of sites B2 and B8. The region between curves 1 and 2 indicates the natural fluctuation.

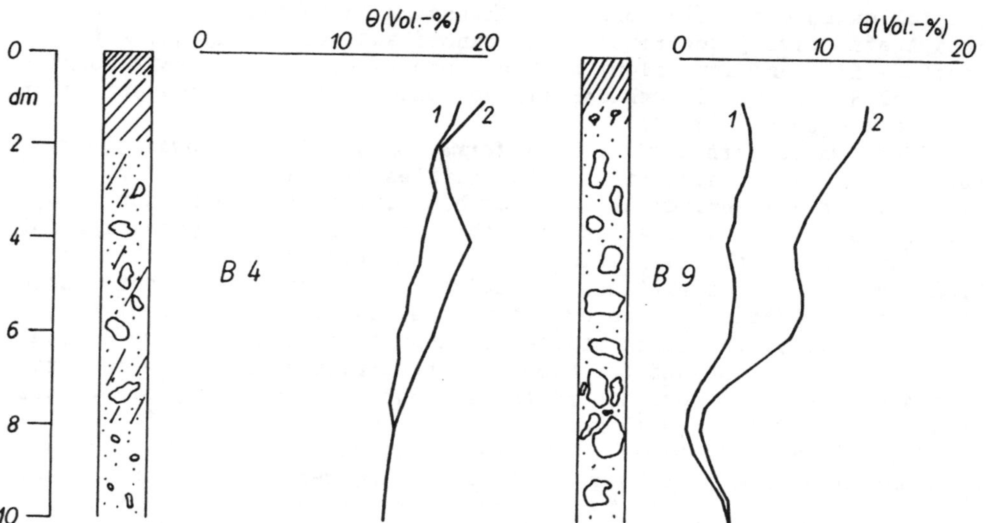

FIG. 3 Soil profile and soil moisture of sites B4 and B9. The region between curves 1 and 2 indicates the natural fluctuation.

sand, 7 % silt, 2 % clay) causes small storage parameters (porosity 21 %, field capacity 6%). The deep position and the small slope (less than 1 %) in the flood land lead to small differences between minimum and maximum moisture distribution with an average of 2 % per volume. Even under very dry conditions an input of about 14 mm moisture and low rain intensities are sufficient for saturation, consequently for formation of surface flow.

B 9 - groundwater recharge: The still greater part of skeleton (92 % skeleton, 3 % sand, 4 % silt, 1 % clay) of the location B 9 (Fig. 3) causes neglectable storage parameters (porosity 15 %, field capacity 5 %) and high values of conductivity (saturated hydraulic conductivity 1 10^{-5} m s^{-1} in the soil matrix, 1 10^{-2} m s^{-1} in the macropores). This small storage is also reflected in the measured moisture variability up today (Fig. 3). Because of this extreme soil properties and in spite of the extreme slope (32 %) this location is a subarea of complete groundwater recharge.

PARTIAL AREA CONTRIBUTIONS TO STORM RUNOFF

The discussed effect on subareas are summarized in the runoff hydrograph of the whole basin. With help of special methods for analyzing of this hydrograph (Schwarze, 1985) it is possible to isolate single flow components, however, without information about their areas of formation. Knowledge can be received only by investigations of the process variability in the basin.

The first step on this way consists in the localization of subareas on which quickflow is formed dependent on the site propereties, on moisture conditions in the basin and on precipitation features. In the following considerations we will use as an auxiliary value the area A effectively contributing to runoff and delivering quick flow (surface flow and interflow) of the storm event with a runoff coefficient of 80 %. The discussion will be concentrated on three groups of the storm events (Fig. 4).

Flood waves with small peakes formed on quickly responding wet subareas (group 1, e.g. sites with profiles similar to B 4) are caused after dry periods by rains of high intensity, short duration and of small amounts. The rising limb of the discharge hydrograph follows immidiately the rain (Fig. 4), so that the areas of runoff formation can be only identified with saturated subareas in the surrounding of the gauge station at the outlet of the basin. The runoff of this subareas reaches the gauge station time-shifted in dependence on the moment of saturation and the time of concentration. Both the investigation of the flood records and the estimation from maps yield values of A of about 0.1 ... 0.15 km^2.

Flood waves with great peakes caused by rains as result of convective and advective processes (group 2) are forced by great amounts and high intensities of rain. The synoptic conditions of formation of floods within this group as well as within group 3 are analyzed by Miegel <u>et al.</u> (1990). Events of group 2 are characterized by relatively steep waves favoured by wet conditions in the basin. Wet conditions and high intensities together with poor infiltration conditions (like B 4) or with compressed horizon (like B 8) are influencing factors contributing to an increasing part of the area on which the quick flow is formed. In dependence on moisture conditions and on precipitation parameters values of A up to 2.0 km^2 are reached during such storm events.

Extreme durations of advective storm events lead also to floods with great peaks (group 3). These events may be connected with the largest areas contributing to quick flow (A up to 3.5 km^2). The high

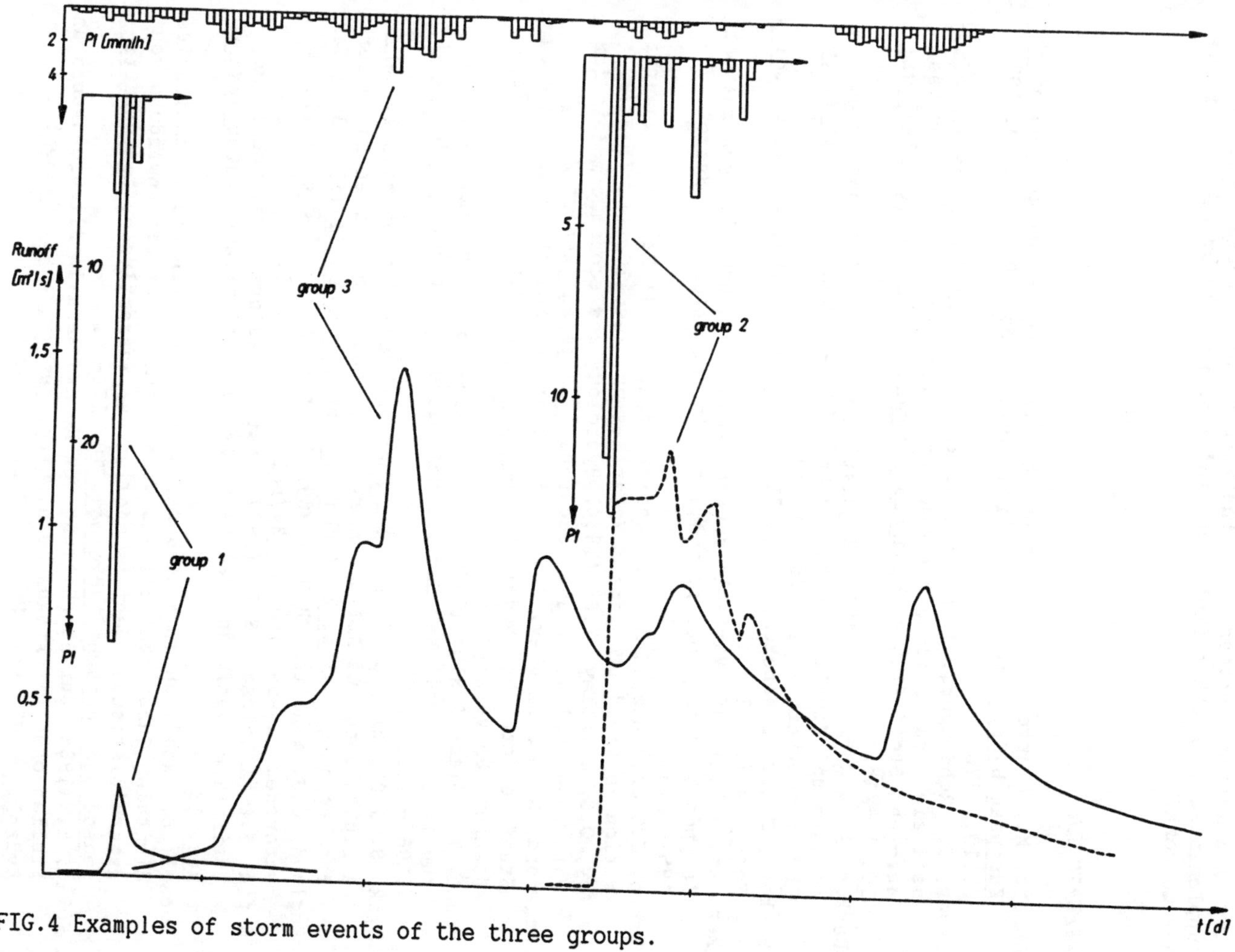

FIG.4 Examples of storm events of the three groups.

soil moisture stored in the basin during such events causes a very similar pattern of the rain record and the discharge hydrograph. Here such subareas, which are characterized by good infiltration conditions, by an unhindered hydraulic connection to the groundwater (B 9) and by very poor slopes (B 2) do not participate in the formation of surface flow and interflow.

These presented first results, concerning the horizontal variability of hydrologic processes in the Wernersbach watershed should be supplemented by further field work and measurements by the aid of the new network.

REFERENCES

Abbott, M., Clarke, R. & Preismann, A. (1978) Logistics and use of the European Hydrologic System. Proc. Int. Sympos. Pisa, 24.10. 1978 - 26.10. 1978.

Bauer, J., Rohdenburg, H. & Bork, H.-R. (1985) Ein digitales Reliefmodell als Voraussetzung für ein deterministisches Modell der Wasser- und Stoff-Flüsse. Landschaftsgenese und Landschaftsökologie 10, 1 - 15.

Becker, A. & Gurtz, J. (1981) Simulation und Vorhersage des Durchflusses und Stofftransports in Oberflächengewässern. Nationalkom. IHP, Sonderheft 2, 2 - 35, Berlin.

Beckett, P.H.T. & Webster, R. (1971) Soil variability: A review. Soils Fert. 34 (1), 1 - 15.

Bernier, P.Y. (1985) Variable source areas and storm-flow generation: An update of the concept and a simulation effort. J. Hydrol. 79, 195 - 213.

Bruch, J.C.Jr., Lam, C.M. & Simundick, T.M. (1974) Parameter identification in field problems. Water Resour. Res. 10 (1), 73 - 79.

Carvey, O.G. & Croley, T.E. (1984) Hydrology and economic models for watershed evaluation and research. IIHR Techn. Report No. 277.

Crawford, N.H. & Linsley, R.K. (1966) Digital simulation in hydrology-Stanford Watershed Model IV. Techn. Rep. 39, Dept. of Civ. Eng., Stanford University.

Dunne, T., Black & R.D. (1970) Partial area contributions to storm runoff in a small New England watershed. Water Resour. Res. 6, 1296 - 1311.

Dyck, S. & Peschke, G. (1982) Das komplexe Wechselverhältnis zwischen Abflußbildung und Abflußkonzentration und Alternativen zu seiner Beschreibung. Wiss. Z. Techn. Univers. Dresden 31 (5), 235 - 242.

England, C.B. & Holtan, H.N. (1969) Geomorphic grouping of soils in watershed engeneering. J. Hydrol. 7, 217 - 225.

Gupta, S.K. & Solomon, S.T. (1977) Distributed numerical model for estimating runoff and sediment discharge of rivers. Water Resour. Res. 13 (3).

Hensel, H., Rohdenburg, H. & Bork, H.-R. (1985) Ein dreidimensionales digitales Substratmodell als Voraussetzung für die Anwendung von deterministischen Gebietsmodellen der Wasserflüsse. Landschaftsgenese und Landschaftsökologie 10, 17 - 62.

Kölla, E. (1986) Zur Abschätzung von Hochwassern in Fließgewässern an Stellen ohne Direktmessungen. Mitt. Versuchsanst. Wasserb., Hydrol. u. Glaziol. Nr. 87, Zürich.

Mc Cuen, R.H., Rawls, W.J. & Brakensiek, D.L. (1981) Statistical analysis of the Brook-Corey and the Green-Amt-parameters across soil textures. Water Resour. Res. 17 (4), 1005 - 1013.

Miegel, K., Peschke, G., Etzenberg, Ch. & Hebentanz, H. (1990) Zur synoptischen Analyse hydrologisch relevanter Starkregenereignisse. Wiss. Z. Techn. Univers. Dresden 39 (im Druck).

Nielsen, D.R., Biggar, J.W. & Erh, K.T. (1973) Spatial variability of field-measured soil-water properties. Hilgardia 42, 215 - 259.

Peck, A.J., Luxmoore, R.J. & Stolzy, J.L. (1977) Effects of spatial variability of soil hydraulic properties in water budget modeling. Water Resour. Res. 13 (2), 348 - 354.

Peschke, G. (1979) Strukturanalyse des Zweistufenmodells zur Berechnung der Infiltration. Wiss. Z. Techn. Univers. Dresden 28 (6), 1603 - 1607.

Peschke, G. (1987a) Die Bedeutung von Regen- und Bodeneigenschaften für die Entstehung von Oberflächen- und hypodermischen Abfluß. Wiss. Z. Techn. Univers. Dresden 36 (6), 183 -186.

Peschke, G. (1987b) Soil moisture and runoff components from a physically founded approach. Acta hydrophys. 31 (3/4), 191 - 205.

Ragan, R.M. (1968) An experimental investigation of partial area contributions. IAHS Publ. 76, 241 - 249.

Reynolds, S.G. (1974) A note on the relationship between size of area and soil moisture variability. J. Hydrol. 22, 71 - 76.

Richter, K.-G. (1987) Vergleichende hydrologische Untersuchungen des Hochwasserablaufes in Testeinzugsgebieten mit unterschiedlicher Bebauungsdichte. Schriftenreihe Hydrologie/Wasserwirtschaft Ruhr-Univers. Bochum 6.

Schilling, W. & Harms, W. (1983) Räumliche Variabilität von Niederschlag und Abflußbildung-Auswirkungen auf den Abflußprozess. DGM 27 (2), 52 - 62.

Schwarze, R. (1985) Gegliederte Analyse und Synthese des Niederschlags-Abfluß-Prozesses von Einzugsgebieten. Techn. Univers. Dresden, Fak. f. Bau-, Wasser- und Forstwesen, Diss. A.

Sharma, M.L., Gander, G.A. & Hunt, C.G. (1980) Spatial variability of infiltration in a watershed. J. Hydrol. 45, 101 - 122.

Tricker, A.S. (1981) Spatial and temporal patterns of infiltration. J. Hydrol. 49, 261 -277.

Hydrology in Mountainous Regions. I - Hydrological Measurements; the Water Cycle
(Proceedings of two Lausanne Symposia, August 1990). IAHS Publ. no. 193, 1990.

Evaluation of evaporation models for alpine tundra, British Columbia, Canada

I. R. SAUNDERS & W. G. BAILEY
Department of Geography, Simon Fraser University, Burnaby, British Columbia, Canada V5A 1S6

ABSTRACT At an alpine tundra site in British Columbia, Canada, hourly latent heat flux density (Q_E) was measured using the Bowen ratio – energy budget (BREB) method, the aerodynamic equation, the Priestley–Taylor model and by treating Q_E as a residual in the energy budget equation. Reliable daytime evaporation measurements were obtained from all four methods. The aerodynamic equation was the most sensitive to errors in input data. The residual method worked well and has potential for operational applications. The Priestley–Taylor model worked well for wet conditions, but problems with the specification of surface moisture availability rendered this method impractical for dry conditions. Future research directed towards refining the residual and Priestley–Taylor approaches to evaporation determination in alpine terrain would be invaluable.

NOTATION

c_p	= specific heat of air at constant pressure	$J\,kg^{-1}K^{-1}$
e	= vapour pressure	Pa
e^*	= saturation vapour pressure	Pa
E	= evaporation	mm
K_V	= eddy diffusivity for water vapour	$m^{-2}s^{-1}$
k	= von Karman's constant	dimensionless
L_v	= latent heat of vapourization of water	$J\,kg^{-1}$
p	= precipitation	mm
Q^*	= net radiation flux density	$W\,m^{-2}$
Q_E	= latent heat flux density	$W\,m^{-2}$
$Q_{E(BR)}$	= Q_E measured with BREB method	$W\,m^{-2}$
$Q_{E(AE)}$	= Q_E measured with aerodynamic equation	$W\,m^{-2}$
Q_{ES}	= equilibrium latent heat flux density	$W\,m^{-2}$
$Q_{E(RE)}$	= Q_E measured with residual method	$W\,m^{-2}$
Q_G	= ground heat flux density	$W\,m^{-2}$
Q_H	= sensible heat flux density	$W\,m^{-2}$
S	= $\partial e^*/\partial T$	$Pa\,K^{-1}$
T	= air temperature	K
T'	= instantaneous deviation from $\overline{T}$	K
u	= horizontal wind speed	$m\,s^{-1}$
w	= vertical wind speed	$m\,s^{-1}$

w'	= instantaneous deviation from $\overline{w}$	$m s^{-1}$
z	= height above surface	m
α	= Priestley–Taylor parameter	dimensionless
β	= Bowen ratio	dimensionless
χ_w	= volumetric soil moisture content	dimensionless
γ	= psychrometric coefficient	$Pa K^{-1}$
Φ_M	= stability function for momentum	dimensionless
Φ_V	= stability function for vapour	dimensionless
ρ	= density of air	$kg m^{-3}$

INTRODUCTION

Physically based latent heat flux modelling procedures explicitly recognize atmospheric and surface controls, but their application to alpine (above treeline) environments has been very limited. The purpose of this study was to compare different physically based evaporation models for an alpine tundra in British Columbia, Canada.

Previous evaporation modelling in alpine tundra environments is limited to the lysimeter-based studies of LeDrew (1975), Isard & Belding (1989), and a one day experiment by Terjung *et al.* (1969). Other studies have described energy budgets from alpine tundra sites, but have not included detailed modelling results or evaluations of surface responses or controls.

THEORETICAL BACKGROUND

Latent heat flux densities were directly computed from the Bowen ratio – energy budget (BREB) method, the aerodynamic equation, the Priestley–Taylor model and as a residual in the energy budget equation. The latent heat flux density equates with evaporation as dictated by

$$Q_E = L_v E \tag{1}$$

The derivation of the BREB and aerodynamic formulae are widely known and need not be described in detail. Assuming all fluxes are positive when directed towards the surface, and *vice versa*, the energy budget may be defined as

$$Q^* + Q_G + Q_H + Q_E = 0 \tag{2}$$

The Bowen ratio is defined as the ratio between sensible and latent heat. If equation (2) is rearranged, then

$$Q_E = \frac{-(Q^* + Q_G)}{1 + \beta} \tag{3}$$

$$\beta = \gamma \frac{\Delta T}{\Delta e} \tag{4}$$

and the assumption is made that the eddy diffusivities for heat and vapour are equal (Dyer & Hicks, 1970).

If zero–plane displacement of the wind speed profile is assumed to be zero (valid for a simple tundra surface), then the aerodynamic equation can be written as (Thom, 1975)

$$Q_E = \frac{\rho c_p}{\gamma} k^2 \frac{\partial e}{\partial(\ln z)} \frac{\partial u}{\partial(\ln z)} (\Phi_M \Phi_V)^{-1} \tag{5}$$

where the Φ functions are introduced to account for non–neutral conditions and are derived from stability measurements (Webb, 1970; Dyer & Hicks, 1970).

Priestley & Taylor (1972) modelled daily potential evaporation as a function of available energy

$$Q_E = \alpha Q_{ES} = -\alpha \frac{S}{S+\gamma} (Q^* + Q_G) \tag{6}$$

where Q_{ES} is the equilibrium evaporation and the parameter α is equal to 1.26 for a diversity of natural surfaces with non–limiting moisture conditions. Once dessication occurs, $\alpha \rightarrow 0$.

If equation (1) is rearranged to isolate Q_E, then the evaporative flux can be found if the other three terms are known. The net radiation and ground heat flux densities were direct measurements. For this experiment, the eddy correlation method was used to measure sensible heat flux density

$$Q_H = -\rho c_p \, (\overline{w'T'}) \tag{7}$$

EXPERIMENTAL PROCEDURES

The study site for this experiment was at an elevation of 2350 m a.m.s.l. on Scout Mountain, in the Cascade Mountains of southern British Columbia. The site was a horizontal grass–sedge tundra developed on the patterned ground typical of the locale and of periglacial tundra in general. Measurements were taken during two field seasons totalling twelve months. The data set used in this paper was derived from snow–free periods during May–July 1987 and April–May 1988. The 1987 season was characterized by frequent light and moderate precipitation events with drying cycles of up to a week in length. The 1988 season was stormy, with persistent snow and rain storms, at times with surface saturation and small amounts of standing water.

Net radiation was measured with a Middleton CN–1 net pyrradiometer. Ground heat flux was measured with an array of five Thornthwaite flux plates buried at $z = -50$ mm and corrected for surface flux divergence. Sensible heat was measured with two Campbell Scientific CA27 sonic anemometers mounted at one metre and interrogated by a compatible Campbell Scientific 21X datalogger. Since this sonic anemometer includes a fragile fine–wire thermocouple and acoustic heads, it could only be used when the field site was supervised, and when no precipitation was falling. Vertical gradients of temperature, vapour pressure and wind speed were derived from four-level measurements of wet and dry bulb temperature from shielded, aspirated thermopiles, and sensitive cup anemometers. Precipitation was measured with three tipping-bucket raingauges. Except for the sonic anemometers, all instruments recorded data continuously on Campbell Scientific CR21 and 21X data aquisition systems. Volumetric soil moisture content was determined gravimetrically from samples taken at intervals of two to five days.

Night-time gradients of temperature and vapour pressure were too small to measure without large errors, and consequently all data considered in the intercomparisons are daytime. The frequent freezing of some or all of the wet bulbs, and the unreliable performance of the anemometers in stormy conditions, compromised the linearity of the vertical profiles, and were excluded from analysis.

RESULTS

The results are summarized in Table 1. Overall, the results were good. Either the aerodynamic or the residual method was capable of estimating hourly mean latent heat to within ±50 W m^{-2} of $Q_{E(BR)}$. Daily totals were within ±1.20 MJ m^{-2}d^{-1}. These represent accuracies of about ±0.54 mm h^{-1} or ±3.60 mm d^{-1} water loss. Hourly $Q_{E(RE)}$ was generally better than $Q_{E(AE)}$ in following the trends of $Q_{E(BR)}$, regardless of ambient weather conditions (Fig. 1).

The results from the Priestley-Taylor model indicated that α was not clearly related to soil moisture content, although the effect of the wet conditions in 1988 is clearly demonstrated by the higher values (Fig. 2). Evaporation rates were observed in the field to be large immediately following precipitation or melt events. At other times the surface dessicated quickly. Therefore, daily Q_{ES} data were stratified according to precipitation totals (Fig. 3). For days with ≥3 mm of rainfall a linear relation between $Q_{E(BR)}$ and Q_{ES} occured, with a regressed slope of 1.08. Dry day α values are exclusively less than 1.00, and the majority are between 0.50 and 0.80. The slope of the regression line through these points was 0.56. Days with 1 or 2 mm of rainfall showed considerable scatter.

DISCUSSION

The physically based methods used in this experiment gave evaporation measurements with accuracies better than those from lysimeters used in alpine tundra studies by LeDrew (1975) and Isard & Belding (1989). Physically based methods have the further advantages that they can be used with accuracy for short time scales, do not disturb the surface and probably give better areal measurements for tundra surfaces.

The good results from the residual method demonstrated the feasibility of determining evaporation without the logistical problems of maintaining lysimeters or vapour pressure measurements. The success of this method was undoubtedly due to the excellence of the eddy correlation measurements of sensible heat flux density. If Q_H could be reliably determined using instruments which are not as sensitive as the sonic anemometer employed here, then a useful operational means of estimating evaporation is available.

TABLE 1 Comparisons between $Q_{E(BR)}$, $Q_{E(AE)}$ and $Q_{E(RE)}$ for hourly mean values and daytime totals.

Observed	Modelled	n	r^2	s.e.	a	b	MAE	MBE	RMSE	d
Hourly Data										
$Q_{E(BR)}$	$Q_{E(AE)}$	239	0.64	44	−24	0.929	35	15	46	0.88
$Q_{E(BR)}$	$Q_{E(RE)}$	430	0.71	34	−46	0.650	36	−9	45	0.90
$Q_{E(AE)}$	$Q_{E(RE)}$	138	0.29	64	−63	0.680	54	−17	68	0.70
Daily Data										
$Q_{E(BR)}$	$Q_{E(AE)}$	19	0.65	1.07	−0.85	0.944	0.99	0.57	1.19	0.86
$Q_{E(BR)}$	$Q_{E(RE)}$	27	0.83	0.65	−0.04	0.918	0.63	−0.44	0.78	0.94
$Q_{E(AE)}$	$Q_{E(RE)}$	13	0.49	0.98	−2.02	0.711	0.96	−0.68	1.19	0.79

Coefficients of determination (r^2), constant (a), slope (b), and standard error of the mean (s.e.) of regression equations are all derived from SPSSX statistical program packages. Mean absolute error (MAE), mean bias error (MBE), root mean square error (RMSE) and index of agreement (d) are derived from the methods described by Willmott (1981). Units are dimensionless for b, r^2, and d, otherwise are $W m^{-2}$ for hourly data and $MJ m^{-2} d^{-1}$ for daily data.

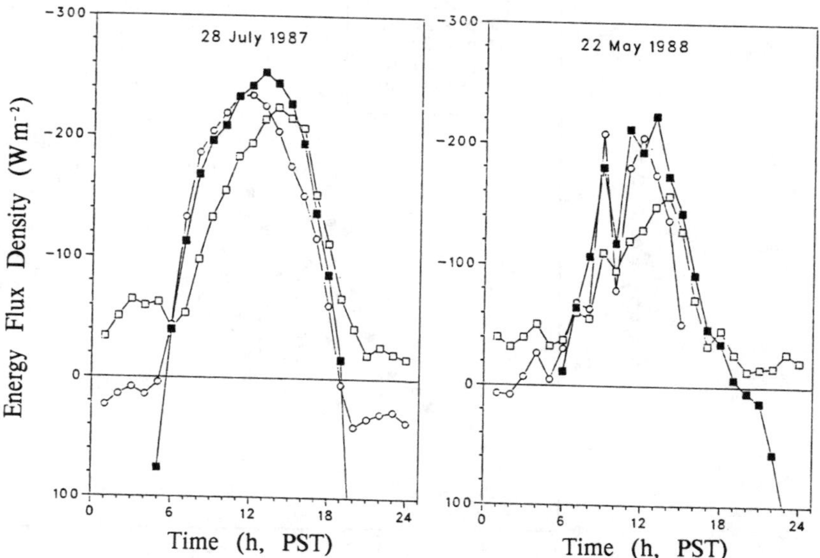

FIG. 1 Hourly mean $Q_{E(BR)}$ (solid squares), $Q_{E(AE)}$ (open squares) and $Q_{E(RE)}$ (open circles) for a cloudless day (28 July 1987) and a day with variable cloud conditions (22 May 1988).

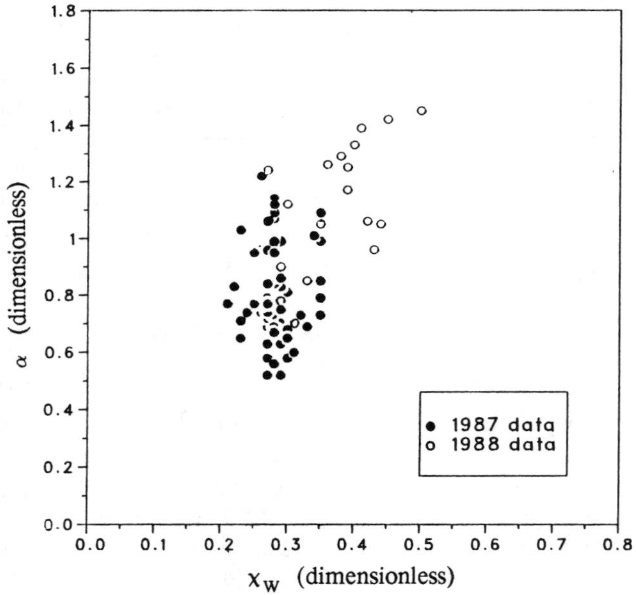

FIG. 2 Relationship between the Priestley–Taylor parameter (α) and volumetric soil moisture content (χ_W).

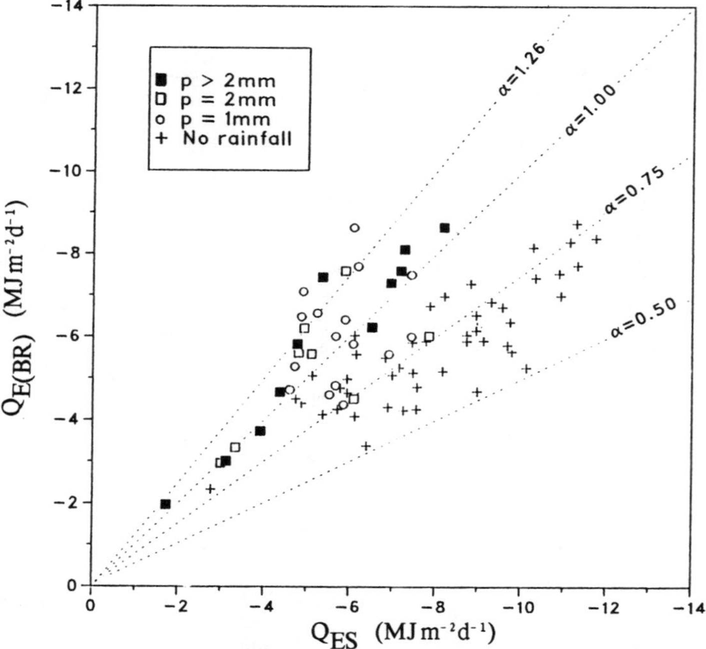

FIG. 3 Daytime totals of Q_{ES} and $Q_{E(BR)}$ stratified by precipitation. Dotted lines show values of the Priestley–Taylor parameter (α).

The Priestley–Taylor model merits further attention for alpine applications. Parameterization of α for dry conditions represents an important research goal for alpine evaporation modelling. For non-saturated conditions at Scout Mountain, α showed no obvious relation with soil moisture content. However, analysis of the coupling coefficient (McNaughton & Jarvis, 1983) showed relations with α and β which demonstrated that the tundra surface does indeed respond systematically to moisture availability through the physiological resistance to vapour transfer (Bowers & Bailey, 1989).

The problem is therefore the objective specification of soil moisture. This was inherently difficult at Scout Mountain because approximately 25% of the tundra surface consists of bare rock. From field observations it was apparent that, except for the periods immediately following precipitation, these rock surfaces dried and did not contribute further to the evaporative flux. This suggests that α should be scaled upwards and a new value, α', used, which represents the value of the parameter that a uniformly evaporating surface would have. The mean value of α at Scout Mountain was 0.93, which becomes $\alpha'=1.20$ when scaled to account for the 25% non-evaporating surface area. This is close to the potential rate, and suggests that the dessication observed in alpine tundra (Bowers & Bailey, 1989) disguises the actual evaporative behaviour of the alpine plant canopy. Determination of the relative microscale heat and vapour fluxes of adjacent vegetated and bare rock surfaces would be of great value in understanding evaporation from mountainous regions.

FUTURE RESEARCH

Further research themes of value for evaporation modelling in alpine tundra environments include:

(a) simple and robust sensible heat models for use in residual methods;

(b) objective specification of surface moisture availability and identification of microscale evaporation sources;

(c) application of physically based evaporation models to complex terrain.

ACKNOWLEDGEMENTS We wish to thank the Natural Science and Engineering Research Council of Canada (Operating Grant A2614) and Simon Fraser University for financial support. Permission to conduct field research was granted by the British Columbia Ministry of the Environment and Parks. The cooperation of Cathedral Lakes Resort greatly facilitated the field work. Mr. J. Bowers assisted in the field. Mr. R. Squirrel assisted with the manuscript production.

REFERENCES

Bowers, J. D. & Bailey, W. G. (1989) Summer energy balance regimes for alpine tundra, Plateau Mountain, Alberta, Canada. Arc. Alp. Res. 21, 135–143.

Dyer, A. J. & Hicks, B. B. (1970) Flux–gradient relationships in the constant flux layer. Quart. J. Roy. Met. Soc. 96, 715–721.

Isard, S. A. & Belding, M. J. (1989) Evapotranspiration from the alpine tundra of Colorado, USA. Arc. Alp. Res. 21, 71–82.

LeDrew, E. F. (1975) The energy balance of a mid-latitude alpine site during the growing season, 1973. Arc. Alp. Res. 7, 301–314.

McNaughton, K. G. & Jarvis, P. G. (1983) Predicting effetcs of vegetation changes on transpiration and evaporation. In: Kozlowski, T. T. (ed.) Water Deficits and Plant Growth, Vol. VII, 1–47, Academic Press, New York.

Priestley, C. H. B. & Taylor, R. J. (1972) On the assessment of surface heat flux and evaporation using large-scale parameters. Mon. Weath. Rev. 100, 81–92.

Terjung, W. H., Kickert, R. N., Potter, G. L. & Swarts, S. W. (1969) Energy and moisture balances of an alpine tundra in mid-July. Arc. Alp. Res. 1, 247–266.

Thom, A. S. (1975) Momentum, mass and heat exchange of plant communities. In: Monteith, J. L. (ed.) Vegetation and the Atmosphere. Vol. I, 57–109, Academic Press, London.

Webb, E. K. (1970) Profile relationships: the log-linear range, and extension to strong stability. Quart. J. Roy. Met. Soc. 96, 67–90.

Willmott, C. J. (1981) On the validation of models. Phys. Geog. 7, 301–314.

Hydrology in Mountainous Regions. I - Hydrological Measurements; the Water Cycle
(Proceedings of two Lausanne Symposia, August 1990). IAHS Publ. no. 193, 1990.

A lysimeter for the measurement of evaporation from high altitude grass

I.R.WRIGHT
Institute of Hydrology, Wallingford, Oxon, OX10 8BB, U.K.

ABSTRACT The design of a lysimeter to measure evaporation in remote regions is described and results of its use as part of a grassland catchment study in the Highlands of Scotland are presented. Direct measurements of evaporation using two such lysimeters show that the Penman equation overestimates the total evaporation from the grass for the early part of the year. It is concluded that for these upland areas modifications to the Penman estimate of evaporation are required to account for the responses of the vegetation to the upland climate.

INTRODUCTION

High altitude grassland is one of the principle vegetation types covering the catchments of impounding reservoirs in Britain. This grassland has a distinctive annual growth cycle, yet little is known about its seasonal water use. For many years, evaporation from grassland in Britain has been estimated using the Penman equation (Penman 1948), which makes the assumption that the vegetation is able to transpire freely: this assumption is not always valid. Whereas the Penman potential rate of evaporation is a satisfactory estimate of water loss for most grassland in Britain (Monteith 1973), at higher altitudes, say over 450 m, temperatures are low enough to affect transpiration and growth, suppressing water use for many months of the year.

Notwithstanding the cold wet climate of the Central Highlands of Scotland, meteorological observations have shown that evaporative demand, as estimated by the Penman equation, can be substantial during the early part of the year (1.5 - 3.0 mm day^{-1} for April - May, Blackie 1987) and increase with altitude as a consequence of higher wind speeds and prolonged sunshine hours at higher altitudes (Blackie 1987, Johnson 1985). It is inevitable that the Penman equation will fail to predict the actual evaporation during those parts of the year when evaporative demand is high and the vegetation is dormant.

The lysimeters described in this paper were designed and installed to investigate the process of evaporation from high altitude grassland and the performance of the Penman estimate of evaporation in an upland environment. Also, the lysimeters were located to complement an upland catchment experiment in the Highlands of Scotland by providing long term measurements of evaporation loss from the grassland at the top of the catchments (Blackie 1987) . The design of the lysimeters addresses the problems of a remote site, the need for continuous measurements, a deep rooted vegetation and a soil which periodically has a shallow water table. No attempt was made to continue measurements during periods of snowfall or subzero temperatures.

BACKGROUND TO LYSIMETRY

For three centuries lysimeters have been designed in many different forms to meet the specific demands of a wide range of ground water investigations. In earlier years, when technology was more limiting, many successful experiments were conducted into the quality and quantity of percolated soil water as illustrated in the extensive review by Kohnke et al. (1940). More recently, extensive research in North America has improved the accuracy of lysimeters by the use of better weighing systems and, more importantly, investigating the causes of error introduced by presence of the lysimeter and ensuring that the sample is fully representative of the surrounding soil. The first accurately weighed and replicated monoliths (undisturbed soil blocks) were installed at Coshocton, Ohio in 1937 (Harrold and Dreibelbis, 1958). The "Coshocton" lysimeters and the comprehensive installation at Davies, California, using back-filled soil blocks of up to 6.1 m in diameter, have contributed much to lysimeter design by investigating the influences of gap size, heat movement and condensation around the sample, wind drag and soil tension control. Notable research into the performance of smaller lysimeters has been reported by McIlroy and Angus (1963), Libby and Nixon (1963) and Dugas and Bland (1989).

EXPERIMENTAL SITE AND INSTRUMENTATION

The lysimeters were located at an altitude of 595 m above mean sea level (AMSL) in the central Highlands of Scotland, 45 km north-west of Stirling, Perthshire (56^{0} 22′ N, 4^{0} 25′ W). Local peak altitudes are typically 900 m AMSL. Although the terrain surrounding the lysimeter site has a 25^{0} slope to the west, the underlying geology has led to the formation of small level terraces by the action of peat deposition. This formation provides a convenient peat depth and level surface for lysimeter installation in a mountainous region having generally shallow soils and where lysimetry would otherwise be very difficult.

The predominant vegetation, which is above the local tree line, is perennial grasses (Festuca ovina and Nardus stricta), marsh plants (Carex and Juncus), and patches of heather (Calluna vulgaris) and bilberry (Vaccinium myrtillus). The soil is dense black peat, 200 mm to 1300 mm deep, over a shale bedrock. Most of the grass roots are in the top 100 mm of soil, but live roots penetrate to at least 400 mm depth. The soil surface is not easily identified; a vertical section of the top 100 mm would reveal a transition of organic material from live vegetation, through matted and decomposing vegetation to the organic peat soil. A backfilled lysimeter sample would not be possible with this soil profile.

Additional instrumentation to the lysimeters included an automatic weather station measuring total solar and net long-wave radiation, air temperature, wet bulb temperature, wind speed and direction, rainfall, soil temperature and soil heat flux. All data, including the signal from the lysimeter load-cells and drainage systems (see below) were recorded on solid-state loggers (Campbell Scientific USA). The loggers also controlled the logic associated with the pumped drainage systems.

Low current power for the load-cells and loggers was provided by a single solar panel for each application, ensuring electrical isolation. Power for the pump systems and all other high current applications was supplied at 12 volts by two 50 Watt wind generators.

DESIGN CRITERIA

Each lysimeter was designed and installed with regard to the following criteria,

(a) There should be no disturbance to the soil or vegetation enclosed by the lysimeter.
(b) There should be no disturbance to the soil or vegetation surrounding the lysimeter hole.
(c) The monolith of soil should be held in a water-tight container.
(d) The soil water status of the monolith should be maintained similar to that of the surrounding soil.
(e) The weighing mechanism should be capable of resolving weight changes equivalent to less than 0.5 mm of water.
(f) The experimental site should be powered by solar and/or wind energy.
(g) The lysimeters should be capable of reliable and accurate, short term (days) and long term measurements of water loss by evaporation.

To satisfy the first three of the above criteria, the soil monoliths were excavated from a similar location to that of the lysimeter sites and placed in a preconstructed water-tight container before being transported to the lysimeter site. In this way the monolith could be carefully cut without regard for the surrounding vegetation, and similarly the hole to receive the lysimeter could be dug without regard for the removed soil.

Within the limitations of cost and constructional difficulty, lysimeter surface area should be as large as possible to maximise sampling and minimise the affects of the surrounding gap. There are several recommendations for minimum lysimeter area for ground cover crops: 4 m^2 by Aboukhaled et al. (1982), 2 m^2 by Samie and Villele (1970). Lysimeter area must be larger for widely spaced row crops and can be smaller for smooth short crops and vegetation that grows to obscure the perimeter gap from the effects of abnormal radiation penetration, ventilation and aerodynamics. Aboukhaled et al. (1982) reported significant overestimates of evaporation from lysimeters of 2 m^2 and 0.25 m^2 when compared with a 5 m^2 lysimeter, yet in contrast to this, Dugas and Bland (1989) conclude that "properly used" lysimeters of 0.75m^2 and 0.18 m^2 were not significantly different in performance when compared to a 3 m^2 lysimeter.

The choice of lysimeter diameter in this study, giving a plan area of 0.5 m^2, was dominated by the available installation equipment. Given this constraint and a requirement to encompass the entire rooting depth, an estimated maximum weight of 450 kg permitted the use of a competitively priced weighing platform: a single 500 kg load-cell (Tedea (USA) model 1250, 600 mm x 600 mm) having a sensitivity of nominally 0.032 mV kg^{-1}. Excluding temperature effects on the weighing system, this gives a resolution of 0.2 mm water when used to measure weight changes. Temperature effects imposed a small diurnal drift in the amplification of the load-cell signal eliminating the possibility of measuring evaporation over a period of less than a day.

Due to the construction method used here (see below), the resultant perimeter gap of 20 mm, giving a gap ratio 11%, is larger than the recommended gap ratio of 5% (Aboukhaled et al. 1982). However, in view of the intended installation period of at least two years and the growth habit of the grass, this was considered to be acceptable once the grass had grown to obscure the gap. In reality, a more important consideration for the lysimeters considered here, was to keep the vegetative growth from bridging the gap and modifying the true surface area of the sample.

LYSIMETER CONSTRUCTION

Two lysimeters were installed on a level terrace 70 m by 30 m, each containing a "undisturbed" monolith of soil and vegetation sampled from a similar area in the vicinity. Each monolith was cut by pushing an aluminium cutting cylinder, 800 mm diameter and 650 mm deep, into the peat. This was achieved using a anchored structure, against which a hydraulic ram could be pushed. The surrounding soil was removed as the cylinder descended to eliminate excessive crushing of the spongy soil at the cutting edge. When the full depth of the monolith had been cut, a steel plate was forced beneath the cutting cylinder and the whole sample was then lifted and inverted for preparation of the base.

With the base of the sample accessible, 50 mm of soil was removed from the base and replaced with 25 mm of washed sand, a nylon gauze filter and a perforated aluminium base to allow percolation of clean water. A central 35 mm diameter access tube was then installed to accommodate a pumped drainage system. Finally, the monolith was reinverted onto a lifting frame and lowered into a water-tight aluminium container, see figure 1. Lifting was achieved using a threaded bar which was inserted down the central access hole and screwed into the lifting frame. The void created by the lifting frame served to equalise soil water potential over the base area of the monolith and provided a sediment trap to prevent gritty water entering the drainage pump.

The hole to receive each lysimeter was prepared with minimum disturbance to the surrounding vegetation by working from a raised walkway supported on short vertical poles. For each lysimeter a cylindrical aluminium hole liner was pushed manually into the peat as the soil was removed from inside. When the top of the liner was level with the soil surface, further soil was removed from the bottom of the hole until the bed-rock was exposed. A concrete foundation was then cast onto the bed-rock giving a flat upper surface to support a load-cell and the hole liner, and incorporating a central well from which water could be extracted to prevent flooding of the weighing system.

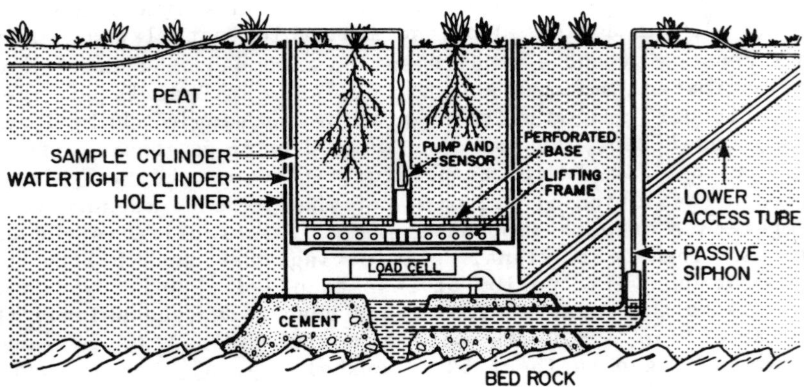

FIG. 1. A vertical cross-section of the lysimeter construction.

Various methods were tried for maintaining the level of the water in the lysimeter at the same level as the water in the surrounding soil. Initially, a sophisticated system of comparative pressure sensors and pumps dynamically kept the water level in the lysimeter never more than 50 mm above that of the surrounding soil. Although this system was accurate, it was prone to calibration drift and rather unreliable. However, observations of soil moisture tension in the root zone of the grass showed that this level of sophistication was not necessary and more reliable and simple systems were developed. The final system used three tiers of liquid level sensors controlling an electric submersible pump to keep the water level in the lysimeter matched to that of the surrounding soil to within three predetermined layers. When the water level in the lysimeter exceeded the control level the excess water, or drainage, was pumped to a tipping bucket flow meter and then to a calibrated storage vessel. It was not necessary to pump water into the lysimeter as prolonged dry periods are rare at this site and depression of the soil water level is soon restored by further rainfall.

ACCURACY

There are two ways in which evaporation from the lysimeters can be evaluated. Firstly, the evaporation can be resolved from the overall water balance, which is the difference between period rainfall recorded by storage raingauge, and the concurrent drainage collected in the final storage bins adjusted for the change in weight of the soil sample. This calculation gives the most reliable and accurate estimate of long term evaporation. Secondly, short term evaporation losses can be evaluated using the rainfall, drainage and weight changes recorded at 20 minute intervals. Assuming a well installed ground-level raingauge is accurate to 5% of the areal input and drainage is measured to 2% then wet period evaporation can be estimated to 15%. Dry period evaporation depends only on the weight changes measured by the load-cell and can be evaluated to +/- 0.5 mm, allowing for temperature distortion of the load-cell signal.

Aboukhaled _et al._ (1982) suggested that small lysimeters may overestimate actual evaporation due to enhanced ventilation and radiation penetration around the lysimeter periphery. Whereas these influences may be significant in the relatively sparse agricultural crops considered by Aboukhaled _et al._ (1982), any possible overestimate by the lysimeters described here is considered to be negligible considering the dense structure of the vegetation and the long installation period allowing full recovery from the disturbance of installation.

No attempt was made to measure evaporation during periods of snowfall or prolonged subzero temperatures. Although the pumped drainage system was able to withstand light frosts, allowing continuous water balance measurements from April to November, the raingauges were not considered accurate enough for snow measurement, especially when required to resolve the concurrent low rates of evaporation.

RESULTS

Figure 2 shows the cumulative measurements of evaporation from the two monolith lysimeters from 24 March 1988 to 28 September 1988 together with the cumulative Penman estimate of evaporation. Total evaporation for the

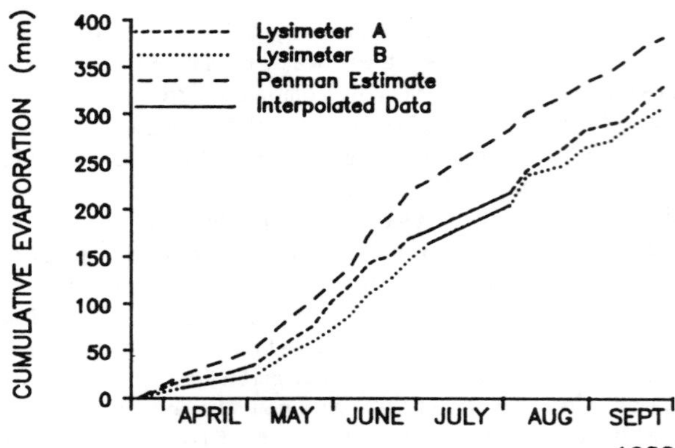

FIG. 2. Cumulative evaporation from upland grass measured by the two lysimeters together with the cumulative Penman potential evaporation for the period 24/3/88 - 21/9/88.

188 day period was measured as 330 mm and 308 mm for lysimeters A and B respectively compared to 397 mm estimated by the Penman equation.

Figure 3 shows the change in mean measured evaporation expressed as a ratio of the Penman estimate of evaporation for the individual periods. Although more detailed data are available from the load-cells these measurements represent the most accurately monitored water balance using volumetric measurements with an adjustment for changes in water storage.

Changes in the live biomass composition for 1987 and 1988 are shown in figure 4. Biomass composition is expressed as the ratio, by weight, of live vegetation to the total biomass. The error bars are an indication of the possible difference between the population mean and the sample estimate of the mean live weight ratio.

DISCUSSION OF RESULTS

Notwithstanding the periods of interpolation in figure 2 necessitated by instrument failures, the performances of the two lysimeters are mutually consistent within the estimated 15% measurement error, and noticeably

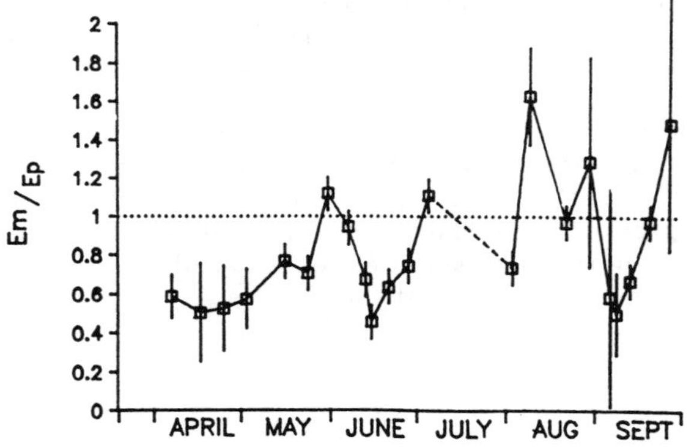

FIG. 3. Mean measured evaporation expressed as a ratio with respect to the Penman potential rate.

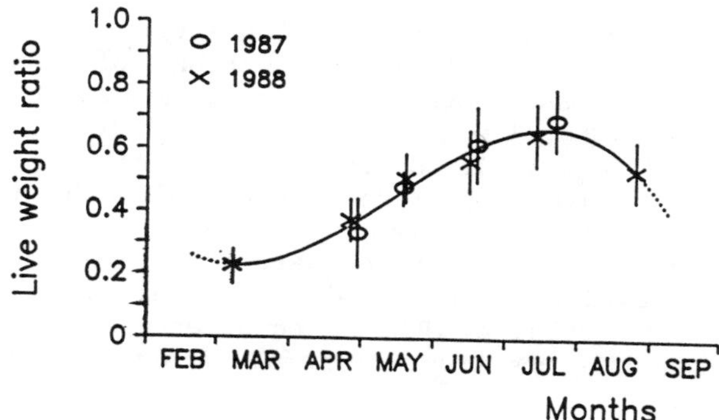

FIG. 4. The ratio of live grass to total biomass for the spring and summer of 1987 and 1988.

different to the cumulative Penman estimate of evaporation for the same period. These data show for the first time that the high altitude grass, typical of the Scottish uplands loses less water than would be estimated by the Penman equation.

When viewed in more detail (figure 3), these data suggest that period evaporation was mostly below the Penman rate at least until the end of June, having a mean ratio of 0.68 +/- 0.19. After this date the loses are not significantly different from the Penman rate, 0.98 +/- 0.32.

The primary influences to the overall shape of figure 3 have not yet been isolated. Both live weight ratio and daily mean temperature are relatively low during the early months of the year and can each suppress transpiration but through different processes. Live weight ratio indicates the proportion of grass that is photosynthetically active whereas low temperature, reduces the transpiration from the live grass. Superimposed upon these processes will be the evaporation of free water from the grass canopy during and after rainfall and the water loss from the underlying mat of decomposing vegetation. For some periods shown in figure 3, the small size of the error bars give confidence to the detailed shape of the figure and indicate the influence of the superimposed processes.

Using the meteorological data recorded by the automatic weather station in combination with the daily measurements of evaporation from the lysimeters, the next step will be to isolate the effects of the controlling processes using a physically based model.

CONCLUSIONS

The lysimeters described in this paper have satisfactorily met their design criteria in returning well replicated estimates of actual evaporation from a remote upland region. During the first complete year of data recovery several refinements have been implemented to ensure the continued return of reliable data: notably, the improved drainage system and the resultant maintenance of realistic soil moisture conditions within the lysimeter. The power requirements of the installation have been satisfactorily supplied by the wind generators and solar panels. For the year studied, the analysis of data has shown that evaporation rates from high altitude grassland are lower than the Penman estimate for the earlier months of the year, i.e., 68% for April - June 1988. During the summer months when a high proportion of the grass is photosynthetically active and ground temperatures are above the threshold for transpiration, then total water loss was much closer to the Penman rate indicating the remarkable performance of the original Penman equation. Further measurements and modelling will show whether abnormally wet periods will follow the same trend.

From this encouraging first year of data it is proposed to develope a simple physically based model of actual evaporation from high altitude grass, based upon the original Penman equation, and to include the modifying influences of temperature, rainfall and plant response.

ACKNOWLEDGMENTS

The author would like to acknowledge the financial support of the Scottish Consortium, also the Director of the Institute of Hydrology for permission to submit this paper. Invaluable assistance was provided by Dick Johnson and Mary Turner, both of the Institute of Hydrology, for site maintenance and logging software respectively.

REFERENCES

Aboukhaled, A. Alfaro, A. & Smith, M. (1982) Lysimeters. FAO Irrig. and Drain. Paper No. 39. Rome.

Blackie, J. R. (1987) The Balquhidder catchments, Scotland: the first four years. Transactions of the Royal Society of Edinburgh: Earth Sciences, 78, 227-239.

Dugas, W. A. & Bland. W. L. (1989) The Accuracy of Evaporation Measurements from Small Lysimeters. Agric. and For. Meteor., 46, 227-239.

Harrold, L. L. & Dreibelbis, F. R. (1958) Evaluation of agricultural hydrology by monolith lysimeters: 1945-1955. USDA Tech. Bull. 1179. Washington, DC.

Johnson, R. C. (1985) Mountain and Glen: climatic contrasts at Balquhidder. J. Meterol. 10, 105-108.

Kohnke, H., Dreibelbis, F. R. & Davidson, J. M. (1940) A survey and discussion of lysimeters and a bibliography on their construction and performance. USDA Misc. Publ. No. 374. Washington, DC.

Libby, F. J. & Nixon, P. R. (1963) A portable lysimeter adaptable to a unique range of site situations. Int. Assoc. Sci. Hydrol. Publ. no. 62, 153-158.

McIlroy, I. C. & Angus, D. E. (1963) The Aspendale multiple weighed installation. CSIRO Div. Meterol. Phys. Tech. Paper No. 14. Melbourne, Australia.

Monteith, J. L. (1973) Principles of environmental physics. Edward Arnold, London.

Penman, H. L. (1948) Natural evaporation from open water, bare soil and grass. Royal Society of London, Proc. Ser. A. 193, 120-146.

Samie, C. & de Villèle, O. (1970) Méthodes et techniques de mesure de l'evaporation et de l'evapotranspiration potentielle. Techniques d'étude de facteurs de la biosphère. INRA, France. 258-266.

Symposium on Improved Methods of Hydrological Measurements in Mountain Areas

Topic C:

Assessment of Snow and Glaciers as Water Balance and River Flow Components

Hydrology in Mountainous Regions. I - Hydrological Measurements; the Water Cycle
(Proceedings of two Lausanne Symposia, August 1990). IAHS Publ. no. 193, 1990.

Bilan hydrologique du bassin versant de la Massa et bilan de masse des glaciers d'Aletsch (Alpes bernoises, Suisse)

M.AELLEN & M.FUNK
Section de glaciologie, Laboratoires de recherches hydrauliques, hydrologiques et glaciologiques (VAW), Ecole polytechnique fédérale, ETH Zentrum, CH-8092 Zurich, Switzerland

ABSTRACT Grosser Aletschgletscher (87 km^2) is the most important glacier within the Massa river basin (195 km^2) and in the Alps. Its mass balance is computed usually as total or mean value for the whole glacierized part (128 km^2) of the river basin, using a fundamentally simple hydrological model applied in a time scale of monthly values for hydrological years (1.10.-30.9.) since 1922. The model, applied in a scale of daily values, provides insight into variability of seasonal water storage in a glacierized high mountain basin of the Swiss Alps in the 56 years from 1931 to 1987. Based on topographical surveys covering the basin as a whole in 1926/27 and 1957, volume change of Aletsch glaciers was determined to calibrate the hydrological balance model. Yearly glaciological measurements are carried out on stake networks in the firn area since 1942 and in the ablation area since 1950 on Grosser Aletschgletscher only. Despite an uneven distribution of the samples in time and in space, the glaciers mass balance is computed from these data by means of a deterministic mathematical model based on the distributive functions of both, glacier surface in 1957 and measured annual mass balance values, versus altitude. Results of a first attempt with a linear concept are presented for 30 hydrological years (1951-1980) in comparison with the results of the hydrological model.

INTRODUCTION

Dans cet article nous présentons avec deux méthodes différentes le bilan de masse des glaciers d'Aletsch, soit de la part englacée du bassin versant de la Massa. Ce bilan est déterminé habituellement en établissant le bilan hydrologique du bassin (Kasser, 1954). Dans le premier chapitre, le modèle hydrologique est présenté avec les résultats obtenus pour la période 1931-1987. Dans le second chapitre, le modèle glaciologique est présenté avec les résultats obtenus pour la période 1950-1980. Cette étude fait partie du programme d'observations à long terme, commun aux VAW et à la Commission des glaciers de l'Académie suisse des sciences naturelles (ASSN), destiné à saisir l'état actuel et les variations des glaciers suisses par des levés annuels.

Le bassin versant de la Massa, situé sur le versant sud (interne) du massif de la Jungfrau et dans la région culminante des chaines septentrionales des Alpes suisses, s'étend sur une surface F de 195 km^2, dont les deux tiers sont recouverts par les glaciers d'Aletsch. Le

Grand glacier d'Aletsch (87 km^2) est le plus important d'entre eux et le plus grand glacier des Alpes. L'étude concernant le bilan hydrologique du bassin versant se fonde sur les observations pluviométriques sur trois stations voisines (situées en dehors du bassin) et sur les mesures du débit de la Massa. L'étude concernant le bilan glaciaire se fonde sur les mesures glaciologiques effectuées sur le Grand glacier d'Aletsch. Les sites de mesure sur le glacier et les stations citées dans ses environs sont indiquées dans la figure 1.

Les observations pluviométriques sont effectuées par le Service météorologique national, depuis 1894 à Grindelwald (situé au nord) et depuis 1900 à Fiesch (au sud-est) et Kippel (à l'ouest). En 1974, la station de Kippel a été déplacée dans le village voisin Ried.

Les débits de la Massa sont enrégistrés par le Service hydrologique national depuis 1922 à la station limnigraphique de Massaboden, déplacée en 1964 à la nouvelle station de Blatten sur Naters.

Les mesures glaciologiques ont commencé en 1918 sur une seule balise d'accumulation installée au Jungfraujoch. Depuis 1942 elles sont effectuées par les VAW. Le nombre de balises a été augmenté jusqu'à 20 dans la zone d'accumulation et jusqu'à 50 (en général alignées sur l'axe médian) dans la zone d'ablation. Les sites de mesure les plus importants sont indiqués dans la figure 1 (un site comprend une ou plusieurs balises). Le nombre ainsi que les coordonnées des balises sur les sites 5-12 ont fortement varié dans la période considérée.

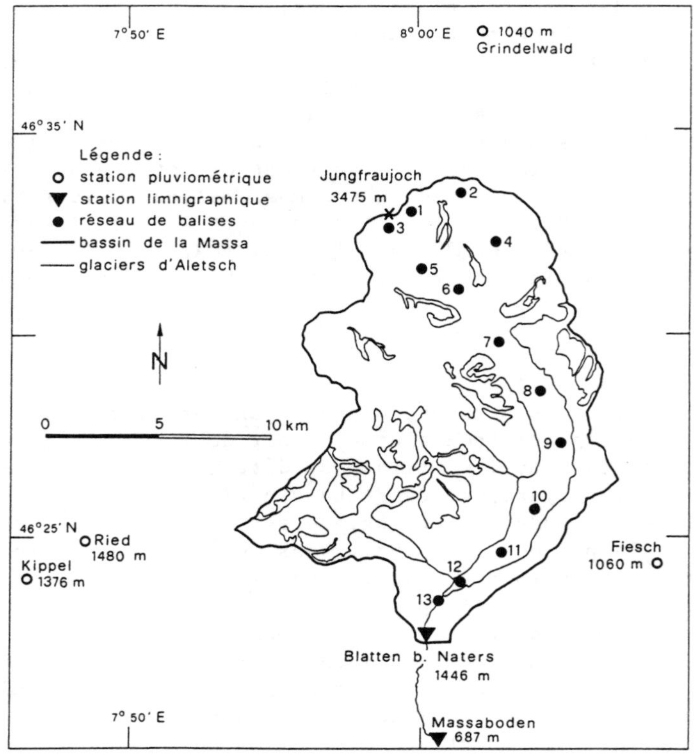

FIG. 1 Bassin versant de la Massa et glaciers d'Aletsch: Situation géographique.

L'Office fédéral de la topographie a restitué la topographie de la région d'Aletsch en 1926/27, dans le cadre des relevés pour la "Carte nationale de la Suisse" (1:50'000, feuille 264, Jungfrau), et en 1957, pour une carte spéciale "Aletschgletscher" (1:10'000, feuilles 1-4b) couvrant le bassin versant de la Massa (Kasser & Röthlisberger, 1966). Des relevés partiels ont été effectués en 1947, 1973 et 1986.

BILAN HYDROLOGIQUE DU BASSIN DE LA MASSA

Ce bilan est établi à l'échelle mensuelle pour les années hydrologiques à partir de 1921/22. Il est calculé à l'aide de valeurs reconstruites pour les années avant 1931, les observations pluviométriques et limnigraphiques étant incomplètes. Le modèle utilisé a été étalonné au moyen de la méthode géodésique sur la base des levés topographiques de 1926/27 et 1947 (Kasser, 1954) ainsi que 1957 (Kasser, 1967). Dans cette étude, nous avons appliqué ce modèle pour calculer les bilans journaliers du 1er octobre 1931 au 30 septembre 1987.

Modèle hydrologique

Le modèle adopté pour établir le bilan hydrologique du bassin de la Massa est défini par l'équation fondamentale qui décrit l'équilibre entre les apports et les pertes en eau:

$$P + D + E + dS = 0 \tag{1}$$

Les quatre termes de cette equation sont:

- P précipitations liquides ou solides
- D débits écoulés
- E évaporation ou condensation (admise invariable)
- dS variation des réserves en eau.

Les caractéristiques de ces termes sont décrites par Kasser (1954).

Résultats

Dans le cadre de cette étude, la quantité dS a été calculée pour chaque jour au moyen de l'équation (1). Pour établir le bilan hydrologique annuel du bassin de la Massa, elle a été cumulée sur les années hydrologiques (1er octobre-30 septembre) de la période 1931-1987. Le bilan de masse annuel b_h des glaciers d'Aletsch est calculé en réduisant la grandeur dS sur la surface englacée G du bassin:

$$b_h = dS \frac{F}{G} \tag{2}$$

La variation annuelle de G est déterminée sur la base des levés topographiques de 1926/27, 1957 et 1973 (Kasser & Aellen, 1967).

Les valeurs annuelles des termes P, D, et dS de l'équation (1) sont présentées pour les années hydrologiques 1932-1987 dans la figure 2 et dans le tableau 1, dans lequel la surface englacée G et le bilan de masse b_h calculé selon l'équation (2) sont également mentionnés.

Les variations journalières, cumulées sur une année hydrologique, sont présentées par des données statistiques (valeur moyenne, écarts-

TABLEAU 1 Bassin de la Massa - Bilans hydrologiques annuels 1931/32-1986/87: Composantes P (précipitations), D (débits), E (évaporation) et dS (variation des réserves en eau), surface englacée G (en km^2) et bilan de masse glaciaire b_h; hauteur des lames d'eau (en mm).

Année	P	D	E	dS	G	b_h	Année	P	D	E	dS	G	b_h
1932	1573	2076	210	-713	136.9	-1014	1960	2217	1828	210	179	129.6	268
1933	1665	1965	210	-510	136.8	-725	1961	2037	2017	210	-190	129.6	-285
1934	1628	2345	210	-927	136.6	-1321	1962	1986	2115	210	-339	129.5	-509
1935	2107	2240	210	-343	136.6	-489	1963	2210	2156	210	-156	129.5	-234
1936	2663	2089	210	364	136.4	519	1964	1597	2307	210	-920	129.4	-1384
1937	2110	2162	210	-262	136.1	-374	1965	2598	1667	210	721	129.2	1086
1938	1934	1891	210	-167	135.8	-239	1966	2345	1771	210	364	129.0	549
1939	1972	1918	210	-156	135.5	-224	1967	2381	2019	210	152	129.0	229
1940	2630	1847	210	573	135.1	825	1968	2303	1699	210	394	128.9	594
1941	2183	1868	210	105	134.7	151	1969	2198	1826	210	162	128.9	244
1942	1696	2614	210	-1128	134.7	-1630	1970	2229	2141	210	-122	128.8	-184
1943	1679	2603	210	-1134	134.2	-1644	1971	1840	2133	210	-503	128.7	-760
1944	1548	2595	210	-1257	133.8	-1829	1972	1685	1665	210	-190	128.7	-287
1945	2673	2660	210	-197	133.6	-287	1973	1964	2143	210	-389	128.6	-589
1946	2365	2273	210	-118	133.4	-172	1974	1941	1728	210	3	128.5	4
1947	1809	3297	210	-1698	132.9	-2487	1975	2296	1785	210	301	128.4	456
1948	2521	1936	210	375	132.8	549	1976	1603	1900	210	-507	128.4	-768
1949	1452	2531	210	-1289	132.6	-1892	1977	2842	1745	210	887	128.4	1345
1950	2077	2784	210	-917	132.5	-1347	1978	2896	1593	210	1093	128.3	1659
1951	2527	2274	210	43	132.2	63	1979	2173	1927	210	36	128.2	54
1952	2081	2413	210	-542	131.8	-800	1980	2844	1716	210	918	128.2	1394
1953	2174	2258	210	-294	131.2	-436	1981	2970	2014	210	746	128.1	1133
1954	2168	1992	210	-34	131.1	-50	1982	2718	2369	210	139	128.1	211
1955	2411	1880	210	321	130.3	479	1983	2396	2160	210	26	127.9	39
1956	2246	1833	210	203	130.2	303	1984	2315	1657	210	448	127.7	682
1957	1952	1817	210	-75	129.8	-112	1985	2192	1945	210	37	127.6	56
1958	2106	2389	210	-493	129.7	-740	1986	2349	2239	210	-100	127.6	-152
1959	1805	2370	210	-775	129.7	-1163	1987	2418	2171	210	37	127.5	56

types et valeurs extrêmes) calculées sur les 56 années observées dans la figure 3. Les précipitations sont présentées pour chacune des trois stations dans la figure 3a, qui montre une tendance croissante des quantités précipitées en direction du versant nord des Alpes, principalement dans la deuxième moitié de l'année hydrologique. Les débits sont présentés sous forme de l'indice du bassin (débits mesurés répartis sur la surface entière F du bassin versant) dans la figure 3b, qui montre le régime typique des bassins englacés (débits faibles et peu variables en hiver, forts et très variables en été). La variation saisonnière des réserves en eau résultant de l'équation (1), présentée dans la figure 3c, montre une variabilité bien plus forte que les précipitations et les débits. Le bilan déficitaire de l'année normale correspond à la tendence générale de décrue glaciaire durant ces 56 années observées.

Les bilans hydrologiques annuels sont résumés par la statistique du tableau 2. Les valeurs moyennes sont présentées dans la figure 4,

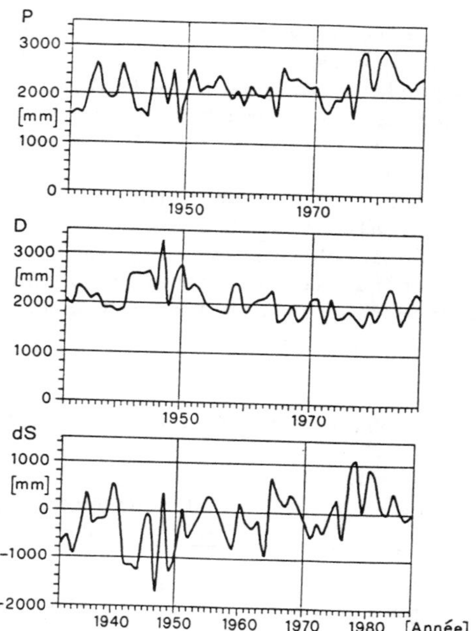

FIG. 2 Bassin de la Massa - Bilans hydrologiques 1931-1987 Variations annuelles de P (précipitations), D (débits) et dS (variation des réserves en eau), en hauteur d'eau (mm).

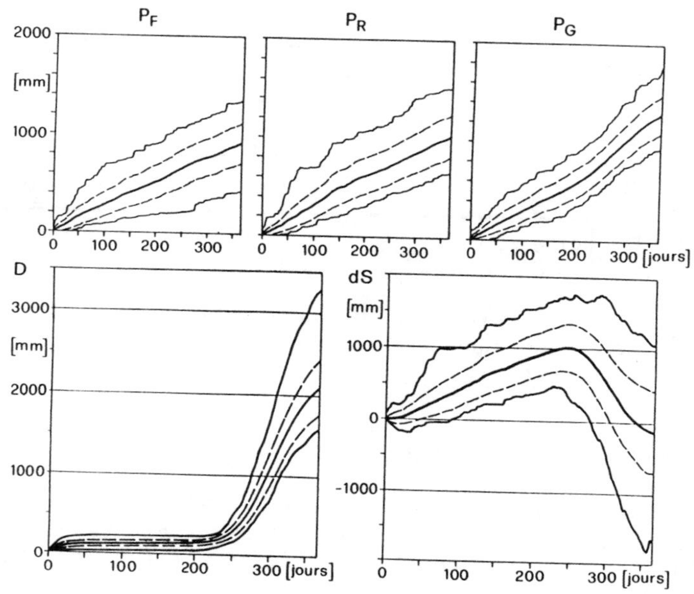

FIG. 3 Bassin de la Massa - Bilan hydrologique 1931-1987: Valeurs statistiques (moyennes, écarts-types et extrêmes) journalières cumulées sur l'année hydrologique, en hauteur d'eau (mm) des précipitations mesurées à Fiesch (P_F), Kippel/Ried (P_R) et Grindelwald (P_G), des débits (D) et de la variation des réserves en eau (dS).

qui montre clairement que l'ordre de grandeur de la valeur dS cherchée est d'un facteur 10 inférieur aux valeurs des précipitations P et des débits D. Ce facteur est cependant fortement variable d'une année à l'autre. En admettant que les erreurs commises sur P et D se situent dans l'ordre de grandeur de la valeur cherchée dS (moyenne), il faut reconnaitre que les résultats présentés ici ont une signification plutôt relative qu'absolue. Une interprétation climatologique fondée sur les variations des valeurs dS calculées et des composantes P et D observées est concevable, tant à l'échelle annuelle de l'évolution saisonnière qu'à l'échelle multiannuelle des tendences à long terme, si l'on admet que toutes les erreurs commises avec cette méthode restent plus ou moins constantes d'une année à l'autre.

TABLEAU 2 Bassin de la Massa - Bilans hydrologiques annuels 1931/32-1986/87: Données statistiques.

Variable		Moyenne	Ecart-type	Minimum (année)	Maximum (année)
P	Précipitations (mm)	2166	375.3	1452 (1949)	2970 (1981)
D	Débits (mm)	2096	332.0	1593 (1978)	3297 (1947)
dS	Variation des réserves (mm)	-140	582.6	-1698 (1947)	1093 (1978)
G	Surface englacée (km^2)	131.0	3.01	127.5 (1987)	136.9 (1932)
b_h	Bilan de masse (mm)	-200	861.2	-2487 (1947)	1659 (1978)

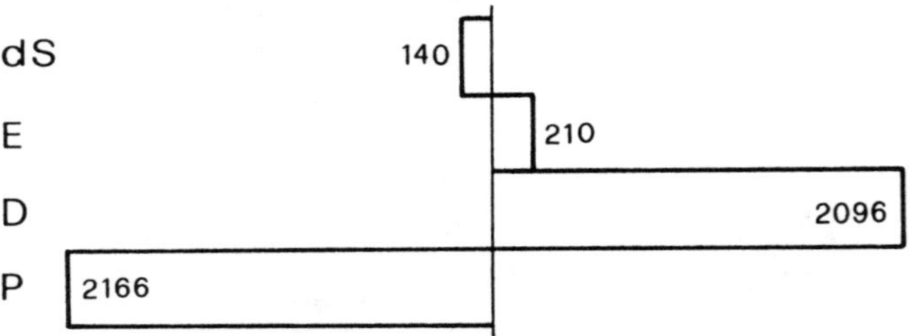

FIG. 4 Bassin de la Massa - Bilan hydrologique 1931-1987: Valeur moyenne des composantes P, D, E et dS, en hauteur d'eau (mm).

BILAN DE MASSE DES GLACIERS D'ALETSCH

Les données utilisées proviennent de l'axe médian du glacier (sites 1, 3, 5-12; v. fig. 1). Les valeurs mesurées ont été réduites à l'année hydrologique et classées par intervalles d'altitude (équidistants de 50 mètres).

Modèle glaciologique

Le modèle adopté pour établir le bilan de masse des glaciers d'Aletsch (ou de la part englacée du bassin versant de la Massa), est défini par le produit des vecteurs **b** et **G** qui décrivent les fonctions distributives par rapport à l'altitude des données de bilan **b** (accumulation ou ablation annuelles nettes) observées sur les balises et des données hypsométriques de la surface glaciaire **G** (tranches d'altitude équidistantes de 100 m) déterminées par les levés topographiques:

$$B_j = \{B_i\}_j = \{b_i\}_j \{G_i\}_j \qquad (3)$$

Les cinq termes de l'équation sont:

- B bilan de masse total (en tonnes de glace ou en m^3 d'eau)
- b bilan annuel net (hauteur d'eau, en m, cm ou mm)
- G surface glaciaire (en km^2)
- i indice des classes d'altitude (tranches de 100 m)
- j indice des unités temporelles (années hydrologiques).

Ce modèle a été décrit et discuté pour le cas du glacier de Gries par Aellen & Funk (1988).

Bilan moyen b_g

Répartie sur la surface englacée G, la quantité B est transformée en une valeur moyenne b_g (appelée bilan moyen net) pour l'ensemble des glaciers d'Aletsch:

$$b_g = \frac{B}{G} \qquad (4)$$

qui est comparable à la valeur b_h déterminée par le bilan hydrologique.

En principe, le vecteur $\{b_i\}_j$ de l'équation (3), comprenant les valeurs moyennes $\bar{b}_{i,j}$ des tranches d'altitude $\bar{H}_{i,j}$, est à déterminer pour chaque année j au moyen d'une régression linéaire des valeurs observées $b_{i,j}$ et $H_{i,j}$:

$$b_{i,j} = c_j + a_j H_{i,j} \qquad (5)$$

Les coéfficients de régression c_j et a_j sont des paramètres caractéristiques pour chaque année j. La solution de l'équation (5) quand $b_{i,j} = 0$ permet d'estimer l'altitude $H_{e,j}$ de la ligne d'équilibre:

$$H_{e,j} = -\frac{c_j}{a_j} \qquad (6)$$

En admettant des gradients invariables ($a_C = 0.5$, $a_A = 1.0$ m/hm) correspondant à une approximation des gradients moyens observés pour les zones respectives d'accumulation et d'ablation, les valeurs moyennes $\bar{b}_{i,j}$ sont estimées au moyen du modèle ainsi simplifié.

Surface englacée G

Le vecteur $\{G_i\}_j$ de l'équation (3) devrait être déterminé chaque année par des mensurations topographiques coûteuses. Tenant compte du fait que les variations de surface sont relativement faibles (diminution de 0.12 pourcent par an, en moyenne), les données hypsométriques du levé topographique en 1957 sont admises invariables.

Modèle hypsographique

Pour des valeurs données des gradients a_C et a_A, il est possible d'établir des courbes qui donnent une valeur probable du bilan annuel net $b_{g,j}$ en fonction de l'altitude $H_{e,j}$ de la ligne d'équilibre (Aellen & Funk, 1988). Dans cette étude, le bilan annuel $b_{g,j}$ est déterminé pour chaque année à partir de la valeur $H_{e,j}$ obtenue des valeurs observées sur les balises selon les équations (5) et (6).

Résultats

Les résultats obtenus pour les 30 années hydrologiques 1951-1980 au moyen du modèle hypsographique sont présentées par l'altitude $H_{e,j}$ de la ligne d'équilibre et le bilan annuel net $b_{g,j}$ dans le tableau 3, qui est résumé par une statistique dans le tableau 4.

Les données de bilan collectées sur les balises situées sur l'axe médian du Grand glacier d'Aletsch sont résumées dans la figure 5 pour les années hydrologiques 1951-1980. Dans la figure 5a, les valeurs mesurées durant ces 30 années observées sont présentées par les valeurs statistiques (moyennes, écarts-types, extrêmes) calculées sur $b_{i,j}$, en fonction de la valeur moyenne de $H_{i,j}$. La droite de régression est définie par les coéfficients c = -2318.16, a = 0.784 avec une variance expliquée par le modèle de 92 pourcent. Les valeurs annuelles de l'altitude $H_{e,j}$ de la ligne d'équilibre déterminées avec les équations (5)

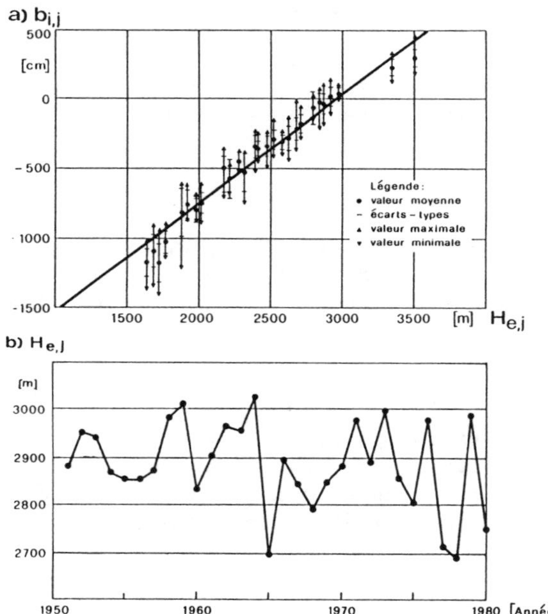

FIG. 5 Glaciers d'Aletsch - Bilan de masse annuel 1950/51-1979/80: Observations sur le réseau de balises
Fig. 5a) Bilans mesurés $b_{i,j}$ (valeurs statistiques, en cm) et altitude $H_{i,j}$ (moyenne, en m) des sites de mesure.
Fig. 5b) Altitude $H_{e,j}$ (en m) de la ligne d'équilibre.

et (6) à partir des valeurs mesurées (en épaisseur de glace, névé ou neige $b^*_{i,j}$) aux sites de mesures ($H_{i,j}$) sont présentées dans la figure 5b. Elles sont comparées aux valeurs $b_{h,j}$ obtenues du bilan hydrologique dans la figure 6. La droite de régression est définie par les coéfficients c = 2101.77, a = -0.729 avec une variance expliquée de 86 pourcent. Les résultats obtenus avec ce modèle correspondent assez bien aux résultats du modèle hydrologique.

TABLEAU 3 Glaciers d'Aletsch - Bilans de masse annuels 1950/51-1979/80 (modèle hypsographique): Altitude observée $H_{e,j}$ (en m) de la ligne d'équilibre et bilan moyen modélisé $b_{g,j}$ (en cm).

Année	$H_{e,j}$	$b_{g,j}$	Année	$H_{e,j}$	$b_{g,j}$	Année	$H_{e,j}$	$b_{g,j}$
1951	2878	20	1961	2904	3	1971	2980	-50
1952	2949	-27	1962	2966	-39	1972	2890	13
1953	2940	-20	1963	2956	-32	1973	2998	-61
1954	2867	28	1964	3024	-77	1974	2858	34
1955	2851	38	1965	2694	138	1975	2807	67
1956	2851	38	1966	2893	11	1976	2976	-46
1957	2870	26	1967	2841	46	1977	2711	128
1958	2985	-52	1968	2792	76	1978	2688	143
1959	3011	-71	1969	2848	41	1979	2988	-54
1960	2833	36	1970	2882	5	1980	2749	105

TABLEAU 4 Glaciers d'Aletsch - Bilans de masse annuels 1950/51-1979/80: Données statistiques.

Variable	Moyenne	Ecart-type	Minimum (année)		Maximum (année)	
$H_{e,j}$ Altitude ligne d'équilibre (m)	2883	93.5	2688	(1978)	3024	(1964)
$b_{g,j}$ Bilan de masse (cm)	16	61.5	-77	(1964)	143	(1978)

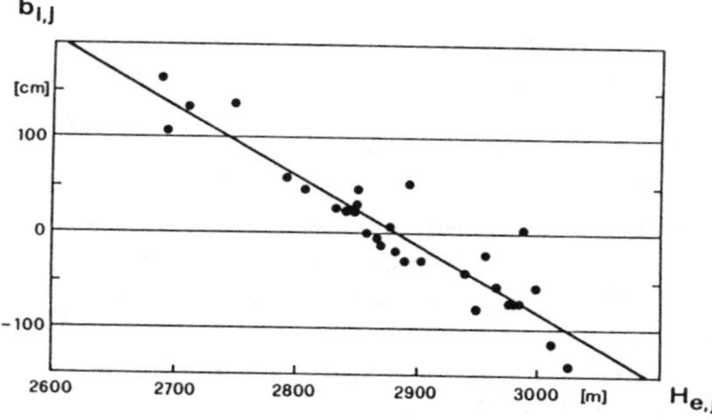

FIG. 6 Glaciers d'Aletsch - Bilan de masse annuel 1950/51-1979/80: Bilan annuel $b_{h,j}$ (cm) du modèle hydrologique, en fonction de l'altitude $H_{e,j}$ (m) de la ligne d'équilibre du modèle glaciologique.

CONCLUSIONS

Cette étude présente les résultats du bilan de masse obtenus pour le plus grand glacier des Alpes au moyen des deux méthodes classiques en glaciologie: la méthode hydrologique et la méthode glaciologique.

Les modèles utilisés ont été crée bien avant l'ère des ordinateurs électroniques et sont par conséquent très simples. Néanmoins, la comparaison des résultats obtenus avec les deux méthodes indépendentes est encourageante. Même si l'incertitude quant aux valeurs absolues due aux erreurs de mesure et à la modélisation reste considérable, les deux séries des bilans de masse ont les mêmes tendances de variations annuelle et pluriannuelle. L'analyse statistique à l'échelle journalière des données hydrologiques montre des différences notables des quantités précipitées aux stations utilisées et révèle ainsi que le bassin versant de la Massa est exposé aux régimes climatiques méridional et septentrional régnant sur les versants sud et nord des Alpes.

Une comparaison des résultats ici obtenus avec le bilan volumétrique basé sur les relevés topographique de 1957 et 1986 permettra d'éstimer la précision absolue des valeurs du bilan de masse calculées et le cas échéant, de modifier les paramètres du modèle hydrologique. Le modèle glaciologique peut être amélioré en considérant les variations annuelles des gradients ainsi qu'en tenant compte plus précisément de la variation non linéaire du bilan de masse avec l'altitude.

REMERCIMENTS Depuis l'installation du réseau de balises sur le Grand glacier d'Aletsch (il y a 40 à 50 ans) par l'équipe des ingénieurs MM. Robert Haefeli, André Roch et Peter Kasser, un grand nombre de personnes a présidé ou assisté aux campagnes glaciologiques annuelles. L'une des plus fidèles parmi tous ces montagnards professionels ou amateurs, Mme Gret Mühlemann, a participé aux campagnes du Jungfraujoch pendant une vingtaine d'années. Nombreuses institutions ont subventionné ce projet mené par les VAW, telles que les Services nationaux météorologique, hydrologique ou de la topographie, la Commission des glaciers de l'ASSN, la Station scientifique du Jungfraujoch et autres, auxquelles les auteurs sont redevables pour toutes sortes d'appuis efficaces.

REFERENCES

Aellen, M. & Funk, M. (1988) Massenbilanz des Griesgletschers von 1961 bis 1986. Vergleich verschiedener Bestimmungsverfahren. Mitt. der VAW/ETH Zürich Nr. 94. Festschrift Hans Röthlisberger, 9-50.

Kasser, P. (1954) Sur le bilan hydrologique des bassins glaciaires avec application au Grand glacier d'Aletsch. Publication No. 39 AIHS, Assemblée générale de Rome, tome IV, 331-350.

Kasser, P. (1967) Fluctuations of glaciers 1959-1965. A contribution to the International Hydrological Decade. IASH (ICSI) - UNESCO, 138 p., (Table 11, p. 70: Aletsch glaciers/Switzerland).

Kasser, P. & Röthlisberger, H. (1966) Some problems of glacier mapping experienced with the 1:10 000 map of the Aletsch Glacier. Canadian Journal of Earth Sciencies, Vol. 3, Nr. 6, 799-809.

Kasser, P. & Aellen, M. (1976) Die Gletscher der Schweizer Alpen 1971/72 und 1972/73. 93. und 94. Bericht. Publikation der Gletscherkommission SNG, 122 S.

Hydrology in Mountainous Regions. I - Hydrological Measurements; the Water Cycle
(Proceedings of two Lausanne Symposia, August 1990). IAHS Publ. no. 193, 1990.

Modelling discharge of glacierized basins assisted by direct measurements of glacier mass balance

L. N. BRAUN
Department of Geography, Hydrology Section, Swiss Federal Institute of Technology (ETH), CH-8057 Zurich, Switzerland
M. AELLEN
Laboratory of Hydraulics, Hydrology and Glaciology (VAW), Swiss Federal Institute of Technology (ETH), CH-8092 Zurich, Switzerland

ABSTRACT When a conceptual runoff model is applied in heavily glacierized areas, calibration of model parameters is a critical task. The calibration procedures usually applied in non-glacierized catchments based on the comparison of measured and calculated discharge may prove to be insufficient. An underestimation of precipitation and consequent snow storage may be compensated for by excess ice melt on one hand, while on the other hand, an overestimation of precipitation can be compensated by an underestimation of icemelt. As a consequence, successful discharge simulations may result despite a poor physical representation of the accumulation and ablation processes.

It is therefore of great value to employ glacier mass balance measurements as a basis for additional criteria of modelling performance. For this purpose direct measurements of specific glacier mass balance (stake readings in the ablation area, snow-pit measurements in the accumulation area) of the Aletsch Glacier have been analysed for the years 1964/65 to 1982/83. For each of the 19 years investigated, 10 to 17 mass balance values at elevations between 1650 and 3500 m a.s.l. are available.

It can be shown that plots of measured and calculated glacier mass balance as a function of elevation can greatly assist the modeller in finding optimal parameter values which yield good simulations of both discharge and glacier mass balance.

INTRODUCTION

Most runoff models described in the literature incorporate some kind of snowmelt routine, not many of them however take explicit consideration of the presence of glaciers. It was of interest to the authors to find out how some of the well-known snowmelt-runoff models that employ meteorological input data that are generally available could be applied to glacierized basins by introducing an icemelt option if necessary. Generally, an assessment of modelling performance is accomplished by the comparison of linear scale plots of simulated and measured discharge and some kind of numerical efficiency criterion. In the case of a glacierized basin, these methods are helpful but not sufficient, because possible shortcomings of the meteorological input-variables or of the melt models may be compensated for by unrealistic changes in the ice storage term in case the simulated and measured seasonal runoff volumes are not equal, for example.

It is felt that a good snow- and icemelt model should be capable of simulating not only discharge but also the glacier mass balance at various elevations to ensure that good discharge simulations are achieved for the right reasons. In this investigation specific mass balance data as well as reliable discharge data were available for the Aletsch Glacier to allow an assessment of both glacier mass balance and discharge simulations (locations see Figure 1). The basin is drained by the Massa River, the area is 195 km², 66 % is glacier-covered, and the elevation range is 1464 m to 4195 m a.s.l. with a mean elevation of 2945 m. Physiographic details concerning the basin can be found in Kasser (1967), and the distribution of the individual elevation zones and their glaciation is given in Figure 2.

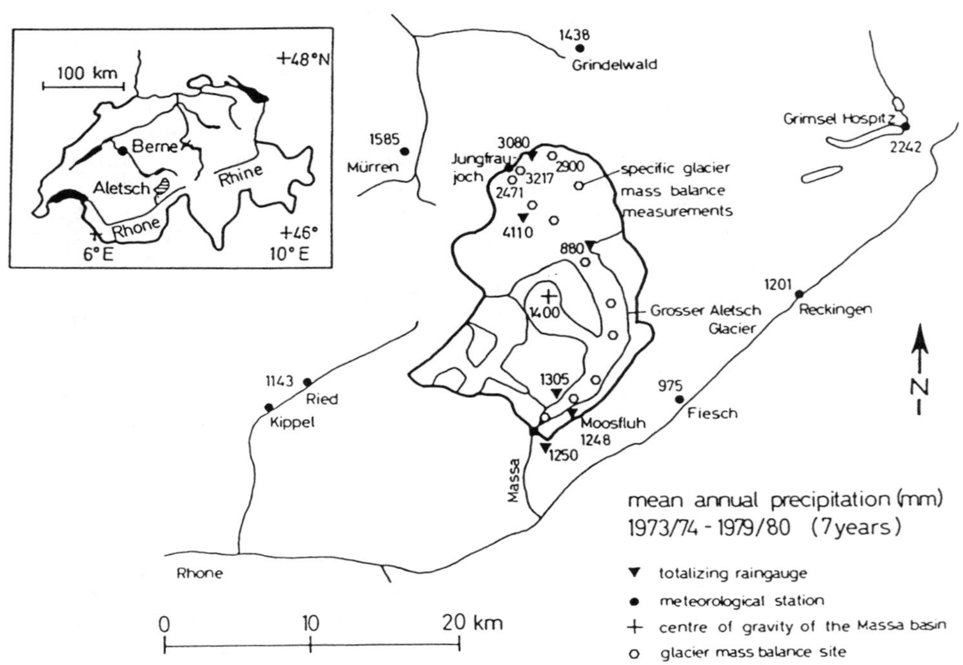

FIG. 1 Map of the Aletsch Glacier region.

METHODS AND DATA

The following melt models are discussed here in more detail:

- The HYMET model (Tangborn, 1984); it requires an estimation of albedo (snow and ice) and uses the diurnal air temperature range as input variable.
- The HBV model (Bergström, 1976); simple temperature-index method.
- The ETH model (Braun, 1988); here, daily ice melt rates M (mm/d) are calculated as follows:

$$M = C(t) * r * (T - T0) \qquad (1)$$

where C(t) is a seasonally varied melt factor (mm/d °C), taking on a value of CMIN on Dec. 21, of CMAX on June 21 and which is interpolated sinusoidally in-between;
r is a multiplicative factor (-) to account for accelerated melt over ice as compared to snow due to the effect of the differing albedo;
T is the mean daily air temperature (°C), and T0 a threshold air temperature parameter.

In order to allow a comparison of the different parameterizations as employed in the various melt models, the same meteorological input data (distributed to 14 elevation zones of 200 m vertical extent) and the same runoff model were used. The experimental layout and results are reported in more detail in Braun (1988). The conceptual runoff model used is based on the HBV-3 model described by Bergström (1976), and it could be applied to this glacierized basin without structural changes. The Nash & Sutcliffe (1970) efficiency criterion R^2 was used to find optimal model parameter values along with linear scale plots of measured and simulated discharge.

A total of 19 hydrological years (1964/65 to 1982/83) were investigated, whereby the years 1971/72 to 1977/78 served as optimization period. These years show highly negative and positive annual glacier mass balances (Kasser et al., 1982).

Specific glacier mass balance data

For each of the 19 years investigated, 10 to 17 specific glacier mass balance values at elevations between 1650 and 3500 m a.s.l. were available (Fig. 1). Measurements in the ablation area were taken at stakes (assuming an ice density of 900 kg/m³), and each value employed in the analysis is taken as the mean of up to 5 individual stakes situated in that elevation range. In the accumulation area, measurements of net accumulation were taken on stakes, in snowpits using the standard gravimetric method, and also using a Neutron sonde in drill holes (core drilling by SIPRE drill, 13 cm diameter, and VAW firn drill, 10 cm diameter). All observed values are reduced to the hydrological year.

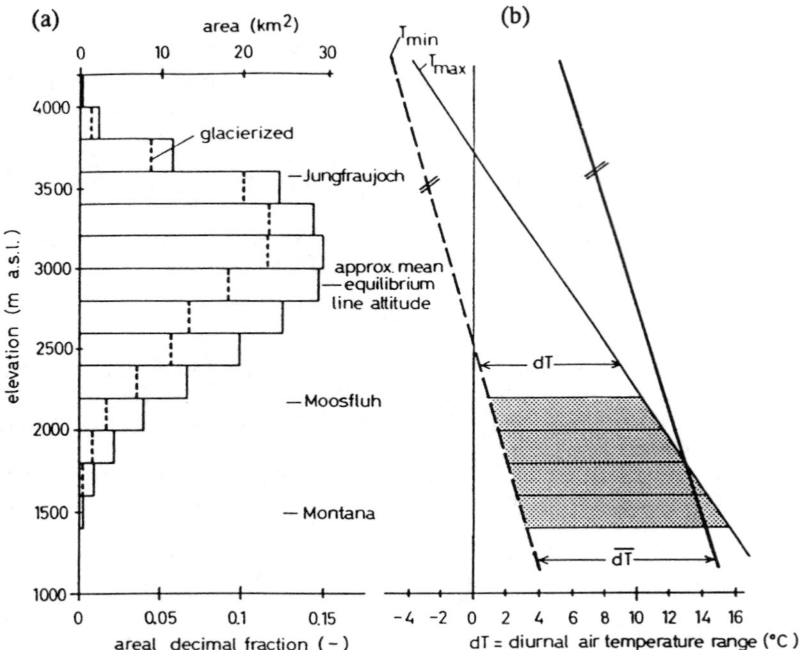

FIG. 2 (a) Area-altitude distribution and glaciation of the Massa basin (area = 195 km²); data based on Kasser (1967).

(b) Schematic representation of the diurnal air temperature range dT typical of a strong radiation day in June, calculated for each zone separately ("previous runs" as reported in Braun, 1988) and as the arithmetic mean of the lowest 4 zones, $\overline{dT}$.

RESULTS

Precipitation in the Aletsch Glacier region

In Figure 1 values of mean annual precipitation for the years 1973/74 to 1979/80 are given based on different modes of measurement: standard (Hellmann) gauges at 6 meteorological stations (elevations between 1040 m and 1959 m a.s.l.), 6 totalizing rain gauges read at the end of the hydrological year, i.e. 30 Sept. (elevations between 2075 and 3810 m a.s.l.) and snow accumulation measurements at 3 locations between 3350 and 3500 m a.s.l. At these elevations, mean melt values are estimated by Aellen (1985) to be about 600 mm/y (1939/40 - 1971/72) using a melt factor of 4.5 mm/d °C. On one hand, melt water contributes to the densification of the firn, on the other hand, it percolates into deeper layers to form a water body in the firn with a water table 14 m to 32 m below the surface (Lang et al., 1977). As a result, the values of net accumulation as given in Figure 1 need to be corrected by about 500 mm to yield total precipitation.

When comparing these figures of mean annual precipitation (the 7 years investigated here were somewhat wetter than the long-term mean), it is evident that they show a very high areal variability. Part of this variability may be caused by measurement problems (in particular the totalizing raingauges excessively exposed to wind), and it is quite a challenge to determine "true" basin precipitation. Kasser et al. (1982) determined this value for the hydrological method to calculate the mass balance of Aletsch Glacier by taking the arithmetic mean of the stations Grindelwald, Fiesch and Ried (Kippel before Sept. 1974) and applying a multiplicative factor of 2 to account for the increase of precipitation with elevation. Braun (1988) used the five meteorological stations surrounding the basin as given in Figure 1 with the exception of Fiesch and determined the weight by an optimal interpolation technique as described in Braun (1985). A mean annual (non-corrected) value of 1400 mm is derived for the centre of gravity. For the modelling exercises daily values were multiplied by the rainfall and snowfall correction factors RCF and SCF, respectively. As described by Braun (1988) these two parameters, in particular SCF, had surprisingly little influence on the calculated discharge volume. One reason for this is that most of the precipitation falls as snow and that a lack of meltwater from the snow cover can be compensated by excess ice melt and vice versa. As a result, the correction parameters could not be optimized alone by minimizing the difference between measured and calculated discharge, but it was necessary to rely on the comparison between specific mass balance as measured on the glacier and simulated by the model. A value of RCF = SCF = 1.8 seems to yield good overall simulation results, and when applied to the (non-corrected) value of 1400 mm, a mean annual basin precipitation of 2520 mm is derived which is somewhat higher than the value of 2443 mm as determined by Kasser et al. (1982) for these years. Their long-term value of basin precipitation is 2166 mm (1931/32 - 1986/87).

Diurnal air temperature range as an index variable for net radiation

Radiation as the main energy source for melt in high alpine regions is seldom available, and it is therefore often necessary to find a practical surrogate variable to calculate melt. A study by Lang (1968) demonstrated that daily mean air temperature data of a valley station (Sion, situated approx. 60 km west of Aletsch Glacier) correlated with measured melt rates on Aletsch Glacier to a better extent than temperatures measured on the glacier, directly outside the glacier and at a high mountain meteorological station (Jungfraujoch, location see Figure 1). Another analysis of air temperature and its information potential

(Lang, 1978) and a recent investigation of 7 years' data of mean daily air temperature, daily temperature range and global radiation of several valley and mountain stations (Braun and Lang, 1988) confirm that the daily temperature range of valley stations represents global radiation to a much higher degree than mean air temperature. The mountain stations, however, also show a rather poor correlation between daily air temperature range and global radiation.

Based on these results, it seemed worthwhile to investigate melt models that require the diurnal air temperatue range as input variable (e.g. the HYMET model). In a first step, the air temperature range was calculated for each zone as observed in nature (general decrease of the range with increasing height, see Figure 2). Figure 3 shows the HYMET model run for the year 1972/73. Generally, very good discharge simulations were obtained (R^2 = 0.925 for this year), however, specific glacier mass balance values were simulated very poorly (case "previous runs", strong overestimation of ablation in the low regions of the glacier, overestimation of accumulation around the equilibrium line). In a second step, the mean daily temperature range of the lowest 4 elevation belts (1500, 1700, 1900 and 2100 m a. s. l.) were used as input at all levels (see Figure 2). The performance of the discharge simulation remained very satisfactory (R^2 dropped slightly to 0.906 for this year), and the simulated glacier mass balance values now follow the measured values very well. It could therefore be demonstrated that the diurnal air temperature range as measured at the lower elevation zones represents radiation conditions across the basin to a better extent than the temperature range as measured at each individual elevation zone.

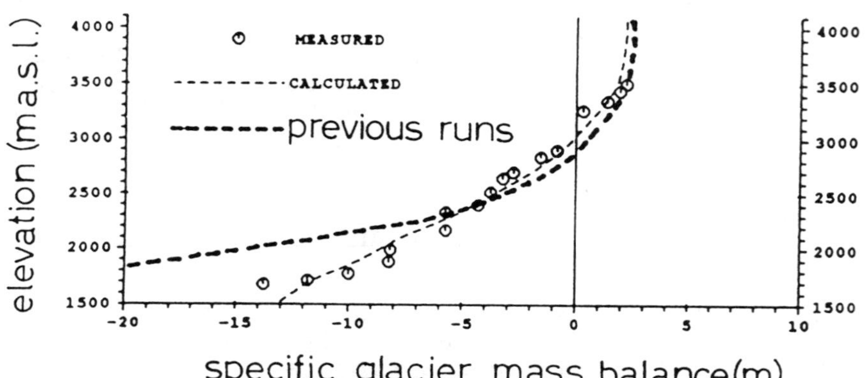

FIG. 3 Comparison of measured specific glacier mass balance (1972/73) and 2 different ways of simulation using the HYMETmelt model; (a) daily temperature range calculated separately for each elevation band ("previous runs"), (b) mean daily temperature range of the lowest 4 elevation belts applied at all levels.

Comparison of the HBV and the ETH snow- and glaciermelt models

Figure 4 shows the performances of the HBV- and the ETH-melt routines in modelling both specific glacier mass balance and discharge for the hydrological year 1977/78. It can be demonstrated that a seasonally varied temperature-index is to be preferred over a simple-temperature index method to reduce possible overestimations of fall melt runoff. Optimal parameter values are: CMIN = 2.0 mm / d °C, CMAX = 5.0 mm / d °C, r = 1.5, T0 = 0.2 °C.

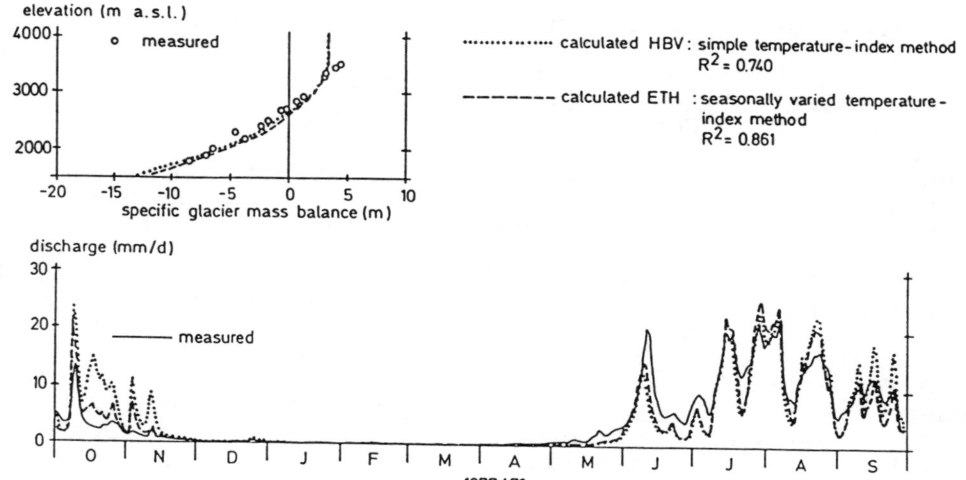

FIG. 4 Performance of the HBV and the ETH snow- and glaciermelt models, 1977/78.

CONCLUSIONS

(a) A realistic assessment of precipitation amounts in high alpine regions strongly relies on direct measurements of snow accumulation and ablation. Snow- and rainfall correction parameters of runoff models cannot be reliably determined without glacier mass balance measurements.

(b) Possible shortcomings of snow- and glaciermelt models or interpolation procedures may be detected by comparing both simulated and measured discharge and specific glacier mass balance.

(c) A seasonally variable temperature-index method is to be preferred over a simple temperature-index method.

The diurnal air temperaure range is a powerful index variable to represent heat available for melt, which is provided mainly by net radiatin in high alpine glacier areas. However, it was found (but not shown here) that inhomogeneities in the data series (e.g. location changes of meteorological stations, changes of measurement systems) may have a more drastic effect than when using daily mean air temperature as input variable.

REFERENCES

Aellen, M. (1985) Niederschlagsbestimmung im vergletscherten Hochgebirge. In: Sevruk, B. (editor), Der Niederschlag in der Schweiz. Beiträge zur Geol. der Schweiz, Nr. 31, Kümmerly und Frey, Bern, 97-105.

Bergström, S. (1976) Development and Application of a Conceptual Runoff Model for Scandinavian Catchments. Dept. of Water Resources Engineering, Lund Inst. of Technology / University of Lund, Bulletin Ser. A no. 52

Braun, L.N. (1985) Simulation of Snowmelt Runoff in Lowland and Lower Alpine Regions of Switzerland. Zürcher Geographische Schriften, Heft 21, Dept. of Geography, Swiss Federal Institute of Technology (ETHZ), Zurich.

Braun, L.N. (1988) Parameterization of Snow- and Glaciermelt. Berichte und Skripten, Heft 34, Dept. of Geography, Swiss Federal Institute of Technology (ETHZ), Zurich.

Braun, L.N. and Lang, H. (1988) Glacier effects on streamflow: some characteristics and modelling aspects with special emphasis on alpine conditions. Proceedings of the Snow Hydrology Workshop held at Manali (H.P.), India, 23 - 25 November 1988, organized by the Central Water Commission & the Himachal Pradesh State Electricity Board. Coordinator: Dr. P.R. Rao, CWC, Director Hydrology North, 514, Sewa Bhawan, R.K. Puram, New Delhi - 110066, India.

Kasser, P. (1967) Fluctuations of Glaciers 1959-1965. A contribution to the International Hydrological Decade. International Commission of Snow and Ice of the IASH - UNESCO.

Kasser, P., Aellen, M. and Siegenthaler, H. (1982) Die Gletscher der Schweizer Alpen 1973/74 und 1974/75, 95. und 96. Bericht. Glaziologisches Jahrbuch der Gletscherkommission der SNG. Published by the Laboratory of Hydraulics, Hydrology and Glaciology (VAW), ETH Zentrum, 8092 Zürich.

Lang, H. (1968) Relations between glacier runoff and meteorological factors observed on and outside the glacier. IASH Publ. no. 79, 429-439.

Lang, H. (1978) Über die Bedeutung der Lufttemperatur als hydrometeorologischer Informationsträger. Arbeiten aus der Zentralanstalt für Meteorologie und Geodynamik, Wien, Heft 31, 23, 1-8.

Lang, H., Schädler, B. and Davidson, G. (1977) Hydroglaciological investigations on the Ewigschneefeld - Gr. Aletschgletscher. Zeitschr. f. Gletscherkunde und Glazialgeologie, 12 (1976), Heft 2, 109-124.

Nash, J.E. and Sutcliffe, J.V. (1970) River flow forecasting through conceptual models. Part I - a discussion of principles. J. Hydrol., 10 (3), 282-290.

Tangborn, W.V. (1984) Prediction of glacier derived runoff for hydro-electric development. Geografiska Annaler, Series A., 66 A(3), 257-265.

Hydrology in Mountainous Regions. I - Hydrological Measurements; the Water Cycle (Proceedings of two Lausanne Symposia, August 1990). IAHS Publ. no. 193, 1990.

Modalités de fonte de neige en moyenne montagne et alimentation du karst sous-jacent

P.CHAUVE,J.MANIA & D.MOINDROT
Université de Franche-Comté , Place Leclerc
25000 BESANCON, France

ABSTRACT-The condition of flow in the hydrologic network of calcareous mountains of the high Doubs(France) corresponds to the influence of the snow covering , during some five months , on hydrologic groundwaters outputs . The winter low flow period of the different springs is twice higher than the summer period .The soil thermal flow at the lower part of the snow cover is one of the possible causes of this phenomenon . This can give ,in winter, a daily snow melting of 0.6 to 0.8 mm water equivalent Under a sufficient thickness of snow the soil is saturated and a little flow of water (5 to 9 l.s-1/km2) can permit the aquifers recharges . During some periods of atmospheric increase of air temperature , the rain added up with the melting snow cover leads to high flow rates . The effect of solar radiation leads to periodic waves of inputs of melting water snow and outputs on hydrograms of springs and rivers . The experimental works give the following results :

-the snow cover (0.8 - 1 m) shows a monthly and an interannual spatial variation . For the studied country (Pontarlier,Mouthe,Le Laitelet and les Fourgs) the snowy precipitations are preponderant during half of the year ,

-the automatic stations of Fourgs and Laitelet , well equiped, can permit the monitoring of the snow cover thickness in middle mountain . It has been possible to improve the relative part of snow and rain in the total precipitation with an hourly time step by the monitoring of several lysimeters . The temperature sensors positioned at different levels in the snow cover record the thermal evolution of snow . The soil thermal flow activity at the snow-soil interface represents 6 to 9% of the total observed melting . The period of atmospheric air thermal increasing is preponderant on the snow cover melting at the Fourgs site and more in lower part of the catchments . The solar radiation (average: 1085 J/cm2) is dominant on the flows of melting water for the stations during the 1986-87 and the 1987-88 winters (38 to 66% of the total flow) ,

-the melting snow simulation with a daily step time , then hourly, with the experimental data issued at the automatic stations is efficient.The use in the numerical model of the temperatures of the snow cover can give a real chronologic study of flow waves from the melting process . The modeling shows that a great part of the solar radiation (30 to 36%) is absorbed by the snow .

EVOLUTION DU MANTEAU NEIGEUX DANS LE HAUT DOUBS

La météorologie nationale contrôle depuis 1969 l'état de l'enneigement sur trois stations situées en moyenne montagne : Pontarlier (837 m),Mouthe (935 m) et Les Fourgs (1100 m) . Sur la période interannuelle 1969-83 les précipitations neigeuses représentent en moyenne , pour un cycle hydrologique annuel débutant en septembre , 30 à 35% des précipitations totales tombant sur le bassin du haut Doubs soit de 470 à 530 mm équivalent eau . Le nombre de jours de neige oscille entre 60 et 85 . Afin d'apprécier l'influence de la fusion de la neige sur l'hydrologie du massif calcaire de Franche-Comté deux sites expérimentaux climatologiques et lysimétriques ont été mis en place et surveillés à partir de 1986 (MOINDROT et al. 1988,MOINDROT,1989) aux Fourgs et au Laitelet avec une étude en parallèle des débits de la source Martin issue du bassin des Fourgs ,du ruisseau du bief des Lavaux à Pontarlier et de la station limnimétrique de Villedieu sur le cours supérieur du Doubs .

ETUDE DE LA FUSION NIVALE SUR LES SITES EQUIPES DE STATIONS AUTOMATIQUES

Deux stations d'acquisition automatique de données hydro-climatologiques "SAD 12-NEOL" (CHAUVE et al. 1987) enregistrent sept paramètres physiques avec douze capteurs répartis dans le sol , la neige et l'atmosphère . Les précipitations neigeuses déposées à la surface du sol forment un stock neigeux qui limite les écoulements vers le sol enregistrés par des lysimètres enterrés et surveillés en continu . Un bilan journalier du stock neigeux est rendu possible par comparaison des entrées (pluies+neige) et des sorties (écoulement lysimétrique) . Nous avons choisi à titre d'exemple les résultats issus des stations des Fourgs (1085 m) et du Laitelet (1193 m) pendant l'hiver 1987-88 . Les figures 1 et 2 montrent une accumulation de neige entre février et avril 1988 avec des valeurs calculées maximum de 348,5 mm (19 mars) aux Fourgs et de 397,9 mm au Laitelet (18 mars) . L'écoulement lysimétrique maximum enregistré en

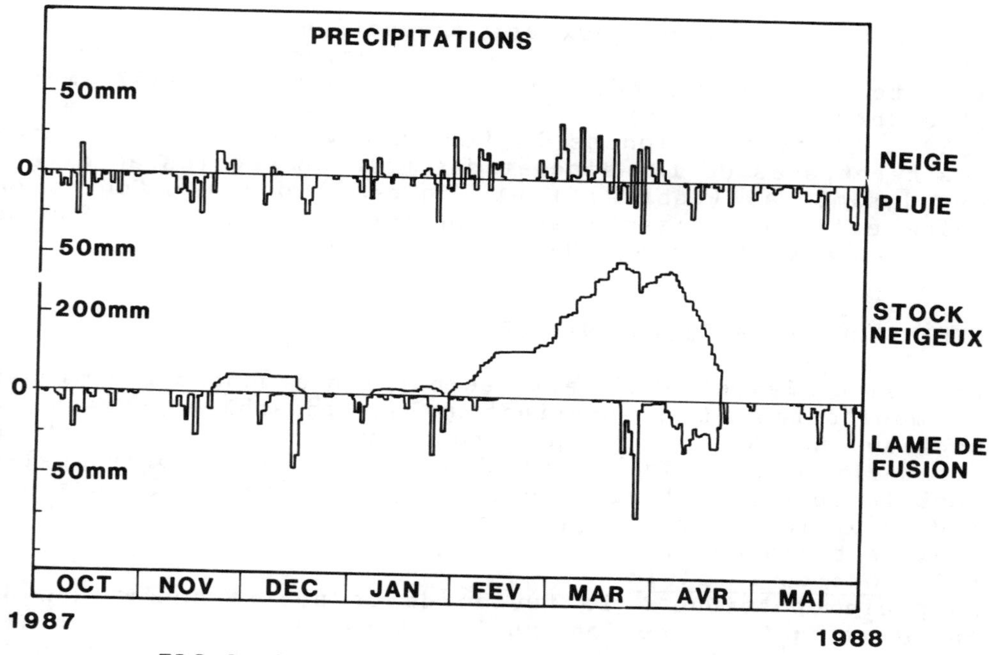

FIG.1 Variation du stock neigeux calculé et écoulement lysimétrique correspondant à la station des Fourgs d'Octobre 1987 à mai 1988.

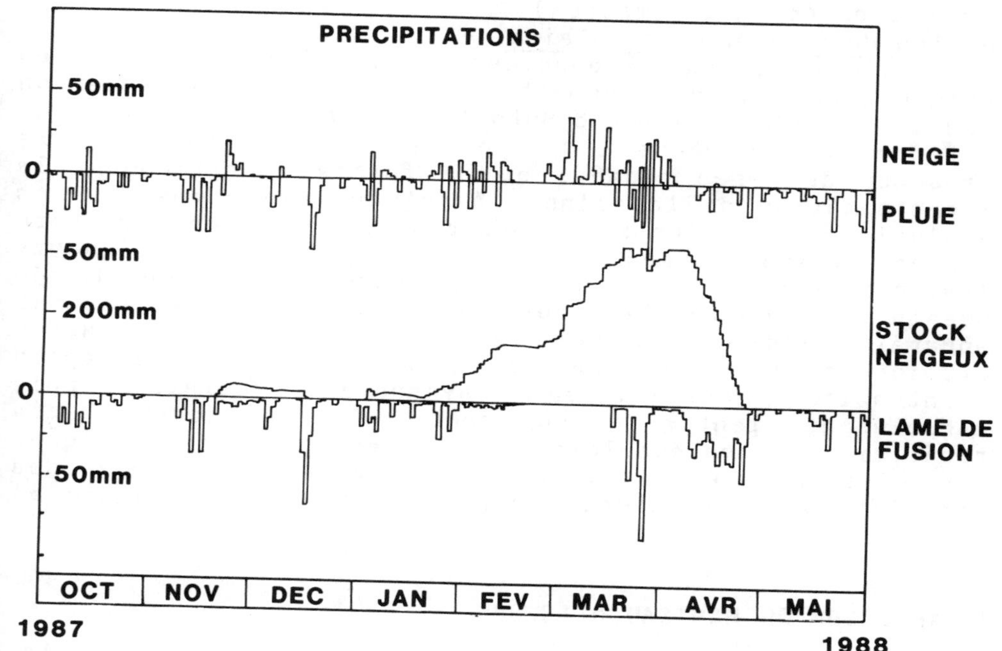

FIG.2 Variation du stock neigeux calculé et écoulement lysimétrique correspondant à la station du Laitelet d'octobre 1987 à mai 1988 .

présence du stock neigeux est respectivement de 73 mm et de 82 mm (25 mars) . La lame de fusion de la neige est importante lors du redoux du mois de mars (18 au 25 mars) et au cours de la fin de fusion nivale à partir du 4 avril 1988 . La corrélation de la fusion nivale théorique issue des carottages de la neige et des volumes écoulés au niveau des lysimètres (tableau 1 et figure 3) dus aux fontes de neige est satisfaisante avec un léger déficit aux Fourgs (station exposée vers l'Ouest) .

MECANISME DE LA FUSION NIVALE

La fusion nivale est déterminée par les échanges thermiques se manifestant à l'interface neige-atmosphère , dans le manteau neigeux (échanges thermiques verticaux) et à l'interface sol-neige . Les sources de chaleur principales sont le rayonnement solaire , la chaleur apportée lors des redoux(pluie ,vent ,température positive de l'air) et le flux géothermique .

Influence de la pluie

La pluie contribue à la fusion de la partie supérieure de la neige qui se burine puis s'affaisse si l'isothermie interne est de 0°C . Dans ce cas les lysimètres répondent de manière synchrone aux pluies . Aux Fourgs , entre le 26 février et le 2 mars (figure 4) on remarque que la totalité de la pluie a traversé le manteau neigeux entrainant de l'eau de fusion (89 mm de pluie pour 131 mm d'eau écoulée au lysimètre) .

Action du rayonnement solaire

La pénétration du rayonnement solaire dans le manteau neigeux varie avec la densité de la neige et sa teneur en eau et la réflexion est d'autant plus intense que la neige est fraiche et sèche . La position topographique et la présence de zones d'ombre ou de forêts conditionnent la transformation de la neige . Ainsi ont été comparées les évolutions des intensités horaires du rayonnement solaire , des températures de l'air , les écoulements lysimétriques et le débits des sources à la sortie du bassin . Une corrélation des différents paramètres mesurés apparait nettement . Les lames de fusion de la neige atteignent leur maximum deux à trois heures après l'intensité maximum du rayonnement solaire puis décroissent lentement au cours de la journée .La répétition de ces écoulements à la base du manteau neigeux sur plusieurs jours se traduit aux exutoires par des oscillations journalières du débit des sources (figure 5).

REPARTITION DU MANTEAU NEIGEUX

Des carottages réguliers au pas hebdomadaire ont permis de suivre l'évolution de l'épaisseur et de la densité de la neige sur différents sites d'exposition et d'altitude

TABLEAU 1 Bilan écoulement lysimétrique - valeur en eau du manteau neigeux en fin de fusion (hiver 1986-1987) aux Fourgs et au Laitelet.

HIVER 1987	Ec Ecoulement lysimétrique	P Pluie cumulée	Ec-P Ecoulement lysimétrique neigeux	N Neige cumulée	Vo Equivalent en eau du stock neigeux	Vo+N Diminution cumulée du stock neigeux
LES FOURGS						
le 31/3	0	0	0	0	192	0
du 31/3 au 7/4	18,5	2,2	16,3	25	192	25
du 7/4 au 11/4	84,9	33,8	51,1	28,5	159	61,5
du 11/4 au 14/4	90,4	33,8	56,6	38,5	152	78,5
du 14/4 au 18/4	170,7	33,8	136,9	38,5	46	184,5
du 18/4 au 19/4	216,2	33,8	182,4	38,5	0	230,5
LE LAITELET						
le 29/3	0	0	0	0	381	0
du 29/3 au 7/4	45,6	6,7	38,9	39,6	383	37,6
du 7/4 au 11/4	111,1	41,7	69,4	43,5	319	105,5
du 11/4 au 18/4	222	41,7	180,3	48,6	234	195,6
du 18/4 au 21/4	315,2	53,8	261,4	48,6	147	282,6
du 21/4 au25/4	419,6	54,8	364,8	48,6	49	380,6
du 25/4 au 27/4	459,5	54,8	404,7	48,6	0	429,6

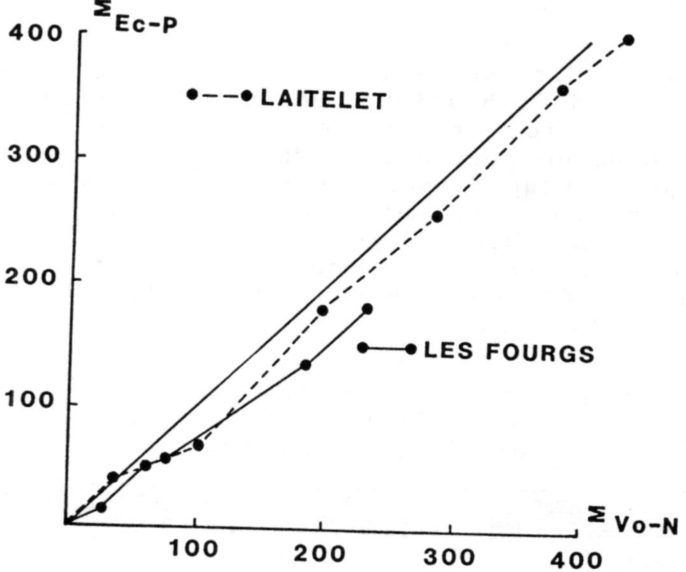

FIG.3 Relation entre les écoulements lysimétriques et la diminution du manteau neigeux calculé aux stations du Laitelet et des Fourgs .

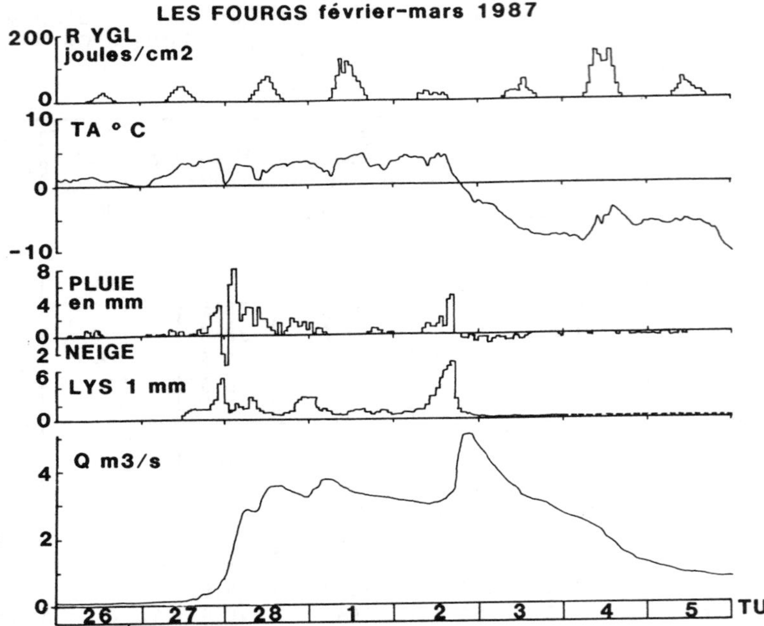

FIG.4 Variations au pas de temps horaire du rayonnement solaire , de la température , des précipitations et des lames d'eau écoulées à la station des Fourgs et du débit des sources Martin (du 26/02 au 5/03/87) .

variée : bassin des Fourgs(1000 à 1250 m),massif du Larmont (823 à 1310 m) et le bassin du Doubs à Villedieu(900 à 1400 m). On a ainsi noté pour les trois cycles hivernaux 1985 à 1988 des Fourgs une permanence des stocks neigeux de 97 , 116 et 71 jours pour respectivement des équivalents en eau respectifs de 106 , 103 et 124 mm .Il apparait que pour tous ces sites (MOINDROT,1989) la neige évolue plus lentement en altitude et un décalage des dates de fusion du stock neigeux a été observé pour chaque tranche d'altitude

TABLEAU 2 Débits journaliers minimum des étiages d'hiver et d'été de 1985 à 1988 (E hiver/E été = rapport des débits journaliers d'étiages d'hiver et d'été).

DEBIT en m3/s	Doubs à Mouthe Etiage	E hiver/E été	Doubs à Villedieu Etiage	E hiver/E été	Sources Martin Etiage	E hiver/E été	Bief des Lavaux Etiage	E hiver/E été
31/10/85	0,071	3,7						
22/2/86	0,262		0,432		0,071			
16/10/86	0,125	2,4	0,122	3,3	0,025	3,4	0,003	2,3
6/2/87	0,306		0,409		0,085		0,007	
23/9/87	0,232		0,229	1	0,072	1,1	0,007	1
11/3/88			0,229		0,078		0,007	

(100 m) . Par ailleurs, le couvert forestier est un facteur non négligeable de libération tardive des réserves en eau accumulées au cours de l'hiver , car la neige est protégée du rayonnement solaire .

RELATIONS HYDROLOGIE SOUTERRAINE - FUSION DE LA NEIGE

Des travaux antérieurs sur les liaisons pluies/débits du haut bassin du Doubs (CHAUVE et al.,1982 ,JACQUEMIN 1984) avaient montré l'importance du phénomène de fusion sur l'hydrologie karstique . La mise au point d'une simulation théorique de la fonte à partir des travaux d'OBLED(1971) et de NAVARRE(1983,1984) intégrée à un modèle hydrométéorologique à pas journalier de type MERO (1978) permettait une bonne restitution des débits . L'analyse de données issues des sites expérimentaux et des mesures de débits sur les exutoires les plus proches a permis d'affiner la compréhension du phénomène hydrologique en dégageant la part relative de trois facteurs thermiques :
-le flux géothermique agissant à la base du manteau neigeux qui fournit une fonte quotidienne de 0,6 à 0,8 mm (soit 6 à 9% de la fusion totale ou de 5 à 9 l/s.km2 à l'échelle du bassin) .Les étiages d'hiver montrent alors des débits supérieurs à ceux de l'été-automne (dans des rapports de 2 à 4 ,tableau 2),
-les redoux hivernaux qui se manifestent épisodiquement et sont accompagnés de pluies qui s'additionnent à l'eau stockée par la neige en fusion occasionnant des débits importants à la base du manteau neigeux comme du 14 au 25 avril 1987 aux sources Martin (figure 5) et du ruisseau du bief des Lavaux (MOINDROT,1989) ,
-le rayonnement solaire qui fournit des lames de fusion journalières cumulées de 20 à 40 mm(soit 38 à 46% de la fusion totale aux Fourgs et de 52 à 66% au Laitelet) . Les débits des sources et des ruisseaux réagissent fortement avec des fluctuations cycliques .

SIMULATION DE LA FUSION NIVALE

Le modèle HELIOS développé par JACQUEMIN (1984) permet de réaliser un bilan thermique du manteau neigeux par des échanges caloriques au niveau des interfaces neige-sol et neige-atmosphère et conduisent au calcul d'une lame de fusion journalière . Un coefficient correcteur de l'énergie absorbée par le manteau neigeux a été intégré compte tenu de l'évolution de la neige en surface(THOMAS,1976) et du gradient thermique journalier du manteau neigeux calculé à partir de la réponse des sondes thermiques placées dans la neige(MOINDROT,1989). Les simulations réalisées au pas horaire ont été testées avec une corrélation significative (r=0,81 pour 113

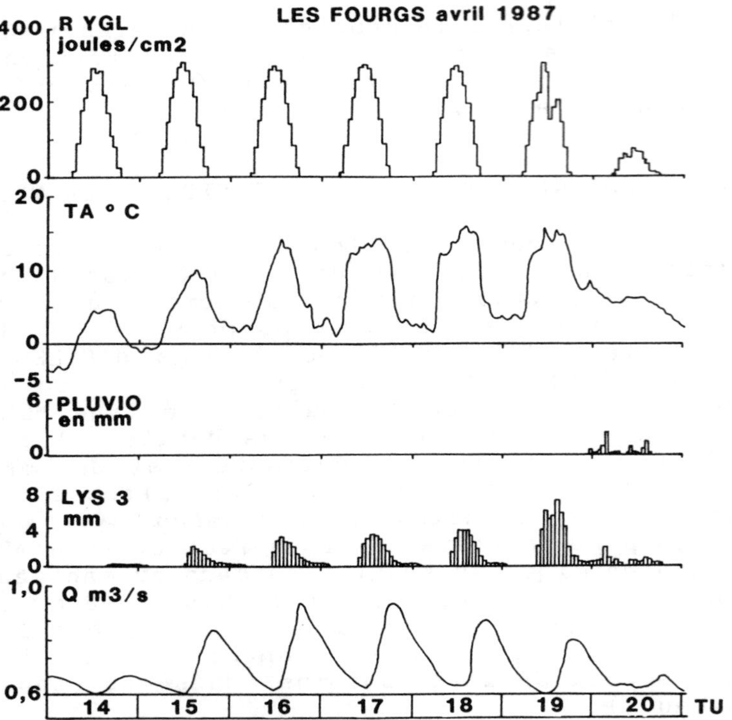

FIG.5 Variations au pas de temps horaire du rayonnement solaire , de la température des précipitations et des écoulements lysimétriques à la station des Fourgs et du débit des sources Martin (du 14 au 20/87) .

valeurs) entre les réponses lysimétriques mesurées et calculées . Ces dernières suivent la loi :

$$L = 1,15.\exp(-0,18.t)+(Lmax-1,15).(1-0,11.t)/(1+0,32.t)$$

avec L:la lame d'écoulement (mm) simulée au temps t (en heures) compté à partir de l'onde de crue ,
Lmax:la lame d'écoulement maximale correspondant au rayonnement solaire maximum .
Le calage du modèle horaire dépend fortement d'un coefficient correcteur héliométrique variant selon l'hiver (C=0,32 à 0,36 en 86-87 et C=0,30 à 0,33 en 87-88 pour respectivement les Fourgs et le Laitelet) .
Une simulation au pas journalier a été effectuée pour l'ensemble des trois cycles annuels hydrologiques dont nous donnons ici un exemple sur la période d'octobre 1986 à mai 1987 aux stations des Fourgs (figure 6) et du Laitelet (MOINDROT,1989). On remarque une simulation correcte de l'évolution du stock neigeux (r=0,92 pour 131 jours aux Fourgs et r=0,98 pour 140 jours au Laitelet)

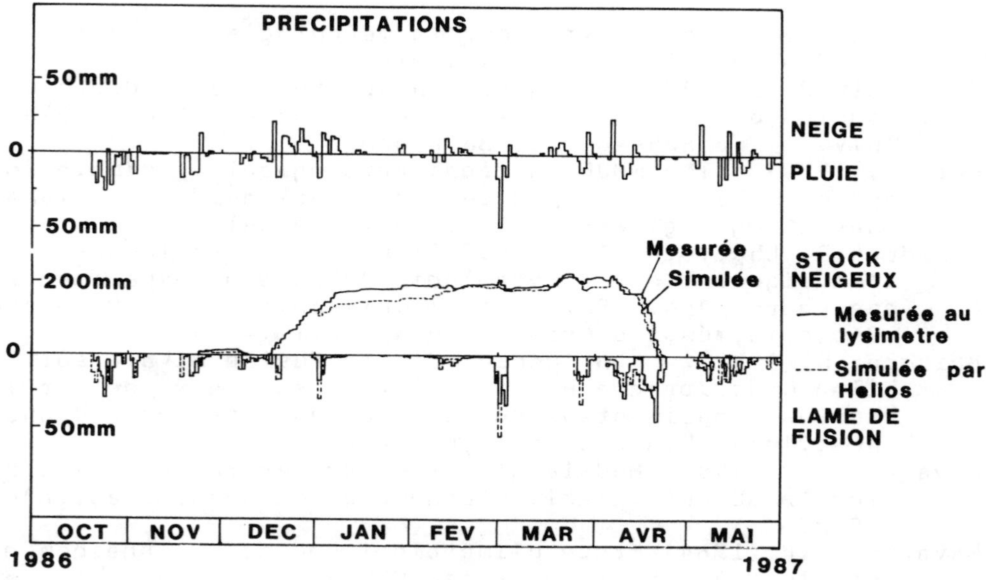

FIG.6 Stock neigeux et lame d'écoulement mesurés et simulés aux Fourgs d'octobre 1986 à mai 1987 .

ainsi que des réponses lysimétriques (r=0,66 pour 41 jours aux Fourgs et r=0,72 pour 43 jours au Laitelet) .

CONCLUSIONS

Les stations automatiques d'acquisition de données des Fourgs et du Laitelet ont permis de suivre l'évolution du manteau neigeux en moyenne montagne (1000-1200m) .L'enregistrement en continu des paramètres physiques régulant le mécanisme de la fusion nivale qui a été comparé aux mesures d'écoulement d'eau sur des lysimétres et sur des stations de jaugeage des sources influencées . Une analyse chronologique précise du rayonnement solaire , des températures atmosphérique ,dans le sol et dans le manteau neigeux,et des écoulements a permis de valider le bilan hydrologique de la fusion de la neige et de tester un modèle de simulation au pas horaire .

REFERENCES

Chauve, P. ,Jacquemin, P. & Mania, J.(1982) Influence de l'enneigement et réponse hydrologique des sous-bassins calcaires du Haut Doubs . Colloque sur les milieux discontinus en hydrogéol .Doc. BRGM45p.193-199,Orléans.

Chauve, P.,Mania, J.,Moindrot,P. et Truche,C.(1987) Un exemple de transmission de données météorologiques sur deux sites expérimentaux de moyenne montagne en

Franche-Comté . Symp. sur la métrologie au service de l'hydrogéologie,mars 1987,Toulouse.

Jacquemin,P.(1984) Réponses hydrodynamiques des hauts bassins du Doubs et de la Loue . Thèse 3ème cycle , Univ. Franche-Comté, Besançon.

Mero,F.(1978) The MM08 hydrometeorological simulation system . Basic concepts and operators guide . Tahal Consulting Engineers LTD,Tel Aviv,Israel.

Moindrot,D.,Chauve,P. & Mania,J.(1988) Influence de l'enneigement sur l'hydrologie du bassin expérimental des Fourgs Ann. Scien. de l'Université de Besançon ,Géologie,mémoire hors série N°6,p.121-129.

Moindrot,D.(1989) Influence de la fusion nivale sur le bilan hydrologique et la qualité des eaux de trois bassins expérimentaux en moyenne montagne (Haut Doubs) Thèse,Univ. Franche-Comté,Besançon.

Navarre, J.P.(1983) Modèle déterministe des fontes nivales ,modèle GENEPI .Etabl. d'Etudes et de Rech.Météo.,n°60 ,39 p.

Navarre, J.P.(1984) Etude climatologique de l'enneigement des Alpes à partir du réseau CEDONGLA . Données et statistiques .Etabl. d'Et. et de Rech.Météo.,n°3.

Thomas, A.(1976) Constitution et évolution d'un manteau neigeux en moyenne montagne : exemple du Col de Porte(massif de la Chartreuse) .Thèse 3ème cycle,Univ. Grenoble I.

Hydrology in Mountainous Regions. I - Hydrological Measurements; the Water Cycle
(Proceedings of two Lausanne Symposia, August 1990). IAHS Publ. no. 193, 1990.

On the influence of Alpine glaciers on runoff

Jiyang Chen & Atsumu Ohmura
Department of Geography, Swiss Federal Institute of Technology, Winterthurerstrasse 190, CH-8057 Zürich, Switzerland

ABSTRACT The hydrological characteristics of partly ice-covered Alpine basins are analyzed on monthly data basis for the sub-basins in the Rhône River and several others in the Alps with respect to the influence of glaciers on runoff. The runoff changes owing to the changes in temperature, precipitation and glacier area are also estimated.

In general, as the basin ice-covered area increases, the ratio of the summer-half year (May-September) to the annual runoff increases and the occurrence of the maximum monthly runoff is delayed. In addition, a moderate ice cover can reduce the year-to-year variation of annual runoff to a minimum.

It is found that the summer temperature is a significant element influencing runoff from a heavily ice-covered basin. As the ice-covered area decreases, the correlation of runoff with annual precipitation increases. Long-term change of annual runoff is analyzed with a simple model whereby the effects of the changes in ice-covered area, summer half-year temperature and annual precipitation on runoff are evaluated. It is shown that the change of ice cover is the most important factor which results in the runoff change of highly glacierized Alpine basins. For forecasting the runoff from a glacierized basin the ice-covered area must be accurately simulated.

INTRODUCTION

A basic aspect of the Alpine hydrology concerns the influence of glaciers on runoff of immediate rivers (Kasser, 1959, 1973, 1981; Aschwanden & Weingartner, 1983; Schädler, 1985; Lang, 1986; Röthlisberger & Lang, 1987). The present work is initiated by an attempt to understand the hydrological significance of the changes of Alpine glaciers since the Little Ice Age and in the near future. The work consists of (1) examining the basic hydrological characteristics of basins with respect to the ratio of basin ice-cover α (the ice-covered area divided by the basin area) and (2) estimating the runoff change of Alpine basins due to the changes in temperature T, precipitation P and α. It is well known that the area of the Alpine glaciers have changed significantly since the 1870s (Vivian, 1975; Müller et al. 1976; Gross, 1985; Chen & Ohmura, 1990). It may change rapidly in a warming scenario of the near future climate. Since the effect of the climatic change is expected to influence our life mainly through changes in the hydrological cycle, it is important to estimate how climatic elements and ice-covered area are related to the basin runoff.

The basins and the corresponding runoff stations used are given in Table 1. These basins mainly cover the central and partly the eastern Alps.

RUNOFF OF A GLACIERIZED BASIN

To clarify the influence of glaciers on the runoff changes of a glacierized basin, it is necessary to understand the relationship between the runoff components and climatic elements in such a basin. Runoff from a partly glacierized basin can be divided into two parts: the runoff from the ice-free part and that from the ice-cover. The ice-covered area is usually the higher part of the basin which has different hydrological behavior than the lower ice-free surfaces. The duration of snow cover is much longer and stable in the ice-covered part. Part of the snow cover in the accumulation area will melt and join the annual water cycle while the rest stays as net accumulation and joins the water cycle in some 10^1-10^2 a.

TABLE 1 The selected runoff stations. H_s: altitude of the runoff station [m a.s.l.]; S: basin area [km^2]; H: mean altitude of the basin [m a.s.l.]; and α: ratio of the ice-covered area to the total basin area. Data source: Swiss National Hydrological Survey unless otherwise specified; 1 Bernath (1980); 2 Moser et al. (1986); 3 Provided by M. Kuhn & G. Markl

No	River/Station	λ [° ' E]	ϕ [° ' N]	H_s	S	H	α	*Period*
Rhône								
1	Rhône/Gletsch	8 22	46 34	1761	38.9	2719	0.52	1894-1903[1], 1920-1928[1] & 1956-1986
2	Rhône/Reckingen	8 15	46 28	1311	215	2306	0.18	1975-1985
3	Massa/Blatten bei Naters	8 00	46 23	1446	195	2945	0.66	1923-1928 & 1931-1985
4	Saltina/Brig	7 59	46 19	677	77.7	2050	0.05	1966-1985
5	Rhône/Brig	7 58	46 19	667	913	2370	0.24	1965-1985
6	Lonza/Blatten	7 49	46 25	1520	77.8	2630	0.37	1956-1985
7	Vispa/Visp	7 53	46 16	659	778	2660	0.30	1965-1985
8	Borgne/La Luette	7 26	46 09	957	231	2620	0.25	1929-1979
9	Rhône/Sion	7 21	46 13	484	3349	2310	0.18	1916-1985
10	Rhône/Branson	7 05	46 07	457	3728	2250	0.17	1941-1985
11	Drance de Bagnes/Le Châble	7 12	46 05	810	254	2630	0.29	1957-1985
12	Drance de Ferret/ Brache d'en Haut	7 06	45 58	1345	66.8	2340	0.12	1956-1973
13	Trient/Trient	6 59	46 03	1273	29.1	2370	0.34	1956-1973
14	Grande Eau/Aigle	6 58	46 19	414	132	1560	0.02	1935-1985
15	Rhône/Porte du Scex	6 53	46 21	377	5220	2130	0.14	1935-1985
Aare								
16	Simme,Oberried/Lenk	7 28	46 25	1096	35.7	2370	0.38	1944-1985
17	Engstligenbach/Engstligenalp	7 33	46 27	1875	14.4	2300	0.11	1949-1966
18	Gornernbach/Kiental	7 45	46 33	1280	25.6	2270	0.17	1949-1982
19	Weisse Lütschine/Zweilütschine	7 54	46 38	650	164	2170	0.21	1933-1985
20	Aare/Brienzwiller	8 05	46 45	570	554	2150	0.21	1954-1985
Reuss								
21	Furkareuss/Realp*	8 30	46 36	1559	60.7	2465	0.15	1957-1985
22	Witenwasserenreuss/Realp	8 29	46 35	1575	30.7	2427	0.13	1957-1985
23	Alpbach/Erstfeld	8 29	46 35	1575	20.6	2200	0.28	1961-1985
24	Isenthal/Isenthal	8 33	46 55	767	43.9	1820	0.09	1957-1985
Rhine								
25	Ferrerabach/Trun	8 58	46 46	1236	12.5	2461	0.17	1963-1985
26	Somvixerrhein/Somvix	8 59	46 40	1490	21.8	2450	0.07	1978-1985
27	Hinterrhein/Hinterrhein	9 12	46 33	1584	53.7	2360	0.17	1945-1985
28	Averserrhein/Campsut	9 29	46 30	1660	124	2424	0.02	1964-1985
29	Dischmabach/Davos	9 52	46 48	1668	43.3	2372	0.02	1964-1985
30	Landquart,Klosters/Auelti	9 55	46 53	1317	103	2332	0.08	1975-1985
Inn								
31	Inn/St.Moritzbad	9 50	46 30	1770	155	2400	0.07	1907-1985
32	Rosegbach/Pontresina	9 54	46 31	1766	66.5	2716	0.30	1955-1985
33	Berninabach/Pontresina	9 55	46 31	1804	107	2617	0.19	1955-1985
34	Chamuerabach/ La Punt-Chamues-ch	9 56	46 36	1719	73.3	2549	0.02	1955-1985
35	Vernagtbach/Pegelstation	10 83	46 86	2640	11.44	3130	0.83	1974-1985[2]
36	Vent/Rofenache	10 88	46 86	1905	98.3	2819	0.43	1967-1985[3]
37	Venterache/Vent	10 88	46 86	1877	164.7	2450	0.40	1951-1982[3]
Adda								
38	Varunasch/Poschiavo	10 23	46 22	1320	4.29	2332	0.02	1970-1985
Ticino								
39	Krummbach/Klusmatten	8 01	46 13	1792	19.8	2276	0.03	1953-1985

A distinct fact is that the runoff of the ice-covered part of the basin correlates positively with temperature and negatively with precipitation (Kasser, 1981; Collins, 1987). In a warm-dry year, increased icemelt compensates for the runoff deficit from the ice-free area, which results from the decrease in precipitation. In a cold-wet year, the melt from the glaciers decreases, while the runoff from the ice-free area increases due to larger precipitation and less evaporation. In this sense, Alpine glaciers are not only water resources but behave as a natural water reservoir which dampen out extreme runoff events. In a warm and dry period, the specific runoff from a basin with glaciers is larger than that from a neighbour ice-free basin if other conditions remain similar.

THEORY

Let us denote the annual total runoff of a partly ice-covered basin as Q_a which consists of a part from the ice cover Q_{ag} and a part Q_{an} from the ice-free area. It follows that $Q_a = Q_{ag} + Q_{an}$. Likewise, the total area of the basin S can be divided into the ice-covered area S_g and ice-free area S_n . The specific annual discharge also consists of two components:

$$q_a = (1-\alpha)\, q_{an} + \alpha\, q_{ag} \qquad (1)$$

where $q_{ag} = Q_{ag}/S_g$, $q_{an} = Q_{an}/S_n$. and $\alpha = S_g/S$. The specific runoff from the ice-covered part q_{ag} is equal to the the specific ablation $<a>$ over the glaciers plus liquid precipitation. q_{ag} is therefore well correlated with the air temperature since temperature is for the Alps a good index of the heat supply for melting on the glacier surface. On a daily basis, the specific ablation is related to the temperature in a power relationship which is implied in Gutersohn's (1936) approach for 8 glaciers in the Swiss Alps and similar formulas are widely used today (Yang, 1988). In another temperature-index method, the $<a>-T$ relationship is sometimes approximated in a linear form on a daily basis (Lang, 1986). On an annual scale, the annual specific runoff from the glacier surface of the basin can be parameterized by the summer half-year temperature T_s:

$$q_{ag} = a_0 + a_1 T_s \qquad (2)$$

where a_0 and a_1 are empirical coefficients. The annual specific runoff from the ice-free part of the basin is considered to be related to the annual precipitation and approximated in a linear form:

$$q_{an} = a_0^* + a_1^*\, P_a \qquad (3)$$

where the coefficient a_0^* and a_1^* are also empirical coefficients and they should be determined from the field work.

For determining the magnitude of changes in the specific runoff resulting from the changes in the ratio of basin ice-cover, differentiating equation 1 with respect to α gives

$$\partial q_a/\partial\alpha = q_a^* + \alpha\, \partial q_a^*/\partial\alpha + \partial q_{an}/\partial\alpha \qquad (4)$$

with $q_a^* = q_{ag} - q_{an}$ being the runoff difference factor, which is the specific runoff from the ice-covered area minus that from the ice-free part. It is shown that the magnitude of q_a^* is in the order of 10^3 mm (Bernath, 1989) and that q_a^* is related to the glacier mass balance The second term on the right is positive but small. The magnitude of $\partial q_{an}/\partial\alpha$ is very small since the change of q_{an} mainly results from precipitation changes. It follows that q_a^* is the most important term to keep.

VARIATIONS OF RUNOFF OF GLACIERIZED BASINS IN THE ALPS

Seasonal distributions of runoff

In glacierized basins, most of the annual runoff occurs in the summer-half year. The summer half-year runoff fraction $\overline{Q}_s/\overline{Q}_a$ increases with α in the following manner:

$$\overline{Q}_s/\overline{Q}_a = 0.74 + 0.43\ \alpha - 0.2\ \alpha^2 \tag{5}$$

with a correlation coefficient of 0.67. For this calculation, basins No. 7, 8, 11 and 12 in Table 1 are excluded since water is artificially transfered out of these basins.

Analysis of the mean monthly runoff data shows that the occurrence of the maximum of the monthly runoff fraction of annual total runoff $\overline{Q}_{mon}/\overline{Q}_a$ is delayed due to the existence of glaciers. Of the considered Alpine basins, the maximum $\overline{Q}_{mon}/\overline{Q}_a$ appears in June by α=0.10 and in July by α=0.24. In the range of α=0.25-0.66, it appears rather stably in July. The maximum $\overline{Q}_{mon}/\overline{Q}_a$ is even delayed to August in Vernagtbach whose α is 0.84.

The year-to-year changes of runoff are usually described by the coefficient of variation v_q, which is defined as

$$v_q = s_q / \overline{q} \tag{6}$$

with s_q being the standard deviation and $\overline{q}$ the mean of q over many years.

The annual march of v_q of monthly mean specific runoff q_{mon} can be partly explained by the change of q_{mon} since v_q is inversely proportional to the mean $\overline{q}_{mon}$ of q_{mon} over time. For a nearly ice-free Alpine basin, the maximum v_q of q_{mon} appears in November with a second peak in February, partly because of the small values for $\overline{q}_{mon}$. The minimum v_q of q_{mon} is in spring when snow-melting runoff leads to a maximum $\overline{q}_{mon}$. For glacierized basins, the maximum v_q occurs in spring and a secondary peak in the fall. The minimum v_q shows up usually in summer for the basins with α>0.24.

The function of a moderate ice cover

The coefficient of variation v_q of the monthly and annual mean runoff are related to the ratio of basin ice-cover α. A moderate glacier cover α_o in a basin can reduce the year-to-year variations of runoff to a minimum. It is found that for the annual mean runoff, α_o takes values of 0.10-0.40 in different regions: 0.30 for the South Cascade Glacier basin (Krimmel & Tangborn, 1974), 0.36 for the North Cascade Mountains of Washington State (Fountain & Tangborn, 1985), 0.10-0.20 for the Himalayan and Karakoram headwaters of the Indus in Pakistan (Ferguson, 1985), 0.20 for Norwegian basins (Tvede, 1983) and 0.21 in Johan Dahl Land of southern Greenland (Braithwaite & Olesen, 1988). For the Alps, α_o is found to be 0.30-0.40 (Kasser, 1959) and 0.30-0.60 (Röthlisberger & Lang, 1987).

In the present analysis, α_o is determined by fitting a square function of v_q with respect to the basin ice-cover α:

$$v_q = a_0 + a_1\ \alpha + a_2\alpha^2 \tag{7}$$

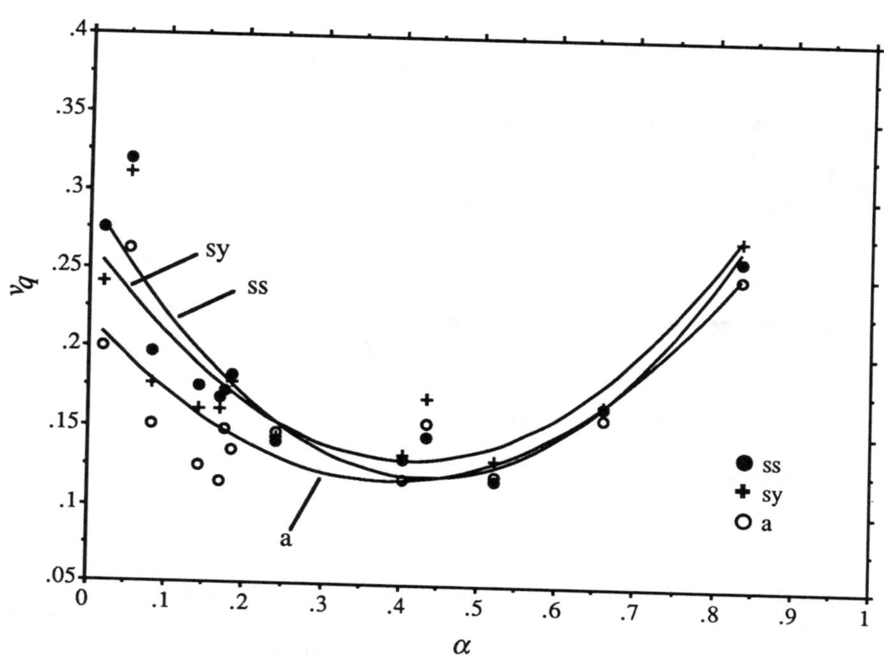

Fig. 1 Relationships between coefficient of variation v_q of mean runoff and ratio α of basin ice-cover. v_q-α curves are determined after equation 7 for the summer season (June-Aug.) *ss*, summer half-year (May-Sept.) *s* and annual (Oct.-Sept.) *a*.

where v_q is the coefficient of variation of the specific runoff. α is the basin ice-cover and a_0, a_1 and a_2 are the coefficients. Differentiating equation 7 with respect to α and setting $dv_q/d\alpha=0$, the basin ice-cover α_o which results in the minimum variability of basin runoff can be obtained:

$$\alpha_o = -a_1/ 2a_2 \quad (8)$$

and the minimum coefficient of variation of runoff v_{qo} is

$$v_{qo} = a_0 - 0.25\, a_1^2/a_2 \quad (9)$$

Equation 7 is statistically significant for the monthly (in the summer-half year), summer seasonal and annual mean runoff by the considered Alpine basins. The moderate ice cover is found to be 0.39-0.44 for the seasonal and annual mean runoff (Fig. 1) which can be compared with the values given by Kasser (1959) and Röthlisberger & Lang (1985).

ESTIMATION OF RUNOFF CHANGE FROM GLACIERIZED BASINS

Formulation of the problem

It is considered that the long-term runoff change from a glacierized Alpine basin consists of three components:

$$\Delta q_a = \partial q_a/\partial \alpha \, \Delta \alpha + \partial q_a/\partial T_s \, \Delta T_s + \partial q_a/\partial P_a \, \Delta P_a \qquad (10)$$

(1) The change due to the change in the basin ice-cover which is represented by the first term on the right side and is estimated with equation 4;

(2) The change caused by the change in temperature. This is represented by the second term which is evaluated by differentiating equation 1 with respect to temperature:

$$\partial q_a/\partial T_s = \alpha \, a_1 \qquad (11)$$

(3) The change resulting from the precipitation change can be deduced from equations 1-3, it is

$$\partial q_a/\partial P_a = (1\text{-}\alpha) \, a_1^* \qquad (12)$$

Now equation 10 becomes

$$\Delta q_a = q_a^* \, \Delta \alpha + \alpha \, a_1 \, \Delta T_s \, + (1-\alpha) \, a_1^* \Delta P_a \qquad (13)$$

This is the first order approximation and the following less significant contributions are neglected: a term $\partial e/\partial T_s$ whereby e is the specific evaporation in the parameterization like equation 11 and a term $\partial e/\partial P_a$ in the parameterization of equation 12. Furthermore, in the analysis above, the changes in the underground water storage is assumed to be small and neglected.

Estimation of the coefficients

The magnitude of the coefficients a_1 in equation 2 and a_1^* in equation 3 are determined on the data base of 13 Alpine glacierized basins: the basin No. 1-5, 10, 14, 15, 30, and 35-37 (see Table 1). A reference meteorological station is selected for each basin: Grimsel (for the basin No. 1), Reckingen (No. 2 and 4-5), Sion (No. 9, 10 and 15), Lysin (No. 14), Davos (No. 30) and Vent (No. 35-37). The coefficient a_1 in equation 2 is determined through the following steps:

(1) A linear relationship between annual runoff q_a of a basin and the summer-half year temperature T_s of a reference meteorological station is calculated;

(2) A linear relationship between the slope A_1 of the q_a - T_s linear relationship and the basin ice-cover α is calculated. Based on data of the 13 Alpine basins mentioned above, it is found that A_1 = 571.037 α - 59.743 (r^2 = 0.92); and

(3) The magnitude of a_1 can be approximated as the value of A_1 at α=1.00 and is therefore 511 mm $^oC^{-1}$.

Similarly, it is found that the slope A_1^* of the linear relationship between annual runoff q_a and annual precipitation P_a is related with the basin ice-cover in the form of A_1^* = -1.605 α + 1.012 (r^2=0.67, N=13). a_1^* is approximated as that of A_1^* at α=0.00. The value of a_1^* is thus 1.012. It is larger than 1 because in most cases, the selected reference meteorological station is situated much lower than the mean altitude of the basin.

As defined, the runoff difference factor q_a^* is an index representing the difference between runoff from the ice-covered area and that from the ice free area, which are averages over the entire basin. q_a^* is of the order of 10^3 mm (Bernath, 1989) and is the largest of the three coefficients in equation 10.

In the following, q_a^* of the Rhône at Gletsch for the period 1894/1903-1970/1975 is determined based on the observed values of $\Delta\alpha$, ΔT_s and ΔP_a. During this period, $\Delta\alpha$ of the Rhône at Gletsch is -0.098. The mean ΔT_s and ΔP_a of Reckingen and Andermatt are +0.5 °C and -125 mm. The estimated runoff changes due to ΔT_s and ΔP_a from the last two terms of equation 13 are 145 mm and -54 mm, respectively. The observed change in mean annual runoff Δq_a is -338 mm. It follows from equation 13 that q_a^* estimated with the data of the Rhône at Gletsch is 4380 mm for this period. This magnitude of q_a^* is therefore 1.884 times of the basin mean annual precipitation (2314 mm), as determined from the isohyetal chart of mean annual precipitation for the period 1901-1940 compiled and revised by Uttinger (1978). Because q_a^* is expected to be proportional to the basin annual precipitation, the following parameterization for q_a^* is proposed:

$$q_a^* = 1.884\, P_a\,. \qquad (14)$$

Estimation of the runoff changes as the result of change in climate and basin ice-cover

The runoff difference factor q_a^* from the Rhône at Gletsch is used to estimate the runoff change of the Massa at Blatten near Naters and the Rhône at Porte du Scex. The processes of the estimation is presented in Table 2. It is found that the mean annual runoff of the Rhône at Porte du Scex has decreased by −231 mm due to the decrease of the basin ice-cover for the period of 1910/1919-1968/1972 and that of the Massa at Blatten near Naters is -69 mm for the period 1922/29-1968/72.

In Table 2, the changes of basin precipitation are deduced from the mean of 17 stations in the Rhône (Lemans, 1981). St Bernhard is used as a reference station for

TABLE 2 Estimation of the change in mean annual runoff Δq_a of the Massa at Blatten near Naters and that of the Rhône at Porte du Scex due to the changes in basin ice-cover $\Delta\alpha$, summer half-year temperature ΔT_s and basin annual precipitation ΔP_a. $\overline{P}_a$ is the long-term mean of the annual precipitation in the basin.

	Massa at Blatten near Naters			Rhône at Porte du Scex		
	1922/29	1968/72	Δ	1910/19	1968/72	Δ
Observed:						
$\overline{q}_a$ [mm]	2090	1891	-199	1066	1003	-63
α	0.709	0.659	-0.050	0.167	0.143	-.024
T_s [°C]	4.62	4.76	0.14	-0.35	0.14	0.47
P_a [mm]	905	853	-52	899	853	
Estimated:						
$q_a^* = 1.884\,\overline{P}_a$ [mm]		4635			2901	
$q_a^*\,\Delta\alpha$ [mm]		−231			−69	
$\alpha\, a_1\, \Delta T_s$ [mm]		49			37	
$(1-\alpha)\, a_1^*\Delta P_a$ [mm]		-17			-39	
Δq_a [mm]		-199			-71	

knowing the change of T_s in the basin Massa. The change of T_s for the basin of the Rhône at Porte du Scex is determined from the mean deviation of T_s from 25 stations in and near the Alps. The mean of P_a in the basin $\overline{P_a}$ is determined from Uttinger's (1978) isohyetal chart.

In a heavily glacierized basin like the Massa at Blatten near Naters, the effects of the glacier surface-area decrease dominates the decrease in runoff. If temperature had not increased during the fifty years, the reduction in discharge could have been larger. In a basin with relatively small ice-cover, such as the Rhône at Porte du Scex, the effect of climatic change becomes larger in comparison with the change in ice-cover. The reason for apparent domination of the effect of the decrease in basin ice-cover is the mutual compensation of the runoff increase due to the increase in temperature and the runoff decrease due to the reduction of the basin precipitation.

COMPARISON WITH PREVIOURS STUDY

Kasser (1959, 1973) has investigated the change in summer runoff due to the change in the ice-covered area for the Rhône at Porte du Scex for the period 1916-1968. His estimation shows that for this period, the change in the ice-covered area is -165 km^2 which is -19% with respect to the area in 1916. The decrease of the ice-covered area has resulted in a runoff reduction of 141 mm in the year 1968 or 16% of the mean summer runoff of 887 mm. Kasser uses the product of the summer ablation and the disappeared ice-covered area as a measure of runoff reduction resulting from change in the ice covered area. His studies show that the mean rate of the change in summer runoff due to the change in the ice-covered area for this period is -71 mm/a. With the method different from Kasser's, the present approach gives a value of -69 mm/a which well agrees with his result. Furthermore, the influence of climatic changes on the change in runoff is considered. The present method allows to take into consideration the discharge change due to climatic changes in addition to that resulting from the changes in the basin ice-covered area.

CONCLUSIONS

The existence of glaciers increases runoff significantly. The ratio of the summer-half year (May-September) runoff to the annual runoff reflects that runoff from a heavily ice-covered basin comes mostly in summer. An ice cover of 0.39-0.44 in an Alpine basin can reduce the variation of seasonal or annual runoff to a minimum.

Summer half-year temperature is a significant element influencing runoff from a heavily ice-covered basin while the correlation of runoff with precipitation increases as the ratio of basin ice-cover decreases. By evaluating the effects of changes in basin ice-cover, the summer temperature and annual precipitation on the total basin runoff, the change in the basin ice-cover is found to be the most important factor. For forecasting the runoff from a glacierized basin the ice-covered area must be accurately simulated.

ACKNOWLEDGEMENT The discussions with Prof. H. Lang, Dr. L. Braun, D. Grebner, H. Jensen and M. Aellen are greatly appreciated. Runoff data for Swiss stations are provided by the Swiss National Hydrological Survey. Meteorological data are from the Klimadatenbank and the Annalen of the Swiss Meteorological Institute. Prof. M. Kuhn and G. Markl of the University Innsbruck kindly provided the runoff and meteorological data of Vent.

REFERENCES

Aschwanden, H. and R. Weingartner. (1983) Die Abflussregimes der Schweiz. Teil 1, Alpine Abflussregimes. Geographisches Inst., Univ. Bern.

Bernath, A. (1980) Gedanken und Beiträge zum Wasserhaushalt eines teilweise vergletscherten Einzugsgebiets in den Schweizer Alpen. Diplomarbeit am Geographischen Institut der ETHZ, Zürich.

Bernath, A. (1989) Zum Wasserhaushalt im Einzugsgebiet der Rhone bis Gletsch. Ph. D. Thesis. Swiss Federal Institutte of Technology. Zürich, no. 9025.

Braithwaite,R.J., and Ole B. Olesen. (1988) Effect of glaciers on annual run-off, Johan Dahl Land, south Greenland. J. Glaciol., 34, 200-207.

Chen, J. and A. Ohmura. (1990) Estimation of Alpine glacier water resources and their change since the 1870s. International Conference on Water Resources in Mountainous Regions. Lausanne.

Collins, D. N. (1987) Climatic fluctuations and runoff from glacierized Alpine basins. IAHS Publ. no. 168, 77-89.

Ferguson, R. I. (1985) Runoff from glacierized mountains: a model for annual variation and its forecasting. Wat. Resour. Res., 21: 702-108.

Fountain, A. G. and W. V. Tangborn. (1985) The effect of glaciers on streamflow variations. Wat. Resour. Res., 21, 579-586.

Gross, G. (1987) Der Flächenverlust der Gletschern in Österreich 1850-1920-1969. Z. Gletscherkd. Glazialgeol., 23, 131-141.

Gutersohn, H. (1936) Ablation und Abfluss - Untersuchungen an Gletschern der Schweizer Alpen. AIHS Publ. no. 22, 401-416.

Kasser, P. (1959) Der Einfluss von Gletscherrückgan und Gletschervorstoss auf den Wasserhaushalt. Wasser- und Energiewirtschaft, 51, 155-168.

Kasser,P. (1973) Influence of changes in the glacierized area on summer runoff in the Porte du Scex drainage basin of the Rhône. AIHS Publ. no. 95, 219-225.

Kasser,P. (1981) Rezente Gletscherveränderungen in den Schweizer Alpen. In: Gletscher und Klima. Jarbuch der Schweizerischen Naturforschenden Gesselschaft, 1978, wissenschaftliche Teil, 106-138.

Krimmel, R. M. and W. V. Tangborn. (1974) South Cascade Glacier: the moderating effect of glaciers on runoff. Proc. the Western Snow Conference. 42nd annual meeting, 9-13.

Lang, H. (1986) Forecasting meltwater runoff from snow-covered area and from glacier basins. In: Kraijenhoff, D. A. and J. R. Moll (ed.): River flow modelling and Forecasting. D Reidel Publ. Company, 99-127.

Lemans A. M. (1981) Klimatologie der Schweiz, E Teil 13: Niedershclag, Schweizerische Meteorologische Anstalt. Zürich.

Moser, H., H. Escher-Vetler, H. Oerter, O. Reinwarth and D. Zunke. 1986. Abfluß in und von Gletschern. Teil 1 und 2. Gesellschaft für Strahlen und Umweltforschung. München.

Müller, F., T. Caflish and G. Müller. (1976) Firn und Eis der Schweizer Alpen. Publ. no. 57. Geographisches Institut der ETHZ, Zürich.

Röthlisberger H. and H. Lang. (1987) Glacier Hydrology. In: Gurnell A. M. and Clark M. J. (eds.): Glacio-fluvial sediment transfer: an alpine perspective. John Wiley and Sons, 207-284.

Schädler, B. (1985) Der Wasserhaushalt der Schweiz (1901-80). Mitteilung der Landeshydrologie, no. 6. Bern.

Tvede, A. M. (1983) Influence of glaciers on the variability of long runoff series. In: Tvede A. M. ed. Effect of distribution of snow and ice on streamflow. Report of Norwegian National Committee for Hydrology, no. 12, 179-189.

Uttinger, H. (1978) Mittlere Niederschlagsmengen in cm. Period 1901-1940. In: Imhof, E., H. Gutersohn, E. Huber, A. Meli, E. Perret, and E. L. Paillard (ed.): Atlas der Schweiz. Edgenösischen Landestopographie, Wabern.

Vivian, R. (1975) Les Glaciers des Alpes Occidentales. Imprimerie Allier, Grenoble.

Yang, Z. (1988) Runoff from glacier melting water in China and its nourishment to rivers. In: Y. Shi, B. Ren and M. Huang (ed.): Introduction to the glaciers in China. Science Press. Beijing. 187-204.

Hydrology in Mountainous Regions. I - Hydrological Measurements; the Water Cycle (Proceedings of two Lausanne Symposia, August 1990). IAHS Publ. no. 193, 1990.

Estimation of Alpine glacier water resources and their change since the 1870s

Jiyang Chen & Atsumu Ohmura
Department of Geography, Swiss Federal Institute of Technology, Winterthurerstrasse 190, CH-8057 Zürich, Switzerland

ABSTRACT An empirical formula relating volume of an Alpine glacier to the surface area is improved based on the data measured by radio-echo sounding and seismic method. The formula is used for calculating the present volume of the Alpine glaciers based on the surface-area data registered in the World Glacier Monitoring Service. The past volumes at several stages are estimated from the surface area and its change.

The ice-covered area of the Alpine glaciers was 4368±54 km^2 in the 1870s, 3541±33 km^2 in the 1930s, and 2909 km^2 in the 1970s. For the period 1870s-1970s, the volume of Alpine glaciers decreased by 57.4±20.4 km^3 with the volume in the 1970s being 140±10 km^3. The mean rate of changes over this period is about -15 km^2/a for the ice-covered area, -0.574 km^3/a for the volume and -0.163 m/a for the mean thickness.

The mass-turnover time of an Alpine glacier, which is important in investigating the water cycle of a basin with glaciers, is estimated to be in the order of 10^1-10^2a.

INTRODUCTION

It is of both scientific and practical importance to know the present amount of and historical changes in the water stored in the Alpine glaciers. The significant decrease in the volume of small glaciers and ice caps may contribute to sea level rise (Meier, 1984). In addition, the Alpine glaciers are of special significance as water resources. As an example, almost 64% of the electricity consumed in Switzerland is from the hydro-power plants and 24% is produced through the reservoirs which collect glacier meltwater (Müller et al., 1976).

The present ice-covered area of the Alpine glaciers is rather accurately known through the glacier inventory (Haeberli et al., 1989). The volume given through the glacier inventory is 67.4 km^3 for the Swiss glaciers (Müller et al., 1976) and 21 km^3 for the Austrian glaciers according to Patzelt (1980) whereby various estimation methods were used. A literature survey suggests that the present ice volume and the changes in the ice-covered area is known only for local regions and not for the whole Alps (Vivian, 1975; Müller et al., 1976; Kasser, 1981; Gross, 1987). In comparison with changes in ice-covered area, the changes in thickness and volume are much poorly understood.

In this work, the volume of the Alpine glaciers in the 1970s are estimated according to an improved empirical volume-area relationship and the data base of the Alpine glacier inventory registered in the World Glacier Monitoring Service. The changes in area and volume of the Alpine glaciers for the period 1870s-1970s are examined. Finally, the mass turnover time of an Alpine glacier is briefly discussed.

THE EMPIRICAL VOLUME-AREA RELATIONSHIP

The volume V of a glacier is well related with its surface area S and a power relationship is commonly applied:

$$V = c_0 S^{c_1} \tag{1}$$

with c_0 and c_1 being the empirical constants which are often deduced from the measured V and S. The common method for finding V of a glacier is to measure its thickness after the grid points or along profiles. A chart of the thickness-isoline is compiled and V can then be calculated. The accuracy of V is therefore strongly influenced by that of thickness soundings. The volume estimation of the Swiss glaciers by Müller et al. (1976) is based on Brückl's (1970) thickness-area relationship:

$$\langle h \rangle = 5.2 + 15.4\, S^{0.5} \tag{2}$$

where $\langle h \rangle$ [m] denotes the mean thickness over the entire glacier and S [km^2] is the surface area. Equation 2 was then the best available formula and used for the Swiss glacier inventory.

Equation 2 was based on the depth measurements by seismic soundings for 16 Alpine glaciers. Recently, a number of mountain glaciers have been measured through radio-echo soundings (Driedger & Kennard, 1986; Zhuravlev, 1988). The experiments on Swiss glaciers show that rather reliable results can be obtained through radio-echo soundings (Wächter, 1981 ; Haeberli et al, 1983). As the measured V data of more glaciers become available, it is possible to improve equation 2. From the data of 63 mountain glaciers (Table 1), it is found that:

$$V = 28.5\, S^{1.357} \tag{3}$$

with the squared correlation coefficient $r^2 = 0.96$ (Fig. 1). The unit of V is in 10^6 m^3 and that of S is 10^6 m^2. The standard deviation of the residuals s_e of equation 3 increases with S. s_e [10^6 m^3] is 0.43 for S [10^6 m^2] ≤ 0.5, 12.9 for $0.5 < S \leq 1.0$, 62 for $1.0 < S \leq 5.0$, 115 for $5.0 < S \leq 10.0$ and 303 for $10 < S \leq 20.0$. From equation 3, the mean thickness $\langle h \rangle$ is

$$\langle h \rangle = 28.5\, S^{0.357} \tag{4}$$

and the change in the volume ΔV of a mountain glacier can be approximated from the change in the surface area ΔS:

$$\Delta V = 38.716\, S^{0.357}\, \Delta S. \tag{5}$$

DISCUSSION ON THE VOLUME-AREA RELATIONSHIP

Equation 3 just concerns the mountain glaciers (except for ice-caps). It is deduced from the measured data of different accuracy and from the glaciers in different regions. The selected glaciers include 15 from the Alps (Brückl, 1970), 23 from the Cascade Ranges, 2 from the Rocky Mts., 1 from Wind River Range, 1 from Sierra Nevada, 1 from Mt. Shasta, 2 from the Kebnekaise Massif (Driedger & Kennard, 1986) and 17 from Svalbard (Zhuravlev, 1988). The $\langle h \rangle_m$ or V of some Svalbard glaciers may be underestimated (Dowdeswell & Drewry, 1984). It is therefore necessary to give some discussions on equation 3 before it is used for the Alpine glaciers.

Firstly, the magnitudes of the coefficients c_0 and c_1 in equation 1 remain within a certain range (Table 2). Except for the V-S relationship for 17 Svalbard glaciers, c_0 is between 17-30 and c_1 is between 1.15-1.52 whereby the difference is due to the fact that various types of glaciers are involved and due to accuracy of V determinations. Furthermore, two parameters which are physically related to the mean thickness are not considered in the V-S relationship: the surface slope and the basal shear stress (Paterson, 1970). The main difficulty in involving them is due to the data availability.

TABLE 1 The measured volume V [$10^6 \mathrm{m}^3$] and area S [km^2] used in this work. $\langle h\rangle$ [m]: the mean thickness. $\langle h\rangle_m = V/S$. $\langle h\rangle_1$: this work (eq. 3). $\langle h\rangle_2$: by eq. 2 after Müller et al. (1976). Data sources: 1 Brückl (1970), 2 Driedger & Kennard (1986), 3 Zhuravlev (1988), 4 cited from 2, 5 Kappenberger (1976), and 6 Wächter (1981) and Haeberli et al. (1983). * Not considered in eq. 3. **V is underestimated (Dowdeswell & Drewry, 1984)

Name	ϕ [° 'N]	λ [° ']	S	V	$\langle h\rangle_m$	$\langle h\rangle_1$	$\langle h\rangle_2$	Sources
Athabasca*	51 40	116 50 W	3.8	574	150	46	35	4
Brandner	47 04	9 42 E	2.08	29.12	14	37	27	1
Carbon	46 56	121 47 W	7.92	710	90	60	49	2
Cascade S.	48 22	121 03 W	3.3	196	59	44	33	4
Coalman	-	-	0.08	1	14	12	15	2
Coe	-	-	1.2	53	43	30	22	2
Collier	-	-	1.1	21	19	30	21	2
Diller	-	-	0.66	13	20	25	18	2
Dinwoody	43 10	109 40 W	1.5	80	55	33	24	4
Eliot	-	-	1.7	91	54	34	25	2
Emmons	46 52	121 41 W	11.17	672	60	68	57	2
Findelen	46 01	7 51 E	19.09	1489.02	78	82	72	1
Gefrorenewand*	47 04	11 40 E	4.59	91.8	20	49	38	1
Gepatsch	10 46	46 51 E	17.69	1328	71	80	70	1
Gosau Gr.	47 29	13 36 E	1.48	42.92	29	33	24	1
Grinnell	48 50	113 50 W	1	62	64	29	21	4
Gurgler	46 48	10 59 E	11.14	401.04	36	67	57	1
Guslar Gr.	46 51	10 49 E	1.76	49.28	28	35	26	1
Hallstaetter	47 29	13 37 E	3.3	108.9	33	44	33	1
Hayden	-	-	0.72	19	26	25	18	2
Hintereis	46 48	10 46 E	9.47	473.5	50	64	53	1
Isfalls	67 55	18 34 E	1.4	92	72	32	23	4
Kesselwand	46 50	10 48 E	4.24	284.08	67	48	37	1
Ladd	-	-	0.9	24	33	27	27	2
Langille	-	-	0.4	8	20	21	5	2
Lost Creek	-	-	0.54	14	21	23	17	2
Maclure	37 40	119 10 W	0.2	4	17	16	5	4
Newton-Clark	-	-	2	39	20	37	27	2
Nisqually	46 48	121 44 W	4.6	220	48	49	38	2
Palmer	-	-	0.13	2	16	14	5	2
Pasterzen	47 06	12 41 E	19.78	1246.14	63	83	74	1
Prouty	-	-	1	16	17	29	21	1
Rabots	67 54	18 33 E	4.1	346	84	47	36	4
Reid	-	-	0.75	18	24	26	19	2
Russell	-	-	3.3	86	26	44	33	2
Sandy	-	-	1.2	25	21	30	22	2
Schladminger	47 28	13 38 E	0.81	7.29	9	26	19	1
Schiedinger	47 12	12 41 E	1.81	45.25	25	35	26	1
Storgl.	67 54	18 34 E	3.12	306	99	43	32	4
Sulztal	47 00	11 05 E	4.14	198.72	48	47	37	1
Tahoma N.-L.	46 50	121 49 W	8.63	457	52	62	50	2
Vernagt	46 53	10 49 E	9.56	583.16	61	64	53	1
White River	-	-	0.54	8.9	16	23	17	2
Whitney	41 25	122 13 W	1.38	26	20	32	23	4
Wilson	-	-	1.4	54	38	32	23	2
Winthrop	-	-	9.2	525	57	63	52	2
Zigzag	-	-	0.78	17	22	26	19	2
Zmutt	46 00	7 38 E	16.98	1341.42	79	78	69	1
Aldegonda	-	-	10.3	710	69	66	55	3
Antonia	-	-	32	4000	125	98	92	3
Bertill	-	-	6	440	73	54	43	3
Boger	-	-	4.5	300	67	49	38	3
Bruegger Bost	-	-	13.3	760	57	72	61	3
Bruegger Zap.	-	-	5.6	240	43	53	42	3
Vöring	-	-	2.1	130	62	37	28	3
Dalfonna	-	-	9.8	860	88	64	53	3
Lein	-	-	4.1	310	76	47	36	3
Loven Srednii	-	-	5.8	370	64	53	42	3
Meryal	-	-	6.4	470	73	55	44	3
Penk**	-	-	83	8850	107	141	146	3
Revtan	-	-	5.9	290	49	54	43	3
Suess	-	-	9	540	60	62	51	3
Finsterwalder**	-	-	38	2800	74	105	100	3
Gess	-	-	7.2	460	64	58	47	3
Erdman	-	-	11.2	1410	126	68	57	3
Laika*	75 55	79 15 W	4.28	223	52	48	37	5
Rhône*	46 37	8 24 E	17.38	1773	102	79	69	6
$\Sigma\lvert\langle h\rangle_c-\langle h\rangle_m\rvert/N$						14.6	16.9	
$\Sigma(\langle h\rangle_c-\langle h\rangle_m)/N$						-2.7	-12.1	

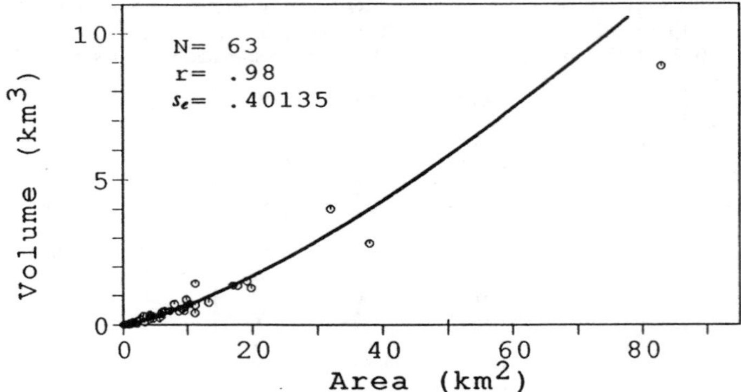

FIG.1 Relationship between the volume [km^3] and the surface area [km^2] of a mountain glacier. Based on the data from 63 glaciers in Table 1 (Brückl, 1970; Driedger and Kennard, 1986; Zhuravlev, 1988). *r*: the correlation coefficient. s_e: the standard deviation of the residuals.

Secondly, the accuracy of different *V-S* relationships can be evaluated by comparing the residual for the calculation of the mean thickness $e = \langle h\rangle_c - \langle h\rangle_m$. It can be shown that the residual is $e = -4.7 + 0.856\ S^{0.357}$ [m] for equation 4 of this work and $e = -19 - 0.554\ S^{0.5}$ for equation 2 (Brückl, 1970). It follows that equation 4 does give better results than the $\langle h\rangle$-*S* relationship applied in the Swiss glacier inventory by Müller et al. (1976).

Thirdly, the measured change in the mean thickness $\langle \Delta h\rangle$ or volume ΔV of a glacier, which is revealed by comparing the large scale topographic maps over relatively long period, are compared with the values calculated from equation 5 based on the known area of the glacier and the measured area change ΔS. From the data of 26 observations for Alpine glaciers (Finsterwalder,1953; Finsterwalder & Rentsch, 1973; Long & Patzelt, 1971; Chen & Funk, submitted), it is found that the standard deviation of the residuals of the linear relationship between the measured and the calculated values is 33x10^{6}m^3 for ΔV and 3.6 m for $\langle \Delta h\rangle$. The calculated and measured values agree fairly well, especially when the considered period is longer.

TABLE 2 Comparison of the values of coefficients c_0 and c_1 of equation 1. The coefficients for No. 2-9 are recalculated. *N*: number of the glaciers; r^2: the squared correlation coefficient; s_e [10^{6}m^3]: the standard deviation of the residuals; *S*: the area range; Method: Sei.-seismic soundings, Rec.-reconstructed from geomorhpological evidence, Rad. - radio-echo sounding, Mix.-seismic or radio-echo sounding, and Est.: estimated. Data source: 1 Erasov (1968) and cited from 6; 2 Brückl (1970); 3 Maisch (1981); 4 & 5 Driedger and Kennard (1986); 6 from 2 & 4; 7 Shi et al. (1981); 8 Zhuravlev (1988); 9 from 2, 4 and 8.

No	*N*	c_0	c_1	r^2	s_e	*S* [km^2]	Method	Mountain glaciers in	Data source
1	-	27.	1.5	-	-		-	Central Asia	1
2	16	16.133	1.520±0.092	0.95	110.9	0.9 -19.3	Sei.	Alps	2
3	63	24.626	1.391±0.033	0.97	35.3	0.4 - 7.5	Rec.	Graubünden, Alps	3
4	32	30.834	1.405±0.071	0.93	105.0	0.1 -11.0	Mix.	Cascade & other areas	4
5	15	21.346	1.145±0.041	0.98	3.3	0.08 - 3.3	Rad.	Cascade, small glaciers	5
6	49	27.551	1.358±0.045	0.95	166.5	0.08 -19.3	Mix.	Alps, Cascade and other areas	6
7	7	36.056	1.406±0.094	1.00	9.4	0.05 -7.02	Est.	Qilian Mountains, China	7
8	17	47.995	1.186±0.070	0.95	374.0	2.1 - 83.	Rad.	Mountain glaciers in Svalbard	8
9	63	28.524	1.357±0.037	0.96	401.4	0.08 - 83.	Mix.	Alps, Cascade and Svalbard etc.	9

ESTIMATION OF THE AREA CHANGE

The measured areas of 324 Swiss glaciers are selected and compared for the period of 1870s-1930s-1970s whereby the data are from Jegerlehner (1902), Rindlisbacher (1954) and Müller et al. (1976). It shows that the area of an Alpine glacier at different times is related with each other in the following manner for 218 glaciers larger than 0.5 km^2:

$$S(1870s) = 0.219 + 1.175\, S(1970s) \qquad (r^2 = 0.98 \;\&\; s_e = 0.593) \qquad (6a)$$

$$S(1930s) = 0.100 + 1.103\, S(1970s) \qquad (r^2 = 0.99 \;\&\; s_e = 0.398) \qquad (6b)$$

and in the forms below for 106 glaciers smaller or equal to 0.5 km^2:

$$S(1870s) = 1.024\, S(1970s)^{0.589} \qquad (r^2 = 0.61 \;\&\; s_e = 0.305) \qquad (6c)$$

$$S(1930s) = 1.006\, S(1970s)^{0.800} \qquad (r^2 = 0.93 \;\&\; s_e = 0.181) \qquad (6d)$$

with the decade in the bracket being the reference time.

A rough estimation of the change in the Alpine ice-covered area since the 1870s can be made under the following assumptions:

(1) The area of Alpine glaciers has not changed much after the inventory time (1970s). This seems to be reasonable (Wood, 1988);
(2) Equations 6 a-d are representative of the Alpine glaciers; and
(3) No glaciers have disappeared since the 1870s. This is not the case (Gross, 1987), but there is not an easy way to estimate.

The changes in the ice-covered area in the Alps are estimated by using equations 6 a-d for single glaciers registered in the data base of the WGMS, that is, using equations 6a and 6b for glaciers with $S > 0.5$ km^2 and equations 6c and 6d for glaciers with $S \leq 0.5$ km^2. The results are summarized in Table 3 for three stages: the 1870s, 1930s and 1970s.

The calculated Swiss ice-covered area is 1580±21 km^2 in the 1930s and 1848±38 km^2 in the 1870s which agrees well with the measured values given by Rindlisbacher (1954). According to Gross (1987), the measured ice-covered area in Austria in 1870/1873 is 995 km^2 which is based on Richter's (1888) work plus the small glaciers not considered by Richter. The area in 1920 calculated by Gross (1987) is 808 km^2 and the method for his calculation was not declared. The ice-covered area in the 1930s can thus be interpolated as 727 km^2 with a mean rate of -5.4 km^2/a for the period 1920-1969. These values are considerably larger than those estimated from equations 6 a-d, which are 782±27 km^2 in the 1870s and 652±15 km^2 in the 1930s. In fact, Richter apparently overestimated the glacier area since the rock area above the snow line was partly counted as glacier area. Moreover, the disappeared glaciers can not be considered in the present work which make a significant portion (6.4%). It may also suggests that the area loss of glaciers is much larger in the eastern Alps than in the Swiss Alps.

TABLE 3 Ice-covered area [km^2] for the period 1870s-1930s-1970s in the Alps. Data sources: 1 Alpine glacier inventory (Haeberli et al., 1989); 2 Rindlisbacher (1954), 3 Müller et al. (1976), 4 Gross (1987); 5 This work; and 6 Estimated from Gross (1987).

Reference period	France	Switzerland	Austria & Germany	Italy	Alps
1870s	640±25 (5)	1818 (2)	995 (4)	915±29 (5)	4368±54
1930s	516±18 (5)	1556 (2)	727 (6)	742±15 (5)	3541±33
1970s	417 (1)	1342 (3)	543 (1)	607 (1)	2909

ESTIMATION OF THE VOLUME AND ITS CHANGE

Equation 3 is applied for the single glaciers registered in the glacier-inventory data base of the World Glacier Monitoring Service to calculate the present ice-volume. For finding the volume change during the 1870s-1970s, equations 6a and 6c are used to estimate the area change ΔS and then the volume change is approximated by using equation 5. The results for the entire Alps are presented in Table 4. The uncertainty intervals are determined at the confidence level of 95%.

The results given in Table 4 are considered to be a rough estimation. However, it covers the entire Alps and it has improved the result of previous studies. Through the inventory, Müller et al. (1976) showed that the ice volume of the Swiss glaciers in 1973 is 67.4 km^3, which is obtained by applying equation 2 for the glaciers with $0.5<S<23$ km^2. A constant of $<h> = 5$ m was assumed for those with $S<0.5$ km^2 and individual estimation was made for those with $S>23$ km^2. It is clear that equation 2 underestimate the mean thickness of a glacier in most cases (Table 1). The present work shows that the total volume of Austrian glaciers is 22 km^3. This can be compared with the 21 km^3 which is given by Patzelt (1980) through glacier inventory and which is obtained by assuming a mean thickness of 40 m for all the Austrian glaciers.

The data in Table 3 suggests that the ice-covered area of the Alpine glaciers has decreased by 1459±54 km^2 or 33% for the period 1870s-1970s. The area loss during the 1870s-1930s (19%) is slightly larger than that during the 1930s-1970s (18%). It is shown that the volume of the Alpine glaciers has decreased by about 29% or 57±20 km^3 for the period 1870s-1970s. The mean rate of changes in the total area, the total volume and area weighted mean thickness of Alpine glaciers for the period 1870s-1970s is -15 km^2/a, and -0.574 km^3/a and -0.163 m/a, respectively.

TABLE 4 Change in area ΔS and volume ΔV of the Alpine glaciers for the period 1870s-1970s S: the present area; V: the volume in the 1970s; $\Delta V/(V+|\Delta V|)$: the relative volume change; and $<\Delta h>/\Delta t$: the mean rate of change in the mean thickness.

Region	S [km^2]	ΔS [km^2]	V [km^3]	ΔV [km^3]	$\Delta V/(V+\|\Delta V\|)$ [%]	$<\Delta h>/\Delta t$: [$m\ a^{-1}$]
France	417	-223±25	17.0±3.2	-8.2±6.4	-33	-0.155
Switzerland	1342	-476	79.3±9.1	-27.9±18.2	-26	-0.177
Austria & Germany	543	-452	21.9±2.0	-9.9±4.0	-31	-0.150
Italy	607	-308±29	22.0±1.9	-11.3±3.8	-34	-0.174
Sum	2909	-1459±57	140.1±10.2	-57.4±20.4		
Mean					-29	-0.163

TURNOVER TIME OF AN ALPINE GLACIERS' MASS

The turnover time of an Alpine glacier's mass τ_g is important in investigating the water cycle of a basin with glaciers. τ_g can be defined as the ratio of the volume to the rate of mass output and it can be expressed as:

$$\overline{<\tau_g>} = \overline{<h>}/\overline{<ma>} \tag{7}$$

with $<h>$ being the mean thickness of the glacier and $<ma>$ the annual mass turnover. A bar specifies the mean over time. $<ma>$ is

$$<ma> = (<b_{ac}> + |<b_{aa}>|) / 2 \quad (8)$$

where $<b_{ac}>$ and $<b_{aa}>$ are the annual balance in the accumulation area and ablation area. Both are averaged over the entire glacier. The specific annual mass turnover $<ma>$ of 14 Alpine glaciers is calculated from the available data (Kasser, 1967, 1973; Müller, 1977; Haeberli, 1986; Haeberli et al, 1988). The mean $<ma>$ of 14 Alpine glaciers is 520 mm w. e./a (mm water equivalent per year) with the standard deviation being 278 mm w. e..

The turnover time of an Alpine glaciers' mass is estimated from equation 7 whereby a reference value of $<ma>$ of 520 mm w. e./a is used. The mean time needed for an Alpine glacier to renew its mass totally is estimated to be 30-60a for a glacier with the surface area S = 0.1-1.0 km^2, 100-120a for one with S = 5.0-10.0 km^2, and 200-240a for one with S = 50.0-100.0 km^2.

CONCLUSIONS AND PERSPECTIVES

The general changes of the Alpine glaciers can be approximately summarized as follows for the period 1870s-1970s: The ice-covered area of the Alpine glaciers was 4368±54 km^2 in the 1870s, 3541±33 km^2 in the 1930s, and 2909 km^2 in the 1970s. For the period 1870s-1970s, the volume of Alpine glaciers decreased by 57±20 km^3 while the volume in the 1970s is 140.1±10.2 km^3. The mean rate of changes in the total area, the total volume and the mean thickness of Alpine glaciers for the period 1870s-1970s are approximately -15 km^2/a, -0.574 km^3/a and -0.163 m/a, respectively. The estimated mass turnover time of an Alpine glacier is in the order of 10^1-10^2a.

At present, the volume - area relationship is widely applied in glacier inventory and water resources estimation due to its simplicity. However, such volume - area relationship should be improved as more accurately measured volume data become available. It is necessary to establish different volume - area relationships according to the type of mountain glaciers (cirque glacier, hanging glacier, valley glacier etc.). In addition, the surface slope of a glacier should be involved in future investigations for estimating the thickness and volume. Because the absolute error of volume estimation increases with the size of the glacier, the volume of larger glaciers (S>20 km^2) should be individually estimated.

ACKNOWLEDGEMENT Dr. W. Haeberli of the World Glacier Monitoring Service has given kind permission for the access to the data base of the Alpine glacier inventory. Dr. P. Müller helped with the transfer of the glacier inventory data. We would also like to express thanks to Mr. M. Aellen and the colleagues of the Department of Geography, Swiss Federal Institute of Technology in Zürich for the discussions and assistance.

REFERENCES

Brückl, E. (1970) Eine Methode zur Volumenbestimung von Gletschern auf Grund der Plastizitätstheorie. Archiv für Meteorologie, Geophysik und Bioklimatologie, Ser.A. 19, 317-328.

Chen J. and M. Funk. (submitted) Mass balance of the Rhône Glacier during 1882/83-1986/87. J. Glaciol.

Dowdeswell, J. A. and D. J. Drewry. (1984) Radio-echo sounding of Spitzbergen glaciers: problems in the interpretation of layer and bottom returns. J. Glaciol., 30, 16-21.

Driedger, C. and P. Kennard. (1986) Glacier volume estimation on Cascade volcanoes - an analysis and comparison with other methods. Annals of Glaciology, 8, 59-64.

Erasov, N.V. (1968) Method to determine the volume of mountain glaciers. Materialy Glyatsiol. Issled. Khronika, Obsuzhdeniya, no.14. Moscow.

Gross, G. (1987) Der Flächenverlust der Gletschern in Österreich 1850-1920-1969. Z. Gletscherkd. Glazialgeol., 23, 131-141.

Finsterwalder,R. (1953) Die Zahlenmäsige Erfassung des Gletscherrückgans an Ostalpengletschern. Z. Gletscherkd. Glazialgeol., 2, 189-239.

Finsterwalder,R., and H. Rentsch. (1980) Zur Höhenänderung von Ostalpengletschern im Zeitraum 1969-1979. Z. Gletscherkd. Glazialgeol., 16, 111-115.

Haeberli, W. (1986) Fluctuations of Glaciers 1980-1985, 4, IAHS (ICSI) /UNEP/UNESCO, Paris.

Haeberli, W., H. P. Wächter, W. Schmid, and G. Sidler. (1983) Erste Erfahrungen mit dem U. S.-Geological-Survey-monopuls-radioecholot im Firn, Eis und Permafrost der Schweizer Alpen. Z. Gletscherkd. Glazialgeol., 19, 61-72.

Haeberli, W. and P. Müller. (1988) Fluctuations of Glaciers 1980-1985, 5, IAHS (ICSI) /UNEP/UNESCO, Paris.

Haeberli, W., H. Bösch, G. Scherler, G. Østrem and C. C. Wallèn. (1989) World glacier inventory status 1988, A contribution to the International Hydrological Programme and the Global Environment Monitoring System. IAHS(ICSI)-UNEP-UESCO.

Jegerlehner, J. (1902) Die Schneegrenze in den Gletschergebieten der Schweiz. Gerlands Beträge zur Geophysik. 5, 486-566.

Kappenberger, G. (1976) Massenhaushalt und Bewegung des Laika Gletschers, Coburg Island N. W. T. 1973/74. Diplomarbeit am Geographischen Institut der ETH Zürich.

Kasser, P. (1967) Fluctuations of Glaciers 1959-1965, 1, IAHS/UNESCO, Paris.

Kasser, P. (1973) Fluctuations of Glaciers 1965-1970, 2, IAHS(ICSI)/UNESCO, Paris.

Kasser, P. (1981). Rezente Gletscherveränderungen in den Schweizer Alpen. In: Gletscher und Klima. Jahrbuch der Schweizerischen Naturforschenden Gessellschaft, 1978, Wissenschaftliche Teil, 106-138.

Lang, H. and G. Patzelt. (1971) Die Volumenänderung des Hintereisferners (Oetztaler Alpen) im Vergleich zur Massenänderung im Zeitraum 1953-1964. Z. Gletscherkd. Glazialgeol., 7, 39-55.

Maisch, M. (1981) Glaziologische und Gletscher-geschichtliche Untersuchungen im Gebiet Zwischen Landwasser- und Albulatal (Kt. Graubünden, Schweiz). Physische Geographie, 3, Geographisches Institut, Univ. Zürich.

Meier, M. F. (1984) The contribution of small glaciers to global sea-level. Science, 226, 1418-1421.

Müller, F. (1977) Fluctuations of Glaciers 1970-1975, 3, IAHS(ICSI)/UNESCO, Paris.

Müller, F., T. Caflish and G. Müller. (1976) Firn und Eis der Schweizer Alpen. Publ. no. 57. Geographisches Institut der ETH Zürich.

Paterson, W. S. B. (1970) The application of ice physics to glacier studies. In: Glaciers. Proc. Workshop Seminar. Canadian National Committee for the International Hydrological Decade. Ottawa, 43-46.

Patzelt, G. (1980) The Austrian glacier inventory: status and first results. IAHS Publ. no. 126, 181-183.

Richter, E. (1888) Die Gletscher der Ostalpen. Handbücher zur Deutschen Landes- und Volkskunde. 3. Bd. J. Engelhorn, Stuttgart.

Rindlisbacher, J. (1954) Flächenstatistik, Planimetrierung der Gletscher (Schweiz u. ausländ. Terriotorium). Bearbeitet auf Landeskarte by Eidg. Amt für Wasserwirtschaft. Vol. 1 & 2.

Shi Yafeng, Wang Zongtai and Liu Chaohai. (1981) Note on the glacier inventory in Qilian Shan Mountains. In: Glacier Inventory of China, 1, Qilian Mountains, Lanzhou Inst. of Glaciology and Geocryology, 1-9.

Vivian, R. (1975) Les Glaciers des Alpes Occidentales. Imprimerie Allier, Grenoble.

Wächter, H. P. (1981) Eisdickenmessungen auf dem Rhonegletscher - Ein Versuch mit Radio-Echo Sounding. Diplomarbeit am Geographischen Institut der ETH Zürich.

Wood, F. B. (1988) Global alpine glacier trends, 1960s to 1980s. Arctic and Alpine Res., 20, 404-413.

Zhuravlev, A. V. (1988) The relation between glacier area and volume. In: G.A. Avsyuk (ed.) Data of Glaciological Studies, no. 40. Russian Translations Series, no.67. A. A. Balkema, Rotterdam. 441-446.

Hydrology in Mountainous Regions. I - Hydrological Measurements; the Water Cycle (Proceedings of two Lausanne Symposia, August 1990). IAHS Publ. no. 193, 1990.

Contribution de la neige et des glaciers dans le débit des rivières: suivi par télédétection spatiale

J.P. DEDIEU
Laboratoire de la Montagne Alpine (LAMA), URA 344 CNRS, Institut de Géographie Alpine, F-38030 GRENOBLE, France

Résumé A partir des connaissances acquises en laboratoire, les données satellitaires peuvent compléter en zone de haute montagne les réseaux de mesure au sol en hydrologie, utiles pour le suivi de la fusion nivale et des bilans glaciaires.

Abstract Founded on laboratory results, Remote Sensing data can provide further informations in high mountains aeras , for hydrological ground network of snowmelt previsions and glacial mass-balance.

INTRODUCTION

La télédétection spatiale et aéroportée, enregistrement à distance du rayonnement électromagnétique émis ou réfléchi par toute surface terrestre, possède un grand nombre d'applications dans le domaine des ressources en eaux continentales (inventaire, suivi multitemporel).

En zone de montagne, la rétention nivale saisonnière ou la capitalisation par les glaciers des lames d'eau précipitées sur les massifs sont des phénomènes suivis par télédétection depuis de nombreuses années, mais essentiellement dans le domaine de la cartographie des surfaces enneigées ou englacées par grand bassin versant.

PRINCIPES

les signatures spectrales de l'eau et de la glace sont nettement différenciables dans le domaine spectral du visible et du proche infrarouge ; domaine de détection du satellite SPOT (10 m et 20 m au sol). Une cartographie des surfaces en neige ou glace est possible dans ce domaine de longueurs d'ondes.
Mais reconstituer l'équivalent en eau complet d'un manteau neigeux est très improbable en raison du faible pouvoir de pénétration de ces rayonnements dans la neige et la glace (20 cm).Seul le canal infrarouge moyen de Landsat (1,55 µm-1,75 µm) permet de distinguer la neige des nuages et identifie l'état qualitatif de la surface d'un manteau neigeux (Dozier, USA, 1987).
Par contre, les longueurs d'ondes lointaines saisies par les radars actifs aéroportés ou satellisés permettent d'espérer plus rigoureusement une estimation quantitative précise des stocks en eau retenus par la neige et les glaciers, et alimentant les cours d'eau en zone de montagne.

CONTEXTE

dans l'attente de la mise en service opérationnelle d'un capteur hyperfréquences (radar) sur un satellite (ERS1 - 1991), le Laboratoire de la Montagne Alpine propose depuis 1987 une méthode de suivi des couvert neigeux et des appareils glaciaires fondée sur une complémentarité entre les analyses d'images numériques SPOT-Landsat TM et les réseaux de mesures existant au sol dans les Alpes francaises.
Un vaste secteur d'étude a été retenu (Figure 1) et les recherches sont effectuées en étroite collaboration avec les organismes qui

suivent :

- Météorologie Nationale. Centre d'Etude de la Neige, Grenoble : analyse d'échantillons de neige en laboratoire (chambre froide)
- Electricité de France. Groupe Production Hydraulique, Grenoble: saisie automatique de mesures terrain (hauteur de neige, **densité**)
- Laboratoire CNRS de Glaciologie, Grenoble : mesures de terrain des variations des bilans glaciaires et modélisation des résultats.

Méthodologies, expérimentations et résultats obtenus reposent sur la collaboration scientifique de ces établissements de Recherche.

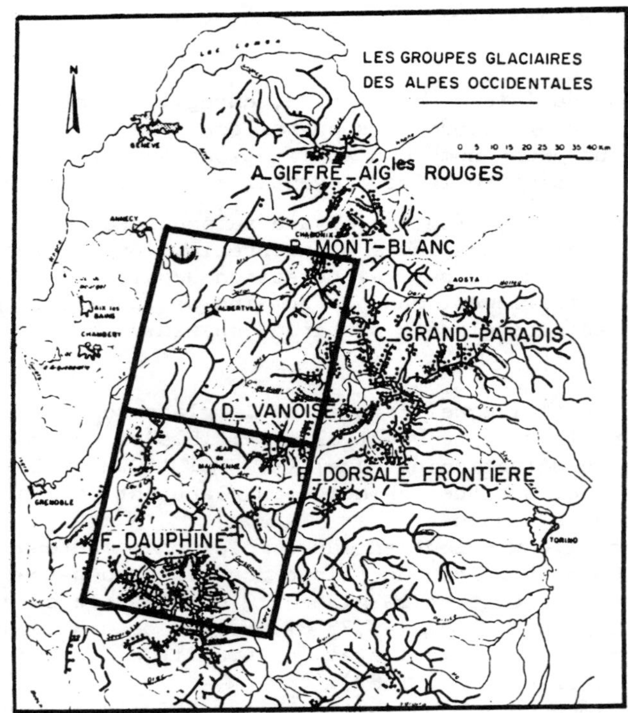

FIG. 1 Zone géographique de l'étude et limites des images satellitaires SPOT et Landsat utilisées: bassin versant de l'Isère (massifs de la Vanoise et Oisans).

1. NIVOLOGIE ET TELEDETECTION

1.1. Mesures de l'équivalent en eau du manteau neigeux

les mesures manuelles ou automatisées d'épaisseur et de densité du manteau neigeux par grand massif montagneux permettent à de nombreux organismes de relier les situations pluviométriques et nivométriques de chaque hiver avec les débits enregistrés lors de la fusion nivale dans les cours d'eau. Des modèles de prévision ont ainsi été constitués sur la base de ces corrélations (DUBAND EDF, 1988). La figure 2

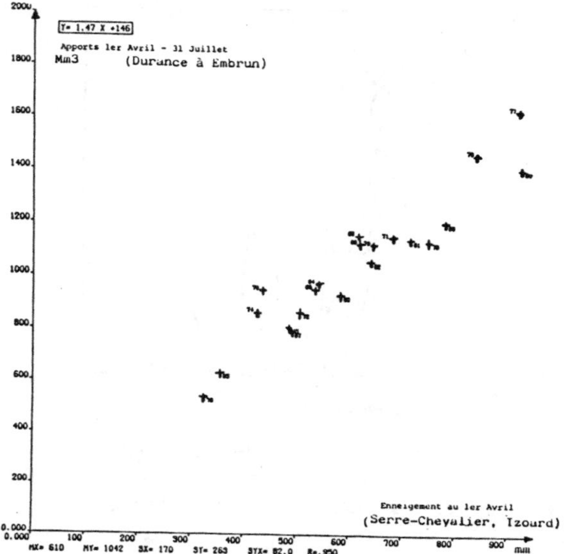

FIG. 2 Comparaison entre les valeurs en eau de la neige en fin d'hiver et le volume d'apports pour le bassin versant de la Durance: période 1970-1989. (Source: EDF, France.)

illustre bien la représentativité des sondages nivologiques, surtout en ce qui concerne les années récentes très déficitaires pour le remplissage des grands réservoirs dans les Alpes francaises. Si les modèles de prévision des débits sont efficaces en période d'accumulation nivale, les estimations des débits restitués s'avèrent plus délicates en période de fusion (juin) en raison de l'inégale répartition des mécanismes locaux de fonte (exposition, pente, altitude).

Dans cet objectif, de nombreux auteurs ont proposé depuis 1975 des modèles de fusion nivale en montagne, à partir de l'interprétation de données télédétection visible et proche infra-rouge (Rango et al, 1980). Il s'agit uniquement d'une délimitation de la ligne inférieure du manteau (altitude) et d'une estimation du pourcentage d'enneigement du bassin versant (surface). Pour efficace que soit cette approche répétitive tout au long de l'hiver en ce qui concerne une cartographie des surfaces enneigées par bassin versant, les auteurs s'accordent pour considérer qu'il n'existe pas de relation directe entre la densité moyenne d'un manteau neigeux (ou son équivalent en eau) et sa réflectance visible ou PIR pour des épaisseurs supérieures à 40 cm (Leprieur, 1987).

1.2. Apports actuels de la Télédétection

en ce qui concerne les propriétés optiques de la neige, l'effet de dimension des grains semble jouer un rôle déterminant dans la réponse radiométrique de l'infra-rouge moyen. Les études de laboratoire (Sergent et al, 1987) ont montré cette influence du rayon des cristaux, peut-être liée également à un effet secondaire de teneur en eau dans la neige de surface.
La figure 3 montre très explicitement ce phénomène à partir de 1 µm.

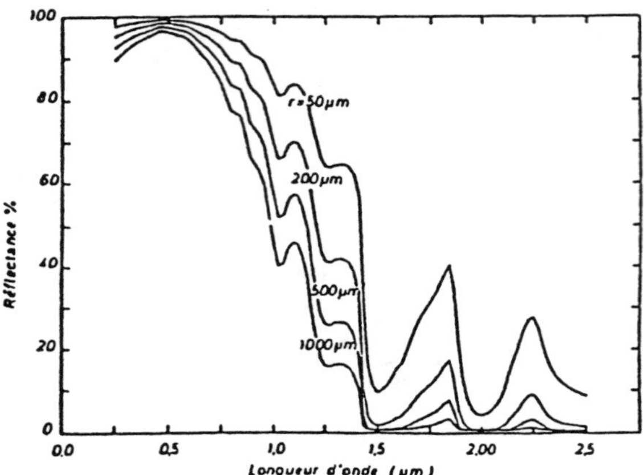

FIG. 3 Signature spectrale de différents rayons de cristaux (50-100 µm) pour un éclairement à 60°: spectre visible et infra-rouge (Dozier, 1988).

Nous avons donc tenté de relier et confronter les analyses radiométriques d'une image Landsat TM sur les Alpes le 18 avril 1984 avec les informations au sol fournies par les stations automatiques EDF le jour même.

METHODOLOGIE :

- .correction des éclairements sur l'image d'hiver (ombre portée des versants) ;
- .correction des effets de déformation du relief sur l'image;
- .traitement de l'image par indice de ratio TM2/TM5 (rapport des indices de réflectance visible et infra-rouge moyen).

RESULTATS :

- . superficie des zones enneigées sur l'image dans le bassin versant de l'Arc (affluent de l'Isère) = 1173 km2, soit 60 % du bassin.

(pour {Débits restitués pour le mois : 5,1 m3)
(information {Débits cumulés du 18.04 au 01.07 : 1200 Mm3)

Cette image se situe donc en fin de période d'accumulation et l'analyse du contexte météorologique a montré une forte élévation des températures depuis le 16.04, avec début de fusion du manteau.

La consultation des informations recueillies par les Télénivomètres EDF en site d'altitude (Figure 4) a été complétée par les rélevés de hauteur de neige et d'état de surface dans quelques grandes stations de ski également présentes sur l'image satellite.

La comparaison entre les paramètres relevés au sol le 18 avril s'est en fait avérée très décevante pour les canaux du visible, de plus le canal thermique de Landsat n'a pu etre utilisé en l'absence de mesure des températures au sol.

Par contre, la confrontation entre le ratio TM2 TM5 et les valeurs de densité de surface du manteau pour 7 postes EDF utilisables ce jour a semblé particulièrement intéressante (Figure 5). On constate une relation étroite entre les deux axes du graphique.

EMPLACEMENT	ALTITUDE	DENSITE de la couche sup. (0 - 10 cm)	HAUTEUR totale de neige (cm)	DENSITE moyenne de la totalité du manteau	EQUIVALENT EN EAU (mm)
SOLAISE	2535 m	0,34	100	0,43	430
CEZANNE	1800 m	0,33	170	0,41	697
CHARDONNET	2455 m	0,27	190	0,39	741
FRAZERE	2545 m	0,21	40	0,35	136
PLAN SETI	2640 m	0,26	220	0,41	902
Ntd. AOUT*	2500 m	0,23	280	0,43	1204
BISSORTE**	2290 m	0,19	210	0,39	819

* mesure le 19/04/1984 (conditions météorologiques identiques)
** reconstitution des données à partir des mesures du 11/04 et 22/04

FIG. 4 Données télénivomètres. (Source: EDF, France.)

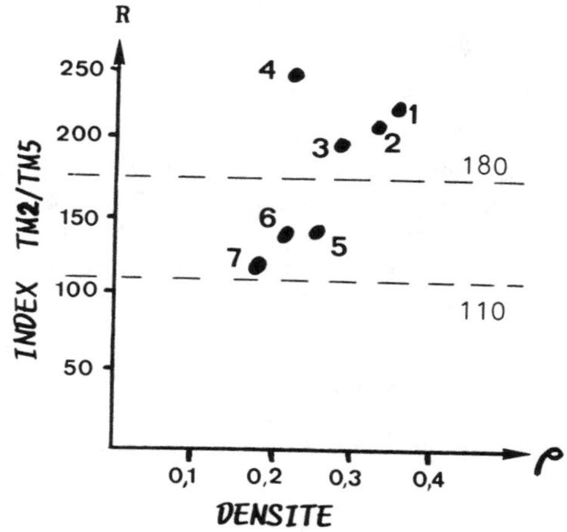

FIG. 5 Comparaison entre le ratio TM2 TM5 et 7 postes de mesure de densité de surface du manteau (0 à -10 cm). (LAMA et EDF)

Nous avons alors étendu ces valeurs de réflectance à l'ensemble de l' image et observé les phénomènes suivants :

- les valeurs les plus faibles de l'indice correspondent aux zones de neiges peu transformées (grains fins ou neige sèche) : versants N. et massifs septentrionaux.

- les valeurs les plus élevées de l'indice correspondent en fait aux neiges à forte teneur en eau liquide dans la couche de surface, et donc en situation de fusion (grains gros et ronds).

En conclusion, cette méthode d'interprétation des données spatiales est issue des expérimentations théoriques de laboratoire, appliquée sur le terrain à une situation concrète, et conforme avec la réalité des mécanismes de fonte sur l'espace géographique couvert par l'image : exposition des versants, latitude du massif, ...

1.3. Perspectives

En télédétection, et à l'échelle de grands bassins versants parfois peu accessibles (pays lointains), les possibilités actuelles et futures sont les suivantes :

- domaine visible et infra-rouge proche : cartographie des zones enneigée et limite inférieure du manteau ;
- domaine infra-rouge moyen et thermique : carractérisation des états de surface d'un manteau et évaluation qualitative d'une situation de fusion ou rétention nivale ;
- domaine hyperfréquences (en prévision) : détection des neiges sèches et profils d'épaisseur du manteau neigeux (en attente de validation sur missions aéroportées durant l'hiver 1989 90).

Une utilisation combinée de l'ensemble de ces capteurs lors de missions aéroportées semble la procédure la plus complète pour confirmer la place nécessaire de la Télédétection en hydrologie alpine.

2. GLACIOLOGIE ET TELEDETECTION

2.1. Procédures actuelles d'acquisition et de traitement des mesures de bilans des glaciers alpins

le suivi des fluctuations et des bilans de masse glaciaires sont des paramètres d'importance, tant en hydrologie qu'en climatologie. Grâce à l'excellente résolution au sol des capteurs SPOT et Landsat TM, les mesures traditionnelles effectuées sur le terrain peuvent être complétées et étendues à l'échelle d'un massif entier.

Les images spatiales offrent en effet une description unique de tous les appareils d'un massif, alors que les missions de terrain ne permettent chaque année la validation que de quelques glaciers-test, régulièrement suivis dans le long terme (Laboratoire CNRS de Glaciologie de Grenoble, Service des Eaux et Forets).

Le bilan de masse d'un glacier alpin est une mesure des variations entre l'accumulation et l'ablation du stock capitalisé (névé et glace) pour une année hydrologique complète (période de référence : septembre à octobre).
Une mesure annuelle de l'altitude des lignes de névé, transition entre la zone d'accumulation (névé) et la zone inférieure d'ablation (glace), permet de cerner la nature du bilan : positif ou négatif.
Ce paramètre est une donnée climatique d'importance, car le glacier va intégrer chaque variation de température et de climat.

En hydrologie glaciaire,l'existence d'une relation entre la position de cette ligne de névé et le bilan de masse du glacier est bien documentée sur de nombreux appareils des Alpes (Reynaud, 1982).

Pour passer d'une variation d'altitude de la ligne de névé à la variation de bilan d'un glacier qui n'a pas fait l'objet de mesures de terrain, toute la clé du transfert repose sur la relation entre le gradient de bilan et le gradient altitudinal : c'est le coefficient d'activité **db / dz** (LLiboutry, 1965).

Pour un appareil glaciaire suivi chaque automne, cette formule est bien confirmée et permet de calculer le volume en eau (mètres) gagné ou per-

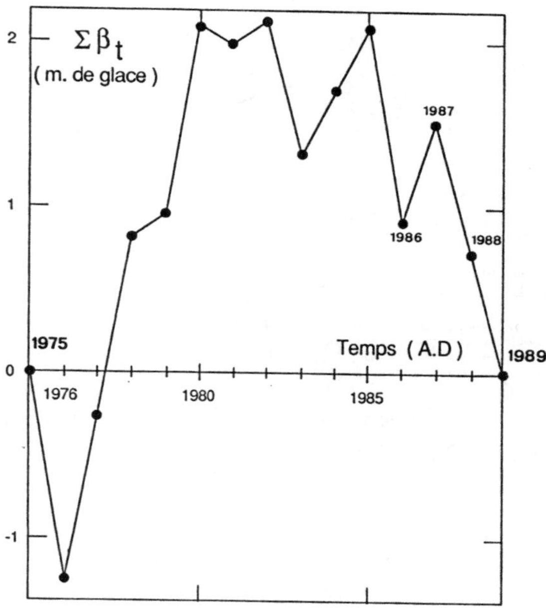

FIG. 6 Variation cumulée des bilans centrés sur la période 1975-1989 pour le glacier d'Argentières (massif du Mt. Blanc, France). (Document Laboratoire CNRS de Glaciologie; Reynaud, 1982.)

du. La figure 6 montre que pour la période considérée, les variations relatives du stock en eau font alterner une séquence positive (1975 - 1980) et une séquence globalement négative (1981 - 1989). Cette tendan-est mesurée également sur d'autres appareils des Alpes francaises.

2.2. Apports de la Télédétection satellitaire

sur le secteur occidental de la chaine Alpin (Mt. Blanc à Oisans), nous avons tenté de 1986 à 1990 de reconstituer par analyse d'images numériques SPOT ou Landsat les bilans glaciaires de chaque année et de confronter les hypothèses de calcul avec la réalité des mesures sur quelques glaciers-test. Le secteur géographique retenu est le massif des Grandes Rousses (Isère), seul massif reproduit chaque année sur une image sans phénomène perturbateur (nuages, neige récente).

METHODOLOGIE :

- usage de deux images cernant une année hydrologique complète S1 et S2 ;
- correction des effet de perturbation radiométrique (ombre) et des déformations radiométriques ;
- créer une image multidate S1+S2 et y définir les sites glaciaires où une identification radiométrique de la ligne de névé et de sa variation altitudinale est possible. Cette identification se fonde sur une analyse de la radiométrie des névés et de la glace vive pour chaque date (Figure 7).

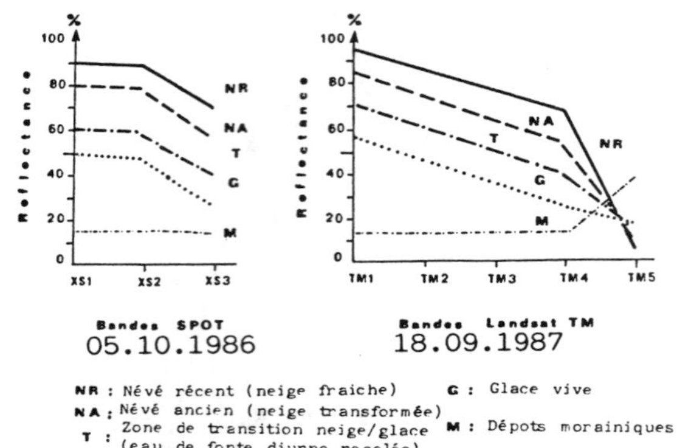

FIG. 7 Réflectances de la neige et la glace pour le glacier St. Sorlin (massif des Grds. Rousses).

.transfert du coefficient d'activité **db dz** sur la variation altitudinale de la ligne de névé entre les deux images.

RESULTATS : à titre d'exemple, l'étude comparative ci-dessous fournit des résultats significatifs entre données satellitaires multitemporelles et mesures de terrain :
Bilan du glacier de St. Sorlin entre 1986 et 1987 =

.variation moyenne d'altitude de la ligne de névé 1986 87 : $\underline{-\ 75\ m}$. (il y a donc extension aval du névé, donc de la zone d'accumulation) ;

.variation globale du bilan :

$$\Delta b = -\frac{db}{dz} \times \Delta z \qquad \frac{0{,}7\ m}{100\ m} \times 75\ m = +\ 0{,}52\ m \text{ d'eau gagnés.}$$

On obtient pour cet appareil un bilan positif entre les années 1986 et 1987, situation confirmée par les mesures effectuées à Argentières pour la meme période (Figure 6).
L'étude comparative menée sur les images SPOT de l'automne 1988 et 1989 donne au contraire une localisation altitudinale de ligne de névé plus haute qu'en 1987, donc des **bilans** à nouveau négatifs (ce que confirme la Figure 6).
Menée sur un très grand nombre de glaciers alpins à chaque année (30) la procédure permet de constater que les bilans sont très homogènes d'un massif à l'autre, quelque soit l'exposition du glacier.

2.3. Conclusion

La qualité de l' imageris SPOT ou Landsat TM permet de proposer un modèle de calcul du bilan glaciaire qui semble reproductible pour les massifs de type alpin très éloignés et difficiles d'accès (Andes, Himalaya) à condition de connaître le rapport moyen **db dz** des glaciers considérés (climat tempéré ou tropical, etc...).

Par contre, de même que pour les images hivernales Landsat en nivologie, un handicap certain réside souvent dans la présence de couvertures nuageuses importantes lors du passage du satellite ; ce qui limite alors les images disponibles pour le chercheur.

REFERENCES

DEDIEU JP., REYNAUD L., SERGENT C. (1989) Apport des données SPOT et Landsat TM pour le suivi de la fusion nivale et les bilans glaciaires dans les Alpes francaise, bull. SFPT n° 115, 49-52.

DOZIER J. (1984) Snow reflectance from Landsat 4 TM, IIEE Geosciences Remote sensing series, vol 22, 323-328.

LEPRIEUR C. (1987) Télédétection de la neige, lien avec les réseaux de mesures existant au sol, Agrométéorologie INRA, Toulouse, 137-145.

LLIBOUTRY L. (1965) Traité de Glaciologie, tome 1, Masson.

RANGO A. (1980) Remote sensing of snow for runoff model, IAHS-AISH n° 129, 291-297.

REYNAUD L. (1982) Glaciers of the french Alpes, USGS vol5, 1386 E.

SERGENT C. et al; (1987) Caractérisation optique de différents types de neige, Journal of Physic, tome 48, 363-367.

Hydrology in Mountainous Regions. I - Hydrological Measurements; the Water Cycle
(Proceedings of two Lausanne Symposia, August 1990). IAHS Publ. no. 193, 1990.

Improving methods for measurement and estimation of snow storage in alpine watersheds

KELLY ELDER & JEFF DOZIER
Center for Remote Sensing and Environmental Optics
University of California, Santa Barbara, CA 93106,USA

ABSTRACT Accurate assessment of snow storage is critical in alpine water balance and glacial mass balance studies. The distribution and quantity of water stored as snow in alpine watersheds is difficult to measure or estimate, because the rugged topography produces a complex pattern of snow accumulation and ablation. New methods for measurement of the spatial distribution of snow water equivalence in alpine basins are needed that are sufficiently accurate and economically feasible. One possible method is to classify a basin into zones of similar snow water equivalence based on topographic and physical characteristics that control the distribution. The necessary sample size to be within a specified error range is evaluated for spatially independent and autocorrelated data. Snow properties, including snow water equivalence, are spatially correlated even in rough topography. Spatial considerations must be considered when designing sampling schemes and in data analysis of snow properties.

INTRODUCTION

The increase and expansion of human population over the surface of the Earth have imposed an increasing importance on understanding of water resources and their management. In arid regions where there is a water deficit attention has recently focussed on the alpine hydrology of nearby or distant mountains that supply needed water from melting seasonal snowpacks or glaciers. A fundamental problem is obtaining accurate assessments of the amount of water stored in a basin or region. This quantity is essential for runoff forecasting, flood control, agricultural planning and hydroelectric considerations. The quantity of interest is snow water equivalence (SWE), the product of the snow depth and the mean snow density at a point.

The distribution and quantity of water stored as snow in alpine watersheds is difficult to measure or estimate. The rugged topography, through controls on snow accumulation and ablation, produces a complex pattern of snow deposition. There are two critical questions that need to be answered about storage of water in basins as snow:

(1) How much water is stored in the basin at the time of peak accumulation?

(2) What is the spatial distribution of SWE?

The total amount of water stored in the basin provides an estimate of the amount of water that will be available for runoff and potential human use. However, this value provides no indication of when the runoff will be produced and become available for use or constitute a potential hazard. Determination of the timing of runoff requires application of a snowmelt model. Many models are currently available and are used in runoff forecasting (WMO, 1986). Some of the models work well at the scale of a field plot (Anderson, 1976), but we lack effective spatially-distributed snowmelt models capable of handling the complex terrain and spatially variable parameters found in alpine basins (Dozier, 1987). There are two reasons for this current void. First, the modeling becomes increasingly complicated when applied to highly variable terrain where parameters such as SWE, temperature, vapor pressure, albedo, and radiation vary greatly over short distances. Second, even if models capable of handling the complex terrain interactions are developed, the data for physical snowpack properties are rare or nonexistent (Dozier, 1987; Leavesley, 1989). An important variable lacking in available data sets used to drive snowmelt models is SWE. These data are scarce because of the high cost, logistical problems, and safety considerations associated with winter field work in alpine basins. The distribution of snow within a basin is a necessary variable to improve snowmelt models for alpine areas because the distribution is irregular and the melt rate is nonuniform. New methods for measurement of SWE in alpine basins are needed that are sufficiently accurate and economically feasible. This paper discusses current methods of measuring SWE and problems with the techniques. An alternate method for measuring and estimating SWE is described and a discussion of sampling strategies and statistical considerations follows.

MEASURING SNOW WATER EQUIVALENCE

The traditional method of measuring SWE is to locate a few snow courses in the basin and sample these sites periodically (U.S. Army, 1956; Dunne and Leopold, 1978). After data have been collected for many years, a statistical relationship can be developed where SWE at the snow course is regressed against measured stream runoff. When the record is long and the snow course represents mean conditions within the basin, adequate forecasts can be made from the statistical relationship. However, when conditions deviate from the norm, the relationship is not as strong and forecasts become more uncertain for years of above- and below-normal accumulation. A further limitation of this method is that since the snow courses are point measurements, they do not provide information that can be used in spatially-distributed snowmelt models.

In an effort to improve the spatial component of data collection and snowmelt modeling, researchers have partitioned basins into different zones based on topography or vegetation. Young (1974, 1975) used elevation, slope angle, and local relief to conduct mass balance studies on a glacier. Woo and Marsh (1978) found that an Arctic basin could be successfully divided into six simple terrain classes that exhibited similar snow distribution characteristics. Rawls et al. (1980) used slope angle, aspect, vegetation, and drift versus non-drift variables to delineate a basin. Elder et al. (1989) found slope, elevation, and net radiation to be effective in modeling the spatial distribution of SWE. Relating these physically-based variables to snow distribution has improved sampling and estimation. These examples are not exhaustive and merely provide a glance at the attempt to improve SWE estimation and measurement. Little work has been done on this problem, especially in alpine basins where SWE is highly variable.

Many topographic and climatological parameters can be derived from static digital elevation data, including net radiation in complex terrain at fine spatial scales (Dubayah et al., 1990). Leavesley (1989) discusses other meteorological variables used in snowmelt modeling. However, we cannot model snow distribution over rugged terrain to acceptable levels of accuracy without extensive field measurements, and it is possible that we will ever be able to do so at a scale useful to spatially-distributed snowmelt models without the support of field or remote sensing data. The problem lies in the stochastic nature of snowfall and redistribution. A complete understanding of atmospheric physics, radiative transfer, three-dimensional wind fields from meso- to micro-scale, and snow transport does not appear to be forthcoming. The picture is further complicated by transfer of previously deposited snow by sloughing and avalanching (Zalikhanov, 1975; Ferguson, 1986; Elder et al., 1989). Deterministic avalanche models with space and time capabilities may never be developed. Although deterministic models exist for special cases of some of these phenomena, they are not applicable over the wide range of conditions occurring in nature.

We need methods of accurately extending point SWE measurements over a basin. Useful spatially-distributed snowmelt models must work at a resolution that can characterize discrete areas of homogeneous behavior: they must operate over a variety of scales where the physical properties and processes are consistent. This constraint means that the model must operate at a scale of the most spatially variable property or process critical to snowmelt that cannot be effectively aggregated to larger scales. Meteorological and radiation balance components may vary greatly over short distances, but methods for sampling the meteorological variables such as wind speed, vapor pressure, air temperature, etc., are not feasible at 25 to 100 m scales and are not likely to be in the near future. However, some of these variables may be averaged over space and time for use in modeling. SWE is a critical variable that can be modeled at high resolutions and one method is briefly described below. The variability in this parameter represents the desirable resolution for modeling snowmelt. Clearly, it is not feasible to measure SWE on a grid of these resolutions on an operational basis because of time, expense and safety. Even in the 120 ha Emerald Lake basin described below this sampling scale required about 115 measurements at the 100 m resolution and over 1800 at 25 m.

Extending Point SWE Measurements Over Space

Common spatial interpolation techniques are not effective for modeling SWE from point measurements in alpine basins because of the variability in the distribution. The correlation length-scale, or length of spatial influence, is small in rugged topography and interpolation does not account for the small-scale variability observed. The exception exists when data are at a resolution approaching the correlation length-scale, but this is rare and not useful operationally.

There are two promising alternatives for obtaining high resolution estimates of SWE. The first involves measuring SWE by use of airborne or spaceborne active microwave remote sensing. This method shows promise for the future, but is not currently capable of measuring SWE on an operational basis in alpine terrain. Remote sensing instruments have resolutions useful for application in alpine areas, and the frequency of coverage is commensurate, or soon will be, with temporal needs in modeling snowpack changes. However, the spatial sampling problem must still be solved on the ground before the electromagnetic signal sampled over the size of a pixel will be useful. If the pixel resolution is 30 m for a particular sensor, we need to know how the snowpack properties being measured vary within that scale, that is from 0 to 30 m. Subpixel information is necessary in in a variety of studies and is needed to understand the integrated electromagnetic signal over the entire pixel. We need to sample snowpack properties on the ground to solve some questions in remote sensing techniques.

Another alternative is to model SWE over the basin using physically-based variables that are known to control the distribution of SWE. Net radiation, slope, azimuth, and elevation are examples. These variables are related to measured SWE from a survey conducted in the basin. If significant relationships can be identified between the observed SWE values and the random variables, the observed SWE can be extended over space with similar topographic characteristics.

An application with field data We attempted extrapolation of point SWE measurements in the Emerald Lake basin located in Sequoia National Park, California, USA, by dividing the watershed into zones of similar physical behavior based on net radiation, slope, and elevation (Elder et al., 1989). Distribution of snow water equivalence was measured in the watershed by taking density profiles at six locations and hundreds of depth measurements throughout the basin during the 1987 and 1988 water years. The peak accumulation for 1987 was 0.67 m SWE, and 1988 was 0.63 m SWE. Elevations in the basin range from 2800 to 3416 m, and the total watershed area is about 120 ha.

Snow depth was measured at up to 354 sites randomly located on a 25-m grid registered to a 5-m resolution digital elevation model (DEM) of the basin. At each site five depth measurements were taken and the mean depth was used in further calculations. Snow pits were dug at selected sites throughout the watershed to obtain density profiles. Locations were chosen to give a range of exposures and elevations characteristic of the basin. Continuous density profiles were taken in 10 cm increments in each pit. Two different approaches were used in the 1987 and 1988 melt seasons to calculate mean snow densities for the basin. During the 1987 water year we were able to dig over fifty pits, giving us density data with high spatial and temporal resolution. Mean density showed an increase from February through June to about 470 kg m^{-3}. From the date of the first survey forward, the standard deviation of the density throughout the basin was always less than 10% of the mean except once, when it reached 11%. A linear model was fitted by correlation of the data after April 1, where mean density was a function of day of year. In the 1988 water year, the early season densities increased asymptotically to about 510 kg m^{-3}. Enough data existed at every site except one, to fit a linear model to the data and have predicted density as a function of date and location. Five linear equations were derived by linear regression to model density as a function of date for the five sites. Predicted density from these equations was interpolated over the entire basin for the peak accumulation survey date.

Point SWE estimates were obtained by combining the density for each survey calculated as described above with the point depth measurements. Mean SWE ($\overline{\text{SWE}}$), total basin SWE volume, standard deviation (SD), standard error of the mean (SE), and the coefficient of variation (CV) for estimate of SWE for the surveys conducted at the peak accumulation in 1987 and 1988 are listed in Table 1.

TABLE 1 Snow Water Equivalence at Maximum Snow Accumulation, Water Years 1987 and 1988.

Year	n	$\overline{\text{SWE}}$ (m)	SWE (m)	SD (m)	SE (m)	CV
1987	256	0.598	718,300	0.372	0.023	62%
1988	354	0.630	750,700	0.395	0.021	63%

n is the number of snow depth measurements (five measurements for each n), see text for other definitions.

When large sample sizes are obtained, as in this work, an accurate estimate of basin SWE volume can be obtained by taking the arithmetic mean of all the point SWE estimates. Using the standard error of the mean as an indicator of our ability to estimate the true sample mean, we found that the SE was less than 4% of the mean for surveys around the date of peak accumulation in both years. However, the standard deviation is high, indicating that the spatial variability of the SWE estimates is high, shown by the coefficients of variation of about 60%.

A stratified sampling scheme was evaluated by identifying and mapping zones of similar snow properties based on topographic parameters that account for variations in both accumulation and ablation. Elevation, slope, and net radiation values calculated from the DEM and some ancillary data were used to determine the zones. These variables were clustered to identify similar classes of physical attributes and then the entire basin was classified into zones of similar topography and radiation. Point SWE estimates from the field data were registered to the classified basin and the mean values from each zone were applied to the entire surface area in the basin belonging to each class. The topographic parameters of the basin used in the classification (slope and elevation) do not change between survey dates. The radiation data vary temporally, providing a physically justified basis for the change in SWE distribution through time.

FIG. 1 Classification results from 20-23 March, 1988 survey using radiation and slope angle variables with six zones. Greatest deposits of SWE are found on the flat areas below the cliffs and at the upper elevations. The southwest-facing wall shows the least amount of SWE, except for the significant drift deposits found on the benches in this area. Black values represent areas of no snow where extent was determined from field notes and oblique photographs. Bar scale length represents a distance of 1200 m.

Field data from the 20-23 March, 1988 snow survey was used to produce an image of estimated SWE based on this model (Figure 1). In this example the basin has been divided into six classes of similar slope angle and net radiation calculated from a 5-m resolution DEM. The mean value of the field samples of SWE registered to the image has been used as the value of SWE for each class. Maximum SWE is correctly classified in zones located on the upper benches and in the high cirque. Significant deposits also lie on the east wall as drifts on the benches, and at lower elevations under the cliffs on the west wall where repeated sloughing produces large accumulations.

The total basin SWE value can be calculated from the modeled distribution by multiplying the mean value of SWE from each zone by the zone area and summing over all zones. Total basin SWE estimated by this method was 726,500 m^3, which is less than a 2% difference from the simple arithmetic mean found in Table 1. This small discrepancy is typical of all the results showing that the method is capable of reproducing an accurate estimate of basin snow volume. Spatial information on SWE is readily available for snowmelt modeling, chemistry loading, or other manipulations because the information is stored spatially as a digital image.

Clustering and classification are not rigorous statistical techniques, and formal statistical approaches for validating results are controversial. The results in this study have been evaluated quantitatively by two methods that may help evaluate the results. First, a single classification analysis of variance (ANOVA) was used where the null hypotheses was stated as: there is no difference between the mean SWE of the groups identified in the classification. If the null hypothesis is accepted, similar information can be found in more than one class and a poor classification has resulted. Rejection of the null hypothesis shows that the classes contain different information or represent different populations, which is the desired result. Second, standard errors (SE) from the classifications were compared to the basin-wide data. In any classification attempt the SE should be reduced for the classified groups when compared to the whole data set, but a significant reduction in SE suggests a successful classification.

ANOVA results for this classification produced an F ratio of 4.48 with 284 degrees of freedom, which was significant at the 95% confidence level, showing that the classification did separate zones of different characteristics. The standard error was reduced from 0.021 m to 0.015 m or about a 30% reduction, also showing that the classification reduced the estimate error and was an improvement over the non-stratified estimate. These results show that a stratified random sample based on physical parameters is superior to a simple random sample for estimating basin SWE. and that SWE could be extended spatially in this watershed using these physical variables to explain the distribution (Elder et al., 1989).

SAMPLING STRATEGIES AND PROBLEMS

Sampling spatial data has specific problems associated with it, which until recently have largely been ignored by researchers. In particular, the problems associated with autocorrelated data are often not addressed and statistical methods applicable only to independent data are used. Classical inferential statistical procedures assume independence in the data. Popular statistical texts suggest that random or stratified random sampling schemes remove bias from sample statistics (Cochran, 1977). Although these sampling methods provide independence in selection of sample locations, they do not remove the spatial dependence or autocorrelation between the locations (Legendre & Fortin, 1989). With recent computer developments that allow easy manipulation of large data sets and matrix manipulations, many advances have taken place in spatial statistical theory and applications. An important example is the development or regionalized variable theory by Matheron (Journel & Huijbregts, 1978). There are many logical applications of spatial statistics in the hydrological sciences. Researchers have used regionalized variables in estimating the spatial distribution of groundwater properties from point data (e.g., Olea, 1984; Loaiciga et al., 1988). Rodriguez-Iturbe & Mejía (1974a, b), Chua & Bras (1982), Creutin & Obled (1982), Bastin et al. (1984), Tabios & Salas (1985), Lebel et al. (1987), and many others have applied spatial statistics to the classic problems of precipitation estimates from point measurements and to the design of optimal networks. Oddly, the problem of extrapolating point measurements of snow over space and optimal sampling schemes for snow distribution have received little attention.

In the design of all sampling schemes, and for SWE in particular, two major questions must be asked:

(1) How many samples do we need to be within a specified error?

(2) How should these sample locations be distributed in space?

The answers to these questions are straightforward for independent, normally distributed data. Measurements $z(x)$ of SWE at point x within a basin for a given date are realizations of the random variable Z, where Z is part of the ensemble of distributions of SWE within the basin. For independent variables, the correlation is defined and equal to zero between $Z(x)$ and $Z(x+h)$, where h is any distance. From standard statistical theory it is easy to show that the error E in estimating the population mean for a given confidence level is

$$E = \frac{\sigma z_{\alpha/2}}{n^{1/2}} \tag{1}$$

where σ is the population variance, z is the standard normal variate, α is the significance level, and n is the number of observations (Bhattacharyya & Johnson, 1977). In reality, σ for SWE will never be known and must be substituted by the sample variance $\hat{\sigma}$, which can be estimated from a pilot survey carried out before hand or from prior knowledge of the behavior of SWE. The number of samples (n) necessary to be $100(1-\alpha)\%$ sure that the error in estimating the population mean from the sample mean does not exceed a specified error (E) is easily obtained by solving equation 1 for n.

$$n = \left[\frac{\sigma z_{\alpha/2}}{E}\right]^2 \tag{2}$$

Although SWE tends to be normally distributed, it is not independent. Snow distribution shows trends on large scales (e.g., increased SWE with increase in elevation), and similar behavior on small scales (e.g., drift accumulation on lee slopes). The result is that a measurement taken at one point will contain information about the SWE at nearby points. Now the value at z(x) may contain information about the value found at z(x+h). The relationship is governed by a covariance function that specifies how distant points are related, commonly plotted in a correlogram or variogram. The distance at which points are no longer considered to be related is called the correlation length-scale. This length can be found from a variogram where the correlation length-scale is the range or distance needed for the covariance function to reach the sill. For further details, the reader is referred to the many publications on the variogram and its interpretation (e.g., Matheron, 1963; Journel & Huijbregts, 1978; Armstrong, 1984)

The minimum sample size required to be within specified error bounds for correlated data is not straightforward as in equation 2 for independent data. Loaiciga & Hudak (1989) present an analysis and derivation for the relationship between the required sample sizes for correlated (n) and uncorrelated (n´) data. They show that the variance of the sample mean ($v(\bar{z})$) for correlated data must be

$$v(\bar{z}) = \left[\frac{1}{n'}\right]\sigma^2\left[n' + 2\sum_{i=1}^{n'}\sum_{j>i}^{n'} r_{ij}\right] \tag{3}$$

where r_{ij} = is the correlation between samples at locations i and j. Substituting $v(\bar{z})$ from equation 3 for σ in equation 1, substituting n´ for n, and collecting terms yields a quadratic equation in n´.

$$(n')^2 - \frac{\sigma^2 z_{\alpha/2}^2}{E^2}n' - \frac{2\sigma^2 z_{\alpha/2}^2 \sum_{i=1}^{n'}\sum_{j>i}^{n'} r_{ij}}{E^2} = 0 \tag{4}$$

Solving this equation for the sample size for correlated data (n´) is complicated and it must be solved numerically because of the dependence of the correlation function on n´. Note that if the samples are all taken at separation distances greater than the range or correlation length-scale, then the covariance term in equation 3 becomes zero and the net effect creates a condition applicable to equation 2.

Estimating Mean Basin SWE

If mean basin SWE is desired without regard to the spatial distribution of SWE, then a sampling scheme that ensures separation of sampling sites by distances exceeding the correlation length-scale will provide the desired sample size using equation 2. In rugged alpine terrain the correlation length-scale is small because the factors controlling the distribution of SWE change over short distances. Experimental variograms from several snow surveys conducted in the Emerald Lake basin showed the range to be less than 100 m. A simulation of pilot surveys (multiple random subsamples of 20 points from the field data) showed the variance to be stable and the required sample size calculated from the simulations by equation 2 had a mean of 10 when rounded to an integer value. These calculations were based on an acceptable error of 0.05 m SWE at the 95% confidence level. This analysis shows that for a sampling scheme with data points separated by a minimum of 100 m, mean basin SWE could be characterized for the stated level of confidence and error with about 10 points for that particular basin, date, and distribution of SWE. This result demonstrates that for optimal sample locations, we can accurately measure and estimate mean basin SWE with a few points.

In basins where the terrain is gentle the snowpack properties vary less with distance, and properties measured at two distant points may contain redundant information. The correlation length-scale for SWE may be greater than 100 m and may approach kilometer scales. If the sampling scheme cannot separate sample locations by distances greater than the correlation length-scale, then the covariance term must be incorporated into the determination of sample size through equation 4. Note that the necessary sample size calculated by equation 4 is a function of sample variance too, and a basin with a homogeneous snow cover will have a small variance, which will reduce the necessary sample size by counteracting the effect of the covariance term. It is important to realize that correlated variables will not necessarily cause an increase in sample size. More work is needed to determine the effect of changes in variance with correlated data on the sample size.

Researchers must be aware of the scale of the basin as it relates to the correlation length-scale. Vast homogeneous areas may not represent mean basin conditions and pilot surveys must be designed to avoid this potential problem. Indeed, this is the case with most snow courses. They are located in areas where local conditions are uniform and samples are taken close to one another. Usually the samples are undoubtably correlated and thus the sample mean and variance affected. This correlation should be considered when these data are used for inferential statistics, but this has been largely ignored in the past. Whether the snow course represents mean basin conditions is a separate question, but one should assume that it does not.

Estimating the Spatial Distribution of SWE

Spatial distribution of SWE can be estimated in several ways. If the distribution is to be used in spatially distributed snowmelt models it must either be at a high resolution or adequately delineate discrete homogeneous regions. High resolution surveys may be carried out in special cases and the data used in model development and testing (e.g., Elder et al., 1989). The point has been made above that high resolution sampling schemes are not practical and will not be operationally successful without the advent of remote sensing techniques. Covariance must be considered in the sampling and analysis of the classification method. When conducting the snow survey to estimate within-zone SWE for each class, both the zone scale and correlation length-scale must be examined. If the zone is small, it may not be possible to adequately sample the zone with all measurements separated by a minimum distance equal to the correlation length-scale. Here it is necessary to increase the sample size according to equation 4 or sample from other zones belonging to the same class. A single large zone may allow the necessary within-zone sampling and the results can then be applied to others of the same class. This procedure must be carried out for each class. Intuitively this requirement creates a paradox for sampling in these zones. If the zone represents an area of homogeneous snow properties, then all the measurements taken in a single zone will be correlated and independent samples will exist only in other zones of the same class. More research is needed to address this problem.

Because of the difficulty in determining n′ and the additional field work that may be required for sampling correlated data, it may be prudent to adopt sampling schemes that ensure that distances between sample locations exceed the correlation length-scale. Once the correlation length-scale is defined, this assurance could be met by sampling from a grid whose resolution exceeds the correlation length-scale. Experience in an area would allow a critical value to be determined after observations of a range of conditions and this value could be adopted and covariance ignored in sampling thereafter.

CONCLUSIONS

Traditional methods of measuring and estimating SWE have done an adequate job for forecasting purposes where long records have been established. An increase in the need for water has placed a greater demand on our understanding of seasonal meltwater volumes and the timing of the runoff release. Traditional methods of measuring SWE must be improved to meet this need. We need accurate spatial information on the distribution of SWE to drive spatially-distributed snowmelt models. In designing new methods for measurement and estimation of SWE, we must be aware of the spatial structure of the distribution and use the appropriate statistical techniques for these data. In particular, we must pay close attention to the dependence of the data in space or the autocorrelation. This property will affect our statistical results and all inferences derived from them.

ACKNOWLEDGEMENTS Comments by Richard Kattelmann and Mark Williams greatly improved the manuscript and their many hours of help in the field will not be forgotten. Portions of this paper were motivated by conversations with Ralph Dubayah and Hugo Loaiciga. This research was supported by grants from the California Air Resources Board, University of California Water Resources Center, and the NASA EOS program.

REFERENCES

Anderson, E. A. (1976) A point energy and mass balance model of a snow cover. Technical Report NWS 19. National Oceanic and Atmospheric Administration, Washington, DC.

Armstrong, M. (1984) Common problems seen in variograms. Mathematical Geology 16 (3), 305-313.

Bastin, G., B. Lorent, C. Duqué & M. Gevers (1984) Optimal estimation of the average areal rainfall and optimal selection of rain gauge locations. Water Resources Research 20 (4), 463-470.

Bhattacharyya, G. K. & R. A. Johnson (1977) Statistical Concepts and Methods. John Wiley, New York.

Chua, S. H. & R. L. Bras (1982) Optimal estimators of mean areal precipitation in regions of orographic influence. Journal of Hydrology 57 23-48.

Cochran, W. G. (1977) Sampling Techniques. 3rd Ed., John Wiley, New York.

Creutin, J. D. & C. Obled (1982) Objective analysis and mapping techniques for rainfall fields: an objective comparison. Water Resources Research 18 (2), 413-431.

Dozier, J. (1987) Recent research in snow hydrology. Reviews of Geophysics 25 (2), 153-161.

Dubayah, R., J. Dozier & F. W. Davis (1990) Topographic distribution of clear-sky radiation over the Konza Prairie, Kansas. Water Resources Research 26 (4), 679-690.

Dunne, T. & L. B. Leopold (1978) Water in Environmental Planning. W. H. Freeman, New York.

Elder, K., J. Dozier & J. Michaelsen (1989) Spatial and temporal variation of net snow accumulation in a small alpine watershed, Emerald Lake basin, Sierra Nevada, California, U.S.A. Annals of Glaciology 13 56-63.

Ferguson, R. I. (1986) Parametric modeling of daily and seasonal snowmelt using snowpack water equivalent as well as snow-covered area. In: Modeling Snowmelt-Induced Processes, International Association of Hydrological Sciences, Publ. no. 155, 151-161.

Journel, A. G. & Ch. J. Huijbregts (1978) Mining Geostatistics. Academic Press, New York.

Leavesley, G. H. (1989) Problems of snowmelt runoff modeling for a variety of physiographic and climatic conditions. Journal of the Hydrologic Sciences 34 (6), 617-634.

Lebel, T., G. Bastin, C. Obled & J. D. Creutin (1987) On the accuracy of areal rainfall estimation. Water Resources Research 23 (11), 2123-2134.

Legendre P. & M. J. Fortin (1989) Spatial pattern and ecological analysis. Vegetatio 80, 107-138.

Loaiciga, H. A., R. H. Shumway & W. Yeh (1988) Linear spatial interpolation: analysis with an application to the San Joaquin Valley, California. Stochastic Hydrology and Hydraulics 2 (2), 113-136.

Loaiciga, H. A. & P. F. Hudak (1989) Correlated versus uncorrelated hydrologic samples. Journal of Water Resources Planning and Management 115 (5), 699-705.

Matheron, G. (1963) Principles of geostatistics. Economic Geology 58 (8), 1246-1266.

Olea, R. A. (1984) Sampling design optimization for spatial functions. Mathematical Geology 16 (4), 369-392.

Rawls, W. J., T. J. Jackson & J. F. Zuzel (1980) Comparison of areal snow storage sampling procedures for rangeland watersheds. Nordic Hydrology 11 71-82.

Rodriguez-Iturbe, I. & J. M. Mejía (1974a) The design of rainfall networks in space and time. Water Resources Research 10 (4), 713-728.

Rodriguez-Iturbe, I. & J. M. Mejía (1974b) On the transformation of point rainfall to areal rainfall. Water Resources Research 10 (4), 729-735.

Tabios, G. Q. & J. D. Salas (1985) A comparative analysis of the techniques for spatial interpolation of precipitation. Water Resources Bulletin 21 (3), 365-380.

U.S. Army Corps of Engineers (1956) Snow Hydrology; Summary of Report of Snow Investigations. PB-151660, North Pacific Division, Portland, Or.

Woo, M. & P. Marsh (1978) Analysis of error in the determination of snow storage for small high Arctic basins. Journal of Applied Meteorology 17 (10), 1537-1541.

Young, G. J. (1974) A stratified sampling design for snow surveys based on terrain shape. Proceedings of the Western Snow Conference 42 14-22.

Young, G. J. (1975) Accumulation and ablation patterns as functions of the surface geometry of a glacier. In: Snow and Ice, (J. C. Rodda, ed.), International Association of Hydrological Sciences, Publ. no. 104, 134-138.

Zalikhanov, M. Ch. (1975) Hydrological role of avalanches in the Caucasus. In: Snow and Ice, (J. C. Rodda, ed.), International Association of Hydrological Sciences, Publ. no. 104, 390-394.

Hydrology in Mountainous Regions. I - Hydrological Measurements; the Water Cycle
(Proceedings of two Lausanne Symposia, August 1990). IAHS Publ. no. 193, 1990.

Improved methods of assessment of snow and glaciers as water balance and river flow components

ANGELA M. GURNELL
GeoData Institute and Department of Geography, University of Southampton, Southampton SO9 5NH, England

ABSTRACT New technologies and techniques are providing detailed information on the hydrological properties of snow and glacier basins. This paper reviews progress in the integration of remote and proximate monitoring techniques for snow and ice hydrology studies; the potential for analysis of these with other geo-referenced data to provide inputs to hydrological models; and the role of multiple-scale hydrological studies and multiple-variable chemical studies for identifying water source areas and routing and for separating hydrographs. Multidisciplinary catchment studies are needed to underpin the development of distributed hydrological models for snow and glacier basins.

INTRODUCTION

The enormous significance of both snow and ice as components of the fresh water balance of the earth (Martinec, 1987) and as major controls upon (Meier, 1983) and responses to (Rango and Martinec, 1987; Martinec and Rango, 1989) world climate and climatic change, render their accurate assessment as water balance and river flow components a very high priority for both researchers and water managers. It is scarcely surprising, therefore, that great emphasis is currently being placed upon improving our knowledge of snow and ice hydrology. This review will consider recent advances in the assessment of snow and glacier ice in the evaluation of catchment water resources (water balance components) and the assessment of temporal variations in catchment water yield (river flow components).

In taking a catchment-based approach to the assessment of snow and glaciers, it is useful to consider more general trends in hydrological research. In particular, the development of catchment-scale distributed hydrological models over the last ten years has now reached a state where applications can be attempted (Anderson and Rogers, 1987). Extensions of such models to incorporate areas of snow and ice would be very profitable (snow, for example, is already incorporated within the Institute of Hydrology Distributed Model; Harding *et al*, 1989) and could build upon the semi-distributed manner in which some current operational methods estimate runoff from glacierised (Fountain and Tangbourn, 1985) and snow covered (e.g. Baumgartner *et al*, 1986) basins.

There are many challenges in working towards the operational use of distributed hydrological models in snow and glacier basins but these challenges fall into two main groups. The first group is the assembly and processing of spatially distributed data on the required variables at a suitable spatial and temporal resolution. Whilst information on static catchment characteristics can be obtained through traditional or remotely sensed sources, information on the hydrological variables is not so easily acquired. Information from well-designed networks of ground data collection sites needs to be efficiently collected and merged with a variety of remotely sensed data from both satellite and airborne platforms, and rapidly processed if the results of modelling are to be useful in the management of all magnitudes and frequencies of hydrological events. These objectives can be achieved with the development of rapid data transmission media and with the integration of complex data sets through the development of geographic information systems. With the increasing capacity and power of microcomputer systems, these data could be processed using hydrological models in remote field offices, although the development of expert systems may be necessary to ensure correct applications of the models (Rango, 1987). The second group of challenges relates to devising ways of calibrating the distributed models for the local routing characteristics of the snow and glacier systems. Both snow and glacier basins exhibit enormous temporal and spatial variability in meltwater storage and routing. In the case of snow, remote sensing techniques are providing increasing detail of snowpack condition which provides a partial solution to the assessment of storage and routing, whereas this has not proved possible in relation to glaciers. Whilst the development of theory provides a basis for modelling englacial and subglacial water storage and routing (Röthlisberger and Lang, 1987) and the storage and routing characteristics of snow, measurement and analysis of the quality and quantity of water draining from snow and glacier basins allows the refinement of such theory to match local catchment circumstances.

REMOTE SENSING OF THE HYDROLOGICAL PROPERTIES OF SNOW AND ICE

There are many excellent technical reviews of the application of remote sensing techniques to the estimation of the physical properties of snow and ice (eg Chang and Rango, 1982; Deutsch *et al*, 1981; Dozier, 1987a; Foster *et al*, 1987; Hall and Martinec, 1985; Rango, 1983; Rees and Squire, 1989; Rott, 1987, Zwally, 1987) and so this discussion will centre on the hydrological content of these applications. The advantages of remote sensing approaches to catchment hydrological studies are threefold. First, if the sensors are mounted on satellite or airborne platforms, they provide detailed, spatially distributed information on hydrological variables over the whole study area. Indeed, with satellite mounted sensors, global monitoring of some variables is possible. Second, these data can be repeatedly collected to provide time series information, although the frequency of repeat survey and the level of interference presented by atmospheric conditions varies enormously between sensors and platforms. Thirdly, whilst the response of the sensor is usually supplying surrogate information for the variable of interest, surrogates can often be identified for hydrological variables which are extremely difficult to measure even at a point using other techniques.

Table 1 provides some examples of published studies which are relevant to catchment-based snow and ice hydrological studies through the monitoring of gamma ray, visible, near infrared, thermal infrared and microwave wavelengths.

Gamma radiation

Sensing of the contrasting emission of natural gamma radiation in the presence and absence of snow cover has been used to estimate the snow water equivalent. Problems of calibration arise if there are major changes in soil moisture content between the pre-snow and snow-covered surveys. Deep snowpacks cannot be accurately monitored using this technique and surveys have to be carried out by using low flying aircraft because of the attenuation of the radiation by the snow and the atmosphere. The requirement for low altitude flying renders the technique expensive. It is also too dangerous for use in very mountainous terrain. Nevertheless, it is a sufficiently effective operational technique to be used for snow water equivalent and soil moisture surveys along 1250 flight lines in North America (Carroll, 1987).

Visible, near infrared and thermal infrared wavelengths

Visible and near infrared images for cloud-free conditions provide good definition of snow cover, and ice cover is also usually clearly-defined where the ice surface is well exposed. In the visible wavelengths, snow reflectance is insensitive to grain size but sensitive to small amounts of impurities, whereas in the near infrared wavelengths, snow reflectance is sensitive to grain size but not to impurities (Dozier, 1987a). These properties are important in assessing the spatial distribution of snow quality and snow metamorphism. Of particular hydrological significance is that ice crystals grow in response to vapour transfer through the snow pack and form clusters within melting snow, the clusters increasing in size through successive melt-freeze cycles (Colbeck, 1987). These changes in crystal and cluster size affect the permeability of the pack. The albedo of the snow pack underpins energy balance calculations from the surface reflectance information gathered by a remote sensor. A model of the bidirectional reflectance distribution of snow is required (Rango, 1983) but "to date, no reliable model for determining the BRDF of snow exists" (Foster *et al*, 1987).

Where snow and glacier ice occur together, it is possible to differentiate various surfaces of hydrological significance. In some circumstances shadow effects can allow surface catchment areas to be defined (eg Thomsen and Braithwaite, 1987). In addition, it is possible to separate snow and ice surfaces (eg Clark *et al*, 1987). Indeed, Williams (1987) distinguishes all the major ice facies on Vatnajökull from Landsat MSS data. At the end of the ablation season, these data may be used to estimate the position of the annual equilibrium line and, if a relationship can be established for a particular glacier or extrapolated from nearby glaciers, the equilibrium line altitude (ELA) may provide a basis for estimating glacier mass balance (Braithwaite, 1984; Østrem, 1975; Pelto, 1987). In the absence of such calibration data, the accumulation area ratio (AAR) is a useful glacial hydrological parameter. The ability to estimate ice surface velocities through the identification of the changing position of features on the ice surface (eg Orheim and Lucchitta, 1987) also provides information relevant to glacier mass balance.

Thermal infrared wavelengths provide information on radiometric surface temperature patterns. This could provide a useful input to energy balance studies, although atmospheric effects and, in the case of snow, effects from the liquid water content and crystal size of the pack (Foster *et al*, 1987), interfere with the temperature relationship.

Microwave wavelengths

Microwave remote sensing is undertaken either by sensing the emission of microwaves (passive microwaves) or the return of a microwave signal (active microwaves). Emission and reflection are both heavily influenced by subsurface properties. Depending upon wavelength, microwave radiation will penetrate clouds and most precipitation, providing an all weather capability (Rango, 1983). The intensity of microwave emmission from snowpacks has been related to many hydrological properties of the pack including the temperature, density, depth, snow water equivalent and grain size characteristics. This sensitivity to a range of snow pack properties means that the provision of detailed ground data for calibration purposes is essential (eg Hallikainen and Jolma, 1986).

Airborne and satellite active microwave studies have differentiated dry from wet snow, have separated a variety of ice facies on glacier surfaces (eg Rott and Mätzler, 1987) and have defined surface morphology and topography, and subglacial topography. Single surveys provide estimates of the hydrological boundaries of glacier basins (from surface and subsurface topography) and repeat surveys can underpin the evaluation of glacier mass balance by indicating changes in surface topography. In addition, the repeated identification of features on the ice surface permits estimation of ice surface velocity. Ground based surveys have also defined subglacial topography and ice thickness as well as internal layering including the identification of cavities.

In summary, a variety of remote sensing techniques employing different wavelengths and platforms are beginning to reveal spatial and temporal variations in the hydrological properties of snow and glacier basins. Some of these techniques are operational whilst others are still at an early stage of research, but in combination they can provide information on the spatial extent, depth, internal and surface hydrological properties of snow and ice and, in the case of glaciers, information on their flow velocity. These are all variables which are of major relevance to hydrological modelling in snow and glacier basins, but in virtually all cases the patterns detected by the remote sensors require calibration using ground data. Thus, the operational application of remote sensing to runoff prediction from snow and glacier basins not only requires further remote sensing research but also the provision of well designed ground data networks to calibrate the remotely sensed information.

TABLE 1
Some examples of applications of remote sensing to snow and ice hydrology studies.

GAMMA RAY SENSORS - SNOW SURVEY

BERGSTRÖM and BRANDT, 1985: experimental comparison of snow water equivalent estimated from gamma radiation in comparison with traditional snow course data and as an input to a catchment flow forecasting model for the Kultsjon catchment, northern Sweden.

CARROLL, 1987: operational airborne surveys of soil moisture and snow water equivalent maintained by the National Weather Service, USA (see also Peck *et al*, 1980).

CARROLL and CARROLL, 1989a: impact of uneven snowcover on snow water equivalent estimates; correction methodology applied to western Canada and Colorado flight line data.

CARROLL and CARROLL, 1989b: impact of forest biomass on snow water equivalent estimates; correction methodology proposed.

KUITTINEN, 1989: comparison of snow water equivalent from ground data, airborne gamma ray spectrometry and NOAA AHVRR data in Finland.

VERSHININA, 1983: assessment of applicability of aerial gamma radiation surveys to snowmelt runoff forecasting in USSR drainage basins.

VISIBLE/NEAR INFRARED/THERMAL INFRARED SENSORS - SNOW SURVEY

BAUMGARTENER *et al* 1987: snow cover determination for different altitudinal zones in the Rhein-Felsberg basin, Switzerland. An assessment of snow cover estimates derived from Landsat MSS (good spatial resolution) and NOAA AVHRR data (good temporal resolution) as inputs to the SRM (Martinec-Rango snowmelt runoff model).

BIRNIE, 1986: snow condition assessed from snow pits and oblique air photos in comparison with Landsat MSS data, to assess the potential of Landsat data for identifying snow condition in Scotland.

DEY *et al* 1983: early April snow cover estimates from NOAA VHRR data for Kabul (88600 km^2) and Indus (162100 km^2) river catchments, Pakistan; seasonal regression of runoff on snow cover for runoff estimation.

DOZIER, 1987a,b; DOZIER and MARKS, 1987: methodologies to distinguish snow cover from cloud cover, compensate for rugged terrain and atmospheric scattering effects; to distinguish snow from other surface covers and to classify snow according to grain size and contamination based upon the combined analysis of digital terrain and Landsat TM data.

GUPTA *et al* 1982: snow cover estimation from Landsat MSS data, snow cover related to subcatchment characteristics, snow area correlated with snowmelt runoff for the Beas catchment (12916 km^2), India.

LUCAS *et al* 1989: a snow mapping scheme based upon unsupervised classification of NOAA AVHRR data (potential operational technique for mapping weekly snow cover in the UK).

RANGO, *et al* 1983: assessment of the suitability of inputs from various remote sensors and platforms to operational snow cover monitoring in drainage basins of different spatial scale.

SØGAARD, 1983: combination of NOAA and ground data to estimate snow water equivalent depletion in Greenland catchments.

SØGAARD and THOMSEN, 1988: combination of NOAA AVHRR data with either a degree-day approach or a hydrological simulation model to assess snow pack water equivalent.

ZHANG SHUNYING and ZENG QUNGZHU, 1986: Low resolution TIROS satellite images were used to map snow extent. Snow cover estimates were combined with air temperature and precipitation observations to provide real-time forecasts of snowmelt in the Qilian Mountains area of China.

VISIBLE/NEAR INFRARED/TEHERMAL INFRARED SENSORS - GLACIER SURVEY

DOWDESWELL, 1987: Landsat MSS and TM data for Spitsbergen; snow/cloud differentiation, glacier mapping, identification of glacier surface features.

FUJII *et al* 1987: identification of bare ice, snow and glazed surfaces in Antarctica from NOAA AVHRR data.

HALL *et al*, 1987: analysis of Landsat TM data for Grossglockner area, Austria and the McCall and Meares glaciers, Alaska. The ice surface was classified into up to three zones (one approximates the ablation area - a basis for estimating AAR, the other two in the accumulation area) and radiometric surface temperature patterns were assessed.

HOWARTH and OMMANNEY, 1986: base mapping to identify areas of glacier change on the Steacie ice cap, Axel Heiberg Island and Kaskawulsh glacier, St Elias Mountains from Landsat MSS data.

NOSENKO, 1986: monitoring of ice/firn/snow boundaries using 600-700nm band black and white and multi-spectral colour photographs from Salyut 6 and 7 space station and Kosmos satellite platforms; inferences about glacier equilibrium line position, glacier mass balance, snow storage and runoff.

ORHEIM and LUCCHITTA, 1987: estimation of surface features and flow rates of Antarctic ice streams from digitally enhanced Landsat MSS and TM images.

PELTO, 1987, 1989: combination of analysis of satellite imagery, local weather records and some mass balance determinations to extrapolate mass balance estimates in time and space, SW Alaska and NW British Columbia.

ROTT, 1988: assessment of potential of Landsat TM data for the estimation of glacier area, snow and ice area and AAR (see also Della Ventura *et al* 1987).

SCHARFEN *et al* 1987: analysis of DMSP, Landsat MSS and NOAA VHRR data to discriminate snow covered from ponded/flooded ice surfaces, Arctic sea ice.

THOMSEN and BRAITHWAITE, 1987: low sun angle Landsat MSS data to identify ice surface morphology, Greenland.

WILLIAMS, 1987: Identification of surface morphology, glacier ice facies (transient snow line, slush zone, wet zone, percolation zone, dry snow) on Vatnajokull, Iceland from analysis of Landsat MSS data.

PASSIVE MICROWAVE SENSORS - SNOW SURVEY

CAMPBELL *et al* 1987: comparison Nimbus 7 SMMR data and ground determination of snow pack properties in the Colorado river basin indicates sensitivity of SMMR data to water equivalent and to the spatial and temporal evolution of crystal size in snow packs.

CHANG ***et al*** **1987a**: snow cover maps for the Northern Hemisphere from Nimbus 7 SMMR data.

CHANG ***et al*** **1987b**: development of snow parameter retrieval algorithm to estimate snow water equivalent in mountainous terrain (Colorado river basin) from Nimbus 7 SMMR data.

GOODISON ***et al*** **1986**: development of algorithms for airborne and satellite (Nimbus 7 SMMR) passive microwave mapping of regional snow water equivalent in Canada calibrated from ground snow survey and airborne gamma-ray surveys. Derived algorithms worked well for dry snow areas without trees.

GRODY, 1986: classification of dry snow, sea ice, dry and flooded land and open water using Nimbus 7 SMMR data.

HALL ***et al*** **1982**: influence of forest cover on analysis of snow cover properties from Nimbus 7 SMMR data.

HALLIKAINEN and JOLMA, 1986: assessment of algorithms to estimate snow water equivalent in Finland from Nimbus 7 SMMR data; requirement for ground data on water equivalent and, in spring, on snow pack surface temperature, to calibrate response.

JOSBERGER and BEAVILLAIN, 1989: comparison of analysis of Nimbus 7 SMMR data with images from visible wavelengths (DMSP) to establish threshold microwave characteristics for snow-free pixels; can then use more frequent SMMR data to monitor detailed temporal change in snow cover (Colorado basin).

ROTT and KÜNZI, 1983: potential of Nimbus 7 SMMR data for monitoring snow areal extent, water equivalent and onset of snowmelt on a global and large river basin scale.

ACTIVE MICROWAVE SENSORS - SNOW AND GLACIER SURVEY

BAMBER, 1987; DOWDESWELL ***et al*****, 1984; KOTLYAKOV and MACHERET, 1987**: airborne suveys; ice thickness and warm/cold ice layers in Spitzbergen glaciers.

BENTLEY ***et al*** **1987**: airborne radar and seismic studies; mapping ice streams, grounding lines of Ross ice streams and shelf; inferences on mass balance and bed conditions.

BINSCHADLER ***et al*** **1987**: identification of surface undulations, ice flow lines, crevasses, icebergs, lakes, streams and possible extent of ablation and wet snow zones from airborne and Seasat SAR data.

BJORNSSON, 1982: drainage basin definition on Vatnajökull from ground survey.

DOWDESWELL, 1986: definition and classification of ice drainage basin characteristics, Svalbard, from airborne surveys of ice surface and bed rock topography.

HALL and ORMSBY, 1983: combined analysis of Landsat MSS and Seasat SAR data to enhance surface features of Malaspina glacier.

JACOBEL and RAYMOND, 1984: changing englacial water conditions during surging of Variegated glacier from ground surveys.

KENNETT, 1989: identification of englacial cavities at Storglaciaren from ground survey.

MUSIL and DOAKE, 1987: ground-based pulsed SAR to determine subglacial topography, Bach ice shelf, Antarctica.

ROTT, 1984: airborne and spaceborne SAR studies of snow and ice; identification of glacier morphology and landforms, differentiation of wet snow from snow-free areas, snow from ice surfaces on glaciers.

ROTT and MÄTZLER, 1987: differentiation of dry firn, wet firn, slush and bare ice from airborne and Seasat SAR data.

THOMSEN ***et al*** **1989**: hot water drilling, photogrammetric mapping and airborne radio echo-sounding to define drainage basins on the Greenland ice sheet.

WALFORD ***et al*** **1986**: interpretation of glacier bed and internal targets, Storglaciären, from ground survey.

ZWALLY ***et al*** **1987**: surface elevation data from Seasat radar altimetry and morphological features from Landsat imagery to define form, boundaries and grounding line for areas of Antarctic ice shelf (see also Partington *et al*, 1987).

PROXIMATE MONITORING TECHNIQUES AND THEIR INTEGRATION INTO DATA GATHERING NETWORKS

The most significant hydrological properties of snow for the estimation of catchment runoff are its areal extent, depth, albedo, water equivalent and the condition of the snow pack, particularly its grain size and water content. Information on all of these properties can be abstracted from remotely sensed data but ground calibration information is essential. Goodison *et al* (1981) describe the commonly used methods for determining snow depth (rulers, boards and stakes), snow fall (precipitation gauges), snow water equivalent (gravimetric techniques using snow samplers, snow pillows, radioisotope gauges, ground natural gamma radiation and microwave monitoring) and Barry (1986) surveys the status of snow cover data and the differences in national practices for the collection of snow cover data for hydrological purposes. Whilst these proximate monitoring techniques provide suitable ground calibration data for remotely sensed surveys, there is a continuing need for: (i) improvements in instrumentation siting and network design (eg Ferner and Wigham, 1987; Galeati *et al*, 1986); (ii) the development of methodologies to combine measurements of hydrological variables from different sampling geometries, densities and levels of accuracy to define spatial patterns and areal averages; particularly the problem of combining proximate monitoring and remote sensing data (Peck *et al*, 1983); (iii) the development and improvement of automatic measuring instruments that can contribute real-time observations via telemetering snow monitoring networks.

Recent advances in ground instrumentation include the development and testing of methods for monitoring the water content, depth and density of snow (eg Akitaya, 1985; Bergman, 1987; Boyne and Fisk, 1987; Denoth *et al*, 1984; Edey *et al*, 1987; Kattelman *et al*, 1983; Siholva and Tiuri, 1986), snow fall (correction and intercalibration of precipitation gauges: Goodison *et al*, 1989; Sevruk, 1983; ground-based radar: Kleppe and Liu, 1983) and components of the energy balance above the snow pack surface (eg Harding, 1986; Strangeways, 1980).

If reliable, automatic, proximate-monitoring systems can be developed then data transmission from these automatic stations by satellite relay can provide real-time inputs to hydrological models (Goodison *et al*, 1983; Rango, 1987). The SNOTEL (SNOw TELemtry) system developed by the US Soil Conservation Service provides an excellent example of such a near real-time snow monitoring system. It is capable of receiving data transmissions from as many as 1000 remote sites using up to 16 digital or analogue sensors at each site. Snow water content, accumulated precipitation and temperature are monitored at each site but transmission of data from the monitoring sites to two ground receiving stations is achieved through reflection of radio signals by ionised meteor trails (Rallison, 1981) rather than by satellite relay.

In addition to the role of snow cover, the hydrology of glacier basins is dependent upon the size and mass balance of the ice mass. The great importance of areas of permanent snow and ice to world climate and water resources has resulted in the development and continuous updating of a world-wide inventory (Haeberli *et al*, 1989), which provides an excellent resource for hydrological studies. The inventory is compiled by the World Glacier Monitoring Service (WGMS) of IAHS/IUGG, which since 1986 has taken over the collection and publication of standardised glacier fluctuation data. The series of publications on "Fluctuations of Glaciers" (of which the most recent volume is Haeberli and Müller, 1988) include information on fluctuations in glacier positions and also mass balance information for some glaciers. These sources provide baseline data for studies of glacier basin hydrology which are invaluable given the laborious and time-consuming nature of the evaluation of a glacier's mass balance (see for example Young, 1981). Methods are urgently required for more rapid methods of mass balance evaluation which are applicable to large and remote glacier basins. Possible approaches include the establishment of regional relationships between easily estimated glacier characteristics and full mass balances evaluated for a sample of glaciers (eg Braithwaite, 1984; Pelto, 1987); the reduction of ablation stake network density coupled with the development of algorithms to assess the balance from the reduced stake network (eg Braithwaite, 1986; Reynaud *et al*, 1986); and estimation of the mass balance from a single sector of a glacier at a location close to the equilibrium line, for which the velocity and cross sectional area are determined (eg Reynaud *et al*, 1986; Young and Schmok, 1989). The last technique can be cross-checked from other information such as the measurement of inter-ogive distances to corroborate velocity measurements (Young and Schmok, 1989) and the estimation of net accumulation at different points in the accumulation area from physical and chemical layering studies in snow pits (eg Wake, 1989). Since the ablation component of the mass balance is of particular importance to river flow (for example Young (1982) illustrates the link between distributed patterns of snow and glacier melt and runoff for the Peyto glacier), it would be extremely useful to develop instruments for continuous monitoring of ice ablation (eg Lewkowicz, 1985) as well as the energy budget above the glacier surface. Such instruments need to be refined to minimise their maintenance. They would then provide invaluable information for mass balance calculations and, if integrated into telemetric networks, would permit refinements of short-term flow forecasting. In the absence of such information, flow forecasting in glacier basins must depend upon the establishment of time series relationships between proglacial river flow and climate variables monitored at any convenient nearby climate stations (eg Lang and Dayer, 1985; Lang *et al*, 1987). A hydrological data system, using satellite data transmission and with local sensing and logging facilities designed for severe climatic conditions (down to -40°C), has been set up by the Greenland Technical Organisation (Thomsen, 1983, 1989) specifically for monitoring and modelling the hydrology of sections of the Greenland ice cap and adjoining glacier and glacier-free basins. This system monitors information from climate stations as well as gathering data on river flow, water and ground temperature, and so provides the bases for effective flow forecasting.

THE COMBINATION OF REMOTELY AND PROXIMATELY SENSED DATA AND OTHER GEO-REFERENCED DATA FOR SNOW AND GLACIER BASINS.

The discussion so far has illustrated that ground hydrological observations are required to calibrate remotely sensed data, and that if proximate monitoring stations are linked through data transmission systems for central processing (with or without remotely sensed data), the observations can be used for flow forecasting as well as for water resource evaluation. The effectiveness of such techniques can be enhanced if other geo-referenced data are combined with the hydrological data. For example, the addition of elevation data can provide a framework for the improved estimation and interpolation of point hydrological processes and for the routing of those processes to the basin outlet. Algorithms to derive topographic landscape units for hydrological modelling from digital elevation data have facilitated the derivation of slope angle, curvature, aspect and upslope contributing area classes (eg Moore et al, 1988). Band (1989) extended this approach in a snow-free and glacier-free context by defining drainage basin structure (ie watershed position, subcatchments and hillslope segments and their relationship to the drainage network through thresholds of drainage area required to support a river channel) from digital elevation data. He then used these data to simulate catchment runoff processes using a distributed hydrological model. Table 2 illustrates the application of similar approaches to snow and glacier basins and shows that the emphasis in undertaking the combined analysis of multiple types of data has been on estimating snow pack rather than glacier hydrological properties.

The combined spatial analysis of proximately and remotely monitored hydrological variables and other catchment characteristics is an area which demands increased research attention but to successfully estimate runoff using this distributed approach, it is essential that information on the temporally dynamic nature of runoff source areas and routing is incorporated. This element can be incorporated using the results of field water balance monitoring studies at different spatial scales, but in the context of snow and glacier runoff, a great deal of additional information can be derived from field studies of water chemistry and from tracer experiments.

TABLE 2 Some examples of the combined use of proximate and remotely sensed data and other geo-referenced data in hydrological studies of snow and glacier basins.

---

1. Purpose of study. 2. Proximate data. 3. Remotely sensed data. 4. Other data. 5. Methods.

BAUMGARTNER *et al*, 1986 1. Estimation of snow-covered areas for river flow estimation. 3. Landsat MSS data. 4. Digital elevation model. 5. Analysis and classification of elevation data to create 205 elevation/aspect/slope classes. Visual classification of cloud covered areas, supervised classification of snow/transition/snow free areas. Analysis of relationship between snow cover and topographic class for interpolation in cloud covered areas and areas without satellite data. Estimation of snow cover in elevation zones for input to SRM (Martinec-Rango snowmelt runoff model).

CAMPBELL *et al*, 1987 1. Snow water equivalent mapping. 2. Snow pit data and snow water equivalent data from SNOTEL stations. 3. Nimbus 7 SMMR data. 5. Analysis of synchronous proximate and remotely sensed data for interpolation of snow water equivalent for different parts of the upper Colorado basin.

DOZIER and MARKS, 1987 1. Snow mapping and classification as a basis for snow-surface energy-balance modelling in alpine areas. 3. Landsat TM data. 4. Digital elevation model. 5. Terrain information provides basis for atmospheric/terrain radiation model. This is combined with calculations of the spectral reflectance of snow to simulate radiance at the top of the atmosphere for different snow grain sizes, levels of contamination and terrain conditions.

ELDER *et al*, 1989 1. Identification of spatial and temporal variation in net snow accumulation in an alpine watershed. 2. Spatial and temporal surveys of snow depth, density profiles, water equivalent. 4. Digital elevation model. 5. Radiation, slope and elevation mapped and clustered for classification of catchment for different time periods; variables and classes assessed for extrapolating snow water equivalent over the basin.

FERRIS and CONGALTON, 1989 1. Estimation of distribution of snow pack properties. 2. SNOTEL snow water equivalent readings synchronous with satellite data. 3. NOAA AVHRR data. 4. Digital elevation data. 5. A GIS containing layers for reflectance in visible, near and thermal infrared, vegetation index, elevation, slope, aspect, shade, sub-basin, SNOTEL sites is used to relate snow water equivalent to other variables and for basin-wide snowpack water volume estimation.

GUNDERSON *et al*, 1987 1. Methodology for spatial estimation of snowpack variables for runoff forecasting. 2. Ground data from 'optimal sites': snow depth, water equivalent, temperature, albedo, free water content. 3. Landsat TM data under snow-free conditions. 4. Digital elevation model. 5. Identification of 'optimal sites' for ground data monitoring from terrain zones (elevation/aspect zones identified from digital elevation model) subdivided into land use/vegetation zones using pattern recognition algorithms applied to multispectral data.

ROSSI *et al* 1986 1. Estimation of distribution and water equivalent of snow for runoff estimation. 2. Meteorological stations, snow depth and water equivalent stations. 3. Classified Landsat images for snow covered, transitional and snow-free ground. 4. Digital elevation model containing basin watershed, elevation, slope and aspect defined for a 'Landsat grid'. 5. Regression of snow depth on elevation and application of mean snow water equivalent to define spatial distribution of snow water equivalent.

SEIDEL *et al*, 1983 1. Snow cover determination in large catchments. 3. Landsat MSS data. 4. Digital elevation model. 5. Derivation of slope, aspect and angle between surface normal and sun direction at time of satellite overpass; registration with satellite data; classification of snow cover in open areas and interpolation of snow line in woodland. Analysis of snow cover in relation to altitude/slope/aspect categories.

SØGAARD, 1983 1. Snow mapping during melt. 2. Snow pack depth, density (water equivalent) and temperature; snow extent from air photos. 3. NOAA satellite data. 4. Digital elevation model. 5. Maximum snow water equivalent modelled from altitude and geographic co-ordinates. Satellite images for different stages of melt registered to common base, used to estimate surface temperature, adjusted for sun angle and topography to derive albedo estimates. Snow cover classified from albedo and temperature (to isolate melting snow) and checked using air photos as 'ground truth'.

WHITING and KISS, 1987 1. Digital terrain model used to refine ground-based snow and runoff measurement. 2. Flow gauging and snow depth sampling (uniform, random, and transects perpendicular to river channels). 4. Digital terrain model. 5. Slope, aspect, slope and contour curvature, elevation, catchment area defined from DTM and used to construct flow lines to basin outlet. Estimated snow water equivalent and flows compared with measured flows indicated redesign of snow sampling in proportion to channel volumes.

THE USE OF RIVER FLOW AND QUALITY SERIES FOR IDENTIFYING RUNOFF SOURCE AREAS AND FLOW ROUTING AT A BASIN SCALE

The analysis of flow quantity

One approach to studying runoff source areas and routing characteristics is to study flow generation processes at nested spatial scales. Such an approach has been adopted in a number of research studies (eg Braun and Slaymaker, 1981; Fitzgibbon and Dunne, 1981; Price, 1987; Woo, 1983) illustrating differences in the runoff regime with spatial scale as well as with the distribution of snow/ice/frozen ground in the catchment.

Studies at different spatial scales have identified different properties of runoff generation processes in snow and glacier basins. Small plot studies illustrate the complexities of water movement through snow pack (eg Harstveit, 1981; Jordan, 1983; Martinec, 1987), including the influences of the melt rate, snow grain size, snow depth and refreezing and redistribution of water through the pack. More than a day of surface melt may be required before any water drains from an initially dry, moderately deep snow pack, whereas a lag of only 1h may occur if the pack is near melting point with a significant initial free water content (Bengtsson, 1986). Water storage and drainage within the snow/firn zone of glacier basins is also complex. Oerter and Moser's (1982) study of water table levels and flow rates within the firn zone of the Vernagtferner glacier illustrate the lengthy (up to 13 day) residence time of water in this zone, whereas Lang *et al* (1979) recorded the peak proglacial discharge of tracer injected into the firn aquifer of the Aletschgletscher approximately 34-36 days after the time of injection.

Hillslope studies reveal details of the role of snow pack properties in the delivery of hillslope runoff to stream channels (eg Bengtsson, 1985 - differences in runoff pathways with vegetation cover; Olyphant, 1984, 1986 - the identification of insolation topoclimates and their impact on snow melt variability; Roberge and Plamondon, 1987 - snowmelt hillslope runoff pathways including role of pipeflow).

Catchment studies identify lags between meltwater release and its transmission to a point on the river network. In the context of snow basins, Kobayashi and Motoyama (1985) show an increase in lag between peak snowmelt and peak runoff of 1.5 to 4 h per 1m increment in snow depth and a power relationship between lag, catchment area and melt rate once the propagation time through the snow pack has been accounted for. Whilst Collins and Young (1981) provide a schematic model for discharge generation from different source areas in snow and glacier basins, Oerter *et al* (1981) compare distributed measurements of meltwater generation and routing from the firn and bare ice areas of the Vernagtferner catchment with the proglacial discharge record and propose and calibrate a four reservoir hydrological model for the basin. Other studies have attempted to identify lags between meltwater generation processes in snow and glacier basins through the analysis of outflow hydrographs. For example, van de Griend and Seyham (1985) use a non-linear optimisation technique to analyse complex hydrographs with pluvial/nival/glacial components.

These hydrological studies at different scales provide fascinating insights into the functioning of snow and glacier basins but more nested, multi-scale studies are needed to formalise the identified relationships and to develop and enhance multiple reservoir models by increasing the detail of the distribution and routing characteristics of the component reservoirs.

The analysis of flow quality

Since water quality is the theme of a separate symposium at this conference, the discussion here will be confined to the monitoring of river quality characteristics to define the role of snow and glacier meltwater as river flow components. The quality of meltwater can be used to separate flow source areas and to estimate routing times in both snow and glacier basins. Natural water quality components (concentrations of individual anions and cations, environmental isotopes) have been used to fingerprint source areas and 'chemographs' have provided information on the phasing of flows from those source areas. Artificial tracer experiments have added precision to estimates of flow timing and to differentiation of flow times between different locations within the same water source area (eg Behrens *et al*, 1983; Hooke *et al*, 1988; Seaberg *et al*, 1988).

Early studies employed only simple indices of water quality and simple models to relate river flow to potential source areas. For example, mixing models can be applied to total discharge and its electrical conductivity to achieve flow separation in glacier and snow basins (eg Collins, 1979), but such models, if they are to remain simple, must assume no evolution of meltwater electrical conductivity either in the source area or during routing. A more useful approach is to allow evolution of water chemistry in the source area by redefining the electrical conductivity characteristics of the source areas during the melt season and by using additional indicators of water source characteristics such as the concentration of particular anions or cations to corroborate the flow separations defined by electrical conductivity fluctuations (Brown and Tranter, 1990). Environmental isotopes, particularly ^{18}O, ^{2}H and ^{3}H, provide conservative tracers which can be used to develop mixing models for water from different source areas in snow basins (eg Bottomley *et al*, 1986; Herrmann *et al*, 1981; Maloszewski *et al*, 1983; Stichler, 1987) and glacier basins (eg Ambach *et al*, 1982; Behrens *et al*, 1979; van de Griend and Arwert, 1983; Theakstone and Knudsen, 1989). The research reported by Behrens *et al* (1979) is particularly interesting because they use a variety of environmental isotopes with electrical conductivity to achieve a four-fold separation of flow in a proglacial river.

Multiple variable approaches to the separation of outflow hydrographs appear to offer the optimum solution to flow separation problems. Anion and cation concentrations may be helpful in some circumstances. For example Hooper and Shoemaker (1986) compared flow separation in a snow basin using both environmental isotopes and the concentration of major cations and anions. They found that an isotopic separation was satisfactory early in the snowmelt period but that the isotopic content of groundwater and meltwater varied through time and became indistinguishable towards the end of the melt period. A comparison of chemical and isotopic separation indicated that dissolved silica was a conservative tracer for the catchment studied.

It is important to note the complexities of snow and glacier meltwater chemistry, which may render flow separation problematical. The 'preferential elution' characteristics of snow meltwater chemistry, which may give rise to 'acid shocks', have been widely reported (eg DeWalle, 1987;

Gjessing and Johanssen, 1987; Goodison *et al*, 1986; Gunn and Keller, 1986; Tranter *et al*, 1986, 1987) and provide a major problem for attempts at chemical flow separation. Similarly, in glacier basins, differential flushing out and leaching of ions from the snow and firn layers, ion exchange mechanisms, selective rejection of ions by regelation processes and selective filtration of ions by particle layers can all affect meltwater chemistry (Souchez and Lemmens, 1987). Of particular importance is the chemical weathering environment at the glacier bed and the associated possibility of variable post-mixing reactions of bulk meltwaters as a result of their closed-system or open-system evolution (Raiswell, 1984). It is clear that multiple conservative natural tracers are required, possibly in combination with artificial tracers, to unravel the source area and routing history of meltwater in snow and ice environments.

CONCLUSIONS

New technologies and techniques have produced significant progress towards the detailed spatial and temporal evaluation of hydrological processes in snow and glacier basins. It is necessary to increase effort in these research areas, particularly in identifying the fundamental hydrological processes and the degree to which they are characterised by new techniques. It is also essential to emphasise multidisciplinary studies which can combine the new research techniques within the same snow or glacier basin since this will underpin the development of realistic distributed hydrological models. Finally, it is essential that the results of research are more rapidly transfered to the development of operational systems and models for evaluating water resources and for flow forecasting, particularly in large drainage basins

ACKNOWLEDGEMENTS Mike Clark, Ted Milton and Martyn Tranter are gratefully acknowledged for their helpful comments on the manuscript.

REFERENCES

Akitaya E. (1985) A calorimeter for measuring free water content of wet snow. Annals of Glaciology 6, 246-247.

Ambach W., Kirchlechner P., Moser H. & Stichler W. (1982) Seasonal variations of deuterium concentration in runoff from a glacierized basin. Hydrol. Sci. J. 27, 29-34.

Anderson, M.G. & Rogers, C.M.M. (1987) Catchment scale distributed hydrological models: a discussion of research directions. Progress in Physical Geography 11, 28-51.

Barry, R.G. (1986) Snow cover data: status and future prospects. In: G. Kukla, R.G. Barry, A. Hecht and D. Wiesnet (Eds) Snow Watch '85, World Data Center A for Glaciology (Snow and Ice) Glaciological Data Report GD-18, 127-139.

Bamber, J.L. (1987) Internal reflecting horizons in Spitzbergen glaciers. Annals of Glaciology 9, 5-10.

Band, L.E. (1989) A terrain-based watershed information system. Hydrol. Proc. 3, 151-162.

Baumgartner, M.F., Seidel, K., Haefner, H., Itten, K.I. & Martinec, J. (1986) Snow cover mapping for runoff simulations based on LANDSAT MSS data in an alpine basin. In: I.A. Johnson (ed), Hydrologic aspects of space technology (Proc. Int. Workshop, Florida, 1985) IAHS Publ. 160, 191-190.

Baumgartner, M.F., Seidel, K. & Martinec, J. (1987) Toward snowmelt runoff forecasts based on multi-sensor remote sensing information. IEEE Trans. on Geoscience and Remote Sensing GE-25(6), 746-749.

Behrens, H., Moser, H., Oerter, H., Rauert, W., Stichler, W., Ambach, W. & Kirchlechner, P. (1979) Models for the runoff from a glaciated catchment using measurements of environmental isotope contents. In: Isotope Hydrology IAEA, Vienna, 829-846.

Behrens, H., Oerter, H. & Reinwarth, O. (1983) Results of tracer experiments with flourescent dyes on Vernagtferner (Oetzal alps, Austria) from 1974 to 1982. Zeits. fur Gletscherkunde und Glazialgeologie 18, 65-83.

Bengtsson, L. (1985) Characteristics of snowmelt induced peak flows in a small northern basin. Nordic Hydrol. 16, 137-156.

Bengtsson, L. (1986) Snowmelt simulation models in relation to space and time. In: E.M. Morris (ed) Modelling snowmelt induced processes (Proc. Budapest Symp.) IAHS Publ. 155, 115-123.

Bentley, C.R., Shabtaie, S., Blakenship, D.D., Rooney, S.T., Schultz, D.G., Anandakrishnan, S. and Alley, R.B. (1987) Remote sensing of the Ross ice streams and adjacent Ross ice shelf, Antarctica. Annals of Glaciology 9, 20-29.

Bergman, J.A. (1987) Accuracy and repeatability of in-situ snow wetness measurements using the newly developed twin-disc capacitance sensor. Proc. Western Snow Conference 1987, 142-145.

Bergström, S. & Brandt, M. (1985) Measurement of areal water equivalent of snow by natural gamma radiation - experiences from Northern Sweden. Hydrol. Sci. Bull. 30, 465-477.

Birnie, R.V. (1986) Pixel mixing effects and their significance to identifying snow conditions from LANDSAT MSS data. Int. J. Remote Sensing 7, 845-853.

Binschadler, R.A., Jezek, K.C. & Crawford, J. (1987) Glaciological investigations using the synthetic aperture radar imaging system. Annals of Glaciology 9, 11-19.

Björnsson, H. (1982) Drainage basins on Vatnajökull mapped by radio echo soundings. Nordic Hydrol. 13, 212-232.

Bottomley, D.J., Craig, D. & Johnston, L.M. (1986) Oxygen-18 studies of snowmelt runoff in a small precambrian watershed. J. Hydrol. 88, 213-234.

Boyne, H.S. & Fisk, D. (1987) A comparison of snow cover liquid water measurement techniques. Wat. Resour. Res. 23, 1833-1836.

Braithwaite, R.J. (1986) Assessment of mass-balance variations with a sparse stake network, Qamanarssup Sermia, West Greenland. J. Glaciol. 32, 50-53.

Braithwaite, R.J. (1984) Can the mass balance of a glacier be estimated from its equilibrium line altitude. J. Glaciol. 30, 364-368.

Braun, L.N., & Slaymaker, H.O., (1981) Effect of scale on complexity of snowmelt systems. Nordic Hydrol. 12, 235-246.

Brown, G.H., & Tranter, M., (1990) Hydrograph and chemograph separation of bulk meltwaters draining the Upper Arolla glacier, Valais, Switzerland. Proc. Lausanne Symp., IAHS, in press.

Campbell, W.J., Josberger, E.G., Gloersen, P. & Chang, A.T.C. (1987) Microwave snow-water equivalent mapping of the upper Colorado River basin, U.S.A. Annals of Glaciology 9, 244-245.

Carroll, T.R. (1987) Operational airborne measurements of snow water equivalent and soil moisture using terrestrial gamma radiation in the United States. In: B.E. Goodison, R.G. Barry & J. Dozier (eds), Large scale effects of seasonal snow cover, IAHS Publ. 166, 213-223.

Carroll, S.S. & Carroll, T.R. (1989a) Effect of eneven snow cover on airborne snow water equivalent estimates obtained by measuring terrestrial gamma radiation. Wat. Resour. Res. 25, 1505-1510.

Carroll, S.S. & Carroll, T.R. (1989b) Effect of forest biomass on airborne snow water equivalent estimates obtained by measuring terrestrial gamma radiation. Remote Sens. Environ. 27, 313-320.

Chang, A.T.C. & Rango, A. (1982) Remote sensing applications in snow hydrology - past, present and future. Proc. Western Snow Conf. 1982, 204-207.

Chang, A.T.C., Foster, J.L. & Hall, D.K. (1987a) Nimbus-7 SMMR derived global snow cover parameters. Annals of Glaciology 9, 39-44.

Chang, A.T.C., Foster, J.L., Gloersen, P., Campbell, W.J., Josberger, E.G., Rango, A. & Danes, Z.F. (1987b) Estimating snow pack parameters in the Colorado River basin. Large scale effects of seasonal snow cover (Proc. Vancouver Symp.) IAHS Publ. 166, 343-352.

Clark, M.J., Gurnell, A.M. & Hancock, P.J. (1987) Ground data inputs to image processing for estimating terrain characteristics for glacio-hydrological analysis. Annals of Glaciology 9, 45-49.

Colbeck, S.C. (1987) Snow metamorphism and classification. In: H.G. Jones and W.J. Orville-Thomas (eds.) Seasonal snowcovers: Physics, Chemistry, Hydrology 1-35, D. Reidel Publ. Co..

Collins, D.N. (1979) Quantitative determination of the subglacial hydrology of two Alpine glaciers. J. Glaciol. 23, 347-367.

Collins, D.N. & Young, G.J. (1981) Meltwater hydrology and hydrochemistry in snow and ice-covered mountain catchments. Nordic Hydrol. 12, 319-334.

Della Ventura, A., Rampini, A., Rabagliati, R. & Serandrei Barbero, R. (1987) Development of a remote sensing technique for the study of alpine glaciers. Int. J. Remote Sensing 8, 203-215.

Denoth A., Foglar, A., Weiland, P., Matzler, C., Aebischer, H., Tiuri, M. & Siholva, A. (1984) A comparative study of instruments for measuring the liquid water content of snow. J. Appl. Physics 56, 2154-2160.

Deutsch, M., Wiesnet, D.R. & Rango, A. (1981) Satellite hydrology Amer. Wat. Resur. Assoc., Minneapolis.

DeWalle, D.R. (1987) Review of snowpack chemistry studies. In H.G. Jones and W.J. Orville-Thomas (eds.) Seasonal snowcovers: Physics, Chemistry, Hydrology 255-268, D. Reidel Publ. Co..

Dey B., Goswami D.C. & Rango A. (1983) Utilization of satellite snow cover observations for seasonal streamflow estimates in the western Himalayas. Nordic Hydrol. 14, 257-266.

Dowdeswell, J.A. (1986) Drainage basin characteristics of Nordaustlandet ice caps, Svalbard. J. Glaciol. 32, 31-38.

Dowdeswell, J.A. (1987) Comparison of Landsat multispectral scanner and thematic mapper radiometric and spatial characteristics over glaciers. Annals of Glaciology 9, 245.

Dowdeswell, J.A., Drewry, D.J., Liestøl, O. & Orheim, O. (1984) Radio echo-sounding of Spitzbergen glaciers: problems in the interpretation of layer and bottom returns. J. Glaciol. 30, 16-21.

Dozier, J. (1987a) Recent research in snow hydrology. Reviews of Geophysics 25, 153-161.

Dozier, J. (1987b) Remote sensing of snow characteristics in the Southern Sierra Nevada. In: B.E. Goodison, R.G. Barry & J. Dozier (eds), Large scale effects of seasonal snow cover (Proc. Vancouver Symp.) IAHS Publ. 166, 305-314.

Dozier, J. & Marks, J. (1987) Snow mapping and classification from LANDSAT thematic mapper data. Annals of Glaciology 9, 97-103.

Edey S.N., Buckley D.J., Lalonde M.J.L. & Nicholls C.F. (1987) Automated monitoring of depth of snow on ground. Agricultural and Forest Meteorology 39, 351-356.

Elder, K., Dozier, J. & Michaelsen, J. (1989) Spatial and temporal variation of net snow accumulation in a small alpine watershed, Emerald lake basin, Sierra Nevada, California, USA. Annals of Glaciology 13, 56-63.

Ferner, S.J. & Wigham, J.M. (1987) The use of snow pillow data for melt rate input on the streamflow synthesis and reservoir regulation watershed model. Canadian J. Civil Eng. 14, 118-126.

Ferris, J.S. & Congalton, R.G. (1989) Satellite and geographic information system estimates of Colorado river basin snow pack. Photogramm. Eng. and Remote Sensing 55, 1629-1635.

Fitzgibbon, J.E. & Dunne, T. (1981) Land surface and lake storage during snowmelt runoff in a subarctic drainage system. Eos 68, 681-684.

Foster, J.L., Hall, D.K. & Chang, A.T.C. (1987) Remote sensing of snow. Eos 68, 682-684.

Fountain, A.G. & Tangborn, W. (1985) Overview of contemporary techniques. In: G.J. Young (ed.) Techniques for the prediction of runoff from glacierized areas, IAHS Publ. 149, 27-41.

Fujii, Y., Yamanouchi, T., Suzuki, K. & Tanaka, S. (1987) Comparison of the surface conditions of the inland ice sheet, Dronning Maud Land, Antarctica, derived from NOAA AVHRR data with ground observation. Annals of Glaciology 9, 72-75.

Galeati, G., Rossi, G., Pini, G. & Zilli, G. (1986) Optimization of snow network by multivariate statistical analysis. Hydrol. Sci. J. 31, 93-108.

Gjessing, E. & Johanessen, M. (1987) Snow chemistry with particular reference for the chemical composition of snow in Scandinavia. In: H.G. Jones and W.J. Orville-Thomas (eds.) Seasonal snowcovers: Physics, Chemistry, Hydrology. 661-672, D. Reidel Publ. Co..

Goodison, B.E., Ferguson, H.L. & McKay, G.A. (1981) Measurement and data analysis. In: D.M. Gray & D.H. Male (eds) Handbook of snow Pergamon, 191-274.

Goodison B.E., Rubinstein I., Thirkettle F.W. & Langham E.J. (1986) Determination of snow water equivalent on the Canadian praries using microwave radiometry. In: E.M. Morris (ed), Modelling snowmelt-induced processes (Proc. Budapest Symp.) IAHS Publ. 155, 163-173.

Goodison, B.E., Sevruk, B. & Klemm, S. (1989) WMO solid precipitation measurement intercomparison: objectives, methodology, analysis. In: J.W. Delleur (ed.) Atmospheric Deposition (Proc. Baltimore Symp.) IAHS Publ. 179, 57-64.

Goodison, B.E., Whiting, J.M., Wiebe, K. & Cihlar, J. (1983) Operational requirements for water resources remote sensing in Canada: now and in the future. In Hydrological Applications of Remote Sensing and Remote Data Transmission (Proc. Hamburg Symp.) IAHS Publ. 145, 647-657.

Goodison, B.E., Louie, P.Y.T. & Metcalfe, J.R. (1986) Investigations of snowmelt acidic shock potential in south central Ontario, Canada. In Modelling snowmelt-induced processes (Proc. Budapest Symp.) IAHS Publ. 155, 297-309.

van de Griend A.A & Arwert J.A. (1983) Mechanism of runoff generation from an alpine glacier traced by oxygen O-18/O-16. J. Hydrol. 62, 263-278.

van de Griend A.A. & Seyhan E. (1985) Determination of resistance parameters of pluvio-nivo-glacial alpine systems by mathematical modelling of runoff. J. Hydrol. 77, 187-207.

Grody N.C. (1986) Snow cover monitoring using microwave radiometry. In: G. Kukla, R.G. Barry, A.D. Hecht & D.R. Weisnet (eds), Snow Watch '85, World Data Centre A for Glaciology, (Snow and Ice) Glaciological Data Report GD-18, 189-192.

Gunderson R.W., Leu C.H., Bowles D.S & Riley P.J. (1987) A classification model for spatial estimation of snowpack variables from satellite data. In: B.E. Goodison, R.G. Barry & J. Dozier (eds), Large scale effects of seasonal snow cover (Proc. Vancouver Symp.) IAHS Publ. 166, 389-401.

Gunn, J.M. & Keller, W. (1986) Effects of acidic meltwater on chemical conditions at nearshore spawning sites. Water, air and soil pollution 30, 545-552.

Gupta R.P., Rao S.N., Sankar G. & Singhal B.B.S. (1982) Snow cover area vs snowmelt runoff relation and its dependance on geomorphology - a study of the Beas catchment (Himalayas, India). J. Hydrol. 58, 325-329.

Haeberli, W. & Müller, P. (1988) Fluctuations of glaciers 1980-1985 IAHS, UNEP, UNESCO, Paris.

Haeberli, W., Bosch, H., Scherler, K., Østrem, G. & Wallén, C.C. (1989) World glacier inventory status 1988. IAHS, UNEP, UNESCO.

Hall, D.K. & Martinec, J. (1985) Remote sensing of ice and snow Chapman and Hall, London-New York. Hall, D.K., Foster, J.L. & Chang, A.T.C. (1982) Modelling microwave emission from forested snowfields in Michigan. Nordic Hydrol. 13, 129-138.

Hall, D.K. & Ormsby, J.P. (1983) Use of Seasat synthetic aperture radar and Landsat multispectral scanner subsystem data for Alaskan glaciological studies. J. Geophys. Res. 88, 1597-1607.

Hall D.K., Ormbsy J.P., Bindschadler R.A. & Siddalingaiah H. (1987) Characterization of snow and ice reflectance zones on glaciers using LANDSAT thematic mapper data. Annals of Glaciology 9, 104-108.

Hallikainen, M.T. & Jolma, P.A. (1986) Retrieval of the water equivalent of snow by satellite microwave radiometry. IEEE Trans. on Geoscience and Remote Sensing, GE-24(6), 885-862.

Harding, R.J. (1986) Exchanges of energy and mass associated with a melting snow pack. In: E. Morris (ed.) Modelling of snowmelt-induced processes (Proc. Budapest Symp.) IAHS Publ. 155, 3-15.

Harding, R.J., Entrasser, N., Escher-Vetter, H., Jenkins, A., Kaser, G., Kuhn, M., Morris, E.M. & Tanzer, E. (1989) Energy and mass balance studies in the firn area of the Hintereisferner. In: J. Oerlemans (ed.) Glacier fluctuations and climatic change, Kluwer Academic Publ., 325-341.

Harstveit K. (1981) Measuring and modelling snowmelt in Drydalen, Western Norway, 1979 and 1980. Nordic Hydrol. 12, 235-246.

Herrmann A., Lehrer M. & Sthichler W. (1981), Isotope input into runoff systems from melting snow covers. Nordic Hydrol. 12, 309-318.

Hooke, R.L., Miller, S.B. & Kohler, J. (1988) Character of the englacial and subglacial drainage system in the upper part of the ablation area, Storglaciären, Sweden. J. Glaciol. 34, 228-231.

Hooper, R.P. & Shoemaker, C.A. (1986) A comparison of chemical and isotopic hydrograph separation. Wat. Resour. Res. 22, 1444-1454.

Howarth, P.J. & Ommanney, C.S.L. (1986) The use of Landsat digital data for glacier inventories. Annals of Glaciology 8, 90-92.

Jacobel, R. & Raymond, C. (1984) Radio echo-sounding studies of englacial water movement in Variegated glacier, Alaska. J. Glaciol. 30, 22-29.

Jordan P. (1983) Meltwater movement in a deep snowpack, 1. Field observations. Wat. Resour. Res. 19, 971-978.

Josberger E.G. & Beauvillain E. (1989) Snow cover of the upper Colorado basin from satellite passive microwave and visual imagery. Nordic Hydrol. 20, 73-84.

Kattelmann, R.C., McGurk, B.J., Berg, N.H., Bergman, J.A. & Hannaford, M.A. (1983) The isotope profiling snow gauge: twenty years of experience. Proc. Western Snow Conf. 51, 1-8.

Kennet, M.I. (1989) A possible radio-echo method of locating englacial and subglacial waterways. Annals of Glaciology 13, 135-139.

Kleppe, J.A. & Liu, S.L. (1983) Quantitative measurements of snowfall using unattended mountain top radar. In: Hydrological applications of remote sensing and remote data transmission (Proc. Hamburg Symp.) IAHS Publ. 145, 335-343.

Kobayshi D. & Motoyama H. (1985) Effect of snowcover on time lag of runoff from a watershed. Annals of Glaciology 6, 123-125.

Kotliakov, V.M. & Macheret, Yu.Ya. (1987) Radio echo-sounding of sub-polar glaciers in Svalbard: some problems and results of Soviet studies. Annals of Glaciology 9, 151-159.

Kuittinen, R. (1989) Determination of snow water equivalents by using NOAA-satellite images, gamma ray spectrometry and field measurements. In: Remote sensing and large-scale global processes (Proc. Baltimore Symp.) IAHS Publ. 186, 151-159.

Lang, H. and Dayer, G. (1985) Switzerland case study: water supply. In: G. Young (ed.) Techniques for the prediction of runoff from glacierised areas, IAHS Publ. 149, 45-57.

Lang, H., Jensen, H. & Grebner, D. (1987) Short-range runoff forecasting for the River Rhine at Rheinfelden: experiences and present problems. Hydrol. Sci. J. 32, 385-397.

Lang, H., Leibundgut, Ch. and Festel, E. (1979) Results from tracer experiments on the water flow through the Aletschgletscher. Zeits. für Gletscherkunde und Glazialgeologie 15, 209-218.

Lewkowicz, A.G. (1985) Use of an ablatometer to measure short-term ablation of exposed ground ice. Canadian J. Earth Sci. 22, 1767-1773.
Lucas, R.M., Harrison, A.R. & Barrett, E.C. (1989) A multispectral snow area algorithm for operational 7-day snow cover monitoring. In: Remote sensing and large-scale global processes (Proc. Baltimore Symp.) IAHS Publ. 186, 161-166.
Maloszewski P., Rauert W., Stichler W. & Herrmann A. (1983) Application of flow models in an alpine catchment using tritium and deuterium data. J. Hydrol. 66, 319-330.
Martinec, J. (1987) Importance and effects of seasonal snow cover. In: Large scale effects of seasonal snow cover (Proc. Vancouver Symp.) IAHS Publ. 166, 107-120.
Martinec, J. (1987) Meltwater percolation through an alpine snowpack. In: Avalanache formation, movement and effects (Proc. Davos Symp.) IASH Publ. 162, 255-264.
Martinec, J. & Rango, A. (1989) Effects of climate change on snowmelt runoff patterns. In: Remote sensing and large-scale global processes (Proc. Baltimore Symp.) IAHS Publ. 186, 31-38.
Meier M.F. (1983) Snow and ice in a changing hydrological world. Hydrol. Sci. J. 28, 3-22.
Moore, I.D., O'Loughlin, E.M. & Burch, G.J. (1988) A contour-based topographic model for hydrological and ecological applications. Earth Surf. Proc. and Landforms 13, 305-320.
Musil, G.J. & Doake, C.S.M. (1987) Imaging subglacial topography by a synthetic aperture radar technique. Annals of Glaciology 9, 170-175.
Nosenko, G.A. (1986) Use of space imagery in the study of mass exchange in glacier systems. Mapping Sci. and Remote Sensing 23, 295-301.
Oerter, H., Baker, D., Moser, H. & Reinwarth, O. (1981) Glacial-hydrological investigations at the Vernagtferner glacier as a basis for a discharge model. Nordic Hydrol. 12, 335-348.
Oerter, H. & Moser, H. (1982) Water storage and drainage within the firn of a temperate glacier (Vernagtferner, Otzal alps, Austria). In: J.W. Glen (ed.), Hydrological aspects of alpine and high mountain areas (Proc. Exeter Symp.) IAHS Publ. 138, 71-81.
Olyphant, G.A. (1984) Insolation topoclimates and potential ablation in alpine snow accumulation basins: Front Range, Colorado. Wat. Resour. Res. 20, 491-498.
Olyphant, G.A. (1986) The components of incoming radiation within a mid-latitude alpine watershed during the snowmelt season. Arctic and Alpine Research 18, 163-169.
Orheim, O. & Lucchitta (1987) Snow and ice studies by Thematic Mapper and Multispectral Scanner Landsat images. Annals of Glaciology 9, 109-118.
Østrem, G. (1975) ERTS data in glaciology - an effort to monitor glacier mass balance from satellite imagery. J. Glaciol. 15, 403-415.
Peck, E.L., Johnson, E.R., Keefer, T.N. & Rango, A. (1983) Combining measurements of hydrological variables of various sampling geometries and measurement accuracies. In: Hydrological applications of remote sensing and remote data transmission (Proc. Hamburg Symp.) IAHS Publ. 145, 591-599.
Pelto, M.S. (1987) Mass balance of South-East Alaska and North-West British Columbia glaciers from 1976 to 1984: Method and results. Annals of Glaciology 9, 189-194.
Pelto, M.S. (1989) Satellite determination of Coast Range, Alaskan glacier mass balance related to atmospheric circulation. In: Remote sensing and large-scale global processes (Proc. Baltimore Symp.) IAHS Publ. 186, 127-137.
Price, A.G. (1988) Prediction of snowmelt rates in a deciduous forest. J. Hydrol. 101, 145-157.
Raiswell R. (1984) Chemical models of solute aquisition in glacial meltwaters. J. Glaciol. 30, 49-57.
Rallison R.E. (1981) Automated system for collecting snow and hydrological data in mountains of the Western United States. Hydrol. Sci. Bull. 26, 83-89.
Rango, A. (1983) A survey of progress in remote sensing of snow and ice. In: Hydrological applications of remote sensing and remote data transmission (Proc. Hamburg Symp.) IAHS Publ. 145, 347-359.
Rango, A., Martinec, J., Foster, J. & Marks, D. (1983) Resolution in operational remote sensing of snow cover. In: Hydrological applications of remote sensing and remote data transmission (Proc. Hamburg Symp.) IAHS Publ. 145, 371-382.
Rango, A. (1987) New technology for hydrological data acquisition and applications. In: Water for the future: Hydrology in Perspective (Proc. Rome Symp.) IAHS Publ. 164, 511-517.
Rees, W.G. & Squire, V.A. (1989) Technological limitations to satellite glaciology. Int. J. Remote Sensing 10, 7-22.
Reynaud L., Vallon M. & Letreguilly A. (1986) Mass balance measurements: problems and two new methods of determining variations. J. Glaciol. 32, 446-454.
Roberge, J. & Plamondon, P. (1987) Snowmelt runoff pathways in a boreal forest hillslope, the role of pipe throughflow. J. Hydrol. 95, 39-54.

Rossi, G., Tomasino, M., Della Ventura, A., Rampini, A., Barbero, S.R. & Rabagliati, R. (1986) Landsat registrations for a snowmelt model of the Piave river basin. In: E.M. Morris (ed) Modelling snowmelt induced processes (Proc. Budapest Symp.) IAHS Publ. 155, 215-229.

Rott, H. (1987) Remote sensing of snow. In: B.E. Goodison, R.G. Barry & J. Dozier (eds.), Large scale effects of seasonal snow cover (Proc. Vancouver Symp.) IAHS Publ. 166, 279-290.

Rott, H. (1988) The use of LANDSAT data for the study of alpine glaciers: Comments on the paper by Della Ventura et al (1987). Int. J. Remote Sensing 9, 1167-1169.

Rott, H. & Künzi K.F. (1983) Remote sensing of snow cover with passive and active microwave sensors. In: B.E. Goodison (ed.), Hydrological applications of remote sensing and remote data transmission (Proc. Hamburg Symp.) IAHS Publ. 145, 361-369.

Rott, H. & Mätzler, C. (1987) Possibilities and limits of synthetic aperture radar for snow and glacier surveying. Annals of Glaciology 9, 195-199.

Röthlisberger, H. & Lang, H. (1987) Glacial Hydrology. In: A.M. Gurnell & M.J. Clark (eds) Glacio-fluvial sediment transfer: an alpine perspective, 207-284, Wiley, Chichester.

Scharfen, G., Barry, R.G., Robinson, D.A., Kukla, G. & Seneze, M. (1987) Large scale patterns of snow melt on Arctic sea ice mapped from meteorological satellite imagery. Annals of Glaciology 9, 200-205.

Seaberg S.Z., Seaberg J.Z., Hooke R.L. & Wiberg D.W. (1988) Character of the englacial and subglacial drainage system in the lower part of Storglaciären, Sweden as revealed by dye tracer studies. J. Glaciol. 34, 217-227.

Seidel K., Ade F. & Lichtenegger J. (1983) Augmenting LANDSAT MSS data with topographic information for enhanced registration and classification. IEEE Trans. on Geoscience and Remote Sensing, GE-21(3), 252-258.

Sevruk, B. (1983) Correction of measured precipitation in the alps using the water equivalent of new snow. Nordic Hydrol. 14, 49-58.

Sihvola, A. & Tiuri, M. (1986) Snow fork for the field determination of the density and wetness profiles of a snowpack. IEEE Trans. on Geoscience and Remote Sensing, GE-24(5), 717-721.

Søgaard, H. (1983) Snow mapping in Greenland based on multi-temporal satellite data. In: Hydrological applications of remote sensing and remote data transmission (Proc. Hamburg Symp.) IAHS Publ. 145, 383-393.

Søgaard, H. & Thomsen, T. (1988) Application of satellite data to monitoring snow cover and runoff in Greenland. Nordic Hydrol. 19, 225-236.

Souchez, R.A. & Lemmens, M.M. (1987) Solutes. In: A.M. Gurnell and M.J. Clark (eds) Glacio-fluvial sediment transfer: an alpine perspective, 285-303, Wiley, Chichester.

Stichler W. (1987) Snowcover and snowmelt processes studied by means of environmental isotopes. In: G.H. Jones & W.J. Orville-Thomas (eds.), Seasonal snowcovers: Physics, Chemistry, Hydrology, 673-726, D. Reidel Publ. Co..

Strangeways I.C. (1984) A cold regions automatic weather station. J. Hydrol. 79, 323-332.

Theakstone, W.H. & Knudsen, N.T. (1989) Temporal changes of glacier hydrological systems indicated by isotopic and related observations at Austre Okstindan, Norway 1976-87. Annals of Glaciology 13, 252-256.

Thomsen H.H. & Braithwaite R.J. (1987) Use of remote sensing data in modelling runoff from the Greenland ice sheet. Annals of Glaciology 9, 215-217.

Thomsen, H.H., Thorning, L. & Olesen, O.B. (1989) Applied glacier research for planning hydro-electric power, Ilulissat?Jakobshavn, West Greenland. Annals of Glaciology 13, 257-261.

Thomsen, T. (1983) Hydrological study in Greenland using the Argos system. In: Hydrological applications of remote sensing and remote data transmission (Proc. Hamburg Symp.) IAHS Publ. 145, 125-133.

Thomsen, T. (1989) Basis of hydro-climatic time series in Greenland. In: Remote sensing and large-scale global processes (Proc. Baltimore Symp.) IAHS Publ. 186, 139-150.

Tranter, M.; Brimblecombe, P.; Davies, T.D.; Vincent, C.E.; Abrahams, P.W. & Blackwood, I. (1986) The composition of snowfall, snowpack and meltwater in the W Scottish Highlands - evidence for preferential elution. Atmospheric Environment 20, 517-525.

Tranter, M.; Abrahams, P.W.; Blackwood, I.; Davies, T.D.; Brimblecombe, P.; Thompson, I.P. & Vincent, C.E. (1987) Changes in streamwater chemistry during snowmelt. In: H.G. Jones and W.J. Orveille-Thomas (eds.) Seasonal snowcovers: Physics, Chemistry, Hydrology, 575-597, D. Reidel Publ. Co..

Vershinina L.K. (1983) The use of aerial gamma surveys of snowpacks for spring snowpack runoff forecasts. In: B.E. Goodison (ed.), Hydrological applications of remote sensing and remote data transmission (Proc. Hamburg Symp.) IAHS Publ. 145, 411-420.

Wake, C.P. (1989) Glaciochemical investigations as a tool for determining the spatial and seasonal variation of snow accumulation in the Central Karakoram, Northern Pakistan. Annals of Glaciology 13, 279-284.

Walford, M.E.R., Kennett, M.I. & Holmlund, P. (1986) Interpretation of radio-echoes from Storglaciären, northern Sweden. J. Glaciol. 32, 39-49.

Whiting, J. & Kiss, J. (1987) Integration of digital terrain models into ground based snow and runoff measurement. In: B.E. Goodison, R.G. Barry and J. Dozier (eds.), Large scale effects of seasonal snow cover (Proc. Vancouver Symp.) IAHS Publ. 166, 375-387.

Williams, R.S. (1987) Satellite remote sensing of Vatnajökull, Iceland. Annals of Glaciology 9, 127-135.

Woo, M-K (1983) Hydrology of a drainage basin in the Canadian High Arctic. Annals of the Assoc. Amer. Geographers 73, 577-596.

Young, G.J. (1982) Hydrological relationships in a glacierized mountain basin. In: J.W. Glen (ed), Hydrological aspects of alpine and high mountain areas (Proc. Exeter Symp.) IAHS Publ. 138, 51-59.

Young, G.J. (1981) The mass balance of Peyto Glacier, Alberta, Canada, 1965 to 1978. Arctic and Alpine Research 13, 307-318.

Young, G.J. & Schmok, J.P. (1989) Ice loss in the ablation area of a Himalayan glacier; studies on Miar glacier, Karakoram mountains, Pakistan. Annals of Glaciology 13, 289-293.

Zhang, Shunying & Zeng, Qunzhu (1986) Forecasting snowmelt runoff using TIROS/NOAA satellite data. In: E.M. Morris (ed) Modelling snowmelt induced processes (Proc. Budapest Symp.) IAHS Publ. 155, 257-268.

Zwally, H.J. (1987) Technology in the advancement of glaciology. J. Glaciol. Spec. Issue, 66-77.

Zwally, H.J., Stephenson, S.N., Binschadler, R.A. & Thomas, R.H. (1987) Antarctic ice shelf boundaries and elevations from satellite radar altimetry. Annals of Glaciology 9, 229-235.

Hydrology in Mountainous Regions. I - Hydrological Measurements; the Water Cycle
(Proceedings of two Lausanne Symposia, August 1990). IAHS Publ. no. 193, 1990.

A lysimetric snow pillow station at Kühtai/Tyrol

R. KIRNBAUER & G. BLÖSCHL
Institut für Hydraulik, Gewässerkunde u. Wasserwirtschaft,
Technische Universität Wien,
Karlsplatz 13, 1040 Vienna, Austria

ABSTRACT For properly forecasting snowmelt-runoff the understanding of processes associated with a melting snow cover may be of primary importance. For this purpose a snow monitoring station was installed at Kühtai/Tyrol at an elevation of 1930 m a.s.l. In order to study individual physical processes typical snow cover situations are examined. These situations include cold and wet snow under varying weather conditions. Based on a few examples the diversity of phenomena occuring at the snow surface and within the snow cover is demonstrated.

INTRODUCTION

Within a short-term flood-forecasting system a snowmelt model should be capable of representing extreme conditions. As Leavesley (1989) points out, a more physically based understanding of the processes involved will improve forecast capabilities. Subjective watching of phenomena together with measuring adequate data of sufficient accuracy and time resolution may form the foundations of process understanding.

Most field studies performed so far concentrated on investigating the energy input to snow, particularly under melting conditions (see e.g. Kuusisto, 1986). Differences in the relative importance of processes during contrasting weather conditions have been reported by numerous authors (e.g. Lang, 1986). Considering these differences some of the authors (e.g. Anderson, 1973) distinguished between advection and radiation melt situations in their models.

In this study meteorological data and snowpack observations from an alpine experimental plot are presented. Following an approach adopted earlier within the context of a model sensitivity analysis (Blöschl et al., 1988), it is believed that individual processes appear more explicitly in typical situations. Therefore, the investigations presented here focus on selected periods of characteristic weather and snow cover conditions.

THE KÜHTAI EXPERIMENTAL PLOT

The snow monitoring station was set up on the site of the Kühtai meteorological station near the Längental reservoir located about 30 km west of Innsbruck at an elevation of 1930 m a.s.l. (see Fig. 1). The research station site was graded prior to the installation of the instruments. Thus the site is flat with a slight slope to the west. It

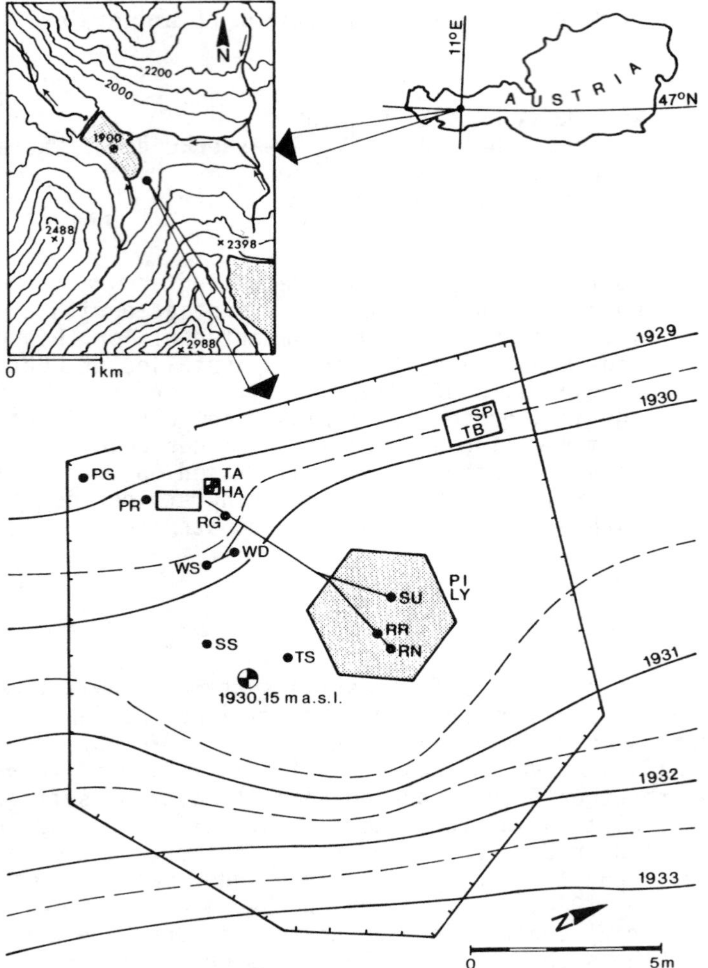

FIG. 1 The lysimetric snow pillow station at Kühtai/Tyrol (for abbreviations see Table 1).

is situated within the high relief environment of the Austrian Alps. In December, therefore, the station is barely met by the sun. The experimental plot is surrounded by typical timber-line vegetation with Alpine roses, meadows and scattered cembra-pines.

The climate is characterized by mean annual precipitation of about 1100 mm, 45% of which fall as snow. The snow cover period typically starts in November and lasts until May. Maximum snow depths of about 150 to 200 cm are reached in March.

The instrumentation comprises meteorological devices as shown in Fig. 1 and listed in Tab. 1. and a lysimetric snow pillow. The design of the lysimetric snow pillow is based on a device described by Engelen et al. (1984). The hexagonal rubber pillow of 10m² in area, filled with antifreeze, is connected to a stand pipe with a floating

TABLE 1 Instrumentation of the Kühtai experimental plot.

Variable	Instrument	Abbrev. in Fig. 1
global radiation	pyranometer (Schenk)	RG
reflected s.w. radiation	pyranometer (Eppley)	RR
net radiation	net radiometer (Swissteco)	RN
air temperature	resistance thermometer	TA
humidity	capacitive sensor	HA
wind speed	cup anemometer	WS
wind direction		WD
precipitation	raingauge	PG
precipitation	recording raingauge, heated, tipping bucket type	PR
snow temperatures at 8 levels above ground	resistance thermometer	TS
snow depth	snow stake	SS
snow depth	ultrasonic device	SU
water equivalent	snow pillow &	PI
	stand pipe	SP
melt rates	snow lysimeter &	LY
	tipping bucket	TB

gauge. The meltwater draining the pillow is collected in a gutter at the edge of the lysimeter and measured by a tipping bucket of 0.05 mm resolution. Lateral inflow to the lysimeter is prevented by a drainage surrounding the device and a 20 cm metal lip. Cross checking of lysimeter and pillow data indicated that lateral inflow was negligible.

During two weeks in April 1989 additional observations of snowpack characteristics were made. These included profiles of snow temperature and liquid water content at intervals of three hours. Snow temperatures were measured by a thermistor. Liquid water content was measured by a capacitive probe designed by Denoth & Foglar (1985). Each time at least two profiles were examined for assessing the horizontal variability of snow cover parameters. Under most conditions this variability was small as compared to temporal fluctuations.

SELECTED PERIODS OF TYPICAL WEATHER AND SNOW COVER CONDITIONS

Mid winter - low humidity conditions

As an example of cold snowpack conditions a period in December 1987 is presented in Fig. 2. It comprises bright and overcast days, horizon shading being most obvious on clear-sky days such as 22 and 24 December. Solar radiation clearly affected the diurnal variations of air temperature. At the beginning of the period humidity gradually decreased to a minimum of 1 mbar vapour pressure equivalent to 20% relative humidity. The snowpack first was at 0°C, subsequently cooled down and only returned to an isothermal state on 27 December. Snow

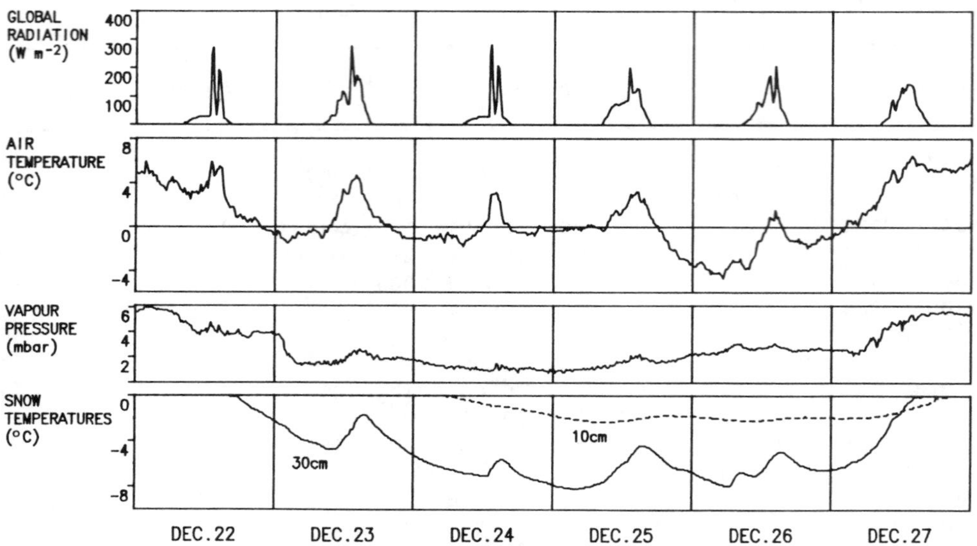

FIG. 2 Meteorological and snow temperature data measured during a mid winter period in 1987.

temperatures were monitored at 10 and 30 cm above ground, the upper sensor being approximately 10 cm below surface.

As may be observed from Fig. 2 the overall cycle of snow temperature at 30 cm is similar to that of air temperature. However, there are tendencies and day-to-day variations (e.g. 23-25 December) which do not correspond to air temperature. These variations indicate the influence of additional variables such as cloudiness and humidity. These influencing factors control surface energy exchange in terms of long wave radiation and latent heat flux. Particularly on fair weather days such as 22 and 24 December one may identify a substantial loss of energy due to long wave radiation. Prevailing evaporation conditions on days of very low humidity (e.g. 24 December) are assumed to significantly accelerate the cooling down of the snowpack. The considerable differences between air and snow temperatures observed during the major part of the period analyzed may be attributed to the combined effect of long wave emission and evaporation.

Melting period conditions

Fundamentally different phenomena may be observed during the melting period. Fig. 3 summarizes results of a 23 day period in April 1989. In this period the snowpack was ripe and experienced night time refreezing at the surface. Snowdepths varied at around 70 cm. Net radiation (in terms of potential melt rates) and lysimeter outflow are compared. For Fig. 3 the daily sum of net radiation is evaluated by integrating hourly values between 1900h and 1900h of the previous day considering the effect of night time radiative loss on the state of the snowpack in the morning. The daily sum of lysimeter outflow is

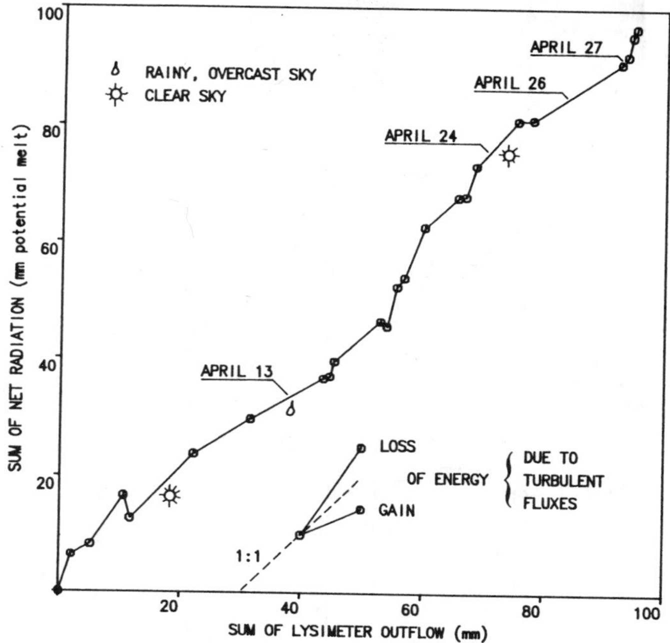

FIG. 3 Melting period 7-29 April 1989. Accumulative lysimeter outflow and radiation on a daily basis.

based on the interval between 1200h and 1200h of the following day due to the well known fact that the melt wave lags behind energy input.

Fig. 3 indicates that cumulative net radiation approximately equals cumulative meltwater outflow over the period considered. Hence one may infere that overall net radiation dominates melting processes. However, this is not true of individual days. Smaller and larger slopes of the graph in Fig. 3 indicate gain and loss of energy due to turbulent fluxes respectively. In the sequel four days within the period are discussed in more detail.

<u>Overcast and clear sky conditions</u> Two contrasting weather conditions are presented in Fig. 4. 13 April represents a typical rainy day whereas 24 April was a fair weather day. On 13 April changes in air temperature and net radiation were small. Humidity was near saturation and approximately 3 mm of mixed rain and snow were observed. The snowpack started draining in the afternoon yielding a maximum melt rate of 2 mm h^{-1}. On 24 April there were pronounced fluctuations in air temperature, low humidity and substantial radiation loss during the night. The melt intensity was about half of that observed on the overcast day.

In analyzing the differences in melt rates one may first look at Fig. 3. The graph shows that the daily net radiation values on 13 and 24 April were 7 and 8 mm whereas the daily melt rates were 12 and 7 mm respectively. On 13 April positive air temperatures along with high wind speeds indicate substantial melt due to sensible heat. On 24

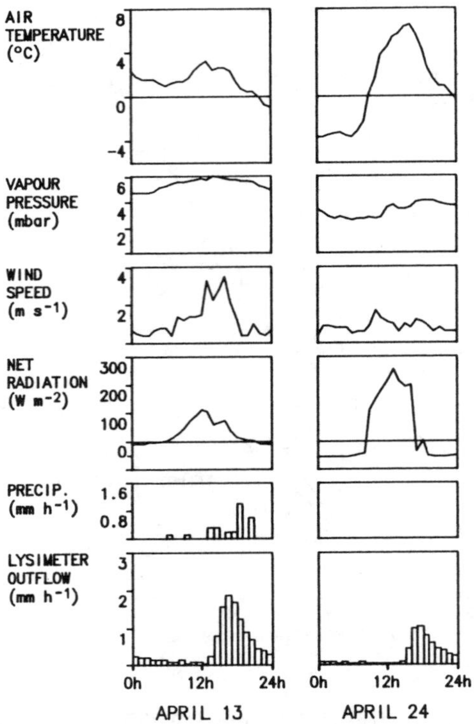

FIG. 4 Comparison of a clear sky and a rainy day in April 1989.

April, however, evaporative heat loss dominated over sensible heat input resulting in a net heat loss due to turbulent fluxes. Additionally, some of the differences may be attributed to (a) rain and (b) differences in the state of the snowpack induced by preceding processes.

Drop of air temperature Fig. 5 illustrates the processes interrupting spring melt. The most striking feature of the weather situation on 26 and 27 April was a sharp drop of temperature during the night (Fig. 5 a). Low values of cloudiness were observed on the first day considered. Subsequently clouds were advected in the early morning of the second day causing overcast conditions on 27 April. A meltwave was produced on the warm and clear day, the trailing limb of which extended to the following cold day.

In order to analyze the processes in more detail snow moisture profiles are presented. Fig. 5 b indicates that in the morning of 26 April the snow surface was frozen in spite of high air temperature and wind speed. This may be attributed to an energy loss due to longwave radiation. The interior of the snowpack was wet. Surface melt, produced between sunrise and 1100h, penetrated the snowpack down to a level of 40 cm above ground (shaded area in Fig. 5 b). The lysimeter hydrograph indicates that the meltwave reached the ground at 1300h. This statement is endorsed by the moisture profile taken at 1400h which shows high liquid water content due to transient water. During

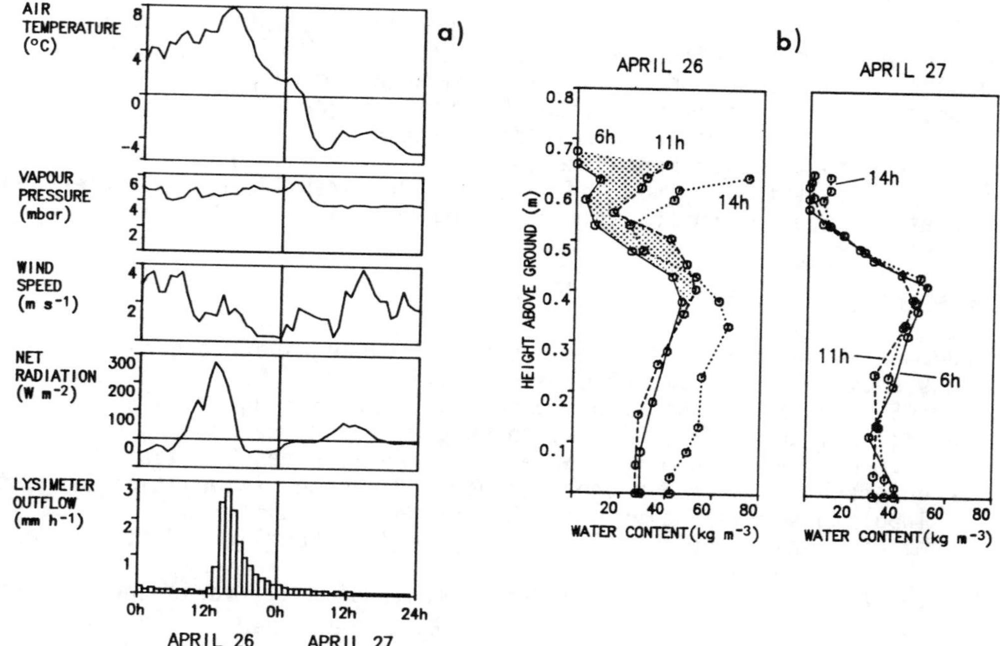

FIG. 5 Drop of temperature on 26 and 27 April 1989.
a) Meteorological data and lysimeter outflow.
b) Liquid water content profiles.

the night melting ceased, and in the morning of 27 April the moisture profile was nearly identical to that of the previous day. This admits the inference that on both mornings the snow was saturated.

CONCLUSIONS

The diversity of phenomena associated with snowmelt in a high alpine environment has been illustrated on the basis of measurements at the Kühtai experimental plot. In order to study individual physical processes typical meteorological and snow cover conditions are examined. During a period of low humidity in mid winter the snowpack cools down to temperatures considerably below air temperature due to longwave radiation and evaporation. During the ablation period snowmelt is dominated by net radiation. Data evidence indicates that turbulent fluxes may significantly increase and decrease melt on rainy and clear sky days respectively. A sharp drop of temperature in the late melt season results in freezing the snow surface but does not affect the moisture profile within the snowpack. If the concept of a snowmelt model is based on physical principles adequate simulation of such phenomena can be expected.

ACKNOWLEDGEMENTS This research was supported by grants from the Austrian Fonds zur Förderung der wissenschaftlichen Forschung under project No. P7002PHY and from the Tyrolean Hydro-electric Power Company (TIWAG). Additionally to the monetary grants the TIWAG provided invaluable support in completing their Kühtai meteorological station with the equipment necessary for snow monitoring. Staff of the Federal Institute for Snow and Avalanche Research (EISLF), Switzerland assisted in designing the snow temperature monitoring device.

REFERENCES

Anderson, E. A. (1973) National Weather Service river forecast system - snow accumulation and ablation model. NOAA Tech. Memo. NWS HYDRO-17, US Dept. of Commerce, Silver Spring, Maryland.

Blöschl, G., Gutknecht, D. & Kirnbauer, R. (1988) Berechnung des Wärmeeintrages in eine Schneedecke - Analyse des Einflusses unterschiedlicher meteorologischer Bedingungen (Simulation of heat input to snow - analysis of the influence of different meteorologic conditions). Deutsche Gewässerkundliche Mitteilungen 32 (1/2), 34-39.

Denoth, A. & Foglar, A. (1985) Measurements of daily variations in the subsurface wetness gradient. Annals of Glaciology 6, 254-255.

Engelen, G. B., van de Griend, A. A. & Valentini, P. (1984) A lysimetric snow-pillow station for continuous monitoring of the snow cover cycle and its processes at the "Seiser Alm", South Tyrol, N. Italy. In: Schneehydrologische Forschung in Mitteleuropa, 129-143. Mitteilungen des Deutschen Verbandes für Wasserwirtschaft und Kulturbau e.V. no.7.

Kuusisto, E. (1986) The energy balance of a melting snow cover in different environments. In: Modelling Snowmelt-Induced Processes (Proc. Budapest Symposium, July 1986), 37-45. IAHS Publ. no. 155.

Lang, H. (1986) Forecasting meltwater runoff from snow-covered areas and from glacier basins. Chapter 5 in: River Flow Modelling and Forecasting (eds. Kraijenhoff, D. A. & Moll, J. R.). D. Reidel Publishing Company, Dordrecht.

Leavesley, G. H. (1989) Problems of snowmelt runoff modelling for a variety of physiographic and climatic conditions. Hydrological Sciences - Journal - des Sciences Hydrologiques 34 (6), 617-634.

Hydrology in Mountainous Regions. I - Hydrological Measurements; the Water Cycle
(Proceedings of two Lausanne Symposia, August 1990). IAHS Publ. no. 193, 1990.

Methods for the computations of onset date and daily hydrograph of the outburst from the Mertzbacher Lake, Tien-shan

V.G.KONOVALOV
Central Asian Regional Research Hydrometeorological Institute, ObservatorsKaya 72, TashKent 700052, USSR

ABSTRACT A method for prediction of the lake outburst date based on application of air temperature, total cloudiness and precipitation data at the Koilju meteorological station is proposed for a simplified and rather regularly repeated model of filling Mertzbacher lake and water break from it.The information about its volume and hydrograph of outburst wave are among the major characteristics of Mertzbacher lake regime. The new method for solving this problem is based on separation of the volume measured at a gauging station into two parts formed by: (a) water break from Mertzbacher lake; (b) usual influx of water due to snow and ice melting in a basin. The algorithm of an outburst wave computation is described.It requires only standard hydrometeorological data.

INTRODUCTION

Mertzbacher lake having the volume of about 0.2 km^3 formed annually in the region of confluence of the northern and southern branches of the Inylchec glacier and outbursts, as a rule, at the end of ablation season. While Mertzbacher lake having been known since 1903, the history of its regular but short-term studies accounts only about 50 years. Assessment of quality of initial information of hydrometeorological regime in the Inylchec river basin and on characteristics of Mertzbacher lake necessary for solving the problems of the present study showed that the following data are the most appropriate in view of their completeness and regularity:
- the results of observations made at the Koilju meteorological station for the period 1951-1988;
- runoff measurements at the Inylchek river (gauging station "Ustje") considering water drop from Mertzbacher lake;
- information on dates of outburst onset and its duration;
- the results of glaciological measurements and computations.

The materials mentioned above were used for development of methods: (a) prediction of the dates of water drop onset from Mertzbaher lake, (b) estimation of the dropped water volume, (c) computation of hydrograph of an outburst wave through gauging station "Ustje" at the Inylchek river. It should be noted that previously Glazyrin G.E. and Sokolov L.N. (Glazyrin and Sokolov,1976) as well as Vinogradov Yu.B.(Vinogradov,1977) have developed mathematical models to compute hydrograph of an outburst wave of the glacier dammed lake. Analysis of the Glazyrin-Sokolov model structure has revealed that initial data necessary for its application is next to impossible to get (namely, cross section area of the bywash inside a glacier before an outburst,lake area as the function of its depth, empirical coefficients), and the results of computations strongly depend on some parameters that are unknown apriori.

PREDICTION OF THE DATE OF AN OUTBURST ONSET

To develop a model for prediction of the onset time of water break from Mertzbacher lake the cases with more or less reliable dates of single outburst have been selected beginning from 1951.

At the first stage of investigation the simple scheme of Mertzbacher lake regime to be as follows:

- fillings of the lake up to critical level begins since the onset of snow and ice melting in the area of the Northern Inylchek glacier bassin limited by an icy dam which blocks Mertzbacher lake;
- break of water is the direct result of exceeding the threshold of an icy dam seeping ability in normal conditions.

It is evident that within the described scheme of the lake regime the meteorological parameters affecting the total layer of melting in the basin of the Northern Inylchek glacier should be the major factors determining the time of the lake readiness to outburst. A formula for computation of the average melting intensity during a pentade as a function of air temperature at the Koilju meteorological station is used to determine the dates of beginning of snow and ice melting period in the Northern Inylchek glacier's basin. The expression:

$$\hat{M}_5 = 0.75\,\bar{T}_5 + 1.2 \qquad (1)$$

based on the measurements at the Inylchek glacier within the altitudial range of 3.2-3.4 km. Here M - is the average layer of melting during a pentade,T - is the mean air temperature for the same pentade. Having taken the left side this formulae to be zero and using the gradient of temperature as 9.0 deg/km we find that the first calendar pentade, when mean air temperature exceeds 2.9 °C at the Koilju meteorological station is considered as the beginning of the snow and ice melting period in Mertzbacher lake basin.

Correlation analysis has revealed quite close relation (r=0.94) between outburst dates (D) and sums of mean air temperature for a pentade at the Koilju meteorological station. But this form of relation D=f(T) can't be used for prediction of the time of an outburst onset. With this connection, all the three potential predictiors used to forecast the date of an outburst have been transformed in the following way. The earliest date of July 25 was selected from the sixteen years set of D. Then 3 days were subtracted and the 22 of July was taken as the date of release a forecast of an outburst. Further, values of mean air temperature T , indices of total cloudiness C and precipitation Q were summed since the 21 of July up to the first pentade of the year with mean air temperature > 2.9 °C at the Koilju meteorological station. The resulted sum for every year were subtracted from the mean long term values of T, C andQ but now they are related to the whole period of time from the first pentade in the year when T>2.9 °C up to the date of an outburst. The described procedure allows to use sums of T , C and Q accumulated by July 21 in a forecast in a case of existing the relation between the sums, their residuals and the date of an outburst.

Multivariate linear regression analysis showed that such a relation actually exists and, finally an equation has been developed to predict D:

$$\hat{D} = 308 - 0.67\Delta T - 0.30\Delta C - 0.11\Delta Q \qquad (2)$$

where $\hat{D}$ - is the numbers of days in a calendar year from January,1; ΔT , ΔC and ΔQ were described above in details. The combined correlation coefficient (r) of the expression (2) is 0.86.

COMPUTATION OF THE VOLUME AND HYDROGRAPH OF AN OUTBURST WAVE

It is quite evident that the volume of daily runoff of Inylchek river in the period of Mertzbacher lake outburst is formed simultaneously owing to the quite different sources:
- regular influx of snow and ice melting water in the watershed basin situated above the outlet;
- catastrophic water break from Mertzbacher lake.

Daily layer of melting of seasonal and long-term reserves of snow and ice in June-September is the only factor determing the Inylchek river runoff before an outburst of the lake and after it.

The problem of separating the Inylchek river runoff in the period of outburst that was formulated above, was solved by means of selecting a multivariant function most effectively describing running average discharge before the onset of water break from the lake. The following data obtained for a number of years have been considered:
- running discharge averages for a pentade with one step backward shift in time, namely, one pentade running average;
- running averages of air temperature, cloud cover indices and atmospheric pressure in current pentade from observations made at the Koilju meteorological station;
- running averages of the same meteorological elements for a pentade but with one step forward shift in time relative to the current mean water discharge in a pentade.

An equation has been derived to compute running averages of discharges ges for pentades in July-August at the Inylchek river which which are not associated with an outburst of Mertzbacher lake.

$$\hat{R}_t = 0.77\,\bar{R}_{t-1} + 3.24\,\bar{T}_t - 14.53 \quad m^3/sec \qquad (3)$$

where $\hat{R}_t$ -is the mean discharge in current pentade; $\bar{R}_{t-1}$ - is the same but shifted one step backward in time; T_t - is the mean air temperature at the Koilju meteorological station in the current pentade. Coefficient r of (3) is 0.95, mean root squre error of computation R is 8.5 m^3/sec.

The equation (3) was used in 1982, 1984-1987 to compute that component of the Inylchek river runoff hydrograph during the lake outburst which had formed due to daily melting of snow and ice in a basin above the gauging station "Ustije". The results of computations are shown in fig.1 by a thick line.

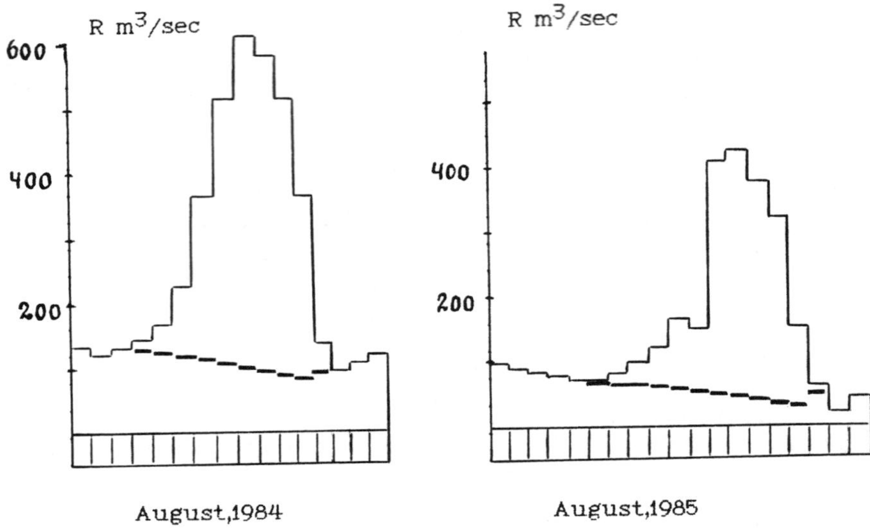

FIG. 1 The samples of average pentade running values of Inylchek river discharges in 1984-1985 (gauging station "Ustije"). Solid thick line on graphs computed pentade averages of running discharges which are not connected with volume of outburst from Mertzbacher lake.

It is seen that the computed hydrograph agrees quite well with run-off measurements after the lake outburst when the usial daily melting of snow and ice becomes again the only source of the Inylchek river nourishment.

Distribution of total volume broken from the lake during the period of outburst is presented in figure 2.

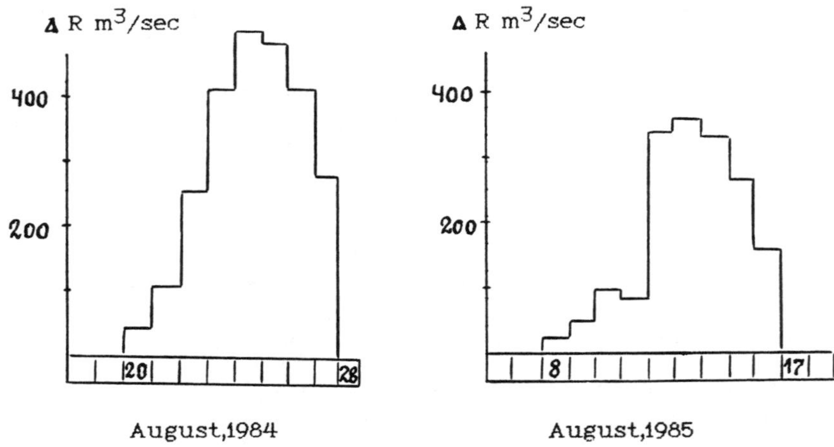

FIG. 2 Average daily discharges of Inylchek river (gauging station "Ustije") related to water break from Mertzbacher lake in the period of its outburst. The abscissa axis shows calendar dates.

Table 1 presents the combined results of computation of water volume during the outbursts. Dimensionless ordinates of empiric differential and integral distribution curves are given here for two cases of an outburst and in general for all the considered years.

It is evident that differential and integral distribution curves in Table 1 represent the typical hydrographs of an outburst wave of Mertzbacher lake. Those hydrographs permit solution of the following important scientific and applied problems:

- to develop modified mathematical model of water break from the glacier dammed lake and to assess its parameters;
- to investigate the process of transformation of an outburst wave on its path from a dam of Mertzbacher lake to the gauging station "Ustje";
- to compute hydrograph of an outburst wave for the gauging station "Ustje" if a volume of water broken from Mertzbacher lake has been estimated by any method at the onset of water break. In any case, this volume could be estimated apriori as 150-180 mln cub.m. The error of this approximation is not more than 10-15 % . It is expedient to present a scheme for solution of the last problem in a form of successive computational operations;

(a) Beginning from the second part of June, average values of discharge for running pentades are computed from daily measurements of discharge at the Inylchek river (gauging station "Ustije"), and a runoff hydrograph is constructed analogous to the graphs in fig.1;
(b) Beginning from the onset of Mertzbacher lake outburst which is estimated by deviations from regularities of daily course level in the river or by any other technique, we calculate continiously during eight days a part of the Inylchek river runoff which is not related to the outburst of the lake using formulae (3) and (9);
(c) A formula:

$$v_t = V_{Lk} [F(t) - F(t-1)] \qquad (4)$$

is used to determine the every day runoff volume passed through the gauging station during the 8-day period after Mertzbaher lake outburst. Here v -is the runoff volume in t-th day, V -is the lake volume at the beginning of its outburst which was computed or prescribed tentatively, F(t) and F(t-1) - are the averaged ordinates of integral distribution function taken from Table 1. So, the quality of the hydrograph of an outburst wave from Mertzbacher lake computed at the gauging station "Ustije" of the Inylchek river depends on reliability of the method for estimation of the lake volume.
(d) Having summed runoff volumes, obtained from computations given in (b)-(c), we will get a total runoff volume of Inylchek river for every day during the period of an outburst.

Thus, the presented in (a)-(c) algorithm of computations allows to get a hydrograph of total runoff of the Inylchek river and, separately, an outburst wave of the Mertzbacher lake without hydromertic measurements during the period of an outburst.

RUNNING AVERAGES IN THE CONSIDERED COMPUTATIONS

Application in the discussed method of running averages of variables during a pentade instead of daily values is intended to smooth random runoff fluctuations due to possible error of hydrometric measurements

TABLE 1 Characteristics of the outburst wave hydrograph of Mertzbaher lake

Month		Runoff	Volume	Increment	Ordinates of distribution curves		The same ordinates averaged for 5 outbursts	
Days	Dates	m^3/sec	$mln.m^3$		differential (d)	integral (I)	(d)	(I)
August 1984								
1	20	40	3	3	0.014	0.014	0.041	0.041
2	21	105	9	12	0.043	0.057	0.067	0.107
3	22	245	21	33	0.100	0.158	0.113	0.221
4	23	395	34	67	0.163	0.321	0.190	0.411
5	24	500	43	110	0.206	0.526	0.191	0.601
6	25	475	41	151	0.196	0.722	0.171	0.773
7	26	410	35	186	0.167	0.890	0.144	0.917
8	27	270	23	209	0.110	1.000	0.082	1.000
August 1985								
1	9	55	5	5	0.033	0.033		
2	10	105	9	14	0.060	0.093		
3	11	90	8	22	0.053	0.146		
4	12	345	30	52	0.200	0.347		
5	13	360	31	83	0.207	0.553		
6	14	330	28	111	0.187	0.740		
7	15	275	24	135	0.160	0.900		
8	16	170	15	150	0.100	1.000		

of extreme discharges of an outburst wave in unstable channels.

Besides that if average water discharges for two successive moving pentades and five values of mean daily discharge at the beginning of a calendar period, over which a running averaging is done are available, it is easy to transfer from presentation of information in the form of pentade averages to daily values. Let's make up a general expression for this procedure.

It is evident that running average values of the first $x_{n,1}$ and second $x_{n,2}$ pentades may be written as follows:

$$\bar{x}_{n,2} = \frac{1}{n}\left(x_1 + \sum_{i=2}^{i=5} x_i\right) \tag{5}$$

$$\bar{x}_{n,2} = \frac{1}{n}\left(x_6 + \sum_{i=2}^{i=5} x_i\right) \tag{6}$$

where n=5 is the number of averaged terms of the initial set, x and x_6 are the first and sixth terms of the initial set. Having subtracted (6) from (5) and write down the result related to the unknown value of x_6, we obtain

$$x_6 = x_1 + n\,(\bar{x}_{n,2} - \bar{x}_{n,1}) \tag{7}$$

and similarily

$$x_7 = x_2 + n(\bar{x}_{n,3} - \bar{x}_{n,2}) \quad (8)$$

then, finally, in general form:

$$x_{i+k} = x_k + n(\bar{x}_{n,k+1} - \bar{x}_{n,k}) \quad (9)$$

$$i = n \div N, \quad k = 1 \div N - n$$

where N - is the total number of terms in the initial set, n=5 is the number of terms in a sample for running averaging.

REFERENCES

Glazyrin, G.E., Sokolov, L.N. (1976) Possibility of forecasting the flood characteristics caused by outburst of glacial lakes. In: Proseedings of Glaciological Researches, Moskow, no. 26, 78-54.

Vinogradov, Yu.B. (1977) Glacial outburst floods and mudflow. Leningrad, Hydrometeorological Publishing Hause.

Hydrology in Mountainous Regions. I - Hydrological Measurements; the Water Cycle (Proceedings of two Lausanne Symposia, August 1990). IAHS Publ. no. 193, 1990.

Role of glacier and snow cover melting in runoff variations from the small basins in Pamir and the Alps

F. I. PERTZIGER
Central Asian Regional Research Hydrometeorological Institute, Observatorskaya 72, Tashkent, 700052, USSR

ABSTRACT Runoff fluctuations from the glaciers and their forefield at two small basins in Pamiro-Alai and Alps (Abramov and Vernagt glacier basins, respectively) are analysed. The method based on parallel hydrometric measurements from neighbouring basins with different extent of glaciation has been applied to subdivide the hydrograph into areas of runoff formation.

Intraannual variations of runoff from the glaciers and forefield in both basins are revealed and compared. It is shown that the first wave of flood forms due to forefield snowmelting; peak of glacier runoff is observed one - two months later.

Relation between annual volume of runoff from the Vernagt glacier basin's forefield and precipitation have been found; as for the Pamir basin such relation has not been discovered: runoff formed by forefield snowmelting shows comparatively small variations. Interannual variability of runoff from Abramov glacier basin as a whole is determined by fluctuations of runoff from the glaciers.

INTRODUCTION

Mountain glacier basin consists of two surfaces generally different in runoff formation - glacier and nonglacier. Generally, the role of each of them is as follows.

There are great runoff losses in the glaciers due to refreezing and firn depth saturation at the onset of ablation period. At the end of the period glaciers output the earlier accumulated water. The first flood wave is related with forefield snowmelting.

As to the annual interval it is considered that runoff from glacier forefield is determined by precipitation, but from glaciers themselves - by energy influx during summer (plus liquid precipitation). The aim of this paper is to assess these schemes in different climatic conditions. As the first step it is necessary to divide runoff from the basin into components, because we couldn't measure it.

METHOD AND INITIAL DATA

A simple, and as we think objective method has been used for subdivision of the measured runoff due to areas of its formation. It is based on comparison of the results of parallel runoff measurements from two or more neighbouring basins greately different by extent of glaciation.

The idea of the method borrowed from Golubev (1976) is as follows: if the glaciers altitudes in adjacent basins are nearly equal, and the ones of forefield also slightly differ, it can be supposed that modules of runoff from the glacier forefield (M_f) are equal, like the ones from the glaciers (M_g) themselves. Then one can define M_g and M_f by solving the set of N linear equations with two unknowns:

$$\begin{cases} S_{g,1} M_g + S_{f,1} M_f = Q_1 \\ S_{g,2} M_g + S_{f,2} M_f = Q_2 \\ \dots\dots\dots\dots\dots\dots \\ S_{g,N} M_g + S_{f,N} M_f = Q_N \end{cases} \qquad (1)$$

where: N is the total number of the basins; S_g and S_f - area of glaciers and their forefields, respectively; Q - water discharge. Digit is the watershead number. Value of Q should be taken for long enough period to exclude an effect of probably different lag times. Moreover, set (1) as well as its every element is true only for flood period on glacier rivers when it is possible to neglect the underground feeding of a river. For that period we shall apply it taking an effort to divide average within the year hydrographs. Moreover, we shall assess applicability of the method to annual intervals.

The results of runoff measurements during 1968 - 1975 (eight years in a whole) in the Abramov glacier basin (at Koksu river), and in two sub-basins situated within the boundaries of the first one at right side of the valley have been used in the study. Runoff data as well as S_g and S_f for main basin have been taken from (Suslov et al, 1978). Sub-basin areas have been defined from the map, scale 1 : 25 000. The difference between mean altitude of glaciers as well as their forefields are no more than 150 m. At Alps, runoff data from Oerter and Zunke (1986) for Vernagt glacier basin that is sub-basin in Oetztaler river watershead were used together with records from three gauges placed in the lower parts of the river. The period of parallel observations is 1974 - 1980 (seven years). Following the authors (Oerter & Zunke, 1986) let's name the topmost gauge as VB, but the lower ones as RA, VA and OA. The difference between mean watershead altitudes for the gauges VB and OA equals to 0.7 km, but annual runoff depth from the highest to the lowest decreases slightly - from 1 250 to 1 100 - 1 150 mm, as it is seen from small - scale figures in (Oerter & Zunke, 1986). It is obviously suggests similarity of runoff modules from different parts of the basins.

Let's first consider the results obtained by the described method and discuss below their reliability.

INTRAANNUAL HYDROGRAPH

Here we shall speak about a mean within-the-year hydrograph.

We haven't data on runoff distribution through the months for the RA gauge, so we have used the results of measurements at three other gauges (during May - October, six months in a whole). Thus, the set (1) at N = 3 was solved six times for Alps.As to the Pamir,it was solved four times by measurements during June - September, respectively. The obtained modules are given in fig. 1.

It is clearly seen, that in Alps variations of runoff modules from both surfaces have more smooth character. Already in June specific yield from the Vernagt glacier is greater than from the forefield, however such sharp decrease of M_f as in the basin of Abramov glacier does not take place. Evidently, great amount of liquid precipitation (summer maximum) and more smooth character of within-the-year variation of air temperature in the Alps adjacent to the ocean decrease the range of modules and difference between them. Extreme summer minimum of precipitation is characteristic for the Abramov glacier region. Decrease of snow covered area on glacier forefields in July is nearly a jump (extreme irregularity of snow cover distribution promotes such a jump). Moisture income to the slopes during the rare summer snowfalls is most probably lossed for evaporation.

Despite of this differences the obtained results in a whole support common notions about the role of every considered zones in flood hydrograph formation. Really, both in Pamir and Alps the first relatively low flood wave is the result of snowmelting on nonglaciated part of watershead. Glaciers give back the earlier accumulated water at the end of melting period. Regulative role of glaciers is especially evident when analysing the results related to Pamir, - in September when air temperature equals in average to 1.7°C, runoff from the glaciers is greater (!) than in July at air temperature of 6.1°C.

Evidently, asynchronous change of runoff from different surfaces in some degree levels the intraannual runoff variations from the whole basin. Another important conclusion: during the second half of flood even in Pamir basin having 40% of the area free from ice, one can consider quite accurately the measured runoff as the glacier one.

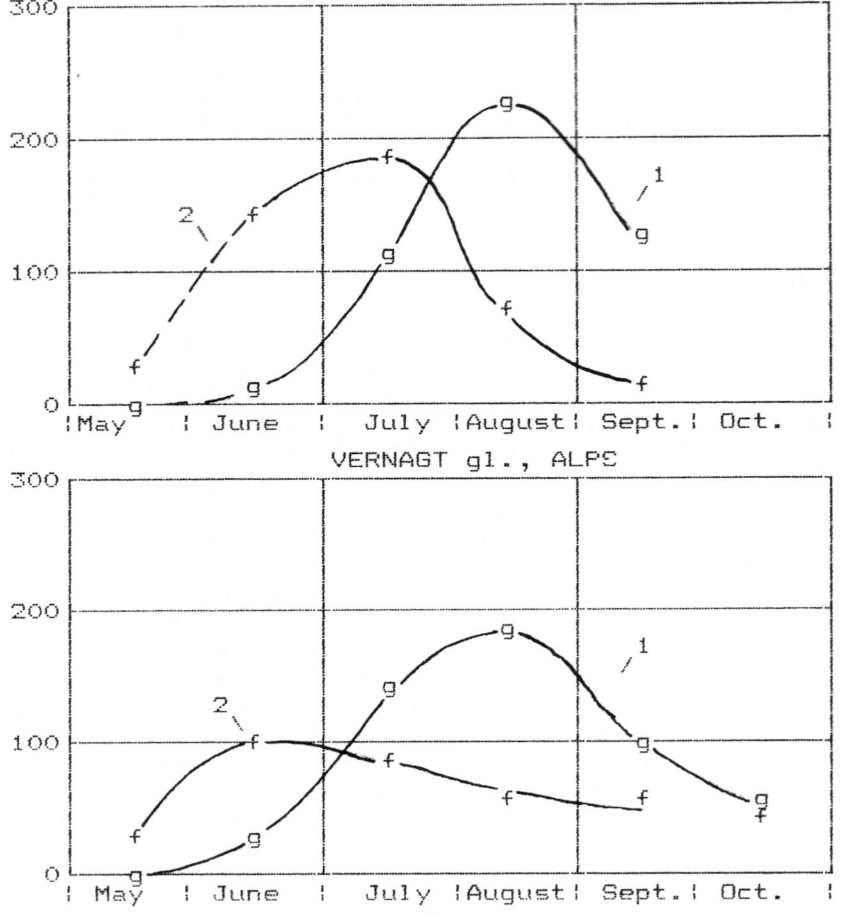

FIG. 1. **Within the year changes of runoff modules from the glaciers (1) and their forefields (2).**

Thus, operating with a small set of parameters in mathematical model of daily runoff formation it is possible to obtain high similarity between measured and computated values (Pertziger, 1990).

INTERANNUAL HYDROGRAPH

Fig. 2 compares annual runoff values from the concidered surfaces with variables, that are believed to determine them. Let's specify the way these graphics were plotted.

Having analysed the results of set (1) application at $N = 4$ to estimate the annual M_g and M_f, we discovered that the runoff norm for each of four Alpine watersheads was defined quite correctly, but annual values had errors.

That is why to evaluate annual modules for Vernagt glacier basin it was decided to use data from two topmost gauges VB and RA only. To be more simple, the two following equations were solved together with changing Q seven times (seven years):

$$S_{g,VB} M_g + S_{f,VB} M_f = Q_{VB}$$

$$S_{g,RA} M_g + S_{f,RA} M_f = Q_{RA}$$

where: Q is mean annual water discharge, lower indices indicate belonging to one or another watershead. We havn't information about the contribution of moisture to different surfaces (sign them W_g and W_f) in the basin of the Alpine glacier. That is why data of Reinwarth (1986) were used to compute those indices:

$$W_g^* = P - B_g \quad \text{and} \quad W_f^* = P$$

where: P is the annual precipitation depth, averaged over a basin; B_g is the annual specific balance of glacier. Relations of $M_g(W_g^*)$ and $M_f(W_f^*)$ are given at fig. 2 for Alpine basin. To comfort the comparison arguments and functions are conversed into dephs.

As to Abramov glacier we managed to define the depths of runoff only for June - September, because through the frost season runoff measurements at two sub-basins were not carried out. However, Koksu river runoff during June - September equals in average 86 % to annual one. It seems possible to consider the obtained values as slightly decreased annual ones. Glacier melting and precipitation data were taken from (Suslov et al., 1978).

One can see from fig. 2 that a close relation between annual input and runoff from the glacier surface is traced in both basins. It is of interest, that for Vernagt glacier the relation is more close, although too rough index was used to estimate the sum of ablation and liquid precipitation.

It is another thing with runoff from the glacier forefield. The results for Alpine basin are within the common notions (close relation between runoff and precipitation was found), but it is not the case for the Pamir one. It is not of great importance that in some years runoff is greater than input; it might be explained by unfavorable selection of relation between precipitation and altitude. The major point is that runoff reflects variations of precipitations in general; correlation being practically absent. Runoff varies less or more around some constant value.

Such results, as we believe, may be explained by differences of precipitation distribution within the year. In the Abramov glacier basin as already was mentioned, the prevailing amount of precipitation falls in cold season.

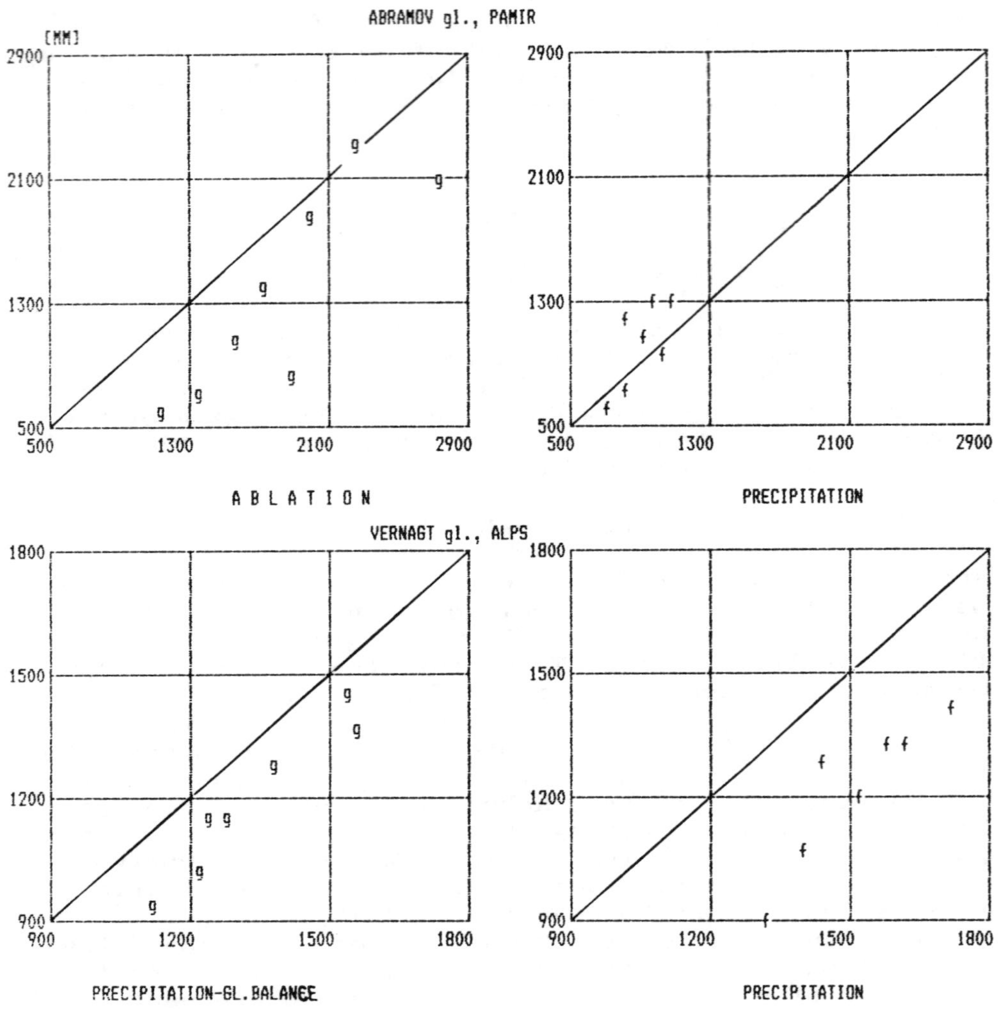

FIG. 2 Comparison annual runoff from the glaciers (g) and their forefields (f) and water income at these surfaces.

Snow is intensively redistributed by strong wind; it is blown off the slopes and concentrated on the glaciers. Perhaps, there is some "snow holding capacity" of the slopes, after which snow storage varies too insignificantly not depending on the amount of continuously falling precipitation. Direct measurements of snow accumulation intensity made on a small site confirm this assumption (Pertziger, 1986). In the Alps a significant part of summer maximum of precipitation, evidently, falls as rain and immidiately supplies runoff. Summer snow melts at the same surface, that it has fallen down.

Thus in conditions of summer precipitation minimum the interannual runoff variations from the entire mountain glacier basin are defined, mainly, by variation of glacier melting. It simplifies reconstruction of long-term runoff variations from the basin and makes it possible to estimate numerical parameters of annual values spectrum for hydrotechnic engineering. It is reached through reconstruction of air temperature series, that is not difficult (Gerasimova & Pertziger, 1986). At great contribution of summer precipitation the role of unglaciated part of the basin is evident even at such high glaciation extent of watershead as for the Vernagt glacier basin (83 %). In such conditions it is impossible to estimate the runoff trends without precipitation series reconstruction,the procedure being too problematic.

Note one more important moment. It is too difficult to evaluate snow accumulation on unglaciated part of the basin in the region where greater part of precipitation falls during cold season. Direct measurements are often impossible because of avalanche danger. Errors are great because commonly applied computational schemes are based on the data of precipitation amount alone.

RELIABILITY OF RESULTS

The method applied for runoff subdivision into areas of it's formation seems to be rather symplified, so doubts may arise on reliability of results. Thereby let's list a number of indirect evidences, confirming realibility of the results.

According to Escher-Vetter et al (1986) rate of the runoff volume increase from the Vernagt glacier forefield is the greatest in June - July, then it decreases but slowly.By the author's visual observations during the last 16 years in Abramov glacier basin at the beginning of August snow cover on slopes melts at all altitudes. These facts are in agreement with the changes of water yield from the slopes found within the year.

The following facts support the results obtained by annual estimations:

a) existence of the relations given in fig. 2;

b) analysis of fig. 2 allows to evaluate runoff losses from different surfaces of Alpine basin. They are numerically equal to vertical distance from the line of connection till the graphic bisector. One can see lower losses from glacial surface. It is believed that for conditions of Alps there is a reasonable correlation; runoff losses by water refreezing within the "warm" glacier are less than evaporation from the its forefield;

c) according to 20 - year measurement data there is nearly functional relation between annual runoff from the entire Pamir basin and summer air temperature. Correlation ratio is equal to 0.98, use of precipitation as the second argument does not make the relation closer. It confirms the conclusion about much greater glacier runoff variability compared with the forefield one in such climatic conditions.

CONCLUSIONS

Parallel hydrometric measurements in neighbouring basins with variable extent of glaciation make it possible to obtain new interesting information about the laws of runoff formation. It should be considered in programmes of field investigations.

A mountain glacier basin, as a system of runoff formation has features of selfregulation. It is expressed in redistribution of runoff by glaciers and incoincidence between glacier runoff peak and the forefield one.

Unlike the Alps in Pamir climatic conditions, interannual variations of runoff from the basin with signinificant glaciation are connected first of all with variations of glacier melting, precipitation role being less evident.

REFERENCES

Escher-Vetter, H., Oerter, H., Zunke, D. & Reinwarth, O. (1986) Glacier discharge modelling - A comparison between measured and calculated values of the runoff from the Vernagtferner (Oetztal Alps, Austria) Data of Glaciol. Studies, Publ. 58 , 65-69, Moscow, USSR.

Gerasimova, Z., A. & Pertziger, F., I. (1986) Raschiot statisticheskih haracteristic stoka s gornolednikovogo basseina (Calculations of statistical parameters of runoff from the mountain glacier basin) Data of Glaciol. Studies Publ. 54 , 87-92, Moscow, USSR.

Golubev, G., N., (1976) Gidrologiya lednikov (Glacier hydrology) Hydrometeoizdat, Leningrad, USSR.

Oerter, H. & Zunke, D. (1986) Study of the runoff from drainage basins with variable extent of glaciation. Data of Glaciol. Studies Publ. 58 , 59-65, Moscow.

Pertziger, F., I., (1986) Mnogoletniy rejim naveyannogo snejnika. (Regim of several years of rewind neve) SARNIGMI Proc. Issue 117(198) , 117-123, Leningrad.

Pertziger, F., I. (1990) Schema raschiota stoka s lednikov s uchiotom vremeni dobeganiya (Scheme of glacier runoff computation with accounting lag time) SARNIGMI Proc. Issue 140(221) , 36-42, Leningrad, USSR.

Reinwarth, O. (1986) Combined ice and water balance investigations at an Alpine glacier (Vernagtferner, Oetztal Alps) Data of Glaciol. Studies Publ.57 , 116-120 Moscow, USSR.

Suslov, V., F., Acbarov, A., A., Nozdrjukhin, V., C. & al (1978) Lednik Abramova (Alaisky chrebet) (Abramov glacier) Hydrometeoizdat, Leningrad, USSR.

Hydrology in Mountainous Regions. I - Hydrological Measurements; the Water Cycle (Proceedings of two Lausanne Symposia, August 1990). IAHS Publ. no. 193, 1990.

Point modelling of snow cover water equivalent based on observed variables of the standard meteorological networks

M. B. ROHRER & H. LANG
Department of Geography, Hydrology Section, Swiss Federal Institute of Technology (ETH), CH-8057 Zürich, Switzerland

ABSTRACT For several stations of the automatic network (ANETZ) of the Swiss Meteorological Institute (SMI) the temporal variation of the water equivalent of the snow cover was modelled. The following operationally measured variables with a resolution of one hour were used: air temperature, precipitation, wind-speed, water-vapour-pressure, global radiation and cloud cover (term readings). Snow water equivalents measured twice per month were used as verification. It is shown that modelled snow water equivalents during accumulation as well as during melting periods are a good estimate for measured ones. The snow water equivalent as a predictor gives optimum coefficients of determination for seasonal runoff of basins situated in high Alpine zones if they are assessed in the late accumulation phase. It is shown that daily available modelled snow water equivalents are very useful as input in seasonal runoff-forecast procedures.

INTRODUCTION

The knowledge of the snow water equivalent (SWE) of the seasonal snow cover in the Swiss Alps is of primary importance not only for catchment scale or national water management studies, but also e. g. for the management of the IJsselmeer (the Netherlands), which is an important fresh water reservoir used for the supply of drinking water. The summer flow conditions of the whole Rhine River down to the Netherlands depend significantly on the SWE-storage in the Swiss Alps [Vischer (1976)] at the end of the winter. Moreover, in recent years, much concern has been expressed on deleterious effects that anthropogenic activities have on ecosystems. Often there is a concentration effect of pollutants (eg. acid pulse), when the seasonal snowcover is melting, as shown e.g. by Bergström et al.(1985). In this context it is of primary interest to be able to estimate e.g. 'cold content' or the liquid water content of the snow cover and the moment of onset of snow cover runoff.

It was therefore appropriate to develop a model that is suited for quantitative and qualitative problems on one hand, on the other hand it should use only operationally measured variables as input so that it is widely applicable.

In the last twenty years several models using an energy and mass balance approach have been developed, eg. by Morris (1983), however it is a main drawback of most of these models, that they are based on a research type of instrumentation. In this investigation we used only operationally measured variables as available in Switzerland on an hourly time step from the automatic network (ANETZ) of the Swiss Meteorological Institute (SMI).

At the Swiss Federal Institute of Technology (ETH), seasonal runoff forecasts have been issued for over 30 years. They are mainly based on regression type equations using time series of SWE-measurements as regressors (among other variables). The applicability of selected point measurements of SWE for the estimation of summer-season runoff forecasts for various alpine catchments between about 10 km^2 and 35000 km^2 has been confirmed by time series of considerable length of successfull forecasts up to 36 years, cf. Vischer (1975) or Vischer und Jensen (1978). It has been shown by Vischer und Jensen (1978) that seasonal runoff forecasts based on SWE are significantly better than those simply based on winter-runoff and winter precipitation measured with storage gauges. Unfortunately a lot of the SWE- stations do not observe until the end of the accumulation season. This was a point leading to the requirement of modelled point-SWE as surrogate for measured ones that could serve as an important additional information for appropriate runoff-forecasts in these situations.

One of the pollution problems in Switzerland is the application of liquid manure on snow covered soils. When the snow cover is melting there is a great danger that a nitrate pulse is poisoning the water fauna. With the help of the model described here, the situations and the exact timing of this pollution pulse was successfully modelled, based on operationally measured variables, as shown by Braun (1990).

METHODS AND DATA

Snow cover model

Braun (1985) presented a point energy and mass balance model for a melting snow cover which is further developed here. This model is mainly based on three equations: The snowcover energy balance equation, the equation describing the mass transfer within the snowpack and the mass balance equation. Energy available for the melting process of snow and for changes in the internal energy of the snow cover is equal to the energy absorbed by the snow cover. The energy fluxes across upper and lower boundaries of the snowcover can be expressed as given in equation (1)

$$Q_M + Q_q = Q^* + Q_H + Q_E + Q_R + Q_G \qquad (1)$$

where:

- Q_M: Energy flux available for melting of snow
- Q_q : Change of internal energy of the snowpack
- Q^*: Net all-wave radiation energy flux
- Q_H: Sensible heat flux at the snow-air interface
- Q_E: Latent heat flux at the snow-air interface
- Q_R : Rainfall heat flux
- Q_G : Heat flux from the ground

All of these components apart from the heat flux across the snow-ground interface Q_G are modelled explicitly. Details on the parameterization are given in Rohrer (1990)

Meteorological Data

As meteorological data input the following variables measured at hourly intervals at stations of the automatic network (ANETZ) of the SMI are used:

- air temperature (ventilated)
- precipitation (tipping bucket, heated)
- wind speed
- vapour pressure
- incoming solar radiation
- cloud cover (eye observation, term readings)

Data used as verification of the model

As verification data the measurements of stations of the ETH snow cover measurement network. Every two weeks there are density measurements of the snowcover and daily observations of snowdepth at a snowstake.

Parameter values

Great importance was attached

1. to use physically meaningful parameter values only.
2. to have only one parameter set for all stations
3. to derive parameter values externally, if possible

a comprehensive discussion of these values can be found in Braun (1985), Rohrer (1989) and Braun and Rohrer (1990).

Output Data:

The model will give for the entire snowpack on an hourly basis:

- snowcover water equivalent
- liquid-water content
- cold content (negative heat storage)
- albedo for solar radiation

- Energy balance components (some components given only during melt conditions)
- liquid water outflow

Sites

Snow cover measurement sites

The following sites all situated in the Swiss Alps (cf. FIG. 1) were selected on the basis of the proximity to an ANETZ station of the SMI and the availability of several years of SWE measurements: Montana(1500m a.s.l.), Disentis (1100m), San Bernardino(1600m) and Davos(1600m).

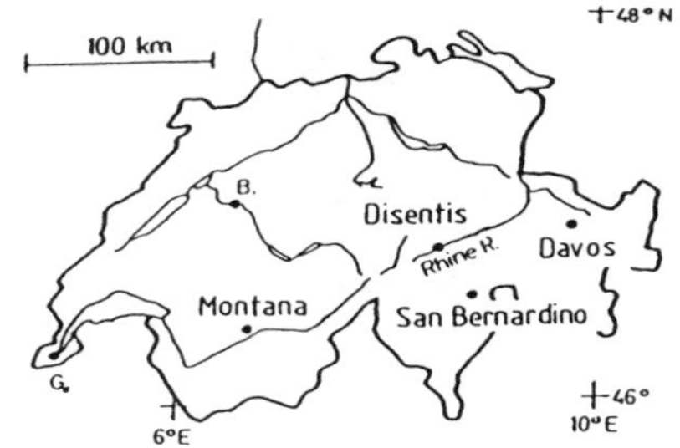

FIG.1 Location map of the four SWE stations selected for simulation.

Measurement sites of the meteorological data

The measurement sites of the meteorological data are within a few tens of meters of the one of snow cover and can therefore be regarded as representative for the snow cover measurement sites. There are some pecularities that need to be considered however, to avoid implications on model results. For example at Montana the measurement of the incoming solar radiation is taken on the roof of a nearby building. At a certain time of the year the sunshine hours can divert as much as two hours between the SWE measurement site and the radiation measurement site.

RESULTS

Measured and simulated point snow water equivalents (SWE) for different sites

Measured and simulated SWEs at the San Bernardino and the Montana site for the winter 1981/82 are presented in FIG. 2 as examples. Generally the simulated snow water equivalents can be considered as satisfactory for the applications suggested in the introduction of this paper. One problem that needs further attention is the parameterization of the albedo for solar radiation. There are only few investigations presenting valuable albedo measurements of the seasonal snow cover in the Swiss Alps. For examples the excellent albedo measurements at Davos (1600 m a.s.l.) of Eckel and Thams (1939) and of Prohaska and Thams (1940) show no dependence of solar incidence angle. However, the same authors could identify such a dependence at the Weissfluhjoch site at 2540m, particularly at 'firnspiegel' conditions.

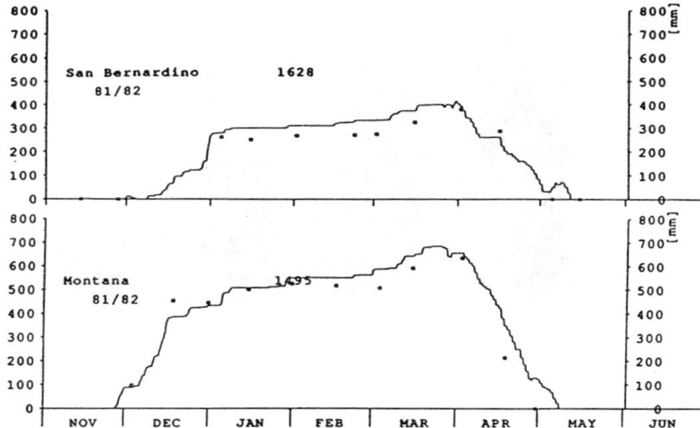

FIG.2 Measured (squares) and simulated water equivalent (through lines) for the winter 1981/82 and the sites San Bernardino and Montana.

Relation between point snow cover water equivalents and long term runoff

To obtain seasonal runoff forecasts (1 to several months, from April to September) for catchments in the Swiss alpine region several techniques can be applied. It is clear that based on the location and above all the hypsography of the catchment a smaller or a greater part of the expected summer runoff is stored in the snowcover at the end of the accumulation season. One technique is to calculate explicitly the stored snow cover water equivalent (SWE) for the whole catchment summing SWEs over unit areas characterized by a certain range of elevation, slope and aspect. Such a technique is actually used to compute water storage of the snow cover for the Wägital basin in the lower Swiss Alps (890-2300 m a.s.l.). Another technique is to correlate time series of SWEs of one or several index locations with the corresponding time series of the runoff. In FIG. 3 the latter technique was used to demonstrate the predictive capabilities of one single SWE measurement station (Weissfluhjoch 2540 m a.s.l.) for two alpine catchments of different elevation ranges and areas. The portions of total variation of the accumulated monthly runoff that can be accounted for by a linear relationship are presented in this figure. In the Dischma catchment, there are no significant anthropogenic influences on runoff, therefore discharge data could be used directly. The Rhine/ Rheinfelden catchment, however, shows considerable anthropogenic influences and 'natural' runoff-values had to be derived on the basis of reservoir manipulations (H. Jensen, pers. communication).

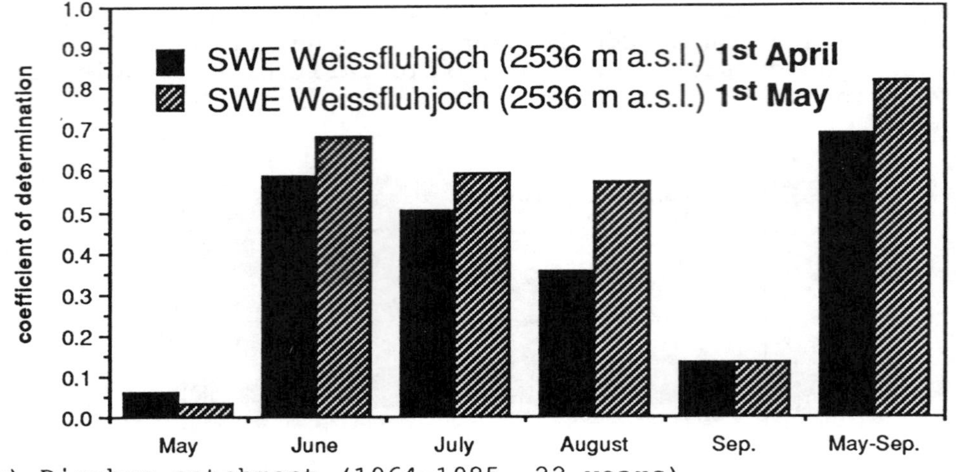

a) Dischma catchment (1964-1985, 22 years)

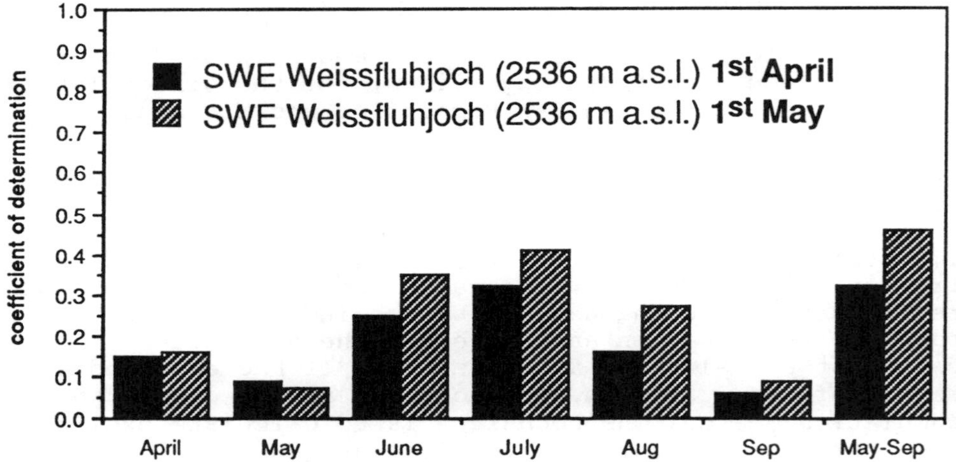

b) Rhein/Rheinfelden catchment (1948-1989, 42 years)

FIG. 3 Portions of the total variation (coefficients of determination) in the values of the accumulated monthly runoff of two different catchments that can be accounted for by a linear relationship with the values of the snow water equivalent (SWE) of the station of Weissfluhjoch (2540 m a.s.l.) situated in the high alpine region (data partly taken from Hydrologisches Jahrbuch).

Some characteristics of the two catchments are listed in TAB 1. The coefficients of determination for summer season runoff sums are significantly higher in the Dischma catchment than in the Rhine/Rheinfelden catchment. The reason for this lies mainly in the different hypsography of the two catchments. In the Dischma catchment 88.8% of the area is

TABLE 1 Characteristics of two alpine catchments of different size and elevation range.

Catchment:	**Dischma**	**Rhine/ Rheinfelden**
area:	43.3 km^2	34 550 km^2
highest point:	3146 m	4277 m
lowest point:	1668 m	258 m
mean elevation:	2372 m	1085 m
area above 2000m:	88.8%	12.7%
glaciated:	2.6%	1.8%
lakes:	0.13%	3.6%
mean ratio winter runoff/ yearly runoff	0.21	0.45

situated above 2000 m a.s.l., in the Rhine/ Rheinfelden catchment it is only 12.7% (cf. TAB. 1). The mean portion of precipitation falling as snow at 2000m a.s.l. is about 90%. The glaciated portions of the catchments are small. As a longterm mean about 43% of the precipitations are falling from the begining of October to the end of April, but only about 21% of total yearly runoff occurs during this period. The conclusion is that a great part of summer runoff of the Dischma catchment is derived from snow cover storage. The coefficients of determination for accumulated summer season runoff are considerably higher for the SWE of the 1st May than for the SWE of the 1st April.

CONCLUSIONS

Previous investigations by Vischer and Jensen (1978) demonstrate that for alpine catchments snow cover water equivalent (SWE) is a better predictor for summer season runoff than winter gauges precipitation measurements only. It is shown here that SWE modelled by an energy and mass balance model using operationally measured meteorological variables are a valuable surrogate for measured SWE. These modelled SWE are particularly useful in the late accumulation season, when some stations do not measure SWE anymore. This time of the season is of particular interest because the coefficients of determination for runoff of SWE are highest for accumulated monthly runoff for the months June to September and for the total accumulated runoff from May to September.

ACKNOWLEDGEMENTS The authors wish to thank H. Jensen and L. Braun for valuable support, as well as M. Bantle and M. Merlo of the SMI for their support in the usage of the meteorological data bases.

REFERENCES

Bergström, S., Carlsson, B., Sandberg, & Maxe, L.(1985) Integrated modelling of runoff, alkalinity and pH on a daily basis. Nordic Hydrol. 16 (2), 89-104.

Braun, L. N.(1985) Simulation of Snowmelt-Runoff in Lowland and Lower Alpine Regions of Switzerland. Zürcher Geographische Schriften, 21, Zürich 1985.

Braun, L. N. & Rohrer, M. (1990) Einige Gesichtspunkte bei der Regionalisierung der Schneedeckenverteilung im mikro- bis mesoskaligen Bereich. In: Deutsche Forschungsgemeinschaft (DFG). Rundgespräch vom 1./2. Feb. in Bonn-Bad Godesberg. (in press).

Braun, M. (1990) Zusammenhänge zwischen Schneedecke, gefrorenem Boden und Güllenabschwemmung. PhD-thesis at the Swiss Federal Institute of Technology (in preparation).

Eckel und Thams (1939) Untersuchungen über die Dichte-, Temperatur- und Strahlungsverhältnisse der Schneedecke.in:Beiträge zur Geologie der Schweiz,- Geotechnische Serie-Hydrologie, Lieferung 3, Kümmerly und Frey Bern. 275-340.

Hydrologisches Jahrbuch (several years). Landeshydrologie und -geologie. Eidg. Dep. des Inneren, BUWAL. Bern.

Jensen, H. (1974) Anwendung der Regressionsanalyse. In: VAW-Mitteilung Nr. 12: Hydrologische Prognosen für die Wasserwirtschaft, Zürich, 1974, 17/1-17/10.

Morris, E.,M.(1983) Modelling the flow of mass and energy within a snowpack for hydrological forecasting. Ann. Glaciol.,4, 198-203.

Prohaska und Thams (1940) Neue Untersuchungen über die Strahlungseigenschaften der Schneedecke. Tagungsber. d. Schweiz. Ges. f. Geophys., Met., Astron. 21-44.

Rohrer, M. (1989) Determination of the transition air temperature from snow to rain and intensity of precipitation. IASH/WMO/ETH International Workshop on precipitation Measurement, St. Moritz, Switzerland,1989, 475-482.

Rohrer, M. (1990) Punktmodellierung des Auf- und Abbaus der Schneedecke mit Stundendaten des automatischen Netzes der Schweizer. Meteorologischen Anstalt SMA, Zürich. PhD-thesis at the Swiss Federal Institute of Technology (in preparation).

Vischer, D. (1976) Abflussprognosen für die Wasserwirtschaft. Wasser, Energie, Luft, 68. Jahrgang,5, 113-118.

Vischer, D. & Jensen, H. (1978) Langfristprognosen für den Rheinabfluss in Rheinfelden, Wasserwirtschaft, 68. Jahrgang, 9, 1-6.

Symposium on Improved Methods of Hydrological Measurements in Mountain Areas

Topic D:

Improved Methods of Measuring Discharge in Mountain Rivers, Including Problems of Bed Load

Hydrology in Mountainous Regions. I - Hydrological Measurements; the Water Cycle
(Proceedings of two Lausanne Symposia, August 1990). IAHS Publ. no. 193, 1990.

Acoustic sensors (hydrophones) as indicators for bed load transport in a mountain torrent

R. BÄNZIGER & H. BURCH
Swiss Federal Institute for Forest, Snow and Landscape Research (FSL), 8903 Birmensdorf, Switzerland

ABSTRACT In a small prealpine torrent the Swiss Federal Institut for Forest, Snow and Landscape FSL operates a hydrological station. Besides other instruments it has also been equipped with acoustic sensors since autumn 1986 which allow to get information about frequency and intensity of sediment transport. To work up raw data and to interpret the verified data - sets raises some difficulties, but some statements can already be made. For example, amount of water runoff in the moment of beginning sensor activity is dependent on season. It is low in spring and autumn but high in summer. It is independent of the length of the preceding flood - free period. For the relativeley low floods in the available data the sum of recorded hydrophone impulses correlates with total sediment load. It is planned to continue the measurements over a long period.

INTRODUCTION

It is still very difficult to measure the amount of sediment load actually transported in rivers and torrents.
It is highly desirable to achieve the ability to measure this value, for only exact measurements give the possibility of calibrating the mathematical transport - models and thus being able to use them for predictions. Predictions of the amount of sediment load are important as a basis for dimensioning control works such as debris retention ponds.

The idea that the sound generated by moving particle collision might serve as a parameter indicative of bedload transport rates is more than 50 years old. Numerous attempts to measure bedload with hydrophones (submarine microphones) have been made, but only limited success has been achieved (Jonys, 1976).

A NEW, DIFFERENT ATTEMPT

In the Erlenbach, a prealpine torrent situated in a flysch - zone of Switzerland, the Swiss Federal Institute for Forest, Snow and Landscape Research (FSL) operates a hydrological station. The catchment area of this torrent is 0.7 km^2, its average inclination 30%, with its highest point at 1655 m.a.s.l., its lowest at 1110 m.a.s.l. Average precipitation is 2300 mm/year. Rate and chemical and physical parameters of runoff are continuously measured as well as a set of meteorological data. 2 - 3 times yearly the total sediment discharge is measured by surveying the volume increase of the sediment accumulation in the sediment basin.

Since autumn 1986 this station has been equipped with an installation which could be designated as an acoustic sensor for sediment movement.
The core of such a sensor is a piezoelectrical crystal. This crystal generates a small electrical potential whenever it is deformed. It is fixed to the underside of a steel plate, which is flushmounted in a transverse structure above the sediment basin. In case of sediment transport, moving gravel bumps against the steel plate. The plate transmits the shock to the crystal , which becomes deformed and thus produces an electrical potential. The magnitude of this potential is measured. Whenever it exceeds a certain, chooseable amount, the shock is recorded as an impulse. These impulses are counted in minute - intervals. Whenever the counted number exceeds a certain value, the equippment starts to record this information on magnetic tape. In the cross section of the torrent nine of these sensors are distributed at different altitudes.

Once the installation has started its recording, the following parameters every minute are stored: date, time, sum of the impulses from each of the nine hydrophones during the respective minute, water runoff, and precipitation intensity. Since February 1989 a remote - controlled video camera has also been in operation, which starts taking pictures as soon as the hydrophones become active. Furthermore 2 - 3 times yearly the total sediment discharge is measured by surveying the volume increase of the sediment accumulation in the basin.

WORKING UP DATA

To work up the raw data sets raises some difficulties. Not only moving sediment can start hydrophone activity. Events like bangs of supersonic airplanes, hail, thunder, transport of fragmented ice sheets or playing children can produce recordings. The video recording can be a help in detecting such events, which must be eliminated from the data.

FIG. 1 Gauging station Erlenbach. The Erlenbach river flows in this photo from the top to the bottom. It passes a first gauging station, flows down a shooting channel and flows over a transverse structure before it falls into the sediment retention basin. In this transverse structure the acoustic sensors are flushmounted . Out of the sediment basin the water passes a standardised V-notch weir before it returns to its original bed.

Furthermore, little is actually known about the interrelation between sediment parameters such as particle size distribution, density, shape, or actual sediment runoff on the one hand and the number of recorded impulses on

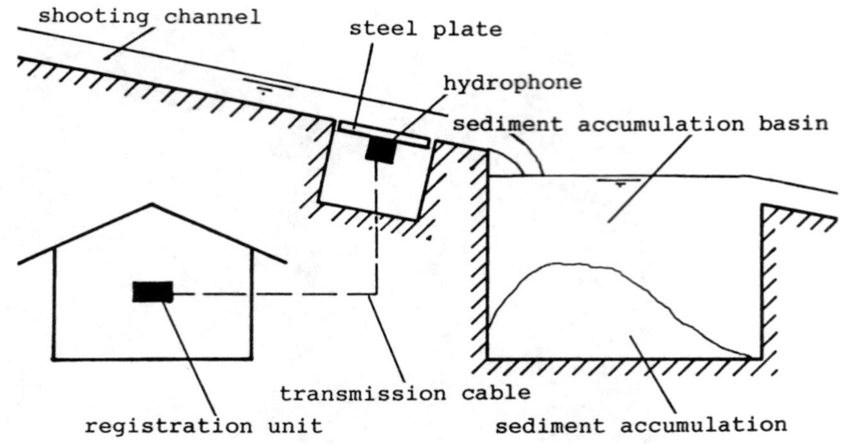

FIG. 2 **Principle of the hydrophone - set up.**

the other. Accordingly the strength of shocks leading to recorded impulses has been fixed to the best of our knowledge and belief, but all the same arbitrarily. Experiments show that small amounts of fine - grained material might remain undetected.
Therefore a very critical check of the raw data is of eminent importance. All the same one cannot always be sure of eliminating all the bad data sets or retaining all the good ones.
If the actual water - runoff is around the one causing the first sediment transport, several events might be recorded within a short time. For this analysis, such events are linked together whenever the intervall between them is less than 20 minutes.

To date we have compiled such verified data - sets from 177 bed - load transporting floods occuring between 20. Oct. 1986 and 19. Dec. 1989.

FIRST RESULTS

In the following some first analyses are presented:
Investigation of single data - sets shows that maximum hydrophone activity and peak of water - runoff very often do not coincide (for example see Figure 3). Deviation of the two peaks are found on either side. Also it may be observed that the amount of water runoff in the moment of the first recorded hydrophone impulse of a data - set (in the following called "critical runoff") and at the end of a flood often differ considerably.

This critical runoff is dependent on the season. As Figure 4 shows, it amounts to an average of about 200 l/s towards the end of winter, increases continuously to

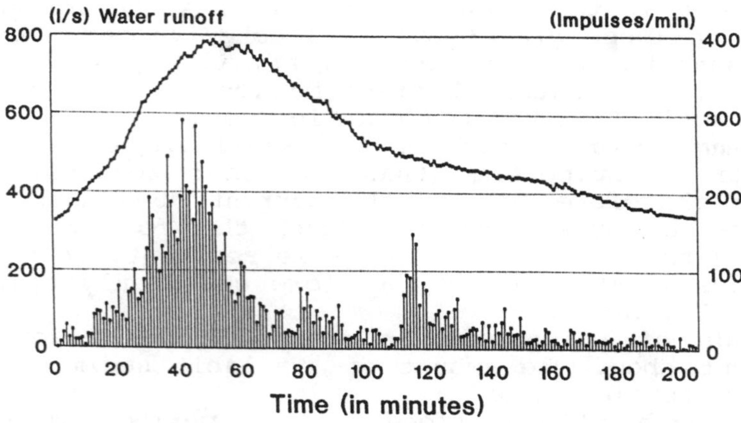

FIG. 3 Example of an event. It can been seen that most intensive hydrophone activity does not coincide with highest water runoff. Around the 120th minute of the event a second peak of hydrophone activity was recorded, though water runoff sank continuoulsy.

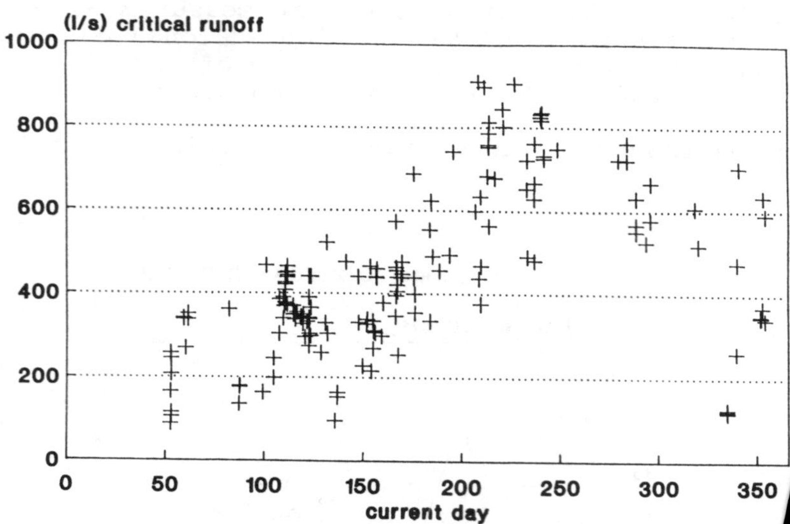

FIG. 4 Water runoff at in the moment of the fi[illegible] hydrophone impulse at the beginning of a flood (criti[illegible] runoff). Around the 100th day of the year (spring - t[illegible] it amounts to about 200 l/s, increases till end of su[illegible] (around 220th day) to an average amount of about 700 [illegible] and decreases again in autumn and winter.

almost 700 l/s in late summer, and decreases agai[illegible] autumn and winter. Though dispersion is quite high[illegible] trend seems to be obvious. The following causes [illegible] partly explain this behaviour:

The geological conditions (the whole catchment area is situated in the flysch - zone) causes the torrent not to flow on loose gravel but on a cohesive bed. In times of frequent but not permanent frost, i. e., spring and late autumn, this material might be loosend and consequently more easily transported than in summer.

Maximum water runoff in the available data - sets is higher in summertime than in other seasons. A summer flood therefore scoured the torrents bed much more than floods in other seasons. Thus the following (summer) floods found much less available sediment; they had first to loosen material and therefore could only start transportation later.

Periods of rainy weather cause slides, also near the torrents bed. The amount of available sediment rises in such a situation.

The length of the flood - free period preceding the actual event could also influence the magnitude of the critical runoff. The longer such a period lasts, the more sediment can accumulate in the river-bed. The longer a dry period lasts, the more transportable sediment is available, hence critical runoff decreases. Figure 5 hows that this last hypothesis has to be rejected. No orrelation can be found between these two parameters.

other interesting question is how far the hydrophone ulses can be seen as a direct measurement of sediment ff. Figure 6 gives the impression that there is a ng correlation between the sum of recorded hydrophone ses and the total transported sediment load.

emarks have to be made as to this assumption:

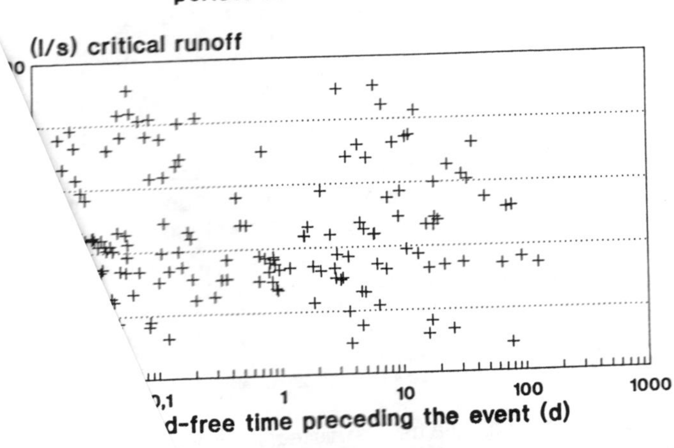

e is no interrelation between the length of free period preceding the event and the cal runoff.

The highest flood to be found in the available data - sets amounts to 4 m^3/s. For only less than 30 minutes (0.36% of the total time of all recorded events) did water runoff exceed a limit of 2 m^3/s. In contrast to this a high flood with a recurrence interval of 100 years amounts to some 12 m^3/s near the gauging station. This shows that only relativly small floods are represented in our data - material. In such events the transported sediment flows in a single layer. Every single stone can therefore produce a hydrophone impulse. Were the flood higher, the sediment would flow in several layers and not every single sediment particle could come into contact with the hydrophone steel - plates. In such a case we would have to expect relatively fewer impulses. For this reason there are nine sensors placed at different heights in the torrent's cross section. We hope that the data from these other sensors will help us to interpret and measure sediment runoff (for example the thickness of the transported sediment layer) in higher floods.

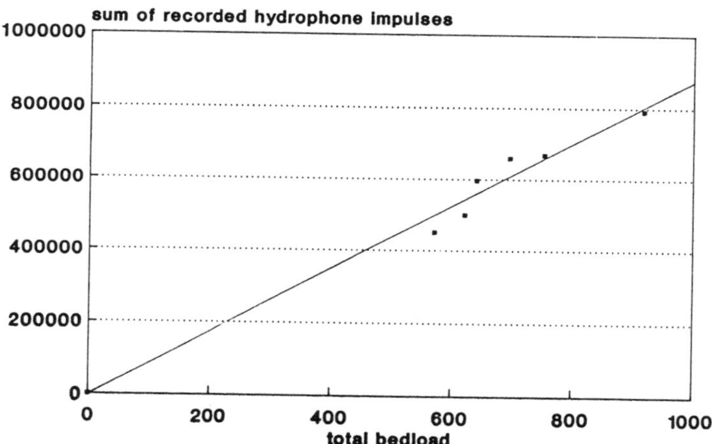

FIG. 6 For the recorded floods with relatively low peaks an interrelation between total bedload and sum of recorded hydrophone impulses seems to be obvious.

Hence the graph in Figure 6 allows us to estimate the total sediment load if we have measured a sum of hydrophone impulses, but only as long as there has not been a flood with a high recurrence interval.

FUTURE WORK

This article presents the first results of a reasearch project which is planned to last a long period. Actually we hope to obtain data on very high floods sooner or later. Such data would make interpretation of the recordings even more interesting than it is already. However until we are able to formulate the interrelation between hydrograph and bed - load transport and especially can generalize such interrelations there is still a long way to go.

REFERENCE

Jonys, C. K. (1976) Acoustic measurement of sediment transport. Scientific series No. 66, Inland Waters Directorate, CCIW Branch, Burlington, Ontario 1976.

Hydrology in Mountainous Regions. I - Hydrological Measurements; the Water Cycle
(Proceedings of two Lausanne Symposia, August 1990). IAHS Publ. no. 193, 1990.

Determination of discharge rates in turbulent streams by salt tracer dilution applying a microcomputer system. Comparison with current meter measurements

R. BENISCHKE & T. HARUM

Institute for Geothermics & Hydrogeology, Joanneum Research, Elisabethstr. 16/2, 8010 Graz, Austria

ABSTRACT The attempt to determine exactly discharge rates of turbulent streams in mountainous regions based on current meter measurements can lead to serious problems rising from a badly defined runoff channel geometry and irregular flow patterns. Therefore systematic errors influence the results and make it sometimes impossible to get reliable stage-discharge relations at gauging stations.

The development of commercially available computerized systems made it possible to apply the salt tracer dilution method with instantaneous or continuous injection and to monitor the tracer passage in the time-concentration or time-conductivity mode directly at the field site. The result of the measurement is available immediately at the end of the measuring procedure. The experience showed that the salt tracer dilution method is the appropriate method in almost all cases of turbulent flow conditions and irregular channel geometry.

The article describes the theoretical basis of the method, the used measuring system and compares the results with current meter data from streams, where the latter method can be applied with sufficient precision and accuracy.

In many cases both methods can be applied with good results within a 2% average deviation, but both methods have limitations, which will be discussed too. Salt tracer dilution and current meter do not exclude each other, they are complementary methods.

INTRODUCTION

Hydrological investigations sometimes suffer the lack on quantitative data. Beside meteorological data also discharge rates of a catchment runoff are needed. An often applied method to determine this is the current meter method, but in runoff channels with turbulent flow or irregular flow pattern some errors will influence the reliability of the results.

As the current meter method depends strongly on a defined channel geometry for the calculation of flow velocities this fact is frequently the source of erroneous data particularly when using such data to evaluate stage-discharge relations for gauging stations.

A possible way to overcome these difficulties offers the long known tracer method (Rimmar, 1960, André, 1964, Behrens, 1971). This method can be applied in various forms, which will be described below. Up to now the method was hardly used comparing it with the well known current meter method. The reason was the necessary equipment to monitor the tracer passage or the uncertain results when collecting water samples for the difficult and time consuming subsequent analytical procedure.

Now these problems could be reduced because of a great variety of computerized, handy, components with high precision and accuracy and the possibility to evaluate and calculate immediately the results after the measurement procedure (Benischke & Harum, 1984). This gives also the opportunity for the immediate decision in the field to repeat a doubtful measurement.

In this article the focus is on the tracer method with instantaneous injection using salt tracer and conductivity measurement to monitor the tracer passage.

THEORETICAL CONSIDERATIONS

Types of the Tracer Method

There are three types:

- Dilution method with constant injection
- Integration method with instantaneous injection
- Hydraulic integration method

The basis is the measurement of the passage of an upstream continuously or instantaneously injected known amount of tracer substance. The most important demand on the method is a complete mixing of the tracer with the water at least at the site of measurement assuming that all the tracer will pass the site during the observation period.

In the case of the dilution method with continuous injection a tracer solution with known concentration (C_0) is added to the stream at a defined constant rate (Q_0). This is carried out normally by application of a Mariotte flask or similar equipment (Bundesamt f. Umweltschutz, 1982). Because of dilution the tracer solution has at the measuring site the concentration C_m under the unknown discharge Q_m.

$$C_0 \cdot Q_0 = C_m \cdot Q_m \tag{1}$$

Thus giving $$(C_0 \cdot Q_0)/C_m = Q_m \tag{2}$$

The integration method with instantanteous injection means that a previously dissolved tracer is poured into the stream at the moment. It is assumed in the calculation formula that this really happens at a moment. Practically this procedure will take some time - possibly some seconds - but this does not affect the result. It is also assumed that the absolute dry mass (M) of tracer is suddenly injected and not the dissolved tracer substance. Practically the volume of the solution does not affect the result as long as the discharge (Q) to be measured is not too small. The tracer passage is monitored or measured by collecting distinct water samples. A possible natural background (C_0) has to be substracted. For the evaluation also the time of first arrival (t_0) and of disappearance (t_1) is needed. Between this time marks is the observation period and during this period the monitored concentration (C_1) is integrated over the time

$$Q = M / \int_{t_0}^{t_1} (C_1 - C_0).dt \tag{3}$$

The integration method with instantaneous injection can be altered to the so-called hydraulic integration. This means that starting with time t_0 a constant volume of the measured water is pumped or siphoned into a container until t_1. At the end there is a composite sample with an average concentration (C_m). The product of the average concentration and the total time interval has the same value than the above mentioned integral. Therefore the unknown discharge (Q) is

$$Q = M/C_m \cdot (t_1 - t_0) \tag{4}$$

The assumption is, that the water to be measured must be pumped or siphoned very exactly and the begin and end of pumping must be exact at the times t_0 resp. t_1. This assumption makes it more difficult to measure a discharge, because of often not exactly working components of the "hardware".

Types of Tracers

Various tracer substances have been investigated for a possible use in that method:
(a) anorganic salts: NaCl, KCl, LiCl, $CaCl_2$, KBr, NaBr or even $Na_2Cr_2O_7$.
(b) organic dyestuff: Sulphorhodamine G, Na-Fluorescein
(c) particle tracers, physical influences: cork particles, magnetic particles, radioactive decay.

All the tracers injected should be non-toxic, should have a good solubility even in cold water and determinable quantitatively in the field or in the laboratory with high sensitivity. Last not least the costs should be a minimum.

From the anorganic salts all Chlorides offer a more or less good solubility and sensitivity and the detectability is cheap and easy. For high discharge rates (above 10 $m^3.s^{-1}$) some problems may arise when dissolving an amount of tens of kg for the injection or at low temperature near the freezing point. With exception of LiCl, $CaCl_2$ and K_2CrO_3 all these tracers are harmless.

Organic dyestuffs have some advantages over the salt tracers. The amount to be injected can be reduced because of the high sensitivity and big rivers can be measured. But the use of such tracers is only possible when there is a suitable analytical equipment. This is normally very expensive.

Particle tracers like cork particles are well known and have been the first tracers for estimation of mean flow velocities but the accuracy was very poor. Radioactive substances would be one of the best tracers but their use is restricted with regard to environmental protection.

Types of Sampling, Monitoring and Analytics

The tracer to be measured can be analyzed by collecting water samples or by monitoring with tracer-selective and sensitive probes.

The collection of water samples can be carried out by sampling manually, with pre-programmed automatic samplers or by continuous pumping or siphoning into a container. Another way is to monitor the tracer passage as mentioned above and to collect data with a recorder, printer, laptop-computer or data-logger.

Several analytical methods depending on the used tracer can be applied: physical methods like the measurement of temperature and conductivity (for salt tracers), others are the titration, polarography (for metal ions), ion-selective probes or electrodes for monitoring in the field or determination in the laboratory, ion-chromatography and atomic absorption or emission, photometric or fluorometric procedures for dyes and other spectrometric methods.

The application of the appropriate analytical method depends on the type of the tracer and the possibilities of the laboratory.

Types of Evaluation and Results

Depending on the used analytical procedure and data collection method it is possible to evaluate the measurement after analysis in the laboratory or immediately in the field at the site of measurement. The latter option requires a portable computer (pocket format, laptop or similar).

The evaluation of the primary electronic signals (voltage, current, resistance, frequency) may give discharge rates, flow velocities, characteristic time marks of the tracer passage or even dispersion parameters. This is only a matter of the used software. An advantage is the possibility to recalculate stored data.

Tracer Dynamics in a Channel

The assumption of a complete mixing is very important. In the above mentioned formulas there is no term regarding good mixing. Partial mixing give rise for significant errors. Mathematically this means, that a complete mixing is reached if the time-concentration integral is constant all over a distinct section of the channel.

If the mixing process was not complete two cases have to be taken into consideration: at first the conductivity probe is in that part of the channel bed where the tracer concentration is high. Then the result of the measurement will give too low discharge, secondly if it is in the less concentrated part, i.e. if there is too high dilution, the result will give too high values.

For the estimation of the appropriate mixing distance several formulas exist but they are not applicable in every case. For a particular discharge measurement it is better to estimate the correct mixing length visually with a small amount of dye tracer or with one or more previously performed tests using the salt tracer in the same way than in the later experiment.

The mixing depends on the flow pattern (laminar or turbulent), the channel geometry like width and depth, regions with retentions, diversions, water intakes or losses into the underground (Fig. 1).

Integration Method with Instantaneous Injection Using a Conductivity Probe

As the title implies the basis of the method is the measurement of the tracer passage during a limited observation period.

The tracer is commercially available salt (NaCl), which is dissolved depending on its solubility at a certain temperature in a suitable amount of water. The water for the dissolution should be the same as to be

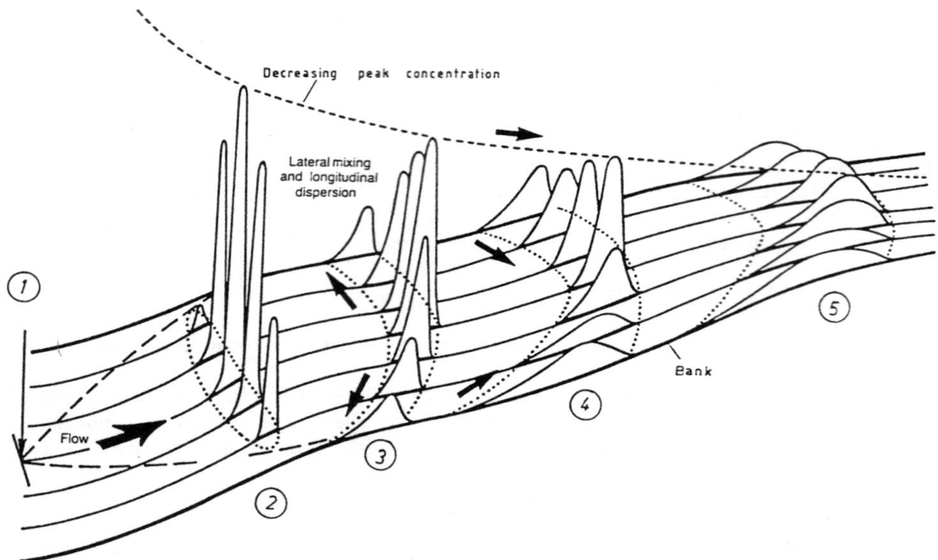

Fig. 1 Possible model of lateral and longitudinal mixing of an instantaneously injected tracer (after Hubbard et al., 1982, Kilpatrick et al., 1989).
1= Injection point of the tracer, 2= Tracer distribution immediately after injection, 3= Tr reaches banks of the channel, 4= Backward directed flow from the banks to the center with succesive lateral and longitudinal mixing, 5= Lateral mixing is complete.

measured and it should be also the same for the instrument calibration. The reason is to match the natural matrix of the water and to avoid systematic errors originating from such matrix effects. The amount of injected salt (absolute value of mass) should be known exactly but the weight is normally within an intervall of ± 2 % . A deviation of 2 % of the nominal weight will cause also a 2%-deviation of the measured discharge, if this would be the only influence. This assumption was true for commercial salt we used for the experiments. The same type of salt must be used for the calibration standard and must be prepared analytically. Because of the impossibility for drying the salt before injection and weighing it analytically also the salt used for preparation of the standard solution need not to be dried prior to weighing in. At this point it is assumed that the moisture content of the salt prepared for injection and that used for the standard is the same. Practical measurements showed that a significant error will arise when using undried salt for injection and dried salt for the standard.

A calibration before starting the measurements is recommended and the calibration function should cover the expected range of conductivity during the tracer passage. With the calibration the measuring system will be compensated for some sources of errors (varying matrix, temperature dependence of conductivity, aging of electrodes etc.). The calibration is recommended each time a change of the water or measuring conditions is expected, i.e. after sewage outfalls and water intakes, or if the matrix has changed during the day for example during snowmelt in alpine regions or excessive rainfall in the catchment area.

THE MICROCOMPUTER SYSTEM

The system (Fig. 2) used for the study is based on a commercially available microcomputer (CPU 80C88, 512 kB RAM, 3.5" disk drive 720 kB) which acts as a system controller. It is linked via the standard RS 232C interface to a data logger (with separate clock, conductivity electronics and a 14 bit analog/digital converter to the probe). All the components are mounted in a portable case and the conductivity probe can be connected from outside. The energy supply is a chargeable battery for about six hours working time. With the same instrument also the application of a current meter is possible, plugged in the same socket as the conductivity probe.

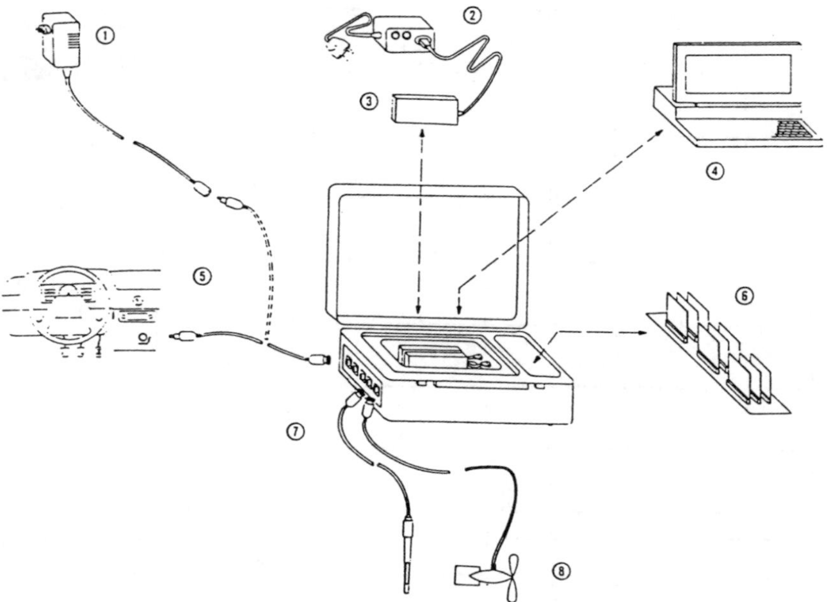

Fig. 2 Scheme of the used equipment.
1= main supply, 2= quick charge device, 3= battery, 4= laptop computer, 5= plug for car cigarette-lighter , 6= electronics, 7= conductivity probe, 8= current meter.

The system is run by a special software, which allows data acquisition and process control for the tracer method and the current meter. Here the focus is on the tracer software.

In a first step the system will be calibrated. A small fixed volume (here 250 ml) of the water to be measured is filled into a beaker, the conductivity probe is submerged and the background conductivity will be monitored until a stable signal is read from the display. In several steps a fixed volume (here 0.5 ml) of the standard is added, well mixed up and after each step and stabilzation of the signal the conductivity is measured again. The standard addition is repeated as often until the expected conductivity range is covered. This procedure is partially a little empirical and depends on the experience of the analyst. Then the relation conductivity/tracer-concentration is evaluated by a least square fit of the form

$$C = E_0 + k \cdot E \tag{5}$$

The intercept E_0 represents the natural background conductivity, E the measured conductivity after each calibration step and later on the monitored conductivity during the tracer passage. The slope k is called the calibration coefficient and is put into the integration formula (3).

The tracer response curve is displayed during passage and after return to the background conductivity the procedure is stopped and the response curve can be evaluated (Fig. 3).

For the evaluation some charcteristic points on the curve are important: start of measurement, first arrival of tracer, point of return to background, end of measurement. The data points between start of measurement and first arrival resp. point of return to background and end of measurement define the trendline of the background conductivity during the passage. The further evaluation is a conversion of the conductivity data on the basis of the calibration and a simple integration of the calculated concentration over the time, which gives finally the discharge.

But the program is more flexible and allows to shift the markers according to the reliability of the data points excluding erroneous results, moreover the discharge can be recalculated and in the case of an accidentally break off before reaching the background an extrapolation of the response curve toward the background is possible.

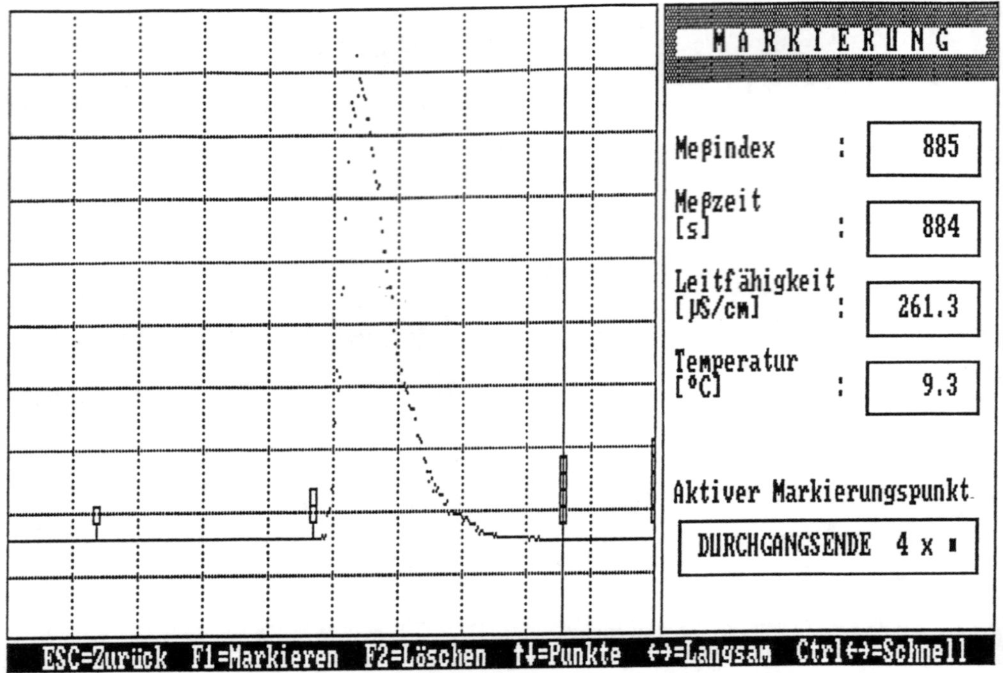

Fig. 3 Example of a tracer response curve displayed during the passage. The shown markers will be added after evaluation automatically but can be altered manually.

APPLICATIONS

This method was applied successfully in hydrogeological projects in alpine catchment areas for several years. The magnitude of the measured discharge rates was between 1 $l.s^{-1}$ and 15 $m^3.s^{-1}$. The method was used not only for individual discharge measurements but also for calculation of stage-discharge relations at gauging stations.

Tab. 1 Comparison of discharge measurements ($l.s^{-1}$) with salt tracer dilution (Q_T) and current meter (Q_C) at selected gauging stations resp. with flow meter (Q_F) at a laboratory model, D (%) deviation from Q_T (= 100 %).

Site	Q_T	Q_C	D	Site	Q_T	Q_C	D
Gößbach	271	260	4.2	Section 11	7.4	7.2	2.7
Gößbach	273	281	2.8	Section 11	11.3	10.8	4.4
Gößbach	2178	2183	0.2	Section 11	14.1	13.6	3.5
Gößbach	517	523	1.1	Section 11	19.9	19.2	3.5
Radmerbach	1264	1273	0.7	Section 2	3.8	3.84	1.1
Radmerbach	1156	1125	2.8	Section 2	6.9	7.2	4.3
Radmerbach	1313	1343	2.2	Section 2	11.0	10.8	1.8
Bodenbach	68	68	0.0	Section 2	13.1	13.6	3.8
Bodenbach	46	47	2.1	Section 2	19.0	19.2	1.1
Bodenbach	107	105	1.9	Section 3	3.7	3.84	4.1
Bodenbach	109	105	3.8	Section 3	7.0	7.2	2.9
Piburger See	20	19.7	1.5	Section 3	10.5	10.8	2.9
Piburger See	55	52	5.8	Section 3	13.0	13.6	4.6
Mosergraben	277	288	3.8	Section 3	18.6	19.2	3.2

We carried out a number of experiments to test the method and to compare it with current meter and flow meter measurements (Tab. 1). Some experiments were carried out at a river model built up in a laboratory to measure travel time and to compare calculated predicted runoff conditions with tracer data. The results obtained with the tracer method were in good agreement with the data from current meter and flow meter. In almost all cases the range of deviations was within a 5 %-interval.

REFERENCES

André, H. (1964) Hydrométrie pratique des cours d'eau. Tome 1: Jaugeages par la méthode de dilution.- E.N.S.E.H.R.M.A., Section Hydraulique, Grenoble.

Behrens, H. (1971) Tracermethoden in Oberflächengewässern.- GSF-Bericht R 38, München.

Benischke, R., Harum, T. (1984) Abflußmessungen mit dem EPSON HX-20 und WTW-LF 91 nach der Integrationsmethode.- In: Bergmann, H., Zojer, H. (1984) Neu- und Weiterentwicklung hydrologischer Methoden für Haushaltsuntersuchungen in Versuchsgebieten, Teil 3.-, Unpubl. Report, Forschungsges. Joanneum, Graz.

Benischke, R., Harum, T. (1984) Computergesteuerte Abflußmessungen in offenen Gerinnen nach der Tracerverdünnungsmethode (Integrationsverfahren).- Steir. Beitr. z. Hydrogeologie, 36, 127-137, Graz.

Bundesamt für Umweltschutz, Landeshydrologie (1982) Handbuch für die Abflußmengenmessung.- Bern.

Hubbard, E. F., Kilpatrick, F. A., Martens, L. A., Wilson, J. F. (1982) Measurement of time of travel and dispersion in streams by dye tracing.- Techniques of Water-Resoursces Investigations of the US Geological Survey, Book 3: Applications of Hydraulics, Washington.

Kilpatrick, F. A., Wilson, J. F. (1989): Measurement of time and travel in streams by dye tracing.- Techniques of Water-Resoursces Investigations of the US Geological Survey, Book 3: Applications of Hydraulics, Washington.

Rimmar, G. M. (1960) Use of electrical conductivity for measuring discharges by the dilution method.- Trudy GGI, 36 (90), 18-48.

Hydrology in Mountainous Regions. I - Hydrological Measurements; the Water Cycle
(Proceedings of two Lausanne Symposia, August 1990). IAHS Publ. no. 193, 1990.

Experiences and results from using a big-frame bed load sampler for coarse material bed load

K.BUNTE
Institut für Physische Geographie, Grunewaldstr. 35,
1000 Berlin 41, Federal Republic of Germany

ABSTRACT In a mountain river coarse material bed load was sampled with a 1.6 m x 0.3 m opening net sampler. Consecutive samples varied in transport rates and grain-size composition. The results of a grain-size analysis suggest that the mode of bed load transport at Squaw Creek switches between selective and equilibrium transport.

INTRODUCTION

The predictive value of bed load formulas for coarse material is still not satisfactory. The processes occuring during coarse material bed load transport have not yet been clarified. Particle interaction and its impact on initial motion have been investigated by various researchers but their findings seem to be contradictory.

One of the main problems regarding transport modes is that during a transport event under natural conditions processes on the river bottom would have to be observed and measured which still cannot be achieved. Even measuring coarse material bed load transport in mountain rivers is still a difficult task. Ordinary hand held samplers do not provide representative samples of the typically very widespread grain-size distribution of mountain river sediments and measuring efforts are hampered by the extreme force of flow during floods with coarse material bed load transport. A practicable and cheap method of measuring not only the quantity but also the grain-size distribution of coarse particles in transport has to be employed.

METHOD OF SAMPLING

Sampling conditions at Squaw Creek

At Squaw Creek, Gallatin Range, Montana (USA) a bed load sampler had to be used that was suitable for the prevalent conditions (ERGENZINGER & CUSTER 1982, 1983; BUNTE et al. 1987; CUSTER et al. 1987; BUGOSH & CUSTER 1989). Grain-size distributions of the gravel bar and the river bottom range from sand to cobbles with a D_{50} of the gravel bar of 20 mm and 120 mm at the river bed (before truncation). Sampling was carried out during bankfull discharge of a snow-melt high flow ranging between 4 - 6 m^3/s with its typical diurnal fluctuations of flow. With flow velocities approaching 2 m/s and water depths of about 0.7 m it is nearly impossible to use a 3 by 3 inch or 6 by 6 inch hand held Helley-Smith sampler. Needless to say, those samples would not have represented the coarser fraction of the river sediments.

The big-frame net sampler

The big-frame net sampler used at Squaw Creek has a wooden frame 0.3 m by 1.6 m with a fisherman's net attached. The length of the net is 3 m and the mesh width was chosen to be 10 mm to reduce the pressure of flow on the sampler. At the measuring site the river is 8 m wide and spanned by a bridge under which a catwalk crosses the river at a distance of about 1 m above the river bottom, exactly above a small artificial water fall made by three logs to protect the bridge. Two vertical bars are wedged into these logs and fastened on the catwalk on their upper end to provide support for the sampler. Once lowered onto the river bottom the frame is pressed onto the bars by the flow. After sampling, the frame is vertically winched up. When the frame is just out of the flow one of the vertical bars is removed. The frame floats downstream on the water surface dragging the net behind. Held by a thick rope the sampler is maneuvered to the next shallow bank where it can be emptied. One measuring cycle (the actual sampling time not included) takes about half an hour and three persons to handle it.

Sample sizes and time resolution

This sampling device provides bed load samples representing a fairly wide part of the active cross-section. The grain-size distributions sampled range from 10 - 180 mm, thus covering the coarser part of mountain river sediments. Time resolution is such that one five-minute sample can be taken every half hour. Sample weights reached 90 kg, thus providing (nearly) enough coarse bed load material for a grain-size analysis. Owing to unpredictable transport rates the sampling durations were kept rather short so that sample weights did not reach the standards set by IBBEKEN (1974) and CHURCH et al.(1987).

Time and location of samples taken

The bar sediments were taken as a bulk sample from a gravel bar that begins to be flooded at $Q_{1.8}$. The river bed was analyzed by an areal sample. At spring high flow 24 samples of bed load were taken with the big frame net sampler. In order to investigate temporal variations of bed load transport the grain-size properties of serial samples were analysed. During one nocturnal flow five consecutive samples of bed load were taken within a seven-hour interval. During the other night another series of seven samples was gained over a twelve-hour period.

DATA ANALYSIS

Sieving and grain-size distribution

All samples (bed load, gravel bar and bed surface) were sieved at half phi intervals. In order to compare grain-size properties of the river bed and the bar with actually transported bed load all samples were commonly truncated at 11.2 mm (-3.5 phi) because particles smaller than 10 mm passed through the mesh width of the net. The grain-size frequency distribution of the three sediment units are shown in fig.1.

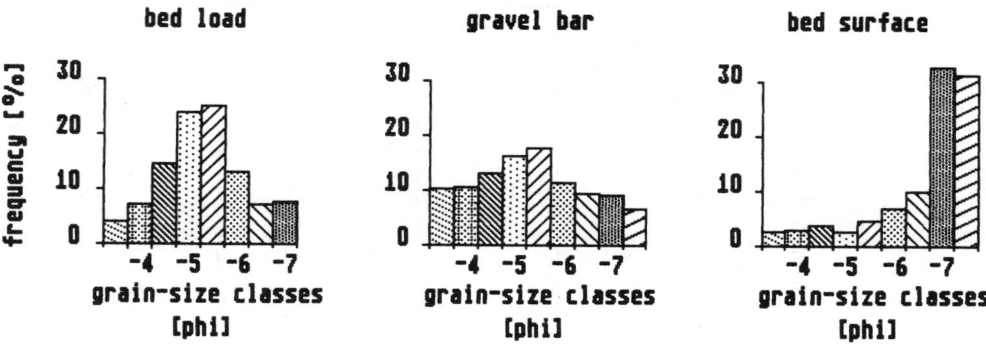

FIG. 1 Grain-size frequency distributions of the sediment units bed load material, gravel bar and bed surface layer.

The bed surface layer

The grain-size distribution of the surface layer of the river bed is typically skewed towards the coarser grain-sizes as indicated by SUTHERLAND (1987), while all the other grain-sizes are about equally well represented by weight. Some of the big particles are blocky and wedged into the surface layer, improving its stability. Nevertheless, according to the definition by ANDREWS & PARKER (1987) the surface layer of Squaw Creek should be called rather pavement than armour, as the bed, though seemingly stable, changed its form during "normal" high flows with a recurrence interval of less than two years and developed a pronounced pool-riffle situation within the measuring reach.

The gravel bar

The grain-size distribution of the gravel bar as a depositional structure of a former (large?) transport event shows that all the particles present in the pavement can be transported, but favourably, the transport concentrates on pebbles. The grain-size composition of the gravel bar is symmetrical and Gaussian distributed. Most of the gravel bar's coarse material is in the pebble range between 32 and 45 mm.

Bed load material

The average grain-size distribution of the seven consecutive samples of current coarse bed load material taken during typical high flow in the night of May 24 - 25 basically has the same grain-size composition as the gravel bar. The concentration of pebbles is more pronounced showing their high and preferential mobility. These pebbles seemingly have the least chance of settling in a "hiding place" between two cobbles. Thus, given a sufficient competence of flow, it is pebbles that are transported most frequently.

Comparison of consecutive bed load samples

The temporal variation of bed load transport rates and the grain-size composition of consecutive samples is plotted on the hydrograph (fig. 2). Transport rates and grain-size distributions fluctuate most

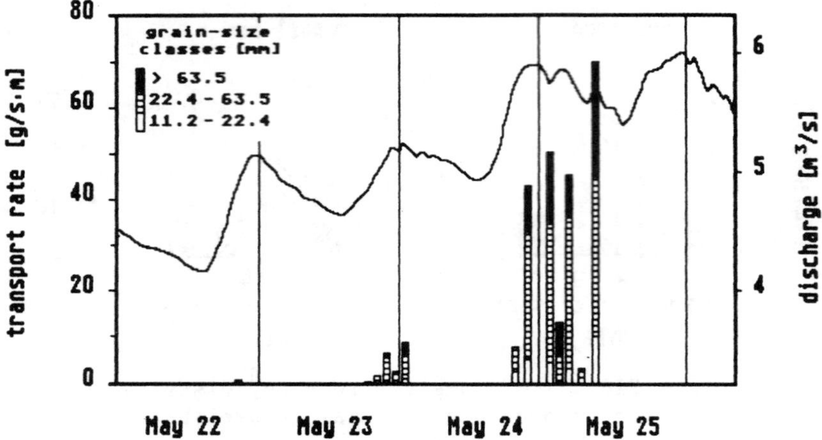

FIG. 2 Consecutive samples of bed load during high flow.

strongly during the falling limb of a daily high flow (see the morning of May 25, 1988). Though discharge was not stationary its variation between 5.5 and 6 m^3/s cannot be made responsible for such strong variations of transport rates, especially as high transport rates do not necessarily coincide with high discharges but show the typically wide scatter (1 order of magnitude) on a plot bed load transport rate versus discharge (fig. 3). The fluctuation of transport

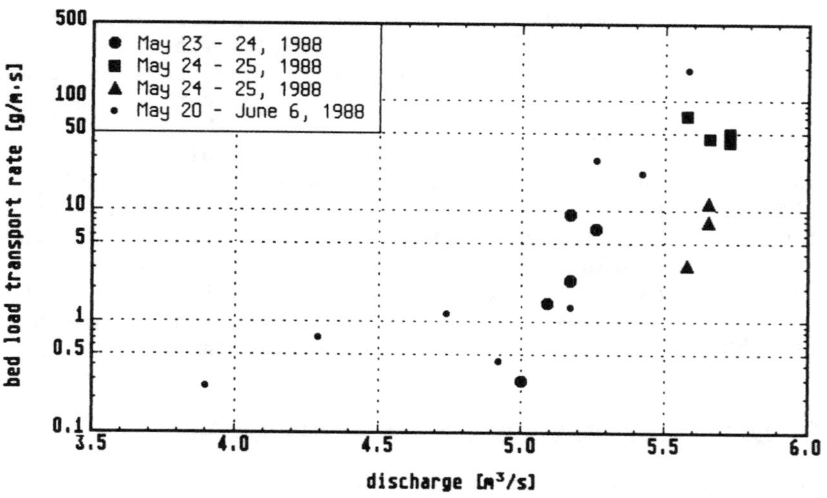

FIG.3 Bed load transport rates versus discharge.

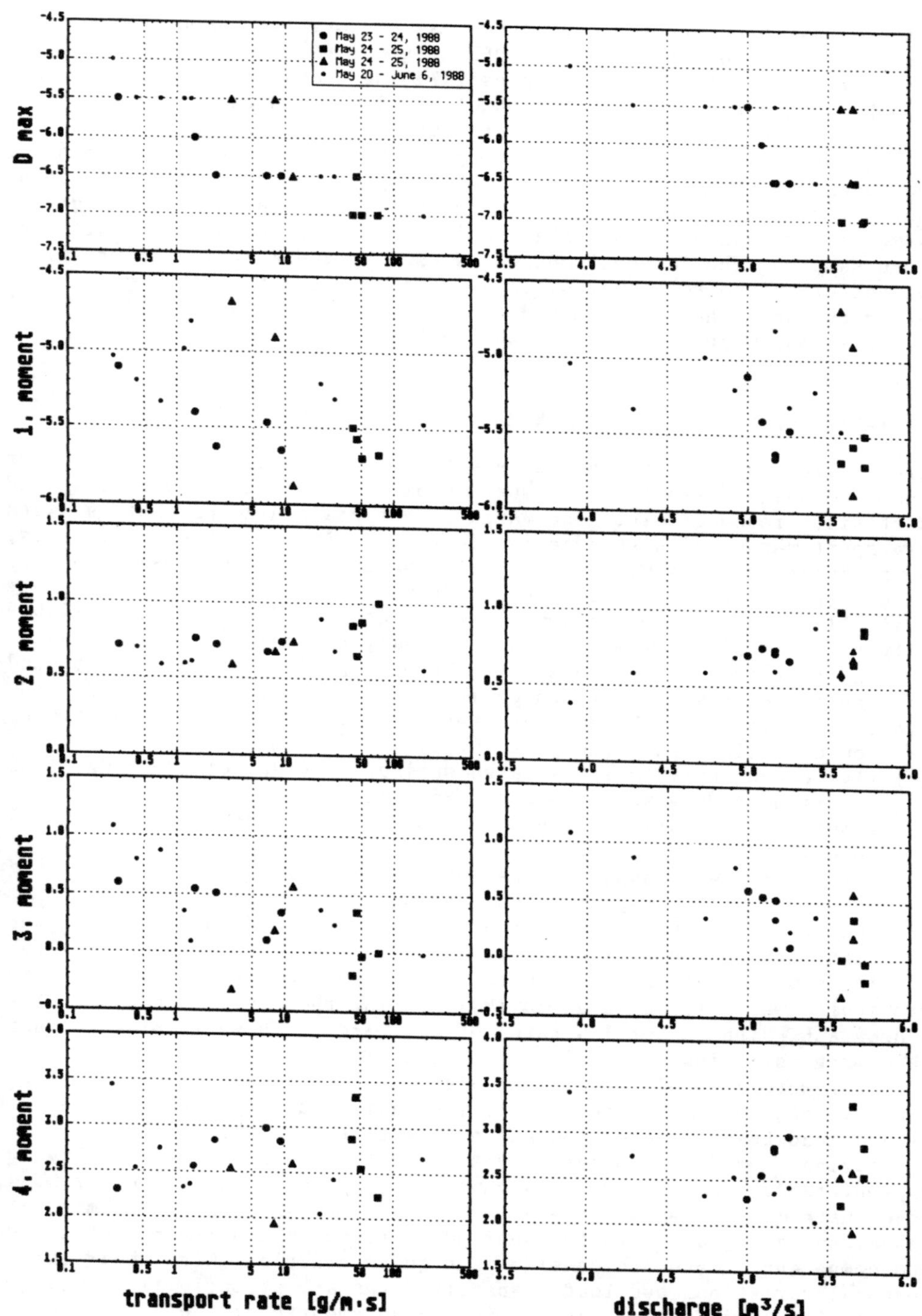

FIG. 4 The variability of grain-size parameters with bed load transport rate and discharge.

rates has been described by numerous authors representing several theories for bed load waves (GOMEZ et al. 1989). In order to gain an insight into processes causing oscillating transport rates at Squaw Creek the grain-size distribution of bed load samples was analyzed.

The grain-size frequency distributions revealed that the spectra of consecutive samples varied strongly. While some spectra seemed to be evenly Gaussian distributed, others gave the impression of being cut off at their coarse part. To quantify these variations in grain-size distribution a grain-size analysis was carried out for all bed load samples. The "moment" method as used by SCHLEYER (1987) proved to be better suited to the problems associated with truncated grain-size distributions than the method proposed by FOLK & WARD (1957). All calculations were based on 1/4 phi units.

Variation of grain-sizes and grain-size parameters

Grain-size parameters examined are the D_{max} size class and the four moments which correspond to mean diameter, sorting, skewness and kurtosis, respectively. The variation of grain-size parameters with transport rates and discharge is plotted in fig. 4. D_{max} size class, mean, sorting and symmetry generally increase with bed load transport rate, though the data scatter widely. The grain-size parameters basically show the same tendency with discharge. However, the variability of grain-size parameters is especially obvious for large flows.

In order to clarify the scatter between grain-size parameters and transport rates or flow respectively and to try to identify the processes involved, the data are separated into four groups according to flow conditions and transport rates:

(1) five consectutive samples taken during the night of 23-24 May 1988 at discharges between 5.0 and 5.26 m^3/s.

(2) samples taken during the night of 24 - 25 May 1988 with discharges between 5.58 - 5.73 m^3/s

    (a) and large transport rates between 41 - 72 g/m·s.

    (b) and small transport rates ranging from 3 - 12 g/m·s.

(3) the rest of the samples from the beginning and the end of the high-flow period with discharges ranging between 3.9 and 5.8 m^3/s.

The samples of group # 1 with relatively small rates of bed load transport were taken consecutively during the rising limb of the hydrograph with rather low rates of discharge. These samples do not show much variation in sorting (2nd moment), but all the other grain-size parameters, their D_{max}, mean diameter (1st moment), symmetry (3rd moment) and kurtosis (4th moment) increase regularly with the amount of bed load being transported and even with the amount of flow.

During heavier flow (group # 2) bed load transport is highly unpredictable. Not only the amount but also the composition of bed load material varies extremely with flow. Though the upper limit of the amount and grain-size transported is fixed by the river's capacity and competence, everything else is highly variable. With their large temporal variations bed load transport rates are strongly fluctuating.

Samples of group # 2a comprising large amounts of bed load have a large D_{max} and mean, moderate sorting but good symmetry. These samples resemble an equilibrium transport (ANDREWS & PARKER, 1987). By contrast, samples of group # 2b with small bed load transport rates have a dearth of coarse material and a low mean particle diameter.

They are better sorted and more strongly skewed in either direction than the bigger samples of the previous group 2a. As the bedload of group 2b was moved within the same range of discharges as the large bed load samples, these small samples indicate a selective transport of finer material (GOMEZ, 1983). Those abrupt changes in bed load quantity and quality that are not matched by discharge variations were observed in consecutive samples of bed load spaced in 1-2 hour intervals. At Squaw Creek they correspond with wavelike transport measured continuously by the magnetic tracer technique. Bed load waves are especially conspicuous on the falling limbs of the daily high flows (ERGENZINGER et al. 1983; CUSTER et al. 1987; BUNTE et al. 1987).

CONCLUSION

During rising discharge of moderate flows the quantity and the grain-size distribution of bed load increases regularly according to the river's growing competence and capacity. The force of the flow is the main factor controlling the amount and quality of bed load.

After the discharge has exceeded a threshold value of about 5.5 m^3/s at Squaw Creek the river's capacity is high enough to transport most of the bed material present. But though the strength of flow is sufficient cobbles and bulks of gravel are only transported temporarly because interactions between grain-sizes (hiding, exposure) hamper the direct conversion of stream flow energy into motion of bed load.

According to the findings described above the fluctuating transport at Squaw Creek can be interpreted as the result of switching between selective transport and equilibrium transport. The reason for this alternation may be partly explained with reference to ANDRREW'S & PARKER'S (1987) theory.

During the rising stage the pavement is coarsened by selectively transporting the finer material (small skewed samples of group 2b). This roughening of the surface is a prerequisite for the onset of equilibrium transport. When the fines are winnowed out the cobbles become fully exposed to flow and are transported, leaving smaller material below them unprotected and thus exposed to flow and transported as well (large symmetrical samples of group 2a). In contrast to ANDREWS & PARKER (1987) equilibrium transport at Squaw Creek is not a self-supporting continuously sustained process but an intermittent process uneven in space and time.

For rivers like Squaw Creek the process of coarse material bed load transport may be explained as follows: when the local scour is deep enough erosion will cease owing to a decrease in shear stress or even owing to a smoothing of the surface by a depletion of cobbles. Having reached an area of reduced shear stress somewhere downstream, the big particles will settle and locally provide a rougher surface in which the smaller material can come to rest as well. Owing to this deposition the river bottom locally aggradates decreasing the flow depth and increasing shear stress. A cyclic process of local deposition and erosion is produced which in the case of a slightly supply-limited river like Squaw Creek might be responsible for wave-like bed load transport phenomena. To test this hypothesis more serial representative samples of coarse bed load material have to be analysed. Future work needs to concentrate on dimensions and speed of bed load waves as well as on classifications of rivers regarding their bed load availibility.

ACKNOWLEDGEMENTS Earlier parts of this project have been funded by the German Research Council. I would like to thank P. Carling, M.Glaister, C. Berry and L. Tuck for their tremendous help with the field work. P. Ergenzinger and S. Custer contributed to this paper by stimulating discussions. A. Bartholomä provided much help with the calculation of the grain-size parameters. All the work could not have been done without the Swingle family in Bozeman, Mt. (USA) who with unlimited helpfulness provided solutions to the continuously arising problems.

REFERENCES

ANDREWS,E.D. & PARKER,G.(1987): Formation of a coarse surface layer as a response to gravel mobility. - *Sediment Transport in Gravel Bed Rivers.* C.R.Thorne; J.C.Bathurst & R.D.Hey (eds.). John Wiley & Sons, New York.

BUGOSH,N. & CUSTER,S.G. (1989): The effect of a log-jam burst on bedload transport and channel characteristics in a headwaters stream. - Proceedings of the Symposium on Headwater Hydrology, held at Missoula, Mt., W.W.Woessner & D.F.Potts (eds.).

BUNTE,K.; CUSTER,S.G.; ERGENZINGER,P. & SPIEKER,R.(1987): Messung des Grobgeschiebetransportes mit der Magnettracertechnik. *Deutsche Gewässerkundliche Mitteilungen.* **31**, 2/3: 60-67.

CHURCH,M.A.; McLEAN,D.G. & WALCOTT,J.F. (1987): Bed load sampling and analysis. - *Sediment Transport in Gravel Bed Rivers.* C.R.Thorne; J.C.Bathurst & R.D.Hey (eds.), John Wiley & Sons, New York.

CUSTER,S.G.; ERGENZINGER,P.E.; BUGOSH,N. & ANDERSON,B.C. (1987): Electromagnetic detection of pebble transport in streams: A method for measurement of sediment transport waves. - *Recent Developments in Fluvial Sedimentology* (F.Ethridge & R.Flores eds.) *Society of Paleontologists and Mineralogists, Special Publication* **39**: 21-26.

ERGENZINGER,P. & CUSTER,S.G.(1983): Determination of bedload transport using naturally magnetic tracers: First experiences at Squaw Creek, Gallatin County, Montana. - *Water Resources Research*, **19,1**: 187-193.

FOLK,R.L. & WARD,W.C. (1957): Brazos River Bar: a study in the significance of grain size parameters. - *Journal of Sedimentary Petrology*, **27,1**: 3-26.

GOMEZ,B. (1983): Temporal variation in bedload transport rates: the effect of progressive bed-armouring. - *Earth Surface Processes and Landforms*, **8**: 41-54.

GOMEZ.B.; NAFF,R.L. & HUBBLE,D.W. (1989): Temporal variations in bed-load transport rates associated with the migration of bed-forms. - *Earth Surface Processes and Landforms*, **14**: 135-156.

IBBEKEN,H.(1974): A simple sieving and splitting device for field analysis of coarse grained sediment. - *Journal of Sedimentary Petrology*, **44,3**: 939-946.

SCHLEYER,R. (1987): The goodness-of-fit to ideal Gaus and Rosin distribution: a new grain size parameter. - *Journal of Sedimentary Petrology*, **57,5**: 871-880.

SUTHERLAND,A.J. (1987): Static armour layers by selective erosion. - *Sediment Transport in Gravel Bed Rivers.* C.R.Thorne; J.C. Bathurst & R.D. Hey (eds.), John Wiley & Sons, New York.

Hydrology in Mountainous Regions. I - Hydrological Measurements; the Water Cycle
(Proceedings of two Lausanne Symposia, August 1990). IAHS Publ. no. 193, 1990.

Mesures des débits solides et liquides sur des bassins versants expérimentaux de montagne

J.P. CAMBON
Centre National du Machinisme Agricole, du Génie Rural, des Eaux et des Forêts, B.P. 31, Le Tholonet, 13612 Aix-en-Provence Cédex
N. MATHYS, M. MEUNIER, J.E. OLIVIER
Centre National du Machinisme Agricole, du Génie Rural, des Eaux et des Forêts, 2 rue de la Papeterie, B.P. 76, 38402 Saint-Martin-d'Hères Cédex

RESUME Les bassins expérimentaux de Draix étant situés dans une zone à climat contrasté et dans des terrains particulièrement érodables, les installations de mesure ont été conçues en tenant compte de ces contraintes. Malgré les précautions prises il s'avère qu'aucun des dispositifs mis en place à l'heure actuelle ne donnent une entière satisfaction. De nouveaux appareils sont actuellement en cours d'étude en vue d'améliorer la pérennité et la fiabilité des mesures.

PRESENTATION DU BASSIN VERSANT DE DRAIX

Le bassin versant de Draix est implanté dans les Préalpes françaises du Sud à quelques kilomètres de Digne. Destinées plus particulièrement à l'étude des phénomènes d'érosion, les installations comprennent essentiellement un réseau de pluviographes et un réseau de stations hydrométiques orientés tant vers la mesure des débits liquides que solides (Mura et al. 1988).

Les stations s'étagent à une altitude comprise entre 850 m et 1200 m. De ce fait, les appareils mis en place en vue de la mesure des phénomènes hydro-météorologiques sont soumis à un climat assez contrasté puisqu'on a relevé des températures extrêmes de - 26°C et + 65°C à l'intérieur des abris destinés à recevoir les appareillages, tandis que les amplitudes journalières y sont assez fréquemment de l'ordre de 40 °C au cours d'une même journée.

Les hivers y sont assez rigoureux pour entraîner un gel permanent pendant plusieurs journées consécutives, pouvant atteindre le mois, en particulier dans les fonds de vallées peu ensoleillés. En revanche, l'été typiquement méditerranéen connait des sécheresses sévères avec de longues périodes où l'écoulement est nul. Par contre des évènements pluviométriques intenses, caractéristiques de ce climat, peuvent se produire. Ils entrainent de brutales variations de débits : d'un écoulement nul à plusieurs m3/s en quelques minutes. Ces brutales variations de débits associées à la nature du terrain particulièrement érodable provoquent des transports solides importants.

Ce dernier point a été une des raisons qui ont présidé au choix du bassin de Draix pour mener à bien une expérimentation en milieu érodé. En revanche, il entraine des problèmes au niveau de la mesure des paramètres de l'écoulement. Chaque station d'observation hydrométrique (Mura et al., 1988) est constituée essentiellement par :
(a) un contrôle hydraulique autojaugeur (déversoir à mince paroi ou canal) ;
(b) un enregistreur de la hauteur d'eau à l'amont de ce contrôle ;
(c) un piège à sédiment du type plage de dépôt situé à l'amont des installations hydrométriques destiné d'une part à la protection de ces installations et à la mesure de ces mêmes sédiments ;
(d) un préleveur automatique d'échantillon permettant de mesurer la quantité de sédiments échappant à la plage de dépôt.

CONTROLE HYDRAULIQUE AUTOJAUGEUR

Dans le milieu torrentiel où sont situées les stations du bassin les transports solides sont contradictoirement le pôle d'intérêt et un facteur perturbant pour la mesure des autres paramètres. Pour assurer ces mesures, on procède au piégeage des sédiments à l'amont des points d'observation des autres paramètres. L'expérience a montré que les canaux autojaugeurs de type Parshall sont alors suffisamment autodégravant.

Quand est apparu l'intérêt d'effectuer des mesures à l'amont des plages de dépôt, un seuil à fond horizontal mais à berges inclinées a été utilisé. Il est en fait inadapté aux forts transports solides et va être remplacé par un canal à fond incliné, rejoignant ce qui existe ailleurs, notamment sur le Rio Cordon en Vénétie (Fattorelli et al., 1988) et sur l'Alptal près de Zurich (Zeller, 1987).

TEST DE LIMNIGRAPHES EXISTANTS

Limnigraphe à flotteur

Bien que simple et robuste, il se révèle mal adapté aux conditions des torrents de montagne pour deux raisons :

(a) en période de gel le flotteur se prend dans la glace et reste bloqué ; de plus, lorsque la glace fond, il peut arriver que le fonctionnement redémarre mais qu'une gaine de glace persistante fausse le libre jeu du flotteur. Le diagnostic de mauvais fonctionnement est alors difficile.

(b) la présence de transport solide est quasi rédhibitoire : pour assurer la flottaison, il faut une garde au fond de l'ordre de 10 cm ; et pour suivre les basses eaux, il faut l'établir en dessous du lit du cours d'eau, constituant ainsi une zone privilégiée de dépôts. Lorsqu'il y a colmatage, la décrue est évidemment faussée (cf. fig. 1 - hydrogrammes à la station du Francon). De plus, le colmatage peut conduire le flotteur à se coucher sur le flanc, faussant ainsi les mesures ; ce détarage est difficile à déceler et à corriger.

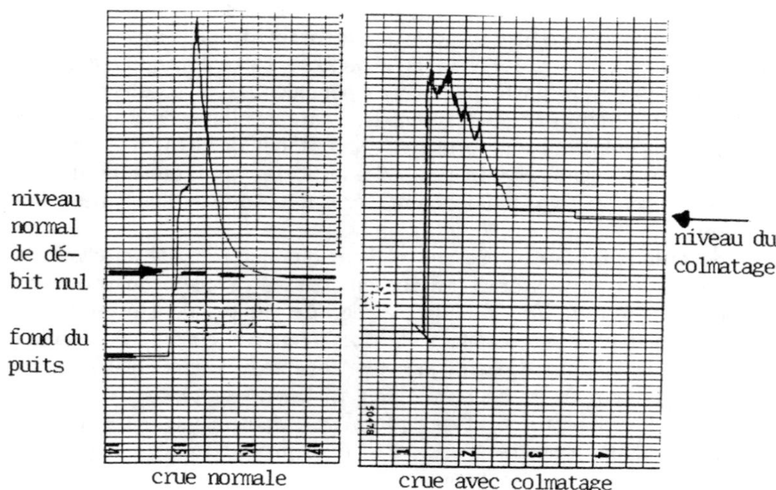

FIG. 1 Exemples de crues enregistrées sur appareil à flotteur.

Malgré ces problèmes, nous avons maintenu ce type d'enregistreurs sur diverses stations du bassin. Pour pallier les inconvénients, nous nous astreignons à un nettoyage hebdomadaire du puits de protection. En outre on a disposé à sa base un trépied sur lequel le flotteur vient se poser pendant l'étiage ce qui l'empêche de se coucher sur le flanc. Avec ces précautions, les mesures par appareils à flotteur sont une référence pour les autres méthodes. Mais la gestion en reste lourde et le risque de perte d'information lors de certaines décrues n'est pas totalement éliminé.

Limnigraphes à mesures de pression par injection d'air

Ce type d'appareil semblait, à l'origine, tout indiqué pour équiper à terme les différentes stations du BVRE. En effet, l'injection d'air assurant une purge du point de mesure, il semblait susceptible de chasser les dépôts et de permettre les mesures dès le zéro. Cet espoir s'est révélé illusoire, pour les raisons suivantes :

(a) en période de gel, la prise en masse entraîne, si la fourniture d'air se poursuit, une montée de la pression qui perturbe la mesure et peut même détériorer le capteur (fig. 2) ;

(b) l'effet de chasse est insuffisant à chasser les dépôts qui créent des obstructions et des turbulences ; le capteur les enregistre et le tracé devient aberrant (voir fig. 2) jusqu'au nettoyage de la prise et du canal jaugeur. Cet inconvénient est d'ailleurs noté assez souvent (Callede et al., 1989).

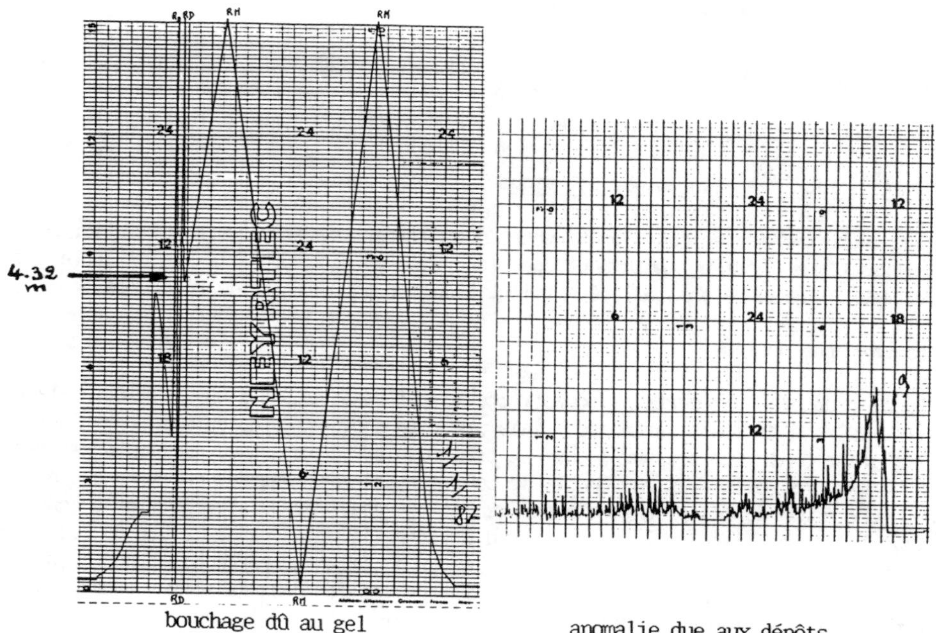

FIG. 2 Exemples de crues enregistrées sur l'appareil à injection d'air.

Limnigraphe à ultrasons aériens

Ce type de limnigraphe présente le gros avantage de n'avoir aucun élément en contact avec l'écoulement. Mais la célérité d'une onde ultrasonique dépend des paramètres climatiques. Sur le capteur utilisé, seule l'influence de la température est prise en compte par une mesure au niveau du capteur. Les hydrogrammes obtenus sont en fait entachés d'incertitude : on constate ainsi une baisse systématique de niveau (fig. 3) avant la montée de crue dont l'explication est encore problématique (refroidissement, humidité ?).

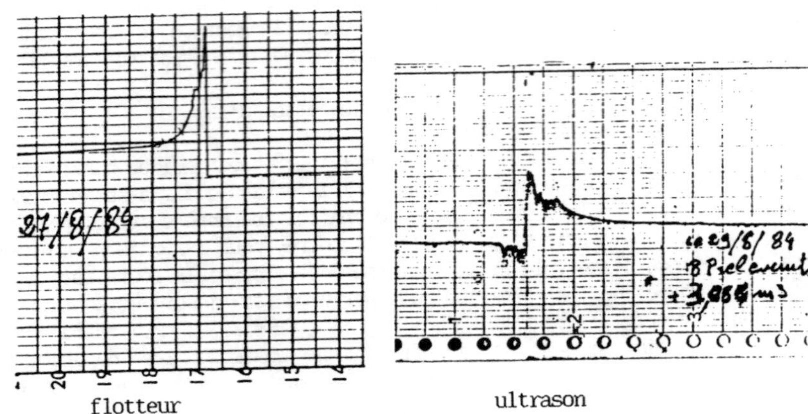

FIG. 3 Comparaison d'enregistrements par flotteur et ultrason aérien.

RECHERCHE DE SOLUTIONS

Quelques solutions possibles sont en cours de tests à l'heure actuelle.

Amélioration des mesures par ultrasons

Une recherche est en cours pour tenter d'améliorer la mesure par un émetteur-récepteur ultrasonique aérien, notamment par la prise en compte de la température à divers niveaux. Une autre possibilité est l'utilisation d'un étrier de référence.

Limnigraphe optique

Déjà proposée par certains constructeurs, l'utilisation d'un télémètre laser est intéressante dans son principe, mais présente a priori plusieurs inconvénients : la réflexion de la lumière sur l'eau est très faible, l'interface air-eau n'est pas plan mais est une surface en mouvement, le coût des télémètres laser est très élevé.

Une étude de ces problèmes a été réalisée (Pebay-Peyroula, 1989) et a conclu à la faisabilité de l'appareil à condition d'utiliser le principe de mesure du temps de vol ou du déphasage, de ne mesurer que le retour du faisceau réfléchi et non celui de la lumière diffusée (en eaux agitées, les intensités des deux faisceaux peuvent avoir le même ordre de grandeur, soit 10^{-4} à 10^{-5} fois l'intensité incidente). Un tel limnigraphe présenterait de nombreux avantages par rapport au limnigraphe ultrasonique aérien, essentiellement dus à la constance de la vitesse de la lumière ; par contre, il semble difficile d'obtenir un coût inférieur à 2 ou 3 fois celui des appareils existants.

ELLAN - Echelle Limnigraphique à Lecture Automatique et Numérique

Appareil entièrement nouveau et breveté, cet appareil semble très prometteur pour les écoulements fortement chargés car il ne comporte aucune pièce mobile ; il est composé d'une échelle limnimétrique graduée par des électrodes qu'on fait parcourir en séquences par un générateur d'impulsions. L'eau conduisant mieux l'électricité que l'air, le courant passe uniquement par les électrodes immergées qu'il suffit de compter pour obtenir le niveau de l'eau. Diverses astuces permettent de réduire le nombre de fils de connexion (Pebay-Peyroula, Meunier, 1989).

Ce principe offre un grand nombre de possibilités tant pour la réalisation électronique que pour la forme, la taille des appareils ainsi que la précision des mesures donnée par la distance entre électrodes (quand l'appareil est en position verticale). Testé successivement au laboratoire, sur rivières torrentielles, sur les torrents de Draix, cet appareil constitue un espoir sérieux de fournir une possibilité de mesures de niveaux sur les torrents difficiles dès lors qu'une berge rigide en permet l'installation.

LES TRANSPORTS SOLIDES

Le dispositif de mesures a été décrit par ailleurs (Mathys, Meunier 1988, Mura et al. 1988) ; nous ne présenterons donc que les améliorations nouvelles ou les pistes de recherche en cours.

Mesure du transport en suspension à partir de capteurs de pression

La relation fondamentale de l'hydrostatique qui relie la hauteur de l'écoulement à la pression quand on connaît la masse volumique du fluide, pourrait être utilisée pour relier la pression à la masse volumique si l'on connaît la hauteur de l'écoulement (Meunier, 1987). En fait la relation qui relie ces trois variables dépend du profil de concentration sur la verticale et vraisemblablement également du mode de transport. La figure 4 montre en effet que la prise en compte de la densité du mélange, calculée à partir de mesures de concentration au fond, donne des hauteurs (donc des débits) plus faibles que ce qui est mesuré avec le limnigraphe ultrasonique. Les

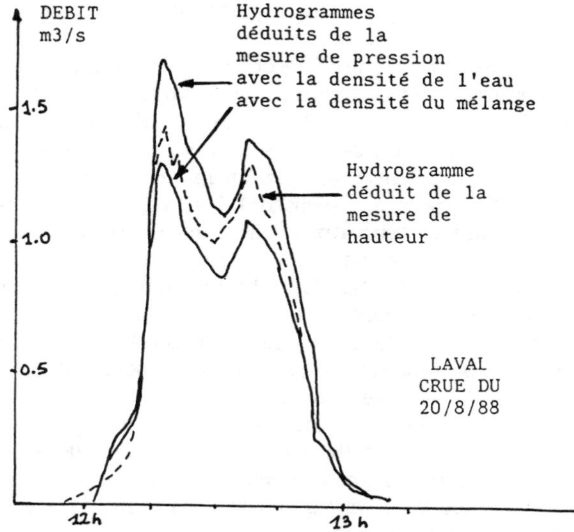

FIG. 4 Hydrogramme tenant compte de la densité du fluide et hydrogramme déduit de la mesure de hauteur.

concentrations calculées à partir de ces mesures sont d'ailleurs assez systématiquement inférieures aux valeurs mesurées (fig. 5). Les essais au laboratoire (Callede et al, 1989), confirment la possibilité de mesurer des transports en suspension par capteurs de pression différentiel dans le cas d'un écoulement ascendant, à la condition que les capteurs de pression soient très précis. Il ne semble pas encore certain que ceci sera possible in situ (Meunier, 1990). Une expérimentation sur le site de Draix va donc être entreprise pour connaître la réponse à cette question.

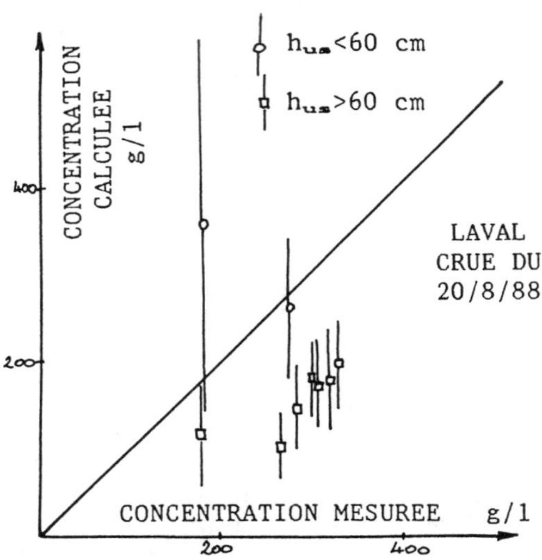

FIG. 5 Comparaison des concentrations calculées et mesurées en site réel.

Méthode simplifiée de mesure des concentrations à partir des prélèvements

La mesure des matières en suspension par prélèvements automatiques, est asservie à la fois au niveau de l'écoulement et au temps. Ces appareils ont un fonctionnement capricieux, mais lorsqu'ils marchent, ils donnent une bonne description de l'évolution de la concentration au cours des crues (Fig. 6, Mathys et al. 1989). Par contre le recueil des échantillons, leur transport et la mesure de la concentration au laboratoire (mesure de volume, pesage, séchage à l'étuve, pesage, etc...) est une opération contraignante et lourde. Nous avons donc mis au point une méthode plus simple permettant la mesure de la concentration à partir de celles des hauteurs de mélanges Hm et du sédiment décanté Hs. La relation qui lie le rapport des deux hauteurs et la concentration a été obtenue de la façon suivante :

(a) A partir de flacons de mélanges à la concentration préétablie, on a déterminé les courbes de décantation en fonction du temps pour deux séries de volumes (250 et 500 ml) et on a vérifié que les résultats ne sont pas significativement différents entre les deux séries, ce qui a déjà été constaté ailleurs (LCHF, 1987). Par contre les rapports Hs/Hm mesurés après cette décantation statique diffèrent de ceux constatés sur les prélèvements recueillis à Draix. Une nouvelle mesure, après transport de quelques heures, confirme que la différence provient du tassement supplémentaire provoqué par un transport en voiture.

(b) Une analyse statistique des rapports Hs/Hm pour les concentrations mesurées à Draix donnent les résultats suivants :

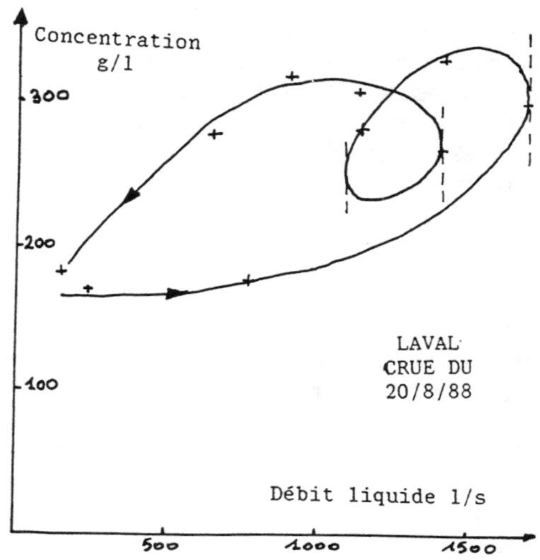

FIG. 6 Relation entre la concentration et le débit.

- il ne faut pas prendre en compte les faibles concentrations inférieures à 30 g/1 à cause des effets liés à la forme arrondie du fond des flacons de prélèvement (Hs inférieur à 0,5 cm) ;
- on obtient une excellente corrélation entre la concentration et le rapport Hs/Hm sur les 108 points restants de l'échantillon : c = 1064 (Hs/Hm) - 28 R^2 = 0,981 Ecart Standard = 12,9
- cette formule est valable pour les deux types de flacons utilisés : leurs formes diffèrent peu, il est vrai.

(c) Les deux séries de valeurs (concentrations constituées au laboratoire et concentrations recueillies à Draix) sont concordantes. En les agglomérant, on obtient une nouvelle relation statistique très proche de celle qu'on a obtenue ci-dessus.

(d) Pour les concentrations supérieures à 50 g/1 (Hs > 1 cm si Hm = 15 cm), on peut donc calculer la concentration en mesurant simplement les deux hauteurs Hs et Hm à condition que la décantation soit suffisamment avancée. On utilise alors soit la relation :

$$c = 874\ (Hs/Hm) - 22,\ R^2 = 0{,}985$$

si on fait les mesures sur place (sans transport), soit la relation :

$$c = 1070\ (Hs/Hm) - 30$$

si on fait les mesures au laboratoire après quelques heures de transport.

SYNTHESE ET CONCLUSIONS

Les mesures de débits solides et liquides sur des torrents de montagne aux écoulements éphémères sont difficiles et aléatoires. Aucun appareil classique ne donnant entièrement satisfaction, des recherches ont été entreprises pour mettre au point des appareils basés sur des principes nouveaux (ELLAN), pour améliorer des appareils existants et des pistes de recherches nouvelles ont été explorées (limnigraphe optique et mesures des MES par capteurs de pression différentiels).

Certaines de ces recherches peuvent améliorer la situation actuelle, notamment en matière de mesure des débits liquides ; par contre la mesure des débits solides reste un problème très difficile à résoudre.

REFERENCES

CALLEDE, CHARTIER, JACCON (1989) Contribution à la mesure des écoulements très chargés. Utilisation de capteurs de pression pour la détermination en continu des transports en suspension. Rapport. Convention MRT/CEMAGREF/ORSTOM, Novembre 89, ORSTOM, Montpellier - France.

FATTORELLI, LENZI, MARCHI, KELLER (1988) An experimental station for automatic recording of water and sediment discharge in a small alpine watershed. Journal des Sciences Hydrologiques. 33.6.12/1988.

L.C.H.F. (1987) Synthèse des connaissances sur le tassement et la rhéologie des vases. Rapport. Service Technique Central de la Direction des Ponts et des Voies Navigables, Compiègne - France.

MATHYS, MEUNIER, GUET (1989) Mesure et interprétation du processus d'érosion dans les marnes des Alpes du Sud à l'échelle de la petite ravine. La Houille Blanche. N° 3/4/1989.

MEUNIER (1987) Etude des écoulements très chargés. in : Compte rendu de recherche n° 1 en érosion et hydraulique torrentielle. BVRE de Draix. Rapport. Septembre 87. CEMAGREF/ONF/RTM, Grenoble - France.

MEUNIER (1990) Examen de la possibilité de mesures du débit des matières en suspension par l'utilisation de capteurs de pression. Février 90. Note interne CEMAGREF, Grenoble - France.

MURA, CAMBON, COMBES, MEUNIER, OLIVIER (1988) La gestion du bassin versant expérimental de Draix pour la mesure de l'érosion, Porto Alegre, Décembre 88, AIHS Public. N° 174, 1988.

PEBAY-PEYROULA (1989) Limnimètres optiques, faisabilité en fonction des caractéristiques de la surface d'un cours d'eau relatives à la réflexion et à la diffusion d'un faisceau lumineux. Rapport. UJF. Laboratoire de Spectrométrie Physique, Septembre 89, CEMAGREF, Grenoble - France.

PEBAY-PEYROULA, MEUNIER (1989) Etude, réalisation et essais d'une échelle limnigraphique à lecture analogique et numérique ELLAN. Rapport. CEMAGREF/UJF, Laboratoire de Spectrométrie Physique, Décembre 89, CEMAGREF, Grenoble - France.

ZELLER (1987) : Hydraulic research at the Swiss Federal Institute of Forestry Research. Wasser Energie Lüft, 79 Jahrang, 1987. Heft 7/8.

Hydrology in Mountainous Regions. I - Hydrological Measurements; the Water Cycle (Proceedings of two Lausanne Symposia, August 1990). IAHS Publ. no. 193, 1990.

Seuil jaugeur adapté aux petits bassins versants à fort transport solide

O. CAYLA & P. JEHANNO - Société d'Etudes et d'Applications Hydrauliques, 6 rue de Lorraine, 38130 Echirolles, GRENOBLE, FRANCE

M. OUAAR - Agence Nationale des Ressources Hydrauliques, Clairbois, Avenue Mohammadia, Bir Mourad Rais, ALGER, Algérie

RESUME On propose un seuil composite dont la loi hauteur-débit est contrôlée par les nombreux jaugeages effectués sur une station existante. Il est constitué :

(a) d'un seuil épais rectangulaire de 3 m de large échancré d'un Parshall 1,6". Cet ensemble de base permet la mesure des débits à moins de 7 % près si les cotes sont lues à 1 cm près, dans la gamme 90 l/s à 2 m³/s. Les débits inférieurs à 90 l/s sont très correctement mesurés également,

(b) d'un seuil épais rectangulaire de mesure des crues, échancré du dispositif de base. Les débits sont estimés à 5 à 7 % près suivant la longueur du seuil (à optimiser en fonction du débit maximal à mesurer).

Le dispositif est calé sur le profil en long de la rivière de façon à éviter l'engravement et l'ennoiement en crue.

INTRODUCTION

Le problème se pose en Algérie de mesurer correctement les débits et les transports solides de petits bassins versants (moins de 20 km²) situés en général en zone de collines ou de montagnes.

Le réseau hydrologigue algérien comporte systématiquement :

(a) un limnigraphe à bulles et une batterie d'échelles lue régulièrement,

(b) des jaugeages au moulinet en étiage et en crue,

(c) des prélèvements à la bouteille pour mesure des transports solides en suspension et pour analyse chimique (salinité).

Pour les petites rivières, cette procédure générale est mise en défaut par l'impossibilité de jauger des crues fugaces.

Divers types de seuils précalibrés ont été installés au cours des années, dont certains ont été jaugés régulièrement ; on dispose ainsi d'une abondante matière pour étudier le problème général des seuils jaugeurs dans le cas de rivières à fort transport solide.

Le choix du type de seuil jaugeur a été effectué sur la base des éléments suivants :

(a) l'analyse des stations hydrométriques sur petits bassins versants algériens, après visite des stations et mise au point des lois hauteur-débit qui s'y rattachent,
(b) une analyse bibliographique sur les seuils jaugeurs de toute nature.

OBJECTIFS ET CRITERES DE CONCEPTION

L'objet du seuil jaugeur est, bien sûr, la mesure en continu (limnigraphe) ou discrète (échelle) du débit de la rivière. La mesure du débit est indirecte, c'est-à-dire que la valeur du débit est déduite de la mesure du niveau auquel on fait ensuite correspondre un débit au moyen de la loi hauteur-débit. En conséquence, le seuil doit répondre aux critères ou contraintes de la liste suivante :

(a) la loi hauteur-débit du seuil doit être constante dans le temps,
(b) le seuil doit permettre de mesurer toute la plage de débits attendus, avec une sensibilité acceptable, notamment les faibles débits qui représentent souvent une part importante de l'apport annuel,
(c) la loi hauteur-débit doit être prédéterminée afin d'éviter les jaugeages nécessaires à la calibration du seuil,
(d) le seuil doit être capable de faire transiter les matériaux solides afin d'éviter les dépôts susceptibles d'obturer la prise du limnigraphe ou de détarer la station par modification des sections d'écoulement. Le problème est particulièrement aigu en Algérie : on a observé l'écoulement de boues (1 kg/litre !) sur lesquelles flottent des blocs rocheux,
(e) pour que la loi hauteur-débit soit prédéterminée, on peut choisir soit un seuil standard ayant fait l'objet d'essais et connu par bibliographie, soit un type de seuil existant, équipant une des stations visitées qui offre satisfaction du point de vue de son fonctionnement et dont la loi hauteur-débit est connue par une série de jaugeages fiables,
(f) le seuil ne doit pas être équipé de parties mobiles (par exemple plaque avec échancrure pour mesure des faibles débits), ce type de dispositif entraînant souvent des erreurs (périodes de changement de gamme inconnues, etc.).

ANALYSE DES SEUILS EXISTANTS EN ALGERIE

Les seuils concernés représentent un large éventail de types de seuils : des seuils normalisés (Parshall, Neyrpic) ou des seuils particuliers (seuils plats à une ou plusieurs échancrures).
On déduit de l'analyse de ces seuils les conclusions suivantes :

(a) La pelle, située à l'amont immédiat de certains seuils, ne joue pas son rôle car elle est rapidement colmatée par les sédiments transportés par la rivière. Les seuils comprenant une pelle à l'amont sont donc à rejeter pour les futures stations (par exemple : seuils Neyrpic).

(b) Pour mesurer toute la plage de débits, un seuil composé d'un élément unique (Parshall, seuil plat) n'est pas suffisant. On est donc amené à considérer un seuil constitué d'une combinaison de seuils simples.

(c) Le seuil doit être placé suffisamment haut par rapport au lit de la rivière d'une part pour être hors de l'influence aval pour toute la gamme des débits attendus, d'autre part, pour être hors de la frange de "respiration" du lit de la rivière (c'est-à-dire des fluctuations de niveau dues à la succession de dépôts et de reprise des sédiments).

(d) La partie aval doit être convenablement protégée contre les érosions (plusieurs exemples de stations endommagées).

ETUDE BIBLIOGRAPHIQUE

Trois publications au moins présentent une synthèse intéressante sur les ouvrages de jaugeages (voir références).

Il se confirme que les dispositifs existant actuellement en Algérie représentent bien la gamme des possibilités, à l'exception du seuil triangulaire épais sans pelle. Ce seuil ne semble pas avoir été l'objet d'expérimentations en laboratoire ou sur le terrain. Après étude, il s'avère d'ailleurs que sa construction revient nettement plus chère que celle du dispositif préconisé dans cet article.

SEUILS RETENUS

Parmi les stations existantes, 2 types de seuil ont été retenus comme base de conception des futurs seuils jaugeurs : le seuil épais plat, sans pelle, et le canal Parshall.

1. Seuil épais rectangulaire

La pelle amont du seuil est nulle (radier amont au même niveau que le seuil ou colmatage du bassin amont au niveau du seuil).

Le point délicat de ce type de seuil est la mesure de la cote. Suivant l'emplacement des échelles, on mesure une hauteur d'eau comprise entre la hauteur critique (échelle sur le seuil) et la charge totale (échelle à l'amont du seuil).

Les seuils correctement jaugés présentent une loi hauteur-débit qui peut s'écrire :

$$Q = 1,5\ b\ z^{1,5} \quad \text{si } z = Z$$

$$Q = 2,75\ b\ z^{1,5} \quad \text{si } z = z_c$$

avec :

- Q Débit en m³ s^{-1}
- z Cote de l'eau mesurée à l'échelle, en m
- Z Charge hydraulique sur le seuil
- z_c Hauteur d'eau critique
- b Longueur du seuil, en m

2. Seuil combiné Parshall - seuil épais

Une station algérienne, Ain Berda sur l'oued Ressoul (100 km²), est construite sur ce principe ; de nombreux jaugeages au moulinet y ont été effectués.

La définition géométrique de ce seuil est donnée par la figure 1 ci-dessous :

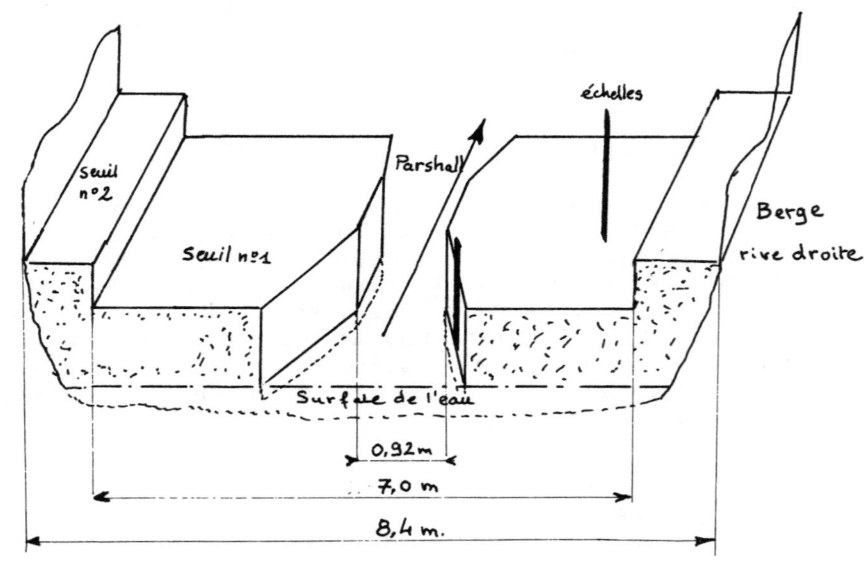

FIG. 1

La mesure des débits faibles à moyens est assurée par le Parshall, alors que les débits plus importants passent par un seuil plat.

La loi du seuil est alors une combinaison de deux lois : loi du Parshall et loi de seuil plat.

Dans le cas précis d'Ain Berda, on a raisonné, pour le calcul, en supposant un écoulement en tranches verticales indépendantes.

Les résultats des calculs sont les suivants :

. Parshall 3' :
Loi théorique :
$Q = 2,184\ z^{1,566}$ (pour $0,04 < z < 0,76$)

. Seuil épais :
Loi théorique : en prenant l'hypothèse que $z = z_c$ (hauteur critique) :
$Q = 2,75 \times b \times (z - 0,88)^{1,5}$
Si $0,88 < z < 1,20$ $b = 7 - 1 = 6$ m (seuil n° 1)

Si 1,20 < z, il faut rajouter un second seuil plat de largeur b' = 1,4 m (seuil n° 2).

Les résultats sont les suivants :

TABLEAU 1

z (m)	$Q_{Parshall}$ (m3/s)	Q seuil plat		Total (m3/s)	Mesures par jaugeages
		1	2		
0,88	1,788	0	-	1,79	1,67
0,96	2,049	0,37	-	2,42	-
1,00	2,184	0,68	-	2,86	2,8
1,20	2,906	2,99	0	5,90	5,8
1,30	3,294	4,49	0,12	7,90	7,8
1,40	3,70	6,19	0,34	10,23	10,4
1,50	4,12	8,05	0,63	12,80	13,0
1,70	5,01	12,25	1,36	18,62	19,0
2,00	6,47	19,56	2,75	28,78	28,5

En définitive, l'accord entre le calcul (colonne "total") et les mesures (colonne "mesures") est excellent. Les hypothèses prises en compte (cote échelle = cote critique, etc.) sont donc confirmées.

DIMENSIONNEMENT DU DISPOSITIF JAUGEUR

1. Critère de précision à obtenir

Il faut que l'on puisse mesurer toute la gamme des débits, de quelques litres par seconde à la crue rare (temps de retour 20 à 50 ans) avec une précision acceptable.

La mesure de cote est effectuée au mieux au cm près. Pour les très faibles débits, les jaugeages présentent une dispersion qui équivaut à une incertitude un peu supérieure au cm. Au-delà, l'erreur sur la courbe de tarage est de l'ordre de 10 %.

Nous allons donc baser notre calcul de dispositif jaugeur sur le principe suivant :

La lecture à 1 cm près doit conduire à une erreur inférieure à 10 % sur le débit

Pour les débits inférieurs à 10 l/s, on admettra une incertitude supérieure : des jaugeages au seau préciseront, si nécessaire, les écoulements très faibles.

En effet, on est limité par la dimension minimale "raisonnable" d'un Parshall de mesure des débits d'un bassin versant naturel : il ne faut pas que des objets divers (cailloux, branchages) puissent facilement se coincer dans le chenal jaugeur. La dimension minimale d'un Parshall 1'6" est de 46 cm, ce qui nous paraît la limite inférieure de cette dimension "raisonnable".

2. Conception du dispositif

La mesure d'étiage sera effectuée au moyen d'un Parshall 1'6".

Or, on dispose d'un tarage de contrôle pour la station d'Ain Berda constituée d'un Parshall de 3' enchâssé dans un seuil épais de 6 m.

Nous avons donc basé nos calculs sur un dispositif de base de mêmes proportions mais divisé par 2 :

Le dispositif de base est un Parshall 1'6" noyé dans un seuil épais de 3 m

Pour mesurer les crues, on ajoute à ce dispositif de base un seuil épais de longueur variable tel que le débit maximal à mesurer déverse sur le seuil, sous une charge inférieure ou égale à 3 m (par rapport à la base du Parshall).

Enfin, pour éviter tout problème d'engravement, on placera la base du Parshall 0,40 à 0,50 m au-dessus du lit de la rivière.

L'ensemble du dispositif intéressera donc une hauteur maximale de 3,50 m.

Une surélévation peut être nécessaire pour éviter l'ennoiement du seuil par l'aval.

3. Dimensionnement

La figure 2 ci-dessous montre le dimensionnement du seuil :

- le seuil du dispositif de base est calé à la cote 0,54 m (le zéro de référence est la base du Parshall), ce qui permet de mesurer 400 l/s dans le Parshall seul,
- le seuil de mesure des crues est calé à la cote 0,94 m : il passe alors 3 m³/s dans le dispositif de base, avec incertitude de 6 à 7 % en deçà,
- la longueur du seuil de mesure des crues varie de 6 à 12 m.

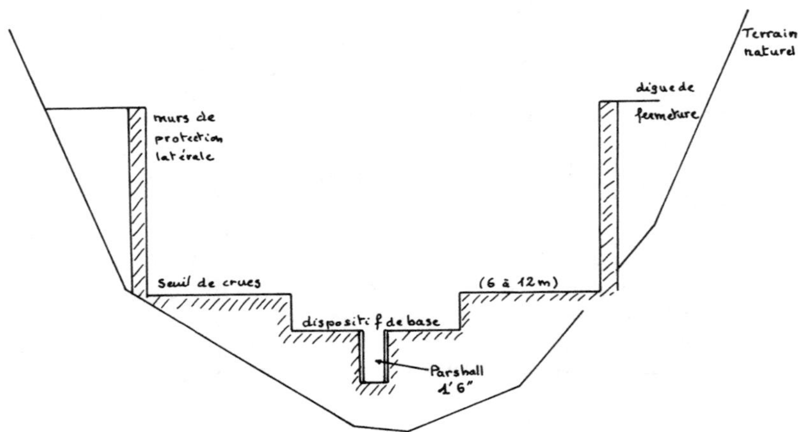

FIG. 2

Pour une longueur de 6 m, on mesure les débits jusqu'à 40 m³/s (pour une cote de 2 m) à moins de 5 % près. Pour cette cote mesurée de 2 m, la charge amont est 2,73 m : on doit prévoir des protections jusqu'à la cote 3 m. Pour une longueur de 12 m, on mesure dans les mêmes conditions de cote et de charge tous les débits de 3 à 60 m³/s avec une incertitude inférieure à 7 %.

L'ouvrage s'étend le long de la rivière sur une longueur de 6 m, plus un tapis aval de protections en enrochements. Cette longueur de 6 m correspond à la dimension du Parshall normalisé (4 m), protégé à l'aval par une structure de protection en béton (2 m).

Suivant la forme du lit de la rivière, l'ouvrage peut être symétrique (seuil de crues disposé de part et d'autre du dispositif de base) ou dissymétrique (seuil de crues disposé latéralement).

CONCLUSION SUR LES SEUILS JAUGEURS

Le dispositif proposé ici permet d'équiper, à un coût raisonnable, les petits bassins versants qu'il n'est pas envisageable de jauger au moulinet.

La précision est aussi bonne que celle que l'on obtient aux moyens de jaugeages de bonne qualité, à condition de caler le dispositif assez haut pour être sûr que le Parshall ne sera jamais engravé.

Le système fonctionne de façon satisfaisante en Algérie à l'échelle double (station d'Ain Berda), ce qui garantit l'adéquation de sa conception aux bassins algériens.

Les seuls problèmes de fonctionnement envisageables sont :

(a) l'obstruction du Parshall par des corps flottants ou des gros galets : l'observateur doit être chargé de l'entretien,

(b) une mauvaise réalisation du Parshall : on utilisera des Parshall préfabriqués en tôle (comme ceux qui sont installés sur les bassins expérimentaux) qui seront noyés dans le béton du seuil inférieur,

(c) une cote mesurée aux échelles du seuil qui ne soit pas la cote critique. Deux précautions seront prises. D'une part, placer les échelles, comme à la station d'Ain Berda, au droit de l'échelle du Parshall et les sceller au milieu des seuils et non pas sur les murs latéraux. D'autre part, on installera une batterie d'échelles amont, sur la berge (comme pour une station hydrométrique ordinaire), 4 m à l'amont de l'angle amont du seuil. Cette batterie d'échelles sera lue par l'observateur en crue supérieure à 0,54 m : on doit y observer la charge, ce qui permettra de confirmer que la hauteur critique est effectivement observée sur le seuil (au limnigraphe et aux échelles principales.

On lèvera également les laisses de grandes crues derrière la digue de fermeture pour contrôler la cote lue à l'échelle de crue.

Les transports solides peuvent être mesurés de façon classique, par prélèvement dans la zone très turbulente située en aval du seuil (là ou tous les matériaux sont mis en suspension).

On peut également, après tarage, utiliser une sonde nucléaire disposée dans le Parshall. Il faut alors un tirant d'eau minimal de 30 cm, ce qui correspond à 160 l/s.

Des essais entrepris en Algérie ont soulevé un problème à résoudre : si la zone d'exploration de la sonde est située trop bas, les mesures sont faussées par le charriage de fond.

REFERENCES

(1) Discharge measurement structures, publié par le laboratoire de Delft, en coopération avec l'"International Institute for Land Reclamation and Improvement".

(2) Ackers, P., White, W.R., Perkins, J.A. & Harrison, A.J.M. Weirs and flumes for flow measurement. John Wiley & Sons.

(3) Article "Débimétrie: dispositifs jaugeurs". La houille blanche, 4/5, 1987.

Hydrology in Mountainous Regions. I - Hydrological Measurements; the Water Cycle
(Proceedings of two Lausanne Symposia, August 1990). IAHS Publ. no. 193, 1990.

Refinements in dilution gauging for mountain streams

KELLY ELDER & RICHARD KATTELMANN
Center for Remote Sensing and Environmental Optics
Computer Systems Lab, 1140 Girvetz Hall
University of California, Santa Barbara, CA 93106 USA
ROB FERGUSON
Department of Geography, University of Sheffield
Sheffield S10 2TN, England

ABSTRACT Dilution gauging has become a common technique for measuring stream discharge in high gradient channels with boulder beds. During a three-year study of the hydrology of an alpine basin in the Sierra Nevada of California, USA, a few hundred measurements were made with the slug injection method. This work led to a few refinements in the general techniques and identified some problems. A lightweight, compact kit and simple operating procedure were developed to permit dependable measurements by one or two hydrographers. Although the replicate measurements were nearly identical in most cases, measurements made at the same stage several days apart were different in several cases. An alternative technique that calculates discharge from a mass balance after injecting salt in solid form was used and found to closely match results from slug injections of brine. This method is very simple in its field application. A continuous injection method suitable for remote use was also developed.

INTRODUCTION

Accurate determinations of discharge in mountain streams are needed for a growing number of purposes. In the past, mountain streams were gaged primarily as part of short-term research projects in such fields as snow hydrology, runoff generation mechanisms, glaciology, geomorphology, fisheries, and biogeochemistry. Increasing use and development of mountain areas have expanded the need for knowledge about mountain runoff quantities into such areas as water supply development for rural communities and recreational areas, micro-hydroelectric generating facilities, water rights disputes, instream flow requirements, environmental impact assessment, and monitoring effects of land use change.

The turbulent flow regime and irregular channel geometry of mountain streams make traditional velocity-area gauging difficult or impossible. Velocity varies dramatically with depth and distance from the rough channel boundary. The velocity at any point can fluctuate wildly over time in the turbulent conditions. Current meters have also been found to over-register velocity in high-gradient streams (Jarrett, 1988). Therefore, sampling the velocity distribution over a cross-section will produce an average with a high degree of uncertainty. Adequate surveying of the cross-sectional area of a boulder-bed channel is also problematic. A substantial part of the active flow area may lie underneath the uppermost surface of rocks along the bed. Although the profile and geometry of step-pool and riffle-pool channels change markedly along any given reach, ideal cross-sections for velocity gauging are rare in most mountain streams. Streams below glaciers involve further measurement difficulties such as high sediment load, rapidly fluctuating discharge, and shifting channels (Bergmann and Reinwarth, 1977).

These same characteristics of high-gradient, boulder-bed streams that make traditional river gauging ineffective enhance the suitability of dilution gauging. "In rock-strewn shallow streams, the dilution method may provide the only effective means of measuring flow" (Herschy, 1985:363). "... a high degree of turbulence in the river makes the results [of dilution gauging] more accurate than those of most other methods of discharge measurement" (Østrem, 1964:21). Stream discharge measurement employing the dilution of a chemical tracer has become a common hydrographic procedure. It was developed more than 80 years ago (Stromeyer, 1905) and has been thoroughly described in the literature (e.g., Aastad and Søgnen, 1954; Østrem, 1964; Church and Kellerhals, 1970; Browne and Foster, 1978; Bjerve and Grøterud, 1980; Kite, 1989). During a detailed study of the hydrology of an alpine basin in the Sierra Nevada of California, we further adapted the general techniques for greater ease-of-use and portability in remote areas.

The basic principle behind dilution gauging is mass conservation of a chemical tracer before and after dilution by a flowing stream. Measurement of the concentration of a tracer after it has become dispersed uniformly downstream of an injection point allows calculation of the discharge required to achieve the measured dilution. In practice electrical conductivity is substituted for mass conductivity. There are two primary alternatives in dilution gauging: the tracer can be injected in a single dose, or it can be introduced at a constant rate over several minutes.

CONTINUOUS INJECTION METHOD

The continuous injection method is the conceptually and computationally simpler of the two versions of dilution gauging, but it traditionally requires more elaborate equipment to introduce the tracer into the stream. With this method, the tracer is added to the stream at a constant rate until an equilibrium concentration is reached downstream. A simple mass balance provides the basis for calculating discharge:

$$Q\,C_B + R_T\,C_S = C_E\,(Q + R_T) \tag{1}$$

where Q = discharge, R_T = injection rate of the tracer solution, C_B = background concentration of the stream, C_S = concentration of the tracer solution, C_E = equilibrium concentration of the tracer downstream. Solving for Q yields

$$Q = \frac{R_T\,(C_E - C_S)}{C_B - C_E} \tag{2}$$

The measurement can be stopped as soon as the observer is satisfied that the concentration of the tracer in the stream is constant both along the reach and over time. In steep, swift mountain streams, equilibrium is usually achieved within a couple of minutes. Measurement accuracy tends to increase as the difference between the background and equilibrium concentrations increases. Bjerve and Grøterud (1980:125) provide a table of conductivity differences needed at various ranges of background conductivity to minimize error.

This technique has been extended to larger rivers by taking advantage of natural differences in specific electrical conductance ("conductivity") between a tributary and the main river (Kite, 1989). If a river's conductivity is significantly different above and below the confluence with some tributary and the flow in the tributary is small enough to measure by dilution or other means, then the above equations can be applied. In this case, Q = discharge of main stream above confluence, R_T = discharge of tributary, C_B = conductivity of main stream above confluence, C_S = conductivity of the tributary, C_E = equilibrium concentration of main stream below confluence. Where conditions are favorable, this method has the potential of measuring discharges of several tens of $m^3 s^{-1}$, which would otherwise require radioisotopes and/or elaborate equipment (e.g., Raja, et al., 1982; Herschy, 1985).

SLUG INJECTION METHOD

The slug injection method involves the injection of a slug of tracer in solution of known volume and conductivity into the stream. From measurement of the conductivity wave as it passes downstream, and the background conductivity, discharge can be calculated from

$$Q = C_S \frac{V_s}{\int_0^T (C_C - C_B)\,dt} \tag{3}$$

where V_s = volume of salt solution slug, C_C = channel conductivity, t = time, and T = final time of conductivity wave passage.

Since conductivity is a ratio in this equation the result is independent of the units used to measure conductivity, and discharge is given in $m^3\ s^{-1}$. The dilution method requires that complete mixing has occurred. This requires that the measurement site is downstream from the slug injection site at a point greater the mixing length. The measurement-time resolution must be fine enough to capture variations in the conductivity wave as it passes.

Although this method has high precision when applied carefully, it has certain disadvantages compared with the method described below. Each gauging, even at the same site on the same day, requires an individual calibration, which is time consuming. Accurate volumetric measurements must be made, both of V_s and of the small quantities during the calibration procedure; this measurement is more difficult in the field than in lab conditions. Two large containers are needed, plus fragile volumetric glassware for the calibration. The set-aside sample for calibration must be representative of V_s; this requirement is difficult to achieve if the solution is almost saturated so that precipitation and stratification are occurring (this problem is more acute at lower temperatures since the saturation concentration is lower).

MASS BALANCE METHOD

The alternative approach uses a mass balance, rather than a volumetric balance. A measured mass M of salt is injected and its mass concentration M_C in the stream is monitored as the tracer wave passes, using a calibrated relationship between M_C and the conductivity y. If M, M_C, Q, and the wave duration T are in commensurate units, the mass balance is

$$M = \int_0^T Q M_C\,dt \tag{4}$$

so that, for steady flow

$$Q = \frac{M}{\int_0^T M_C\,dt} = \frac{M}{T \langle M_C(t) \rangle} \tag{5}$$

where < > denotes the arithmetic mean over time. This method has been used by Ferguson since 1984, and has been discovered independently by other workers (e.g., Hongve, 1987; C.R. Fenn, personal communication, 1988). It has the immediate advantage that M can be measured in the lab in advance, e.g. by preparing preweighed packages of salt labeled with the mass M. It is also possible to inject dry salt without preparing a primary solution. Comparative studies by Ferguson (1988, unpublished) and Hongve (1987) found no systematic difference between the salt waves or discharges calculated using dry salt or using a solution. Dissolution on the stream bed need not be instantaneous, so long as the tracer salt does not remain solid long enough to be washed past the conductivity measurement point in suspension or as bedload rather than in solution.

A further advantage is that the calibration can be done in advance in the lab, or just once in the field, for any number of gaugings using the same combination of conductivity meter and batch of salt. The relationship between measured conductivity C_C at time t and water temperature W_T is

$$C_C(t, W_T) = C_B(W_T) + K\,C(t)\,f(W_T) \tag{6}$$

where C_B = natural background conductivity, K = proportionality constant, and $f(W_T)$ = temperature correction factor that allows for the increase in C_C with W_T for a given C. To a close approximation

$$f(W_T) = 0.50 + 0.02\,W_T \tag{7}$$

(Østrem, 1964; Hongve, 1987). The constant K depends on the type of tracer used, the accuracy and cell constant of the conductivity meter, and to a small extent the ionic activity of the streamwater to which the tracer is introduced. The constant K is equal to 0.214 for pure NaCl in otherwise ion-free water, and an accurate meter of cell constant equal to unity measuring conductivity in units of $mS\,m^{-1}$ ($1\ mS\,m^{-1} = 10\,mS\,cm^{-1}$) (Hongve, 1987). Hongve recommends using this value with an empirical correction of -0.0003 per $mS\,m^{-1}$ of background conductivity. Ideally K should be estimated from lab calibration, rather than relying on the purity of the salt and the accuracy of the conductivity meter and cell constant. This calibration involves preparing standard solutions of different concentration, measuring their temperature and conductivity, and regressing $C_C(W_T)$ on $Cf(W_T)$ (cf Eq. 6). An alternative is to take the standard solutions into the field, immerse them in the edge of the stream to eliminate any temperature difference, measure their conductivity, and regress $C_C(W_T)$ on C to obtain an estimate of $Kf(W_T)$ (A. Jenkins, U.K. Institute of Hydrology, personal communication, 1988).

Once K or $Kf(W_T)$ has been estimated by one of these calibration procedures, the same value holds for all gaugings using this particular combination of salt and conductivity meter. Discharge is calculated by combining Eqs. 5 and 6:

$$Q = \frac{M\,K\,f(W_T)}{T\,[\langle C_C(t, W_T)\rangle - C_B]} \tag{8}$$

The only field measurements required are of the background conductivity, temperature and salt wave. The mass balance approach therefore minimizes the time required for a gauging and maximizes the accuracy.

TRACERS

A variety of tracers are available and the choice depends on factors such as cost, accessibility, contamination of natural waters, worker safety and availability. Tracers should be soluble in water at the ambient temperature of application, have density and viscosity properties similar to water, be nonreactive with the chemistry of the natural water, exhibit stability in light, organic materials and suspended sediments, and be conservative regarding sorption losses. Further, a tracer should not be found in the natural streamwater except at low concentrations that will not effect its use, and should be detectable at very low concentrations, e.g., less than one part per million. Lastly, the tracer must not be detrimental to the stream biota or unacceptable to water users, and must not have lasting effects (Church, 1975).

Major classes of tracers include chemicals, electrolytes, fluorescent dyes, radioactive substances, and the natural waters themselves (Church, 1975). Many chemicals are available for almost any application and usually can be applied at acceptable dilution levels if careful laboratory calibration is carried out. Electrolytes use electrical properties (conductance) as a surrogate for concentration. A variety of common salts are popular and work well in field situations. Fluorescent dyes are also good for field applications because the fluorometry is carried out in the lab and they have the added advantage of providing a visual verification of mixing. Sorption losses must be considered for some dyes. Rhodamine WT dye was found to be inadequate in a mountain stream because of sorption of the dye onto natural stream features and observed concentrations were as low as 45% of the expected measurements (Bencala, et al., 1983). Radioactive tracers have been widely studied and are detectable at low concentrations, but have some noteworthy disadvantages. Safety of researchers, acquisition and transport of material, and regulations governing their use make them prohibitive in many cases. Although some are available with short half-lives, their effect on the biota in streams is cumulative and must be considered. Short half-lives also mean rapid transport and use are necessary and limits their application in remote field areas. The natural physical properties of water may be used as well. Temperature and natural background chemistry have been used as tracers.

It is important that the tracer selected be conservative in the environment it is being applied. A tracer that is conservative in one environment may be nonconservative in another where the chemical constituency is different. For example, salt was an effective tracer in the Sierra Nevada where background conductivities were low (5-10μS cm^{-1}), but other tracers are better in saline streams where it is difficult to introduce a tracer with conductivity above the background value. This example is simplistic and more subtle problems may arise with other tracers.

Researchers should be aware that introduction of tracers to natural waters may have effects on the biota of the aquatic ecosystem. The obvious disadvantages of radioactive tracers have been identified above. Salt is relatively harmless as a tracer, although its effect has not been well quantified. At Emerald Lake researchers found an increase in macroinvertibrate drift after an increase in solutes in the stream. The amount of drift is a function of the intensity and duration of the solute shock wave. The most sensitive organisms drift first but they also recolonize most rapidly. Recolonization is also a function of intensity and duration because a greater drift will result in slower recolonization. There is little doubt of an effect, the question is how much of an effect there is and what the implications are. The effect of changes in the solute chemistry on large organisms such as fish is not as drastic in this context because of the greater mobility of these organisms.

APPLICATION OF DILUTION METHODS AT EMERALD LAKE

Adaptation of the slug injection technique

During a three-year study of the hydrology of an alpine basin in the Sierra Nevada of California, a few hundred measurements were made with the slug injection method. A lightweight, compact kit and simple operating procedure were developed to permit dependable measurements by one or two hydrographers. The practical experience gained during this field program may be helpful in other studies. Listed below are details of the equipment used and the basic procedure.

Equipment All the equipment listed is available from a variety of sources at a range of prices. Individual needs should be considered when selecting products. The following items are required:
1) A lightweight digital conductivity meter with a submersible probe.
2) A timing device.
3) Two plastic containers, with a volume of about 10 L each.
4) Two plastic graduated cylinders, volumes 1000 mL and 10 mL
5) An adequate supply of common table salt.

The type of conductivity meter selected will depend on the natural background conductivity and the discharge being measured. At most of the flows we observed, a 0-200 $\mu S\,cm^{-1}$ meter scale was adequate. At moderate flows (0.05 $m^3\,s^{-1}$) 250 g of salt mixed with 8 L of stream water produced a slug conductivity of 40,000 $\mu S\,cm^{-1}$ and an effective conductivity wave. This mixture was varied depending on flow.

Procedure Choose a channel reach for measurement. An adequate injection and measurement site should be located and should allow the slug to be dumped into the main channel flow and allow placement of the conductivity probe in the main current without movement after placement. The distance between the two sites should not be too close or the wave will pass too quickly as a sharp peak. If they are too far apart, attenuation from mixing will provide a poorly defined peak that is difficult to measure. Stream stage should be measured and recorded. Measure and record the background conductivity of the stream. Fill one plastic bucket with the appropriate amount of stream water. Record the volume of the water and the amount of salt added to make the slug mixture. After mixing thoroughly, measure 10 mL slug solution and 1000 mL of stream water and mix in the second bucket and measure and record the diluted slug conductivity and the dilution factor (e.g., 100/1). The conductivity of the undiluted salt slug (C_S) is computed by multiplying the diluted slug conductivity C_{dil} by the dilution factor (x) and removing the background conductivity (C_B):

$$C_S = C_{dil}(x - 1) - C_B \tag{9}$$

After placing the probe and meter at the measurement site, inject the slug and record the wave passage as conductivity. Conductivity should be recorded at 5 to 10 second intervals. The procedure takes 15 minutes or less to complete for experienced personnel. Two measurements should be taken for quality assurance and error estimation. Calculation of discharge can be done in the field with an inexpensive calculator capable of simple integration.

Continuous injection for backcountry use

Because of the heavy and bulky equipment traditionally used for the continuous injection technique, this option has rarely been used in the backcountry. In our study in Sequoia National Park, we experimented with two transportable injection systems: small constant-speed pump and siphon. The battery-powered pump allowed injection of up to 250 ml min^{-1} of brine. Because of low background conductivities (3-5 $\mu S\,cm^{-1}$) in the basin's streams, this injection rate was sufficient to double the conductivity at discharges up to about 0.2 $m^3\,s^{-1}$. Conductivities reached equilibrium within 5 minutes of the start of injection. This time is probably much shorter than the time to equilibrium in most other streams (Church and Kellerhals, 1970). The pump with 8 D-cell batteries weighed about 3 kg and was completely reliable. A few comparisons between this method and the slug injection method at discharges of 0.1 to 0.2 $m^3\,s^{-1}$ resulted in equivalent values except for one discrepancy of 20 percent. Discharge determined from simultaneous current meter measurements were up to 60 percent greater than the dilution measurements.

A siphon tube attached to a float in a large container also provides a constant flow rate. A lightweight cylinder or tank with cross-sectional area of 0.1 to 0.2 m^2 can be easily carried in a rucksack and can hold up to 100 l of brine. A couple of siphon tubes of different diameter allow a range of injection rates. Two or more tanks can be used simultaneously in larger streams. A few observations of the water level at different times provide the injection rate. The tank should be shaded if the solution must stand for more than 10 minutes to minimize temperature change. A simply-designed Mariotte vessel (Browne and Foster, 1978; Herschy, 1985:382) constructed of lightweight material could also be suitable for backcountry use.

Problems and considerations

Almost every dilution measurement was replicated immediately. Although the replicates were nearly identical in almost all cases, measurements made at the same stage several days apart were different in several cases. This discrepancy may result from difficulty in defining the shape of the tails in the final decline of the conductivity wave, a problem that we encountered and others have reported (Day, 1976). The problem may result from sampling at too course of a resolution or from changes in the background conductivity during a measurement. Background conductivity should not change during a measurement under normal circumstances, but will often change with changes in discharge. The problem we encountered at Emerald Lake was a result of the low background conductivities that ranged between 3-6 μS. At this level a change of a few μS represented about 100% of the background conductivity. We observed long tails as the solution from all the eddies and entire channel reach finally washed through the system past the measurement point. In some cases, the area under these tails was a significant portion of the entire conductivity wave. In calculating the discharge with Eq. 3 there was a considerable difference in the resultant discharge depending on the final value of time t_f used in the integral. Not all field measurements were continued until the measured conductivity returned to the background level. This leaves the data analyst with the problem of estimating the behavior of the tail and produces an unknown error. Some researchers have used exponential decay and linear least-squares models to extrapolate the tail to the background level. Model fitting involves subjective choices of model type and the portion of the data to which it is fit thus producing error. The error will be minimized when a the area under the tail is a small portion of the total integral therefore, using a strong solution that maximizes the peak and area under the bulk of the curve will produce the best results.

The stream reach should be as turbulent as possible to maximize mixing and be free of tributaries, bifurcations, vegetation, and back-water areas or dead zones (Herschy, 1985). The minimum length of stream required for thorough mixing depends on the hydraulics of the particular stream reach. A variety of empirical equations for estimating mixing length have been developed (e.g., Day, 1977; Herschy, 1985:376). A study of mountain streams in New Zealand showed that complete mixing is achieved in a reach 25 times as long as the average channel width (Day, 1977). Day found that mixing lengths in his study reaches tended to be considerably shorter than lengths predicted with the various equations. He attributed these discrepancies to the greater roughness of the beds of mountain streams. With the continuous injection method, the mixing length can be determined by successively measuring the specific electrical conductance downstream of the injection site until the values become constant with distance downstream. In the turbulent streams at our study site in the southern Sierra Nevada, we found that Day's criteria was conservative and that complete mixing appeared to occur in as little as 15 times the mean channel width.

ACKNOWLEDGEMENTS Jim Sickman and John Melack of U.C. Santa Barbara provided the idea and the equipment for the small pump for our experiments at Emerald Lake. Kim Kratz provided valuable information regarding the biological implications of salt tracers. Dave Clow, Steve Petersen, and Mark Williams made many of the dilution measurements during the associated study. D. Marks introduced salt dilution gaging to the Emerald Lake project.

REFERENCES

Aastad, J. & R. Søgnen (1954) Discharge measurements by means of a salt solution: the relative dilution method. General Assembly of Rome International Association of Hydrological Sciences Publ. no. 38, 289-292.

Bjerve, L. & O. Grøterud (1980) Discharge measurements by a new-formed relative salt-dilution method in small turbulent streams. Nordic Hydrology 11 (3/4), 121-132.

Bencala, K., R. Rathbun, A. Jackman, V. Kennedy, G. Zellweger & R. Avanzino (1983) Rhodamine WT dye losses in a mountain stream environment. Water Resources Bulletin 19 (6), 943-950.

Bergmann, H. & O. Reinwarth (1977) Die pegelstation Vernagtbach (Ötztaler Alpen): planung, bau, und messergebisse. Zeitschrift für Gletscherkunde und Glazialgeologie 12 (2), 157-180.

Browne, T. & I. D. L. Foster (1978) The measurement of low streamflow by dilution gaging. Revue de Geomorphologie Dynamique 27 (1), 21-28.

Church, M. & R. Kellerhals (1970) Stream gauging techniques for remote areas using portable equipment. Inland Waters Branch, Department of Energy, Mines and Resources, Ottawa, Technical Bulletin No. 25.

Church, M. (1975) Electrochemical and fluorometric tracer techniques for streamflow measurements. Published for the British Geomorphological Research Group by Geo Abstracts, Norwich, England, Technical Bulletin no. 12.

Day, T. J. (1976) On the precision of salt dilution gaging. Journal of Hydrology 31 293-306.

Day, T. J. (1977) Observed mixing lengths in mountain streams. Journal of Hydrology 35 125-136.

Herschy, R. W. (1985) Streamflow Measurement. Elsevier, London.

Hongve, D. (1987) A revised procedure for discharge measurement by means of the salt dilution method. Hydrological Processes 1 267-270.

Jarrett, R. D. (1988) Hydraulic research of mountain rivers. Eos, Transactions of the American Geophysical Union 69 (44), 1217.

Kite, G. (1989) An extension to the salt dilution method of measuring streamflow. International Journal of Water Resources Development 5 (1), 19-24.

Østrem, G. (1964) A method of measuring water discharge in turbulent streams. Geographical Bulletin 6 21-43.

Raja, R. K., A. K. Agarwal, O. P. Jain & S. S. Chhabra (1982) Measurement of hydrological elements in mountainous regions. Proceedings of International Symposium on Hydrological Aspects of Mountainous Watersheds School of Hydrology, University of Roorkee, Roorkee, UP, India, II-39—II-46.

Stromeyer, C. E. (1905) The gauging of streams by chemical means. Proceedings of the Institute of Civil Engineers 160 349-363.

Hydrology in Mountainous Regions. I - Hydrological Measurements; the Water Cycle (Proceedings of two Lausanne Symposia, August 1990). IAHS Publ. no. 193, 1990.

Flow measurement under difficult measuring conditions: field experience with the salt dilution method

A. GEES
Institute of Geography - Hydrology, University of Berne, Hallerstrasse 12, CH-3012 Berne, Switzerland

ABSTRACT First of all, flow measurement by salt dilution method is described as well as the record and analysis of data by means of a microcomputer. The next chapter includes a vice-versa comparison of the salt dilution method, the flow meter measurement and the dilution method by fluorescence dye tracer on field experiments. Finally the use as well as the advantages and disadvantages of the three methods are discussed.

INTRODUCTION

In the last years many discharge measurements by the salt dilution (integration) method have been carried out. The comparison of those discharge measurements with other methods were missing. In cooperation with the Swiss National Hydrological and Geological Survey (SNHGS) a field campagne took place to get first information about the quality of the different methods. Eight river gauging stations of the monitoring network of the SNHGS were chosen for discharge measurements with the following three methods:
a) integration (gulp) method (salt dilution method, tracer: NaCl)
b) constant-rate injection method (tracer:sulforhodamine)
c) hydrological current meter (SNHGS-type)
The results presented of the three different methods in this paper are directly comparable, because the measurements were carried out at the same time.

PRINCIPLES

The main points of the three methods are described in a short form. The integration (gulp) and the constant-rate injection method are the two basic dilution gauging methods. The current meter method is used worldwide and therefore well known.

INTEGRATION (GULP) METHOD: In the integration method of dilution gauging, a simple gulp of tracer solution is added to the river. At the sampling station the passage of the entire tracer cloud is monitored to determine the relationship between the concentration and time.
The discharge is calculated of the equation:

$$M_1 = c_1 V_1 = Q \int_{t_1}^{t_2} (c_2 - c_0) \, dt$$

Where M_1 is the quantity of tracer, c_1 the concentration and V_1 the volume of the initial tracer solution, t_1 is a time before the leading edge of the tracer cloud arrives at the sampling point, and

t_2 is a time after all the tracer has passed this point. The background tracer concentration is c_0 and c_2 is the recorded tracer concentration [5].
In our case salt (NaCl) was used as a tracer. The detection of the salt in the small rivers is very easy, because a conductivity meter can measure the throughflow of the tracer. A microcomputer monitors the results from the conductivity meter. When the entire tracer cloud has passed the sampling point the runoff can be calculated from the concentration-time diagram. The microcomputer makes the result of the discharge measurement available in the field. Therefore the check of the results whether plausible or not can be made [7].
If the salt dilution method (integration) is used for discharge measuring then some conditions should be fulfilled:

a) the exact quantity of tracer must be known
b) the tracer added to the river must be competely diluted
c) the runoff should be constant
d) all the tracer must pass the sampling cross section
e) flow must be turbulent between the injection and the sampling point
f) no dead water between the injection and sampling point
g) in order to get a good mixture of the tracer over the whole cross section it must be diluted homogenously
h) the tracer must be stable
i) the background level (conductivity) of the river should be stable

The tracer used was salt (NaCl) which is available in every food shop. The salt concentration in the river water was measured with a WTW LF 91 conductivity meter at a one second interval. The monitoring, interpretation and plot of the discharge measurements were available in the field. The whole measuring equipment (Fig. 1) is build in a synthetic suitcase (microcomputer, printer, conductivity meter, A/D-converter and battery).

CONSTANT-RATE INJECTION METHOD: In the constant-rate-injection method an exactly known tracer solution, of a determined concentration is injected continuously, at a fixed volumetric rate, for a certain time, so that an equilibrium concentration is established for a limited time at a sampling station downstream. The sampling time has to be chosen in a way that the tracer concentration at the sampling point is constant. The total discharge can be

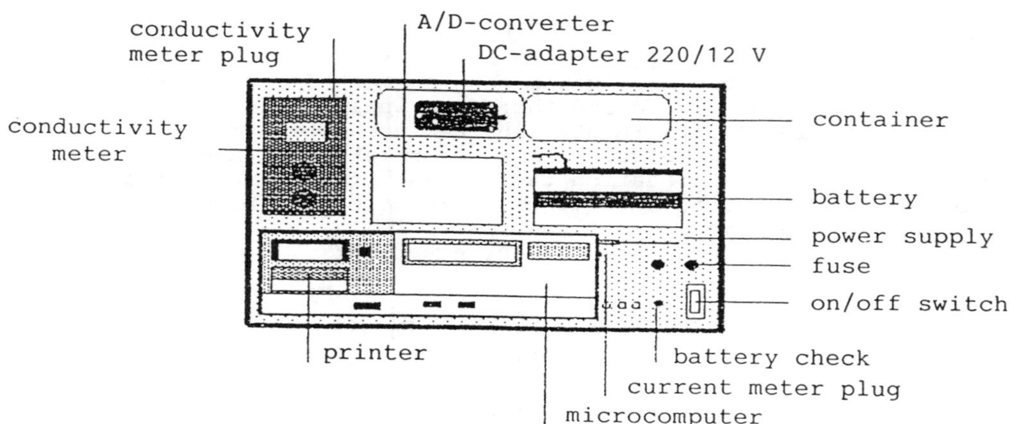

FIG. 1 Measuring equipment for salt dilution and current meter.

calculated from the dilution of the injected tracer concentration and the tracer concentration at the sampling point [5]. Some conditions must be fulfilled:

a) the amount of tracer injection must be constant during the measurement
b) the flow must remain steady for the measuring time
c) the method requires that the same amount of tracer per time passes the sampling cross section as was injected
d) the tracer must be stable (no sorption)
e) turbulent flow between the injection and the sampling point
f) the tracer must be completely mixed with the river water and at the sampling cross section distributed homogenously
g) the background level of the river water must be stable [3]

For the constant tracer injection a "Mariott'sche Flasche" was used [6]. The bottle contains 12 litres. The applied tracer was sulforhodamine. (Fig. 2)

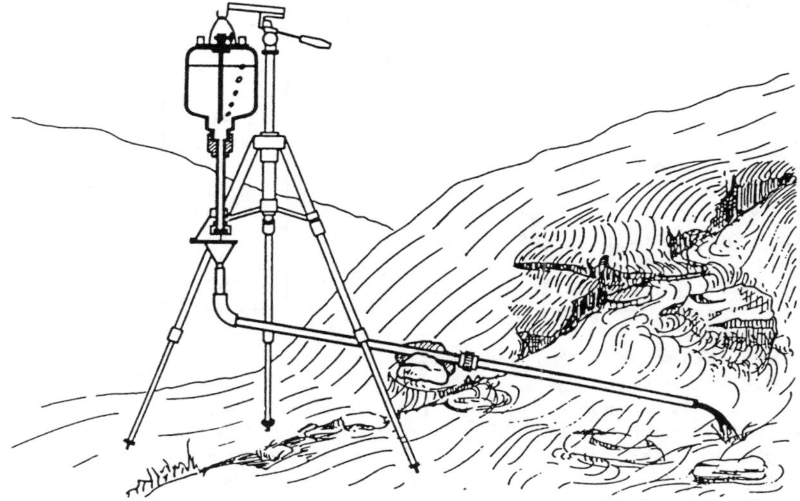

FIG. 2 Mariott'sche Flasche (constant-rate injection equipment).

CURRENT METER METHOD: The principle of discharge measurements with common current meter are known. The flow velocity is measured by a cross section of the river at different points. We used the 5-point method of the SNHGS [6]. This method takes about 20 profiles over the transsection of the river and at every profile 5 vertical measuring points. The total runoff is calculated with a double integral calculus on the wet area and the time.

Some conditions have to be considered at current meter measurings:

a) The runoff must be constant during the measuring time
b) stable discharge area (the best results are known from solid measuring cross sections)
c) laminar flow conditions
d) measuring cross section free of vegetation
e) calibration of the current meter at regular intervals

The shovels of the used current meter from the SNHGS have a diameter of 8 cm.

TEST STATIONS

The selection of the discharge test stations was based on the following criterions:
a) runoff not more than 4 m^3 s^{-1}
b) monitoring station of the SNHGS
c) long term water gage relation curve
d) turbulent flow between the injection point and the sampling cross section for the dilution methods

Therefore we chose eight stations in Central Switzerland for a field campaign. (Table 1)

TABLE 1 Test station parameter and injected tracer amount.

gauging station	m.a.r	temp.	cond.	velocity	dist.	amount of trac	
	m3 s-1	°C	µS cm-1	m s-1m	m	const. g	integr kg
Grossthalbach	1.84	9.2	260	2.40	300	3	6.1
Alpbach	1.80	6.5	86	2.60	200	3	10.0
Walenbrunnen	0.25	10.6	237	0.27	300	-	2.1
Schächen	5.39	10.4	221	1.50	450	10	15.0
Erlenbach	1.63	6.3	216	1.73	250	5	10.3
Engelberger Aa	4.64	8.9	146	1.10	400	10	11.5
Chli Schliere	0.75	15.1	304	0.05	450	2	2.5
Würzenbach	#	14.6	461	0.50*	200	1	1.7

- no value
monitoring less than one year
* estimated velocity
m.a.r. : mean annual runoff, periode 1986-1988,
velocity: mean velocity at the monitoring cross section
dist. : distance betweent injection and sampling point
const. : constant-rate injection (Mariott'sche Flasche), sulforhodamine
integr. : integration (gulp) method, salt (NaCl)

RESULTS

Table 2 shows the results of the tests. The reference for the comparison of the three different measuring methods was the water gage relation curve (1989). This reference was chosen because the water gage relation curve is derived from many discharge measurings with the current meter and therefore the influence of incorrect values could be eliminated. The relationship of the water gage and the runoff is a mean value and therefore is suitable as a reference value.

The results can be interpretated as follows:

The **integration (gulp) method** with salt dilution measurement gave differences between -7.0 and +21%. The highest negative deviation was -7% (Erlenbach). This effect is very unusual, mostly the measurements are too high because of tracer loss between the injection point and the measuring point.

The greatest difference to the water gage relation resulted at the Chli Schliere. It was 0.019 m^3 s^{-1} or +21%. At the time of our field campaign the measuring conditions in the large and braced riverbed with treshold and pools were very difficult. It might be

TABLE 2 Test results.

gauging station	Runoff				Differences from w.g.r.		
	w.g.r	corr.m	const.	integr	curr.m	const.	integr
	m^3s^{-1}	m^3s^{-1}	m^3s^{-1}	m^3s^{-1}	%	%	%
Grossthalbach	1.310	1.319	1.341	1.312	+0.7	+2.4	+0.2
Alpbach	1.880	1.890	1.952	1.923	+0.5	+3.8	+2.3
Walenbrunnen	0.260	0.280	-	0.266	+7.7	-	+2.3
Schächen	4.700	4.555	4.537	4.566	-3.1	-3.5	-2.9
Erlenbach	1.850	1.862	1.560	1.720	+0.7	-15.7	-7.0
Engelberger Aa	3.620	3.696	3.424	3.598	+2.1	-5.4	-0.6
Chli Schliere	0.090	0.074	0.090	0.109	-17.8	0.0	+21.1
Würzenbach	0.120	-	0.094	0.118	-	-21.7	-1.7

- : no value
w.g.r. : water gage relation (1989)
curr. m : current meter method
const. : constant-rate injection method, sulforhodamine
integr : integration (gulp) method, salt (NaCl)

possible, that a certain amount of the salt was lost in the pools of the riverbed due to higher specific density of the brine.
The other variations are less than ±3%, that lays in the accurancy of the conductivity meter.
By another test we made 7 discharge measurements one after the other (from 13.45 until 16.15 hours), to show the variation of the results. The test rivulet was the Luterbach near Berne. The first measuring was 15.3 l s^{-1} and the last was 15.8 l s^{-1}. That means that the difference of the results is not more than 0.5 l s^{-1} or less than 3%.

To consolidate those few results we must get more data from field measurements.

The **constant-rate injection method** with sulforhodamine as tracer shows similar results. The variations are between -21.7% (Würzenbach) and +3.8% (Alpbach). This result lays in the accurancy of the method (Alpbach). The mixing conditions between the injection point and the sampling point were excellent.
The Würzenbach had a background conductivity of 461 µS cm^{-1}, that means that the water is possibly contaminated with wast water. The background level of sulforhodamine was 0.2 mg m^{-3} in the blank samples, what influenced the fluorescence analysis. Therefore the value of this streamlet differs so much from the water gage relation.
The other results vary from -5.4 to +2.4%. A negative result means that we measured too much of the tracer, positive differences are from a loss of tracer. Usually the results have a positive difference because of little tracer loss by sorption or exfiltration.

The **current meter** measurings varied between -17.8% and +7.7% to the actual water gage relation. The negative difference of -17.8% was measured at the Chli Schliere. Due to the large riverbed (6.6m) and the low runoff (about 13% of the mean annual runoff, Tab. 3), where the mean streamflow velocity with 0.05m s^{-1} was also very low for a correct measuring. The natural bottom of the river bed at the measuring cross section makes it more difficult to measure with the current meter (Tab. 2). The low water discharge measurements are in general very difficult to realize with the

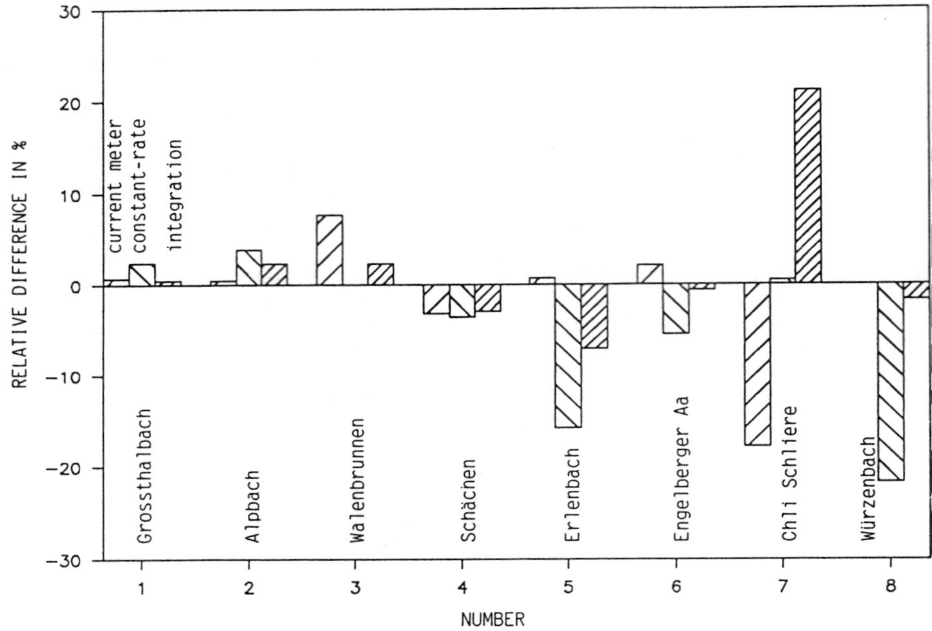

FIG. 3 Relative difference of the three methods (cf. Tab. 2).

current meter if the cross section is not concrete and therefore not stable.
The next highest positive difference was at the Walenbrunnen with +7.7%. The reason of this variation is not known.
The other differences are between -3.1% (Schächen) and +2.1% (Engelberger Aa). That lays in the accurancy of the method.

A comparison of the differences of the three involved methods shows that the Chli Schliere gave the greatest variation. The relative difference between the current meter and the salt dilution method was 38%. This difference is partly a result of the low runoff and the large riverbed and the reasons metioned above.
The smallest relative variation was measured at the Schächen with only 0.6% difference between the three methods. This results are equal with the tree involved methods.
Mostly the relative differences are not more than 8% (cf. Tab. 2). Therefore the three methods are similar, at good mixing conditions for the dilution methods (salt, sulforhodamine) and concrete cross sections for the current meter, to each other.

OUTLOOK

The aim of this investigation was to have basic information about discharge measurement with the three different methods under the same conditions. Those first results allow an estimation about the reliability of the three methods; as there is only little data available, we can not get a final conclusion. The next step must be collecting more data for statistical analysis.

The advantages of the **integration (gulp) method** is that it can be applied to natural rivulets with turbulent flow. The use of a bridge or some other installation is not necessary. The limit of the salt dilution method is the amount of tracer to be added (about 5 kg per m^3 runoff) to increase the conductivity about 100 µS cm^{-1} at the peak of the tracer flow-trough curve. If the background level of the conductivity is less than 100 µS cm^{-1} a smaller amount of salt per cubicmeter runoff can be added. If the background conductivity is more than 500 µS cm^{-1} then more than 5 kg salt per cubicmeter should be used. An advantage of the method is that the measuring equipment is in a suitcase (about 10 kg) and therefore it is very easy to move. The salt can be dissolved in a vessel (bucket, barrel) and from this it can be injected. The microcomputer records the data and plots the result after the monitoring is finished. The plausibility check can be made in the field and if the result seems to be incorrect an other measurement can be made immediately. A disadvantage of this method is that only a runoff less than 4 m^3 s^{-1} can be made easily, because the amount of salt to be dissolved is difficult to handle (about 20 kg for 4 m^3 s^{-1} runoff). In the literature a discharge measurement of 14 m^3 s^{-1} is mentioned [1], but such a runoff needs a great amount of salt and some heavy injection equipment.

For the **constant-rate injection method** (sulforhodamine) a special injection equipment is necessary (Mariott'sche Flasche or similar constant-rate injection equipment). The analysis of the samples must be done in a laboratory by a costly spectral fluorometer. The results of the measurements are therefore not available in the field and the plausibility check can not be made there. The advantage of the method is that only a small amount of the tracer (about 5 g per cubicmeter) is used. Therefore the limiting factor for this method is not the runoff but the distance of the complete mixing of the tracer, because the tracer must be distributed homogenously at the measuring cross section. By rule of thumb we can say that the amount of tracer to be injected is about:
- 5 g SR per cubicmeter, constant-rate injection
- 5 kg salt per cubicmeter, integration (gulp),

Therefore the transport of the tracer for the constant-rate injection is no problem, but for the salt dilution method it could be one.

An advantage of the **current meter method** is that the amount of runoff to be measured is not a limiting factor. In mountainous rivulets with only a few cubicmeter runoff and a concrete cross section for the measurement, the current meter gives good results. A disadvantage of this method is the calibration of the current meter every 10 to 20 operations with a lot of technical installation needed. Another problem is that at low water at natural cross sections the discharge measurement is very difficult. The question of measuring high water runoff, with a lot of suspended matter is not yet solved, because the current meter is very sensible about suspended matter in its moving parts.

ACKNOWLEDGEMENTS The discharge measurements have been possible thanks to the Swiss National Hydrological and Geological Survey, especially Mr. Bichsel J., Burla A. and Luder B. Then our thanks go to Mr. M. Gossauer and Mr. Th. Wagner of the University of Berne for the help to collecting the data.

REFERENCES

[1] BENISCHKE, R., HARUM, T. (1984) Computergesteuerte Abflussmessungen in offenen Gerinnen nach der Tracerverdünnungsmethode (Integrationsverfahren), in Steir'sche Beiträge zur Hydrogeologie 36, S. 127 - 137.

[2] ESTERMANN, H. (1990) Die Auswertung von Abflussmengenmessungen auf einem Kleincomputer. Hausarbeit am Geographischen Institut der Universität Bern, Physische-Geographie Hydrologie (unveröffentlicht).
[3] GASPARS, E. (1987) Modern trends in tracer hydrology, CRC Press Inc. Boca Raton, Florida
[4] HERSCHY, R. W. (1986) New Technology in Hydrometry, Adam Hilger Ltd, Bristol and Boston.
[5] HERSCHY, R. W. (1978) Hydrometry: Principles and Practices, Wiley, Chichester.
[6] LANDESHYDROLOGIE UND -GEOLOGIE (1982) Mitteilungen Nr. 4, Handbuch für die Abflussmessung (Bundesamt für Umweltschutz, Bern).
[7] LUDER, B. (1986) Ein Messgerät zur Bestimmung des Abflusses nach dem Verdünnungsverfahren, Geographisches Institut der Universität Bern, Physische-Geographie Hydrologie (unveröffentlicht).

Hydrology in Mountainous Regions. I - Hydrological Measurements; the Water Cycle (Proceedings of two Lausanne Symposia, August 1990). IAHS Publ. no. 193, 1990.

Reliability of bed load measurements in mountain rivers

B.V. GEORGIEV
Institute of Water Problems, Bulgarian Academy of Sciences, 1113 Sofia, Bulgaria

ABSTRACT The applicability and reliability of some equations for bed load discharge is tested by means of collected data using sediment trap technique. Data from six gaging sites in mountain rivers are used for the test. The best prediction of bed load discharge for this set of data has been obtained by the equations of Schamov and Schoklitsch. The effect of unsteady flow in flood conditions on the bed load discharge is estimated by comparing the measured sediment volume trapped and the summarized volume from the calculation of bed load discharge.

INTRODUCTION

Most of the mountain rivers are characterized by very high variations of water and sediment discharges. In these circumstances the bed load transport takes place mainly during flood waves possessed short duration and rapid increase of the water levels. The river flow in these conditions is unsteady and nonuniform with relatively high velocities.

The accuracy of sediment load data obtained in these steep gravel-channel streams is not known, and there are no direct and exact techniques by which the accuracy can be evaluated.

Because of the increasing importance of research and management problems in water development and environmental protection the knowledge of errors in sediment data and reliability of the bed load measurements and formulas assume great importance.

With regards to the severe complication of direct measurements of river bed load some authors make an attempt to establish relations between bed- and suspended-load and to give certain transition coefficients for practical purpose. However, the comparison between annual yields of bed and suspended load fluctuates in very large bounds and depends on many natural factors. Data from Soviets authors (Karaushev, 1977) give the values of this relation from 50 to 300 per cent for mountain rivers with a slope more than 0.02 m/m and from 1 to 5 per cent for foothill or plain rivers with a slope less than 0.002. From field investigation on an experimental river reach,Papazov & Georgiev, (1969) set up the mean value of the bed-and suspended-load relation as 18 per cent for a river slope 0.00125 m/m and considered that this relation has to vary from year to year and to a great extent it depends on the annual variation of runoff, river turbidity, etc.

The general purpose of this paper is to present some results by which the reliability of bed load measurements and empirical relations for streams flowing in very steep and rough channels can be evaluated.

The studied streams are characterized by very irregular discharges with short flood waves and long periods with low levels. Intensive bed-load transport has been observed only during the flood waves.

MEASURING METHOD

Many problems arise when we have to measure the water and sediment discharges in complicated conditions of rapid flowing floods in steep irregular channels. Most of the methods and equipment used in the ordinary conditions of flat alluvial channel flow cannot be employed in high-velocity flood flows in mountain rivers.

Some appropriate field measurement techniques developed to suit flood conditions have been developed in the Institute of Water Problems (Georgiev & Papazov, 1970). The essence of these techniques is accumulation and volumetric measurements of the trapped bed load. Other flow parameters such as velocity, water level, energy slope, suspended sediments, are measured simultaneously.

The techniques have used two approaches: first, the so called "summary-striped method" represent specially designed sediment traps with one meter wide front edge, dug in river bottom or flood plain (Fig.1, Papazov & Georgiev, 1978), the second approach applicable in very small streams, uses special concrete weirs with sharp steel edge crossing the river profile (Fig. 2). These trap techniques detain and store all bed load transported by short flood waves.

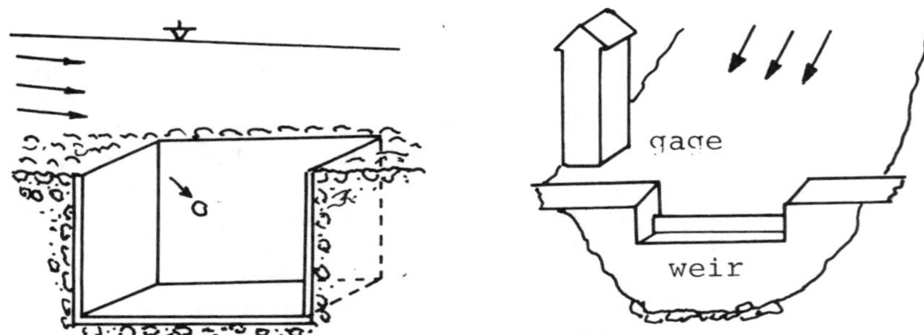

FIG.1 Trap dug in flood plain or in main channel of river. FIG.2 Weir for bed load collection in small creek.

The trap efficiency was investigated in laboratory conditions (flume experiment) on six various types of traps. The main conclusions from these experiments are:

- all bed load reaching the front edge of the trap is accumulated up to 80 per cent of the trap height;
- the smallest fractions of bed load is possible to move transitly over the trap if it is filled about 80-85 per cent;
- there are possibilities to enter bed load from side edges, but so far no quantitative information on this effect has been obtained;
- the type described here was chosen for field applications because of its simplicity, convenience and foolproof.

BASIC DATA

Gaging sites

The techniques described above have been tested at two various types of mountain rivers. The data from six gaging stations:the Varbitza river at Dgebel and five tributaries of the Bistritza creek near Sofia, have been used.

The Varbitza river gaging station is situated on the end of experimental river reach. The cross section has 110 meters total width including a single adjacent flood plain about 70 m wide and main channel for medium and low flow about 25 - 30 m wide. The river channel has a longitudinal slope of about 0.0125 m/m and is a normal pool and riffle type. The pools are generally full of sand that erodes relatively not so easily during low and medium flow, and riffles are fairly stable gravel bars. The sediment bed material consists of well-mixed sand and gravel covers the flood plain and conforms in size grading to the bed load which has entered the traps.

The shape of the river channel in the end of the experimental reach was relatively stable during the entire period of investigations (about four years, Fig.3).

The surface-water stage was determined by the use of stilling-well type gages, which were equipped with continuous analog record that operates from the float.

High-water measurements (levels, velocities and suspended load samples) were made from the road bridge. Two concrete piers in river channel support the bridge and some effects on velocity distribution could be expected.

The stage-discharge relation was relatively stable at all flows. The major factor that contributes to the slow fluctuating of stage-discharge relation is scouring and filling in the controlling reach of the river but the effect is mainly in low waters.

Four sediment traps were set up uniformly in the flood plain cross section (Fig.3). The sizes of the traps were considered by expected floods and bed load.

The gaging sites in the Bistritza creek basin are equiped by measuring weirs, bed load traps and outomatic water-stage recorders. The main hydrological features of these gaging sites are given in Table 1.

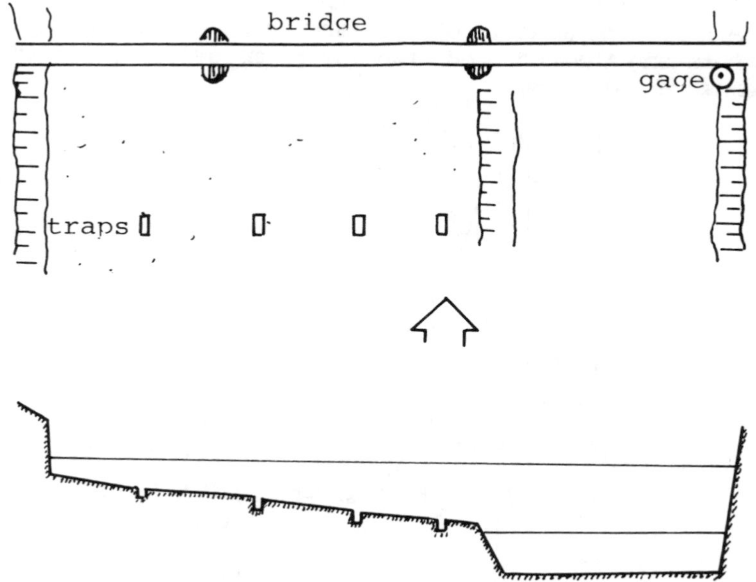

FIG.3 Gaging site and bed load traps in Varbitza river.

TABLE 1 Hydrological characteristics of measuring sites in the Bistritza creek experimental basin.

Site	Area of watershed km^2	Mean slope of a river m/m	slope at gaging site m/m	Mean annual disch. m^3/s	Maximum water disch. m^3/s	Bed load measuring device
Gabeshnitza	23.35	0.134	0.114	0.486	34.60	trap
Monastirska	8.08	0.142	0.101	0.099	4.14	trap
Liava	10.76	0.094	0.065	0.087	2.80	trap
Stara	9.40	0.216	0.125	0.162	3.76	weir
Ianchevska	6.74	0.177	0.135	0.113	2.95	weir

DATA PROCESSING

To obtain the relation between the total volume of bed load trapped during the flood and the characteristics of river flow the following data analysis techniques have been adopted. The flood hydrographs are divided in time-intervals with constant flow characteristics equal to the time-step averages (Fig. 4). The bed material size distribution obtained by samples from the river bottom and from traped sediments (Fig. 5) are developed in series of grading curves in dependence of the maximum sediment size, transported by a given mean velocity over the trap according the following relation $d_{max} = 0.0113\ u/\sqrt{D}$.

The flow over a bed load trap is considered as steady during each time step. The mean velocities are obtained on the basis of the measurements and the adopted two-layer model for velocity distribution (Samage et al., 1986).

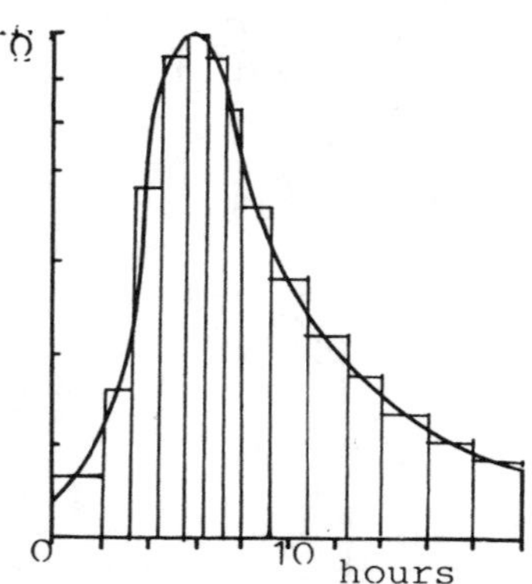

FIG. 4 Flood Hydrograph.

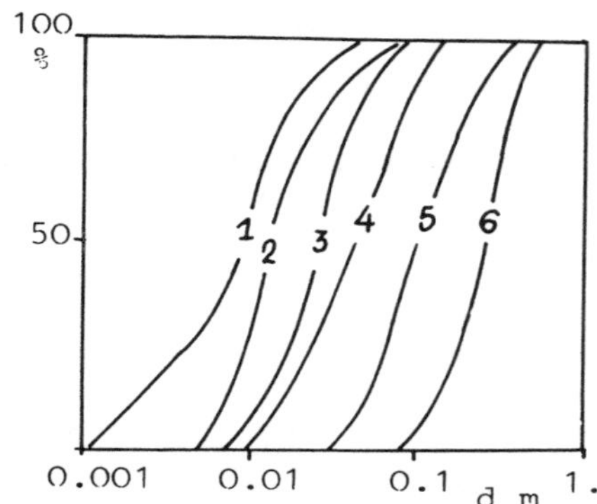

FIG. 5 Bed material size distribution for the gaging sites: 1. Varbitza, 2. Liava, 3. Manastirska, 4. Gabeshnitza, 5. Stara 6. Janchevska.

On the base of a composed approximated space-time model of flood flowing and using all the data obtained by measurements and hydraulic computations some comparative analyses for the bed load discharge have been made. The following equations have been used:

First, the bed load equation of Levi (Karaushev, 1977)

$$q_{sb} = 0.002 \left(\frac{u}{gd}\right)^{3} d(u - u_o) \left(\frac{d}{D}\right)^{0.25} \tag{1}$$

where u is mean velocity over the trap; D is the water depth; uo is the critical velocity for an incipient motion; d = mean bed load diameter, qsb = bed load discharge [kg/s.m']

Second, the bed load equation of Egiassaroff (Karaushev, 1977)

$$q_{sb} = 24\, q\, I \left(\frac{RI}{1.6 f_o d} - 1\right) \tag{2}$$

where, qsb is bed load discharge for unit width [kg/s.m']; q = water discharge per unit width; R = hydraulic radius [m]; d = mean size of moved bed sediments; fo = resistance coefficient of moved sediment channel determined by procedure suggested by Egiassaroff; I = energy slope.

Third, the bed load equation of Schamov (Karaushev, 1977) for sand-gravel beds

$$q_{sb} = k\left(\frac{u}{u_{st}}\right)^{3} d(u - u_o) \left(\frac{d_m}{D}\right)^{0.25} \tag{3}$$

where qsb is bed load discharge for unit width [kg/s.m']; k is a coefficient for the bed material distribution according to Schamov's procedure; u = mean velocity; u_{st} = mean flow velocity when the sediments of given size stop to move; dm = mean size of moved bed sediments; D is the water depth.

Fourth, the bed load equation of Schoklitsch (1962)

$$q_{sb} = \frac{2.5}{\rho_s/\rho} S^{3/2} (q - q_c) \tag{4}$$

where qc is the critical unit water discharge at which bed load transport begins to be determined according to Schoklitsch's version of the Shields equation;

Fifth, the bed load equation of Meyer-Peter and Mueller (Graf, 1971)

$$q_{sb} = 8[(Ks/Kr)^{3/2} \tau_* - \tau_{*c}]^{3/2} [g(P_s/P - 1)D^3]^{1/2} \tag{5}$$

where Ks/Kr is a correction factor for bed load roughness; τ_* is dimentionless shear stress according to Shields.

Sixth, the bed load equation of Smart (1984) which is a modified version of Meyer-Peter and Mueller equation for steep slopes:

$$q_{sb} = 4[(d_{90}/d_{30})^{0.2} S^{0.6} u/u_*(\tau_*-\tau_{*c})\tau_*^{0.5} [g(\rho_s/\rho - 1)D^3]^{1/2} \qquad (6)$$

Six equations were tested using all data only for those floods covering the criterion of trap filling not more than 80% of total volume. The measured volume of traped sediments, Vs, is compared with the sum of calculated volumes by the equations of bed load discharge, q_{sbi}, for every time step, t_i, i. g.

$$Vs = \Sigma(q_{sbi} \cdot t_i) \qquad (7)$$

For each equation the mean error in prediction was calculated as:

$$\epsilon m = \frac{1}{n}\sum_{j=1}^{n}\frac{1}{T}[Vs_j - \sum_{i=1}^{m}(q_{sbi} \cdot t_i)]_j \qquad (8)$$

and the root mean square error, ϵr, which gives an indication of the scatter, was calculated as:

$$\epsilon r = \left[\frac{1}{n}\sum_{j=1}^{n}\frac{1}{T}\{Vs_j - \sum_{i=1}^{m}(q_{sbi} \cdot t_i)\}_j^2\right]^{1/2} \qquad (9)$$

where Vsj is measured volume of traped sediments in j-th flood, T is the total time of every flood, subscript i denotes a time step, and n = 55 is a number of used measurements in the test.

TABLE 2 Errors in predictions of the bed load discharge equations based on 55 field measurements.

Equation	mean error ($10^{-5}m^3/s.m'$)	Root mean square error ($10^{-5}m^3/s.m'$)
Schoklitsch	- 1.21	3.29
Schamov	- 0.05	0.75
Egiassaroff	46.82	182.15
Meyer-Peter & Mueller	- 3.19	6.83
Levi	5.78	18.55
Smart	2.42	5.86

DISCUSSION

The models for bed load evaluation have been elaborated mainly in experiments in steady flow conditions. Their application for the real flood conditions poses the problem for the acceptability of a hypothesis for equivalent sediment transport at steady and unsteady flows.

Bathurst et al. (1987) give some results from tests of six equations (Ackers & White, Meyer-Peter & Mueller, Smart, Mizuyama, Bagnold and Schklitsch) with the conclusion that the Schoklitsch equation provides the most accurate predictions for the EPFL flume data. Here as it was mentioned above some of these equations along with the equations given by Levi, Egiasaroff and Schamov are used for the comparisons of specially proceeded field data from the traps.

Since the bed material gradation in mountain rivers is extremily wide, the bulk sediment movement may not occur even at very high flows which are observed at strong floods. Very often the bed material forms quite stable bottom structures which destruction time to time leads to a temporarily increasing of bed load discharge. This phenomenon is observed in small mountain streams and it is dificult to be comformed to the bed load discharge equations which are an idealization of the real field situation.

The overestimation of bed load discharge by some of equations could be explained with the differences between equilibrium sediment transport conditions with permanent material supply and the real deficit of sediments in real condition of bed armoring.

The results also indicate that the differenced in stream bed conditions at the beginning of each flood can explaine the wide range of bed load discharge connected with initial sediment motion. The inportance of each factor determining the history of flow and bed state is not easily quantified. Here one can mention the sediment storage in stream channel which is a very important factor especially at small steep creeks. For this reason the scater of obtained results is very large.

CONCLUSIONS

Measuring methods for the bed load discharge in mountain rivers are still far from required perfection. The sediment trap method described in the report can be used only in a case of flood waves with short duration. Its labour consuming operations do not allow wide application but can be used to collect data for the applicability estimation of the existing equations for a bed load discharge in the specific mountain river conditions and their reliability.

Tested equations of bed load discharge in the flood conditions show that a fairly good prediction can be obtained by the equations of Schamov and of Schoklitch. In the case of very coarse bed material (boulders, cobbles) the discrepancy is very large because the sediment availability is limited and the stochastic effect of bed load transport from flood to flood is considerable.

The magnitude of unsteady flow effect on the bed load discharge depends on the flood wave steepness or the relation D/ t.

REFERENCES

Bathurst, J.C., Graf, W.H. & Cao, H.H. (1987) Bed Load Discharge Equations for Steep Mountain Rivers. In: Sediment Transport in Gravel bed Rivers, Ed: C.R. Thorne, J.C. Bathurst & R.D. Hey, John Wiley & Sons.

Georgiev, B.V. & Papazov, R. (1970) Measuring Method for Bedload Discharge at short Flood Waves, Symposium on Hydrometry IHD, Coblence,

Proceeding of IAHS, No 92.

Graf, W.H. (1971) Hydraulics of Sediment Transport, McGraw-Hill.

Graf, W.H. & Suszka, L. (1985), Unsteady Flow and its Effects on Sediment Transport, XXI Congress of IAHR, Melbourn.

Papazov, R. & Georgiev, B. (1969) Investigation on the Bed load Transport in Varbitza river, Proc. of Institute of Water Problems, BAS, vol. XI, (in bulg.).

Papazov, R. & Georgiev, B. (1978) Investigations on the Bed load Transport, An. Report of Inst. of Water Problems, BAS, (in bulg.).

Paul, T.C. & Dhillon, G.S. (1987) Effect of Unsteady Flow on Sediment Transport, XXII Congress of IAHR, Lausanne.

Samaga, B.R., Ranga Raju, K.G. & Garde R.J. (1986) Velocity Distribution in alluvial channel Flow, J. of Hydraul. Res. IAHR, vol. 24, No4.

Smart, G.M. (1984) Sediment transport Formula for steep Channels, Proc. ASCE, J. of Hydr. Div. vol. 110, No 3.

Hydrology in Mountainous Regions. I - Hydrological Measurements; the Water Cycle
(Proceedings of two Lausanne Symposia, August 1990). IAHS Publ. no. 193, 1990.

Utilisation de mesures journalières de la turbidité pour l'estimation des flux de matières en suspension. L'exemple des fleuves andins de Bolivie

J.L. GUYOT
ORSTOM, C.P. 9214, La Paz, Bolivie
H. CALLE
SENAMHI, C.P. 996, La Paz, Bolivie

RESUME En zone montagneuse, les concentrations en matières en suspension (MES) présentent de grandes variations dans le temps, qui sont souvent très rapides. Dans les Andes de Bolivie, les flux de matières en suspension sont estimés à partir des données journalières de turbidité, en utilisant une courbe d'étalonnage MES = f(Turbidité). Cette méthode de mesure est illustrée par les résultats de trois stations du réseau PHICAB qui contrôlent des bassins andins aux caractéristiques hydrologiques différentes.

INTRODUCTION

L'étude hydrologique du bassin versant amazonien de Bolivie, menée par le programme PHICAB (Convention ORSTOM/SENAMHI/UMSA), s'intéresse à la mesure des flux de matières dissoutes et particulaires à partir d'un réseau de 15 stations hydrométriques situées en plaine amazonienne, depuis le piedmont des Andes. Compte tenu de l'étendue du bassin étudié (744.000 km²) et de l'absence de voies de communication, les échantillons sont acheminés au laboratoire du SENAMHI à La Paz par frêt aérien. Afin de maintenir un échantillonnage journalier, compatible avec les contraintes budgétaires du PHICAB, une méthode basée sur la mesure de la turbidité, a été developpée.

TABLEAU 1 Caractéristiques des bassins étudiés, 1983-1987. D'après Guyot et al., 1988, 1989.

Station	Rio	Sup. km²	Alt. m	Pluviom. mm	Débit m3.s-1	MES mg.l-1
AB	Béni	68.000	280	1.700	2.200	1.100
PV	Ichilo	7.600	170	3.000	560	220
AP	Grande	59.000	450	750	330	7.500

Trois bassins andins sont controlés par des stations du réseau PHICAB (Fig. 1). Au Nord, le Rio Béni draine une région de hautes montagnes culminant à 6.500 mètres, puis les vallées tropicales humides des Yungas. Plus au Sud, le Rio Ichilo est alimenté par les reliefs du Chaparé, qui est la zone la plus humide de Bolivie. Enfin, le Rio Grande draine une région de montagnes semi-arides (Tableau 1).

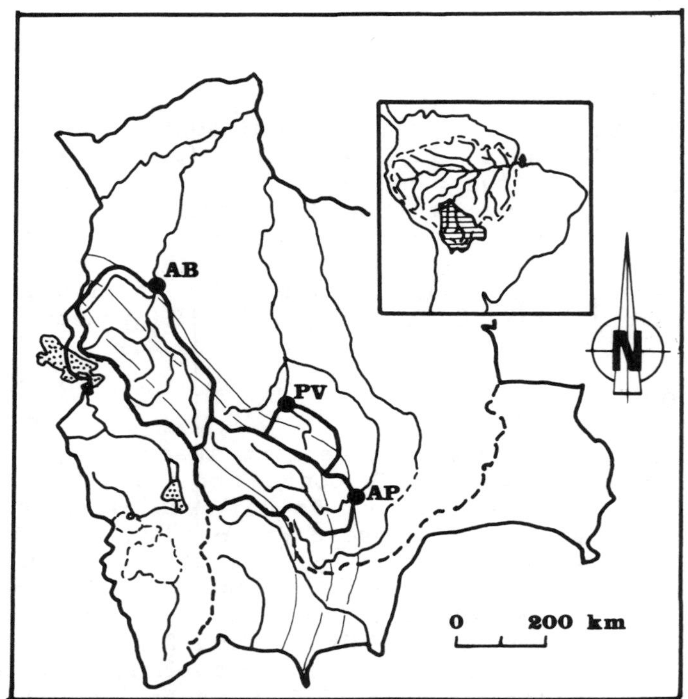

FIG. 1 Localisation des bassins étudiés. AB = Rio Béni à Angosto del Bala, PV = Rio Ichilo à Puerto Villarroel, AP = Rio Grande à Abapo.

L'ECHANTILLONNAGE

Les teneurs en sédiments varient fortement d'un jour à l'autre, dans ces cours d'eau andins. L'autocorrélation effectuée sur les données de turbidité journalières (Fig. 2) montre que la liaison entre des données successives diminue rapidement. Pour un décalage de 10 jours, les coefficients de corrélation sont de 0.25 à AB, 0.17 à PV et 0.47 à AP. Pour un décalage de un mois, ces mêmes coefficients passent respectivement à 0.03, 0.05 et 0.16.

Compte tenu de cette forte variabilité temporelle, un échantillonnage journalier, de faible volume (125 ml) a été mis au point. Ces échantillons font l'objet de mesures de turbidité (Turbidimètre Hach) et de conductivité. Ensuite, des prélèvements d'un litre sont réalisés tous les dix jours, pour analyses physico-chimiques et détermination des MES par filtration-pesée.

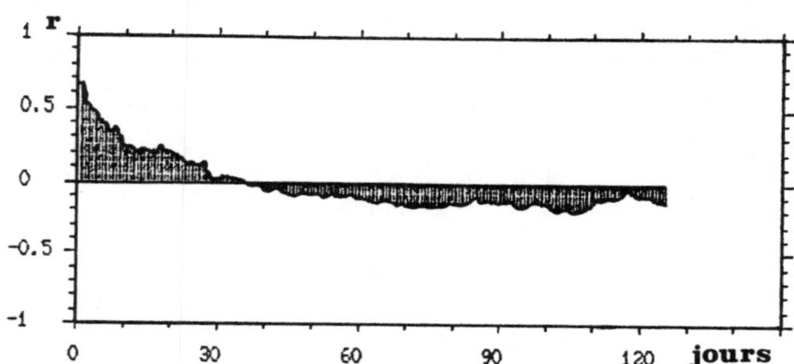

FIG. 2 Coefficients d'autocorrélation des turbidités journalières sur le Rio Béni.

Les prélèvements journaliers et décadaires sont effectués par des observateurs en bordure des cours d'eau. Une étude récente a montré que la distribution des turbidités, sur plusieurs verticales dans la section de mesure, était homogène compte tenu des fortes vitesses observées aux stations du piedmont andin (Guyot et al., 1988).

EVALUATION DU FLUX DE SEDIMENTS

A partir des données de MES et de turbidité des échantillons décadaires des trois stations, une courbe d'étalonnage MES = f(Turbidité) a été construite (Fig. 3).

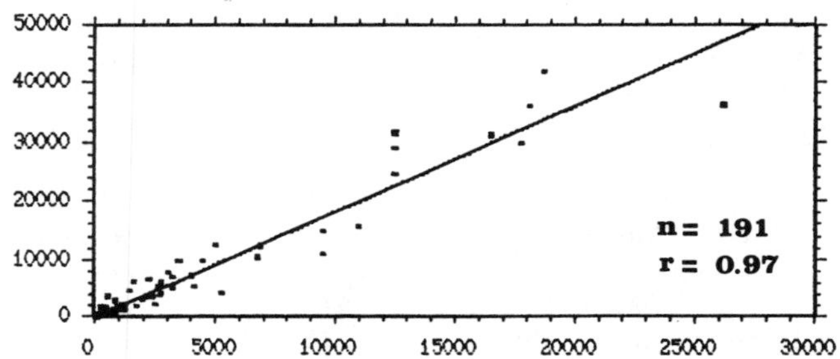

FIG. 3 Courbe d'étalonnage MES ($mg.l^{-1}$) = f (Turbité FTU).

La figure 4 montre l'évolution saisonnière au cours du cycle hydrologique 1986-1987, des MES mesurées et déduites de la turbidité. Il apparait clairement que les prélèvements décadaires ignorent les maxima enregistrés grâce aux mesures journalières. Un échantillonnage à pas de temps supérieur (décadaire, mensuel) entrainerait une sous-estimation sensible des flux de sédiments, à ces stations andines.

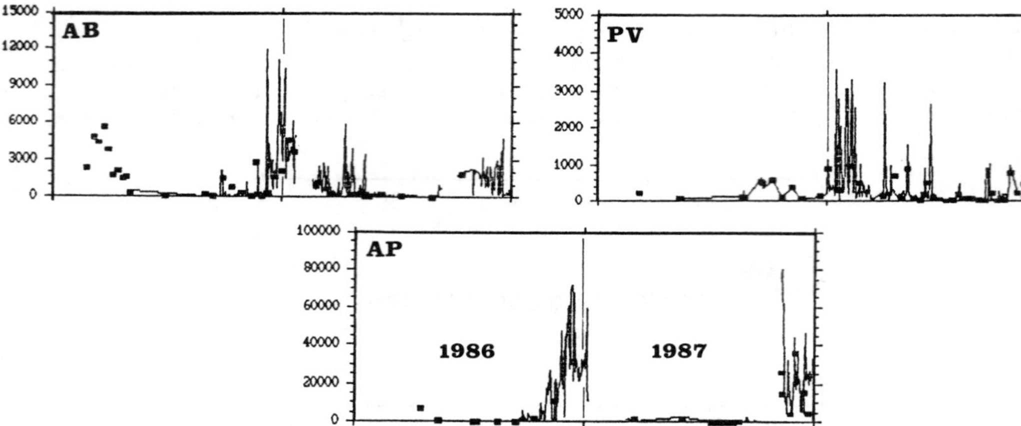

FIG. 4 Evolution au cours du cycle hydrologique 1986-1987 des MES (mg.l-1) mesurées (■) et déduites de la turbidité.

CONCLUSION

Dans les Andes de Bolivie, l'estimation des flux de sédiments n'est possible qu'à partir de mesures journalières. La bonne corrélation obtenue entre la turbidité et les MES a permis l'élaboration d'une courbe d'étalonnage MES = f(Turbidité). A partir d'une mesure journalière de la turbidité, les flux de sédiments peuvent être estimés de manière plus précise sur l'ensemble des stations du réseau PHICAB.

REFERENCES

Guyot, JL., Bourges, J., Calle, H., Cortes, J., Hoorelbecke, R. & Roche, MA. (1989) Transport of suspended sediments to the Amazon by an andean river : the River Mamore, Bolivia. In : River Sedimentation (Proc. Beijing Symp., November 1989).

Guyot, JL., Bourges, J., Hoorelbecke, R., Roche, MA., Calle, H., Cortes, J. & Barragan, MC. (1988) Exportation de matières en suspension des Andes vers l'Amazonie par le Rio Béni, Bolivie. In : Sediment budgets (Proc. Porto Alegre Symp., December 1988), IAHS Publ. 174, 443-451.

Guyot, JL., Bourges, J. & Roche, MA. (1989) Transporte de sedimentos y materias disueltas en la cuenca amazónica de Bolivia. In : La Investigación Francesa en Bolivia (Proc. Santa Cruz Symp., Junio 1989), PHICAB Publ., 3-8.

Guyot, JL., Roche, MA. & Bourges, J. (1989) Etude de la physico-chimie des eaux et des suspensions des cours d'eau de l'Amazonie bolivienne : l'exemple du Rio Béni. In : Journées Hydrologiques de l'ORSTOM (Proc. Montpellier Symp., Septembre 1988), 13-41.

Hydrology in Mountainous Regions. I - Hydrological Measurements; the Water Cycle
(Proceedings of two Lausanne Symposia, August 1990). IAHS Publ. no. 193, 1990.

Choice and calibration of streamflow structures for two mountain experimental basins

J.A. HUDSON, R.C. JOHNSON & J.R. BLACKIE
Institute of Hydrology, Maclean Building, Crowmarsh Gifford, Wallingford, Oxon., OX10 8BB, U.K.

ABSTRACT In 1981, an experiment was set up to investigate the differences between evaporative loss from the 40% forested Kirkton catchment and the heather/grass covered Monachyle catchment, at Balquhidder in Central Scotland. Precise estimates of streamflow from the two main catchments, and from the nested Upper Monachyle catchment, were required for the water balance, and also to calculate loadings of solutes and sediment in the streams. Two Crump weirs and a Flat-V weir were chosen, to be deployed in conditions near to or exceeding design recommendations. Calibration of the Crump weirs using dilution gauging and current metering indicated significant, systematic deviations from the theoretical rating. Alternative ratings are presented which rely on empirical corrections to the velocity head that take account of sediment accretion and unusual velocity distributions.

NOTATION

- b weir width (m)
- Cd discharge coefficient
- H total head above weir (m)
- h static head (m)
- p weir height (m)
- Q discharge (cumecs)
- Qcm current metering Q (cumecs)
- Qx discharge xth iteration (cumecs)
- Va approach velocity (m/sec)
- Vmax maximum point velocity (m/sec)
- α, β velocity head correction coeffs.

INTRODUCTION

A number of catchment land use studies have been established in upland Britain over the last 30 years, a process fraught with difficulties in this inhospitable rugged terrain. In upland Britain, determination of the small evaporation term is critically dependent on the accuracy of measurement of the large precipitation and streamflow terms. Conventional techniques of measuring these terms have therefore come under increasing scrutiny. Accurate flow gauging is essential also for other studies of upland hydrology affected by land use change such as floods and droughts, accurate assessment of solute and sediment losses and for the calibration of rainfall/runoff models.

In theory, suitable flow gauging techniques can be selected from those in the hydraulic literature, many of which are the subject of British or International Standards giving precise design and calibration guidelines. In practice, it has proved difficult to adapt conventional techniques to cope with the wide range of flows in the steep, sinuous, irregular and often unstable channels common in upland areas. Whilst specialised designs such as the steep stream critical depth flume (Harrison, 1965) are available, other constraints on the size and location of experimental catchments often preclude the siting of structures in reaches with the required profiles and approach conditions. In many cases the reaches to be gauged have gradients exceeding the conventional 1:200 upper limit specified for trapezoidal flumes or triangular profile weirs, yet the large flood flows preclude the use of channel width restricting steep stream flumes.

In 1981, two upland catchments at Balquhidder in Central Scotland were instrumented with a view to estimating evaporation rates from both the indigenous vegetation and plantation forestry in this area and comparing these rates with those from previously studied areas in upland Wales and England. This paper uses the Balquhidder flow gauging structures as examples in assessing the feasibility of using independent calibrations for conventional structures built in reaches exceeding British Standard limits to provide integrated flow estimates of sufficient accuracy for use in water balance studies.

CHOICE OF STRUCTURES FOR THE BALQUHIDDER CATCHMENTS

The structures chosen for the two main catchments at Balquhidder, the Kirkton (6.85 sq. km) and the Monachyle (7.70 sq. km), were simple Crump weirs. Despite the steep stream gradients, potential sediment problems and the wide range of flows to be gauged, this design was preferred to others such as steep stream structures, trapezoidal flumes or compound Crumps on the basis of experience gained in the Plynlimon catchments in mid-Wales (Smart, 1977).

Potential problems with this choice existed at both extremes of the flow range but the need to deal with these, through field calibration checks at high flows and the use of temporary, pre-calibrated small flumes in series to check low flow performance, was considered an acceptable cost against the benefits of simple, speedy, low cost installation in difficult conditions.

The Kirkton and Monachyle Crump weirs were both installed in 1982; the layout of the Kirkton is shown in Fig. 1. They both have a nominal 0.7m crest height, and predicted 50 year discharges of 30 cumecs and 26 cumecs dictated crest widths of 7m and 5m respectively. Pre-installation inspection of the size of bedload in the Kirkton suggested that the major movement would probably comprise large calibre material which would cause problems only during and after extreme events. In practice, regular accretion of gravel and sand size fractions occurs in the stilling pool, caused by erosion from forest ditches and roads (Stott et al., 1986). Accretion has reduced the effective weir height from 0.7m to around 0.4m, the level at which the sediment equilibrates. Regular clearance was attempted, but was abandoned to avoid the need to vary the rating for different effective weir heights. It was decided to define a unique independent calibration for the weir, at the lower crest height of 0.4m.

Fluvial geomorphologists have found that up to five times less sediment tends to move in moorland streams than in forest streams (Leeks & Roberts, 1987). Consequently, the reduced sediment problem at Monachyle compared to Kirkton comes as little surprise, and increases the chances of obtaining a rating close to the theoretical. Sediment does build up in the stilling pool, mainly on the left bank where velocity is reduced by a slight left hand bend, but the shoal does not encroach on the weir crest to the extent that occurs at Kirkton. The weir height of 0.7m is maintained but the possibility remains that approach conditions are adversely affected.

The nested Upper Monachyle sub-catchment, scheduled to remain under heather moorland, has a low gradient and sluggish flow through a deep peat area in the approach to the rock bar outfall. A 1:10 Flat Vee design of 0.6m crest height and 3.2m width was considered suitable. The remoteness of the site led to this being prefabricated in duralumin and transported in kit form by helicopter. Confidence in the theoretical rating has been justified by dilution gauging checks. There have been operational problems, due to the freezing conditions common at this altitude. Pressure transducers, installed in the forecourt of the weir, now substitute for the conventional float and counterweight system when this is frozen into the stilling well.

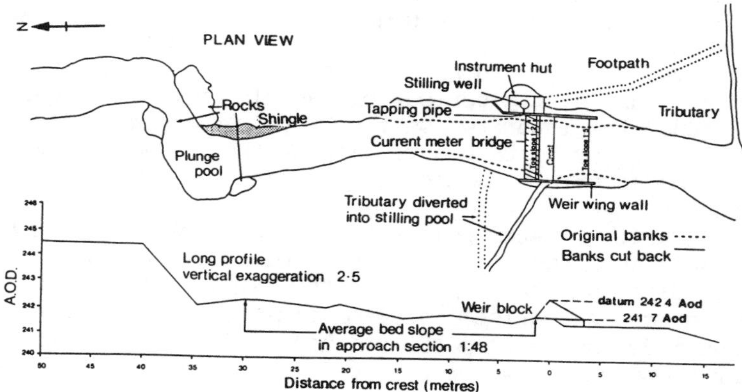

FIG. 1 Channel layout around Kirkton Crump weir.

CALIBRATION METHODS

Dilution gauging using sodium iodide as the tracer (Gilman, 1984) suggested that the Kirkton discharge was being underestimated by the theoretical rating by up to 36% at high flows. A current metering programme was instigated to provide further evidence for this discrepancy, and to provide data from which revised ratings could be derived. The layout is shown in figure 2, and the calculation of discharge is performed as specified by the British Standards Institution (1980).

Meterings were done in a plane parallel to the crest line and adjacent to the tapping point, using an array of up to 6 current meters set at 10cm or 20cm intervals, on a rod which could be moved between each of 15 verticals (11 on Monachyle). To ensure a rigid geometry, a bridge was erected between the wing walls. The cradle, bobbin and clamp system of locating the meter rod (Fig. 2) was subsequently replaced by a simplified system which could be slid more rapidly between verticals. Given adequate safety precautions, this modified system is suitable for one man operation.

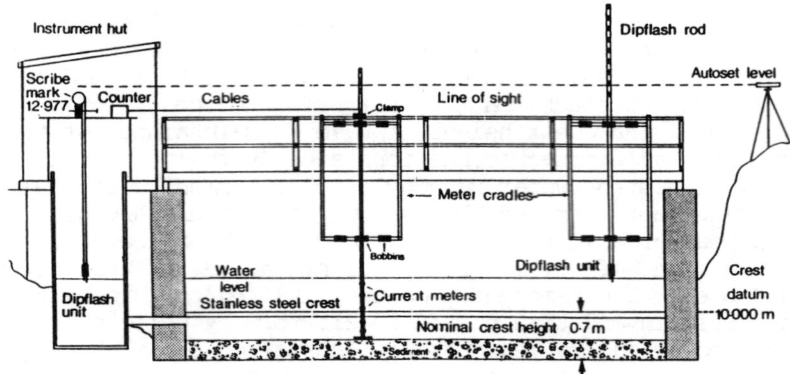

FIG. 2 The current metering rig.

On Kirkton, 53 meterings were performed over a large range of flows, of which nine were subsequently discarded because of meter malfunction; 47 successful meterings were performed at Monachyle. Consecutive runs were done in reverse order of verticals in order to preclude bias during periods of rapidly changing stage. During the later runs the lower two of the Braystoke meters were replaced by miniature meters, to take advantage of their lower velocity threshold. No systematic errors in the final rating were evident as a result of this change.

The current meter pole was used to check the varying sediment level and hence the effective weir height at each vertical. A rod-mounted dipflash provided the water levels used to calculate water depth and cross-sectional area of flow. This also provided a measure of stage independent from the stilling well and allowed identification of any slope on the water surface across the weir after allowing for changing stage. At low to medium flows only small, random deviations were evident. However, at the top end of the flow range, precision was severely limited by the choppiness of the water surface. Discharges were calculated in the field using a BASIC program written for a battery driven EPSON HX-20 computer.

CALIBRATION THEORY

The general discharge equation for Crump weirs is given by Ackers *et al.* (1978) as:

$$Q = Cd\ b\ g^{0.5}\ H^{1.5} \tag{1}$$

where $$H = h + \alpha Va^2/2g \tag{2}$$

$$Va = Qcm/((h+p)b) \tag{3}$$

and $$\alpha = 1 + 3e^2 - 2e^3 \tag{4}$$

where $$e = (Vmax/Va) - 1 \tag{5}$$

The theoretical rating is usually produced by inferring velocity head from iterations on discharge:

$$Qx = Cd\ b\ g^{0.5}\ (h + (\alpha\ Qx\text{-}1^2/2\ g\ ((h+p)b)^2))^{1.5} \qquad (6)$$

The coefficient of discharge (Cd) for the Crump weir has been derived from a combination of hydraulic theory and laboratory studies backed up by extensive field calibrations (British Standards Institution, 1969; Herschy et al., 1977). A constant value of 0.633 is recommended, as it should not vary significantly with head.

To ensure accurate stage measurement, the Froude Number should be less than 0.5 and Alpha, the Coriolis coefficient (or energy flux correction), should be less than 1.25. Alpha used to be the accepted method for correcting velocity head for the effects of mildly unusual approach velocity distributions. However, more extreme velocity distributions can suffer from both skewness and kurtosis, so it is unreasonable to expect one index of asymmetry to cover all eventualities. The velocity profiles for Kirkton, shown in Fig. 3a, indicate that flow is skewed towards the right bank at low flows and towards the left bank at high flows. Alpha ranges up to a value of 2 at a stage of 0.4m on Kirkton, and therefore tends to overestimate the impact of asymmetry on velocity head.

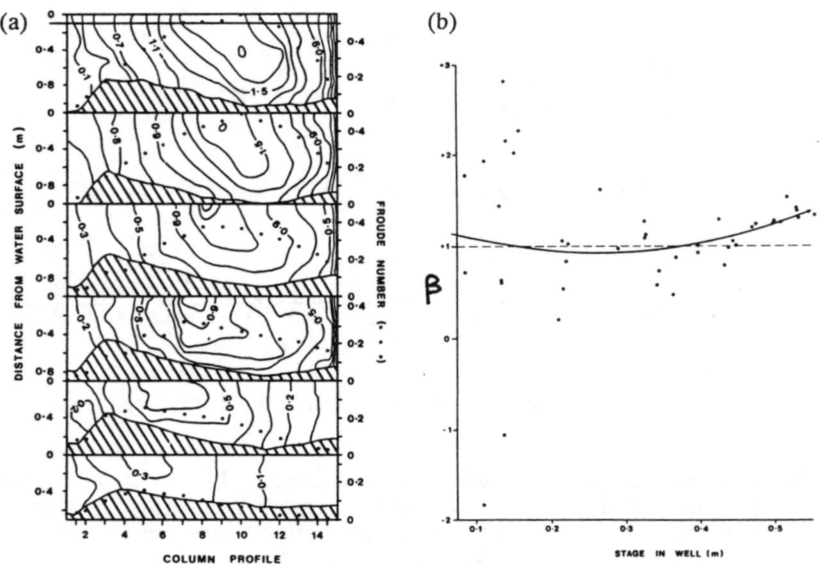

FIG. 3 (a) Velocity profiles for Kirkton (m/sec).
(b) Relationship between Beta and stage.

Fitting new ratings

Mean approach velocity having been calculated from current metering discharges (equation 3), a stage-velocity rating can been derived using a polynomial function fitted by a least-squares technique:

$$Va = 1.1589h^2 + 1.4302h - 0.0236 \qquad (7)$$

As alpha is inapplicable, a new index of velocity asymmetry, Beta, can be derived by rearranging equation 1 and substituting Qcm:

$$\beta = ((Qcm/(Cd\ g^{0.5}\ b))^{0.6667} - h)\ (2g/Va^2) \qquad (8)$$

Beta varies with stage (see Fig. 3b) and can be described thus:

$$\beta = 5.381h^2 - 2.866h + 1.3140 \qquad (9)$$

A rating can now be fitted to the current metering discharges as shown in Fig. 4a. Two theoretical iterative ratings have also been fitted in figure 4a, one using the design weir height (p) of 0.7m and the other using the equilibrium weir height of 0.4m.

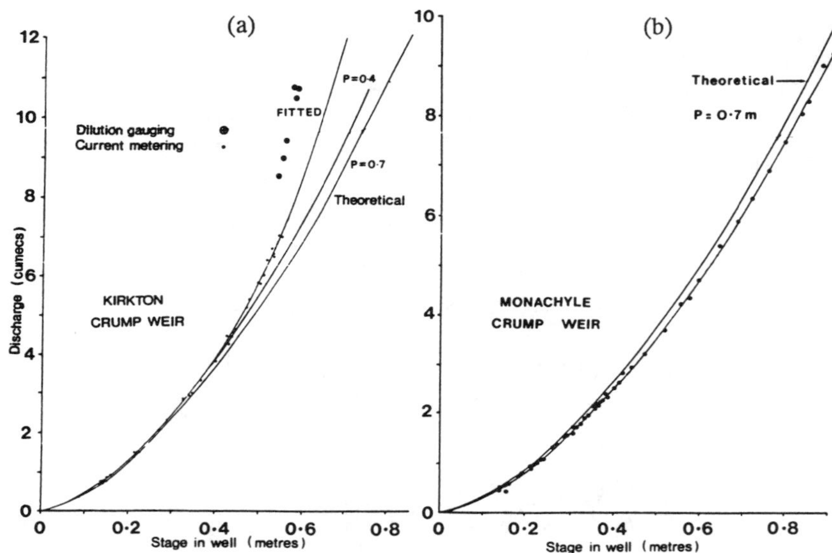

FIG. 4 Theoretical and current meter ratings.

A similar technique was used on the Monachyle, the result being shown in Fig. 4b. Unlike Kirkton, the current metering discharges are less than the theoretical throughout the range, suggesting that either:

(a) the weir height is greater than 0.7m
(b) stage is being overestimated, possibly due to a lateral slope on the water surface. A lag in the response of the well is unlikely as there is no significant difference between ratings done on rising and falling stages.
(c) the shoal developing upstream is reducing approach velocities, possibly by increasing flow resistance. This would make it reasonable to adopt a negative value for Beta.

DISCUSSION OF RESULTS

Both of the new ratings fit the current metering discharge estimates well, with little scatter at low heads. The increasing scatter at the higher flows is probably due to a decreasing precision in stage measurement in turbulent conditions. Flow computation using the mean stage over each gauging, for both rising and falling stages, does not appear to result in significant bias. The two flow values at 0.533m stage in figure 4a were obtained in rising and falling conditions.

The channel configuration upstream of Kirkton weir (Fig. 1) affects approach velocity distributions. Average Froude numbers are less than the maximum value of 0.5 allowed by the British Standard. If column Froude numbers are considered, however, a process which takes more account of the extreme kurtosis of the velocity distribution (Fig. 4a), then the Froude number threshold is reached at a stage of 0.502m. This represents a maximum H/p ratio of 1.4, compared to a ratio of 3.0 - 3.5 that is normally attainable. It is noteworthy that significant deviation of the current meter rating from the p = 0.4m theoretical rating, starts to occur at a stage of 0.4m, 0.1m lower than the Froude number threshold. This may be due to the added impact of skewed flow distribution, and indicates the importance of obtaining a velocity head correction factor that takes both forms of maldistribution into account.

Use of the empirical factor, Beta, has made the recomputation of the rating easier, by removing the need for iteration on discharge. It may also provide the basis for the future development of a correction factor that has a more physical basis. Plotting Beta against stage (Fig. 3b) reveals a parabolic curve, showing considerable scatter particularly at low flows. A minimum value of 0.94 is evident at a stage of 0.250m, with Beta rising to above unity at both lower and higher stages. Comparing this with the velocity profiles in figure 3a, shows that Beta equals 1.0 when the maximum column Froude number is in the centre of the stream (0.375m stage) and departs from unity when the flow distribution is skewed in either direction. The fact that the sediment is not evenly distributed on the approach apron obviously complicates the matter, particularly at low flows, and casts doubt on the fit of the curve at the bottom end. However, errors in velocity head estimation tend not to be so important at low flows.

CONCLUSIONS

The check calibrations performed on the Balquhidder Crump weirs show that accurate operation of Crump weirs is feasible in non-standard conditions provided that their calibrations do not rely solely on British Standard recommendations. The provision of unique independent ratings becomes particularly important for research studies using water balance techniques, where the accuracy of flow estimation is critical.

Dilution gauging has a part to play in this, although the experience at Balquhidder suggests that it is not a technique that should be used in isolation. Velocity-area methods, in contrast, provide a reliable means of estimating discharge independently and also have features suitable for an analytical approach to re-rating structures. These include:

(1) Measurement of the "true" water depth at the tapping pipe, from which it is possible to calculate cross-sectional area of flow and to keep a check on the variation in effective weir height due

to the build up of sediment in the stilling pool.

(2) Independent estimation of stage, at low to medium flows, to compare with the stage measured in the well.

(3) Quantification of the impact of unusual velocity distribution on velocity head.

When further calibrations of this type have been done, on a range of Crump weirs, it may be possible to derive a more physically-based correction factor that relates deviation of Beta to both the skewness and kurtosis of velocity distribution.

The errors found in the ratings of both Kirkton and Monachyle Crump weirs can be directly attributed to the configuration of the channel upstream of the weirs and the varying degree of sediment accretion in the weir pools. For Kirkton, any channel modification made to improve the pattern of flow over the weir would be a step that precludes improvement of the historical data record. Clearing sediment from Kirkton to increase weir height would result in having to use multiple ratings. Channel improvement is unnecessary on the Monachyle, yet clearing sediment would be beneficial as this will build up only slowly in future.

REFERENCES

Ackers, P., White, W.R., Perkins, J.A. & Harrison, A.J.M. (1978) Weirs and flumes for flow measurement. John Wiley and Son Ltd.

British Standards Institution (1969) Long base weirs. Methods of measurement of liquid flow in open channels: No. 3680, Part 4B.

British Standards Institution (1980) Velocity area methods. Methods of measurement of liquid flow in open channels: No. 3680, Part 3A.

Gilman, K. (1984) Errors and uncertainties in dilution gauging. Nordic Hydrological Programme Seminar on methods of water flow measurement with the emphasis on new methods., Trondheim, 16-18 October, 1984.

Harrison, A.J.M. (1965) Some problems concerning flow measurement in steep rivers. J. Inst. Wat. Engs. Vol 19, No. 6, 469-477.

Herschy, R.W., White, W.R. & Whitehead, E. (1977) The design of Crump weirs. Technical Memorandum No. 8., Water Data Unit, Reading.

Leeks, G.J.L. & Roberts, G. (1987) The effects of forestry on upland streams - with special reference to water quality and sediment transport. In Environmental Aspects of Plantation Forestry in Wales. J.E.G. Good (ed), Institute of Terrestrial Ecology, Symp. No. 22, 9-24.

Smart, J.D.G. (1977) The design, operation and calibration of the permanent flow measuring structures in the Plynlimon experimental catchments. Institute of Hydrology Rept. No. 42. Wallingford, Oxon, U.K.

Stott, T.A., Ferguson, R., Johnson, R.C. & Newson, M.D. (1986) Sediment budgets in forested and unforested basins in upland Scotland. In Drainage Basin Sediment Delivery. R.F. Headley (ed). Int. Ass. Hydrol. Sci., Publ. No. 159, 57-68.

Hydrology in Mountainous Regions. I - Hydrological Measurements; the Water Cycle (Proceedings of two Lausanne Symposia, August 1990). IAHS Publ. no. 193, 1990.

Measurement of coarse sediment transport in a small Alpine stream

M.A. LENZI
University of Padova, Department of Land and Agroforest Environments, Water Resources and Soil Conservation Division, Via Gradenigo 6, 35131 Padova, Italy
L. MARCHI
CNR, Institute of Applied Geology, Corso Stati Uniti 4, 35020 Padova, Italy
G.R. SCUSSEL
Experimental Centre for Avalanche Control and Hydro-geological Defence, Veneto Region, 32020 Arabba di Livinallongo (Belluno), Italy

ABSTRACT The paper illustrates the results of early years' operation of an experimental station for the automatic recording of water discharge and coarse sediment transport (Rio Cordon, northeastern Italy, 5 km^2). Coarse sediment is separated from water and fine sediment and is measured by ultrasonic gauges installed on an overhead travelling crane that moves over the storage area where sediment deposition occurs. The paper provides data recorded during two flood events with remarkable sediment transport and illustrates the results of some measurements on artificial sediment accumulations. The possibility is also discussed of using the same approach for coarse sediment measurement in other recording stations.

INTRODUCTION

In recent years, continuous measurements of coarse sediment deposition during flood events have been carried out at an experimental station on the Rio Cordon, a small stream of the Italian Alps, whose watershed drains an area of 5 km^2 (Fig. 1).

The experimental station of the Rio Cordon has been designed, realized and intended for a research project started by the University of Padova and developed in co-operation with Veneto Regional Authority. The recording station of the Rio Cordon was detailly described in a previous paper (Fattorelli <u>et. al</u>, 1988).

The basic components of the station are shown in Fig. 2 and, briefly, it works as follows. A grille has been installed to separate coarse sediment from water and fine sediment (with minimum size < 20 mm). Coarse sediment then accumulates in an open storage area (Fig. 3). The height of accumulated debris during a flood event is evaluated by means of ultrasonic gauges fitted on an overhead travelling crane that moves over the storage area. The ultrasonic sensors record the distance from the travelling crane to accumulated debris: based on these measurements, height and volume of deposited material can easily be assessed. The distance among the sensors fitted on the travelling crane is 1.10 m. The devised approach avoids damages from direct contact between the measuring devices and the remarkable volume of coarse sediment occurring in the Rio Cordon.

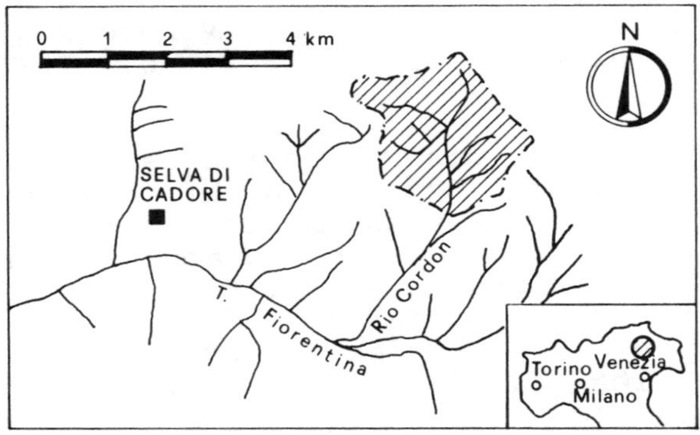

FIG. 1 Geographical location of Rio Cordon watershed.

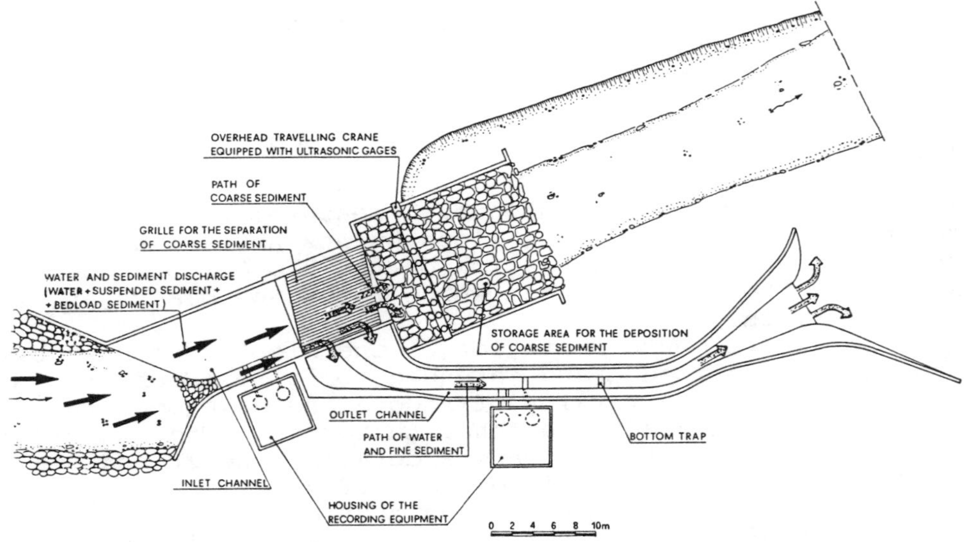

FIG. 2 Plan of the experimental station.

FIG. 3 Sediment accumulation after a flood (3 July 1989).

Water and fine sediment passing through the grille are diverted to an outlet channel. Gauges for recording water discharge and water quality parameters have been installed both in the inlet and in the outlet channels. Suspended sediment is measured in the outlet channel by means of a turbidimeter based on light absorption. Data acquisition from the various gauges of the experimental station is managed by a data logger. The ultrasonic gauges for sediment accumulation measurement work when the water level exceeds a given value. In order to ensure an adequate flexibility in the station operation, the possibility has been provided to modify the water stage value at which the ultrasonic gauges start working, the channel in which the threshold water level is measured and the distance between subsequent stops of the travelling crane. Present settings are 0.3 m for the water stage in the outlet channel (corresponding to 0.943 m^3s^{-1}), 0.5 m between each stop of the travelling crane and the subsequent one for the first ten stops and 1.0 m for the remaining stops.

ANALYSIS OF EXPERIMENTAL DATA

In order to test the consistency and the accuracy of the recordings of the ultrasonic gauges, a set of experimental measurements was performed on artificial sediment accumulations.

Five artificial sediment accumulations, differently shaped, were placed in the open storage area. One of these accumulations (main accumulation) was similar to the debris cone that accumulates in the open storage area during flood events. The other accumulations were cone- or mound-shaped. Four measurements of the accumulation heights were performed using the ultrasonic gauges fitted on the overhead travelling crane. Table 1 reports mean and standard deviation of the height of the accumulations.

TABLE 1 Height of artificial accumulations.

		Measurement set			
		1	2	3	4
Mean	a)	61.16	61.47	61.31	61.04
	b)	62.44	61.79	62.35	62.46
Standard	a)	34.42	34.73	35.02	34.91
deviation	b)	46.07	45.85	45.82	45.85

a) main accumulation
b) measurement on the whole storage area

It should be pointed out that the values reported in Table 1 for the whole storage area also include areas where no accumulations were present. Possible causes of variability among measurements could be due to variations in air temperature and to differences in the points where the overhead travelling crane stopped. The absence of significant differences among the four sets of measurements appears clearly from the values reported in Table 1. Besides, it was tested using Friedman's test (Statistical Graphic System, 1987): the obtained significance level was 0.878 for the whole storage area and 0.997 for the main accumulation.

A manual measurement was also performed of the distance from the sensors to the surface of the accumulations. The values of the height of the accumulations recorded by the ultrasonic gauges resulted to be somewhat higher than the respective manual measurements. The values measured by the ultrasonic sensors are represented by the distance between the gauges and the nearest point of the accumulation area exposed in the wave beam. On a sloping surface, as the sediment cone accumulated in the open storage area during flood events, this record results in an overestimation of the accumulation height. The difference between the values recorded by the ultrasonic gauge and the distance measured on the sensor vertical depends upon the slope and the height of the accumulation and upon the sensor characteristics. For the main accumulation (14 m^3), the automatic measurement made using ultrasonic gauges resulted in a volume overestimation of 20%. Thanks to the reduced distance between the gauges and deposited sediment, minor discrepancies are expected for final values of larger accumulations from major floods. The inaccuracy of continuous sediment accumulation measurements at the experimental station may be considered comparatively limited. The comparison of automatic and manual measurements just described and the topographic evaluation of the total debris volume deposited allows to correct the values recorded during flood events.

The experimental station has been working since the summer of 1986. In the early years of its operation, four flood events occurred with remarkable sediment transport. During the first event (19 July 1987), the grille used to separate coarse sediment from water and fine sediment was damaged by the passage of large boulders: this fact affected the accuracy of bed load measurement both for this flood and for the subsequent one (24 August 1987). The grille was then reinforced and a more complete and satisfacory recording of sediment deposition was available for the remaining events (11 October 1987 and 3 July 1989). Figs 4 and 5 show precipitation, flood hydrograph and coarse sediment accumulation for the events of 11 October 1987 and of 3 July 1989. These events resulted in a deposition in the storage area of about 50 m^3 and 75 m^3 respectively. During the event of 3 July 1989, about 10 m^3 of sediment stopped at the grille end and were prevented from reaching the storage area. Thus they were not recorded by the gauges fitted on the overhead travelling crane.

The recorded data seems to indicate a behaviour in the event of October 1987 different from the one of July 1989. In the October 1987 flood, sediment deposition occurred mainly during the rising limb of the hydrograph. This can possibly be referred to the availability of loose sediment in the channel reach immediately upstream the recording station. The event of July 1989 seems to be characterized by a more continuous sediment supply.

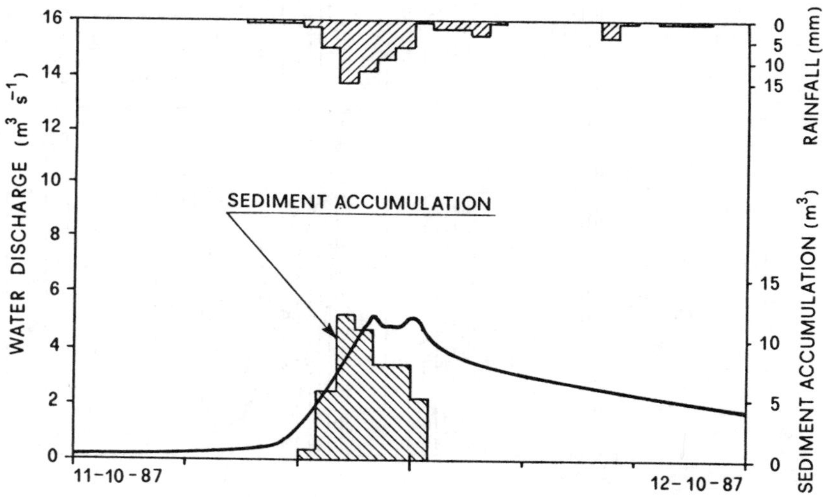

FIG. 4 Water discharge and sediment deposition for the flood of 11 October 1987.

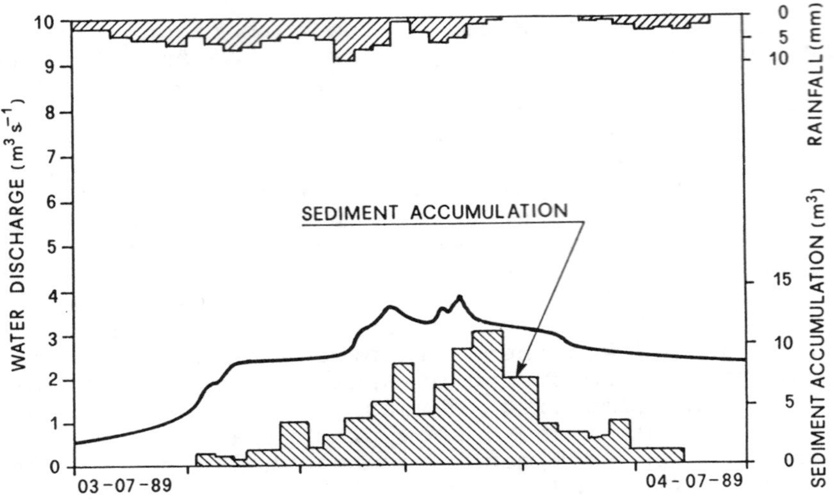

FIG. 5 Water discharge and sediment deposition for the flood of 3 July 1989.

A detailed analysis of the relationships between hydrologic flood characteristics, sediment storage in the channel and sediment transport, apparently needs more experimental data. In addition, it goes beyond the objective of this contribution, that deals essentially with the operation of instruments for coarse sediment measurement.

The particle size distribution in the sediment from the event of 3 July 1989 is shown in Fig. 6.

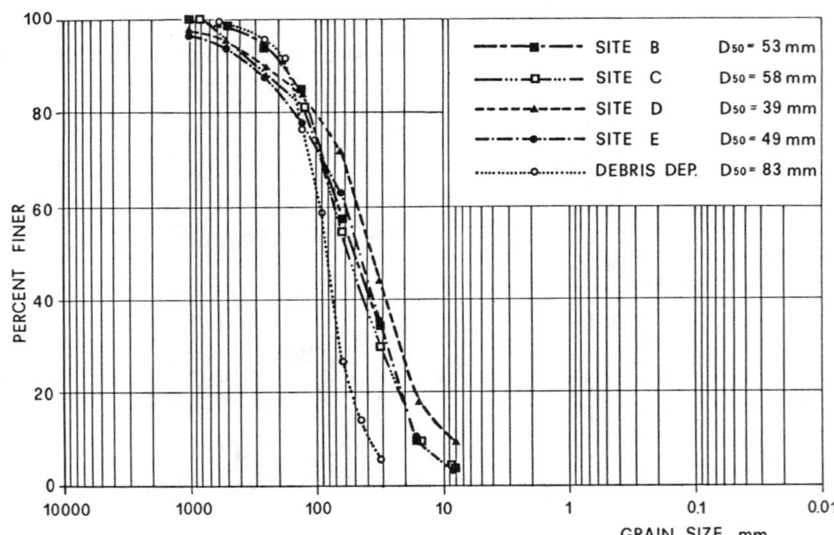

FIG. 6 Particle size distribution for debris deposition and for four sites on the stream.

The coarser sediment in the accumulation and its uniform distribution, in comparison with four sites located on the main stream upstream the experimental station, can be referred mainly to the selection by the separating grille.

A bottom trap has been installed in the outlet channel to measure fine sediment moving as bed load. The need for a larger bottom trap emerged from the early years of station operation and it will be built at the end of the outlet channel. This would ensure a reliable and complete (even if not continuous) measurement of fine bed load.

CONCLUSIONS

The satisfactory resolution of sediment measurement at the experimental station appears from Figs 4 and 5. From more data, it is expected that useful information can be obtained for an improved understanding of sediment transport processes in small alpine streams. In this connection, it should be reminded that data on coarse sediment transport are still scanty for this kind of streams and, in most cases, only total volume of sediment deposited during a flood is available. In the Rio Cordon station, on the contrary, debris accumulation data for time increments of about one hour have proved available.

The recording devices do not require the operator's presence during flood events and this represents a valuable characteristic of the Rio Cordon automatic station. However, due to the complexity of the station, the maintenance both of hardware and of software requires steady care: in addition to an ordinary maintenance, a special intervention is performed after every significant flood event, in order to remove accumulated sediment from the storage area and to check the proper operation of various instruments and of the power supply system in the station (a hydraulic turbine, a diesel engine and a standby battery.

In spite of some initial difficulties, the basic operation principle of the experimental station of the Rio Cordon, based on the separation of coarse sediment by means of a grille and on the measurement of the accumulated volume using ultrasonic gauges, has proved rational and suitable. In the opinion of the authors, the approach developed and tested on the Rio Cordon could be adopted in other recording stations where a continuous measurement of coarse bed load transport is required. In smaller streams, or in the cases in which a comparatively minor precision can be accepted, ultrasonic gauges could be installed on fixed structures without the need of increasing their number. In this way, it would be possible to remove problems from moving and stopping the overhead travelling crane.

AKNOWLEDGEMENTS The authors wish to thank Prof. Sergio Fattorelli, Head of the Water Resources and Soil Conservation Division of the Departement of Land and Agroforest Environments - University of Padova and Mr. Alberto Lucchetta, Director of the Experimental Centre for Avalanche Control and Hydro-geological Defence - Veneto Region for the valuable suggestions and for the support given in the development of the study. The work was partly funded by the Italian Ministry of Public Education (60% Funds - Prof. G. Benini, University of Padova).

REFERENCES

Fattorelli, S., Keller, H.M., Lenzi, M. & Marchi, L. (1988) An experimental station for the automatic recording of water and sediment discharge in a small alpine watershed. Hydrol. Sci. J. 33 (6), 607-617.

Statistical Graphics System (1987) STATGRAPHICS - User Guide, 14.1-14.19.9.

Hydrology in Mountainous Regions. I - Hydrological Measurements; the Water Cycle
(Proceedings of two Lausanne Symposia, August 1990). IAHS Publ. no. 193, 1990.

Overflow weirs as gauging stations in mountain brooks

H. MOSCHEN
Tiroler Wasserkraftwerke AG, Abt. BaH, Landhausplatz 2, A-6020 Innsbruck, Austria

ABSTRACT The measuring profiles in mountain brooks are subject to constant alterations due to the movement of bed load. A frequent countermeasure is the construction of channels in order to create steady measuring conditions. Another good solution is the construction of two successive drop sills.

HISTORY OF DEVELOPMENT

The thorough knowledge of the regime of mountain brooks is a basic requirement not only for the planning and design of any hydropower development there, but also for the estimation of possible environmental effects. Subsequently it is necessary to prove the officially ordered minimum flow downstream of an intake weir or dam and to demonstrate the development of discharge along the residual water brook section.

In these brooks water-stage measurements presents a variety of difficulties so that for a long time no continuous measurements were performed. The most frequent problem is the variability of the measurement profile. The relation between water-stage and discharge often remains stable for a short time only (hours, days). In order to overcome this disadvantage gauging stations had to be built, where the mean velocity curve remains approximately stable for a longer period of time. To obtain reliable gauge records in mountain brooks considerable constructional measures are necessary.

In 1975 there were already some examples of mountain brook gauging stations in the Alps, where attempts at the stabilization of mean velocity curves were made.

Following experiments at the ETH Zürich the Swiss National Hydrology (3) constructed a gauging station on the Massa below the Aletsch Glacier and started to operate it in 1965. The building costs amounted to 850,000 SFr. The gauging station consisted in principle of a concentrating drop sill below which a basin was formed. The outflow of this basin was conducted by a well-formed intake into an approximately 9 m long paved channel, in which no bed load remained, and then at the end of the channel it fell down again into the natural brook bed. The measuring profile was situated in the lower third of the channel. With this construction the measuring area was hydraulically separated from upstream and downstream and thus hydraulically clearly defined conditions prevailed.

In 1963 the Hydrographic Service of the Tyrolian government likewise established a gauging station on the Rofenache, a headwater of the Ötztal Ache (A = 98 Km², 1900 m above sea-level). This station was essentially a channel without sills, paved with granite (length 14.5 m, width 6.5 m, depth 2.5 m). The purpose was to stabilize the measurement profile and to create steady flow conditions for current measurements. Local hydraulic phenomena and occasional backwater due to downstream sedimentation, however, influenced the water-stage measurements.

With the construction of the gauging station Vernagtbach in 1973 (1), also in the Ötztal, (A= 11.4 Km², 2640 m above sea-level) the disadvantages of the gauging station Rofenache were improved by building a drop structure at the end of the channel.

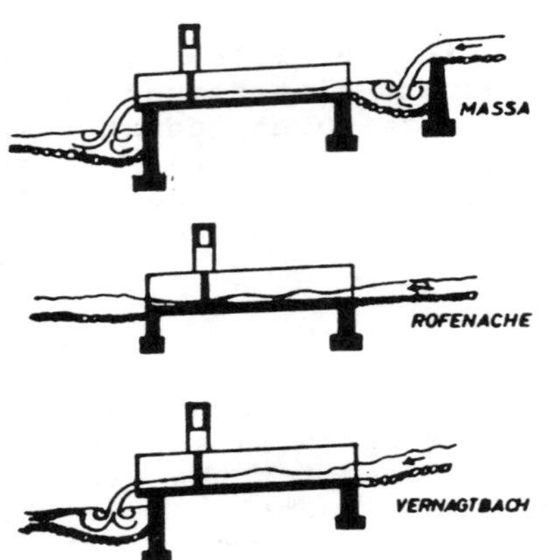

FIG. 1 History of development.

THE TIWAG TWIN OVERFLOW WEIR TYPE

L = length of basin
w_1 = horizontal weir section
w_2 = section inclined 1:10
H = differential head between the weirs
h = measured gauge over the weir

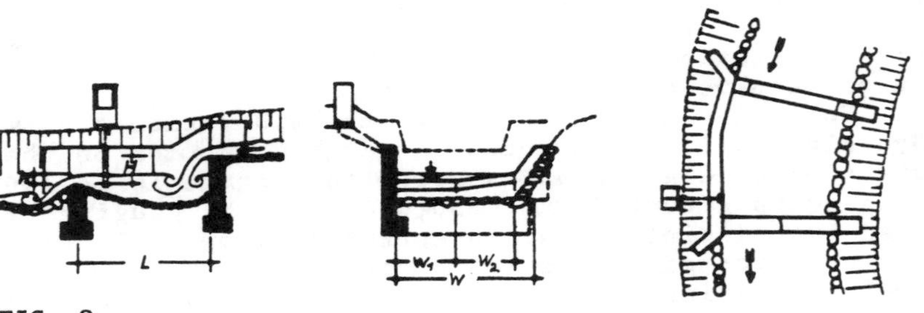

FIG. 2

Based on the hydraulically correct constructional principles of the gauging station Massa, Drobir (Tiroler Wasserkraftwerke AG, Innsbruck- TIWAG) considered lowering the enormous construction costs while maintaining the hydraulic effectiveness.

If current measurements in the immediate area of the gauge profile are abandoned in favor of discharge measurements according to a dilution method, the measuring channel, which has been used up to now and is not unproblematic from the hydraulic point of view (local hydraulic phenomena), becomes unnecessary. It is replaced by a bottom sill with a rounded crest as control section for the discharge from the basin formed between the two sills. This form of measuring sill with a rounded crest and steel-plated against abrasion was chosen for hydraulic reasons. It also facilitates the removal of sedimentation from the basin. A guidewall at one bank allows a simple and convenient installation of the measuring equipment (pneumatic gauges, pressure sensors, rarely gauges shafts).

The distance between the basin-forming overflow weir and the control section is a compromise between sufficient removal of bed load and necessary distance of water-stage measurement from the control section (<= 3h). In residual water brook sections with smaller discharges a short distance is chosen. These short basins remain largely free of bed load. However, during floods they show irregular and disturbing wavy surfaces due to the approaching roller, thus reducing the accuracy of measurement.

Gauging stations, where the measurement of large discharges is required are provided with suitable long basins, which with the receding flood regularly fill up with bed load. Thus, with small or average discharges, i. e. during 90 % of the year, the effect of the twin overflow weir type is diminished with correspondingly poor measurement results during this period.

Dimensions and characteristic data of the described twin overflow weir gauges:

No.	Name	Year of const.	Constr costs in 1,000 ÖS	A-Rest / A-nat. km^2	Discharge NQ ($m^3 s^{-1}$)	Discharge HQ_1 ($m^3 s^{-1}$)	Dimensions H (m)	L	W	w1	w2
1	Kühtai	1979	500	12.3 6.8	0.12 0.05	2.5 1.5	0.9	6.5	4.9	-	4.0
2	Längental	1980	500	9.7	0.07	2.0	1.1	6.3	4.3	1.3	2.5
3	Jaßsteg	1982	500	16.7 172.0	0.15 1.7	8.0 32.0	0.2	7.0	1.3	-	8.0
4	Mühlbach	1977	280	13.9	0.20	2.8	1.0	6.0	5.0	-	3.2
5	Grundache	1976	400	17.0	0.12	3.4	1.1	6.0	3.0	1.5	-
6	Milders	1987	600	39.1 62.1	0.20 0.35	8.0 12.0	1.0	7.0	9.0	3.0	4.5
7	Platz	1981	1200	40.0 188.5	0.20 0.60	8.0 30.0	1.3	9.0	9.4	2.0	7.0
8	Ochsen-garten	1980	700	14.6 43.0	0.10 0.30	3.0 9.0	0.8	6.8	7.5	2.0	3.0
9	Pfunds	1980	400	50.6 91.6	0.25 0.50	7.5 16.0	0.4	7.0	5.0	4.9	-
10	Kniepiß	1978	500	22.7 52.0	0.12 0.30	5.0 11.0	0.8	6.3	11.0	-	6.0
11	Gepatsch*	1981	1000	55.0	0.10	16.0	1.8	8.5	8.0	3.0	3.5
12	Niederthai	1975	350	30.4 56.0	0.25 0.40	6.0 11.0	1.0	9.5	9.5	1.6	6.0
13	Koflerkreuz	1978	600	32.7 64.4	0.17 0.40	6.5 13.0	1.2	6.0	6.5	2.5	-
14	Ritzenried	1978	600	132.6 220.0	1.0 1.6	26.0 45.0	3.0	9.8	15.5	3.5	15.0
11	Gepatsch* rebuilt	1989		55.0	0.10	16.0	0.5	8.5	8.0	3.0	3.5

THE TIWAG SINGLE OVERFLOW WEIR TYPE

As with the twin overflow weir type the control section in the single overflow weir type is also constructed with a rounded crest. This type of gauge should preferably be used for brook reaches with low or average surface slopes. Sites just below sediment deposit sections are also favorable. The main flow should be along the guidewall. This is achieved by installing the gauging stations in a slight bend of the brook. Particular attention should be paid here to upstream debris deposits, which naturally modify the conditions of approach and thus influence the water-stage. Temporary test gauges of round timber sealed with foil are also used upstream.

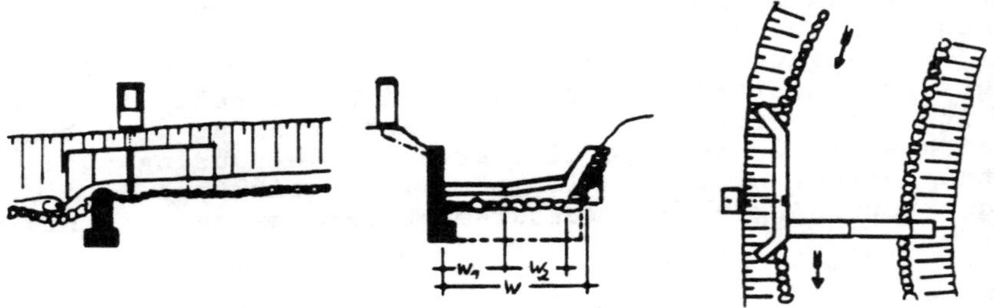

FIG. 3

Dimensions and characteristic data of the described single overflow weir gauges:

No.	Name	Year of const.	Constr. costs in 1,000 ÖS	A-Rest / A-nat. km²	Discharge NQ m³ s⁻¹	Discharge HQ1 m³ s⁻¹	Dimensions H m	W	w1	w2
1	Urgen	1989	400	2.8 22.4	0.02 0.20	3.5 4.0	0.7	6.0	-	4.2
2	Finstermünz	1985	100	73.4	0.50	11.0	0.6	4.5	4.0	- timber
3	Achenkirch	1989	500	7.4 125.7	0.01 1.00	5.0 25.0	0.3	11.0	1.0	10.0
4	Schalklhof	1985	80	107.0	0.50	17.0	0.6	7.5	7.0	- timber
5	Eggeberg	1987	420	35.2	0.14	6.4	0.4	6.3	-	6.3
6	Pigerbach	1989	500	191.0	1.50	33.0	0.3	7.0	-	5.8
7	Plangeroß	1985	400	15.5 102.9	0.06 0.40	2.3 16.0	0.5	9.0	3.5	4.0
8	Wenns	1984	700	187.6 275.0	1.0 1.5	28.0 55.0	0.4	20.0	7.5	8.0
9	In der Au	1989	600	140.5 201.5	0.5 0.8	4.7 6.5	0.5	12.0	2.5	9.5
10	Hopfgarten	1984	800	287.5	1.5	45.0	0.6	17.5	5.0	9.5
11	Rabland	1988	1000	374.0	2.9	40.0	0.5	15.0	5.0	6.7
12	Hof	1986	800	8.2 430.0	1.1 3.0	30.0 50.0	0.5	17.0	2.5	13.5
13	Lienz	1988	1100	669.0	5.0	70.0	0.5	21.0	7.0	11.0

HYDRAULIC PRINCIPLES

The planning and design of a gauging station of the twin overflow weir type is performed in a similar way as the installation of sills for the stabilization of a course of a river (3). When determining the length of the basin, as already mentioned, the requirements of the gauging stations should be taken into consideration and the validity of the initial estimations should be examined. The calculated tolerable lengths show a great range of variation.The basin should be kept as short as possible for a better removal of bed load.

The mean velocity curve can be estimated in advance. With small discharges it follows the curve the energy head (HE) and depending on the the distance between the gauge and the sill it approaches more or less rapidly the curve of the critical depth (t_{Gr}). With large discharges the mean velocity curve cuts the h-line due to the lowering of the water surface. A distance of a <= 3 h_{max} has proved favorable.

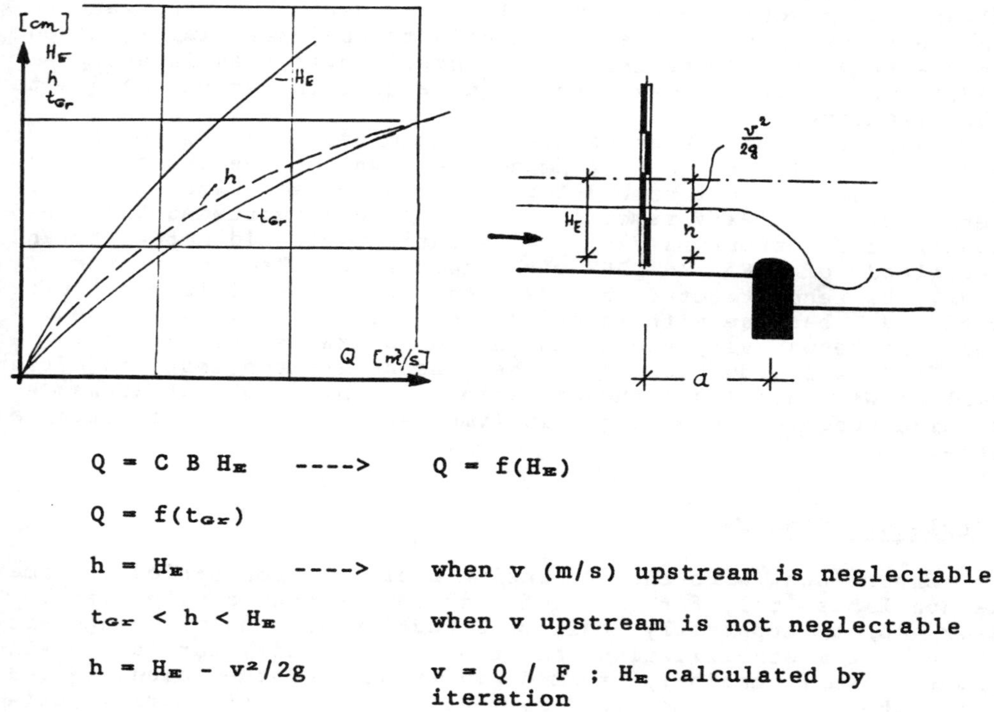

$Q = C\ B\ H_E$ ----> $Q = f(H_E)$

$Q = f(t_{Gr})$

$h = H_E$ ----> when v (m/s) upstream is neglectable

$t_{Gr} < h < H_E$ when v upstream is not neglectable

$h = H_E - v^2/2g$ $v = Q / F$; H_E calculated by iteration

PRACTICAL EXPERIENCE

From 1975 to 1981 the TIWAG built 13 gauges of the twin overflow weir type and subsequently in order to save expenses 14 more gauging stations of the single overflow weir type.

All these gauging stations cover mountain brooks, glacier

brooks or mountain rivers with characteristically high discharge fluctuations (low water 3-8 l s^{-1} Km^{-2}, flood 300-1000 l s^{-1} Km^{-2}). They are all situated at an altitude of 1000 to 2000 m above sea-level. The catchment areas vary from 6 to 200 Km^2, with single overflow weir types even 350 or 650 Km^2.

Characteristic for all these brooks is their coarse bottom (particle diameter > 100 mm), which again and again undergoes great changes during floods due to the movement of bed load.

At all gauge stations of this type a long-term stabilization of the relation between water-stage and discharge has been achieved. The scatter of results corresponds to the accuracy of measurement in mountain brooks, i.e. it varies between +/- 10 %.

Twin Overflow Weir Type

During exceptional floods the entire station may be inundated. Its effect then equals that of a single overflow weir, where the peek discharge can still be calculated from traces of the maximum upstream surface.

Occasionally basins had to be cleared mechanically after floods (Grundache, Platz, Kühtai). The costs, however, were relatively low. Due to the easy access to the measuring equipment water-stage recordings have so far hardly ever been interrupted. Defective equipment was more frequent than interruptions due to the discharge.

The basin of the gauge Gepatschalm proved to be too short. Since it is situated on the immediate front of the Gepatsch Glacier a large amount of bed load is transported there. In consideration of an easy removal of bed load a shortened basin was constructed. Unfortunately the measuring weir did not withstand the floods of 1985 and 1987 with their strong bed load force. It had to be reconstructed in 1989. The conditions of approach were modified, because with larger discharges (< 12 m^3 s^{-1}) the water surface was very uneven in the immediate measuring area.

In Kühtai and Grundache the basins are too long and often fill up with bed load, the conditions in the catchment areas (e. g. high sediment discharge in lime) are probably of importance here.

Single Overflow Weir Type

Experience with the operation over a longer period of time is available only for few of the constructed single overflow weir gauges. Apparently this construction also helps to achieve a long-term stabilization of the mean velocity curves. In all cases a small basin is formed in front of the round-crested weir. The occuring bed load is mostly carried off. During periods of flood occasionally some boulders remain or are slowly transported through the measuring area. Due to the decentralized organization of our measuring crews these boulders with their influence on the water-stage can be removed within a short time, thus restoring the former relation between water-stage and discharge within a short time. Two gauging stations (Plangeroß and Wenns, both on the brook Pitzbach) disappeared in the bottom of the brook due to bed load deposits during the flood of 1987 and had to be elevated.

Gauge Gepatschalm

Gauge Kniepiß

Gauge Platz

Gauge Wenns

CONCLUSION

Without exception the use of overflow weirs as gauging stations can be considered successful irrespective of the occasional impairment due to the chosen length of the basins. The planning and design of a gauging station also require a certain amount of "luck". Nature does not always follow the considerations and calculations of man, especially not if the catchment areas present special conditions which are difficult to estimate.

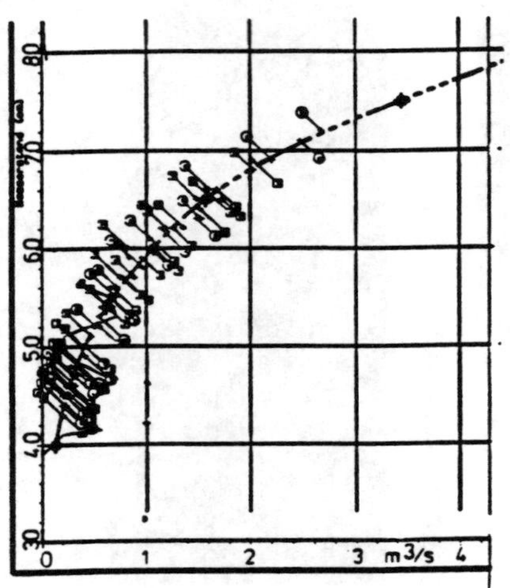

FIG. 4 Observation points (Kniepiß gauge 1983-1989).

REFERENCES

(1) Bergmann u. Reinwarth (1976) Zeitschrift für Gletscherkunde und Glazialgeologie, 157-180
(2) Volkart P. (1972) Stabilisierung von Flußläufen mittels Einb von Querschwellen. Mitt. Nr.6, der Versuchsanstalt für Flußbau, Hydrologie und Glaziologie, ETH Zürich
(3) Walser, E. (1971) Besondere Mitteilungen zum Deutschen Gewässerkundlichen Jahrbuch 35. 225-232, Koblenz.

Hydrology in Mountainous Regions. I - Hydrological Measurements; the Water Cycle
(Proceedings of two Lausanne Symposia, August 1990). IAHS Publ. no. 193, 1990.

Hydrological and sediment monitoring in mountainous pilot watersheds in Sefid Rud basin in Iran

R. PAVLOVIC
Food and Agriculture Organization of the United Nations, C/o UNDP Res. Rep., P.O.Box 15875-4557, Tehran, Iran
S. PROHASKA
FAO-Consultant, Jaroslav Cerni Institute for Development of Water Resources, P.O.Box 530, Belgrade, Yugoslavia
M. BEHBEHANI, B. BABAKHANLOH & S. DAMAVANDI
Bureau of Soil Conservation and Watershed Management, Forest & Range Org., Min. of Agriculture, Tehran, Iran

ABSTRACT A monitoring network which was established in pilot watersheds in the Sefid Rud basin in Iran is presented in this paper. The watersheds, ranging in size from 10 ha to 10 km2, were equipped for monitoring of various climatological, hydrological, soil erosion and sediment transport parameters. The data are collected for later analyzis of relationships between rainfall, runoff, landuse practices, soil erosion and sediment yield. The results will be used for replication to other watersheds with similar physiographic characteristics.

INTRODUCTION

The UNDP/FAO project entitled "In-service training in watershed management techniques" has been implemented in the Sefid Rud basin in Iran since 1988. The basin covers an area of 56 700 km2 and is drained into the country's largest same named reservoir. Although the precipitation rate is low in most of the basin, the steep topography and heavy rains in spring and fall, when the soil cover is poor, produce intensive erosion which results in reservoirs siltation; so, for example, the volume of the Sefid Rud reservoir was reduced during the first 20 years of its life from 1 800 million to 900 million m3. Similar problems are faced in other areas of the country, and the government has undertaken an extensive soil conservation programme.

The main development objective of the project is to increase the trained manpower needed for these activities. It is implemented in two training centers, in Tehran and Zanjan; field works are carried out on small training and demonstration watersheds near Zanjan, which is the center of the basin. Some of the training areas were equipped in 1989 as pilot catchments, for systematic monitoring of hydro-meteorological parameters as well as for measurements of soil erosion and sediment transport. The data collected will be used for analyzing relationships between rainfall, runoff, landuse practices, soil erosion and sediment yield; the results should then be replicated to other watersheds with similar physiographic characteristics. The paper gives first basic information on pilot watersheds, and then describes the monitoring network and makes remarks on data collection and processing methods.

WATERSHEDS AND THEIR TREATMENT

The Sefid Rud basin is settled up in the northwestern part of the country. It has two main river systems, Qezel Owzan covering 90% of the total area, and Shah Rud covering the remaining 10%. The climate in the basin is dry and harsh. The temperature may range from - 35°C to 44°C, with the mean annual values between 5 and 14°C. Mean annual rainfall varies between 300 and 400 mm. However, along the northern boundary of the Elburz Range annual rainfall is as high as 700 to 1000 mm. There is a dry period from July to October. The erosion rate is high and the estimated value of the average sediment yield is approximately 1000 t/km2/year.

The pilot watersheds are located near Zanjan; four areas were selected and they will be briefly described in this section.

Barut Aghaji pilot watershed

The catchment is 16 km Zanjan off the highway to Bijar. It covers 10.56 km2 and is north facing. The central stream divides the catchment equally and the village of Barut Aghaji is centrally located (Fig. 1). Altitude ranges from 1 800 m in the main valley to 2 045 m at the highest point on the north side of the catchment. Slopes are moderate (15-20 degrees) with steep areas occurring adjacent to streams. The geology consists of the older Pre-Cambrian to Permian rocks (shales, dolomites, limestones). Quarternary alluvium in fans and terraces and landslide colluvium occur in the valley floors and on side slopes.

The central basin in which the village is located is used for intensive cropping (wheat, barley, potatoes, peas), forage (alfalfa), and fruit (grapes, apricots, mulberry). The steeper perimeter slopes are used for rainfed cultivation of wheat and barley. Those slopes which are difficult to cultivate are used for extensive grazing by sheep, goats and cattle.

The Barut Aghaji catchment is used to demonstrate and evaluate short-term and long-term responses of treatment practices including simple gully control measures, conservation and dry farming practices, improved irrigation and other land management and rehabilitation measures, range management and water harvesting.

Two sub-catchments were selected as pilot areas (paired watersheds B1 and B2 in Fig. 1), with areas of 74 and 77 ha, respectively. They are located opposite on both catchment sides. The sub-catchment B2 will be treated with appropriate conservation and gully control measures, such as:

(a) reduction of surface runoff by contour farming and terracing;
(b) elimination of grazing and extension of agricultural land;
(c) gully control by building checkdams.

The sub-catchment B1 will remain in its present state and serve as a control.

Bijar road pilot watershed

This catchment is located 5 km east of Barut Aghaji, and covers an area of 28 ha. The topography is steep, with altitudes ranging between 1 880 and 2 120 m. The catchment is severely degraded and eroding rangeland, with rills and gullies which are up to 10 m deep. The area will be used for demonstration of improved rangeland management using reseeding with improved species, grazing control, and rill, gully and stream bank erosion control. The catchment will also be adapted to well designed water harvesting and spreading techniques for providing sufficient irrigation water for forage crop on bench terraces and fruit trees on contour furrows and banks. The adopted measures of the catchment treatment are shown in Fig. 2.

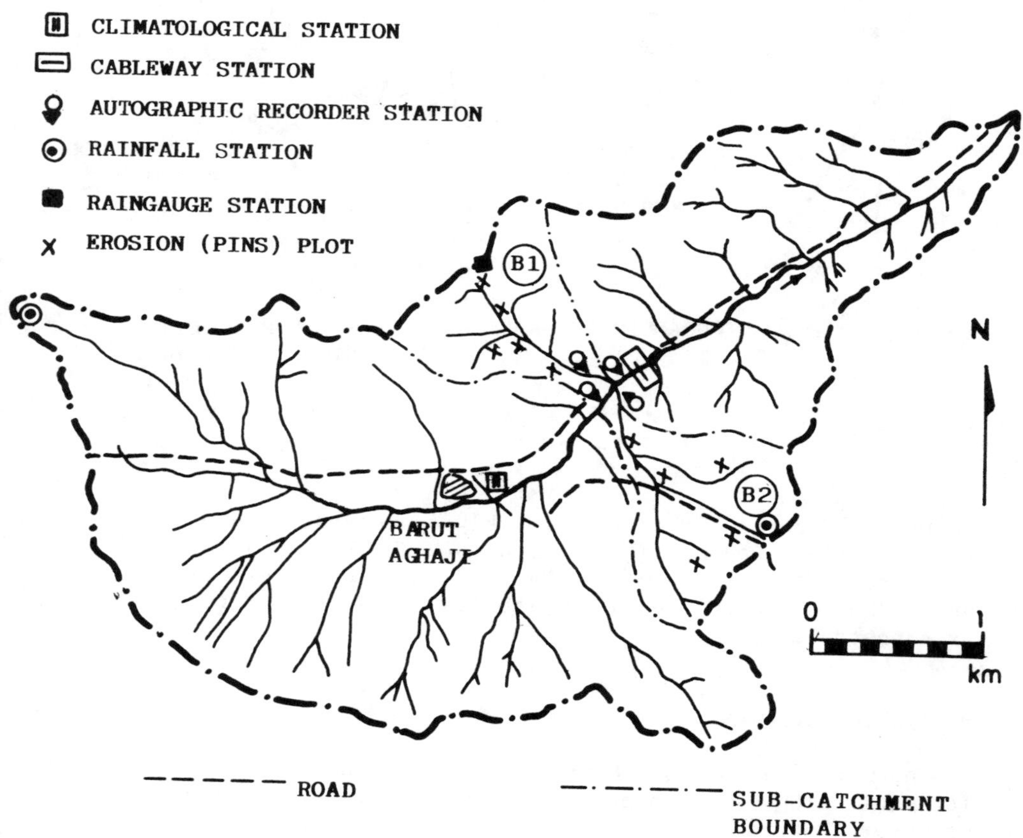

FIG. 1 Layout of monitoring sites in Barut Aghaji pilot watershed.

Sarcham pilot watersheds

These are two localities near the village of Sarcham, 75 km from Zanjan on the road to Miyaneh (S1 and S2 in Fig. 4). Both localities contain 4 year old earth sediment retention dams. The size of the areas is 10 and 11 ha. The geology and physiography is similar with badlands developed on flat-lying Miocene marls of different colors, with no organic soil except where marls are covered by alluvial

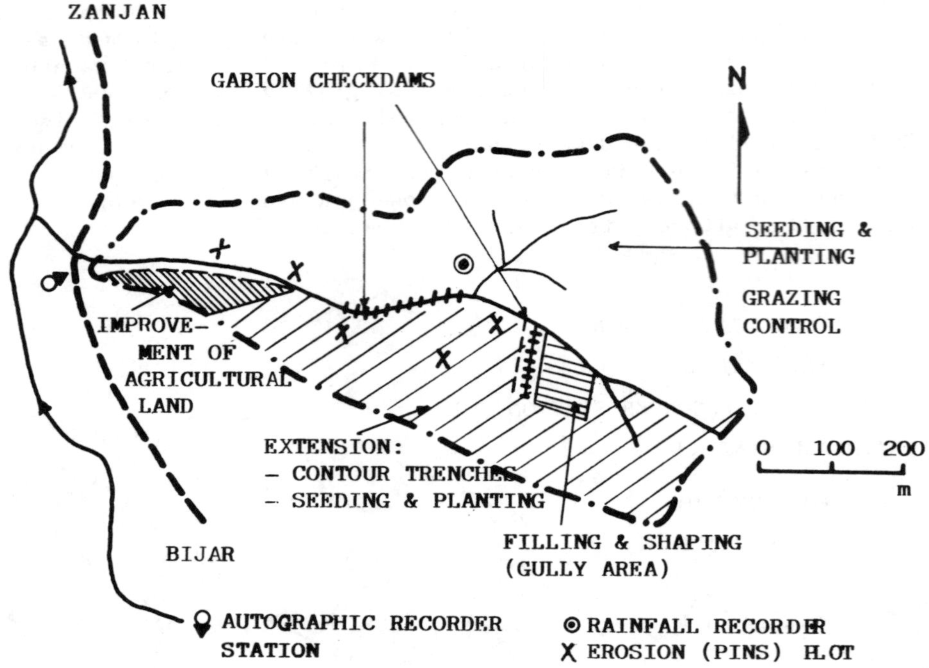

FIG. 2 Monitoring sites and treatment measures of Bijar road pilot watershed.

material. Since the runoff is quickly concentrated into rills and small gullies, the surface erosion is high. The areas will be used as paired watersheds; the catchment S1 will be treated with erosion and sediment control measures, whereas the other one (S2) will serve as a control.

MONITORING NETWORK

The network consists of stations equipped with various instruments for monitoring of hydro-meteorological parameters, and measurements of water flow, sediment transport and soil erosion.

Hydro-meteorological network

Barut Aghaji catchment The following stations were established in this catchment (Fig. 1):

(a) one climatological station for observation of: air temperature, soil temperature, humidity, rainfall, sunshine, wind run and evaporation; the station is accordingly equipped with: thermometers, thermohygrograph, raingauge and rainfall recorder, wind recorder and evaporation balance;
(b) two stations with rainfall recorder and one with raingauge;
(c) one station for flow measurements on the main stream, located

downstream from the tributaries draining sub-catchments B1 and B2 (Fig. 1). The station consists of a cable way installation and a steep-floored self cleaning flume built upstream from it; the flume is equipped with a water level recorder (it is called autographic recording station and is the same is the one shown in Fig. 3). The cableway installation is used for fast measurements of flow as well as for flume calibration;

(d) one autographic recording station for flow measurements on the main stream upstream from B1 and B2 tributaries;

(e) two autographic recording stations on tributaries draining the sub-catchments B1 and B2.

Bijar road watershed In this catchment only one rainfall station was established and equipped with rainfall recorder and a raingauge. The other needed climatological data will be taken from the Barut Aghaji station. Flow measurements are carried out by a steep floored self cleaning flume (Fig. 3) which was built at the end of the main stream, on the Bijar road bridge. The flume is suitable for mountainous streams with heavy load. The discharge is determined from the flow depth which is measured immediately upstream the structure, by using water level recorder.

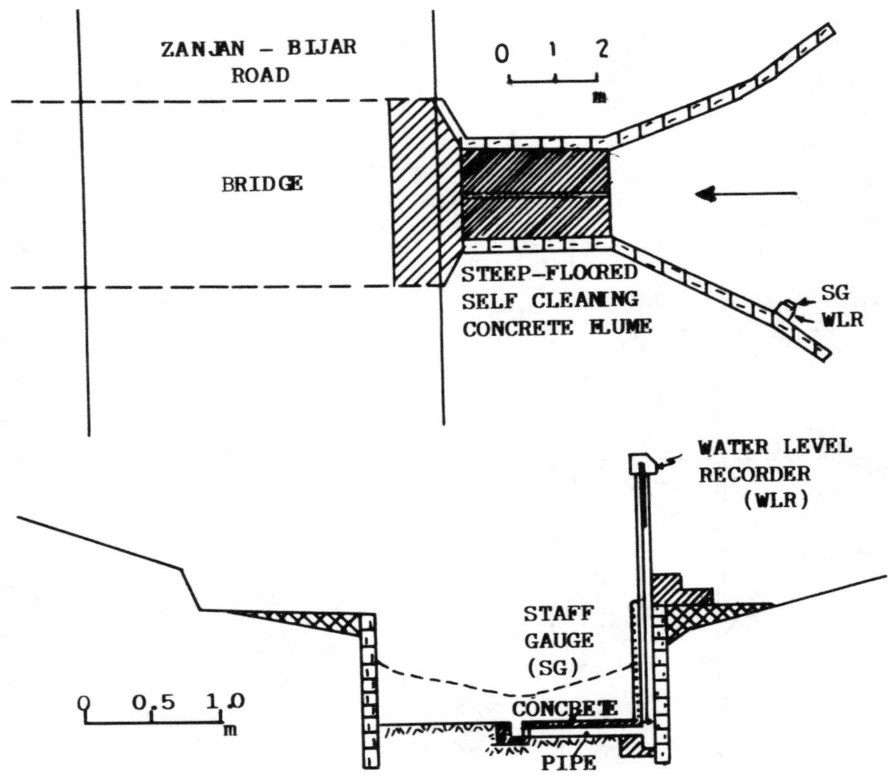

FIG. 3 Steep-floored self cleaning flume for flow measurements in Bijar road watershed.

Sarcham watersheds One station was here established for rainfall measurements, consisting of rainfall recorder and a raingauge. The other climatological data will be taken from the station installed by the project on two (paired) watersheds some 30 km away.

Each retention pond is equipped with a water level recorder, installed on a special bridge construction (Fig. 4). The continuously recorded water level in the reservoirs will enable the determination of the inflow hydrographs by applying a special procedure which is based on the flood routing (through the pond) technique. The method needs also the continuous record of the overflow discharge through the spillway channel, and this is carried out on a precalibrated structure built in the spillway.

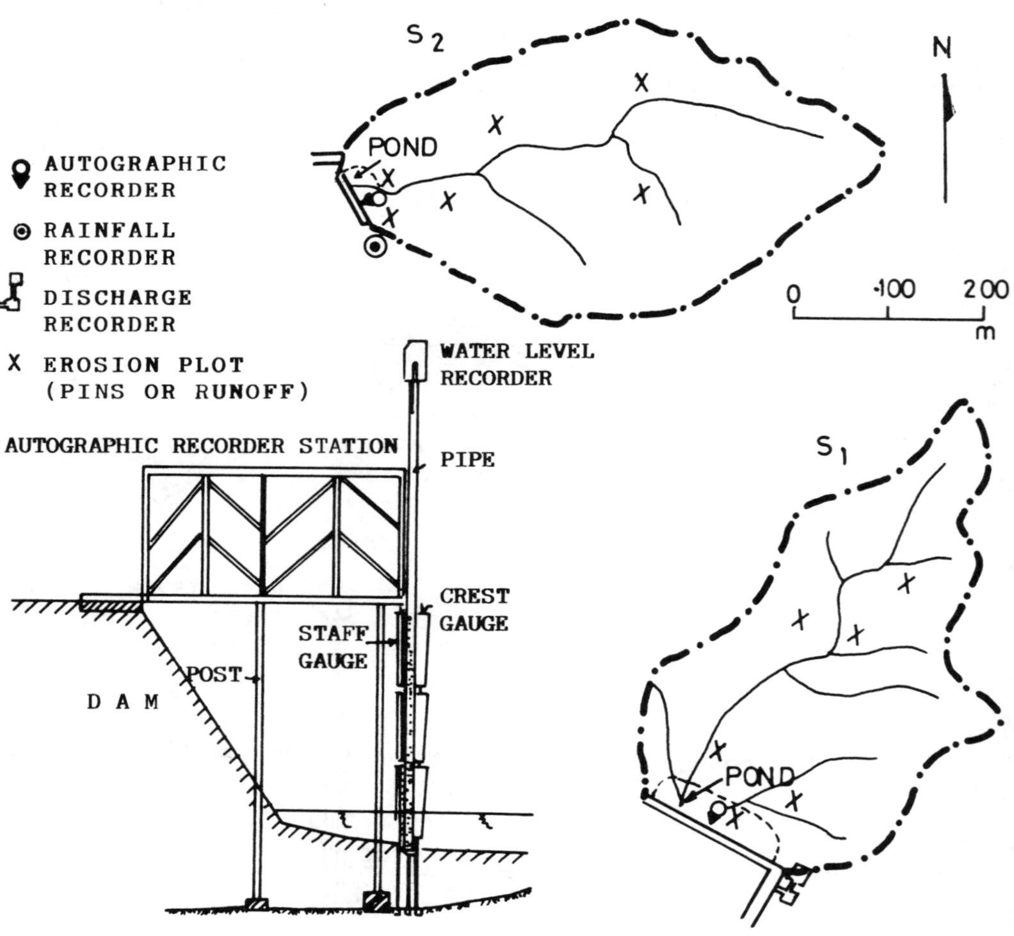

FIG. 4 Monitoring sites in pilot watersheds in Sarcham.

Sediment transport observations

Suspended sediment and bed load are measured in Barut Aghaji and Bijar road catchments. In all flow measurements sites suspended sediment samples are taken daily, or more frequently after storms and increased water discharge in the streams. The samples are later processed in the laboratory to obtain sediment concentration needed for sediment discharge calculation.

Bed load is measured in traps built downstream from the flow measurement sections. The main measuring section in Barut Aghaji catchment is located some 400 m downstream from the cable way; an old reservoir (established at times for storring of irrigation water) was partly dredged and a trap for bed load obtained. All traps are re-surveyed regularly, ie before and after rainy periods in fall and spring, as well as after every storm in the catchments.

In Sarcham catchments the total load is measured after every storm by surveying the bottom of the retention ponds. The bottom increase between two surveys corresponds to the total load delivered from the catchment during this period.

Soil erosion monitoring

Soil erosion is measured on plots equipped with erosion pins, on small runoff plots, or by standard surveying methods. In Barut Aghaji soil erosion is monitored in both sub-catchments B1 and B2 (Fig. 1). Six experimental sites were established on each sub-catchment. Sheet erosion and shallow rill erosion is measured by erosion pins at 5 m centers of squared grids varying in size from 20 X 20 m to 50 X 50 m. Deep rills and gullies are monitored along several cross sections at approximately 25 m intervals and along one longitudinal profile. In addition, several small plots of erosion pins at 1-2 m centers are installed to measure surface erosion on the stream banks.

In Bijar road catchment five experimental sites were established. Three of them are in form of 50 X 50 m plots for measuring of sheet and shallow rills erosion, with pins at 5 m centers. Gully erosion is measured by surveying cross sections and the longitudinal profile of the gully. Besides, some erosion pins were installed also on gully side slopes.

Each of Sarcham catchments has 6 experimental sites. These are either grids 30 X 30 m to 50 X 50 m with erosion pins, or runoff plots 2 X 1 m, on steeper slopes. The main streams are surveyed at cross sections at 20 to 50 m intervals. In ponds, fixed cross sections were established, and surveying is carried out along them to assess the total delivery of sediments from the catchments.

On selected experimental sites, in all catchments, photo points were established to carry out repeated photography; this is aimed at both semi-quantitative erosion assessment and extension purposes.

DATA COLLECTION AND PROCESSING

All observations and measurements are carried out by the project office in Zanjan. Only climatological station in Barut Aghaji is monitored by the Zanjan meteorological service, which uses data for its own purposes and delivers copies of all records to the project.

Detailed manuals were prepared for all kinds of monitoring and observation sheets for daily, monthly and yearly data drawn up for every station. Since the most of stations is equipped with the recording instruments, more care is required from technicians and observers only for timely flow measurements in the main stream of Barut Aghaji catchment, as well as for taking of suspended sediment samples. Also surveying activities for soil erosion assessment have to be carried out timely, ie soon enough after a rainfall event.

The basic processing of the data is carried out in the Zanjan office. Data are written on floppy disks and transferred to the main office in Tehran. They are there stored into a data base created on the IBM-PS/2-80 computer. This computer was configurated as a system with multi-user access and equipped adequately (6 terminals, printer, plotter, digitizer, etc.).

Collection of hydrological data is limited to two rather short rainy periods. First of them is at the end of November, before the snowfall, and the second one in March and April, during snowmelt and spring rainfalls. Only the main streams in Barut Aghaji and Bijar road watersheds have some water discharge over the whole year, requiring therefore continuous monitoring.

Processing of the data collected during the rainy season 1989/90 and a first analyzis are planned for summer 1990.

ACKNOWLEDGMENTS The project is jointly funded by the United Nations Development Programme (UNDP) and the Government of the Islamic Republic of Iran, executed by the Food and Agriculture Organization of the United Nations (FAO) and implemented by the Bureau of Soil Conservation and Watershed Management within the Forest and Range Organization of the Ministry of Agriculture. These organizations are thanked for their continuous support enabling the conduction of the presented research programme.

REFERENCES

FAO (1989) Project IRA/86/004; Consultancy report on hydrological monitoring.

FAO (1989) Project IRA/86/004; Consultancy report on watershed management.

FAO (1989) Project IRA/86/004; Consultancy report on erosion assessment.

FAO (1989) Project IRA/86/004; Consultancy report on conservation structures and earth dams.

UNESCO (1970) Representative and experimental basins.

Hydrology in Mountainous Regions. I - Hydrological Measurements; the Water Cycle (Proceedings of two Lausanne Symposia, August 1990). IAHS Publ. no. 193, 1990.

Spatial and temporal variation of flow resistance in an Alpine river

P. E. STÜVE
Institut für Physische Geographie, Freie Universität Berlin, D-1000 Berlin 41, Germany

ABSTRACT River morphology for coarse material bedload was measured in a mountain river, the Lainbach, at the Bavarian Alps. In an 140 m long experimental reach roughness and flow resistance variations were measured during low, average and high discharge. The river morphology of this reach is surveyed with the photogrammetric system Rolleimetric MR2. Two techniques were employed to determine the grain size. Volume samples with the help of the sieving and splitting device at several sites was shifted. The grain size spectrum of the armoured layer was surveyed by photo-sieving. The average value of grain roughness elements (D_{50}) at each step and pool sequence was compared with the slope of the energy line and the Darcy-Weisbach flow resistance at each cross profile. For low discharges energy losses and roughness are extremely variable between different cross sections. The higher stages shows a good relationship between the measured and calculated parameters.

INTRODUCTION

It is only recently that investigations of channel morphology in mountain streams have met with interest. These are necessary, however, in order to analyse the transport and deposit of boulders during and after high floods. An important role in this process is played by the elements of roughness in the riverbed and the flow resistance.

By first qualitative classifications of riverbed roughness were made by Leopold (1964). Bathurst (1982), Whittaker & Jaeggi (1982) and Bray (1988) provide description of the roughness of gravel beds in mountain torrents. Both authors review numerous friction equations, check the results in each case with the help of a data record, and, after statistical tests, suggest the most suitable empirical equation for each data record. The present data records for riverbed roughness describe only mean values. The more precise obsevational and measurement values necessary for the spatial and temporal friction of rivers are lacking.

The Lainbach, the hydrological catchment of Munich University's Geographical institute, has, with its two tributary streams, Kotlaine and Schmiedlaine, a catchment area of 18.8 km^2. Maximum discharges occur during periods of melting snow and after heavy summer rain. The experimental reach specially chosen to investigate channel morphology lies directly below the mouth of the Kotlaine and Schmiedlaine streams. The middle channel slope of the experi-

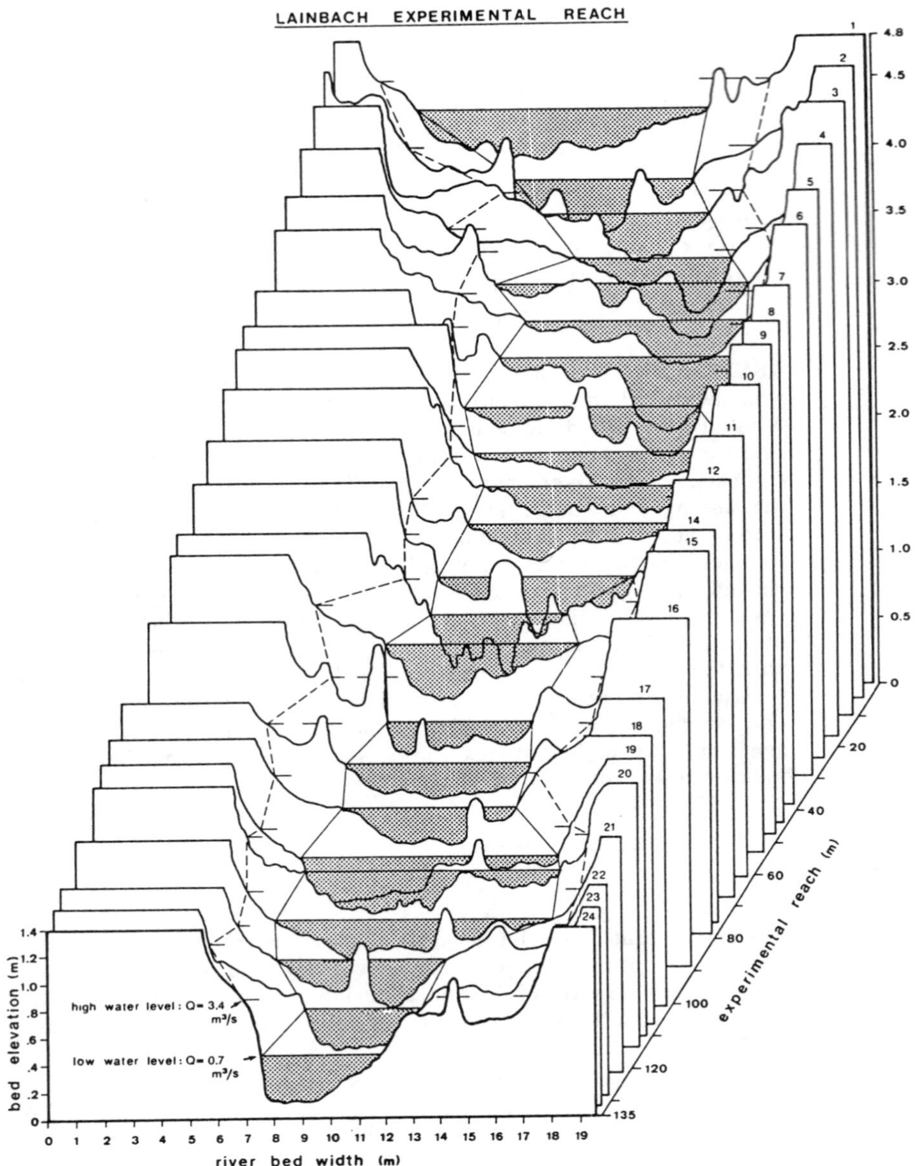

FIG. 1
The experimental reach at the Lainbach. Cross profiles with no. 1 to 24, which were surveyed, were used for the calculation of hydraulic parameters. A water line with a discarge of 0.7 and 3.4 m^3/s is represented. The measurements for discharge were taken at profile 10 (pool section), profile 14 (step section) and profile 20 (pool section).

mental reach comprises roughly 2.8%. The steepness of the mountain stream slope varies from place to place on account of its typical step-pool profile from 0.6% to 8.7%. The parameters of the riverbed geometry, the channel hydraulics, and the flow resistance, all vary accordingly.

The variability of flow resistance was measured along an experimental reach of the Lainbach and in 24 cross sections. Details shows figure 1. The experimental reach is 140 m long and the investigation of the spatial variation of flow resistance took place in summer of 1988 and 1989 by low, normal and high water discharge. The temporal development of discharge and variation of channel shape was measured in cross sections no. 10, 14 and 20.

ANALYSES OF RIVER MORPHOLOGY AND COARSE GRAINED SEDIMENT

In order to determine the spatial variation of flow resistance an exact description is necessary. It is therefore important that the investigation should be based on geomorphological and granulometric analyses of the riverbed using geodetical photogrammetric photographs. The length section is characterised by a continuous succession of steps and pools (Fig. 1 and 3a), so called step-pool system (Whittaker & Jaeggi, 1982). The pools are eroded in the bedrock and under low flow conditions are visible in the form of flat basins. The steps can be recognized in the outline of the riverbed by the more frequent occurence of boulders.

Changes in the grain size distribution of the sediment layer occur in both the longitudinal and the cross sections. A typical example is the armouring of low flow beds with pebbles and cobbles. Finer material can be found lying on the riverbed and boulders of approximately one metre in size strewn along the steeper reaches. The grain size spectrum of the river is therefore extremely large. Various techniques were employed to determine the grain size. With help of the sieving and splitting device (Ibbeken, 1974), a volume sample from the beginning and the end of the reach respectively was shifted. The grain size spectrum of the armoured layer was photographed in to cross sections by means of the photo-sieving process (Ibbeken & Schleyer, 1986).

TABLE 1 Grain size parameters from sieving and photo-sieving.

Testsite	Technique	Grain size parameter D_{50} (mm)	D_{84} (mm)
Reach at 5 m	Volume sample	75	135
Reach at 5 m	Photo-sieving	160	280
Reach at 105 m	Volume sample	60	120
Reach at 105 m	Photo-sieving	120	205

The different grain size analyses led, even in the same cross section, to very different results. The shifted volume sample reflects the grain size spectrum of heavy flood bedload. The grain size spectrum of the armoured bed is reproduced by means of the photo-sieving process. Both results are therefore of importance for the investigation. As long as there is no erosion or bedload transport, the roughness is determined, to a large extend by the armouring. Where bedload transport occurs, and where the river bed is mobile, there is an increase in the amount of slightly smaller sizes in the grain sample. In table 1 the parameters frequently used to describe the grain roughness D_{50} and D_{84}, are compared to show the results of the various analyses.

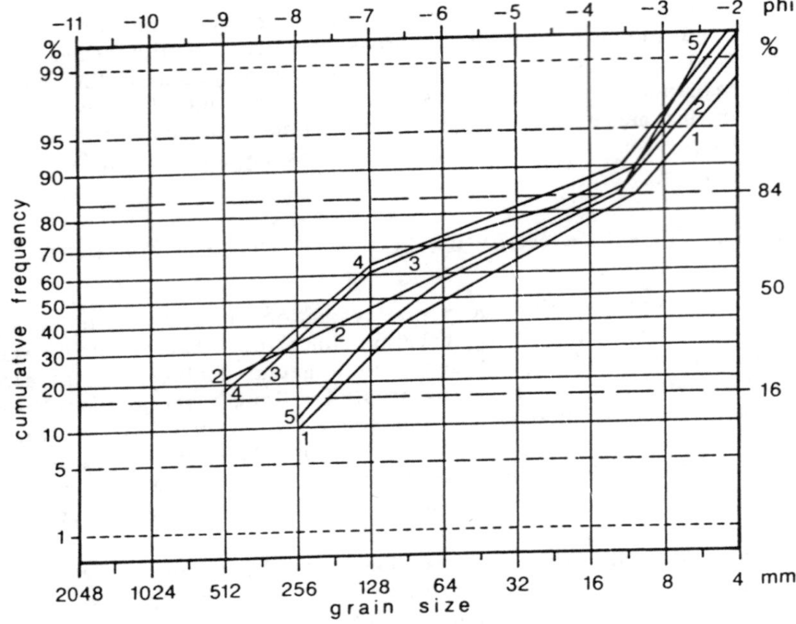

FIG. 2
Grain size distribution for distinctive parts at Lainbach and the test reach:
1 - Lainbach, near main gauge
2 - Schmiedlaine
3 - experimental reach at 105 m
4 - experimental reach at 5 m
5 - Kotlaine

The above values were taken from a longitudinal section of pool areas. Whereas the range of the grain size spectrum is considerable, the difference in grain sizes in the longitudinal section is relatively insignificant. A marked displacement is to be observed in the grain size spectrum of the armoured bed. The values after photo-sieving of the grain size parameters D_{50}, correspond to the values obtained through sieving D_{84}.

These grain size spectra are still incomplete; the boulders typical of the steps are absent. Boulders with a b-axis of 600 mm can be found among the bedload in the Lainbach. Nevertheless, a smaller boulder with a b-axis of 490 mm moved a distance of 4 metres during the highest summer flow level of 1988. The discharge amount was approximately 19 m^3/s. In order to complete the evaluation of the test reach, oblique photos were taken from the bank and perpendicular photos were taken from a cable suspended above the entire experimental reach. The photo measurements were evaluated using the photogrammetric system Rolleimetric MR 2, of the Technische Fachhochschule in Berlin (Prof. G. Schulz). The aim of these analyses was to photograph the location of all bedload with a b-axis of 120 mm. The 27 boulders with a b-axis of greater than 700 mm take up 4.1% of the entire area of the experimental reach with 994 m^2. These boulders appear as large roughness elements projecting above the water at a flow level of approximately 8 m^3/s and remain visible above the water until the onset of exeptionally high floods, when, in certain cases, they are transported along the riverbed.

In order to determine the representative grain size parameters the experimental reach was divided into four sections. The first slope steps end after 30 metres and are succeeded in the second section by a pool area. The next channel slope begins at the cross section no. 11 at 55 metre and ends after two sharply sloping steps at a distance of 85 metres. The lowest pool area with the cross profiles no. 17 - 21 ends after 120 metres. The following section is a step until to 136 metres.

TABLE 2 Representative grainsizes D_{50} and D_{84} for steps and pools along the experimental reach.

Area (m)	Grain size analysis	Grain size parameter D (mm)	D (mm)
0 - 30 step	MR 2 + splitting device at 5 m	650	1380
30 - 55 pool	MR 2 + splitting device at 5 m	320	645
55 - 85 step	MR 2 + splitting device at 105 m	805	1710
85 - 120 pool	MR 2 + splitting device at 105 m	290	535

The representative grain size spectrum was assembled from the surface area of the boulders and their grain size spectrum (MR2 -analysis), and the spectrum of nearest respective photo-sieve analysis. The areas not filled by boulders were filled with the data from the neighbouring grain size analyses. The curves recording the sum of the grains for the individual river sections and the sieve curves are shown in Fig. 2. There is a close connection between the grain size distribution and the bed slope, i.e. in the longitudinal profile the grain roughness alters over short reaches. These conditions need to be more closely investigated by means of further grain size analyses.

ANALYSES OF THE SPATIAL VARIATIONS OF FLOW RESISTANCE

The influence of the armouring layer to channel hydraulic were tested at low discharge with $Q=0.69\ m^3/s$ to medium discharge with $Q=3.39\ m^3/s$ and $Q=5.3\ m^3/s$. The measured and calculated parameters for each cross profile are:

- topographic altitude: z
- lowest points along the channel: z_0
- width of cross profile: w
- velocity profile at z_0

At known discharge (Q) following parameter are calculated:

- cross sectional area: A
- hydraulic radius: R
- average velocity: $\bar{v}$
- average depth: d
- energy height, Bernoulli equation: $H_e = z + d + \bar{v}^2 \cdot 2g^{-1}$
- energy slope: J_e
- energy loss: E_e
- Froude number: $F = \bar{v} \cdot (g R)^{-0.5}$
- Darcy-Weisbach friction factor: $f = 8 g d J_e \cdot \bar{v}^{-2}$
- relative roughness: R/D_{84}

The corresponding parameters for the low and normal flow discharge are shown in Table 3. On the longitudinal average the flow resistance by a discharge increase of 0.69 to 5.3 m^3/s drops in accordance with Darcy-Weisbach factor ($f^{-0.5}$). The causes are to be found less in the velocity differential than in the energy slope. It is very difficult to locate the points where average roughness occurs in the cross section. The corresponding points vary according to the different discharges. In order to determine representative roughness for mountain streams, taking into consideration differences in slope, pools and average discharge velocity, at least more hydraulic measurements of different cross sections are necessary.

Essential measurement results are shown in Figs. 3b and 4. Of decisive importance are the already mentioned large differences in the longitudinal profile of of the bed in Fig. 1 and 3a and the high variability of the average flow velocity in Tab 3. The highest velocities do not always occur at the steepest points in the longitudinal profile. They are also to be found , under conditions of low discharge $\bar{v}_1$ and high discharge $\bar{v}_2$, under the slope steps in the area of pools. There is no point which provides representative values for all discharges.

By means of the Bernoulli analysis it was possible to determine the energy heights (H_e) and the energy slopes (J_e)for both discharges. The energy slopes follow a different course under the different flow conditions in the experimental

TABLE 3 Measured and calculated hydraulic parameters at a discharge of:

		Q = 0.69 m^3/s						and	Q = 5.3 m^3/s			
no.	dist.	J_s	R	$\bar{v}_1$	J_{e1}	F	$f^{-0.5}$	R	$\bar{v}_2$	J_{e2}	F	$f^{-0.5}$
1	2	3	4	5	6	7	8	9	10	11	12	13
2	9	0.0573	0.25	0.41	0.0467	0.26	0.43	0.35	1.11	0.0520	0.60	0.93
3	15	0.0078	0.19	0.98	0.0157	0.72	2.03	0.25	1.63	0.0196	1.04	2.63
4	21	0.0362	0.16	0.78	0.0435	0.62	1.06	0.30	1.45	0.0309	0.85	1.70
5	26	0.0123	0.16	0.81	0.0123	0.65	2.06	0.25	1.47	0.0278	0.94	1.99
6	34	0.0268	0.18	1.18	0.0110	0.89	2.99	0.28	1.58	0.0126	0.95	3.00
7	42	0.0340	0.23	0.72	0.0500	0.48	0.76	0.46	1.03	0.0300	0.48	0.99
8	50	0.0005	0.16	0.51	0.0109	0.41	1.38	0.37	1.23	0.0056	0.65	3.05
9	58	0.0099	0.14	0.56	0.0132	0.48	1.47	0.40	1.22	0.0067	0.62	2.66
10	65	0.0073	0.16	0.51	0.0018	0.41	3.39	0.40	1.18	0.0091	0.60	2.21
11	70	0.0211	0.14	0.64	0.0250	0.55	1.22	0.40	1.21	0.0213	0.40	1.25
12	74	0.0218	0.19	0.55	0.0109	0.40	1.36	0.35	1.34	0.0264	0.72	1.57
13	78	0.0633	0.21	0.63	0.0567	0.44	0.65	0.44	1.14	0.0400	0.55	0.97
14	84	0.0083	0.16	0.99	0.0125	0.79	2.50	0.30	2.03	0.0167	1.18	3.24
15	91	0.0245	0.23	0.43	0.0208	0.29	0.70	0.42	1.09	0.0340	0.54	1.13
16	97	0.0256	0.12	1.05	0.0317	0.97	1.92	0.34	1.40	0.0280	0.77	1.62
17	103	0.0136	0.20	0.51	0.0114	0.36	1.21	0.39	1.09	0.0136	0.56	1.69
18	108	0.0167	0.17	0.71	0.0167	0.55	1.50	0.34	1.53	0.0152	0.84	2.40
19	113	0.0147	0.16	0.47	0.0179	0.38	0.99	0.37	1.19	0.0160	0.62	1.75
20	119	0.0089	0.19	0.36	0.0044	0.26	1.41	0.35	1.21	0.0182	0.65	1.71
21	123	0.0081	0.14	0.50	0.0161	0.43	1.19	0.31	1.25	0.0097	0.72	2.57
22	129	0.0165	0.19	0.64	0.0066	0.47	2.04	0.26	1.87	0.0149	1.17	3.61
23	132	0.0429	0.23	0.82	0.0397	0.55	0.97	0.38	1.29	0.0349	0.67	1.26
24	136	0.0676	0.20	0.74	0.0648	0.53	0.73	0.39	1.30	0.0479	0.66	1.07

reach (Fig. 3b). The range lies between 6% and nearly 0%. Distinct fluctations in the area of both steep channels, and even the little shallows in the lowest pool area, cause considerable changes in the energy slope. A more regular energy slope is reached under higher flow conditions (J_{e2}). Energy heights (H_e) and energy loss (E_e) were calculated for all crosssections and are reproduced in Tab. 3 and Fig. 4. The values of energy height have a natural tendency to increase at all points during the transition from low to middle and higher flow. However it was simultaneously observed that the differences between the observation points decrease, and that consequently, as nearly as the normal flow stage, an energetic flow begins which runs more regulary than during low water discharge. In the course of this compensation the enrgy loss at the end of the steep reaches increase.

The root of the reciprocal value of the Darcy-Weisbach friction was used to measure the flow resistance. The corresponding values are shown in Fig. 5. On the whole the values vary between 1 and 5. In general the highest values, i.e. the least friction, occur in areas with small differences in the energy slope. The pool areas have, in places, a lower friction than the steep channels.

CONCLUSIONS

By reason of the observations on the spatial variation of flow resistance the causes for the recorded differences can, in essence, be traced back to the differences in the bed slope. Futher conclusions would require a corresponding analysis during a high flow discharge. Furthermore the slope conditions, and above all the grain size distribution, must be surveyed in greater detail. The Bernoulli analysis revealed a tendency towards flow standardization when the

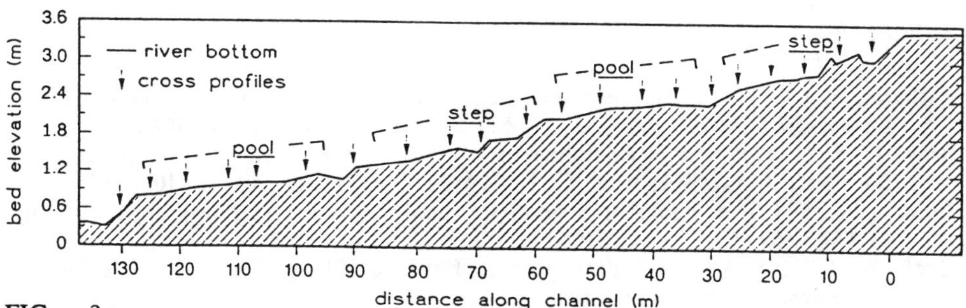

FIG. 3a
Length section of the river bottom of the experimental reach Lainbach.

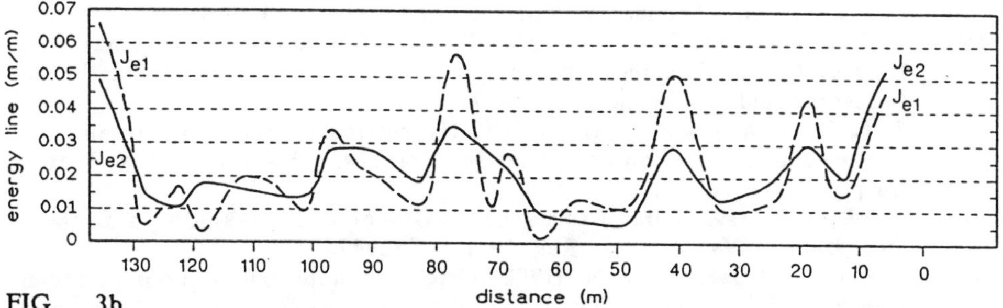

FIG. 3b
Energy slope J_{e1} and J_{e2} at low ($Q=0.69\ m^3/s$) and high ($Q=5.3\ m^3/s$) discharge.

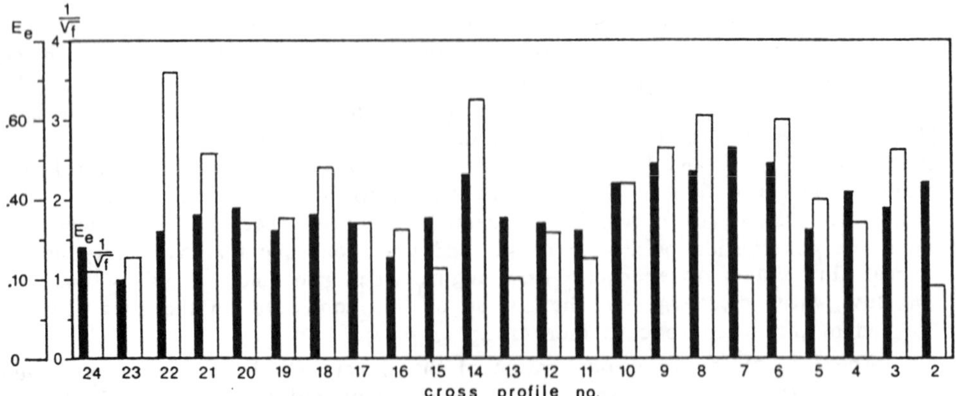

FIG. 4
Energy loss (E_e) and Darcy-Weisbach roughness ($f^{-0.5}$).

amount of water increases. It is assumed that the river energetically standardizes its flow under high flow conditions and that the large roughness elements on the riverbed then produce the required flow resistance in the steep reaches.

ACKNOWLEDGEMENTS This work was supported by the Deutsche Forschungsgemeinschaft. Thanks to the field group for assistance.

REFERENCES

Bathurst, J. C. (1982) Theoretical Aspects of Flow Resistance. In: Hey,R.D., Bathurst,J.C. & Thorne,C.R. (1982) Gravel Bed Rivers, 83-108.

Bray, D. I. (1982) Flow Resistance in Gravel-Bed Rivers. In: Hey, R. D., Bathurst, J. C. & Thorne, C. R. (1982) Gravel-Bed Rivers. 109-137.

Chin, A. (1989) Step Pools in Stream Channels. Process in Physical Geography 13 (3), 391-407.

Graf, W. L. (1988) Fluvial Processes in Dryland Rivers. Springer Series in the Physical Enviroment (3).

Griffiths, G. A. (1981) Flow Resistance in Coarse Gravel Bed Rivers. J. Hydr. Div. ASCE 107, 899-918.

Ibbeken, H. (1974) A Simple Sieving and Splitting Device for Field Analysis of Coarse Grained Sediments. Journ. of Sed. Petrol. 44, 939-946.

Ibbeken, H. & Schleyer, R. (1986) Photo-Sieving: A Method for Grainsize Analysis of Coarse-Grained, Unconsolidated Bedding Surfaces. Earth Surface Processes and Landforms (11), 59-77.

Leopold, L. B. & Maddock, T. (1953) The Hydraulic Geometrie of Stream Channels and some Physiographic Implications. US Geol. Survey. Water Supply Paper 282-B.

Prestegaard, K. L. (1983) Bar Resistance in Gravel Bed Streams at a Bankfull Stage. Wat. Resour. Res. 19 (2), 472-476.

Whittaker, J. G. & Jaeggi, M. N. (1982) Origin of Step-Pool Systems in Mountain Streams. J. Hydr. Div. ASCE 108 (6), 758-773.

Hydrology in Mountainous Regions. I - Hydrological Measurements; the Water Cycle (Proceedings of two Lausanne Symposia, August 1990). IAHS Publ. no. 193, 1990.

Comparison of bed load yield estimates for a glacial meltwater stream

J.WARBURTON
Department of Natural Resources Engineering, Lincoln University, Canterbury, New Zealand

ABSTRACT Estimates of bed load yield in mountain streams can be made using three principal methods: sediment traps, sediment rating curves and sediment transport formulae. This paper compares these three techniques for estimating the bed load yield in the Bas Glacier d'Arolla proglacial stream (Valais, Switzerland) for May-September 1987. This stream is a steep (0.07 m m^{-1}), coarse-bed, boulder and cobble channel. Bed load yield estimates are provided by a self-purging sediment trap; a bed load rating curve constructed from a program of Helley-Smith bed load sampling; and loads calculated using the Schoklitsch sediment transport formula. The sediment trap estimate is taken as a reference for the evaluation of the site-specific bed load rating curve and the Schoklitsch formula. Results for 1987 show that both methods over-predict yields; the bed load rating curve by 36% and the Schoklitsch formula by 111%. These discrepancies arise due to temporal and spatial variation in transport rates, problems in defining "active bed" width and difficulty in characterising a representative particle size for the critical threshold of bed material movement.

INTRODUCTION

Bed load transport rates in mountain rivers tend to be high when compared with their lowland counterparts (Bathurst et al. 1985). Engineering projects involved with mountain rivers are therefore required to manage a large flux of coarse bed material. This is especially true of projects involved with run-of-the-river water extraction, sediment control structures built to protect dwellings, cultivated land and communications, and reservoir and dam storage schemes. Such projects usually involve excluding sediment from intakes, minimising changes in local bed topography, planning to avoid downstream aggradation problems and predicting the functional life of the structure. Therefore, an estimate of bed load yield is essential. Understanding bed load transport in mountain rivers is also important in fluvial hazard prediction and estimating rates of denudation in mountain catchments.

However, estimation of bed load yield in mountain rivers is difficult due to temporal and spatial variability in transport processes and the wide range of sediment sizes involved. Although no standard estimation technique is agreed upon, three general methods are used (Fig. 1). Bed load yield can be estimated from sediment traps (e.g. Lauffer & Sommer 1982), bed load rating curves (e.g. Hollingshead 1971) and computations involving sediment transport formulae (e.g. Hean & Nanson 1987). Fig. 1 shows the general relationship between these three estimation techniques and the data requirements of each. Sediment trap estimates are the simplest and involve the collection of the total amount of bed load moved in a given period. Survey of the trap volume together with an estimate of the trapped sediment packing density provide a gross bed load yield (Fig. 1). Rating curve estimates are based on the assumption that a quantifiable relationship exists between bed load discharge and water discharge.

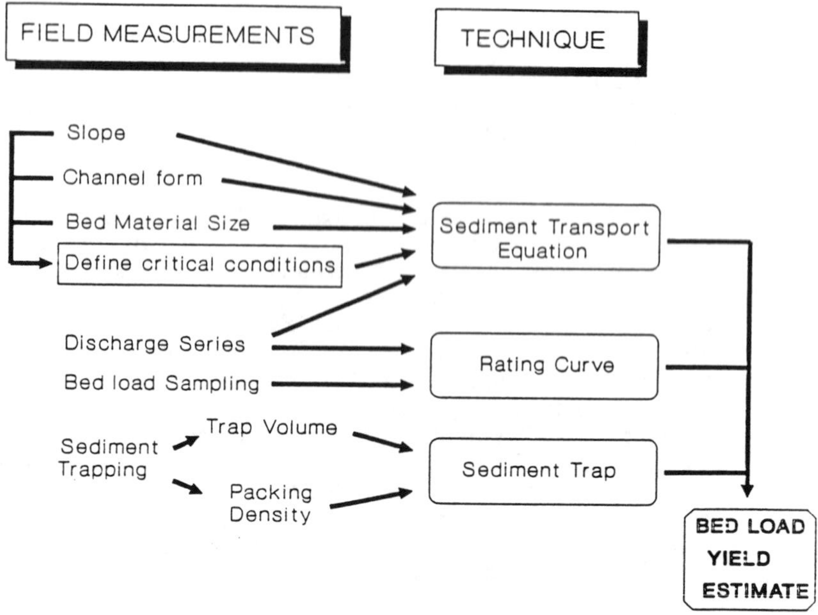

FIG. 1 Interrelationships amongst field variables involved in the estimation of bed load yields.

Such a relationship when combined with continuous discharge data can be used to estimate bed loads (Fig. 1). The rating curve is usually constructed from pairs of intermittent observations of bed load transport and water discharge, measured simultaneously. Alternatively, bed load yields can be estimated using bed load transport formulae based on the assumption of a relationship between fluvial hydraulics, sediment characteristics and bed load transport rate. Bed load yield is computed using the transport formula together with the flow series (discharge or a derivative of that). Application of bed load transport formulae usually involves a limited amount of field data used to define critical conditions for initial motion of the bed material (Fig. 1).

The aim of this paper is to compare estimates of bed load yield derived from these three methods for the Bas Glacier d'Arolla proglacial stream (May 29 - September 4 1987), and to discuss the limitations of these methods in relation to field evidence of bed load transport at this site.

STUDY SITE AND METHODS

The Bas Glacier d'Arolla proglacial stream (Valais, Switzerland) extends 300m downstream of the snout of the Bas Glacier d'Arolla to a meltwater intake/gauging structure. The stream is part of a multiple glacier basin, which is managed by the Grande Dixence S.A. hydro-electric company. The catchment has an area of 21.5 km^2, of which 55% is glacierized. Bedrock is dominantly gneiss and schist.The proglacial stream has a steep (0.07 m m^{-1}), coarse, boulder and cobble bed channel. The stream is confined by bluffs to a valley train which is approximately 30-40 m wide. Channel widths vary between 4-7 m but can be as great as 12 m. Channel pattern is generally low sinuosity single-thread with nodes of braiding. In steep single-thread sections a step-pool morphology is developed. Median sediment sizes for the channel bed surface were 60-80 mm, and 128-430 mm for bed material clusters and steps.

Gravel trap

The intake structure, located at the outlet from the catchment, incorporates two "self-purging" sediment traps (one for gravel and one for sand). These traps have been field calibrated and can be used to estimate bed load and suspended load yield (Gurnell et al. 1988). Streamflow is diverted through the gravel trap and then through an underground sand trap. Discharge is gauged continuously at the outlet from the sand trap by means of a weir and stage recorder. A sensor in the trap automatically purges the sediment at a pre-determined level of accumulation. Periodic automatic purging of the two sediment traps is registered, on the stage record, as a fall to two different levels depending on which trap is purged. Bed load transport was monitored by surveying the accumulation of sediment in the gravel trap and estimating packing density of the accumulating sediment using cartons suspended in the trap. Given the frequency of gravel trap purging, determined by a characteristic "purge signature" on the stage record, these data can be used to estimate bed load yield. Suspended sediment monitoring at the inlet and outlet of the gravel trap showed that no appreciable amounts of suspended sediment were deposited in the gravel trap and therefore the material trapped was exclusively bed load. This estimate is a minimum because at the end of August 1987 a large flow event caused prolonged intermittent purging of the intake over a 24 h period. To ensure comparability of all the bed load yield estimates this period was omitted from the analysis.

Rating curve

Field measurements of instantaneous bed load transport were obtained using a 152mm orifice Helley-Smith bed load sampler. These measurements were made at a stable cross section approximately 100m upstream of the gravel trap between May 25 and July 30 1987. Instantaneous bed load transport measurements were used to construct a rating relationship and illustrate the variability of the bed load transport process. Between 3-10 measurements were taken in each traverse of the stream to determine the composite bed load transport rate through the cross section. Based on 64 determinations a rating relationship was constructed from a least squares log-log regression of instantaneous bed load transport rate on discharge. The relationship had the form:

$$\log BLT = -1.36 + 3.86 \log Q \quad (1)$$

where BLT is the instantaneous bed load transport rate (kg s^{-1}), Q is the water discharge (m^3 s^{-1}), $r^2 = 0.75$ and standard error = 0.72. The simple correction factor proposed by Ferguson (1986) is used to remove the bias associated with the log-transformation regression used to derive the rating relationship. This simple correction factor has recently been criticised (Walling & Webb, 1988) on the basis that bias correction procedures do not provide accurate estimates of sediment yield alone and other sources of error are more important in producing inaccurate estimates. Nevertheless bias correction is still necessary before other sources of error in the rating relationship can be considered.

Schoklitsch bed load transport formula

Sediment transport formulae give the rate of discharge of sediment in terms of sediment properties and the hydraulic properties of the flow. Several formulae are available for predicting sediment transport in steep mountain rivers (Bathurst et al. 1987; Jaeggi & Rickenmann 1987). The choice of formula is somewhat arbitrary as long as the formula chosen has been developed for flow conditions and sediments typical of mountain streams. Of the available formulae, that of Schoklitsch (1962) is attractive since it is suitable for steep, coarse-bed mountain streams where sediment supply is high (Bathurst et al. 1985). Also it is based on discharge rather than shear stress or stream power, which from a practical point of view is important, as discharge is frequently measured at hydro-electric sites.

The Schoklitsch (1962) form of the transport formula is:

$$g_b = 2500\ S^{3/2}\ (q - q_{cr}) \quad (2)$$

where g_b = specific bed load discharge kg m^{-1} s^{-1}; S = channel slope; q = specific water discharge m^2 s^{-1}; and q_{cr} = critical specific water discharge for initial movement m^2 s^{-1}. Critical conditions for the initiation of bed load movement (qcr) are given using the following expression (Schoklitsch, 1962):

$$q_{cr} = 0.26\ (\rho s/\rho\ -1)^{5/3}\ \frac{d_{40}^{\ 3/2}}{S^{\ 7/6}} \quad (3)$$

where: ρs = sediment density; ρ = water density; and d_{40} = size of particle median axis for which 40% of the sediment is finer. Alternatively, where data exist, the critical threshold discharge can be determined from a scatter-plot of the relationship between discharge and measured instantaneous bed load transport rate as shown in Fig. 2.

BED LOAD YIELDS

Table 1 shows the bed load yield estimates based on the gravel trap, rating curve and Schoklitsch formula.

TABLE 1 Bed load yield estimates Bas Glacier d'Arolla proglacial stream, May 29 - September 4 1987.

Estimation method	Yield in tonnes	Discrepancy*
Gravel trap	31210	
Schoklitsch formula	65898	+ 111%
Rating curve (bias corrected)	42636	+ 36%
Rating curve (no bias correction)	10794	- 65%

* Discrepancy is the departure of the bed load yield estimate from the bed load yield measured in the gravel trap. This is expressed as a % underestimation (-) or overestimation (+).

The bias corrected rating curve is superior to the Schoklitsch formula in predicting the bed load yield and produces an estimate within 36% of the gravel trap yield. However, a rating relationship without bias correction under-predicts the load by 65%

(Table 1), a result which is expected given log transformation of the data and the relative high standard error of the relationship (Ferguson, 1986). At first sight, the Schoklitsch estimate appears to be tolerable given the rapid and inexpensive nature of the technique. However, application of this formula, to date, has met with only limited success. For example, during a period of snow melt flooding on the Roaring River, Colorado, Bathurst et al. (1985) predicted transport rates 3 orders of magnitude greater than actual measured transport rates. But this is not true only of the Schoklitsch formula; Lauffer & Sommer (1982) used the Meyer-Peter formula to estimate bed load transport on the Pitzbach (Austria) and found that calculated transport rates exceeded average measured transport rates by 10-fold. Hean & Nanson (1987) in a test of 8 bed load transport formulae, including that of Schoklitsch, at gauging sites on 11 eastern Australian rivers found the formulae inherently unreliable under field conditions, concluding that using formulae to determine absolute bed load yields was a futile exercise. In these cases, where sediment availability is supply-limited, formulae (including Schoklitsch 1962) which predict bed load transport capacity are unlikely to produce bed load transport estimates of the correct order of magnitude (Bathurst et al. 1987). However, before these results can be fully accepted further testing is required: namely consideration of bed load transport rate variations and testing the sensitivity of the Schoklitsch formula to input data.

Table 2 shows bed load yields estimated by the Schoklitsch formula for various combinations of input data.

TABLE 2 Bed load yield estimates based on the Schoklitsch formula showing the sensitivity to input data.

	Values used in the formula			Yield in tonnes	Discrepancy*
	Discharge series	Slope $m\ m^{-1}$	Critical discharge $m^3\ s^{-1}$		
A	Hourly	0.07	2.4	65898	+ 111%
B	Hourly	0.088	2.4	92904	+ 198%
C	Hourly	0.052	2.4	42200	+ 35%
D	Hourly	0.07	0.85	328289	+ 952%
E	Hourly	0.07	0.65	385528	+ 1235%
F	Mean daily	0.07	2.4	47307	+ 52%

* Discrepancy as defined in Table 1.

Estimate A is considered the "best estimate" using the Schoklitsch formula. The input data for estimate A include channel slope surveyed in the field and critical discharge determined from the water discharge bed load transport plot (Fig. 2). Loads are calculated using the mean hourly discharge series gauged at the meltwater intake structure. In order to test the sensitivity of the formula to slope, 1° was added to and subtracted from the actual channel slope (estimates B and C respectively). The yield estimates, B and C, are altered by between 76 and 87% of the actual bed load yield. Calculating critical discharge using formula (3) rather than determining the value from Fig. 2 causes an even worse discrepancy. Critical discharge calculated using the mean d_{40} from grid samples of bed material produces an over-estimate (D) of 952% using the d_{16} (as recommended by Bathurst et al. 1987) is even worse over-estimating by 1235% (estimate E). Given these large discrepancies the critical discharge formula (3) cannot be used in this type of channel. Finally the estimate will also vary with the nature of the flow series used to calculate loads. Estimate F based on a mean daily discharge series produces an improved bed load yield estimate by reducing the influence of the more extreme discharges in the load calculations. Based on the results in Table 2 it appears the Schoklitsch formula is difficult to apply to field conditions in a physically meaningful manner.

VARIATIONS IN BED LOAD TRANSPORT

Bed Load - Water Discharge Relationship

Bed load transport measurements collected from the field site (Fig. 2) with a Helley-Smith bed load sampler do not show a clear linear relationship with discharge.

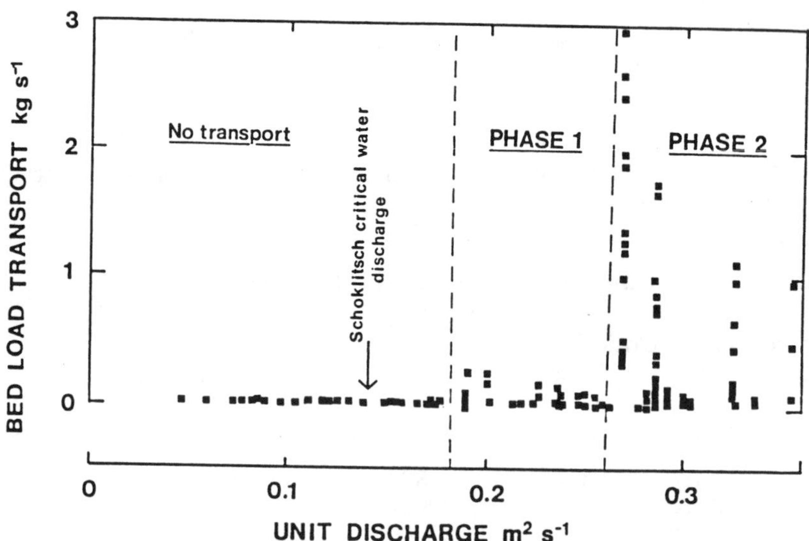

FIG. 2 Variation of bed load transport rate with unit water discharge for the Bas Glacier d'Arolla proglacial stream. Sampling period June-July 1987.

Below 0.26 $m^2 s^{-1}$ bed load transport is negligible but above 0.26 $m^2 s^{-1}$ there is a very rapid increase in transport rate. This applies up to 0.36 $m^2 s^{-1}$. There is thus a critical threshold discharge of approximately 0.26 $m^2 s^{-1}$ (2.4 $m^3 s^{-1}$) for the initiation of bed load transport at this site. The theoretical critical discharge for the bed material at the measurement site, based on the Schoklitsch formula (Schoklitsch, 1962) Wolman grid surface sampling, was 0.142 $m^2 s^{-1}$. The lack of correspondence between the predicted threshold of motion and the observed bed load movements suggests that the Schoklitsch critical water discharge formulae is of limited value in this case.

The lack of correspondence between observed and calculated thresholds may also be partly caused by the problems of determining a representative grain size. Bed materials vary considerably in mountain streams so the threshold of motion would be better represented by an envelope of curves. Furthermore, calculations based on a single representative grain size are unrealistic since both the conditions for the initiation of motion and transport itself will be affected by other sizes in the mixture. For example, the threshold water discharge calculated for the boulder and cobble cluster bed forms (for a representative grain size of 263 mm), which form the channel bed steps, was 1.7 m^2 s^{-1}. This corresponds to a critical discharge of approximately 10 m^3 s^{-1} for the Bas Glacier d'Arolla proglacial stream. Discharges of this magnitude only occur during extreme floods. Whittaker (1987) suggests that bed steps (clustered bed forms) of step pool streams are relatively stable over the usual flow conditions. This is certainly true of the Bas Glacier d'Arolla proglacial stream since it is only after large floods that the channel pattern is substantially altered.

For gravel bed rivers Jackson & Beschta (1982) divide bed load transport into two phases. Phase 1 movement involves the flushing out of sands deposited in the channel during low discharges. The bed structure is unaltered and thus initial transport rates are low. This condition is probably similar to bed conditions under which the "running bed load" described by Lauffer & Sommer (1982) is transported. With increased flow, bottom velocities and associated shear stresses increase; the armour layer is disrupted as gravels are entrained and erosion of bed sediments proceeds rapidly as smaller relative particle sizes are exposed. This disruption of the armour layer is phase 2 transport. In mountain streams, and the example studied here, the bed structure alternates between reaches of armoured bed and step pool sequences of clustered boulders. This will have the effect of producing a third threshold for bed load movement which involves the break up of clustered bed forms. This hierarchy of bed material motion thresholds suggests extreme discontinuity of transport in phase 1 to almost continuous transport in phase 3. Therefore, bed load transport formulae will be less reliable at lower discharges when a greater proportion of the bed is stable and transport is supply-limited. Although each phase may become supply-limited as armouring occurs. Recognition of various thresholds of motion in mountain streams is essential. Application of bed load transport formulae, such as Schoklitsch, must be made for each size fraction in turn since it cannot be assumed that when the stream discharge exceeds the critical discharge, all the bed is in motion.

Short-term temporal variations in bed load transport

Variations in transport rates occur over relatively short timescales. Measurement of bed load transport at hourly intervals on July 6 1987, between 0920 h and 2010 h, reveal marked fluctuations in the maximum transport rate even though the minimum transport rate is relatively stable. Peak transport rates (>0.27 kg s^{-1}) do not correspond directly to discharge peaks, rather variations in bed load transport correspond to variations in discharge whether increasing or decreasing. This suggests that flow variability is more important than discharge magnitude in regulating bed load discharge (although this needs further investigation). Indeed, over very short timescales (seconds), fluctuations in bed load transport can be related to turbulent velocity bursts. Alternatively, supply factors such as bank erosion along the channel margin or sporadic inputs of sediment from outside the channel can produce variability. In fact during this period of observation the local bed elevation at the measurement site changed little, which suggests that supply was not from the immediate channel bed but from upstream.

Intensive bed load sampling at 10 min intervals on July 8 1987 showed even more pronounced variations in transport rates during a period of almost constant discharge (0.3-3.1 kg s^{-1}). During the two-hour sampling period both minimum and maximum transport rates increased although fluctuations were very marked. Survey of the channel bed before, during and after the sequence of measurements showed the bed elevation to increase between 1020 h - 1120 h and decrease from 1120 h -

1200 h which suggests the possible passage of a bed sediment wave or load pulse because by 1150 h bed load transport was declining.

Cross section variations in bed load transport

Substantial variations in transport also exist in the cross-channel dimension with bed load moving as threads along the channel bed (Bathurst et al. 1985). This bed load "streaming" effect varies markedly between days. Generally peak bed load peak transport rate roughly corresponds to the central thread of flow. Transport rates can vary by as much as 10 times in the space of 1 m. Pitlick (1988) also found considerable variation in bed load transport rates; cross-section mean values were found to be of the same order of magnitude as the standard deviation of the measurements.

These observations have implications for sampling and for the calculation of mean transport rates and bed load yields (Hubbell, 1987). Given the high variance of observed transport rates, estimation of mean bed load transport rates from cross section traverses, based on a few cross-channel samples, are likely to have large errors associated with them. Surveys of cross-section variation in transport rate are also useful in determining the "active" bed width over which bed material movement takes place. In the Bas Glacier d'Arolla channel the active width is fairly stable and can be approximated by 0.6-0.7 channel width (for within channel flow).

CONCLUSIONS

Where estimates of bed load yield are required for management of glacial meltwater streams the indiscriminate use of the Schoklitsch sediment transport formula is not recommended, and bias corrected rating curves should only be used where a clear relationship exists between sediment transport and discharge at a particular site. Predictions of bed load yield will be even more unreliable in mountain streams where permanent stream flow gauging structures do not exist. Sediments traps, whether man-made or natural, provide the "best" estimate of bed load yield.

The Schoklitsch bed load transport formula does not realistically model bed load transport in mountain streams. If used at all it is recommended that the critical threshold discharge (q_{cr}) be determined from field measurements, where possible.

Variability in bed load transport is very marked in short-term bed load transport series, cross section surveys and in the relationship between bed load transport and discharge (Fig. 2). Bed load moves in "threads" with transport rates varying by a factor of 10 in the space of a metre. Sediment supply and storage are important factors in determining the strength of the bed load transport relationship. Sediment storage related to a hierarchy of bed elements within the channel appears to be an important control on the release of bed sediment. A 3 phase model of bed load transport may be appropriate to mountain streams but this needs to be verified.

Finally, bed load transport processes in the Bas Glacier d'Arolla proglacial stream, although generally characteristic of steep, coarse bed mountain streams should be considered site specific. Each mountain stream will require a specific solution in estimating bed load yield.

ACKNOWLEDGEMENTS Financial support was provided by a research studentship provided by the U.K. Natural Environment Research Council. Grande Dixence S.A. kindly provided the discharge data and access to field installations. Tim Davies and Bill Young reviewed the manuscript.

REFERENCES

Bathurst, J.C., Leeks, G.J.L. & Newson, M.D. (1985) Field measurements for hydraulic and geomorphological studies of sediment transport - The special problems of mountain streams. In: Symp. Measurement Techniques Hydraul.Res. (Delft April 1985) 137-151.

Bathurst, J.C., Graf, W.H. & Cao, H.H. (1987) Bed load discharge equations for steep mountain rivers. In Sediment Transport in Gravel-bed Rivers, (Eds) Thorne, C.R., Bathurst, J.C. & Hey, R.D., John Wiley & Sons, 453-491.

Ferguson, R.I. (1986) River loads underestimated by rating curves. Wat. Resour. Res. 22 1, 74-76.

Gurnell, A.M., Warburton, J. & Clark, M.J. (1988) A comparison of the sediment yield characteristics of two adjacent glacier basins, Val d'Hérens, Switzerland. Sediment Budgets (Proc. Porto Alegre Symp. December 1988). IAHS Publ.no. 174, 431-441.

Hean, D.S. & Nanson, G.C. (1987) Serious problems in using equations to estimate bedload yields for coastal rivers in NSW. Aust. Geogr. 18, 2, 114-124.

Hollingshead, A.B. (1971) Sediment transport measurements in gravel river. J.Hydraul.Div.ASCE 97, 1817-1834.

Hubbell, D.W. (1987) Bed load sampling and Analysis. In Sediment Transport in Gravel-bed Rivers, (Eds) Thorne, C.R., Bathurst, J.C. & Hey, R.D., John Wiley & Sons, 89-118.

Jackson, W.L. & Beschta, R.L. (1982) A model of two-phase bedload transport in a Oregon Coast Range stream. Earth Surf. Processes Landforms 7, 517-527.

Jaeggi, M.N.R. & Rickenmann, D. (1987) Application of sediment transport formulae in mountain streams. Proc. IAHR Congress, (Lausanne 1987), 98-103.

Lauffer, H. & Sommer, N. (1982) Studies of sediment transport in mountain streams of the Eastern Alps. Proc. 14th Congress Intl. Commission on Large Dams, Rio de Janiero, Brazil, 431-453.

Pitlick, J. (1988) Variability in bed load measurement. Wat.Resour.Res. 24, 1, 173-177.

Schoklitsch, A. (1962) Handbuch des Wasserbaues, 3rd edn, Springer-Verlag, Vienna.

Walling, D.E. & Webb B.W. (1988) The reliability of rating curve estimates of suspended sediment yield: some further comments. Sediment Budgets (Proc. Porto Alegre Symp. December 1988). IAHS Publ.no. 174, 337-350.

Whittaker, J.G. (1987) Modelling bed-load transport in steep mountain streams. Erosion and Sedimentation in the Pacific Rim (Proc. Corvallis Symp. August 1987). IAHS Publ.no. 165, 319-332.

Symposium on Quantitative and Qualitative Water Cycle Aspects in Heterogeneous Basins

TOPIC A:

QUANTITATIVE SPACE-TIME WATER VARIABILITY

Hydrology in Mountainous Regions. I - Hydrological Measurements; the Water Cycle (Proceedings of two Lausanne Symposia, August 1990). IAHS Publ. no. 193, 1990.

Méthodes d'étude de la variabilité spatiale du cycle hydrique dans le petit bassin du Ringelbach

B. AMBROISE
Centre d'Etudes et de Recherches Eco-Géographiques
(CEREG, URA 95 du CNRS), Université Louis Pasteur,
3 rue de l'Argonne, F 67083 Strasbourg Cedex, France

ABSTRACT This paper presents a brief synthesis of methodological studies made since 1975 in the small (36 ha) granitic Ringelbach research catchment on the spatial variability of the water cycle components in temperate middle mountains. Simple but physically-based methods and models have been tested to estimate and to map input (precipitations) and output (evapotranspiration) fluxes, flux-controlling parameters (soil hydric properties), hydrological processes (streamflow generation). These results help us to assess the spatial representativeness of any point measurement, and to improve the precision of water balance and hydrological modelling in a mountainous area.

INTRODUCTION

En montagne, les composantes du cycle de l'eau, les paramètres qui les contrôlent, les processus qui les génèrent, présentent en fonction de la topographie des variations qui rendent difficiles leur mesure ou leur estimation. Cette variabilité spatiale, qui se manifeste à différentes échelles, pose le problème de la représentativité spatiale de toute mesure ponctuelle de ces variables et paramètres, et donc de leur interpolation à l'échelle d'un bassin.

Afin d'améliorer la précision des bilans hydriques et hydrologiques en montagne et de leur modélisation, des méthodes cartographiques et des modèles simples mais à bases physiques, applicables à l'échelle de tout un bassin, peuvent être élaborés en tirant parti à la fois des acquis théoriques pour le choix des variables et paramètres pertinents, et des méthodes naturalistes pour établir une typologie d'unités spatiales relativement homogènes dans leur fonctionnement (Ambroise et al., 1982).

Cet article présente une brève synthèse des recherches méthodologiques menées en ce sens depuis 1975 dans le petit bassin du Ringelbach, qui par sa taille et sa topographie se prête bien à des études fines de variabilité. La démarche employée sera illustrée par des exemples d'application portant sur des variables d'entrée (précipitations) et de sortie (évapotranspiration), sur des paramètres (propriétés hydriques des sols) et sur des processus (génération des débits).

PRESENTATION DU BASSIN

Le bassin du Ringelbach se trouve sur le versant alsacien des Vosges centrales, dans la commune de Soultzeren (Haut-Rhin), à 18 km à l'ouest de Colmar. Les altitudes de ce petit bassin de 36 ha s'échelonnent entre 748 m et 1000 m, avec une pente moyenne de 20° et une gamme d'expositions allant du SSE au WNW. Il est entaillé dans 2 granites hercyniens recouverts sur les sommets (Hurlin, Heidenkopf) par des lambeaux de grès triasique. L'arène granitique est recouverte de formations de pente peu épaisses, et de sols bruns à texture très grossière. La végétation est une pelouse pâturée sur granite, une pineraie sur grès. Dans le fond du vallon une nappe permanente en surface ou à faible profondeur est drainée par trois ruisseaux pouvant localement et temporairement s'assécher. Le climat est de type transitoire océanique, avec des températures moyennes mensuelles variant de 0° à 15.6°C. Bien réparties sur toute l'année, les précipitations sont en moyenne de 1230 mm/an (Paul, 1982), dont environ 40% est évapotranspiré. Les débits à l'exutoire varient de moins d'1 l/s à plus de 150 l/s, autour d'un module d'environ 7.4 l/s (Humbert, 1982).

L'équipement climato-hydrologique permanent comporte depuis 1975 2 abris météorologiques standard petit modèle (avec thermohygrographe, évaporimètre Piche et thermomètres à minima et maxima) et 2 pluviographes situés en des sites représentatifs l'un du climat régional, l'autre du topoclimat du fond plus abrité et humide du vallon; 1 limnigraphe à l'exutoire, dans un chenal calibré de 9 m de long fermé par un déversoir triangulaire (28°) en mince paroi, permet une grande précision de mesure dans toute la gamme des débits. Depuis 1987, une station météorologique automatique (irradiation globale, humidité, températures, vitesse et direction du vent, précipitations) enregistre en continu le climat régional, et le bilan hydrique du sol est suivi en 4 sites équipés de tensiomètres et de tubes neutroniques. Des réseaux complémentaires de mesures topoclimatologiques ont été utilisés durant plusieurs années.

PRECIPITATIONS

La quantité d'eau effectivement reçue par le sol (pluie "hydrologique") varie selon la pente et l'orientation du versant, et selon la vitesse et la direction du vent local - elles-même influencées par la topographie. En montagne, cette quantité peut donc être très différente de la quantité collectée, selon les normes météorologiques, par des pluviomètres à ouverture horizontale (pluie "météorologique"). Cette forte variabilité spatiale des précipitations en montagne -même à l'échelle de petits bassins- rend difficile une estimation précise et spatialisée des lames d'eau précipitées.

Un modèle trigonométrique simple mais encore peu testé en montagne (Serra, 1952; Sharon, 1980) permet d'estimer et d'expliquer ces différences, en reliant en tout point à la topographie locale le vecteur-pluie au niveau du sol, défini par 3 composantes: son module R, son angle d'incidence Ir (par rapport à la verticale descendante), l'azimuth Zr d'où vient la pluie (par rapport au Nord, dans le sens horaire). La lame d'eau (Pc), par unité de surface horizontale, recueillie dans un pluviomètre incliné est reliée à ce vecteur par la relation de trigonométrie sphérique:

$$Pc = R\ [\cos Ir + \tan It\ \sin Ir\ \cos(Zt-Zr)]$$

où S est la surface de réception du pluviomètre, It sa pente et Zt son orientation. Le vecteur-pluie local au niveau du pluviomètre peut donc être estimé en tout point à partir de mesures faites avec un ensemble de 3 pluviomètres d'inclinaisons différentes, chacun fournissant une telle équation à 3 inconnues (R, Ir, Zr).

Pour estimer ces variations spatiales et tester ce modèle dans le bassin du Ringelbach, un réseau de 14 stations pluviométriques a été installé le long de transects repésentatifs, équipées chacune de 3 pluviomètres à 40 cm du sol et d'inclinaisons différentes -dont un à ouverture horizontale pour la mesure des précipitations météorologiques (PH), et un à ouverture parallèle au versant pour la mesure des précipitations hydrologiques (PPc).

Le traitement des 60 épisodes pluvieux ainsi collectés en 1987 et 1988 a permis (Ambroise & Adjizian-Gérard, 1989; Adjizian-Gérard & Ambroise, 1990):

(a) de mettre en évidence des différences pluviométriques importantes entre les sites selon leur position topographique (altitude, exposition), mais aussi entre les précipitations météorologique et hydrologique en chaque site (Fig. 1);

(b) d'expliquer ces différences locales à partir du modèle trigonométrique, dont la validité a été vérifiée par comparaison des vecteurs-pluie estimés et des vecteurs-vent mesurés à la station météorologique;

(c) de préciser par cartographie la structure topopluviométrique du bassin, fortement liée à celle du vent, et variable selon les types de circulation atmosphérique.

Cette approche vectorielle et cartographique semble prometteuse pour estimer en montagne la représentativité spatiale des stations pluviométriques en fonction de la topographie locale, et en déduire des estimations plus précises des lames d'eau précipitées sur un bassin: ainsi, la lame d'eau hydrologique effectivement reçue par le bassin du Ringelbach est de 7% supérieure à la lame d'eau météorologique.

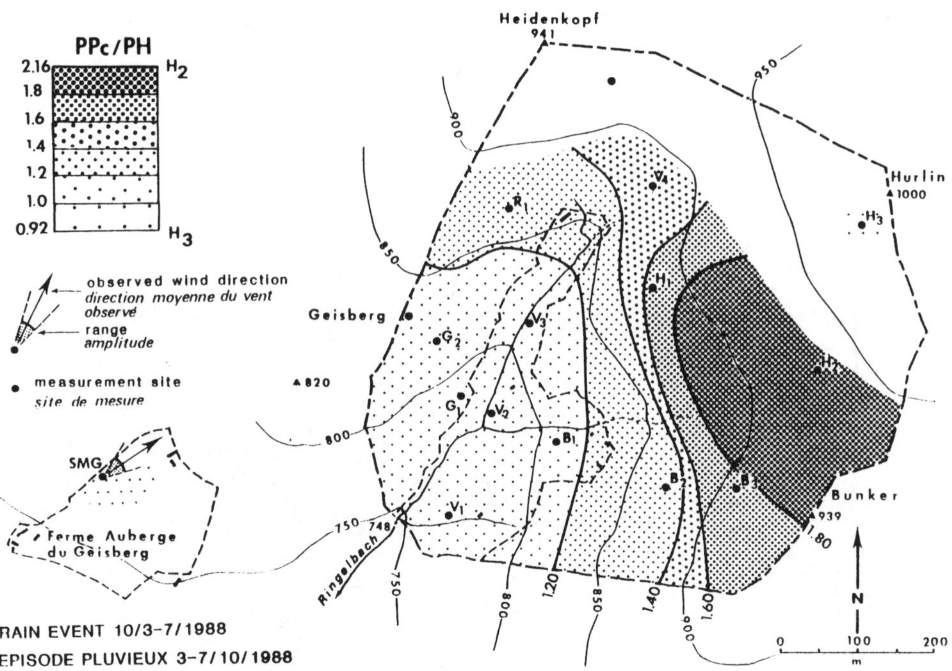

FIG. 1 Exemple de carte du rapport PPc/PH des lames d'eau précipitées (par unité de surface horizontale) mesurées sur pente PPc et horizontalement PH (In: Ambroise & Adjizian-Gérard, 1989).

EVAPOTRANSPIRATION

Bien que composante importante de tout bilan hydrologique, l'évapotranspiration à l'échelle d'un bassin est difficile à évaluer, surtout en montagne où le relief provoque d'importantes variations spatiales de l'énergie disponible -tant radiative (provenant du rayonnement solaire) qu'advective (liée aux caractéristiques physiques des masses d'air en mouvement). Les méthodes d'estimation généralement utilisées en hydrologie fournissent des valeurs globales assez peu précises et à des pas de temps trop longs (décade, mois) pour permettre une véritable compréhension des mécanismes en jeu. Inversement, les méthodes et modèles physiques -qui mesurent et simulent avec précision et à des pas de temps courts (heure) les échanges radiatifs, énergétiques et hydriques- donnent des résultats dont la représentativité spatiale est limitée, et sont trop lourds pour être mis en oeuvre à l'échelle de tout un bassin.

Une méthode simple mais à bases physiques d'estimation et de cartographie, au pas de temps journalier, des évapotranspirations potentielle ETP (dépendant de l'énergie disponible) et réelle ET (dépendant aussi de l'eau disponible et de l'état de surface) a été élaborée et testée dans le bassin du Ringelbach. ETP est estimée à partir de la relation de Brochet & Gerbier (1972), dérivée de l'équation de Penman; et ET, à partir d'une approximation -valable localement- de la relation de Bouchet (1963) combinée à la relation de Priestley & Taylor (1972):

$$ETP = m\ Rg + n\ Ep \quad , \quad ET = EP_o - r\ (ETP - EP_o) \quad , \quad EP_o = 1.26\ m\ Rg$$

où m et n sont des coefficients tabulés dépendant de la saison, de la latitude et du type d'abri; l'irradiation globale Rg et l'évaporation Piche sous abri Ep sont bien plus simples à mesurer que les variables intervenant dans l'équation de Penman, dont r est un coefficient; EP_o est l'évapotranspiration potentielle climatique limite.

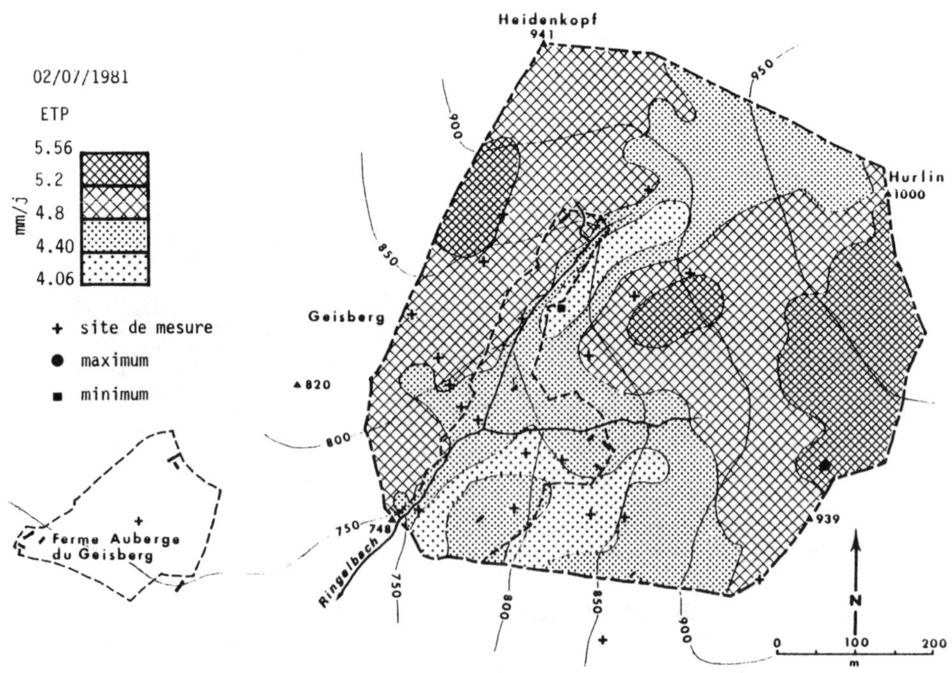

FIG. 2 Exemple de carte d'évapotranspiration potentielle journalière ETP par la formule de Brochet & Gerbier (In: Ambroise & Najjar, 1983).

Des cartes d'ETP et d'ET journalières peuvent ainsi être obtenues, en combinant selon les relations précédentes:

(a) des cartes de la composante radiative, obtenues en calculant Rg en tout point à partir de mesures pyranométriques de référence en une station horizontale et d'un modèle numérique de terrain, en tenant compte des pentes, orientations et masques orographiques au lever et au coucher du soleil;

(b) des cartes de la composante advective, obtenues à partir des mesures d'Ep faites en implantant dans le bassin un réseau d'évaporimètres Piche dans de petits abris peu coûteux spécialement conçus.

Cette méthode cartographique a été testée dans le petit bassin du Ringelbach à partir des données recueillies au cours de plusieurs campagnes de mesures topoclimatiques intensives (20 sites de mesure). Elle a donné des résultats très satisfaisants pour l'estimation d'ETP et d'ET, par comparaison avec les bilans hydrique local et hydrologique global. Mais elle a de plus permis de mettre en évidence et de quantifier d'importantes différences dans la répartition spatiale de l'énergie et de l'évapotranspiration dans ce bassin pourtant petit (Fig. 2): variables selon la saison et le type de temps, ces différences sont bien fonction de la topographie et de l'état hydrique des versants (Ambroise & Najjar, 1983). Cette méthode -qui doit encore être testée sur une plus grande région- fournit ainsi une approche intéressante pour caractériser par type de temps la structure topoclimatique de bassins montagneux.

PROPRIETES HYDRIQUES DES SOLS

Les transferts d'eau à l'interface sol-plante-atmosphère sont largement conditionnés par les propriétés hydriques (rétention hydrique, conductivité hydraulique) des sols. Ces propriétés dépendent de la structure et de la texture des milieux poreux, dont l'organisation spatiale dépend de leur mode de mise en place -fortement conditionné en montagne par le relief. Elles sont donc très variables, tant verticalement (selon les horizons dans un profil de sol), que latéralement (suivant les types de sol, mais aussi à l'intérieur d'une même unité de sol). Pour pouvoir estimer la représentativité spatiale de toute mesure locale de ces propriétés et limiter leur échantillonnage toujours coûteux, il est important d'élaborer des méthodes simples de stratification de l'espace, de déterminer par type de milieu poreux la distribution statistique de ces propriétés et de dégager des corrélations avec d'autres propriétés plus faciles à mesurer.

La démarche adoptée dans le petit bassin granito-gréseux du Ringelbach a consisté à tester, par un échantillonnage stratifié, l'hypothèse que des levers morpho-pédologiques permettaient de définir des unités hydrodynamiques relativement homogènes et significativement différentes. A partir de plusieurs critères naturalistes simples, le bassin a donc été découpé en 4 unités morpho-pédologiques: 2 sur granites, 1 sur grès, 1 sur les colluvions hydromorphes du fond de vallon. Plus de 400 échantillons de sol non remanié ont été prélevés dans ces unités, et traités au laboratoire (courbe de rétention hydrique, conductivité hydraulique à saturation, densité, granulométrie).

Le traitement statistique de ces données a permis (Ambroise & Viville, 1986; Viville et al., 1986):

(a) de caractériser du point de vue hydrique ces formations superficielles, dont le matériel est très grossier: faible rétention hydrique, conductivité hydraulique forte à saturation mais décroissant très rapidement quand le sol se draine -d'où un fonctionnement hydrique en "tout ou rien";

(b) de vérifier la pertinence, du point de vue hydrodynamique aussi, de ce découpage de l'espace en unités morpho-pédologiques: des classifications hiérarchiques et des analyses discriminantes pas à pas ont souligné le rôle prépondérant de la teneur en matière organique dans cette typologie;

(c) d'estimer les distributions statistiques de ces propriétés dans une même unité et un même horizon, et leurs variabilités inter-unité et intra-unité (verticale, latérale) (Fig. 3): distributions normales pour les rétentions hydriques et les fractions texturales, lognormales pour les conductivités hydrauliques; variabilité faible à moyenne des fractions texturales et des rétentions, forte des éléments grossiers et des conductivités; variabilité locale importante, surtout en surface.

Toutes ces données ont également permis de tester plusieurs méthodes indirectes d'estimation de ces propriétés hydriques difficiles à mesurer:

(a) obtention, à l'aide d'un modèle simple de mélange, de corrélations très significatives entre la rétention hydrique et diverses fractions granulométriques: rôle prépondérant joué dans ce milieu par les fractions organiques fine et grossière et les éléments minéraux grossiers (Ambroise et al., 1990);

(b) vérification -par comparaison avec des courbes expérimentales obtenues au laboratoire sur des monolithes de sol non remanié- de la validité pour ce type de milieu des modèles proposés par Van Genuchten (1980) pour ajuster les courbes expérimentales de rétention hydrique et en déduire une bonne estimation des courbes de conductivité hydraulique (Reutenauer & Ambroise, 1990).

Cette démarche, testée également avec de bons résultats à l'échelle de plus grands bassins, fournit ainsi des informations de base sur un type de formations superficielles largement répandu dans la région et des méthodes d'estimation et de cartographie utilisables à l'échelle régionale pour caractériser au moindre coût le comportement hydrique des sols et leur variations spatiales, et paramétriser des modèles hydrologiques spatialisés à bases physiques (Perrin et al., 1990).

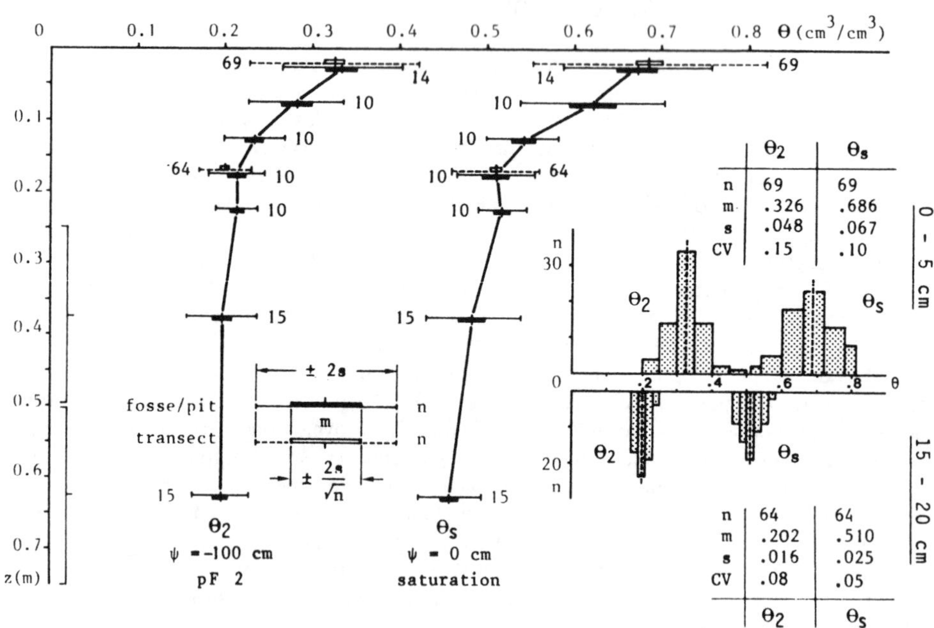

FIG. 3 Exemple de variabilités verticale et latérale des rétentions hydriques à saturation (θ_s) et à pF2 (θ_2) dans une même unité de sol: moyenne, dispersion et intervalle de confiance de la moyenne par niveau z (In: Ambroise & Viville, 1986).

ROLE HYDROLOGIQUE DES SURFACES SATUREES

La nature très filtrante de ses formations superficielles sur granite et grès, ainsi que la continuité de sa couverture végétale permanente font que dans le bassin du Ringelbach -comme d'ailleurs dans tout le massif vosgien- le ruissellement est généralement absent sur les versants: l'eau peut s'y infiltrer et s'écouler de façon hypodermique ou profonde. Il est généralement limité aux surfaces imperméables ou aux surfaces déjà saturées, situées dans les fonds de vallon à proximité du réseau de drainage. Ces surfaces saturées, dont l'extension peut varier largement au cours de l'année, jouent donc un rôle essentiel dans la formation des débits, notamment lors des crues: dans ce type de milieu, le concept de "zone contributive variable" pour chaque forme d'écoulement (Cappus, 1960) s'applique très bien.

Des cartographies répétées de l'extension des surfaces saturées en eau de ce bassin ont permis de mettre en évidence (Ambroise, 1986, 1988):

(a) une bonne corrélation entre leur extension et le débit de base à l'exutoire: cette extension est donc un bon indicateur de l'état hydrologique du bassin;

(b) une bonne concordance entre les coefficients de ruissellement (au sens strict) et l'extension relative de ces surfaces saturées dans le bassin (le plus souvent comprise entre 1% et 8%): le volume ruisselé correspond bien au volume des précipitations sur ces seules surfaces saturées;

(c) une bonne concordance entre le volume des oscillations journalières des débits observées par beau temps chaud et le volume de l'évapotranspiration (au taux potentiel) sur ces seules surfaces saturées;

(d) le rôle tout à fait symétrique joué dans la génération des débits par les précipitations et l'évapotranspiration sur ces surfaces saturées: la courbe de tarissement non influencé apparaît comme la courbe d'équilibre dynamique vers laquelle tend à revenir le débit après toute perturbation par évaporation ou par précipitation sur ces surfaces.

Ainsi, bien que recouvrant une faible superficie, les surfaces saturées jouent, dans le bassin du Ringelbach comme dans de nombreux autres bassins, un rôle climato-hydrologique très important, à l'interface eaux souterraines/eaux superficielles. Ces résultats confirment bien l'intérêt d'une approche spatialisée et non plus globale du fonctionnement de tels bassins: pendant une large part de l'année, les variations de débits à l'exutoire sont contrôlés par les processus actifs sur cette petite portion du bassin, les versants ne contribuant directement que lors des épisodes pluvieux importants. Extension des surfaces saturées et courbes de tarissement semblent pouvoir fournir des indicateurs synthétiques très utiles pour caractériser globalement le fonctionnement des bassins élémentaires dans ce type de milieu. D'où l'intérêt de développer des méthodes de cartographie rapide (par télédétection) de ces surfaces saturées, et des modèles hydrologiques permettant de simuler leur dynamique.

CONCLUSIONS

Ainsi, même à l'échelle d'un petit bassin de 36 ha comme celui du Ringelbach, les échanges hydriques (précipitations, évapotranspiration) entre le sol et l'atmosphère, les propriétés hydriques des sols et les processus de génération des débits présentent en montagne des variations spatiales importantes, bien reliées à la topographie et fonction également -pour les variables climatiques- des types de temps. Les modèles simplifiés et méthodes cartographiques à bases physiques proposés -dont la validité à l'échelle de plus grands bassins est en cours de test- devraient être utiles pour mieux évaluer la représentativité spatiale de toute mesure locale de ces variables et paramètres, et ainsi améliorer la précision des bilans hydrologiques et de leur modélisation physique et spatialisée en région montagneuse.

REMERCIEMENTS J'exprime toute ma reconnaissance à Richard Braun, technicien du CEREG, qui assure depuis 1978 le suivi du réseau de mesure. Ces recherches ont été financées par le Programme PIREN-Eau/Alsace (CNRS, Ministère de l'Environnement, Région Alsace) et l'ATP CNRS-INRA-ORSTOM-CIRAD 1986-89.

REFERENCES

Adjizian-Gérard J., Ambroise B. (1990) Application d'un modèle trigonométrique à la mesure des précipitations sur pente dans le petit bassin du Ringelbach (Hautes Vosges, France). Publ. Assoc. Int. Climatologie (à paraître).

Ambroise B. (1986) Rôle hydrologique des surfaces saturées en eau dans le bassin du

Ringelbach à Soultzeren (Hautes-Vosges), France. Recherches sur l'Environnement dans la Région du Rhin supérieur. O. Rentz, J. Streith, L. Zilliox (Eds), Univ. Louis Pasteur - Conseil de l'Europe, Strasbourg (F), 620-630.

Ambroise B. (1988) Interactions eaux souterraines - eaux de surface dans le bassin du Ringelbach à Soultzeren (Hautes Vosges, France): rôle hydrologique des surfaces saturées. Interaction between Groundwater and Surface Water (Proc. IAHR Symp., Ystad (S), 30/5-3/6/1988). P. Dahlblom, G. Lindh (Eds), Univ. Lund (S), 231-238.

Ambroise B., Adjizian-Gérard J. (1989) Test of a trigonometrical model of slope rainfall in the small Ringelbach catchment (High Vosges, France). Precipitation Measurement (Proc. WMO/IAHS/ETH Workshop, St. Moritz (CH), 3-7/12/1989). B. Sevruk (Ed), ETH, Zurich (CH), 81-85.

Ambroise B., Gounot M., Mercier J.L. (1982) Réflexions sur la modélisation mathématique du cycle hydrologique à l'échelle d'un bassin versant. Rech. Géogr. à Strasbourg 19/20/21, 5-24.

Ambroise B., Najjar G. (1983) Cartographie de l'évapotranspiration journalière en région montagneuse - Application au petit bassin du Ringelbach, Hautes Vosges (France). Les Colloques de l'INRA n°15, 187-200.

Ambroise B., Reutenauer D., Viville D. (1990) Estimation of soil water retention from mineral and organic fractions of natural coarse soils (Vosges Mountains, France). Indirect Methods for Estimating the Hydraulic Properties of Unsaturated Soils (Proc. Int. Workshop, Riverside (Ca, USA), 11-13/1O/1989), USDA (à paraître).

Ambroise B., Viville D. (1986) Spatial variability of textural and hydrodynamical properties in a soil unit of the Ringelbach study catchment,Vosges (France). Z. Geomorph. N.F. Suppl.-Bd 58, 21-34.

Bouchet R.J. (1963) Evapotranspiration réelle et potentielle: signification climatique. IAHS Publ. n°62, 134-142.

Brochet P., Gerbier N. (1975) L'évapotranspiration, aspect agrométéorologique - Evaluation pratique de l'évapotranspiration potentielle. Monographie n°65, Météorologie Nationale, Paris, 95 p.

Cappus P. (1960) Bassin expérimental d'Alrance - Etude des lois de l'écoulement. La Houille Blanche n°A, 493-520.

Humbert J. (1982) Cinq années de bilan hydrologiques mensuels sur un petit bassin versant des Hautes Vosges (1976-1980): le bassin du Ringelbach. Rech. Géogr. à Strasbourg 19/20/21, 105-122.

Paul P. (1982) Le climat de la vallée de la Fecht - Aspects généraux. Rech. Géogr. à Strasbourg 19/20/21, 65-78.

Perrin J.L., Ambroise B., Humbert J. (1990) Application du modèle couplé à discrétisation spatiale au bassin de la Fecht (Vosges, France). Les Ressources en Eau en Régions Montagneuses (Actes AIH/AISH Conf., Lausanne (CH), 27/8-1/9/1990) (Soumis pour publication).

Priestley C.H.B., Taylor R.J. (1972) On the assessment of surface heat flux and evaporation using large-scale parameters. Month. Weath. Rev. 100 (2), 81-92.

Reutenauer D., Ambroise B. (1990) Validation of the Van Genuchten-Mualem model of water hydraulic properties for natural coarse soils (Vosges Mountains, France). Indirect Methods for Estimating the Hydraulic Properties of Unsaturated Soils (Proc. Int. Workshop, Riverside (Ca, USA), 11-13/1O/1989). USDA (à paraître).

Serra L. (1952) Interprétation des mesures pluviométriques - Lois de la pluviosité. La Houille Blanche n° spécial B, 491-504.

Sharon D. (1980) The distribution of hydrologically effective rainfall incident on sloping ground. J. Hydrol. 46, 165-188.

Van Genuchten M.T. (1980) A closed-form equation for predicting the hydraulic conductivity of unsaturated soils. Soil Sci. Soc. Am. J. 44, 892-898.

Viville D., Ambroise B., Korosec B. (1986) Variabilité spatiale des propriétés texturales et hydrodynamiques des sols dans le bassin versant du Ringelbach (Vosges, France). Z. Geomorph. N.F. Suppl.-Bd 60, 21-40.

Hydrology in Mountainous Regions. I - Hydrological Measurements; the Water Cycle
(Proceedings of two Lausanne Symposia, August 1990). IAHS Publ. no. 193, 1990.

The importance of hydrological networks for estimating average flows in Alpine regions

H. ASCHWANDEN
Swiss National Hydrological and Geological Survey, Berne, Switzerland

ABSTRACT The planning of water economy measures on running waters is based on the assumption that the local flow conditions are suitably known. This is often not the case in small and medium-sized catchments. Engineers are then compelled to estimate the flow conditions. In mountainous regions in particular however the necessary data for the development or application of complex runoff models are not available. The procedures of regional transfer offer one means of solving this problem. They consist of transferring discharge values to ungauged areas through statistical procedures, on the basis of the physiographic characteristics of the catchments. The present study shows how estimates of average flows may be obtained in this way. Hydrological networks have an important part to play in this. On the one hand they form the basis for the required analyses and on the other they help the application of the procedures. Further progress in the modelling of runoff processes in mountain areas may not be expected until it is possible to identify the relevant affecting factors and to spot them in greater detail regarding both space and time. Hydrological networks are indispensable for this purpose.

NOTATIONS

A	catchment area [km^2]
E	mean elevation of the catchment [m a.s.l.]
LHG	Swiss National Hydrological and Geological Survey
o	observed
P	mean annual precipitation depth over area [mm]
q	mean annual specific discharge [$l\ s^{-1}\ km^{-2}$]
Q	mean annual discharge [$m^3\ s^{-1}$]
SANW	Swiss National Academy of Natural Sciences
SLF	Swiss Federal Institute for Snow and Avalanche Research
SMA	Swiss National Meteorological Institute
u	ungauged

INTRODUCTION

Planning, projecting and controlling water economy measures and constructions needs optimum information on flow conditions at any given location. Runoff data are frequently available for the larger streams thanks to the measuring networks of national hydrological surveys. But everyday experience often shows a lack of such data for small and medium streams with catchment areas of about 1-100 km². Therefore the engineer has to estimate the flow conditions by means of a wide range of hydrological models and procedures. However it may be noticed that in mountainous regions the necessary input data for hydrological modelling are often not available or can only be obtained through considerable efforts. Moreover not all of the runoff processes are well known in detail so that some significant factors affecting the runoff are unknown or cannot be described in a quantitative manner. After a period of euphoric belief in the possibilities of hydrological modelling these limiting aspects mentioned above have led to a certain stagnation. It is therefore preferable to use the information of existing measuring networks or to estimate average flows by means of short-term measurements.

The present study shows by way of example how discharge estimates may thus be obtained in mountain areas at reasonable expense. Descriptions are limited to catchment areas in the Swiss Alps with a mean catchment altitude of over 1550 meters above sea level. The runoff regime of such catchment areas is governed mostly by the snow and ice melt (Aschwanden et al., 1986).

ESTIMATE OF DISCHARGE MEAN VALUES

Background

Any attempt to assess the significance of snow and ice and their effects on discharge, e.g. in the context of the climatic changes which are to be expected, must be based on the question which of the many available runoff models may be operative in the whole of the Alpine region. For a long time, it was considered that the description of the runoff by means of models consisted in fact almost exclusively in reconstituting exactly the discharge variations of a given catchment and in explaining these through relevant factors of influence. There was no need to transfer the results to other catchments. As models became more complex, input data for calibration and validation had to be more accurate. The effort required for measuring in view of calibration and for the application of deterministic models may often be possible for research purposes only, but not for field application. For estimates in the mean water level range the procedures mostly used are therefore those of the water balance and regression analysis. In both cases, the relevant affecting factors to be considered are varying climatic elements such as precipitation, temperature and radiation. In this field however, there is a lack of data regarding mountain areas, both for small time and space units.

Measuring network situation in the Swiss Alps

Figure 1 shows the density of networks for various climatic elements and for runoff in the Swiss Alps. The precipitation, which is the most important affecting factor, has the largest density of networks. For daily values it amounts to 125 km^2 per station; there are only very few continuous recordings of the precipitation. Other climatic elements, in particular temperature and radiation, are measured by one station each over surfaces of 345 and 670 km^2 respectively. The density of these measuring networks is already markedly inferior. The assessment of the time distribution of the snow cover growth and the recording of the melting processes present insuperable difficulties of interpolation owing to the compartmentation of the landscape and the considerable differences in altitude. There are no more than five stations in the whole of the Alps to measure the mass balances of glaciers.

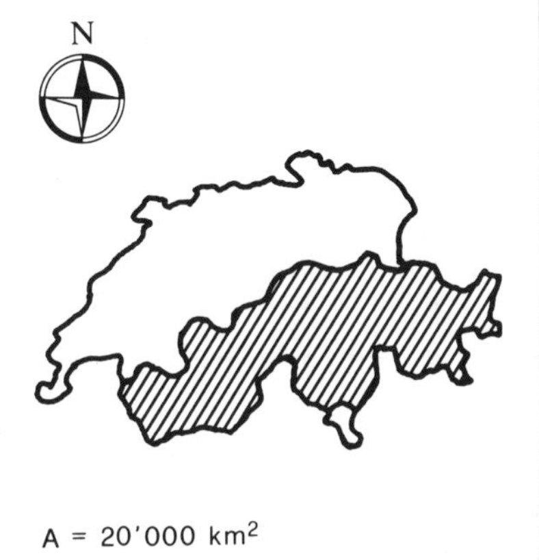

N

A = 20'000 km^2

Network	Time interval	Number of stations	density [km²/station]
C l i m a t e (SMA)			
- Automatic network	10 min	30	670
- Meteorological stations	3/day	28	715
Total		58	345
R a i n f a l l (SMA)			
- Automatic network	10 min	30	670
- Meteorological network	2/day	28	715
- Precipitation network	1/day	105	150
Total		163	125
- Annual storage gages	1/year	129	155
- Radar	10 min	2	
S n o w (SLF)			
- Base network	1/day	67	300
- Additional network	1/day	29	690
Total		96	210
G l a c i e r s (SANW)			
- Fluctuations in the length	1/year	120	
- Mass balance	1/year	5	
D i s c h a r g e (LHG)	continuous	95	210

FIG. 1 Measuring networks for the recording of various elements of the water cycle in the Alpine area.

It is obvious that this density of the measuring networks is not adequate for the development and application of a deterministic model to assess mean average flows in catchment areas in the range from 1 to 100 km^2. The problems become even more apparent when the distribution of the measuring stations per levels of altitude is considered. Figure 2 shows that from about 1500 meters above sea level upwards the density of stations for the application of discharge models becomes insufficient for both the meteorological and the rain gauges networks. While recording gauges are practically inexistent, the network of annual storage gauges, which give little information regarding short periods of time, is increasing strongly. Müller (1980) moreover shows that the density of stations in all slope and hollow positions is above average.

The procedure of regional transfer provide a solution out of this situation. They include statistical procedures which, as a result of the physiographic characteristics of the catchment, enable measured discharge values to be transferred to ungauged areas. Since the climatic and hydrological networks in Switzerland are operated by various institutions and since measuring sites are selected according to varying criteria, the use of data from hydrometrical networks is therefore a notable improvement of the information and must be considered as necessary for the development of such statistical procedures for the estimates of flows. This solution moreover appears to be the only possible way to ensure accuracy of measurement, since the determination of the precipitation over area in high Alpine conditions for example constitutes a major problem. For annual values of precipitation at the station alone a systematic error of over 25% has to be reckoned with (Sevruk, 1985), whereas mean annual discharge values may be determined with a 5% precision margin. The network density of stations measuring the discharge must also be viewed from this angle: it covers 210 km^2 per station and is therefore not much below that of the precipitation network; moreover, the quality of information is better, since in the case of discharge values it covers an area, whereas for the station precipitation it is only punctual.

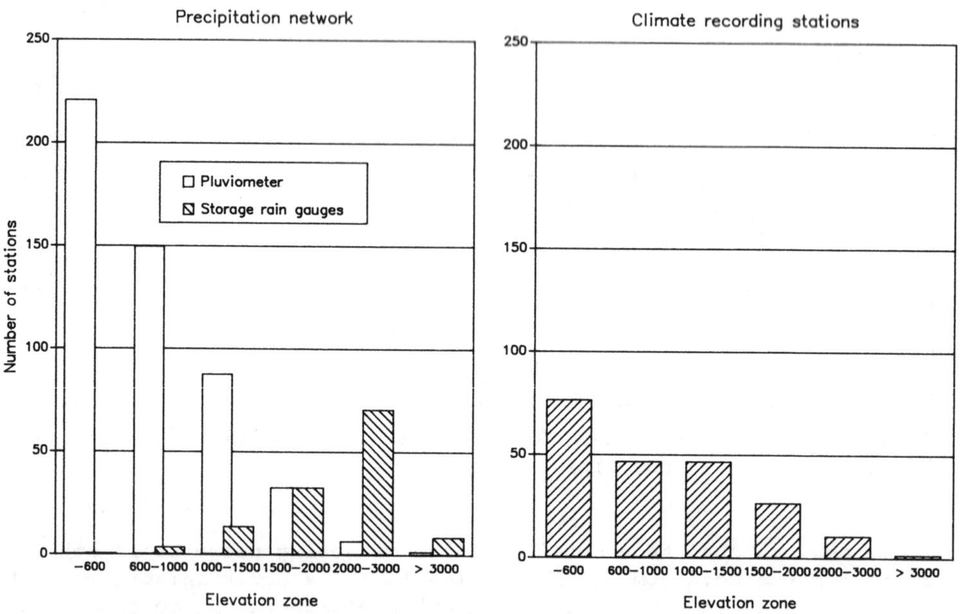

FIG.2 Respective heights of climatological and precipitation measuring stations in Switzerland.

Long-term mean annual discharge

The discharge processes of alpine catchments are determined by snow and ice melt. Snow fall in winter and clear sky conditions in summer are climatic elements of great constance. Aschwanden et al. (1986) examined the runoff regimes in Switzerland and arrived at the conclusion that the mean seasonal runoff regime in the Alps may be described with only four different types of regimes (Fig. 3). The runoff regime is recorded by means of 12 dimensionless coefficients resulting from the quotients from the monthly discharges and the annual discharge. The variation of annual discharges is small and dependent on the regime type. The coefficients of variation amount to an average of 10 to 20%: they are lower in glacierized catchments than in those which are characterized by the snow melt process. The conditions are therefore favourable for determining the long-term mean discharge values through short-term measurement. Thus in heavily glacierized areas, an accuracy of 20% may already be obtained for the annual mean value with a measuring period of two years, and of 15% after three years. In snow melt areas the respective periods are four and six years. Problems of measuring techniques should not however be disregarded in this case. As is shown in figure 3, there are considerable seasonal differences as regards discharge. While during the low water period the discharge represents only a few per cent of the mean annual amount, the maximum discharge during a summer day under cloudless sky is a multiple of it.

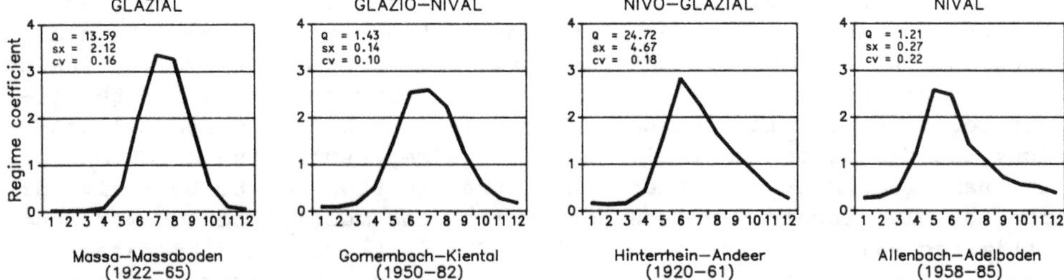

FIG.3 Types of discharge regimes in the Swiss Alpine region: regime curve, mean annual discharge (Q), standard deviation (s_x) and variation coefficient (c_v).

Comparable results as regards accuracy may be obtained more quickly with estimate procedures. A frequent means of determining annual discharges consists in transferring to the catchment under investigation the values measured in an hydrologically similar catchment (Formula 1). This simple model may be noticeably improved if rainfall conditions are included (Formula 2). In this cases, the main problem is to assess the hydrological analogy of two catchments.

$$Q(u) = \frac{A(u)}{A(o)} Q(o) \tag{1}$$

$$Q(u) = \frac{A(u)\ P(u)}{A(o)\ P(o)} Q(o) \tag{2}$$

A procedure based on the measured values of a downstream measuring station is however more appropriate. This restriction has the advantage of not giving too much importance to local peculiarities, since the specific discharges are transferred merely inside one single and hence relatively homogenous catchment area. It is assumed that the discharge differences between the total catchment and the subcatchment are due mainly to the different conditions of altitude and precipitation. In this case the model based on regression analysis for Swiss conditions would be as follows (Formula 3):

$$q(u) = (0.6617 \frac{E(u)}{E(o)} + 0.3904 \frac{P(u)}{P(o)})\ q(o) \tag{3}$$

The standard error is 10%. Care should be taken during application that the specific discharges of glacierized areas should not be transferred to non-glacierized area sections (Aschwanden et al., 1986).

Long-term mean monthly discharge

The assessment of monthly mean discharge values may be obtained indirectly through classification of the runoff regimes. In the case of dimension the idea of representative basins is taken up. The area to be analysed is attributed to a regime type on the basis of its physiographic characteristics with the help of the "Runoff regimes map of Switzerland" (Weingartner, 1990). In the Alpine region this attribution is based on the mean elevation of the catchment and its glacierization. The identification of the regime type moreover indicates the catchments which may be considered as representative for the given regime type. With the help of conclusions based on spatial analogy the dimensionless regime curve of a representative catchment of the same regime type is then transferred to the area to be analysed; the monthly discharge values result from the multiplication with the estimated value for the annual flow. The fact that this transfer takes place inside a given regime type reduces the error resulting from the use of non-representative coefficients. This procedure has a mean accuracy of 10 to 20%.

The long-term 95%-quantile of daily discharges

To ensure appropriate residual flow below water derivation Swiss legislation has set the latter on the basis of the discharge quantity Q_{347}, which is equivalent to the 95%-quantile of the daily discharges. The relevant article of the law (Bundeskanzlei, 1987) thus defines this amount of water that characterizes the low water regime:"A quantity of water which over a ten-year period is present or exceeded during 347 days a year and which is not significantly influenced through storing, derivation or conduction."

In areas where no measurements take place this quantity must be estimated. In the Alpine region the precipitation in the winter semester is stored at the surface in the form of snow and ice. The low flow is registered during this time. The extent and the duration of the low flow period are governed by radiation and temperature as climatic factors, by the slope, the exposition and the elevation level as physiographic characteristics of the area. Given the present knowledge and database the complex imbrication of these factors and the mechanisms of storage can however not be recorded with sufficient accuracy through simple statistical procedures. Owing to the strong spatial variability of this discharge quantity the application of procedures covered under the name "regional transfer" is made difficult. It expresses itself in the fact that the extreme dry year periods in various catchments do not occur simultaneously, but with varying duration and extent (Figure 4). Aschwanden and Schädler (1988) showed that in the Alpine region an estimate of this discharge value is possible through classification and regionalisation procedures. Although the average accuracies in the range of 20 to 25% which may be obtained are acceptable in the light of the known natural variations the authors recommend checking through short-term measurement. Aschwanden (1990) comes to the conclusion that a more reliable estimate of the long-term low flow discharge Q_{347} may only be obtained through short-term measurement.

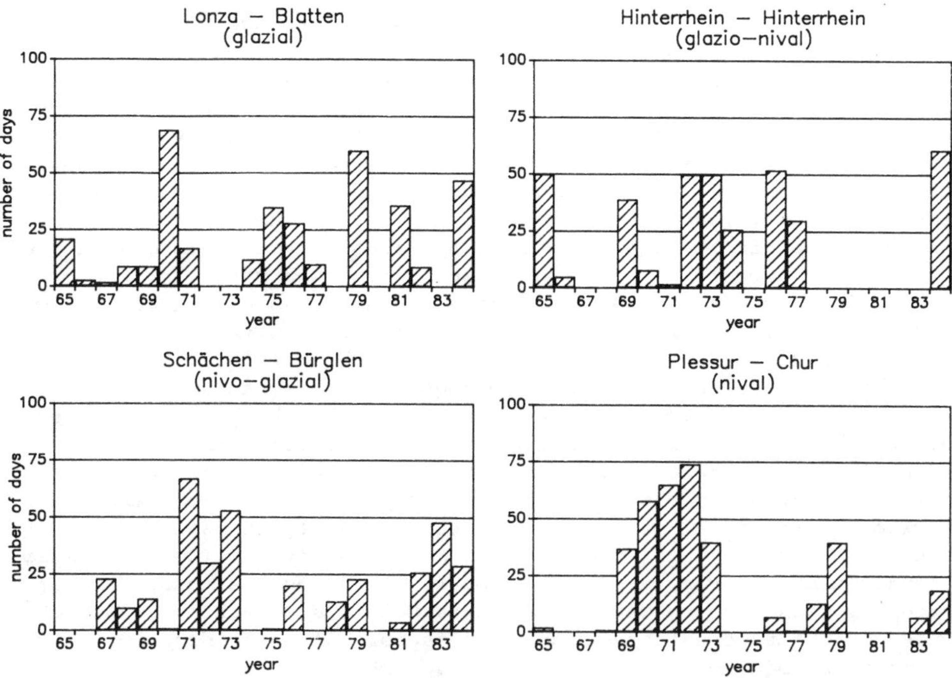

FIG. 4 Distribution of the days with a smaller or equal runoff than the mean discharge quantity Q_{347} during the period 1965 to 1984.

With a measuring period of two to three years and observation periods from October to April it is possible to determine the mean discharge quantity Q_{347} with great accuracy. It amounts to an average of 5 to 10%, but maximum derivations of up to 20% may occur in individual cases. In this case, short term measurement proves to be better than estimate procedures. The small amounts of water which may be expected in comparison with the annual average moreover facilitate the measurement techniques of this procedure.

THE SIGNIFICANCE OF HYDROLOGICAL NETWORKS

The experience gathered with the procedures mentioned goes to show that even with simple estimate procedures good results may be achieved. These are the better the smaller the space-time variability of the parameter under investigation. In this respect Alpine regions offer good conditions. It can be seen that in many cases the space and time variability of discharge values is very small. This is due to the fact that water resources are continuously available in the form of snow and ice and that temperature and radiation as important relevant factors show far smaller local fluctuations than the precipitations for example. The prevailing conditions thus on the one hand permit to draw conclusions from the results of the short-term measurements for the long-term flow regime of a measured amount while, on the other hand, information gathered in one area may be transferred to other hydrologically similar areas. The one thing all these procedures have in common is that they use already available measuring data. Existing hydrological networks are an excellent basis in this respect. They contain information which may be useful for many questions. This usefulness is twofold: on one hand the networks constitute the data basis for studies and analyses. In connection with the development of assessment procedures the space-time analysis of the discharge variations is the most important. The information thus gained often also serves to improve previously known methods. On the other hand, hydrological networks also serve as a basis for the procedures of regional transfer, whereby discharge values themselves or derived quantities are transferred to catchments without measurements. The denser the networks, the larger the possibilities to improve and deepen the state of knowledge on the mechanisms of runoff processes in mountain areas. Despite the far-reaching possibilities offered by the runoff models measurement of runoff amounts in the mountains is a more urgent task than ever. Together with the procedure for estimating flood peaks (Naef et al., 1985), there are workable statistical procedures for the Swiss Alpine region for assessing the mean runoff processes of mountain rivers. The obtainable standards of accuracy are sufficient for many applications. Further progress cannot be reached until it is possible to achieve a better grasp of the relevant space and time factors of influence. For this purpose we require the hydrological networks.

ACKNOWLEDGEMENTS The present paper was drawn up in the "Studies and Forecasts Section" of the Swiss National Hydrological and Geological Survey. I thank Mr B. Schädler for a critical reading of the manuscript.

REFERENCES

Aschwanden, H. (1990) Einsatz von Kurzzeitmessungen zur Bestimmung der Abflussmenge Q347. Gas-Wasser-Abwasser 70 (2), 20-28.

Aschwanden, H., Schädler, B. (1988) Die Abflussmenge Q_{347} als Grundlage zur Bestimmung der Restwassermenge. Gas-Wasser-Abwasser 68 (9) 491-496.

Aschwanden, H., Weingartner, R., Leibundgut, Ch. (1986) Zur regionalen Übertragung von Mittelwerten des Abflusses. Dt. Gewässerkundl.Mitt. 30 (2/3 and 4), 52-61, 93-99.

Bundeskanzlei (1987) Botschaft zur Volksinitiative "Zur Rettung unserer Gewässer" und zur Revision des Bundesgesetzes über den Schutz der Gewässer. Eidg. Drucksachen- und Materialzentrale, Bern.

Naef, F., Zuidema, P., Kölla, E. (1985) Abschätzung von Hochwassern in kleinen Einzugsgebieten. Beitr. zur Geologie d. Schweiz-Hydrologie 33,195-233.

Müller, G. (1980) Die Beobachtungsnetze der Schweizerischen Meteorologischen Anstalt - Konzept 1980. Arbeitsber. d.Schweiz. Meteor. Anstalt 93, Zürich.

Sevruk, B. (1985) Systematischer Niederschlagsfehler in der Schweiz. Beitr. zur Geologie d. Schweiz-Hydrologie 31, 65-75.

Weingartner, R. (1990) Hydrologischer Atlas der Schweiz - Ein erster Bericht. Geographica Helvetica 45 (2) in print.

Hydrology in Mountainous Regions. I - Hydrological Measurements; the Water Cycle
(Proceedings of two Lausanne Symposia, August 1990). IAHS Publ. no. 193, 1990.

Investigations of the precipitation conditions in the central part of the Tianshan mountains

FELIX P. BLUMER
ETH Zurich, Hydrology Section, Department of Geography, 8057 Zurich, Switzerland

ABSTRACT The climate of the Xinjiang Province in northwestern China is charaterized by low precipitation amounts and large seasonal temperature differences as a consequence of its innercontinental position. The flat areas are deserts (Tarim Basin) or prairies (Dzungarian Basin) with 20-250 mm precipitation per year. For this reason precipitation falling in the mountainous regions of the Tianshans (about 500 mm/year) is very important for the people and economy in this region. Most of the annual precipitation falls during the summer months under the influence of the Indian monsoon system. At this time about 70% of precipitation is influenced by cyclone activity and only 30% results from local convection. Two zones with considerably more precipitation can be found, one at an elevation of about 2000 m a.s.l. and one at an elevation of about 3800 m a.s.l.

INTRODUCTION

In the summers 1986 and 1987 extensive precipitation measurements at 11 observation sites in the uppermost part of Urumqi River Valley were carried out by the Climatology and Hydrology Group of ETH Zurich and a Group from Lanzhou Institute of Glaciology and Geocryology of Academia Sinica.

The Tianshan is a high mountain ridge more than 1500 km long extending from 75°E to 95°E along 42°N latitude. It divides the Chinese Autonomous Province Xinjiang Uigur in two parts. In the south are the desert areas of the Taklamakan and in the north the great plains of the Dzungarian Basin. The Urumqi River rises in the mid-part of the Chinese Tianshan (90 km south of Urumqi, the capital of the province) and it runs from south to north. Mountains in this area reach an altitude of 4500 m a.s.l. and glaciers are located in regions higher than 3700 m a.s.l..

The climate of northwestern China

The climate of the Xinjiang Province is characterized by its innercontinental location. For this reason temperature differences between summer and winter seasons are high and the yearly precipitation amounts are low. The corresponding values of the three stations, Kucha, Kashgar and Urumqi are given in Tab. 1. The pressure conditions are different between the summer and winter seasons. During the winter a cold anticyclone in the lowest layers covers the Asian continent north of the Himalayas and the Tibetan Plateau. It is formed already in September and does not normally disappear from the mean monthly pressure maps before May. During the summer months, the entire Asian continent is influenced by the seasonal depression of the Indian monsoon system. During this time most of the annual precipitation amount falls in the Tianshans.

TABLE 1 Temperature differences and annual precipitation of Kucha, Kashgar and Urumqi (Müller, 1983).

Station	Altitude m a.s.l.	Geographical Site	Mean Temperature January	July	Annual Precipit.
Kucha	970	41°40'N/83°06'E	-12.6°C	24.1°C	91 mm
Kashgar	1309	39°24'N/76°07'E	-5.3°C	26.7°C	86 mm
Urumqi	913	43°54'N/87°28'E	-15.8°C	23.9°C	273 mm

General precipitation conditions in the Xinjiang Province

In general, precipitation amounts in the Xinjiang Province are very low. In Fig. 1 annual precipitation results for some stations in the Xinjiang Province are given.

FIG. 1 Map of the Xinjiang Province with annual precipitation amounts (mm).

Stations north of the Tianshans in the Dzungarian Basin have distinctly more precipitation than stations south of it in the Tarim Basin even if the altitude is higher in the south. Because of the shortness of the observation period the precipitation values are not totally reliable, but the differences in precipitation amounts can be also seen in vegetation characteristics. The Tarim Basin is a desert and the Dzungarian Basin a prairie.

In Tab. 2 the seasonal variation of precipitation amounts for different stations in the Xinjiang Province is given.

TABLE 2 Monthly precipitation amounts (mm) for several stations in the Xinjiang Province: Urumqi 913 m a.s.l., Kucha 970 m a.s.l., Hero Bridge 1920 m a.s.l., Houxia (Tianshan Glaciological Station) 2130 m a.s.l. and Daxigau Valley (Meteorological Station) 3450 m a.s.l..

Stations	Monthly Precipitation Amounts													Observati. Period
	Jan	Feb	Mar	Apr	May	Jun	July	Aug	Sep	Oct	Nov	Dec	Year	
Urumqi	6	4	19	23	25	29	16	19	14	17	15	7	195	7 years
Kucha	3	3	5	3	3	33	18	8	5	0	2	8	91	2 years
Hero Bridge	8	10	15	63	67	143	110	20	43	25	13	9	526	1987
Houxia	1	4	5	29	56	78	134	29	26	20	6	1	388	1987
Daxigau Valley	2	5	6	25	38	73	160	42	47	25	1	2	426	1987

Stations in the centre of Xinjiang Province normally have their precipitation maximum during the three summer months (June - August); this is true as well for the Dzungarian Basin, the Tarim Basin and also in the mountainous regions of the Tianshan. During these months warm air currents are coming from the southeast in the lower atmosphere and cold and wet air masses are coming from the north and the northeast in the upper atmosphere. In autumn cold and wet air masses in the lower atmosphere moving from the arctic sea produce orographical rain showers on the northern slope of the Tianshans. At this time the winterly high pressure core over Central Siberia is only weakly developed (Grebner, 1990 a). For this reason the annual precipitation maximum can exist in October for stations near the northern slope of the Tianshan Mountains. The year-to-year variability for precipitation in October for these stations is very high because precipitation depends on the exact position of the high pressure core and its development. This is the reason that Tab. 1 does not show this maximum for October but in Tab. 3 (NOAA, 1984) this maximum can be found for a different time period.

TABLE 3 Monthly precipitation amounts (mm) for Urumqi (654 m a.s.l.) (NOAA, 1984).

Station	Jan	Feb	Mar	Apr	May	Jun	Jul	Aug	Sep	Oct	Nov	Dec	Year	Obs. Per.
Urumqi	6	15	15	33	25	33	16	35	15	47	22	11	273	1961-70

Stations near the western border of the Xinjiang Province also have different precipitation systems. Kashgar has nearly no seasonal differences in its precipitation.

TABLE 4 Precipitation conditions for Kashgar (1309 m a.s.l.) for a 18 years period.

Precipitation	Jan	Feb	Mar	Apr	May	Jun	Jul	Aug	Sep	Oct	Nov	Dec	Year	Ob.Period
Amounts (mm)	15	3	13	5	8	5	10	8	3	3	5	8	86	18 years
Days	1	<1	1	1	1	1	1	2	1	<1	1	<1	13	18 years

The precipitation days are also divided over the whole year in Kashgar. Urumqi shows a slight maximum of days with precipitation (p > 0.1 mm) during the winter months even if at that time the seasonal precipitation amount has its minimum (Tab. 5). In mountainous regions the maximum of days with precipitation is at the same time as the maximum of precipitation amount (Tab. 6).

TABLE 5 Precipitation days in Urumqi (Müller, 1983).

Precipitation	Jan	Feb	Mar	Apr	May	Jun	Jul	Aug	Sep	Oct	Nov	Dec	Year	Ob. Period
Days	10	11	7	8	5	6	7	5	4	9	12	11	95	7 years

TABLE 6 Number of days with precipitation for Hero Bridge (1920 m a.s.l.), the Tianshan Glaciological Station in Houxia (2130 m a.s.l.) and the Meteorological Station in Daxigau Valley (3539 m a.s.l.).

Station	Jan	Feb	Mar	Apr	May	Jun	Jul	Aug	Sep	Oct	Nov	Dec	Year	Ob. Period
Hero Bridge	6	5	10	9	11	18	13	6	8	13	6	7	112	1987
Houxia	3	4	8	10	16	15	20	10	8	10	3	4	111	1987
Daxigau Valley	6	5	10	13	22	25	23	18	16	12	3	6	159	1987

In flat areas year-to-year variabilities are much higher than in mountainous regions in the Tianshans where the annual precipitation amount is about 500 mm.

TABLE 7 Annual precipitation at the Meteorological Station in Daxigau Valley (3539 m a.s.l.) (Zhang, 1981 and Blumer, 1990).

Year	58/59	59/60	60/61	61/62	62/63	63/64	64/65	65/66	66/67
Precipitation (mm)	472.8	422.4	434.5	444.2	495.5	444.2	502.3	373.8	428.0
Year	67/68	69/70	70/71	72/73	74/75	76/77	77/78	1987	aver.
Precipitation (mm)	377.6	471.0	380.5	465.5	490.3	354.0	418.4	427.0	435.4

For a seventeen year period at the Meteorological Station in Daxigau Valley (3539 m a.s.l.) the annual precipitation average is 435.4 mm. The standard deviation is 44.9 mm or 10% which indicates that the year-to-year variability is less, especially with regard to the arid climate of the Tianshan Mountains. The amount for the three summer months in particular seems to be very constant, although there is a considerable variability between the different months.

For the stations in Urumqi River Valley two thirds of the annual precipitation falls between June and August.

METHODS

11 observation sites including the existing permanent stations maintained by the Tianshan Glaciological Station were selected and analyzed to understand the characteristics of the precipitation regime in the Urumqi River Valley and especially on Glacier N° 1 at the source of the Urumqi River.

TABLE 8 Network of the observation sites.

	Observation Site	Altitude	Precipitation gauge
A	Accumulation area of Glacier N° 1	4020 m a.s.l.	H, St
B	Equilibrium line of Glacier N° 1	3910 m a.s.l.	H, Ch, UR
C	Near the tongue of Glacier N° 1	3750 m a.s.l.	H, 2 Ch, St
D	Moraine on the northside of Glacier N° 1	3860 m a.s.l.	H, Ch
E	Ablation area of Glacier N° 1	3860 m a.s.l.	St
F	Daxigau Valley	3450 m a.s.l.	St
G	Empty Cirgue	3825 m a.s.l.	St
H	Tianshan Glaciological Station in Houxia	2130 m a.s.l.	Ch
I	Runoff Station Urumqi River	3350 m a.s.l.	Ch
K	Runoff Station near Glacier N° 1	3750 m a.s.l.	Ch
L	Runoff Station in the Empty Cirgue	3800 m a.s.l.	Ch

Abrevations of the precipitation gauges:
H: Hellmann gauge; Ch: Chinese Standard gauge
St: Storage gauge; UR: Universal Recording raingauge (Belfort type)

The Hellmann gauges were cleared every morning at six o'clock Local Standard Time (LST). The Chinese Standard gauges were cleared after each precipitation event. This was necessary to impede evaporation because there was no funnel in the gauge. The Swiss storage gauges were measured twice a month, on the 1st and the 16th day of the month.

The Universal Recording raingauge (Belfort type) operates on the weighing principle. In this precipitation gauge the beginning, the end and also differences in the cumulative precipitation are recorded. The resolution of the records is 0.3 mm/h. The capacity of the gauge is 300 mm.

The 11 observation sites were chosen in such a way that the precipitation characteristics on the whole glacier should be well represented. Sites A, B and C are considered to represent the middle axis of the glacier. Together with the other permanent stations, they supply good information about the precipitation conditions along the upper part of the Urumqi River Valley on the north slope of the Tianshan Mountains.

Results of the precipitation measurements in Urumqi River Valley

The precipitation conditions in summer 1987 in the mid-part of the Tianshans were characterized by a normal June (values near the year-long average). Strong cyclonic activities were responsible for the above-average precipitation in July, while August was very dry, influenced by anticyclonic circulation (Grebner, 1990 b). In an analysis of the precipitation regime of the Xinjiang Province and especially the regime of high mountain areas in Tianshan, it is important to differentiate between convective precipitation and cyclonic precipitation. Using the structure of the clouds, the form of precipitation and air pressure values, it was possible to determine the type of precipitation for the period from June 15th to August 31st 1987. Tab. 9 gives information about the cyclonic precipitation events. Precipitation events were classified as cyclonic according to the synoptic weather conditions even if the structure of precipitation seemed to be convective.

TABLE 9 Contribution of cyclonic precipitation to total precipitation in 1987.

Month	Precipitat. Amount (mm)	Cyclonic Precipitation Amount (mm)	Cyclonic Precipitation Amount (%)	Precipitat. Events (count)	Cyclonic Precipitation Events (count)	Cyclonic Precipitation Events (%)
June 87	62.8	36.6	58.2	19	5	26.3
July 87	175.7	129.6	73.7	28	5	17.9
August 87	34.7	33.2	95.7	13	8	61.5
Total	273.2	199.4	73.0	60	18	30.0

In the summer months 1987 only 30-60% of the precipitation events were of cyclonic origin, but 70-95% of the monthly precipitation amounts were produced by cyclonic influence. This accords well with the literature. Lu (1944) (Watts, 1969) found that only 30% of the annual precipitation is brought by the local convection. The high percentage values for August are also a result of low moisture in low evening convective activity. For the same reason the number of days with precipitation was decreasing in August but the percentage value of cyclonic events was higher than in the other months. At the same time convection was dominant for stations in the lower part of Urumqi River Valley. Convective clouds climbed only up to an elevation of about 2000 m a.s.l..

On Glacier N° 1 60 isolated precipitation events with 309 precipitation hours were observed for the period from June 15th to August 31st. About 80% of these precipitation events took not more than 8 hours. This is the result of the dominance of the convective typus.

Precipitation intensities in the Tianshans are very low. The highest intensity was measured with 5.5 mm/h. Nearly half of all 309 hours with precipitation had intensities of less than 0.5 mm/h, although 70% of the precipitation events have a cyclonic origin. This is a result of low moisture content in the air.

Dependence of precipitation on the altitude

In Tab. 10 the measurement results of different altitudes are compared.

TABLE 10 Precipitation amounts for the various observation sites in the Urumqi River Valley in summer 1987.

Observation Site	Altitude	June (mm)	July (mm)	Aug. (mm)	Total (mm)
A	4020	.	151.3	27.3	.
B	3910	.	175.7	34.7	.
D	3860	.	193.0	40.0	.
L	3800	80.4	162.3	31.9	274.6
C	3750	.	179.9	35.7	.
I	3350	71.3	154.9	22.9	249.1
H	2130	79.4	132.3	31.2	242.9

It is obvious that the general precipitation conditions do not change with the altitude under the aspect of the short horizontal distance and the dominant influence of cyclonic events to precipitation amounts. For all stations the maximum value is in July and the minimum in August.

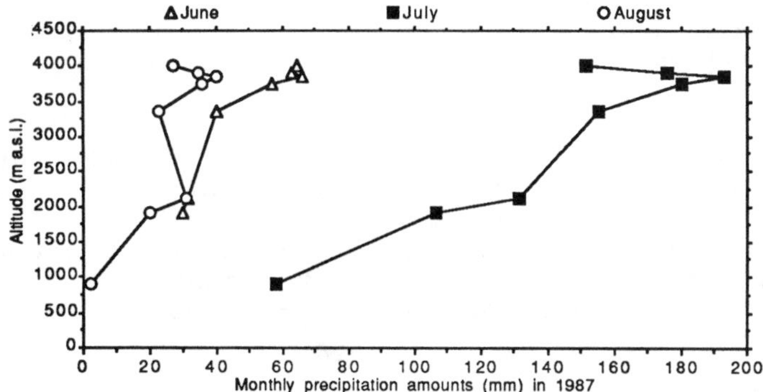

FIG. 2 Dependence of monthly precipitation on the altitude in Urumqi River Valley in 1987.

Fig. 2 shows that the maximum precipitation amount for all three summer months is not over 3900 m a.s.l.. Similar results were found by Yang (1989) for summer 1986 and by Wang and Zhang (1985) for the summer months 1959. This result is very remarkable because the measurement sites in the upper Urumqi River Valley in 1986 and 1959 are not identical with those of 1987. Wang and Zhang gave a result for the south slope of the mountain ridge as well, where the maximum precipitation amount was also below 3900 m a.s.l..

For summer 1986 and summer 1959 a second maximum can be found at an elevation of about 2000 m a.s.l.. This peak can also be seen for August 1987. It seems to be a result of convective precipitation events, reaching up to only about 2000 m a.s.l.. For the same reason it could not be seen in June and July 1987 because cyclonic influence was extremely dominant. In August 1987 this result could be analyzed very well. On Glacier N° 1 at 3700 m a.s.l. precipitation was falling in the first half of the month as a result of slight cyclonic activity. At the Glaciological Station in Houxia (2130 m a.s.l.) precipitation days appeared in the second half of August and were a result of some convective events. This zone of maximum precipitation for convective events is at about the same altitude as precipitation maximums that can be found in other convective regions on earth (Lauscher, 1976).

CONCLUSIONS

About 70% of the annual precipitation in the Tianshan Mountains falls during the three summer months under the influence of Indian monsoon system. During this time about 70% of the precipitation amount is of cyclonic origin and only 30% is from local convection. The altitudinal distribution of precipitation through the Tianshan Mountains shows two zones with relative high precipitation amounts, one at an elevation of about 2000 m a.s.l. and one at an elevation of about 3800 m a.s.l.. The lower zone seems to be primarily influenced by local convection, while the upper zone, where mountains reach up to 4500 m a.s.l., seems to have a maximum of cyclonic precipitation amount.

ACKNOWLEDGEMENTS Thanks are extended to the Lanzhou Institute of Glaciology and Geocryology for scientific cooperation and logistic support. At the Geography Department of ETH Zurich my thanks are also extended to H. Lang, A. Ohmura and L. N. Braun for their valuable comments and Mrs. S. Braun-Clarke for proofreading.

REFERENCES

Blumer, F. (1990) Precipitation Conditions in Xinjiang Province. Glacial Climate Research in the Tianshan. Zürcher Geographische Schriften, 38, 76-107.

Grebner, D. (1990 a) Climate in Northwestern China. Glacial Climate Research in the Tianshan. Zürcher Geographische Schriften, 38, 21-26.

Grebner, D. (1990 b) Synoptical Conditions during the Summers 1986 and 1987. Glacial Climate Research in the Tianshan. Zürcher Geographische Schriften, 38, 29-36.

Lauscher, F. (1976) Weltweite Typen der Höhenabhängigkeit des Niederschlages. Wetter und Leben, 28/2, 80-90.

Lu, A. (1944) Chinese climatology. Collected Sci. Papers (Meteorology) Academia Sinica, Peking, 1954, 441-466.

Müller, M. J. (1983) Handbuch ausgewählter Klimastationen der Erde, Trier.

NOAA, (1984) U. S. Department of Commerce. World Weather Records 1961-70, Vol. 4, Asia.

Wang, D. & P. Zhang (1985) On the valley climate of Urumqi River in the Tianshan Mountains. Journal of Glaciology and Geocryology, 7, 239-248.

Watts, I. E. M., (1969) Climates of China and Korea. Climates of Northern and Eastern Asia. World Survey of Climatology, H. Arakawa, Ed., 8, 1-117.

Yang, D., Y. Shi, E. Kang & Y. Zhang (1989) Research on analysis and correction of systematic errors in precipitation measurement in Wulumqi River Basin, Tianshan. Precipitation Measurement. WMO/IAHS/ETH Workshop on precipitation measurement St. Moritz, 3. - 7. Dec. 1989, 173-179.

Hydrology in Mountainous Regions. I - Hydrological Measurements; the Water Cycle
(Proceedings of two Lausanne Symposia, August 1990). IAHS Publ. no. 193, 1990.

Evolution spatio-temporelle des débits et des matières particulaires sur un bassin des Andes boliviennes: le Rio Béni

J. BOURGES & J.L. GUYOT
ORSTOM, C.P. 9214, La Paz, Bolivie
M. CARRASCO & M.C. BARRAGAN
UMSA-IHH, C.P. 303, La Paz, Bolivie
J. CORTES
SENAMHI, C.P. 996, La Paz, Bolivie

RESUME Drainant un bassin de 68000 km² situé sur le flanc oriental des Andes, le rio Béni est un affluent du rio Madera. L'influence du relief, jusqu'à plus de 6000 m, provoque une hétérogénéité des précipitations qui se traduit au niveau des apports, par des différences selon les zones du bassin. Les transports de sédiments, donc l'érosion, sont également affectés par cette variabilité spatiale. Au niveau interannuel, les variations relevées sont plus faibles pour les grands bassins, alors qu'au niveau annuel, la répartition des apports laisse apparaitre l'influence des glaciers.

INTRODUCTION

L'étude du rio Béni fait partie d'un projet plus vaste s'intéressant à tout le bassin versant amazonien de Bolivie (744000 km²), et mené dans le cadre du programme hydrologique et climatologique - PHICAB - en collaboration avec plusieurs entités nationales de Bolivie. Les observations de terrain utilisées pour cette étude ont été effectuées par le Service National de Météorologie et d'Hydrologie (SENAMHI).

LE BASSIN VERSANT

Le bassin du Beni à sa sortie des Andes, à Angosto del Bala, est situé entre 66° et 69° de longitude Ouest et 14° et 18° de latitude Sud. D'une superficie de 68000 km² (Espinoza, 1985), il présente une forme allongée, d'axe NW-SE parallèle à la Cordillère Royale dont la crête forme sa frontière Sud-Ouest. Malgré l'altitude et l'importance de ces reliefs, une partie de la frange Sud du bassin se situe au delá de la ligne de crête, bénéficiant ainsi d'un régime climatique particulier.

Le Rio Beni, aprés avoir reçu l'appoint substanciel du rio Madre de Dios, se joint au rio Mamoré pour former le rio Madeira qui est un des principaux affluents méridionaux de l'Amazone. Depuis les glaciers de la cordillère de Tres Cruces (5500 m.) où il prend sa source, jusqu'à sa rencontre avec son principal affluent, le rio Kaka, il change plusieurs fois de nom pour finalement s'appeller rio Beni et faire son entrée dans la plaine amazonienne à moins de 300 m. d'altitude.

Le réseau de drainage, caractéristique du relief, est trés dense. Dans la partie haute du bassin, les axes de drainage sont des vallées orientées SW-NE, perpendiculairement à la cordillère, et qui se jettent à l'aval dans trois grandes gouttières orientées SE-NW parallèlement aux plissements. Le principal collecteur, celui de

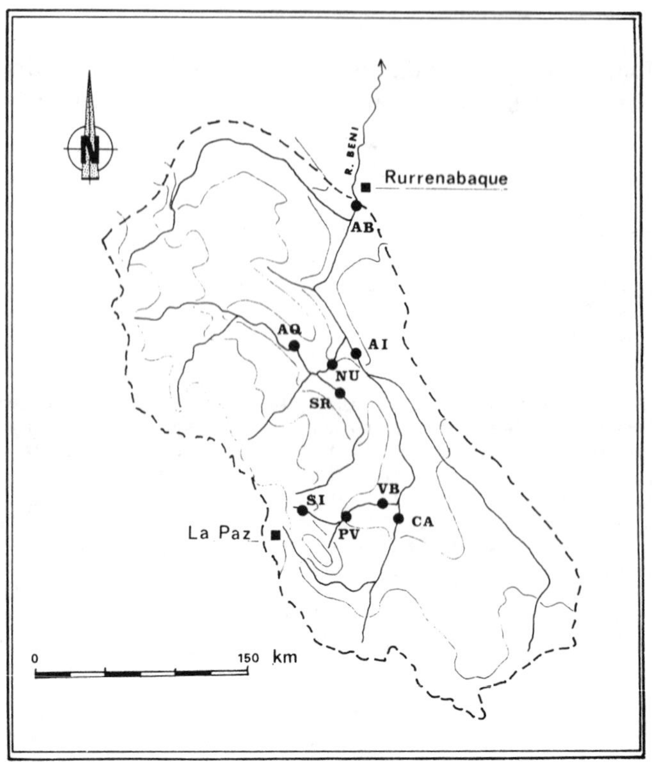

FIG. 1 Carte de situation des stations. Voir tableau 1 pour le code des stations.

l'Alto Beni ne reçoit, sur un bief quasi rectiligne de plus de 300 km., des affluents que sur sa rive gauche.

La végétation, inexistente sur les sommets se manifeste, vers 4.000 m. d'altitude, en présence de sols rares et peu profonds, par une couverture herbacée qui progressivement cède la place dans les

TABLEAU 1 Caractéristiques des stations, modules interannuels.

Code	Rio	Station	Alt. m	Sup. km²	débit moyen m3.s-1	mini m3.s-1	maxi m3.s-1
SI	Unduavi	Sirupaya	1700	270	12	8	16
PV	Tamampaya	Pte Villa	1190	950	48	37	61
VB	Tamampaya	V.Barrientos	1050	1900	69	43	86
CA	La Paz	Cajetillas	760	6500	78	30	110
SR	Coroïco	Santa Rita	440	4700	240	150	350
AQ	Mapiri	Ang.Quercano	500	9400	430	280	560
AI	Alto-Béni	Ang.Inicua	420	29900	850	610	970
NU	Kaka	Nube	380	19600	970	840	1100
AB	Béni	Ang. del Bala	280	68000	2200	1900	2600

vallées à une végétation plus épaisse, de type tropical, d'autant plus exhubérante que les sols sont profonds. La partie basse du bassin est recouverte de forêt.

La totalité de ce bassin versant de zone tropicale est soumis au même régime pluviométrique, d'origine atlantique, avec une saison des pluies bien marquée de novembre à mars qui représente plus de 70% de la lame d'eau précipitée. Les masses d'air chaud et humide amazonien qui, au cours de l'été austral, viennent heurter les contreforts orientaux de la cordillère provoquent au contact des reliefs importants des précipitations très inégales selon l'orographie (Roche et al., 1990).

Les précipitations peuvent varier, en moyenne, de 1500 mm par an dans le centre du bassin à 2000 mm sur sa bordure orientale et même jusqu'à plus de 3000 m sur certains reliefs du Sud-Ouest. Exceptionnellement elle atteignent 4000 mm à l'extrémité de certaines vallées, et sont inférieures à 500 mm sur le haut bassin du rio La Paz au Sud, ou de l'ordre de 700 mm sur le haut bassin du rio Mapiri à l'Ouest du fait de leur situation à l'abri de la Cordillère (Roche et al., 1990). Les chutes de neige au dessus de 4500 m durant l'été et la présence de glaciers au dessus 5000 m influencent les réponses des bassins.

Par suite de l'inaccessibilité de certaines régions du bassin, la répartition spatiale des neuf stations étudiées est inégale. En particulier les extremités Sud-Est et Nord-Ouest du bassin restent quasi inobservées. La période de référence, identique pour huit de ces stations, s'étend sur dix ans de 1974 à 1983. Ces stations, étagées de 1700 m à 280 m d'altitude, controlent des bassins versants allant de 270 à 68000 km².

EVOLUTION TEMPORELLE

Conséquence de la saison des pluies estivales dans cette région, la période de hautes eaux dure de novembre à mai sur l'ensemble du bassin à l'exception des deux sous bassins moins arrosés pour lesquels elle ne dure que de décembre à avril.

Bien que le mois le plus abondant soit, sur toutes les stations, le mois de février, on remarque qu'en amont, sur les bassins inférieurs à 2000 km², les plus forts apports mensuels sont observés en janvier et février, alors que pour des bassins supérieurs à 5000 km², les mois de plus hautes eaux sont février et mars (Fig. 2) ce qui paraît être simplement une conséquence de la propagation des crues le long de ce réseau dont certaines branches mesurent jusqu'à 550 km de longueur.

D'une façon générale, plus de la moitié des apports annuels transitent de janvier à mars. Mais, sur l'Alto Beni, cet apport estival peut varier de 58% en tête de bassin à 56% avant sa confluence, alors que sur le rio Kaka il ne représente que 48% du côté du Mapiri-Tipuani, et 52% sur le Coroico. Cette différence vient de la présence, sur le bassin du rio Kaka, de hauts sommets recouverts de neiges éternelles, en particulier de l'imposant massif de l'Illampu (6600 m) qui fournit un débit de base important lors de la fonte des neiges durant la saison sèche aux rios Tipuani et Mapiri. Moins élevés dans l'ensemble, les reliefs situés au Sud du bassin ne peuvent jouer ce rôle de château d'eau.

A l'échelle interannuelle, la variabilité dans le temps des modules annuels diffère selon la taille des bassins versants. Si l'on évalue cette variabilité par le coefficient Kv, rapport de l'écart entre les valeurs extrêmes ramené à la moyenne, il apparaît que pour les bassins supérieurs à 20000 km², ce coefficient est inférieur à 0.36 et semblerait diminuer légèrement avec la taille du bassin.

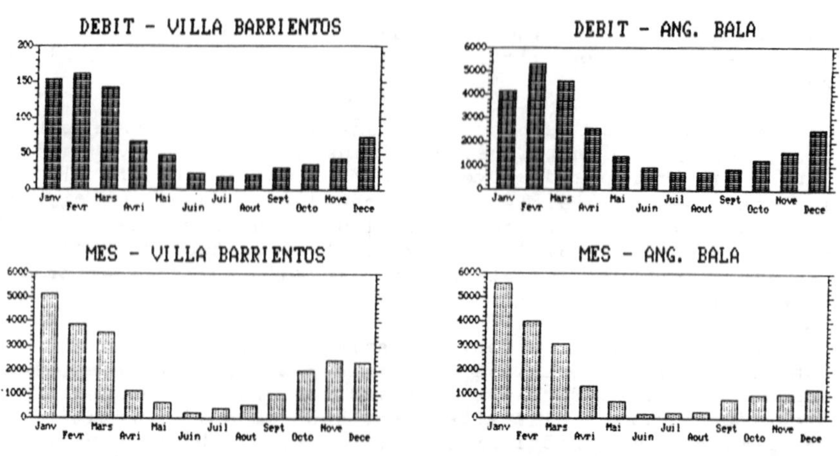

FIG. 2 Histogramme des débits moyens mensuels (m3.s-1) et des concentrations en MES (mg.l-1) aux stations de Villa Barrientos et d'Angosto del Bala.

Pour les bassins inférieurs à 20000 km², il est compris entre 0.5 et 0.8 sans qu'il soit possible de le corréller à la taille du bassin ou à sa pluviomètrie. Enfin dans la zone plus aride du haut rio La Paz, il atteint 1.0.

Cette régularité relative des modules à l'aval du bassin peut s'expliquer par l'occurence aléatoire des maximums ou minimums. Sur la période considérée, n'apparaît aucune synchronisation des modules maximums entre stations, tout au plus remarque-t-on que la plupart des étiages les plus sévères ont eu lieu en 1983, et ont surtout affecté le Sud et le Nord du bassin. Il est probable que la forme très allongée du bassin formant un front de 450 km perpendiculaire au déplacement des perturbations accroît l'hétérogénéité des précipitations à l'échelle annuelle.

L'évolution des teneurs en matières en suspension (MES) suit sensiblement l'évolution des débits (Fig. 2). Les maxima de débit solide coïncident donc avec les maxima hydrologiques, les périodes de hautes eaux fournissant ainsi la plus grande partie des sédiments. Les trois mois de janvier; février et mars, fournissent de 69% (Rio Tamampaya à Puente Villa) à 86% (Rio Alto-Béni à Angosto Inicua) du volume annuel de sédiments. Par contre, lors de la période de basses eaux, de mai à novembre, ces sept mois ne participent que de 5% (Rio Coroïco à Santa Rita) à 14% (Rio Tamampaya à Villa Barrientos) du débit solide annuel (Guyot et al, 1988).

REPARTITION SPATIALE

Les fortes variations spatiales de la pluviométrie dues aux effets orographiques vont être à l'origine de régimes hydrologiques particuliers (Fig.3).

Le calcul des débits spécifiques moyens fait ressortir deux zones à forte hydraulicité: les bassins du Coroico, Tipuani et Challana au centre et celui de l'Aten et du Tuichi au Nord pour lesquels les débits sont supérieurs à 50 l.s-1.km-2. Sur plus de la moitié du bassin, le débit spécifique est supérieur à 40 l.s-1.km-2.

Deux sous bassins situés à l'abri de la cordillère présentent des débits beaucoup plus faibles: le haut rio La Paz avec moins de 10 l.s-1.km-2 et le haut rio Mapiri estimé à 20 l.s-1.km-2. Cette influence

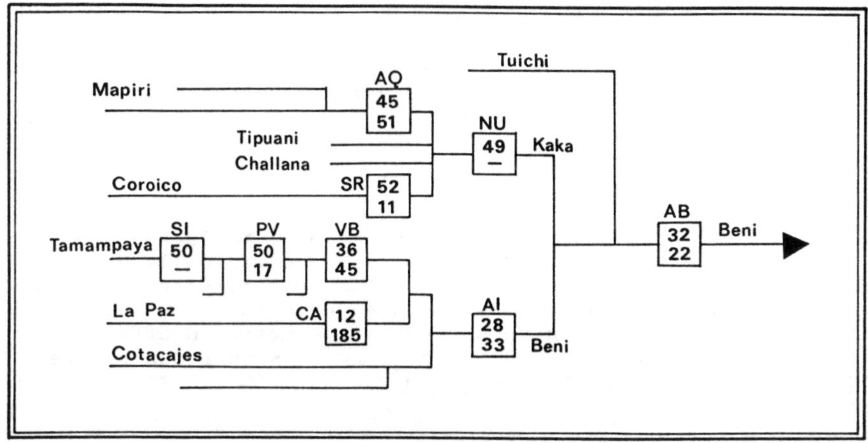

FIG. 3 Schéma du réseau de drainage, débit spécifique (l.s-1.km-2), taux d'érosion (10^2 t.km-2.an-1).

des zones les plus arides du bassin se répercute à l'aval malgré l'apport d'affluents plus abondants puisque avant sa confluence avec le Tamanpaya, le rio La Paz ne fournit que 12 l.s-1.km-2, tandis que, avant de rejoindre le rio Kaka, l'Alto Beni ne dépasse pas 28 l.s-1.km-2. Les apports du rio Kaka avec 49 l.s-1.km-2 donnent une moyenne à la sortie du bassin de 32.6 l.s-1.km-2. Dans la plaine, à sa confluence avec le Madre de Dios, Le rio Beni ne présente plus qu'un débit de 25 l.s-1.km-2 (Bourges, 1989).

L'étude d'un transect allant des sommets de la Cordillère jusqu'au pied des Andes, dans une zone homogène telle que le centre du bassin, ne met en évidence aucune relation entre le débit spécifique et l'altitude, du moins en dessous de 2.000 m. Les variations remarquées le long de la vallée du Tamanpaya et jusqu'au Beni sont dues aux apports des zones semi-arides et non à l'influence de l'altitude.

Le flux maximum de sédiments est observé à la sortie des Andes à Angosto del Bala (tableau 2), ce qui représente un taux moyen d'érosion mécanique de 2200 t.km-2.an-1, pour la période considérée. Des taux nettement supérieurs sont observés sur des bassins plus petits, tels ceux des rios La Paz, Tamampaya, Mapiri et Alto-Béni, c'est à dire dans la partie amont du système qui correspond à une zone

TABLEAU 2 Transport de matières en suspension.

Code	Période	Nbre éch.	MES mg.l-1	débit solide 10^6 t.an-1	taux d'érosion t.km-2.an-1
PV	1975-1985	320	800	1.6	1700
VB	1975-1984	353	1950	8.6	4500
CA	1973-1975	332	19500	120	18500
SR	1976-1977	49	590	5.1	1100
AQ	1975-1979	351	1930	48	5100
AI	1975-1983	157	1920	100	3300
AB	1969-1989	454	1630	150	2200

à plus faible pluviosité et couvert végétal réduit, donc à plus forte érodabilité potentielle. Le maximum est obtenu à Cajetillas sur le rio La Paz (18500 t.km-2.an-1), et le minimum sur le rio Coroïco à Santa Rita (1100 t.km-2.an-1). Les cours d'eau à faible débit spécifique présentent des taux d'érosion élevés.

CONCLUSION

Qu'il s'agisse de l'hétérogénéité spatiale ou de l'influence des glaciers, les résultats de l'étude hydrologique comme celle des transports solides corroborent les observations climatologiques. La poursuite des mesures et la comparaison avec un bassin versant voisin très différent, celui du rio Mamoré, devrait permettre d'affiner l'analyse des phénomènes et d'améliorer la connaissance des régimes hydrologiques et de l'érosion dans cette région.

REFERENCES

Bourges, J. (1989) La investigación hidrológica en el Beni : infraestructuras y previsión de crecidas. In : La Investigación Francesa en Bolivia (Proc. Santa Cruz Symp., Junio 1989), 9-22.

Espinoza, O. (1985) Balance hídrico superficial de la cuenca del Río Beni, Amazonía, Bolivia. Tesis de grado, UMSA, PHICAB Publ., 181 p.

Guyot, J.L., Bourges, J., Hoorelbecke, R., Roche, M.A., Calle, H., Cortes, J. & Barragan, M.C. (1988) Exportation de matières en suspension des Andes vers l'Amazonie par le Rio Béni, Bolivie. In : Sediment budgets (Proc. Porto Alegre Symp., December 1988), IAHS Publ. 174, 443-451.

Roche, M.A., Aliaga A., Campos, J., Cortes, J., Peña, J. & Rocha, N. (in press) Hétérogénéité des précipitations sur la cordillère des Andes boliviennes. In : Aspects quantitatifs et qualitatifs du cycle de l'eau en bassins inhomogènes (Proc. Lausanne Symp., Septembre 1990).

Hydrology in Mountainous Regions. I - Hydrological Measurements; the Water Cycle (Proceedings of two Lausanne Symposia, August 1990). IAHS Publ. no. 193, 1990.

Synthèse régionale pluviométrique en région montagneuse

O. CAYLA - Société d'Etudes et d'Applications Hydrauliques, 6 rue de Lorraine, 38130 Echirolles, GRENOBLE, FRANCE

M. TAIBI - Agence Nationale des Ressources Hydrauliques, Clairbois, Avenue Mohammadia, Bir Mourad Rais, ALGER, Algérie

RESUME En s'aidant de la théorie du Processus de Poisson et au moyen d'un système d'études (méthodologies, logiciels) appelé SPEED (Système Probabiliste d'Etudes par Evénements Discrets), on définit la méthodologie de la Synthèse Régionale. La synthèse régionale est un outil de résolution du problème de la prédétermination, en tout point d'un espace géographique appelé zone d'études, des valeurs à attendre d'une grandeur physique accidentelle.
On présente l'exemple de la pluviométrie analysée à partir des relevés d'observations aux stations de la zone d'études. L'incertitude sur le résultat ne dépend que de l'incertitude sur la moyenne de chaque série et de la densité du réseau d'observations : la synthèse régionale élimine, en effet, l'incertitude sur la variance des séries observées.

INTRODUCTION

La synthèse régionale est une méthode de résolution du problème suivant :

(a) la variable à étudier, ici la pluviométrie (journalière ou annuelle) varie dans l'espace et dans le temps,

(b) les valeurs observées sont de trop courts et trop rares échantillons extraits de populations-mères, a priori inconnues, et variables dans l'espace (surtout en région montagneuse),

(c) on désire obtenir en chaque point une prédétermination fiable des pluies, c'est-à-dire une bonne approximation de la répartition spatiale des populations-mères.

La méthodologie complète a été mise au point de 1987 à 1989 dans le Nord-Est de l'Algérie, après plusieurs tentatives partielles dans l'Ouest et dans le centre. La zone d'études considérée s'étend sur 26 000 km² et comprend, du Nord au Sud :

(a) une suite de plaines côtières séparées entre elles par des caps montagneux,

(b) un relief côtier dépassant par endroits l'altitude 1 500 m (petite Kabylie),

(c) des hautes plaines d'altitude proche de 1 000 m (Constantinois).

Plus au Sud, les hauts plateaux à climat semi-aride font la transition avec le désert saharien.

Le climat de la zone d'études est méditerranéen, c'est-à-dire qu'il comporte une saison sèche de trois mois (15 juin-15 septembre) en été et un maximum pluviométrique en hiver.

PROCESSUS DE POISSON

Il faut constater tout d'abord que le problème n'a de solution que dans le cadre d'une théorie, ce qui n'a rien de surprenant scientifiquement.

La théorie adoptée, le processus de Poisson, doit être considérée comme valide tant qu'aucune vérification expérimentale ne viendra démontrer le contraire.

On considère un événement aléatoire A qui peut se réaliser (par exemple : il pleut) ou ne pas se réaliser (il ne pleut pas). A chaque réalisation de A, on attache un nombre x (la mesure de la pluie cumulée depuis l'origine des mesures par exemple).

Un processus <u>discret</u> est défini :

. soit par représentation des valeurs de x : X_n est la variable aléatoire attachée au énième événement. Le processus est <u>simple</u> si $X_n < X_{n+1}$ pour toute valeur de n et $X_n \longrightarrow \infty$ si $n \longrightarrow \infty$,

. soit par comptage du nombre d'événements de 0 à x : N_n est la variable aléatoire du nombre d'événements.

Un processus discret est <u>stationnaire</u> si la structure probabiliste du processus n'est pas affectée par un changement d'origine des x (c'est-à-dire, en pluviométrie, si le climat est stable).

Un processus de Poisson est un processus discret, simple et stationnaire qui satisfait à l'axiome de base :

> La probabilité que A se réalise dans l'intervalle Δx, sous la condition qu'il ne soit pas réalisé de 0 à x, est proportionnelle à Δx.

Cet axiome exprime qu'il n'y a pas "usure" de l'événement au sens où une usure provoque, dans une pièce mécanique, une modification de sa "mesure" en fonction des événements antérieurs. Il paraît évident que cet axiome est adapté à l'événement "pluie" comme à beaucoup d'événements météorologiques accidentels (coups de vent, cyclones, orages, etc.). Cette apparence d'évidence n'est pas une preuve scientifique.

Avec ces définitions et si l'on admet cet axiome de base, on démontre mathématiquement les propriétés suivantes.

Si l'événement A suit un processus de Poisson, alors :

. la variable aléatoire X des mesures x de A suit la loi exponentielle,

. le nombre K d'apparitions de A dans un intervalle (X_1 ; X_2) donné suit la loi de Poisson,

. les maximums annuels (ou saisonniers) Z de la mesure attachée au phénomène A suivent une loi de Gumbel, les totaux annuels (ou saisonniers) S de la mesure attachée à A suivent une "loi des fuites" qui est très proche de la distribution √Gauss (les racines carrées de valeurs de S suivent une loi normale).

Intérêt de cette théorie

Cette théorie permet de lever les principaux obstacles habituels des études statistiques.

(a) Ajustement statistique

Les distributions probabilistes des diverses catégories d'événements sont définitivement connues.

Si quelques échantillons semblent anormaux, l'anomalie peut être expliquée par des particularités physiques de phénomènes locaux. Par exemple, dans de nombreuses régions où les maximums annuels de pluies journalières semblent ne pas bien s'ajuster à une loi de Gumbel, il est possible de trouver deux types d'événements pluvieux mélangés (cyclones et orages tropicaux). Avant toute analyse statistique, ils doivent être séparés.

(b) Cohérence interne de l'étude

Il y a une relation logique et prouvée entre les divers types de variables aléatoires hydrologiques. Par exemple, les maximums annuels de pluies journalières sont effectivement liés aux totaux annuels.

(c) Synthèse régionale

Certains paramètres des distributions ont une signification physique. Par exemple, un de ceux-ci est le nombre annuel moyen d'événements. Dans le cas des pluies, il est lié au nombre de perturbations météorologiques qui ne doit pas varier sur une vase zone.

(d) Cohérence avec un faible volume de données observées

Les relations internes et les constantes de ces distributions peuvent être utilisées pour tirer de bons résultats de séries d'observation courtes ou incomplètes. Par exemple, il est possible de déduire des valeurs de projet cohérentes de la seule analyse probabiliste, même en l'absence de réseau d'observation ; une enquête de terrain adaptée peut apporter les informations nécessaires.

Il est évident que le résultat sera plus précis si on utilise une longue série de données fiables. Il est à noter que les mêmes méthodes probabilistes sont utilisées de la même façon que l'on dispose de pauvres ou de riches séries d'observations, ce qui justifie que les résultats obtenus avec des données fragmentaires soient fiables.

Enfin, notons que les valeurs de projet sont des valeurs probabilistes. Les méthodes hydrologiques probabilistes vont directement des données de bases aux résultats demandés.

SYSTEME PROBABILISTE D'ETUDES PAR EVENEMENTS DISCRETS EN HYDROLOGIE

SPEED (Système Probabiliste d'Etudes par Evénements Discrets) est un système probabiliste mis au point à partir de la théorie du processus de Poisson et de la théorie de l'échantillonnage.

SPEED, appliqué à l'hydrologie (SPEED HY), couvre tout le domaine des études, depuis l'acquisition de données (réseau d'observations) jusqu'au modèle de simulation d'un barrage. Il est matérialisé par des logiciels, créés spécialement, qui concernent :

(a) la saisie, le prétraitement et l'édition des données observées,
(b) le traitement statistique, en synthèse régionale, des paramètres d'études,
(c) la génération des apports et des crues les plus vraisemblables sur un nombre arbitraire d'années,
(d) la simulation du fonctionnement d'un ouvrage d'aménagement en rivière (barrage par exemple) de façon à optimiser ses dimensions et son exploitation.

L'élaboration des logiciels, associés à SPEED, a obéi aux principes suivants :

(a) distinction claire entre les fichiers en l'état (conformes aux originaux d'observations), les fichiers opérationnels (obtenus après prétraitement et analyse critique des fichiers en l'état) et les fichiers de travail (créés pour une étude particulière),
(b) utilisation systématique de la visualisation sur écran graphique de chaque étape de la saisie et du traitement des fichiers : l'ordinateur propose, l'opérateur juge et décide,
(c) strict respect des théories du processus de Poisson et de l'échantillonnage,
(d) fichiers et simulation d'ouvrages sont à pas de temps variable.

Nous énumérons ci-dessous les logiciels d'aide à la synthèse régionale.

. OCCOR de critique systématique de l'homogénéité des échantillons (corrélations et doubles cumuls),
. CALSTAT de calcul des paramètres statistiques des phénomènes étudiés et de leur incertitude d'échantillonnage à 80 %,
. OCSYNT d'aide à la synthèse régionale proprement dite,
. OCAJU de présentation des ajustements comparés,
. OCARAJ de corrélation et comparaison entre deux variables

FICHIER DE DONNEES

On dispose, après critique et homogénéisation des données, des fichiers de totaux annuels et maximums annuels de pluie journalière de 88 stations totalisant près de 3 000 années. Les séries sont de longueur variable.

Le programme CALSTAT calcule automatiquement sur chacune des stations les paramètres statistiques suivants, affectés de leur intervalle de confiance à 80 % :

. totaux annuels S : moyenne $\bar{S}$, écart type s_s, coefficient de variation $C_v = s_s/\bar{S}$, coefficient $\lambda = 2/C_v^2$, maximums annuels Z : moyenne $\overline{Z}$, écart type s_z, gradex α, pivot y_p (la définition de α et de y_p est donnée ci-dessous).

LOI DES TOTAUX ANNUELS ASSOCIEE A SPEED

La loi √Gauss des totaux annuels S(T) de temps de retour T s'écrit :

$$\sqrt{S(T)} = m_v + s_v\, u(T) \qquad (1)$$

avec :

- m_v Moyenne des racines des valeurs de pluie annuelle S
- s_v Ecart type des racines
- u(T) Variable réduite de Gauss pour le temps de retour T

Une bonne approximation de u(T) est :

$$u(T) = 2{,}84\ \mathrm{Log}\ [-\mathrm{Log}\ (-\mathrm{Log}\ (1 - 1/T)) + 2{,}95] - 3{,}40$$

$$\text{si } T > 2 \text{ ans} \qquad (2)$$

et, pour les temps de retour secs, utilisation de la symétrie de la loi de Gauss.

En utilisant le paramètre $e = (m_v/s_v)^2$, on peut écrire la loi √Gauss sous la forme directe :

$$S(T) = \frac{\overline{S}}{1+e}\,[\sqrt{e} + u(T)]^2 \qquad (3)$$

$$\text{avec } 1 + e = \lambda\,(1 + \sqrt{1 - \tfrac{1}{\lambda}}) \text{ très proche de } 2\lambda = 4/C_v^2 \qquad (4)$$

La loi est donc à deux paramètres :

- . la moyenne $\overline{S}$,
- . le coefficient $\lambda = 2/C_v^2$.

On démontre que λ est un nombre d'événements indépendants. Il s'agit du nombre annuel d'"épisodes pluvieux", c'est-à-dire du nombre de perturbations météorologiques intéressant chaque année le poste pluviométrique à analyser. Ce nombre étant évidemment le même dans toute la région, on peut s'attendre à la constance dans cette région du paramètre λ.

LOI DES MAXIMUMS ANNUELS ASSOCIES A SPEED

La loi de Gumbel s'écrit :

$$Z(T) = \alpha\, y(T) + M \qquad (5)$$

avec :

- M Mode de la distribution
- α Gradex de la distribution
- y(T) Variable réduite de Gumbel pour le temps de retour T

Par définition de la loi de Gumbel :

$$y(T) = -\mathrm{Log}\ (-\mathrm{Log}\ (1 - \tfrac{1}{T}) \qquad (6)$$

α et M se déduisent de la moyenne $\overline{Z}$ et de l'écart type s_z par :

$$\alpha = s_z\ \sqrt{6}/\pi$$

$$M = \overline{Z} - C\,\alpha \text{ avec } C = \text{constante d'Euler} = 0{,}57721566490..$$

On appelle y_p le pivot de la distribution, c'est-à-dire la valeur de y pour laquelle la droite de Gumbel coupe l'axe Z = 0 :

$$y_p = -M/\alpha = C - \frac{\pi\overline{Z}}{\sqrt{6}\ s_z} \qquad (7)$$

La loi de Gumbel se met alors sous la forme utile :

$$Z(T) = \overline{Z}\,\frac{y_p - y(T)}{y_p - C} \qquad (8)$$

Les deux paramètres de la loi sont la moyenne $\overline{Z}$ et le pivot y_p.

Or, on démontre que :

$$\nu = e^{-y_p} \qquad (9)$$

est le nombre moyen d'événements indépendants d'où sont tirés les maximums annuels. Ce nombre ν est proportionnel au nombre de perturbations météorologiques et on peut s'attendre à son invariance dans une région géographique, donc à l'invariance de $y_p = -\text{Log}\ \nu$.

On notera que $\nu < \lambda$ pour des raisons qu'il serait trop long d'exposer ici.

PROCEDURE DE MISE EN OEUVRE DE LA SYNTHESE REGIONALE

A l'aide du programme OCSYNT, on cherche dans la zone d'études à délimiter des régions homogènes du point de vue du second paramètre, λ pour les totaux annuels et y_p pour les maximums.

Cette recherche est purement statistique ; OCSYNT visualise sur écran les diverses ellipses (une ellipse par station) fabriquées de la façon suivante :

(a) centre de l'ellipse de coordonnées (moyenne, second paramètre),

(b) axes de l'ellipse de longueur égale ou double de l'incertitude à 80 % sur chacune des coordonnées.

La recherche d'une région homogène en λ consiste à définir une valeur de λ, par exemple $\lambda = 50$, et à supprimer toutes les ellipses qui coupent la droite horizontale correspondante.

La valeur de λ est bien choisie si l'on obtient in fine :

. 80 % des ellipses supprimées,

. 10 % d'ellipses restantes au-dessus de la droite,

. 10 % d'ellipses restantes en dessous de la droite.

Procédure identique pou y_p.

En fin d'opération sur le second paramètre, on tente la régionalisation sur le premier paramètre, la moyenne. Si l'on peut mettre en évidence des sous-régions homogènes du point de vue de la moyenne, grandes plaines par exemple, la pluviométrie est considérée comme constante sur chacune de ces sous-régions. Dans le cas de l'étude effectuée dans l'Est algérien, le relief est trop chahuté pour que de telles sous-régions aient pu être isolées.

La moyenne est alors représentée par cartographie d'isovaleurs, comme sur les cartes pluviométriques classiques.

Le second paramètre étant régionalisé, la carte des moyennes permet de déduire, pour chaque point de la carte, les lois probabilistes complètes de la pluie : il suffit d'utiliser les relations (3) et (8).

VALEURS ABERRANTES

En réalité, beaucoup d'échantillons de la zone d'études présentent des valeurs "aberrantes" : les plus fortes valeurs sont situées très nettement au-dessus de la droite d'ajustement.

On peut démontrer que l'existence de telles valeurs aberrantes, quelle que soit leur origine, a une influence négligeable sur la moyenne mais augmente considérablement l'écart type calculé.

Par conséquent, pour tous les échantillons contenant de telles valeurs :

. λ est trop faible,
. y_p est trop fort.

ou encore, le nombre de valeurs indépendantes que l'on calcule sur ces échantillons est sous-évalué.

Ceci ne change pas le principe de la procédure de mise en oeuvre de la synthèse régionale mais complique un peu les calculs.

NATURE DES VALEURS ABERRANTES DES MAXIMUMS ANNUELS DE PLUIES JOURNALIERES

On peut démontrer que la grande majorité des valeurs aberrantes provient de l'instabilité des sous-régions homogènes (un petit nombre de ces valeurs est du à des erreurs de mesure ou de fichiers).

Il est bien connu et vérifié dans la zone d'études que la pluviométrie augmente par effet orographique. Ce que montre la synthèse régionale, c'est que cette augmentation est due à une variation des moyennes mais pas à une variation du nombre d'événements.

Or, cet effet orographique n'est pas identique d'un événement à l'autre : un poste situé en piedmont d'une chaîne montagneuse sera affecté par des pluies :

(a) de la plaine pour certains événements (moyenne faible),
(b) de la montagne pour d'autres événements (moyenne forte).

Il y a donc, en ce poste, mélange de deux lois de Gumbel différentes.

Si ce mélange est en proportions à peu près égales, on obtient un échantillon qui ne suit pas la loi de Gumbel (courbe à concavité tournée vers le haut sur papier de Gumbel). Si les proportions sont très inégales, on obtient des valeurs aberrantes.

Il faut bien voir que ces valeurs aberrantes s'ajustent sur une loi de Gumbel de même pivot y_p que les valeurs "normales" mais de moyenne supérieure. Il est faux (l'erreur est considérable à l'extrapolation) d'ajuster à l'ensemble une loi à forte courbure, loi de Frechet par exemple : la synthèse régionale confirme que ces échantillons sont constitués de pluies qui obéissent au processus de Poisson et permet d'effectuer un ajustement correct du mélange de deux lois de Gumbel.

RESULTATS DE LA SYNTHESE REGIONALE SUR LA ZONE D'ETUDES ALGERIENNE

Nous résumons ci-dessous les principaux résultats :

Il y a deux régions homogènes, la région côtière (plaines et reliefs) et les hautes plaines constantinoises.

Les valeurs de y_p, ν et λ sur chacune des régions sont :

. région côtière $y_p = -3,10$ $\nu = 22$ $\lambda = 50$,
. Constantinois $y_p = -2,85$ $\nu = 17$ $\lambda = 43,5$.

On montre en outre qu'il y a une relation entre $\bar{Z}$ et $\bar{S}$:

$$\bar{Z} = 50\left(\frac{\bar{S}}{1000}\right)^{1,3} + 20 \qquad (10)$$

On peut donc déduire toutes les valeurs de temps de retour T des pluies journalières et des pluies annuelles de la seule carte pluviométrique classique (isovaleurs de pluies annuelles).

Une synthèse régionale sur les lois intensité-durée-fréquence a également été établie qui permet de calculer les pluies de durée t et de temps de retour T à partir de cette même carte.

Hydrology in Mountainous Regions. I - Hydrological Measurements; the Water Cycle (Proceedings of two Lausanne Symposia, August 1990). IAHS Publ. no. 193, 1990.

Variability of runoff from partially-glacierised Alpine basins

DAVID N. COLLINS & DAVID P. TAYLOR
Alpine Glacier Project, Department of Geography, University of Manchester, Manchester M13 9PL, U.K.

ABSTRACT Records of streamflow measured at gauging stations on rivers draining basins in the Swiss Alps between 0 and 84% glacierisation are examined. Effects of ice cover on year-to-year variability of seasonal and annual runoff are considered in relation to precipitation and summer air temperature. Coefficient of variation of runoff declines rapidly, with a few per cent of ice cover having a marked impact. At higher levels, considerable spread masks slight increases in coefficient of variation above 30 per cent ice cover.

INTRODUCTION

The presence of even a small glacier can reduce year-to-year variability of runoff from a high mountain basin. In an ice-free basin, annual runoff is directly related to, and always less than, the total quantity of precipitation. Runoff from a basin partially covered by perennial snow and ice may be more than, equal to, or less than total precipitation, according to changes in the amount of water stored in the solid form. Variation in runoff is moderated by the interaction of thermal conditions for the melting of snow and ice with precipitation. In warm dry summers, enhanced meltwater production offsets the scarcity of flow arising from liquid precipitation, and conversely melt is reduced in cool wet years, so compensating for year-to-year variations in precipitation (e.g. Meier and Tangborn, 1961).

Evidently, the variance of summer runoff declines considerably in basins with a few per cent of the area covered with glacier ice. This is of practical importance in water resources with respect to the reliability of flow in dry years. Whilst variance might be expected to decline further in basins with greater proportions of ice cover, the actual effect is unclear, largely as a result of paucity of measurements, particularly for more highly glacierised basins. In the North Cascade Mountains, Washington, only one gauged basin has a glacier extent greater than 14 per cent, and at 53 per cent glacierisation, has the observed minimum of variance for summer discharge (Fountain & Tangborn, 1985). For annual flow, and unspecified, but shorter, lengths of stream flow record, observed minimum variance occurs at 14 per cent ice cover (Krimmel & Tangborn, 1974). There is an indication, however, that glaciers most effectively moderate variability of annual and summer totals of runoff at about 20 per cent ice cover, below and above which variance increases, as demonstrated by measurements in basins within the range 0-40% glacierisation in western Norway (Tvede, 1982). In the European Alps, minimum variance of annual river flows of fifty years length in Switzerland was observed at 24.4% glacierisation (Walser, 1960), but for July runoff, minimum variance occurred around 16% ice cover (Kasser, 1959).

The aim of this study is to describe the influence of glaciers on year-to-year variability of seasonal and annual runoff in basins in which ice covers up to 83.7% of the drainage area, by comparison with ice-free basins, and with a view to determining whether, at higher levels of glacierisation, variance of runoff actually increases. The effects of variability of precipitation and thermal energy characteristics on runoff in basins with differing proportions of glacier cover are also assessed.

MEASUREMENT RECORDS FROM PARTIALLY-GLACIERISED BASINS IN SWITZERLAND

Records of streamflow measured at gauging stations draining basins in Alpine catchments of the Rhone above Lac Leman and of the Aare above the Thunersee, in Switzerland, have been examined (Fig. 1). With the exception of the Grande Eau at Aigle, which has been slightly influenced by hydropower adduction since 1957, the basins listed in Table 1 have uninterrupted homogeneous records of natural flow regime of considerable length. The geological substrate of the headwaters of the Simme may not be watertight.

Meteorological stations at Sion (Aeroport) (482m a.s.l.) in the trunk Rhone valley, Sion (Couvent des Capucins) (542m), Zermatt (1632m), and Saas Almagell (1669m) provide information concerning seasonal and annual variations of precipitation in the area. Positive degree days between May and September are used as an indicator of year-to-year variability in thermal energy availability. Degree days are calculated from measured air temperature at Sion (Couvent) to 1977 and subsequently from Saas Almagell (Collins, 1987; 1989).

VARIABILITY OF RUNOFF

Variability of runoff was calculated for several periods selected with the intention of maximising both duration and number of contemporaneous gauging records of uniform length. For comparative purposes, between months, and between basins, coefficient of variation c_v is used here as a measure of dispersion, rather than standard deviation. c_v is the ratio of standard deviation to the mean. The calendar year from 1 January to 31 December has been utilised rather than the hydrological year, as recession flows in Alpine basins between October and December relate to conditions before the build-up of the stable winter snowpack (see Collins, 1984).

Variability of both annual (Q_{1-12}) and summer (May through September, Q_{5-9}) totals of runoff declines considerably with even a small percentage of ice cover to minima sustained between 20 and 30 per cent glacierisation (Fig. 2). There is a slight increase in c_v between about thirty-five and fifty per cent glacier cover. Variations of summer and annual runoff totals are closely-parallel above about 4 per cent glacierisation, although the proportion of annual runoff occurring in summer extends from as low as 60 per cent to 95 per cent, over the range of percentage glacierisation represented in Fig. 2, and changes considerably from year to year for any one basin. Glacial moderation

TABLE 1 Characteristics of ice-free and partially-glacierised basins in Alpine Aare and Rhone catchment areas.

River/Gauge	Glacierisation %	Elevation range (m a.s.l.)	Basin area (km^2)
Allenbach/Adelboden	0.0	1297-2762	28.8
Grande Eau/Aigle	1.9	414-3124	132.0
Simme/Oberwil	3.7	777-3244	344.0
Saltina/Brig	5.1	677-3553	77.0
Gornernbach/Kiental	17.3	1280-3437	25.6
Simme/Oberreid-Lenk	34.6	1096-3244	35.7
Lonza/Blatten	40.6	1520-3897	77.8
Kander/Gasterntal	43.5	1470-3709	40.7
Truebbach/Ralziburg	53.7	1430-3244	19.5
Rhone/Gletsch	56.4	1754-3634	38.9
Massa/Blatten-bei-Naters	66.0	1446-4195	195.0
Findelenbach/ Findelengletscher	76.7	2500-4190	24.9
Gornera/Gornergletscher	83.7	2005-4634	82.0

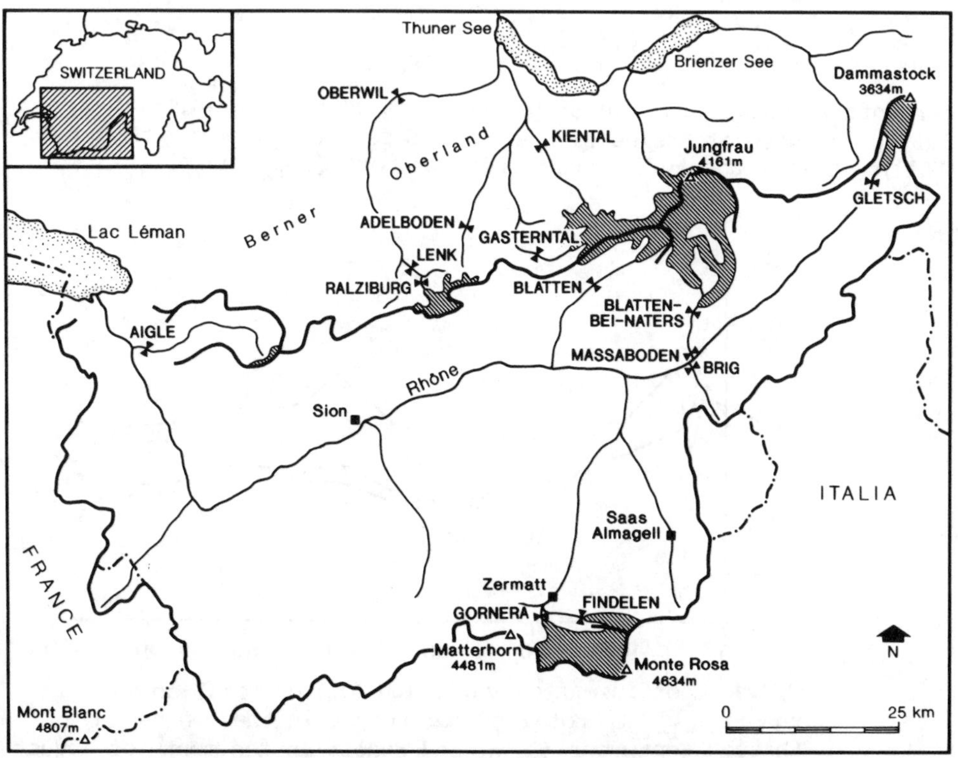

FIG. 1 Location of gauging stations and meteorological stations in the Alpine Aare and Rhone basins, Switzerland, from which records have been analysed. Glacierised areas are shown only within the gauged basins.

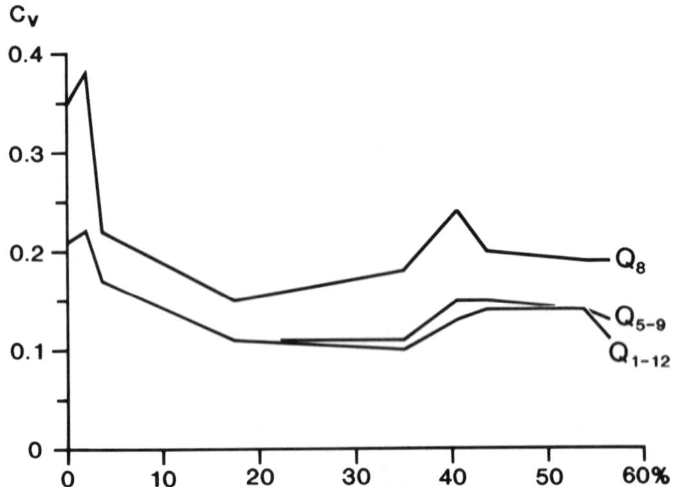

FIG. 2 Coefficient of variation (c_v) of total annual runoff (Q_{1-12}), total summer runoff in the months May through September (Q_{5-9}) and runoff in the month of August (Q_8) from ice-free and partially-glacierised basins of up to 56.4% ice cover for the period 1956-1982. Each inflexion in the curves represents an actual measurement.

of runoff is enhanced above 55 per cent ice cover, to minima of c_v similar to those of basins with around 35 per cent glacierisation (0.10 - 0.11). This tendency is maintained for both Q_{1-12} and Q_{5-9} above 60

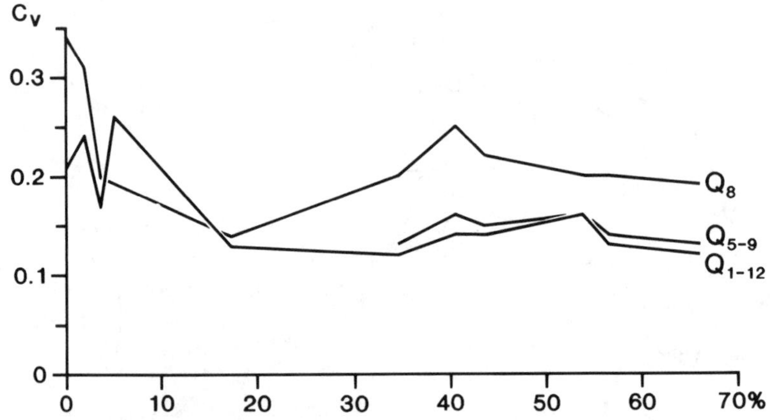

FIG. 3 Coefficient of variation (c_v) of total annual runoff (Q_{1-12}), total summer runoff in the months May through September (Q_{5-9}) and runoff in the month of August (Q_8) from ice-free and partially-glacierised basins of up to 66.0% ice cover for the period 1966-1982. Each inflexion in the curves represents an actual measurement.

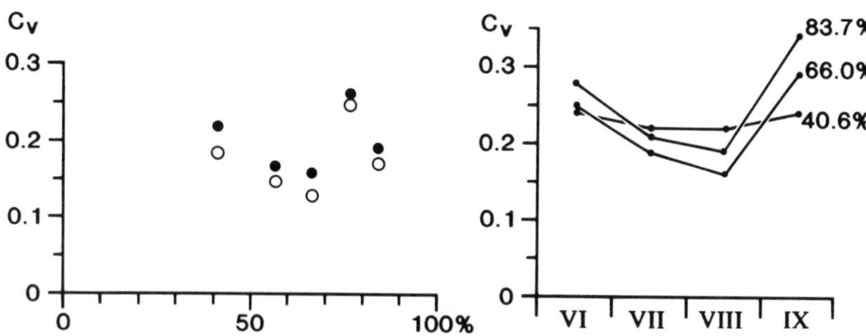

FIG. 4 Coefficient of variation (c_v) of total summer runoff in the months June through September (Q_{6-9} open circles), and runoff in the month of August (Q_8 closed circles), from partially-glacierised basins of between 40.6 and 83.7% ice cover (left) and coefficient of variation of total monthly flow in each of the months June through September in basins of 40.6, 66.0 and 83.7% glacierisation (right), for the period 1971-1988.

per cent glacierisation (Fig. 3). Differences in detail between the curves of c_v of both Q_{1-12} and Q_{5-9} as shown in Figs. 2 and 3 result from the reduced (17 years) length of the time base used in the calculations of variability, and the inclusion of additional basins with records of insufficient length to cover the 27 year 1956-1982 span in the dataset on which Fig. 3 is based. Above 70 per cent glacierisation, variation of summer (June-September (Q_{6-9})) runoff is increased, suggesting similar behaviour for the unmeasured annual flow (Fig. 4).

Coefficient of variation itself shows considerable variation between basins with small differences only in per cent ice cover throughout the range of glacierisation up to 83.7% for both summer and annual runoff for Q_{6-9}. For example, the coefficient of variation of runoff in Findelenbach (0.25) differs significantly from that of the Gornera (0.17) and Massa (0.13) draining from the other highly-glacierised basins.

Summer discharge is always slightly more variable from year to year than annual total flow, the months May through September having monthly total discharges generally higher than those of other months in more highly glacierised basins. For individual months in summer, variability of monthly runoff is greater than that for summer total of discharge, and minimum variability is associated with lower percentage glacierisation (under 20%), as illustrated by the month of August in Figs. 2-4. The influence of percentage glacierisation on variation of summer monthly flows is shown in Fig. 4. At 40.6% ice cover, c_v in June and September is 0.24, reducing to 0.22 in July and August. June and September variation increases with increasing glacierisation, whereas c_v is substantially reduced in July and August. Considerably reduced variability of monthly flow in May through September, by comparison with winter months, is introduced in basins containing a glacierised fraction (Fig. 5). In the ice-free Allenbach basin, reduced variance occurs in May only, during snowmelt. The more

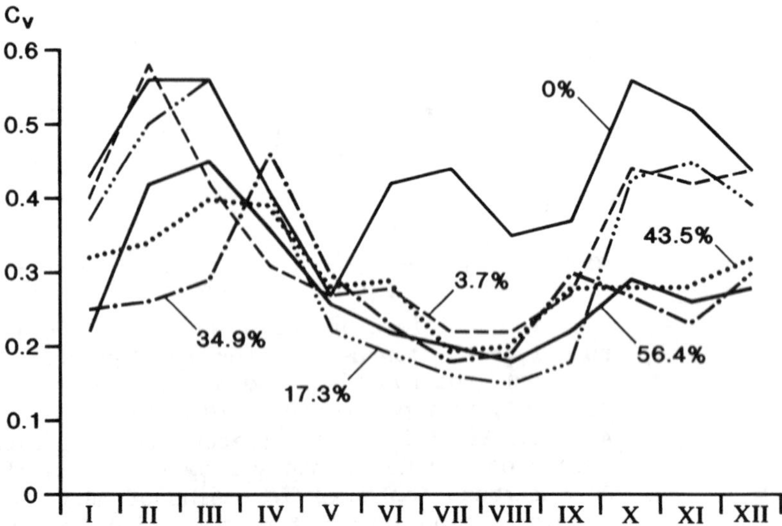

FIG. 5 Coefficient of variation (c_v) of monthly runoff from an ice-free basin, and partially-glacierised basins of 3.7 17.3, 34.9, 43.5 and 56.4% ice cover for the period 1956-1982.

glacierised the basin the less important volumetrically is the highly variable runoff in the winter months between October and April.

VARIABILITY OF CLIMATIC CONDITIONS

Coefficients of variation of annual total precipitation, between 1 October and 30 September, for periods of years equivalent to those of the runoff measurements, are presented in Table 2. Except at glacierisation levels of under about 5 per cent, c_v of precipitation exceeds those of annual and summer runoff. Variation of monthly precipitation is greater still (c_v in the range 0.47 - 1.18 at Saas Almagell 1971-1988), with the least variability in July and August. Year-to-year variability in summer energy availability is low by comparison with precipitation and runoff.

Between 1956 and 1988, summer air temperature variations were superimposed on an underlying downward trend (from 17.9°C average for 1958-1962 to 16.7° for 1977-1981) before recovering to a mean of 17.51°C in 1982-1986. Precipitation was above the average of the overall period in the late 1970s. These secular trends influence c_v values for the same variable and station over differing lengths of time and periods. Between 1956 and 1988, long glaciers, such as Aletsch- and Gornergletscher continued to retreat, whereas smaller glaciers stabilised or, as Findelengletscher, advanced.

CLIMATIC INFLUENCES ON RUNOFF VARIABILITY

Annual runoff from a basin with α per cent glacierisation is determined by a balance between precipitation over the non-glacierised portion of

TABLE 2 Year-to-year variability of hydrometeorological characteristics recorded at Sion, Saas Almagell and Zermatt.

Characteristic	Station	Period	c_v
Precipitation (October-September)	Zermatt	1956-1982	0.199
		1966-1982	0.211
		1971-1988	0.225
	Saas Almagell	1971-1988	0.269
	Sion Aeroport	1956-1982	0.176
		1966-1982	0.196
Degree days (May-September)	Sion Couvent des Capucins/Saas Almagell	1966-1982	0.038
		1971-1988	0.045

the basin and the interaction between precipitation and thermal energy availability over the glacier surface:

$$Q_t = f_1[(1-\alpha)P] + f_2[\alpha(T_\wedge P^{-1} + P)] \qquad (1)$$

where Q_t is total annual runoff, P precipitation in the appropriate hydrological year, and $T_\wedge P^{-1}$ an interaction representing the meltwater produced when available energy for melting T is reduced by the precipitation accumulated as snow in winter and falling during summer. P increases with altitude in high mountain basins. Runoff from a basin with low percentage glacierisation is influenced largely by precipitation in the ice-free area, and, in years when precipitation is low, to some extent by the glacier interaction term in which energy will dominate. Increasing glacierisation leads to further dependence on the glacier interaction term, influence of which is weighted more heavily than α would suggest on account of higher specific discharge from melting ice than from precipitation. At the higher levels of glacierisation runoff influenced by the interaction term dominates that arising from relatively small ice-free area with low specific discharge. This is indicated by the explanation of 85 per cent of runoff variance by temperature at 66 per cent glacierisation (Collins, 1989). Increased variability of runoff at higher percentage glacierisation might be expected therefore to result from the impact of high precipitation on the glacier precipitation-energy interaction with little compensation from the part of the basin within which all precipitation received runs off in the same year.

A simple model by Braithwaite & Olesen (1988) in terms of ratios of standard deviations of precipitation and net ablation (the latter being a direct measure of the glacier interaction term used here) predicts that variability of runoff will increase with both higher levels of glacierisation, and higher ratio of variance of ablation to that of precipitation. However, decline of variation of runoff with a few per cent glacierisation is not reflected in the model curves. An approach by Fountain & Tangborn (1985), utilising specific runoff from basins of different glacier cover, increases the steepness of the sag in the curve of c_v against glacierisation in the region 0-40% ice proportion, followed by an increase at higher percentages.

CONCLUSION

There is a considerable spread in the coefficients of variation obtained for the basins in the Aare and Rhone catchment areas within ranges of a few per cent change in glacierisation. The fitting of a curve relating c_v to percentage glacierisation through these data would be invidious, especially at the upper end of the glacierisation range represented. Precipitation is more variable than air temperature and considerably modifies runoff through the interaction effect in the glacierised area of a basin.

ACKNOWLEDGEMENTS The authors wish to thank Landeshydrologie und-geologie, Schweizerische Meteorologische Zentralanstalt and Grande Dixence SA for making available hydrometeorological and discharge records; S. Braun-Clark, L. Braun and A. Ohmura for assistance in and around Geographisches Institut, Eidg. Technische Hochschule, Zurich.

REFERENCES

Braithwaite, R. J. & Olesen, O. B. (1988) Effect of glaciers on annual runoff, Johan Dahl Land, south Greenland. Journal of Glaciology 34(117), 200-207.

Collins, D. N. (1984) Climatic variation and runoff from Alpine glaciers. Zeitschrift fur Gletscherkunde und Glazialgeologie 20, 127-145.

Collins, D. N. (1987) Climatic fluctuations and runoff from glacierised Alpine basins. International Association of Hydrological Sciences Publication 168, 77-89.

Collins, D. N. (1989) Influence of glacierisation on the response of runoff from Alpine basins to climate variability. Publications of the Academy of Finland, 9/89 Vol. 1, 319-328.

Fountain, A. G. & Tangborn, W. V. (1985) The effects of glaciers on stream-flow variations. Wat. Resour. Res. 21(4), 579-586.

Kasser, P. (1959) Der Einfluss von Gletscherruckgang und Gletschervorstoss auf den Wasserhaushalt. Wasser- und Energiewirtschaft 6, 155-168.

Krimmel, R. M. & Tangborn, W. V. (1974) South Cascade Glacier: the moderating influence of glaciers on runoff. Proceedings of Western Snow Conference 42, 9-13.

Meier, M. F. & Tangborn, W. V. (1961) Distinctive characteristics of glacier runoff. USGS Prof. Pap. 424, B14-B16.

Tvede, A. M. (1982) Influence of glaciers on the variability of long runoff series. Fourth Northern Research Basins Symposium, 179-189.

Walser, E. (1960) Die Abflussverhaeltnisse in der Schweiz waehrend der Jahre 1910 bis 1959. Wasser- und Energiewirtschaft, 8/9/10, 197-214.

Hydrology in Mountainous Regions. I - Hydrological Measurements; the Water Cycle
(Proceedings of two Lausanne Symposia, August 1990). IAHS Publ. no. 193, 1990.

Interêt de la densité de drainage pour régionaliser les données hydrologiques en zone montagneuse

J. HUMBERT
Centre d'Etudes et de Recherches Eco-Géographiques
Université Louis Pasteur
3, rue de l'Argonne, 67083 STRASBOURG Cedex, France

RESUME On présente ici quelques résultats d'une étude qui a pour but de hiérarchiser les principaux facteurs de l'écoulement sur le massif des Hautes Vosges (N-E France), à partir d'un ensemble de 45 bassins-versants. Une analyse en régressions multiples "pas à pas" a été effectuée sur plusieurs variables complémentaires : écoulement direct de crue et débit de pointe, écoulements annuels et mensuels de saison froide. Les résultats montrent le rôle déterminant des facteurs climatiques dans la variabilité spatiale de l'écoulement. Parmi les facteurs propres aux bassins, seuls les paramètres relatifs à la densité de drainage (parfois corrigés de la lithologie) se montrent toujours très significatifs et améliorent nettement les régressions. Celles-ci révèlent aussi l'influence de la densité maximale des drains élémentaires en période de crue. On montre enfin le rôle-clé de la densité de drainage en tant que paramètre de synthèse entre les facteurs climatiques, lithologiques et hydrologiques.

Importance of drainage density for hydrological data regionalisation in mountainous area

ABSTRACT Some results of a study which aims to hierarchise the main factors of streamflow in the High Vosges Mountains (N-E France), are commented on. A stepwise regression analysis from a sample of 45 catchments has been used on complementary variables : direct runoff and peak discharge, annual and cold season monthly streamflows. Results point out the essential role of climatic factors for explaining the areal variability of streamflow. Amongst the catchment variables, the drainage density parameters (sometimes corrected by lithology) are only very significant and clearly improve the regressions. The influence of maximum density of elementary streams is also shown in flood period. Drainage density has a key-role, as a synthesis parameter among the climatic, lithologic and hydrologic factors.

INTRODUCTION

Toute synthèse des caractéristiques hydrologiques régionales comporte en général une étape permettant de hiérarchiser les facteurs contrôlant l'écoulement et sa variabilité spatiale. L'un des outils les plus couramment utilisés pour y parvenir est la régression linéaire multiple. A condition d'être interprétée avec prudence, cette méthode est suffisamment souple et efficace pour établir les bases d'une régionalisation. Le travail présenté ici s'appuie sur cette démarche et constitue un élément d'une étude plus vaste menée sur les Hautes Vosges (N-E France). Les variables étudiées sont l'écoulement direct de crue et le débit de pointe correspondant, les modules et les débits mensuels de saison froide. En incluant ceux réservés à la validation, un ensemble de 45 bassins a été utilisé, couvrant une surface de 2 300 km^2

environ. Les principales régressions sont discutées et on montre la part respective des facteurs climatiques et des paramètres propres aux bassins, en faisant ressortir, parmi ces derniers, le rôle très significatif de la densité de drainage.

ZONE D'ETUDE

La région étudiée s'étend essentiellement sur le versant oriental des Hautes Vosges : elle représente un secteur d'environ 100 km de long sur 20 à 25 km de large. Ce massif constitue un milieu forestier de moyenne montagne (altitude max. = 1 424 m), typique du domaine tempéré humide. La pluviométrie montre des contrastes spectaculaires : 2 400 mm/an sur la crête principale et environ 650 mm/an sur le piedmont longeant la plaine d'Alsace. Sur le plan géologique, il s'agit d'un massif ancien composé de roches variées (granites, schistes et grauwackes du faciès Culm, gneiss ...) ; localement affleurent des lambeaux de la couverture gréseuse du Trias. Le socle à tendance imperméable est cependant recouvert de formations superficielles filtrantes, à faible rétention. A saturation, la conductivité hydraulique présente assez peu de différences spatiales et atteint plusieurs dizaines de cm/h (par ex. Reutenauer, 1987). Le régime de la majorité des cours d'eau appartient au type pluvial océanique, légèrement influencé par la fonte nivale en mars-avril. Les débits de crue décennaux peuvent atteindre 1.7 $m^3/s/km^2$.

METHODE UTILISEE

Les différentes équations présentées sont issues d'une analyse en régression multiple "pas à pas" (Draper & Smith, 1983). Afin de minimiser la multicollinéarité, seules ont été retenues les régressions incluant des variables indépendantes faiblement intercorrélées. Une transformation logarithmique (log 10) des variables a permis de linéariser les relations et d'assurer une plus grande homoscédasticité des résidus. Toutes les équations se présentent donc sous une forme multiplicative :

$$y = a \; x1^b \; x2^c \; x3^d \ldots$$

où y = variable dépendante ; x1, x2, x3 ... = variables indépendantes ; a = constante de régression ; b, c, d ... = coefficients de régression. Chaque régression a été testée sur divers groupes de bassins non utilisés dans le calcul de l'équation.

DONNEES UTILISEES

Globalement on disposait d'un ensemble de données concernant 45 bassins, dont la surface varie de 0.36 à 447 km^2. Sachant que les informations disponibles n'étaient pas identiques sur la totalité de l'échantillon, les régressions ont été calculées sur des sous-ensembles de taille variée. Les variables dépendantes étudiées concernent des pas de temps différents et complémentaires :

a) des caractéristiques relatives à l'épisode de crue : écoulement direct (LC mm) et débit de pointe (QP $l/s/km^2$) ;

b) des caractéristiques moyennes : débits moyens mensuels (octobre à mai, QMM mm) et débit moyen annuel (QMA mm).

Les variables indépendantes collectées au départ ont été nombreuses et il n'est pas possible de les détailler ici. Notons simplement que pour ce qui est des variables climatiques on disposait toujours des précipitations totales, solides et liquides en moyenne sur le bassin, de la lame d'eau de fonte nivale (Humbert, 1986) ; des intensités pluviométriques maximales sur divers pas de temps, à l'échelle de la crue ; de l'ETP Turc en moyenne sur le bassin, à l'échelle mensuelle. Concernant les paramètres propres aux bassins-versants, 17 variables ont été utilisées. Outre les paramètres facilement accessibles (lithologie, occupation du sol, altitude, pente ...), plusieurs données du réseau hydrographique ont été introduites à partir de mesures sur cartes au 1/25 000, complétées par des observations in situ sous différentes conditions d'humidité. Ce sont : les densités de drainage (réseaux permanent, temporaire, maximal), les densités de drains d'ordre 1 et 2 (classification Strahler), et la fréquence des drains élémentaires d'ordre 1. Le tableau 1 fournit la liste des variables intervenant dans les régressions discutées ci-dessous.

TABLEAU 1 Signification des symboles utilisés dans les régressions.

DDM	densité de drainage en extension maximale (km/km^2)
DDM12	densité des drains d'ordres 1 et 2 en extension maximale (km/km^2)
DDP	densité de drainage du réseau permanent (km/km^2)
DDT	densité de drainage du réseau temporaire (km/km^2)
DPDM	DDP / DDM
ETP	évapotranspiration potentielle moyenne du bassin (mm), méthode de Turc
FN	lame d'eau de fonte nivale (mm)
GRA	surface relative des affleurements de granite (%)
GRE	surface relative des affleurements de grès (%)
HM	altitude moyenne du bassin-versant (m)
LC	lame d'eau d'écoulement direct de crue (mm)
LM	longueur du réseau en extension maximale (km)
LP	longueur du réseau permanent (km)
P	précipitations moyennes sur le bassin-versant (mm)
PFN	FN / (PL + FN) (%)
PL	précipitations liquides moyennes sur le bassin-versant (mm)
PN	précipitations solides moyennes sur le bassin-versant (mm)
QB	débit de base initial au départ de la crue (l/s/km^2)
QMA	écoulement moyen annuel (mm)
QMM	écoulement moyen mensuel (mm)
QP	débit maximum d'une crue (l/s/km^2)
QPB	QP – QB (l/s/km^2)
RMI	paramètre d'intensité moyenne max. d'un épisode pluvieux (Humbert, 1990)
RPI	paramètre de régularité d'un épisode pluvieux (Humbert, 1990)
S	surface du bassin-versant (km^2)
SCHI	surface relative des affleurements de schisto-grauwackes (%)

RESULTATS ET DISCUSSIONS

Régressions obtenues au niveau de l'épisode de crue

Pour cette étude on a utilisé un échantillon de 228 crues de saison froide enregistrées sur 9 bassins bien équipés. Toutes les crues ont été analysées automatiquement. Les différents modes de calcul et les résultats détaillés de cette étude sont décrits ailleurs (Humbert, 1990). Parmi l'ensemble des régressions obtenues, 3 sont considérées ici pour illustrer notre propos, et sont rassemblées dans le tableau 2, les variables expliquées étant ici LC, QP et QPB (cf. tabl. 1). On peut résumer les principaux résultats de la manière suivante :

a) En incluant le débit de base initial QB, les variables d'ordre climato-hydrologique contrôlent largement la variance : 85% pour LC, près de 70% pour QP et 55% pour QPB ; on notera que le paramètre d'intensité pluviométrique (RMI) intervient sur le débit maximum,

TABLEAU 2 Régressions obtenues sur les caractéristiques de l'écoulement au niveau de l'épisode de crue.

y	a	Coefficients des variables indépendantes								σr	r	ε	VARD
		PL + FN	PFN + 1	RPI	RMI	QB	DDM	DDM12	DPDM				
LC	0.077	0.936	-	1.26	-	0.346	-	0.433	-	0.116	0.935	20.1	2.2
QP	5.22	0.495	−0.03 *	-	0.531	0.293	-	0.68	1.27	0.109	0.890	19.2	10.3
QPB	3.56	0.609	-	-	0.813	-	1.2	-	2.0	0.139	0.853	25.4	18.1

** Significatif au seuil de 2% . Les autres coefficients sont significatifs à un seuil < 0.001%*

alors que le volume de crue est plutot influencé par un paramètre de régularité de l'averse (RPI).

b) Les variables propres aux bassins jouent un rôle beaucoup moins important ; parmi elles, seuls les paramètres de densité de drainage se montrent très significatifs, et surtout la densité du réseau élémentaire en condition d'extension maximale (DDM12). En outre, le

TABLEAU 3 Régressions obtenues sur les écoulements moyens mensuels et annuels.

Période d'étude	a	Coefficients des variables indépendantes						σr	r	ε	VARD	VARL	r partiel (DD)
		P	P - ETP	DDM	DDP	SCHI + 1	GRE + 1						
Octobre	0.137	-	1.267	0.365	-	-	−0.104	0.067	0.978	8.8	1.2	6.7	0.428
Novembre	0.080	1.287	-	0.521	-	-	−0.066	0.075	0.970	11.7	4.0	1.7	0.518
Décembre	0.312	1.085	-	0.476	-	0.033	-	0.068	0.970	9.2	3.0	1.0	0.526
Janvier	1.103	0.814	-	0.520	-	0.056	-	0.078	0.943	11.5	3.2	2.4	0.485
Février	2.406	0.702	-	0.641	-	0.052	-	0.078	0.948	13.1	5.6	1.8	0.602
Mars	0.569	0.972	-	0.685	-	0.041	-	0.061	0.970	7.8	4.8	1.1	0.688
Avril	15.67	-	0.410	-	0.654	0.050	-	0.057	0.976	7.9	9.8	2.0	0.789
Mai	18.53	-	0.296	-	0.439	0.071	-	0.077	0.930	12.3	6.4	13.6	0.533
Année	3.993	-	0.742	0.410	-	0.031	-	0.040	0.987	6.1	2.2	1.0	0.663
Année (33 obs.)	2.083	-	0.881	.	0.190	-	-	0.033	0.988	5.6	1.5	-	0.587

Tous les coefficients sont significatifs à un seuil < 5%

avec a = constante de régression : σr = écart-type résiduel ; r = coefficient de corrélation multiple ;
ε = erreur moyenne d'estimation en % ; VARD et VARL = pourcentage de variance expliquée par un paramètre de densité de drainage (DD) ou par un paramètre lithologique (L) ;
r partiel (DD) = coefficient de corrélation partielle de la densité de drainage (DDM ou DDP)

rapport DDP/DDM semble être un descripteur intéressant : en effet, pour une DDM donnée, plus ce rapport est élevé, plus la réponse du bassin est importante. L'introduction des paramètres de drainage entraîne une nette réduction de l'écart-type résiduel : 7.2% pour LC, 18.4% pour QP et 23.6% pour QPB.

c) Les erreurs d'estimation sont de l'ordre de 18% pour LC et QP et de 26% pour QPB ; testées sur un échantillon de 28 crues enregistrées sur 4 bassins voisins, les régressions sur LC et QP ont fourni une erreur moyenne de 19% dans les deux cas.

D'autre part, afin de vérifier l'influence des paramètres de drainage sur le coefficient d'écoulement direct KEC (= LC / (PL + FN)), on a constitué pour 12 bassins, un échantillon de 20 crues engendrées par les mêmes épisodes météorologiques. La relation entre DDP et la moyenne de KEC est montrée sur la fig. 1 : on constate une liaison très étroite confirmant les résultats précédents. Dans ce cas, le graphique révèle qu'un doublement de DDP correspond en moyenne à un doublement de la réponse du bassin.

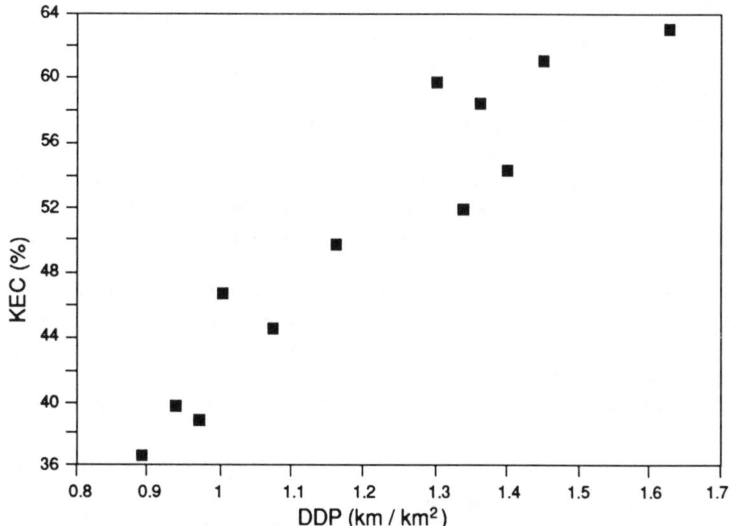

FIG. 1 Relation entre la moyenne des coefficients d'écoulement de crue (KEC) obtenus pour chaque bassin et la densité de drainage du réseau permanent (DDP).

Régressions obtenues pour les écoulements mensuels (QMM) et annuels (QMA)

Une étude complémentaire a été effectuée sur les variables QMM et QMA. Dans un premier temps, on a retenu un groupe de 23 bassins pour lesquels on a calculé les régressions expliquant les QMM d'octobre à mai (période 1974-1983), soit 8 mois pour lesquels on vérifie la relation P > ETP. Les 4 mois de saison chaude pour lesquels ETP > P sur de nombreux bassins ont été écartés car les relations pluie-débit sont plus floues et font intervenir des paramètres de stockage non pris en compte ici. Les résultats sont consignés dans le tableau 3.

On constate que les variables climatiques s'approprient 82 à 90% de la variance, ce taux tombant à 66.4% au mois de mai, annonciateur de la période estivale. Pour la période novembre-mars, l'introduction de la variable P seule entraîne des résultats aussi satisfaisants sinon meilleurs, que si des variables telles que PN, PL ou FN sont présentes ;

l'évolution des précipitations solides et de la fonte est alors incorporée dans le coefficient de P : supérieur à 1, il signifie un accroissement du rendement à mesure que P augmente ; inférieur à 1 (de janvier à mars), il implique une baisse du rendement avec une hausse de P, ce qui est logique puisque dans ce cas la proportion des précipitations solides augmente d'autant.

Parmi les facteurs physiques, seuls les paramètres de drainage (DD), puis les données lithologiques sont significatifs au seuil de 5% ; la part de variance qui leur revient est assez faible (de 4 à 12% et 20% en mai), celle revenant à DD étant nettement majoritaire. Durant la période octobre-mars, pendant laquelle le réseau hydrographique fonctionne souvent à un niveau d'extension élevé, on note que DDM prédomine par rapport à DDP. Cette importance croissante de DDM dans le fonctionnement hydrologique est aussi attestée par la progression de son coefficient de régression et par celle de son coefficient de corrélation partielle. En moyenne, on estime qu'un doublement de DDM entraîne une hausse de QMM de 30 à 60% selon le mois.

Le rôle lithologique paraît moins décisif (cf. VARL, tabl. 3), mais toujours significatif et en corollaire de DD. On notera le rôle différenciateur des variables GRE et SCHI. L'influence du grès ressort clairement durant les mois de recharge (octobre et novembre), avec un coefficient négatif lié à sa capacité de stockage. Dès décembre, cette influence s'estompe et fait place à celle des schisto-grauwackes, devenant plus discriminants de par la perméabilité moyenne plus faible des formations qui les surmontent.

Les équations présentent un écart-type résiduel satisfaisant et l'erreur d'estimation varie de 7.8 à 13.1% ; testées sur 8 bassins et sur différentes périodes, les erreurs restent toujours dans la même gamme.

On a effectué d'autre part 2 séries de calcul sur QMA, l'un reprenant l'échantillon étudié ci-dessus, l'autre considérant un groupe de 33 bassins. Les résultats (tabl. 3) confirment l'influence écrasante des facteurs climatiques : la variable P – ETP s'approprie 94 à 95% de la variance et ne laisse qu'une part très faible aux paramètres de bassin. Mais parmi eux, seuls les paramètres de densité de drainage (DDP ou DDM) se révèlent très significatifs (seuils $< 0.5\%$). L'influence lithologique paraît moins évidente au niveau annuel. La régression établie sur 33 observations a été vérifiée sur un autre échantillon de 11 bassins : l'erreur moyenne d'estimation est de l'ordre de 6% avec un maximum de 10%. Une régression construite avec la seule variable P – ETP fait passer l'erreur de 6 à près de 10%.

Estimation de la densité de drainage

A partir des mesures et observations effectuées sur 29 bassins-versants, sous différentes conditions d'humidité, on a calculé un ensemble de régressions estimant les longueurs de drains du réseau permanent (LP) et du réseau en extension maximale (LM). Calculées pour une surface donnée, on peut facilement évaluer DDP, DDM, et DDT par déduction. Les résultats sont rassemblés dans le tableau 4.

Deux groupes de régressions ont été calculés, selon que l'on introduit ou non une caractéristique de l'écoulement. Dans le premier cas, l'introduction du déficit d'écoulement P – QMA entraîne un gain systématique d'environ 17% sur l'écart-type résiduel. Ce terme intervient à la fois comme un facteur de causalité et comme une résultante ; il est relié de manière inverse à DD : une hausse du déficit d'écoulement est significative d'une diminution de la densité de drainage, tout autre facteur restant constant. D'autre part, en l'absence d'un paramètre d'écoulement, DD est positivement reliée au terme P – ETP et de manière plus significative que si P ou ETP sont introduits isolément.

A l'échelle considérée, cette influence climatique est modulée par la lithologie (Morgan, 1973 ; Gregory & Gardiner, 1975). Le poids respectif des variables GRA et SCHI reste cependant difficile à mettre en évidence ; le granite semble plutôt favoriser le réseau permanent. Par contre DDM est fortement contrôlée par la présence de grès, de manière inverse : les drains temporaires s'y développent peu. Par exemple, un bassin totalement granitique possède un taux moyen d'extension de son réseau d'environ 85%, alors que pour un bassin comportant environ un tiers de grès, ce taux tombe à 45%. Autrement dit, dans le milieu étudié, la présence pourtant mineure de grès est très différenciatrice.

Enfin, testées sur 8 bassins, les équations du tableau 4 ont fourni une erreur moyenne variant de 9 à 14%.

TABLEAU 4 Régressions obtenues sur les longueurs de drains, en extensions maximale (LM) et permanente (LP).

y	a	Coefficients des variables indépendantes							δr	r	ε
		S	HM	P - ETP	P - QMA	GRA + 1	SCHI + 1	GRE + 1			
① LM	114.1	0.968	0.390	-	−1.028	-	0.023	−0.072	0.050	0.997	8.4
LP	2016.5	0.914	-	-	−1.188	0.065	0.048	-	0.069	0.995	11.8
② LM	0.838	0.957	-	0.136	-	0.045	-	−0.075	0.060	0.997	9.8
LP	0.383	0.947	-	0.147	-	0.073	-	-	0.084	0.993	13.9

Tous les coefficients sont significatifs à un seuil < 5%

① = avec connaissance de l'écoulement moyen annuel (QMA)

② = sans connaissance de l'écoulement moyen annuel

CONCLUSION

Au terme de ce travail, il apparaît que dans les Vosges, milieu à lithologie variée et aux précipitations très contrastées, la variabilité spatiale de l'écoulement s'explique essentiellement par des facteurs d'ordre climatique. Les facteurs physiques propres aux bassins jouent un rôle moindre, malgré leur grande gamme de variation. Parmi eux, seuls les paramètres de densité de drainage, éventuellement associés à la lithologie, se montrent toujours très significatifs. Les régressions obtenues soulignent l'intérêt d'opérer une distinction entre les différents niveaux d'extension du réseau de drainage et un effort important reste à faire pour bien comprendre sa dynamique (par ex. Gregory & Walling, 1968 ; Ambroise, 1986). En outre une bonne connaissance du réseau de drains élémentaires améliore nettement les équations au niveau de l'épisode de crue. Finalement, en région humide, la densité de drainage semble être un puissant descripteur du milieu, en tant que paramètre-charnière entre les éléments climatiques, hydrologiques et lithologiques ; ce rôle essentiel tient au fait qu'elle est à la fois une résultante et un agent de l'écoulement.

REMERCIEMENTS Ce travail a été financé par le programme PIREN-Eau/Alsace (CNRS, Ministère de l'Environnement, Région Alsace).

REFERENCES

Ambroise, B. (1986) Rôle hydrologique des surfaces saturées en eau dans le bassin du Ringelbach (Hautes Vosges, France). In Actes du 1er Coll. Sci. des Univ. du Rhin Supérieur, ULP, Conseil de l'Europe, Strasbourg, 27-28/6/86, 620-630.

Draper, N.R. & Smith, H. (1981) Applied regression analysis. Snd Ed., Wiley, New York.

Gregory, K.J. & Walling, D.E. (1968) The variation of drainage density within a catchment. Int. Assoc. Sci. Hydrol. Bull. 13, 61-68.

Gregory, K.J. & Gardiner, V. (1975) Drainage density and climate. Z. Geomorph. N.F. 19 (3), 287-298.

Humbert, J. (1986) Estimation et rôle de la fonte nivale dans l'écoulement de crue des rivières des Hautes Vosges. Revue Géogr. de l'Est 26, (1/2), 27-56.

Humbert, J. (1990) Factors controlling cold season stormflow in humid forested mountains : a case study in North-Eastern France. Soumis pour publ. à J. Hydrol.

Morgan, R.P.C. (1973) The influence of scale in climatic geomorphology : a case study of drainage density in West Malaysia. Geografiska Ann. 55 A, 107-115.

Reutenauer, D. (1987) Variabilité spatiale des propriétés physiques et hydriques des sols et des formations superficielles du bassin-versant de la Fecht en amont de Turckheim (Haut-Rhin). Thèse de Doct. de l'Univ. Louis Pasteur, ULP/CEREG, Strasbourg.

Hydrology in Mountainous Regions. I - Hydrological Measurements; the Water Cycle (Proceedings of two Lausanne Symposia, August 1990). IAHS Publ. no. 193, 1990.

Hétérogénéité des précipitations sur la Cordillère des Andes boliviennes

M.A. ROCHE
ORSTOM, PHICAB, C.P. 9214, La Paz, Bolivia
A. ALIAGA, J. CAMPOS, J. PENA
IHH-UMSA, C.P. 303, La Paz, Bolivia
J. CORTES & N. ROCHA
SENAMHI, Ed. La Urbana, La Paz, Bolivia

RESUME Du désert chilien, le plus aride du monde (1 mm an^{-1} sur la côte), la traversée des Andes vers l'Est conduit à des sites amazoniens dont la pluviométrie est très élevée (6000 à 7000 mm an^{-1}). Il existe une tendance à une diminution des précipitations en direction du Sud-Ouest. La masse d'air humide orientale, d'origine atlantique et amazonienne, envahit la Bolivie durant l'été (oscillation de la ZITC) en débordant fréquemment sur l'Altiplano jusqu'aux sommets de la Cordillère Occidentale. Des masses d'air froid, d'origine polaire, remontent jusqu'au nord de la Bolivie en créant des fronts froids au contact de la masse d'air précédente. Des conditions de stabilité extrêmement fortes sont engendrées sur la côte ouest par l'anticyclone sud pacifique et le courant froid de Humboldt. Outre l'influence de la dynamique des masses d'air, l'orographie des Andes et les vastes étendues d'eau et de sel (Lac Titicaca, Salar d'Uyuni) contribuent à l'échelle régionale et locale à déterminer l'hétérogénéité des précipitations.

INTRODUCTION

Les Andes boliviennes, situées entre 10 et 20°S, sont un domaine montagneux intertropical soumis à une forte hétérogénéité des précipitations. En un seul pays, depuis la plaine orientale (200 m), jusqu'aux hauts sommets andins (6800 m) et l'Altiplano (3600 à 4100 m), une variété de climats parmi la plus ample de la planète régle la distribution des ressources renouvelables.

La carte en courbes isohyètes présentée (fig.1) constitue le document actuel le plus détaillé existant pour la région sur les précipitations moyennes pluriannuelles. Elles provient d'un document offset couleur au 1/4 000 000 établi sur la base d'un total de 348 stations pluviométriques . Les données les plus anciennes remontent à 1945; l'année limite prise en considération étant 1984.

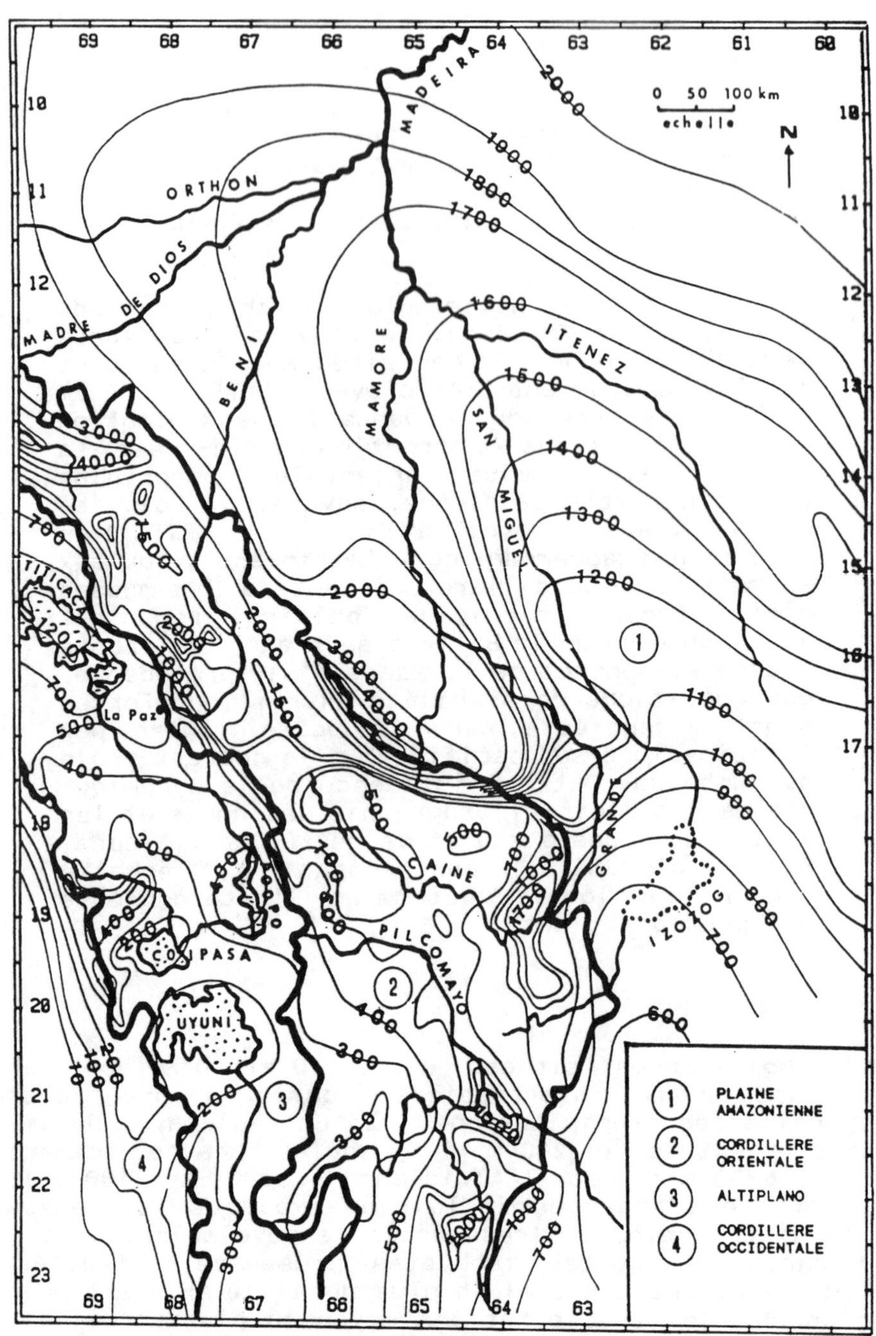

FIG. 1 Carte des précipitations moyennes inter-annuelles (mm an^{-1}) dans la région andine bolivienne.

L'homogénéisation des données n'a pas été effectuée. Malgré les critiques qui peuvent être portées à cet aspect méthodologique, on se rend compte que les gradients spatiaux accentués l'emportent largement sur l'hétérogénéité des séries d'observation. Le détail du tracé des courbes a tenu compte de la carte topographique et d'une carte écologique existantes.

La similitude des hyétogrammes mensuels interannuels sur toute la région montre l'appartenance à un même régime pluviométrique.

Ces travaux ont été menés dans le cadre du Programme Hydrologique et Climatologique de la Bolivie -PHICAB- (Roche & Canedo, 1984), selon des accords de coopération entre les Organismes sus-mentionnés.

DISTRIBUTION SPATIALE ET SAISONNIERE DES PRECIPITATIONS

A partir de sites amazoniens du piémont des Andes remarquablement arrosés (6000 à 7000 mm an^{-1}), la traversée de la cordillère sur 400 km conduit au désert chilien et péruvien, le moins pluvieux du monde (1 mm an^{-1}) sur la côte de l'Océan Pacifique.

Dans la plaine amazonienne adjacente aux Andes, les valeurs croissent depuis 600 mm au Sud jusqu'à 2000 mm au Nord ,selon des isohyètes en forme de gouttière. La pluie augmente ainsi en direction des Andes où sont observés les maximums du pays, peu avant ou sur les premiers reliefs. Dans la Cordillère Orientale même, se rencontre des zones isolées à pluie inférieure à 500 mm. C'est le cas général dans le sud de la chaine où des minimums de 300 mm sont identifiés. Le vaste plateau de l'Altiplano reçoit des précipitations supérieures à 500 mm au nord de la latitude de La Paz, avec un maximum de 1200 mm sur le Lac Titicaca. Ainsi, les pluies décroissent depuis le centre du lac jusqu'au Salar d'Uyuni. Les cimes de la Cordillère Occidentale correspondent à un léger accroissement des précipitations jusqu'à des valeurs de 300 à 500 mm. Les hauteurs de pluie deviennent ensuite rapidement décroissantes sur le versant pacifique, avec des valeurs inférieures à 1 mm en bordure de mer.

La Bolivie peut être divisée en trois grands bassins versants qui s'étendent totalement ou en partie sur les Andes, et aussi partiellement dans les pays limitrophes (Roche & Fernandez, 1988, Bourges, 1989, Guyot <u>et al.</u>, in press). Le tableau 1 indique la précipitation interannuelle évaluée pour chaque sous-bassin andin. Les valeurs varient de 200 à 3000 mm, illustrant ainsi les fortes différences pouvant exister entre zones voisines.

La saison des pluie est centrée sur l'été avec un maximum en janvier, secondairement en février. La saison sèche est en hiver, avec un minimum de mai à juillet. L'année hydrologique est considérée commencer le 1er octobre. Un total de 60 à 75% tombe durant les quatre mois les plus pluvieux et 0 à 15% durant les quatre mois les plus secs, la période sèche étant d'autant plus sévère que le total annuel est faible.

TABLEAU 1 **Précipitations moyennes interannuelles sur les grands bassins versants andins de Bolivie.**

	Superficie (km^2)	Pluie (mm)
Amazonie		
Madre de Dios (Andes+plaine)	125 000	2 380
Beni	73 670	1 720
Grande	59 480	750
Bassins orientaux Mamoré	28 870	2 990
Parapeti	14 750	950
Altiplano		
Titicaca	56 740	680
Desaguadero	29 480	410
Poopo	27 740	370
Coipasa	30 170	240
Uyuni	46 625	200
Rio de La Plata		
Pilcomayo	81 320	480
Grande y Bermejo	16 050	1 070

LES PRECIPITATIONS ET LA DYNAMIQUE DES MASSES D'AIR

La distribution des pluies s'explique par la dynamique des principales masses d'air actives sur cette partie de l'Amérique du Sud, et par le rôle orographique des Andes, aussi bien à l'échelle du continent qu'à celle de la vallée.

Les masses d'air atlantique et amazonienne

Le bassin amazonien est généralement le siège de basses pressions par rapport aux anticyclones sud pacifique et atlantique. La dynamique de l'ensemble est réglée pour une part essentielle par l'inclinaison apparente du soleil qui détermine l'oscillation saisonnière de la Zone Intertropicale de Convergence (ZITC) et des anticyclones précités.

Pendant l'hiver austral, la ZITC atteint les Antilles et les anticyclones tropicaux sud rejoignent leurs latitudes les plus septentrionales, voisines du bassin amazonien de Bolivie. C'est la saison sèche, caractérisée par une meilleure stabilité de l'air et une moindre disponibilité de vapeur d'eau.

Pendant l'été austral, la ZITC oscille sur l'Amazonie bolivienne où sa remarquable inflexion vers le Sud étend largement les basses pressions tropicales. C'est alors la saison des pluies qui détermine finalement la distribution spatiale des précipitations, compte tenu de l'importance relative de la lame précipitée durant cette période.

L'alizé de secteur nord-est dévie le long des Andes selon une inflexion nord-nord-ouest. Il apporte sur la Bolivie l'essentiel de la vapeur précipitable originaire de l'Atlantique, mais qui s'est en fait amplement recyclée à partir de l'évapotranspiration de la forêt et des vastes zones inondées, lesquelles seulement dans la plaine bolivienne couvrent de l'ordre de 100 000 km2 en fin de saison des pluies. L'alizé de secteur sud-est contribue à l'apport d'humidité directement depuis l'Est et le Sud-Est. La convection diurne, dans la plaine, et encore plus dans les Andes, est responsable d'une grande part des précipitations. Elle correspond alors essentiellement au recyclage de la vapeur d'eau.

Les masses d'air polaire

Ce système est perturbé fréquemment par l'intrusion, dans la plaine adjacente aux Andes, d'air plus froid et sec venu du Sud (Surazo), avec la formation d'un front froid au contact des masses d'air humides et généralement plus chaudes qui occupent la région. La progression des masses d'air froid a été expliquée par Leroux (1987) selon le mécanisme d'anticyclones mobiles peu épais qui se détachent de l'anticyclone antartique et progressent jusqu'aux basses latitudes en écartant les autres masses d'air. La distribution des pluies dans la plaine, selon une inflexion des isohyètes en gouttière allant de pair avec un fort accroissement des valeurs du Sud (600 mm) au Nord (2 000 mm), dénote l'interférence des deux masses d'air. L'air sec en provenance du Sud se trouve canalisé par la dépression topographique (500 à 150 m) située entre les Andes et le Bouclier brésilien (1500 m). L'abaissement des températures accompagnant les fronts froids peut atteindre 10°C d'un jour à l'autre, et les chutes de pluies sont notables, pour les plus fortes intrusions d'hiver, au-delà de 10° de latitude Sud dans la plaine et le sud des Andes boliviennes (Ronchail, 1988). Ces masses d'air froid traversent fréquemment les Andes du sud du Chili, en y abandonnant leur humidité, puis suivent la bordure orientale de la cordillère.

Oscillations de la ZITC et des alizés associés, perturbations du système par les fronts froids provoqués par l'intrusion d'air polaire, sont les grands mécanismes qui intéressent le sud des Andes et tout le piémont oriental de la cordillère. L'Altiplano ne serait pas concerné par ces masses d'air froid (Ronchail, 1988). L'épaisseur du flux amazonien, selon l'importance des basses pressions, la convection produite dans la plaine et sur le versant est , et le soulèvement éventuel par l'air méridional, détermine son débordement par dessus les lignes de crêtes.

La masse d'air pacifique

A l'opposé, le versant occidental des Andes est soumis à ces latitudes à des conditions de stabilité atmosphérique de plus en plus fortes, depuis la crête qui le sépare de l'Altiplano jusqu'à la côte. Ces conditions sont engendrées par la présence permanente de l'anticyclone sud pacifique et par le courant froid de Humboldt qui lui est associé. Bien que l'humidité atmosphérique dans les 1000 premiers mètres soit très élevée, une subsidence permanente de l'air, et une inversion dans la stratification thermique de la troposphére aux alentours de 1300 m, empêchent l'ascension de l'air humide et les précipitations. En hiver, une couche de stratocumulus, peu épaisse (200 à 300 m), s'établit au-dessus de cette inversion, accompagnée de brouillard la nuit et tôt le matin. En hiver, elle disparaît fréquemment l'après-midi et s'avére souvent inexistante en été. Les isohyètes sur ce versant suivent les courbes topographiques. Si l'on peut concevoir, comme cela est signalé au Pérou, une ascension diurne de la vapeur du Pacifique le long des versants à l'occasion du réchauffement du sol, il n'apparaît pas cependant dans le paysage chilien d'effets marqués de ce phénomène.

La barrière de la Cordillère Occidentale constitue ainsi la limite de l'antagonisme des influences atmosphériques de secteurs atlantique et pacifique. Cependant, le régime des précipitations, estivales au-dessus de l'isohyète 10 mm, soit sensiblement au-dessus de 1200 m, et une pluviométrie croissante jusqu'à la crête (200 à 500 mm) en continuation des précipitations de l'Altiplano, indique un débordement des alizés orientaux sur ce versant. Ceux-ci subissent alors une subsidence forcée qui fait décroître rapidement les pluies vers l'Ouest. Sur la côte même, les rares pluies observées se produisent généralement en hiver. Dans l'extrême sud de la zone considérée (au-delà de 22°S), l'incursion accidentelle des Westerlies en hiver peut occasionner des pluies sur le versant occidental de la cordillère, comme cela est fréquent à partir de 27°S.

LE ROLE DE L'OROGRAPHIE DES ANDES

Les facteurs orographiques jouent pleinement. La déviation des alizés en provenance d'Amazonie par la barrière des Andes orientales dont les sommets s'échelonnent de 4500 à 6500 m, jusqu'à une direction nord-nord-ouest, présente une ampleur régionale. Les masses d'air humide, coincées fréquemment entre l'air méridional plus sec et le massif andin, viennent balayer en long ce versant oriental où elles abandonnent préférentiellement leur humidité. Les maximums de 5000 à 7000 mm sont observés, dans le Chaparé à l'est de

Cochabamba et dans le bassin du Madre de Dios au Pérou, pour des altitudes basses en regard de celles de la chaine. En effet, le premier maximum signalé se produit entre 400 et 800 m d'altitude alors qu'aucun relief marqué n'est apparant; l' épicentre du second est repéré à 620 m. Il est à noter que des zones de fortes pluies, de 2000 à plus de 4000 mm, existent ainsi tout au long des Andes, depuis la Colombie jusqu'à la Bolivie, pour des altitudes très basses comprises entre 150 et 700 m. Ces sites boliviens correspondent à l'accentuation du gradient négatif de température (1,50 m du sol), de la plaine vers la montagne. Cependant, la variation reste faible, les isothermes évoluant de 23 à 21°C à l'épicentre. Dans le sud de la Bolivie, la carte fait également apparaître des zones de précipitations maximums de 1500 à 2200 mm sur les premiers reliefs orientaux, à des altitudes de 400 à 900 m.

On remarque que les précipitations se produisent dans des "baies" de relief, parties concaves vers la plaine de la limite des Andes, alors que les parties convexes reçoivent des précipitations moindres. La disposition concave favoriserait la convection à l'abri du vent.

Certaines extrémités de vallées ouvertes au vent de la plaine, notamment au nord-est de La Paz, reçoivent également à des altitudes bien supérieures aux précédentes (3000 m), de fortes précipitations, de l'ordre de 2000 à 4000 mm. Le profil longitudinal de ces vallées, qui se termine souvent en amont par une véritable falaise (exemple d' une dénivelée de 3500 m sur 35 km) force en bout de course les masses d'air à une rapide ascension.

Ainsi n'existe-il pas dans les Andes de relation générale entre précipitation et altitude. Après les zones de piémont, la pluviométrie tend généralement à décroître. Le blocage fréquent de l'air oriental par la cordillère met à l'abri de vastes zones à l'intérieur des Andes, les nuages plafonnant à l'Est en dessous de la ligne de crête. C'est le cas de l'Altiplano mais aussi de toute la moitié sud des Andes boliviennes où s'enfoncent de vastes vallées et zones déprimées d'origine techtonique (exemple des vallées de Cochabamba). Ces dépressions topographiques provoquent une subsidence de l'air oriental qui arrive latéralement après avoir perdu une grande partie de son humidité sur le flanc est du massif. Ces zones semi-arides (600 à 400 mm) se développent encore plus vers le Sud où l'humidité originelle de l'air atteignant les Andes est plus faible qu'au Nord, et l'influence pacifique plus intense. Les vallées de Cochabamba, du Rio Grande et Pilcomayo, du Rio La Paz et de Luribay sont ainsi nettement semi-arides.

LE ROLE DES ETENDUES D'EAU ET DE SEL

L'influence des grandes masses d'eau et surfaces de sel apparaît également sur la carte pluviométrique. Dans le nord de l'Altiplano, l'effet du Lac Titicaca (8600 km^2) se traduit par une forte augmentation concentrique des pluies, les valeurs décroissant de 1200 mm en son centre à 700 mm à quelques dizaines de kilomètres de ses rives. l' influence sous le vent, est plus étendue.

Le Lac Poopo, de superficie plus réduite (3600 km^2) et fluctuante, n'induit qu'une légère augmentation des pluies (400 mm).

Par contre, il apparaît que les vastes étendues de sel des Salars d'Uyuni (9100 km^2) et de Coipasa (2000 km^2), correspondent à une diminution des pluies qui n'y dépassent pas 200 mm. La même constatation est faite pour le Salar d'Atacama au Chili (25 mm). Les bilans d'énergie et l'évaporation des lacs sont très différents de ceux des salars. Le Lac Titicaca permet une importante convection et recyclage de la vapeur d'eau.

CONCLUSION

L'hétérogénéité des précipitations sur la Cordillère des Andes est due à la rencontre en cette région de grandes masses d'air dont la dynamique régle les échanges atmosphériques méridiens et latitudinaux de l'hémisphère sud. Cependant les variations spatiales sont encore accentuées par les effets du relief et des vastes étendues d'eau et de sel constituées par le Lac Titicaca et les Salars. Les Andes, par leur orographie exceptionnelle, contribuent à provoquer des précipitations extrêmes, soit maximums ,soit minimums, selon les zones. La chaine montagneuse met fin à l'influence pluviogène des masses d'air tropical humide d'origine atlantique et amazonienne.

BIBLIOGRAPHIE

Bourges, J. (1989) La investigación hidrológica en el Beni: ejemplos de aplicación para el desarrollo de infraestructuras y previsión de crecidas. III Simp. invest. francesa en Bolivia, Santa Cruz, junio :9-22.

Guyot, J.L., Roche, M.A., Quintanilla, J., Calliconde, M., Noriega, L., Calle, H. & Cortés, J. (in press) Salinities and sediment loads on the Bolivian Highlands. <u>J. Hydrol.</u>

Leroux, M. (1987) L'anticyclone mobile polaire, relais des échanges méridiens : son importance climatique. <u>Géodynamique 2</u> (2): 161-167

Roche, M.A. & Canedo, M. (1984) Programa Hidrológico y Climatológico de la Cuenca Amazoníca de Bolivia. Folleto de presentación del PHICAB, offset color.

Roche, M.A. & Rocha, N. (1985) Mapa pluviométrico de Bolivia y regiones vecinas, 1/4 000 000. PHICAB, offset color.

Roche, M.A. & Fernández, C. (1988) Water Resources, Salinity and Salt Exportations of the Rivers of the Bolivian Amazon. <u>J. Hydrol.</u>, 101 : 305-331.

Ronchail, J. (1988) Variabilidad del tiempo en Bolivia : la anomalía climática del invierno 1988. PHICAB.

Hydrology in Mountainous Regions. I - Hydrological Measurements; the Water Cycle
(Proceedings of two Lausanne Symposia, August 1990). IAHS Publ. no. 193, 1990.

New findings from the investigation of the runoff regime in the Police Cretaceous basin in the Bohemian Massif

K. SARGA, F. SLEPIČKA
Department of Hydrogeology and Engineering Geology, Faculty of Sciences, Albertov 6
128 43 Praha 2, Czechoslovakia

ABSTRACT Using new approaches to solve the increasingly more complex hydrogeological problems, modern hydrological methods for evaluating time and space-related ground-water regime are developed which are focused to rational and optimum development of ground-water resources and of surface flow. Several examples of application are presented.

INTRODUCTION

A detailed investigation and analysis of complex processes (including the origin of stream - bed flow with the contribution of the ground-water flow and relations of both components in time and space) are a significant part of hydrogeological studies.

New approaches to solution of complex problems create new methods based on a single independent input value, i.e. the stream- bed flow, which is a result of a complex dynamic process in the underground, on the surface of the territory as well as between both of them. This is an advantage of the methods. Appropriate methods and reliable input data ensure correct results.

We present some basic results from the area of our investigation in the basin of Police nad Metují in Eastern Bohemia.

AN OUTLINE OF THE GEOLOGICAL SETTING, HYDROGEOLOGY AND HYDROLOGY

From the regional geological point of view, the basin of Police nad Metují is a Mesozoic filling of the Intrasudetic depression within the Bohemian Massif, with a brachysynclinal closure in the NW at Adršpach along the border with Poland. It extends, about 25 km long and 10 km wide, from the NW to the SE as far as the town of Hronov. Its area is about 250 square kilometers.

The bedrock consists of Cretaceous sandstones overlying Triassic sandstones and / or Permo-Carboniferous sedimentary rocks. The valley bottoms are filled with alluvial sediments.

The uppermost member of the sequence is thick-bedded pure sandstone forming labyrinths at Adršpach and Teplice, the tops of which reach the altitudes of more than 750 m a.s.l.

The lowest surface form is the valley of the Metuje River, the main surface recipient of the basin within the watershed of the Labe (Elbe) River. In the NW, in the spring area at Horní Adršpach, the streambed of the Metuje is 350 m a.s.l. The 50-year average of precipitation is about 800 mm per year.

Within the hydrogeologically significant structure of the Police Basin, there are several independent aquifers. First of all, it is the lowest artesian aquifer in the Cenomanian. The Lower Turonian is water-bearing along the edges of the basin at the villages of Dřevíč and Hlavňov and in the valley of Židovka with substantial springs.

In the Middle Turonian, there is one aquifer in the sandstones of its lower part and another one in calcareous and spongilitic sandstones at the niveau of the erosion level. Above the erosion level, there ar two more aquifers with unconfined water level in the thick-bedded sandstones of the rock labyrinths of Adršpach and Teplice and of Broumovské Stěny.

Detailed investigation indicates that the size of the yield and the origin of runoff in the basin of Police nad Metují are controlled directly by the tectonic exposure in its partial areas. The originally continuous sedimentary unit is considerably tectonically disrupted. Among others, the longitudinal faults of Police nad Metují and Bělá are significant; along these, the NE blocks subsided. A system of transversal fault lines in the southern edge of a fault zone at Teplice nad Metují is significant from the hydrogeological point of view. Due to a vertical shift of the blocks of aquicludes in front of aquifers, a natural impermeable barrier originated which impounds ground water within the town limits of Teplice nad Metují and which, at the same time, separates the upper Adršpach - Teplice part of the basin that is rich in ground water from the central part which in fact is without any surface influent streams. The closing Police n.M. - Hronov part of the basin in the SE is again remarkable from the hydrogeological point of view. It consists of the water-rich left-bank affluent streams of Ledhuje and Židovka and of the right-bank tributary Dřevíč upstream from Hronov with a developed spring area at the Dřevíček mill; one part of its water which it contributes to the Metuje River comes from the Permo-Carboniferous.

USED METHODS AND NEW APPROACH

It has been very difficult if not impossible to solve hydrogeological and water - management problems in a satisfactory way in applying methods which, while using various simplifications, are based on hydrological, physical and mathematical simulation of the mentioned complex process, apart from the fact that it requires, at the same time, a difficult determination of independently variable input data, the values of which mainly have the character of average estimations.

The new approach to solution is based on using only one independently variable value, the stream-bed flow, measured in streams and springs. From the correspondent set of outflow values we construct basic hydrological curves for further analyses. For solving the time-related problems, these are the curves of discharges subsequent in time, usually annual hydrographs of daily discharges (outflows) from the watershed measured in a representative hydrological profile for the particular period of years. For solving the space-related problems, these are the curves of discharges subsequent in space measured once in a series of successive measuring profiles along the streams, usually in several hydrologically characteristic measuring periods. The measuring profiles are determined according to the geomorphological, lithological, tectonic and hydrographic circumstances in the watersheds to achieve an appropriate expression of the hydrological conditions and a truthful solution of the hydrological problems.

Such curves are a graphic record of the studied time or of a space-related hydrological regime. The course of the basic outflow curves reflects the influences and effects of all factors, which subsequently participated in the pertinent process. Using an adequate analysis of the curves, they can be decoded, i.e. to determine the occurrence of influences, to determine the nature and size of effects, site and time of acting of factors which caused the changes in the water resources, to derive further information, including complex hydrological balance in waterheds and sustainable utilizable yields, long-term forcast, etc.

ANALYSIS OF THE TIME-RELATED REGIME

After the culmination of the runoff, as a rule during the autumn or winter period, it is the declining section, the so-called outflow curve. In hydrogeology, its lowest and extreme rear part, the so called drainage curve is of special interest. In fact, it is a graphical representation of the gradual decrease of water resources in the watershed. In the semilogarithmic seale, the whole outflow line becomes a bending line with some linked abscissas each of which represents an independent genetic section. The lowest of the abscissas pertains to the forming of outflow solely from the deep ground-water resources. Its analytical form is a pure exponential function. In its expression

$$Q = Q_0 \cdot e^{-\alpha t} \qquad (1)$$

there are two parameters Q_0, the outflow at the beginning of the validity of the equation, and the coefficient of decrease of α. For a certain case and situation, the equation of the decreasing water resources or the equation of the drainage curve can be concretized by determining the values of the parameters. The values Q, t for two outflow events in the solved case are inserted into the equation converted to a logarithmic form. By solving a system of two linear equations the values of both parameters are obtained. The concretized form of the drainage equation makes it possible to solve numerically many tasks.

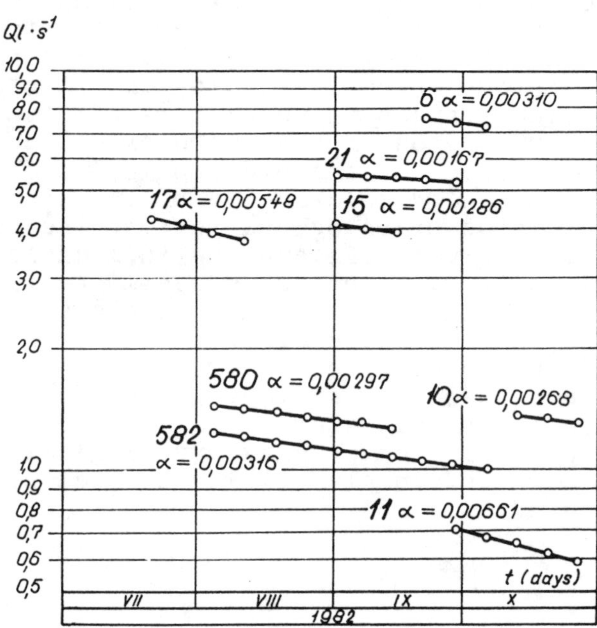

FIG. 1 Recession curves of springs.

In fig. 1, there are some recession curves presented in semilogarithmic plot for outflow of springs measured systematically in the studied area of the Cretaceous basin of Police nad Metují. The tab. 1 converts the group of values of parameters in their exponential equations, Q_0 and α. The inclination of the lines expressing the value of the coefficient of decrease α by means of the tangent is little different.

TABLE 1 Values of parameters

Spring	1982	Q_o	Q_t	t	α
		$l.s^{-1}$		days	
6	22. 9. - 6. 10.	7,54	7,22	14	0,00310
10	13.10. - 27. 10.	1,36	1,31	14	0,00268
11	29. 9. - 27. 10.	0,71	0,59	28	0,00661
15	1. 9. - 15. 9.	4,08	3,92	14	0,00286
17	21. 7. - 11. 8.	4,23	3,77	21	0,00548
21	1. 9. - 29. 9.	5,47	5,22	28	0,00167
580	4. 8. - 14. 9.	1,46	1,28	42	0,00297
582	4. 8. - 6. 10.	1,22	1,00	63	0,00316

It expreses a very similar hydrogeological quality of the aquifers in the watersheds of the springs. The difference of the Q_o indicates differences in the initial saturation in individual cases.

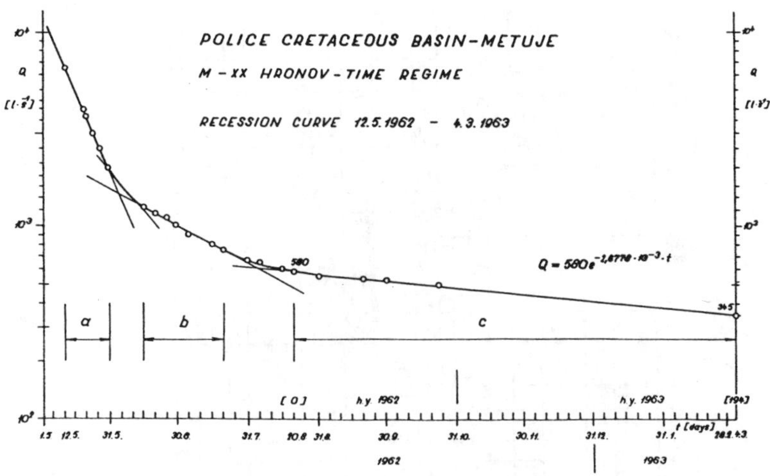

FIG. 2 Recession curve - M XX - Metuje.

In fig. 2, the drainage curve is presented in a semilogarithmic plot for the gaging station M - XX on the Metuje River at the closure of the Cretaceous Police Basin in Hronov for a period of low discharge. Of the three sections of the broken line, the lowermost abscissa pertains to the period of emptying the proper deep ground-water reservoirs in the pertinent part of the hydrogeological watershed. The evaluation of the exponential form concretizes the equation of the decrease of ground-water resources in the pertinent ground-water reservoir. It facilitates to solve numerous practical tasks. E.g. by integration of the equation in the limits $Q = Q_0$, $t = 1$ and $Q = 0$ at $t = \infty$, the total volume of the ground-water accumulation is expressed numerically. Forecasts data for certain time limits can be determined, etc.

From analyses of the time- related regime, a regular relation was established between the m - day values of the total outflow $Q_{(m)}$ and the m - day values $P_{(m)}$ of the pertinent excess of ground water, which were determined after separation of the outflow hydrograph, i.e. after separating the daily values P of ground water from the hydrograph of surface runoff Q. In a bilogarithmic plot, the correlation plot, the relation is reflected in the form of a broken line with three linked abscissas; the lowermost abscissa pertains to the genetic range of origin of the total outflow exclusively of the surplus of ground-water resources, the middle one to the mixed waters (mainly to the hypodermic outflow) and the uppermost abscissa represents the post-culmination outflow period. The regular relations have a form of an exponential function:

$$Q_{(m)} = a \cdot P_{(m)}^{\ b} \qquad (2)$$

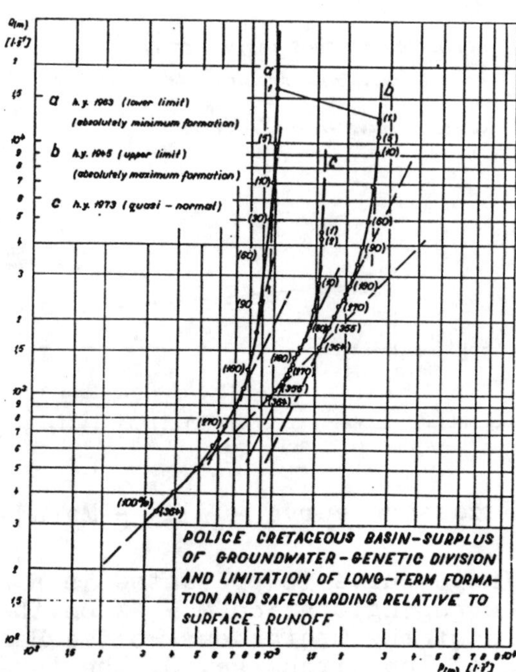

FIG. 3 Formation of outflow in the closing discharge profile M XX.

In fig. 3, the relations are plotted for the years with the lowest and highest formation of outflow in the closing discharge profile M - XX in Hronov;they are the limiting lines of the natural origin in both categories of the water resources in the Police-Basin in the long-time period of time, i.e. of the origin of the stream-bed flow Q under the influence of the contribution of ground water P, in m-day values. They limit a large field of natural posibilities for the forming of Q and P at different levels of the pertinent degree of security. Concrete data can be derived easily from the graphs. Both mentioned methods of evaluation of both components of the water resources evidently offer a possibility how to derive in a simple way reliable numerical data for deciding about the optimum use of water resources of the studied regions while respecting significant hydrological relations of both categories of water.

ANALYSIS OF THE SPACE-RELATED REGIME

The basis for solving the problems of space-related water regime is the line of successive discharges measured along the stream of the studied watershed in suitably situated gaging profiles. The successive discharges are related as ordinates either to the increasing length L of the stream on to the increasing area A of the partial watersheds pertaining to the individual discharge profiles, i.e. as

$$Q = f(L), \quad \text{or } Q = f(A) \qquad (3)$$

In complex watersheds with tributaries, the reduced values of outflow are considered after subtracting the successive values of inflow of tributaries, i.e. the values of the outflow of the proper watershed of the stream (with the area A_u), without the watershed areas pertinent to the tributaries (subsequently ΣA_p), i.e. the values Q_u.

The line of the successive discharges Q is the mass curve of the subsequent contributions of discharge occurring along the stream from its upper reaches to its mouth into the recipient of higher order. It is virtually an irregular analytically non definable line. Because of this, we deduce its derivative line, the contribution line P, by graphical derivation. The ordinates of the derivative contribution line P indicate the local value of the contribution to the discharge of the stream (positive in the case of outflow of ground water and negative in the case of leakege of water from the streambed into the ground).The intersections of the P-line with the axis of abscissas L are zero points in the section where the functional interval ends. The peaks and lows of the P-line express the culmination of the effect ($\pm P$) in the positive or negative interval of the stream which is limited by the zero points. They correspond to the points of inflexion on the Q-line. The zero points of the P-line correspond to the peaks and lows of the Q-line (the tangent of the Q-line there is horizontal, tg $\alpha = 0$). By numerical demarcating of the existence of the individual phenomena and of their effects, a detailed hydrological balance of the watershed with numerical positive and negative values in the delimitated functional intervals can be carried out in this way and sections significant for water development along the valley can be determined. The points of inflexion on the Q-line correspond to the intersections with tectonic lines with the stream; the same relates to the culminations of the P-line

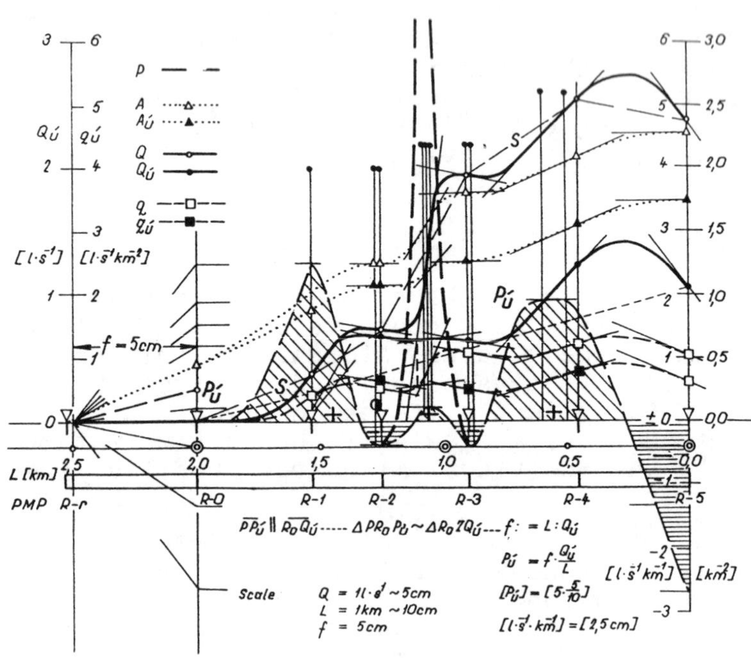

FIG. 4 Small stream Rohový potok -9.6.1982 - spatial regime

In fig. 4, a simple case of a small stream is solved. It deals with the creek Rohový potok, the left-hand tributary of the Adršpašský potok in the upper reaches of the Metuje River which is short and has a small waterhed area (L = 2 km, A = 2 km^2); an example of calculating the scale for the values of contributions P (l.s^{-1}. km^{-1}) is given.

A very interesting case of the space regime is that in the Teplice outflow district. Here in the about 500 m long reach of the river Metuje, the increase of the river flow attains 240 l.s^{-1}. From this amount, 130 l.s^{-1} come from the Jezírko spring area within a river section only 300 m long. The basic yield of the spring area itself is about 60 l.s^{-1}. The graphic method provides a precise localization and the value of the effects of hydrotectonics which have been verified by hydrogeological logging and thermometry.

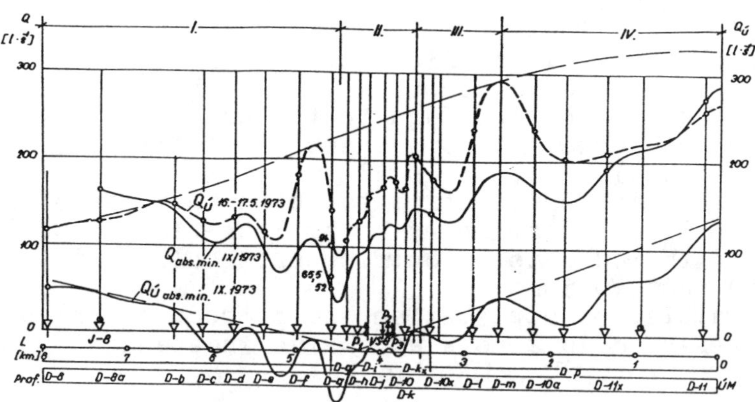

FIG. 5 Dřevíč discharge area - spatial regime (Q_u = f (L))

In fig. 5, the graphical solution of the space-related regime at the Dřevíč Creek, a right - hand tributary of Metuje is given by analysis of lines of reduced outflows Q_u, in the section Stárkov - Hronov. The lines are valid for two intervals, partly for the time with a higher discharge on 16. 5. 1973, partly for the time of the absolute discharge minima in September 1973. The outflow line during the low-discharge intervals proves an especially high negative effect of the fault tectonics. The generally declining tendency of the origin of outflow in the upper part of the river section is changed for a generally rising tendency in the lower part. It follows, that if there were not the right-hand tributary at the beginning of the mentioned section at Stárkov (already from the Permocarboniferous formation), the streambed of Dřevíč between Stárkov and the Dřevíček Mill in the middle of the section would be left without any discharge during periodic dry intervals. The discharge would renew only in the lower half of the section due to the contribution of ground water, beginning with the Dřevíček spring area with a stable yield of about 80 $l.s^{-1}$. The conclusions of solution show the significance of the tributary Jívka for the hydrogeological conditions at the Dřevíček - spring water - supply area and indicate the necessity to ensure the existence of the contribution of the Jívka tributary at Stárkov. This should eliminate the endangering of the hydrogeological conditions in regard of capacity as well as of quality of ground water due to hydrostatic relations between the surface and underground net of outflow lines.

CONCLUSIONS

Appropriate analyses of time and space-related regime of ground water scientifically justified and based on reliable input data (collections of outflow data) show in practical application reliable results of solution even in complex cases. In this short report, the principles of the method could be presented which are based on new approaches which are adequate to the complexity of the solved problems, and some examples of illustrative simple quantitative solutions could be given.

The method can contribute to further research as well as to application by using long-time as well as newly gathered sets of outflow data collected in numerous institutions.

Examples of application and methodological details are presented in a more extensive independent publication (Anton et al., in press).

REFERENCE

Anton, Z., Sarga, K., Slepička, F.
Moderní hydrologické metody pro hydrogeologické testování a bilancování. MON, Praha (in press)

Hydrology in Mountainous Regions. I - Hydrological Measurements; the Water Cycle
(Proceedings of two Lausanne Symposia, August 1990). IAHS Publ. no. 193, 1990.

Factors controlling the spatial variability of direct annual runoff as a percentage of total runoff

L.SOLIN
Institute of Geography, Slovak Academy of Sciences,
Stefanikova 49, 814 73 Bratislava, Czechoslovakia

ABSTRACT The paper deals with the quantitative expression of the dependence of the annual percentage values direct runoff of total runoff on selected 10 catchment characteristics. The results attained with the help of linear multiple correlation and regression analysis are further tested by comparing the testing values F with the table values of the F distribution. The logic justification of the dependence ascertained was judged in the light of the general knowledge of the runoff process.

INTRODUCTION

The spatial variability of hydrological characteristics of surface streams has been declared for decades primarily to the spatial variability of the climate Kolacek (1925), Lvovich (1946), Parde (1946), Dub (1954). More thorough research and new konwledge gained have gradually given rise to the view that, in addition to climate, other components of the landscape also exert an important effect upon runoff depth: the relief, the soil, the substrate, the vegetation and man who alters these landscape elements with his activity.

The classic geographic approach to elucidating spatial variability of hydrological characteristics is based upon the mutual comparison of their values in a priori separated physical geographic regions and upon Horton's runoff conception. Under the complexity of the interrelations, the basic assumption that different values of selected hydrological characteristics tally with different physical geographic regions, is not always confirmed. In many cases an equal value of hydrological characteristics tallies with different physical geographic regions or one type of physical geographic region may acquire different values of a selected hydrological characteristics Sopper & Lull (1965), Tarabek <u>et al</u>. (1984).

Another mode of elucidating spatial variability of hydrological characteristics is based on the exact analysis of the measure of their dependence on the individual basin characteristics. However not all basin characteristics affecting the degree of dependence are measurable, or is their effect sufficiently scientifically clarified. Hence their selection is mostly limited to those landscape element characteristics that are to be easily ascertained from accessible maps Woodruf & Hewlett (1970), Acreman (1965).

An exact spatial analysis of the variability of hydrological characteristics apart from expressing the degree of their dependence on basin characteristics may also be based on the clustering of catchments on the basis of an exact expression of similarity or congruence degree of both the hydrological and basins characteristics respectively Mosley (1981), Acreman & Sinclair (1986).

This paper aims at attemting to elucidate the spatial variability of hydrological response which is expressed as annual percentage direct runoff of total runoff on the territory of Slovakia (49 000 km^2) on the basis of the exact expression and analysis of its dependence on selected basin characteristics.

ANALYTICAL PROCEDURE

To estimate the annual value of hydrological response characteristic it is necessary to determine in addition to the annual absolute total runoff depth, the direct runoff depth as well. Its size was estimated from the underlying analysis of flood wave hydrographs in terms of the formula

$$RD = \frac{\sum_{j=1}^{k} \sum_{i=1}^{n} Q_i - \frac{Q_{oj} + Q_{nj}}{2}}{A} \; 86,4 \qquad (1)$$

in which

RD annual direct runoff depth (mm)

Q_o streamflow value in which the flood wave begins ($m\ s^{-1}$)

Q_n streamflow value in which the flood wave ends ($m\ s^{-1}$)

Q_i streamflow value in the i-th day of flood wave duration ($m\ s^{-1}$)

i 1,2,3,...,n number of days in which the flood wave lasted

j 1,2,3,...,k number of flood waves in hydrological year

A basin area (km^2)

86,4 conversion constant arisen after rearranging the formula in order to have the RD value indicated in mm.

Such point on the recession limb of the hydrograph has been chosen for the termination point of the flood wave (Q_n) from which the difference between the values of mean daily streamflows acquires an approximately constant character.

The dependence of the hydrological response characteristic has been expressed and analysed on the following basin characteristics:

(a) basin area (km^2)

(b) maximal altitude above sea level (m)

(c) mean altitude above sea level (m)

(d) relative basin altitude (m). Difference between the maximal altitude above sea level of the basin and the above sea altitude of the water level recorder

(e) basin gradient. Ratio of relative basin altitude to the river valley length

(f) basin shape. Ratio of the basin area to the second power of the side of the square whose perimeter is equal to the basin area perimeter

(g) river network density ($km\ km^2$). Ratio of the blue line length to the basin area

(h) percent forest (%). Percentage of basin under forest cover
(i) precipitation depth (mm). In those basins in which there were more rain recorders and their distribution hitting off the altitude range of the basin well, the precipitation depth for corresponding period was determined as the average from these recordes. In basins with several rain recorders inadequtely distributed in terms of the altitude of the basin, the precipitation depth was determined from the recorder with the highest altitude above sea level. In basins with a single rain recorder, the precipitation depth within the basin was determined from the underlying depth measured by that recorder
(j) permeability of the soil-rock complex expressed by ordinals from 1 to 8 (1 least permeable, 8 most permeable). The basic sequence of order was determined by soil texture defined for the particular basins from underlying rock according to Saly (1962). The sequence was also influenced by mineral strength of soils, structure and porosity, similarly exibiting a strong bond with the rock. If the basin is heterogenous in terms of the soil-rock complex, its resultant value was estimated by weighted arithmetic mean.

The determination of the dependence degree annual percentage value direct runoff of total runoff on selected basin characteristics as well as of their combinations and the mathematical description of these dependences was carried out by the method of multiple correlation and regression analysis within the selected set of basins of two hierarchic levels. First within the set of 192 basins representing the variability of physical geographic conditions of Slovakia's entri territory, and subsequently within the frame of selected sets of basins representing four of the areally largest soil-rock complexes. The selection of basins subjected to analysis was made by intentional selection. Their size ranging from 1 to 200 km^2 and maximal altitude above sea level from 300 up to 2600 m.

The statistical significance of the identified dependences was analysed by testing the zero hypothesis: there is no dependence between the given hydrological response characteristic and selected basin characteristics, through the mutual comparison of the testing quantity F with the table values F distribution.

As a result of the catenation of cuases and effects the given hydrological response characteristic may exibit a similar degree of quantitative dependence upon several basin characteristics. Hence basin characteristics which refuted the zero hypothysis with a respectively 99% or 95% security, were further analysed with the help of the partial coefficients of the correlation. The logic evaluation of correlation dependences was similarly appraised from the underlying knowledge of the runoff process. Such an analysis aims at discerning the causal correlation dependence from pseudocorrelational one.

Only those basin characteristics are regarded as a fators of the spatial variability annual percentage value direct runoff of total runoff that refuted the zero hypothysis and their dependences are causal.

RESULTS AND DISCUSSION

Within the <u>first hierarchic level</u> the zero hypothesis was refuted for the 99% significance level by the permeability of soil-rock complex (correlation coefficient -0.73), the basin area (0.45), the precipitation depth (0.22) and by the mean basin gradient (-0.19). It followed from the appraisal of the trend of these dependences from the aspect of contemporary knowledge related to the runoff process and from results of analysing these dependences with the help of partial coefficients of correlation as well as that the dependence on the permeability of the soil-rock complex and on the precipitation depth is the causal one. The permeability of the soil-rock complex accounts for 53% and the precipitation depth for 5% out of the total scatter of of the annual percentage values direct of total runoff.

Relying upon the correctness of the statement that out of possible functions it is exactly the linear regressive function that optimally embodies the dependence between the characteristic expressing basin response and the basin characteristics, than those one which did not refute zero hypothesis are considered insignificant in terms of their influence upon the spatial variability of the annual percentage direct runoff of total runoff.

It follows from the presented analysis that the permeability of the soil-rock complex is the dominant factor of the spatial variability of the annual percentage value direct runoff of total runoff within the entri territory of Slovakia.

Within the <u>second hierarchic level</u> the effect of the dominant factor has been excluded and subsequent examination is focussed upon elucidating the spatial variability of the given hydrological response characteristic within the frame of four soil-rock complexes, namely the crystaline complex, flysch with the preponderance of clay soils, neovolcanites and limestones and dolomites which are most widespread areally on the territory of Slovakia. The crystaline soil-rock complex is represented by 39 basins, the flysch with preponderance of clay, soils 22, neovolcanites 23, and the soil-rock complex of limestones and dolomites by 24 basins.

Out of selected basin characteristics, it is the basin afforestation percentage which refutes the zero hypothesis in the crystaline soil-rock complex, and even this a 95% certainty only. The correlation coefficient has the value -0.36 and the corresponding equation of regression accounts for 13% out of the total scatter of the annual percentage direct runoff of total runoff. The analysis of the set basins within which the dependences are identified, points at the fact that the afforestration percentage is lower in basins with the a maximal altitude above sea level from 1700 to 2600 m. Thence follows that it is not the outcome of human intervention but the result of primarily climatic-soil conditions limiting the natural incidence of forest in above sea level altitudes exceeding 1600 m. Above that limit the zone with shallow and skeletal soils sets in, without tree and continuous shrub vegetation and the zone with a rocky glacial relief. These surfaces become active very quickly from the aspect of direct runoff formation and causing so a slight increase of annual percentage value direct runoff of total runoff.

Thence follows that the slight degree of the negative correlation dependence of the annual percentage direct runoff of total runoff on the afforestation percentage of the basin, is probably mediated by the attribute of the altitude above sea level the depth of deluvia.

In the soil-rock complex of flysch with the preponderance of claystones the zero hypothesis was not refuted with a 99% certainty by any of the selected basin characteristics. With a 95% certainty it was refuted by the precipitation depth and basin shape (the correlation coefficient having the values of 0.47 and 0.48 respectively), further by maximal altitude above sea level and the mean gradient of the basin (-0.50 and -0.43 respectively). Dependence on precipitation depth is a causal dependence because the greater the precipitation depth, the greater the probability of occurence direct runoff in view of the specific properties of clayey soils (swelling). This basin characteristic accounts for 22% out of total scatter of the annual percentage values direct runoff of total runoff. Also the dependence on the shape of the stream pattern, accouting for 23% of the total scatter of values, is similarly in agreement with the general knowledge relative to the runoff process. The more streched the basin is, the more elongate it is with a feather structured stream pattern, the lower is the share direct runoff of total runoff, and conversely, the more the basin shape gets closer to a square or circle with a fanwise stream pattern, the greater is the share direct runoff of total runoff. The cause lies in the different mode of flood waves cumulation. A negative trend of the dependence on the mean gradient of the basin is illogical from the aspect of the general knowledge about the runoff process. The expression of the dependence of the annual percentage value direct runoff of total runoff on the mean gradient of the basin, assuming the maximal altitude above sea level of the basin to be constant (the partial coefficient value of the correlation being -0.21) indicates that in case of a simple paired coefficient the dependence in question is mediated by the maximal altitude above sea level. The negative direction of the correlation dependence on the maximal altitude above sea level lacks logic justification either. The dependence is probably the outcome of a definite heterogenity of the selected basins in terms of the permeability of the soil-rock complex. It is the flysch-claystone soil-rock complex with a major admixture of sandstones that is bound to basins with a higher maximal altitude above sea level. As a result, in these basin areas the conditions are more favourable for enlarging the direct runoff depth that entails lower proportion values direct runoff of total runoff.

In the soil-rock complex of neovolcanites the zero hypothesis is rejected only by basin size with a 95% security. The moderate degree of positive correlation dependence indicated by the simple paired correlation coefficient (0.47) is in contrast to the general knowledge about the transformation of flood waves with the rising size of the basin. Since a subsequent analysis into this dependence, either with the help of partial coefficients of correlation, or by a more detailed analysis of the set of basins examined, did not reveal the possible causes of the dependence referred to, it is probable that this is the result of a random numerical congruence of both variables.

In the soil-rock complex of limestones and dolomites, the value of annual percentage direct runoff of total runoff exhibits only a very low degree of dependence on selected basin characteristics. The zero hypothesis has not been rejected, either with 99% or 95% certainty, by any of the basin characteristics. From the underlying results achieved it is thus impossible to draw serious conclusion about spatial variability of the annual percentage values direct runoff of total runoff in the given soil-rock complex.

ACKNOWLEDGEMENT I am indebted to S. Polacik for his assistance in statistic data processing.

REFERENCES

Acreman, M. C. (1985) Predicting the mean annual flood from basin characteristics in Scotland. Hydrol. Sci. J. 30 (1), 37-49.

Acreman, M. C. & Sinclair, C. D. (1986) Clasification of drainage basins according to their physical characteristics, an aplication for flood frequency analysis in Scotland. J. Hydrol. 84 ,365-380.

Dub, O. (1954) Vseobecna hydrologia Slovenska (General hydrology of Slovakia). SAV, Bratislava, CSFR.

Kolacek, F. (1925) System vodnych toku (System of rivers). Prir. Fakulta Brno, CSFR.

Lvovich, M. I. (1946) Elementy vodnogo rezima rek zemnogo sara. Gidromet, Leningrad.

Mosley, M. P. (1981) Delimitation of New Zealand hydrological regions. J. Hydrol. 49, 173-192.

Parde, M. (1955) Fleuves et rivers. Paris

Sopper, W. E. & Lull, H. W (1965) Stream flow characteristics of physiographic units in the Northeast. Wat. Resour. Res. 1 (1), 115-124

Tarabek, K., Mazur, E. & Porubsky, A. (1984) Stanovenie kriterii pre regionalizaciu povrchovych a podzemnych vod a vypracovanie map vo vybranych uzemnych celkoch na Slovensku (Criterions for regionalisation rivers and groundwaters, maps elaboration of. the selected regions in Slovakia). Sprava za kon. etapu 04, Geograf. ustav, Bratislava, CSFR.

Woodruf, J. F. & Hewlett, J. D. (1970) Predicting and maping the average hydrological response for the eastern United States. Wat. Resour. Res. 6 (5), 1312-1325.

Hydrology in Mountainous Regions. I - Hydrological Measurements; the Water Cycle (Proceedings of two Lausanne Symposia, August 1990). IAHS Publ. no. 193, 1990.

Estimation of monthly precipitation by geographical factors and meteorological variables

Keiichi Yamada
Department of Civil Engineering College of Engineering Hosei University Koganei Tokyo Japan

ABSTRACT For water resouces in Japan,it is very important to estimate spatial distribution of precipitation during winter months particulariy In mountainous areas where precipitation varies widely, due to both topographic and meteorologic conditions.
In this paper, the monthly precipitation data from 107 stations was analysed in Kinki District,Japan for the period of 1967-1982. During winter months NW or WNW winds are prevailing,along these directions three geographycal factors were measured; L is the distance between the coastal line and gauging station along wind direction, S is the land slope along this wind direction. E is the elevation above sea level at the station.
The mean precipitation amounts for each of the stations averaged over a period of time were related to these factors. From these considerations, it has been clarified that in the area L≦80km the mean precipitation amount is related to L and S, and in the area L>80km it is related to L and E. These facts were explained by meteorological aspects. Precipitation amounts for each month and station were multiple correlated with the independent variables of L and S in the area L≦80km, L and E in the area L>80km respectively. Except for some cases, high multiple correlation coefficients were obtained. Partial correlation coefficients were related to the mean temperature and mean wind velocity for each month, averaged over a area. From these generalized formulae for the estimation of monthly precipitation amount were developed.

INTRODUCTION

Winter(Dec.to Jan.)and summer(Jun. to Sept.)are the wet seasons in Japan. In winter, almost all of precipitation is due to snow falling,and the snow-melt runoff which occurs as a result lasts two to five months. Water resources for irrigation of paddy fields in spring and summer, and for municipal water use during summer peak, depend on the amount of winter precipitation. On the other hand,in winter NW or WNW monsoons are prevailing and spatial distribution of precipitation is strongly affected by the winter monsoons. It is the major factor in the climatical classification in Japan.
Due to the accumulation of heavy snow,especially in mountainous areas, obser-

vation of precipitation is very difficult as often we cannot be available to collect sufficient date from the mountainous areas.

As mentioned above,from the macroscopic view point,spatial distribution of precipitation is simple,but mean precipitation amounts for each month averaged over an area are varied, with wide ranges and spatial distribution patterns,which are changed year after year.

Many papers were presented about annual,monthly and daily precipitation distribution considering meteorological and topographical conditions. From these various geographycal factors were proposed. But these were not explained from a meteorological view point, the author investigated to estimate, spatial distribution of precipitation using geographycal factors, measured along prevailing wind direction.

This paper considers the meteorological mechanism of winter precipitation in Japan, and precipitation amounts for each of the months and stations were estimated from geographycal factors and meteorological variables.

METEOROLOGICAL ASPECTS OF WINTER PRECIPITATION IN JAPAN

In winter, due to the strongly developed Siberian High Pressure, cold dry air masses(about -20℃) flow into Japan with a NW or WNW wind direction. When the dry cold air crosses the Japan Sea,the lower part of the air mass is heated by the warm sea surface water (about 15℃) and a large amount of vapor is evaporated from the sea surface to dry air. Then warmed and wet air mass is drafted to the upper layer by convection. These processes are called "modification of air mass". When the wet and warmed air mass reaches the coastal line, strong convective precipitation is induced by even the small relief and friction of land surface. Flowing into the leeside, moist air becomes dry, and along this wind direction the precipitation amount decreases rapidly. When the air reaches mountainous areas precipitation is then affected by orography, and in the inland areas the lower part of air mass is very dry, so only in high elevation zones does precipitation occurs. These processes are shown in Fig.1.

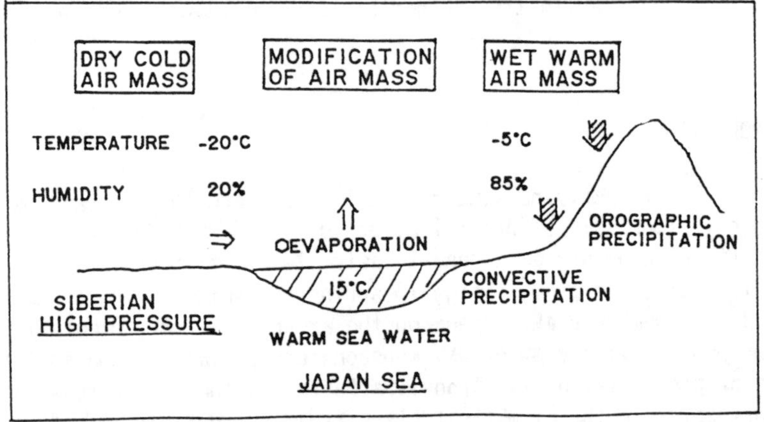

FIG.1 Meteorolgical aspects of winter precipitation in Japan.

MONTHLY PRECIPITATION AND GEOGRAPHYCAL FACTORS

Estimation of monthly precipitation amount is carrried out as follows.

1)To investigate macroscopic features,geographycal factors which can be considered to affect mean monthly precioitation amount over a period are selected by correlation analysis. This procedure is described in this chapter.

2)Considering basic relationship between mean monthly precipitation amount over a period and geographycal factors, monthly precipitation amounts are estimated by multiple correlation method with independent variables of geographycal factors selected 1). Obtained parameters are related to meteorological variables,then generalized fomulae are developed. This procedure is described in next chapter.

Monthly precipitation data in Kinki District from 107 stations for period of 1967 to 1982 are analysed(Fig.2).

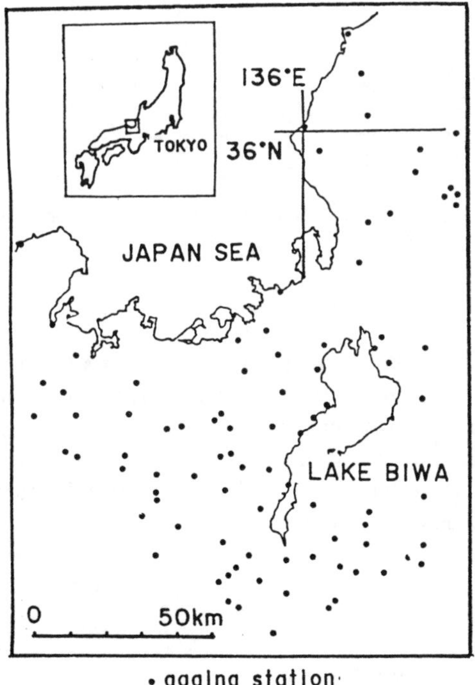

FIG. 2 Location map.

Geographycal factors measured along WNW direction are more highly correlated to mean monthly precipitation amount averaged over a period than those measured other directions. Three geographycal factors are selected which are strongly related to mean monthly precipitation amount and independent each other. These geographycal factors L,S and E are defined as follows.

L; distance from coastal line to station along WNW direction (km)

S; land slope (ΔH/Lo)。 ΔH is the difference in elevation between the station and point which is Lo on the windside of the station. Lo is unit length(5km). In cases where a ridge top is 500m higher than neigbouring valley,spill over zones are a setting 5km or10km behind the ridge top.

E; elevation above sea level of the station (m)

L is major factor which affects mean monthly precipitation amounts for each of the station averaged over a period and correlation coefficients are around - 0.8. Shown in Fig.3, the mean monthly precipitation amount is rapidly decreased with the increasing of L.

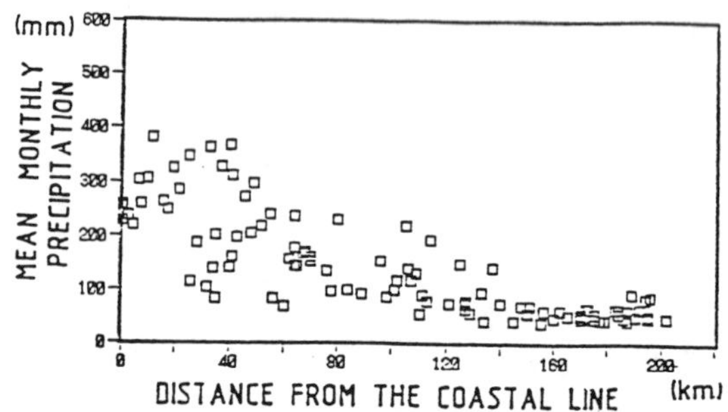

FIG. 3Mean Monthly precipitation and distance from the coastal line.

Listed at Table-1,S and E are not strongly related to mean monthly precipitation amounts compaired with L. But dividing this area into two areas by L, S and E get relatively high correlation coefficient.In the area L≦80km,mean monthly precipitation amounts are related to S, on the other hand in the area L>80km they are related to E. (Shown in Fig.4-5.9 These facts coincide with meteorological aspects mentioned above.

TABLE 1Correlation coefficients between mean monthly precipitation (Jan. and Dec.) and siope(S),elevation(E).

Area	Slope Jan.	Slope Dec.	Elevation Jan.	Elevation Dec.
Total Area	0.04	0.17	0.14	0.05
L≦80km	0.29	0.31	0.01	0.18
L>80km	0.09	0.10	0.36	0.39

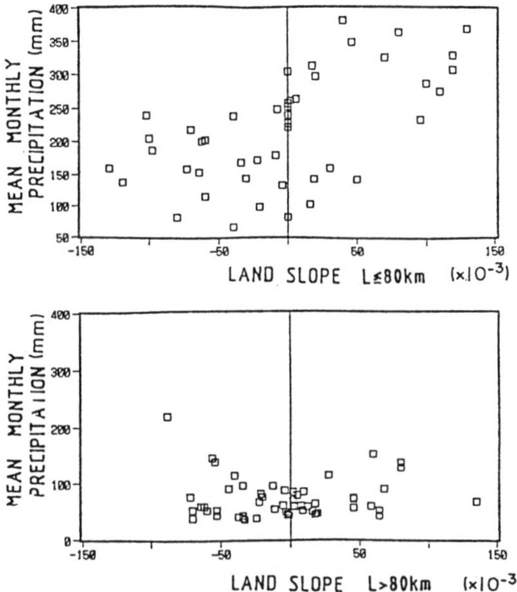

FIG. 4 Mean monthly precipitation (Jan.) and land slope.

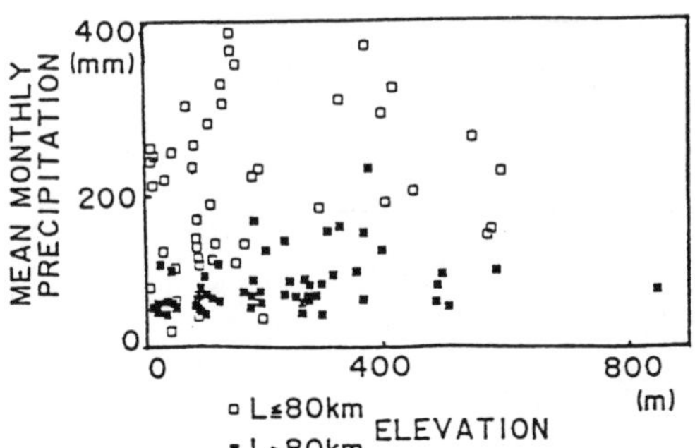

FIG. 5 Mean monthly precipitation (Jan.) and elevation.

MULTIPLE CORRELATION ANALYSIS USING GEOGRAPHYCAL FACTORS

According to the above investigation of macroscopic features, monthly precipitation amounts are analysed by the multiple correlation method with the independent variables of L,S(L≦80km) and L,E(L>80km), from these analyses we obtained following formulae.

$$R(L \leqq 80km) = \alpha L + \beta S + C \qquad (1)$$

$$R(L > 80km) = \alpha' L + \gamma E + C' \qquad (2)$$

where C and C' are constant vaiues.

Multiple correlation coefficients of these analyses are around 0.8 except a few cases which are not available sufficient data, but partial correlation coefficients are widely varied. Not only geographycal factors but also meteo/rological variables affect spatial distribution of precipitation amount. However,its mechanism is very complex,so it is not easy to evaluate a statistical relationship. If from a weather forecast for long periods we can get adequate meteorological variables and estimate spatial distribution of precipitation,it is very useful for water resources management. Then partial correlation coefficients for each month are plotted with mean temperature and mean wind velocity for each month averaged over an area.(Fig.6)

Much stronger WNW monsoons cause more moist air mass to flow into the area with decreasing of air temperature and increasing of instability of air column. Then convective precipitation is induced and mean monthly precipitation

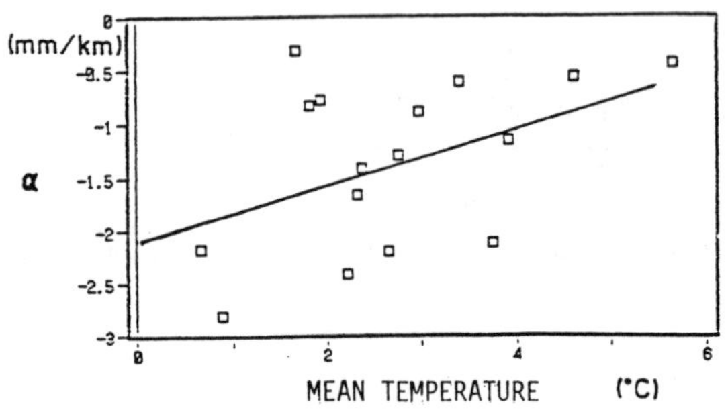

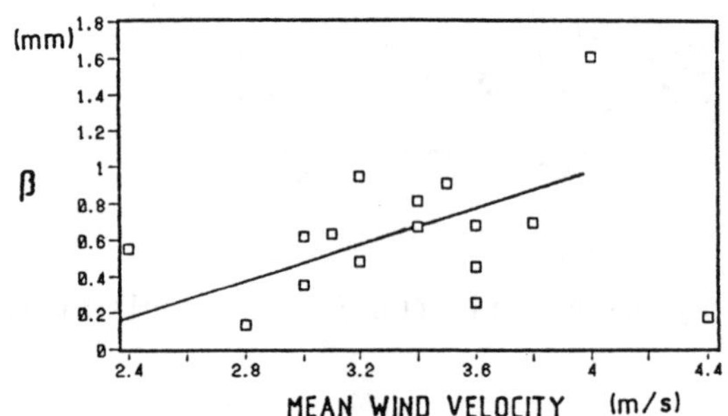

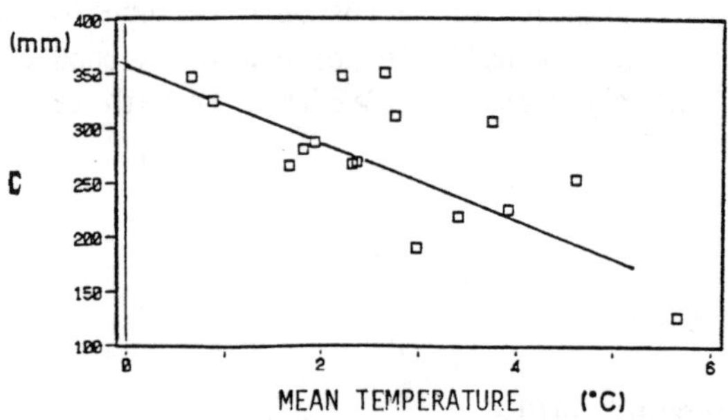

FIG.6 Parameters and meteorological variables.

is increased. From these consideration following facts are explained. "α" which indicates convective effect is related to mean temperature. "C" which depends on mean monthly precipitation averaged over an area is related to temperature. On the other hand, "β" which indicates orographic effects is related to wind velocity, "α'" is nearly 0.1α. "γ" and "C'" can be assumed 0.05,100 respectively. Considering these relationships we obtain following generalized formulae.

$$R=(0.234T-2.12)L+(0.12V+0.23)S+(362.0-32.6T) \quad \text{(Jan)} \quad L\leqq 80\text{km} \tag{3}$$

$$R=(0.357T-4.10)L+(0.87V-1.84)S+(426.6-25.6T) \quad \text{(Dec)} \quad L\leqq 80\text{km} \tag{4}$$

$$R=0.1\alpha L+0.05E+100 \quad (L>80\text{km}) \tag{5}$$

Results from these equations are shown in Fig.7.

As correlation cofficients between estimated value and observed values are around 0.85, these equations have a sufficient accuracy for a practical purpose. Shown in fig.8 ,estimated values are fitted with observed value at almost all of the stations, but at a few stations the differences of them are

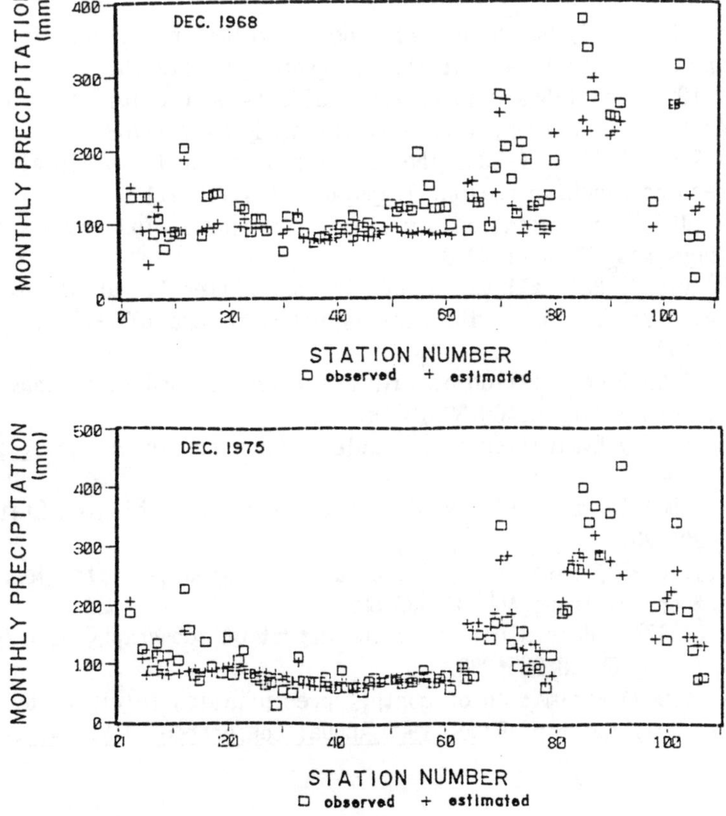

FIG.7 Results from these equations.

not small.At these stations, non-linear and two dimensional effects must be considered.

CONCLUSIONS

Three geographycal factors L,S snd E are selected which affect mean monthly winter precipitation amounts over a period in Kinki District,Japan. Dividing the investigated area by L,relationships between these factors and mean precipitation amounts are explained by meteorological aspects. Monthly precipitation amounts are analysed by the multiple correlation method with the independent variables of L,S(L≦80km) and L,E(L>80km),and partial correlaton coefficients are related to temperature and wind velocity. From these analyses,generalizd fomulae to estimate monthly precipitation amounts are developed. To extend this method,non-linear and two dimensional effects must be considered.

REFERENCES

Barrows,H. (1933) Precipitation and runoff and altitude relation for Connecticut river. Trans.AGU 396-405.

Bernardson, R. (1987) On the use of cross correlation analysis in studies of patterns of rainfall variability. J. Hydrol. 93 113-134.

Burns,J. (1953) Small-Scale topographic effects on precipitation distribution in San Dimas experinental forest. Trans.AGU 34 761-768.

Donley,D .& Mitchell,R. (1939) The relation of rainfall to elevation in the southern Appalachian region. Trans.AGU pt.4 710-721.

Hovind,E. (1965) Precipitation distribution around a windy mountain peak. J.Geophys.Res. 70 3271-3278.

Kutiel, H. (1987) Rainfall variations in the Galilee 1. Variations in the spatial distribution in the periods 1931-1960 and 1951-1980. J. Hydrol. 94 331-344.

Linsley,R. (1958) Correlation of rainfall intensity and topography in northern California. Trans.AGU 39 15-18.

Paulhus,J. (1953) Evaluation of probable maximum precipitation. Trans.AGU 34 701-708.

Small,R. (1966) Terrain effects of precipitation in Washington State. Weathewise 204-207.

Smallshaw,J. (1953) Some precipitation-altitude studies of the tennessee valley authority. Trans.AGU 34 583-588.

Spreen,C. (1947) A determination of the effect of topography upon precipitation. Trans.AGU 28 285-290.

Yamada, K. (1989) Estimation of monthly precipitation in winter by geographycal factors. Proc. 1989 Annual Conference, J.S.H.W.R, 167-170.

Hydrology in Mountainous Regions. I - Hydrological Measurements; the Water Cycle (Proceedings of two Lausanne Symposia, August 1990). IAHS Publ. no. 193, 1990.

Tracking rainfall impulses through progressively larger drainage basins in steep forested terrain

ROBERT R. ZIEMER & RAYMOND M. RICE
USDA Forest Service, Pacific Southwest Forest and Range Experiment Station, Arcata, California 95521, USA

ABSTRACT The precision of timing devices in modern electronic data loggers makes it possible to study the routing of water through small drainage basins having rapid responses to hydrologic impulses. Storm hyetographs were measured using digital tipping bucket raingauges and their routing was observed at headwater piezometers located mid-slope, above a swale, and near the swale. Downslope, flow was recorded from naturally occurring soil pipes draining the 0.8-ha swale. Progressing downstream from the swale, streamflow was measured at stations gauging nested basins of 16, 52, 156, 217, and 383 ha. Peak lag time significantly ($p = 0.035$) increased downstream. Peak unit area discharge decreased downstream, but the relationship was not statistically significant ($p = 0.456$).

INTRODUCTION

The processes involved in the delivery of rainfall from hillsides, to swales, and through progessively larger stream channels in steep forested watersheds are not fully understood. Most hydrologic concepts concerning the routing of flood hydrographs have developed from observations on large rivers. It is usually assumed that downstream hydrographs are lagged in time and flattened to produce later peaks and smaller unit area peak discharges (Chow, 1964). There are few reports of hydrograph routing in small, steep upland watersheds.

Researchers working in steep forested watersheds generally agree that classic Hortonian overland flow (Horton, 1933) rarely occurs because the infiltration rate of forest soils usually exceeds precipitation rates. Despite several studies conducted in the past 20 years, the pathways of routing rainfall into and through hillslope soils in forested basins remain poorly understood. The presently favored theory of subsurface drainage is that of an expanding and contracting saturated wedge--that is, during the course of a storm, the saturated zone expands up the soil profile from an area of permanent soil saturation at the base of a slope (Hewlett & Hibbert, 1967; Dunne, 1978). When rainfall infiltrates the surface, water is displaced downward into the saturated zone. Further upslope, the soil is drier and the distance to saturation is greater. Therefore, one would expect piezometric levels to rise earlier at the base of the slope.

However, the presence of large, non-Darcian macropores dramatically changes the manner in which precipitation is routed to a stream channel. Where piping occurs, the hydraulic conductivity of the soil matrix is of secondary concern for generating stormflow (Mosley, 1982; Tsukamoto et al., 1982; Ziemer & Albright, 1987). These subsurface conduits can transport water several orders of magnitude more quickly than the saturated hydraulic conductivity of the soil matrix. Saturation of the soil was thought to be necessary for water to flow through macropores and influence streamflow. However, Mosely (1982) and others have reported that large macropores permit rapid movement before the deficit in soil water storage is satisfied. These processes must be understood in order to predict the timing of water delivery from hillslopes to progressively larger streams.

THE STUDY AREA

Our study was conducted in the 483-ha drainage basin of the North Fork of Caspar Creek in northwestern California. The basin is located about 7 km from the Pacific Ocean at 39°22'N 123°43'W. The orientation of the watershed is southwest. Topographic development of the area is youthful, with uplifted marine terraces deeply incised by antecedent drainages. About 35% of the basin's slopes are less than 17° and 7% are steeper than 35°. The hillslopes are steepest near the stream channel and become more gentle near the broad rounded ridgetops. The elevation ranges from 37 to 320 m.

The soils in the North Fork basin are well-drained clay-loams, 1 to 2 m in depth, and are derived from Franciscan graywacke sandstone and weathered, coarse-grained shale of Cretaceous age. They have high hydraulic conductivities and subsurface stormflow is rapid, producing saturated areas of only limited extent and duration (Wosika, 1981).

The climate is typical of low-elevation watersheds on the central North American Pacific coast. Winters are mild and wet and summers are moderately warm and dry. About 90% of the average annual precipitation of 1200 mm falls during the months of October through April. Snow is rare and rainfall intensities low.

The watershed supports a 90- to 110-year-old second-growth forest composed of coast redwood (*Sequoia sempervirons* (D.Don) Endl.), Douglas-fir (*Pseudotsuga menziesii* (Mirb.) Franco), western hemlock (*Tsuga heterophylla* (Raf.) Sarg.), and grand fir (*Abies grandis* (Dougl. ex D.Don) Lindl.). The forest contains about 700 $m^3 ha^{-1}$ of stem wood.

OBJECTIVES

The purpose of our investigation was to verify that the commonly held assumptions concerning the routing of storm hydrographs were valid in a small, steep, forested watershed. Specifically, we investigated the lag of the start of storm runoff, its peak, and the time at which half of its volume had passed the gauging stations. This was facilitated by our ability to precisely synchronize the electronic instrumentation installed at our gauging sites. We also tested whether unit area peak discharge decreased downstream.

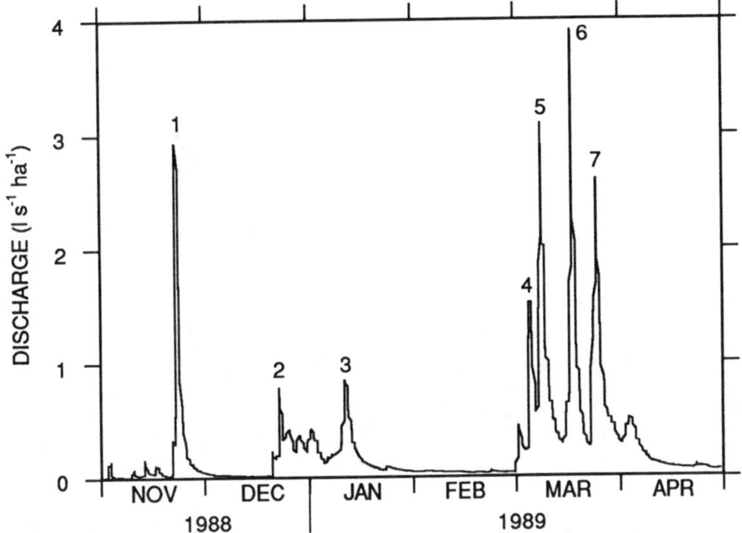

FIG. 1 Streamflow at station N during the winter of hydrologic year 1989. The 7 storms selected for analysis are numbered.

METHODS

Hydrologic year 1989 was a typical year at Caspar Creek. The basin received 1217 mm of rainfall. The seven storms that we analyzed produced peak flows in the 483-ha basin ranging from 0.8 l s^{-1} ha^{-1} to 3.5 l s^{-1} ha^{-1} (Fig. 1).

Measurements

Rainfall was measured using digital tipping bucket raingauges located at the bottom of the watershed near station N and on a ridge at the top of the watershed (Fig. 2). The raingauges were interrogated every 5 min. The watershed's response to precipitation was first monitored as a change in piezometric level measured using pressure transducers positioned in the bottom of three piezometers. They were located near the upper raingauge on a hillside approximately 6, 9, and 14 m upslope from the axis of a small swale. The transducers were interrogated every 15 min. Next, flow from three naturally occurring soil pipes was measured every 10 min. The pipes drained a 0.8-ha swale and were located about 100 m downhill from the piezometers. Downstream from the swale, streamflow was measured at 10-min intervals at gauging stations K, J, L, F, and A that monitor basins of 16, 52, 156, 217, and 383 ha, respectively. Discharge at the upper two stream gauging stations (K and J) was measured using Parshall (1953) flumes and the next three stations (L, F, and A) were individually-rated rectangular flumes. The internal electronic clocks of the data loggers at all stations are synchronized within a few seconds.

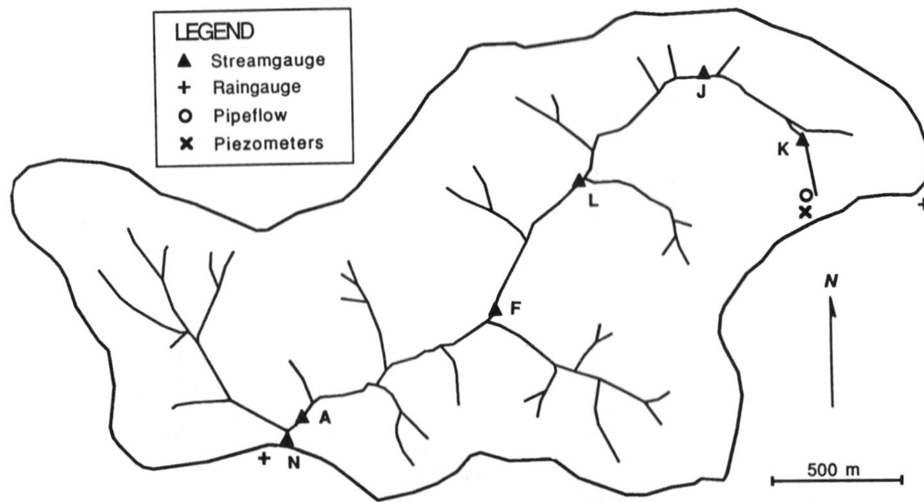

FIG. 2 The location of perennial streams, streamgauges, raingauges, pipeflow station, and piezometers within the North Fork Caspar Creek watershed.

Station N is located a short distance downstream from station A, but was not included in this analysis because a tributary that enters between stations N and A (Fig. 2), representing about 20% of the drainage area of station N, was clearcut logged in 1985 and 1986. We anticipated that logging might affect hydrograph transit time at station N relative to the unlogged areas, making its inclusion in our analyses inappropriate.

We used the mean length of the flow paths (MFP) of a station's tributaries (Fig. 2) as a measure of its location in the drainage network. This seemed to be an adequate surrogate for the time of concentration for the watershed above each streamgauge. For example, the value of MFP at streamgauge K is merely the length of the channel originating below the piping site (Fig. 2); MFP at station J is the average of the length of the K channel extended to J, the length of the channel originating northeast of K to J, and the length of the small channel joining the main channel just above J. MFP was highly correlated with the square root of the drainage area ($r^2 = 0.94$), a variable commonly used to estimate the size of flood peaks in a region (Jarvis, 1942; Izzard, 1954).

Antecedant precipitation

An antecedant precipitation index (API) "hyetograph" was constructed from each precipitation record. API at any time (i) was calculated as:

$$API_i = API_{i-1}\, c^t + P_i \quad (1)$$

where c is the decay constant characteristic of the particular recession, t is the time interval, and P_i is the precipitation that occurred during the ith interval of duration t. Using regression analysis, we determined that the best predictor of Caspar Creek peak discharge was a decay constant (c) equal to 0.9966 when 5-min precipitation intervals (t) were used. This is equivalent to a daily decay constant of 0.375.

The timing of rainfall at the lower end of the watershed was not very different from that at the top of the watershed. API peaked at the raingauge near station N an average of 7 min earlier than at the raingauge at the upper watershed near the piezometer site. This difference ranged from 0 to 20 min. The differences in rainfall timing were always more than an order of magnitude smaller than any computed streamflow lag times. Furthermore, these differences approximate the 5-min sampling interval of the raingauges. It is unlikely that there are any effects on streamflow timing due to such small differences in precipitation timing at the two raingauges. For convenience, therefore, lag times were computed from the headwaters raingauge only. The lag time was the difference between the time of peak API calculated at the headwaters raingauge and the time of the feature of interest on the hydrograph from each station.

RESULTS AND CONCLUSIONS

The dependent variables we tested were: the time of the start of rise of the storm hydrograph (SR), the time of the peak (Tp), the time

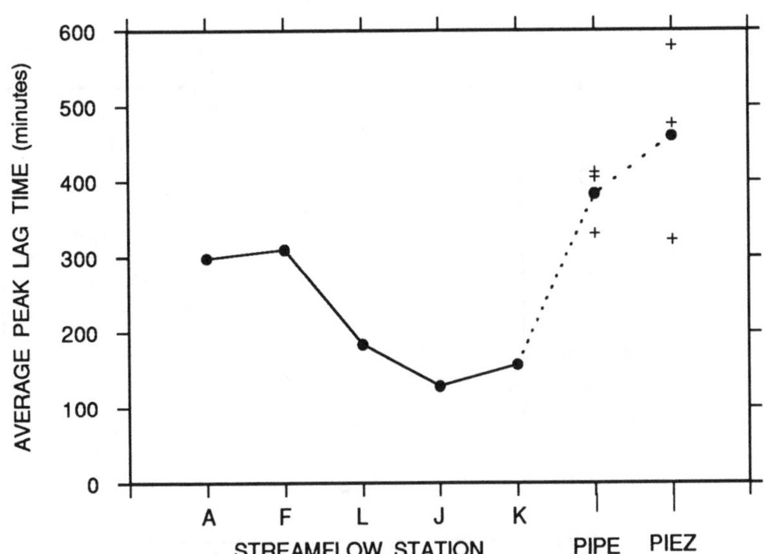

FIG. 3 The average difference between the time of peak antecedant precipitation and the time of peak streamflow, pipeflow, and piezometric level at each station from the bottom of the watershed (A) to the top (PIEZ). The (+) symbols mark the average lag times of individual soil pipes and piezometers. The line connects the average of the seven storms at each site.

when half of the volume of runoff had passed each gauging station (0.5Q), and the magnitude of the peak unit area discharge (Qp). Regression analysis was used to test the relationship between these variables and the mean length of the longest flow paths (MFP).

- Our data show that for streamflow routing, there is a generally increasing lag in the time of the peak downstream (Fig. 3). However, streamflow peaks at even the farthest downstream station (A) arrived earlier than pipeflow peaks in a headwater swale, and the peaking of piezometric level on hillsides is delayed further.

  Pipeflow is delivered by capturing the groundwater macropore flow and matrix flow. In addition, the roughness and sinuosity of the pipeflow channel is probably much greater than that of open channel streamflow. Consequently, the timing of peak pipeflow is retarded relative to that of streamflow.

  Lag times of peak piezometric levels were more delayed than that for pipeflow. A piezometer near the swale peaked 94 min later than the peak of pipeflow measured about 100 m downslope. A piezometer higher up the slope was delayed 197 min. A shallower piezometer even higher up the slope peaked 61 min earlier than the pipeflow. The rise of piezometric levels is a function of matrix infiltration rate, the soil depth, and the flow rate downslope. Much more time is required for water to move through the soil matrix to a restricting layer than is required for the turbulent, non-Darcian movement of water in subsurface soil pipes. Much more work needs to be done on the flow nets of subsurface water before we can make conclusions about the linkages between piezometric levels, pipeflow, and channel flow.

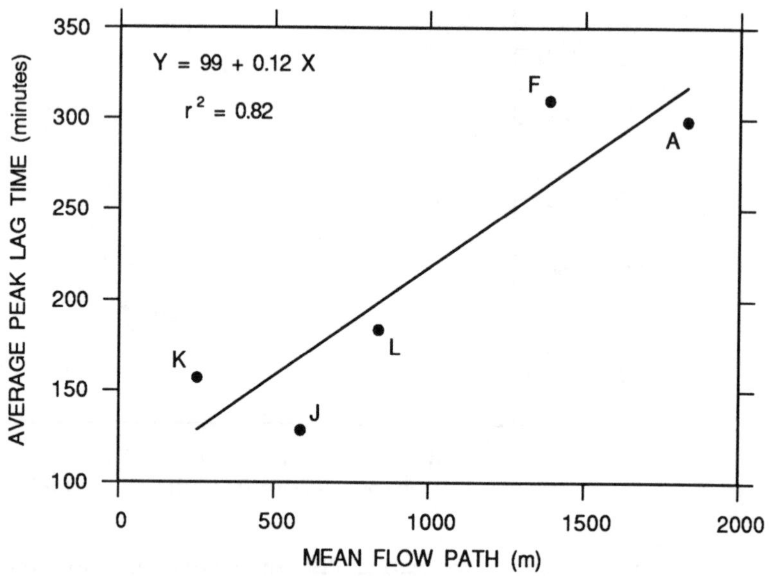

FIG. 4 Relationship between average lag time and mean flow path at the 6 streamgauges on the mainstem of North Fork Caspar Creek. Lag time is the difference between the time of peak antecedant precipitation and the time of peak streamflow.

- There is a significant positive relationship ($p = 0.035$) between average peak lag time (Tp) in the mainstem (stations K, J, L, F, and A) and MFP (Fig. 4). A smaller watershed with MFP = 250 m (such as station K) on average peaked about 155 min earlier than a larger watershed with MFP = 1800 m (such as station A). This follows conventional wisdom that it takes longer to route a peak through larger watersheds.

- There was a negative, but statistically insignificant ($p = 0.575$), relationship between the lag time of 0.5Q and MFP. This implies that the shape of the hydrograph was not shifted by drainage path length. Sendek (1985) reported that logging the South Fork did not influence 0.5Q lag time.

- There was no relationship ($p = 0.998$) between the lag time of start of rise (SR) and MFP. When the smallest storm is excluded, the relationship improved ($p = 0.457$), but was still insignificant.

- There was a negative, but statistically insignificant ($p = 0.456$), relationship between unit area peak discharge at the stream gauging stations and MFP (or square root of drainage area). Even if the relationship were significant, the decrease in unit area discharge would be much less than that predicted either by Jarvis (1942) or Izzard (1954).

Considering the above findings, it appears that the North Fork of Caspar Creek is behaving like a "small" watershed according to Chow's (1958) classification. That is, it is responding mainly to watershed conditions and fails to show channel storage effects.

The precision timing capabilities of modern data loggers provide a resolution that is a tiny fraction of the travel time of flow between even very closely spaced gauging stations. This capability allows various assumptions about the hydrologic responses of small steep basins to be tested. Our preliminary findings suggest that hydrologists concerned about small mountainous drainage basins should avail themselves of the capabilities of modern electronic instrumentation to determine how their basins are actually performing.

ACKNOWLEDGEMENTS The Caspar Creek studies are a suite of cooperative studies conducted jointly since 1962 by the USDA Forest Service, Pacific Southwest Research Station and the California Department of Forestry and Fire Protection on the Jackson Demonstration State Forest. The authors especially thank Peter Cafferata for his contribution to the piezometric study.

REFERENCES

Chow, V. T. (1958) Frequency analysis in small watershed hydrology. Agric. Engng 39 (4), 222-231.

Chow, V. T. (1964) Runoff. Section 14 in: Handbook of Applied Hydrology. McGraw-Hill, New York, USA.

Dunne, T. (1978) Field studies of hillslope flow processes. Chapter 7 in: Hillslope Hydrology (M.J. Kirkby, ed). John Wiley & Sons, London, UK.

Hewlett, J. D. & Hibbert, A. R. (1967) Factors affecting the response of small watersheds to precipitation in humid regions. In: Forest Hydrology (W. E. Sopper & H. W. Lull, eds), 275-290. Pergamon Press, Oxford, UK.

Horton, R. E. (1933) The role of infiltration in the hydrologic cycle. Trans. Amer. Geophys. Union 14, 446-460.

Izzard, C. F. (1954) Peak discharge for highway drainage design. Trans. Amer. Soc. Civil Engng, CXIX, 1005-1015.

Jarvis, C. S. (1942) Floods. Chapter XI-G in: Hydrology (O.E. Meinzer ed). McGraw-Hill, New York, USA.

Mosley, M. P. (1982) Subsurface flow velocities through selected forest soils, South Island, New Zealand. New Zealand J. Hydrol. 55, 65-92.

Parshall, R. L. (1953) Parshall flumes of large size. Colorado Agric. Exp. Sta. Bull. 426A. Colorado State Univ., Ft. Collins, Colorado, USA.

Sendek, K. H. (1985) Effects of timber harvesting on the lag time of Caspar Creek watershed. MS thesis, Humboldt State Univ., Arcata, California, USA.

Tsukamoto, Y., Ohta, T. & Nagochi, H. (1982) Hydrological and geomorphological studies of debris slides on forested hillslopes in Japan. In: Recent Developments in the Explanation and Prediction of Erosion and Sediment Yield. (Proc. Exeter Symp., July 1982), 89-98. IAHS Publ. no. 182.

Wosika, E. P. (1981) Hydrologic properties of one major and two minor soil series of the coast ranges of northern California. MS thesis, Humboldt State Univ., Arcata, California, USA.

Ziemer, R. R. & Albright, J. S. (1987) Subsurface pipeflow dynamics of north-coastal California swale systems. In: Erosion and Sedimentation in the Pacific Rim. (Proc. Corvallis Symp., August 1987), 71-80. IAHS Publ. no. 165.

Symposium on Quantitative and Qualitative Water Cycle Aspects in Heterogeneous Basins

Topic B:

Qualitative Space-Time Water Variability

Hydrology in Mountainous Regions. I - Hydrological Measurements; the Water Cycle
(Proceedings of two Lausanne Symposia, August 1990). IAHS Publ. no. 193, 1990.

Polycyclic aromatic hydrocarbons as pollutants of the aquatic environment in the Sudety Mts, southwestern Poland

T.BĄBELEK & J. GROCHMALICKA-MIKOŁAJCZYK
Department of Inorganic and Analytical Chemistry, Medical Academy, Grunwaldzka 6, 60-780, Poland

ABSTRACT Results of determination of the natural background concentration of PAH in aquatic environment of Sudety Mts. (South - West Poland) are presented.

Generally, 78 underground and 11 surface water sources in Sudety Mts. were selected for PAH analysis. In a period from 1983 to 1989 235 underground and 46 surface waters from this region were analysed.

Fourteen compounds of the polycyclic aromatic group have been found in the analysed waters. Different chemical composition of the analysed waters from different sources have been noted.

The highest concentration of PAH, according to the WHO standards, in underground waters does not exceed the total allowed amount of these compounds in drinking water. The determined natural background of six PAH in underground waters of Sudety Mts. is 60 - 160 ng/dm^3. The mean value for the same compounds in surface waters is 366 ng/dm^3.

The high level of PAH in surface waters and occasionally also in underground waters can result from the activity of industry localised in this region.

INTRODUCTION

Polycyclic aromatic hydrocarbons (PAH) are present in the environment from both natural and anthropogenic sources. As a group, they are widely distributed in the environment, having been detected in sediments, soils, air and various water sources. Some PAH, including benzo(a)pyrene - B(a)P, indeno(1,2,3-c,d)pyrene - IP and benzo(b)fluoranthene - B(b)F were shown cancerogenic both to animals and to man (Neff, 1979).
The level of PAH in surface water is influenced by industrial discharges. These compounds tend to accumulate in the aqueous environment. Investigational works on PAH in waters (Borneff & Kunte, 1969) have mainly been confined to six compounds (including B(a)P) which are relatively easily detected and can serve as indicators for the whole group.

Previous European and international standards for drinking water proposed a limit of 200 ng/dm^3 for the sum of six named indicator PAH in drinking water (WHO, 1971).

The concentration of the indicator PAH in different types of water were typically 10-50 ng/dm^3 in underground waters, 50-250 ng/dm^3 in relatively unpolluted river waters and higher in polluted rivers and effluents.

WHO in 1984 (WHO, 1984) based on the application of the linear multistage extrapolation model to the available toxicological data for B(a)P and taking account of the fact that this substance is associated in water with other PAH of known carcinogenity, a limit value at 10 ng/dm^3 for this compound was fixed.

Grochmalicka et all (1979) showed the appearance of six PAH in selected drinking waters in Poland. Studies by Bąbelek and Ciężkowski (1989) showed the necessity of analysis water samples from South-Western Poland for their PAH content.

Results of the analysis of PAH content in the underground waters in the Sudety region were some of the first, and therefore there were difficulties in interpreting them. The level of the natural background impurities was still unknown in the underground waters of that region. That was the reason why the studies were performed in the Sudety region. Basing on this results it was possible to determine the natural background concentration of PAH in underground waters of South - Western Poland.

EXPERIMENTAL PART

In a period from 1983 to 1989 235 underground and 46 surface waters samples from Sudety Mts. were analysed. Generally 78 underground and 11 surface water sources from this region were selected for PAH analysis (Fig.1).

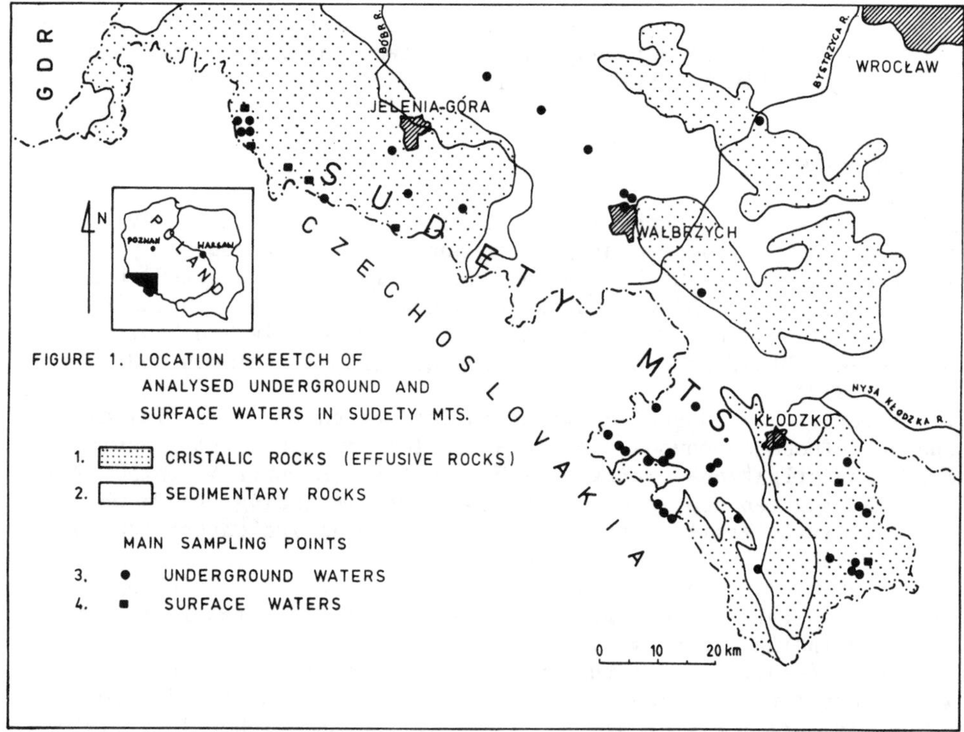

FIGURE 1. LOCATION SKEETCH OF ANALYSED UNDERGROUND AND SURFACE WATERS IN SUDETY MTS.

FIG. 1

Analysis of water samples consists of three stages:
(a) extraction with cyclohexane as a solvent and two dimensional thin-layer chromatographic separation
(b) qualitative analysis; spectrofluorometry at 77 K
(c) quantitative analysis; spectrofluorometry at room temperature.
The content of six representative PAH was determined (Table 1).

TABLE 1 PAH identified in underground and surface waters in the Sudety Mts.

Number	Name of compound	Abbreviation
1	Anthracene	An
2	Benzo(a)anthracene	B(a)A
3*	Benzo(b)fluoranthene	B(b)F
4	Benzo(j)fluoranthene	B(j)F
5*	Benzo(k)fluoranthene	B(k)F
6*	Benzo(a)pyrene	B(a)P
7	Benzo(e)pyrene	B(e)P
8*	Benzo(g,h,i)perylene	B(g,h,i)P
9	Coronene	COR
10	Dibenzo(a,h)anthracene	Db(a,h)A
11*	Fluoranthene	FL
12*	Indeno(1,2,3-c,d)pyrene	IP
13	Perylene	Per
14	Pyrene	Pyr

* Compound included in WHO Standards for Drinking Water (1971)

RESULTS AND DISCUSSION

Qualitative analysis of water samples after chromatographic separation revealed the presence of 14 compounds of the PAH group as shown in table 1. All of these compounds were present both in sources of analysed underground and surface waters. Different chemical composition of the analysed underground and surface waters from different sources have been noted. The growth of the number of identified compounds from 1983 to 1989 can suggest the progressive contamination of waters by the egzogenous hydrocarbons.The smallest number of the identified polycyclic compounds in one source was 5. Two hydrocarbons i.e. anthracene and benzo(a)pyrene were found in all analysed waters, but benzo(k)fluoranthene, benzo(g,h,i)perylene and indeno(1,2,3-c,d)pyrene were detected periodically. Benzo(e)pyrene, perylene, pyrene and coronene belong to compounds which were present in the smallest number of analysed sources. The presence of B(a)P (the most cancerogenic compound of the PAH group) in all analysed kinds of waters was very important.

TABLE 2 Content of 6 representative PAH and B(a)P in underground and surface waters in the Sudety Mts.

Analysed water	Number of analysed sources	Number of samples	The Sum of 6 PAH			B(a)P		
			ng/dm^3					
			min/max	$\bar{x}$	σ	min/max	$\bar{x}$	σ
Under-groud waters	78	235	52/444	162	79	1/22	8	4
Surface waters	11	46	96/1172	366	143	5/80	24	16

Table 2 shows the mean contents of B(a)P and the sum of 6 representative PAH determined in water samples from the period 1983 to 1989. The mean content of the analysed compounds was very high. The highest concentration of PAH was determined in surface waters.

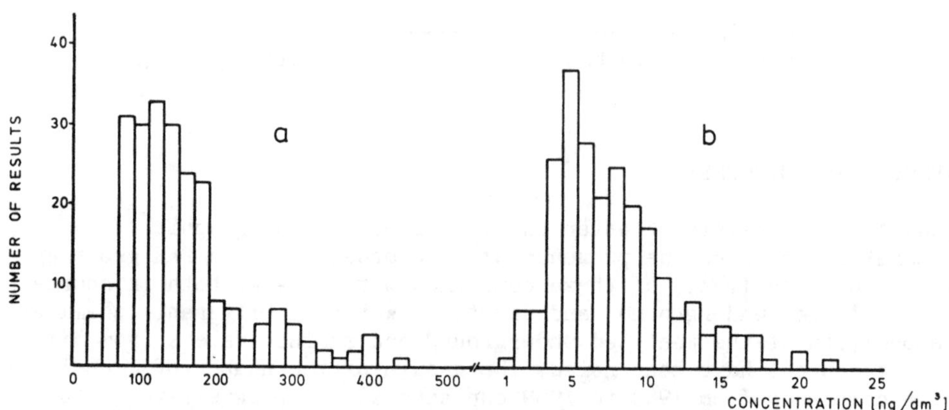

FIG. 2 Frequency distribution of B(a)P and 6 PAH content in underground waters in the Sudety Mts.
a - sum of 6 PAH b - B(a)P

According to WHO standards the total admissible amount of six typical hydrocarbons in drinking water is 200 ng/dm^3 and the concentration of B(a)P is allowed to be up to 10 ng/dm^3. The results of PAH determination in the underground waters in most cases do not exceed the mentioned values. However, there were sources in which the quantities of PAH were higher than the upper limit value. The mean content of the sum of PAH in underground waters was 162 ng/dm^3 and B(a)P 8 ng/dm^3. The same data for surface waters were 366 and 24 ng/dm^3.

On figure 2 the frequences of B(a)P and the sum of 6 PAH content in analysed underground waters are presented. Figure 3 shows the cumulative curves of the distribution of B(a)P and 6 PAH determined in the underground waters from Sudety region. Basing on these curves it was possible to determined the natural background of six representative PAH (60-160 ng/dm^3) and B(a)P (3-8 ng/dm^3) in underground waters from this region.

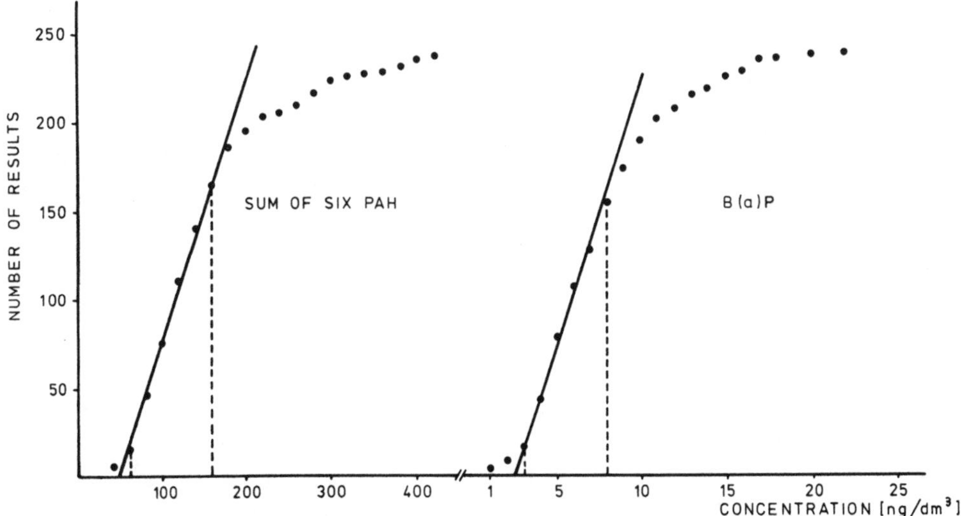

FIG. 3 Cumulative curves of the distribution of B(a)P and 6 PAH determination in underground waters in the Sudety Mts.

The high level of PAH in surface waters and also in underground waters in the Sudety Mts. can be connected with the activity of industry which is localized in this region. Results presented above showed the necessity of analysis of underground waters for their PAH content. PAH can serve as a sensitive indicators of underground water pollution.

REFERENCES

Bąbelek, T., Ciężkowski, W. (1989) Polycyclic aromatic hydrocarbons as an indicator of contamination of medicinal waters in the spas in the Sudetes mountains of South - Western Poland. Environ. Geol. Water Sci. 14 (2), 93-97.

Borneff, J. & Kunte, H. (1969) Kanzerogene Substanzen in Wasser und Boden. XXVI. Routinmethode zur bestimmung von polyzyclischen Aromaten im Wasser. Arch.Hyg. 153 (3), 220-229.

Grochmalicka-Mikołajczyk, J., Ochocka, J.R. & Lulek, J. (1979) Polycyclic aromatic hydrocarbons (PAH) in the municipal waters in the towns above 100.000 of population. Problemy Higieny 8, 125-136.

Neff, J.M. (1979) Polycyclic aromatic hydrocarbons in the aquatic environment. Sources, fates and biological effects. Applied Science Publishers, England.

World Health Organisation. (1971) International Standards for Drinking Water Quality, Geneva.

World Health Organisation. (1984) Guidelines for Drinking Water Quality, Geneva.

Hydrology in Mountainous Regions. I - Hydrological Measurements; the Water Cycle
(Proceedings of two Lausanne Symposia, August 1990). IAHS Publ. no. 193, 1990.

Hydrograph and chemograph separation of bulk meltwaters draining the upper Arolla Glacier, Valais, Switzerland

G. H. BROWN & M. TRANTER
Departments of Geography and Oceanography,
University, Southampton, SO9 5NH, UK

ABSTRACT A new method of the hydrograph separation of bulk meltwaters into englacial and subglacial components is examined. Diurnal bulk meltwater discharge, conductivity and calcium cycles in June and July demonstrate that the composition of the subglacial component is not constant, and is dissimilar to the season's highest recorded conductivity or calcium concentration.

INTRODUCTION

The separation of the hydrograph of Alpine glacial meltwaters into even two components is problematical, because of the dynamic nature of the hydroglacial system. There are likely to be seasonal variations in the distribution and efficiency of the drainage network and the seasonal variation in discharge is well documented (Rothlisberger and Lang, 1987). These factors effect the residence time of water within the hydroglacial system, and hence the chemical composition of the various components of bulk meltwater discharge are likely to vary throughout the season (Tranter and Raiswell, in prep). Collins (1978, 1979) suggested that the composition of bulk meltwaters can be explained by the mixing of two components. The first, the subglacial component, is concentrated and dominates bulk discharge at low flow, while the second, the englacial component, is dilute and dominates bulk discharge at high flow. Collins (1978, 1979) adopted a pragmatic approach to hydrograph separation based on conductivity determinations. He suggested that the composition of both components is constant, corresponding to the season's highest and lowest bulk meltwater values. In this paper, we compare this pragmatic approach with the results of a new method of hydrograph separation (Tranter and Raiswell, in prep).

STUDY AREA

Haut Glacier d'Arolla is located in the Val d'Herens, Valais, Switzerland (Fig.1.). The Haut Arolla basin comprises an area of 11.74 km^2 of which 6.33 km^2 (54%) is glacierized. A compound firn basin (max. elevation 3838 m) feeds the main ice tongue which terminates at 2560 m. The tributary Glacier de la Mitre joins the main ice tongue in

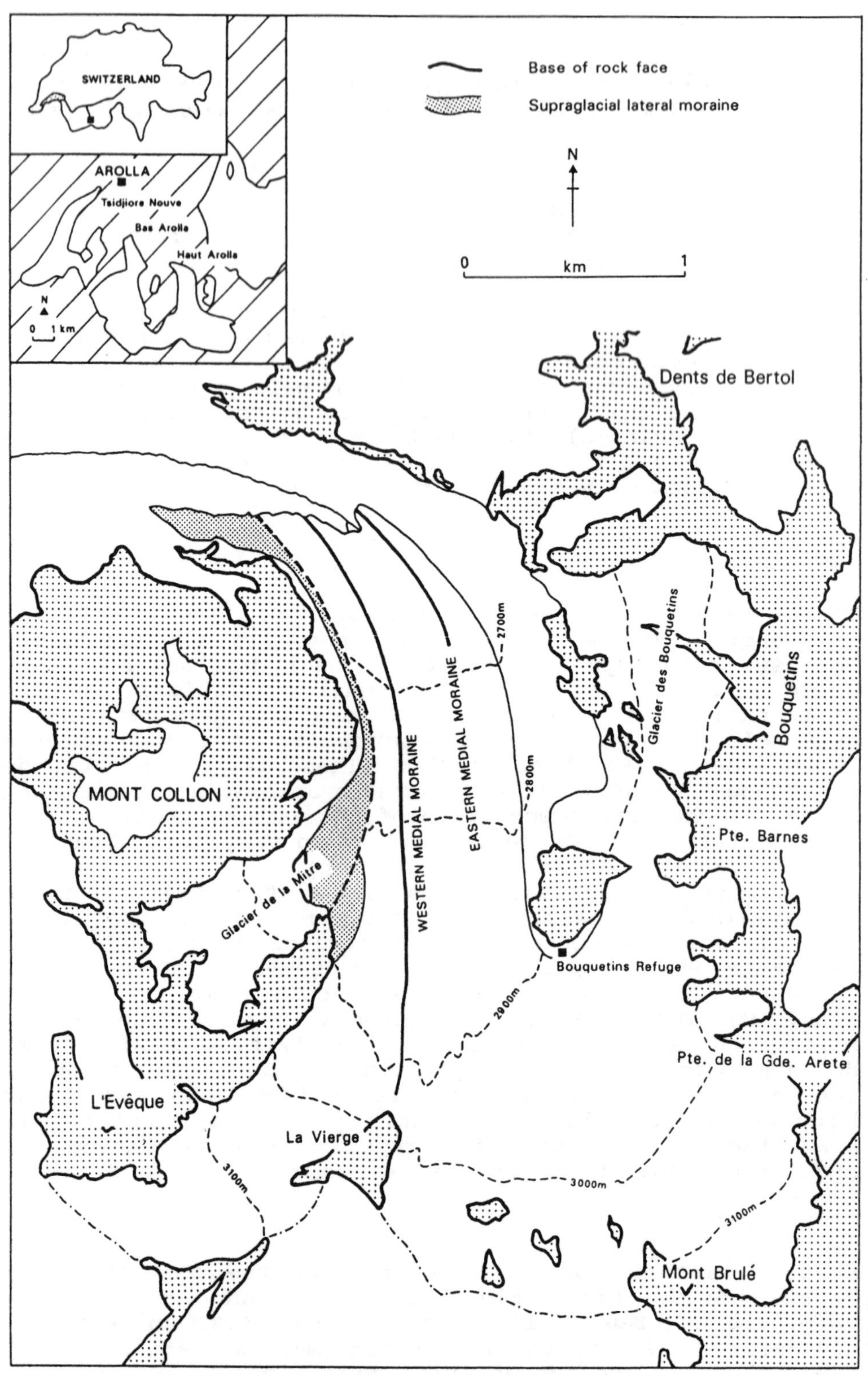

FIG. 1 The Haut Arolla catchment.

the west, though the compound Glacier de Bouquetins remains distinct and supplies meltwater and sediment only to the Haut Arolla system. Despite recent periods of advance by other glaciers in the area (eg. Tsidjiore Nouve and Bas Arolla), Haut Arolla has shown a marked contraction (520 m 1967 - 1977, 200 m 1977 - 1989). The catchment is underlain by schist and gneiss of the Arolla series. It forms part of the Grande Dixence, S.A. hydroelectric power scheme. Extraction of water is effected 950 m from the snout, downstream from the sampling site, which is located some 100 m from the snout.

METHODS

Sampling was undertaken hourly between consecutive minimum flow conditions, during two 24h periods in June and July. Samples were also collected near to minimum and maximum discharge on most days throughout the field season. Bulk meltwaters were filtered immediately through a 0.45 μm membrane, under vacuum, in a pre-washed apparatus and decanted into clean 60 ml plastic bottles. Samples for Ca^{2+} analysis were acidified with 1 ml of Analar HNO_3 in the field. Discharge data was obtained from Grande Dixence measurements taken at an intake structure approximately 1 km from the snout. The accuracy of the data is $\pm$ 4%. Conductivity values were continuously recorded at the sampling site using a pHOX 57 (Mk.2) meter with a resin carbon electrode probe (cell constant 1.0). Accuracy is $\pm$ 3%. Temperature compensation was not employed. The temperature of the bulk meltwaters was 0.7 $\pm$ 0.7 ^{o}C throughout the sampling season. Hence, since temperature correction is approximately 2% per degree, an error of $\pm$ 5% is associated with the measurements. Calcium concentrations were determined on a Pye-Unicam flame spectrometer (model SP9) with an air-acetylene flame. Accuracy was $\pm$ 5%, as determined by standard additions. Precision was also $\pm$ 5%.

RESULTS

The 24h cycles discussed here fit into a run of hydrochemical data that cover virtually the whole of the 1989 melt season for the Haut Arolla catchment. Seasonal traces for discharge, conductivity (representing total dissolved solids) and calcium (the major cation) are shown in Fig.2. Low early season discharge levels soon develop into a regular diurnal cycle showing the characteristic inverse relationship between discharge and solute concentration. The maximum amplitude of all three variables occurs in July which is characterised by a long period of uninterrupted diurnal cycles. Major disruptions to the pattern occur at 23/6, 02/7, and 30/8 when snowfall covered the glacier. The two diurnal cycles examined here are from 22nd - 23rd June and 17th - 18th July.

Maximum conductivity values and calcium concentrations occur at the start of the season, when values of 38 μS/cm

(a)

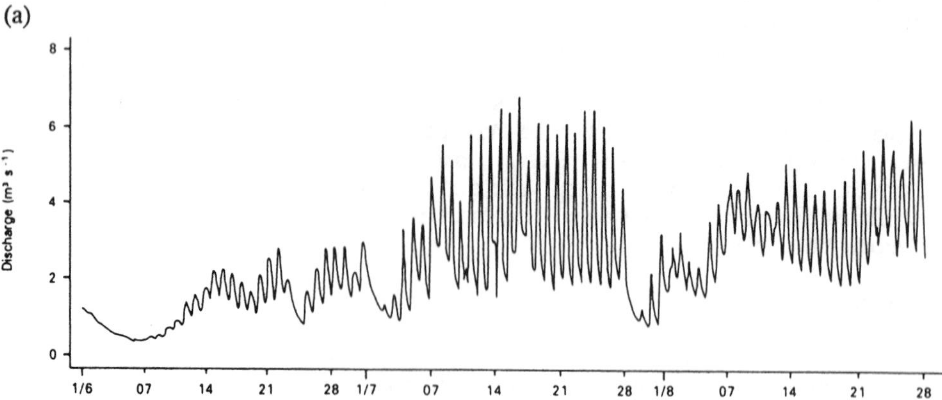

(b)

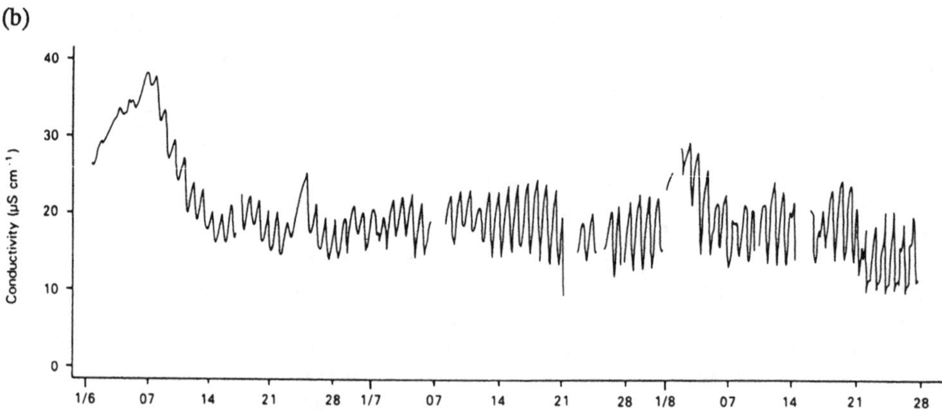

(c)

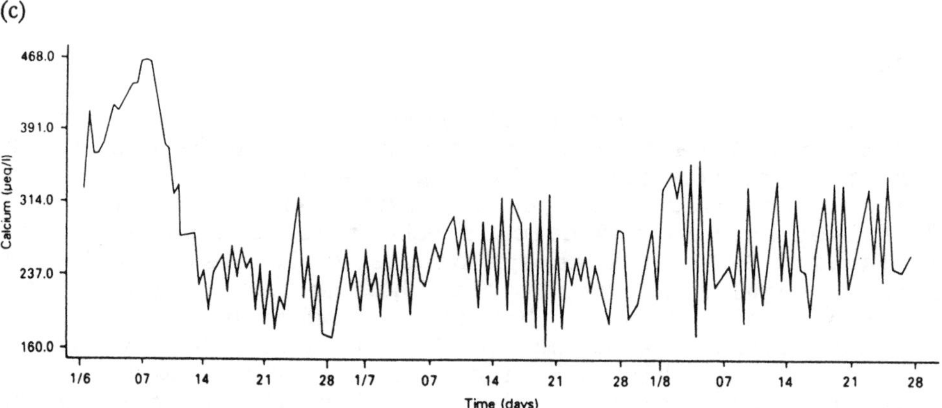

FIG. 2 Variations in (a) discharge, (b) conductivity and (c) calcium concentration throughout the 1989 ablation season.

and 470 μeq/l were recorded. Minimum values occur during July, when values of 10 μS/cm and 165 μeq/l were recorded.

DISCUSSION

Figure 3 shows that for each of the diurnal cycles sampled during June and July, calcium and conductivity show strong linear associations with discharge, which explain between 89% to 97% of the variance. This linear association can be exploited to find the composition of the subglacial component. We follow the method of Tranter and Raiswell (in prep).

Let Qb be the bulk discharge, and let Qs and Qe be the contribution to the bulk discharge of the subglacial and englacial components respectively. Let C denote the conductivity or calcium concentration of the bulk meltwater (b), subglacial (s) and englacial (e) component. Conservative mixing of the englacial and subglacial components requires that

$$\frac{Qe}{Qb} = \frac{(Cs - Cb)}{(Cs - Ce)} \qquad (1)$$

Since there is a linear association between Cb and Qb,

$$Cb = mQb + k \qquad (2)$$

where m and k are constants.

Substituting equation 2 into equation 1 and rearranging gives

$$\frac{Qe}{Qb} = \frac{- mQb + Cs - k}{(Cs - Ce)} \qquad (3)$$

We will assume that Cs and Ce are constants. Therefore, the bulk discharge, Qb, is a simple, linear measure of the mass fraction of the englacial component in the bulk meltwater, (Qe/Qb). The value of Cs is defined when the mass fraction of the englacial component is zero. Given this condition, from equation 3,

$$Qb = \frac{Cs - k}{m} \qquad (4)$$

Remembering that m is a negative value, Cs cannot be greater than k, since Qb cannot be a negative value. If Cs is less than k, this implies that at some value of Qb, let us say Qx, the discharge consists entirely of subglacial waters. At bulk discharge lower than Qx, the subglacial component must become more concentrated to satisfy equation 4. This

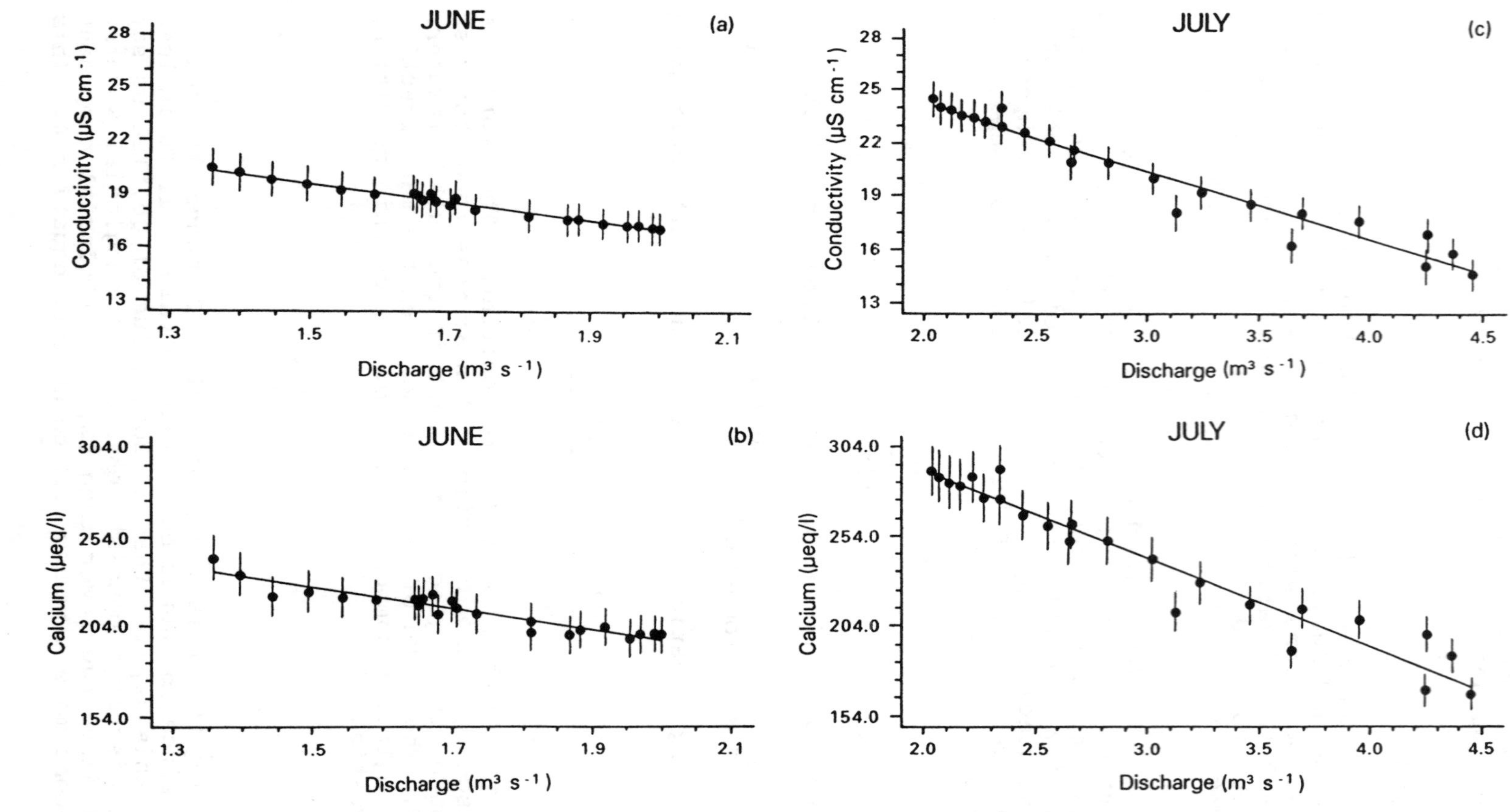

FIG. 3 Scatterplots of bulk meltwater conductivity or calcium and bulk meltwater discharge. Regression equations:

a) $C_b = -5.2 * Q_b + 27$ ($R = -0.987$, $n = 24$) c) $C_b = -3.8 * Q_b + 32$ ($R = -0.976$, $n = 23$)

b) $C_b = -58 * Q_b + 310$ ($R = -0.945$, $n = 24$) d) $C_b = -49 * Q_b + 390$ ($R = -0.969$, $n = 23$)

condition is not permissible given that we are assuming that the end-member compositions are constant. An alternative explanation is that if Cs is less than k, there must be a constant discharge of subglacial water of fixed composition. In other words, a third component. This is also not permissible in a two component mixing model. Hence, Cs must equal k.

Since Cs = k, the regression equations of Cb against Qb define the composition of the subglacial component. Fig. 3a and 3b show that for the June diurnal cycle, the conductivity and calcium concentration of the subglacial component is 27 μS/cm and 310 μeq/l respectively, while for July, Fig. 3c and 3d show that the values are 32 μS/cm and 390 μeq/l. The conductivity and calcium concentration of the subglacial component are clearly not constant, and the values are dissimilar to the maximum recorded values for the season.

Methods to define a unique composition for the englacial component are presently being explored. The englacial component is likely to have a composition bounded by the composition of supraglacial meltwaters and the season's minimum bulk meltwater values for much of the ablation season. We have separated the hydrograph assuming that the composition of the englacial component is 1) that of more concentrated supraglacial meltwaters (conductivity = 2.7 μS/cm; calcium = 16 μeq/l) and 2) that of the season's minimum recorded bulk meltwater values (conductivity = 10 μS/cm; calcium = 165 μeq/l). Fig. 4a and 4b illustrate the range of errors associated with the englacial component being poorly defined. Clearly, greatest discrepancies occur when the bulk meltwaters are dilute and approach the composition of the englacial component. This is clearly illustrated in Fig. 4b, a hydrograph separation for the July diurnal cycle based on calcium concentrations. By assuming that the composition of the englacial component is that of supraglacial water, rather similar discharge of each of the components at maximum bulk discharge is produced. By assuming that the englacial component has the season's lowest recorded calcium concentration of the bulk meltwaters, a much different separation is produced. In this case, the subglacial component is cut off at maximum discharge.

Hydrograph separations based on conductivity and calcium produce broadly similar patterns of hydrograph separation. However, the ratio of the values calculated or chosen for each of the components differs. Hence, the exact values for the discharge of each component varies. The best agreement between the calcium and conductivity based separation is for June, assuming that the composition of the englacial component is approximated by the composition of supraglacial waters. Regression analysis of Qe determined by calcium and conductivity values gives a slope of 1.06 and an intercept of 0.01. The correlation coefficient is 0.990. Perfect agreement between the different methods of hydrograph separation would produce a slope of 1.00 and an intercept of

(a)

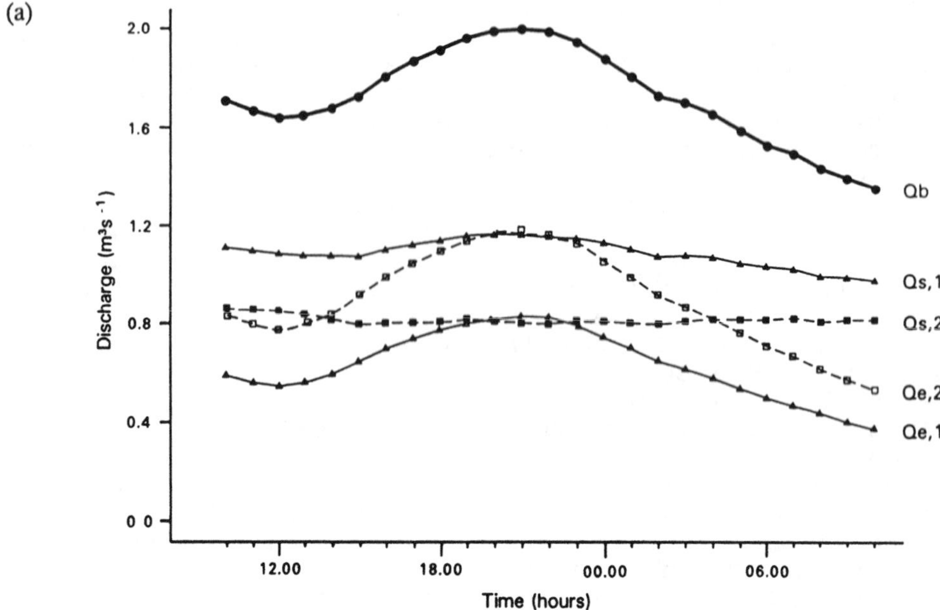

(b)

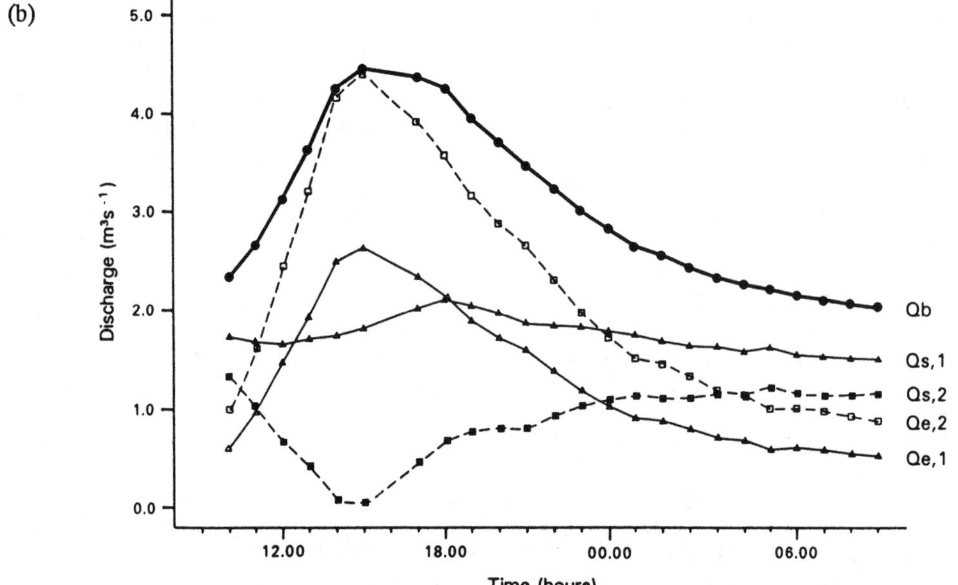

FIG. 4 Hydrograph separation of bulk meltwater discharge. Subscripts 1 and 2 denote the assumptions made in determining the composition of the englacial component (see text).
a) The June hydrograph, separated by conductivity values.
b) The July hydrograph, separated by calcium concentrations.

0.00.

CONCLUSIONS

The composition of subglacial waters may vary throughout the melt season. Their composition is therefore not best represented by the season's highest recorded values in bulk meltwaters. The composition of the englacial component must be determined accurately if the hydrograph separation of dilute bulk meltwaters is to be determined with confidence.

ACKNOWLEDGMENTS

This work is part of an integrated study of hydrology and water quality in glacierised catchments, conducted by the Departments of Geography at the Universities of Cambridge and Southampton. Mr. C. T. Hill is thanked for his efforts in the field, and Dr. A. M. Gurnell provided critical commentary on the manuscript. The work was sponsored by NERC Grant no. GR3/7004, and NERC studentship (GHB) no. GT4/88/AAPS/56.

REFERENCES

Collins, D. N. (1978) Hydrology of an Alpine glacier as indicated by the chemical composition of meltwater. Zeit. Glets. Glaz., Bd. 13 (1977), 219-238.
Collins, D. N. (1979) Quantitative determination of the subglacial hydrology of two Alpine glaciers. J. Glaciol., 23, 347-362.
Rothlisberger, H. & Lang, H. (1987) Glacial hydrology. Chapter 10 in: Glacio-fluvial sediment transfer, eds. A. M. Gurnell and M. J. Clark, John Wiley and Sons, Chichester.
Tranter, M., and Raiswell, R. (in prep) The composition of the englacial and subglacial component in bulk meltwaters draining the Gornergletscher. Submitted to J. Glaciol.

Hydrology in Mountainous Regions. I - Hydrological Measurements; the Water Cycle (Proceedings of two Lausanne Symposia, August 1990). IAHS Publ. no. 193, 1990.

Seasonal and annual variations of suspended sediment transport in meltwaters draining from an Alpine glacier

DAVID N. COLLINS
Alpine Glacier Project, Department of Geography, University of Manchester, Manchester M13 9PL, U.K.

ABSTRACT Suspended sediment content of meltwaters in the Gornera, draining from Gornergletscher, Pennine Alps, Switzerland, was determined at hourly intervals throughout the ablation seasons of 1983 through 1988 in order to assess year-to-year variability of sediment yield. Considerable variations in seasonal patterns of sediment flux and in annual total yield result from the incidence of periods of instability in the basal drainage system brought about during hydraulic integration at the initiation of the network in spring, as a result of temporary constrictions to flow in major subglacial arteries, by emptying of the ice-dammed Gornersee and by precipitation-enhanced high discharges. During these spatial instabilities, meltwaters gain access to areas of bed in which fine sediment has accumulated, and flush large quantities of suspended material to the portal. Annual sediment yield is influenced by the pattern of seasonal discharge and by the occurrence, scale, timing and order of spatial instabilities.

INTRODUCTION

Each year, following closure under ice overburden pressure during winter, the drainage system beneath an Alpine glacier becomes re-established as surface meltwaters penetrate the glacier subsole in spring and early summer. Initiation and subsequent evolution of the subglacial drainage network in an ablation season are influenced not only by seasonal patterns of hydrometeorological conditions in that year but also by the timing, magnitude and sequence of hydrological events during which large quantities of suspended sediment are evacuated from under the glacier to the portal in meltwater. Such events are indicative of sudden, one or several day, spatial instabilities of the basal hydrological passageways. Instabilities allow meltwaters to come into contact with areas of bed which have remained hydraulically-isolated from flowing meltwaters for a sufficiently long time for large quantities of glacially-eroded sediment to have accumulated (Collins 1989).

Year-to-year changes in seasonal pattern of suspended sediment transport in meltwaters and differences in annual total yields of fine sediment from Alpine glaciers might be expected to result from variations in spatial stability of the basal drainage net. Less sediment transport will occur in a year in which the subglacial drainage system develops to cover only a limited area of subsole and remains spatially-stable within that zone, than when the area of subsole integrated with meltwater flow progressively enlarges during an ablation season. Patterns of seasonal variations of discharge and suspended sediment transport in meltwaters draining from Gornergletscher, Pennine Alps, Switzerland, during the six summers 1983 through 1988, are examined in this study with a view to assessing year-to-year variability of sediment yield. Impacts of spatial stability of the subglacial hydrological system and of levels of discharge on evacuation of suspended sediment from beneath the glacier are evaluated.

MELTWATER-SEDIMENT INTERACTION BENEATH ALPINE GLACIERS

Glacial erosion processes will occur throughout the year, and debris will accumulate over all areas of bed in direct contact with sliding ice and become incorporated in the thin debris-rich basal ice layer. Small quantities of fine sediment are continually supplied to meltwaters during the ablation season through frictional melting of the basal ice layer above flowing threads of water and of the margins of passageways, allowing meltwater to move laterally onto stored basal sediment. Some sediment will be deformed into meltwaters at channel margins and glacier sliding will position further debris-rich basal ice over flowing meltwater and transfer ice-walled conduits onto unworked areas of bed.

Spatial instabilities suddenly inject much larger quantities of suspended sediment to meltwaters. In spring, pulses of suspended sediment in portal meltwaters are consistent with flushing of large areas of subsole as drainage is initiated (Collins 1988, 1989). These may relate to progressive simplification of a diffuse cavity drainage system to fewer, larger conduits, as suggested by Walder (1986), with sediment swept from fresh partial areas of bed in a series of episodes, which have been called spring events by Rothlisberger and Lang (1987). After the initial hydraulic integration of much of the bed, large quantities of sediment are acquired on only those occasions when meltwater penetration extends to further outlying areas of subsole. This can occur as a result of exceptional precipitation-enhanced discharge levels, ponding back of meltwater behind a blockage or constriction to flow in a major subglacial artery which raises water pressure, and drainage of marginal ice-dammed lakes. Otherwise in the later part of an ablation season meltwaters largely flow within the confines of areas of bed from which sediment has already been flushed. Sediment may be restocked in areas where inundation has been temporary. These areas may then be subject to subsequent purging.

MEASUREMENTS IN THE GORNERGLETSCHER BASIN

About 83.7 per cent of the area of 82 km^2 upstream of the gauging structure on the Gornera, the only proglacial stream emerging from Gornergletscher, is currently covered with permanent snow and ice. The gauge is located 0.75 km from the present terminus of the glacier. An ice-dammed marginal lake, Gornersee, forms in the apex of the junction between trunk Gornergletscher and tributary Grenzgletscher, at an axial distance of about 6 km from the portal (see Collins 1986).

TABLE 1 Mean summer air temperature at Saas Almagell and total discharge and suspended sediment transport in the Gornera 1983-1988.

Year	Saas Almagell	Gornera		
		27 June - 11 September		
	T_{5-9}	Q_{5-9}	Sediment yield	mean sediment concentration
	(°C)	(10^6 m^3)	(10^3 tonne)	(kg m^{-3})
1983	10.67	127.44	136.64	1.259
1984	8.62	99.10	88.99	1.050
1985	9.93	119.52	90.43	0.974
1986	10.56	135.50	94.98	0.949
1987	9.92	131.60	134.81	1.302
1988	10.17	133.08	79.91	0.748

Samples of meltwater were collected by a Manning automatic pumping sampler at the gauge, every hour, 24h day^{-1} throughout the six ablation seasons. The volume (between 110 and 300 ml) of each sample was measured, and the samples filtered through individually pre-weighed numbered Whatman No. 1 papers. Clean filter papers and those laden with sediment were dried at 105°C, and the quantity of sediment in a sample was determined gravimetrically to a precision of 1 mg, by subtraction of the original filter weight from the weight of sediment-laden filter. Suspended sediment flux was obtained as the product of sampled suspended sediment concentration and hourly average instantaneous discharge. Daily totals of suspended sediment load were calculated from the hourly suspended sediment flux values, except on days with fewer than 24 sediment samples when total load was estimated from the mean of the available values. The load data presented here are effectively suspended sediment flux at the position of the sampler-hose intake in the cross section of the river, and as such are only indicators of actual transport in the Gornera. Nevertheless, these homogeneous data allow interpretation of relative variations in sediment flux through time.

YEAR-TO-YEAR VARIATIONS OF RUNOFF AND SEDIMENT YIELD

Mean summer air temperature for the months of May through September (T_{5-9}) measured at Saas Almagell, about 16 km north of Gornergletscher, and at an elevation 400m lower than the snout, provides a crude index of relative energy availability between years for melting snow and ice (Table 1). 1983 ranked as the second warmest summer (after 1982) and 1988 third in the period since the record commenced in mid-1967. In contrast 1984 was the fourth coolest ablation season ($\bar{x}$ = 9.60°C). Total runoff from Gornergletscher between May and September was well above the 1970-1988 average (107.89 x $10^6 m^3$) in all years except 1984, reflecting annual precipitation as well as thermal energy characteristics.

Comparison of annual suspended sediment yields from Gornergletscher is complicated by length of measurement period varying between years and by missing data particularly in 1984 and 1985. Suspended sediment yield has therefore been computed for 77-day periods from 27 June to 11 September each year. Data have been estimated for those days on which sampling apparatus failed to operate satisfactorily, as the mean of the daily sediment transport on the three days before and the three days after the interruption. It should be noted that should hydrological events have occurred during the periods for which data have been approximated the suspended sediment yields given in Table 1 will under-estimate the true values. Similarly, the occurrence of events producing high sediment loads in the three days before/after missing data may lead to some over-estimation.

Considerable variation in suspended sediment yield arises from year to year (coefficient of variation = 0.22, $\bar{x}$ = 104.29 x 10^3 tonne). Substantially above average yields in 1983 and 1987 were accompanied by high but not the highest summer discharge totals. There is no simple relationship between total discharge and either suspended sediment yield or mean sediment concentration (sediment transport/discharge in the 77-day periods). This points to the importance of spatial stability of the basal drainage system and occurrence of hydrological events within each summer season.

SEASONAL PATTERNS OF DISCHARGE AND SUSPENDED SEDIMENT FLUX

Contrasting seasonal patterns of discharge in the years 1983-1988 result from the interaction of thermal conditions, solid and liquid precipitation events, and the drainage of the Gornersee (Fig. 1). Temporal fluctuations of suspended sediment flux can occur both related to discharge variations and also independent thereof. In 1983, flow in the Gornera increased suddenly between 7 and 10 July, followed by a rising trend to 1 August, after which warm dry conditions returned only between 10 and 16 August. Snowfall over the glacier from 10 September finally reduced flow. Throughout August and September 1983, the drainage system appears to have remained stable, maintaining only background levels of sediment flux. Two major drainage network instabilities during July account for 59 per cent of the total sediment transport. Between 8 and 10 July, much of the glacier bed appears to have undergone massive hydraulic re-organisation, a possible spring event. Maximum hourly discharge of the season was next exceeded on 18 July at the onset of the second event, and exceeded again each day to 23 July, the day with the season maximum sediment flux. Further increases in flow to 1 August failed to expand further the area of bed integrated with drainage.

Two major spatial instabilities resulted in sediment transport events in 1984, accounting for a large proportion of the relatively small annual suspended sediment load. Rising discharge to levels not reached since July 1983 from 8 to 14 July dramatically increased

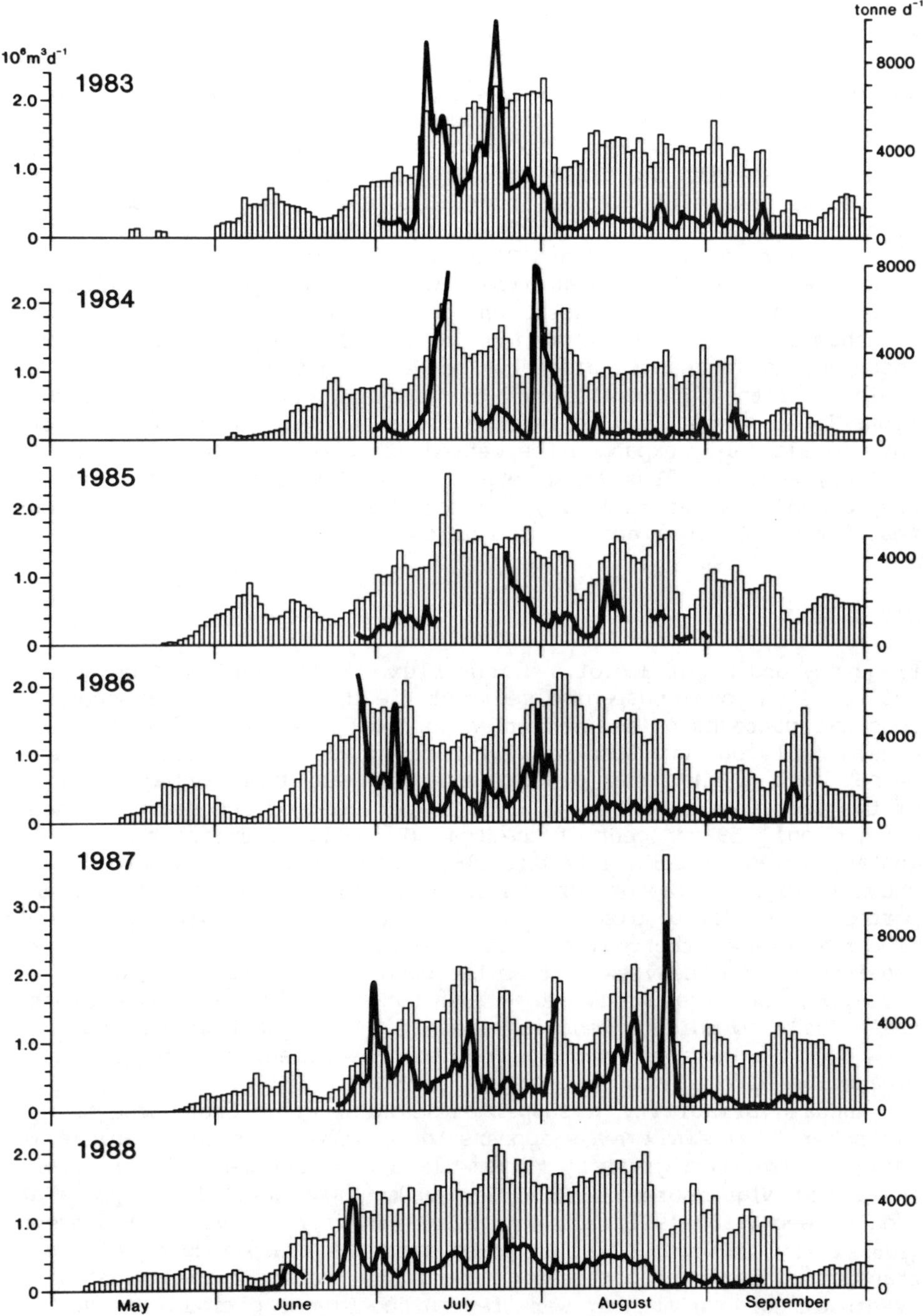

FIG. 1 Seasonal variation of daily total discharge of the Gornera (bars) and daily total suspended sediment transport by meltwaters in the Gornera (curves) between May and September in the years 1983 to 1988.

sediment flux. Although hourly average discharges remained lower than earlier in the season, a second event on 30-31 July 1984 probably resulted from temporary blockage of a subglacial drainage artery. In 1985, drainage of the Gornersee from 12-14 July produced the highest daily total discharges of the year, and since 1982, but no measurements of flux are available. Rising flows after snow in early August produced a small sediment flux response. A major spatial instability occurred also with the first rise of discharge of the season in late June 1986, but related to an arterial blockage, as discharge remained high throughout the night of 27-28 June. Events with no expression in runoff occurred also on 4 and 31 July. Meltwaters emptying from Gornersee on 23-24 July must have remained in the previously-flushed areas of subsole. Sediment-releasing events characterise 1987. The sequence comprises a major spring event on 30 June, followed by events accompanying increasing discharge between 5 and 7, and 14 and 16 July, drainage of the Gornersee from 2 to 4 August, unusually high overnight flows 16-18 August, and an intense storm on 24-25 August which must have considerably expanded the wetted subsole area (see Collins 1989). In 1988, sediment flux was generally low. The Gornersee drained unspectacularly before 4 July, and small flux events relate to partial restrictions to subglacial throughflow.

DISCUSSION

Frequency and magnitude of sediment flux events exert considerable influence on total suspended sediment yield from Gornergletscher. The seasonal patterns of sediment transport of 1983 and 1987 differ considerably but produced similar total yields. In 1983, by 2 August, 50 per cent of the total discharge had already transported 77 per cent of the load, but by 6 August 1987, 50 per cent of the discharge had carried only 59 per cent of the load (Fig. 2). The impact of instabilities in 1983, 1984 and 1986, independent of discharge, is shown in Fig. 2. The proportion of total annual sediment load transported leads that of discharge throughout every year with the exception of a few days at the beginning of a season. This observation is consistent with the view that as the subglacial drainage system develops, the first meltwaters flush out stored sediment from areas of the subsole to which access is possible. Later, meltwaters confined to flow in the same area are much reduced in sediment content, an exhaustion effect noted by Østrem (1975).

Annual variability of suspended sediment yield from Gornergletscher for the six years appears to be lower than for glaciers in Norway. From data given by Østrem (1975), coefficient of variation for 4 years at Nigardsbreen (1968-1971; 40 km^2) was 0.48; for 5 years at Erdalsbreen (1967-1971; 11 km^2) 0.34; and for 3 years at Engabreen (1969-1971; 39 km^2) 0.22. At these glaciers, rain-induced floods transported large proportions of the load, whereas rain-dominated events at Gornergletscher were few in the 6 year period. However, the highest flow of the period, in late August 1987, was rain-induced. The scale of that event may have been sufficient to flush such a wide area of subsole, late in the ablation season and so reducing the time available for debris production that no matter where on the bed the drainage system developed in 1988, little sediment would be available for removal in the spring events and other spatial instabilities.

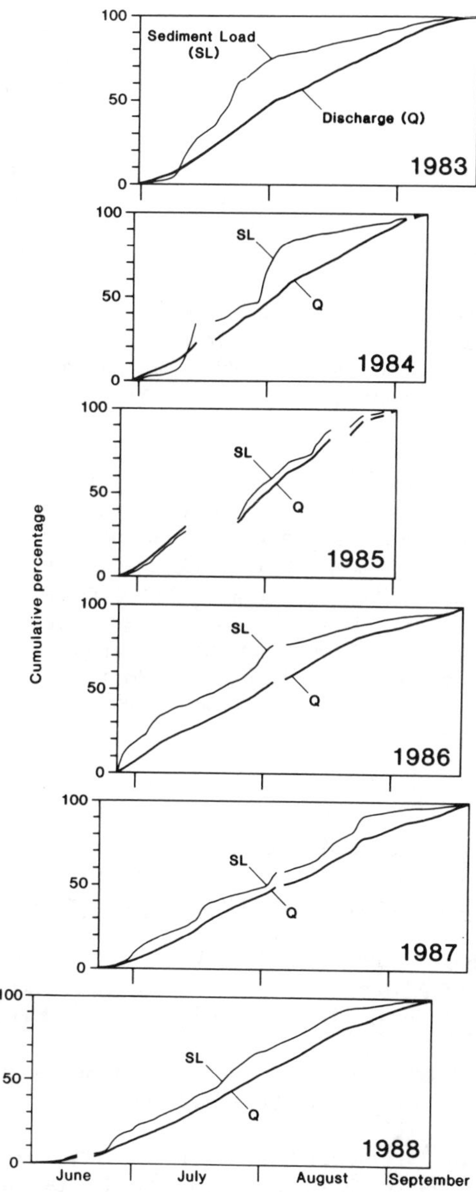

FIG. 2 Graphs for each of the years 1983 through 1988 of the cumulative percentages of the season totals of discharge (Q) and suspended sediment load (SL) of the Gornera which have passed the gauging station plotted by day through the measurement period. Where suspended sediment measurements are missing, the concurrent discharge has not been included in the accumulating runoff total.

CONCLUSION

There is no simple relationship between total annual discharge and suspended sediment yield in meltwaters draining from Gornergletscher. In an ablation season, spatial instabilities of the basal drainage network from time to time permit meltwater access to new areas of bed, from which sediment is flushed to the portal. In most years, largest instabilities occur during June, July or early August, after which background levels of sediment are transported. A large sediment transport event at the onset of an ablation season probably results from the initiation of a major conduit drainage system. Instabilities later in summer result from meltwaters spreading out over wider areas of bed during drainage of the Gornersee, when major conduits become partially blocked, ponding back water under the ice, and following large-magnitude rainfall events. The occurrence, scale, timing and order of events influencing the areal contact of the subsole drainage system determine annual sediment yield from an Alpine glacier.

ACKNOWLEDGEMENTS The assistance of A. Bezinge, A. Kronig, H. Kronig and J.-P. Perreten, Grande Dixence, S.A., with logistical support and in supplying discharge records, is gratefully acknowledged. Members of the University of Manchester Alpine Glacier Project assisted with collection of the samples. Schweizerische Meteorologische Zentralanstalt provided meteorological data. Grant support was received in 1983 and 1984 from the Natural Environment Research Council (GR3/4787) and in 1987 and 1988 from the Royal Society (Overseas Research Grants).

REFERENCES

Collins, D. N. (1986) Characteristics of meltwaters draining from the portal of an Alpine glacier during the emptying of a marginal ice-dammed lake. Mater. Glyatsiol. Issled. Khron. Obsuzhdeniya 58, 224-232.

Collins, D. N. (1988) Suspended sediment and solute delivery to meltwaters beneath an Alpine glacier. Eidg. Tech. Hochschule, Zurich, Versuchsanst. Wasserbau, Hydrol., Glazio. Mitt. 94, 147-161.

Collins, D. N. (1989) Seasonal development of subglacial drainage and suspended sediment delivery to meltwaters beneath an Alpine glacier. Ann. Glaciol. 13, 45-50.

Østrem, G. (1975) Sediment transport in glacial meltwater streams. In: Jopling, A. V. & McDonald, B. C. (Ed.) Glaciofluvial and Glaciolacustrine Sedimentation. Tulsa, OK, Society of Economic Paleontologists and Mineralists Special Publication 23, 101-122.

Rothlisberger, H. & Lang, H. (1987) Glacial hydrology. In: Gurnell, A. M. & Clark, M. J. (Ed.) Glacio-fluvial sediment transfer: an Alpine perspective. John Wiley & Sons, Chichester, 207-284.

Walder, J. S. (1986) Hydraulics of subglacial cavities. J. Glaciol. 32(112), 439-445.

Hydrology in Mountainous Regions. I - Hydrological Measurements; the Water Cycle
(Proceedings of two Lausanne Symposia, August 1990). IAHS Publ. no. 193, 1990.

Image synchrone de la composition isotopique de la couverture neigeuse des Alpes de Suisse occidentale

M. DRAY
Centre de recherches géodynamiques, Université Pierre et Marie Curie, Thonon les Bains, et Laboratoire d'hydrogéologie de l'Université d'Avignon, France
A. PARRIAUX & J.D. DUBOIS
Ecole Polytechnique Fédérale de Lausanne, Laboratoire de Géologie, 1015 Lausanne, Suisse

RESUME: Le milieu montagneux joue souvent le rôle d'un cas très particulier dans les règles scientifiques générales qu'on établit en étudiant les phénomènes hydrologiques sur des territoires à faible relief. Notamment, l'usage de certains paramètres comme indicateurs des zones d'alimentation doit être évalué d'une manière critique dans des chaînes de montagne. L'analyse des eaux du réseau "Stock neigeux" confectionné dans les Alpes de Suisse occidentale dans le double but isotopique et hydrochimique permet de situer les limites des méthodes, sans pouvoir à l'heure actuelle conduire à des conclusions définitives. Il ressort toutefois clairement qu'en ce qui concerne les isotopes stables liés à l'altitude, les gradients obtenus sont éminemment variables, allant même parfois pratiquement à l'inverse des modèles classiques. Les calculs d'altitude des bassins versants doivent donc être considérés comme très délicats. La nécessité d'observations à échelle réduite, avec la prise en compte de plusieurs cycles hydrologiques, s'impose pour les calculs hydrologiques à venir. La présente étude constitue le premier pilier encore bien imparfait de cette approche méthodique.

I. INTRODUCTION

Parallèlement à l'étude hydrochimique de la neige effectuée en mai 1988 dans les Alpes de la vallée du Rhône en amont du lac Léman (Parriaux et al., 1990), un échantillonnage particulier pour l'analyse isotopique des éléments stables ^{18}O et ^{2}H et radioactifs ^{3}H a été réalisé. Les points du réseau sont reportés à la figure 1.

La collecte des échantillons a été faite durant la même journée, les déplacements d'un site à l'autre effectués par hélicoptère.

Le ^{18}O, isotope constitutif de la molécule d'eau, montre un fractionnement lié à la température. Aussi va-t-il servir de marqueur des précipitations neigeuses en altitude qui permettra de calculer un gradient altimétrique. Nous utiliserons ce gradient pour déterminer les zones de recharge et par là, l'origine des écoulements de surface, comme des écoulements souterrains, en aval des zones d'accumulation de neige.

Le deutérium, autre isotope stable de la molécule d'eau, servira de témoin des phénomènes d'évaporation ou de sublimation.
Quant aux concentrations de tritium dans la neige, la comparaison de ses différentes valeurs analytiques avec celles effectuées sur les pluies et/ou les neiges (au minimum mensuelles) doit permettre de

préciser les périodes de précipitations hivernales à relier aux différentes accumulations neigeuses.

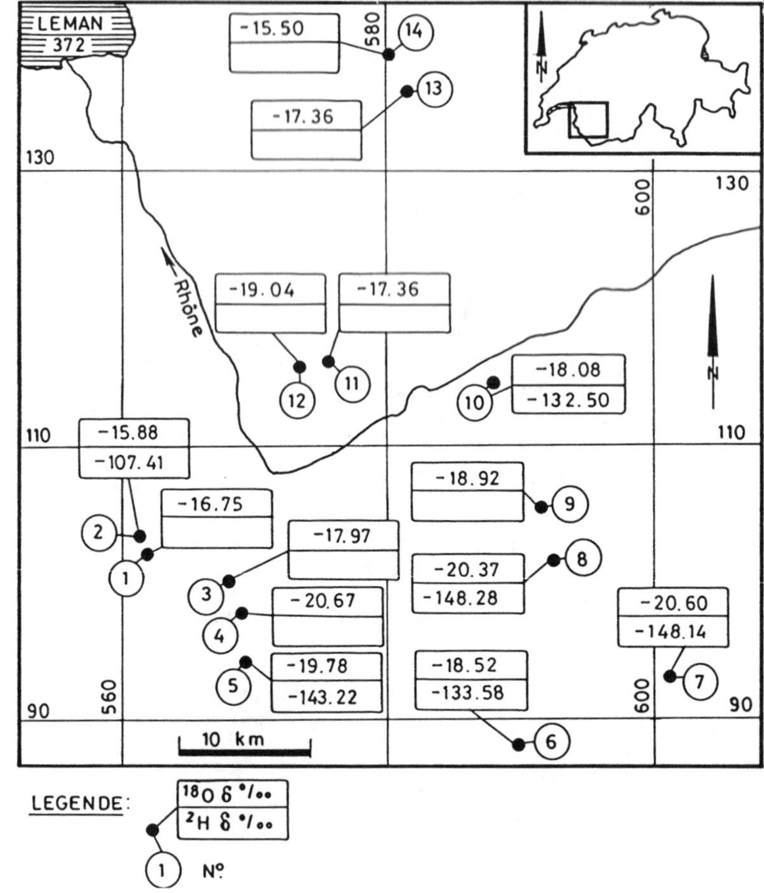

FIG. 1 Situation des points du réseau "Stock neigeux" et répartition spatiale des valeurs d'oxygène 18 et deutérium.

II. LES ISOTOPES STABLES

Les données sur échantillons globaux

Les figures 1 et 2 donnent la répartition spatiale en ^{18}O et ^{2}H ainsi que la relation deutérium - oxygène 18.

La figure 3 matérialise le gradient altitude - oxygène 18.

En prenant tous les échantillons moyens de neige, excepté les échantillons 10 et 6, qui se révèlent être des cas particuliers, les valeurs s'échelonnent entre -15 et -21 δ ‰ pour des altitudes entre 1'600 et 3'700 m. Le gradient trouvé est de 0,35 δ ‰ par 100 m. Les échantillons de surface portant sur des prélèvements de 3 cm d'épaisseur donnent la même tendance.

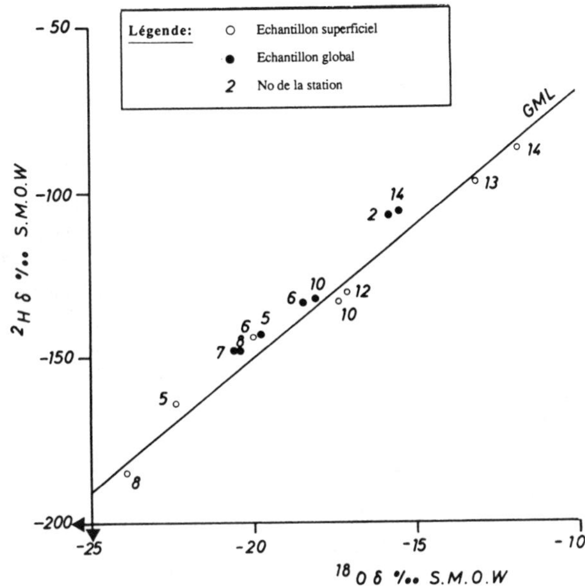

FIG. 2 Relation entre deutérium et oxygène 18 en regard de la droite de Craig.

Cas particuliers: L'échantillon 6 (figure 1) pris sur un sommet secondaire du Grand Combin correspond à une épaisseur de neige de 70 cm alors que presque partout ailleurs elle est supérieure à 170 cm. Cela résulte du fait que cette neige est en partie soufflée et par là n'est pas représentative de la totalité du manteau neigeux annuel.

L'échantillon 10 (figure 1) de faible altitude montre cependant une valeur très négative qui est à rapprocher des derniers événements neigeux comme semblent le montrer les profils détaillés de neige de Rosa Blanche (voir ci-dessous). Il correspond à une neige récente et très froide.

Quand on compare ces gradients à ceux rapportés dans la littérature (Blavoux, 1978), soit 0,20 à 0,25 δ‰ par 100 m, on constate que ces derniers sont relativement plus faibles. Moser & Stichler (1975) ont montré des gradients de 0,50 dans les Alpes.

Pour nous assurer de la représentativité des échantillons, nous la contrôlons par la relations $^{18}O/^{2}H$ (figure 2). Au vu des résultats en ^{18}O, nous avons choisi sept échantillons moyens et sept échantillons de surface. La référence étant la droite des eaux météoriques mondiales (Craig et al, 1965), on peut assurer que les prélèvements ne sont pas évaporés, les deux droites étant très voisines, soit pour l'échantillon moyen $^{2}H_{moyen} = 8,53 \cdot {}^{18}O + 25,4$ (r = 0,99) et $^{2}H_{surface} = 7,77 \cdot {}^{18}O + 5,37$.

Etude d'un profil de sondage

Sur un profil de neige carotté sur le glacier du Grand Désert de la Rosa Blanche (point 8 figure 1) comportant sept prélèvements entre 0 et 170 cm, on note une grande dispersion en ^{18}O (9 δ‰) (figure 4). Tout se passe comme si cette neige n'était pas évaporée à quelque profondeur que ce soit, comme le montre la droite deutérium-oxygène

18 très proche de la droite de Craig. Ou bien il peut s'agit d'une compensation entre l'évaporation de la neige pendant le jour et la condensation de l'humidité atmosphérique pendant la nuit. Ce carottage de neige met clairement en évidence le fait que si une série est incomplète soit par évaporation, soit par ablation, l'échantillon moyen perd de sa représentativité et de ce fait rend plus difficiles les comparaisons des manteaux neigeux entre eux à une période donnée.

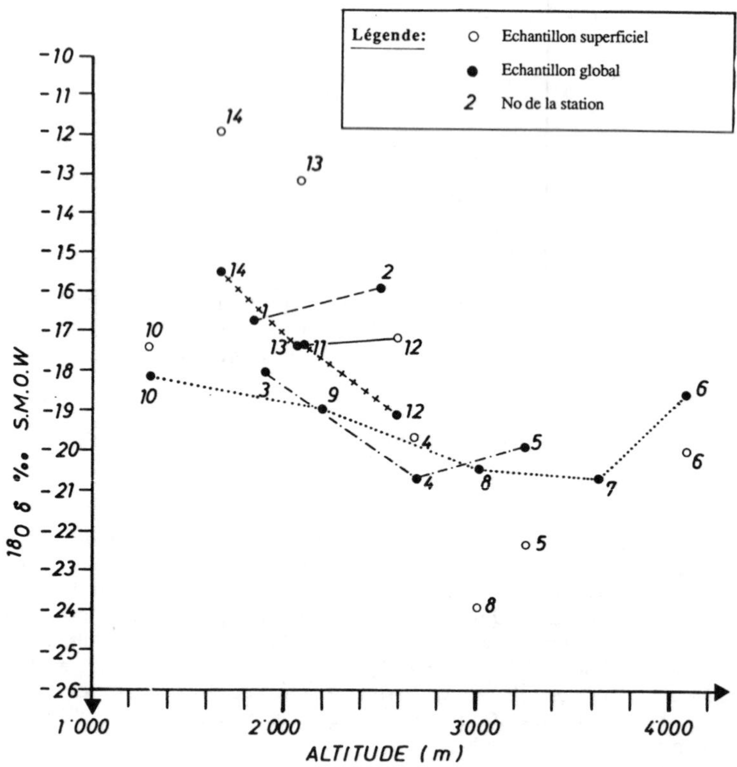

FIG. 3 Relation oxygène 18 - altitude. Les liaisons entre les points symbolisent les différents profils d'altitude choisis.

Interprétation globale des données en isotopes stables

L'ensemble des données disponibles permet de séparer deux différents domaines:

- Les massifs externes en rive droite du Rhône (nord de la chaîne), où l'on trouve un stock neigeux composite avec une neige ancienne plus positive.
- La zone pennique en rive gauche du Rhône (centre et sud de la chaîne), qui montre une neige plus récente et plus négative.

Valeurs des gradients d'altitude

Si l'on prend l'ensemble des valeurs on doit considérer plusieurs groupes (figures 1 et 3).

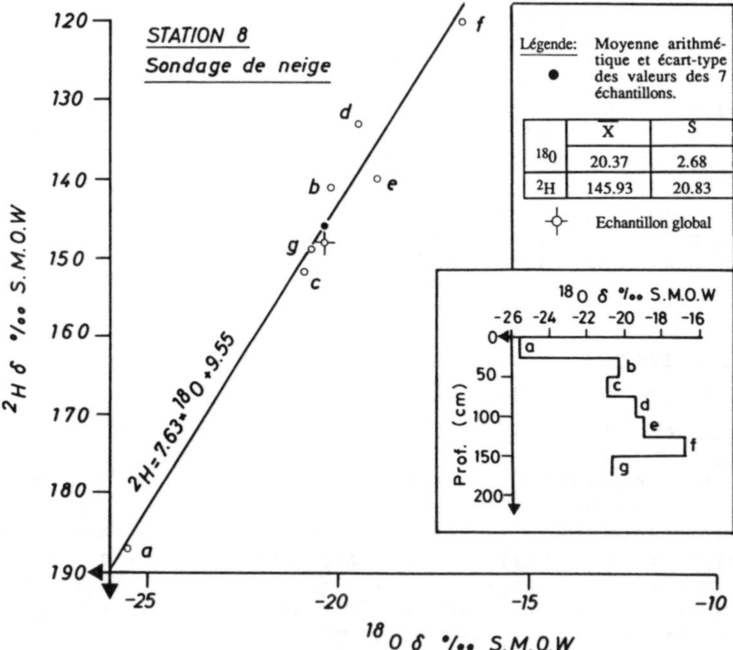

	X	S
^{18}O	20.37	2.68
^{2}H	145.93	20.83

FIG. 4 Répartition de l'oxygène 18 et du deutérium des échantillons carottés dans la neige de la Rosa-Blanche (point 8).

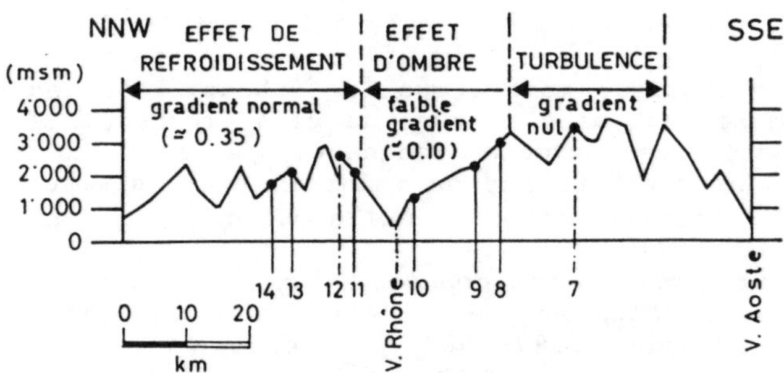

FIG. 5 Profil schématique à travers la région étudiée et perturbations liées au relief.

- Les échantillons 1-2 de la zone des Aiguilles Rouges où il n'y a pas de gradient ou même celui-ci est inversé. Sur ces versants en situation exposée au vent du nord (bise), la neige peut remonter depuis les basses altitudes. C'est une zone de turbulences maximum marquées par un mélange de neiges de diverses altitudes et une forte ablation ou parfois une accumulation dans les dépressions protégées.
- Les échantillons 3-4-5 de la zone du Mont-Blanc, où le gradient altimétrique est normal, mais l'échantillon 5 plus positif subit encore les effets turbulents éoliens ("wind drift")
- Les échantillons 11-12 et 13-14 en rive droite du Rhône, qui montrent un gradient normal proche de celui de la zone du Mont-

Blanc; 0,42 δ ‰ par 100 m.

- Les échantillons 7-8-9-10, profil en plein Pennique, qui forment un gradient normal mais très faible, de l'ordre de 0,125 δ ‰ par 100 m. On peut voir là probablement un "shadow effect" (figure 5) lié au "filtrage" des précipitations par les reliefs externes qui eux, montrent un gradient altimétrique normal.

De l'ensemble de ces résultats, on voit qu'à l'exception de la partie septentrionale de la chaîne, il est difficile de préciser un gradient dans cette région des Alpes.

III. LES ISOTOPES RADIOACTIFS

Les données

Pour des questions d'encombrement, il n'a pas été possible de prélever suffisamment de neige pour permettre l'analyse du tritium par enrichissement électrolytique de tous les échantillons. Tous ont en revanche été l'objet d'un comptage direct avec l'imprécision qui en découle. Ces comptages ont été réalisés parallèlement au CRG Thonon et au GEOLEP Lausanne. Afin de diminuer la dispersion et les erreurs systématiques liés au comptage direct, une corrélation a été, établie entre ces derniers et les quatre mesures par enrichissement. Les valeurs brutes de tritium ont été ainsi corrigées.

Tous les échantillons contiennent du tritium. On doit considérer trois groupes (fig. 6):

< 17 UT	échantillons 7, 8, 9
≈ 25 UT	échantillons 1, 2, 5, 6, 10, 11
≈ 30-40 UT	échantillons 3, 4, 12, 13, 14

La répartition spatiale montre que les échantillons les plus riches en tritium se situent dans la zone la plus proche du Léman (12, 13, 14). Les échantillons les moins radioactifs en sont les plus éloignés (7, 8, 9). On ne constate pas de relation entre altitude et concentration en ^{3}H, contrairement à ce qui a été noté par certains auteurs (Merlivat et al. 1977).

Si l'on veut comparer ces données avec les mesures en tritium des précipitations les plus proches, c'est-à-dire la station de Thonon-CRG pendant l'hiver 1987-1988, on trouve les concentrations suivantes:

1987:		1988:	
septembre	10 UT	janvier	20 UT
octobre	25 UT	février	17 UT
novembre	22 UT	mars	20 UT
décembre	18 UT		

Interprétation

On ne peut corréler directement les concentrations en tritium trouvées dans la neige avec celles des précipitations d'un mois bien précis. La gamme des valeurs mesurées dans la neige alpine est sensiblement plus élevée que dans les précipitations de Thonon durant la même période.

La zone du Plateau suisse semble être la source de pollution potentielle, avec une contamination maximale en bordure (12, 13, 14)

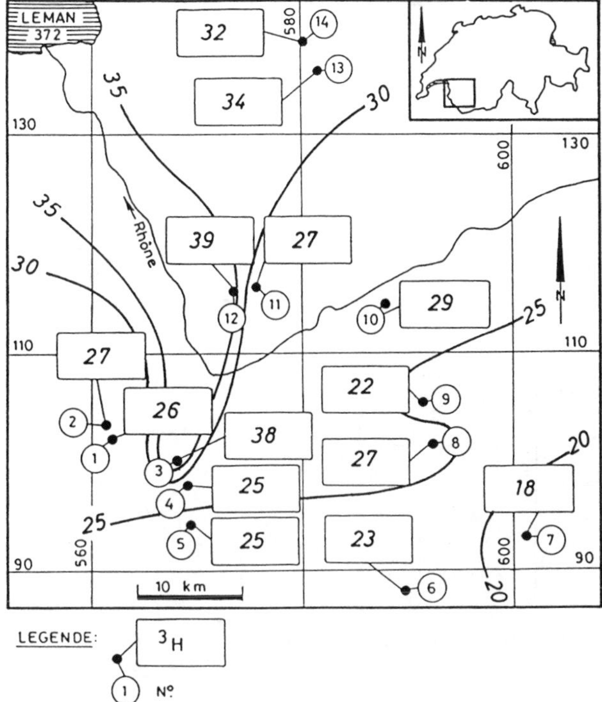

FIG.6 Répartition spatiale du tritium.

et minimale dans les zones les plus éloignées (7, 8, 9) (fig. 6).

Cette observation rejoint l'étude chimique des neiges du même réseau (Parriaux et al. 1990). En effet, une forte corrélation tritium - total des sels dissous (fig. 7) conforte l'idée d'une origine anthropique d'une majeure partie de la minéralisation.

3. CONCLUSION

Cette campagne de mesures isotopiques de la neige dans les massifs de la vallée du Haut-Rhône nous a permis de mettre en évidence:

1. la quasi-absence de phénomène d'évaporation ou de sublimation de la neige,
2. la difficulté d'utiliser des gradients isotopiques d'altitude simples, vu la complexité des précipitations liées aux directions principales des vents qui provoquent des mélanges et d'autres effets perturbateurs associés à la succession de chaînes et de vallées,
3. l'extrême variabilité isotopique dans l'épaisseur de la couche de neige d'où la relativité de la représentativité de l'échantillon moyen,
4. enfin, par les concentrations en tritium, une origine de contamination en provenance de la bordure nord de la chaîne des Alpes.

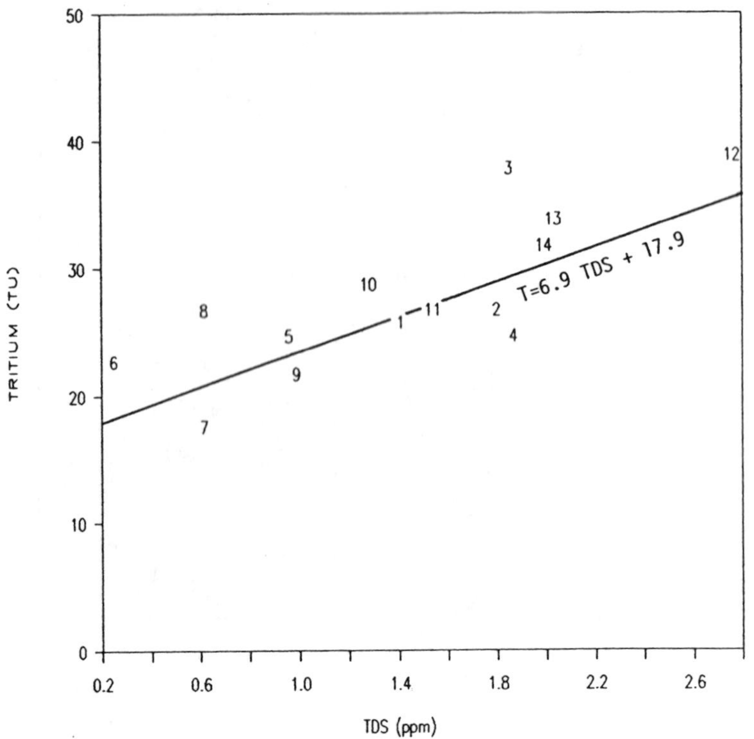

FIG. 7 Corrélation tritium et minéralisation totale (TDS = total des sels dissous).

REMERCIEMENTS: A l'Armée suisse qui a permis cet échantillonnage synchrone en mettant à notre disposition un hélicoptère, et au personnel technique du CRG qui a assuré les analyses isotopiques.

REFERENCES

Blavoux, B. (1978) Etude du cycle de l'eau au moyen de l'oxygène 18 et du Tritium. Thèse de doctorat d'Etat, Paris.

Craig, G. & Gordon, L.J. (1965) Deuterium and Oxygen 18 variations in the ocean and the marine atmosphere. Proc. Conf. Nuclear Geology, Spoleto, 1965.

Merlivat, L., Jouzel, J., Robert, J. & Lorius, C. (1977) Distribution of artificial tritium in firn samples from East Antarctica. IASH Publ. 118.

Moser, H. & Sticher, W (1975) Deuterium measurements on snow samples from the Alps. IAEA-SM-129/4, 43-57.

Parriaux, A., Dubois, J.D. & Dray, M. (1990) Chemical composition of snow cover on the west Swiss Alps. Proc. & Rep. IAHS Conf. Lausanne.

Hydrology in Mountainous Regions. I - Hydrological Measurements; the Water Cycle (Proceedings of two Lausanne Symposia, August 1990). IAHS Publ. no. 193, 1990.

Qualitative determination of drainage basin storage in nine drainage basins of the Basque Country, northern Spain

J. GARCIA MUÑIZ
Diputación Foral de Bizkaia, 48001 Bilbao, Spain
I. ANTIGUEDAD AUZMENDI
Area Geodinámica, Universidad del País Vasco, 48080 Bilbao, Spain
J. LLAMAS SIENDONES
Dép. Génie Civil, Faculté des Sciences, Université Laval, Québec, Canada

ABSTRACT The relationship between physical and hydrological characteristics of differents drainage basins is tried to know in this work. Nine drainage basins from the Basque Country (Spain) were selected to determine the influence of physical characteristics over their hydrological response. The methodology used, factorial analysis, has let know that five physical parameters are enough to characterize, qualitatively, the self-regulator power of an ungaged drainage basin. A second methodology applied to several basins from the Basque Country and Quebec (Canada), linear regressions, has let stablish simple and stable relationships between drainage network parameters and hydrological parameters. This analysis has let stablish two types of drainage basins according to their nordicity.

INTRODUCTION

The search of relationships between hydrological and natural environmental characteristics in drainage basins is the goal of this work. The methodologies used have let stablish the influence of the physical characteristics on the hydrological response of a drainage basin. The first methodology, factorial analysis (P.C.A.), has been applied to nine drainage basins from the Basque Country (N. of Spain). The first analysis was made with nineteen parameters, but in differents stages of the analysis the number of parameters was reduce to five. These five parameters have enough information to determinate qualitatively the regulator power of a drainage basin. The second methodology, linear regression, applied to basins in Quebec (Canada) and Basque Country has let stablish simple and stable relationships between drainage network characteristics and the residual hydrogram corresponding to a mean hydrological year and to ten hydrological years. The results obtained are comented along this paper.

QUALITATIVE DETERMINATION OF REGULATION POWER IN DRAINAGE BASINS

The hydraulic potential of a drainage basin depends on the rainfall on it, but its natural characteristics bring about the rainfall distribution. Some of these characteristics have been taken into account in this work, refered to the physical parameters that control the regulation power and the filter of the hydrological system.

The natural characteristics selected were compared with some hydrological parameters that inform about the self-regulation power and the filter of a hydro(geo)logical system.

The statistical analysis applied to these parameters lets select five of them to define qualitatively, more detailed than the others, the self-regulator power and the filter in the nine studied basins of the Basque Country, using pluriannual flow time series.

METHODOLOGY

The parameters procesed have been calculated in nine drainage basins from the Basque Country (North of Spain).They, being considered as variables, were grouped as: variables to be explained and explanatory variables.

a) Variables to be explained: They are the hydrological parameters defined by Mangin (1982) as indicatives of the regulation power and the filter of a hydrological system over the rainfall. These variables have been obtained from the correlatory and spectral analysis of rainfall and flow time series (Box and Jenkins,1976). These are: Memory effect (ME), Cut Frecuency (CF) and the highest peak value of the cross correlogram rainfall-runoff (PCC).

b) Explanatory variables: We have grouped here the natural parameters that refer to the physical characteristics of the drainage basins. The form, drainage network and permeability of the geology are the physical characteristics considered here.

.- *Form characteristics*: Form factor (FF).

.- *Network characteristics*: Drainage density(DD); Bifurcation ratio (BR).

.- *Permeability characteristics*: Low permeability (LP); High permeability (HP) and Medium permeability (MP). We have considered as areas with HP those who are so senso stricto, plus the ones which are artificially regulated.

Nineteen parameters were initially selected as global characteristics of the studied basins, but the nine mentioned above have enough information to let us go on with the analitical process. Table 1 shows the drainage basins with the parameters used in this analysis.

The analitical process applied to all the variables, factor analysis (Principal Components Analysis), has shown the influence that the physical characteristics have on the self-regulator power of the hydrological systems considered in this work.

STATISTICAL ANALYSIS

According to the hydrological parameters, memory effect and cut frecuency (table1), Arratia, Bidasoa and Urola hydrological systems have the highest self-regulator power, while the Urumea, Ibaizabal and Deba systems have medium self-regulator power, and the Urkiola, Oiartzun and Herrerias ones are distinguished for their low regulator capacity.

The P.C.A. shows high correlations between some variables to be explained and explanatory variables (Fig. 1). This will let us reaffirm the influence that the natural characteristics have on the hydrological response to the rainfall in hydrological systems. The correlation values obtained are:

R >	0.6	between	ME	and	HP
		"	CF	"	DD
R >	0.7	"	CF	"	LP
R >	0.8	"	CF	"	BR
R <	-0.7	"	ME	"	DD,BR
R <	-0.8	"	CF	"	HP

Figure 1.a. shows in the I-II factorial plane, 69% of accumulated variance, the distribution of the nine parameters and the studied drainage basins.

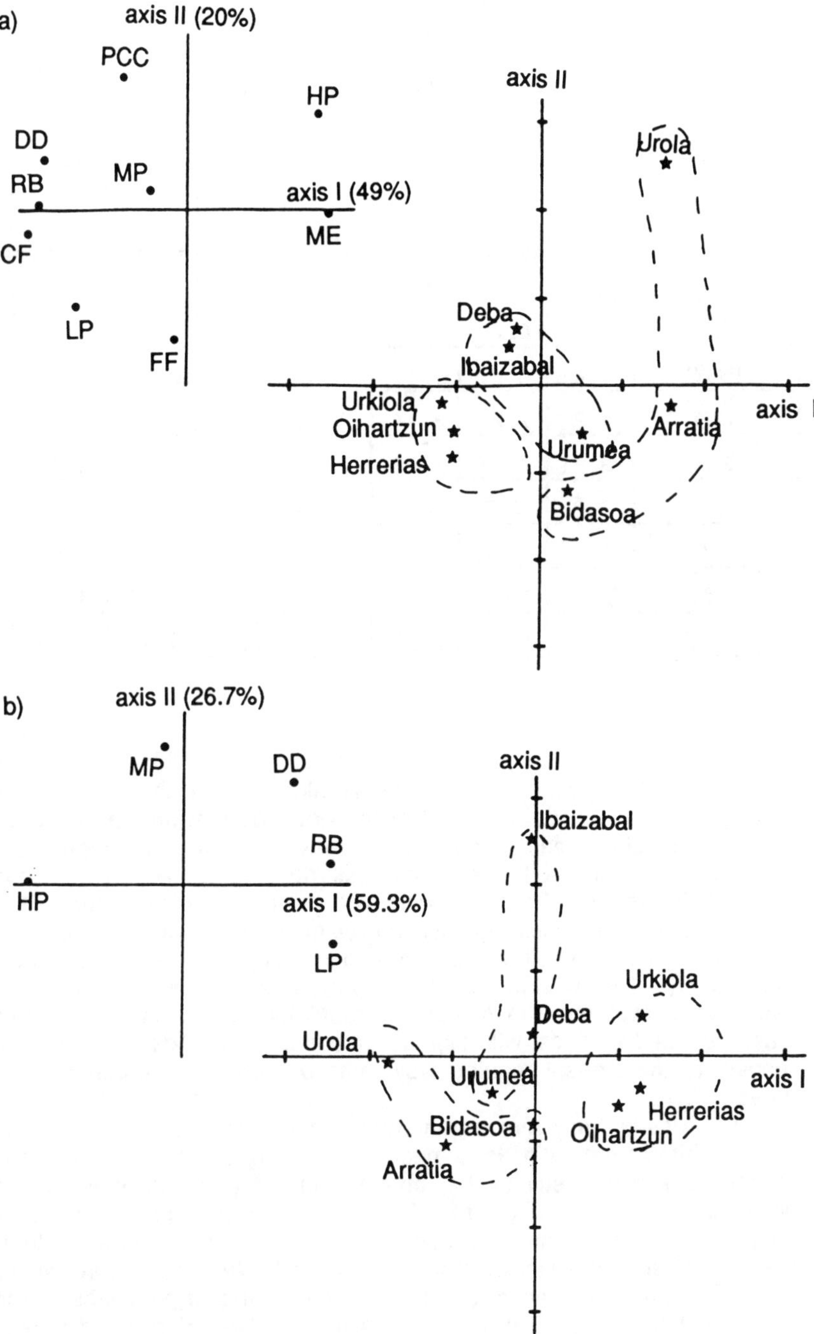

FIG. 1 Basins distribution in I-II factorial plane

a) using nine parameters
b) using five physical parameters

TABLE 1 Drainage basins and parameters.
(ME=Memory effect; CF=Cut frequency; DD=Drainage density; BR=Bifurcation ratio; PCC= Highest peak of the cross-correlogram; HP=High permeability; MP=Medium permeability; LP=Low permeability; FF=Form factor. Basins: 1=Bidasoa; 2=Oiartzun; 3=Urumea; 4=Urola; 5=Deba; 6=Ibaizabal; 7=Urkiola; 8=Arratia; 9=Herrerias)

Parameters	1	2	3	4	5	6	7	8	9
M.E.	23	13	17	26	16	17	14	40	3
C.F.	0,17	0,22	0,17	0,14	0,2	0,2	0,2	0,15	0,2
P.C.C.	0,49	0,66	0,37	0,66	0,66	0,52	0,7	0,42	0,47
D.D.	1,89	2,26	2,14	1,89	2,26	2,71	3,16	1,39	2,43
B.R.	3,59	4,96	3,86	3,47	4,32	4,29	5,27	3,85	5,17
H.P.	8,6	2,7	29	52,92	19,1	15,7	12,3	33,4	1,8
M.P.	1,5	0	0	2,18	5,8	20,4	0	0	0
L.P.	89,9	97,3	71,0	44,9	75,1	63,9	87,7	66,6	98,2
F.F.	0,7	0,48	0,58	0,26	0,43	0,44	0,67	0,56	0,44

The relative position of parameters along axis I shows this as indicative of the self-regulator power, development of the drainage network and importance of high and low permeability areas. Figure 1.a. shows that the drainage basins with higher regulator power have the network less developed and /or the low rates of low permeability and /or the areas with high permeability are bigger. On the other hand the basins with less self-regulator power have the network well developed and/or the rates of high permeability areas are low, being more important the areas with low permeabilty. The basins position along axis I shows, in the positive side, the hydrological systems with higher self-regulator power, and, in the negative side, the least regulated systems, with high cut frecuency. The Bidasoa system is desplaced with respect to the highest regulated systems because of importance of low permeability areas.

The use of only five parameters, refered to physical characteristics (drainage density, bifurcation ratio, low, medium and high permeability), in the factor analysis reaches a similar result to that obtained in the previous analysis, but with 86% of accumulated variance (Fig. 1b). The distribution of hydrological systems along axis I, on the I-II factorial plane, is according to the drainage network development and/or the rate of permeable litologies of the drainage basins. The basins which have the least developed drainage network and/or the highest rates of permeable litologies are located in the negative side of axis I. The basins with well depeloped network and/or small permeable areas are placed in the positive side.

Along axis II the basins are distributed according to the importance of medium permeable litologies.

The Bidasoa drainage basin characterized by the important of areas with low permeability and by a bad developed drainage network, that determine its high self-regulator power, is displaced to the coordinates origen because of the high rate of low permeability.

RESULTS AND DISCUSSION

The control that the natural environment, specially the drainage network and the permeability characteristics of the geology, performs on the runoff distribution in a drainage basin is demostrated in this work.

We have been able to demonstrate that five physical characteristics of a drainage basins let determine qualitatively its self-regulator power. These parameters are easily known from topographical and geological maps with an appropiate scale.

The physical parameters used are: drainage density, bifurcation ration, high, medium and low permeability of basins' litologies. The results obtained let say that the systems with less developed network regulate the runoff in the same way as a drainage basin with big areas of high permeability does.

The validity of these affirmations is corroborated by the significance of high permeability. It is refered to areas with natural, aquifers, and, in some cases, artificial regulation, dams.

The methodology used in this work seems applicable to environmental planning politics and to some aspects of civil engineering.

The fact of knowing the self-regulator power of a drainage basin from five physical characteristics is quite interesting to be applied to ungaged basins in order to estimate their hydraulical potential. It also provides the possibility of determining the hydrological system sensibility to ground-water pollution and selecting the basins or sub-basins to be protected against harmful activities, which is another tool in the territorial politics.

The erosive capacity in a drainage basin is related to the stage of drainage network development; we have considered this development using drainage density and bifurcation ratio as network parameters. In this way we can know which basins need to be protected against erosion and denudation, by direct actions on them. It is also known the influence of solids from erosive process in extraordinary flood events. The methodology is useful to select the points where a dam to laminate the flood is necessary.

Using this methodology basins and sub-basins to build dams can be selected. In these basins the flow must be enough to different uses and their erosive capacity must be low, to avoid the dam fill up too early.

SEARCHING A SIMPLE RELATIONSHIP BETWEEN PHYSICAL AND HYDROGRAPHYICAL CHARACTERISTICS OF A DRAINAGE BASIN.

The goal of this study is the search of a simple and stable relationship between some physical characteristics of a basin, easly measurables on topographyc maps, and its hydrological response. The selected factor to define the physical characteristics is the frequency hystogram of river lenght, while the residual annual and pluriannual hydrogram has been selected as hydrological factor.

The study has been developed (Llamas et al., in print) for two well differents situations and scenes: one of them without nordicity an the otherone with nordicity. This term defines the situation in which most of the meteorological conditions are dominated by snow. The snowmelt, together with rainfall, gives the characteristical annual flood hydrogram.

Firstly eight nordic basins in Quebec (Canada) and seven basins in the Basque Country (Spain), lacking of any nordicity, were selected for this study. The residual hydrogram corresponding to a mean hydrological year (1974-1975) was chosen for every case. The study was completed, secondly, with sixteen basins from Quebec and five from Basque Country, taking into account the average residual hydrogram which belongs to ten hydrological years. We must also point out that the nordical basins are bigger than those in the Basque Country.

METHODOLOGY

In order to detect and to quantify the dependence between the physical and hydrological characteristics the following comparative parameter has been taken, deduced and improved from that used by Rogers (1972, in Llamas et al., in print) to concentrate the hydrological information.

$$C = \ln\left(\frac{K\,A_{max}}{S^2}\right)$$

where: -K is a surface parameter with the following values :
K=1 in the hydrogram
K=B in the frequency hystogram of river lenght.
B= Basin area (Km2).
-Amax= Stand for the hydrogram mode and frequency hystogram mode.
-S represents the area under each curve.
According to all this the parameters to be used in the study are:

- *Physical characteristics* (relative hystogram frequency)

$$C = \ln\left(\frac{B\,A_{max}}{S^2}\right) = \ln\left(B\,A_{max}\right) - 2\ln S$$

where : $-A_{max}=f_{max}=n_{max}/N$.
$-n_{max}$= number of class in the mode of the hystogram.
-N= total class in the hystogram.
-S= cumulative frequency hystogram =1.
Therefore the parameter is:

$$C_{fr} = \ln\left(B\,A_{max}\right) = \ln\left(\frac{B\,n_{max}}{N}\right) = \ln\left(\frac{n_{max}}{D}\right)$$

where : -D= River density= N/B.

-*Hydrological characteristics* (residual annual hydrogram)
The selected factor to represent the hydrological character of a drainage basin is the residual annual hydrogram,obtained, using the logarithmic method, substracting the base hydrogram from the annual hydrogram. Therefore the residual hydrogram characterizes the basin annual response, exclusively due to its physical characteristics. The parameter corresponding to this factor is:

$$C_H = \ln\left(\frac{A_{max}}{S^2}\right)$$

STATISTICAL ANALYSIS

Table 2 shows the C_{fr} and C_H values of the sixteen basins in Quebec and of the seven basins in the Basque Country. Two linear regressions have been obtained with the C_H values, the first one using a mean hydrological year (1974-1975) and the second one using the average hydrogram obtained from ten hydrological years. The regressions have been developed together with all the avalable basins and separately with the Quebec basins and Basque basins. The equations of the regression lines are:

a) Mean hydrological year:

-Total	$C_{fr}=9.718-0.448\ C_H$	r=-0.693
-Basque Country	$C_{fr}=8.084-0.358\ C_H$	r=-0.847
-Quebec	$C_{fr}=11.308-0.548\ C_H$	r=-0.903

b) Average ten hydrological years:

-Total	$C_{fr}=10.722-0.522\ C_H$	r=-0.602
-Basque Country	$C_{fr}=14.052-1.113\ C_H$	r=-0.990
-Quebec	$C_{fr}=11.863-0.643\ C_H$	r=-0.877

TABLE 2 Parameters of the studied basins.

Basin name	Gauging site number	Area km^2	Cfr	CH 1 year	CH 10 years
Quebec					
Portneuf	50701	355	5.56	10.81	10.013
Petite Cascapédia	10901	1390	6.40	9.72	8.530
Du Sud	23106	821	5.68	-	8.350
York	20401	1010	6.06	8.96	8.908
Trois Pistoles	22301	958	5.86	8.52	8.818
Coulonge	41301	5150	7.74	7.32	7.214
Chaudière	23402	5830	7.48	6.74	6.839
Romaine	73801	13000	8.17	6.07	6.163
Etchemin	23301	1130	6.34	-	8.270
Beaurivage	23401	707	5.55	-	9.052
Famine	23422	686	5.84	-	8.921
Nicolet S-O	30101	544	5.99	-	9.457
Massawippi	30220	619	5.98	-	10.038
Eaton	30234	642	6.12	-	9.372
Yamaska	30302	1270	6.33	-	8.840
Noire	30304	1470	6.41	-	8.745
Godbout	71401	1570	6.53	8.72	-
Basque Country					
Oiartzun	107	38	3.46	9.34	9.400
Herrerías	175	247	5.16	8.63	8.200
Ibaizabal	164	256	5.32	7.75	7.850
Deba	103	450	5.86	7.17	7.390
Bidasoa	106	716	6.28	6.47	6.860
Urkiola	-	37	3.29	14.48	-
Urola	109	303	5.33	7.24	-

RESULTS AND DISCUSSION

The correlation coefficients obtained are quite high showing the stable statistical dependence between the physical and hydrological characteristics of a basin.

The dependence is lower when all the basins are considered together, but if the basins of the two regions (Quebec and Basque Country) are separately considered the dependence is higher, where the coeficients range between 0.847 and 0.990. The minus sign , in the correlation coeficients, means that the angular coefficient is less than zero in the regression lines. We have to indicate that when using exponential or parabolical regressions the coefficients increase.

The results obtained show that:

-There is a stable relationship between physical and hydrological characteristics of a basin; the parameters C_{fr} and C_H concentrate the relation.

-The more uniform the studied region is, the higher relationship is. The basin area does not seem to affect the statistical dependence order.

-Eventhoug the dependence, considering two different hydrological regions (nodicity), is significant, it is smaller than when considering the two regions, separately. The different laminator effect of the basins in both regions can be cause of the small dependence. This point will be investigated in following stages of this study.

CONCLUSIONS

The results presented in this paper corroborate the environmental influence, particularly those refered to physical characteristics, on the hydrological response of a drainage basin. The drainage network development and the high permeable litologies regulate the flow in the same way than the dams.

The principal components analysis, applied to nine drainage basins in the Basque Country, has shown that five physical characteristics are enough to know, qualitatively, the filter capacity and regulator power of an ungaged basin. The utility of this analysis can be extended to territorial politics, environmental protection and extraordinary floods lamination.

Simple and stable relationships between drainage network characteristics and annual and pluriannual hydrogram have been stablished using linear regressions. The chosen basins, belonging to two differents meteorological conditions (Basque Country and Quebec), can be gruped according to their nordicity. This parameter reflects the different natural laminator effect of the basins in both regions.

ACKNOWLEDGEMENTS This article is a part of the Investigation Proyect code 121310-9/88 (Hydrological Investigation of the Drainage Basins) of the Basque Country University.

REFERENCES

Box, G.E.P. & Jenkins, G.M. (1976) Time series analysis: Forecasting and control. Holden Day. San Francisco.

Llamas, J., Antiguedad. I., Alain, D., García, J. & Díaz, C. (in print) Relación entre las características físicas e hidrográficas de una cuenca. Ingeniería Hidráulica en Mexico.

Mangin, A. (1982) Mise en évidence de l'originalité et de la diversité des aquifèrs karstiques. Ann. Sci. Université Besancon. III Colloque d'hydrologie en Pays Calcaire 159-172.

Hydrology in Mountainous Regions. I - Hydrological Measurements; the Water Cycle (Proceedings of two Lausanne Symposia, August 1990). IAHS Publ. no. 193, 1990.

The significance of suspended sediment pulses for estimating suspended sediment load and identifying suspended sediment sources in Alpine glacier basins

A.M. GURNELL & J. WARBURTON*
Department of Geography, University of Southampton, Southampton SO9 5NH, England
*present address: Department of Natural Resources Engineering, Lincoln College, Canterbury, New Zealand.

ABSTRACT Variability in the suspended sediment concentration of proglacial streams is often attributed to the existence of temporal lags between suspended sediment concentration and discharge; and to the existence of sediment supply/exhaustion effects which underly hysteresis in the relationship between the two variables at diurnal, sub-seasonal, seasonal and interannual timescales. This paper considers another component of the variability in suspended sediment concentration; the occurrence of frequent pulses or flushes of suspended sediment. Although these flushes are small both in duration and magnitude, some events transport sufficient sediment to make a significant contribution to the sediment yield. They have characteristic shapes, which appear to be related to their source area; and their occurrence is associated with particular transport conditions. Subsampling of continuous turbidity records to simulate the effect of a discrete interval sampling strategy (e.g. pump sampling) 'smooths' the record so that the detail of the flushes is quickly lost. Turbidity measurements are thus required to give accurate estimates of suspended sediment and precise definition of suspended sediment flush characteristics on proglacial streams.

INTRODUCTION

Many studies have described and analyzed the relationship between suspended sediment concentration and discharge, illustrating the low level of linear correlation between the two variables (e.g. Østrem, 1975; Fenn *et al.* 1985). This is often attributed to temporal lags between the two series and sediment supply / exhaustion effects which underly hysteresis in the relationship between the two variables at diurnal, sub-seasonal, seasonal and interannual timescales (e.g. Gurnell, 1987). Variability in suspended sediment concentration is also caused by non-periodic events: meltwater flood events (high magnitude - low frequency) and pulses or flushes, short-lived bursts in suspended sediment concentration (low magnitude - high frequency). This paper considers the latter component of suspended sediment concentration variability. Flushes of suspended sediment which occur with no apparent variation in discharge of the proglacial stream have been attributed to tapping of sediment sources in a variety of glacial and proglacial locations (Bøgen, 1980; Hammer & Smith, 1983; Richards, 1984; Gurnell, 1987) and their causes have been ascribed to rapid changes in glacial motion (Humphrey *et al.* 1986), failure of channel banks (Hammer and Smith, 1983), channel erosion (Gurnell, 1982), inputs from tributaries and hillslopes (Bathurst *et al.* 1986), and surges in discharge caused by fluid instabilities in steep channels (Heggen, 1986).

Sediment flushes are usually small in duration and in the magnitude of sediment transported, but some events transport a significant proportion of the sediment yield from the glacier basin. Their brevity is of great significance in relation to suspended sediment concentration estimates from pumped water samples, since the highest frequency of published pump sampling in the proglacial environment is one hour (Gurnell, 1987, Table 12.2). Sediment pulses are of interest to studies of the hydrology and sediment yield from glacier basins since they may provide indications of glacial and fluvial activity both within the glacial and proglacial zones of the drainage basins.

This paper addresses the significance of sediment flushes as a component of suspended sediment transport in proglacial streams in three ways. First, 571 flush events observed from 22 days of turbidity records for the proglacial stream of Glacier de Tsidjiore Nouve are analysed to identify their size, shape and frequency characteristics in relation to the background suspended sediment concentration and discharge regime. Second, the causes of flushes are explored in relation to parameters of their size and shape using: (1) field observations at Glacier de Tsidjiore Nouve; (2) pulses derived from simulated bank instability on the proglacial streams of the Bas Glacier d'Arolla and Glacier de Tsidjiore Nouve; (3) observations of sediment pulses routed through the Bas Glacier d'Arolla. Third, the significance of flushes as a component of total suspended sediment transport is investigated using turbidity records from the proglacial stream of the Bas Glacier d'Arolla. The degree to which pumped/hand sampling of glacial meltwaters can account for sediment transport flushes is estimated by subsampling a continuous turbidity record according to various simulated sampling frequencies.

THE STUDY BASINS AND INSTRUMENTATION

Glacier de Tsidjiore Nouve and Bas Glacier d'Arolla occupy adjacent valleys in the Val d'Herens, Switzerland, have similar catchment characteristics (Gurnell *et al.* 1988), and have short proglacial streams which are diverted into meltwater intake structures, forming part of the Grande Dixence S.A. hydro-electricity scheme, within 300m of the glacier snouts.

Flow gauging stations within the intake structures provide accurate discharge records. Suspended sediment concentration was monitored using turbidity meters (Partech 7000 3RP MKII suspended solids monitors with a single gap (SDM-10) probe) located in the water intake structures, which provide an environment free from ambient light and with a stable power supply. Suspended sediment concentrations were estimated from the turbidity record using standard gravimetric calibration procedures (400ml USDH-48 samples filtered through Whatman 40 papers). The same instrumentation, was also used in artificial pulse experiments.

AN ANALYSIS OF SEDIMENT FLUSH EVENTS IN THE PROGLACIAL STREAM OF GLACIER DE TSIDJIORE NOUVE DURING A 22 DAY PERIOD

All flush events were abstracted from a turbidity record for the proglacial stream of the Glacier de Tsidjiore Nouve over a 22 day period, 26 July to 16 August 1986. Parameters of each flush were abstracted from the turbidity chart, including the time of rise of each flush (t), the turbidity immediately preceding the flush (Tb), turbidity at the flush peak (Tp), and the turbidity at a lag equivalent to the time of rise after the flush peak (Tf). A calibration curve converted the turbidity values Tb, Tp, Tf into suspended sediment concentration estimates Sb, Sp, Sf. This analysis yielded 571 flush events with a temporal resolution of 1.5 minutes and a calibrated suspended sediment concentration resolution of 90 mg l^{-1}. Further flush parameters were derived including the peak suspended sediment concentration (Spk = Sp - Sb), the slope of the rising limb (Srl = (Sp-Sb)/t), the slope of the falling limb (Sfl = (Sp-Sf)/t), the shape of the flush (Sfl/Srl) and the time of occurrence of the flush (to the nearest hour). Descriptive statistics for the flush parameters, which were all strongly skewed, are presented in Table 1. Of particular interest is the very short time of rise of the flushes (maximum, 36 minutes; median, 6 minutes) which may be important in causing poor linear correlation between suspended sediment concentration and discharge in proglacial streams. Although many of the flush peak suspended sediment concentrations are small, the upper quartile of events with peak concentrations in excess of 450 mg l^{-1} could have a strong effect on the total suspended concentration and could introduce scatter to the suspended sediment - discharge relationship if intercepted by a pump sampler.

TABLE 1 Descriptive statistics of measured and calculated flush parameters, Glacier de Tsidjiore Nouve, 26 July to 16 August 1986.

	t	Spk	Srl	Sfl	Shape
Median	6.0	270	60	30	0.8
Upper Quartile	7.5	450	90	60	1.0
Lower Quartile	3.0	180	30	20	0.5
Maximum	36.0	9810*	660	540	5.0
Minimum	1.5	90	3	0	0

* This event is not included in Figures 2 or 3 because it is almost double the size of the second largest event and so it would distort the graphs.
t is expressed in minutes; Spk in mg l^{-1}, Srl and Sfl in mg l^{-1} min^{-1}; Shape is dimensionless.

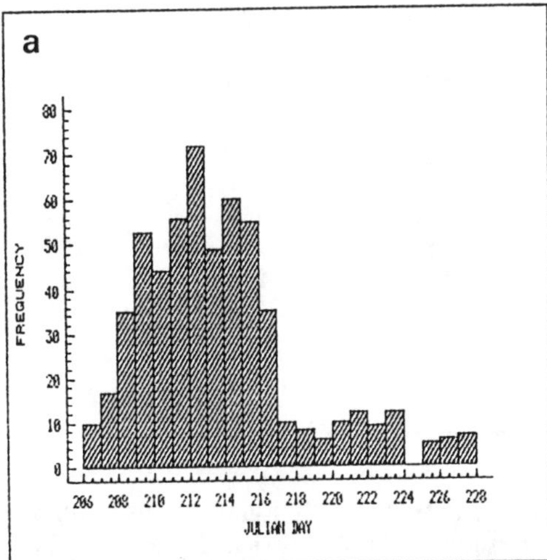

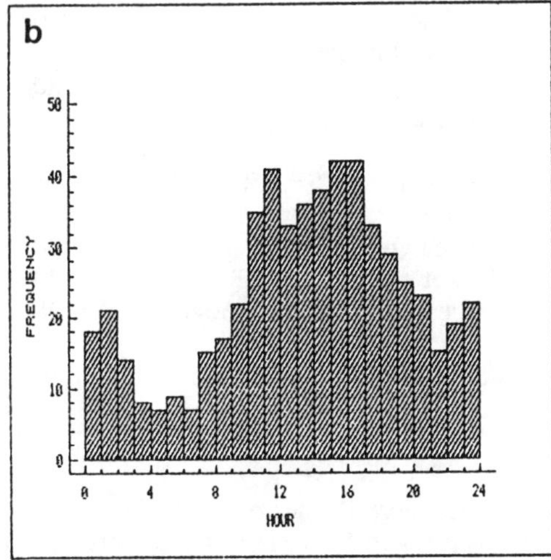

FIG. 1 Flush frequency characteristics in association with a) Julian day, b) time of day, Glacier de Tsidjiore Nouve 26 July - 16 August 1986.

The first 11 days of the study period were subject to considerably higher discharges and background suspended sediment concentrations than the final 11 days. Flush frequency was greatest in the first 11 days of the study period (Figure 1a) and was also greatest between 11.00h and 20.00h (Figure 1b). Suspended sediment concentration and discharge were relatively high prior to the flush events when compared with the frequency distributions of these variables for the whole study period. Small flushes occurred throughout the study period, but the upper quartile of flush peaks occurred mainly in the first 11 days and between 11.00h and 20.00h, were associated with preceding suspended sediment concentration in excess of 1500 mg l^{-1} and with discharges over 1 m^3 s^{-1}. Large flushes had shorter times of rise than smaller flushes so that their rising limbs were also steeper. Variations in the shape parameter (Sfl/Srl) show that large flushes have a steeper rising than falling limb (shape parameter < 1), whereas smaller flushes vary across the range from slightly steeper to substantially less steep rising than falling limbs.

In order to explore the relationships between flushes and discharge in more detail, the discharge associated with each flush event was allocated to one of four flow classes. Class 1 was on the rising limb of the discharge hydrograph but at a flow less than the previous day's peak flow. Class 2 was on the rising limb and exceeded the preceding day's peak flow. Class 3 was on the falling limb but exceeded the previous day's peak flow. Class 4 was on the falling limb and at a flow less than the previous day's peak flow. Table 2 compares the frequency and flood peak magnitude characteristics of flushes occurring in the flow classes with the percentage of time over the 22 day period occupied by each of the classes.

TABLE 2 Comparison of the frequency and magnitude characteristics of suspended sediment flushes, by flow class, Glacier de Tsidjiore Nouve, 26 July to 16 August 1986.

	Flow Class			
	1	2	3	4
Spk for all flushes ($mg.l^{-1}$)				
Median	270	360	270	180
Upper Quartile	450	720	450	180
Lower Quartile	180	180	180	360
% total flushes	31	21	12	36
Flushes with Spk >= 450 $mg.l^{-1}$				
Median	630	720	630	540
Upper Quartile	900	1080	990	1080
Lower Quartile	540	540	450	540
% flushes with Spk >= 450mgl^{-1}	28	32	13	28
% study period in flow class	30	8	6	56

2.6 times more flushes occur in class 2 than would be expected with a uniform distribution of flushes with flow class. The observed/expected ratios for classes 3, 1 and 4 are 2.0, 1.0 and 0.6 respectively. In the case of the upper quartile of flushes (according to the magnitude of Spk), the ratios of observed to expected flush frequency for classes 2,3,1 and 4 are 4.0, 2.2, 0.9 and 0.5, respectively, showing a more marked contrast between classes. The median time of flush rise does not vary with flow class but the maximum time of rise is higher in classes 1 and 4 than in 2 and 3, providing some further evidence of the more attenuated shape of some of the flushes with smaller peak suspended sediment concentrations.

Thus over the 22 day turbidity record flush events occurred preferentially during periods of high discharge and particularly during rising flow in excess of the previous day's peak flow. The largest flushes had steeper rising limbs and shorter times to peak than the majority of flushes and occurred between 11.00 and 22.00h. Although individual flushes may not be particularly large in either their peak suspended sediment concentration or the magnitude of the sediment load they transport, together they form a very significant component of suspended sediment transport during the 22 day period: 46% (1891 tonnes) of the total suspended sediment load transported by the proglacial stream was transported during flush events and 9% (369 tonnes) of the total suspended sediment load was transported as part of a flush peak rather than as part of the background suspended sediment load underlying the peak.

CAUSES OF FLUSHES

Field Observations at Glacier de Tsidjiore Nouve

During the early part of the 22 day study period in 1986 and during a hydrologically similar period in 1983 (29 July - 3 August), when large numbers of flushes were associated with a period of gradually increasing diurnal peak discharge, the progressive encroachment of the proglacial stream across its floodplain appeared to have an influence on flush generation. During 1983, hand sampling of meltwater was undertaken on tributary streams at the glacier snout and at various sites along the main proglacial stream. These were used to determine suspended sediment concentration at different points on the proglacial stream network and, if flushes were recorded on the turbidity chart during hand sampling, it was possible to attribute the flushes to approximate source areas.

The proglacial stream of the Glacier de Tsidjiore Nouve is steep, has a boulder bed and step-pool sequences in its long profile. As discharge increases, distributaries develop as water spills from the pools to occupy previously dry areas of the valley train. These increases in the area of active stream flow are often associated with the flushing out of fine sediments. High flows are also associated with bank erosion and collapse, which can also produce pulses in the turbidity chart (as was observed on both the 31 July and 2 August 1983). None of these proglacial sources of suspended sediment have been observed to produce very large turbidity pulses and they have a characteristic timing, being most noticeable during rising discharge and particularly when flows exceed the previous day's peak discharge.

Two types of event have been observed to generate large, asymmetrical, peaked sediment pulses with steep rising limbs. On 5 August 1984, a large boulder collapsed down the snout of Glacier de Tsidjiore Nouve revealing an area of fine sediments at the snout and releasing water from the ruptured ice to two small streams. The tributary streams became highly charged with suspended sediment (4600 and 40700 mg l^{-1}) and produced a very peaked sediment pulse on the turbidity chart. On 2 August 1983, high suspended sediment concentrations (2900 and 24000 mg l^{-1}) were observed in two different streams draining from the snout of the glacier and were associated with sediment flushes on the turbidity chart. There had been a heavy thunderstorm the previous night, major cracks had developed across the glacier snout and the two tributaries transporting high concentrations of sediment had moved their point of exit from the glacier snout since the preceding day. In this case the peaked flushes tapped sediment sources upstream of the glacier snout.

These limited field observations indicate that major, asymmetrical, peaked sediment flush events can be generated from the glacier-covered part of the catchment and so support the results of hand sampling in the proglacial stream in 1981 reported in Gurnell (1982). Gurnell noted flush events from single tributaries and simultaneously from multiple tributaries but turbidity records were not available to describe the form of the 1981 flush events. No major peaked pulses have been observed to be generated proglacially in the Tsidjiore Nouve catchment, but this may be a function of insufficient field observations. Experiments to simulate the impact of proglacial bank collapse were, therefore, undertaken to investigate the role of proglacial sources in generating sediment flushes.

Suspended sediment flushes produced by simulated bank collapse - a field experiment

In the field the effects of individual sediment supply events can rarely be studied directly, therefore field experiments involving either the artificial generation of a supply event (e.g. use of explosives in initiating cliff collapse - Bathurst *et al.*, 1986) or simulation of sediment supply (e.g. bed disturbance experiments - Lambert and Walling (1988)) are necessary. In the Bas Glacier d'Arolla, Haut Glacier d'Arolla and Glacier de Tsidjiore

Nouve proglacial zones two major sediment sources may contribute to sediment flushes: valley train bluff erosion and eluviation of the valley floor. Sediment transport experiments were carried out to determine the nature of suspended sediment pulse transport in proglacial channels using sediment derived from these sources.

Stream bank collapse and valley train eluviation were simulated by injecting a known weight of sediment (in units of approximately 15 kg) into the proglacial channel. Downstream of the injection point, turbidity was monitored using a Partech suspended solids monitor. The sediment was collected from proglacial streambanks and bluffs but some finer sediment was also injected to allow comparison between the passage of coarse sediment (bank material) and finer sediment pulses.

The experiments showed that sediment introduced at increasing distances from the turbidity monitoring station induced an increased time to peak and an attenuation of the turbidity trace so that after a short distance pulses were symmetrical in shape and even tended towards a steeper falling than rising limb. Increasing the amount of injected sediment resulted, over a fixed distance, in an increase in peak turbidity; finer sediment induced larger and slightly earlier turbidity peaks, supporting the view that more peaked sediment flushes are likely to be subglacial in origin. However, variations in turbidity response by a factor of two occurred for apparently similar samples collected from the same source. Differences may be attributable to inadequate mixing or to variations in source material.

These experiments demonstrate the variability of suspended sediment transport, but the small-scale of the experiments is also significant. The study reaches were short (less than 50 m), sediment volumes were small (less than 75kg) and the experiments were carried out over a restricted discharge range (0.6 - 1.0 $m^3 s^{-1}$), giving very short flush durations (30-110 seconds) which would only just be recognisable on the turbidity charts used in the analysis of prototype events. It is questionable whether these results can be scaled to prototype pulses. However, the results suggest that it is unlikely that large sediment pulses would be generated from valley train sediment sources and that if flushes are generated they are likely to have an attenuated shape. Given the coarse nature of valley train sediments (average silt/clay content of bank and bluff materials at Bas Glacier d'Arolla is only 4% by weight) and that proglacial suspended sediment is dominantly silt-sized, it would be necessary to erode over 130 m^3 of valley train sediments to generate a flush transporting approximately 10 tonnes of suspended sediment.

The identification of sediment pulses routed through the Bas Glacier d'Arolla

Field observations at Bas Glacier d'Arolla suggested that large asymmetrical sediment flushes in the turbidity chart (with steeper rising than falling limbs) recorded on the proglacial stream, originate from source areas upstream from the glacier snout. The turbidity record for the Bas Glacier d'Arolla for June to August 1987 was characterised by suspended sediment flushes. The times of purging of the Haut Glacier d'Arolla meltwater intake sediment trap were found to closely correspond with the large asymmetrical sediment pulses. Haut Glacier d'Arolla is a high-level glacier occupying an adjacent valley 1.5 km to the southeast of Bas Glacier d'Arolla. Virtually every pulse or pulse complex is linked with a purge of the Haut Arolla sediment trap, suggesting that sediment charged meltwater purged from the upper glacierised catchment is very rapidly routed through the Bas Glacier d'Arolla. Analysis of the full turbidity record for Bas Glacier d'Arolla 1987 (25 May - 4 September), identified 256 pulses. 91 of these flushes had a steep rising limb and marked asymmetrical form, and 85% of these flushes were matched with Haut Glacier d' Arolla purges. The remaining asymmetrical flushes, when observed in the field, were seen to also come from the glacier.

The nature and frequency of flush events at Bas Glacier d'Arolla and Tsidjiore Nouve are very different. The Bas Glacier d'Arolla turbidity record is relatively simple with large flushes dominating (2.5 flushes/day - 1987 season). At Tsidjiore Nouve the record is much more complex with more, smaller pulses, the majority of which occur with negligible variations in discharge. It is interesting to speculate whether the differences in the frequency of flushes is indicative of processes acting at the bed of these glaciers. Could this mean that the glacier drainage system at Bas Glacier d'Arolla is more stable and accesses few sediment stores? Bezinge *et al.* (1988) and Gurnell *et al.* (1988) suggested that at Glacier de Tsidjiore Nouve enhanced sediment yield is associated with glacier advance and Humphrey *et al.* (1986), for the Variegated Glacier, Alaska, showed that discharges of turbid water were related to mini-surge activity.

SIGNIFICANCE OF PULSES

The significance of suspended sediment flushes can be evaluated in terms of their contribution to the proglacial meltwater streamload and the loss of information that results if the flush events are not adequately characterised. The contribution of suspended sediment flushes to total suspended sediment yield has been determined for the Bas Glacier d'Arolla catchment for the period 25 May - 30 July 1987. The total amount of sediment contributed by purging of the Haut Glacier d'Arolla sediment trap was 1903 tonnes (i.e. 28.8% of the suspended sediment (turbidity) load and 8.8% of the total basin sediment output during this period) whilst other 'natural' flushes contributed 630 tonnes to the suspended sediment yield. Thus, a total of 37% of the suspended sediment yield was derived from flush events. This is probably an underestimate of the importance of these events since flushes in suspended sediment may also be accompanied by pulses in bedload transport.

Identifying suspended sediment flushes is important in the design of glacio-hydrological sampling strategies. Simulated sampling experiments were conducted on two continuous suspended sediment series (23 June - 27 June 1986 and 11 July - 11 September 1986) from the Bas Glacier d'Arolla proglacial stream. An hourly sampling strategy resulted in respectively, 84% and 64% reduction in the number of pulses identified; implying a potential underestimation of suspended sediment yields and the loss of diagnostic information regarding the sediment origins. The two series represent, respectively, a period of frequent small-scale flushes (11.4 flushes/day) and a longer period of less frequent but larger flushes (1.8 flushes/day). The loss of information for the two glaciers reported here is quite large. Continuous turbidity records are, therefore, required to give an accurate measure of suspended sediment yield and a precise definition of the nature of the suspended sediment transport events. This supports the conclusion of Olive and Rieger (1988). Where turbidity meters are not available, probability based sampling methods (Thomas, 1988) can improve estimates of sediment load and increase the representation of suspended sediment flushes which, at Tsidjiore Nouve, have an increased frequency with higher background discharges.

CONCLUSIONS

Proglacial suspended sediment concentration series are characterised by frequent short flushes. They form an important component of suspended sediment load (46% and 37% of suspended load was transported in association with sediment flush events during the study periods at Glacier de Tsidjiore Nouve and Bas Glacier d'Arolla, respectively) but have different frequency - magnitude characteristics in the two basins. Detailed analysis of size and shape parameters of flushes at Tsidjiore Nouve, field observations of specific events and their causes in both glacier basins, and small-scale field experiments simulating proglacially-generated flushes, indicate that the size and shape of flushes may be indicative of their source area. Peaked, asymmetrical flushes with steeper rising than falling limbs appear to be predominantly glacial in origin, whereas smaller, more symmetrical flushes can be generated from proglacial sediment sources. However, a better understanding of the genesis of suspended sediment flushes would be gained if measurements of glacial motion, particle size determinations and sediment tracing studies were carried out concurrently with proglacial stream turbidity monitoring. Particle size characteristics offer valuable information on sediment source areas and pathways (Bøgen, 1988; Fenn and Gomez, 1989) and a quantitative knowledge of source areas is essential to understanding suspended sediment transport variability (Van Sickle and Beschta, 1983).

ACKNOWLEDGEMENTS NERC are gratefully acknowledged for the provision of a studentship to support J. Warburton during this research. The generous provision of discharge data and logistical support by Grande Dixence S.A. is also very gratefully acknowledged.

REFERENCES

Bathurst J.C., Leeks G.J.L. and Newson M.D. (1986) Relationship between sediment supply and sediment transport for the Roaring River, Colorado, USA. In Drainage Basin Sediment Delivery, (Proc. Albuquerque Symp, Aug. 1986) IHAS Publ. 159, 105-117.

Bezinge A., Clark M.J., Gurnell A.M. and Warburton J. (1988) The management of sediment transported by glacial meltwater streams and its significance for the estimation of sediment yield. Annals of Glaciology, 13, 1-5.

Bøgen J. (1980) The hysteresis effect of sediment transport systems. Norsk Geografisk Tidsskrift, 34, 45-54.

Bøgen J. (1988) A monitoring programme of sediment transport in Norwegian rivers. In Sediment Budgets (Proc. Porto Alegre Symp., Dec. 1988) IAHS Publ. 174, 149-159.

Fenn C.R., Gurnell A.M. and Beecroft I. (1985) An evaluation of the use of suspended sediment rating curves for the prediction of suspended sediment concentration in a proglacial stream. Geografiska Annaler, 67A, 71-82.

Fenn C.R. and Gomez B.(1989) Particle size analysis of the sediment suspended in a proglacial stream: Glacier de Tsidjiore Nouve, Switzerland. Hydrological Processes, 3, 123-135.

Gurnell A.M. (1982) The dynamics of suspended sediment concentration in a proglacial stream. In Hydrological Aspects of Alpine and High Mountain Areas (Proc. Exeter Symp. July 1982) IAHS Publ. 138, 319-330.

Gurnell A.M. (1987) Suspended sediment. In A.M. Gurnell and M.J. Clark (Eds) Glaciofluvial Sediment Transfer: An Alpine Perspective, John Wiley & Sons, Chichester, 305-354.

Gurnell A.M., Warburton J. and Clark M.J. (1988) A comparison of sediment transport and yield characteristics of two adjacent glacier basins, Val d'Hérens, Switzerland. In Sediment Budgets (Proc. Porto Alegre Symp., Dec. 1988) IAHS Publ. 174, 431-441.

Hammer K.M. and Smith N.D. (1983) Sediment production and transport in a proglacial stream: Hilda Creek, Alberta, Canada. Boreas, 12, 91-106.

Heggen R.J. (1986) Periodic surges and sediment mobilization. In Drainage Basin Sediment Delivery, (Proc. Albuquerque Symp, Aug. 1986) IHAS Publ. 159, 323-333.

Humphrey N., Raymond C. and Harrison . (1986) Discharges of turbid water during mini-surges of Variegated glacier, Alaska, USA. Journal of Glaciology, 32, 111, 195-207.

Olive L.J. and Rieger W.A. (1988) An examination of the role of sampling strategies in the study of suspended sediment transport. In Sediment Budgets (Proc. Porto Alegre Symp., Dec. 1988) IAHS Publ. 174, 259 - 267.

Østrem G. (1975) Sediment transport in glacial meltwater streams. In A.V. Jopling and B.C. MacDonald (Eds) Glaciofluvial and Glaciolacustrine Sedimentation, Society of Economic Palaeotologists and Mineralogist Special Publication 20, 101-122.

Richards K.S. (1984) Some observations of suspended sediment dynamics in Storbregrova, Jotunheim. Earth Surface Processes and Landforms, 9, 101-112.

Thomas R.B. (1988) Measuring sediment yields in storms using PSALT. In Sediment Budgets (Proc. Porto Alegre Symp., Dec. 1988) IAHS Publ. 174, 315 - 323.

VanSickle J. and Beschta R.L. (1983) Supply-based models of suspended sediment transport in streams. Water Resources Research, 19, 3, 768-778.

Hydrology in Mountainous Regions. I - Hydrological Measurements; the Water Cycle
(Proceedings of two Lausanne Symposia, August 1990). IAHS Publ. no. 193, 1990.

Environmental contamination and other anthropogenic impacts on Otamiri and Nwaore rivers, Owerri, Nigeria

K. M. IBE Sr., A. H. O. SOWA & O. C. OSONDU
Federal University of Technology, Dept. of Geosciences, Owerri, Nigeria

ABSTRACT The study has been carried out by conducting short-term surface water (Otamiri and Nwaore rivers) and land pollution survey of Owerri urban area and environs, Imo state, in order to establish the current levels of pollution. An attempt has been made to show the relationships between pollution levels, population density, industrial and agricultural activities. The spatial distribution of pollutants due to poor land use system and human activities were investigated, thus emphasizing integrated planned development as a preventive measure for arresting pollution levels in fast-growing urban centres.

INTRODUCTION

The importance of environmental quality in Imo State (southeastern Nigeria) generally, and in Owerri urban area in particular has recently attracted a great deal of interest. The population density of the study area in 1969 was about 102,800, in 1976 about 149,000, and in 1982 about 400,000. By the year 2000, it may exceed 1,000,000 (Egboka & Uma, 1985). Water and land, the vital resources of life, are increasingly being contaminated in the wake of popular growth, poor land use system, agricultural activities, industrialization and anthropogene impact on the study area.

The study area is the water-shed of Otamiri and Nwaore rivers both in Owerri and the surrounding villages with a radius of about 20 km. Due to urbanization, rapid population growth in Owerri, the extension of surface water contamination along the downstream of the rivers ranges from moderate to serious. The principal objective of this study is to delineate pollution levels and their spatial distribution especially along the rivers, and to look into the causes and sources of surface water pollution.

GEOLOGY

The study area is underlaid by the sedimentary sequence of the Benin formation (Miocene to recent), and the underlying Asaba formation (Oligocene). The Benin formation is made up of friable sands with minor intercalations of clay. The sand units are mostly coarse-grained, pebbly, poorly sorted, and contain lenses of fine-grained sands (Short & Stäuble, 1967; Onyeagocha, 1980). The formation starts as a thin edge at its contact with Ogwashi-Asaba formation in the north of the area and thickens southwards (seawards). The average thickness of the formation at the study area is 800 m (Avbovbo, 1978).

The terrain of the study area is characterized by two types of land forms: highly undulating ridges in the northeast, and nearly flat topography in the southwest.

METHODS OF ANALYSIS

A short term field survey of Otamiri and Nwaore rivers was carried out in order to locate the important sources of pollution. Plant, stream sediment, and water samples were collected and analysed in order to determine the extent of possible contamination of surface water arising from human activities and urbanization. The plant ash and sediment samples were analysed at the Institute of Mineralogy, University of Erlangen, West Germany, using XRF. The hydrochemical analyses of the water samples (Tab. 1) were carried out in the geological laboratory of Federal University of Technology, Owerri, using a portable Hach DR-EL/4 Laboratory Kit. The values were determined within confidence limits of +/- 5%.

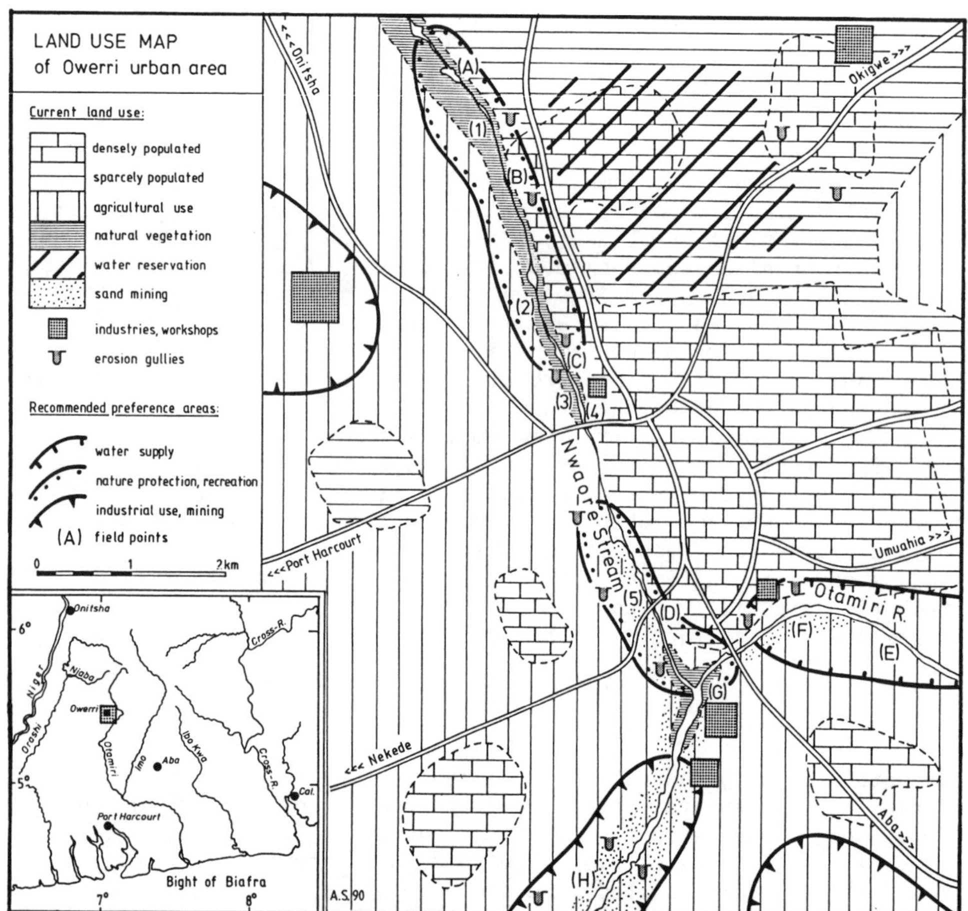

FIG. 1 Map of land use and usage claim of Owerri urban area.

Basing on a map with the scale 1 : 20,000, a proper land use map was produced (Fig. 1) that presents spatial distribution and concentration of population, industry, agriculture, untouched nature, and other features related to environmental considerations. The evaluation of hydrochemical analyses and map was to bring out the impact of rapid population growth, human activities and urbanization in degrading the quality of surface water resources.

RESULTS AND DISCUSSION

The results of the plant sample analyses are graphically presented in Fig. 2. The concentration of total lead detected (80 - 420 ppm) is well above the geochemical background (<10 ppm) of lead in plants (Kloke, 1974). The local variation of lead and zinc concentrations shows that the maximum values were recorded at field point 4, i.e. down-stream of the zinc industry.

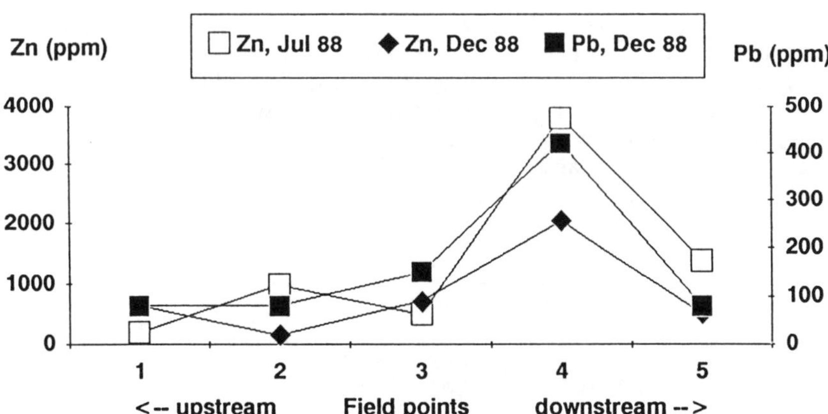

FIG. 2 Heavy metal content of plant ash samples taken along Nwaore Stream, Owerri, during rainy (July) and dry season (December), 1988; see Fig. 1 for the location of the field points. A zinc factory is situated between points 3 and 4.

The total concentrations of cations and anions from Otamiri and Nwaore rivers (Table 1) are graphically presented in Fig. 3. The generalized concentration trend of dissolved solids shows a slight but steady increase following the course of the rivers (field points A --> D --> H for Nwaore, and E --> H for Otamiri river; see Fig. 1). This counts especially for the typical indicators of anthropogene pollution, i.e. nitrate, phosphate and chemical oxygen demand (COD). The pH values, on the other hand, decrease continuously. The concentrations of sodium, magnesium, calcium, iron and sulfate are relatively low and constant.

TABLE 1 Hydrochemical analyses of water samples from Nwaore (A-D) and Otamiri streams (E-H), Owerri, collected on 28/5/1989. Confidence limits +/- 5%.

No.	Na^{+} mg/l	Mg^{++} mg/l	Ca^{++} mg/l	Fe^{++} mg/l	HCO_3^{-} mg/l	PO_4^{--} mg/l	NO_3^{-} mg/l	SO_4^{--} mg/l	Total mg/l	pH	COD mg/l
A	6.3	8.0	5.6	0.0	16.5	2.3	56.3	8.0	103.0	6.5	80
B	6.4	10.0	5.6	0.0	16.5	2.3	56.7	8.0	105.5	6.6	105
C	6.4	10.2	5.7	0.1	18.6	3.1	57.3	8.1	109.5	5.1	170
D	6.4	10.3	5.7	0.1	16.6	4.2	60.2	8.2	111.7	5.0	172
E	6.3	3.4	2.3	0.0	18.0	1.1	50.0	4.0	85.1	6.0	40
F	6.4	3.4	2.4	0.0	18.0	1.1	50.8	4.0	86.1	6.3	50
G	6.4	3.4	2.4	0.0	19.1	2.0	51.2	4.2	88.7	6.3	100
H	6.5	10.4	5.7	0.1	16.6	4.2	61.2	8.3	113.0	5.0	180

The results gained, however, show that the concentrations of several critical parameters are outside the recommended range as provided by World Health Organization (WHO). For comparism, the guidelines for drinking water quality of European Community (1980) provide reference values of 25 mg/l for nitrate, 0.35 mg/l for phosphate, and maximum admissible limits of 50 mg/l for nitrate, 6.1 mg/l for phosphate, 20 mg $KMnO_4$/l for COD.

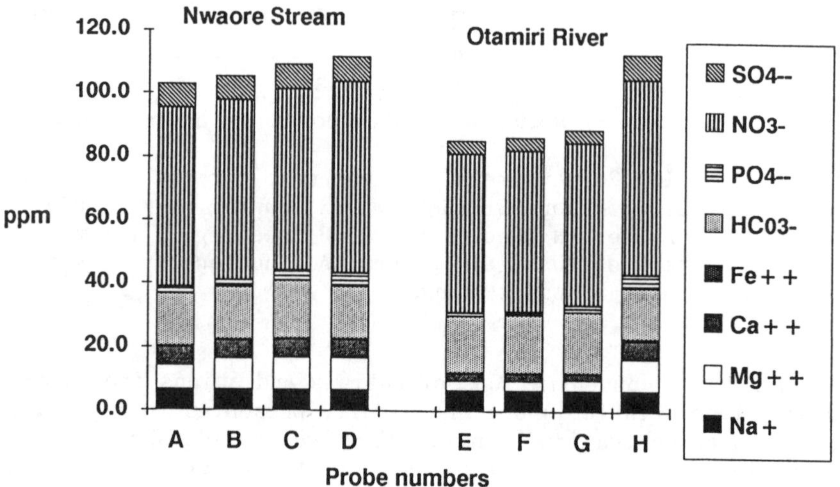

FIG. 3 Hydrochemical analyses of water samples from Nwaore and Otamiri streams, Owerri; see Fig. 1 for the location of the field points.

It has been evident from the findings that the causes and sources of water pollution in the study area are due to agricultural land use, human activities and industrialization: The land use map produced (Fig. 1) reveals that the entire course of the two rivers is accompanied by agricultural activities. This is seen as the main source for the high nitrate and phosphate contentrations. Industries like FAUSON Industries (Nig.) Ltd., that manufactures zinc products, discharge their waste water directly into Nwaore river and are probably responsible for the observed high heavy metal contamination.

Additional water pollution problems like entrophication, or high oxygene demand could be partly due to sand dredging activities along the rivers, and the uncontrolled disposal of saw dust by timber producing saw mill industries into the river-beds. Of course, relatively high COD, and low pH-values, may be partly due to a high content of humic acids in the water, too.

FUTURE WORK

Efforts will be made to define the project area on a map with the primary objective of producing the following maps of the area at a reasonable scale as the research advances: geological, topographic, geomorphologic, soil and erosion bar maps. It is essential to measure and to monitor levels of pollution due to environmental and other anthropogene impacts on a continuing basis. It is suggested that the State Government should enact a law that should control the use of areas for agriculture, deforestation and sanitary land fill sites.

ACKNOWLEDGEMENTS

The authors are grateful to Prof. Dr. W. Bausch and Dipl.-Min. W. Köhler from the Institute of Mineralogy, University of Erlangen (FRG) for invaluable assistance with the geochemical analyses of the samples. Field work was financed through a Federal University of Technology, Owerri Research Grant, and we are grateful for this.

REFERENCES

Avbovbo, A. (1978) Tertiary Lithostratigraphy of Niger Delta. Bull. Amer. Ass. Petr. Geol. 62, 295 - 305.

Egboka, B. C. E. & Uma, K. O. (1985) Water resources of Owerri and its Environs, Imo State. Nig. Journ. Min. Geol. 22,, 57 - 62.

European Community (1980). Official Gazette No. L 229/11-229/29.

Ibe, K. M. (1988) Environmental Contamination of Otamiri and Nwaore rivers, Owerri, Nigeria. (in press)

Onyeagocha, A. C. (1980) Petrography and Depositional Environment of the Benin Formation. Nigerian Journ. Min. Geol. 17, 147 - 151.

Kloke, A. (1974) Blei - Zink - Cadmuim, Anreicherung in Böden und Pflanzen. VDI-Bericht 203, 71 - 74.

Short, K. & Stäuble, J. (1967) Outline of the Geology of the Nigerian Delta. Bull. Amer. Ass. Petr. Geol. 51, 661 - 779.

Hydrology in Mountainous Regions. I - Hydrological Measurements; the Water Cycle
(Proceedings of two Lausanne Symposia, August 1990). IAHS Publ. no. 193, 1990.

Extreme conditions of streamwater chemistry in a partly forested mountainous region

HANS M. KELLER
Swiss Federal Institute for Forest, Snow and Landscape Research, CH-8903 Birmensdorf, Switzerland

ABSTRACT The chemical composition of streamwater in mountainous regions is mainly influenced by non-point sources. Based on weekly flow proportional samples the inorganic chemistry of streams in the Flyschzone of the northern Prealps is analysed for extreme (95% percentile) concentrations of solutes. It is typical for all 3 basins considered - regardless of size and land use - that mineral concentrations (Ca, Mg, Na, K, Si, S) show maximum levels during low flows. Such hydrologic conditions are most frequent in autumn at the end of prolonged rainfree periods and in winter when freezing temperatures and a nonmelting snowpack prevail. Nitrates and ammonia show peak concentrations during the dormant season and at medium flow rates. Suspended sediment concentrations are highest in mid summer during the times when intensive thundershowers occur. The respective streamflow volumes however are moderate indicating that isolated individual intensive storms yield higher concentrations than prolonged rain events. In order to explain the suggested mechanisms more detailed studies on a storm basis are necessary.

INTRODUCTION

Water Resources in mountainous regions can consider many different aspects. With respect to water quality most often average or frequent conditions are of utmost importance, since the use of these waters from mountainous areas often affects groundwaters and water supply systems. As long as good quality of these waters prevail, little has to be done to improve the situation in the catchment areas of the mountains.

If however extreme situations occur, one is often caught by surprise, because there is a lack of studies which focus on extreme concentrations and the respective hydrological situations.

In this study we have attempted to look at the water chemistry of three mountain streams which have been monitored continuously since 1982, 1984 and 1985 respectively. Average and seasonal conditions, export fluxes and general chemistry have been published elsewhere (Keller et al. 1989a, Keller 1989b) and are not considered here. The following discussion focuses on the top 5% maximum concentrations of 14 elements and suspended sediment. This study should give some insight into climatic and hydrologic situations during which these maximum concentrations occur. Since the 3 basins are located in the same general region, but each with different proportions of the various land use types (forest, open wetlands, pasture, extensive agriculture, permanent housing, access roads) the comparison was thought to bring some light also on the possible effects of the various land use practices.

THE STUDY AREA

The 3 streams and their respective catchment basins are located in the Alptal, a north-south oriented valley in the central prealps, Switzerland. The geologic parent material is Flysch, consisting of alternating calcareous sandstones with argillite and bentonite shists. The weathering of these rocks results in very heavy and impervious soils of low permeability. Wetlands (meadows, bogs) are frequent, however in some locations artificial open drainage ditches have been dug to improve the stability of the slopes and the possibility of natural regeneration of the local forest (montane to subalpine spruce-fir forest).

Annual precipitation in the basins with elevations between 1100 and 1550 m.a.s.l. is usually around 2200 mm per year. In years with cold winters, up to 40% of that falling as snow. The recent years (since 1988) however have brought only 10 to 20% of that stored in a winter snowpack. In the summer thundershowers are frequent and intensive rains produce short but pronounced peaks in streamflow with elevated rates of suspended sediment and bed load transport.

The basin characteristics are summarized in table 1.

TABLE 1 Main Characteritstics in 3 Basins of the Alptal.

	Basin		
	3 Vogelbach	4 Lümpenenbach	10 Erlenbach
Size, km^2	1.5	0.9	0.7
Mean elev.masl	1365	1340	1350
Forest, %	65	20	40
Pasture, %	10	60	-
Wetlands, %	25	25	60
Perm.housing	no	yes	no
Accessroads, m'	~1000	~4300	~500
Continous sampling, since	May 85	April 84	Feb 82
No of samples	216	265	371

METHODS

Sampling

In order to get continuous information on the chemistry of

streamflow from the 3 basins, flow proportional samplers have been installed at the gauging sites. This sampler is connected to the water level recording system. At intervals set by the flow rate, a small sample (approx 10 ml) is automatically pumped from a protected bypass at the gauging site to the sample container placed in a refrigerator cooled to $4^{o}C$. In this fashion samples are drawn 4 to 10 times daily during low flows and up to once a minute during high flows. The sample container can take up to 1500 samples. At the weekly visits subsamples are taken for suspended sediment determination and for chemical analysis. They are taken in a cool box to the laboratory where the chemical analysis is done as follows (see also Keller et al. 1989a): ICP analysis for Al, Cu, Fe, Zn, Si, K, Mg, Na, Ca, and S. HPLC is used for NO_3-N^-, SO_4^{--} and Cl^- and a Technicon II Auto-Analyzer for NH_4^+. The detection limits are given in Table 2.

This sampling procedure is appropriate to estimate the total loads of dissolved substances on a continuous basis. It is therefore well suited to monitor concentrations of dissolved minerals and nutrients, which seep to the stream continuously. Point sources of pollution however can easily pass through the gauging site without being detected. This can be the case particularly during low flows, when only once every few hours a sample is taken. The subsequent interpretation of the data from this sampling system should therefore take into account these limitations.

Statistical Procedure

For each the three basins two sets of data have been assembled to find prevailing patterns of climatic and hydrologic conditions at which extremely high concentrations (> 95% percentile level) occur. The first is a set of the 4 to 7 year sampling period (see table 1) which was used to look at the frequency pattern with respect to season and to the level of stream flow. It also was used to determine the 95% percentile level of the extreme maximum concentrations.

The second was a data set which included all samples for each basin exceeding the 95% percentile value (see also Table 2). In such a way the large database was reduced to sample-data considering situations of extreme conditions only.

RESULTS

Accuracy

From table 2 it is obvious to see, that **Al, Zn, Cu and Fe** are found on average close to the detection limit of the analytical instrument used (ICP). Considering the lowest quantitatively determinable concentrations given for the 4 metals (Al 0.2; Zn 0.005; Cu 0.02; Fe 0.03 mg/l), only in rare cases does one of these concentrations reach a significant level to make any interpretations with respect to hydrological conditions or differences between the basins.

TABLE 2 Detection limits (DL), arithmetic mean ($\bar{x}$) and 95% percentile concentrations of 14 chemical substances and suspended sediments in basins 3, 4 and 10, Alptal.

Substance	DL	Basin 3		Basin 4		Basin 10	
mg/l	mg/l	$\bar{x}$	95%	$\bar{x}$	95%	$\bar{x}$	95%
Al	0.05	0.06	0.11	0.06	0.10	0.06	0.11
Zn	0.001	0.006	0.015	0.004	0.009	0.006	0.015
Cu	0.005	0.009	0.016	0.008	0.015	0.007	0.016
Fe	0.005	0.02	0.05	0.01	0.04	0.02	0.07
Si	0.012	1.4	2.5	1.2	2.0	0.7	0.9
NH_4^+-N	0.005	0.11	0.35	0.07	0.24	0.02	0.04
K	0.2	0.7	1.4	1.0	1.8	0.8	1.5
Mg	0.005	2.4	5.2	2.6	4.2	2.8	4.7
Na	0.03	2.0	4.4	2.5	5.4	2.5	5.4
Ca	0.02	42.4	71.2	54.0	80.7	43.3	66.4
S	0.05	2.9	5.5	3.7	7.5	4.4	9.0
SO_4^{--}	0.8	8.3	14.9	10.4	20.9	12.4	25.3
Cl^-	0.3	0.8	1.7	1.2	2.8	0.7	1.9
NO_3^--N	0.15	0.5	1.0	0.5	0.9	0.2	0.5
Susp.Sed.	3	297	965	264	1236	391	1585

From these data we have therefore to conclude that more accurate analytical procedures have to be used to make inferences on the behaviour of these elements.

Another problem is found with ammonia, NH_4^+-N. The well aerated and oxygen saturated mountain streams often show very low ammonia-concentrations. The sampling procedure described earlier and the storage as composite samples however could also be responsible for low ammonia concentrations. This paper however deals with extreme high concentrations only, for which we are confident about the signifant accuracy.

The observation periods

An anylsis at basin 10 with the longest continuous sampling period shows the majority of all extreme concentrations (>95% percentile) occurring during the years 85 through 89. Exceptions are a few high values of nitrate in 1982, of suspended sediment in 1984 and a few of Zn and Si in the years 1982 through 1984. In basin 4 ammonia shows some high concentrations in 1984; all other extreme values were observed later. This allows a comparison of the 3 basins considering the extreme values between 85 and 89 eventhough the original database originates from different observation periods.

The seasonal frequency of streamflow

All 3 basins show repeatedly a typical seasonal behaviour

of streamflow. It is characterized by a period of elevated flow in spring and early summer. An example based on the first data set is given in Figure 1.

On the other hand we observe the lowest flows in mid winter (January /February) and in late autumn (October/November).

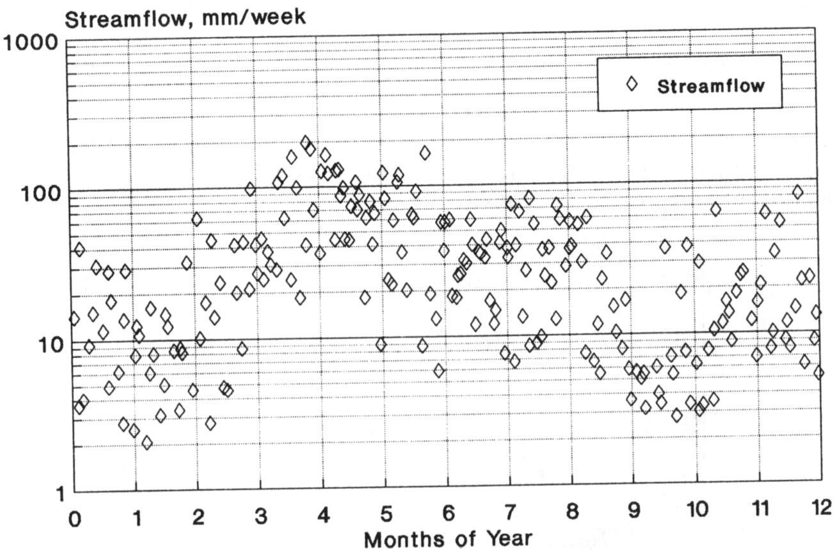

FIG. 1 Weekly streamflow volumes through the seasons of the year in basin 3, Alptal, 1985-89.

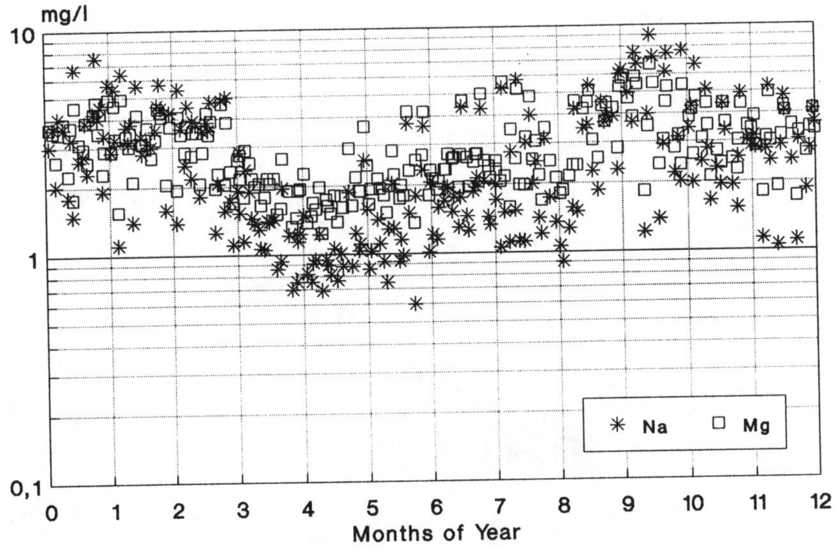

FIG. 2 Seasonal Distribution of Na and Mg in Basin 10.

Maximum Concentrations at Low Flow

This analysis includes only information of the second data set described earlier. A number of mineral concentrations show a seasonal distribution symmetric to that of streamflow volumes, e.g. Na and Mg in Fig. 2. Figure 3 shows the very pronounced inverse relationship of sodium to weekly streamflow and hence explaining that pattern.

A more detailed analysis is given in the correlation matrix for the 3 basins (Table 3). It is interesting to note, that Si has a very different behaviour in basin 10 with much lower correlation coefficients than in basin 3 and 4. This may be due to the low concentration levels of Si in basin 10, which is only about half of that in the basins 3 and 4 (see Table 2).

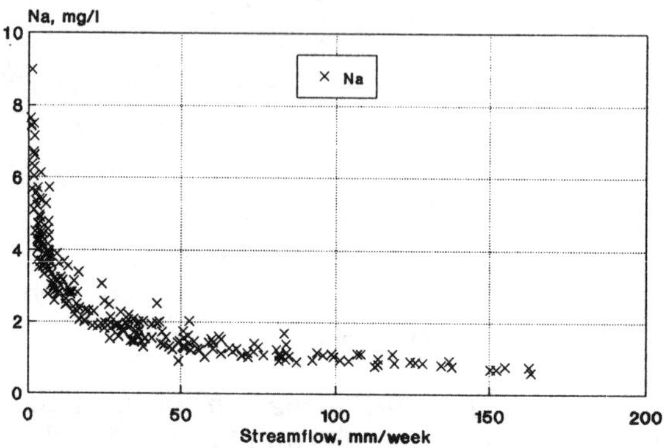

FIG. 3 Sodium and Streamflow volumes in Basin 10, Alptal.

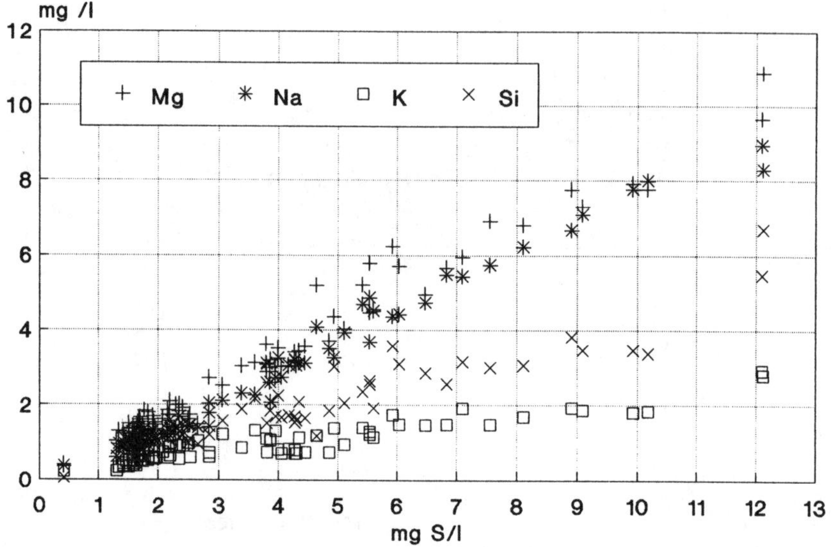

FIG. 4 The interrelationship of extreme mineral concentrations, Basin 3, Alptal.

rals as related to sulfur in basin 3. We concluded therefore that extremely high mineral concentrations occur at winter or autumn low flows, conditions which are highly influenced by the hydrology of the area: periods of low precipitation which are most frequent in autumn and low flows related to snow and frozen winter conditions. High mineral concentrations are therefore always linked to low streamflow (Feller and Kimmins, 1979).

Nitrate and Ammonia

From earlier work (e.g. Reynolds et al. 1989, Keller 1989b) it is known that high nitrate fluxes occur in the dormant season, when a wet front passes through the soil profile.

TABLE 3 Correlations Coefficients r for maximum concentrations of 6 minerals in basins 3, 4 and 10, Alptal.

		Na	Mg	K	Ca	Si
S	Basin 3	.99	.98	.92	.81	.93
	Basin 4	.96	.97	.92	.75	.92
	Basin 10	.93	.90	.72	.83	.24
Na	Basin 3		.98	.90	.81	.91
	Basin 4		.93	.88	.73	.89
	Basin 10		.95	.66	.90	.29
Mg	Basin 3			.93	.83	.95
	Basin 4			.91	.80	.95
	Basin 10			.71	.97	.35
K	Basin 3				.75	.93
	Basin 4				.68	.90
	Basin 10				.67	.26
Ca	Basin 3					.81
	Basin 4					.69
	Basin 10					.39

The analysis of extremely high (top 5%) nitrate concentrations in the basins shows that they - like the minerals -occur in early spring and late autumn (Fig. 5, left). However streamflow conditions are not always as low as they are for extreme mineral concentrations and may in some cases be as high as 50 mm /week and more (Fig. 5, right).

Ammonia concentrations show a similar pattern with maximum concentrations early and late in the year (Fig. 6). For this nutrient we find considerable differences between basins: Almost no variability in basin 10, moderate levels and definite seasonalities in basin 3 and very pronounced seasonalities with the highest peaks in basin 4; the only basin with permanent housing and noticeable pasture areas.

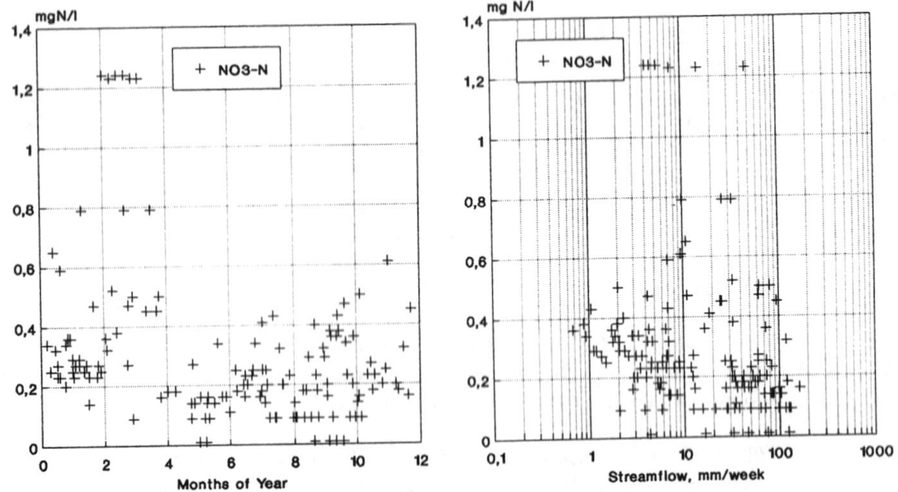

FIG. 5 Extreme Nitrate Concentrations with respect to Season (left) and Streamflow volumes (right) in Basin 10, Alptal.

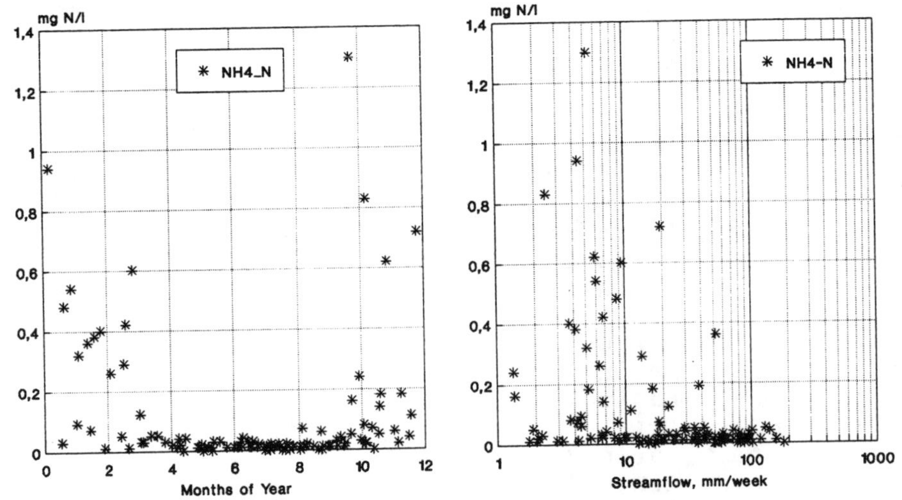

FIG. 6 Extreme Ammonia Concentrations with respect to Season (left) and Streamflow (right) volumes in Basin 4, Alptal.

As an illustration of the relationship among the minerals Figure 4 shows the extreme concentrations of 5 mine-

Suspended Sediment Concentrations

Many mechanisms are responsible for suspended sediment transport. The results from the 3 basins show, as expected, very variable results. Only with respect to seasonal occurrence are the basins similar and show during the summer season (thundershowers) maximum suspended sediment concentrations. Basin 3 had few but high peaks in the middle of the season, basin 10 however (see Fig 7) shows a longer season with many intermediate concentration levels. The respective streamflow levels however are usually intermediate, ranging from 50 to 100 mm/week in basin 4 to 30 to 110 mm/week in basin 10 and from 20 to 60 mm/week in basin 3.

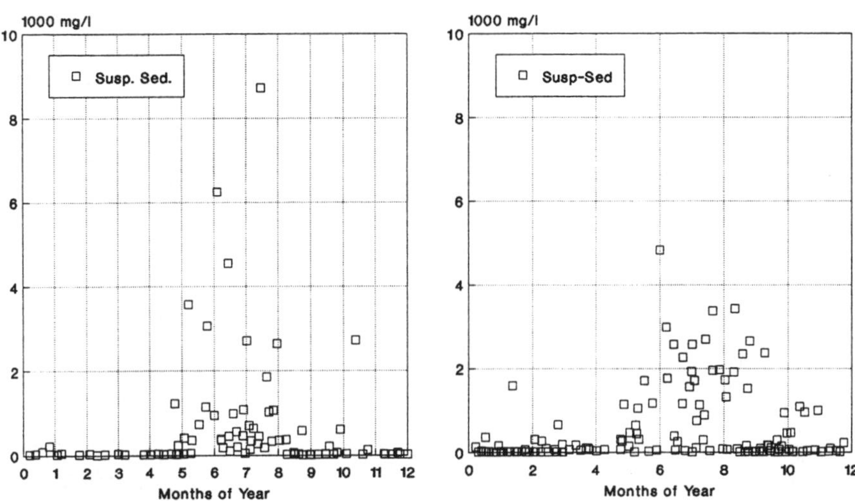

FIG.7 Seasonal Distribution of Extreme Suspended Sediment Concentrations in Basins 3 (l) and 10 (r).

CONCLUSIONS

The hydrology of low flows, the geology of the substrata and maximum mineral concentrations have shown clear relationships in all basins. The behaviour of maximum nutrient concentrations (nitrate, ammonia) however needs more detailed eco-hydrological research.

ACKNOWLEDGEMENTS The help and support of W. Hofstetter, P. Weibel, M. Guecheva, P. Klöti, H. Burch in the field, laboratory and office is gratefully acknowledged.

REFERENCES

Feller, M.C. & Kimmins, J.P. (1979) Chemical Characteristics of small Streams Near Haney in Southwestern British Columbia.**Water Resources Research**, 15(2),p.247-258.

Keller, H.M., Burch H. & Guecheva, M.(1989a) The variability of water quality in a small mountainous region. IAHS Publication, no. 182, p. 305 - 312.

Keller, H.M. (1989b) Seasonal Characteristics of flow regime and water quality in small mountainous basins. Conference on Headwater Control; Proceedings IUFRO and World Ass.of Soil and Water Cons., Prag, 1989, Vol 1, 122-129.

Reynolds, B., Hornung M. & Hughes S. (1989) Chemistry of streams draining grassland and forest catchments at Plynlimon, mid Wales. **Hydrological Sciences Journal** 34, 6, p. 667-686.

Hydrology in Mountainous Regions. I - Hydrological Measurements; the Water Cycle (Proceedings of two Lausanne Symposia, August 1990). IAHS Publ. no. 193, 1990.

Principal characteristics of fold-mountain hydrogeology

A.V.KUDELSKY
Institute of Geochemistry and Geophysics, BSSR Academy of Sciences, Minsk, 220600, U.S.S.R.

ABSTRACT In view of optimization of regional water supply systems, hydrological conditions of fold-mountain areas are examined. A basic model of the dynamics of underground waters on monoclinal structures is characterized. A new type of hydrogeological reservoirs — accumulative microbasins of underground waters of alluvial deposits being of great importance for water supply of mountainous countries is described.

INTRODUCTION

The theoretical concepts of classical hydrogeology which result from the experience obtained in this field of science in the eighteenth-nineteenth centuries in pre-Alpine countries, considered mountainous structures including fold-mountain ones as areas of "catchment" and "pressure creation" for water-bearing horizons of the entire sedimentary rock profile of adjacent hydrogeological basins. The directions of movement of underground waters were considered to be centrifugal relative to fold-mountain systems.Along with this, the washing out down to the basement and homogeneity of the hydrogeochemical profile represented mainly by fresh waters were attributed to the latters. Such ideas neglecting frequent and widely known shows of mineral and thermal waters, the presence of oil-gas fields in the profiles of intramountain depressions and on subsided fold-mountain depressions and on subsided fold-mountain megastructures disoriented for many decades the development of theoretical hydrogeology and hydrogeochemistry and, naturally, did not promote the elaboration of rational water supply systems on the territory of mountainous countries and foothills.

DISCUSSION

The validity of the ideas about the dominant of fold-mountain structures in hydrogeology of associated geological structures was firstly doubted by A.M.Ovchinnikov (1946). Further special hydrogeological studies of mountainous countries (Kolodiy & Kudelsky, 1972; Kudelsky,

1964; Kudelsky et al., 1972) that fold-mountain structures are characterized by hydrodynamic and hydrogeochemical independence, spatial coincidence of the so-called "catchment" and "leakage" areas of water-bearing horizons underlying the groundwater levels, normal hydrogeochemical zonality with a minor-depth (usually up to 200—500m) fresh water belt. A rapid movement of underground waters involves there only the heads of exposed monoclinal strata. The subsided parts of these typically show the regimes of low and extremely low water exchange and highly mineralized underground waters and brines characteristic of these regimes, accumulations of hydrocarbons and metal and nonmetal mineralogical associations.

A good exposure and a high hypsometric position are favourable to the atmospheric water infiltration to the sedimentary rock masses forming ranges of mountains. A rapid movement of underground crack-confined waters involves water-bearing horizons of steep and highly raised slopes. The underground waters show the fastest velocity along the rock stratification, and the filtration rate sharply decreases in a direction perpendicular to this stratification. Therefore, the "washout" of anticlinal structures of ranges of mountains made up of sedimentary rocks occurs "scalewise". The vertical filtration of atmospheric waters in anticlinal arches is quite feeble. Deposits in the central parts of even very large and highly raised anticlines which are not exposed by erosion, are often not washed out and contain highly mineralized chloride waters (Fig. 1).

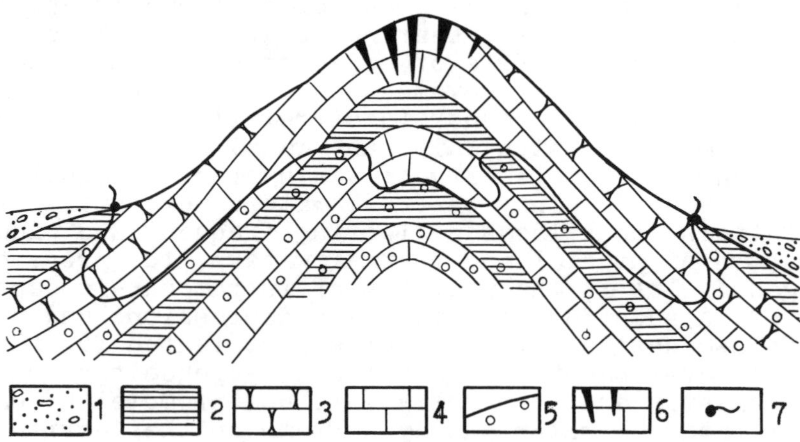

FIG. 1 Peculiarities of hydrogeology of anticlinal structures of fold-mountain systems.
1 - coarse detrital alluvial-proluvial deposits of river valleys and side canions; 2 - relatively low-permeable aleurolite-argillite formations; 3 - sand rocks; 4 - lime rocks; 5 - conditional divide between infiltration and saltish and salt waters of the low water exchange zone; 6 - sedimentary rock cracking in anticlinal arches; 7 - springs.

Infiltration waters of the slopes of mountain ranges migrate to short distances and a major portion of them leaks in situ, on monoclines, as hillside contact springs, or those confined to the contact lines of water-bearing rocks with water-resisting ones at the foot of the slopes. The association of the leakage centres (springs) with the contact lines of rocks having different filtration properties is a characteristic feature of hydrogeology of all the mountain structures without exception and may be attributed to the absence of sufficiently rapid groundwater outflow in the subsided parts of water-bearing horizons. Indeed, underground waters of relatively deep horizons of intermountain depressions and synclines are in most cases highly mineralized (more than 20-25 g/l) methane chloride sodium or calcium (intrafold basins of the Urals, Caucasus, Kopet-Dag, etc.) and, therefore, do not look promising for obtaining fresh potable water.

Long since thick regional leakage areas of fresh underground waters have been known in the outlying areas of the Alpine, Kopet-Dag, Caucasian, Altaian and other fold zones. Basing on this fact, some researchers concluded that there was a connection between the underground waters of folded regions and the middle waters of associated areas of alluvial, intermountain troughs and depressions. However, the question turned out to be more complicated. Field investigations of many years in the Kopet-Dag area, as well as special analysis of hydrogeology of mountainous countries (Kudelsky, 1964) have revealed the following: 1. Outlying regional fresh water leakage areas carry out drainage of not the entire mountain system as a whole, but only of its individual hydrogeological structures and basins situated in the area of high and, to a lesser extent, low water exchange; 2. Fresh waters of mountain structures do not replenish the horizons of deeply subsided edge waters of associated tectonic depressions. Highly mineralized chloride waters of various cation composition often with a high content of microcomponents occur in the immediate vicinity of fresh water discharges within alluvial troughs and depressions. Therefore, the leakage of fresh underground waters at the boundary of mountain structures and associated depressions should be considered not as an evidence of the relationship between the former and the latter, but as an indication of their hydrodynamic disconnection and hampered water exchange within depressions.

A few words about the so-called accumulative microbasins of undergroundwaters of alluvial sediments of river valleys discovered and described in the 1970s on the territory of the West Kopet-Dag (Kudelsky, 1969).The structural-morphological signs of such microbasins are reflected by an anomalous (up to 10 times the background values) and fragmentary increase in the depth of coarse detrital alluvial water-bearing deposits in limited areas of river valleys. The accumulative microbasins are associated with the intersection of axial parts of synclines by river valleys at the points of negative maxima of the youngest (relative to the time of the formation of valleys) undulations (Fig. 2).

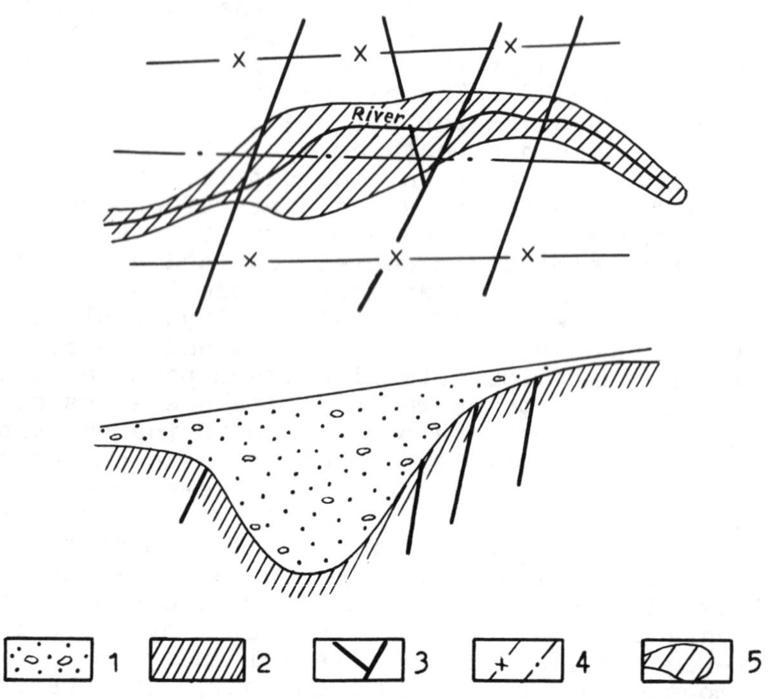

FIG. 2 Accumulative microbasin of underground waters of alluvial deposits: 1 - coarse detrital water-bearing alluvial formations of river valley; 2 - relatively water-resisting underlying deposits; 3 - tectonic disturbances; 4 - anticlinal and synclinal axes; 5 - accumulative microbasin of alluvial deposits and its longitudinal (along the River) geological profile.

The water-bearing horizons of alluvial deposits of river valleys play an important part in the water supply system on the territory of fold-mountain regions. A major portion of the underground water used through wells represent dynamic and capacity (statistical) reserves of the water-bearing horizon. Significant capacity reserves of underground waters is also a characteristic feature of microbasins of alluvial deposits of river valleys, their replenishment during floods being proportional to the decrease during low waters. The seasonal replenishment of water-bearing horizons of alluvial deposits due to the flow water infiltration makes it possible to use the underground waters "for decrease" to the extent exceeding the flow (dynamic) and statistical reserves of the horizons.

CONCLUSIONS

It results from the aforesaid that:

1. Mountain structures as a whole present a wide variety of conditions favourable for the accumulation of fresh underground water, namely, high hypsometric level of the territory, rather high precipitation, good exposure and intensive cracking of rocks in the arches and on the wings of positive structural forms, etc.

2. The areas of catchment, main leakage, outcrop of water-bearing horizons superimpose and are, in the majority of cases, in the same hydrodynamic zone of rapid water exchange. Exceptions are water-bearing horizons of alluvial-proluvial Neogene-Quaternary deposits whose leakage may occur far beyond the mountain structures (valleys of rivers and temporary water courses, debris cones and undermountain benches, etc.).

3. Within the mountain structures the leakage of water-bearing horizons occurs in numerous valleys and canions, the final leakage takes place at contacts of layers with different water permeability on monoclinal structures of rocks.

4. A rapid water exchange, intense washing involve mountain structures from the tops of mountain ranges to the hypsometric contact lines of water-bearing materials with relatively water-resisting ones on monoclinal structures and in outlying areas of mountainous countries. Water-bearing horizons subsiding under impervious beds are weakly washed and contain saltish and salt waters, even though they are in the immediate vicinity of infiltration areas.

5. The lower boundary of the area of rapid water exchange and fresh hydrocarbonate waters is at the contact of water-bearing horizons with water-resisting deposits at the foot of mountain ranges. It should be noted that due to the "scalewise" washing of anticlinal ranges, deposits not exposed by erosion in the central parts of folds can preserve highly mineralized groundwaters.

The area of extremely low water exchange and highly mineralized chloride waters is associated with the most deeply subsided portions of water-bearing horizons, it is the thickest one and typical of all the fold-mountain regions without exception. Hydrocarbons dominate, and nitrogen, carbonic acid, rare elements and, more seldom, hydrogen sulphide are present in the gas composition of underground waters of this area.

6. Fold-mountain structures in the overwhelming majority of cases are not catchment areas for deeply subsided artesian aquifers within the neighbouring depressions, including oil-gas fields (OGF). It has been established by comprehensive hydrogeological studies of fold-mountain structures and large OGF (Kolodiy & Kudelsky, 1972; Kudelsky et al., 1972) that: (a) OGF are hydrodynamically independent of the associated mountainous countries; (b) there is no transbasin movement of underground water masses

along the profile "highly raised — deeply subsided parts" of water-bearing strata underlying the horizons of ground and, partially, confined waters; (c) hydrodynamic peculiarity of productive OGF systems depends on a series of factors independent or slightly dependent on the intensity and direction of infiltration processes and strata hydrodynamics in sections of the upper floors of sedimentary sequences.

REFERENCES

Kolodiy, V.V. & Kudelsky, A.V. (1972) Gidrogeologiya gornykh stran, smezhnykh progibov i vpadin (Hydrogeology of mountainous countries, associated troughs and depressions). Kiev, Izd. Naukova dumka, U.S.S.R. (in Russian).

Kudelsky, A.V. (1964) Osobennosti gidrogeologii gornykh stran na primere zapadnogo Kopet-Daga (Peculiarities of hydrogeology of mountainous countries examplified by the West Kopet-Dag).in: Geologiya i polezniye iskopayemiye Turkmenii. Trudy Gosudarstvennogo proizvodstvennogo geologicheskogo komiteta TSSR. Vyp. 2. Ashkhabad, 307— 320 (in Russian).

Kudelsky, A.V. (1969) Podzemniye vody rykhlykh otlozheniy mezhgornykh dolin Zapadnogo Kopet-Daga (Underground waters of loose deposits of intermountain valleys of the West Kopet-Dag). in: Problemy osvoyeniya pustyn'. Moscow, Izd. Nedra, N 4, 70— 73 (in Russian).

Kudelsky, A.V., Akmamedov, A., Milkis, M.P., et al. (1972) Zapadno-Turkmensky arteziansky bassein. Skladchataya oblast' Kopet-Daga i Malogo Balkhana (The West Turkmenian artesian basin. Folded area of the Kopet-Dag and Minor Balkhan). in: Gidrogeologiya S.S.S.R., vol. 37, 121— 187 (in Russian).

Ovchinnikov, A.M. (1946) Osobennosti gidrogeologii gornykh stran (Hydrogeological peculiarities of mountainous countries). Doklady AN SSSR, vol. 54, 3, 259— 262 (in Russian).

Hydrology in Mountainous Regions. I - Hydrological Measurements; the Water Cycle
(Proceedings of two Lausanne Symposia, August 1990). IAHS Publ. no. 193, 1990.

Chemical composition of precipitation in a prealpine area of eastern Switzerland

O. LANGENEGGER
Riesern 1561, CH-9056 Gais, Switzerland

ABSTRACT The purpose of this paper is to present some results of precipitation analyses which have been conducted in the project area since 1986. The main objective of the investigations has been to study the physico-chemical composition of wet depositions, especially snow, as a function of time, meteorological conditions, and dry precipitation, in order to assess the potential of snow with regard to storing information on air pollution. The majority of the samples considered in this paper originate from the village of Gais, which is located in a prealpine area of the Canton of Appenzell AR in Eastern Switzerland at an altitude of about 940 m above sea level. Snow samples have also been collected in the surroundings of Gais and in the nearby mountains of the Alpstein (Säntis) up to an altitude of 2500 m above sea level. The results presented illustrate a high degree of variability of the physico-chemical composition of precipitation as a function of time, space, and meteorological conditions. Furthermore, an example of mapping air pollution on a local scale by means of the parameter electrical conductivity of snow samples is depicted.

INTRODUCTION

Air pollution has become one of the major problems of our age both in terms of potential health hazards for human beings and adverse effects on local, regional, and global ecological systems. The state of the atmosphere related to air pollution is reflected in the physico-chemical composition of precipitation. Therefore, precipitation analyses represent an important means of monitoring air pollution and determining deposition rates of air pollutants. The investigations partially presented in this paper were initiated in 1986 and have been conducted by the author since. The main part of the investigation area is located between Lake Constance and the Alps in Eastern Switzerland (Fig. 1). It is a typical prealpine area between 900 and 1500 m above sea level. The yearly precipitation is in the range of about 1200 - 1500 mm predominantly originating from the west.

Regular precipitation samples have been taken in the village of Gais having a population of about 2000 people since late 1988. The nearest bigger settlements, Appenzell (population of about 5400), is 5 km southwest, and the town of St.Gall (population of 70'000), is about 9 km northwest of Gais.

The parameters taken into consideration are: pH, electrical conductivity, turbidity, ammonium, nitrite, nitrate, sulfate, as well as, but to a smaller extent, total hardness, calcium, dissolved carbon dioxide, lead, iron, cadmium, and zink. The methods/equipment for analysis comprise: pH-, conductivity-, nephelo-, and spectrophotometers.

Different methods for collecting precipitation samples have been applied, namely: (1) Single snow samples from snow profiles, (2) weekly bulk deposition samples (open collector), and (3) daily wet deposition samples (open collector).

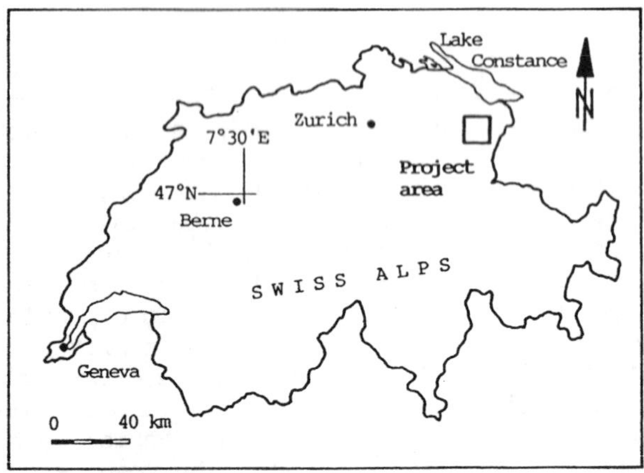

FIG. 1 Map showing the location of the project area.

RESULTS

The volume-weighted values of some selected parameters (pH, electrical conductivity, ammonium, nitrate, and sulfate) of daily wet depositions at the station in Gais for 1989 are listed in Table 1. These results indicate a relatively low level of air pollution and might be taken as typical of the country side of the region. On the other hand, however, they show a wide range of variations. As an example, the mean monthly pH-value varied between 4.2 and 6.1 while the lowest pH-value measured was 3.8. The frequency distribution of the data set of wet depositions for 1989, which comprises 114 samples, is depicted in Table 2.

Figure 2 shows the frequency distribution of the parameters electrical conductivity and ammonium versus the amount of precipitation. A relationship between wind direction and composition of wet deposition is indicated in Figure 3 suggesting that a large proportion of the air pollutants obviously originates from the densely populated and industrialized zones northwest to northeast of the observation station.

Frequency distibutions of the pH-value and the electrical conductivity are presented in Figure 4. These diagrams reveal a superposition of different frequency distributions which are thought to reflect the effect of the wind direction, as shown in Figure 3.

The variations of the composition of wet deposition and, thus, of air pollution, as a function of space is illustrated in Figures 5 and 6. The profile depicted in Figure 5 shows the concentration of ammonium in fresh snow. It clearly demonstrates a high degree of variation within short distances, that is in the range of several hundred meters.

TABLE 1 Volume weighted average values of the pH, electrical conductivity (EC), ammonium (NH_4), nitrate (NO_3), and sulfate (SO_4) of daily wet depositions at the sample site in Gais for 1989.

Month	Precipitation mm	pH	EC $uScm^{-1}$	NH_4 mgl^{-1}	NO_3 mgl^{-1}	SO_4 mgl^{-1}
January	19.0	5.0	26.3	0.9	4.0	
February	38.3	5.8	27.1	1.6	0.9	
March	100.5	5.5	17.8	0.6	1.3	0.2
April	136.9	4.7	23.1	0.6	1.9	1.7
May	70.7	5.6	21.4	1.6	1.4	0.1
June	162.1	5.0	25.5	1.5	2.2	2.3
July	266.7	5.6	17.9	1.3	1.5	1.2
August	164.9	5.1	15.5	0.8	0.9	0.6
September	132.3	4.2	41.4	1.7	2.9	3.3
Oktober	119.3	4.6	25.9	0.9	2.0	0.4
November	72.4	5.1	15.8	0.6	1.2	0.3
December	77.9	6.1	10.9	0.6	0.4	0.8
1989	1361.0	5.1	22.1	1.1	1.7	1.5

TABLE 2 Frequency distribution of the wet deposition samples considered in Table 1 and Figures 2-4.

Range of precipitation mm	Number of samples	Precipitation mm
0- 1	3	1.9
1- 2	10	14.9
2- 5	23	84.4
5- 10	26	184.4
10- 20	31	435.4
20- 50	19	539.2
50-100	2	102.8
0-100	114	1361.0

The map in Figure 6 contains the electrical conductivity of old snow. The time elapsed between snow fall and sampling was about 3 weeks (22 November - 10 December 1989) and characterized by nice but cold weather. Therefore, these results seem to reflect the bulk precipitation, that is both wet (snow) and dry depositions for the period of time mentioned. This example illustrates an interesting application

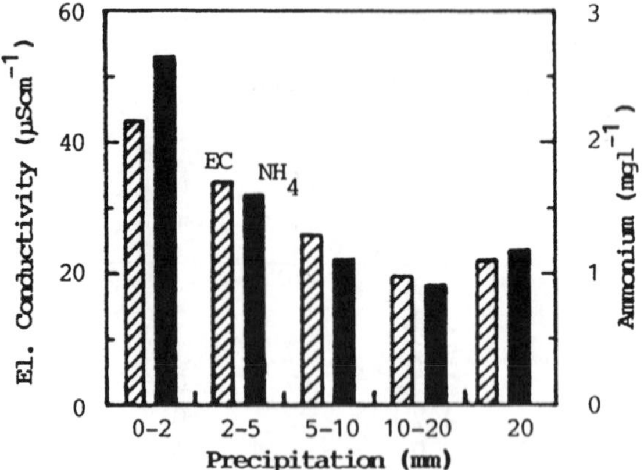

FIG. 2 Frequency distribution of the electrical conductivity (EC) and of ammonium (NH_4) versus the amount of precipitation.

of physico-chemical analyses of precipitation.

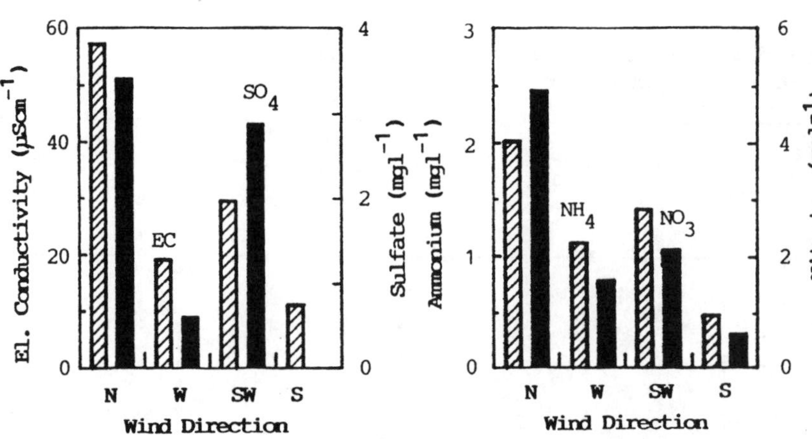

FIG. 3 Average values of the electrical conductivity (EC), sulfate (SO_4), ammonium (NH_4), and nitrate (NO_3) versus wind direction.

The pH-value, the electrical conductivity (EC), and the concentration of ammonium (NH_4) of samples from various snow profiles taken in the surroundings of the Säntis at altitudes between 1300 and 2450 m above sea level were in the ranges of 4.3-6.1 (pH), 3-32 μScm^{-1} (EC), and 0.01-0.65 mgl^{-1} (NH_4). In general, these values are lower than those measured in Gais. However, they also show a high degree of variation.

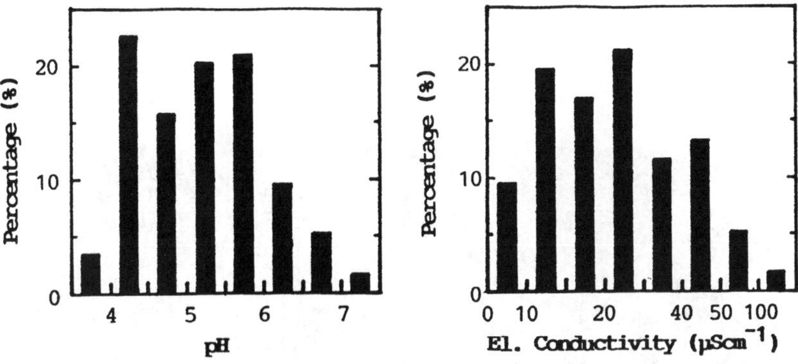

FIG. 4 Frequency distributions of the pH and the electrical conductivity (EC) of wet deposition samples in Gais (1989).

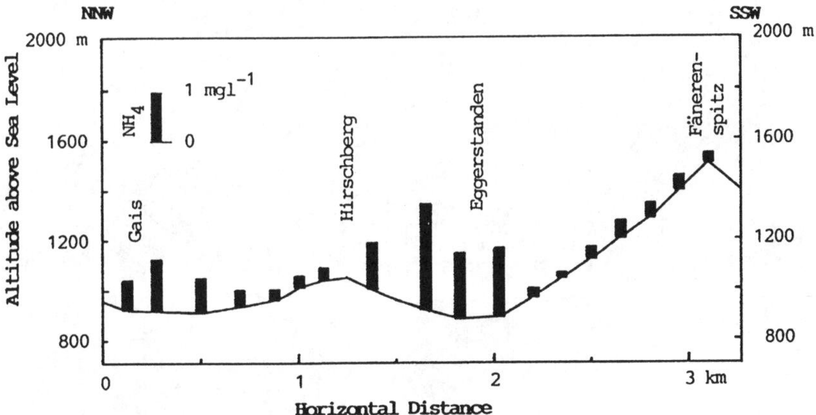

FIG. 5 Ammonium concentration of fresh snow along a profile (19 March 1989).

CONCLUSIONS

Physico-chemical analyses of precipitation play an important role in the fields of air pollution control and research. They are of particular interest in view of determining deposition rates of air pollutants as well as with regard to mapping and monitoring air pollution. Applications vary within a wide range, and that not only regarding sampling intervals, which can be daily, weekly or, particularly in the case of snow, even longer periods, but also in terms of the parameters to be taken into account.

Although both methods of measuring air pollution (the one being based on determining the gaseous pollutants, and the other one being based on determining the pollutants in depositions, as presented in this paper) can be applied independently and considering that each of them has advantages and disadvantages, in many practical applications they can and should be applied in a complementary way in order to get optimal results.

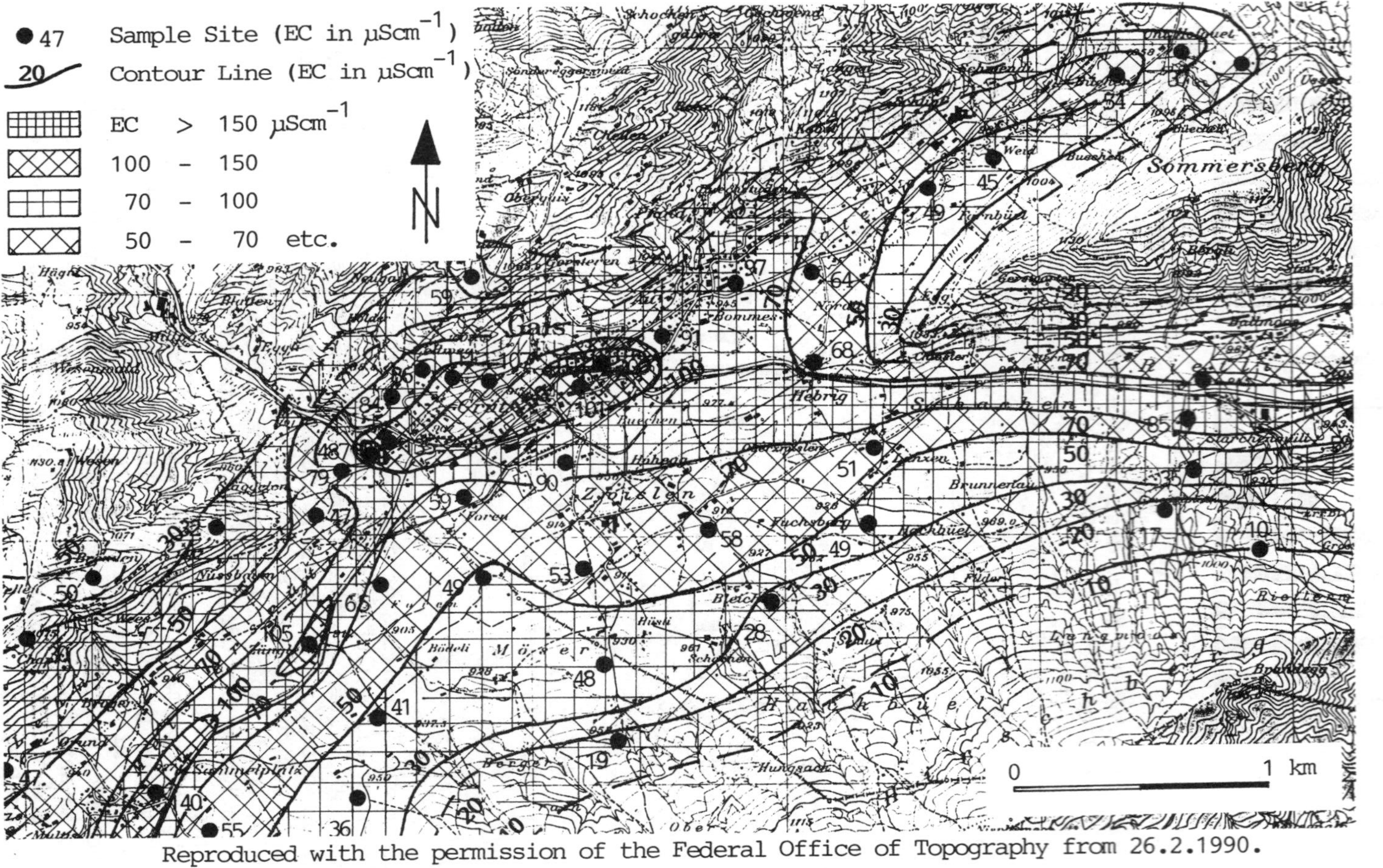

Reproduced with the permission of the Federal Office of Topography from 26.2.1990.

FIG. 6 Map showing the electrical conductivity (EC) of about 3 weeks old snow which is suggested to represent bulk deposition predominantly originating from local sources.

REFERENCES

Fuhrer, J. (1986) Study of acid deposition in Switzerland: Temporal variation in the ionic composition of wet precipitation at rural sites during 1983-1984. Environmental Pollution (Series B) 12 (1986) 111-129.

National Atmospheric Deposition Program, NADP/NTN Instruction Manual-Site Selection and Operation (1984) and Instruction NADP/NTN Site Operation (1988). Natural Resource Ecology Laboratory, Colorado State University, Fort Collins/Illinois State Water Survey, University of Illinois, Champaign/U.S.Geological Survey.

Keller, B.J., Peden, M.E. & Skowron, L.M. (1988) Methods for collection and analysis of precipitation: Trace metals. Illinois State Water Survey, Champaign.

Peden, M.E. (1986) Methods for collection and analysis of precipitation. Illinois State Water Survey, Champaign.

Sverdrup, H., de Vries, W. & Henriksen, A. (1989) Mapping critical loads - criteria, calculation methods, input data, and calculation examples for mapping critical loads and areas where they have been exceeded.

Zürcher, F. (1987) Ionenchromatographie von hochalpinem Schnee - Auswirkungen der Luftverschmutzung im Alpenraum. Labor 2000.

Hydrology in Mountainous Regions. I - Hydrological Measurements; the Water Cycle
(Proceedings of two Lausanne Symposia, August 1990). IAHS Publ. no. 193, 1990.

Chemical composition of snow cover on the western Swiss Alps

Aurèle PARRIAUX & Jean-Daniel DUBOIS
Federal Institute of Technology, Laboratory of Geology, 1015 Lausanne, Switzerland
Martial DRAY
Centre de recherches géodynamiques, Université Pierre et Marie Curie, Thonon les Bains, France

ABSTRACT The AQUITYP project studies the geochemical imprint given to the water by the aquifers through which it has passed. A complete analysis of the output of flow systems has been analyzed, yielding the major and minor mineral components. The interpretation of the role of the underground environment implies a knowledge of the composition of the input, especially for aquifers which have low reactivity with groundwater. In this case, priority has been given to accessing the composition of recharge groundwater in mountainous regions. The amount of snow accumulated before the spring thaw is a practical method of determining the composition of the winter deposits. A network of 14 points was established at the end of the 1987-88 winter season. These points are distributed in various regional profiles at altitudes between 1000 and 4000 m. The laboratory analyses show a variability of parameters mainly according to the distance from urban zones.

1. PRINCIPAL AIMS

The study of the composition of snow accumulation in the Alps is linked to the AQUITYP project, which was started several years ago to study systematically the typology of aquifers (Parriaux & Lutz, 1988, Parriaux & Dubois, 1990). The principal aims can be summarized in the following manner:

a) Quality of groundwater recharge: The study of the geochemical regime at the output of a typical aquifer necessitates information concerning the composition of the surface water. This is even more important when the groundwater is slightly mineralized (Dubois & Parriaux, 1990) and when an analysis of the trace components is carried out. The isotopic composition is also important. This subject is treated in a second article (Dray et al., 1990) in these proceedings.
b) Chemical image of precipitation in mountainous regions: Even though the "Snow cover" network was not conceived with this aim in mind, it enables an average image of the spatial dispersion of the snow composition during the winter period. The dispersion of natural mineral substances, as well as those linked to human activity at the foot of the mountain chains, is described. This image does not pretend to treat the time variability at the scale of pluviometric events, as this would necessitate a different sampling concept which would become much too complicated in the framework of this project.

2. OBSERVATION NETWORK

The mesh was made up of 14 points distributed in and around the Alpine catchment basin of the AQUITYP network. These points were situated in the Prealps and the west Swiss Alps, in the interior of the Rhone basin and on its edge. Their altitudes varied between 1330 and 4080 m. Generally, they were grouped by increasing altitude in transversal formation, as is shown by the Mont Blanc and Pennic Alps profiles (Fig. 1 and Table 1). The number of points is limited by the cost of one day of helicopter time per year.

The present article analyzes the results of snow accumulated during the 1987-88 winter season. Those of the 1988-89 season are still undergoing analysis.

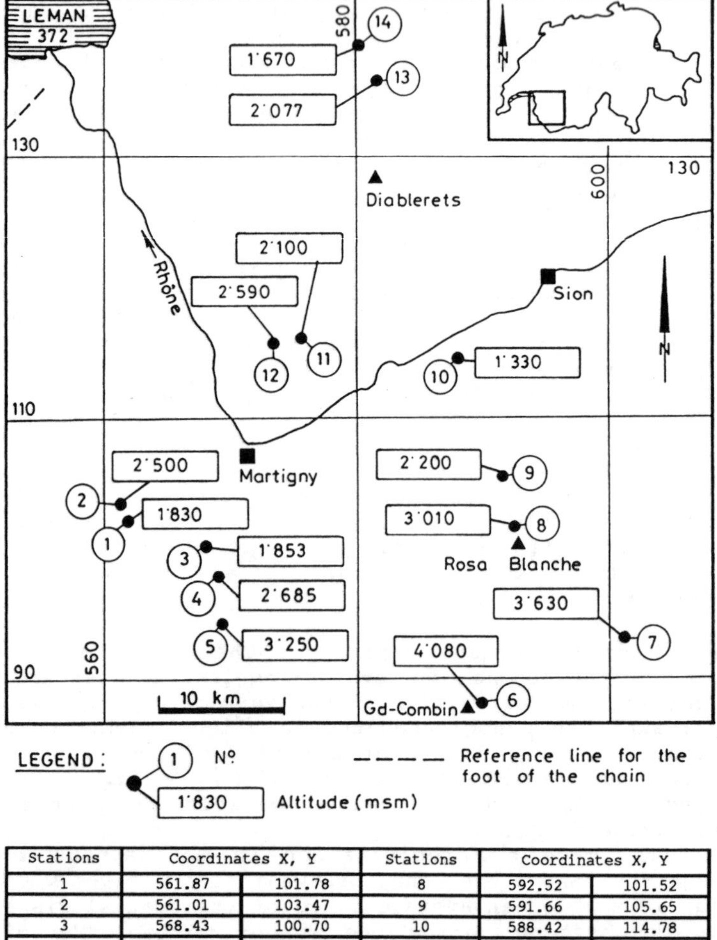

Stations	Coordinates X, Y		Stations	Coordinates X, Y	
1	561.87	101.78	8	592.52	101.52
2	561.01	103.47	9	591.66	105.65
3	568.43	100.70	10	588.42	114.78
4	569.03	097.32	11	575.13	116.32
5	569.23	092.96	12	573.05	116.15
6	589.86	088.00	13	580.97	136.22
7	600.73	092.96	14	580.11	138.05

FIG. 1 & TABLE 1 Situation of the sampling stations of the snow cover.

3. SAMPLING TECHNIQUE

Sampling by helicopter has the advantage of being able to insure synchronized samples (in one day) of relatively inaccessible regions. However, this must be carried out rapidly for financial reasons. The sampling process was the following:

<u>Standard scenario:</u>

a) Non-tubed boring with an auger (140 mm in diameter, 1.7 m maximum depth)
b) Placement of the snow sample in a plastic (PVC) case
c) Mixing of the sample for homogenization
d) Filling of polyethylene bottles with the "average snow"
e) Slow melting in the laboratory, followed by analysis

<u>Stratification scenario</u>: Identical to the standard scenario except the sampling was carried out by 25 to 35 cm runs. Three parallel borings were executed at 0.5 m from each other in order to obtain enough snow.

4. ANALYSES

The samples were analyzed according to classical methods of mineral hydro-chemistry: emission and atomic absorption spectrometry, graphite furnace, ionic chromatography. A process of ion concentration on a 8-hydroxyquinoline resin was necessary due to the weak mineral content of the snow.

5. RESULTS

The analytical results have been synthesized and are presented on maps of spatial distribution for each parameter (Fig. 2). Their interpretation is carried out as a function of the fixed goals (Chap. 1).

<u>5.1 Groundwater recharge</u>

The geochemical comparison of the water from snow with that of groundwater found in crystalline massifs is meaningful. Figure 3 shows that the geochemical input of the precipitations is totally negligible for the major cations. However, a large number of anions is already present in the recharge water in quantities of percents for the sulfates and of several tens of percents for the nitrates and especially the chlorides. On the basis of the major components, it can be concluded that the water-rock interaction is predominant. Further trace analysis of the groundwater will verify if this conclusion is valid for the minor components as well.

<u>5.2 Chemical image of the precipitations</u>

Table 2 regroups the average parameters analyzed as well as their variability in the observation network. These values are compared to those found in the literature for similar sites.

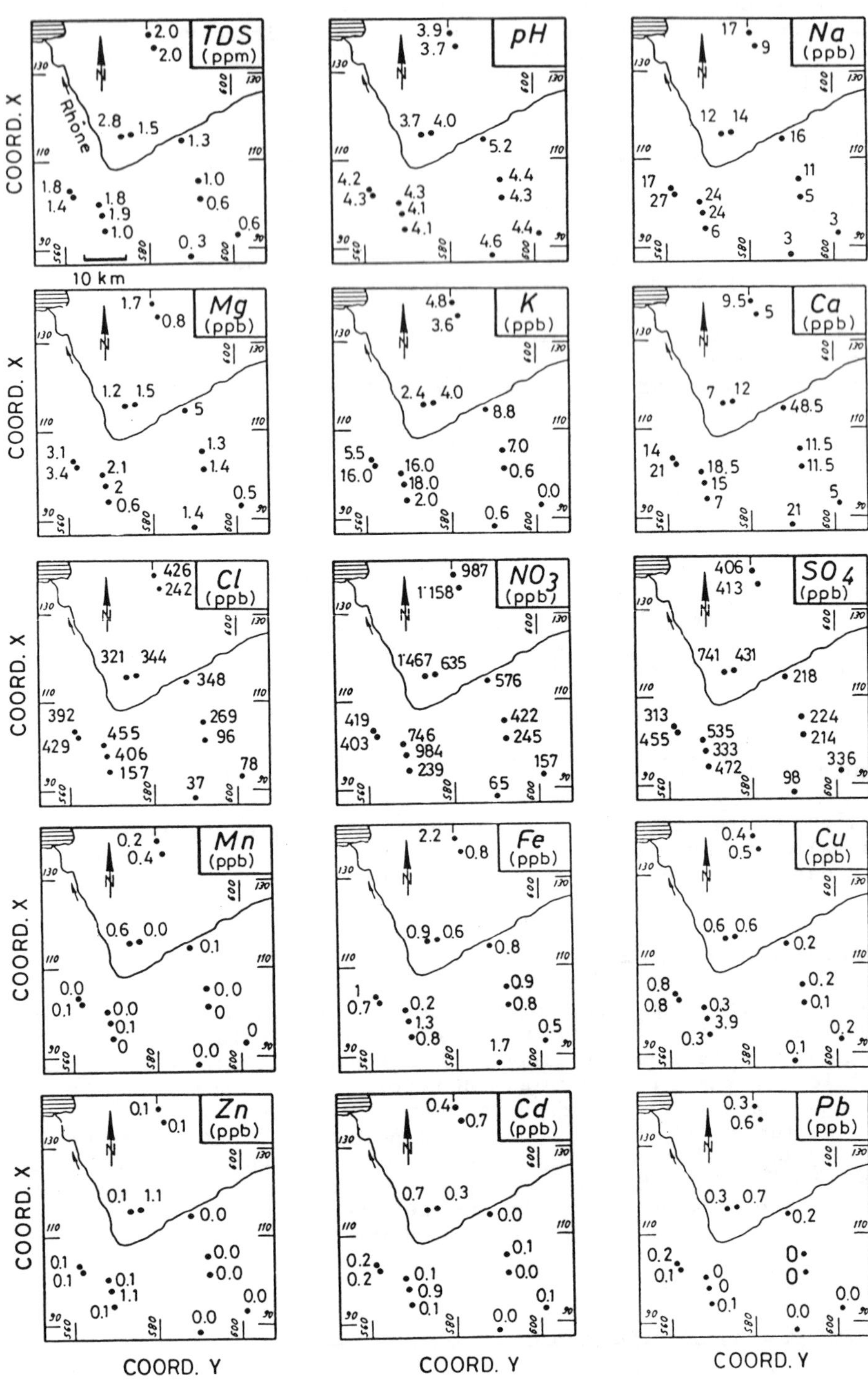

FIG. 2 Spatial variability of the physico-chemical parameters.

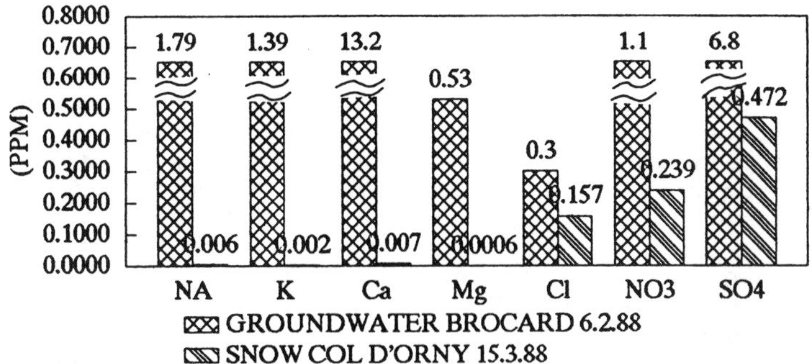

FIG. 3 Comparison of concentrations of major ions in a groundwater of Mont-Blanc massif and in a snow sample.

TABLE 2 Average and variability of physico-chemical parameters.

	TDS (ppm)	pH	Na (ppb)	Mg (ppb)	K (ppb)	Ca (ppb)	Cl (ppb)	NO3 (ppb)	SO4 (ppb)	Mn (ppb)	Fe (ppb)	Cu (ppb)	Zn (ppb)	Cd (ppb)	Pb (ppb)
$\bar{x}$	1.43	4.2	13.4	1.9	6.4	14.8	286	607	371	0.11	0.96	0.64	0.15	0.27	0.18
s	0.66	0.38	7.6	1.2	5.9	10.7	137	399	155	0.18	0.48	0.93	0.27	0.28	0.20
X_{min}	0.3	3.7	3	0.5	0	5	78	157	214	0	0.7	0.1	0	0	0
X_{max}	2.8	5.2	24	3.4	18	48.5	426	1467	741	0.4	2.2	0.8	1.1	0.9	0.7

Analyses carried out in the French and Austrian Alps (Page, 1987) give comparable orders of magnitude for the major cations. Their variability with time is increased by taking into account various snow events of the season.

The comparison with the analyses in the Mont Blanc massif (Batifol and Boutron, 1984) is more complex. Overall, the concentrations obtained in our study are 10 to 100 times less, with the exception of calcium, manganese, copper and cadmium. The reason for these differences can probably be found in the treatment of the sample with nitric and fluorhydic acid that these authors used, which tends to put the eolian particles in the accumulated snow in solution.

Spatial arrangement: Generally speaking, the concentrations of the parameters seem to be influenced by the altitude as well as by the distance from urban and industrial zones.

Zoning by altitude: The graphical representations of the different parameters (Fig. 4) show a vague negative correlation between the concentrations and altitude. These distributions can be separated into two groups:

- a domain below 2800 m where the values are dispersed without any clear pattern,
- a domain at high altitude where the concentrations are low.

Zoning according to distance from urban regions: The situation at each point is represented with respect to the large urban region found on the Swiss plateau, situated to the NW of the investigation area. A reference line with a N45E azimuth was selected as the schematic border of this region. A value was then assigned to each station, corresponding to the distance from this populated area.

The behaviour of various parameters according to this distance is given in Figure 5.

The majority of the following concentrations appear to be rather distinctly negatively correlated with distance: TDS (Total Dissolved Solid), Na, Cl, NO_3, SO_4, Mn, Cu, Zn, Cd and Pb, even though the correlation coefficient is low.

An improvement of the correlation can be observed on certain graphs of Figure 5 if the urbanization of the Rhone valley is taken into account. This is the case for Mn, Cu, Cd, Pb with station numbers 11 and 12, which are close to the industrial zones of the lower Rhone in the Valais canton.

To access the origin of these components, the example of the NaCl-HCl couple was examined:

- NaCl: natural meteoric origin,
- HCl: essentially anthropogenic origin.

The concentration of Na^+ and Cl^- clearly shows that for 1 meq. of sodium, there exists approximately 10 meq. of chlorides. It can be concluded that in this case, about 90% of the mineral charge comes from human activity.

These observations indicate that the concentrations of the principal components depend directly on the distance from the major centers of pollutant emissions.

The relations observed as a function of altitude (Fig. 4) are therefore illusory, as high-altitude zones are also far from human activity.

6. DISCUSSION OF THE RESULTS

The results obtained must be reviewed to evaluate various causes which may have altered the quality of the measurements.

Contamination:

- Chemical influence of the sampling instruments on the snow.
- Snow-soil chemical exchanges at the base of the snow layer.
- Accidental contamination in the laboratory.

The behaviour of points 4 and 10 could be linked to contamination.

Time dependent representativity: The samples do not reflect the entire snow accumulation during the 1987-88 winter season for the following reasons:

- Only 4 samples include measurements from the complete snow layer. For the others, the profile is incomplete and the first snows are missing.
- An important snow event occurred after the samples were taken (second half of March).

Spatial representativity: The points were chosen on profiles with altitudes corresponding to the basins studied in the AQUITYP project. They were found to be in extremely varying morphological conditions. This means that there were great climatic differences during snow-falls. Eolian transport of the snow on the ground tends to increase

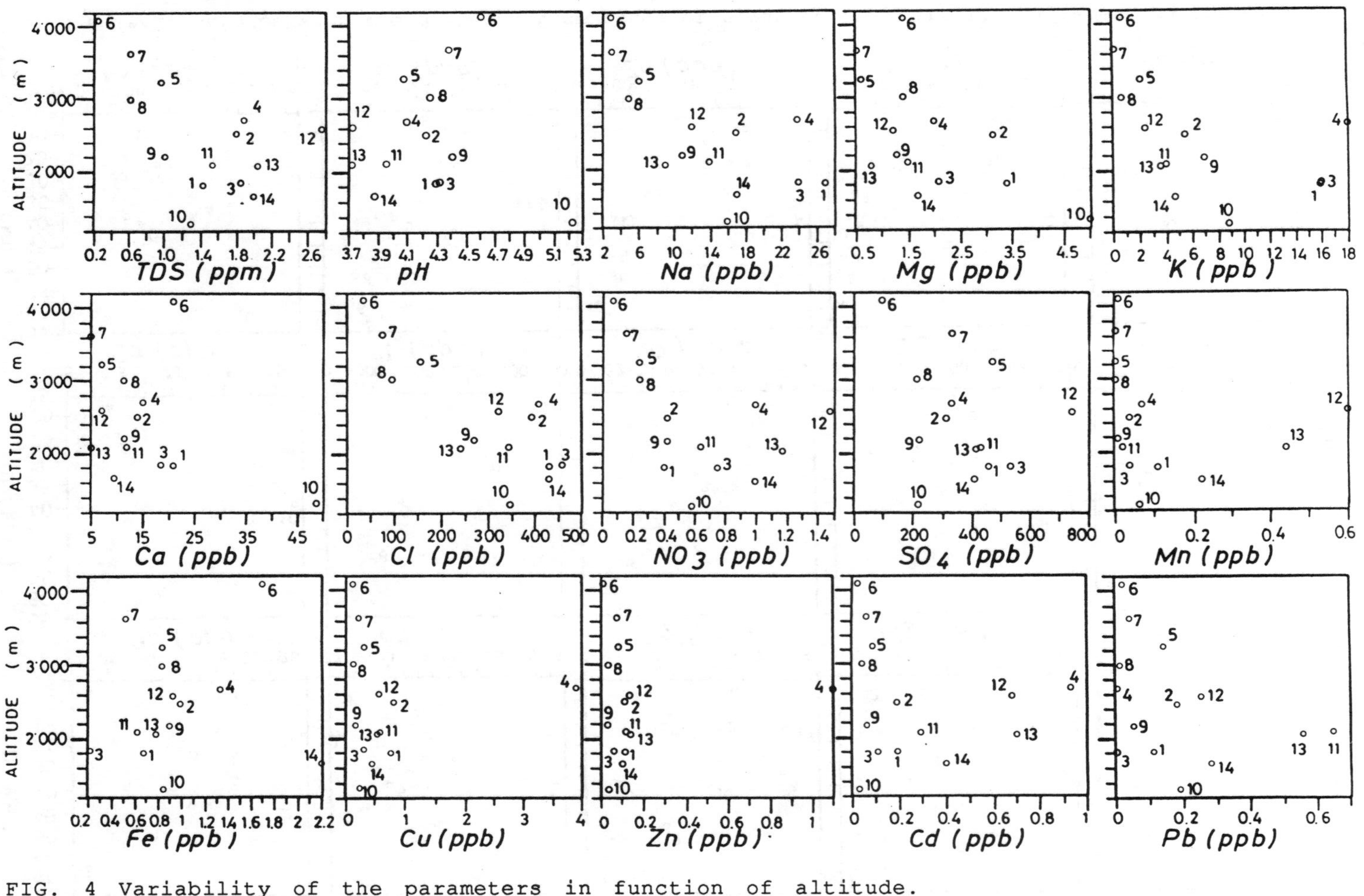

FIG. 4 Variability of the parameters in function of altitude.

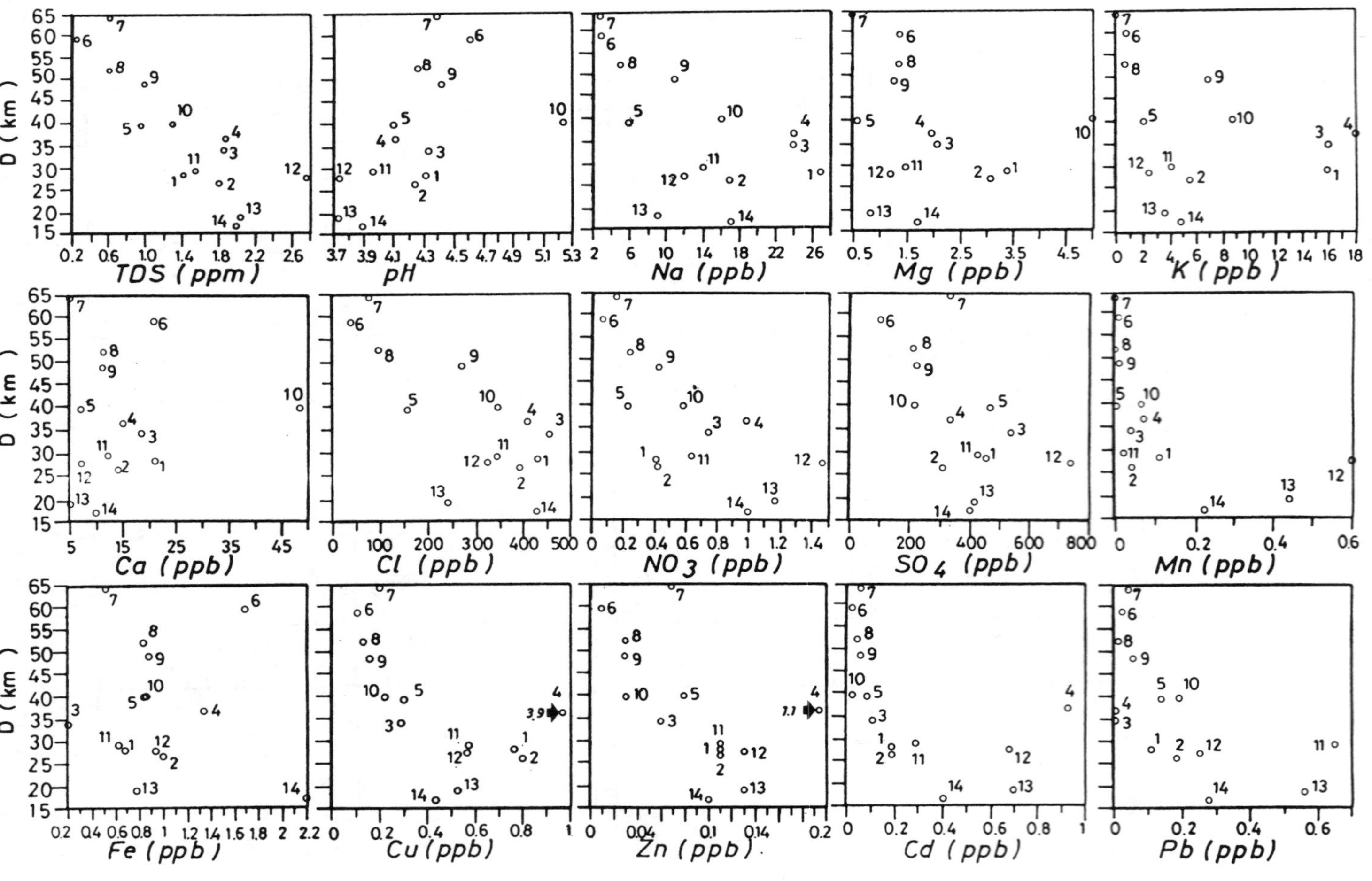

FIG. 5 Relationship between the distance from zones of human activity and the different parameters.

this variability, as the stable isotopes of the same region seem to indicate (Dray et al., 1990).

In spite of these limitations, the results follow certain rules, especially the correlation with zones of pollutant emissions.

7. CONCLUSIONS

The two main goals of the study were realized:

1. Infiltration water resulting from snow thaw has a weak mineral content (major components), very inferior to that of groundwater, even in the crystalline massifs. Therefore, a systematic bias does not seem to exist in the geochemical interpretation of groundwater. Trace studies remain to be carried out.
2. The spatial distribution of the components shows that they are principally of anthropogenic origin and that their concentration is linked to zones of human activity.

The samples from the 1988-89 season are still undergoing analysis and this analysis should provide the information necessary to complete these first observations.

ACKNOWLEDGMENTS go to the Swiss Army for having provided us with the necessary helicopter transport, without which this study would not have been possible. Also, we thank the GEOLEP personnel for the analyses and the layout of the article.

REFERENCES

Batifol, F.M. & Boutron, C.F. (1984) Atmospheric heavy metal in high altitude surface snows from Mont Blanc, French Alps. Atmospheric Environment, 18/11, 2507-2515.

Dray, M., Parriaux Aurèle & Dubois Jean-Daniel (1990) Image synchrone de la composition isotopique de la couverture neigeuse des Alpes de Suisse occidentale. Proc. & reports IAHS Conf. of Lausanne 1990.

Dubois, J.D. & Parriaux, A. (1990) Spatial and time-dependent variations of the springs of crystalline aquifers of the Mt.Blanc and Aguilles Rouges massif (Switzerland, France and Italy): first results. Proc. of 22nd IAH Congress Lausanne 1990.

Page, Y. (1987) Meteorology, chemistry, acidity of mountain snowfalls and snowpack chemistry. Journal de physique, Colloque CI, Tome 48.

Page, Y. (1987) The chemical evolution of a seasonal snowcover at midland-high altitude. In: H.G. Jones & W.J. Orville-Thomas (Eds) Seasonal snowcovers: Physics, chemistry, hydrology, 281-288.

Parriaux, A., Lutz, T. (1988) Contribution of an informatized concept to the chemical analysis of groundwater series. Proc of 21st IAH Congress in Guilin (China).

Parriaux, A. (1990) The AQUITYP project: towards typology of aquifers in the alpine orogen. Proc. of 22nd IAH Congress Lausanne 1990.

Parriaux, A. & DUBOIS, J.D. (1990) Groundwater typology before and after the introduction of the ICP-MS. Chimia, Birkhäuser AG, Basel.

Hydrology in Mountainous Regions. I - Hydrological Measurements; the Water Cycle (Proceedings of two Lausanne Symposia, August 1990). IAHS Publ. no. 193, 1990.

Acidification studies at northern Black Forest cirque lakes

H. THIES
Zoological Institute University Hohenheim,
P.O. Box 700562, D-7000 Stuttgart 70, FRG

ABSTRACT The study is focussing on qualitative aspects of the actual acidification of small dystrophic lakes and their inlets. Acidic pulses during snow melt and after heavy rainfalls cause strong pH depressions together with a depletion of buffer capacity. Differing types of acidic pulses are showing different reaction patterns of acid anions (NO_3, SO_4, DOC) and cations (Al, Na, K, Ca, Mg).

INTRODUCTION

The drainage basins of the Northern Black Forest lakes (fig.1) are situated on an extremely low buffered Bunter sandstone bedrock formation. Stands of Norway spruce and fir affected by the "Acid Rain" induced Central European forest decline are growing on podzols, (spodo)-dystric cambisols and dystric planosols which cover the drainage basins of the lakes. Poorly buffered rocks and soils as well as high annual rainfall rates (up to 2000 mm) and a fairly strong acidic deposition (0.5-1.5 kmol H^+, 0.3-0.6 keq Cl, 0.5-1.5 keq NO_3 and 0.6-1.8 keq SO_4 in the open and in canopy throughfall, resp.) meet the requirements for enhanced susceptibility for surface water acidification (UBA, 1987).

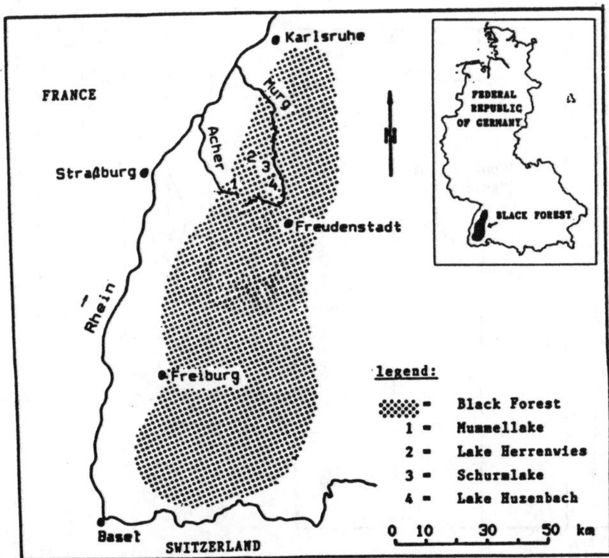

FIG.1 Lakes in the Northern Black Forest. Inset: Black Forest in FRG.

MATERIALS AND METHODS

A first monitoring program was carried out in 1985/86 at the dystrophic cirque lakes Mummellake, Schurmlake, Lake Herrenwies and Lake Huzenbach with monthly sampling (considering as well snow melt events as heavy rain falls). Covered parameters were pH value, ANC, conductivity, temperature, O_2, u.v. extinction 240/260 nm, nutrients (PO_4, TDP, part. P, NH_4, SiO_2), cations (Na, K, Ca, Mg, Fe, Al) by atomic absorption spectroscopy and anions (Cl, NO_3, SO_4) by ionic chromatography in inlets, outlets and vertical profiles of the lakes (THIES, 1987). Precipitation was sampled as open bulk and canopy throughfall and analysed for pH value, conductivity, Cl, NO_3, SO_4. New isobathic maps of the lakes were made by using echosound equipment and aerial photos in order to determine the actual lake volume. In 1988 an intensivied case study started at Lake Huzenbach with regard to mass balances including the continuous registration of pH, conductivity, temperature and water level in constructed gauging stations in the inlet and outlet of the lake.

RESULTS AND DISCUSSION

The historical development of lake water pH values was reconstructed by palaeolimnological studies regarding subfossil diatom and cladoceran remains in sediment cores (ARZET et al., 1986; ARZET & STEINBERG, 1987; STEINBERG et al., 1987), which prove a rapid acidification of lake water during the latest 100 years. The example of Lake Huzenbach gives evidence to the fact, that this recent pH depression is the most pronounced one in its history of more than 10.000 years (STEINBERG et al., 1987; see fig. 2).

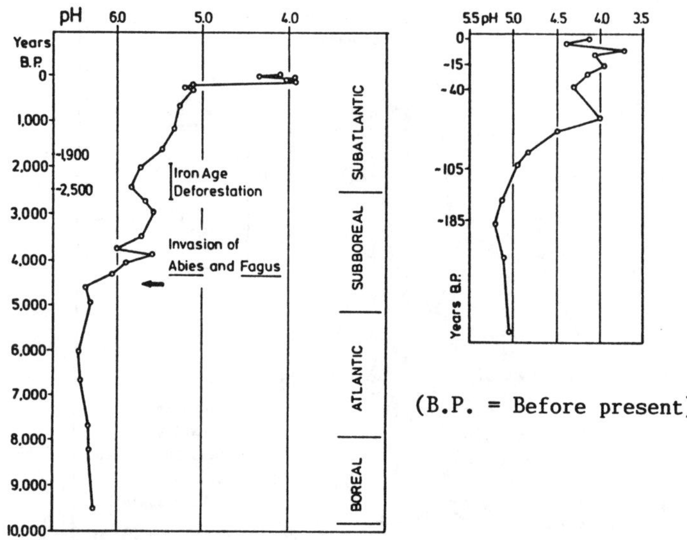

FIG. 2 Reconstruction of acidification of Lake Huzenbach by subfossil diatom analysis in lake sediment cores, latest decades are shown in amplification (right), after STEINBERG et al. (1987).

In order to characterize the lakes a small set of a data is shown in table 1, for details cf. THIES (1987).

TABLE 1 Morphometric data and mean annual surface values of northern Black Forest lakes (1985/86). (data from THIES, 1987)

parameter/lake	Mummellake	Schurmlake	L. Herrenwies	L. Huzenbach
[m a.s.l.]	1027	790	830	747
max. depth [m]	17.7	13.0	9.5	8.0
surface [ha]	3.7	1.4	1.1	2.0
volume [m^3]	277.500	114.000	69.000	65.200
watershed [ha]	18	64	32	63
crt* [days]	473	63	71	36
delog pH	5.64	4.27	4.17	4.33
NO_3 [µeq/l]	53	34	27	9
SO_4 [µeq/l]	143	131	150	105
UV 240 nm [1/m]	11.9	21.1	31.8	29.8

(note: crt* = calculated retention time)

The actual acidification is taking place in the inlets and in the pelagic zone of the lakes due to surface flow controlled flash floods during the time of snow melt and after heavy rains. The discharge curve (fig. 3) of the river Murg (fig. 1) may characterize such events for the year 1986, as in the drainage basins of the lakes numerous acidic pulses were flushing downhill within a few hours time.

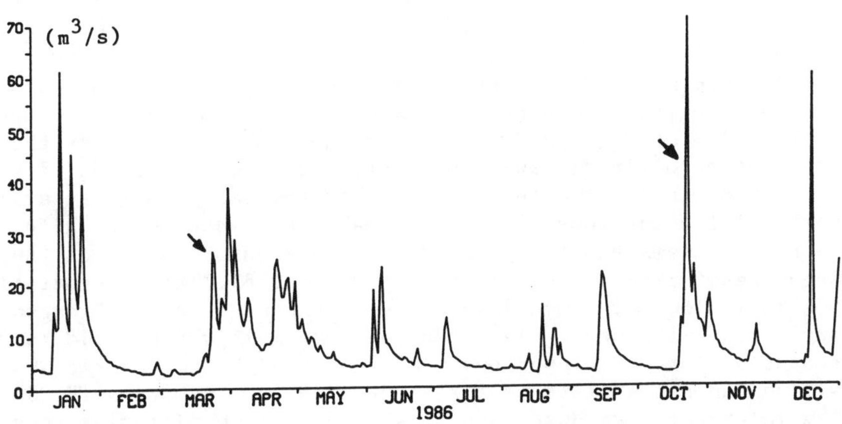

FIG. 3 Discharge curve of river Murg (gauging station Schwarzenberg) in 1986, (daily mean discharge in m^3/s) from THIES, 1987.

During snow melt acidic pulses show reduced contact with the top soil layer and are entering the lakes in the course of their inverse stratification phase underneath the ice cover, where often dense strata of phytoplankton are living due to better light conditions. The influence of acidic input on these organisms is currently examined. Strong pH depressions occur together with a depletion of buffer capacity (ANC) (see fig. 4, at 23.03.1986 in 0 m depth and at 24.10.1986 in 0-5 m depth; cf. with fig. 3, where arrows indicate these pulses).

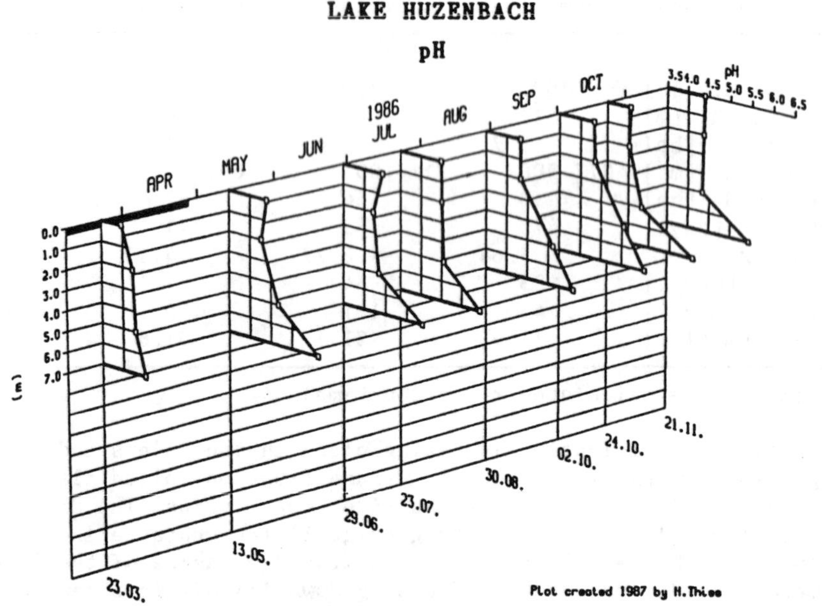

FIG.4 Lake water pH in vertical profiles of Lake Huzenbach (1986), dark bar = ice cover; after THIES (1987).

The effects of acidic flushes are also detectable in the inlets of the lakes where strong pH depressions (pH_{min}= 3.66) occur together with a rise of NO_3 and SO_4 concentrations. Whereas SO_4 is the predominant anion in all surface water samples of the lakes, its concentration in inlet waters of Lake Herrenwies exhibits less distinct seasonal fluctuations. This is probably connected with sulfur retention mechanisms and changing redox conditions in soils of the drainage area (FEGER, 1986, EINSELE et al., 1988). The concentration for NO_3 in inflows of Mummellake shows an enhanced level throughout the whole year with peak release during snow melt which could be representative for a drainage basin with both high atmospheric NO_3 deposition and a high rate of forest decline (cf. tab. 1 & THIES, 1987). The inlets of Lake Huzenbach do show a somehow differing reaction: rising concentration of NO_3 during snow melt but close to detection limits during summertime. This behaviour could be an indicator for a still functioning biotic uptake within the drainage area. Especially in such inlets with a greater proportion of surface flow a supposed seasonality of dissolved organic matter could emphasize its higher significance after heavy rains than during snow melt (e.g Lake Huzenbach). The drainage basin of Lake Herrenwies exhibits a greater influence of humic substances on inlet water quality than that of

Mummellake (cf. tab. 1). The proportion of organic versus mineral acid derived anions in lake inlets seems to depend as well on the type and size of the drainage basin, on the season and special climatic conditions as on the proportion of discharge components of inflowing waters. In most lake inlets the cations Na, K, Ca, Mg are subject to dilution during acidic pulses (with exception of Mummellake because of the use of street deicing salts on a nearby road). The cations Fe and Al show an inverse behaviour. Even the baseflow concentrations of Al do exceed the critical value of 200 µg/l which is suspect to harmful effects on waterorganisms like amphibia and fish (LfU, 1988).

ACKNOWLEDGEMENT This work was kindly supported by the Federal Environmental Protection Agency (Berlin, FRG) within the project "Water 102 04 342".

REFERENCES

ARZET, K., KRAUSE-DELLIN, D. & STEINBERG, C. (1986) Acidification of four lakes in the Federal Republic of Germany as reflected by diatom assemblages, cladoceran remains and sediment chemistry. In: SMOL, J.P., BATTARBEE, DAVIS, R.W. & MERILÄINEN, J. (eds.) Diatoms and Lake Acidity. Developm. in Hydrobiology 29, 227-250.

ARZET, K. & STEINBERG, C. (1987) The anthropogenic influence on four humic acid lakes in the northern Black Forest as reflected by diatoms in the sediment. (unpubl.)

EINSELE, G., EHMANN, M., IROUSCHEK, T. & SEEGER, T. (1988) Boden und Gewässerversauerung sowie Stoffbilanzierung für verschiedene Abflusskomponenten und Einzugsgebiete im Buntsandstein-Schwarzwald. Projekt Europäisches Forschungszentrum für Maßnahmen der Luftreinhaltung (PEF), 4. Statuskolloquium vom 8.-10.03.1988, Kernforschungszentrum Karlsruhe, 49-60.

FEGER, K.H. (1986) Biogeochemische Untersuchungen an Gewässern im Schwarzwald unter besonderer Berücksichtigung atmogener Stoffeinträge. Freiburger Bodenkundl. Abhandl. 17.

LfU (1988)(Landesanstalt für Umweltschutz, ed.) Immissionsökologisches Wirkungskataster Baden-Württemberg. Jahresbericht der LfU Baden-Württemberg, 203-213.

STEINBERG, C., ARZET, K., KRAUSE-DELLIN, D., SANIDES, S. & FRENZEL, B. (1987) Long core study on natural and anthropogenic acidification of Huzenbachersee, Black Forest, FRG. Global Biogeochemical Cycles 1, 89-95.

THIES, H. (1987) Limnochemische Untersuchungen an vier Karseen des Nordschwarzwaldes unter Berücksichtigung von sauren Niederschlägen sowie der Makrophytenvegetation. Diploma thesis at the Limnological Institute Lake Konstanz, University of Freiburg.

UBA (1987) (Umweltbundesamt, ed.) Gewässerversauerung in der Bundesrepublik Deutschland, Teil I: Kartierung der zur Gewässerversauerung neigenden Gebiete in der Bundesrepublik Deutschland sowie des aktuellen Standes der pH-Wert-Situation (< pH 6.0) in Oberflächengewässern. Texte 22/87, Umweltbundesamt Berlin.

Symposium on Quantitative and Qualitative Water Cycle Aspects in Heterogeneous Basins

Topic C:

Hydrological Modelling in Regions of Rugged Relief

Hydrology in Mountainous Regions. I - Hydrological Measurements; the Water Cycle
(Proceedings of two Lausanne Symposia, August 1990). IAHS Publ. no. 193, 1990.

The effect of space-time rainfall variability on unit hydrograph parameters

Š. BLAŽKOVÁ
Water Research Institute, Prague, Podbabská 30, Praha 6, Czechoslovakia 160 62

ABSTRACT Unit hydrographs of direct runoff expressed in the form of simple conceptual models contained in PICOMO program (Dooge & O'Kane, 1977) have been identified on the Sputka Catchment (100 km^2) using both the areal average and one of the available rain vectors at a time. For the areal average it was possible to derive three different dimensionless pulse-responses, each connected to certain space-time characteristics of rainfall. The CLSX nonlinear time-variant model for total runoff (Todini, 1980) has been used both with the areal average as a single input and with three rain inputs at different stations. Although the accuracy of modelling with the areal average is satisfactory the introduction of more rain inputs provides a better description of the runoff process.

NOTATION

A,B,C	- types of dimensionless UH
A20,B20	- parameters of model 20
API	- antecedent precipitation index
N,K	- parameters of model 16
k	- coefficient in API
CLSX	- Constrained Linear Systems Extended
Dur	- duration of net rain (h)
S,V,CH,L	- rainfall stations at the altitudes of 555, 740, 1122 and 835 m a.s.l., respectively
Q_{max}	- maximum discharge (m^3 s^{-1})
S_R	- Rth shape factor
t_L	- lag of the catchment
UH,UH 16,UH 20	- unit hydrograph, UH of models 16 (Nash) and 20 (convective diffusion reach)
ε_p	- error in maximum discharge (%)
Δ_p	- error in time to peak (h)
450,70,etc.	- set of net data, estimate of UH
310777,etc.	- event to be modelled with CLSX (date of beginning)

INTRODUCTION

The objective of the present contribution is to discuss the implications of the space-time variability of rainfall when deriving both the pulse-response of the direct runoff models and the response functions of a nonlinear time-variant total runoff model.

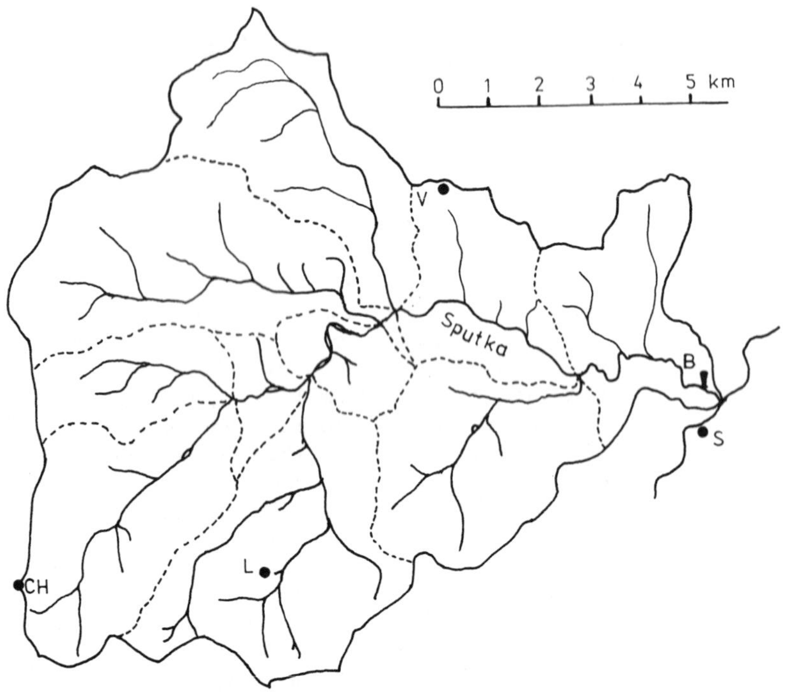

FIG. 1 The Sputka Catchment.

Data of isolated rainfall-runoff events from the 1970s on the Sputka Catchment were used (Janoušek et al., 1979). The catchment area is 104.3 km² (Fig. 1).

DIRECT RUNOFF MODELLING

As examples of simple conceptual models the Nash model and the convective diffusion wave, contained in the PICOMO program (Dooge & O'Kane, 1977), have been chosen. It has been shown before (Blažková, 1988) that a dimensionless pulse-response function (A in Fig. 2) can be derived on the Sputka Catchment using the areal average of rainfall from storm events with the duration of net rain longer than 6 hours if it rains on the whole catchment and if the hyetographs and hydrographs are not too complex. The t_L, however, doesn't depend on the rainfall intensity (compare Dooge, 1977).

The model parameters computed from individual events fulfilling the above stated conditions are very close and in the dimensionless plot of the unit hydrographs the scatter is unimportant (Fig. 2). For example the Nash's N ranges from 2.1 to 2.6 and the K from 2.8 to 4.2, the parameters A20 and B20 from 2.5 to 3.5 and from 0.3 to 0.4, respectively. Also in the shape factor diagram the events plot close to each other. In Fig. 3 the shape factors of three of the five hydrographs used for deriving the curve A (Fig. 2) are shown. The rain of the event 450 is remarkable by its uniformity over the catchment, the event 70 is a five-year flood. During the event 381

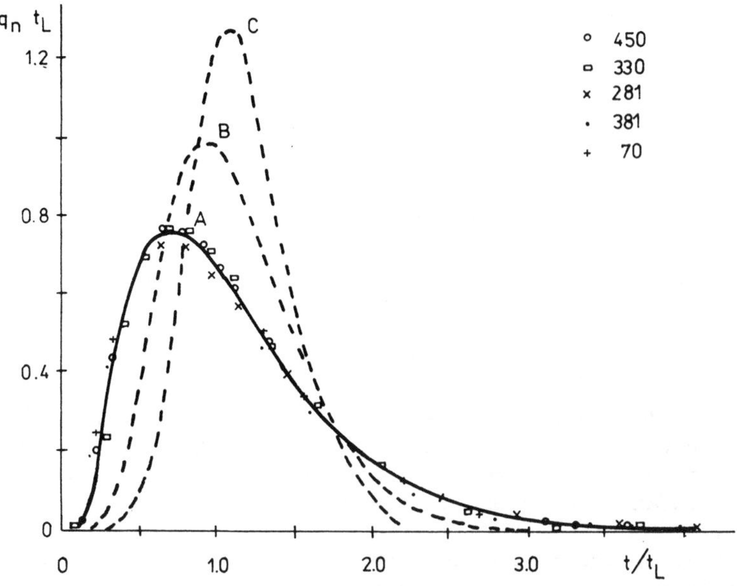

FIG. 2 Dimensionless pulse-responses of UH 16 for different types of storms (q_n - normalized direct runoff).

TABLE 1 Variation of parameters of UH 16 and UH 20 when using individual rain vectors.

Data	Rain	Dur (h)	t_L (h)	N	K	A20	B20
450	aver.	6	9.0	2.5	3.6	3.4	0.4
	S	6	9.2	2.7	3.4	3.5	0.4
	V	6	8.9	2.5	3.6	3.3	0.4
	CH	6	9.2	2.7	3.4	3.5	0.4
70	aver.	12	8.5	2.4	3.6	3.2	0.4
	V	12	8.3	2.0	4.2	2.9	0.4
	CH	12	8.9	3.0	2.9	3.7	0.4
381	aver.	19	10.0	2.4	4.2	3.5	0.4
	S	5	20.7	6.7	3.1	8.3	0.4
	V	13	8.8	1.5	6.0	2.6	0.3
	CH	11	9.0	1.7	5.4	2.7	0.3
30	aver.	5	9.0	5.0	1.8	4.8	0.5
	CH	5	8.8	4.9	1.8	4.6	0.5

the storm was moving over the catchment.

The dimensionless UH B (Fig. 2) has been derived from the events with shorter net rain which was much heavier in the upper parts of the catchment (station CH) and the curve C from the events with rain grossly nonuniform both in space and time. The scatter in these cases was bigger and depended more strongly on the parameters of net data

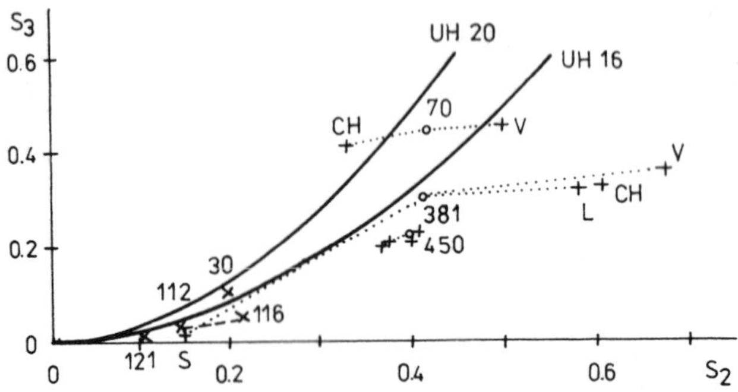

FIG. 3 Shape factor diagram.

computation (112 and 116 in Fig. 3 are two versions of the same set of data) but, all the same, the shapes B and C were distinct. Also the events from the 1960s grouped along similar shapes A, B and C. In Fig. 3 events 30 and 116 belong to the curve B and the event 121 to the curve C.

Further, pulse-responses have been identified using only one of the available rain vectors at a time. The model parameters as well as the lags for selected events are shown in Table 1 and the shape factors in Fig. 3. Various estimates of t_L computed with the average rain and with individual rain vectors are quite close except the event 381, vector S. The rain started there but stopped soon and the total was small. The big difference can be seen in Fig. 3.

Fig 4 shows that it would be more difficult to derive the dimensionless UH A having only one rain station at one´s disposal even if it was station CH which characterizes the storms very well.

TOTAL RUNOFF MODELLING

The CLSX (Todini, 1980) is a threshold model of black-box type. The use of more rainfall inputs is made possible. For each input one, two

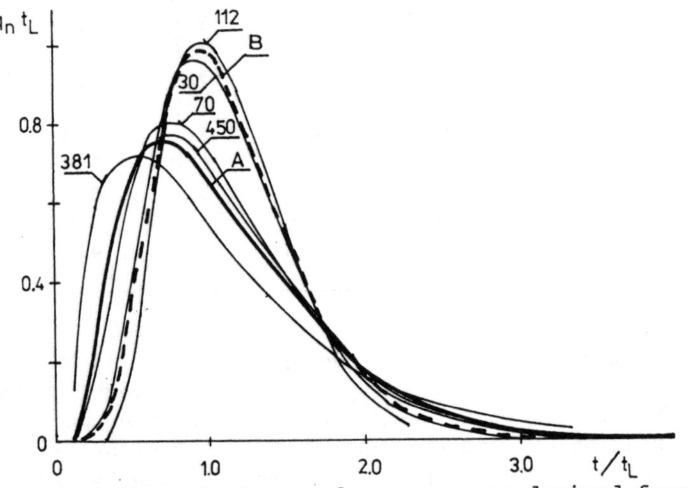

FIG. 4 Dimensionless pulse-responses derived from rain vector at CH.

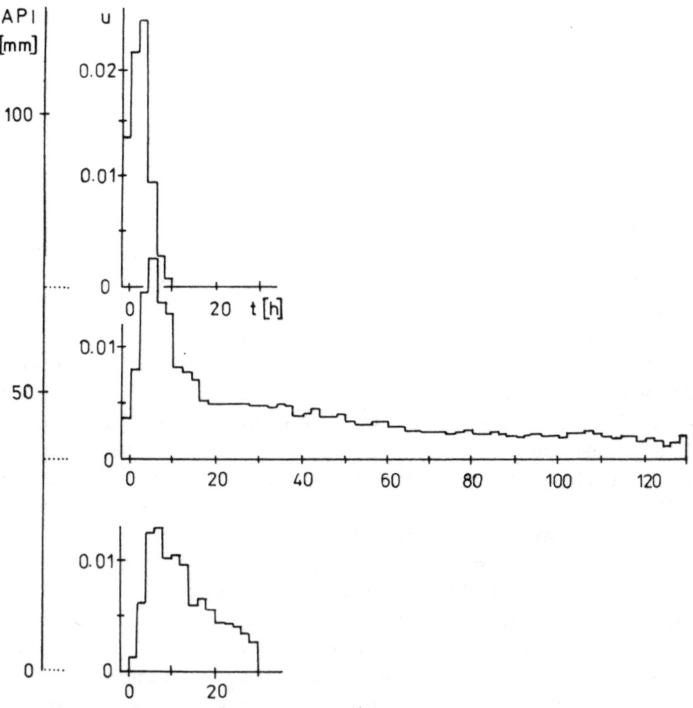

FIG. 5 Response functions u(t) of CLSX derived with areal average as a single input.

TABLE 2 Accuracy of total runoff modelling using CLSX with more rain inputs.

Date	Q_{max} ($m^3\ s^{-1}$)	Q_0 ($m^3\ s^{-1}$)	average ε_p (%)	average Δ_p (h)	3 inputs ε_p (%)	3 inputs Δ_p (h)	comment
310777	40.8	0.3	+2	-4	+13	0	70
	6.4		+22	+2	-14	+2	
	3.6		+64	0	+45	0	
	8.3		-3	0	+3	-2	112,116
	5.6		-	-	-7	-1	121
	3.2		+29	+2	-84	+6	
	3.1		+32	+2	-9	+4	
	4.6		+13	0	-6	+1	
	8.5		+6	-2	-5	-1	
	9.2		+22	-8	+11	-4	
250776	5.4	0.6	+6	0	-3	0	
	9.7		-6	0	+16	0	30
170679	17.8	0.7	-7	0	+3	+2	381
	17.1		-26	-4	-5	0	

or three response functions can be identified. The model switches to the right ones according to the threshold values of API. The area under a particular response function is equal to the runoff coefficient.

First the model has been calibrated on two events using the areal average of rainfall. The results proved quite comparable taking into account different API conditions. The response functions derived from the 310777 event are in Fig. 5 and the accuracy achieved on the same event and two control ones in Table 2. The record of data was three weeks long and contained a five-year flood (event 70 of previous paragraphs) and nine other peaks.

Next the calibration has been carried out with three rain inputs (S, V and CH) both on the same event and on the other two from Table 2 (each of about one week of length). In the 310777 event the causal rain before the five-year peak was reasonably uniform in space but some of the other peaks were strongly influenced by space non-uniformity. In the 250776 event the total at the station CH was dominant (2.15 times bigger than the average) and in the 170679 event the storm moved over the catchment.

For each event two sets of parameters (i.e. responses, thresholds and k) obtained with different numbers of thresholds or different time units of modelling have been found by trial and error. The differences were bigger than when calibrating with the average rain and even some spurious responses appeared. In general, however, it was possible to put together a physically meaningful set of functions (Fig. 6). Each function was obtained from at least two sets by adjusting them graphically. This rather subjective procedure could have been avoided had the data been continuous. It would have enabled also the use of a cosine function for the k and would have made the responses longer (they get truncated due to numerical reasons). As it is the k´s and the thresholds are only an estimation. The set of parameters in Fig. 6 fits all three events with accuracies given in Table 2. Not all the functions are always used. For example the five--year flood is modelled by the middle functions at S and CH (comparatively dry catchment).

There is some improvement in fitting some of the peaks, especially the second peak of the 170679 event and the Q_{max} = 5.6 m^3 s^{-1} (310777) where no modelled peak appeared when using the average rain, but there is also some deterioration.

All the original parameter sets had a zero or a very small first function at the V station and a small second function. This station lying on the divide (Fig. 1) doesn´t seem to represent the Sputka Catchment although its Thiessen coefficient is high.

CONCLUSIONS

From both direct and total runoff modelling it is apparent that the most representative rain vector is at the CH station. For more accurate identification of the UH, however, at least one more station (in the lower part of the catchment) is desirable. The accuracy of total runoff modelling with the CLSX program on the Sputka Catchment using the average rain vector seems satisfactory but the introduction of more rain inputs makes the description of the catchment behaviour clearer for research purposes.

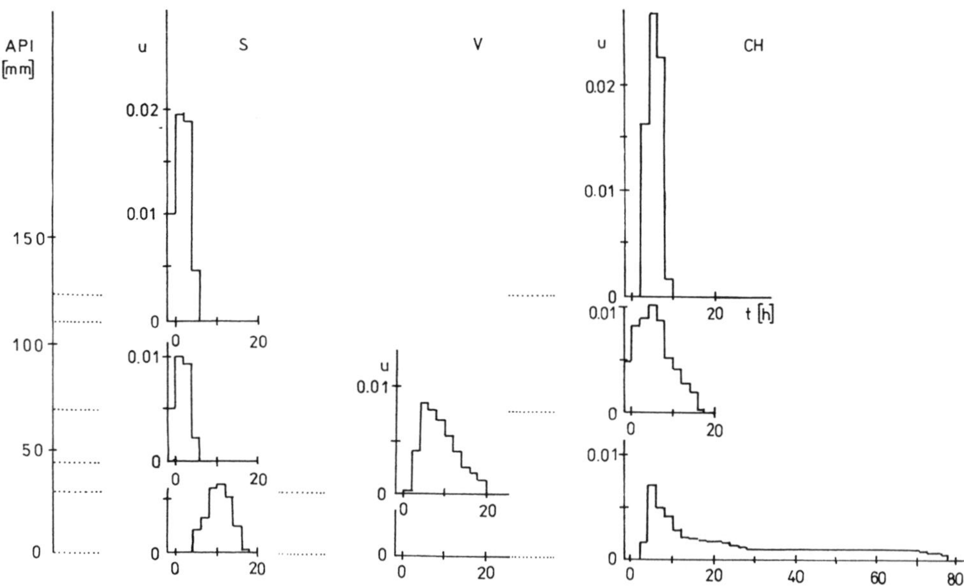

FIG. 6 Response functions of CLSX derived with three rain inputs.

REFERENCES

Blažková, Š. (1988) Flood hydrograph analysis of the Sputka catchment with the help of simple conceptual models. In: Hydrology of mountainous areas (Proc. Štrbské Pleso Workshop, June 1988), 4.11-4.12, Documents in Hydrology.

Dooge, J. C. I. (1977) Problems and methods of rainfall-runoff modelling. In: Mathematical Models for Surface Water Hydrology. Ed. Ciriani, Malone & Wallis. Wiley, Chichester, 71-108.

Dooge, J. C. I. & O´Kane, J. P. J. (1977) PICOMO: A program for the identification of conceptual models. In: Mathematical Models for Surface Water Hydrology. Ed. Ciriani, Malone & Wallis. Wiley, Chichester, 277-294.

Janoušek, M., Mates, K. & Urban, J. (1979) Srážkoodtokový proces v experimentálních povodích (Rainfall-runoff process in experimental catchments). Report. Water Research Institute, Prague.

Todini, E. (1980) CLSX, HOMS component, WMO, Geneve.

Hydrology in Mountainous Regions. I - Hydrological Measurements; the Water Cycle (Proceedings of two Lausanne Symposia, August 1990). IAHS Publ. no. 193, 1990.

Modélisation des petits bassins versants au moyen de lois probabilistes: exemple des crues

O. CAYLA - Société d'Etudes et d'Applications Hydrauliques, 6 rue de Lorraine, 38130 Echirolles, GRENOBLE, FRANCE

M. DEMMAK & M. TOUAT - Agence Nationale des Ressources Hydrauliques, Clairbois, Avenue Mohammadia, Bir Mourad Rais, ALGER, Algérie

RESUME On a mis au point, à partir des données de pluies et de débits observés sur une vingtaine de bassins versants de moins de 100 km² en Algérie, une méthode probabiliste d'élaboration de relations pluie-débit. Cette méthode est basée sur la théorie du Processus de Poisson et utilise le système SPEED, théorie et système qui sont décrits dans l'article "Synthèse Régionale Pluviométrique en région montagneuse". Connaissant par synthèse régionale ou par analyse directe les pluies sur un bassin versant non mesuré et connaissant par mesures sur carte et par enquête de terrain les caractéristiques physiques du bassin, on déduit de ces relations les lois de probabilité des crues, donc les caractéristiques des "crues de projet" ou crues de temps de retour donné. SPEED permet, en outre, d'en déduire une chronologie vraisemblable de crues sur autant d'années que l'on veut, par méthode Monte-Carlo modifiée.

INTRODUCTION

On désire résoudre au mieux le problème de la prédétermination des crues et des apports solides et liquides d'un petit bassin versant, c'est-à-dire que l'on désire calculer les "crues de projet" de ce bassin. Par "crue de projet", on entend les crues de temps de retour donné. Une crue est, de ce point de vue, un débit de pointe, un volume (et un hydrogramme type), un apport solide et une date d'apparition.

Un bassin versant est caractérisé par deux catégories de paramètres :

(a) des paramètres mesurables (ou supposés tels) comme la surface, la pente du thalweg principal, la climatologie,

(b) des paramètres non mesurables que l'on appelle les paysages, comme la végétation, la nature des sols et des sous-sols, l'aspect du lit des rivières.

L'étude se déroule en deux temps. Une première étape concerne l'analyse des relations pluie-débit sur les bassins où l'on dispose de mesures concomitantes de ces deux grandeurs. La seconde étape concerne la corrélation entre les paramètres probabilistes de ces relations et les paramètres physiques des bassins versants, c'est-à-dire la mise au point de formules.

On se reportera à l'article "Synthèse Régionale Pluviométrique en région montagneuse", contribution au Symposium 2, thème 2A pour la description résumée du Processus de Poisson et celle de SPEED.

FICHIERS D'ETUDE

On dispose au départ, en Algérie du Nord, de 33 stations hydrométriques sur lesquelles les crues sont mesurées au limnigraphe, avec contrôle à l'échelle. Les transports solides en suspension sont mesurés par prélèvements à la bouteille. Cinq de ces stations sont inexploitables pour des raisons diverses, en particulier parce que les mesures sont faites sur seuil jaugeur inadapté (voir article "Seuil jaugeur adapté aux petits bassins versants à fort transport solide", Symposium 1, thème 1.D).

Sur les 28 stations restantes, les mesures pluviométriques sont absentes de huit bassins versants. On a donc établi les relations pluie-débit sur vingt stations.

Les mesures s'étendent, en moyenne, sur une douzaine d'années (1970-1987 avec lacunes).

On a défini une crue par les paramètres d'études suivants :

(a) le débit de pointe Q en m³/s,

(b) le volume de crue V, en Mm³ ou 10^6 m³,

(c) le temps de base de la crue triangulaire équivalente T_B en heures. T_B est <u>déduit</u> de Q et V par la relation :

$$T_B = \frac{1\,000\ V}{1{,}8\ Q} \qquad (1)$$

(d) la concentration solide C, en g/l. C est le quotient de la masse solide transportée par la crue au volume liquide V,

(e) la date d'apparition de la crue dans l'année (instant du débit de pointe).

Le fichier de travail des crues est le tableau des mesures de ces divers paramètres pour toutes les crues observées dont le débit de pointe dépasse le seuil Q_o. Q_o est choisi de façon à disposer de trois à cinq crues par an, en moyenne, sur chaque station. Pour l'étude des relations pluie-crue, on n'utilise de ce fichier que la partie qui correspond aux périodes de mesure de la pluie.

On définit la pluie du bassin versant par la mesure de la pluie journalière en un point particulier du bassin que l'on appelle poste caractéristique.

En ce poste caractéristique, on doit vérifier les trois propriétés suivantes :

(a) à chaque crue importante de la rivière, on observe une pluie, même faible au poste,

(b) à chaque forte pluie au poste correspond une crue, même faible, à la station hydrométrique,

(c) la loi probabiliste des pluies au poste est proche de la loi probabiliste moyenne des pluies sur le bassin versant.

Cette dernière condition ne peut se vérifier qu'au moyen d'une synthèse régionale sur la pluviométrie journalière.

Si le poste caractéristique du bassin existe, on construit le fichier de toutes les pluies journalières supérieures au seuil P_o, sur la période commune d'observations des pluies et des crues.

On définit enfin le fichier des caractéristiques physiques mesurables de chaque bassin versant. On a retenu les grandeurs suivantes :

(a) la superficie du bassin versant A, en km²,
(b) la longueur du thalweg principal L, en km,
(c) la pente globale i, rapport de la dénivelée brute à L. i est exprimé en %,
(d) la pluie annuelle moyenne Pa au poste caractéristique, en mm.

LOIS PROBABILISTES DES PARAMETRES D'ETUDES

1. Paramètre T_B : contrairement à notre attente, T_B est une variable aléatoire à part entière. On a adopté une loi de Galton (loi Gaussologarithmique) comme approximation de la loi probabiliste de T_B. Pour l'ensemble des bassins versants, l'écart type du logarithme des temps de base est constant et vaut 0,72.

On peut probablement rattacher ces deux résultats aux caractéristiques de la loi probabiliste des pluies journalières en Algérie, mais ceci est une autre étude.

On démontre également que les variables Q et T_B sont statistiquement indépendantes. Sur le fichier des crues de chaque station, on calcule le coefficient de corrélation $r(Q, T_B)$. L'ensemble des coefficients r obtenus s'ajuste approximativement à une loi de Gauss de moyenne zéro, ce qui prouve l'indépendance de Q et T_B.

2. Paramètre Q : la théorie du Processus de Poisson prévoit que les maximums annuels de débit suivent une loi de Gumbel et que les échantillons tronqués, les débits de pointe Q du fichier, suivent une loi exponentielle.

On a vérifié ce résultat par la méthode des stations années.

3. Paramètre V : partant des deux variables indépendantes Q et T_B, on peut calculer, crue par crue, les valeurs de la variable V. On montre ainsi que V ne suit pas les lois du Processus de Poisson. La loi suivie par V, combinaison de la loi de Gumbel de Q et de la loi de Galton de T_B, n'a pas été recherchée de façon théorique. Elle n'est pas nécessaire à l'étude.

4. Paramètre date de crue : la date de crue s'ajuste assez bien à une loi normale de moyenne le 31 janvier et d'écart type 55 jours (pour l'Algérie du Nord).

5. Concentration solide C : la loi probabiliste de C n'a pas été recherchée. On désire seulement, dans cette étude, déduire de la moyenne de C l'apport moyen interannuel (envasement de barrages par exemple).

6. <u>Pluie journalière P</u> : elle obéit aux lois du Processus de Poisson. Les valeurs supérieures au seuil P_o s'ajustent à la loi exponentielle ; les maximums annuels suivent la loi de Gumbel. Ceci est démontré par synthèse régionale.

RELATIONS P-Q

Il y a deux façons de mettre en relation deux variables aléatoires dont on connaît la loi de distribution : la relation équifréquence et la corrélation en valeurs classées. Ces deux méthodes fournissent théoriquement le même résultat, mais les erreurs d'échantillonnage ne sont pas les mêmes dans les deux cas. On les utilise donc conjointement en posant, en principe, que la relation qui ajuste en même temps les deux graphiques correspondants est la plus précise.

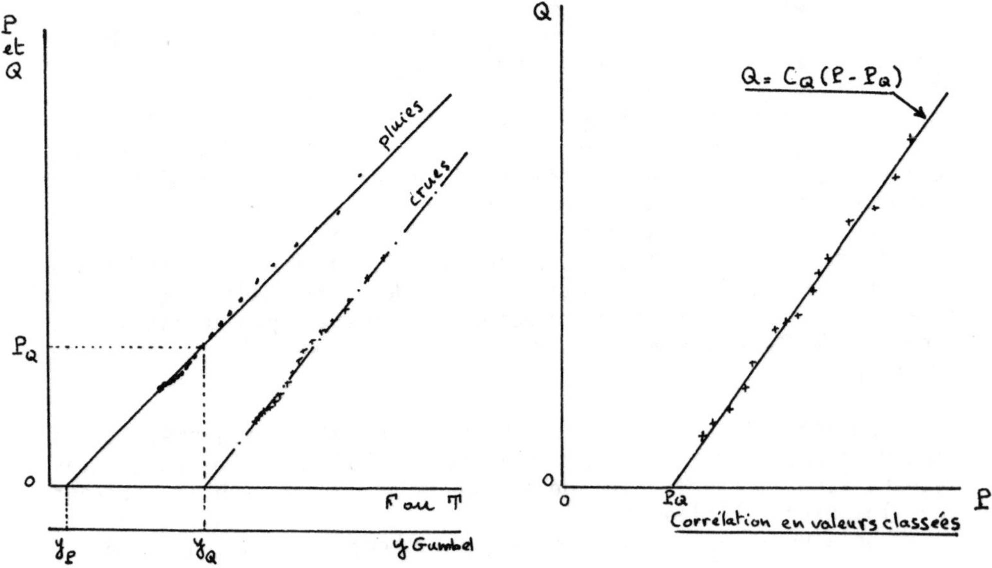

Les schémas ci-dessus expliquent ces deux méthodes.

Dans la relation équifréquence, on place sur un papier probabiliste (logiciel OCAJU de SPEED, ici le papier de Gumbel) les échantillons P et Q. Les lois probabilistes sont représentées par les droites (voir O. CAYLA, M. TAIBI, 1990) :

$$P(T) = P \frac{y_P - y(T)}{y_P - C} \tag{2}$$

$$Q(T) = Q \frac{y_Q - y(T)}{y_Q - C} \tag{3}$$

avec :

- T Temps de retour, en année (relié à la fréquence de non dépassement)
- $y(T)$ Variable réduite de Gumbel pour T
- y_p Pivot associé à la loi des pluies
- y_Q Pivot associé à la loi des débits de pointe
- C Constante d'Euler = 0,5772...

REMARQUE

Il existe une méthode d'ajustement des échantillons tranqués qui fournit directement la loi de Gumbel des maximums annuels, seule loi intéressante du point de vue pratique. Voir O. CAYLA, 1986.

L'élimination de y(T) dans les relations (2) et (3) conduit à la relation équifréquence qui est évidemment linéaire :

$$Q = C_Q\ (P - P_Q) \qquad (4)$$

avec :

- C_Q Coefficient statistique de ruissellement en débit de pointe de crue
- P_Q Seuil statistique de ruissellement en débit de pointe de crue

La corrélation en valeurs classées met en corrélation les échantillons classés de P et Q. Le logiciel OCORAJ de SPEED effectue le graphique correspondant. Il faut, bien entendu, classer les valeurs en ordre décroissant pour que l'opération ait un sens. Le résultat est un autre estimateur de la relation (4).

Nous n'insistons pas ici sur les justifications théoriques de ces deux méthodes d'analyse des corrélations lâches. L'expérience montre que, même si la période de mesure est très éloignée d'une période normale (c'est-à-dire si l'erreur d'échantillonnage sur P est très grande), la relation P-Q obtenue est très peu affectée d'erreur d'échantillonnage (l'erreur d'échantillonnage sur Q "suit" celle sur P). L'étude théorique de cette propriété expérimentale reste à faire.

FICHIER DE RESULTATS STATISTIQUES

On construit les relations (4) pour chacune des stations hydrométriques.

On dispose alors d'un ensemble de paramètres C_Q et P_Q que l'on joint au tableau des caractéristiques physiques des bassins versants.

On construit de la même façon les relations afférentes aux volumes de crues (ou aux lames ruisselées). Bien entendu, puisque V ne suit pas la loi de Gumbel, on doit résoudre cette petite difficulté supplémentaire.

On termine le tableau en écrivant, pour chaque station, les valeurs de T_B, moyenne du temps de base et de C, concentration moyenne en crue.

REGRESSIONS MULTIPLES

On cherche à expliquer, de la façon la plus satisfaisante possible, les valeurs de T_B, C_Q, P_Q et C au moyen des caractéristiques du bassin versant. On procède en deux étapes :

(a) une corrélation multiple en fonction des caractéristiques physiques mesurables du bassin versant,

(b) une explication des résidus obtenus au moyen d'une analyse des paysages.

On est limité dans le choix des variables explicatives par le faible nombre de stations disponibles (une vingtaine) : on ne peut garder que quatre à cinq variables dont la variable "paysages".

Le logiciel utilisé, ARMORE, effectue les calculs classiques de régression multiple et visualise les diverses étapes du calcul (graphiques de corrélations totales et partielles), ce qui permet la critique objective des résultats.

Un tel logiciel ne fournit pas directement la "vraie" formule. Le calcul en régression réduit la variance, c'est-à-dire que la variance des valeurs calculées à partir de la formule brute est inférieure à la variance des valeurs observées.

On corrige ce biais en effectuant, au moyen de OCORAJ, la corrélation en valeurs classées entre valeurs observées et valeurs calculées brutes : la correction consiste à multiplier toutes les valeurs calculées brutes par le coefficient qui amène à une pente 1 la corrélation en valeurs classées.

On effectue enfin la corrélation normale entre valeurs calculées définitives et valeurs observées de façon à visualiser le résidu, station par station.

C'est ce résidu qui peut être expliqué par l'analyse en paysages.

RESULTATS DE LA CORRELATION MULTIPLE EN ALGERIE DU NORD

La variable de base des formules est T_B, temps de base moyen des crues.

On obtient une formule provisoire :

$$T_B = 2,33 + L^{1,7} (Pa \sqrt{i})^{0,577}/1000 \qquad (5)$$

La formule est provisoire parce que, par un malencontreux hasard, il existe une très forte corrélation entre les variables explicatives Pa et i sur la vingtaine de stations disponibles. On ne peut donc pas départager, de façon fiable, l'influence respective de ces deux variables.

La variable P_Q peut être considérée comme constante, égale à 20 mm.

La variable C_Q peut se mettre sous deux formes :

(a) en fonction de la seule superficie A du bassin versant, on retrouve la formule classique :

$$C_Q = 1/12\ A^{0,75} \qquad (6)$$

dont on sait qu'elle peut s'extrapoler aux grands bassins versants,

(b) le meilleur résultat en corrélation multiple est la formule :

$$C_Q = A\ T_B^{0,77}/6 \qquad (7)$$

On a vérifié que cette formule donne d'aussi bons résultats avec T_B calculé au moyen de la formule (5) qu'avec T_B observé.

Enfin, la concentration moyenne en crue peut se calculer par :

$$C = \frac{8\ i^{0,7}}{T_B\ (Pa/1000)^2} \qquad (8)$$

Cette formule est provisoire, pour la même raison que la formule (5).

Elle ne peut pas être extrapolée à des bassins de superficie supérieure à 100 km².

La concentration moyenne annuelle est le tiers de la concentration en crue.

ANALYSE PAR PAYSAGES

Cette analyse ne permet pas d'améliorer les formules (5) à (7) qui sont déjà très précises : l'incertitude obtenue est très proche de l'incertitude sur les données de base.

Elle permet, par contre, d'expliquer la relative mauvaise qualité de la formule (8) qui fournit les concentrations en crue avec une erreur de 1 à 10 (ce qui est déjà un progrès par rapport aux formules appliquées couramment en Algérie. Les concentrations moyennes en crue des bassins mesurés varient de 1,5 à 300 g/l).

Par essais successifs, on a défini les "paysages" du tableau ci-dessous : pour chaque paysage, un bassin versant appartient à l'une des quatre classes -2, -1, 1, 2.

TABLEAU 1

FACTEURS DU PAYSAGE ET CLASSIFICATION					
N° de paysage	Intitulé	Classe -2	Classe -1	Classe 1	Classe 2
A	Roche et substrat : taux de roches tendres	inférieur à 40 %	de 40 % à 60 %	de 60 % à 80 %	supérieur à 80%
B	Contrastes topographiques	plaine ou plateau	faibles	marqués	vallées encaissées
C	Pression anthropique	très faible	faible	forte	très forte
D	Formes d'érosions visibles	pas d'érosions visibles	traces localisées, faibles ou anciennes	érosions localisées actives	érosions actives généralisées
E	Lits mineurs	pas de lit	lit envégété	lit marqué	sapement de berges

L'influence des paysages se traduit par un facteur multiplicatif MP à appliquer à la formule (8).

(a) calcul de l'indice global IP : IP = A + 2B + C + D + 2E
(b) si IP inférieur à -10 : MP = 0,25
(c) si $-2 \leq IP \leq 2$: MP = 1
(d) si $+3 \leq IP \leq +4$: MP = 2
(e) si $+5 \leq IP \leq 10$: MP = 3
(f) si IP > 10 : MP = 4

Les concentrations ainsi calculées et les concentrations observées sont dans un rapport un à trois, au pire un à quatre, sur les trente bassins pour lesquels on dispose de données.

CONCLUSIONS

Axes de recherches complémentaires :

On propose deux catégories de recherches :

1. Une reprise de l'étude en Algérie ou dans le Maghreb en étoffant l'échantillon des stations, de façon à détruire la corrélation apparente entre Pa et i (formules (5) et (8)).

On utilisera toutes les stations sur bassins mesurés de superficie inférieure à 1 000 km² et on cherchera la limite supérieure de superficie pour laquelle T_B est une variable aléatoire. On définira ainsi ce que l'on appelle "petit" bassin versant. Il est évident que la méthodologie s'applique à d'autres régions que l'Afrique du Nord.

2. Des recherches fondamentales sur certains points qu'une étude de recherche appliquée ne peut approfondir. Par exemple :

(a) Etude des liaisons lâches : définition du poste caractéristique, erreurs d'échantillonnage de la liaison équifréquence et de la corrélation en valeurs classées.

(b) Etude des relations entre la loi probabiliste des pluies (lois intensité-durée-fréquence) et la loi du temps de base des crues. En déduire pourquoi les débits de pointe de crue s'accordent à la théorie du processus de Poisson.

REFERENCES

O. CAYLA, M. TAIBI (1990) Synthèse Régionale Pluviométrique en région montagneuse. Conférence internationale sur les ressources en eau en régions montagneuses. Symposium 2, thème 2A.

O. CAYLA (1986) Contribution à la Connaissance de l'Hydrologie Yéménité. Etude hydrologique par événements. Société Hydrotechnique de France (pour prix Henri MILON, 1986).

Hydrology in Mountainous Regions. I - Hydrological Measurements; the Water Cycle (Proceedings of two Lausanne Symposia, August 1990). IAHS Publ. no. 193, 1990.

Application of the Preissmann scheme on flood propagation in river systems in difficult terrain

K.W. CHAU
Department of Civil & Structural Engineering, Hong Kong Polytechnic, Hong Kong

ABSTRACT This paper presents the application of an accurate as well as efficient Preissmann type implicit finite difference solution to approximate flood propagation in a river network system of difficult terrain, tailored on the IBM/PC/XT or PC/AT or their compatible personal computers. With the use of this mathematical model, the hydrograph at any point on the river and hence the probable extent of flooding can be estimated in advance. The potential flood hazard in Shing Mun River and Sham Chun River in Hong Kong have been studied.

INTRODUCTION

A flood hydrograph changes as storm water flows from upstream to downstream of a river channel, including the magnitude and timing of the peak. It is imperative to estimate the hydrograph at any point on the river channel during a rainfall or flood event and to know in advance the probable extent of flooding.

Apart from the development of efficient, high-speed computer program, two alternatives are available in modelling free surface flow: (i) analytical solutions, and (ii) physical hydraulic models. Despite providing the most accurate results, analytical solutions are extremely rare and apply only in highly simplified situations. Physical models have the drawbacks of expensive, time-consuming and lack of flexibility for adaptation to different uses.

In this paper an accurate as well as efficient numerical solution for use on the IBM or compatible personal computers is implemented to simulate unsteady flood propagation in a river system of difficult terrain. The program is written in Fortran and is compiled by PC software Microsoft Fortran Version 4.0. The model developed is based on the 4-point operators Preissmann implicit finite difference scheme (Cunge, 1980 & Preissmann, 1960). As a yardstick against which the model performance can be compared, an explicit scheme has also been coded (Dronkers, 1969) which is conditionally stable. Real hydraulic features, including branched channels and tidal flats, are also simulated.

THE UNSTEADY FLOW EQUATIONS

The governing equations of mass and momentum transport, the de Saint-Venant Equations, are utilized to describe unsteady constant density flow in an open channel which may be subject to tidal forcing and/or upstream freshwater inflows. The de Saint-Venant Equations can be derived from the general equations for fluid flow by integrating the governing equations over the cross section and making certain valid approximations (Abbott, 1980).

The governing equations of unsteady open channel flow are expressed as:

Continuity equation
$$bs\frac{\partial z}{\partial t} + \frac{\partial Q}{\partial x} = q \tag{1}$$

Momentum equation
$$\frac{\partial Q}{\partial t} + \frac{\partial}{\partial x}(uQ) + gA\frac{\partial z}{\partial x} + gA\frac{Q|Q|}{K^2} = 0 \tag{2a}$$

or its linearized version

$$\frac{\partial Q}{\partial t} + gA\frac{\partial z}{\partial x} + \tau Q = 0 \tag{2b}$$

where Q = flow discharge, u = velocity, z = water stage above a datum, bs = storage width, q = lateral inflow, A = area of the channel, g = acceleration due to gravity, K = conveyance factor of the channel and τ = constant linearized bottom friction coefficient.

The unknown variables involved are the discharge Q and the height of the free surface above a datum z, or equivalently the water depth h(z) and the horizontal velocity u = Q/A(h), as shown in Fig. 1.

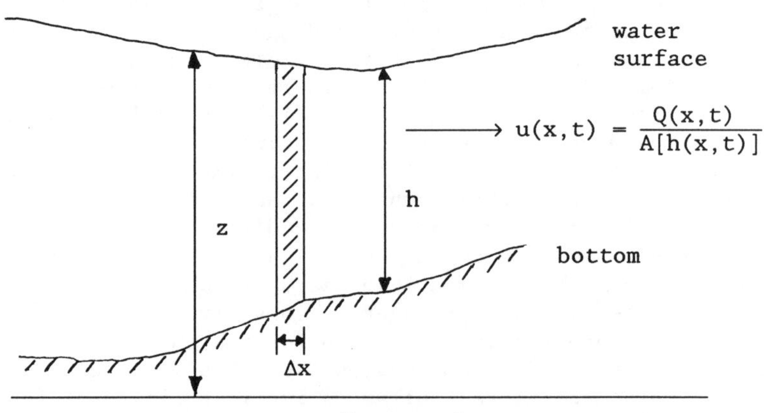

FIG. 1 Definition sketch for unsteady flow equations.

For an explicit finite difference scheme a stability analysis usually results in the Courant-Friedrichs-Lewy (CFL) stability criterion, equation 3, in choosing Δt for given Δx.

$$\left| C\frac{\Delta t}{\Delta x} \right| \le \gamma, \qquad C = \sqrt{gh} \tag{3}$$

often $\gamma = 1$

The stability limit γ is equal to 1 or or a certain number below unity. The value $(C\Delta t/\Delta x)$ is called the Courant number, Cr. One needs to use smaller Δt than that specified by the Courant and other analogous conditions to assure stability. The limitation on Δt for a selected Δx may require a lengthy computation, subsequently making the method impractical (Dronkers, 1969). As such, implicit finite difference scheme is chosen in the mathematical model.

THE PREISSMANN TYPE IMPLICIT FINITE DIFFERENCE SCHEME

Amongst the two implicit finite difference schemes most widely used in engineering practice, Preissmann scheme has advantages over Abbott-Ionescu scheme since it allows non-equidistant grids and computes discharge Q and elevation z at the same point. Thus the Preissmann type of implicit finite difference scheme was chosen in the mathematical model.

The salient features of the Preissmann scheme are as follows :

(a) The Preissmann scheme is unconditionally stable as long as $\Theta \geq 0.5$. Consequently, the time step is only a function of the required accuracy. The time step Δt used can be chosen freely to be comparable with the particular physical phenomena under consideration.

(b) The space intervals Δx_j may be variable. This enables a more flexible schematization of the river, especially in the case of strongly varying cross sections.

(c) Both unknown flow variables are computed at the same computational grid points. Stage/discharge rating curves and similar relationships may be introduced at the same locations with no particular difficulty.

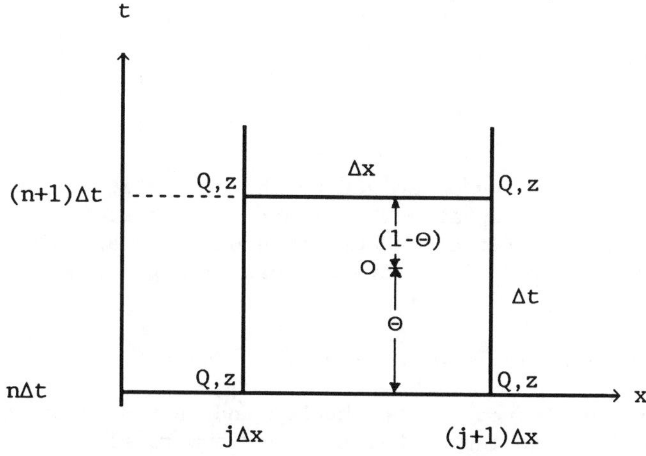

FIG. 2 Data layout of the Preissmann type implicit scheme.

Fig. 2 and equations 4 show the actual discretization of dependent derivatives according to Preissmann (Cunge et al., 1980):

$$f(x,t) \approx \frac{\Theta}{2}\,(f_{j+1}^{n+1} + f_{j}^{n+1}) + \frac{1-\Theta}{2}\,(f_{j+1}^{n} + f_{j}^{n})$$

$$\frac{\partial f}{\partial x} \approx \Theta\,\frac{f_{j+1}^{n+1} - f_{j}^{n+1}}{\Delta x} + (1-\Theta)\,\frac{f_{j+1}^{n} - f_{j}^{n}}{\Delta x}$$

$$\frac{\partial f}{\partial t} \approx \frac{f_{j+1}^{n+1} - f_{j+1}^{n} + f_{j}^{n+1} - f_{j}^{n}}{2\Delta t} \tag{4}$$

where f is the flow variable, discharge Q or water elevation z, and Θ is a time weighting coefficient, $0 \le \Theta \le 1$, introduced in the spatial derivatives to aid in the numerical solutions.

For single channels with one boundary condition given at each end, the coefficient matrix contains elements only in the band along the main diagonal. A computational point j is not linked directly to all other points, but only to adjacent points j-1 and j+1. The discretized form of continuity and momentum equations, written for each adjacent pair of the N computational points in the model, together with the two boundary conditions constitute the following penta-diagonal system of equations in matrix form:

$$\begin{bmatrix} -E_1 & 1 & & & & & & & \\ -C_1 & -D_1 & H_1 & B_1 & & & 0 & 0 & 0 \\ -C'_1 & -D'_1 & H'_1 & B'_1 & & & & 0 & 0 \\ & & -C_2 & -D_2 & H_2 & B_2 & & & \\ & & -C'_2 & -D'_2 & H'_2 & B'_2 & & & \\ & & & & \cdot & \cdot & \cdot & & \\ & 0 & & & \cdot & \cdot & \cdot & & \\ & 0 & 0 & & & -C_{N-1} & -D_{N-1} & H_{N-1} & B_{N-1} \\ & & 0 & & & -C'_{N-1} & -D'_{N-1} & H'_{N-1} & B'_{N-1} \\ & & & & & & & -E_N & 1 \end{bmatrix} \begin{bmatrix} \Delta z_1 \\ \Delta Q_1 \\ \Delta z_2 \\ \Delta Q_2 \\ \Delta z_3 \\ \cdot \\ \cdot \\ \cdot \\ \Delta z_N \\ \Delta Q_N \end{bmatrix} = \begin{bmatrix} F_1 \\ G_1 \\ G'_1 \\ \cdot \\ \cdot \\ \cdot \\ \cdot \\ G_{N-1} \\ G'_{N-1} \\ F_N \end{bmatrix} \tag{5}$$

Thus this system may be solved by the conventional double-sweep method for any time step Δt. The amount of core storage is minimized by taking advantage of the banded nature of the coefficient matrix, which is not destroyed by the branch channel algorithm.

RIGOROUS ANALYTICAL TESTS ON RECTANGULAR CHANNEL

All numerical models need to be checked and tested to ensure that the physical boundary problem is being solved numerically with sufficient accuracy to provide useful and worthwhile engineering results.

The numerical model is tested against several carefully chosen representative analytical solutions :i) a standing wave in a short rectangular channel with constant depth and in the absence of bottom friction, ii) a co-oscillating tide in a rectangular channel with quadratic bottom bathymetry and linearized bottom friction (Lynch,

TABLE 1 Comparison of water elevations at t/T = 0.25 computed by implicit scheme with analytical solution for frictionless flow in rectangular channel with constant depth.

x/ℓ	Exact Solution	Θ = 0.6 Cr=1.990	Θ = 0.6 Cr=8.957
0.0000	0.1011E-0	0.1011E-0	0.1011E-0
0.4000	0.1009E-0	0.1009E-0	0.1009E-0
0.8000	0.1004E-0	0.1004E-0	0.1004E-0
1.0000	0.1000E-0	0.1000E-0	0.1000E-0

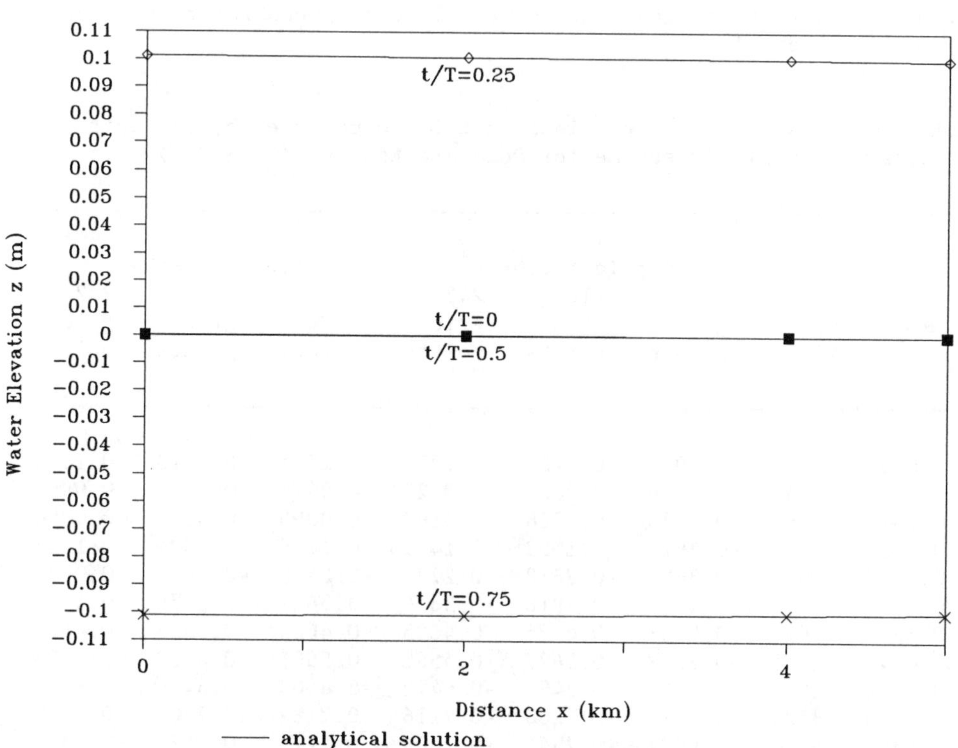

FIG. 3 Comparison of water elevations along the channel computed by implicit scheme with analytical solution for frictionless flow in rectangular channel with constant depth.

1978). These tests also give guidelines on mesh size and length of time step in prototype applications. Table 1 and Fig. 3 show the comparison of elevations along a rectangular channel computed by the scheme and the analytical solution for frictionless flow with constant depth. It can be observed that excellent agreement are obtained for the linearized analytical cases.

VERIFICATION ON REAL PROTOTYPE CASES

In the development of a numerical model, apart from the analytical test cases, it is worthwhile to investigate its effectiveness in real prototype cases (Chau, 1990). As such, the mathematical model has also been verified on tidal hydraulics of two prototype estuaries, namely, the Delaware Estuary and the Chincoteague Bay in the United States, where enormous information was available (Harleman & Lee, 1969 & Ippen, 1966) and where irregular geometries occur.

Table 2 gives the comparison of elevations at t/T = 0 computed by implicit scheme with explicit scheme for Delaware Estuary while Fig. 4 shows the results of velocities over the periodic cycle at different locations of the channel computed by implicit scheme in Chincoteague Bay. It can be noted that the finite difference solutions are in good agreement with historical data of tidal range, mean water level and high/low water times.

TABLE 2 Comparison of elevations at t/T = 0 computed by implicit scheme with explicit scheme for Delaware Estuary (Cr = 0.5).

		Explicit Scheme			**Implicit Scheme**		
x/ℓ	bed width	17 grid points	116 grid points	248 grid points	34 grid points	133 grid points	232 grid points
0.0303	433	-0.0060	0.1159	0.1271	0.1521	0.1413	0.1398
0.0909	543	-0.0516	0.0623	0.0729	0.0979	0.0867	0.0851
0.1515	681	-0.1325	-0.0268	-0.0169	0.0095	-0.0031	-0.0050
0.2121	854	-0.2519	-0.1552	-0.1461	-0.1166	-0.1321	-0.1344
0.2727	1070	-0.3681	-0.2818	-0.2736	-0.2498	-0.2617	-0.2634
0.3333	1342	-0.4657	-0.3918	-0.3846	-0.3682	-0.3754	-0.3764
0.3939	1683	-0.5338	-0.4745	-0.4685	-0.4609	-0.4623	-0.4625
0.4545	2111	-0.6029	-0.5627	-0.5582	-0.5505	-0.5529	-0.5533
0.5152	2648	-0.6645	-0.6495	-0.6472	-0.6403	-0.6434	-0.6440
0.5758	3320	-0.7027	-0.7206	-0.7216	-0.7162	-0.7204	-0.7213
0.6364	4164	-0.6927	-0.7444	-0.7496	-0.7477	-0.7523	-0.7533
0.6970	5222	-0.6095	-0.6712	-0.6789	-0.6753	-0.6849	-0.6857
0.7576	6549	-0.4703	-0.5065	-0.5106	-0.5167	-0.5151	-0.5148
0.8182	8213	-0.3450	-0.3680	-0.3711	-0.3761	-0.3746	-0.3745
0.8788	10300	-0.2304	-0.2398	-0.2418	-0.2459	-0.2444	-0.2441
0.9394	12918	-0.1225	-0.1170	-0.1180	-0.1198	-0.1192	-0.1191
1.0000	16200	0.0000	0.0000	0.0000	0.0000	0.0000	0.0000

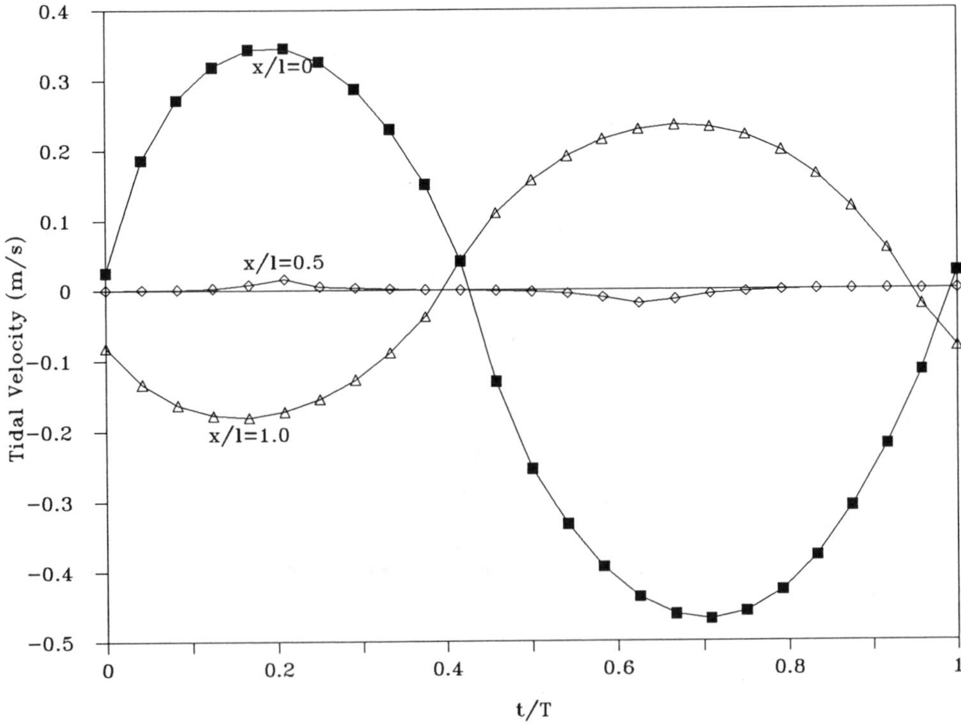

FIG. 4 Variation of tidal velocities over the periodic cycle at different locations of the channel computed by implicit scheme in Chincoteague Bay.

APPLICATION ON FLOOD PROPAGATION

The model is then applied to study the potential flood hazards in Shing Mun River together with its three tributary branches — Tin Sam Nullah, Fo Tan Nullah and Siu Lek Yuen Nullah (Maunsell, 1979). The effect of a proposed river training scheme in River Indus on the flood propagation in the future Sham Chun River network along the Hong Kong/China border is also evaluated (Maunsell, 1988). Both channels are of trapezoidal shape.

Fig. 5 depicts the computed water velocities along the Shing Mun River due to the effect of flood hydrographs applied at the upstream end of the river channel with tidal forcing of amplitude 1.05 m at the ocean end. It is found that the areas adjacent to the two river channels are protected against flooding if a severe storm surge does not occur. However, flooding is possible in the event the following combination occurs, i.e. 50-year Rainstorm + High Tide + Storm Surge.

CONCLUSIONS

It is useful to predict, accurately and efficiently, water stages and

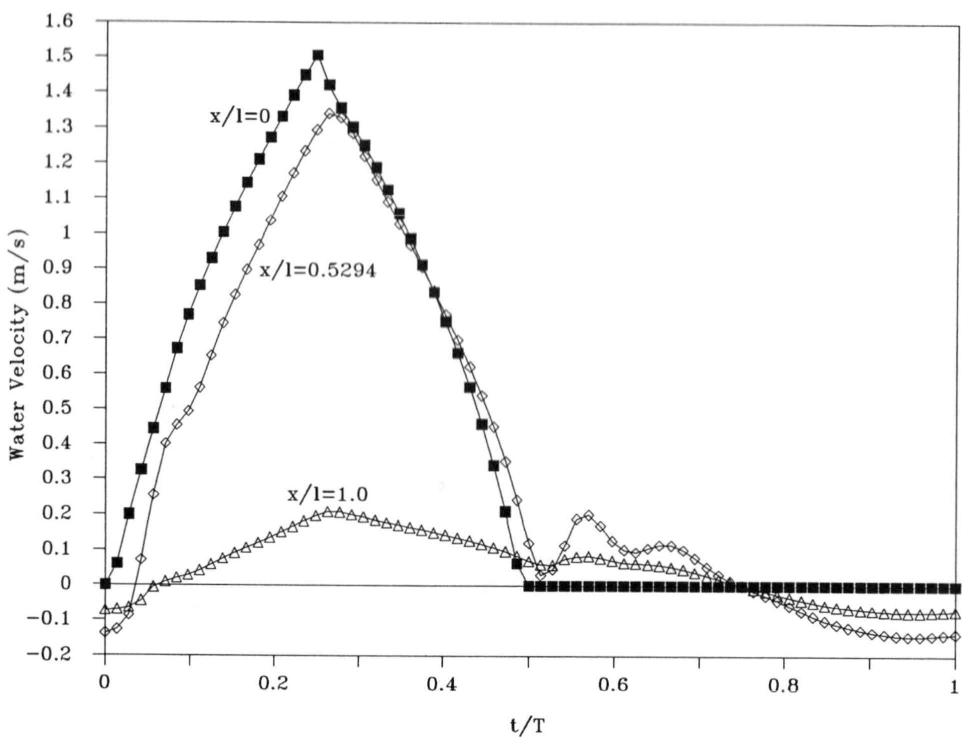

FIG. 5 Variation of water velocities computed by implicit scheme due to the imposition of a 50-year stormwater discharge coincident with high tide in Shing Mun River Channel.

flow quantities in river channels, particularly during heavy rainstorm, since the prediction of the time and magnitude of flood peaks can give alarm signals to the people at the downstream end. Appropriate measures to alleviate the effect of flooding can hence be made accordingly.

The model is able to describe the physical processes correctly and, for comparable accuracy, is more convenient and reliable than the explicit scheme. Solution features attributable to the nonlinearity of the equation can be noted. The accuracy of the implicit model is good at the Courant Number up to 10. The rigorous verification for the analytical test cases and the successful applications of the model to various prototype cases with different characteristics provide confidence for its capability as predictive tools in situations involving complex bathymetry and/or nonlinear bottom frictional effects, which pure analytical models is not able to incorporate.

The PC based mathematical model for simulation of unsteady flood propagation in an open channel network system is useful for predictive purposes and, as well, for design of proper urban stormwater drainage schemes to cope with different rainstorm runoffs or to carry off the surplus water.

REFERENCES

Abbott, M. B. (1980) Computational Hydraulics, Elements of the Theory of Free Surface Flows.

Chau, K. W. (1990) Verification of an efficient PC based numerical model of river network, Proc. of the VIII International Conf. on Computational Methods in Water Resources, Venice, Italy.

Cunge, J. A., Holly, F. M. & Verwey, A. (1980) Practical Aspects of Computational River Hydraulics.

Dronkers, J. J. (1969) Tidal computations for rivers, coastal areas, and seas, J. Hydraul. Div. ASCE, January, HY1, 29-77.

Harleman, D. R. F. & Lee, C. H. (1969) The computation of tides and currents in estuaries and canals, Tech. Bulletin No. 16, U.S. Army Corps of Engrs.

Ippen, A. T. (1966) Estuaries and Coastal Hydrodynamics, McGraw-Hill Book Co.

Lynch, D. R. & Gray, W. G. (1978) Analytical solutions for computer flow model testing, J. Hydraul. Div. ASCE, vol. 104, HY10, 1409-1428.

Maunsell Consultants Asia (1979) Tolo Harbour Rivers, Pollution & Sedimentation Study Part 1 — Shing Mun River.

Maunsell Consultants Asia Ltd. (1988) River Indus Study — Working Papers.

Preissmann, A. (1960) Propagation des intumescences dans les canaux et riviers, 1er Congrès d'association Française de calcul, 433-442, Grenoble, France.

Hydrology in Mountainous Regions. I - Hydrological Measurements; the Water Cycle (Proceedings of two Lausanne Symposia, August 1990). IAHS Publ. no. 193, 1990.

Snowmelt assessment in a complex system of reservoirs (Comunidad de Madrid)

FRANCISCO CUBILLO
Statistic and Model Division, Planning Department
Engineering and Development Directorate,
Canal de Isabel II
Santa Engracia, 125, 28003-Madrid, Spain

ABSTRACT The management of a water supply system based on 98% surface water, with all its reservoir basins located at an elevation of around 2000 m requires the use of a tool for the prediction of the runoff that each reservoir will receive, especially from snowmelt. This tool is a phenomenologic mathematical model for the daily simulation of runoff,and takes into account the snowcover in the basin, climatological conditions, geomorphological, vegetation cover, soil moisture, groundwater outflows, etc. This paper shows the method used for the calibration and development of the model for the main reservoir basins of the Comunidad de Madrid.

REASONS FOR THE CONSTRUCTION OF A WATERSHED MODEL

The Comunidad de Madrid gets its water supply from 12 main reservoirs (Fig.1). The management of this system, carried out by the Canal de Isabel II, needs to establish operation rules to minimize the spillouts and maximize the water supply reliability as well as hydroelectric power generation. In order to do this, it is necessary to seek evaluation techniques for runoff prediction, with specific attention to snowmelt since the regulated basins are located at an average elevation of 1500 m.

These operation rules must be defined for long, medium and short terms. For long term, these methods do not represent any more of an advantage than the possibility to estimate, in planning tasks, the total runoff variations as a consecuence of different soil uses. For medium term (1 to 3 years) the results become more useful for management since they help in the prediction of runoff based on existing conditions and sthocastic information (rainfall, themperature, etc). All of this, allows for the evaluation of the volume of snowmelt as a total monthly resource. But in the short term (1 to 20 days) its utility is most evident in facilitating decision making when the reservoirs are nearly full, as in flash flood management, and of course, in optimizing hydroelectric power generation.

The Canal de Isabel II as manager of the water supply for around 5.000.000 inhabitants, also has a communications network which transmits, in real time, hydraulic, hydrologic and climatologic information from its reservoirs, basins and conveyances which would facilitate the use of this kind of model in the short term.

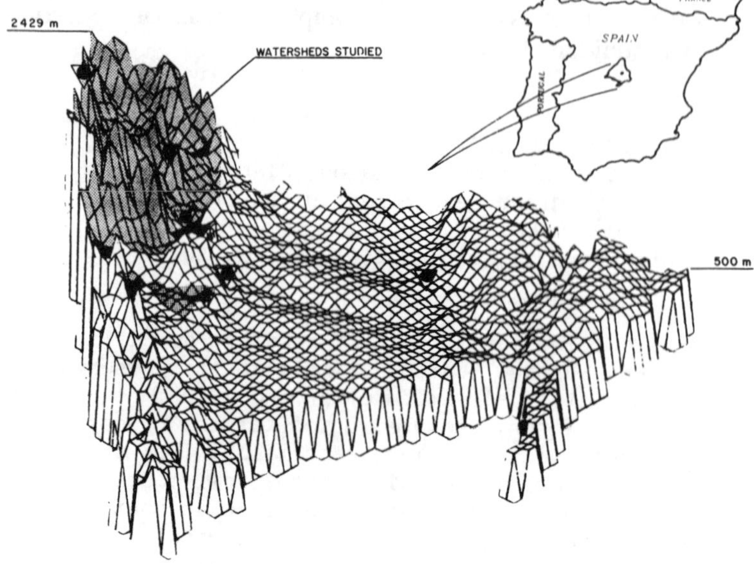

COMUNIDAD DE MADRID

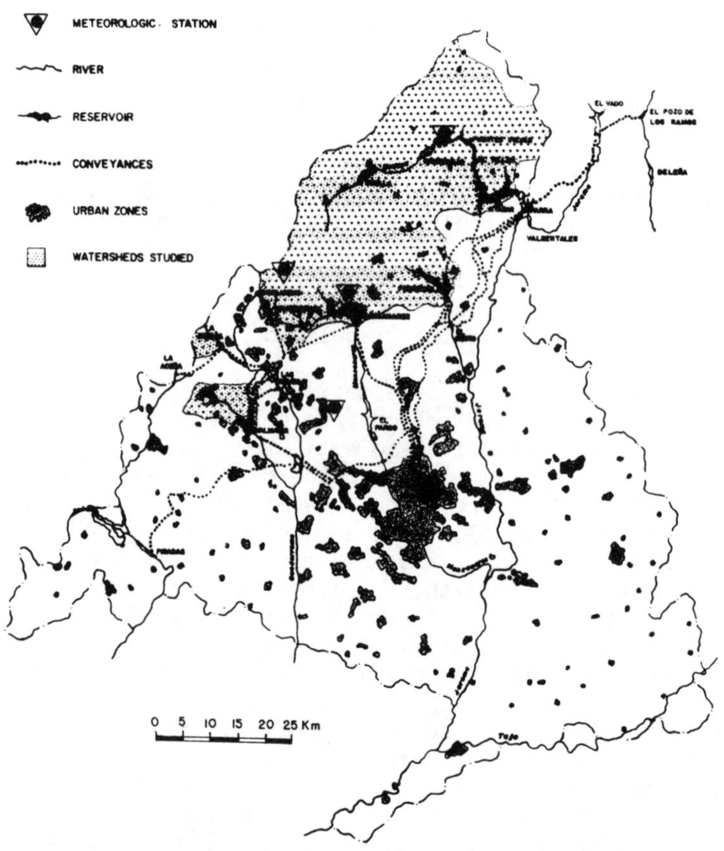

FIG. 1 Scope of the study.

SCOPE

The scope considered for the study correspons to the basins of the main reservoirs of Madrid, and included some of the smallest in order to get more widely useful results.

All the basins studied are located in a range of elevations from 800 to 2429 m. (Fig. 1).

The climate in the zone is continental mediterranean at its mountain level, detecting a clearly altitudinal variation in the main thermopluviometric variables. This variation can be established in a generic manner, with a thermometric gradient of -0.55 ºc/100 m. and a pluviometric gradient of 0.46 mm/100 m.

The average yearly rainfall in the Comunidad de Madrid is 758 mm/year, varying from 650 mm at the lower zones and up to 1.500 mm at the summits.

MODEL USED

The model used has been the Hydrological Simulation Program Fortran HSPF developed by the U.S. Environmental Protection Agency. This program can simulate continuously the hydrologic, and associated water quality processes, on pervious and impervious land surfaces and in streams and well mixed impoundments. It is a conceptual type model and can analyse intervals from 5 minutes to 1 week. One of the phenomenon that this model can simulate with accuracy is the fall, accumulation and melt of the snow, and which was fundamental in selecting it for application to our study.

Model description

Considering the basins' characteristics which the model was applied to, we will limit the model description to the section that can simulate the quantitative hydrologic processes in zones were the infiltration rate is high enough to have an influence on the water budget.

The hydrologic behaviour in the pervious zones is studied according to the method developped in the Standford Watersheds Model (Crawford and Linsley, 1966) and simulates the different processes of interception, infiltration, runoff, percolation and evapotranspiration, where it is possible to include, optionally, the accumulation and melt of snowpack, using for its evaluation the heat budget method.

The more relevant sections of the model related to this study are:

(a) ATEMP. This section permits the user to correct the air temperature depending on the different elevations on the basin. The lapse rate for air temperature is dependent upon precipitation during the time interval. If precipitation occurs, a wet lapse rate of 0.0035 degrees F per foot difference in elevation is assumed. Otherwise, a dry lapse rate, that varies with the time of day, is used. A table of 24 hourly dry lapse rates varying between 0.0035 to 0.005 is built into the system. The user can modify these rates.

(b) SNOW. This section can simulate accumulation and melting of snow and ice. The algorithms used are based on the work by the Corps of Engineers (1956) Anderson and Crawford (1964), and Anderson (1968). Empirical relationships are employed when physical ones are not well known. The snow algorithm uses meteorologic data to determine whether precipitation is rain or snow, to simulate an energy balance for the snowpack, and to determine the effect of the heat fluxes on the snowpack.

- Five types of meteorological data are required in this section: precipitation, air temperature, solar radiation, dewpoint and wind velocity.
- Air temperature is used to determine when snow is falling. Once snow begins to accumulate on the ground, the snowpack accumulation and melt calculation occurs and takes into consideration five sources of heat which influence the melting of snowpack.
  (1) net radiation heat, both longwave and shortware.
  (2) convection of sensible heat from the air.
  (3) latent heat transfer by condensation of moist air on the snowpack.
  (4) heat from rain, sensible heat from rain falling and latent heat from rain freezing on the snowpack.
  (5) conduction of heat from the underlying ground to the snowpack.

  Other heat exchange processes such as latent heat from evaporation are considered less significant and are not simulated. Fig. 2. Shows the processes considered.

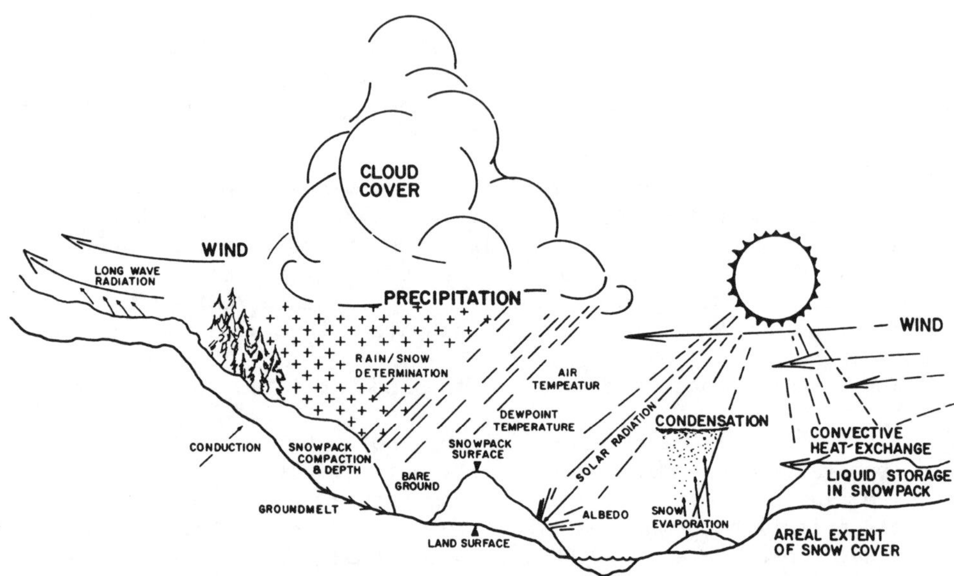

FIG. 2 Snow accumulation and melt processes (Johanson et al. 1984).

- For uniformity and accounting, energy values are calculated in terms of the water equivalent which they could melt. It takes 202.4 calories per square cm on the surface to melt one inch water equivalent of snow at 0ºC.
- All the sources of heat are considered to be positive (incoming to he pack) or zero, except the net radiation heat which can also be negative (leaving the pack).
  Net incoming heat from the atmosphere is used to warm the snowpack. The snowpack can be further warmed by the latent heat released upon rain freezing. Any excess heat above that required to warm the snowpack to 0ºC is used to melt the pack. Likewise, net loss of heat is used to cool the snowpack producing a negative heat storage. Furthermore, incoming heat from the ground melts the snowpack from the bottom, independent of the atmospheric heat sources except that the rate depends on the temperature of the snowpack.

(c) PWATER. This section is used to calculate the components of the water budget, primarily to predict the total runoff from a pervious area. The main aspects considered in this section are:
- It simulates the interception of moisture by vegetal or other ground cover. Moisture is supplied by precipitation or under snow conditions, it is supplied by the rain not falling on the snowpack plus the water yielded by the snowpack.
- It determines what happens to the moisture on the surface of the land. It my infiltrate, go to the upper zone storage or interflow storage, remain in surface detention storage, or run off.
- It determines the amount of interflow and it updates the water storage. Interflow can have an important influence on storm hydrographs particularly when vertical percolation is retarded by a shallow, less permeable soil layer. Additions to the interflow component are retained in storage or routed as outflow from the land segment. Inflows to the interflow component may occur from the surface or from upslope external lateral flows.
- It calculates the water percolating from the upper zone. Water no percolated remains in upper zone storage available for evapotranspiration.
- It determines the quantity of infiltrated and percolated water which enters the lower zone.
- It determines the amount of the inflow to groundwater that is lost to deep or inactive groundwater and to determine the amount of active groundwater outflow.
- It simulates evaporation and evapotranspiration fluxes from all zones of the pervious land segment since in most hydrologic regimens the volume of water that leaves a watershed as evapotranspiration exceeds the total volume of streamflow, this is an important aspect of the water budget.

MODEL CONSTRUCTION FOR THE COMUNIDAD DE MADRID RESERVOIRS

Model construction was based on calibrations ordered from the smallest subbasins to the biggest ones while assigning and comparing the values that were a result of the parameters in the different hypothesis.

The first calibration was carried out with daily flows registered in three gage stations, that drain 32,33 and 90 Km2 of subbasin, the rest of the calibrations were perfomed for the total watershed of every reservoir the bigest of which has a surface of 275 Km2.

In order to construct these models a detail collection of basic necessary data was made. The geomorphological and vegetation information was collected with 1 Km2 of precision. The meteorological information was based on daily precipitation, potential evapotranspiration, average daily temperatures, wind velocity solar radiation and dewpoint. The precipitation and temperature were taken from the weather station on the dams while the rest of the variables were calculated from the only two complete weather stations in the area (Fig. 1).

Contrasting data were selected from the period June 1986 to march 1988 since this period produced variyng climatological conditions which could represent wide range of scenarios which the model would simulate.

Calibration

Calibration was focust on three levels of tasks:

- Analysis of the validity of the flows registered.
- Definition of homogeneous meteorological subzones for each basin.
- Assigning values to the model parametres.

The first two levels are basic for considering the third and in some cases it is impossible to consider any one of them without taking into account the other two.

The inflow calibration data were always sufficient for the records corresponding to the total reservoirs basins, thanks to the excellent system of measurement and control that the Canal de Isabel II has installed at every reservoir. On the other hand, some series of recorded values were rejected at gage stations probably due to an inaccurate debit curve.

For the definition of homogeneous meteorological subzones it was very helpful to compare the results obtained from each basin and the totality of them, and to analyse their similitudes and revise their discrepancies.

The numerous parameters contemplated in the model were adjusted by means of the methodology described in the HSPF calibration manuals (Donigian et al. 1982). The ranges of values obtained coincided in general with the suggested ones.

The calibration results were satisfactory and produced the best similitudes between values observed and the values simulated, for the smallest subbasins. This is probably a consecuence of the necessity to define subzones with homogeneous vegetation, geomorphologic and climatological characteristics.

As an example we can see in fig. 3. the differences between the values observed and simulated in Manzanares Reservoir.

The results represented in terms of flows frecuency distribution and accumulated runoff are specially good.

Two of the more significant aspects detected during the calibration process were the low capacity of ground infiltration and low discharges of groundwater.

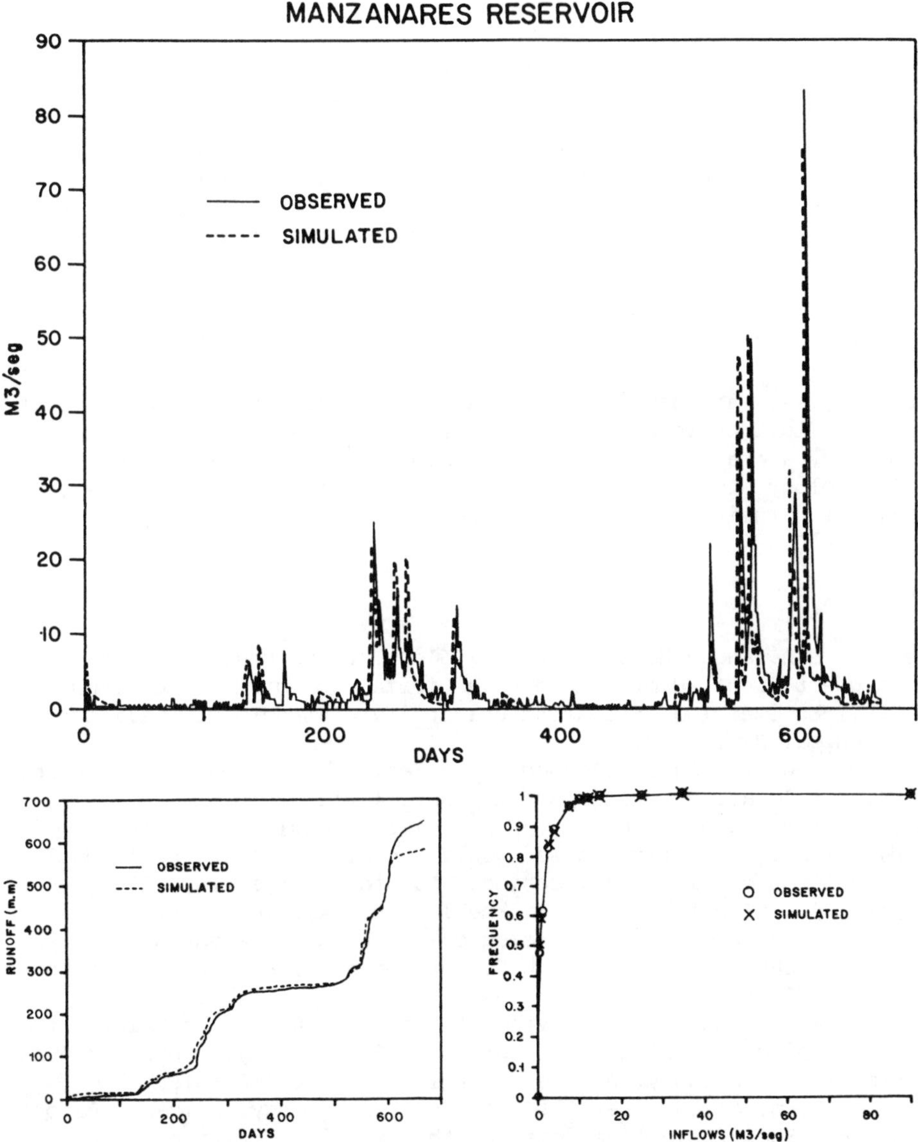

FIG. 3 Some significant calibrations results for Manzanares reservoir basin.

It was also proven that the infiltration capacity diminished during frost periods and reached values of 0,5 mm/h.

In summary, and although it sounds contradictory the worst local adjustments corresponded to the peak flows coinciding with spring snowmelts. In any case the differences were always lower than the 10%. This is probably due to the scarce meteorological information on snow precipitation and snow cover (1 station for the total zone), and the model assumes average values for some very heterogeneous climatic zones.

CONCLUSIONS

The model developed is sufficient accurate in the simulation of dayly inflows to the reservoirs and it is perfectly possible to consider its use for the runoff prediction in the short term management.

Incorporation of new weather stations, that transmit daily information through the Canal de Isabel II communications network and a better knowledge of the snow accumulation process and snowmelt with mesures of snowpack depth will instil more confidence in the use of this model.

ACKNOWLEDGEMENTS

This study was made possible thanks to the Cooperative Project with the U.S. Environmental Research Laboratory (E.P.A.) partially financed by a grant from the U.S.-Spain Joint Commettee for Science and Technology. Special thanks is given to Tom Barnwell and Victor Castillo for their colaboration in model construction.

REFERENCES

Anderson, E.A. and N.H. Crawford. (1964) The Synthesis of continuos Snowmelt Runoff Hydrographs on a Digital Computer. Department of Civil Engineering, Standford University. Standford, California. Technical Report No. 36.

Anderson, E.A. (1968) Development and Testing of Snow Pack Energy Balance Equations. Water Resour. Res. 4 (1), 19-37.

Crawford, N.H. and Linsley, R.K. (1966) Digital Simulation in Hydrology: The Stanford Watershed Model IV, Tech. Rept No.39. Department of Civil Engineering, Standford University, 1966.

Donigian, A.S. Imhoff, J.C., Bicknell, B.R. Kittle, J.L. (1984) Aplication Guide for Hydrological Simulation Program -FORTRAN (HSPF), EPA- 600/3-84-065. U.S. Environmental Research Laboratory Athens, Georgia.

Johanson, R.C. Imhoff, J.C. Davis, H.H. (1984) Users Manual for the Hydrological Simulation Program-FORTRAN (HSPF). Environmental Research Laboratory, Athens, Georgia. EPA-600/9-80-015.

U.S. Army Corps of Engineers (1956) Snow Hydrology, Summary Report of the Snow Investigations. North Pacific Division. Portland Oregon.

Hydrology in Mountainous Regions. I - Hydrological Measurements; the Water Cycle (Proceedings of two Lausanne Symposia, August 1990). IAHS Publ. no. 193, 1990.

Application of the Kennessey method for the determination of the runoff coefficient and evaluation of aquifer recharge in mountain regions

D. FARINA
Progettambiente s.r.l.-Pesaro, Italy
A. GASPARI
Fabriano, Italy

ABSTRACT The Kennessey method, a phisiography-based indirect method for the determination of the Runoff coefficient, has been applied to the calcareous massif of M. Cucco (1566 m a.s.l., Umbria-Marche borderline) and verified with experimental Runoff data. The value of the Runoff coefficient calculated with such method, Rc(Kenn.), is 0.587, compared to a value of 0.580, obtained from experimental data (Pantana stream-gauge station). The measured Infiltration rate is 29% of precipitation.

DETERMINATION OF Rc WITH THE KENNESSEY METHOD

The determination of the Runoff coefficient by means of the Kennessey method (Tardi & Vittorini, 1977), Rc(Kenn.), is obtained by the following procedure:

(a) drafting of three different thematic maps: acclivity (slope), vegetational cover of the soil and permeability. The three parameters are quantified by numerical coefficients in function of the Index of Aridity (Ia,see Table 1).Intermediate coefficients have been attributed to a wide belt corresponding to the south western outcrops of Scaglia Rosata and Cinerea Fs showing values of Ia on the limits(36÷40);

(b) calculation of the weighed average of the distribution of coefficients from each map. Three "components" are obtained (Ca,Cv,Cp).The addition of the three components yelds to the value of the Runoff coefficient, which in this case is:

$$Rc\ (Kenn.) = Ca + Cv + Cp = 0.272 + 0.112 + 0.193 = 0.587$$

(c) the overlapping of the three maps evidences a set of several combinations of the coefficients whose addition leads to the drafting of a Rc(Kenn.) map,representing a zonization of this parameter. In this case,the over 50 combinations where gathered in 16 classes of values,differing by 0.05. Due to graphical reasons,only 6 classes were differenced in the map of fig.1/a.

The acclivity map has been drawn on the basis of the standard IGM 1:25000 map following the four-classes differentiation suggested by the method. Vegetation has been analyzed on aereophotographs and drawn on the derived orthophotomaps 1:10000 of Regione Marche.

As for the choice of attribution of the permeability classes to the various rock-formations,the assessment has been based on thorough meso-structural analysis of many outcrops in the area, along with hydrologic information on aquifer productivity.

A 16 Km^2 rappresentative area of the Sentino basin has also been tested in order to check any possible difference. The value found was 0.589.

TABLE 1 Coefficients utilized in the Kennessey method.

	SLOPE (Ca)	COEFFICIENTS Ia < 25	Ia 25÷40	Ia > 40	INTERMEDIATE COEFFICIENTS OF THE WESTERN ZONE		VEGETATION (Cv)	COEFFICIENTS Ia < 25	Ia 25÷40	Ia > 40	INTERMEDIATE COEFFICIENTS OF THE WESTERN ZONE
1	> 35%	0,22	0,26	0,30	0,28	1	bare rock	0,26	0,28	0,30	0,29
2	10÷35%	0,12	0,16	0,20	0,18	2	grassland	0,17	0,21	0,25	0,23
3	3,5÷10%	0,01	0,03	0,05	0,04	3	farmland, reafforestation	0,07	0,11	0,15	0,13
4	< 3,5%	--	0,01	0,03	0,02	4	forest land	0,03	0,04	0,05	0,04
ROCK FORMATIONS							PERMEABILITY (Cp)	COEFFICIENTS Ia < 25	Ia 25÷40	Ia > 40	INTERMEDIATE COEFFICIENTS OF THE WESTERN ZONE
MARNE A FUCOIDI, SCAGLIA CINEREA						1	very poor	0,21	0,26	0,30	0,28
ROSSO-AMMONITICO, MARNE DEL SENTINO, CALCARI DIASPRINI						2	poor	0,17	0,21	0,25	0,25
SCAGLIA ROSSA: CALCARI AD APTICI						3	moderate	0,12	0,16	0,20	0,18
CORNIOLA: MAIOLICA, BUGARONE						4	good	0,06	0,08	0,10	0,09
CALCARE MASSICCIO						5	very good	0,03	0,04	0,05	0,04

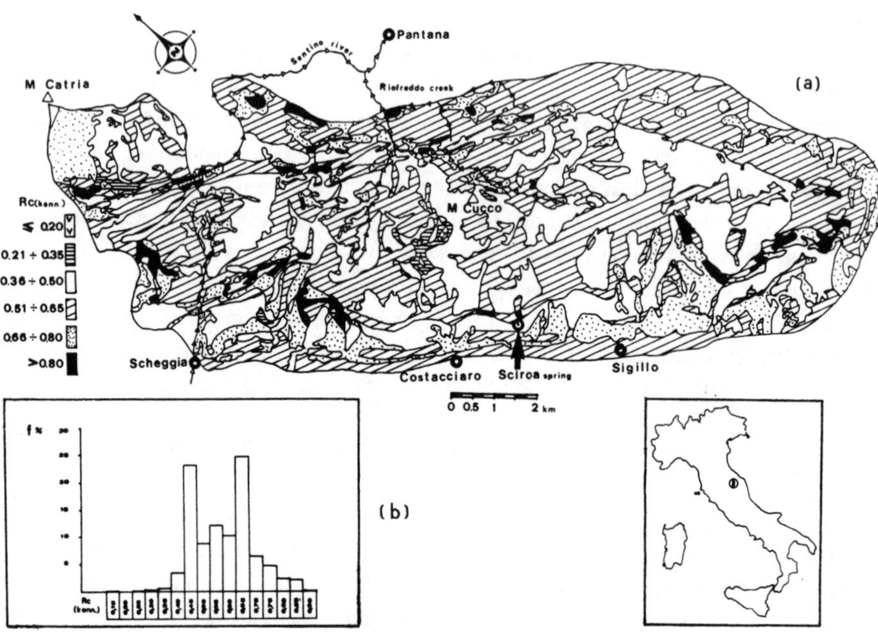

FIG.1 Map of Rc(Kenn) (a);Frequency % of Rc(Kenn) (b).

pertinent to Pantana station.

We conclude that the determination of the Runoff coefficient with the Kennessey method gives a value which is fairly close to the Rc = 0.580, calculated from experimental hydrologic data

GROUNDWATER RUNOFF

The extimation of the groundwater runoff is based on the amount of the total average discharge occurring though well defined springs plus the average seepage into the Sentino-Riofreddo streams.

While the first component gives a fairly reliable value of Q = 0.3 m^3/s,the determination of seepage, which appears to be considerably more relevant,takes a particular consideration.

Sentino's average base flow in dry periods (June-September) ranges from 0.89 m^3/s in June to 0.26 m^3/s in August with a summer average of approximately 0.6 m^3/s,almost completely attributable to groundwater seepage into the streams.

Differential yeld measurements carried out on Sentino river during a 15 days-long dry period in October 1974 (Servizio Geol. Ital.,1975) evidenced an increasing yeld of a total 2.0 m^3/s (18 l/s/Km^2).This runoff is 16% higher than the average 15.5 l/s/Km^2 for the same month.

The highest Specific runoff values were recorded at the crossing of the M.Cucco anticline (P.Calcara-Valdorbia sud-basin) and in the Riofreddo tributary basin (45 and 30 l/s/Km^2 ,respectively) with a total 1 m^3 /s. These values corresponds to high Runoff coefficients (1.09 and 0.65 respectively,on annual basis) showing that most of the runoff is due to seepage flow.

Qsp and Rc data decrease dramatically in the sector downvalley Valdorbia (14 l/s/Km^2 ; Rc = 0.31) and upvalley Ponte Calcara (7 l/s/Km^2;Rc = 0.11).

The first sector may represent a recharge area to outer units due to the deepening of Catria' anticline's flank and heavy karstification of Corno Gorge (470 m o.s.l.). The upvalley sector would simply represent the predominance of surficial runoff due to the lower permeabilities of "Scaglia" formations.

These data confirm that a large part of the seepage flow evidenced in the Sentino basin has its recharge area in the M.Cucco massif , which contribute with an average runoff of approximately 0.8 m^3/s .This value represents the discharge measured on the sole Riofreddo creek,which has a basin thoroughly internal to the massif.It corresponds to the 50% of the average runoff of Sentino in October,as suggested by the 1974 differential flow measures.The high pertinent Specific runoff value, 28 l/s/Km^2 ,typical of discharge basins,show the wider extension of the hydrological basin.

In conclusion, the total groundwater runoff amounts to 1.1 m^3/s corresponding to specific value of 14.2 l/s/Km^2 on the total area.

For checking purposes, averaging Sentino's June + October Specific runoff and applying it to the permeable part of the basin (83.8 Km^2) we obtain a value of 14 $l/s/Km^2$. Comparable values are represented by Scirca spring's value of Qsp determined on the basis of its most probable hydrogeological basin (12.5 $l/s/Km^2$). A lower value (11.5 $l/s/Km^2$) is obtained by considering the average increase in spring's yeld between base-flow and average flow (+60%) and extrapolating this value to the Sentino's base flow.

The average value chosen is 13 $l/s/Km^2$.

WATER BUDGET

We can quantify the hydrologic cycle of the area by expressing its average water budget :

	P = I + R + E + Q
in mm/y	1420 = 409.5 + 424 + 535 + 51.5
in % of P	100 = 28.8 + 29.8 + 37.6 + 3.6

where: P = Precipitation
R = Surficial Runoff (= Q-I);Q(Total Runoff) = P*Rc
I = Groundwater Runoff (measured)
E = Turc's Actual Evapotranspiration
ΔQ = Deficit to the balance

ACKNOWLEDGEMENTS Many thanks to Progettambiente s.r.l. for supporting this study. A special thanks to Paola Giammattei and Andreina Leporoni who did most of the drawing work.

REFERENCES

Bertuccioli, M.,Reichenbach, G. & Salvatori, F.(1975) Relations between M. Cucco underground hydrography and Scirca spring. Ann. Speleol. 1975, 30, 4.

Calamita, F. & Deiana, G. (1986) Geodinamica dell'appennino Umbro-Marchigiano. 73° Congr.Soc.Geol.It., Roma.

Castany, G. Prospection et exploration des eaux souterraines, Dunod, Paris.

Mouton, J. (1970) Evapotraspirazione reale ed infiltrazione efficace in Italia meridionale. E.S.A., A.I.H. Atti del I Convegno Inter. sulle acque sotterranee, Palermo.

Servizio Geologico d'Italia (1975) Carta Geologica d'Italia - Fogli 301, 291; Note illustrative della Carta Idrogeologica F. 291, Pergola, a cura di E. Centamore, Idrotecno, M. Valletta.

Hydrology in Mountainous Regions. I - Hydrological Measurements; the Water Cycle
(Proceedings of two Lausanne Symposia, August 1990). IAHS Publ. no. 193, 1990.

Annual precipitation and regional effects on daily precipitation model parameters

C. L. HANSON
US Department of Agriculture, Agricultural Research Service, Northwest Watershed Research Center, 270 South Orchard, Boise, Idaho 83705, USA

D. A. WOOLHISER
US Department of Agriculture, Agricultural Research Service, Aridland Watershed Management Research Unit, 2000 East Allen Road, Tucson, Arizona 85719, USA

ABSTRACT In mountainous areas, most precipitation measurements are taken at valley sites that do not necessarily represent conditions at higher elevations. However, daily precipitation estimates are needed for the higher elevations to estimate precipitation-related watershed variables. The Markov chain-mixed exponential model (MCME) was developed to simulate daily precipitation. This model was developed using data from five widely dispersed stations in the United States and a relatively well-spaced network that covered most of the state of South Dakota (196,726 km^2). These locations do not represent the mountainous western United States. In this paper, data from sites throughout the state of Idaho and the Reynolds Creek Experimental Watershed in southwest Idaho were used to investigate the relationships between mean annual precipitation and parameters in MCME that can be used to simulate daily precipitation in ungauged, mountainous areas.

INTRODUCTION

Daily precipitation data are often necessary for hydrologic, natural resource, and agricultural planning and development projects. This information is frequently used to estimate expected rates and amounts of runoff, vegetation yields, and other precipitation-related watershed variables. A daily climatic simulation model (CLIMATE.BAS) has been developed to simulate daily precipitation, maximum and minimum air temperature, and solar radiation (Woolhiser et al., 1988). The temperature and radiation submodel in CLIMATE.BAS was developed using data from widely dispersed stations in the United States and daily precipitation is simulated in CLIMATE.BAS by the Markov chain-mixed exponential (MCME) model that was tested on a well-spaced precipitation network in South Dakota (196,726 km^2).

It would be useful to extend this model to other states. However, in the western United States most precipitation measurements are from valley stations which do not necessarily represent conditions at higher elevations. Therefore, to extend the model to mountainous regions, relationships between model parameters and annual precipitation must be developed so that parameter sets for valley stations can be adjusted to provide simulated data for any location on mountainous watersheds.

The effects of elevation on precipitation occurrence and amount have been investigated by several scientists and engineers (Hanson et al., 1989). Most of these efforts concentrated on annual and seasonal precipitation rather than daily precipitation. Hanson et al. (1989) showed that there were relationships between mean annual precipitation and parameters in the MCME model that could be used to simulate daily precipitation series for the Reynolds Creek Experimental Watershed in southwest Idaho.

In this paper, daily precipitation data from climatological stations in Idaho and from the precipitation gauge network on the Reynolds Creek Experimental Watershed (henceforth called Reynolds) were used to evaluate the effect of mean annual precipitation on parameters in MCME and to suggest parameter-mean annual precipitation relationships that may be developed to simulate daily precipitation in other mountainous areas.

MODELING DAILY PRECIPITATION

Occurrence of wet days

Daily precipitation was described by the Markov Chain-mixed exponential (MCME) model (Woolhiser and Roldan, 1986). Precipitation occurrence was described by a first-order Markov chain specified by parameters $P_{00}(n)$, the probability of a dry day on day "n" given that day n-1 was dry, and $P_{10}(n)$, the probability of a dry day on day "n" given that day n-1 was wet. The pertinent relationships between parameters are:

$$P_0(n) + P_1(n) = 1 \tag{1}$$

$$P_{11}(n) + P_{10}(n) = 1 \tag{2}$$

$$P_{00}(n) + P_{01}(n) = 1 \tag{3}$$

where $P_0(n)$ and $P_1(n)$ are the unconditional probabilities of a dry day or wet day on day n.

The probability of precipitation on day "n" equals the sum of conditional probabilities of precipitation following a "wet" and "dry" day:

$$P_1(n) = P_{11}(n) \cdot P_1(n-1) + P_{01}(n) \cdot P_0(n-1) \tag{4}$$

and the unconditional probability of a wet day on day "n" can be approximated by:

$$P_1(n) \cong \frac{(1 - P_{00}(n))}{1 - P_{00}(n) + P_{10}(n)} \tag{5}$$

Amount of precipitation on wet days

The amount of precipitation on a "wet" day is simulated with a mixed exponential distribution:

$$f(x) = \frac{\alpha(n)}{\text{ß}(n)} \exp\left[\frac{-x}{\text{ß}(n)}\right] + \frac{1-\alpha(n)}{\delta(n)} \exp\left[\frac{-x}{\delta(n)}\right] \tag{6}$$

where the mean precipitation per "wet" day, $\mu(n)$, equals $\alpha(n)\text{ß}(n)$ + $[1-\alpha(n)]\delta(n)$. The parameter α is usually assumed constant throughout the year, but ß and μ may vary seasonally. Note that if $\alpha(n) = \alpha$ = a constant and ß(n) and $\mu(n)$ are specified by Fourier series, $\delta(n)$ is determined by the above relationship.

The seasonal variations in the parameters P_{00}, P_{10}, ß, and μ can be described by the polar form of a finite Fourier series (Woolhiser and Pegram, 1979).

DATA BASE

The data for this study were from 25 National Weather Service stations located throughout Idaho. These daily precipitation records were as close to a 40-year period starting March 1, 1940 as was available for each station (Table 1). Also, data from 16 gauges located on the Reynolds Creek Experimental Watershed with 22 to 25 years of records were included in the analysis (Hanson et al., 1989).

Constant terms in the Fourier series, $\bar{P}_{00}$, $\bar{P}_{10}$, significant amplitudes and phase angles as determined by the Akaike information criterion (Akaike, 1974), and the number of wet days were all determined for the occurrence (Markov chain) portion of the MCME model for each climatological site. The constant terms $\bar{\alpha}$, $\bar{\text{ß}}$, and the mean precipitation per wet day, $\bar{\mu}$, and significant amplitudes and phase angles were determined for the mixed exponential portion of the MCME model. Constant terms in MCME are shown in Table 1. MCME parameters were estimated by maximum likelihood techniques described by Woolhiser and Roldan (1986) who also discussed data requirements for obtaining reliable parameter estimates.

DISCUSSION

As mentioned earlier, it is generally observed that there is an increase in mean annual precipitation with increasing elevations in the intermountain region of the Pacific Northwest USA. This concept may hold for individual watersheds or areas but, as can be seen in Fig. 1, there is no relationship between elevation and mean annual precipitation for an area the size of the state of Idaho. In fact, a nonsignificant relationship with a negative slope was obtained from linear regression analysis of the data from Idaho. Also shown in Fig. 1 are the results of analysis of data given by Hanson et al., 1989 indicating that two regression equations are required to represent the relationships between elevation and mean annual precipitation for leeward and windward sites on Reynolds, a watershed of only 234 km^2.

TABLE 1 Station Information and Constant Fourier Series Terms for the MCME Model.

Station	Year*	Elev. (m)	Prec. (mm)	Wet days/ year	$\bar{P}_{00}$	$\bar{P}_{10}$	$\bar{\alpha}$	$\bar{\beta}$ (mm)	$\bar{\mu}$ (mm)
Aberdeen	1940-80	1343	223	68.3	.863	.595	.541	1.135	3.185
Boise USFO	1940-80	865	294	90.6	.831	.512	.141	.533	3.061
Burley	1944-84	1267	253	77.7	.848	.560	.274	.751	3.162
Cambridge	1940-80	808	514	80.5	.855	.511	.201	3.376	5.799
Coeur d'Alene	1940-80	658	660	120.4	.777	.452	.146	1.355	5.100
Driggs	1944-80	1864	410	93.8	.829	.493	.315	2.986	4.217
Grange-ville	1940-80	1024	593	121.1	.761	.482	.223	.972	4.816
Grouse	1948-85	1859	319	68.9	.864	.585	.362	1.659	4.419
Howe	1950-83	1469	223	56.5	.889	.607	.626	1.635	3.778
Idaho City	1940-80	1209	622	99.5	.834	.443	.235	1.633	5.853
Idaho Falls	1940-80	1442	240	82.7	.839	.545	.320	.548	2.826
Island Pk.	1940-80	1917	779	123.3	.780	.430	.317	2.823	6.015
Kooskia	1940-80	390	645	115.9	.767	.500	.245	2.302	5.514
Lifton	1940-80	1806	257	86.1	.826	.563	.376	.636	2.861
May	1944-84	1557	202	61.2	.869	.649	.398	1.217	2.937
McCall	1944-84	1532	722	108.9	.804	.460	.266	5.472	6.251
Moscow	1940-80	811	602	123.9	.784	.420	.198	.986	4.658
Nez Perce	1952-85	959	562	131.3	.749	.447	.224	1.056	4.226
Oakley	1943-83	1402	287	79.1	.842	.570	.520	1.389	3.514
Orofino	1950-81	402	649	125.5	.777	.426	.141	1.731	4.937
Payette	1948-85	655	287	76.5	.853	.553	.286	1.093	3.522
Porthill	1940-80	541	520	113.9	.779	.487	.350	2.467	4.340
Riggins	1940-79	549	429	97.7	.804	.535	.200	1.444	4.256
Swan Falls	1948-82	709	198	65.5	.872	.586	.113	.662	2.842
Wallace Woodland	1952-85	896	986	159.0	.750	.324	.188	.939	5.859

*Year = March-February

Occurrence of wet days

Because values of P_{00}, P_{10}, and α vary between 0 and 1, the logit transformation (Hanson <u>et al.</u>, 1989) of their values was used to develop relationships between each of them and mean annual precipitation. This transformation was used to prevent computing unrealistic values of the variables at sites where mean annual precipitation is considerably more or less than that at sites in Idaho and Reynolds. As can be seen in Figs. 2 and 3, the parameters $\bar{P}_{00}$ and $\bar{P}_{10}$ decreased with increasing mean annual precipitation for both sets of data. For both $\bar{P}_{00}$ and $\bar{P}_{10}$, the slope of the regression lines for Idaho were significantly different from the Reynolds regression line. This indicates that local climate has an effect on

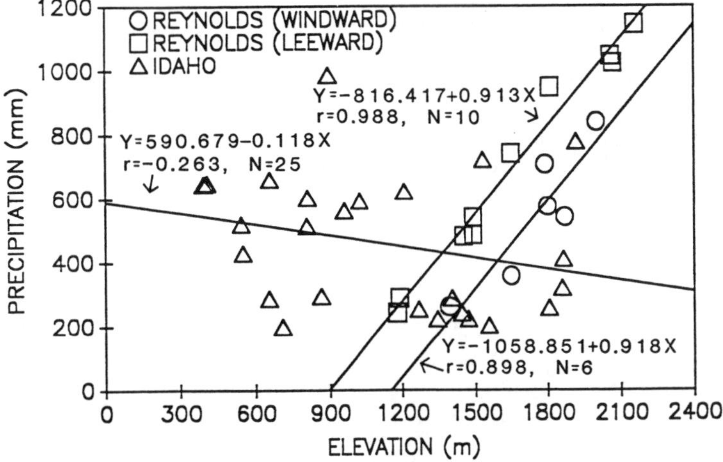

FIG. 1 Linear relationships between mean annual precipitation and elevation.

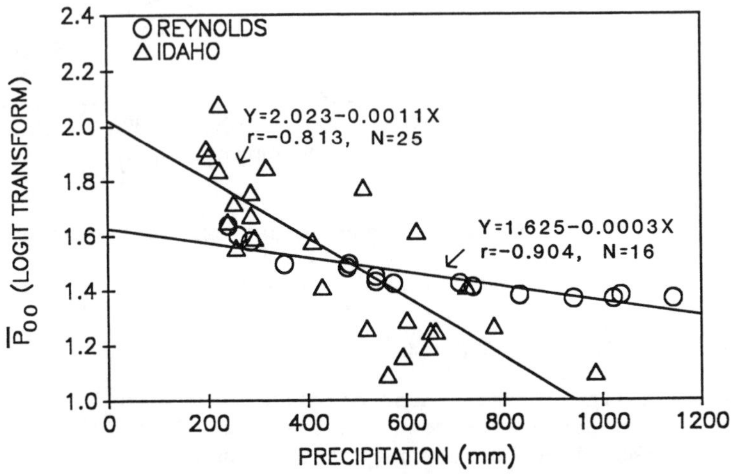

FIG. 2 Effect of mean annual precipitation on $\bar{P}_{00}$.

the relationship of these two parameters to mean annual precipitation. However, the means of $\bar{P}_{00}$ and $\bar{P}_{10}$ for both the Idaho and Reynolds data were about the same, so tests of MCME would have to be run to determine if the values of $\bar{P}_{00}$ and $\bar{P}_{10}$ from the Idaho data could be used to represent the Reynolds watershed.

For Idaho, P_{00} varied seasonally with the first five harmonics being significant and the amplitude of the first two harmonics increased as annual precipitation increased. The other amplitudes and all phase angles associated with P_{00} in Idaho were not related to mean annual precipitation. At Reynolds, P_{00} varied seasonally with the first, second, and fourth harmonics being significant. The amplitude of the first harmonic increased as mean annual precipitation increased. The other two amplitudes and the three phase angles associated with P_{00} were not related to mean annual precipitation.

P_{10} varied seasonally with the first three harmonics being significant in Idaho. The amplitudes and the phase angles were not related to mean annual precipitation. At Reynolds, P_{10} varied seasonally with only the first harmonic significant. The amplitude of the first harmonic was related to mean annual precipitation.

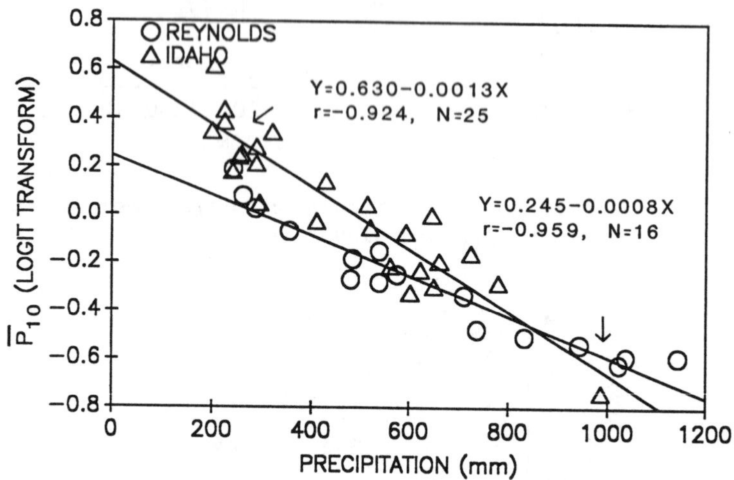

FIG. 3 Effect of mean annual precipitation on $\bar{P}_{10}$.

Amount of precipitation on wet days

There was a significant linear decrease in $\bar{\alpha}$ with increasing mean annual precipitation for both the Idaho and Reynolds data sets (Fig. 4). Both the slopes of the regression equations and the means of $\bar{\alpha}$ for Reynolds and Idaho were not significantly different from each other. Because of the large scatter in the values of α for each site, it could not be shown that α varied seasonally.

As shown in Fig. 5, values of $\bar{\beta}$ for Idaho indicate a small but significant increase with increasing values of mean annual precipitation. Values of $\bar{\beta}$ for Reynolds show no relationship to mean annual precipitation. β varied seasonally for both the Idaho and Reynolds data, with the first harmonic being significant for the Idaho data and the first two harmonics being significant for the Reynolds data. There was no relationship between mean annual precipitation and the harmonics of β for either of the data sets.

There was a significant positive increase of $\bar{\mu}$ with mean annual precipitation for both Idaho and Reynolds as shown in Fig. 6. The slope of the regression equations and the means of $\bar{\mu}$ for Idaho and Reynolds were not significantly different. μ varied throughout the year with the first three harmonics significant for the Idaho data and the first and sixth harmonics significant for the Reynolds data.

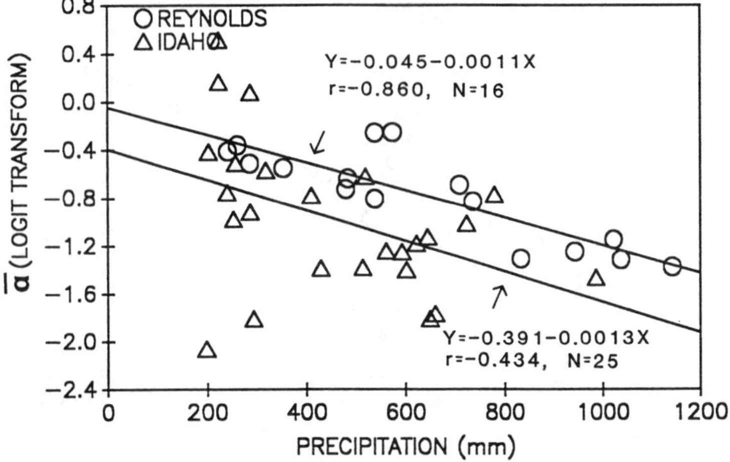

FIG. 4 Effect of mean annual precipitation on $\bar{\alpha}$.

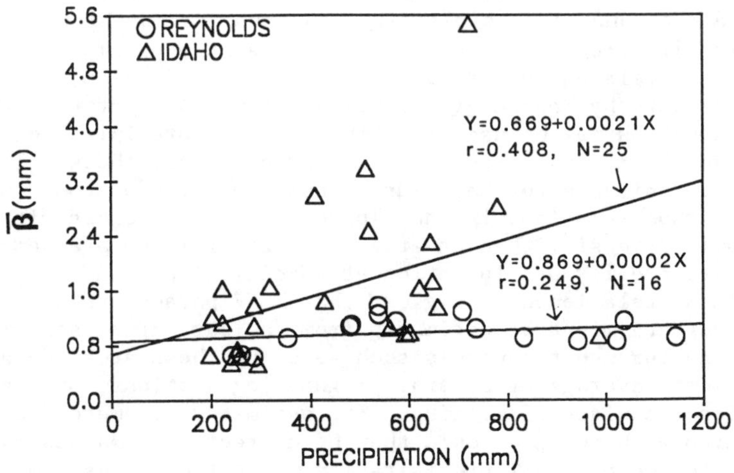

FIG. 5 Effect of mean annual precipitation on $\bar{\beta}$.

SUMMARY

This study was conducted to determine which parameters in the Markov chain-mixed exponential model (MCME), a daily precipitation simulation model, were related to mean annual precipitation and which could be kept locally constant when estimating precipitation at ungauged mountain locations. There was a linear relationship between mean annual precipitation and $\bar{P}_{00}$ and $\bar{P}_{10}$ with both $\bar{P}_{00}$ and $\bar{P}_{10}$ decreasing as mean annual precipitation increased. Both parameters P_{00} and P_{10} varied throughout the year.

$\bar{\alpha}$ decreased with increasing mean annual precipitation, but α was assumed constant throughout the year. There was a small but significant increase in $\bar{\beta}$ with increasing mean annual precipitation for the Idaho locations but no relationship for the Reynolds locations. β varied throughout the year. There was a positive linear

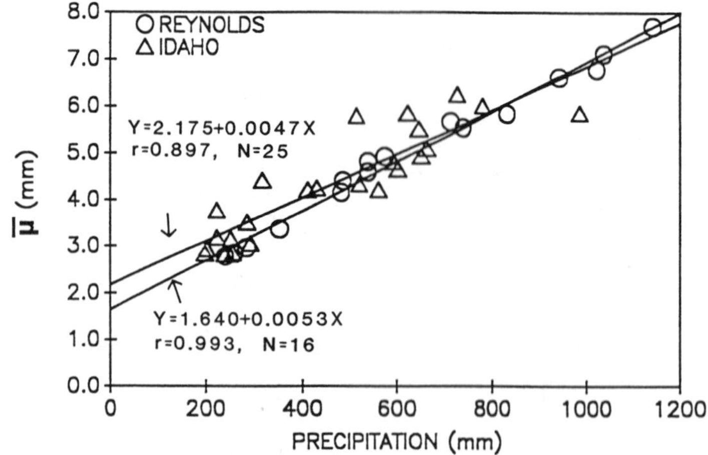

FIG. 6 Effect of mean annual precipitation on $\bar{\mu}$.

relationship between the mean amount of precipitation on a wet day, $\bar{\mu}$, and mean annual precipitation. μ also varied throughout the year.

Results from this study indicate that the parameters in the MCME model are related to mean annual precipitation which, based on earlier work by Hanson et al. (1989), would suggest that these relationships may be used to simulate daily precipitation amounts at ungauged locations. Results also indicate that these relationships are more suitable for Reynolds, a small watershed, than the state of Idaho, thus relationships developed for smaller areas with less climatic diversity than an area the size of Idaho are better for simulating daily precipitation at specific locations.

These relationships suggest that MCME parameters at a location with no data might be estimated from the parameters at neighboring stations through techniques such as using the nearest neighbor, arithmetic average of several neighboring stations, or the regionalization technique of kriging. The estimated parameter values at the location with no data could then be corrected to maintain the estimated mean annual precipitation using techniques similar to those used by Woolhiser et al. (1988).

REFERENCES

Akaike, H. (1974) A new look at the statistical model indentification. IEEE, Trans. on Automatic Control AC-19 (6), 716-723.

Hanson, C. L., Osborn, H. B. & Woolhiser, D. A. (1989) Daily precipitation simulation model for mountainous areas. Trans. Am. Soc. Agric. Engrs. 32 (3), 865-873.

Woolhiser, D. A. & Pegram, G. G. S. (1979) Maximum likelihood estimation of Fourier coefficients to describe seasonal variations of parameters in stochastic daily precipitation models. J. Appl. Meteor. 18 (1), 34-42.

Woolhiser, D. A. & Roldan, J. (1986) Seasonal and regional variability of parameters for stochastic daily precipitation models: South Dakota, U.S.A. Water Resour. Res. 22 (6), 965-978.

Woolhiser, D. A., Hanson, C. L. & Richardson, C. W. (1988) Microcomputer program for daily weather simulation. U.S. Dept. Agric., Agricultural Research Service, ARS-75, Dec.

Hydrology in Mountainous Regions. I - Hydrological Measurements; the Water Cycle (Proceedings of two Lausanne Symposia, August 1990). IAHS Publ. no. 193, 1990.

A comparative assessment of two approaches to evaluate anthropogenic effects on flood events in mountainous regions

J.-P. JORDAN, V. LAGLAINE & PH. HOHL
Institute of Soil and Water Management, EPFL, Switzerland

ABSTRACT As a result of the extensive damages created by catastrophic flood events in some Alpine valleys of Switzerland during the summer of 1987, concerns about the impact of human activities on the hydrologic cycle in small alpine watersheds were raised. Two modelling approaches are compared. The first one is the Soil Conservation Service Curve Number method (SCS-CN) which is included in the hydrologic model OTTHYMO. This approach is empirical and does not account explicitly for the various phenomena involved in the process of flood generation. The second relies on a simple physically based model, TOPMODEL, which takes into account the variable source area concepts. Comparison of results obtained given by models with measurements will allow to validate the basic principles behind each of them. It is shown that the saturation overland flow process is the most important one for the covered land area of the studied watersheds. The SCS method is able to simulate this process. However, the use of the well known CN tables is not recomended. A more suitable physically based approach with minimum input data requirements is prefered.

INTRODUCTION

The 1987 summer was particularly devastating in Switzerland. Three months with high rainfalls followed by extreme events generated extensive flooding in various regions of Switzerland, especially in the Alps, provoking damages up to 1.2 billion swiss francs. The political authority decided that a part of the money for compensations should be invested in research to investigate the causes of extreme floods in order to prevent future disasters. Some fifteen research topics were defined from rainfall to mudflow studies.

The Institute of Soil and Water Management was asked to evaluate anthropogenic effects on flood events for small rural watersheds. An answer had to be given in a relatively short period of time. Therefore, the development of new concepts was not attempted, and the study emphasized on sound application of existing knowledge. Within the study of extreme floods, it was possible to use the results of another investigation on the effects of forestry on the hydrologic cycle at a daily time step, conducted by the Swiss Federal Institute of Forestry, Snow and Landscape (FSL) in Birmensdorf.

This paper presents the main results obtained for one of the three selected watersheds where flooding occured in 1987.

METHODOLOGY

Deterministic simulation techniques were prefered to statistical analysis since the sample of monitored floods is too small to solve our problem.

Hydrological models can be classified according to their degree of conceptualization. Physically based models allow a better representation of the system. However, practical implementation of this type of models remains difficult (Jordan, 1987), especially in the calibration and validation processes due to the complexity of the different phenomena involved. Too many parameters have to be estimated from limited information with respect to the behaviour of the catchment. Those are the reasons for which we decided to follow a more empirical approach as a first attempt to solve the problem.

The OTTHYMO model (Jordan & Wisner, 1983) was selected because of the good experience gained by our Institute with its application. Input requirements are limited and the model is flexible and easy to use. OTTHYMO applies the SCS modified method to compute infiltration losses :

$$Q = (P - Ia)^2/(P - Ia + S)$$

Where P and Q are total rainfall and runoff respectively. Ia are initial abstractions and S is maximum soil storage related to the curve number CN by the formula (in metric system) $S = (25400/CN) - 254$.

The SCS provides tables with CN values for various soil types and land uses. OTTHYMO converts rainfall excess into runoff hydrographs by means of a unit hydrograph approach.

Because of the low level of conceptualization of this model, we felt that a comparison with a more physically-based technique was necessary to prove the adequacy of the various assumptions. The TOPMODEL developed by Beven and Kirby (1979) is based on the Variable Source Area Concepts. This model can predict the spread of a variable saturated area on the basis of catchment topography and soil characteristics (fig.1).

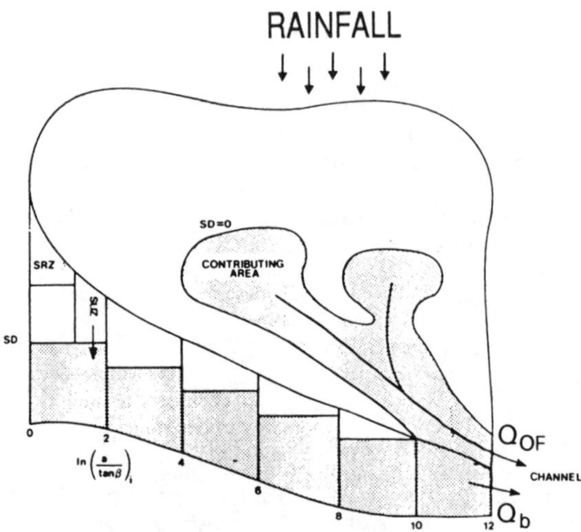

FIG. 1 Schematic diagram of TOPMODEL like used in our simulations (after Hornberger et al.).

The hydrological behaviour is related to the topography derived variable ln $(a/\tan\beta)$, where a is the area drained by unit contour and β is the local slope. Both infiltration excess and saturation excess mechanisms of runoff production are simulated. The subsurface flow Qb is computed by the formula :

$$Qb = SZQ\ e^{(-S/SZM)}$$

where S is the average saturation deficit distributed according to the topographic distribution function. The saturated storage deficit SD for any value of ln $(a/\tan\beta)$ is related to S by :

$$SD = S + (SZM/A) \int_A \ln(a/\tan\beta)\, dA - SZM \ln(a/\tan\beta)$$

Model simplicity is definitively an advantage due to the limited amounts of information available for the catchment.

Moreover, simulations conducted by FSL with the BROOK model (Federer C.A.; Lash D., 1978) are an interesting sources of informations. Three reservoirs included in the model :EZONE, UZONE and GWZONE for the root, unsaturated and permanently saturated zones.are used to determine some parameters of OTTHYMO and TOPMODEL.

WATERSHED DESCRIPTION

The watershed of the Witenwasserenreuss (31 km^2) is located in the Alps in the Swiss Canton of Uri. The outlet is located at Realp (fig.2). The flow gauge of the Hydrology and Geology National Service was destroyed by the extreme flood of 1987. Although flow data is available from 1974, we only have rainfall measurements close to the watershed from 1980 at Bedretto, a station located in a parallel valley. Spatial variability of rainfall could be evaluated with three other pluviographs located within a 20 km range

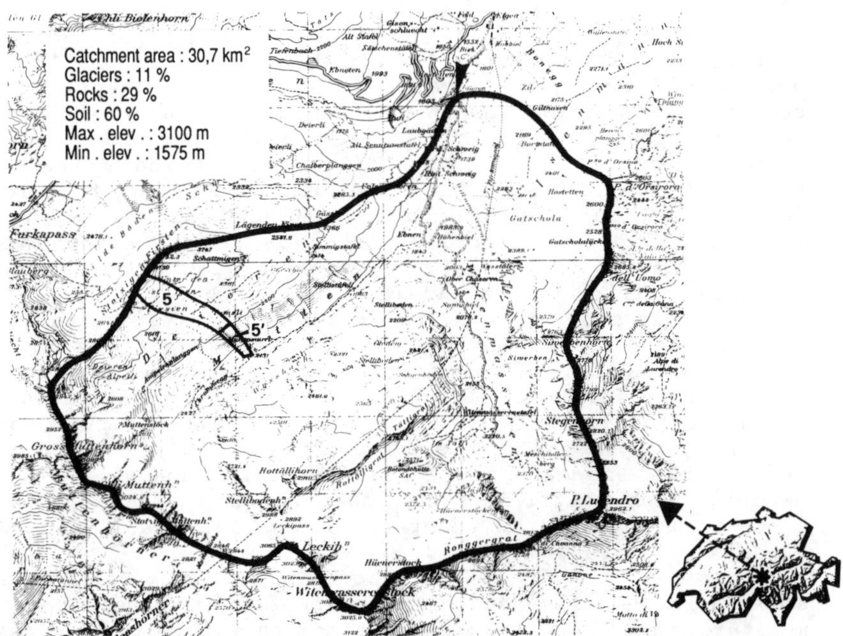

FIG. 2 Catchment map and situation.

The upstream area of the catchment (40 %) is covered mainly by glaciers and rocks. The rest of the watershed is covered by grassland with sometimes emerging rocks or debris. Soil properties have been studied by FSL in five pits and are relatively homogeneous : low thickness (around 1 m) and acid brown to podzolic. In most cases sandy loams are encountered with high hydraulic conductivities (10 - 40 mm/hr). Hillslopes are high in the order of 30 to 60 %. The stream network is dense.

Only eight observed floods could be selected for calibration and validation of the models because the period, during which snow does not affect significantly the flood generating mechanisms, is very short (July to September). However, the contributions from snowmelt and glaciers are an important component of the hydrograph even during this period of the year. This phenomena is difficult to evaluate. Since the scope of the study is to analyze the response of areas covered with vegetation, it was decided to perform an arbitrary separation of flow components, which, in our opinion, should not lead to significant errors.

MODELING

The Witenwasserenreuss watershed is relatively small with high slopes and considerable flow velocities. Therefore, the runoff mechanisms are more important than the routing processes. As a matter of fact, simulation results will show that, as a first approximation, routing can be neglected. Thirteen subwatersheds were schematized. A constant lag is applied for river routing. The time lag is a function of the distance to the outlet and an estimated average velocity.

Otthymo

In the SCS method, Ia is not an important parameter for extreme events and was arbitrarily fixed to a value of 1.5 mm. CN is dependant upon soil characteristics and antecedent moisture conditions. A relationship between lumped observed CN values and moisture conditions is investigated assuming a time invariant system (some floods for which only daily rainfall was available could be used to establish such a relationship). The CN is afterwards modified for each sub-basin according to land use and imperviousness ratio. This procedure is arbitrary since, as we will show later, the CN values from the table are not reliable. High values are adopted for the upper part of the catchment

The main problem consists of defining a representative parameter for moisture conditions. A commonly used index is API (Antecedent Precipitation Index) which is based on previous rainfalls. In our case, API is only able to explain 13 % of the total variance of CN. A linear regression between the values of UZONE (computed by the BROOK model) the day before the event and the corresponding CN was found to be the best model to predict the curve numbers. The corrected determination coefficient is equal to 82 % (fig. 3), while it was close to zero when the other two reservoirs (EZONE and GWZONE) were used.

This result seems to indicate that the stock of free water in the soil has more influence on the quick flow response than the topsoil moisture conditions. It appears that the infiltration excess overland flow mechanism is not predominant in this watershed. This conclusion will be confirmed with the simulation results of TOPMODEL.

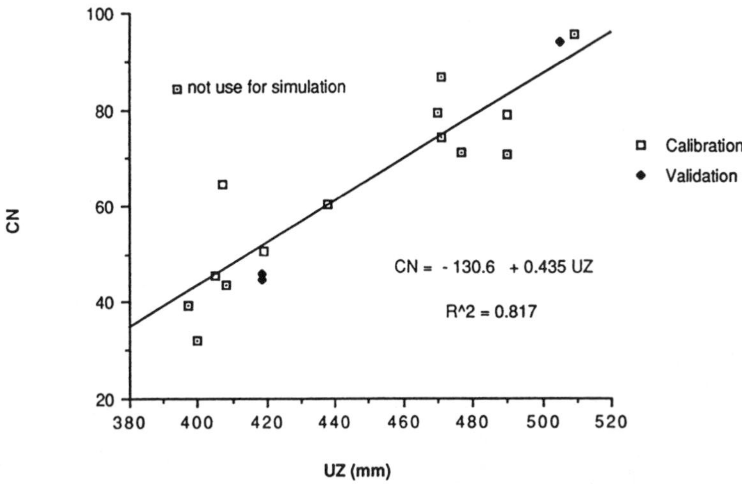

FIG. 3 Relation between lumped CN and UZONE.

Topmodel

Parameters for TOPMODEL were selected in order to minimize as much as possible the assumptions with respect to catchment response. Special consideration was given to parameters with the most significant spatial variability. Only the areas of the watershed covered with soil were simulated with TOPMODEL. The hydrograph from the remaining area are those simulated by OTTHYMO. As a matter of fact, for the three events selected for validation, the contribution of these areas is larger than 65 % of the peak flow. Finally, even if TOPMODEL is a continuous model, we applied it on a single-event basis to facilitate calibration.

Eight parameters describe the runoff mechanism in TOPMODEL. Most of them can be evaluated from the Digital Terrain Model (DTM : 40 m grid from maps 1/25'000) or from simulation results at daily time steps of the BROOK model.

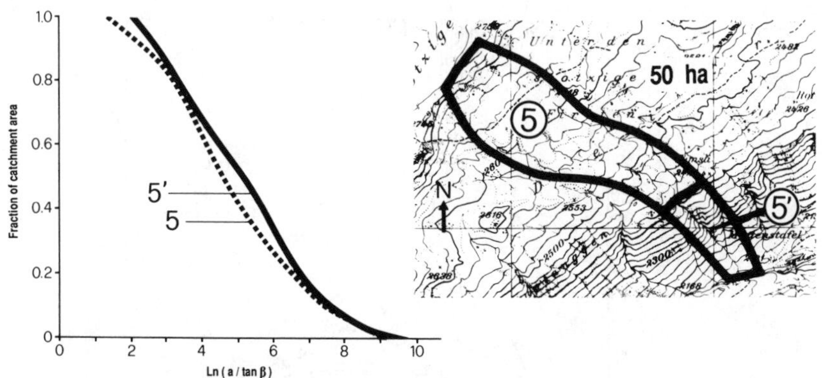

FIG. 4 Topographic distribution functions for two sub-catchments and map (cf. fig. 2).

The topographic distribution functions have been calculated for various representative sub-watersheds. Figure 4 shows the computed relationships for sub-basin no 5 which was splited in order to account for differences in moisture conditions (snowmelt in the upstream area).

Distributions are close. Similar conclusions can be drawn for the other sub-watersheds. Therefore, it was decided to model all catchments with a single representative function. This relationship corresponds to the one which characterizes the right hillsides are not particularly propitious to the formation of saturated areas.

Soils, with low thickness, have a small storage capacity and can easily promote saturation. In TOPMODEL, two parameters SZM and SZQ are closely related to soil characteristics. This two parameters can be determined from the storage-outflow relation of the UZONE reservoir.

To compute infiltration excess overland flow, saturated hydraulic conductivities have been measured in situ. Values are high and rainfall intensities generally do not exceed infiltration capacities. Therefore this component should not be significant and we will verify that flood generating mechanisms can be well explained by subsurface flow and saturation excess overland flow.

BROOK simulation results have shown that moisture content is seldom higher than the field capacity. Therefore the reservoir that simulates the deficit below field capacity was not considered (SRZ =0) The TD parameter which represents flow from the unsaturated to the saturated zone was definitively calibrated with the first simulated event. The value of initial subsurface flow Qo could not be completely explained by subsurface flow simulated by the BROOK model. TD and Qo were the only parameters estimated from the observed hydrographs.

SIMULATION RESULTS

Simulations were conducted at 15 min. time steps with the eight observed events. Results show that both models are able to simulate satisfactorily observed hydrographs. With one exception, relative errors on peak flows and volumes are not higher than 30 %. Because of uncertainties on precipitation data and spatial variability of watershed characteristics, it is not realistic to expect better

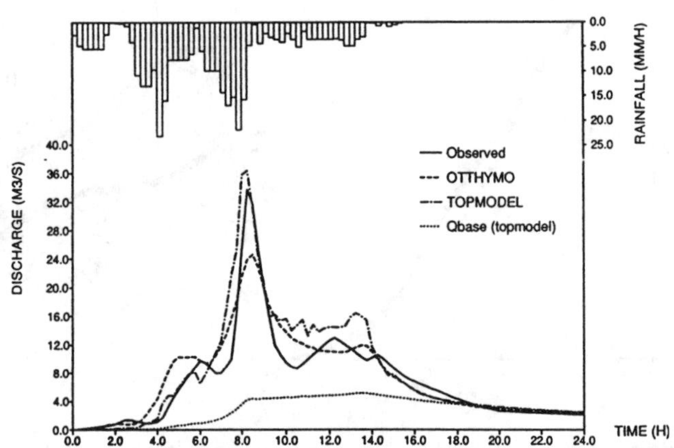

FIG. 5 Hydrographs for the event of the 5 th sept. 1982

results. Figure 5 shows an example for a validation event (highest observed peak flow).

Even if TOPMODEL performs better in this particular case, it is not possible to select any of both models on the basis of the single criteria of comparison of observed and simulated flows. However comparison of both models leads to interesting conclusions. TOPMODEL results confirm that the spreadout of saturated areas (maximum of 55 % of the soil area for the event above) can explain entirely the hydrologic response of land covered areas. The subsurface flow is not significant for great events. The OTTHYMO response is very similar to that of TOPMODEL. Although the SCS method was developed according to the Hortonian concept, this method seems to be able to simulate the mechanism of saturation excess overland flow. However we do not recommend the use of the SCS tables for CN values as a function of soil type and land use, seen they are based on infiltration tests.

The overland routing, for instance the unit hydrograph, is not important and contributes only to smoothing slightly the outlet hydrograph.

Simulation of complex hydrographs (two or more peaks) shows that both models tend to overestimate the response to rainfall at the end of the event. To explain this behaviour, some assumptions have to be made. TOPMODEL has definitively the advantage of its physical basis. Therefore, an increase in return flow speeding up the drainage of the saturated areas or deep losses could be considered as possible explanations for this excess of volume at the end of the event.

The superiority of a physically based approach can also be realised when it is required to evaluate impact on floods of land use changes.

In OTTHYMO, only the CN value can take these modifications into account. Therefore, it is not possible to differentiate between land use changes and antecedent moisture condition variations. On the other hand, TOPMODEL includes enough parameters to account explicitely for the various conditions. TOPMODEL also provides interesting information regarding the expansion of saturated areas and moisture conditions at any time step.

We will only describe some of the results from the wide range of situations considered in conjonction with the effects of deforestation. The historical storm of August 1987 was used as a design storm. The location of the maximum intensity at the end of the event is critical for the watershed. This explains the reason why a 40 mm/hr intensity over 1 hour period with a return period less than 5 years generates an extreme flood higher than 200 years. On the other hand, to generate such a flow from an isolated thunderstorm, a 90 mm/hr intensity over an hour (T > 400 years) would be required.

Simulated hydrographs for that storm are similar for both models (peak flow 20 % higher for TOPMODEL but shapes positively similar). The sensitivity analysis showed that variation of initial moisture conditions did not affect significantly the results (< 5 % on peak flow). In other words, the beneficial function of the forest which consists of reducing the initial water stock of the watershed is not relevant for the peak flow of this extreme event.

TOPMODEL also showed that increasing water storage in the litter or improving the drainage network did not have any effect on the peak flow. The expansion of the saturated areas just before the occurence of the maximum intensity (80 % of the total area of the catchment) is not very sensitive to the various modifications considered (less than 5 % of the soil area.). Moreover the remaining sectors of the watershed (20 %) where the excess infiltration overland flow mechanism is possible, are too small for the modifications of land use to produce changes in the peak flow.

CONCLUSIONS

This study has only covered a few aspects concerning the assessment of anthropogenic effects on flood generating mechanisms. Extrapolation of results to different watersheds to different scales or to frequent floods can not be done. Moreover, several questions were not analysed, for instance : non-linearity of hydrologic response, effect of flooding or solid transport. It is also necessary to recognize that hydrology of mountainous regions has to deal with several unknowns, for instance : uncertainties on snowmelt during high rainfalls. However this study had as a primary objective to provide a quick answer to public concern following the catastrophic floods of 1987. From this point of view, a certain number of results have been obtained.

A simple physically based modeling approach (TOPMODEL) taking into account the available and usefull information has allowed to support the argument that land use has minimum impacts on extreme floods. Application of TOPMODEL has shown that the saturation excess overland flow mechanism is predominant in land covered areas. In this case, the CN method worked well. However, it is suggested that the application of this method should be done with care because of its empirical basis. We do not recommend to use directly values coming from standard tables.

REFERENCES

Beven, K.J., Kirkby, M.J., Schofield, N. & Tagg, A.F. (1984) Testing a physically-based flood forecasting model (TOPMODEL) for three U.K. catchments. J. of Hydrol. 69, 119-143.

Beven, K.J. & Kirkby, M.J. (1979) A physically-based, variable contributing area model of basin hydrology. Hydrol. Sci. Bull. 24 (1), 43-69.

Federer, C.A. & Lash, D. (1978) BROOK : A Hydrologic simulation model for eastern forest. Water resource research center, University of New Hampshire, Durham, New Hampshire, USA.

Forster, F. & Keller, H.M. (1988) Hydrological simulation of forested catchments using the BROOK-Model. In Proc. of Nato: "advances study institute on recent advances in the modeling of hydrologic systems".

Hawkins, R.H. (1984) A comparison of predicted and observed runoff Curve Numbers, ASCE 702-709.

Hornberger, G.M., Beven, K.J., Cosby, B.J.& Sappington, D.E. (1985) Shenandoah watershed study: calibration of a topography-based, variable contributing area hydrological model to a small forested catchment. Wat. Resour. Res.12 (21), 1841-1850.

Jordan, J.-P. & Hohl, Ph. (1990) Influence des modifications anthropologiques sur les débits de crues extrêmes. Rapport final. EPFL, IATE-HYDRAM, Lausanne, Switzerland.

Jordan, J.-P., Bathurst, J.C.& Musy, A. Modelisation hydrologique à base physique sur un bassin versant rural en climat tempéré (1987), communication présentée à l'assemblée générale de l'AISH, Vancouver. EPFL, IATE, Switzerland.

Jordan, J.-P. & Wisner, P. (1983) Description du modèle OTTHYMO et exemples d'application. Université d'Ottawa et EPFL, IATE no 172.

Petrascheck, A. (1989) Die Hochwasser 1868 und 1987, ein Vergleich. Wasser, Energie, Luft, Heft 1-3, 1-8.

Soil conservation service (1972) National Engineering Handbook. Sec. 4. Hydrology, Washington D.C.

Hydrology in Mountainous Regions. I - Hydrological Measurements; the Water Cycle
(Proceedings of two Lausanne Symposia, August 1990). IAHS Publ. no. 193, 1990.

Use of satellite data for hydrologic modelling of a mountain watershed

G. W. KITE
Hydrometeorological Research Div., AES, 11 Innovation Blvd, Saskatoon, Saskatchewan S7N 3H5, Canada

ABSTRACT Satellites offer the only practical way of obtaining the vast amounts of distributed data needed for hydrologic models. Because of the difficult terrain and the expense of operating in remote areas, mountainous watersheds have always been difficult to instrument and satellite data are particularly appropriate. The SLURP hydrologic model was applied to the Kootenay watershed in the Rocky Mountains of Canada first without satellite data and then using cloud cover and snow cover from a NOAA satellite. Results are compared and preliminary conclusions are drawn on the utility of present satellite data for hydrologic modelling.

INTRODUCTION

Developments in hydrologic models include more watershed physics, smaller scales and, often, more data than are available from existing groundbased stations. One solution to this problem is to use satellite data. This paper describes the use of satellite data in the SLURP (Simple LUmped Reservoir Parametric) model for the 7100 km² Kootenay watershed in British Columbia (Fig. 1). This work is part of a larger study in which two different models are being applied to watersheds in western Canada to investigate the utility of satellite data for hydrologic modelling in different physiographic zones.

The choice of satellites with hydrologically useful data included SPOT, Landsat, NOAA and GOES. Considering the resolution, frequency and cost of the images available, it was decided to use daily NOAA imagery for snow and cloud cover analyses and to use one Landsat image per watershed for land-use classification. One AVHRR image (5 channels) per watershed per week is obtained on magnetic tape and data for the intervening days are video-digitized from black and white visible and near-IR photographs.

DATA

The SLURP model uses daily precipitation, evaporation and temperature data to simulate streamflow. In addition, recorded streamflow data are needed for calibration. Optionally, satellite-based cloud and snow-cover data and recorded snowcourse data may be used. A PC database combines the ground-based point data with areally-distributed physiographic and land-use data and the satellite data. The model accesses it's data directly from this databank. Watershed daily mean temperature and precipitation are derived within the database by averaging up to five climate stations; missing data are accounted for in the averaging process. Evapotranspiration, E_a, is derived using Morton's (1983) complementary relationship areal evapotranspiration (CRAE) model:

$$E_a = 2E_w - E_p \tag{1}$$

where E_w is evapotranspiration under wet conditions and E_p is potential evapotranspiration. CRAE uses monthly mean air and dewpoint temperatures and hours of bright sunshine to calculate E_p using an iterative solution of the energy-balance and vapour transfer equations for dry conditions and, hence, E_a. Daily evapotranspiration is interpolated from the monthly CRAE values using equal weight for daily hours of bright sunshine and wind-run as:

$$DE_{i,j} = (ME_j/2)\left[(DS_{i,j}/MS_j)+(DW_{i,j}/MW_j)\right] \qquad (2)$$

where $DE_{i,j}$, $DS_{i,j}$ and $DW_{i,j}$ are the evapotranspiration, hours of sunshine and windrun on day i of month j, and ME_j, MS_j and MW_j are the mean evapotranspiration, sunshine hours and windrun for month j.

Snow and cloud cover are calculated from a supervised classification of NOAA AVHRR images using a UTM grid square over the watershed. Snow water equivalent data are the averages, on a given day, of the figures reported from available snow courses.

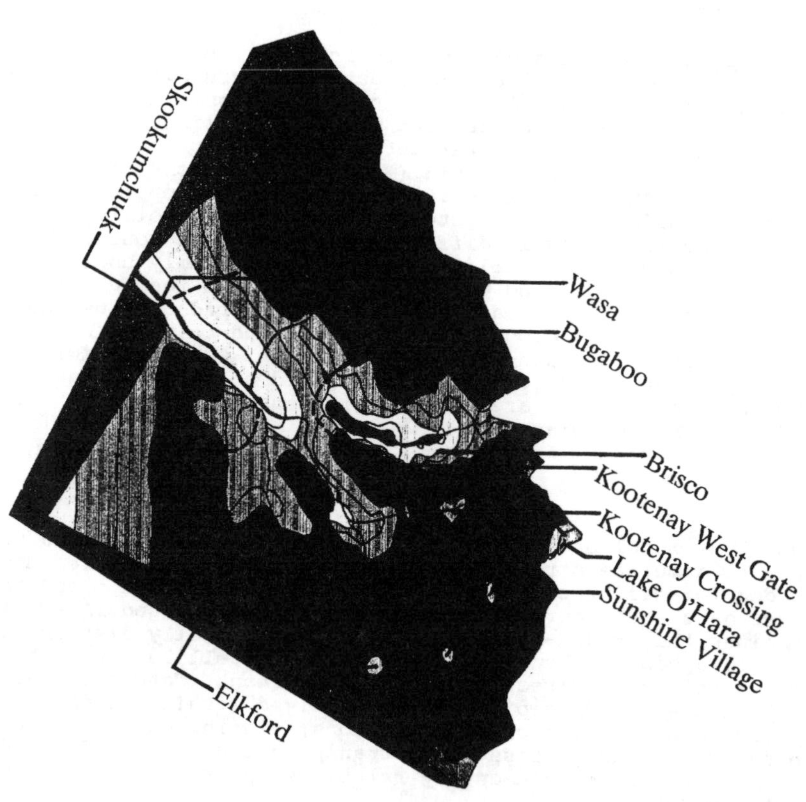

FIG. 1 Kootenay watershed, British Columbia, showing locations of meteorologic and hydrometric stations.

THE MODEL

The latest version of SLURP uses a microcomputer with menu system, full-screen data entry and on-screen graphics (Kite, 1989). The watershed is represented in the model by three tanks, one for snowpack, one for a combined surface storage and top soil layer and the third for groundwater. The three tanks have specified initial contents and maximum allowable depths. The model operates on a daily time interval and, on a particular day, the sequence of operations would be as follows:

(a) Daily precipitation is adjusted to compensate for using point data as an areal average.
(b) Optionally, precipitation data may be modified according to the percentage of the watershed covered by cloud, as observed from satellite.
(c) If the daily mean temperature, T °C, is above a specified temperature, TS °C, then the precipitation is added as rainfall to the surface storage tank. If the supplemented depth, D_s, exceeds the maximum allowable depth, D_{smax}, the excess runs off. The surface storage is depleted to infiltration at a rate depending on it's depth and also on the availability of storage in groundwater, D_g, as a fraction of it's allowable depth, D_{gmax}:

$$Q_i = k_{s1}(1.0 - D_g/D_{gmax}) D_s^{(1.0+D_s/D_{smax})} \qquad (3)$$

where k_{s1} is a specified constant, and to runoff, Q_s, as:

$$Q_s = k_{s2}\ D_s^{(1.0+D_s/D_{smax})} \qquad (4)$$

where k_{s2} is also a constant. At the same time, the snowpack (if it exists) is depleted by snowmelt to the surface tank and to the groundwater tank. The snowmelt is governed by the temperature excess and by a meltrate, in mm°C^{-1}.
(d) If, on the other hand, the daily mean temperature is below the specified level, then the precipitation is assumed to be snow and is added to any snowpack. In this case, there is no snowmelt but the surface storage would contribute to runoff and groundwater as above.
(e) If snow-course data are available then the calculated snow water equivalent on any day may be adjusted to agree with the measured data.
(f) Snowmelt may, optionally, be modified by the areal extent of snowcover measured from satellite image.
(g) Evapotranspiration demand is satisfied, if possible, first from the snowpack and then from the surface storage and, finally, from the groundwater tank.
(h) The groundwater tank contributes to runoff, Q_g, at a rate depending on its depth and on the temperature ratio:

$$Q_g = k_g\ D_g^{[0.5+k1(D_g/D_{gmax})+(1-k1)(T-TS)/TS)]} \qquad (5)$$

(i) Runoff from groundwater is passed through a variable length moving average filter.

When running the model, the user specifies the watershed name and the program will display the latest set of run-control options for that watershed. There are options to control the data input and the program output. Flows from an upstream watershed may be read in and combined with the simulated streamflows for writing to another data file. The user accepts or modifies the default options and then specifies, on screen, the operational parameters for the model. Each parameter has three values; an initial value and a maximum and minimum value to specify the range for optimization. If the user specifies a grid-search or an optimization, a screen will display the initial and optimized values of the 14 parameters and the corresponding function values; these may then be saved back to the command file.

For each year of simulation a hydrograph is displayed (Fig. 2). The screen shows the daily rainfall along the top of the graph and a plot of the difference between the recorded and observed daily runoffs along the bottom. If the computed runoff is greater than the observed, the difference is shown in grey while, if the observed runoff is greater than the computed, the difference is shown in black. Statistics for total precipitation, observed runoff, computed runoff and evapotranspiration, in mm, are shown on the screen as well as the sum of squares of deviations and the standard error of daily flows.

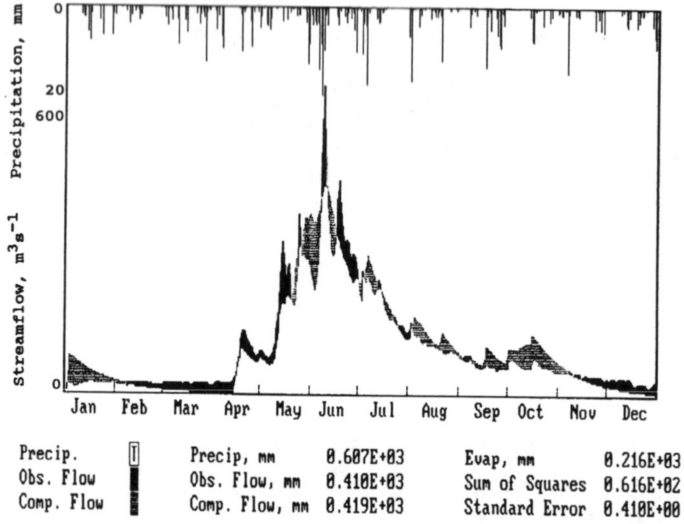

FIG. 2 Precipitation, recorded streamflow and computed streamflow, Kootenay River at Skookumchuck, 1988.

The final screen of a simulation shows statistics for the entire period including three measures of efficiency. These are the Nash/Sutcliffe (1970) efficiency:

$$F^2 = \frac{F^2{}_m - F^2{}_d}{F^2{}_m} \tag{6}$$

where

$$F^2{}_m = \frac{1}{n} \sum_{i=1}^{n} (Q_i - \bar{Q})^2 \tag{7}$$

and

$$F^2{}_d = \frac{1}{n} \sum_{i=1}^{n} (Q_i - C_i)^2 \tag{8}$$

Q_i is the observed flow and C_i is the calculated flow on day i. This criterion compares the simulation to a "forecast" consisting of the average flow.

Secondly, the efficiency measure of Garrick et al. (1978) in which F^2_m in equation 6 is replaced by:

$$F^2_m = \frac{1}{n} \sum_{i=1}^{n} (Q_i - \bar{Q}_i)^2 \qquad (9)$$

where $\bar{Q}_i$ is the long term mean flow on day i. This criterion compares the model simulation on a particular day to a "forecast" consisting of the long term mean flow for that particular day.

Taking advantage of the persistence component of river flows, a simple forecast of the flow on day i might be the flow on the previous day, Q_{i-1}. A criterion based on this forecast replaces F^2_m in equation 6 with:

$$F^2_m = \frac{1}{n-1} \sum_{i=2}^{n} (Q_i - Q_{i-1})^2 \qquad (10)$$

METHOD

The model was calibrated using daily data for January 1 to December 31, 1988. Daily areal evapotranspiration was estimated using data from Cranbrook airport. Daily mean temperature and daily total precipitation were averaged from four climate stations, Kootenay Crossing, Brisco, Elkford and Wasa. The daily streamflow used for calibration was measured at Skookumchuck.

Snow water equivalent data were averaged from four snowcourses and compared with those computed within the model (Table 1). The mean difference is 9% and, although there are large differences on particular days, no consistent bias appears. Since the average snowcourse data didn't appear to add any information, they were omitted from the model except for January 1 which was needed for initialization. Rango (1990) also found that snow water equivalent data are not necessary for simulation. No satellite data were used in the initial calibration.

The volume of runoff calculated in the model is close to that recorded and the total evapotranspiration extracted is about 70% of the theoretical areal evapotranspiration (column 2 of Table 2). A comparison of the hydrographs is given in Fig. 2.

TABLE 1 Comparison of Snow Water Equivalents, Kootenay Watershed, 1988.

Date	SWE from precip & temp. mm	SWE from snow courses mm	Difference %
Jan 1	97	100	+ 3
Feb 1	135	123	- 9
Mar 1	135	147	+ 9
Apr 1	174	224	+29
May 1	165	157	- 5
May 15	110	140	+27

TABLE 2 Model Calibration and Verification, Kootenay Watershed.

Statistic	No Satellite Data	With Sat. Snowcover Data	With Sat. Snowcover & Cloud Data
a) Calibration, Jan 1 - Dec 31, 1988.			
Total adjusted precip., mm	606	606	526
Total observed runoff, mm	410	410	410
Total computed runoff, mm	421	440	424
Total evapotranspiration,mm	204	210	199
Nash/Sutcliffe criterion	0.85	0.87	0.86
Garrick et al. criterion	0.46	0.51	0.47
Previous-day criterion	-2.94	-2.57	-2.86
b) Verification, Jan 1 - Jul 31, 1989.			
Total adjusted precip., mm	312	312	202
Total observed runoff, mm	323	323	323
Total computed runoff, mm	286	272	251
Total evapotranspiration,mm	193	183	184
Nash/Sutcliffe criterion	0.83	0.85	0.79
Garrick et al. criterion	0.40	0.46	0.25
Previous-day criterion	-6.68	-5.96	-8.66

The monthly change in watershed storage, dS, can be computed as:

$$dS = P - Q - E \tag{11}$$

where P is precipitation, Q is streamflow and E is evapotranspiration, all in mm over the watershed, either recorded data or data calculated in the model. A comparison of the two series gives a measure of the performance of the model (Fig. 3).

The model was then run incorporating satellite snowcover; this gave a slight improvement in the criteria (column 3 of Table 2). All the parameters remained as in the first run except for the initial snow storage. The third run (right-hand column of Table 2) used both satellite-observed snow cover and cloud cover. The parameter values remained the same but, this time, the criteria showed a slight decrease.

Daily data for January 1 to July 31, 1989, were used to verify the calibration of the model. The parameter values were maintained for the same three runs as before, i.e. no satellite data, satellite snow cover, and satellite snow and cloud cover. The statistics (lower half of Table 2) show that the best results are obtained when using satellite snow cover data, next is the run with no satellite data and, last, is the run using both satellite snow and cloud cover data. The standard error of the verification runs averages about 50% greater than for the calibration runs.

DISCUSSION

The results indicate that some improvement is achieved using satellite data snowcover andit is anticipated that further improvements can be made in future steps. The modification to precipitation using cloud cover was not successful, as might have been expected for a mountain watershed. Further work is needed to devise a better method, perhaps incorporating cloud-top temperature (see, for example, Negri et al., 1984). The availability of satellite data was good. In the period

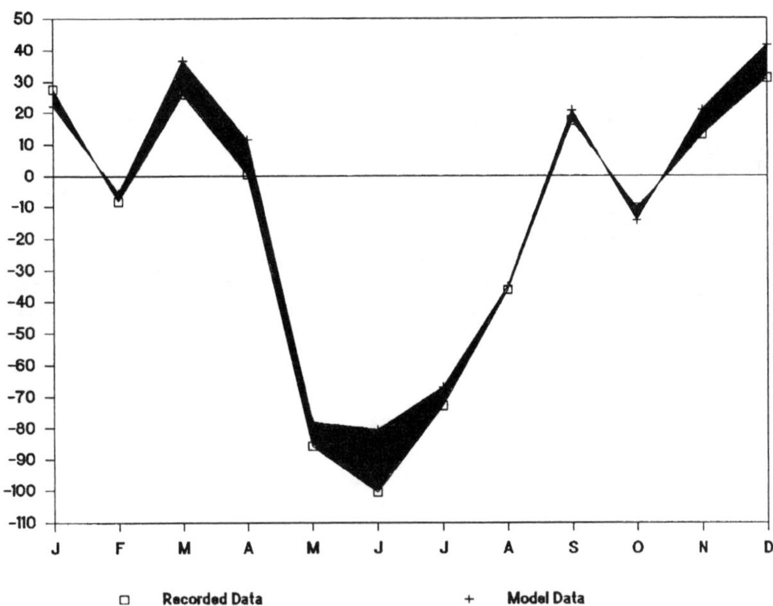

FIG. 3 Monthly change in storage, Kootenay watershed, 1988.

January 1, 1988, to October 31, 1989, the number of digital images received was 71% of expected and, of those received, 72% were useable (i.e. could be geometrically corrected and calibrated). Similarly, for black & white hardcopy images, for the two years 1988 and 1989 85% of possible images were received and 91% of those were useable.

There is an advantage in computing evapotranspiration from the complementary relationship since this is independent of soil moisture conditions. However, this still uses air temperature as a substitute for surface temperature; the next step is to use microwave data as a direct estimate (see, for example, Bussieres et al.).

Because data were used in near real-time, the meteorological and hydrological data were preliminary with many missing values. This undoubtedly influenced the model simulation. It is expected that better results will be obtained when quality-controlled data are available.

The lumped model has been used to test the data and get a feel for the response of the watershed. More verification of this model is needed in different watersheds but, further ahead, the project will use a more physically-based distributed model to make better use of the satellite data.

REFERENCES

Bussieres, N., Louie, P.Y.T. & Hogg, W. (1990) Progress Report on the Implementation of an Algorithm to Estimate Regional Evapotranspiration Using Satellite Data. In: Workshop on Application of Remote Sensing in Hydrology, Proc. Saskatoon Workshop, February 1990, National Hydrology Research Centre, Saskatoon, Saskatchewan.

Garrick, M., Cunnane, C. & Nash, J.E.(1978) A criterion for efficiency of rainfall-runoff models. J. Hydrol. 36, 375-381.

Kite, G.W. (1989) Hydrologic modelling with remotely sensed data. Proc. 57th Annual Western Snow Conference. Ft. Collins, Co., April 18-20, 1-8.

Morton, F.I. (1983)Operational estimates of areal evapotranspiration and their significance to the science and practice of hydrology. J. Hydrol. 66, 77-100.
Negri, J.E., Adler, R.F. & Wetzel, P.J. (1984) Rain estimation from satellites: an examination of the Griffith-Woodley technique. J. Climate & Appl. Meteorology, 23, 102-116.
Nash, J.E. & Sutcliffe, J.V. (1970) River flow forecasting through conceptual models; part I - a discussion of principles. J. Hydrol. 10(3), 282-290.
Rango, A. (1990) Effective Use of Satellite-Observed Snow Cover Data in the Snowmelt-Runoff Model (SRM). In: Workshop on Application of Remote Sensing in Hydrology, Proc. Saskatoon Workshop, February 1990, National Hydrology Research Centre, Saskatoon, Saskatchewan.

Hydrology in Mountainous Regions. I - Hydrological Measurements; the Water Cycle
(Proceedings of two Lausanne Symposia, August 1990). IAHS Publ. no. 193, 1990.

Estimation des débits moyens mensuels sur cours d'eau alpins non mesurés: application à la Dranse de Bagnes

G. LUYET
BTF Etudes techniques et forestières S.A., Besse-Surgat, 1971 Grimisuat, Suisse

RESUME Dans le cadre d'une étude de gestion des eaux en Valais, nous avons essayé de définir les débits moyens mensuels des affluents latéraux non mesurés de la Dranse de Bagnes (VS). Nous avons tout d'abord réparti les débits totaux en fonction de la surface, puis du volume de stockage (Grâce à la géologie de la région, à l'estimation de la porosité et de la profondeur de stockage). Enfin, nous avons effectué une répartition analogique. Cette dernière se base d'abord sur des relations empiriques de détermination du module annuel des bassins versants non mesurés. L'étude des régimes alpins et leurs caractéristiques principales permettent ensuite de classer tel ou tel cours d'eau dans tel ou tel régime et de répartir le module annuel selon les indices de Pardé des stations de référence. Les résultats ont été comparés pour les sous-bassins composant le bassin versant d'études.

INTRODUCTION

D'un point de vue hydrologique, les renseignements les plus importants pour la gestion de l'eau dans une région demeurent les débits moyens mensuels. Dans le cas de la Dranse de Bagnes, qui possède une station de mesures des débits au Châble, il s'agit de déterminer les apports des affluents latéraux non mesurés (voir Fig. 1). Ce travail a été effectué dans le cadre d'un travail de recherches ponctuant le cours postgrade en hydrologie et hydrogéologie 1988-1989, de l'Ecole Polytechnique Fédérale de Lausanne et UNI-Neuchâtel. Lorsque les sources et détails ne sont pas mentionnés, voir Luyet, 1989.

HYDROLOGIE DESCRIPTIVE (VOIR FIG. 1)

Le bassin versant de la Dranse de Bagnes se situe dans la partie orientale des Alpes Pennines et fait partie du bassin versant du Rhône. Jusqu'au site de mesures limnigraphiques au Châble, il occupe une superficie de 254 km^2, et s'étage de 800 à 4314 m d'altitude. Son altitude moyenne se situe à 2630 m et son taux de glaciation est actuellement de 31.6%.

La limite des forêts se situe aux environs de 2000 m, et occupe une surface de 16.4 km^2.

Le barrage de Mauvoisin, propriété des Forces Motrices de Mauvoisin (FMM), a été construit de 1951 à 1958 au voisinage de la cote 2000 m, là où la vallée se referme de manière significative. Ce barrage collecte en aval des eaux supplémentaires par deux galeries, une sur chaque rive. Les eaux du barrage sont turbinées à Fionnay, avant de s'accumuler dans un bassin-tampon, d'où elles partiront pour la plaine du Rhône (usine de Riddes) et pour l'usine de Champsec (dotations).

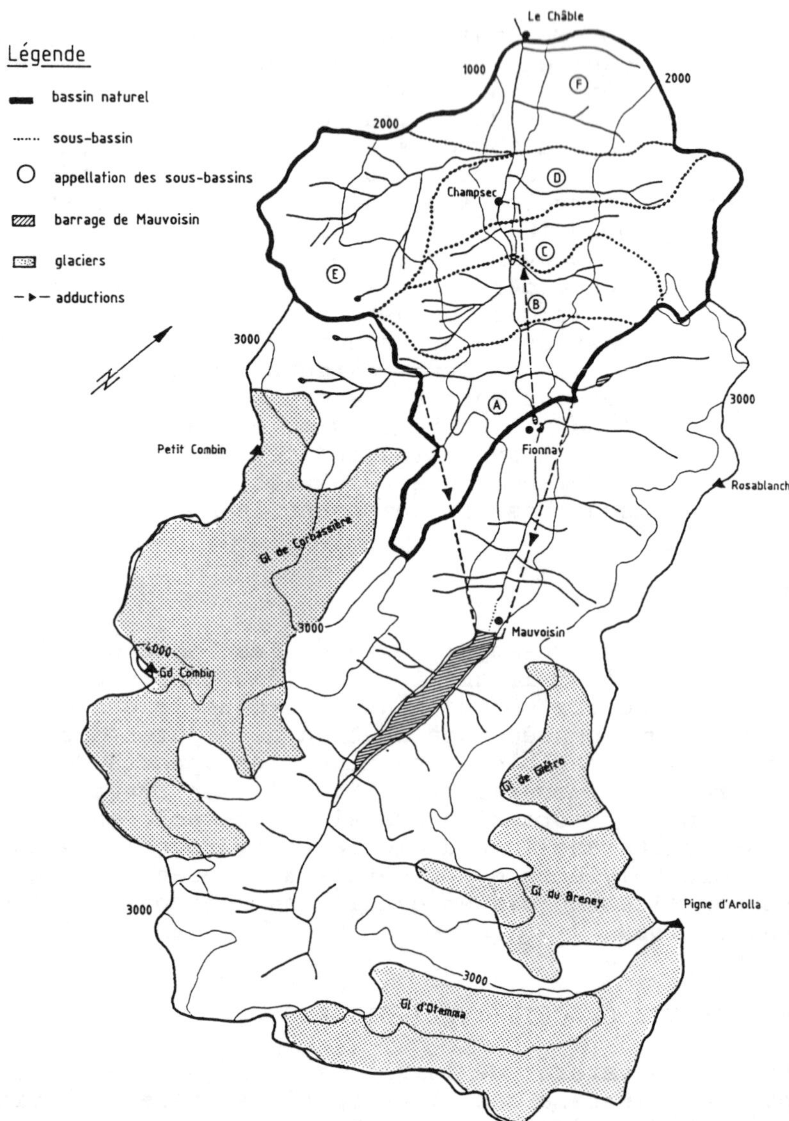

FIG. 1 Bassin versant de la Dranse de Bagnes au Châble, avec le bassin "naturel" d'études et ses sous-bassins d'investigation.

Mesures débitmétriques et bassin versant d'études

La station limnimétrique du Châble mesurait jusqu'en 1951 les apports en eau du bassin versant total. Depuis la création du barrage de Mauvoisin et du bassin-tampon de Fionnay, les mesures ne concernent plus qu'une part du bassin versant total (voir Fig. 1). Ces valeurs ne représentent pas seulement les apports latéraux, mais aussi les débits exogènes au bassin versant Le Châble-Fionnay, suppléments apportés par les purges, les dotations, les mises hors service des galeries latérales. Ces valeurs "d'influence" étant connues quotidiennement depuis 1962 (statistiques FMM), il a été possible de les soustraire aux mesures du Châble, pour obtenir les quantités naturelles apportées par les cours d'eau du bassin versant d'études Le Châble-Fionnay. Les statistiques des débits moyens mensuels pour les années 1962-1988 sont présentées dans le tableau suivant.

TABLEAU 1 Statistique des débits "naturels" moyens mensuels au Châble pour la période 1962-1988.

Mois	Moyenne (m^3/s)	Ecart-type (m^3/s)	Minimum (m^3/s)	Maximum (m^3/s)
Janvier	0.67	0.12	0.49	0.99
Février	0.68	0.18	0.48	1.29
Mars	0.84	0.26	0.56	1.68
Avril	1.48	0.52	0.70	3.13
Mai	3.38	0.86	1.79	5.01
Juin	4.60	1.42	1.76	7.83
Juillet	3.46	1.19	1.28	6.64
Août	2.24	0.70	1.00	4.82
Septembre	1.44	0.39	0.84	2.65
Octobre	1.09	0.34	0.60	2.17
Novembre	0.89	0.16	0.61	1.32
Décembre	0.76	0.14	0.52	1.04

Ayant réussi à déterminer les limites des apports naturels du bassin versant Le Châble-Fionnay à la station limnimétrique du Châble, nous avons pu définir les surfaces entrant en ligne de compte. Ce bassin d'études occupe une surface de 65.05 km^2, et son altitude moyenne est de 1890 m.

ESTIMATION DES DEBITS MOYENS MENSUELS LATERAUX

Lorsque nous devons estimer les débits moyens mensuels de cours d'eau sans mesures en n'ayant que les renseignements qui figurent sur des cartes topographiques et géologiques,

les méthodes ne sont pas légion, surtout dans le domaine alpin. Nous en proposons trois qui sont:
(a) Répartition en fonction de la surface.
(b) Répartition en fonction du volume.
(c) Répartition analogique.

Compte tenu des objectifs à atteindre, il a été décidé de se fixer une dimension minimale de bassin versant en dessous de laquelle les résultats risquaient de ne plus être significatifs. Cette valeur, d'environ 10 km^2, permettant aussi la comparaison des méthodes, a été choisie pour plusieurs raisons:

(a) Bien que les deux premières méthodes n'aient pas de limites d'applications bien définies, on se rend compte que, plus la surface est petite, plus les apports "parasitaires", tels les sources temporaires non captées jouent un rôle important. De surcroît, l'homogénéité globale peut ne plus être valable.
(b) Quant à la méthode analogique, elle a été établie après une étude effectuée sur une centaine de bassins versants représentatifs en Suisse (Aschwanden, 1985), dont les surfaces sont comprises entre 10 et 500 km^2.

Les six sous-bassins versants d'études sont représentés sur la Fig. 1, ainsi que leurs différentes surfaces sur le Tableau 2:

TABLEAU 2 Surface et volume des sous-bassins versants d'études.

Sous-bassin	A	B	C	D	E	F
Surface(km^2)	13.94	9.80	9.79	6.54	14.90	10.08
Volume(dam^3)	10 81	11 10	7 53	7 87	13 69	12 14

Répartition des débits selon la surface

Un renseignement que l'on peut toujours tirer d'une carte topographique est la surface des bassins versants. Une règle fondamentale en hydrologie est celle de la proportionnalité entre les débits et la surface. Intuitivement, on se rend compte que, plus la surface d'un bassin versant est grande, plus son débit sera important. Cette répartition est d'autant plus réaliste qu'elle intervient sur un phénomène global à pas de temps mensuel. Nous avons réparti les débits moyens mensuels du bassin total en proportion des surfaces des sous-bassins A à F.

Répartition des débits selon le volume

Le volume d'un réservoir de sol est donné par sa surface A, sa profondeur de stockage h, et sa porosité ρ. Pour deux bassins versants, nous avons:

$$\frac{Q_1}{A_1\ h_1\ \rho_1} = \frac{Q_2}{A_2\ h_2\ \rho_2} \qquad (1)$$

En hydrologie, on suppose habituellement que $h_1 = h_2$ et $\rho_1 = \rho_2$ ce qui revient à faire une répartition selon les surfaces.

Nous avons estimé les profondeurs de stockage moyennes pour des tranches altimétriques de 500 m, ainsi que les porosités des sols en place. Connaissant déjà les surfaces, il était alors possible de définir des volumes de stockage pour chaque sous-bassin (voir Tableau 2).

L'idée de base de cette répartition est celle du réservoir. Au printemps, le stock neigeux accumulé durant l'hiver va commencer à fondre. Une faible partie va s'écouler directement dans le réseau hydrographique, alors que la majorité de l'eau va s'infiltrer dans le terrain et remplir le réservoir du sol. Les écoulements de l'année, au niveau mensuel moyen, représentent le résultat de la vidange de ces réservoirs. En juin, lorsque la quasi-totalité de la neige a fondu, le réservoir est à son maximum. Des mesures ont été faites en période d'étiage (octobre 1989) et donnent de bons résultats pour la vidange lente (septembre à décembre). La répartition des débits selon le volume repose sur l'hypothèse que le comportement du sol sera le même lors de la vidange rapide (juin à septembre). Comme pour la répartition selon les surfaces, nous avons réparti les débits moyens mensuels du bassin total en proportion des volumes des sous-bassins A à F.

Répartition analogique

Quand on veut quantifier des débits pour un cours d'eau non mesuré, il est possible d'utiliser les données d'un autre bassin versant présentant des similitudes géomorphologiques et climatiques avec notre bassin d'études, et de procéder par analogie. Un facteur important d'analogie est le régime hydrologique.

La limite de la zone alpine est donnée par l'altitude moyenne, qui doit être supérieure à 1500 m. Les courbes des débits moyens mensuels des régimes alpins présentent un seul maximum, les processus décisifs se déroulant durant l'été (mai à septembre). Dans les régions alpines, la transposition spatiale est effectuée par le biais de la surface glaciaire et de l'altitude moyenne. Le classement par ordre décroissant des coefficients de Pardé des mois d'été fournit quatre types principaux de régimes alpins, dont leur dénomination conceptuelle se base principalement sur le rang des mois glaciaires ou nivaux (voir Tableau 3).

Selon ces caractéristiques spatiales, les cours d'eau mesurés des Alpes suisses ont été classés par régime, et leurs coefficients de Pardé ont été traités de manière statistique. Cela nous donne, pour chaque régime et chaque mois, des valeurs maximales et minimales des coefficients de Pardé.

TABLEAU 3 Les régimes hydrologiques des Alpes et leur classement spatial. L'ordre indique le classement décroissant des débits moyens mensuels d'été.(Aschwanden & Weingartner, 1985)

Régime-type	Sous-régime	Ordre	H_{moy} (m)	% de glacier
Glaciaire	a	7>8>6>9	> 2400	> 36
Glaciaire	b	7>8>6>9	> 2100	22-36
Glacio-nival	a	7>6>8>5	> 2000	12-22
Glacio-nival	b	6>7>8>5	> 1900	6-12
Glacio-nival	b	6>7>8>5	> 2300	1-12
Nivo-glacial		6>5>7>8	1500-1900	3-12
Nivo-glacial		6>5>7>8	1900-2300	1-6
Nival alpin		6>5>7>8	1500-1900	≤ 3
Nival alpin		5>6>7>8	> 1900	≤ 1

<u>Transfert régional du débit moyen annuel</u> En 1985, Aschwanden a établi, après une étude réalisée sur une centaine de bassins versants des Alpes suisses, une formule d'estimation du module annuel pour un bassin versant non mesuré, en fonction d'un bassin versant mesuré de référence. Cette formule, applicable sur des bassins versants d'une surface comprise entre 10 et 500 km^2, et dont la précision est d'environ 90%, est la suivante, avec Mq le débit spécifique moyen annuel (l/s km^2), $\bar{h}$ l'altitude moyenne (m), $\bar{P}$ les précipitations annuelles moyennes (mm/an), réf le bassin versant de référence, i le bassin versant d'études:

$$Mq_i = \left(0.6617 \frac{\bar{h}_i}{\bar{h}_{réf}} + 0.3904 \frac{\bar{P}_i}{\bar{P}_{réf}}\right) Mq_{réf} \tag{2}$$

Cela nous permet de transférer les débits spécifiques à des bassins versants non mesurés, à partir des rapports de précipitations et d'altitudes.

<u>Méthodologie</u> La première étape consiste à définir Mq de chaque bassin versant non mesuré en utilisant la formule (2). L'altitude moyenne se détermine sur une carte

topographique, et les précipitations se calculent avec un gradient pluviométrique. Dans un deuxième temps, le bassin d'études doit être classé dans un régime hydrologique type, selon les paramètres de sélection. L'estimation des débits moyens mensuels peut se faire alors de deux manières:

(a) La première méthode consiste à repérer dans les stations représentatives du régime hydrologique concerné une station ayant de fortes analogies géomorphologiques avec le bassin d'études. Ces facteurs analogiques sont, par ordre d'importance, le taux de glaciation, l'altitude moyenne, puis la surface. Dès qu'une station représentative est repérée, nous transférons ses coefficients de Pardé. Cette manière de faire ne fournit qu'une seule valeur de débit par mois.

(b) La deuxième méthode consiste à utiliser les valeurs maximales et minimales des coefficient de Pardé de l'ensemble des stations représentatives du régime hydrologique, et de les transférer au bassin d'études. Cette façon de faire nous fournit une fourchette d'estimation des débits moyens mensuels.

En général, les sources d'erreurs possibles se situent dans la précision d'estimation de la formule de corrélation pour le module moyen annuel, dans l'incertitude de la détermination du régime hydrologique type, et dans le choix d'une mauvaise station représentative.

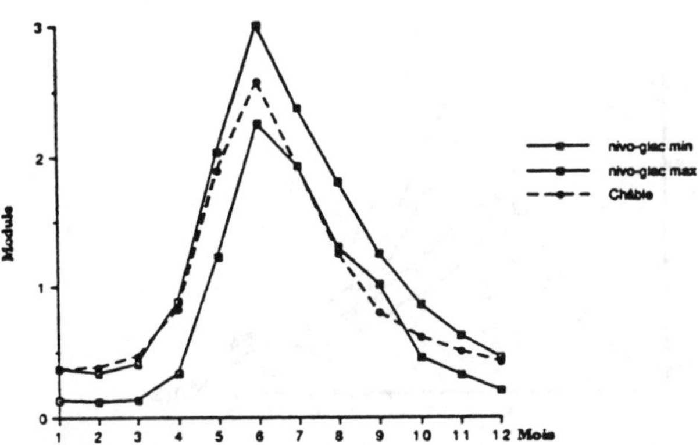

FIG. 2 Régime hydrologique du bassin versant d'études Le Châble-Fionnay: nivo-glaciaire.

<u>Application au bassin versant d'études</u> Avec une altitude moyenne d'environ 1900 m et un taux de glaciation proche de 1%, le régime hydrologique du bassin d'études Le Châble-Fionnay est de type nivo-glaciaire (Fig. 2). Après avoir déterminé pour chaque sous-bassin (de A à F) son régime hydrologique, nous avons estimé les modules moyens annuels latéraux des sous-bassins en appliquant la formule (2), et en utilisant le bassin global d'études Le Châble-

Fionnay comme station de référence. La somme des modules moyens annuels de chaque sous-bassin diffère de 5% de ce qui est mesuré au Châble.

COMPARAISON DES METHODES

Les Figs 3 et 4 donnent un exemple des résultats obtenus par les trois méthodes décrites plus haut, pour les sous-bassins A et F. Ces figures nous amènent à faire quelques remarques à leur sujet:

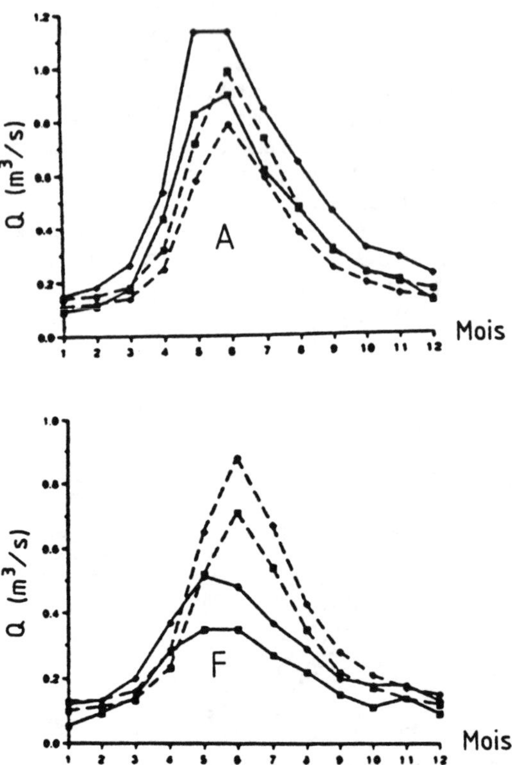

FIGS. 3-4 Estimation des débits moyens mensuels pour les sous-bassins A et F (méthode analogique en traits pleins, méthode surfacique en traitillé et rond, méthode volumique en traitillé et carré).

(a) Globalement, les mois d'étiage (hiver) concordent assez bien d'une méthode à l'autre.

(b) De grands écarts existent entre les méthodes "simples" et la méthode analogique, surtout pour les sous-bassins de basse altitude, où le régime hydrologique est très différent de celui du bassin global naturel, qui génère les répartitions surfacique et volumique.

(c) La répartition en fonction de la surface fournit, par rapport aux variations de la méthode analogique, de meilleurs résultats que la répartition selon le volume. Ils se situent soit à l'intérieur, soit plus près de cet intervalle.

Remarquons enfin, sur la Fig. 5, que la somme des débits moyens minimums et maximums de chaque sous-bassin (A à F) donne une autre plage de variation, dans laquelle s'inscrivent les débits moyens mensuels "naturels" mesurés au Châble. Cette figure représente en quelque sorte un moyen de contrôle pour la technique analogique.

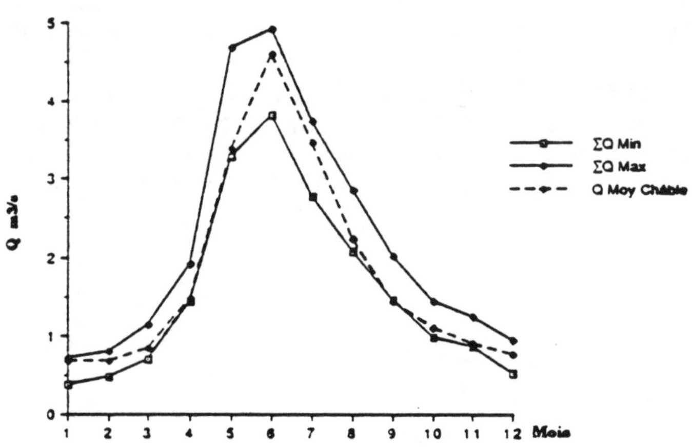

FIG. 5 Comparaison entre les valeurs moyennes mensuelles mesurées au Châble et la plage de variation des estimations.

CONCLUSIONS

Les répartitions surfacique et volumique ne peuvent s'appliquer qu'à des sous-bassins dont le bassin total est lui-même mesuré. Ceci est évident, car les contributions des bassins versants non jaugés sont distribués au prorata de la surface et du volume total. Ces deux répartitions ne tiennent pas compte du facteur altimétrique qui, en régions alpines, est déterminante, autant du point de vue du stockage des précipitations que du moment de la fonte.

Si la théorie des réservoirs s'applique de manière très satisfaisante pour la vidange lente, leurs comportements peuvent être très différents les uns des autres lors de la vidange rapide, où une plus grande précision dans l'estimation de la porosité et de la profondeur de stockage (paramètre le plus difficile à évaluer) devient nécessaire. Il faut donc être prudent avec l'utilisation de cette technique, et être critique quant aux résultats des mois d'abondance, ces derniers étant surestimés ou sous-estimés par rapport aux deux autres méthodes.

C'est la répartition analogique, ne nécessitant que des paramètres d'ordre topographique et utilisant des stations mesurées,qui introduit le moins d'éléments aléatoires. C'est aussi la seule méthode qui prenne en compte le facteur "altitude" des bassins versants.

REFERENCES

Aschwanden, H. (1985) Zur Abschätzung der Abflüsse in ungemessenen schweizerischen Einzugsgebieten. Geogr.Institut, Publ. Gewässer Kunde no. 66, Bern.

Aschwanden, H & Weingartner, R. (1985) Die Abflussregimes der Schweiz. Geogr.Institut, Publ. Gewässerkunde no. 65, Bern.

Luyet, G. (1989) Etude hydrologique des cours d'eau non influencés de la Vallée de Bagnes. Mémoire de recherches de fin du 3e Cycle inter-universitaire en Hydrologie et Hydrogéologie, UNI-Neuchâtel et EPF-Lausanne.

Hydrology in Mountainous Regions. I - Hydrological Measurements; the Water Cycle (Proceedings of two Lausanne Symposia, August 1990). IAHS Publ. no. 193, 1990.

Runoff modelling in complex three-dimensional terrain

I.D. MOORE
Centre for Resource and Environmental Studies, The Australian National University, Canberra, ACT, 2601, Australia
R.B. GRAYSON
Centre for Environmental Applied Hydrology, The University of Melbourne, Parkville, Victoria, 3052, Australia
J.P. WILSON
Department of Earth Sciences, Montana State University, Bozeman, Montana, 59717, U.S.A.

ABSTRACT Contour-based methods of partitioning landscapes and structuring hydrologic models permit the effects of topography to be efficiently included within these models in areas of rugged terrain. The method uses a "stream-tube" approach that allows the governing flow equations to be reduced to a series of coupled one-dimensional equations. A saturation overland flow and subsurface flow model based on this approach produced good agreement between observed and predicted runoff hydrographs on a small, steeply-sloping forested catchment in southeastern Australia. The model predicts the location of the variable source areas and the depths and velocities of surface and subsurface flow throughout the catchment.

INTRODUCTION

In mountainous catchments with steep hillslopes and complex topography runoff is principally generated by subsurface stormflow and/or saturation overland flow. Surface saturation generally occurs at the foot of converging hillslopes and in near-channel areas. These saturated zones expand and contract in response to precipitation and the movement of subsurface water from upslope, giving rise to the variable source area concept of runoff generation. Zavlavsky & Sinai (1981) brought together these concepts with considerable insight and found the topographic structure of a catchment to be the controlling factor in the mechanism of lateral subsurface flow and soil water distribution in a catchment.

Numerous models have been developed to simulate these processes on hillslope segments and in idealized landscapes (e.g., Sloan & Moore, 1984), but few are capable of predicting distributed runoff behaviour throughout complex landscapes. Notable exceptions are the three-dimensional saturated-unsaturated flow model of Freeze (1972), SHE-Systeme Hydrologique Europeen (Abbot et al., 1986), and TOPMODEL (Beven & Kirkby, 1979). Both Freeze's model and SHE are very detailed and computationally and data intensive. TOPMODEL represents the basin structure in detail, but simplifies many processes and is most applicable to large catchments. In this paper we present a model that represents a compromise between these two approaches. It permits detailed representation of basin topography, represents the physical processes of subsurface storm flow and saturation overland flow in considerable detail, but simplifies the vertical flow processes in the soil profile. In its present form it is a storm event model.

CATCHMENT PARTITIONING AND TERRAIN ANALYSIS

TAPES-C, Topographic Analysis Programs for the Environmental Sciences - Contour (Moore et al., 1988; Moore & Grayson, 1990), provides a method of partitioning a catchment into a series of interconnected elements using a contour-based digital elevation model (DEM) in the form of digitized contour lines (see Fig. 1). The method uses a "stream-tube" analogy (Onstad & Brakensiek, 1968) and assumes contour lines are equipotentials and water flows orthogonal to these equipotentals along streamlines. Each element is bounded by adjacent equipotential lines (which are curvilinear) on two sides and adjacent streamlines (assumed to be straight lines) on the other two sides. This form of partitioning provides a "natural," phenomena-based structure on which to build hydrologic models. It allows the complex two-dimensional water flow equations to be reduced to a series of coupled quasi-one-dimensional equations for each element. The equations can be solved using one-dimensional finite-difference numerical schemes and can handle complex boundary conditions.

For each element, TAPES-C computes the following topographic attributes: (1) element area; (2) total upslope contributing area; (3) connectivity of upslope and downslope elements; (4) x,y,z-coordinates of the element centroid; (5) x,y,z-coordinates of the midpoint on the downslope contour bounding the element; (6) the average land surface slope and channel slope, if one exists; (7) the widths of the element on the upslope and downslope equipotential lines bounding the element; (8) the flow distance across the element; and (9) aspect or azimuth of the element. These attributes are commonly required parameters in many hydrologic, water quality, snowmelt, and geomorphic models. TAPES-C also predicts the stream channel network using a

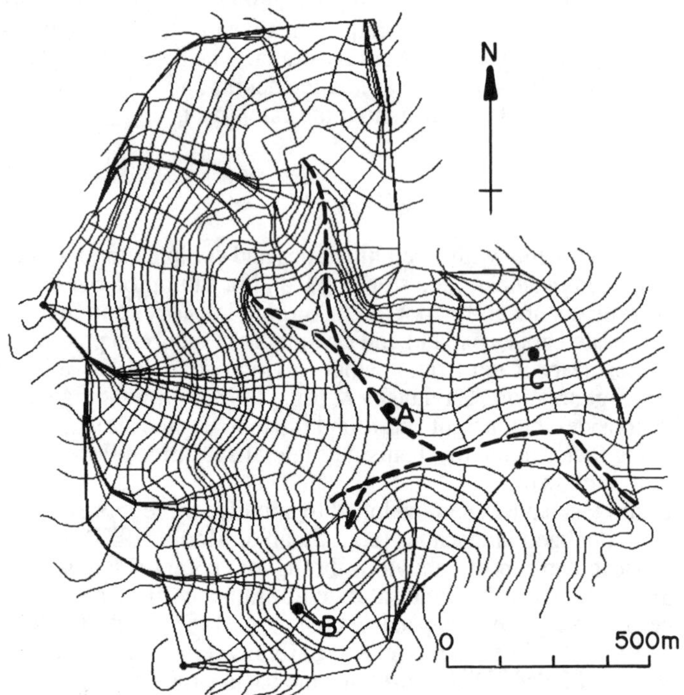

FIG. 1 Subdivision of the Geebung Creek catchment into elements using TAPES-C. Shown are the 5 m interval contour lines (average base width=75 m), and the predicted channel network (dashed line -assumes a critical area of 8 ha).

method based on the critical upslope contributing area criteria proposed by Band (1986). The channel network shown in Fig. 1 was predicted using this technique.

SATURATION OVERLAND FLOW AND SUBSURFACE FLOW MODEL

The catchment subdivision computed by TAPES-C, and shown in Fig. 1, is used as the basis for structuring the saturation overland flow and subsurface flow model. In applying this technique to modelling subsurface flow, there is an inherent assumption that the potential gradient of the flow can be approximated by the slope of the ground surface. Anderson & Kneale (1982) found this assumption to be satisfactory in catchments with steep slopes (> 6°) because the elevation potential dominates the total soil water potential in such cases. The model structure allows each element to have different soil and vegetation characteristics, however, this is usually not practical because of the large data requirements. In most of our applications of the model we measure, for example, the drainage parameters for each soil type on a catchment and make the crude approximation that these parameters do not vary within each soil type. We then numerically overlay a soil survey map over the element map of the catchment and assign a soil type to each element based on the soil type at the centroid of the element. A similar approach is used for other soil and vegetation characteristics. Spatial variability in catchment characteristics can therefore be at least partially represented in the model with the level of accuracy determined by the available data.

In the model, surface runoff is generated from rain falling on areas that are saturated and from exfiltration of subsurface flow. Interception is simulated using O'Loughlin's (1982) interception model, which requires three parameters: the maximum canopy storage, S, the throughfall coefficient, p, and the evaporation rate from a saturated canopy, E (Moore et al., 1986b). The infiltration capacity is assumed to exceed the rainfall intensity at all points in the catchment so that Hortonian overland flow is ignored. In the application we present here, the hydraulic response of the soil is dominated by preferential flow through macropores (Moore et al., 1986a) and the perched water tables respond rapidly to rainfall (Durham et al., 1986). Therefore, as a first approximation of soil-water processes in the unsaturated zone we assume that infiltrating water immediately penetrates to the perched watertable or an impermeable layer at shallow depth without attenuation or delay in the unsaturated zone. Because it is currently a storm event model, the model neglects evapotranspiration.

We have adapted the combined surface-subsurface kinematic modelling approach described by Takasao & Shiiba (1988) which does not require the explicit calculation of exfiltration. The one-dimensional form of the continuity equation that is applied to each element is

$$\frac{\partial A}{\partial t} + \frac{\partial Q}{\partial x} = \frac{i\,A_e}{\Delta x_e} \tag{1}$$

where A is the "apparent" cross-sectional flow area (Takasao & Shiiba, 1988), Q is the discharge, i is the rainfall intensity at the soil surface or the drainage rate from the unsaturated zone to the saturated zone in the soil profile, A_e is the plan area of the element, and Δx_e is the flow distance along a streamline through the element. The "apparent" cross-sectional flow areas for the two cases of subsurface flow only, and combined subsurface and saturation overland flow are, respectively:

$$A = \omega\gamma H \qquad \text{for } 0 \le A < \omega\gamma D \text{ or } 0 \le H < D \tag{2a}$$

and

$$A = \omega\gamma D + A_c \qquad \text{for } A > \omega\gamma D \tag{2b}$$

where ω is the width of the element orthogonal to the streamlines, γ is the effective porosity (total porosity - field capacity soil water content), D is the thickness of the hydrologically active soil profile (above an impermeable layer), and H is the depth of flow above the impermeable layer. In (2b) $A_c = \omega(H-D)$ for broad sheet flow, where H-D is the overland flow depth (H>D), and A_c is the channel cross-sectional area when the flow concentrates in rills or defined channels.

The resistance equations or kinematic forms of the momentum equations for subsurface flow only, and for combined subsurface flow and saturation overland flow can be expressed in terms of the Darcy and Manning equations. They are, respectively:

$$Q = K\frac{A}{\gamma}\sin\beta = \omega HK\sin\beta \qquad \text{for } 0 \le A < \omega\gamma D \text{ or } 0 \le H < D \qquad (3a)$$

and

$$Q = \omega D\,K\sin\beta + \alpha A_c^{\,m} \qquad \text{for } A > \omega\gamma D \qquad (3b)$$

where K is the effective hydraulic conductivity of the soil, β is the local slope angle, and α and m are parameters that depend on the type of flow (laminar or turbulent; broad sheet or channelized) [Moore & Foster, 1990].

Brakensiek's (1967) four-point, implicit, finite difference solution of both the kinematic overland flow and channel flow equations is used to route the subsurface and surface flow between elements. The values of A_e, Δx_e, ω, and β for each element are estimated by TAPES-C. Parts of the model are described more fully by Moore & Grayson (1990).

STUDY SITE

The study area (Fig. 1) is the 79.6 ha forested Geebung Creek catchment in the Yambulla State Forest in southeastern New South Wales, Australia (37°18' S and 149° 40'E). This catchment was selected because its runoff producing mechanisms are dominated by subsurface stormflow and saturation overland flow (Moore et al., 1986b). The total relief is 174 m and 18% of the catchment has slopes of 0-5%; 32% 6-10% slopes; 27% 11-15% slopes; and 23% has slopes in excess of 15%.

The soils consist predominantly of coarse-textured profiles, strongly duplex soils, and deep, uniform coarse-textured soils overlying a thin band of clay . Soils are generally shallow being less than one metre deep in upslope areas and somewhat greater than one metre deep in lower-slope areas and overlie weathered granite in all cases (Moore et al., 1986a, 1986b).

The vegetation consists of dry sclerophyll forest, having a tall open structure, with a sparse understorey, except along drainage lines and other wet areas. The distribution and location of the different vegetation species appears to have developed in response to differences in radiation input and soil water content variations across the catchment (Moore et al., 1988).

The precipitation averages about 900 mm per annum and is highest during summer and early autumn (80-85 mm per month) and lowest during mid-winter to early spring (55-60 mm per month). Much of the rainfall occurs as long-duration, low intensity storms, but isolated thunder storms are also common in summer (Moore et al., 1986b). The hydrologic characteristics of the Geebung Creek catchment have been described in more detail by Moore et al. (1986a, 1986b).

Runoff from the catchment is measured using a 140° V-notch weir constructed on a rock outcropping so that combined surface and subsurface flow is recorded. Precipitation is measured at the stream gauging site by a tipping bucket pluviometer with a 0.2 mm bucket capacity.

RESULTS AND DISCUSSION

Because of the limited space available we only present results from one storm event - the 27 July-2 August, 1984 event in which the catchment had a high average antecedent soil water content and a low potential evapotranspiration (Moore et al., 1986b). TAPES-C produced 956 elements, and these are shown in Fig. 1. The canopy parameters, such as the throughfall coefficient, etc., used in the model were the same as those used by Moore et al. (1986b). Preferential flow through macropores dominate the hydraulic behaviour of the soils, so a saturated hydraulic conductivity of 500 mm h^{-1} and a drainable porosity of 0.10 were assumed. The hydrologically active soil depth (D in Eqs. 2 and 3) was assumed to be 0.75 m thick. For simplicity, the model parameters were held constant and not varied from element to element, with the exception of Manning's roughness coefficeint, n, which was assumed to be 0.15 where overland flow occurs and 0.05 where channel flow occurs. To establish the antecedent conditions for the model, the height of the water table was assumed to be proportional to the "wetness index" $\ln(A/b\tan\beta)$, where A/b is the specific catchment area (m^2 m^{-1}) and β is the local catchment slope, wherever the wetness index was less than WETI and equal to D whenever it was greater than WETI. The value of WETI was selected using a trial and error proceedure so that the initial observed and predicted runoff rates at the catchment outlet were the same. The model was operated using a 5 minute internal time interval. Observed hourly precipitation and runoff rates at the catchment outlet were available for input into the model and for comparison of observed and predicted hydrographs, respectively.

The predicted and observed hydrographs at the catchment outlet (Fig. 2) show good agreement. The total runoff volumes, the peak runoff rate and the time to peak are all similar. These results are somewhat poorer than those obtained from the much simpler lumped model described by Moore et al. (1986b) that assumes successive steady-state conditions at each time interval of the simulation for describing the expansion and contraction of the zones of surface saturation. The simulated hydrograph recessions occur faster than the observed because no drainage of water from the soil in the unsaturated zone to the perched water tables is represented in the model. At the end of the third day of the simulation (72 hours) the predicted hydrograph is flatter than the observed. This occurred because evapotranspiration is also neglected. Over a period of days and weeks evapotranspiration processes are very important. These neglected processes obviously need to be included in the model if it is to be more generally applicable to a range of environments.

The model described in this paper has significant advantages over the lumped model: (1) it can predict runoff hydrographs and flow depths and velocities at any point in the catchment; (2) the zones of surface saturation can be specifically identified, rather than simply the fraction of total catchment area that is saturated; (3) it is capable of accounting for spatially variable soil and vegetation conditions, although this capability was not used in the present application; and (4) the effect of spatially and temporally varying precipitation patterns on catchment hydrology can be examined relatively easily. Advantages (3) and (4) are related to the availability of input data for the model and will not be demonstrated here. Precipitation data were only available from one gauge and the soil and vegetation data were not detailed enough to reliably differentiate between elements. We will attempt to demonstrate (1) and (2), although no validating data are available. In practice this type of distributed data is extremely rare and for the most part the capabilities of our models have now out-stripped the availability of such data.

Figure 3 shows the areal extent of the predicted zones of surface saturation at three different times during the storm event: initially, at the time of the peak runoff rate and immediately before the initiation of the small secondary peak. Initially only 13 % of the catchment was saturated, but this expanded rapidly to 67 % at the time of the peak. The saturated zones then quickly contracted to 44 % 9 hours later. Figure 3 shows that in this steeply-sloping catchment with relatively thin soils, the saturated source areas of

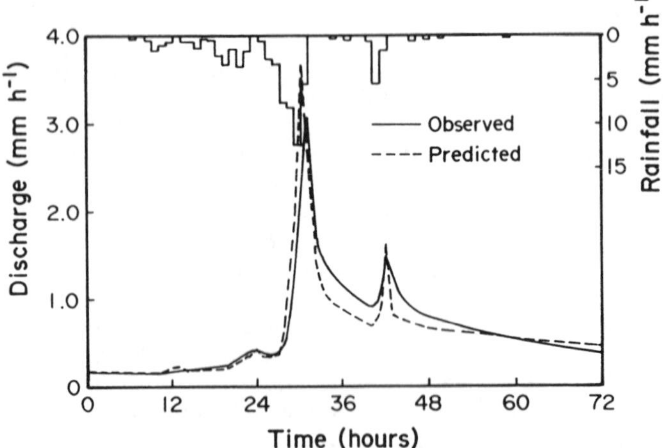

FIG. 2 Predicted and observed hydrograph at the catchment outlet for the July, 1984 storm event.

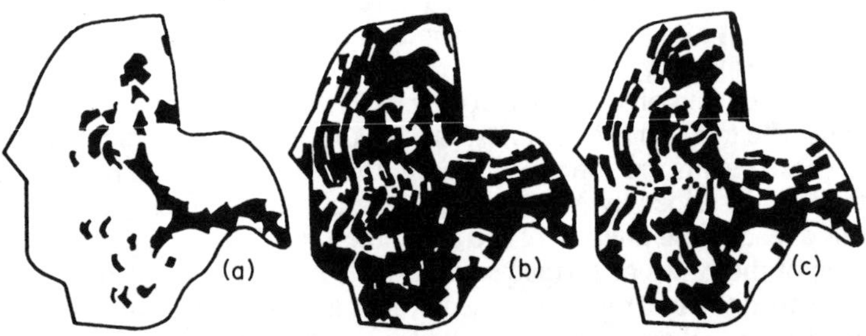

FIG. 3 Predicted location of the zones of surface saturation at three times during the storm event: (a) initially; (b) at the time of the peak runoff rate; and (c) immediately before the initiation of the secondary peak.

runoff respond rapidly to precipitation. Futhermore, the saturated zones are not continuous so that surface runoff from a saturated zone may reinfiltrate into the soil profile further downslope if unsaturated conditions exist there. Figure 3 shows that saturated zones form where the local slopes are the flattest and in areas of convergent topography. Observations on the catchment confirm this general behaviour.

Figure 4 presents the predicted surface runoff rates at the three locations on the catchment shown on Fig. 1. Location A is in the main channel; B is in a zone that remains saturated throughout the event, where overland flow occurs; and C is on an element that is only saturated for a short time during the event. For these simulations we assumed that concentrated flow occurred in the channel(s) could be represented in the model by the channel flow equations. In the non-channel areas we assumed that overland flow could be described by the shallow flow (sheet flow) equations. In many natural catchments sheet flow is rare. Rather, shallow overland flow tends to occur as flow concentrations in rills or due to flow concentrations caused by the effects of vegetation at the surface and micro-variations in the topography (Moore & Foster, 1990). Grayson (1990) demonstrated that these assumptions have a large impact on predicted depths and velocities of flow at specific points within a catchment, but has a smaller impact on the predicted runoff at the catchment outlet.

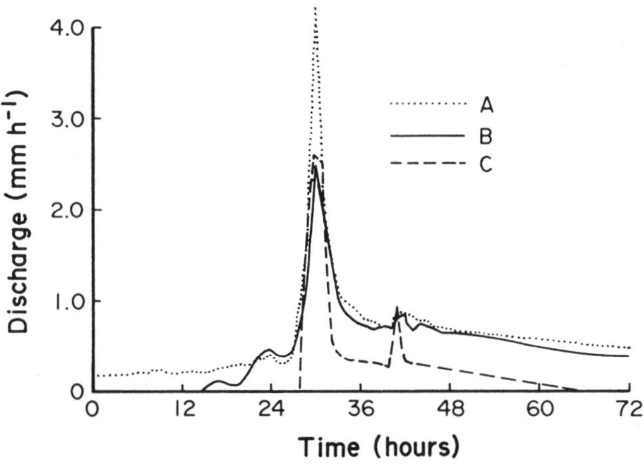

FIG. 4 Predicted surface and subsurface flow at the locations A, B, and C shown in Fig. 1.

CONCLUSIONS

The contour-based terrain analysis method, TAPES-C, permits a realistic representation of the three-dimensional nature of natural landscapes for dynamic hydrologic modelling under the constraints of maintaining physical realism and reducing computational requirements. While the saturation overland flow and subsurface flow model simulates the general hydrologic response of the steeply sloping Geebung Creek catchment to rainfall, the model has two inadequacies. The storage-delay and attenuation provided by soil in the unsaturated zone needs to be represented in the model and evapotranspiration algorithms are needed.

In future developments of the hydrologic model it is proposed to simulate the spatial variability of evapotranspiration that occurs in mountainous terrain using a daily radiation ratio which is a function of the topographic attributes of slope and aspect, and solar declination, terrestrial latitude and the ratio of the earth-sun distance to its mean (Moore et al., 1988).

ACKNOWLEDGEMENTS This study was funded in part by grant NSF/SES-891204? from the National Science Foundation and by the Minnesota Agricultural Experiment Stations. This work was largely carried out while I.D. Moore and R.B. Grayson were with the Dept. Agricultural Engineering, University of Minnesota, St. Paul, Minnesota, USA.

REFERENCES

Abbott, M.B., Bathurst, J.C., Cunge, J.A., O'Connell, P.E., and Rasmussen, J. (1986) An introduction to the European Hydrological System - Systeme Hydrologique Europeen, "SHE," 2: Structure of a physically-based, distributed modelling system. J. Hydrol. 87, 61-77.

Anderson, M.G. and Kneale, P.E. (1982) The influence of low-angled topography on hillslope soil-water convergence and stream discharge. J. Hydrol. 57, 65-80.

Band, L.E. (1986) Topographic partitioning of watersheds with digital elevation models. Wat. Resour. Res. 22 (1),15-24.

Beven, K.J. and Kirkby, M.J. (1979) A physically based variable contributing area model of basin hydrology. Hydrol. Sci. Bull. 24, 43-69.
Brakensiek, D.L. (1967) Kinematic flood routing. Trans. Am. Soc. Agric. Engrs. 10 (3), 340-343.
Durham, I.H., O'Loughlin, E.M. and Moore, I.D. (1986) Electronic acquisition of hydrologic data from intensively instrumented hillslopes. Hydrological Processes 1, 79-87.
Freeze, R.A. (1972) Role of subsurface flow in generating surface runoff, 2. Upstream source areas. Wat. Resour. Res. 8 (5), 1272-1283.
Grayson, R.B. (1990) Terrain based hydrologic modelling for erosion studies. Ph.D. thesis, Dept. Civil and Agric. Engr., Univ. of Melbourne, Australia.
Moore, I.D., Burch, G.J., and Wallbrink, P.J. (1986a) Preferential flow and hydraulic conductivity of forest soils. Soil Sci. Soc. Am. J. 50 (4), 876-881.
Moore, I.D. and Foster, G.R. (1990) Hydraulics and overland flow. In: Process Studies in Hillslope Hydrology (eds: M.G. Anderson and T.P. Burt). John Wiley & Sons, Sussex, England (in press).
Moore, I.D. and Grayson, R.B. (1990) Terrain-based prediction of runoff with vector elevation data. Wat. Resour. Res. (in press).
Moore, I.D., Mackay, S.M., Wallbrink, P.J., Burch, G.J., and O'Loughlin, E.M. (1986b) Hydrologic characteristics and modelling of a small forested catchment in southeastern New South Wales. Pre-logging condition. J. Hydrol. 83, 307-335.
Moore, I.D., O'Loughlin, E.M., and Burch, G.J. (1988) A contour-based topographic model for hydrological and ecological applications. Earth Surf. Processes and Landforms 13 (4), 305-320.
O'Loughlin, E.M., Cheney, N.P., and Burns, J. (1982) The Bushrangers experiment: hydrological response of a Eucalypt catchment to fire. Inst. Engrs., Aust., Publ. No. 82/6, 132-138.
Onstad, C.A. and Brakensiek, D.L. (1968) Watershed simulation by the stream path analogy. Wat. Resour. Res. 4 (5), 965-971.
Sloan, P.G. and Moore, I.D. (1984) Modeling subsurface stormflow on steeply sloping forested watersheds. Wat. Resour. Res. 20 (12), 1815-1822.
Takasao, T. and Shiiba, M. (1988) Incorporation of the effect of concentration of flow into the kinematic wave equations and its application to runoff system lumping. J.Hydrol. 102, 301-322.
Zaslavsky, D. and Sinai, G. (1981) Surface hydrology: I Explanation of phenomena, II Distribution of raindrops, III causes of lateral flow, IV Flow in sloping layered soil, V In-surface transient flow. J. Hydraul. Div. ASCE 107 (HY1), 1-93.

Hydrology in Mountainous Regions. I - Hydrological Measurements; the Water Cycle
(Proceedings of two Lausanne Symposia, August 1990). IAHS Publ. no. 193, 1990.

Hydrological modeling in regions of rugged relief

Ch. OBLED
Institut de Mécanique de Grenoble, Groupe Hydrologie, B.P. 53 X,
38 041 Grenoble Cedex, France

ABSTRACT This paper reviews the present status of hydrological modeling in mountainous or hilly regions. The two major sources of problems seem to be the spatial variability of input variables, mainly rainfall, influenced by orography and enhanced convection, and the description of runoff generating mechanisms, themselves strongly related to slope and topography. The lumped, the semi- and the fully distributed approaches try to cope with these problems in different ways that are briefly analyzed. Field experiments are increasingly used through hydrograph separation to help in the identification of dominant processes. Although all approaches seem to progress smoothly, none can claim for a definite advantage, and the major criterion for choice remains the external objectives and overall context of the modeling problem.

INTRODUCTION

A first point is to illustrate what we mean by hydrology in regions of rugged relief. Such regions may be found in various geographical and climatological contexts. So if we look first at the watersheds considered, the major ingredient is slope gradient. Commonly, one thinks mostly of mountainous watersheds at medium or high elevations, although low elevation hilly watersheds can also be included. And, as will be stressed below, the absolute elevation is more related to the climatic forcing while the internal functioning of the watershed is mostly related to slope and morphology.

These watersheds may be either small or large. On one hand, they may consist either of headwater basins, located near the crest lines, with mostly steep slopes. On the other hand, larger watersheds usually drop down to lower elevations and may display in their bottom part wide and flat valleys with locally low gradients. However, other cases are possible, such as a fairly flat upper plateau followed by a steep and narrow valley downstream. So to summarize, we shall consider basins with either marked slopes or significantly varying slopes, whatever their absolute elevation, with varied soil types, often of shallow depth, and varied vegetation cover and land uses.

Climatic environments

As for the climatic forcing of such watersheds, any type may be found, from desert to glacial, although these two extremes have very little liquid water available. So most problems are encountered in climates like, on one hand, arid (eg. Northern Africa, Middle East, etc...), mediterranean (eg. Southern Europe), and even temperate (eg. Western and Northern Europe) with dominant convective rainfall yields, or on the other hand in alpine, and cold climate(e.g. Northern latitudes) with dominant snowyields.

For the first type, the interaction between rugged relief and climatic environment is characterized by orographic effects, enhanced convection, and intense localized rain events. For the second type, precipitation may be either rain or snow depending on the elevation, and slope aspects may be important on other variables, like wind or radiation, themselves strongly influencing snowmelting or water delivering.

Globally, this means more variability than in watersheds of similar size in flat homogeneous regions. According to the climatic environment, basin forcings may be quite different, as will be the appropriate input data, and also the dominant mechanisms controlling the generation of runoff.

Modeling aims and approaches

Both the watershed characteristics and its climatic environment should be taken into account when entering into a modeling process. However, modeling purposes can be quite different, ranging from fully operational to purely cognitive.

Operational problems can themselves be split between short-term real time problems like flood forecasting or water management, and longer-term problems like land use changes, impacts of new water works or estimation of design flood or drought from rare meteorological events. Conversely, cognitive modeling is often oriented towards testing of hypotheses on the watershed response or improvement of algorithms for the description and simulation of physical processes. Recent interest in water quality problems have also induced new requirements in hydrological modeling in order to simulate pollutant transfer.

These differents aims have lead to the development of different types of model, that can be classified in different ways. A first one is based on the basin subdivision: models can range from fully lumped to fully distributed. Another criterion based on the description of hydrological processes distinguishes conceptual from physically-based models.

Lumped models consider the basin as a whole, as a unique entity, and simulate a single output from a single, or sometimes multiple, but lumped inputs. In this approach, everything is averaged at the basin scale, so that the spatial variability of the phenomenum seems often ignored. Usually, the complexity of the phenomena is reduced to a very simple "conceptual" analog, like a few reservoirs pouring into each other, although some loss functions call upon physically-based infiltration equations. Usually considered as very crude and held in contempt by researchers, they has nevertheless proved their robustness in many operational situations.

At the opposite, fully distributed models attempt to include the whole spatial variability by gridding the domain into small homogeneous elements. The physically-based approach consists in applying at the mesh size scale the governing equations derived from laboratory experiments on soil columns for infiltration, sheet or overland flow, etc... The underlying assumption is that if everything is included in the modeling scheme at the microscale, any possible integrated output, however unlikely its value may be, can be simulated if proper input data are made available. However, in practice, these models often encounter problems in their calibration, due to the difficulty of allocating proper parameter values to each mesh element objectively, not to speak of the limitations caused by their needs in computer memory and running time. In spite of a rather poor record in operational applications, these models are usually thought as being the unique future of hydrological modeling...

Intermediate approaches are many and multifaceted. Often based on a "reasonable" splitting of the watershed, they are then termed "semi-distributed". The simulation algorithms range from quasi-conceptual at the scale of the land unit, to quasi-physically-based. However, the subdivision selected is often related to one particular problem or process considered as dominant.

Model review and intercomparison

The reflections in the following section will try to present a state of the art and to address the problems currently encountered in the modeling of small to medium sized mountain watersheds. However, this is not an easy task to handle so many different approaches. Usually, authors are experienced in only one type of modeling, since it requires a long time to get fully acquainted with a given modeling approach.

So, previous papers in this direction must be acknowledged, mainly those by Todini (1988) and Beven (1989). In the particular case of snowmelt runoff modeling, G.H. Leavesley has recently given a very detailed paper (1989).

Actual intercomparisons of different models, with similar effort for each ones, and possibly over a variety of watersheds, are rare and extremely costly in time and money. Some attempts have been performed by individual authors like Charbonneau et al. (1981) or Loague and Freeze (1985). However the most exhaustive intercomparisons have been organized by WMO, particularly in its 1986 report on "Intercomparison of Models of Snowmelt Runoff" and will often be referred to.

ROLE OF THE INPUT/OUTPUT VARIABLES

In rugged relief, the basin itself is often far from homogeneous, and even uniform rainfall for example could generate strongly varied responses from one place to another. But as suggested in the introduction, external meteorological input variables are themselves very affected by the relief, and a major problem, at the very beginning of any simulation run, is to cope with their spatial variability, which may itself be strongly time varying.

Another problem, which is not unique to rugged terrain, is the quality of output variables, mainly discharges, and their crucial role in calibrating the models. We shall consider these successively.

Precipitation inputs

Liquid precipitation

For rainfall, the role of relief is often described in an oversimplified way as a general increase with altitude. This may be true in terms of annual or seasonal totals, at least for a rather common elevation range (0 - 4000 m), but it is no longer true when instantaneous rainfalls or short time step totals (up to several hours) are considered. When the rainfall is convective, it seems that statistically the largest intensities are observed more often near the bottom or the middle of the slope, close to the triggering of convection, rather than near the ridges. This has been observed in mediterranean regions (Obled and Creutin 1982) but also elsewhere, and this is now reasonnably reproduced in refined mesoscale meteorological models. This is mainly true for windward slopes, while the spatial distribution of rainfall on leeward slopes is still more complex.

On the other hand, daily or event totals (over several days, e.g. 2 to 5) tend to show again the rule of a regular increase with elevation. However, this is not due to higher intensities but rather to longer lasting rainfalls at higher elevation, where the number of wet hours may be twice as much than at lower elevation.

This space-time variability rises 2 questions :

i - If the generation of runoff is a rather rapid process (i.e. some 10 minutes to a few hours), then, the modeling scheme must fit this intrinsic time step. Consequently, rainfall patterns must be provided at this time step and may be quite different from the daily total pattern.

ii - Furthermore, if runoff generating processes are non-linear and more sensitive to high intensities, then these high intensities must be located properly.

These requirements are hardly met by the commonly available raingauge networks. An example is given in fig. 1 and 2. Figure 1 concerns the Real Collobrier research basin (71 km^2) equipped with 21 raingauges. Simulation have been performed with a lumped model on an half hourly basis. Although the basin average input was based on 5 well scattered raingauges which were considered as representative, problems did occur for some time steps. And if one compares, for these time steps, the hyetograph of basin average based on the 5 gauges on one hand, and on the 21 gauges on the other hand, significant differences appear. Coming back to the isohyets, it can be seen that this is due to a rain kernel moving in between the 5 gauges without hitting any of them.

However, even high density networks may not be sufficient to get a good idea of the actual rainfall pattern. For another region located in the South East of France, Figure 2 displays an hourly total as seen from the dense available ground network, together with the calibrated radar image at the same hour. Although the patterns look qualitatively similar, the quantitative basin averages computed from both informations on a test watershed (the Gardon d'Anduze - 545 km^2) differ significantly.

In the future, it is hoped that mesoscale meteorological models may help in better understanding the rainfall pattern. But at present, good rainfall input data on a watershed may only be obtained by direct observation, and Radar imagery seems the only way to get full coverage and proper time-steps. Unfortunately, the problem of calibration of radar images, particularly in mountain environments, is tractable only at the cost of a huge computational burden, and will not be available soon on wide and regular basis (Andrieu et al. 1989).

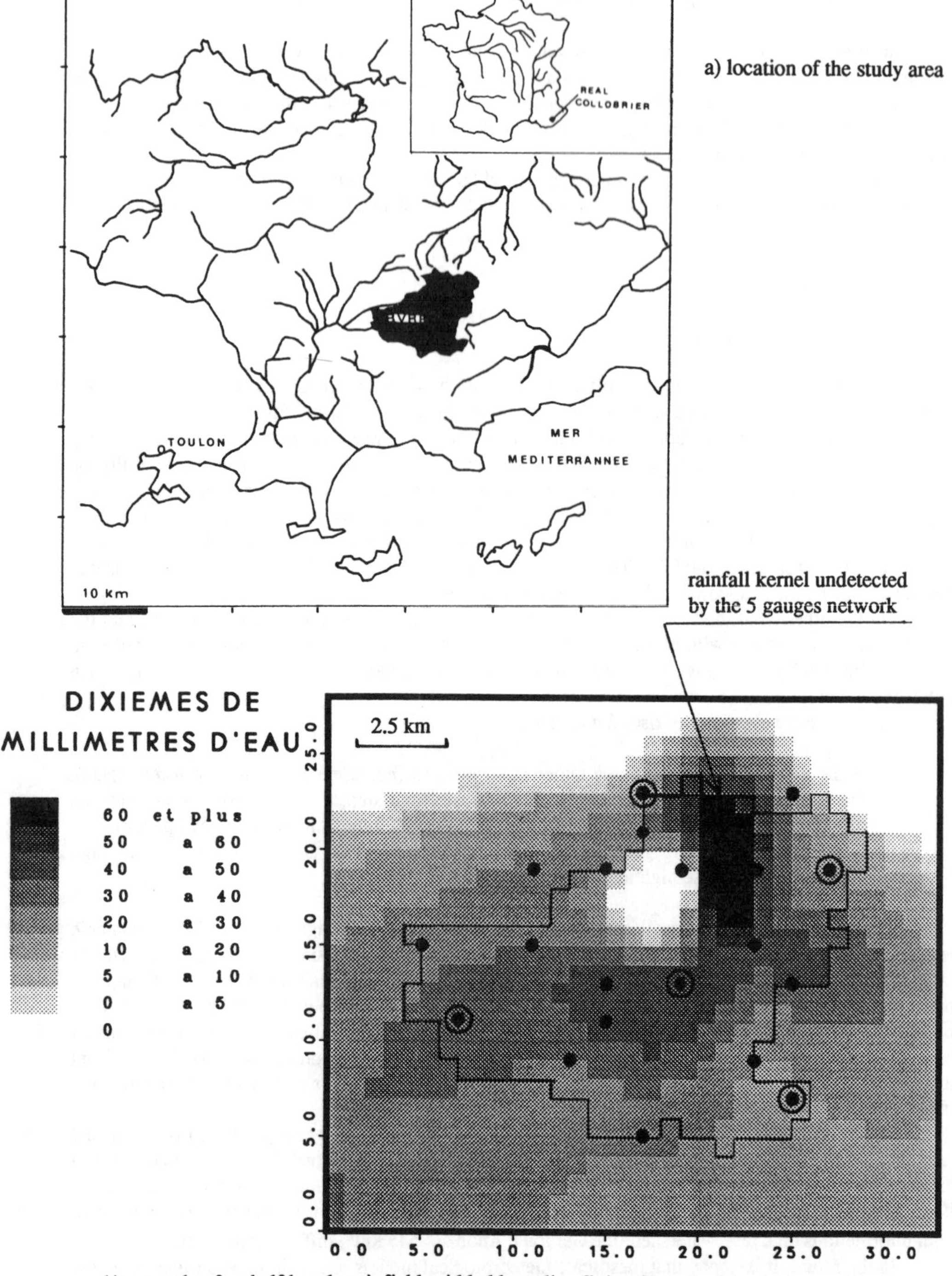

a) location of the study area

b) example of an half hourly rainfield gridded by spline fitting from the 21 raingauges (dots).
(The 5 circled dots correspond to the representative stations used for estimating the average rainfall .)

FIG. 1 Real Collobrier research basin.

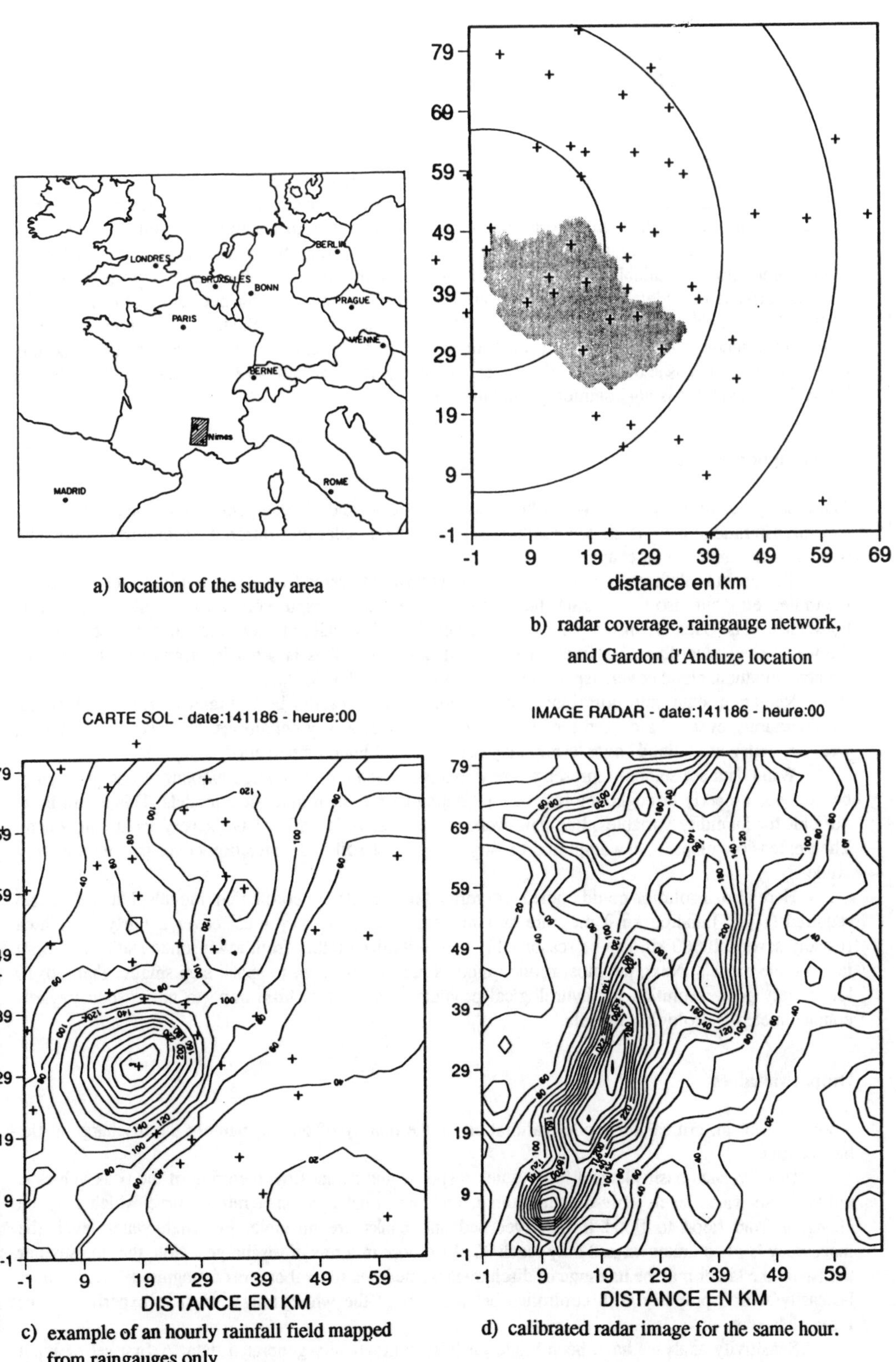

a) location of the study area

b) radar coverage, raingauge network, and Gardon d'Anduze location

c) example of an hourly rainfall field mapped from raingauges only

d) calibrated radar image for the same hour.

FIG. 2 The CEVENNES 86-88 experiment and the Gardon d'Anduze basin.

So far, input rainfall must thus be considered a variable carrying large uncertainty, particularly at the short-time steps and small elemental areas used by distributed models... (Obled 1989).

Solid precipitation

The problem of solid precipitation is much different. Time steps are less critical since the water is not immediately involved in hydrodynamic processes and just accumulates. Snowstorm are rarely convective, and usually the within storm spatial distribution is smoother than for rainfall.

However, a first problem is to decide the transition altitude between rain and snow, when no direct observation is available. Furthermore, in spite of a rather regular within storm deposition pattern, this regularity is considerably modified by after storm wind transport, by between storm differential melt, or by avalanches which, in small alpine watersheds, accumulate packed snow in valley bottoms.

So a major problem remains to monitor at any time the snow water equivalent, and hopefully other variables such as snow depth, albedo, cold content, etc..., throughout the watershed. According to Leavesley (1989) this is not commonly available already.

Other input variables

These are mostly concerned with the thermal budget, and further with snowpack melting or evapotranspiration, such as air temperature, radiation, both solar and infrared, incoming or outgoing, wind data and humidity or evaporation data.

Temperature data is very important for snow covered basins (rain/snow transition, estimation of melt rates, etc), but also for all other basins to estimate evapotranspiration and soil moisture depletion between storms. Usually, air temperature is measured at a few valley bottom locations, and spread over the wathershed according to a fixed or estimated lapse rate. This is often in error depending on the weather situation, cloud cover, aspect and cover of the basin slopes, etc...

Radiation data are often lacking but may rather easily be estimated from geometrical considerations, even on a rugged topography, at least for clear sky conditions. However, for disturbed weather, with partial cloud cover, errors may rise to several hundred percent.

Wind data are seldom representative, if available, and require a huge amount of computation to be extended properly throughout a rugged topography by means of numerical models. This is still more difficult for humidity variables, like pan evaporation data, which often have a very local component. Their extension in space, elevation and to varying types of soil and vegetation cover is generally very crude.

Here also, a solution could come from refined mesoscale meteorological models, but at the scale required (a few hundred km^2) they are still of poor help. First they must cover a fairly large area (usually several 10000 km^2) to be reasonnably well initialized either from rawinsonde stations or from larger scale models. Next, the most refined models hardly get down to space step smaller than 10x10 km, a very poor resolution for hydrological problems. So there is little hope to move soon towards coupled meteo-hydrological models.

Output variables

Another problem, critical for model calibration, is the quality of output, namely the discharge at the basin outlet.

Usually, such basins have a fairly quick response and actual flow metering of the peak values is unlikely. So water levels only are monitored, and one must rely on a rating curve which may be changing from flood to flood if the river bed and banks are unstable. For high water level, the inaccuracy is often unknown and may reach 30 % or more in terms of discharges. Note that the smaller the basin, the larger may be its range of discharges, sometimes several orders of magnitude. This cannot be easily sensed properly with controlled accuracy, over the whole range, even in experimental or research basins.

Sensitivity analyses have been made on fully synthetically generated data. A first set of input data is used to generate outflows from a given model with a priori fixed parameters. Conversely, based on these inputs and on the produced outflows, models parameters can be identified and fall close to the a priori fixed values. However, when the outflows are polluted by no more than 5 to 10 % in variance with white or colored random noise, then the identified values of the parameters may become erratic and far from those used in generating the data (Nalbantis et al.1988).

This is also observed in operational cases when random noise is added to the observed discharge, within the range of its expected accuracy, causing also the parameters to change significantly. The problem is that usually the calibration of models is optimized, either manually or automatically, on this only one uncertain data.

The only reasonable way would be to consider discharge data with a given confidence interval and to stop the calibration when the simulated run falls within this confidence band. Recent works based on such a concept have been published in urban and pollutant hydrology (Baffaut and Chameau 1990).

Partial conclusions

So a general conclusion about input variables is that it will remain very difficult to know precisely point values everywhere in the watershed, especially for the purpose of fully distributed modelling. Meteorological forcing variables are very difficult to obtain, even from remote sensing, and tedious to extend numerically from a few point values. This appears particularly critical for snowmelt modeling.

The only hope is for short time-step rainfall, which could become soon available from radar imagery at the km^2 scale. This can be interesting for flood event management, as long as the other required state variables can be estimated with sufficient accuracy. But between events, the accuracy of spatial evaporation estimates will remain poor.

Finally, as all the models even those termed "physically-based" have to be calibrated to fit the output data, the accuracy of these data must be considered carefully, as well as their effect on model calibration.

DISTRIBUTED AND SEMI-DISTRIBUTED MODELING

If the first problem is what kind of data shall be entered in the model, another challenge is what processes should be included in the model description of the watershed functionning.

It is known that a basin as a whole has a certain integrating capacity, in that the observed discharges display a much smoother pattern than the rainfall for example. However, it is hard to predict a priori what part of the rainfall or meltwater space-time variability will still appear in and influence the outflow.

The answer put forwards by the physically-based distributed approach is that entering the whole known physics at the point or element scale, then prescribing the expected links between neighbouring elements will describe completely the system, so that smoothing or dampening effects, storages, etc... need not be predicted explicitly but will appear in the results and could be just observed and interpreted afterwards. Taken to extremes, this approach requires no intuition or creativity, nor any critical choices from the modeler, but only call on his carefulness and exhaustivity, as well as on his working and computing capacity !...

Generally, a so-said physically-based approach usually consists of several steps.

Dividing the watershed

Two major sources of spatial variability are usually distinguished :

- one comes from the input variables, more precisely the incoming water (either rainfall, as discussed in a previous chapter, or snowmelt arriving at the ground)
- and, the other originates from the watershed characteristics (mainly topography and soil, but also vegetation cover, etc).

And the question is: Which one must be given the major role? It appears in the published literature that most fully distributed models have been developed and tested on small watersheds, where more or less extensive field studies had shown the strong variability of soil properties. So rainfall is often considered as slowly varying as compared to soil properties, and basin subdivision in then based essentially on soil characteristics.

However, the question needs further attention (see for example Loague (1988)).

As pointed out by different authors, but well summarized by Beven (1989), hydrodynamic or even geometrical morphological features have a very small correlation scale, mainly a few tens meter or so. So their description would require a subdivision of the watershed into very small mesh element, 100 x 100 m at the most, which is hardly tractable at the present time, not only because of the memory size and computation required, but also because of the impossibility of measuring and filling in the proper values of soil characteristics on such a grid. Furthermore, as pointed out by Beven (1989), variability decreases when block average values are considered instead of point values, at least as long as the soil type does not change drastically.

Although less often adressed, other basin characteristic may play a significant hydrological role, although having a different scale of space variation. This is the case in fully forested basins, where the tree cover may store and delay the rainwater, according to cover density, tree species, etc...

But coming back to spatial variability of input rainfall, it has been observed, in mediterranean regions, that convective rainfall pattern often displays an average correlation length in the order of :

$$d_{km} = 20 \times (\Delta t_{hours})^{1/2}$$

So the average size of the raincells can be estimated as d, or d/2 for their intense part. It can thus be inferred that for a 10 min time step, the rainfield is reasonnably smooth at scales of some tens km^2 (d ~ 8 km). This appears consistent with radar observations, and even if raincells are not fully circular, the rainfield can be considered as slowly varying over small watershed of a few km^2.

But this is no longer true when working at 1 hour or half an hour time steps over a basin of a few hundred km^2 (cf. figure 2) where the point values of rainfall may range from 1 to 100 mm/h., as shown by radar imagery, with a meshsize or 1 or 2 km...

So it appears that the scale of variations are about one or 2 orders of magnitude for rainfall and for soil characteristics (some km compared to some 10 m). Furthermore, precipitation variability tends to increase if watershed size increases, while basin variability tends to reach a plateau (since a small watershed of some km^2 already displays all the complexity of a large one), or may even decrease relatively if watershed size still increases.

Consequently, the basin subdivision should depend on the dominant processes, which themselves could depend on the watershed size. The space step used up to now in refined watershed modeling (a few hundred meters) falls in between the scales that have been observed, and looks much as a compromise.

Describing the runoff generating mechanisms

As it is difficult to review in detail all existing models, this part will remain rather general. Usually most general purpose distributed models have in mind a very one-dimensional scheme for water movement in the soil. The most sophisticated ones use at the grid element scale an infiltration equation (eg. Richard's equation in the SHE model) which assumes that water either infiltrates or generates overland flow. When infiltrated, it percolates vertically to the underlying aquifer and flows to the river as saturated ground water.

However, it may still be far from really physical, since the soil is rarely considered as multilayered, and there is little opportunity for soil water to flow laterally either as subsurface flow in macropores or temporary saturated zones at soil layer interfaces. Nor is the aquifer allowed to rise up enough to cause saturation from below over large areas.

So apart from the difficulty of allocating proper parameter values once the land divisions have been chosen, the type of possible processes described in the model appears to be determining. For long, Hortonian processes of overland flow generation by infiltration excess have been considered as the only source of quick runoff. But it has now been observed that subsurface stormflow may display a rather quick response also, especially in regions with permeable and sloping topsoil. And so does the groundwater flow response, which had been considered for years as slow in responding. Although such choices are apparent in any model, they can hardly be made on the basis of theoretical considerations or visual inspections of a watershed, but would rather needs detailed hydrological experimentation.

Furthermore, some existing "physically-based" distributed models are so parametrized that a process that has not been explicity described can easily be transferred to and taken into account by another one, but at the cost of very unexpected parameter values. For example, subsurface flow in macropores may be actually represented by the proposed overland flow component, but with a surface roughness coefficient which can hardly be explained by the surface and vegetation cover.

These parameters values are often accepted as "effective" values, and considered as resulting from the spatial averaging of the processes over a land unit. For example, very low hydraulic conductivities of a few mm/h are accepted for a model to be able to generate quick runoff, while measured point values are sometimes several 10 or 100 mm/h... Obviously such field measurements may be biaised (sites often chosen over flat area, or for easy access, etc...), but nobody knows how to measure or to derive representative values at the element scale. All this weakens considerably an often put forward argument in favour of physically-based modeling, mainly their capacity of using physical parameters that can be actually measured...

Another trend, that has appeared rather recently with the advent of radar imagery and of digital terrain models, could be termed conceptual but over-distributed. It consists in using a very simple water accounting routine but a very refined subdivision to enter the rainfall data and to route the excess water. A recent exemple is given by Wyss et al. (1990).

Role of intermediate or internal state variables

As already suggested, a major way to decide whether a modeling approach is appropriate or not is to measure continuously some intermediate variables. Here, two examples will be given.

i) Looking only to a rainfall-runoff transformation, most models separate the sources of water into two or more components (overland flow or direct runoff, subsurface stormflow, groundwater flow, etc...). These are assumed to have followed different pathways and set in action different types of water, either "new" rainfall water or "old" water stored over various durations in the soil. This could be more or less easily recognized by hydrochemical or isotopic analyses, to provide an estimated time series of each component. An example, taken from Mac Donnell et al., is given in figure 3, but others may be found in recent papers by Caine (1989) or Swistock et al. (1989). It is then hardly acceptable to have the model producing most of its runoff through overland flow when most of the observed discharge displays groundwater characteristics.

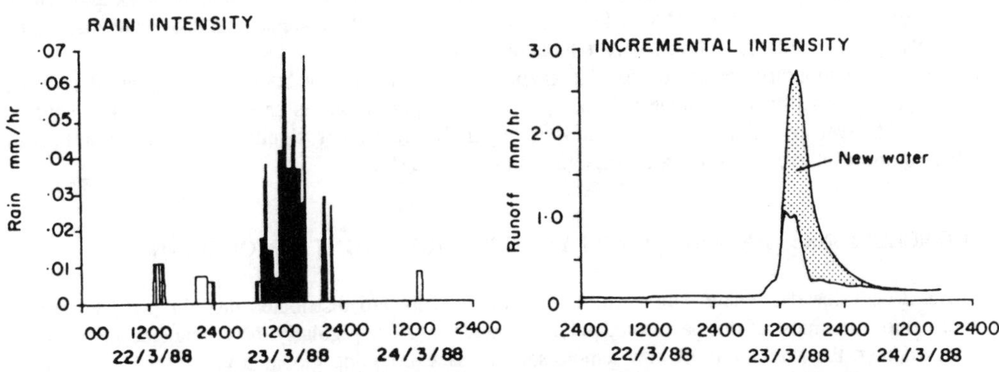

FIG. 3 Exemple of hydrograph separation (from Mc Donnell et al.1990).

In a rather similar way, models are often fitted to the data of an outlet gage while intermediate gages may exist. It is here also hardly acceptable that a model could be good at the outlet and completely wrong for intermediate basins data, for which it has not been optimized.

However apart from these two types of cross checking with field data, it is hard to monitor more directly the moisture status of a watershed, particularly in a rugged topography. Usually local soil moisture data (neutron probe or tensiometers) are not representative, nor are groundwater data since aquifers, if any, may develop only locally and temporarily.

ii) Another example is in the case of a snow covered watershed. Even if the buildup of the snowpack has been well represented in the model, or if it has been properly monitored, usually snowmelt water is computed from meteorological variables only. Just note that this wateryield can be spatially varying as much as rainfall inputs, due to the presence or not of snow at any given location, to the temperature distribution, and to the aspects and orientation of the slope considered, etc..

So a good cross-checking is to compare (every week, or month) the model status for internal variables like snow depth, water equivalent etc.. with actual data. The most easily available one is the snowline contour, when the basin is no longer fully covered. This usually leads to interesting conclusions... Just remember that a wrong estimation of the rain/snow transition leads on one hand to adding fresh snow, that does not runoff, with a high albedo that prevents the underlying snowpack from melting, while on the other hand, the actual precipitation has been in the form of rain that has flowed immediately, while increasing the snowpack ripeness...!

So these types of cross-checking are essential in testing the adequacy of models with respect to reality.

From distributed to semi-distributed modeling

For many good reasons, among which to avoid keeping track of the water budget on many land segments, people have often preferred to manage a reasonable number of subunits, usually a few tens. However, their choice is critical, and strongly influenced by some assumption on a dominant mechanism for generating the runoff.

In the case of snow covered watersheds, it seems obvious to divide first the watershed into elevation bands, which will usually appear to fit also a vegetation subdivision. Eventually the orientations will be considered, assuming a major role for clear weather snowmelt processes.

In other cases, the basin will be subdivided into large units based on soil types, either permeable or not, thus stressing Hortonian processes, etc...

An intermediate compromise between semi-distributed and "physically-based" consists in splitting the watershed into a collection of sloping planes, draining into each other untill reaching the main tributary. Usually, the runoff is generated by Hortonian processes: Overland flow originates mainly from infiltration excess while infiltrated water percolates down to an aquifer that drains directly to the river, assuming that the overland flow is quickly collected by the drainage network and cannot reinfiltrate on the lower plane (Morel-Seytoux 1987). However, there are several such semi-distributed models, and it is thus difficult to compare them objectively.

As a temporary conclusion for this chapter, let us remark that both physically-based or more conceptual semi-distributed models do not provide high performances as can be got in neigbouring fields like riverflow modeling or groundwater hydrodynamics, nor significantly better results than those of more simple lumped models (Loague and Freeze 1985).

CONCLUSIONS : PRESENT TRENDS AND NEW DIRECTIONS IN MODELING

After 2 or 3 decades where major efforts were directed toward distributed modeling, it has seemed normal to focus most of this paper on this type of modeling. The regularly increasing size and capacity of computer, the availability of new remote sensing data providing global coverage of the watershed have pushed in this way. However, it is also worth to review briefly all the modeling approaches together and to see where they are now.

Lumped and semi-lumped modeling

First of all, it must be noted that lumped modeling has not been abandoned as it might have been expected from the advent of easy accessible distributed models. They still remain very economical in terms of implementation effort, data and computer requirements. Their calibration can be easily optimized and automatized, since they do not need more than a few (3 to 6) lumped parameters.

Next, they can be run on an event basis, as currently done for example in flood forecasting. In this case, at the price of a proper initialisation of the model, it may be run only during the most critical part of the event. This avoids a refined simulation of the processes that are little activated, or of secondary effect during the event, like evapotranspiration for example. And this reduces consequently the data requirements for other variables than precipitation. Furthermore, lumped models are often calibrated by rather objective, statistically-based identification methods. This allows, even if overall performances are limited, the knowledge of their uncertainty, which may be quantified and prove of great help in decision making.

BVRE REAL COLLOBRIER
RELIEF

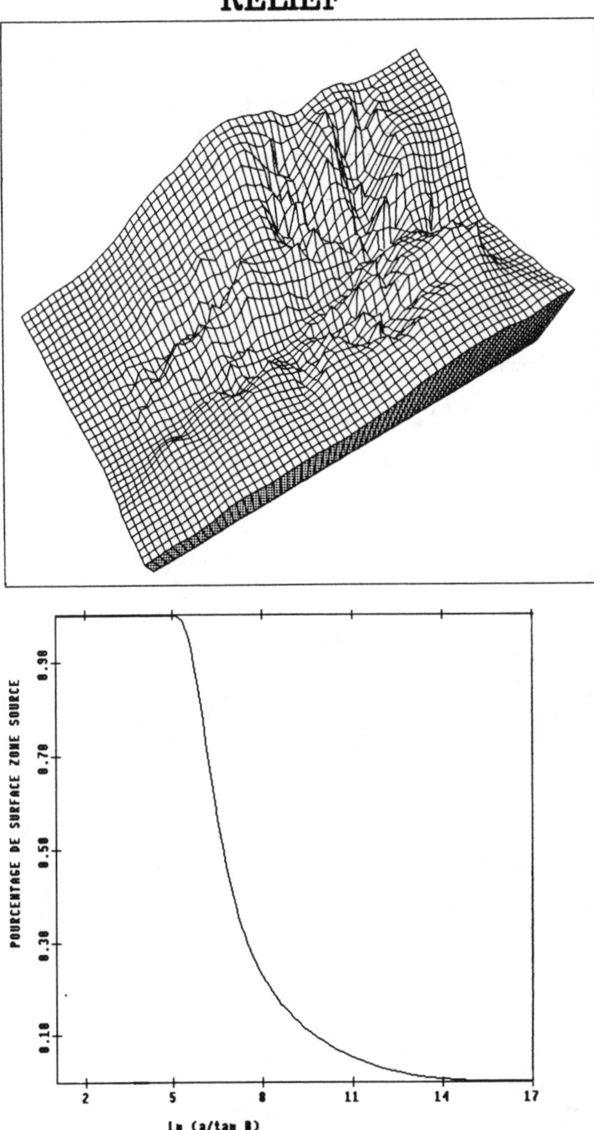

FIG. 4 Exemple of a Digital Terrain Model for a watershed and of the derived distribution function for the topographic index .

Furthermore, lumped models do not necessarily mean single input, nor that spatial variability is completely neglected. First, when calibrated on a multiple event set, a lumped input does not mean that the model assumes fully uniform rainfall, but rather that the model is calibrated for the most frequent (but not necessarily uniform) rainfall pattern over the watershed. Precipitation can even be measured at several locations, thus considered as several inputs, but this approach has not proved significantly better than using a single averaged input. The problem is that describing the spatial variability by including many point measurements as input variables considerably decreases the robustness of the model. However, with the coming of new sensors, such as radar, other lumped indexes can be easily computed and tested to represent spatial variability. First, better estimates of the average rainfall can be got, but also the variance of the field, the location and extension of rainfall above some threshold value, the departure from the usual pattern, etc... These indexes can be easily tested as correctors, superimposed to the average model, to refine the production of runoff water (Sempere 1990).

Conversely, a similar lumped approach may also be used for the watershed mechanisms. If a given process has been identified as dominant in generating the runoff, then a simplified form, preserving its dynamic, can be adapted to a lumped model. An example is the saturation excess runoff caused by the development of time varying source areas. It has been promoted mainly by K. Beven (1979,1989) and E.O'Loughlin (1981,1986) mainly in a distributed modeling context. The major ingredient is a topographic index representing the local saturation potential as the ratio of the upstream

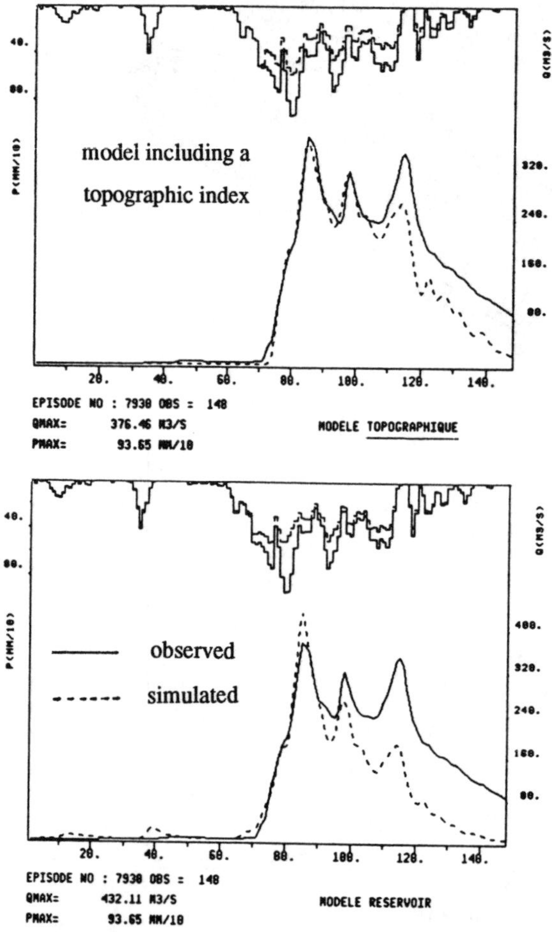

FIG. 5 Exemple of improvement caused by the inclusion of a simple routine for variable source area simulation based on the topographic index distribution curve.

drainage area, providing water to that point, to the local topographic slope, indexing its capacity to evacuate this water as subsurface flow.

Although this index was first derived for use in a distributed model, it may well be used in a lumped way by considering only its distribution function over the watershed, in connection with an index of the basin moisture status. According to this moisture index, the percentage of basin units exceeding their transit capacity is estimated from the topographic index distribution curve. This percentage of area is considered as saturated and generates direct runoff, thus adding a time varying dynamics to the basin response. Although the computation of the topographic index and of its distribution function requires a Digital Terrain Model, it is done offline, once and for all (Figure 4), and there is no need to keep track of the moisture budget of each unit. This has been successfully included by Ormsbee and Khan (1989) in the HEC1 model framework. Similarly, Sempere (1990) showed that adding this component to an existing lumped model with a reservoir like loss function improves significantly the dynamics (Figure 5), and increases by 10% the variance explained by the simulated discharges.

This is a good example of what could be called semi-lumped modeling. Usually, the term semi-distributed involved a splitting of the watershed in a rather small number of homogeneous units or subwatersheds. Here semi-lumped means that the model remains lumped, but includes the use of complementary indexes of input variables or of basin characteristics that summarize the spatial variability sources without needing a water budget accounting for each separate units.

However, a general problem remains about the type of spatial variation to include. Is it the spatial distribution of rainfall that is important in the generation of runoff, or the spatial variation of soil characteristics, of soil moisture status, or is it actually their combination? Both approaches seem to improve the performances of semi-lumped models, but may be the answer would come from distributed modeling sensitivity analyses ?...

Furthermore, identification methods for lumped models have been improved, for example by transferring some techniques used in Automatic and Systems Control. An example can be found into the DPFT-ERUHDIT method developed for simultaneous identification of Unit Hydrograph and of the sequences of Excess Rainfall on a multi event data set (Sempere et al., this symposium). Another advantage is that they can easily be made adaptive. Although distributed models can also, it is much more difficult and seldom practised. This relaxes somewhat the claim that only "physically based" models could deal with progressive basin changes.

All these little but significant improvements, once combined together, probably explain the continuing interest for this type of modeling in operational applications.

Distributed modeling

A first trend towards "over-distributed" models has already been been addressed in a previous paragraph. A more lasting trend over the last ten years has been to reconsider some underlying hypotheses such as "quick overland flow", vertical percolation and "slow groundwater response", and to admit that there could be quick lateral unsaturated subsurface flow and quick groundwater response, particularly through the building up of quickly developing saturated area.

So progress does not always come from taking smaller time or space steps, but from a different description of the processes at work within the basin. This makes use of new available data, such as DTM and GIS. However, except for rainfall estimation by radar, teledetection products like satellite imagery has not played a critical role.

This evolution has raised a renewed interest in field experiments at the basin scale, mainly through tracer experiments that have illustrated and strengthened the hypotheses about such a separation into components. These experiments are very usefull since the monitoring of internal state variables considerably curtails the collection of possible pathways to generate runoff water when dealing only with the discharge at the outlet.

However, even when the processes at work are clearly established, like in snowmelt generation where the parameters can be derived directly from thermodynamics, problems then arise from the inability to extend properly the external meteorological input variables, and this may cancel any improvement expected from a more "physically based" description.

Thus it is the author opinion that no major breakthrough can be expected from either lumped, distributed, physically based modeling, nor from current or future experiments alone. Progress will probably come little by little, from a constant dialogue between all these complementary approaches...

ACKNOWLEDGEMENTS

These opinions have emerged from the careful exploratory works done by several Ph.D. students, among whom I. Nalbantis, Y. Rodriguez and D. Sempere must be thanked. Many discussions with local and foreign colleagues like B. Ambroise, J.M. Grésillon, Ph. Mérot, J.P. Jordan, J. Lavabre, P.Matias, and some others have also fed this reflexion. Obviously, through his anterior works and various discussions with the author, K. Beven have strongly influenced the author opinions, and kindly revised this paper...

REFERENCES

Baffaut C. and Chaumeau J.L. (1990)
Estimation of pollutant load with fuzzy set.
Civil Engineering System (in press).

Beven K.J. (1989)
Changing Ideas in Hydrology: the case of physically-based models.
J.of Hydrol., vol. 105, pp. 157-172.

Beven K.J., and Kirkby M.J.(1979)
A physically based variable contributing area model of basin hydrology
Hydrol. Sci. Bull. , vol. 24, n° 1, pp. 49-69.

Caine N. (1989)
Hydrograph separation in a small alpine basin based on inorganic solute concentrations.
J. of Hydrol., vol. 112, pp. 89-101.

Charbonneau R., Lardeau J.P., and Obled Ch. (1981)
Problems of modelling a high mountainous drainage basin with predominant snowyields.
Hydrol. Sci. Bull. , vol. 26, n° 4, pp. 345-361.

Creutin J.D. and Obled Ch. (1982)
Rainfall related problems in operating the Gard flood warning system.
Symposium on Hydrometeorology (Denver Co USA). Publ. Amer. Wat. Res. Assoc., pp. 159-169.

Andrieu H. , Creutin J.D., Delrieu G., Leoussoff J., and Pointin Y.(1989)
Radar data processing for hydrology in the Cevennes Region
IAHS 3rd Int. Assembly, Baltimore MD USA , May 1989, Proc. pp 105-115.

Leavesley G.H. (1989)
Problems of snowmelt runoff modelling for a variety of physiographic and climatic conditions.
Hydrol. Sci. Journ., vol 34, n°6, pp 617-634.

Loague K.M. and Freeze R.A. (1985)
A comparison of rainfall-runoff modelling techniques on small upland catchments
Water Ress. Res. vol. 21, pp. 229-240.

Loague K.M. (1989)
Impact of rainfall and soil hydraulic properties information on runoff predictions at the hillslope scale.*Water Ress. Res.* vol. 24, n°9, pp. 1501-1510.

Mac Donnell J.J,Bonell M., Stewart M.K., and Pearce A.J. (1990)
Deuterium variations in storm rainfall: Implications for stream hydrograph separation.
Water Ress. Res., vol. 26, n°3, pp. 455-458.

Morel-Seytoux H.J. (1987)
SWATCH: The Swiss watch rainfall-runoff model for prediction of surface and subsurface flows
Hydrology Days Publ., Fort Collins Co.-USA.

Nalbantis I.,Obled Ch. and Rodriguez Y.(1988)
Modélisation Pluie-Débit: validation par simulation de la méthode DPFT
La Houille Blanche, n° 5/6, pp. 467-474.

Obled Ch. (1989)
Reflexions on rainfall information requirements for operational rainfall-runoff modelling.
Proc. of Int. Symp. on Hydrological Applications of Weather Radar Univ. of Salford U.K.

O'Loughin E. M.(1981)
Saturation regions in catchments and their relation to soil and topographic properties
J. of Hydrol., vol. 53, pp. 229-246.

O'Loughin E. M.(1986)
Prediction of surface saturation zones in natural catchments by topographic analysis.
Water Ress. Res. ,vol. 22, n°5, pp. 794- 804.

Ormsbee L.E. and Khan A.Q. (1989)
A parametric model for steeply sloping forested watersheds.
Water Ress. Res. ,vol. 25, n°9, pp. 2053- 2065.

Sempere -Torres D. (1990)
Calcul de la lame ruissellée dans la modélisation pluie-débit: limitation des approches globales et introduction simplifiée de la topographie et de la variabilité spatiale des pluies.
Thèse de l'Inst. Nat. Poly. de Grenoble.

Swistock B.R.,De Walle D.R., and Sharpe W.E. (1989)
Sources of acidic stormflows in an appalachian headwater stream.
Water Ress. Res., vol. 25, n°10, pp. 2139-2147.

Todini E. (1988)
Rainfall-runoff modelling: past, present and future.
J. of Hydrol., vol. 100, pp. 341-352.

W.M.O.
Intercomparison of models of snowmelt runoff.
WMO Operational Hydrology report n°23- WMO publ. n°646. Geneva (Switzerland).

Wyss J. , Williams E.R., and Bras R.L.
Hydrologic modeling of New England river basins using radar rainfall data.
J. of Geophys. Res., vol. 95,n° D3, pp. 2143-2152.

Hydrology in Mountainous Regions. I - Hydrological Measurements; the Water Cycle
(Proceedings of two Lausanne Symposia, August 1990). IAHS Publ. no. 193, 1990.

Application du modèle couplé à discrétisation spatiale au bassin de la Fecht, Vosges (France)

J.L. PERRIN, B. AMBROISE & J. HUMBERT
Centre d'Etudes et de Recherches Eco-Géographiques, Université Louis Pasteur, 3 rue de l'Argonne, F-67083 Strasbourg Cedex, France

ABSTRACT The MC-Model (Girard et al., 1981), a spatially-distributed conceptual model which uses functional relationships, has been tested on the Fecht catchment (Vosges mountains, France), where large spatial variations of precipitations and soil water properties are well related to topography. A topography-based discretization of the catchment and a physically-based parametrization of the model have permitted to reduce significantly the calibration process. Five years of daily simulations at four gauging stations were used for the validation. The results are quite good: observed and simulated water balances and hydrographs compare well for all years and subcatchments, with efficiencies better than 80%. These results show the regional validity of the modelling assumptions made in this mountainous environment.

INTRODUCTION

En montagne, le relief provoque de fortes variations dans la distribution spatiale des précipitations et de l'énergie disponible pour l'évapotranspiration; il joue aussi sur la répartition spatiale des sols et de la végétation et sur leurs propriétés hydriques. Aussi est-il nécessaire d'adopter une approche spatialisée dans la modélisation hydrologique de bassins versants montagneux, et de disposer de méthodes simples pour caractériser ces variations spatiales. Une telle étude a été tentée en milieu de moyenne montagne tempérée: le Modèle Couplé (MC) à discrétisation spatiale (Girard et al., 1981) a été appliqué dans les Vosges au bassin versant de la Fecht, où les nombreuses informations climato-hydrologiques et morpho-pédologiques disponibles permettent de tester des méthodes de spatialisation du milieu et de paramétrisation à base physique du modèle.

LE MODELE COUPLE

Le modèle couplé est un modèle conceptuel à discrétisation spatiale utilisant une grille à mailles carrées. Il est constitué de trois modules simulant respectivement l'écoulement de surface, l'écoulement souterrain et les échanges nappes-rivières. Pour cette application, seul le premier module a été utilisé, aucune grande nappe n'étant présente sur le domaine considéré.

Ce modèle de surface est constitué de trois fonctions distinctes interconnectées:

La fonction d'entrée

La fonction d'entrée est constituée par :

(a) un module de chute de neige permettant de différencier les précipitations solides des précipitations liquides,

(b) un module de fonte lente de la neige utilisant une formule de type degrés/jour,
(c) un module de fonte brutale de la neige liée aux redoux de printemps.

La fonction de "production"

La fonction de production (Fig. 1) gère l'eau disponible sur chacune des mailles ainsi que l'écoulement de l'eau, du versant vers le drain principal. Elle est constituée d'un modèle à quatre réservoirs comportant sept paramètres habituellement calibrés:

(a) le premier réservoir conditionne le bilan global. Il est contrôlé par deux paramètres, DCRT et RMAX, qui permettent de déterminer la quantité d'eau disponible pour l'écoulement (EAU).
(b) le deuxième sépare l'écoulement superficiel de l'infiltration dans le sol. Il est contrôlé par le paramètre FN (lame d'eau maximale pouvant s'infiltrer en profondeur durant un pas de temps).
(c) le troisième régule le ruissellement de surface et l'écoulement hypodermique; le quatrième, l'infiltration profonde vers les nappes (dans ce cas, l'eau infiltrée est perdue pour l'écoulement en rivière) ou l'écoulement de base (dans ce cas, l'eau infiltrée est rendue à la rivière). Les paramètres QRMAX et QIMAX (niveaux de débordement) et CQR et CQI (coefficients de vidange) contrôlent ces réservoirs qui, dans la version originale du modèle, suivent une loi de vidange exponentielle.

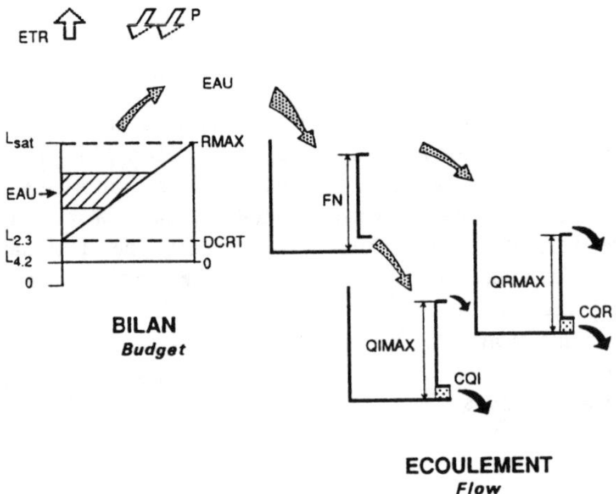

FIG. 1 Fonction de production (d'après Girard et al., 1981).

La fonction de transfert de surface

Cette fonction assure le transfert de l'eau à l'intérieur du bassin en tenant compte de la durée du trajet d'une maille jusqu'à l'exutoire. Ce calcul implique une discrétisation du bassin en zones isochrones regroupant les mailles présentant une durée de trajet identique jusqu'à l'exutoire.

LE BASSIN VERSANT DE LA FECHT

Le bassin versant de la Fecht (Fig. 2) a une superficie de 450 km² à Ostheim. Ce bassin se situe dans les Vosges moyennes près de Colmar. Il est formé de deux vallées principales : celle de la Fecht elle-même (Vallée de Munster), et celle de la Weiss, son affluent le plus important (Vallée de Kaysersberg). Les altitudes sont comprises entre 1362 m, sur la crête vosgienne, et 190 m à la confluence de la Fecht et de la Weiss.

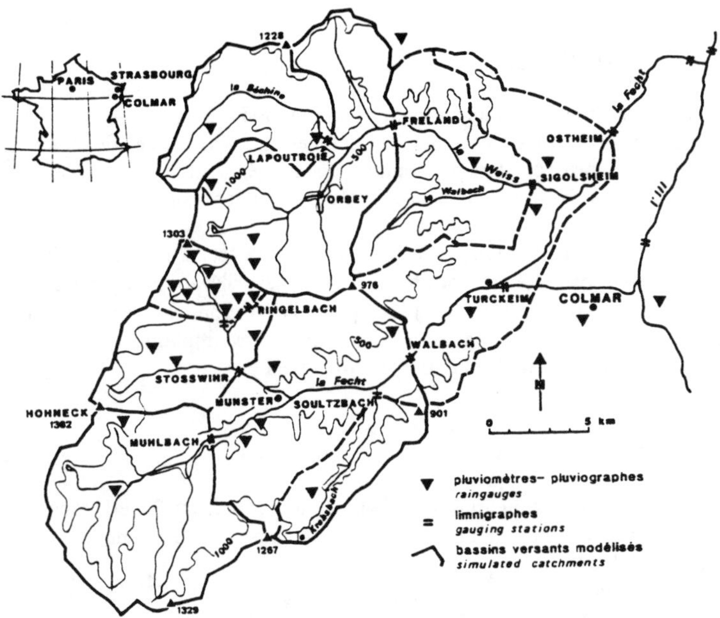

FIG. 2 Equipement climato-hydrologique du bassin versant de la Fecht.

Le substrat est essentiellement granito-gneissique, grauwackeux et gréseux. Les versants ont été façonnés par les actions glaciaires et périglaciaires. Les sols sont généralement très grossiers et riches en matière organique.

Le climat est de type tempéré océanique sur la crête et à tendance continentale dans la plaine. On note l'existence d'un important gradient pluviométrique lié à un effet de foehn entre la crête vosgienne (2000 mm/an) et la plaine d'Alsace (550 mm/an à Colmar). L'étude du champ pluviométrique de cette région (Humbert & Paul 1982) a nécessité l'implantation d'un réseau dense de stations sur le bassin.

Sur les 11 stations limnigraphiques présentes sur le bassin, seules cinq d'entre elles ont été modélisées : Stosswihr (44 km²), Muhlbach (74 km²) et Walbach (211 km²) sur la Fecht; Lapoutroie (38 km²) et Fréland (117 km²) sur la Weiss.

DISCRETISATION DES BASSINS VERSANTS

Pour tenir compte de la grande hétérogénéité spatiale des variables dans ce bassin de montagne, trois types de discrétisation ont été utilisés :

Discrétisation géographique

Elle s'opère au moyen de trois tailles de mailles carrées emboîtées de 1000, 500 et 250 m de côté. Le maillage comprend 739 éléments pour le bassin de la Fecht en amont de Walbach, et 557 pour celui de la Weiss en amont de Fréland.

A chaque maille, sont affectées des valeurs de températures, de précipitations et d'évapotranspiration potentielle, ainsi que des informations physiographiques. La structure du modèle impose la discrétisation du bassin en zones climatologiques et physiographiques homogènes.

Discrétisation climatologique

(a) Définition de zones homogènes de précipitation
16 zones de précipitations ont été définies sur le bassin de la Fecht et cinq sur celui de la Weiss en tenant compte de la répartition des isohyètes et du relief sur chacun des bassins. A chacune de ces zones correspond une station de mesure.
(b) Définition de zones homogènes de température et d'évapotranspiration
Ces 21 zones ont été regroupées en 4 zones d'évapotranspiration, affectée chacune à une station de mesure; de plus, pour la gestion du stock de neige, la température en chaque maille a été estimée en appliquant un gradient altimétrique de 0.5°C/100 m à l'intérieur de ces 4 zones.

Discrétisation physiographique

La discrétisation physiographique des bassins a été effectuée en tenant compte de trois critères importants conditionnant, dans cette région, l'écoulement de l'eau dans le sol (Reutenauer, 1987) :
(a) Un critère géologique et géomorphologique.
Cinq types de formations ont été retenues : les formations superficielles sur granite, sur grauwackes et sur grès, les alluvions fluviatiles et les moraines.
(b) Un critère phyto-pédologique.
En tenant compte de l'augmentation avec l'altitude du taux de matière organique des sols qui contrôle leur rétention hydrique, trois étages phyto-pédologiques ont été définis : un supérieur (au dessus de 1000 m), un moyen (entre 700 et 1000 m) et un inférieur (en dessous de 700m).
(c) Un critère d'occupation des sols.
Il permet de différencier les forêts, les zones non boisées et les lacs.

En tenant compte de ces trois critères, 14 types de fonction de production ont été définis, chacune caractérisée par un jeu de paramètres.

LA PARAMETRISATION DES FONCTIONS D'ENTREE ET DE PRODUCTION

La fonction d'entrée

(a) Le module chute de neige
Considérant la variabilité spatio-temporelle de l'isotherme 0°C au cours de la journée, une relation linéaire entre -1°C (100% de neige) et +1°C (100% de pluie) a été appliquée afin d'estimer le pourcentage de précipitations solides à chaque pas de temps.

(b) Le module fonte de neige
Des températures-seuils de fonte de neige de +1 et +2°C ainsi que des taux de fonte de 3.5 et 4.0 mm/°C/jour (respectivement sous couvert forestier et hors couvert) admis pour le massif vosgien (Humbert, 1986) ont été appliqués.

(c) L'évapotranspiration potentielle
Compte tenu des difficultés pour estimer l'évapotranspiration potentielle (ETP) en milieu de moyenne montagne, celle-ci a été calculée au pas de temps décadaire avec la formule de Turc à partir d'un site de mesures de rayonnement et de quatre sites de mesures des températures. Pour compenser la sous-estimation de l'ETP Turc par rapport à l'ETP Penman (prise comme référence en l'absence de mesures directes d'évapotranspiration), un facteur correctif de 1.2 a été appliqué (Najjar, 1982).

La fonction de production

Les courbes de rétention hydrique des sols étant connues sur le bassin (Reutenauer, 1987), certaines hypothèses ont pu être formulées en tenant compte des analogies qui existent entre le réservoir où s'effectue le bilan hydrique et les sols. En effet, ce réservoir est conditionné par trois limites importantes :

(a) la limite inférieure (en dessous de laquelle l'évapotranspiration est nulle) peut être associée au point de flétrissement, c'est-à-dire à la rétention hydrique à pF4.2 .
(b) la limite intermédiaire (en dessous de laquelle l'écoulement est nul) peut être associée à la capacité au champ c'est-à- dire à la rétention hydrique à pF2.3 .
(c) la limite supérieure qui peut être associée à la rétention hydrique à saturation.

En intégrant les valeurs de rétention hydrique mesurée sur l'ensemble du profil racinaire à saturation, à la capacité au champ et au point de flétrissement, on obtient les valeurs L_{sat}, $L_{2.3}$ et $L_{4.2}$ et, par un simple changement d'origine (Fig. 1):

$$DCRT = L_{2.3} - L_{4.2} \qquad RMAX = L_{sat} - L_{4.2}$$

Pour les fonctions de production de versants, le quatrième réservoir, qui simule l'écoulement de base, peut faire l'objet d'une paramétrisation à base physique. Ce réservoir utilise habituellement une loi de vidange exponentielle. Or, la courbe de tarissement (reliant le débit (Q) au temps (t)) de la Fecht à Walbach, obtenue à partir des périodes de récession en régime non influencé, est de type hyperbolique:

$$Q(t) = Q_r/(1+X_r t)^2 = 90/(1+0.19t)^2$$

L'intégrale de cette formule permet d'estimer la lame d'eau équivalente des réserves (L) du bassin versant et leur coefficient de tarissement (X):

$$L(t) = L_r/(1+X_r t) = 194/(1+0.19t) \qquad X(t) = X_r/(1+X_r t) = 0.19/(1+0.19t)$$

Q_r (m^3/s), X_r (j^{-1}), L_r (mm) étant respectivement un débit, un coefficient de tarissement et une lame d'eau équivalente de référence. Le coefficient de vidange (CQI) du réservoir peut donc être estimer à partir des équations précédentes:

$$CQI = X = (X_r/L_r)\ L = (0.19/194)\ L \qquad (j^{-1})$$

Ce type de courbe de tarissement, caractéristique de nappe peu profonde et bien drainée par la rivière, semble être valable pour ce milieu, puisqu'il a aussi été mis en évidence sur un autre sous-bassin de la Fecht : le Ringelbach (Ambroise, 1988).

Pour la fonction de production des fonds alluviaux des vallées, une forte infiltration profonde vers la nappe (admise dans ce type de matériel alluvial) a été permise, générant ainsi des pertes pour la rivière.

RESULTATS ET INTERPRETATION

Afin de valider au mieux les hypothèses de discrétisation des bassins, de paramétrisation des fonctions du modèle, de calcul de certaines variables, le modèle a été testé sur cinq bassins emboîtés pour une période de cinq ans (1983-1987) rassemblant un éventail très varié de situations climatiques et hydrologiques. Les paramètres DCRT, RMAX, QIMAX et CQI n'ont pas été calibrés : leurs valeurs ont été directement déduites des mesures de terrain ou de laboratoire. Les paramètres FN, QRMAX, CQR qui n'ont pas été l'objet d'une interprétation physique ont été calibrés sur les données d'une seule station (Walbach), pour une seule année très contrastée (1983 - crues exceptionnelles et étiage très marqué).

Globalement, les bilans annuels sont corrects. En effet, l'écart entre les débits observés (Qo) et les débits calculés (Qc) est généralement inférieur à 5% (Tableau 1). La variation de stock pour les cinq années modélisées représente environ 1% de la lame d'eau précipitée: il n'y a donc pas de divergence du bilan hydrologique lors de la modélisation en continu. L'évapotranspiration réelle (ETR) est très proche de l'évapotranspiration potentielle, ce qui est normal dans ce type d'environnement. L'infiltration (I) vers la nappe alluviale est inférieure à 50 mm/an à Walbach soit moins de 5% des précipitations, ce qui semble correct compte tenu de la faible extention des formations alluviales sur le bassin.
La simulation des hydrogrammes au pas de temps journalier est satisfaisante (Fig. 3). Les phénomènes de chute et de fonte de neige sont assez bien pris en compte par le modèle. Deux critères d'efficacité du modèle ont été calculés :

$$E \;=\; \Sigma(Qc - Qo)^2 \;/\; (Qc - \overline{Qo})^2$$

$$LE \;=\; \Sigma(Log_{10}Qc - Log_{10}Qo)^2 \;/\; (Log_{10}Qc - Log_{10}\overline{Qo})^2$$

Le critère E nous permet d'apprécier globalement l'efficacité du modèle, le critère LE relativise l'importance des hautes eaux. Les efficacités sont généralement supérieures à 80%. Les résultats de deux simulations sont présentées ici (Tableau 1) : la première (1) utilise pour simuler l'écoulement de base la loi de vidange exponentielle du modèle originel, la seconde (2) utilise une loi de vidange hyperbolique. L'amélioration du critère LE (et donc de la simulation des tarissements et des étiages) entre l'essai 1 et l'essai 2 est très nette.

Quelques imperfections subsistent encore dans cette modélisation.
Certaines sont liées aux données utilisées. Ainsi, pour la station de Stosswihr, où la validité de la courbe de tarage en basses eaux est douteuse pour cette période, on note un écart important entre les débits observés et les débits calculés. Les valeurs de LE y sont particulièrement faibles. De même, pour l'année 1986, on constate une sous-estimation marquée des débits calculés et ce, quelle que soit la station considérée. Cette sous-estimation est due à une valeur trop importante de l'évapotranspiration potentielle (liée à une surestimation du rayonnement global mesuré). De plus, la comparaison entre les hydrogrammes calculés et observés en valeurs logarithmiques montre, et ce quelle que soit l'année, un décalage peu important mais systématique entre les décrues observées et calculées (Fig. 3b). Ce phénomène est en partie lié au décalage temporel qui existe entre les données de débits (collectées de 0 à 24h) et les données de précipitations (collectées de 8h à 8h).

TABLEAU 1 Bilans hydrologiques annuels et efficacités du modèle.

	Stations	S km²	P mm	I mm	ETR mm	Qc mm	Qo mm	Qc/Qo	E-1 exponent.	LE-1	E-2 hyperbol.	LE-2
1	Walbach	211	1572	57	623	938	905	1.04	0.91	0.67	0.91	0.87
9	Muhlbach	74	2036	31	616	1393	1340	1.04	0.88	0.64	0.87	0.87
8	Stosswihr	44	1767	42	599	1164	1290	0.90	0.92	-0.83	0.91	0.27
3	Fréland	117	1580	49	615	915	935	0.98			0.83	0.70
	Lapoutroie	38	1653	52	619	1021						
1	Walbach	211	1360	32	575	754	780	0.97	0.84	0.82	0.89	0.88
9	Muhlbach	74	1760	18	557	1222	1218	1.00	0.80	0.48	0.82	0.79
8	Stosswihr	44	1462	23	554	923	1110	0.83	0.79	0.22	0.80	0.65
4	Fréland	117	1377	33	575	766	745	1.03			0.82	0.82
	Lapoutroie	38	1516	41	577	925	825	1.12			0.57	0.61
1	Walbach	211	1074	20	573	492	514	0.96	0.80	-0.11	0.80	0.72
9	Muhlbach	74	1415	13	607	808	770	1.05	0.72	0.01	0.73	0.69
8	Stosswihr	44	1232	18	597	637	646	0.88	0.30	-1.69	0.36	-0.60
5	Fréland	117	1060	20	596	496	520	0.95			0.75	0.28
	Lapoutroie	38	1162	25	609	601	572	1.05			0.62	0.67
1	Walbach	211	1622	40	638	895	1010	0.89	0.86	0.69	0.86	0.86
9	Muhlbach	74	2136	23	638	1462	1560	0.94	0.81	0.45	0.80	0.75
8	Stosswihr	44	1754	29	635	1087	1270	0.86	0.72	-0.79	0.75	0.19
6	Fréland	117	1579	37	649	812	897	0.91			0.71	0.68
	Lapoutroie	38	1677	44	650	971	1068	0.91			0.59	0.79
1	Walbach	211	1495	33	608	881	920	0.96	0.82	0.84	0.80	0.88
9	Muhlbach	74	1945	21	582	1393	1450	0.96	0.79	0.67	0.79	0.84
8	Stosswihr	44	1694	29	586	1121	1160	0.97	0.47	0.24	0.52	0.58
7	Fréland	117	1571	40	603	942	960	0.98			0.73	0.81
	Lapoutroie	38	1679	48	606	1077	1140	0.94			0.62	0.78

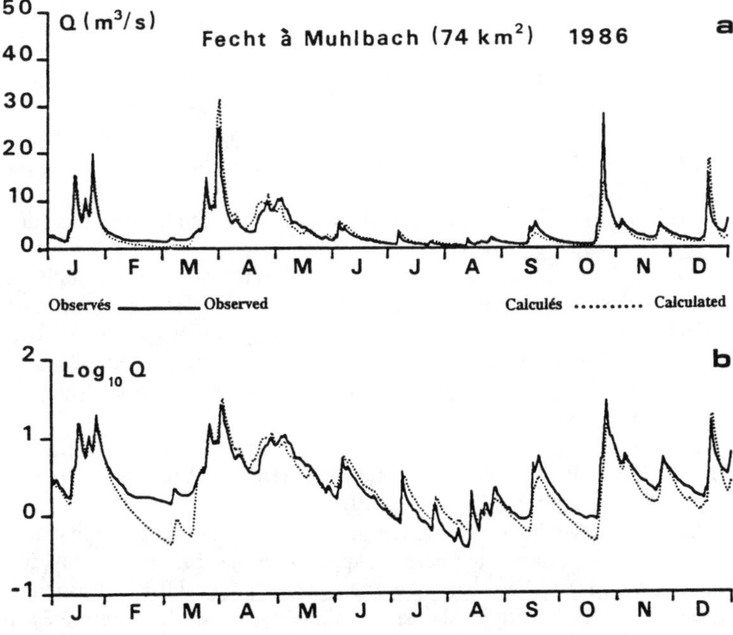

FIG. 3 Exemple d'hydrogrammes observés et calculés.

D'autres sont plus directement liées à la modélisation des processus. Ainsi, la forte augmentation de la pente de la courbe de tarissement lors de périodes caniculaires n'a pu être modélisée. Ce phénomène est d'autant plus sensible sur les hauts bassins que l'on y note très souvent la présence de surfaces saturées en eau. Le deuxième processus qui n'a pu être modélisé est aussi directement lié à l'existence de ces surfaces saturées. En effet, lors des précipitations orageuses d'été, le ruissellement observé sur les surfaces saturées (1% du bassin de la Fecht en amont de Walbach), représente une part importante du débit observé à l'exutoire, les précipitations tombées sur le reste du bassin ne servant qu'à recharger le profil pédologique -concept de zones contributives variables (Cappus, 1960).

CONCLUSION

La reconstitution satisfaisante des bilans annuels et des hydrogrammes montrent la validité régionale, dans ce milieu de moyenne montagne, du découpage naturaliste du bassin en unités homogènes en fonction du relief, ainsi que des hypothèses nous ayant permis d'interpréter de façon physique certains paramètres du modèle. Cette démarche nous a permis de limiter sensiblement la part de la calibration dans les simulations. Cependant, l'une des limites de ce modèle est de ne pas tenir compte de la dynamique des zones saturées lors de la simulation des processus de génération du débit ainsi que de l'évapotranspiration durant les périodes estivales.

REMERCIEMENTS Nous exprimons toute notre reconnaissance à M. Georges GIRARD (ORSTOM, Ecole des Mines de Paris) pour la mise à disposition du Modèle Couplé.
Ce travail a été réalisé dans le cadre du Programme PIREN-Eau/Alsace (CNRS, Ministère de l'Environnement, Région Alsace) et de l'Action Thématique Programmée CNRS-INRA-ORSTOM-CIRAD 1986-89.

REFERENCES

Ambroise, B. (1988) Interactions eaux souterraines - eaux de surface dans le bassin versant du Ringelbach à Soultzeren (Hautes Vosges, France) : Rôle hydrologique des surfaces saturées. Interaction entre eaux souterraines et eaux de surface, (Proc. IAHR Symp., Ystad (S), 30/05-3/06/1988). P. Dahlblom et G. Lindh (Eds), Lund Univ., 231-238.

Cappus, P. (1960) Bassin expérimental d'Alrance - Etude des lois de l'écoulement. La Houille Blanche n°A, 493-520.

Girard, G., Ledoux, E. & Villeneuve, J.P. (1981) Le modèle couplé, simulation conjointe des écoulements de surface et des écoulements souterrains sur un système hydrologique. Cah. ORSTOM, série hydrologie, vol. XVIII, n°4, 191-280.

Humbert, J. (1986) Estimation et rôle de la fonte nivale dans l'écoulement de crue des rivières des Hautes Vosges (bassin de la Fecht, Haut-Rhin). Rev. Géogr. de l'Est (1-2), 27-56.

Humbert, J. & Paul, P. (1982) La répartition spatiale des précipitations dans le bassin versant de la Petite Fecht à Soultzeren (Hautes Vosges) : Premiers résultats. Rech. Géogr. à Strasbourg, 19/20/21, 105-122.

Najjar, G. (1982) Méthode de cartographie de l'évapotranspiration journalière moyenne en moyenne montagne tempérée. Application au bassin versant du Ringelbach (Hautes Vosges). Thèse de doctorat de 3e cycle, ULP, Strasbourg.

Reutenauer, D. (1987) Etude de la variabilité spatiale des propriétés physiques et hydriques de sols et des formations superficielles du bassin versant de la Fecht, en amont de Turckeim (Haut-Rhin).- Thèse de doctorat de ULP, Strasbourg.

Hydrology in Mountainous Regions. I - Hydrological Measurements; the Water Cycle (Proceedings of two Lausanne Symposia, August 1990). IAHS Publ. no. 193, 1990.

Simulation of daily runoff in a mountainous catchment using the Tank model

K. S. RAMASASTRI
National Institute of Hydrology
Roorkee, 247667, India

ABSTRACT Tank model developed by Sugawara has been used to simulate daily streamflow of Malaprabha. The catchment area of Malaprabha upto discharge measuring site Khanapur is 326.0 sq.km. Using daily observed flow data of Malaprabha at Khanapur for the period 1981 to 1985, the tank model has been calibrated. The calibrated model has been used to simulate daily streamflows during 1984 and 1985 which were found to be within 10% of observed streamflows.

INTRODUCTION

Different rainfall runoff models are in use in India for simulation of daily runoff. Tank model is a simple conceptual rainfall runoff model developed in Japan by Sugawara (1967). Application of tank model for hydrological studies in India has been rather limited. 4 x 4 tank model for daily analysis was used by Datta (1984) for simulating daily streamflows in two sub-basins in Central India. Kandaswamy et al (1989) applied tank model for simulation of daily stream flows in two mountainous rivers in Southern India.

In this paper the application of tank model for simulation of daily streamflows of a mountainous river in western India is described.

STUDY AREA

The Malaprabha rises in the western ghats in southern India at an elevation of 793 m and joins river Krishna at an elevation of 488 m. Average annual rainfall over Malaprabha catchment is 675 mm. The South west monsoon(mid June to mid October) accounts for nearly 80% of the normal annual rainfall. The catchment of Malaprabha upto the gauge site Khanapur and location of raingauges is shown in Figure 1.

DATA

Data of daily rainfall and discharge for the period 1981 to 1985 and mean vaues of 'evapotranspiration were used in the analysis. The observed daily dischare data for the years 1981, 1982 and 1983 was used for calibration and the data for the years 1984 and 1985 was used for testing.

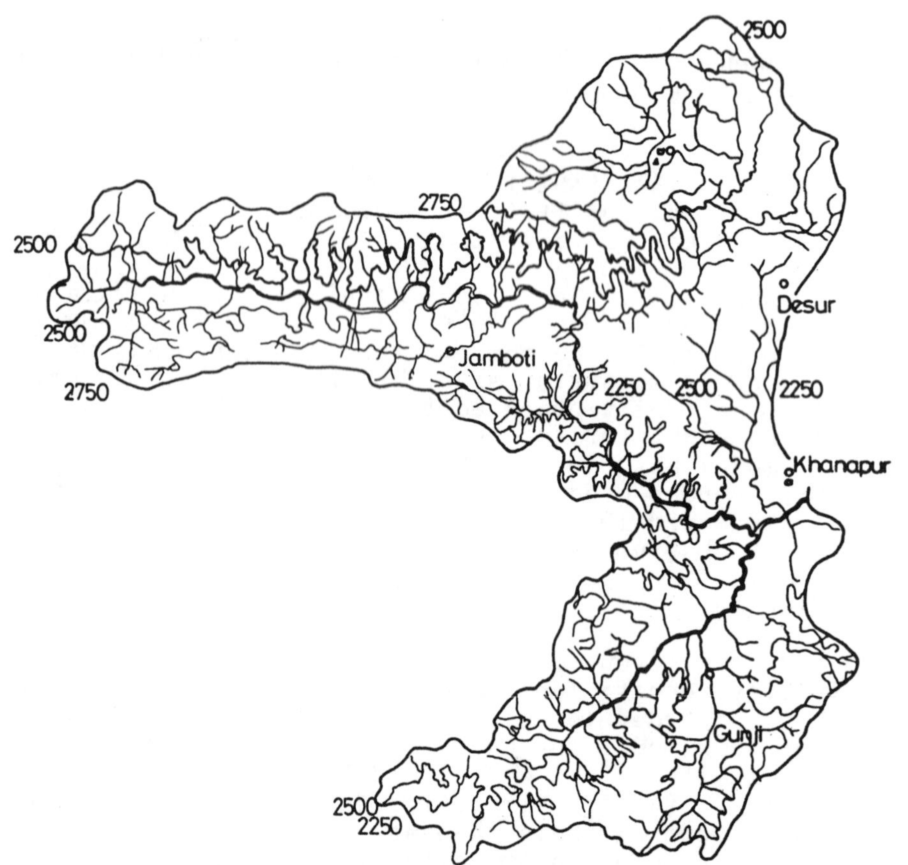

FIG.1 Catchment plan of Malaprabha upto Khanapur.

APPLICATION OF TANK MODEL

From the recession slopes of observed flood hydrographs, average value of recession coefficient (α)was calculated and the initial set of values of parameers for different tanks have been selected as

Top Tank .. $A_o=A_1=A_2=0.115$ HA1=15, HA2=40

2nd Tank .. $B_o=B_1=0.023$ HB=15

3rd Tank .. $C_o=C_1=0.0046$, HC=15

Primary and secondary soil moisture were taken as 50 and 250 mm respectively. The correction factors for precipitation CP and WE were taken as equal to 1.0. Initial storage of four tanks were assumed to be zero.

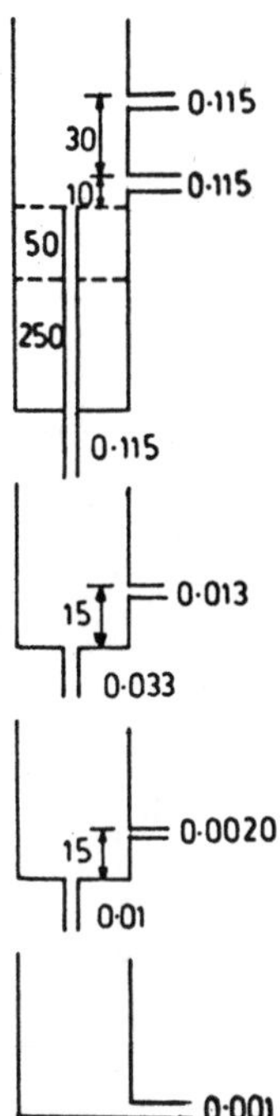

FIG.2 Tank Model for Daily Analysis of Malaprabha Basin.

Calibration of the Model

The tank model for the catchment was calibrated using the daily rainfall and streamflow during the years 1981, 1982 and 1983.

The coefficient of discharge and initial loss head parameters were adjusted starting from the top tank. The calibration of the model was done by trial and error by matching the computed daily flows with the observed flows. The parameters of the calibrated model are shown in Fig.2.

Testing of the Model

The calibrated model has been tested with observed flow data of 1984 and 1985. The computed hydrograph for 1985 together with the observed is given in Fig.3.

DISCUSSION

The model simulated the flows satisfactorily during 1984 and 1985. The performance of the model was relatively better in 1985 due to the fact that the model is a continuous model and the antecedant conditions are well represented in the second year. There is appreciable variation in surface flow and comparatively less variation in the interflow and sub-baseflow.

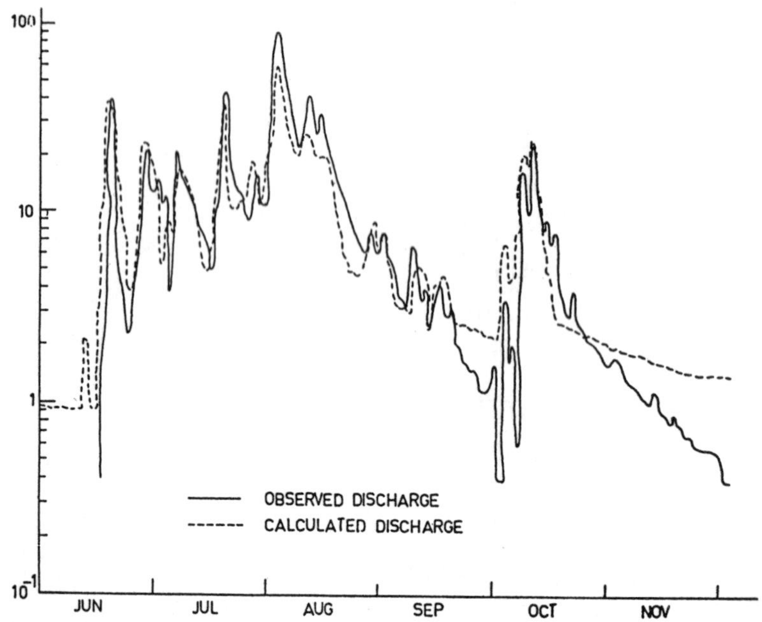

FIG.3 Daily Flow Hydrographs of Malaprabha Basin for 1985 obtained by Tank Model for Daily analys

CONCLUSIONS

The tank model though simple is quite versatile with wide range of applicability. The model is best suited to catchments with data availability limited to a few parameters like rainfall and streamflow. The model simulated high flows better than the flow flows. From the experience of the application of the Tank model to mountainous catchments in different parts of India it can be said that the model is suited to Indian catchments.

REFERENCES

Datta,B (1984) Runoff analysis of two Indian basins using tank model. Research note 55, National Research Center f Disaster Prevention, Japan.

Sugawara,M (1967) On the analysis of runoff structure about several Japanese rivers. Japanese Journal of Geophysics 2 (4).

Hydrology in Mountainous Regions. I - Hydrological Measurements; the Water Cycle
(Proceedings of two Lausanne Symposia, August 1990). IAHS Publ. no. 193, 1990.

Snowmelt runoff forecasts in Colorado with remote sensing

A. RANGO & V. VAN KATWIJK
USDA Hydrology Laboratory, Agricultural Research Service,
Beltsville, Maryland 20705 U.S.A.
J. MARTINEC
Federal Institute for Snow and Avalanche Research,
CH-7260 Weissfluhjoch/Davos, Switzerland

ABSTRACT Some evidence exists to indicate that remote sensing of snow cover areal extent can be used to improve the performance of snowmelt runoff models. The Snowmelt Runoff Model (SRM) already accepts snow covered area and several additional models are being revised to accept this remote sensing input. Modified snow cover depletion curves have been developed to permit SRM snowmelt runoff forecasts of three types, namely, seasonal volume, short-term daily flows, and long-term daily flows. The method of forecasting was tested on the Rio Grande basin in Colorado for 1987. The method was evaluated to be successful in producing useful SRM forecast hydrographs. Forecast improvements resulted when the forecasted discharge was updated with actual observations every seven days.

INTRODUCTION

The transition from snowmelt runoff simulations to operational forecasts in real time is outlined by examples from basins in the Rocky Mountains. In order to forecast runoff using the Snowmelt-Runoff Model (SRM), air temperatures and precipitation amounts are required for the forecasting period. The third variable, the areal extent of the seasonal snow cover, is currently measured by satellites. The depletion curves of the snow coverage are projected into the future by using temperature forecasts and a set of so called modified depletion curves which should be derived for the basin in question.

EXAMPLES OF AN OPERATIONAL FORECAST

When a flood situation developed in the Spring of 1983 in Cache La Poudre basin (2732 km^2, 1596-4133 m a.s.l.) of Colorado, a private company was asked by the local water authority to forecast the time and magnitude of the flood peak to allow sufficient time for instituting adequate protective measures. Special short-term meteorological forecasts of temperature and precipitation were prepared and aircraft flights over the basin were carried out in order to evaluate the snow covered areas separately for three elevation zones. The authors of the forecast reported (Jones et al., 1984) that the 1-3 day forecasts during the critical period by SRM were within 20% of the measured streamflow values. These short term forecasts do not require an extrapolation of the depletion curves of the snow coverage to an extended future period. Such extrapolation, however, is necessary if the day-by-day forecast should extend to several weeks or to the whole snowmelt season. Therefore, a method was developed (Martinec, 1985), to derive the course of the depletion curves from the forecasted trends of air temperatures.

ROLE OF SNOW COVER MAPPING IN RUNOFF MODELLING

The gradual decline of the areal extent is a typical feature of the seasonal snow cover in the ablation period. Before the advent of remote sensing it was difficult to measure this variable in remote mountain basins. In addition, measurements must be repeated periodically. Consequently, in order to minimize measurement problems, the first attempts were limited to small experimental basins. In view of this situation, most developers of snowmelt runoff models adapted rainfall runoff models to snow conditions without paying special attention to the actual areal extent of the snow cover. In a worldwide intercomparison of snowmelt runoff models conducted by the World Meteorological Organization (WMO) (1986) this proved to be a disadvantage.

Only one model in the WMO intercomparison, SRM, used remote sensing input (satellite snow cover extent) for producing the simulations of snowmelt runoff. SRM achieved a better overall accuracy than the non-remote sensing models in the WMO study, especially when maximum inaccuracies for all years tested are considered as shown in Fig. 1. The definitions of the accuracy criteria in Fig. 1 are given in the WMO report (WMO, 1986).

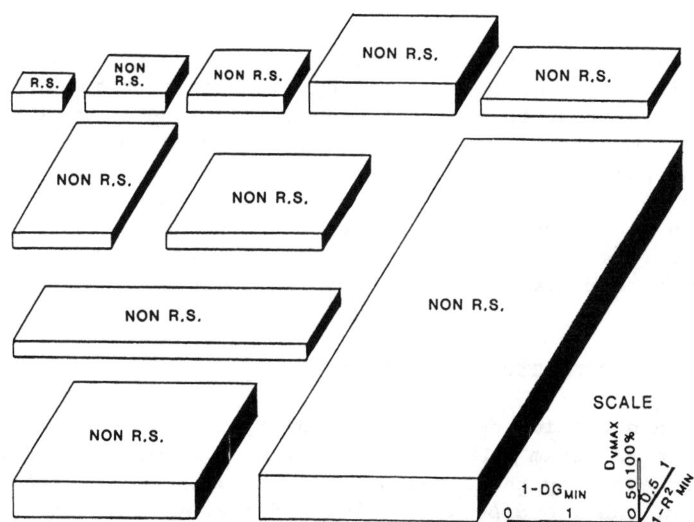

FIG. 1 Combined representation of model performance with regard to the coefficient of determination, R^2, the coefficient of gain from daily means, DG, and the runoff volume deviation, D_v. The volumes of the prisms indicate the maximum inaccuracies of the respective models from results listed in the WMO snowmelt season tables. R.S. refers to a model with remote sensing input and NON R.S. to models without remote sensing inputs (after Martinec & Rango, 1989).

Thus, the areal extent of the seasonal snow cover has proved to be a powerful tool in snowmelt runoff modelling. It is therefore worthwhile to reinforce the position of snow cover mapping in planning future remote sensing programs. At the same time, it is necessary to develop methods for using satellite snow cover data without delay and even with a projection to the future. In fact, several modellers participating in the WMO intercomparison are now incorporating remote sensing inputs into their models (Leavesley and Stannard, 1990; Fortin et al., 1990).

FORECASTS OF SNOW COVERED AREAS

As was explained elsewhere (Hall & Martinec, 1985), the conventional (snow cover versus time) depletion curves of snow covered areas do not unequivocally reveal the initial accumulation of snow. The future course of these curves cannot be forecasted because a shallow snow cover will decline rapidly and a deep snow cover slowly, with the same forecasted air temperatures. Modified snow cover depletion curves have been proposed (Martinec, 1985) to determine the snow accumulation at the start of the snowmelt season in terms of the areal average water equivalent. Figure 2 shows a set of these curves derived for the Rio Grande basin above Del Norte, Colorado (3419 km^2, 2432-4215 m a.s.l.) (Rango & van Katwijk, 1990). If only a single year is available, with no direct measurements of the water equivalent, a modified depletion curve indicates the initial snow accumulation only after the snowmelt season is completed. With a set of curves, it is possible to compare, in real time, snow covered areas from satellites with the corresponding totalized snowmelt depths and thus determine, several weeks after the beginning of the snowmelt season, which modified depletion curve is valid in the current year. If the water equivalent of snow is measured in the basin, the proper modified depletion curve can be selected at the start of the snowmelt season by using these measurements as an index of the snow accumulation in the given year. It should be remembered that the effect of intermittent snowfalls during the snowmelt period is excluded. In other words, the energy input (represented by degree-days) spent for melting new snow does not count in computing the cumulative snowmelt in Fig. 2.

SNOWMELT RUNOFF FORECASTS

When an appropriate modified depletion curve for the current year is identified, it is possible to issue the following runoff forecasts:

(a) Seasonal forecast of the runoff volume.
The initial water volume stored in the snow cover corresponds to the area below the curve. The resulting water volume must be reduced by a runoff coefficient and increased by an expected contribution from precipitation. The seasonal forecast can be repeated on later dates according to the cumulative computed snowmelt depth to date or if snow coverage data becomes available.

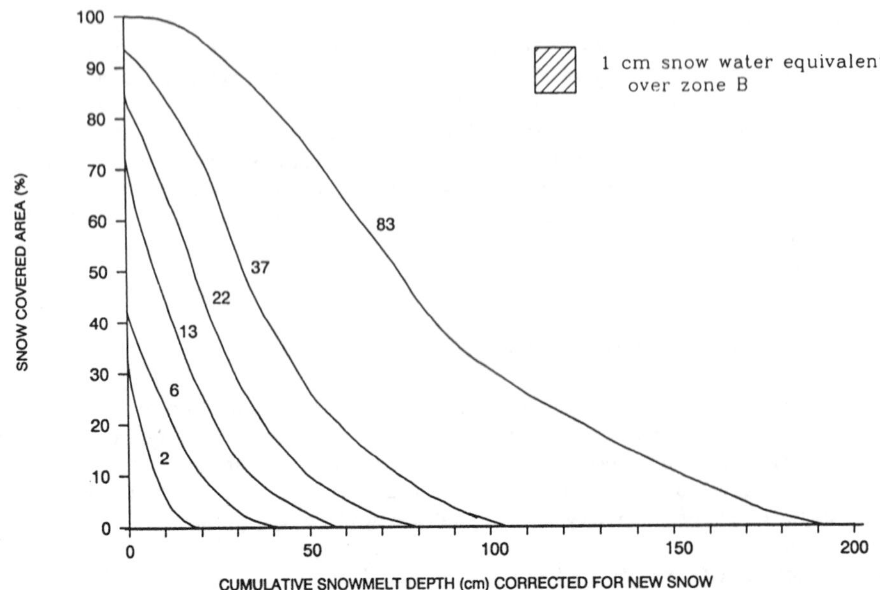

FIG. 2 Nomograph of modified snow cover depletion curves indicating the estimated areal average water equivalent of snow (cm) on 1 April in elevation zone B (2925-3353 m a.s.l.) of the Rio Grande basin above Del Norte, Colorado.

(b) Periodical short term forecast (e.g., weekly) of daily flows. Predetermined SRM parameters are used (Martinec & Rango, 1986) together with forecasted temperatures and precipitation. The future course of the conventional depletion curve of the snow coverage is evaluated from the modified depletion curve and from the temperature forecast. The model computations can be updated weekly by taking into account the actual discharge instead of the computed discharge.

(c) Seasonal forecast of daily flows. Predetermined SRM parameters are again used. The seasonal hydrograph can be computed for the following assumptions: average temperatures and precipitation to be expected, or various combinations of minimum and maximum values to be expected, or probable stochastic series of these two variables.

For each temperature series to be applied, the modified depletion curve is again used to forecast the snow covered areas for the entire snowmelt season so that the daily values can be used in running the model.

RUNOFF FORECASTS IN THE RIO GRANDE BASIN

Apart from the three mentioned variables and the area-elevation curve of the basin, the following parameters must be predetermined to run the SRM model:

degree-day factor [a]
runoff coefficients for snow and rain [c_S, c_R]
temperature lapse rate [LR]
critical temperature for snow/rain [T_c]
time lag [TL]
recession coefficient as a function of the current discharge [k]

With SRM, runoff simulations with historical data are not used for arithmetical optimizing or calibration of the parameters, but rather to verify values which can be expected from the hydrological and physical point of view. Figure 3 shows a SRM simulation for the year 1983 which is one of the 10 years of historical simulations on the Rio Grande basin. After this historical verification, the following average parameter values are ready to be used in a forecast year:

$a = 0.32\text{-}0.57\ cm^{o}C^{-1}day^{-1}$; $c_S = 0.24\text{-}0.68$; $c_R = 0.15\text{-}0.60$;
$LR = 0.65\text{-}0.95^{o}C/100\ m$; $T_c = 0.75\text{-}2.5^{o}C$; TL = 14 hrs; and
$k = 0.9823\ Q^{-0.0214}$. To demonstrate the real time conditions, it would be appropriate to use temperatures and precipitation forecasts as they are issued by meteorological offices. Such data were not available in Colorado. They were also not available in a recent WMO project (Askew, 1989) which aimed at demonstrating real time conditions. The measured temperatures and precipitation were used, so that the only simulation of real time conditions consisted in data being distributed at the same time to model operators and the model runs had to be done without delay.

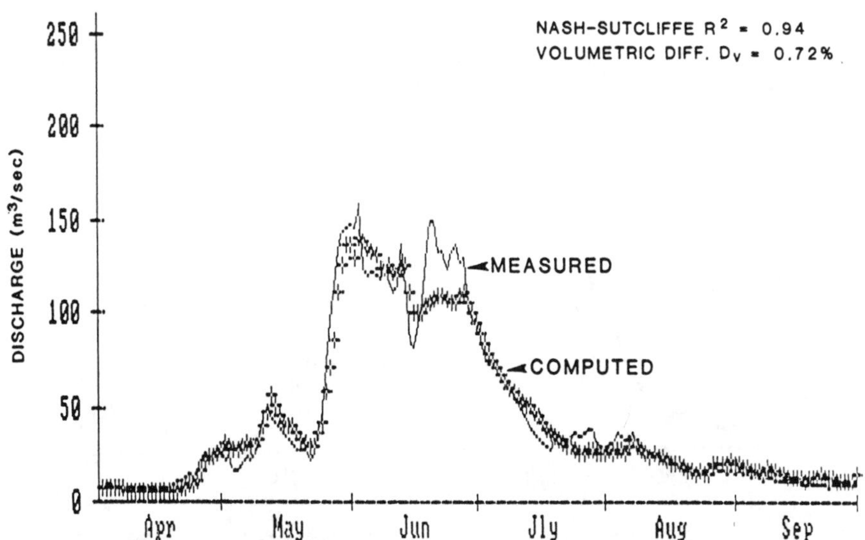

FIG. 3 Snowmelt runoff simulation for 1983 on the Rio Grande basin above Del Norte, Colorado using SRM.

In this paper, in order to come closer to real time conditions, the U.S. Soil Conservation Service was consulted to furnish what could be considered as forecasted temperatures and precipitation for the test forecast year 1987. They directed us to use long term average daily

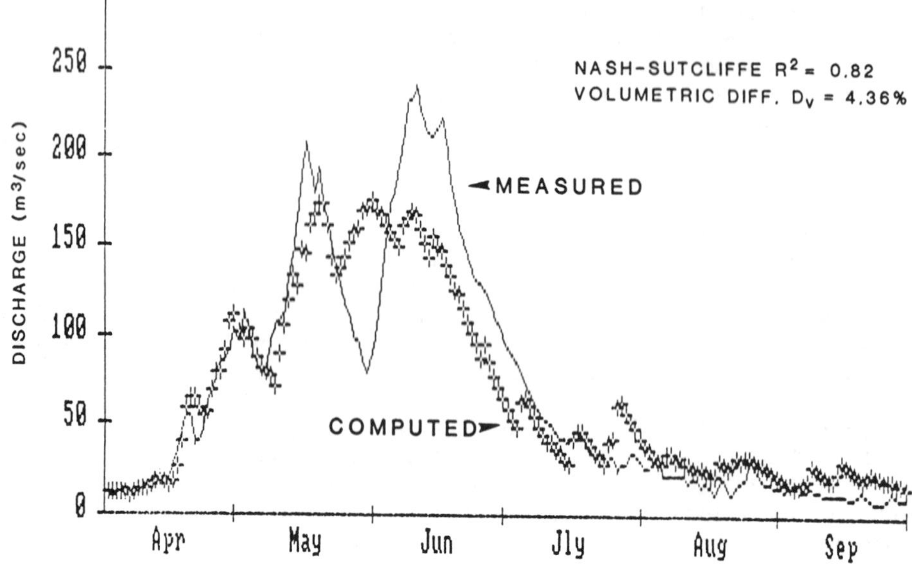

FIG. 4 Snowmelt runoff forecast for 1987 on the Rio Grande basin using SRM.

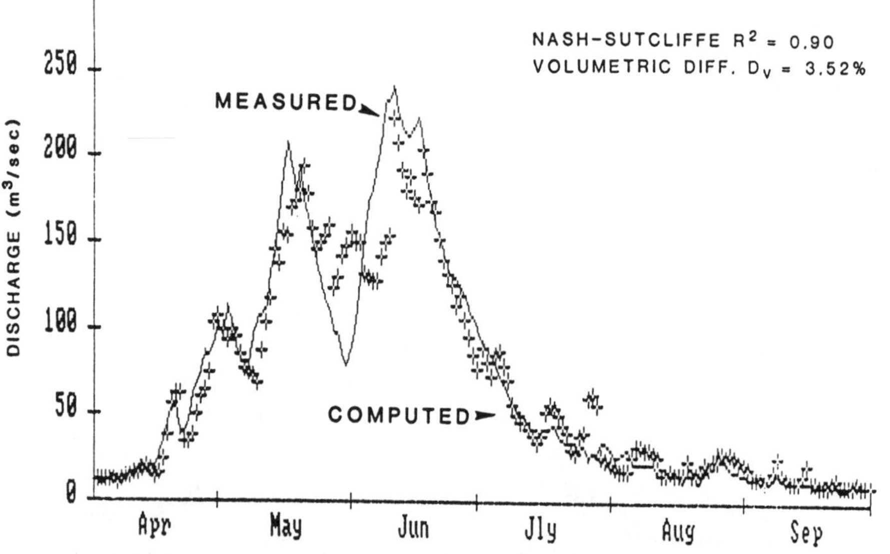

FIG. 5 Snowmelt runoff forecast for 1987 on the Rio Grande basin using SRM and updates with actual streamflow every seven days.

minima and maxima for temperature and 110% of average monthly precipitation totals scattered randomly through the respective months. Thus the snow covered areas had to be extrapolated, using the nomograph in Fig. 2 and long term average temperatures for each day of the year instead of correct temperatures.

In view of this deteriorated quality of input variables, the "forecasted" hydrograph is less accurate than the simulated hydrograph, as shown in Fig. 4. It is possible, however, to improve it by a weekly updating, that is to say by starting each forecast for the next seven days using the last measured discharge (Rango & van Katwijk, 1989). Figure 5 shows that the agreement of daily flows in late May and June has been improved with this very limited kind of updating.

CONCLUSIONS

At the moment, few snowmelt runoff models include the areal distribution of the snow as obtained from remote sensing as an input. SRM profited from such remote sensing input in a WMO intercomparison of snowmelt runoff models when simulated hydrographs were required. In order to provide forecasts with SRM, it is necessary to develop modified snow cover depletion curves. When combined with temperature forecasts, the modified depletion curves can be used to project the snow cover extent into the forecast period. This makes possible three types of runoff forecasts, namely, seasonal forecasts of snowmelt volume, periodical short term forecasts of daily flows, and seasonal forecasts of daily flows. The method of forecasting was tested on the Rio Grande basin in Colorado for 1987. SRM was evaluated to be successful for producing forecast hydrographs. Forecast improvements resulted from updating the forecasted discharge with actual observations every seven days.

REFERENCES

Askew, A. J. (1989) Real-time intercomparison of hydrological models. New Directions for Surface Water Modeling (Proceedings of the Baltimore Symposium), IAHS Publication No. 181, 125-132.

Fortin, J-P., Villeneuve, J-P, Bocquillon, C., Leconte, R. & Harvey, K. D. (1990) HYDROTEL - A hydrological model designed to make use of remotely sensed and GIS data. Proceedings of the Workshop on Application of Remote Sensing in Hydrology, National Hydrology Research Institute, Saskatoon, Saskatchewan.

Hall, D. K. & Martinec, J. (1985) Remote Sensing of Ice and Snow. Chapman and Hall, London, U.K.

Jones, E. B., Frick, D. M., Barker, P. R. & Allum, J. (1984) Application of a snowmelt runoff model for flood prediction. Unpublished report, Resource Consultants, Inc., Fort Collins, Colorado.

Leavesley, G. H. & Stannard, L. G. (1990) Application of remotely sensed data in a distributed-parameter watershed model. Proceedings of the Workshop on Application of Remote Sensing in Hydrology, National Hydrology Research Institute, Saskatoon, Saskatechewan.

Martinec, J. (1985) Snowmelt runoff models for operational forecasts. Nordic Hydrology 16, 129-136.

Martinec, J. & Rango, A. (1986) Parameter values for snowmelt runoff modelling. Journal of Hydrology 84, 197-219.

Martinec, J. & Rango, A. (1989) Merits of statistical criteria for the performance of hydrological models. Water Resources Bulletin 25, 421-432.

Rango, A. & van Katwijk, V. (1990) Development and testing of a snowmelt-runoff forecasting technique. Water Resources Bulletin 26.

World Meteorological Organization (1986) Intercomparison of models of snowmelt runoff. Operational Hydrology Report No. 23, Geneva, Switzerland.

Hydrology in Mountainous Regions. I - Hydrological Measurements; the Water Cycle
(Proceedings of two Lausanne Symposia, August 1990). IAHS Publ. no. 193, 1990.

Prise en compte de la variabilité spatiale des pluies efficaces par un modèle semi-global: extension de la méthode DPFT à des cas bi-entrées

J.Y. RODRIGUEZ
EDF-DTG. Sce Ressources en Eau B.P. 4348, 31029 Toulouse Cx, FRANCE
Ch. OBLED
Institut de Mécanique de Grenoble. B.P. 53X, 38041 Grenoble Cx,FRANCE

ABSTRACT The DPFT-ERUHDIT approach (Excess Rainfall and Unit Hydrograph by Deconvolution and Identification Technique) is a Unit Hydrograph approach which supplies **both** the average transfer function and a set of consistent excess rainfall, without any prior assumption concerning the production function. The excess rainfall is subsequently used together with the raw rainfall data to fit the parameters of any kind of production function which may be suitable for the case-study at hand. Even if this operational approach provides good results on more than 20 basins, the lumped structure is far from be valid on some others, particulary in mountainous regions. This assumption is first briefly reviewed in a Unit Hydrograph context, in order to extend the the DPFT-ERUHDIT approach to bi-inputs cases, for which it provides two averages responses and two sets of excess rainfalls, one for each basin. The results of a case study (the Petite Creuse basin, 840 km^2) comparing the classical single-input, single-output model and this new double-input extension show the little improvements offered by taking into account the rainfall distribution in a semi-lumped manner.

INTRODUCTION

D'un point de vue opérationnel, les modèles simples, et souvent globaux, sont préférés aux modèles plus complexes, distribués, qui nécessitent une quantité d'information difficile à satisfaire.

La méthode DPFT (Différence Première de la Fonction de Transfert) est une technique d'identification adaptée à l'approche globale de type Hydrogramme Unitaire, où la transformation pluie-débit se représente par un modèle associant une fonction de production suivie d'un modèle de transfert.

Son principal intérêt est de fournir **simultanément** une fonction de transfert **et** la série des pluies efficaces de chaque épisode, sans faire d'hypothèses préalables sur la structure du modèle de production. Dans un deuxième temps, cela permet de choisir et d'ajuster les paramètres de la fonction supposée représenter correctement la production du bassin. Le problème ainsi posé se ramène alors à une simple ajustement de type entrée-sortie.

Une dizaine d'applications issues de l'approche DPFT sont exploitées couramment par Electricité de France dans des systèmes d'annonce de crues, donnant des résultats opérationnels satisfaisants. Néanmoins, sur des bassins où l'on peut craindre que la variabilité spatiale du processus de transformation pluie-débit est prépondérante, les performances de l'approche globale sont moins bonnes.

Cet article s'intéresse donc à une spatialisation simple des modèles de type Hydrogramme Unitaire. Il présente d'abord très brièvement la méthode DPFT, et évoque les situations où l'on commet, en admettant que la pluie efficace est uniforme, une erreur d'appréciation importante. Parmi les différentes solutions envisagées pour inclure des informations sur la distribution spatiale des champs de pluie dans le modèle, le choix d'une version bi-entrées est proposée. A titre d'illustration, on comparera sur le bassin de la Petite Creuse à Puy-Rageaud (840 km^2) les résultats de l'approche globale et ceux de cette approche bi-entrée.

PRESENTATION SOMMAIRE DE LA METHODE DPFT

S'appuyant sur une approche de type Hydrogramme Unitaire, elle suppose donc que la pluie reçue sur le bassin, appelée pluie brute (PB), se transforme en débit par passage successif à travers deux fonctions:

- Une fonction de production, transformant la pluie brute PB en pluie efficace PE, qui se retrouve sous forme de débit de ruissellement à l'exutoire. Cette fonction généralement non-linéaire dépend aussi des conditions antérieures du bassin.
- Une fonction de transfert H, linéaire et invariante, qui étale dans le temps la pluie efficace PE sous forme de débit de ruissellement Q. Un débit de base Q_B lui est habituellement ajouté pour donner le débit total mesuré à l'exutoire Q_T.

Dans les approches classiques de type Hydrogramme Unitaire, la fonction de production est souvent imposée au préalable, avant identification de la fonction de transfert . Dans le meilleur des cas, seuls les paramètres de la fonction de production sont remis en question. Il va de soi que les résultats obtenus par ce procédé dépendent fortement du concept qu'on s'est fait "a priori" du mécanisme de production.

L'approche DPFT s'affranchit de ce préjugé en identifiant simultanément la fonction de transfert moyenne H **et** la série de pluies efficaces PE de chaque épisode, à partir des simples mesures disponibles de pluie brute PB et des débits à l'exutoire Q_T. Elle utilise pour cela l'algorithme itératif alterné proposé initialement par Newton et Vinyard (1967), amélioré depuis par Guillot et Duband (1980), puis par Versiani (1983), Nalbantis (1987) et Rodriguez (1989). Le principe en est le suivant :

A chaque itération (i) , on résout alternativement :

- *L'identification de la fonction de transfert* $H_{(i)}$: partant d'un estimateur des pluies efficaces $PE_{(i-1)}$ pour chaque épisode, (obtenu à l'itération précédente), et de la série de débits Q_T, on identifie les nouveaux coefficients $H_{(i)}$ de la fonction de transfert moyenne du bassin, cela sur un jeu **multi-événements** (Mays et Coles, 1980). Un algorithme de moindres carrés est souvent employé, mais cette identification peut aussi se faire par d'autres techniques: ARMAX, programmation quadratique, ...

Pour satisfaire les caractéristiques physiques attendues de H : positivité des coefficients, intégrale conservative, aspect lisse, des contraintes sont appliquées "a posteriori".

- Puis, on procède à *l'identification des séries de pluies efficaces* : On utilise alors les coefficients de la dernière fonction de transfert $H_{(i)}$ et la série des débits Q_T pour résoudre le problème inverse, cette fois-ci **épisode par épisode**. Cette identification, plus délicate que la précédente, tend à être numériquement instable. Elle peut cependant se faire par moindres carrés, en utilisant une version originale de la technique de Ridge Regression, ou par programmation Linéaire ou Quadratique. Nalbantis (1987) préconise, après de nombreux essais sur des données synthétiques incluant des erreurs simulées, la technique de Ridge Regression adaptée par Versiani (1983). Ce résultat rejoint ceux d'études analogues, portant sur l'identification des pluies efficaces, menées par Hino (1986).

Cet algorithme itératif est initialisé à l'aide des pluies brutes, considérées comme une première approximation des pluies efficaces du bassin. La convergence est obtenue en général au bout de 3 à 5 itérations.

La méthode DPFT travaille en différences premières de débit (Guillot et Duband, 1980), pour des raisons de stabilité dans la procédure d'identification et de déconvolution, mais aussi pour diminuer l'influence du débit de base éventuel, sans faire appel à des modèles de filtrage.

Le bien-fondé et la robustesse de cette approche ont été établis sur données synthétiques (Nalbantis et al. 1988, Rodriguez et al., 1988), et vérifiés sur de nombreuses applications pratiques. En fin de traitement, la méthode fournit une fonction de transfert moyenne, et une série de pluies efficaces, optimale au sens des moindres carrés pour la reconstitution des variations de débits observées.

Le calage d'une fonction de production peut alors être abordé. Le problème se ramène à une identification d'un modèle non-linéaire de type Entrée(la pluie brute PB)-Sortie(la pluie efficace PE identifiée par l'approche DPFT). On dispose ainsi d'un critère objectif pour déterminer si une fonction s'adapte mieux qu'une autre au bassin étudié.

Quelques tentatives d'adaptation de fonctions de production courantes ont été abordées sans donner entière satisfaction. Selon Rodriguez et al. (1989a), seul 50 % de la variance des variations de débits sont expliqués en mode simulation, et 80 % de celles de débits. L'utilisation de modèles plus physiques comme le 'ponding time' (Morel-Seytoux, 1988) n'a cependant pas permis d'obtenir des résultats plus probants (Sempere et al., à paraître). On peut alors suspecter, non pas seulement le mécanisme retenu pour évaluer les pertes, mais plutôt l'effet d'une uniformisation abusive dans son extension au bassin.

INFLUENCE DE LA REPARTITION SPATIALE DES PLUIES EFFICACES DANS UN MODELE DE TYPE HYDROGRAMME UNITAIRE

L'analyse cartographique des champs de pluie (par exemple Obled et Rodriguez, 1988, Andrieu et al. 1988) a permis de vérifier la non-uniformité spatiale des précipitations dans des bassins montagneux, soumis à de fortes intensités. A moyenne spatiale identique, le champ (a) de la Figure 1, aura vraisemblablement une capacité de production différente de celui du champ (b).

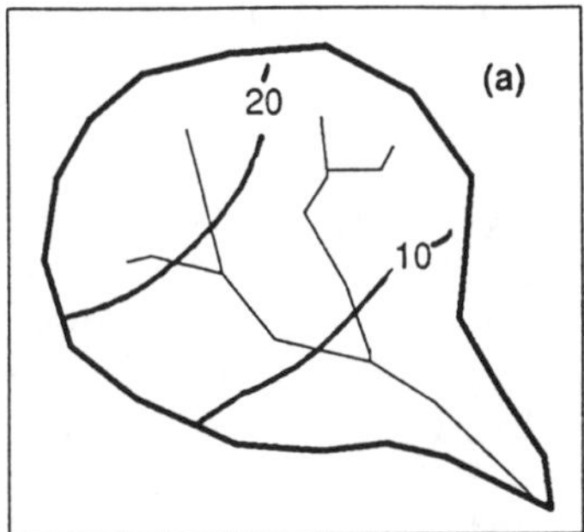

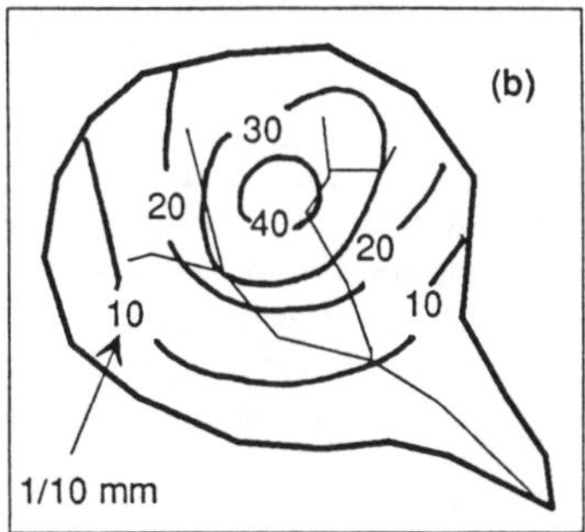

FIG. 1 Champs de pluie de moyenne semblable, mais de répartition spatiale fortement différente.

On peut alors penser qu'une partie importante des erreurs commises par les modèles globaux est due à la globalisation: la simple valeur "pluie moyenne" (point de départ de beaucoup de modèles), même acquise avec un réseau de mesure très dense, ne suffit pas à traduire suffisamment le type d'excitation auquel le bassin est soumis. On trouvera chez Hromadka II et McCuen (1989) une revue des auteurs arrivant à cette même conclusion. Parmi eux, Schilling et Fuchs (1986) établissent par simulation que l'erreur commise sur les pluies efficaces, surtout dans sa distribution spatiale, est plus importante que celle commise sur les temps de transfert de chaque maille.

Plus généralement, d'autres éléments prépondérants dans la transformation pluie-débit, comme la topographie, la pédologie, les aménagements d'origine humaine, ... sont tout aussi variables spatialement. Pour inclure cette réalité physique dans les modèles, plusieurs solutions sont envisagées:

-1) *La modélisation distribuée.* Elle peut privilégier la morphologie du terrain (Beven et Kirkby, 1979), supposé être le facteur déterminant du processus de production; ou bien la distribution spatiale des pluies mesurées (Corradini et Singh, 1985), ou encore l'ensemble des processus physiques connus et traduisibles par des relations physiques (comme le modèle SHE, Abbot et al. 1986).

-2) *Une modélisation encore globale*, mais où certains paramètres traduiraient, globalement, les éléments les plus caractéristiques de la variabilité spatiale considérée. Pour ce faire, on peut chercher à prendre en compte la morphologie des champs de pluie par des indices de forme, tout en faisant abstraction de leur localisation géographique. On conserve alors le caractère global du modèle de transfert et du modèle de production, mais ce dernier prend en compte plusieurs variables d'entrées, comme des indices de forme (cf. ceux présentés par Obled et Rodriguez (1988), ou Obled

(1989)), cherchant à décrire sommairement la forme de l'averse sur un pas de temps par rapport à la valeur moyenne sur le bassin.

- 3) *Une modélisation semi-globale* . Elle comporte un découpage limité du bassin. On privilégie alors l'aspect localisation géographique de la pluie. On peut aussi chercher à identifier les zones de capacité de production différentes soumises à des précipitations suffisamment peu corrélées pour affiner sensiblement la réponse du bassin.

Ces deux dernières démarches représentent une alternative. Elles ont été donc analysées parallèlement car il est difficile de déterminer "a priori" laquelle des deux est prépondérante. En attendant de pouvoir éventuellement les combiner, l'une peut être préférée à l'autre selon le cas particulier d'étude.

La deuxième démarche ne sera pas traitée dans cet article. Elle est discutée par Sempere et al. (1990, dans ce même symposium). Nous nous intéresserons ici à la troisième.

VARIABILITE SPATIALE DES CHAMPS DE PLUIE EFFICACE ET HYDROGRAMMES UNITAIRES

Revenons à l'une des hypothèses de l'Hydrogramme Unitaire. Selon ce concept, la fonction de transfert est définie comme la réponse à une lame de pluie efficace dite "unitaire" uniformément répartie sur le bassin.

En pratique, lorsqu'on effectue une identification de fonctions de transfert épisode par épisode, on s'aperçoit, même en utilisant les pluies efficaces les plus "objectives" possibles, que les réponses obtenues peuvent différer les unes des autres. Ce résultat bien connu permet donc d'interpréter chaque fonction de transfert propre à chaque épisode comme la réponse moyenne à la pluie efficace d'intégrale 1 ayant la distribution spatiale particulière à l'épisode. Ainsi, si nous avons sur un bassin une distribution spatiale moyenne différente sur trois épisodes (Fig. 2), nous serions amenés à identifier, pour chaque événement, les trois fonctions (a), (b) et (c).

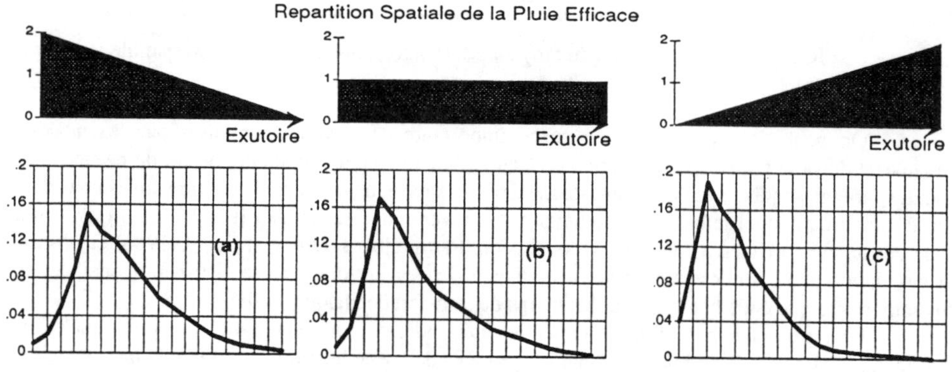

FIG. 2 FT selon la répartition moyenne des PE dans l'épisode.

La fonction de transfert moyenne sur l'ensemble des épisodes est, en conséquence, la réponse à la distribution moyenne de la pluie efficace, i.e. la plus fréquente.

Prenons l'exemple du Gardon d'Anduze (545 km^2) situé sur le flanc Sud-Est des Cévennes (Fig. 3.a). La fonction de transfert moyenne des épisodes d'Automne identifiée par l'approche DPFT (Fig 3.b) avec un pas de temps d'une heure présente un délai de 2 heures avant de croître significativement. Cette particularité est justifiée par la distribution moyenne des pluies brutes, seules à être réellement accessibles par la mesure directe, et qui est loin d'être uniforme. En général, on a plutôt de fortes précipitations sur les zones à fort relief du haut bassin (nous donnons sur la figure 3.a les pluies décennales au pas de temps d'1 heure de quelques stations à l'intérieur du bassin).

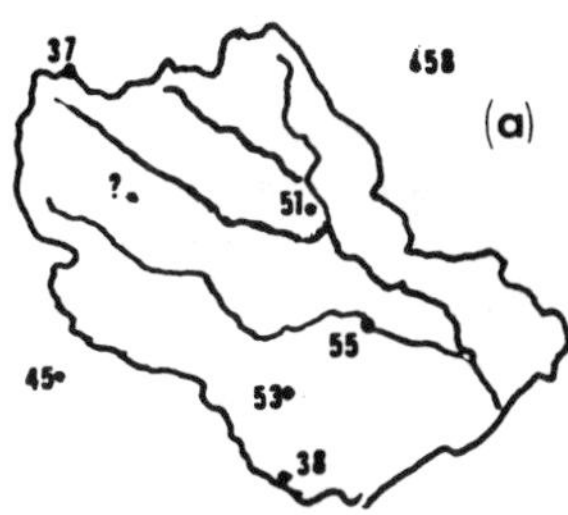

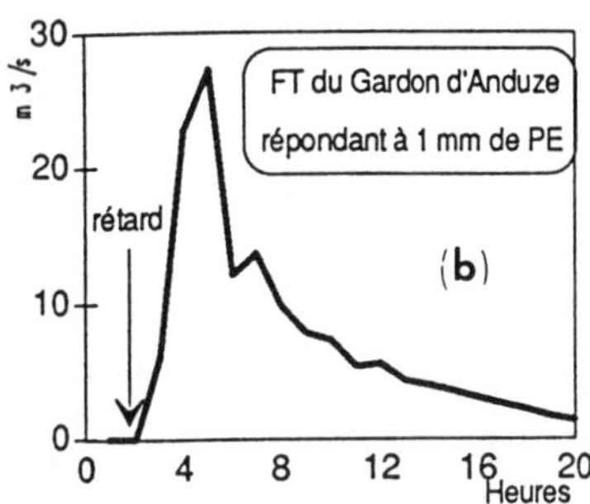

FIG. 3 (a) Bassin du Gardon d'Anduze, (b) FT résultante.

Rappelons d'autre part que dans ces régions, plus les précipitations sont intenses, plus leur répartition spatiale est non-uniforme, et plus elle peut s'éloigner du champ moyen. Si on admet donc que le champ de pluie efficace résultant possède une variabilité similaire, ou même supérieure, il devient intéressant d'agir directement sur le transfert pour traduire au mieux la configuration de l'averse.

Deux solutions peuvent alors être envisagées. La première consisterait à déformer continûment l'Hydrogramme Unitaire en fonction de la localisation de l'épicentre de la pluie, ou d'un autre indice géographique.

L'autre à identifier des fonctions de transfert relatives aux zones sensibles du bassin, au sens de la distribution de pluies efficaces, en particulier dans le cas de bassins aux caractéristiques contrastées (par exemple, un sous-bassin rural et un autre urbain).

Plus généralement, il est bien admis que la réponse d'un bassin versant est la résultante de sous-hydrogrammes élémentaires. Pour illustrer cela, on peut s'appuyer sur Pinte (1989) qui identifie sur le bassin de la Creuse au barrage d'Eguzon (2400 km^2, Fig. 4) une fonction de transfert globale sur la totalité du bassin. Dans ce cas particulier, la disponibilité supplémentaire de 3 limnigraphes contrôlant les apports des trois sous-bassins principaux à l'amont de la retenue, a permis de réaliser une étude plus fine, en identifiant sur chaque affluent une fonction de transfert spécifique (Fig. 4.b).

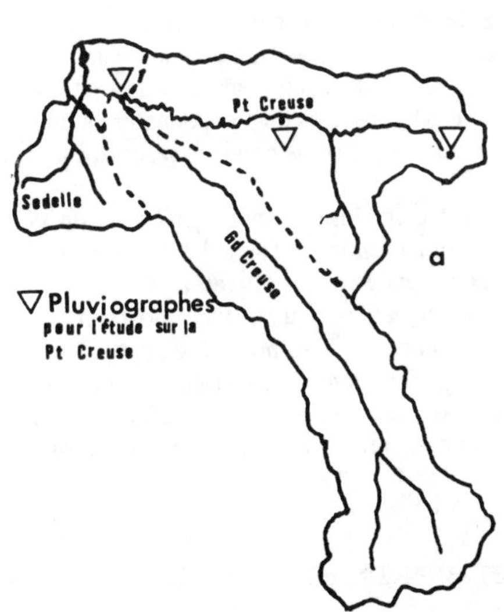

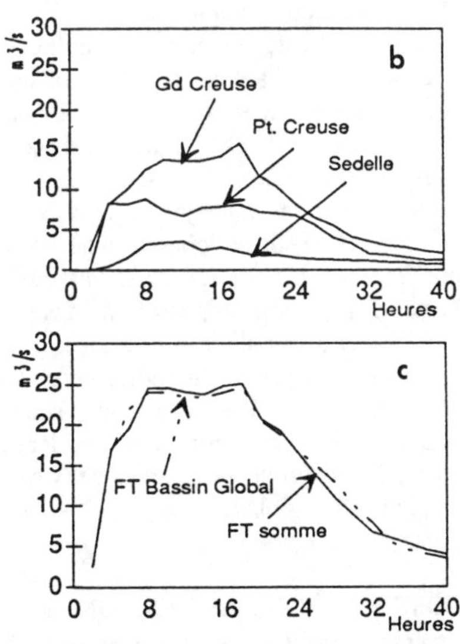

FIG. 4(a) Situation du bassin de la Creuse à Eguzon, (b) FTs sur chaque sous-bassin, (c) FT globale et somme des 3 FT des sous-bassins.

Il est remarquable de voir sur la figure 4.c. que la somme des trois fonctions de transfert moyennes sur les sous-bassins coïncide avec la fonction de transfert moyenne obtenue directement. Ainsi, quand la pluie efficace sur l'ensemble du bassin est proche de la "pluie efficace moyenne", le modèle utilisant la réponse globale suffit à modéliser correctement la réponse de tout le bassin. Mais si les répartitions des pluies efficaces sont concentrées sur l'un ou l'autre sous-bassins, alors le modèle semi-distribué fournit des détails opérationnellement importants.

Notons que non seulement il est important d'identifier des fonctions de transfert plus fines, mais aussi, et surtout, de se donner les moyens d'identifier des modèles de production propres à chaque sous-bassin.

Schilling et Fuchs (1986) ont analysé cette question en générant, à partir d'une grille radar de 81 mailles sur 729 ha. et d'un modèle fortement distribué, des débits dits de référence. Ensuite, ils ont globalisé d'une part la pluie efficace, et d'autre part les composantes du transfert, pour conclure que la connaissance du champ de pluies efficaces était plus importante que la connaissance exacte des paramètres de transfert. Corradini et Singh (1985) démontrent de leur côté que la connaissance plus fine de la répartition spatiale de la pluie brute n'apporte pas de véritable amélioration au modèle si la même fonction de production est appliquée sur chaque sous-bassin.

On voit donc l'intérêt d'effectuer une tentative de développement d'une méthode opérationelle, donc faiblement distribuée, capable de fournir simultanément la fonction de transfert et surtout les séries de pluies efficaces de chaque sous-bassin, afin de caler dans un deuxième temps, et de façon indépendante, des modèles de production locaux. Par contre, on ne dispose généralement pas de mesures de débit appropriée sur les sous-bassins, et il faut travailler avec le seul débit global. C'est pour résoudre ce problème que la méthode DPFT a été étendue à des cas bi-entrées (pluies), mono-sortie (débit).

EXTENSION DE LA METHODE DPFT A DES CAS BI-ENTREES

L'algorithme est similaire à celui de la version mono-entrée. Il a été détaillé par Rodriguez (1989) et présenté sommairement par Rodriguez et al. (1989b). Schématiquement, il résout alternativement :

- L'identification simultanée des deux fonctions de transfert moyennes (celles des bassins supérieur et inférieur, par exemple), en s'appuyant sur une technique de pseudo-orthogonalisation, afin de limiter les effets dus à l'intercorrélation des deux réponses. La résolution se fait en utilisant la Programmation Quadratique sur un jeu multi-événements.

- La déconvolution simultanée par événements des deux séries de pluies efficaces, propres à chaque sous-bassin. Ici, le problème d'identifiabilité se pose à cause du nombre d'inconnues recherchées par rapport aux nombre d'équations disponibles. C'est la raison pour laquelle l'extension s'est limitée à des cas bi-entrées. Des contraintes traduisant des hypothèses de comportement entre les pluies efficaces de chaque sous-bassin par rapport à la valeur moyenne deviennent nécessaires pour pallier le manque de degrés de liberté.

Ces deux phases alternatives d'identification-déconvolution sont itérées jusqu'à la convergence. L'initialisation se fait, comme dans la version mono-entrée, à l'aide des séries de pluies brutes disponibles, supposées être des premiers estimateurs des vraies pluies efficaces.

Les simulations effectuées sur des données synthétiques (Rodriguez, 1989) montrent que le biais introduit par les hypothèses de comportement reste important, et se manifeste surtout sur les séries de pluies efficaces de chaque sous-bassin. Par contre, les fonctions de transfert de chaque sous-bassin peuvent être robustement identifiées. Néanmoins, sur des crues générées avec une forte variabilité de production sur les deux sous-bassins, l'approche bi-entrée fournit des meilleurs résultats que la version globale.

COMPARAISON DES VERSIONS MONO-ENTREE ET BI-ENTREES SUR LE BASSIN DE LA PETITE CREUSE A PUY RAGEAUD (840 KM^2)

Ce bassin, soumis essentiellement à des régimes atlantiques d'Ouest, se situe à l'ouest du Massif Central français. Cette rivière, affluent de la Creuse, la rejoint quelques km à l'amont du barrage d'Eguzon (Fig. 4.a) L'exutoire est situé à 210 m. d'altitude, tandis que les lignes de crêtes varient entre 350 et 530 m. L'échantillon de travail comporte 19 épisodes de crues, avec des débits de pointe allant de 45 à 230 m^3/s. Trois pluviographes servent à mesurer la pluie brute (fig 4.a). Le pas de temps de l'étude est de deux heures.

Pour l'application de la version bi-entrées de la DPFT, le découpage s'est fait entre bassin supérieur et bassin inférieur. Le premier représente 66 % de la surface totale, et le deuxième 34 % . La forme particulière du bassin, avec un haut bassin récepteur, et un bassin inférieur beaucoup plus étroit et encaissé, justifie en partie cette démarche.

Phase d'identification des fonctions de transfert et des pluies efficaces

Nous donnons, sur la figure 5, les fonctions de transfert identifiées par l'approche globale (a), et bi-entrées ((b) pour le bas bassin, (c) pour le haut). La complexité de la réponse globale, comportant une première pointe, suivie de deux autres fortement éloignées, se retrouve assez bien sur les fonctions de transfert des deux sous-bassins, même si leur somme reproduit incorrectement la décroissance de la réponse globale.

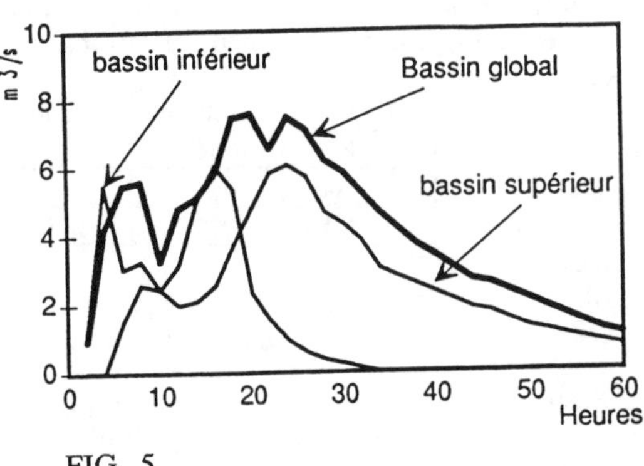

FIG. 5

Sur la figure 6 nous représentons l'épisode du 26 Mai 1977, (plus grande crue de l'échantillon), reconstitué par l'approche globale (a) et par l'approche bi-entrée (b). La nouvelle version reconstitue assez correctement cette crue, tout en permettant de donner l'allure des hydrogrammes provenant de chaque sous-bassin, ainsi que leurs pluies efficaces respectives.

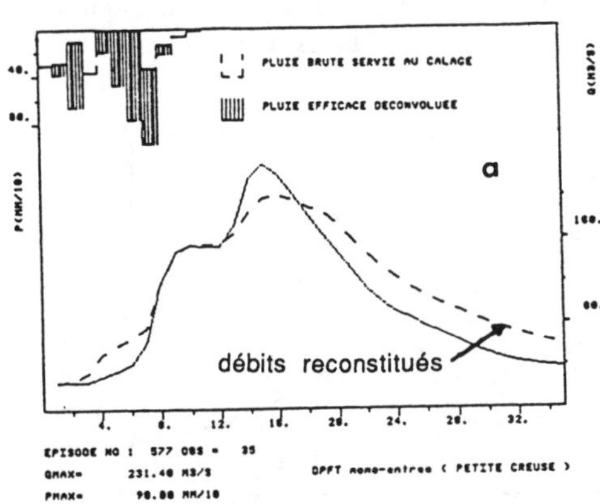

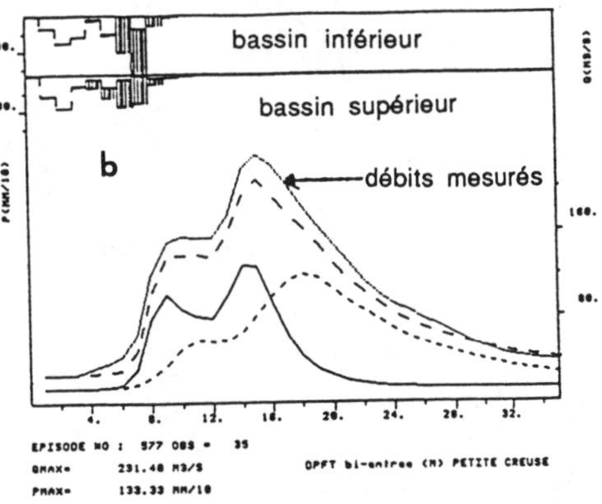

FIG. 6

Par ailleurs, le tableau 1 donne les coefficients de détermination entre les débits reconstitués et mesurés, d'une part, et entre leur variations d'autre part. On note, en calibration, une amélioration non négligeable, surtout sur le critère des variations de débits, apportée par la version bi-entrées.

R2	variations de débits	débits
globale	0,77	0,91
bi-entrées	0,84	0,92

Tableau 1 Coefficients de détermination en calibration.

Phase de calage de modèles de production

Deux modèles de production ont été ajustés, présentés par Rodriguez et al. (1989a), et non détaillés ici. Celui rétenu pour illustrer cette application est un modèle classique à réservoir, comportant deux paramètres communs à tous les épisodes, et un paramètre d'initialisation propre à chaque événement.

Les coefficients de détermination entre les pluies efficaces calculées par le modèle et celles identifiées par une des versions de la méthode DPFT sont donnés dans le tableau 2. On observe d'une part que les coefficients de calage sont équivalents sur les trois jeux (global, bassin supérieur et bassin inférieur), et d'autre part, que ce modèle n'est pas vraiment adapté à reconstituer des pluies efficaces obtenues par l'approche DPFT.

R2	PE modélisées / PE identifiées
globale	0,51
bassin supérieur	0,49
bassin inférieur	0,53

Tableau 2.

Simulation des débits

Nous allons cependant utiliser ces différents modèles de production, avec les paramètres calés, pour calculer les pluies efficaces *modélisées*. Puis, en faisant le produit de convolution avec les FT correspondantes, identifiées par l'une des versions de l'approche DPFT, nous obtiendrons les débits modélisés ou simulés pour les versions respectives.

Les coefficients de détermination entre les débits simulés et mesurés, ainsi qu'entre leurs variations, sont donnés dans le tableau 3 pour les deux versions. Sur l'ensemble des épisodes, la version bi-entrées est sensiblement plus performante que la version globale, mais reste incapable de modéliser très correctement les débits.

R2	variations de débits	débits
globale	0,48	0,65
bi-entrées	0,59	0,81

Tableau 3 Coefficients de détermin en simulation.

Cette capacité de reconstituer les débits dépend d'ailleurs de l'épisode. Par exemple, la version bi-entrées fournit une très bonne simulation sur l'épisode du 5 Janvier 1982 (fig. 7.a), tandis que sur celui du 1 Avril 1987 (fig. 7.b) c'est la version globale qui est meilleure. Dans ce dernier, la version bi-entrées introduit une réponse liée à une variabilité spatiale de la pluie brute, qui ne se manifeste pas visiblement sur les pluies efficaces. Bien évidemment, d'autres crues sont mal simulées par les deux approches.

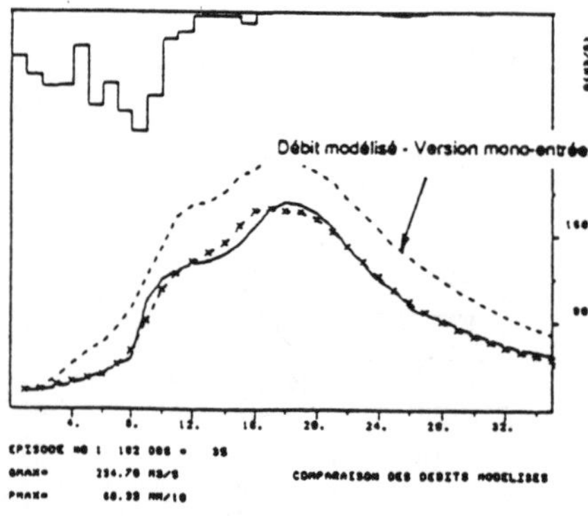

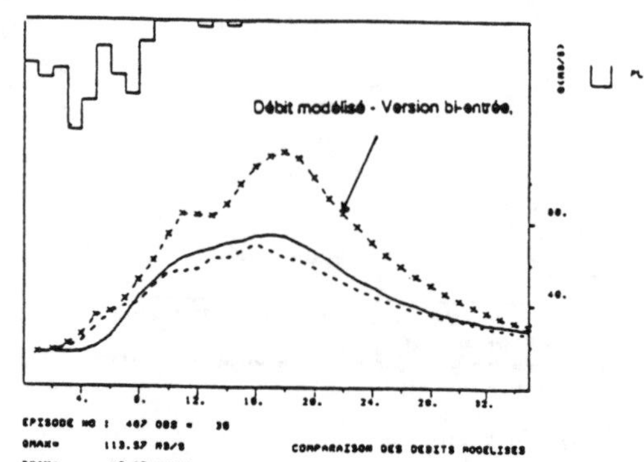

FIG. 7

CONCLUSION

Dans le cadre de modèles de type Hydrogramme Unitaire, nous avons essayé d'analyser l'influence de la répartition spatiale de la pluie efficace sur les hydrogrammes résultants et son éventuelle prise en compte. Quand celle-ci est loin de la pluie efficace spatiale moyenne (celle qui donne lieu à la fonction de transfert moyenne du bassin), les modèles globaux ont tendance à ne plus être satisfaisants.

Or, dans les régions montagneuses, on sait que les précipitations convectives s'écartent parfois beaucoup de la distribution moyenne climatologique, et, d'autre part, que plus la pluie brute est forte, moins elle est uniformement répartie sur le bassin.

Afin de prendre partiellement en compte cet élement, suivant un point de vue opérationnel, l'approche DPFT a été étendue à des cas bi-entrées. Les résultats recherchés - à savoir : identifier deux réponses sur deux sous-bassins à productibilité différente, ainsi que leurs séries de pluies efficaces associées - permettent de calibrer indépendamment deux modèles de production, un sur chaque entité.

Même si les pluies efficaces identifiées sur ces sous-bassins sont moins robustes que celles du bassin total, la version bi-entrée fournit, sur la Petite Creuse, des résultats encourageants. Dans ce cas particulier, le biais introduit pour résoudre le problème inverse est certainement moins pénalisant que le fait de traiter le bassin comme une seule entité.

Notons enfin que les modèles de production utilisés - tant sur les versions globale que bi-entrées - ont du mal à se caler sur des pluies efficaces identifiées, 'optimales' au sens de la reconstitution des variations de débits observés. Des recherches sont en cours sur ce dernier point car, tant que nous serons dans l'incapacité de fournir de bonnes "pluies efficaces", les modèles de type Hydrogramme Unitaire, les plus opérationnels, pourront être difficilement spatialisés.

REFERENCES

Abbot M.B., Bathurst J.C., Cunge J.A., O'Connell P.E. et Rasmussen J. (1986) An Introduction to the European Hydrological System - Système Hydrologique Européen "SHE". J. Hydrol., 87, pp. 45-77.

Andrieu H., Creutin J.D., Delrieu G., Leoussof J. et Pointin Y. (1989) Radar data processing for hydrology in the Cevennes region. Publ IAHS n° 186 pp. 105-115.

Beven K.J. et Kirkby M.J. (1979) A physically based variable contributing area model of basin hydrology. Hydrol. Sci. Bull. 24,1,3, pp. 42-69.

Corradini C. et Singh V.P. (1985) Effect of spatial variability of effective rainfall on direct runoff by a geomorphologic approach. J. Hydrol. 81, pp. 27-43.

Guillot P. et Duband D. (1980) Fonctions de transfert pluie-débit sur des bassins versants de l'ordre de 1000 km2. Publ IAHS n° 129 pp. 177-186.

Hromadka II T.V. et McCuen R.H. (1989) An approximate analysis of surface runoff model uncertainty. J Hydrol. 111, pp. 321-360.

Hino M. (1986) Improvements in the inverse estimation of effective rainfall from runoff. J. Hydrol. 83, pp. 137-147.

Mays L.W. et Coles L. (1980) Optimization on Unit Hydrograph Determination. J. Hydraul. Div. ASCE. Vol. 106, Hy 1, pp. 85-97.

Morel-Seytoux H.J. (1988) Decipe for simple but phisically based modeling of the infiltration and local runoff processes. Proc. 8th Annual Hydrological Days. April 1988. Fort Collins. Colorado. Etats Unis d'Amérique.

Nalbantis I. (1987) Identification de modèles pluie-débit du type Hydrogramme Unitaire: Développements de la méthode DPFT et validation sur données simulées avec et sans erreurs. PhD. INPG. Grenoble. France.

Nalbantis I., Obled Ch. et Rodriguez J.Y. (1988) Modélisation pluie-débit: validation par simulation de la méthode DPFT. La Houille Blanche. 5/6, pp. 415-424.

Newton D.W. et Vinyard J.W. (1967) Computer-Determined Unit Hydrograph from Floods. J. Hydraul. Div. ASCE. Vol. 93, Hy 5, pp. 219-235.

Obled Ch. (1989) Reflexions on rainfall information requirements for operational rainfall-runoff modelling. Int. Symp. on Hydrol. Application of Weather Radar. Univ. of Salford, August, 14-17, paper J4.

Obled Ch. et Rodriguez J.Y. (1988) La distribution spatiale des précipitations et son rôle dans la transformation pluie-débit. La Houille Blanche, 5/6,pp. 467-474.

Pinte J. (1989) Les modèles théoriques et pratiques de mise en place de systèmes de surveillance et de prévision de crues. Rapport interne. EDF-DTG. 4 p.

Rodriguez J.Y., Nalbantis et Obled Ch. (1988) Rainfall-runoff modelling by the DPFT method: testing and validation by generated data. Proc. 4th Int. Symp. on Systems analysis apllied to Management of Water Resources, Octobre 1988. Rabat. Maroc.

Rodriguez J.Y. (1989) Modélisation pluie-débit par la méthode DPFT: développements de la méthode initiale et extension à des cas bi-entrées. PhD. INPG. Grenoble. France.

Rodriguez J.Y., Sempere-Torres D. et Obled Ch. (1989a) Nouvelles perspectives de développement dans la modélisation des pluies efficaces par application de la méthode DPFT. IAHS Publ. no. 181, pp 235-243.

Rodriguez J.Y., Sempere-Torres D. et Obled Ch. (1989b) Extension of Lumped Operational rainfall-runoff models to semi-lumped modelling: the case of the DPFT-ERUHDIT approach. Int. Symp. on Hydrol. Application of Weather Radar. Univ. of Salford, August, 14-17, Paper M2.

Schilling W. et Fuchs L. (1986) Errors in stormwater modeling - A quantitative assessment. J. Hydraul. Div. ASCE. Vol. 112,Hy 2, pp. 111-123.

Sempere-Torres D., Rodriguez J.Y. et Obled Ch. (à paraitre). Using the DPFT approach to improve flash flood forecasting. Natural Hazards.

Sempere-Torres D., Obled Ch. (1990) Modélisation pluie-débit en bassins à relief accidenté: Le rôle de la variabilité spatiale des pluies. Conf. Int. sur les Ressources en Eau en regions montagneuses, Lausanne, Aout 1990.

Versiani B. (1983) Modélisation de la relation pluie-débit pour la prévision de crues. PhD. INPG. Grenoble, France.

Hydrology in Mountainous Regions. I - Hydrological Measurements; the Water Cycle (Proceedings of two Lausanne Symposia, August 1990). IAHS Publ. no. 193, 1990.

Modélisation pluie-débit de bassins à relief accident: le rôle de la variabilité spatiale de la pluie

D. SEMPERE TORRES & CH. OBLED
Institut de Mécanique de Grenoble (Groupe Hydrologie),
BP 53 X,38041 GRENOBLE CEDEX, FRANCE

RESUME Les modèles pluie-débit globaux sont les mieux adaptés aux contraintes de prévision des crues. Néanmoins, l'intensité moyenne de pluie ne suffit pas, dans certains cas, pour bien décrire le champ de pluie. Nous avons exploré l'introduction simplifiée de la variabilité spatiale de la pluie à l'aide des Indices de Concentration de Pluie. Ces indices mesurent la représentativité de la valeur moyenne de la pluie et permettent de corriger la pluie efficace calculée par les modèles globaux. Les résultats obtenus sur un bassin réel montrent l'intérêt de cette démarche.

POSITION DU PROBLEME

Dans le cadre de la modélisation pluie-débit dans un contexte de prévision de crues, les modèles dits globaux (considérant le bassin comme une seule entité homogène, excitée par la séquence temporelle de l'intensité moyenne de la pluie sur le bassin, supposée représentative du vrai champ de pluie) sont ceux qui s'adaptent le mieux aux contraintes operationnelles (simplicité, données peu abondantes, utilisation par évenements...), surtout quand il s'agit de bassins de taille superieure à 100 Km².

Même si ces modèles ne correspondent pas à la réalité physique des processus à modéliser, lorsqu'on les compare dans ce contexte aux modèles dits distribués, prétendant incorporer les lois physiques des processus mis en jeu, les modèles globaux classiques s'avèrent les plus performantes (un exemple intéressant est fourni par Loague & Freeze, 1985). En particulier ceux basés sur l'approche de l'Hydrogramme Unitaire de Sherman (1932) continuent à être les mieux adaptés avec le coût le plus faible (Kirkby, 1988, p. 335).

Malheureusement, cela ne signifie pas qu'on les reconnaîsse la qualité d'une bonne description des processus vraiment mis en jeu, mais bien plutôt la constatation que l'on ne sait pas mieux faire.

Concrètement, dans le cas des bassins à relief accidenté, l'hypothèse que le champ de pluie est bien décrit par la seule valeur de l'intensité moyenne sur le bassin est loin d'être réaliste.

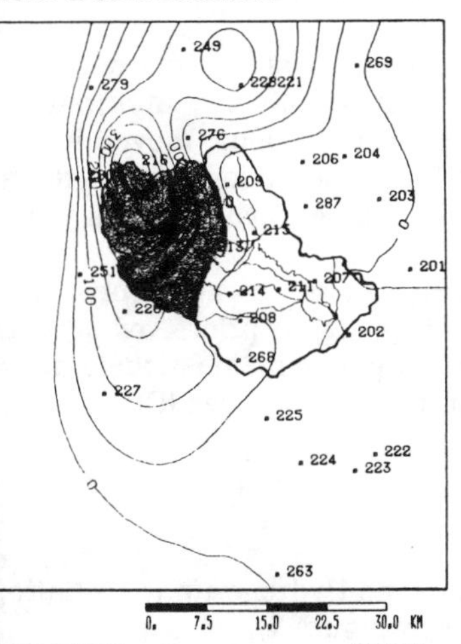

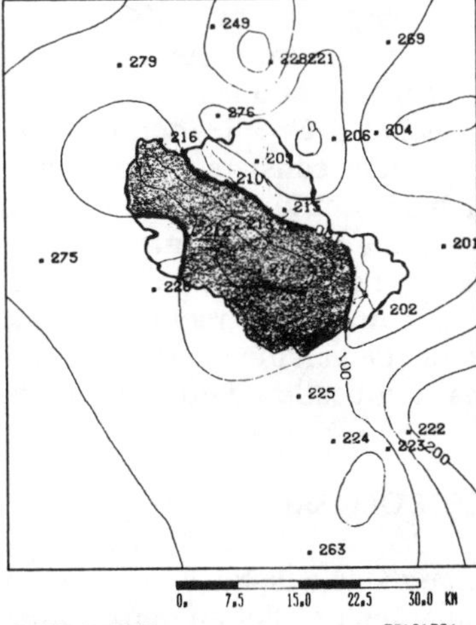

FIG. 1 Isolignes de deux champs de pluie horaires sur le Gardon d'Anduze d'intensites moyennes égales, mais de configurations spatiales differentes.
■ : Surface où la pluie est > PB(t)

A titre d'exemple la Figure 1 nous montre deux champs de pluie horaires sur le bassin du Gardon d'Anduze: tous les deux sont caractérisés par une même valeur de l'intensité moyenne de la pluie brute ($PB(t_1)= PB(t_2) = 11$ mmh^{-1}), mais leurs distributions spatiales sont très différentes.

Or, il va de soi que la configuration spatiale de ces deux champs de pluie doit influencer de façon non négligeable l'efficacité de la lame de pluie brute moyenne tombée sur le bassin, PB(t). Cependant, l'influence de la variabilité spatiale de la pluie n'est pas souvent prise en compte par les modèles pluie-débit.

En effet, même les modèles distribués supposent généralement que la pluie est spatialement uniforme. Et les quelques modèles théoriques visant à introduire cette variabilité spatiale ne le font qu'au prix de grandes simplifications. C'est, par exemple, le cas du développement proposé par Milly & Eagleson (1988), que l'on ne peut pas qualifier de simple, mais où la variabilité spatiale de la pluie est prise en compte en considérant l'intensité de la pluie temporellement constante (!).

Cela est en fait la réconnaissance de la difficulté de ce type d'études, difficulté qui a entraîné la modélisation pluie-débit dans un impasse certainement "frustrante":

Il y a longtemps déjà que l'on est persuadé de l'importance de l'influence de la variabilité spatiale de la pluie sur les processus hydrologiques (voir par exemple Wilson et al., 1979). De plus, on dispose aujourd'hui de moyens pour décrire le champ de pluie d'une façon bien plus complète que par sa simple valeur moyenne, même en temps réel.

Cependant, nous ne disposons pas du corps thèorique capable de relier les caractéristiques mesurables du champ de pluie avec la production du ruisellement à l'échelle du bassin, et par conséquent la plupart des modèles continuent à éviter d'introduire explicitement la variabilité spatiale de la pluie.

Toutefois, quelques auteurs ont proposé des idées pour la prise en compte de cette variabilité spatiale, en général en découpant en sous-unités de modélisation l'entité considérée (voir entre d'autre Rodriguez & Obled, 1990). Mais bien que l'idée du découpage en sous-unités soit séduisante (elle est sentie comme l'unique alternative: reduir le problème en le découpant puisque la description à l'échelle du bassin paraît "inabordable"), nous avons voulu nous cantoner à la prévision des crues, et respecter les contraintes imposées par les besoins opérationnels.

Dans ce contexte, nous avons exploré l'intérêt de l'introduction simplifiée de la variabilité spatiale de la pluie dans les modéles pluie-débit les plus simples: les modèles globaux. Ceci, qui peut paraître paradoxal, est fondé sur l'hypothèse que la façon dont la lame de pluie est répartie spatialement sur le bassin a une influence sur la transformation pluie-débit plus importante que celle de la variabilité de la fonction de production, ou que celle du routage (ou transfert) de la pluie efficace à l'exutoire, comme les travaux de Schilling & Fuchs (1986) le suggérent.

Pour cela, nous allons introduire dans un modèle global classique une sorte de perception diffuse des caractéristiques spatiales qui apportent une information complémentaire, mais globale, à celle donnée par la seule valeur moyenne de l'intensité de pluie brute. L'idée consiste à proposer un Indice de Concentration de la Pluie (ICP) mesurant globalement la représentativité de la valeur moyenne de la pluie par rapport au champ de pluie réellement mesuré.

Pour évaluer l'intérêt de la démarche proposée, nous comparerons les performances obtenues sur un bassin réel par un modèle global, a priori "aveugle" à toute information différente de la lame moyenne de pluie, et par ce même modèle mais nuancé (voire corrigé) par l'utilisation d'un facteur prenant en compte des ICP.

LE MODELE PLUIE DEBIT GLOBAL

Nous avons utilisé comme modèle de base, un modèle de type Hydrogramme Unitaire, où la transformation pluie-débit se fait en deux étapes (voir Figure 2).

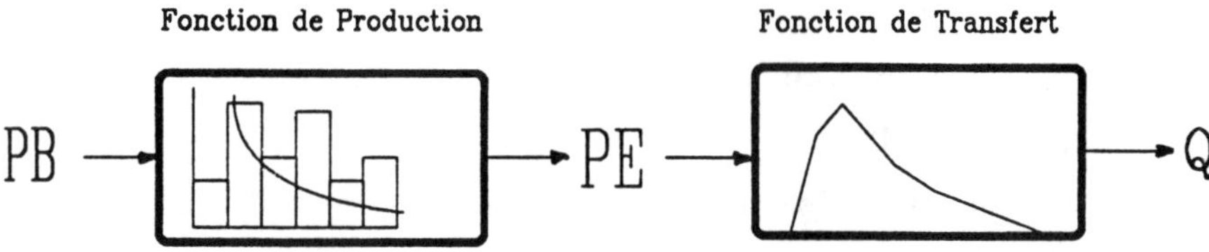

FIG.2 Schéma de la modélisation pluie-débit de type Hydrogramme Unitaire.

a) La pluie brute tombant sur le bassin, PB(t), est transformée en pluie efficace (PE(t), partie de la pluie brute qui est efficace pour le ruissellement), à l'aide d'une Fonction de Production non-linéaire qui prend en compte la modélisation des processus des pertes en volume.

b) Le volume efficace, sous forme de PE(t), est étalé dans le temps à l'aide d'une Fonction de Transfert, ou Hydrogramme Unitaire, supposée linéaire et invariante.

L'utilisation de ce schema requiert donc un modèle de Fonction de Production et une Fonction de Transfert.

Pour identifier la Fonction de Transfert du bassin nous avons utilisé la méthode DPFT (Différence Première de la Fonction de Transfert). Cette méthode, couramment utilisée par Electricité de France dans ses modèles opérationnels de crue, a été proposée par Guillot & Duband (1980,1981) sous forme d'une extension améliorée et opérationnellement orientée de l'algorithme itératif-alterné de Newton et Vinyard (1967). Elle a fait l'objet, depuis sa creation, de nombreux travaux de développement qui ont montré sa stabilité et sa robustesse comme méthode d'identification (Versiani, 1983; Nalbantis, 1987; Rodriguez, 1989...)

A l'aide de cette méthode, la Fonction de Transfert peut être identifiée, dans une première étape, de façon indépendante de la Fonction de Production sur un jeu multi-événement. Ensuite, les pluies efficaces, estimées par déconvolution des débits épisode par épisode, nous serviront de référence pour l'identification du modèle de Fonction de Production et pour l'optimisation de ses paramètres.

La séparation de ces deux étapes est le principal avantage de cette méthode d'identification, qui permet de comparer les performances de différents types de Fonction de Production en utilisant la même Fonction de Transfert, identifiée au préalable (Rodriguez et al., 1989).

Le modèle global est complèté par une Fonction de Production de type Réservoir proposée par Lorent (1975), et qui s'est avérée la plus performante des modèles globaux utilisés dans des études préalables (Sempere Torres, 1990). Cette Fonction de Production permet de calculer la PE(t) comme la différence entre la PB(t) et le volume retenu par le bassin pendant le pas de temps t, W(t).

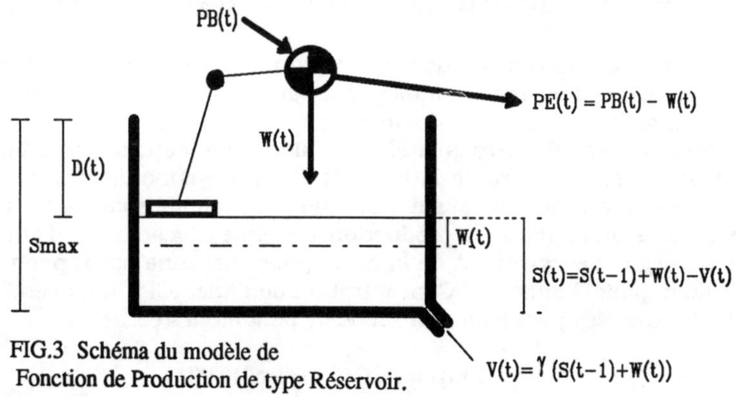

FIG.3 Schéma du modèle de Fonction de Production de type Réservoir.

Avec:

PB(t) : Pluie Brute au pas de temps t (en 10^{-1} mm par pas de temps Δt).

PE(t) : Pluie Efficace au pas t (10^{-1} mm / Δt).

W(t) : Apport au réservoir, taux de pertes, au pas t (10^{-1} mm / Δt).

V(t) : Vidange du réservoir au pas t (10^{-1} mm / Δt).

S(t) : Stockage du réservoir au pas t (10^{-1} mm).
D(t) : Déficit du réservoir au pas t (10^{-1} mm).
SMAX : Stock maximal du réservoir (10^{-1} mm).

L'expression pour le taux de pertes, W(t), est donnée par une équation de type exponentiel contrôlée par le rapport entre la lame de pluie et le déficit d'un réservoir à vidange linéaire (Voir Figure 3).

$$W(t) = [\, SMAX - S(t-1)\,]\ \{1 - \exp[\, -\beta\, PB(t)\, \Delta t \,/\, (\, SMAX - S(t-1)\,)\,]\,\} \,/\, \Delta t$$

Le comportement de ce réservoir, qui répresente l'évolution de l'état hydrologique du bassin, peut être réduit à la gestion du déficit D(t) = SMAX - S(t), qui devient

$$D(t) = D(t-1) + V(t) - W(t) = (\, 1 - \alpha\,)\, D(0) + \alpha\, [\, D(t-1) - W(t)\,]$$

où

$$\gamma = (\, 1 - \alpha\,)$$

Le fait de travailler par événements nous obligera à initialiser ce déficit en début d'épisode, D(0). Par conséquent le modèle possede deux paramètres à calibrer sur l'ensemble des épisodes, α et β, en respectant la condition $\alpha\,,\ \beta \in [\,0,\ 1\,]$, et une variable à initialiser.

Notons enfin que lorsque D=>0, la PE=>PB, et en particulier PE(t)=PB(t) si D(t-1)=0. De même, à partir d'un certain rapport de PB(t)/D(t-1), les pertes ne sont plus fonction que du niveau de remplissage du réservoir (et non plus de l'intensité des pluies).

La PE(t) ainsi calculée est ensuite utilisée pour calculer les séries des débits, $Q^*_1(t)$, par convolution avec la Fonction de Transfert préalablement identifiée.

INTRODUCTION SIMPLIFIEE DE LA VARIABILITE SPATIALE DE LA PLUIE

Notre propos est de trouver un moyen d'introduire l'effet de la variabilité spatiale de la pluie dans un cadre aussi simple que possible, qui soit compatible avec la modélisation globale du bassin versant.

Pour cela, nous modéliserons la PE(t) à l'aide d'une Fonction de Production globale utilisant une bonne mesure de la lame de PB(t) moyenne (le même modèle de type réservoir qu'auparavant), en considérant que la variabilité spatiale de la pluie joue un rôle de second ordre dans la production de pluie efficace. En d'autres termes, la mesure du degré d'éloignement de la description moyenne par rapport à la structure spatiale de la pluie (l'Indice de Concentration de Pluie, ICP) "nuancera" l'effectivité de la PB. La PE calculée par ce nouveau modèle peut alors s'écrire:

$$PE(t) = PEG(t)\, [\delta_1 + \delta_2\, ICP(t)\,]$$

où la pluie efficace calculée par le modèle de production global (PEG(t)) est corrigée par un facteur donné par l' ICP (δ_1 et δ_2 étant deux paramètres à calibrer).

La PE(t) ainsi calculée sera à nouveau routée à l'aide de la même Fonction de Transfert afin de calculer une nouvelle série de débits, $Q^*_2(t)$. Ce deuxième modèle aura donc 4 paramètres à calibrer sur l'ensemble des épisodes de calibration (α , β, δ_1 et δ_2), et une variable à initialiser en début d'épisode (D(0)).

Notre problème consiste maintenant à définir un "bon" Indice de Concentration de Pluie qui nous permette de reproduire au mieux les épisodes observés. Pour cela, nous avons repris les idées proposées par Obled et Rodriguez (1988), et nous avons défini quelques variables mesurant la concentration de la pluie pendant chaque pas de temps, comme par exemple (voir Figure 4):

S(t): Surface du bassin mouillée par des pluies supérieures à la moyenne.
V(t):Volume de pluie tombé sur le bassin, excédant le seuil donné par la PB(t) moyenne.
$V_s(t)$: Volume de pluie tombant sur la surface S.
$V(t)/S_t$: Lame moyenne sur le bassin (S_t= surface totale du bassin) équivalente au volume V.

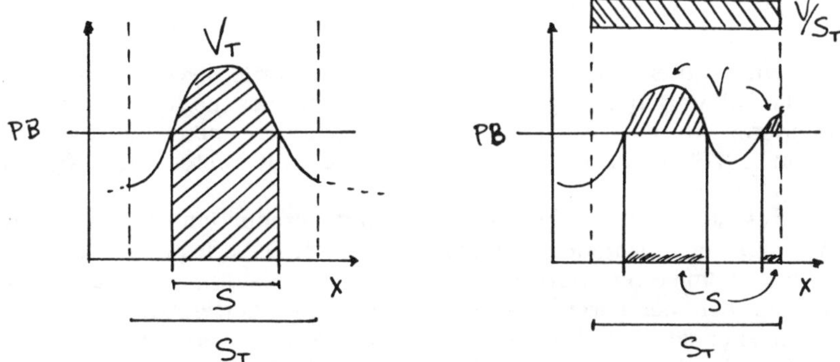

FIG. 4 Schéma unidimensionel des variables mesurant la représentativité de la lame moyenne de pluie sur le bassin, PB(t), utilisées pour définir des Indices de Concentration de Pluie.

Nous avons utilisé ces variables, et des combinaisons de ces dernières, comme des ICP(t). Leur valeur fournit une mesure du manque de representativité de la valeur moyenne de la PB(t). Nous avons ensuite suivi une démarche exploratoire pour choisir l'indice optimisant les résultats du modèle proposé, en cherchant à réproduire au mieux les séries de pluie efficace préalablement estimées. En d'autres termes, nous avons comparé les performances obtenues avec les différents indices et nous avons choisi, parmi la dizaine de combinaisons utilisées, celle qui nous a donné les meilleurs résultats.

Pour le bassin du Gardon d'Anduze, présenté ici, la combinaison retenue comme ICP(t) est:

$$ICP(t) = (V_s(t) \;/\; S_t) \;/\; PB(t) \quad (S_t - S) \;/\; S$$

Il s'agit d'un Indice de Concentration composé de deux facteurs, un rapport d'intensités et un rapport de surfaces, qui varie entre 0.5 et 1.5 en cours de crue.

COMPARAISON DES DEUX MODELES SUR LE BASSIN DU GARDON D'ANDUZE

Le bassin du Gardon d'Anduze (545 Km²), situé dans la région des Cévennes (voir Figure 5), est caractérisé par des épisodes pluvieux d'automne, d'intensités souvent comprises entre 20 et 50 mm h^{-1}, et par de fortes pentes (altitudes entre 200 et 1600 m). Ces deux caractéristiques conditionnent la réponse du bassin (temps de réponse moyen = 5 h) et l'avènement régulier de fortes crues éclairs.

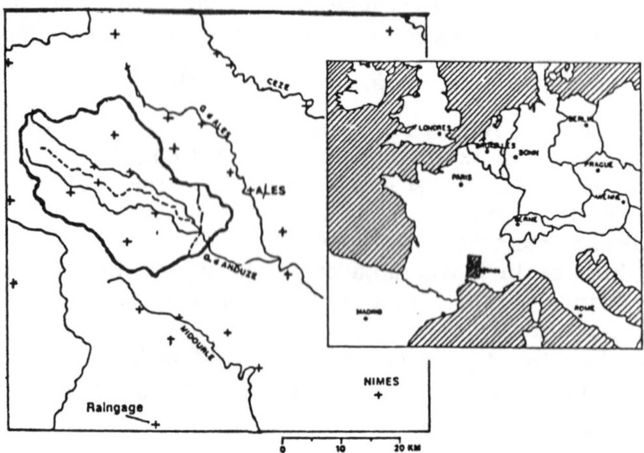

FIG. 5 Localisation du bassin versant du Gardon d'Anduze.

Pour cette étude, nous avons utilisé 16 épisodes de crue, avec un pas de temps horaire pour la calibration des paramètres, et 2 épisodes pour la validation des modèles. Le champ de pluie est calculé par interpolation spline de type "plaque mince" (Duchon, 1976) sur un réseau dense (entre 26 et 36 postes selon l'épisode) de pluviomètres.

Les paramètres des deux modèles de fonction de production ont été calibrés en cherchant à minimiser la somme des résidus au carré. Dans les deux cas, le déficit initial D(0) a été optimisé pour chaque évenement. Les résultats obtenus, presentés dans le Tableau 1, sont comparés à l'aide du coefficient de correlation au carré, R^2, et du critère d'Efficience de Nash, E (Nash & Sutcliffe, 1970; Aitken, 1973), calculés sur les débits Q, et sur les différences de débits, DQ (DQ(t) = Q(t) - Q(t-1)).

	RESERVOIR	INDICE DE CONCENTRATION
E_Q	0.84	0.85
R^2_Q	0.86	0.87
E_Q	0.52	0.58
R^2_Q	0.54	0.59

<u>Tableau 1</u> Résultats des deux modéles sur le jeu de calibration (16 épisodes). Critères E et R^2 calculés sur les débits, Q, et sur les différences de débit, DQ.

RESERVOIR	INDICE DE CONCENTRATION
$\alpha = 0.875$	$\alpha = 0.982$
$\beta = 0.955$	$\beta = 0.982$
	$\delta_1 = 0.59$
	$\delta_2 = -0.59$

<u>Tableau 2</u> Valeurs des paramètres calibrés.

A première vue, l'utilisation des indices de concentration de pluie ne semble pas introduire de gains supplémentaires, et les coefficients de qualité calculés sur les débits sont presque identiques. Cependant, ces mêmes coefficients calculés sur les différences de débits (critère qui mesure mieux la capacité prédictive du modèle)

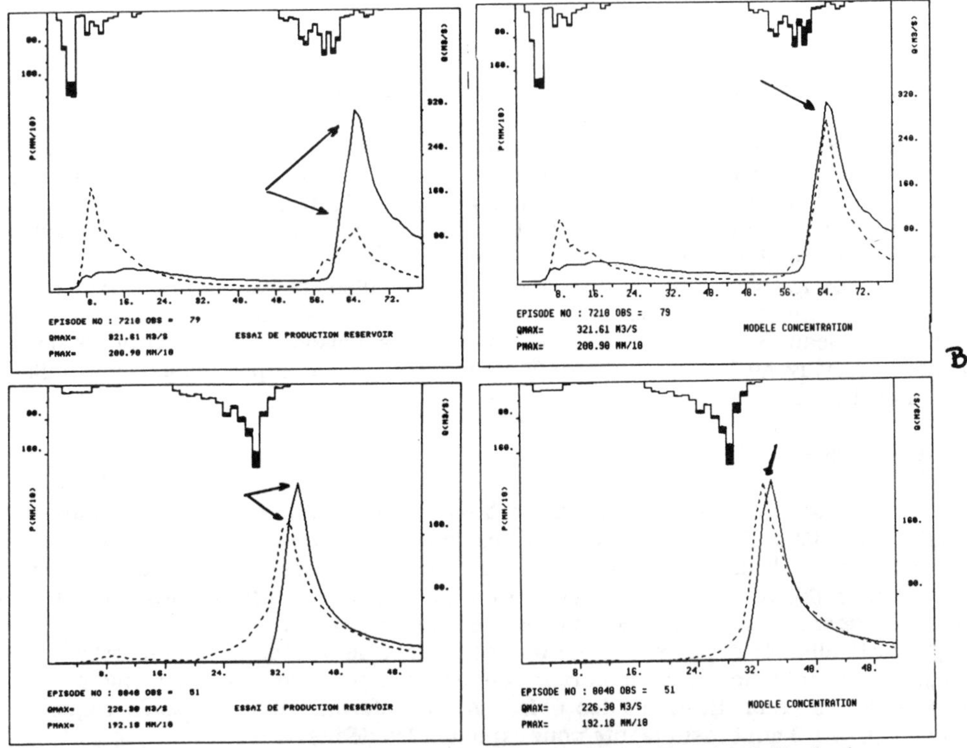

FIG.6 Exemples de reconstitutions fournies par les deux modèles de Fonction de Production **(jeu de calibration)**. A : modèle Réservoir ; B : modèle à Indice de Concentration.
❑❑ : PB ; ■■ : PE ; ---- : Q ; - - - : Q*

	RESERVOIR	INDICE DE CONCENTRATION
E_Q	0.15	0.22
R^2_Q	0.49	0.71
E_Q	0.44	0.66
R^2_Q	0.47	0.68

Tableau 3 Résultats des deux modéles sur le jeu de validation (2 épisodes).

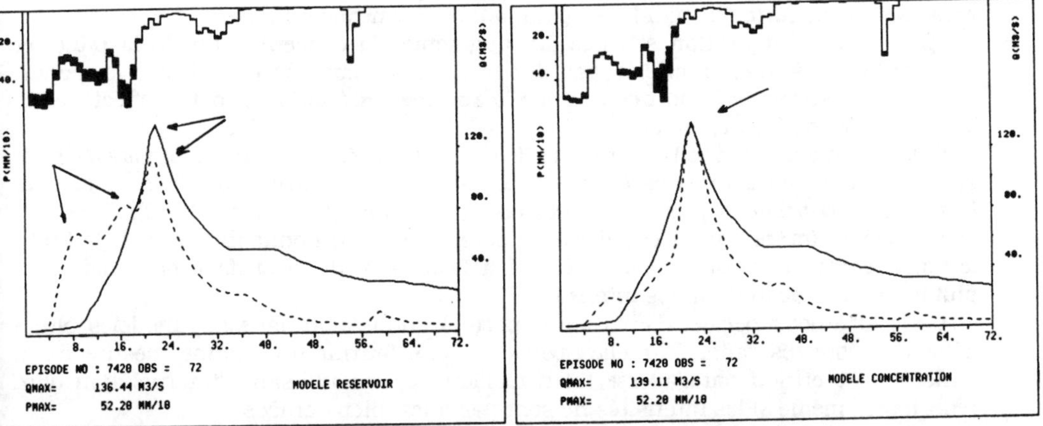

A FIG.7 Exemple de reconstitutions fournies par les deux modèles de Fonction de Production **(jeu de validation)**. A : modèle Réservoir ; B : modèle à Indice de Concentration. B

traduisent un net avantage pour le modèle à Indice de Concentration, qui fournit une dynamique plus adaptée aux épisodes observés.

Néanmoins, ces indices mesurant la qualité des modèles sur l'ensemble des pas de temps ne sont pas suffisants. La comparaison des reconstitutions des épisodes nous montre que l'amélioration de la dynamique, due à l'introduction des indices de concentration, devient surtout très nette quand on compare les pics des épisodes (voir Figure 6), le plus important en prévision de crues.

Enfin nous avons utilisé les deux modèles préalablement calibrés pour comparer leurs performances sur 2 épisodes de validation. Les résultats obtenus, présentés dans le Tableau 3, ainsi que la visualisation des épisodes (voir Figure 7) nous montrent à nouveau la superiorité de la dynamique proposée par le modèle à Indice de Concentration.

CONCLUSIONS

Nous avons exploré l'intérêt d'introduire la variabilité spatiale de la pluie dans un modèle pluie-débit global à l'aide des Indices de Concentration de Pluie, ICP. Bien que les résultats sur l'ensemble des pas de temps ne soient pas très différents de ceux d'un modèle global classique, la dynamique du modèle en utilisant des ICP s'avère plus performante, surtout quand on compare les pics de crue.

En particulier, la prise en compte non seulement de la séquence temporelle de la PB(t), mais aussi d'un indice de la répresentativité spatiale de cette moyenne, permet d'améliorer les reconstitutions des épisodes où l'information de la seule séquence temporelle de PB était insuffisante pour expliquer les débits.

Enfin, les résultats obtenus sur les trois épisodes de validation permettent de conclure l'intérêt de l'amélioration introduite, bien que le paramètre initial ait été optimisé.

Quant à la signification de l'indice, l'ensemble du coefficient correctif peut être interprété, vu les valeurs des paramètres calibrés (voir tableau 2), comme une mesure du pourcentage de la **surface productive** du bassin. En d'autres termes, la PEG(t), donnée par le modèle global, est corrigée par un facteur qui répresente le pourcentage de surface qui est en fait productive à ce taux (Sempere Torres, 1990). Cette **surface productive** oscille dans notre cas entre 0 et 56%, selon la valeur de l'ICP.

-Quand la PB(t) est une bonne mesure du champ de pluie (ICP(t) => 0), la PE(t) calculée est obtenue utilisant le taux de pluie efficace fournie par le modèle global, PEG(t), mais sur une **surface productive** de 60% du bassin. Cette limite superieure est sans doute liée à la configuration spatiale type des averses sur le bassin, qui se présentent sous forme de bande ocupant la moitié centrale du bassin.

-Quand la configuration spatiale fait augmenter la concentration de la pluie, et donc réduit la surface mouillée par des intensités comparables à PB(t), le modèle réduit en conséquence le pourcentage de la **surface productive** et donc l'effectivité de la PE calculée de façon globale.

Cela est en accord avec l'experience: *"le degré de la rélation entre l'intensité de pluie sur le bassin et le taux des pertes est directement liée à la proportion de la surface du bassin ne contribuant pas au processus de production"* (Clark, 1980). Une des conséquences intéressantes est alors que si on utilise une bonne moyenne de la PB(t), le terme correctif à utiliser est plutôt lié à la mesure de la surface non "mouillée" plutôt qu'à la distribution des intensités.

Cette idée nous permet d'ouvrir une porte à l'utilisation dans des modèles pluie-débit des données radar, car elles peuvent nous fournir une bonne mesure de la surface mise en jeu par l'averse (bien meilleure qu'en utilisant l'interpolation d'un réseau sol), même si les intensités ne sont pas aussi bien cernées.

Enfin notons que nous avons suivi une démarche exploratoire, et que l'indice proposé n'est que le meilleur parmi la dizaine d'indices utilisés. Par conséquent, la poursuite des recherches dans ce domaine est nécessaire, notamment pour la définition d'indices plus robustes, issus plutôt de considerations théoriques sur la structure spatiale de la pluie.

REMERCIEMENTS

Cette étude a été financée partiellement par le Ministère de l'Environnement et la DATAR Rhône-Alpes (Action Risques Naturels), ainsi que par une bourse FPI du *Ministerio Español de Educación y Ciencia*. Les donnée utilisées ont été amicalement fournies par la Direction Departamentale de l'Equipement du Gard.

REFERENCES

Aitken, A.P. (1973) Assessing systematic errors in Rainfall-Runoff models. J. Hydrol., **20**,121-136.

Beven, K. (1989) Changing ideas in hydrology. The case of physically based models. J. Hydrol., **105**, 157-172.

Clark, R.D.S. (1980) Rainfall stormflow analysis to investigate spatial and temporal variability of excess rainfall generation. J. Hydrol., **47**, 91-101.

Corradini, C. & Singh, V.P. (1985) Effect of spatial variability of effective rainfall on direct runoff by a geomorphologic approach. J. Hydrol., **81**, 27-43.

Creutin, J.D. (1979) Méthodes d'interpolation optimale de champs hydrométéorologiques. Comparaison et application à une série d'épisodes pluvieux Cévenoles. Thèse de Docteur Ingénieur, INPG, Grenoble (France).

Creutin, J.D. & Barancourt, C. (1988) Pattern and variability analysis of heavy rainfall fields in a mountainous mediterranean region. Proc. Conference on mesoscale precipitation : Analysis, simulation and Forecasting, Endicott House, M.I.T. (USA), Sept. 1988.

Duchon, J. (1976) Interpolation des fonctions de deux variables suivant le principe de la flexion des plaques minces. Revue Française d'Automatique, d'Informatique et de Recherche Opérationnelle, Analyse numérique, **10** (12),5-12.

Hawkins, R.H. (1982) Interprétations of source area variability in rainfall-runoff relations. In : V.P. Singh (Ed.), Rainfall-Runoff Relationships, Water Resources Publications, Littleton, Co. (USA), pp. 303-324.

Lebel, T. (1984) Moyenne spatiale de la pluie sur un bassin versant : estimation optimale, génération stochastique et gradex des valeurs extrêmes. Thèse de Docteur Ingénieur, INPG, Grenoble (France), 339 pp.

Guillot, P. & Duband, D. (1980) Fonction de transfert pluie-débit sur des bassins versants de l'ordre de 1000 km^2, La Houille Blanche, **4/5**,279-290.

Guillot, P. & Duband, D. (1981) Une méthode de transfert pluie-débit par régression multiple. In : Proc. of Oxford Symposium on Hydrological Forecasting, IAHS Publ. n° **129**, pp. 177-186.

Kirkby, M.J. (1988) Hillslope runoff processes and models, J. Hydrol., **100**, 315-339.

Loague, K.M. & Freeze, R.A. (1985) A comparison of rainfall-runoff modeling techniques on small upland catchments. Water Resour. Res., **21**, 229-248.

Lorent, B. (1975) Tests of different river flow predictors. In: G.C. Vansteenkiste (Ed.), Modeling and Simulation of Water Resources Systems, Nort-Holland Publishing Company, Amsterdam (Pays Bas), pp. 233-241

Milly, P.C.D. & Eagleson, P.S. (1988) Effect of storm scale on surface runoff volume. Water Resour. Res., **24** (4),620-624.

Nalbantis, I. (1987) Identification de modèles pluie-débit du type hydrogramme Unitaire : Développement de la méthode DPFT et validation sur données simulées avec et sans erreur. Thèse de doctorat, INPG, Grenoble (France).

Nash, J.E. & Sutcliffe, J.V. (1970) River flow forecasting through conceptual models, 1. A discussion of principles. J. Hydrol., **10**,282-290.

Newton, D. W. & Vinyard J. W. (1967) Computer-determined Unit Hydrograph from flows, J. Hydraul. Division, ASCE, **93**, Hy5, pp. 219-235.

Obled, Ch. (1989) Réflexions on rainfall information requirements for operational Rainfall-Runoff modeling. Paper J4, Proc. of Int. Symposium on Hydrological Applications on weather radar, University of Salford, Salford (UK).

Obled, Ch. & Rodriguez, J.Y. (1988) La distribution spatiale des pluies et son rôle dans la transformation pluie débit. La Houille Blanche, n° **5/6**, pp. 467-474.

Rodriguez, J.Y. (1989) Modélisation pluie-débit par la méthode DPFT. Développements de la méthode initiale et extension a des cas bi-entrées. Thèse de doctorat, INPG, Grenoble (France).

Rodriguez, J.Y. & Obled, Ch. (1990) Prise en compte de la variabilité spatiale des pluies efficaces par un modèle semi-global : Extension de la méthode DPFT à des cas bi-entrées. Proc. International Conference on water resources in moutainous regions, IAHS, Lausanne (Suisse), Août 1990.

Rodriguez, J.Y., Sempere Torres, D. & Obled, Ch. (1989) Nouvelles perspectives de développement dans la modélisation des pluies efficaces par application de la méthode DPFT, Surface Water Modeling-New directions for Hydrologic Prediction, IAHS Publ. n° **181**, 235-244.

Schilling, W. & Fuchs, L. (1986) Errors in stormwater modeling - A quantitative assessement. J. Hydraul. Eng., ASCEE, **112** (2), 111-123.

Sempere Torres, D. (1990) Calcul de la lame ruissellée dans la modélisation pluie-débit : limitations des approches globales et introduction simplifiée de la topographie et de la variabilité spatiale des pluies. Thèse de doctorat, INPG, Grenoble (France).

Sherman, L.K. (1932) Stream flow from rainfall by the Unit-Hydrograph method. Engin. News. Rec., **108**, 801-805.

Versiani, B. (1983) Modélisation de la relation pluie-débit pour la prévision des crues. Thèse de doctorat, INPG, Grenoble (France).

Wilson, C.B., Valdes, I.B. & Rodriguez-Iturbe, I. (1979) On the influence of the spatial distribution of Rainfall on Storm Runoff. Water Resour. Res., **15**(2), 321-328.

Hydrology in Mountainous Regions. I - Hydrological Measurements; the Water Cycle (Proceedings of two Lausanne Symposia, August 1990). IAHS Publ. no. 193, 1990.

Rainfall-runoff modeling of a microcatchment in the western region of Saudi Arabia

ALI U. SORMAN, M.J. ABDULRAZZAK & A.S. ELHAMES
Department of Hydrology and Water Resources Management, Faculty of Meteorology, Environment and Arid Land Agriculture, King Abdulaziz University, Jeddah 21413, Saudi Arabia

ABSTRACT Hydrologically, watersheds in the western region of Saudi Arabia can be classified as highlands with high rainfall, shallow soil, low infiltration and alluvial wadi channels in lowlands with runoff discharge, infiltration with recharge. In this research, mountainous microcatchment was selected in the southwest region to study rainfall-runoff modeling. Two models are selected, eleven storms are collected for analysis during three year period. The selected models are applied to some of the storms for calibrating the input parameters and tested for simulation for the others. The results are compared with the runoff hydrographs. Conclusive discussions for the application of the proposed models are presented.

INTRODUCTION

Arid regions of the world are usually characterized by extremely variable parameters in time and space regarding the depth and distribution of rainfall and runoff. There is also lack of adequate data for modeling and designing the structures.

Arid countries such as Saudi Arabia have expressed vast buildups of infrastructures and have been designed based on crude and empirical methods for runoff estimation. So far designing of future projects with dependable data depends on the accuracy of application models under arid climate conditions. There is an urgent need to calibrate and test the most applicable models to determine their suitability.

The objectives of this study is to determine the shape and characteristics of flood hydrographs from individual observed storms in one of the upper microcatchments located in the Asir mountains near Al-Baha area. Modified Soil Conservation Service (SCS) and distributed runoff-routing (RORB) models are selected to calibrate and test to the historical records, collected recently by the investigators (M.J. Abdulrazzak et al,1985-89). The selection of suitable model will contribute toward the assessment and development of water resources in arid environment like in the Kingdom of Saudi Arabia.

BACKGROUND

A review of early rainfall-runoff models has been provided by Linsley (1971) and subsequent model evolution was described by Papadakis and Preul (1973). The majority of these models were developed for humid regions. The problem of model application in arid zones was recently discussed by Pilgrem et al. (1988).

Rainfall-runoff models in arid regions were reported by Wallace and Lane (1976), Pilgrem et al. (1982), Laurenson and Meis (1983), Morel-Seytoux et al. (1984). Large scale catchment model studies were also reported by Saudi Arabian Dames and Moore (1988), Allam and Sorman (1988) for wadis in the southwestern region of the Kingdom.

Two models are selected to test their applicability under the arid climate. Description and application of the models will be addressed in the following subsections.

DESCRIPTION OF THE STUDY AREA

For model study purposes, an experimental site near Al-Baha is selected in order to determine what percentage of storm depth is transformed into direct runoff and what shape of runoff hydrograph is produced from various rainfall intensity-time distribution histograms.

The catchment site called as USGS is located at the upper Ranyah area with a drainage site of

0.13 km^2. About half of the area is bare ground in the form of rocks and soil. The catchment is a second order drainage basin with a circular in shape and seems to have the same runoff contribution from both tributaries. The area is instrumented with H-type flume to measure discharges. The flume is designed to handle about maximum flow rates up to 1.25 m^3/sec. A tipping bucket recording rainfall station is also installed at the runoff site with a data logger unit. A non-recording daily measuring raingage is also placed next to the recording to check the total precipitation depth since its installment in 1985.

DESCRIPTION OF THE MODELS

Soil Conservation Service (SCS) method

The use of the Soil Conservation Service procedure described in the NEH, 1972 revised in 1985 involves the determination of curve numbers for urban and rural areas with their respective percentage areal coverages where the curve number depends on soil type and land use.

The potential maximum retention capacity (S) for each sub-basin is determined for the selected CN. Land use type in addition to the estimated initial abstraction loss for the determination of excess rainfall. Estimation of runoff is done by a relationship between accumulated storm rainfall depth (P), runoff (Q) and infiltration (F) plus initial abstraction (I_a) as

$$\frac{F}{S}=\frac{Q}{(P-I_a)}$$

where S is the maximum potential abstraction which is related to CN as S = (1000/CN) - 10, I_a = 0.1~0.2S and F = ($P-I_a-Q$)

Runoff-Routing Model (RORB)

This is a distributed model developed by Laurenson and Mein (1983) representing both linear and non-linear basin response. It represents detention, overland flow and channel storage by a model distributed over the area. After losses are subtracted from rainfall on each sub-basin, the excess rainfall is determined and discharge is routed to produce the surface flow at the outlet. Two loss models are incorporated as constant and proportional loss in addition to other two model parameters representing the non-linearity (m) and storm delay coefficient (K_c).

COLLECTION AND ANALYSIS OF DATA

The rainfall depths and stage hydrographs are recorded for each storm between 1986-1988 using datapods DP101 for rainfall and DP115 for runoff. Both electronic recorders are battery operated and data are stored on data storage modules (DSM) which can be processed through computer readers. DP101 module records the time and scans the rainfall sensor according to a preset time interval selected as one minute. Once every 24 hours, an absolute level recording is also stored in the DSM. The water level readings on the other hand were in hundredths of feet of water up to 10 feet by DP115 datapod which varies between zero to 1000 counts. The recording time interval varies from six minutes to one day. The interval is set up to six minutes.

Depths of rainfall and observed runoff peak discharges as well as rainfall intensities and ordinates of discharges are collected in order to use them in the model studies. The water level recordings are converted to discharges of each 6 minutes using the rating table of the respective 3.5 foot flume at the outlet.

APPLICATION OF THE MODELS

There were 11 individual storm events which occurred in the Al-Baha site during the period from March 1986 to March 1988. Five of these events observed in the first year are selected for calibrating the rainfall-runoff models and the rest are used for testing the models. Most of these were single produced storms, two were with double and other two were with multiple peaks. Rainfall events which produce more than 10 mm of precipitation depth are considered for simulation studies. Two models (SCS and RORB) which gave better calibration results are used for predicting the remaining storms left for simulation purposes. The six minute time increment is used in the model simulation studies.

The calibrated and tested input parameters for both models are tabulated in Table 1 and variation in model parameters for single and multiple peak storms are presented in Table 2. Comparison of observed storm characteristics with the simulated hydrographs is done in graphical forms and some of which are presented for discussion in Figure 1.

TABLE 1 INPUT MODEL PARAMETERS FOR CALIBRATED AND TESTED STORMS.

	SCS MODEL						RORB MODEL			
	Q_p UH (cfs)	I_a (inch)	CN Urban	CN Rural	%R	% DCIA	m	K_c	I_L (mm)	R_C
01/03/86*	150	0.10	90	75	20	45	0.50	0.25	5.6	0.04
02/03/86*	150	0.03	95	85	20	52	0.70	0.050	1.5	0.08
03/04/86*	120	0.10	80	70	25	40	0.85	0.050	8.0	0.17
04/04/86*	80	0.10	80	70	25	30	0.80	0.100	10.0	0.17
	250	0.35	70	60	40	35			26.5	0.55
01/03/87*							0.80	0.001		
	150	0.25	80	75	25	30			25.0	0.11
03/03/87**	200	0.20	95	90	20	50	0.50	0.050	25.0	0.37
									13.0	0.71
									22.0	0.97
07/03/87**	240	0.07	90	85	15	60	0.50	0.009	5.0	0.47
29/10/87**	200	0.19	95	85	20	50	0.80	0.010	9.0	0.48
23/12/87**	150	0.19	80	75	25	45	0.50	0.010	8.5	0.62
15/01/88**	150	0.31	80	70	25	45	0.80	0.020	14.0	0.42
24/02/88**	110	0.10	85	75	25	45	0.80	0.060	2.7	0.26

TABLE 2 VARIATION IN INPUT PARAMETERS.

			SCS MODEL				RORB MODEL			
Hydrograph	Q_p UH (cfs)	I_a (inch)	CN Urban	CN Rural	%R	% DCIA	m	K_c	I_L (mm)	R_C
Single*	80	0.03	70	60	20	30	0.50	0.100	1.5	0.04
Multiple*	250	0.35	95	85	40	50	0.85	0.001	25.0	0.55
Single**	110	0.07	80	70	15	45	0.50	0.060	5.0	0.02
Multiple**	240	0.30	95	90	25	60	0.80	0.009	25.0	0.62

* calibrated storms

** tested storms

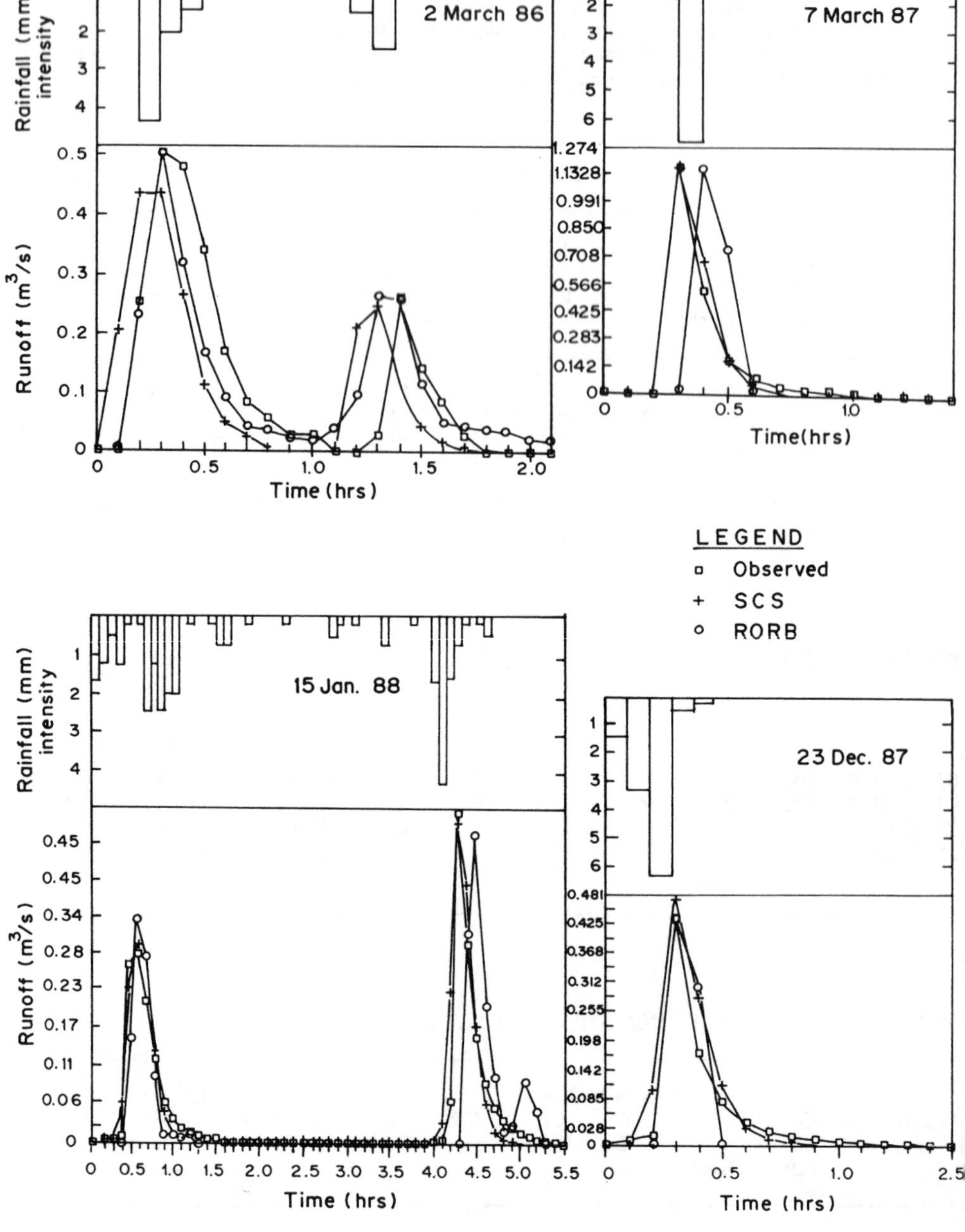

FIG. 1 Rainfall intensity and runoff hydrograph at the Al-Baha USGS site.

DISCUSSION OF RESULTS

During the calibration stage of SCS model, the initial abstraction (I_a) and curve numbers for rural and urban areas (CN_u and CN_r) are found more sensitive in simulating runoff hydrographs. The tested model parameters are found within the range of calibrated input parameters.

Similarly, the results of RORB model showed some consistency in input parameter values of initial loss (I_L) and calculated runoff coefficient (R_C) which are changed between 1.5~25 mm and 4~55 per cent respectively. The values of non-linear parameter (m) ranged from 0.50~0.85. But the storm delay coefficient (K_c) was varying in a wider range between 0.001~0.100 where the pair of parameters for all the storms were not exist to get the optimum simulated model outputs compared with observed runoff hydrograph parameters.

CONCLUSIONS

Reasonable comparative results by simulated models are produced with the actual flood hydrographs some of which are presented graphically. Input model parameters were found in certain ranges depending upon the storm characteristics being multiple, or single peak produced storms as well as the intensity and duration of the rainfalls. The antecedent soil moisture affected on the determination of abstraction and initial losses in conjunction with the runoff coefficient.

When more hydrologic events would be available for the site in Al-Baha area, some more refinements in the input parameters for both models are expected in order to apply other microcatchments which have similar climatologic and hydrologic characteristics.

REFERENCES

Abdulrazzak, J.M., Sorman, A.U. et al. (1985-89) Estimation of Natural Groundwater Recharge, Progress Report Nos.1~8, AR-6-170, supported by KACST, Riyadh.

Allam, M.N. and Sorman, A.U. (1988) Geomorphologic rainfall geomorphologic rainfall-runoff models for infiltrating watershed. Final Report, AR-07-86 supported by KACST, Riyadh.

Laurenson, E.M. and Mein, R.G. (1983) RORB version 3, Runoff routing program user manual, Dept CE, Monash Univ, Australia.

Linsley, R.K. (1971) A Critical Review of Currently Available Hydrologic Models for Analysis of Urban Stormwater Runoff, Dept of the Interior, Office of WRR, Washington, D.C.

Morel Seytoux, H.J., Correia, F.N. et al. (1984) Some recent developments in physically based rainfall-runoff modeling, Frontiers in Hydrology, WR Publications, Colorado, U.S.A.

National Engineering Handbook (1972, 1985), Soil Conservation Service, Section 4, U.S. Government Printing Office, Washington, D.C.

Papadakis, C.N. and Preul, H.C. (1973) Testing of Methods for Determination of Urban Runoff, Journal of Hyd. Div, ASCE, 99 (HY9), p1319.

Pilgrem, D.H., Chapman, T.G. and Doran, D.G. (1988) Problems of rainfall-runoff modelling in arid and semiarid regions, Hydrological Sc. Journal, vol.36(4).

Pilgrem, D.H., Cordery, I. and Boyd, M.J. (1982) Australian developments in flood hydrograph modelling, Water Resources Publications, Rainfall-Runoff Relationship 37-48.

Saudi Arabian Dames and Moore (1988) Representative Basin Study for Wadis. Final Report, vol F8 submitted to Water Resources Dev. Dept of MAW, Riyadh.

Wallace, D.A. and Lane, L.J. (1976) Geomorphic thresholds and their influence on surface runoff from small semi-arid watershed. American Water Resour. Ass. and Arizona Acad of Sc., 6, 169-176.

Hydrology in Mountainous Regions. I - Hydrological Measurements; the Water Cycle
(Proceedings of two Lausanne Symposia, August 1990). IAHS Publ. no. 193, 1990.

The "Hydrograph GGI-90" model and its application for mountain basins

YU. B. VINOGRADOV
State Hydrological Institute, 199053 Leningrad, USSR

ABSTRACT Brief information is given on the "Hydrograph GGI-90" model developed within the framework of creating methods for hydrological computations of a new generation. The problem of its use for mountain basins is discussed.

Deterministic mathematical model "Hydrograph GGI-90" is designed as a universal model with lumped parameters for a continuous computation of runoff hydrograph for any number of years. Regional peculiarities of runoff formation are taken into account parametrically. It is primarily intended for mountain basins. It is supposed to apply the model in the system of probabilistic hydrological computations of a new generation in case of possible changes in climate and topography.

The surface of the Earth may be divided into different areas within which the process of runoff formation may be considered as qualitatively uniform, and the quantitative characteristics may be averaged. We may define this area as a runoff-producing complex (RPC), i.e. a part of a basin which is conventionally uniform hypsometrically, hydrographically, geologically, geohydrologically, geobotanically and pedo-geographically. It is assumed that all the model parameters characterise the RPC as a whole, they are constant within the RPC and they are subject to leap-changes at the RPC boundaries.

Water balance components in a soil-plant column are computed at individual "representative points" (RP), located at the nodes of a hexagonal grid consisting of regular hexagons. Basin area A, number of points n and distance between equispaced points Δl are interrelated by the following ratio $n = 1.1547\ A/\Delta l^2$. A hexagonal plot of $\Delta A = 0.866\,\Delta l^2$ in area corresponds to every RP. Various heterogeneities occurring within this area are neglected. Every RP has its latitude, elevation above m.s.l., exposure and slope.

Since every RP is located within a certain RPC, it gets the parameters of this RPC.

Every RP consists of five "quantile" and one "narrow ravine" design points similar by all the parameters but water equivalent of snow pack, which takes into account the natural heterogeneity of snow pack distribution over territory within one RPC in case of similar precipitation.

Runoff summarizing from all the system of RP with the account of the appropriate time shift explained by the of water travel within the basin leads to obtaining the runoff hydrograph at the outlet.

If the design time interval of the model is a day (24 hours) the input model parameters are: daily precipitation, air temperatures,air humidity deficit and rainfall duration. In general, any reduction of the design time interval is possible, but in this case a coordinated change of the input meteorological information is required.

This model differs from the other models by the following:

- there is no equation of water conductivity (water diffusion) in the model, since it does not correspond to the physics of the process, not provided with information and which makes computations more complicated;
- equations of Saint Venant type or the equations of kinematic wave are not applied, which makes it possible to use more realistic approaches and to reduce nonproductive computations greatly
- universality, i.e. applicacy of the model for any basin in any physiography;
- the model is based on the actual information available;
- all kinds of runoff are taken into account, i.e. snowmelt runoff, rainfall runoff and ground water outflow;
- specific features of mountain terrains are taken into account.

A particular emphasis should be made on the a priori specification of model parameters having a particular physical sense; laboratory and field methods and ways of measurements are developed for the evaluation of these parameters. If the measured characteristics are used as model parameters, it increases the physical validation and efficiency of the model. Proceeding from this, the optimization of the model parameters is not reasonable.

A general idea of the model is given in schematic block (Fig. 1) showing the main features and interrelations of the model.

The model algorithm is arranged in a system of blocks and it is separated into three stages; the names of these stages show their hierarchic level: "Design point", "Representative point", "Basin".

The "Design point" stage corresponds to the ideology of the lumped parameters model almost completely. The system of blocks at this stage provides modeling of some accompanying hydrometeorological events for a plot, which are of an independent interest, i.e. evaporation, soil thaw and freeze-up, soil moisture dynamics, for-

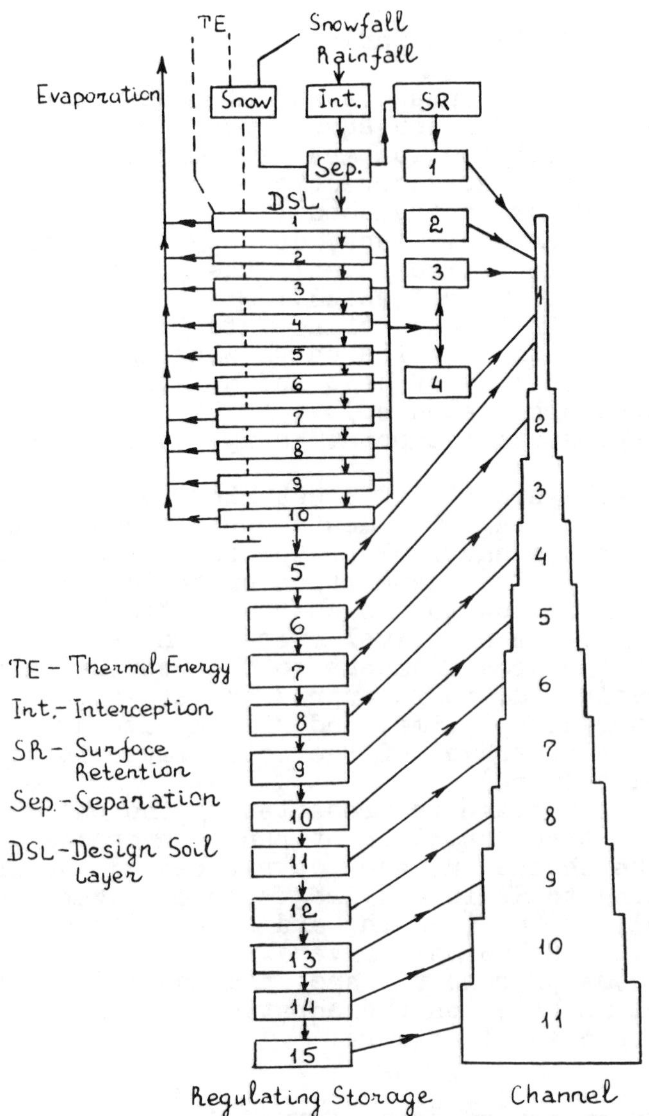

FIG. 1 The "Hydrograph GGI-90" model.

mation, accumulation and disappearence of the snow pack.

The system consists of six blocks:

"Diagnosis" (evaporation from snow pack is computed, diagnosis is made on the formalised presence or absence of the snow pack, the amount of heat energy required for the all the phase transformations in soil and snow is evaluated in the first approximation);

"Parameter" (heat-physical characteristics of snow and soil are computed, i.e. specific volumetric heat capacity, coefficients of heat conductivity and heat exchange);

"Energy" (heat-cold inflow to snow-soil system is computed);

"Precipitation" (phase state of precipitation, humidity and density of fresh snow, amount of thermal energy delivered by precipitation are determined; interception is taken into account; corrections for systematic errors of measurements are introduced);

"Snow" (water equivalent, density, saturation by water, water yield are computed; the processes of freeze-up and snow melt are reflected);

"Soil" (water is subdivided into infiltration and surface runoff; the results on thawing and freeze-up, evaporation, dynamics of heat and moisture, ground runoff formation are evaluated).

The "Representative point" stage consists of two blocks:

"Slope" (layers of different kinds of runoff computed at the previous stage for design points contributing to the system of the particular representative point are averaged; then, after separation of the design time interval, water inflow to the channel network is computed);

"Brook" (time of travel over the hydrographic network within the area adjacent to the representative point is evaluated, it is expressed as a number of design subintervals of time, and sliding averaging is made from the time of travel of the total water inflow to the channel network).

The "Basin" stage is presented by the only block:

"River" (transformation of runoff hydrographs derived at the channel network output beyond the areas corresponding to RP into hydrographs at river mouths successively of the (n-2)th, and of (n-1)th orders and at the outlet of the main river).

The scheme of runoff transformation before reaching the channel is based on the equation of inflow hydrograph to the channel network:

$$R = \frac{S + b}{1 + \frac{S-h}{b+h} \exp\left[-a \cdot \Delta t(S+b)\right]} - b \qquad (1)$$

Where: S, R - intensities of runoff formation and inflow (m^3/s); $a = a^*/A$, $b = b^*A$; a^*, b^* - normalised parameters of runoff transformation before reaching the channel; A - area of the basin or of its part; Δt - design time interval.

The system of runoff components or regulating capacities (in case of other similar conditions) may be characterised by a duration of outflow decrease is compared with the initial value, from R_0 to R_0/e, where $e = 2.72$:

$$\tau^* = 1/(ab) = 1/(a^*b^*) \qquad (2)$$

$$\tau = \tau^* \ln \ (e - R_o/b)/(1 + R_o/b) \qquad (3)$$

where τ^* - characteristic time of regulating capacity response, τ - response time at the particular basin water availability.

Hydraulic parameters a* and b* are connected with the RPC type, moreover a* is clearly determined by the type of flow while b* is to a certain extent a correcting factor. This information is given in Table 1.

At the space interpolation of precipitation in mountains the following two independent problems are separated: interpolation of total precipitation for individual dates and interpolation of distribution curves parameters for total daily precipitation.

The first problem is connected with the hydrograph modeling for particular years during particular meteorological situations. Here a necessity arises to transfer data obtained at meteorological stations to the RP.

The second problem, climatic by its essence, is to get reliable dependences of statistic parameters of total daily precipitation distribution curves upon the appropriate orographic characteristics; thus, this problem is specific and independent.

There are different digital coefficients in the mathematical model algorith. These are:

TABLE 1 System of Runoff Transformation before Reaching the Channel.

Capacity number	Type of flowing	τ^*	Order of a* value	Order of watercourse output
1	surface 1	16.7 min	3	1
2	surface 2	16.7 min	3	1
3	upper soil	52.7 min	2.5	1
4	lower soil	52.7 min	2.5	1
5	rapid ground 1	2.8 hr	2	1
6	rapid ground 2	8.8 hr	1.5	2
7	ground 1	1.2 day	1	3
8	ground 2	3.7 day	0.5	4
9	ground 3	12.0 day	0	5
10	ground 4	1.2 month	-0.5	6
11	deep ground 1	3.8 month	-1	7
12	deep ground 2	1 year	-1.5	8
13	deep ground 3	3.2 year	-2	9
14	deep ground 4	10 year	-2.5	10
15	deep ground 5	31.7 year	-3	11

- conventional constant values (density of water and ice, specific mass heat capacity and coefficients of heat conductivity of water and ice, specific mass heat of vapour formation and heat of ice melt);
- empirical coefficients;
- basin characteristics (length, area and slopes of watercourses of n, n-1 and n-2 orders);
- RPC characteristics (depth of the underlying mountain surface and of genetic soil horizons, depth of ground water table, depth of organogenic layers of the forest litter, depth of moss-lichen top cover, height of plant layers, etc.);

RPC parameters (29 parameters, such as soil porosity, maximum water-holding capacity of soil and plants, hydraulic parameters of runoff transformation before reaching the channel, normalised coefficients of heat exchange, four phenological dates, etc.);

- hydrographic network parameters (18 parameters), such as number of watercourses of the 1st order per unit area, mean length, area and angle of slopes of the 1st order watercourses, ratios of lengths, areas and slopes of flows, channel roughness coefficients, etc.).

Model parameters should be normalised and generalized comprising a definite section of the information data base for runoff modeling. Generalization of parameters is made on the RPC basis corresponding to various physiographic zones and vertical belts of mountain terrains.

A comparison of the observed hydrographs and of those computed by the model for the mountain basin of the Varzob river is given below (Fig. 2).

The basin is located on the southern slope of the Gissarsky Range in Tadzhikistan. The drainage area at

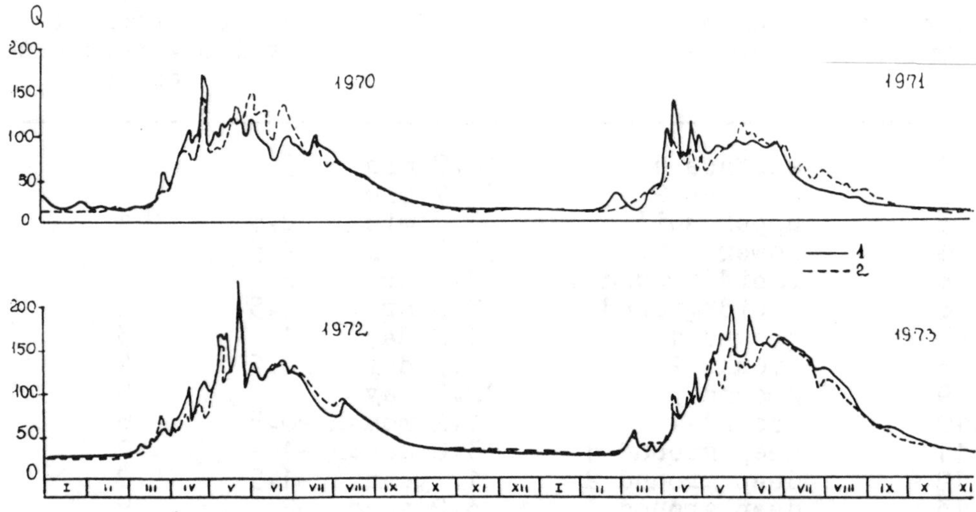

FIG. 2 Computed (1) and observed (2) runoff hydrographs for the Varzob River at Dagana for 1970-1973 (A = 1270 km^2, 8 RPC, 40 RP).

Dagana is 1270 km^2, the order of the main river is 6, the range of elevations is from 982 m to 4881 m, 8 RPC, 40 RP.

Types of the RPC: (1) Glaciers and firn fields; (2) Rocks and talus (contemporary moraines included); (3) Alpine meadows; (4) Subalpine meadows; (5) Archa light forest; (6) Xerophyte bushes and light forest; (7) Broad-leaved forests; (8) Cultivated lands (Fig. 3).

FIG. 3 Runoff-producing complexes and representative points in the Varzob river basin.

CONCLUSION

Hydrological computations by the model make it possible to obtain runoff characteristics of the specified probability. Therefore, synthesis of statistics and determinism is required. A sequence of deterministic-stochastic (DS) modeling is as follows:

- at the output of stochastic model A the sequences of meteorological components are generated, which appear at the input of deterministic model B;
- at the output of model B simulated runoff characteristics appear, and they enter the input of stochastic model C;
- at the output of model C the coordinates of the distribution curves for the required runoff characteristics are obtained.

This chain should be the basis for the methodology of hydrological computations of a new generation. Besides the reliable deterministic model "Hydrograph", the major emphasis of the DS-modeling is focussed on the construction of a stochastic model, which may be named "Weather". All the above problems are given in detail in (Vinogradov, 1988).

REFERENCE

Vinogradov,Yu.B. (1988) Matematicheskoe modelirovanie protsessov formirovania stoka. Opyt kriticheskogo analiza (Mathematical modeling of runoff formation. A critical analysis). Leningrad, USSR.

Hydrology in Mountainous Regions. I - Hydrological Measurements; the Water Cycle
(Proceedings of two Lausanne Symposia, August 1990). IAHS Publ. no. 193, 1990.

Application of the unit hydrograph model to Swiss catchments

R. WEINGARTNER
Institute of Geography-Hydrology, University of Berne,
Hallerstr. 12, CH-3012 Berne, Switzerland

ABSTRACT The analysis of about 350 rainfall/runoff events in seventeen different types of Swiss catchments shows a pronounced dependency of unit hydrographs on events. Moreover, a special stress is laid on the duration of rainfall. The unit hydrograph model can be worked into a coherent method emanating from so-called contributing areas. The method allows a feasible classification of the analyses results, procures isolation of representative unit hydrographs and guides to the estimation of design flood based on a few analysible rainfall-runoff results. Initial steps are being presented for regionalization of unit hydrographs.

INTRODUCTION

In Switzerland, within the field of flood hydrology, many investigations indicate a brisk measurement and analysis activity: The Swiss National Hydrological and Geological Survey above all runs on a comparatively dense runoff-network at an average density of one station per 100 km^2 (surface of Switzerland about 40'000 km^2). Large regional distinctions in the network-density, however, impede a model-fitting and -test, a characteristic fact relevant to the alpine region (cf Aschwanden, 1990). The network-extension taken recently by means of so-called flood-limit-gauges ("Hochwassergrenzwertpegel") indicating the peak-flood-level and designating the discharge by hydraulic calculations proves to be interesting.

For about 130 stations, data series span more than 30 years and facilitate the gaining of extreme values (Q_{50}, Q_{100}) by means of statistical analyses (Spreafico & Stadler, 1986, 1987). Together with extensive statistical analyses of extreme station precipitations, the input- and output-quantities of the rainfall/runoff-process are excellently documented. Actual efforts are orientated on the regionalization of point-rainfall (Geiger et al., 1990) and flood-values.

In Switzerland, empirical flood formulas have been applied for a long time and with varying success. The most often used formulas mainly provide enveloping curves and an overestimation of peakflows up to a factor of 10 becomes apparent. In the last years, special efforts have been made within the range of a "rational formula": Kölla (1986) presented an interesting model considering new recognition on the runoff formation (Zuidema, 1985) and stressing the status of contributing areas:

$$Q_x = r_x(T1_x + T2_x)\ FL_x \tag{1}$$

Q_x: x-year flood
r_x: intensity of x-year rainfall of duration T1+T2
T1: moisture time
T2: time of translation
FL: contributing area

In Switzerland too, conceptual models - detailed models thus - are limited by the documents available for their application. As shown by this very brief outline, wide-spread investigations on flood hydrology have therefore been carried out (details see Weingartner & Spreafico, 1990). For everyday-use, the question rises which approach on flood estimation is to be selected and on what conditions. Aschwanden & Spreafico (1989) help us make a decision:

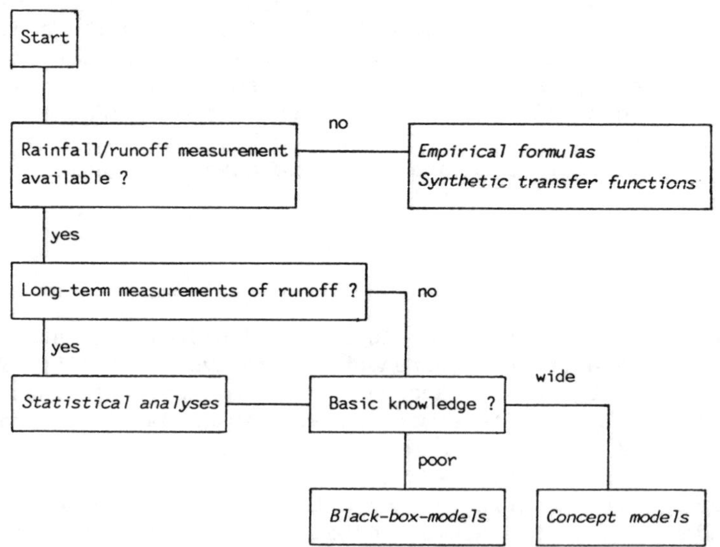

FIG. 1 Method of flood estimation depending on data and knowledge (acc. Aschwanden & Spreafico, 1989).

So far, the unit hydrograph model has not been mentioned yet. As a black-box-model it can be applied for flood estimation on catchments with few runoff events available. On the other hand, there is the possibility to use the unit hydrograph as a synthetical transfer-function. In Switzerland, the unit hydrograph model has been applied mainly to the Swiss Plateau area in the French part until now (i.e. Gloor et al., 1983, Consuegra, 1988).

The present study includes catchments of all Swiss regions. It compiles the most important results of an aptitude test and gives an overview of the analysis of rainfall/runoff events. The final chapter indicates possible applications of the unit hydrograph model.

THE UNIT HYDROGRAPH MODEL

For the unit hydrograph model, the catchment is considered as a "black-box" in the meaning of the systems theory. A complete determination of the systems reaction by both the systems input and -characteristics is demanded. A connection between a systems input and response exists and is generally described as transfer-function. The unit hydrograph represents a linear and time-invariate transfer-function between both the effective rainfall (rainfall excess) and the direct runoff. At a first attempt, the rainfall/runoff process may obviously be sufficiently described by such simplified terms (Aschwanden & Spreafico, 1989).

A unit hydrograph can be derived from an observed hydrograph. After the base flow is separated from the observed hydrograph, the ordinates of the direct runoff hydrograph (QD) at convenient equal time intervals (dt) can be expressed by the following redundant system of linear equations:

$$QD_i = \sum_{k=1}^{m} u_{i-k+1}\, I_k \qquad 0 < i-k+1 < n \qquad (2)$$

m: number of rainfall intervals
n: number of unit hydrograph ordinates

The solution of these equations will give the ordinates of the unit hydrograph (u). The intensity of effective rainfall (I) must be known (cf Ven te Chow, 1964).

ANALYSIS OF SELECTED RAINFALL/RUNOFF EVENTS

The analysis is linked with catchments showing well documented and high resolvable precipitation and runoff gaugings. A catchment surface of 5 to 250 km^2 secures a homogeneity to a certain extent. This homogeneity is significant for both the regionalization (synthesis) and the problem of spatial regularity of rainfall. Seventeen catchments on investigation to comply with such qualification could finally be selected, indicating data series for at least two years and representing the Swiss hydrological spectrum on the whole (Aschwanden & Weingartner, 1985).

To make a selection, single peaked floods were considered primary. This, however, is subjected to some restrictions, multi-peaked floods in fact often leading to the most significant peak flows. Obviously, some stress was laid on a good temporal synchronization between rainfall and runoff. Moreover, events easily to be reconstructed by means of a unit hydrograph are considered only. More than 350 events within the 17 catchments on investigation were available finally.

To determine the direct runoff, a linear separation of base flow was selected. The runoff ratio is determinable by the quotient between the volumes of direct runoff and total rainfall. The calculated runoff ratios reveal the expected wide variation between and within the catchments. Correlation analyses confirm a wide independency of the runoff ratio on parameters such as rainfall total, duration and intensity of precipitation, as well as on parameters by antecedent moisture conditions (antecedent rainfall). These results are corroborated in a study by Naef (1985), based on 170 Swiss catchments. Significant correlations between the runoff ratio and the antecedent moisture conditions as well as the total rainfall are noticed however on investigations in the Swiss Plateau area.

If we compare the closer range of ratio variation (mean ± 1 standard deviation) inferred from "normal" flood events (return period 10 years) with the variation noticed for the ten most extreme floods observed (Naef et al., 1985), the following facts are discerned: The runoff coefficients of extreme events do not significantly differ from those of "normal" events, with the exception of the alpine catchments of Allenbach and Hinterrhein. It is remarkable that in most of the cases the highest flood observed does not result in the widest ratio. Extreme floods can also develop from a superposition of hydrographs from sub-catchments showing mean runoff coefficients as the example of the Langeten proves. Usually the variation-range derived from "normal" flood events provides empirical ratios of extreme floods - empirical ratios, though, varying still considerably.

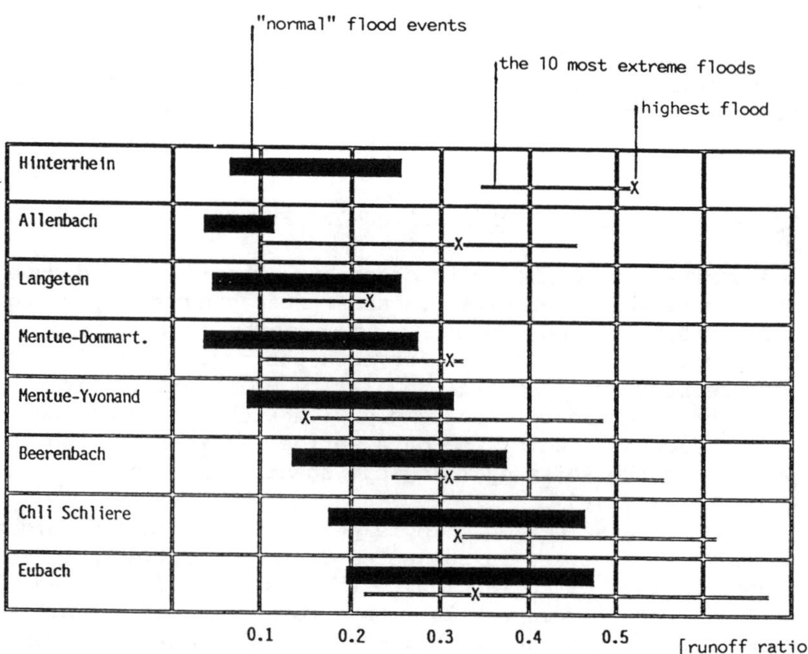

FIG. 2 Variation of runoff ratios of "normal" flood events in comparison with the ten most extreme floods observed

To find out the temporal distribution of effective rainfall, very good experience was gained with an analysis by the variable ratio model by Köhler (1971). The model assumes a runoff ratio of nearly zero at the beginning of rainfall, increasing gradually to attain a constant value.

To characterize initial moisture conditions, great significance is generally attached to parameters representing antecedent rainfall (aP_5, aP_{21}). This fact has not been confirmed for Swiss catchments on investigation. Their extreme slopes might be of great importance: About 60 % of the catchment areas present an average slope gradient of >15°. Therefore we suppose a quick drainage after a rainfall event. For Switzerland, an indicator aligned with the period of 24 to 48 hours before the start of a flood event seems to be more suitable. The fact whether further floods had drained off shortly before the analyzed event is of prime importance (cf Weingartner, 1989).

ANALYSIS OF THE RESULTING UNIT HYDROGRAPHS

Within a catchment we discern a pronounced variation of the unit hydrograph. Based on experience of other authors (i.e. Köhler, 1971 and Lutz, 1984), a variation was to be expected, its extent being significant however (Fig. 3).

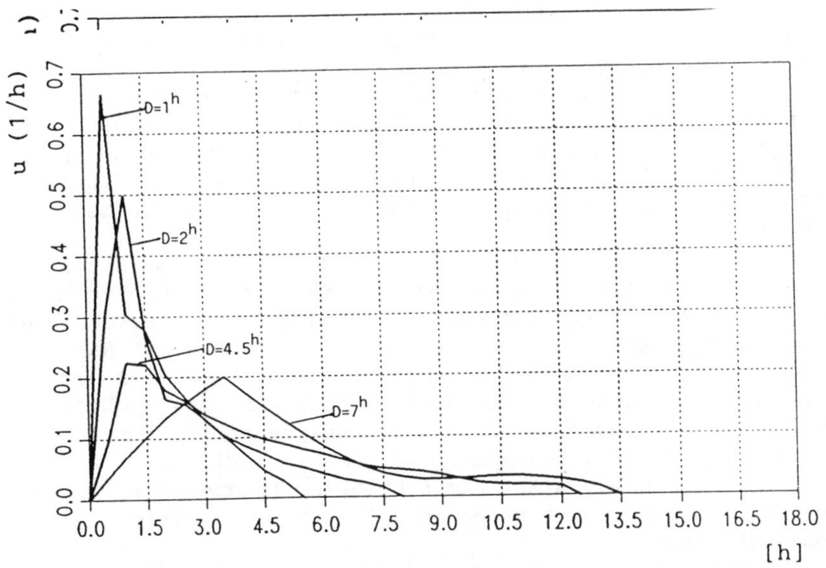

FIG. 3 The variation of the unit hydrographs by the example of Chli Schliere at Alpnach. (D: Total duration of the rainfall event; time interval 0.5^h)

The influence of incorrect gaugings being mostly ruled out by a careful choice of data, we focus on the question of dependency on an event: Short rainfall events generally lead to pronounced and rather short unit hydrographs. As a rule, less pronounced unit hydrographs with a larger base-length are noticed with an increasing duration of the rainfall event (Fig. 3). This general connection between the duration of rainfall and the form of unit hydrographs can be hypothetically explained by the conception of contributing areas. This conception is mainly based on the observation that slopes close to rivers are merely flood relevant, as only the precipitation dropped on these parts reach the control point within a period of time pertinent to flood formation (Kölla, 1986 and Zuidema, 1985).

Within a shorter duration of rainfall, those areas of soils with almost water-saturated conditions mainly contribute to the direct runoff. These conditions are above all observed in areas closest to rivers and lead to a pronounced and short unit hydrograph. Within a longer duration of rainfall the areas close to rivers with initially unsaturated soils also contribute to direct runoff. Due to effects of retention those areas allow a delayed runoff and cause on the whole a more even and longer unit hydrograph. It lies in the nature of flood events that this presentation can only describe a main part of the complex process. For further details cf Weingartner 1989.

For Swiss conditions the unit hydrograph model can in principle be focused on, although its variation can not be too much emphasized, especially when a representative unit hydrograph is to be determined for the application (see below).

SIGNIFICANCE FOR CONCRETE APPLICATION

According to figure 1, both the black-box-models to estimate extreme floods (Q_{20}, Q_{50}, Q_{100}) and the unit hydrograph model in particular as a simple and practicable method are suitable for cases disposing of some rainfall/runoff events. The following paragraphs introduce gradually the method to estimate design floods with a representative unit hydrograph. The model on the whole is described in Weingartner (1989). Fundamental data can also be found in Aschwanden & Spreafico (1989).

1) *Hypothesis*: A x-year flood (x=20,50,100) is initiated by a rainfall of a similar return period. For lack of better knowledge this is to be assumed although it has not been observed in analysis. A constant intensity of rainfall is assumed as well. Rainfalls are transferred from the nearest precipitation station. A decreasing curve has not been considered. Undouptly, an easy application speaks well for this concept. However, we realize the fact that these suppositions are not widely accepted, particularly in view of the uniform design storm. On the other hand, no fundumental improvement has been produced by tests based on differing suppositions relevant to design storms.

2) Determination of the *time of concentration* for the catchment concerned: Previous experience has shown a general underestimation of concentration time by the well known Kirpich (1940) model. Positive experience has been gained however from the model Kölla (1986), focusing on the retention within contributing areas. The time of concentration is estimated iteratively, considering the time of translation and saturation of certain moisture deficits in soils. They are depending on both the return period and the geological and pedological ratios and can easily be investigated from actual maps of Switzerland.

3) Selection of the *representative unit hydrograph*: Due to a variation described before, special attention is to be drawn to the selection of a suitable unit hydrograph. The best results have been achieved with a unit hydrograph originating from an event with a rainfall duration closest to the concentration time as model tests

have shown. Are no events available to obtain an appropriate unit hydrograph, representative unit hydrographs as a synthetical transfer function can be derived from both the catchment form and soil characteristics, the storage capacity in particular (cf Weingartner 1989).

4) The SCS model scheduled for a large dependency of the *runoff ratio* on the rainfall total proved to be unsuitable under Swiss conditions, as our investigations and works by Naef & Moser (1984) have shown. Above all a dependency of the runoff ratio on the rainfall total supposed by the SCS model was not discerned in any of the catchments. The definition of the "curve number" presents an additional difficulty: Small miscalculations will have serious consequences for the runoff ratio. To determine the runoff ratio, another method has been chosen in this case considering the information by Költa (1986) about contributing areas in particular: Assuming a 100 % drainage of the contributing area, an adequate estimation of the runoff ratio based on the relation of the contributing area to the total catchment surface results. In fact, the contributing areas are of central significance in synthesis model. Following Költa (1986) they can be estimated by the total length of the stream channels assuming an average slope length of 100 m.

On the whole, the following estimation formula can be established, developing formulas (1) and (2):

$$QD_i = FL_x/3.6 * dt * r_x(tr_x) * \sum_{k=1}^{m} (u_{i-k+1}) \qquad [0 < i-k+1 < n] \qquad (3)$$

QD_i: ordinates of direct runoff [m^3/s]
FL_x: contributing area of a x-year flood [km^2]
dt: time interval [h]
r_x: (constant) intensity of rainfall [mm/h] of duration tr_x
tr_x: time of concentration [h]
u_i: ordinates of the representative unit hydrograph [1/h]
m: number of rainfall intervals
n: number of unit hydrograph ordinates
i,k: indices

The estimation results based on this model are to be assessed as satisfactory to good. Not only is the result depending on a correct selection of the unit hydrograph but on a correct estimation of the contributing area in particular. The model ought to be interpreted as a possible synthesis concept, ready to pass the test by its application. The significance of contributing areas is to be emphasized. On the one hand, they help to explain a variation of analyzed unit hydrographs, giving rise on the other hand to a guideline for a calculation of the concentration time and with it to both the identification of representative unit hydrographs and the estimation of the runoff ratio.

ACKNOWLEDGEMENTS

I thank Mrs. D. Vuillemin for the English translation.

REFERENCES

Aschwanden, H. (1990) The importance of hydrological networks for the estimate of average flows in alpine regions. IAHS-Proceedings of Lausanne congress 1990.

Aschwanden, H. & Spreafico, M. (1989) Uebertragungsfunktionen Niederschlag-Abfluss in ausgewählten schweizerischen Einzugsgebieten. Mittl. der Landeshydrologie und -geologie 11, Bern.

Aschwanden, H. & Weingartner, R. (1985) Die Abflussregimes der Schweiz. Publikationen Gewässerkunde No. 65, Bern.

Chow, V.T. (1964) Handbook of applied hydrology. New York.

Consuegra, D. (1988) Détermination des caractéristiques d'un hydrogramme unitaire standard applicable aux bassin versants du Plateau suisse. Proceedings of the VIth IWRA World Congress on Water Resources, Vol. 2, Ottawa.

Geiger, H., Zeller, J. & Röthlisberger, G. (1990): Starkniederschläge des schweizerischen Alpen- und Alpenrandgebietes. Bd. 7, Birmensdorf.

Gloor, R., Jordan, J.P., Sautier, J.L. & Wisner, P. (1983) Etude hydrologique de bassin versant de la Seymaz. EPFL-IGR 173, Lausanne.

Kirpich, Y.P. (1940) Time of concentration in small agricultural watersheds. Civil Engeneer 10 (6).

Köhler, G. (1971) Ermittlung massgebender Abflussdaten für kleinere Vorfluter mit Hilfe kurzzeitiger Naturmessungen. Mittl. Inst. f. Wasserwirtschaft .u. Hydrologie., Heft 23, Hannover.

Kölla, E. (1986) Zur Abschätzung von Hochwassern in Fliessgewässern an Stellen ohne Direktmessungen. Mittl. der VAW 87, Zürich.

Lutz, W. (1984) Berechnung von Hochwasserabflüssen unter Verwendung von Gebietskenngrössen. Mittl. Inst. f. Hydrologie. u. Wasserwirtschaft., Heft 24, Karlsruhe.

Näf, F., & Moser, U. (1984) Ermittlung von Hochwasserabflüssen in kleinen Einzugsgebieten ohne Abflussmessungen. Zwischenbericht VAW, Zürich.

Näf, F., Zuidema, P. & Kölla, E. (1985) Abschätzung von Hochwassern in kleinen Einzugsgebieten. Beiträge zur Geologie der Schweiz - Hydrologie 33, 195-233, Bern.

Spreafico, M. & Stadler, K. (1986,1987) Hochwasserabflüsse in schweizerischen Gewässern. Mitt. der Landeshydrologie und -geologie 7,8, Bern.

Weingartner, R. (1989) Das Unit-Hydrograph-Verfahren und seine Anwendung in schweizerischen Einzugsgebieten. Publikationen Gewässerkunde No. 107, Bern.

Weingartner, R. & Spreafico, M. (1990) Analyse und Abschätzung von Hochwasserabflüssen - Eine Uebersicht über neuere schweizerische Arbeiten. Deut. Gewässerkundl. Mittl. Jg. 1990 (2), Koblenz.

Zuidema, P. (1985) Hydraulik der Abflussbildung während Starkniederschlägen. Mittl. der VAW 79, Zürich.

Hydrology in Mountainous Regions. I - Hydrological Measurements; the Water Cycle
(Proceedings of two Lausanne Symposia, August 1990). IAHS Publ. no. 193, 1990.

The formation and calculation of cold region runoff in the Qilian mountains

Z. H. YANG
Lanzhou Institute of Glaciology and Geocryology
Academia Sinica, Lanzhou, China

ABSTRACT The variation of frozen soil existing in the high and cold mountains can change the property of runoff producing and flow concentration of the ground. So the areas and situations of the water source of each runoff component change with the geography and time in this kinds of basin. Under the circumstances the effect of frozen soil on the runoff calculation must be considered. The daily discharge of the Binggou Basin is computed with the variable source model in order to express the influence of the frozen soil on the runoff forming. In the computation of the runoff producing and the flow concentration, the areas and situations of each water sources are adjusted according to the state of frozen soil in order to determine the proportion which rainfall (or meltwater) supplies to the each water source and the discharge velocity of groundwater. By means of above measures, the precision of the runoff computation in this kind of region is improved.

INTRODUCTION

The variation of frozen soil in thaw is one of the key factors that affect runoff forming (Slaughter et al, 1983; Woo et al, 1983; Roulet & Woo, 1986). It is due to the redistribution of rainfall (or meltwater) in vertical and time is closely related with the thawed depth of frozen ground (Kane & Stein, 1983; Brook, 1983). In the high and cold mountains existing frozen soil, because the variation of frozen soil also is affected by topography besides season, the thawing depth of frozen soil is different as well everywhere in basin at any given time, so the runoff forming process and calculation is very complicated in this kind of basin. The differentiation of water source is the key to the runoff calculation in this kind of basin as is other kind of basin. Owing to the area and situation of every water sources relate to the variation of frozen soil in this kind of basin, the dynamic relation between the water source of each runoff component and the frozen soil must be considered in calculation. This relation can be set up through analyzing the kinds of runoff forming areas and their variation in basin. In the first place, all kinds of runoff forming areas in basin are divided according to the thawing depth of frozen soil, and then the area and situation of each kind of runoff forming area is determined according to the distribution of frozen soil in basin. Next the area and situation of each water source in basin is calculated according to the proportion of this kind of water souce in every kind of runoff forming area. Lastly, the runoff process is calculated according to the geographical and temporal distribution of the every water sources in basin. Owing to the variation of frozen soil in basin is considered, the result of the runoff computation of this kind of basin is more close to the actual state, thereby improving the precision of computation.

The Binggou Basin is a second-class branch of headwaters of the Heihe River in northwest China and originates from the northern slope of the Tuolai Mountains in the Qilian Mountains. The study area (Binggou Basin) is located in the upstream area of the Binggou River, between 38°1'-38°4'N and 100°12'-100°18'E. Its drainage area is 30.5 km^2 and its altitude ranges from 3 430 to 4 401 m a.m.s.l.. Data from the Binggou meteorological station (3 452 m a.m.s.l.) shows that the mean annual air temperature is about -2.7°C and the mean annual air temperature of the middle elevation in the Binggou Basin is about -5.6°C. The study (Zhou & Guo, 1982) shows that the Binggou Basin is within the permafrost region.

THE KIND AND VARIATION OF WATER SOURCES IN THE BINGGOU BASIN

In the Binggou Basin, because existing frozen soil, water storage capacity and permeability of the ground are not constant, and the frozen degree of ground formed different kinds of the runoff forming area and the water source. They have been changing with the geography and time in the runoff period.

The kinds of runoff forming area in the Binggou Basin

The water sources of runoff in the Binggou Basin consist of surface water, shallow groundwater and deep groundwater in the main. The existence and quantity of these water sources depend on the state of frozen soil besides the meteorological factors. When the ground where shallow groundwater or deep groundwater exist in is freezing, the appropriate groundwater sources stopped the exchange of water with outside, and were on the state of non-activity. Only when the ground thawed they can return to exchange of water with outside and take the effect of water source. But the surface water just is opposite. When the ground is freezing, all of the rainfall (or meltwater) supplies to surface water as is on the confining layer. Conversely, the groundwater can obtain the nourishment but the surface water can't (with the exception of the confining layer). According to the relationships between the water sources and the frozen soil in the Binggou Basin, the runoff forming area can be divided into three kinds as follows:

(a) When the runoff forming area has been not thawed or the thawed depth is shallow (less than 20 cm), the rainfall (or meltwater) have not or a shallow permeation on the ground. So this kind of runoff forming area only forms surface water, but doesn't form shallow and deep groundwater. It can be called the forming area of the one kind of runoff component (Area 1).

(b) When the thawed depth of the frozen ground is more than 20 cm but is not very deep (compare with the thawed limit), the groundwater has distinguished from the surface water in discharge velocity. Thereby the new water source, shallow groundwater, is formed in this kind of area. Because the deep layer has not been thawed, the deep groundwater also has not been formed. So this kind of runoff forming area forms surface water and shallow groundwater, but doesn't deep groundwater. It can be called the forming area of the two kinds of runoff component (Area 2).

(c) When the thawed depth of the frozen ground approaches or reaches the thawed limit, some rainfall (or meltwater) can permeate to form the deep groundwater in some areas. So this kind of runoff forming area can form surface water, shallow and deep groundwater. It can be called the forming area of the three kinds of runoff component (Area 3).

The variations of each kind of runoff forming area

Because the Binggou Basin is located at the high and cold mountains, the variation of the frozen soil is affected by not only season but also topography, the distribution of the every runoff forming areas also has been changing continuously. In Fig. 1, the line $H_{ss}(t)$ and $H_{sd}(t)$ are the relationships between the altitudes where the 20 cm and the 40 cm thawed depth of the frozen ground are at and the date respectively in the Basin. The lines shaw that before early March the maximum thawed depth of the frozen ground is less than 20 cm in the Binggou Basin, so all of the Basin belong to the Area 1 from the beginning of the runoff period till early March. After this time, the thawed depth of frozen soil begins to exceed 20 cm in low of the Basin. The Area 2 begins to appear and expand from the low to the high in the Basin,

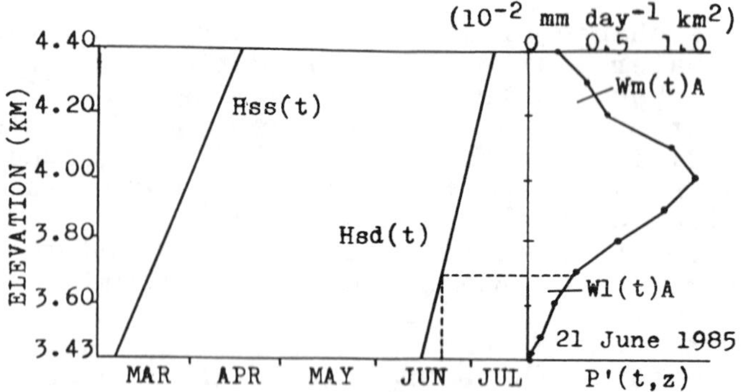

FIG. 1 The calculation of the daily average of nourishment water for each kind of runoff forming area during the runoff period.

but the Area 1 beging to decrease. By this time there are two kinds of runoff forming area in the Basin. After early May, the thawed depth of the frozen ground begins to exceed 40 cm in low of the Basin. The Area 3 appears and also expands from the low to the high. But it does not be clear until early June. As time goes on, the Area 1 and Area 2 disappear one after another before early July. After this, there is only the Area 3 in the Basin and this state continues to the end of the runoff period.

The variations of each kind of water sources

In the each kinds of runoff forming area mentioned above, there are a fixed proportions among the water source areas. In the Area 1, the water source area of the direct runoff is equal to the area of the Area 1, and other water source areas are zero. In the Area 2, the proportions between the water source areas of the direct runoff and the shallow groundwater runoff are 0.1 and 0.9 respectively, and the water source area of the deep groundwater runoff is zero. In the Area 3, the proportions among the water source areas of the direct runoff, the shallow and deep groundwater runoff are 0.1, 0.7 and 0.2 respectively. Thus when the areas and situations of the each runoff forming area change with the frozen soil, the areas and situations of the each water sources also change appropriately. So the sources, the quantities and the discharges of the runoff have close connection with the frozen soil in this kind of basin.

THE CALCULATION OF RUNOFF

When the relationship between the water sources and the frozen soil is obtained, the calculation of runoff can be carried on according to the geographical and temporal distribution of the frozen soil and meteorological factors. First, the net rainfall (or meltwater) with area weighing at some altitudes (the interval is taken in 100 m a.m.s.l.) are calculated (Fig. 1).

$$P'(t,z) = P(t,z)A'(z) \tag{1}$$

In this equation, P'(t,z) is the net daily rainfall (or meltwater) with area weighing, P(t,z) is the net daily rainfall (or meltwater) at z m a.m.s.l. and at the tth day (mm day^{-1}), A'(z) is the rate of area with altitude at z m a.m.s.l. (km^2 m^{-1}).

According to the altitude where the upper limits of 20 and 40 cm thawed depth of frozen soil are at, the net daily nourishment water of every runoff forming areas are calculated respectively by:

$$Wu(t) = \frac{1}{A}\int_{Hss(t)}^{4\ 401} P'(t,z)dz \tag{2}$$

$$Wm(t) = \frac{1}{A}\int_{Hsd(t)}^{Hss(t)} P'(t,z)dz \tag{3}$$

$$Wl(t) = \frac{1}{A}\int_{3\ 430}^{Hsd(t)} P'(t,z)dz \tag{4}$$

In these equations, Wu(t), Wm(t) and Wl(t) are the net daily nourishment water of the Area 1, Area 2 and Area 3 respectively at the tth day (with area weighing; mm day^{-1}), A is the area of the Binggou Basin (km^2), 3 430 and 4 401 are the altitudes of the lowest and highest point in Binggou Basin respectively (m a.m.s.l.).

The nourishments that each water sources obtain are calculated by:

$$Wsu(t) = Wu(t) + a(Wm(t) + Wl(t)) \tag{5}$$

$$Wsg(t) = bmWm(t) + blWl(t) \tag{6}$$

$$Wdg(t) = cWl(t) \tag{7}$$

In these equation, Wsu(t), Wsg(t) and Wdg(t) are the nourishments that the surface water, shallow groundwater and deep groundwater obtain respectively at the tth day (mm), a, bm, bl and c are the nourishment proportions that each water sources obtained from each runoff forming areas in the Basing respectively, theirs values are 0.1,

0.9, 0.7 and 0.2 respectively.

Because the Binggou Basin is smaller, the necessary time for flowing to exit the basin is usually one day for the nourishment that surface water source obtained and several days or even tens of days for the shallow and deep groundwater sources. The discharge of the shallow and deep groundwater coincide with the mechanism of the linear reservoir model. So the each runoff components are calculated as follows:

$$Rsu(t) = Wsu(t) \tag{8}$$

$$Rsg(t) = \frac{bmWm(t) + Dsgm(t)}{Ksgm} + \frac{blWl(t) + Dsgl(t)}{Ksgl} \tag{9}$$

$$Rdg(t) = \frac{Wdg(t) + Ddg(t)}{Kdg} \tag{10}$$

$$R(t) = Rsu(t) + Rsg(t) + Rdg(t) \tag{11}$$

In these equations, R(t), Rsu(t), Rsg(t) and Rdg(t) are total runoff, direct runoff, shallow and deep groundwater runoff respectively at the tth day (mm day^{-1}), Dsgm(t) and Dsgl(t) are the shallow groundwater that are located in the Area 2 and Area 3 respectively before the tth day, Ddg(t) is the deep groundwater before the tth day (mm), Ksgm and Ksgl are the storage constants of the linear reservoir model for the shallow groundwater in the Area 2 and Area 3 respectively, Kdg is the storage constant of the linear reservoir model for the deep groundwater, Ksgm, Ksgl and Kdg are 6, 12 and 60 respectively in the Binggou Basin.

RESULTS AND DISCUSSION

The daily averages of runoff calculated with above mentioned method is showed in Fig. 2. The relative error of model runoff is about 19%. By comparison with the staged variable water source method (Yang & Yang, 1989), the error goes down and the calculated values coincide with the actual runoff process on the whole. This showed that the method above mentioned can improve the shortcoming that the calculated precision is inconsistent in the every stage of runoff producing period.

The problems in this method are that only the altitude is considered but the slope and direction of ground are not in the geographical factors affecting the distribution of frozen ground as a result of shortage of data. So the variation of frozen ground calculated only is the linear function of the altitude. This is the main factors affecting precision of this method. It is

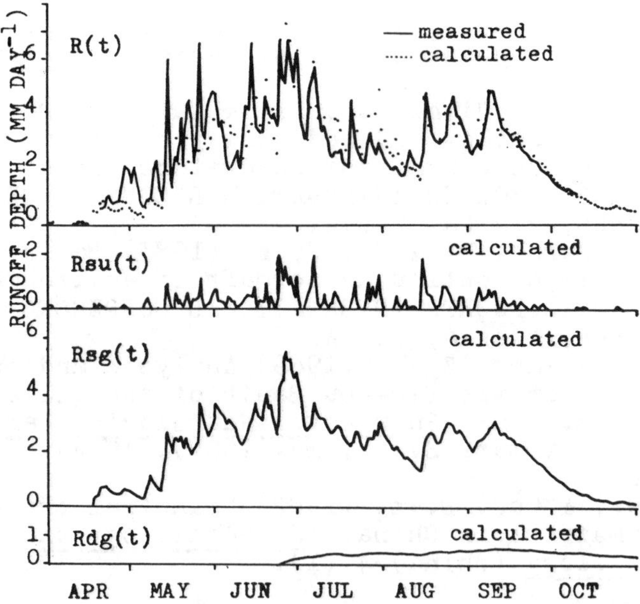

FIG. 2 Daily averages of the calculated and measured runoff values for the whole modelling period in 1985. In addition to the total runoff, the discharge of the different water sources also are plotted.

necessary to calculat the variation of frozen ground on the basis of various geographical factors. Thus the variation process of the every runoff forming areas in frozen region can be determined in precise terms. In addition, the locations where groundwater sources are at in this kind of region are variational, so the discharge velocities of the sallow and deep groundwater also are variational. The improvements in these respects remain to collect more precise data.

ACKNOWLEDGEMENTS I am grateful to Dr. Z. N. Yang for guiding this work and to F. Li for numerical calculation. In addition, I am particularly indebted to numerous other people who helped with the field-work.

REFERENCES

Brook, G. A. (1983) Hydrology of the Nananni, a highly karsted carbonate terrain with discontinuous permafrost. PERMAFROST, FOURTH INTERNATIONAL CONFERENCE, Fairbanks, Alaska, U.S.A.

Kane, D. L. & Stein, J. (1983) Field evidence of groundwater recharge in interior Alaska. PERMAFROST, FOURTH INTERNATIONAL CONFERENCE, Fairbanks, Alaska, U.S.A.

Roulet, N. T. & Woo, M.-k. (1986) Hydrology of a wetland in the continuous permafrost region. J. Hydrol. 89, 73-91.

Slaughter, C. W., Hilgert, J. W. & Culp, E. H. (1983) Summer streamflow and sediment yield from discontinuous permafrost headwaters catchments. PERMAFROST, FOURTH INTERNATIONAL CONFERENCE, Fairbanks, Alaska, U.S.A.

Woo, M.-k., Marsh, P. & Steer, P. (1983) Basin water balance in a continuous permafrost environment. PERMAFROST, FOURTH INTERNATIONAL CONFERENCE, Fairbanks, Alaska, U.S.A.

Yang, Z.-n. & Yang, Z.-h. (1989) Analysis and estimation of runoff in the Binggou Basin of the Qilian Mountains. In: Snow Cover and Glacier Variations (Proc. Baltimore Symp., May 1989), 39-44. IAHS Publ. no. 183.

Zhou, Y.-w., & Guo, D.-x. (1982) Principal characteristic of permafrost in China. J. Glaciology and Cryopedology (china) 4 (1).

Hydrology in Mountainous Regions. I - Hydrological Measurements; the Water Cycle
(Proceedings of two Lausanne Symposia, August 1990). IAHS Publ. no. 193, 1990.

A conceptual distributed model for large-scale mountainous basins

Fumio YOSHINO and Junichi YOSHITANI
Public Works Research Institute, Ministry of Construction
1-Asahi, Tsukuba-shi, Ibaraki-ken, 305 JAPAN

Masayuki SUGIURA
CTI Engineering Co. Ltd.
1-4-7 Honmachi, Chuo-ku, Osaka, 541 JAPAN

ABSTRACT This research aims to develop a distributed model which is able to evaluate the effects of spatial differences of rainfall measured by radar and the prediction of runoff changes due to artificial changes to a basin. The model is applicable to mountainous catchment of sizes in the range of a few hundred square kilometers. This paper describes the development of the model and its application to the Kusaki-dam basin, having a catchment area of 254 km^2. The model is verified by runoff analysis using daily and hourly runoff data and through making a comparison with the results from a storage function model.

INTRODUCTION

River planning and flood prediction today are often based on black-box models such as the storage function models. Since these models analyze rainfall-runoff relationships only, they are unable to predict changes in runoffs due to possible changes in the local geographic and topographic conditions and rainfall characteristics. To solve these problems, it is necessary to produce a physically-based model which can reflect the runoff mechanisms acting in the catchment as precisely as possible.

The SHE Model[1)], which is a physically-based distributed model developed in Europe, can only be applied to a river basin with an area of up to 10km^2 due to difficulty in modeling and computing time limitations.

This paper presents a conceptual-simplified distributed model which is operational and gives the results of its application to a mountainous basin, the Kusaki-dam. The model simulates the major physical processes in a catchment. In future radar rainfall data and satellite data for land-use and soil moisture will be analyzed by the conceptual distributed model.

OUTLINE OF THE CONCEPTUAL DISTRIBUTED RUNOFF MODEL

The conceptual distributed model divides a river basin into fine grids and expresses the various flows as movement between the grids. First, topographical features are expressed using altitude grid-square data, as shown in Fig. 1. Second, analysis of daily runoff data is carried out. Conditions of the model before a flood are set as the initial value for runoff analysis. Finally, analysis of hourly data is carried out.

Digital mapping

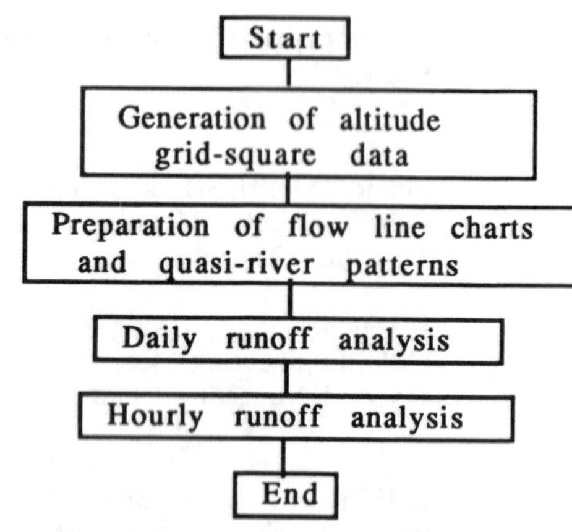

FIG. 1 Flow Chart For Runoff Analysis.

A river basin is divided into grid squares, and the directions of storm water flows are determined. Then, each grid square is classed as river basin or river channel which together form a network of slopes and river channels.

In Japan, altitude grid-square data are readily available from the Geographical Survey Institute of the Japanese Ministry of Construction as standard numerical information. There is also a method of generating them by scanning contour maps. In this paper, the scanning method is used for the digital mapping.

The direction of a specific flow is that direction with the steepest gradient, out of the eight directions in a grid-square consisting of the North, South, East, West directions and the four diagonal directions[2]. A map showing such directions of flow is called a flow line chart. The flow line chart of Kusaki-dam basin is given in Fig. 2.

A threshold is set for the number of grid points above a certain grid point (therefore, the area of a river basin), and grid points below and above the threshold are regarded as slopes and river channels. A flow line chart of a river channel system is called a quasi-river pattern because it represents the outline of a river channel system. The quasi-river pattern of the Kusaki-dam basin (with a threshold value of 15) is shown in Fig. 3.

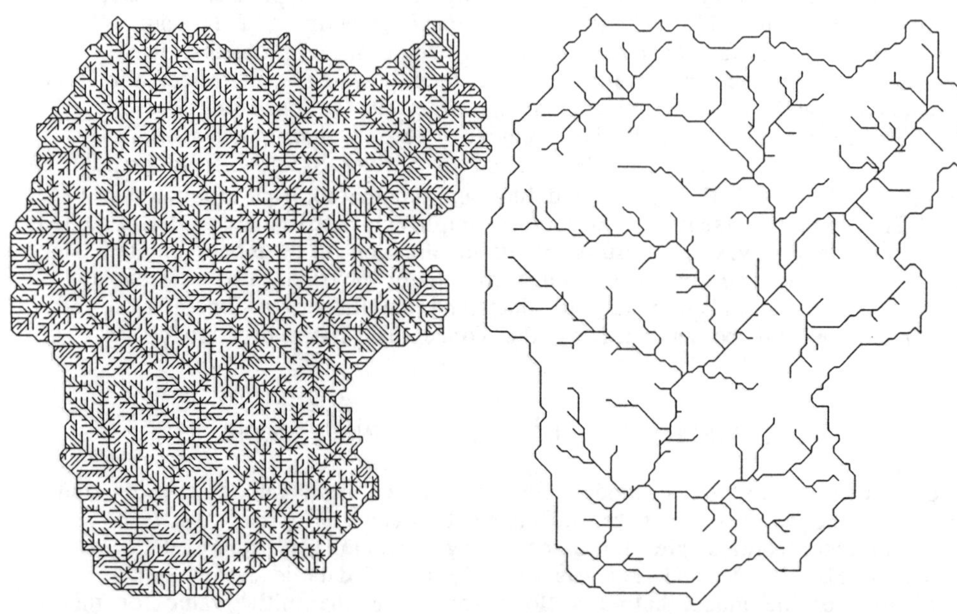

FIG. 2 Flow Line Chart (with a grid of 200m).

FIG. 3 Quasi-River Pattern (Threshold value of 15).

Structure of the model

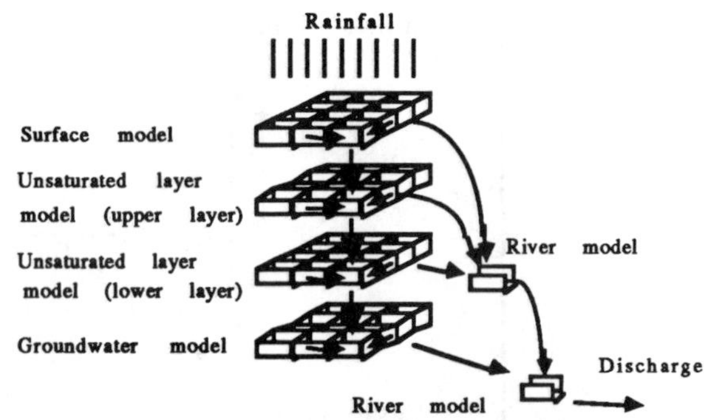

FIG. 4 Concept of the conceptual Distributed Model.

As shown in Fig. 4, the conceptual distributed model consists of a set of four-layered models piled up over the grid points of all grid squares and a river flow model. It is assumed that the vertical flow of water goes straight downward, and the horizontal flow of water only runs toward the lowest neighboring grid point.
Two types of the river flow model has been defined. One has only inflows from the surface and unsaturated-layer models. Another has inflows from all the four kinds of model including the groundwater model. Each of the model performs the following functions:

- Surface model : Surface runoff, prompt subsurface runoff,percolation, surface storage
- Unsaturated layer model : Delayed subsurface runoff, groundwater percolation, storage in unsaturated zones
- Groundwater model : Unconfined groundwater runoff, confined groundwater runoff
- River model : River flow

Fig. 5 illustrates the runoff analysis procedures of these models.

Surface model

It is assumed that surface flow is governed by Manning's formula and that discharge is proportional to water storage to the 3/5th power. Prompt subsurface flow and percolation are assumed to be proportional to soil water storage. This model consists of such constants as surface equivalent roughness and final infiltration capacity.

Unsaturated layer model

Horizontal water flow is represented by delayed subsurface flow. Runoff is calculated on the assumption that it is proportional to capillary hydraulic conductivity and that hydraulic gradient approximates topographical gradient. Percolation of the groundwater model is proportional to capillary hydraulic conductivity, and is calculated based on the hydraulic gradient of 1.

Many researchers have presented their representations of the relation between capillary hydraulic conductivity and water content. To simplify numerical calculation, Equation (1) is used for this model.

$$k = k_s \frac{\exp\{b(\theta - \theta_w)\} - 1}{\exp\{b(\theta_s - \theta_w)\} - 1} \qquad (1)$$

where k : capillary hydraulic conductivity
k_s : saturated hydraulic conductivity
b : constant

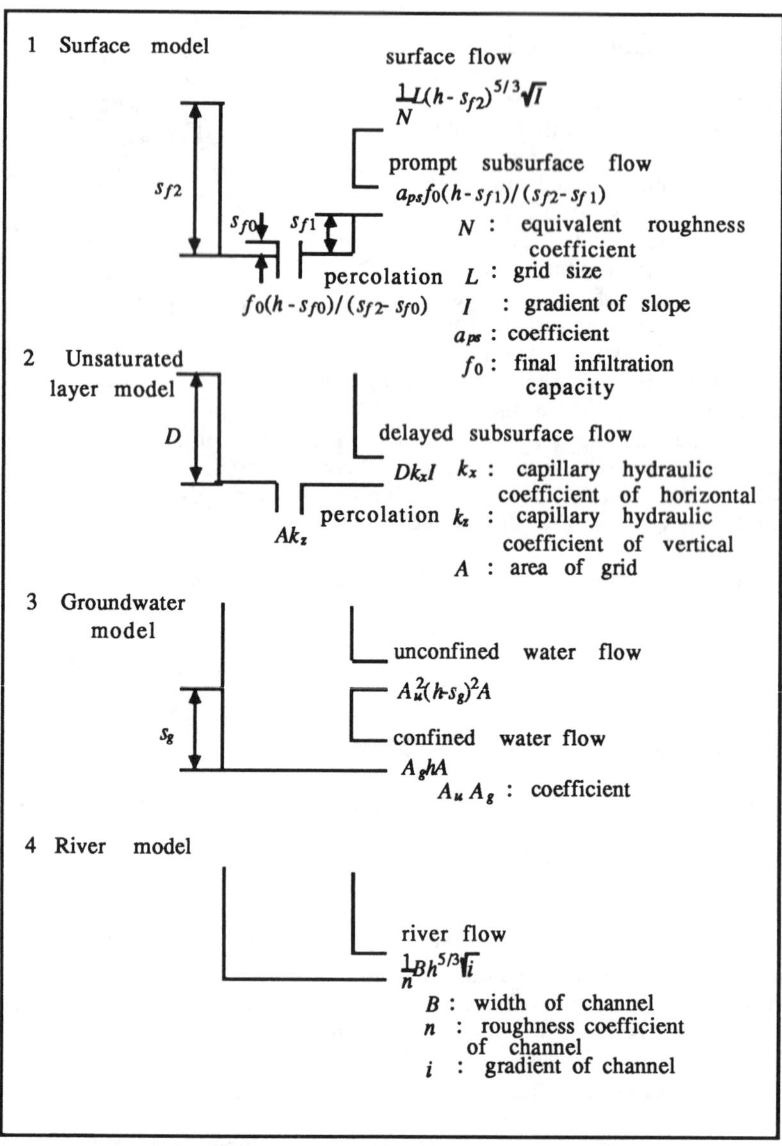

FIG. 5 Model Structure.

θ : water content
θ_s : saturated water content
θ_w : minimum water content

Vertical water flow from unsaturated layers represents percolation. Unsaturated zones are divided into two: overlying layers with higher permeability and underlying layers with lower permeability. The upper and lower layers represent layers A and B of forest soil, respectively. Layer A includes roots of plants and other coarse materials, and is a highly permeable layer. Layer B includes sediments that have leached down from layer A, and therefore is less porous.

Groundwater model

In this model, it is assumed that runoff from the lower outlet is proportional to soil water storage, and that runoff from the upper outlet is proportional to the second power of soil water storage.

River model

In the river model, runoff is assumed to be governed by Manning's formula. Since river channel gradient can be obtained from altitude grid-square data, model parameters can be determined if the width of a river channel is known. In this model, the river channel width is considered approximately as a function of the area of a river basin. Many researchers have performed investigations about constants based on the relationship $B=aQ^b$ (Q: flow, a & b: constants) as a regime theory. If flow is assumed to be proportional to the area of a river basin according to their results, the width of a river channel can be expresses as a function of the area of a river basin as follows:

$$B=cA^s \tag{2}$$

where B: : width of river (m)
A : area of river basin (km^2) c & s : constants

Calculation method

If the runoff model is to be operational, time steps (δt) for daily and hourly analysis should be one day and one hour, respectively. To obtain stable solutions with the method of finite differences , δt needs to be very short. In this model, to ensure stable solutions approximate expressions are used from the practical viewpoint. For example, $h^{5/3}$ is approximated by $a h^2+b h$ (h : depth of water, a & b: : constants). On the assumption that rainfall and inflow in the model during δt are constant, the fundamental expression is written as follows:

$$\frac{\partial h}{\partial t}=f(h) \tag{3}$$

Solving equation (3) analytically gives the following expression:

$$h_{n+1}=g(h_n,\delta t) \tag{4}$$

where g : functio $n, n+1$: suffixes representing time

When $f(h)=a-b\,h$ (a & b : constants), then

$$h_{n+1}=\{a-(a-b h_n)\exp(-b\delta t)\}/b \tag{5}$$

Method of parameterization

As shown in Fig. 5, this model has 23 parameters. The surface flow model represents layer A_0 and thus surface parameters are determined from the soil characteristics of layer A_0. Parameter s_{f2} is determined from the depth of layer A_0 ,and s_{f0} is determined from the initial storm water loss. As for N, general values obtained by the kinematic wave method can be used. However, there is no method for determining the remaining parameters of s_{f1}, f_0 and α_{ps}.

The upper and lower layers of the unsaturated zone model represent layers A and B respectively. Parameter D represents the depth of a layer. Parameter k_z, θ_s and θ_w are assumed to be equal to the generally accepted values. At present there is no method for determining the values of k_x and b .

The three parameters of the groundwater model can be determined from flood recession characteristics.

The two parameters of the river model can be determined if the width of more than one river channel is known.

Trial and error method has been used to determine seven parameters since there is no available method to estimate them.

Input of precipitation distribution

Any precipitation distribution can be inputted into each grid square. It is also possible to directly input radar rainfall data. In practice rain gauge data are used for the Kusaki-dam model and the rainfall data of each grid square is taken to be equal to that of the data of the nearest rain gauge station to the grid-square.

Evapotranspiration

For daily runoff analysis,the actual evapotranspiration needs to be subtracted, as in a tank model. Evapotranspiration is obtained from the annual potential evapotranspiration after adjustment for the annual water balance.

VERIFICATION OF THE CONCEPTUAL DISTRIBUTED RUNOFF MODEL

The conceptual distributed model is applied to the Kusaki-dam basin which is in the upper reaches of the Watarase River, a tributary of the Tone River. This basin is a temperate and humid mountainous area at an altitude between 500 and 2,000m. Daily runoff analysis was performed for a six-year period from 1983 to 1988, and hourly runoff analysis for 11 floods.

Altitude grid-square data with 200 m resolution was generated by scanning topographical maps. The number of grid points was 6,489. In the quasi-river pattern , the threshold for surface flow and subsurface flow into river channels were set at 3, and that for all the inflow at 15.

In determining the model coefficients, efforts were made, including some trial-and-error approaches. The parameters of the model are determined using the 1983 daily data and data from two floods in the same year. Table 1 shows the identified model coefficients.

Results of model verifications based on other data are given in Figs. 6 and 7. Reproducibility acceptable for operational use in obtaining both annual runoff and flood runoff was confirmed.

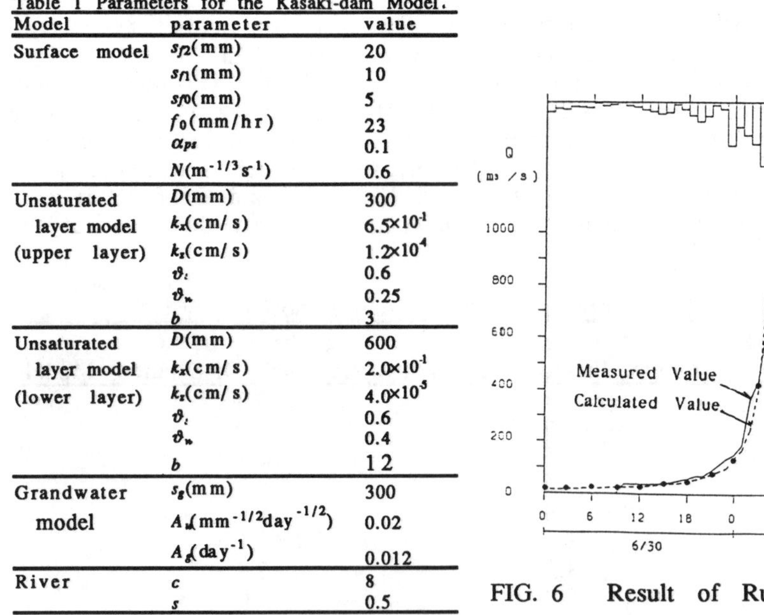

Table 1 Parameters for the Kasaki-dam Model.

Model	parameter	value
Surface model	s_{f2}(mm)	20
	s_{f1}(mm)	10
	s_{f0}(mm)	5
	f_0(mm/hr)	23
	α_{ps}	0.1
	N($m^{-1/3}s^{-1}$)	0.6
Unsaturated layer model (upper layer)	D(mm)	300
	k_x(cm/s)	6.5×10^{-1}
	k_z(cm/s)	1.2×10^{4}
	ϑ_s	0.6
	ϑ_w	0.25
	b	3
Unsaturated layer model (lower layer)	D(mm)	600
	k_x(cm/s)	2.0×10^{-1}
	k_z(cm/s)	4.0×10^{5}
	ϑ_s	0.6
	ϑ_w	0.4
	b	12
Grandwater model	s_g(mm)	300
	A_d($mm^{-1/2}day^{-1/2}$)	0.02
	A_g(day^{-1})	0.012
River	c	8
	s	0.5

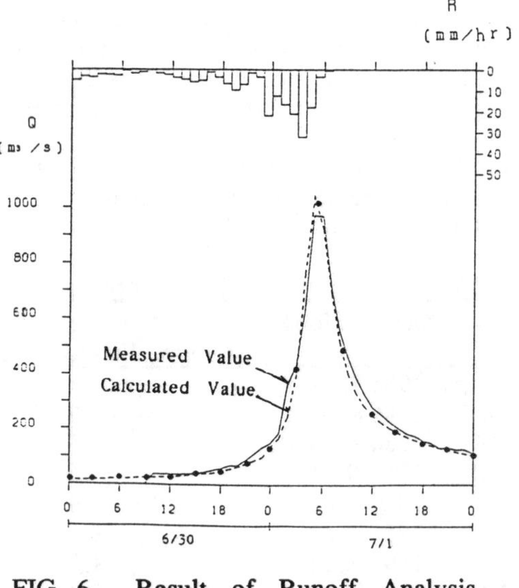

FIG. 6 Result of Runoff Analysis.

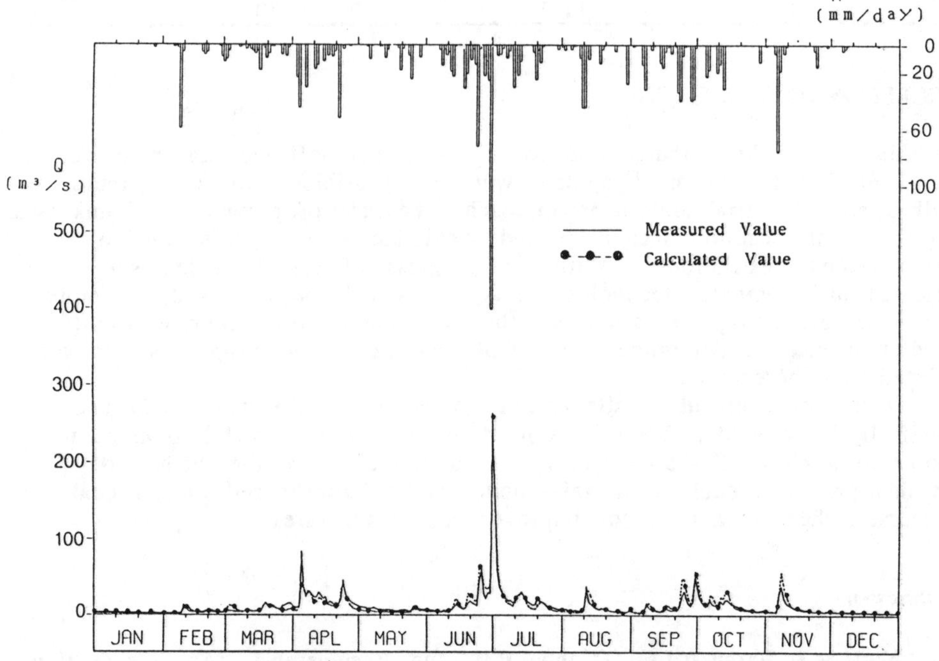

FIG. 7 Result of Annual Runoff Analysis.

COMPARISON WITH THE STORAGE FUNCTION METHOD

The distributed model was compared with a storage function method that uses optimized constants, in terms of flood runoff analysis. In the storage function method, the Kusaki-dam area was regarded as a single basin, and saturated rainfall (Rsa) was determined so that effective rainfall becomes equal to observed runoff. Calculated χ^2 errors are shown in Table 2. Average values obtained from the nine floods used in the verification point to higher accuracy of the distributed model. In the storage function method it is necessary to determine saturated rainfall by trial and error according to the basin's actual humidity. Since the distributed model is equipped with rainfall losses, it permits flood prediction without trial and error effort and produces predictions with accuracy equivalent to or higher than that of the storage function method.

Table 2 Evaluation of Accuracies Obtained from Runoff Analysis.

No.	Date of Flood	χ^2 Errors of Storage Function Method	χ^2 Errors of Conceptual Distributed Model
3	1985.7. 1	32.2	3.5
4	1986.8. 5	4.5	21.0
5	1986.9. 3	5.5	10.1
6	1987.9.11	7.0	5.6
7	1987.9.25	6.4	31.5
8	1888.8.11	9.1	13.1
9	1899.8.24	13.3	2.8
10	1988.9. 9	10.3	1.6
11	1988.9.25	13.0	2.1
	Average	11.3	10.3

PROBLEMS TO BE SOLVED

In this model, the authors tried to represent a runoff mechanism using physically-based conceptual models wherever possible. However, there is still a need for trial and error approaches because of a number of unknown factors in the runoff mechanism and inevitable simplification due to computational restrictions. With the progress of runoff mechanism research and computer technology, this model will be improved for more physically-based representation so that parameters for accurate runoff prediction can be determined by simply analyzing soil properties and other related characteristics.

This model probably falls halfway between a conceptual model and a physically-based model. There is a need to improve this model to make it closer to a physically-based model. In particular, since the method of physical-process modelling in this model is not truly based on physical processes, there is a need for improvements in this area .

REFERENCES

1. Abbott,M.B.,Bathurst,J.C.,O'Connel,P.E. and Rasmussen,J. :An introduction to the European Hydrological System - Systeme Hydrologique Europeen,"SHE", 1: History and philosophy of a physically based distributed modeling system, Journal of Hydrology Vol 87 1986.
2. M.Nogami and Y.Sugiura : Mathematical Geography Exercise by Personal Computer, Kokin Shoin Co.Ltd.,(in Japanese).

Hydrology in Mountainous Regions. I - Hydrological Measurements; the Water Cycle
(Proceedings of two Lausanne Symposia, August 1990). IAHS Publ. no. 193, 1990.

Simulation of daily runoff in the Urumqi River basin with the improved Tank model

ZHANG GUOWEI
Geography Department of Xinjiang University; Xinjiang Hydrological Burean, Urumqi, P.R. of China
SHANG SICHEN & WANG XINQI
Xinjiang Hydrological Burean, Urumqi, P.R. of China

ABSTRACT The Urumqi River Basin of Xinjiang in China, locating in the internal arid area, is a river with multi-water feeds. Ice-snow meltwater feeds the river in a relatively large proportion. Based on the characteristics of Urumqi River Basin, the paper has developed a tank model with glacier and snow components to simulate the daily runoff in YingXiong Qiao hydrometric station of Urumqi River. Through the comparison of simulated and observed values during 1984-1987, the qualification ratio is 90% and more for monthly runoff and the criteran CR value for the simulation of daily runoff is 0.3830. The results are rather satisfied.

INTRODUCTION TO THE RIVER BASIN AND THE ZONE DISTRIBUTION

Origining from Tianger Peak (4486 m a.s.l) in the mid-section of north slope of Xinjiang Tianshan Mountain, Urumqi river acrosses Urumqi City and disappeares in the desert. The mountain area above 1800 m a.s.l. forms the runoff feeding area and below the altitude is runoff loss area. The catchment area above YingXiong Qiao hydrometric station (1920 m a.s.l.) is 924^2km and the river is 53 km long (Fig. 1).

The mountain area of the Urumqi river basin is precipitous. The average slope of the river basin is 48.5%. There are widely distribution of bare rock and developed rock fracture. The low boundary of soil frozen belt ranges between 3000 and 3600 m. The recorded rainfall in the mountain area is 420.0 mm. Annual snowfall accounts for 54% of the total precipitation. The decrease ratio of average annual temperature with the altitude is about 0.4°C/100 m. There are large annual temperature difference and daily temperature difference. The differences are getting less along with the increase of the altitude. Potential evaporation is decreasing with the increase of the altitude. In the high mountain area above 3500 m a.s.l. 38 km^2 is covered by glaciers. The high mountain belt is mainly feeded by glacier and snow melt. The middle mountain belt contains proper vegetation and rainfall is the principal water feed. The average annual runoff depth of the river is 251.4 mm. There are totaly 14 precipitation stations and nine hydrometric stations in the basin. It is one of the experimental river basins in the west of China.

According to the apparent vertical distribution of hydrological belts, the unbalanced distribution of the hydrological elements and

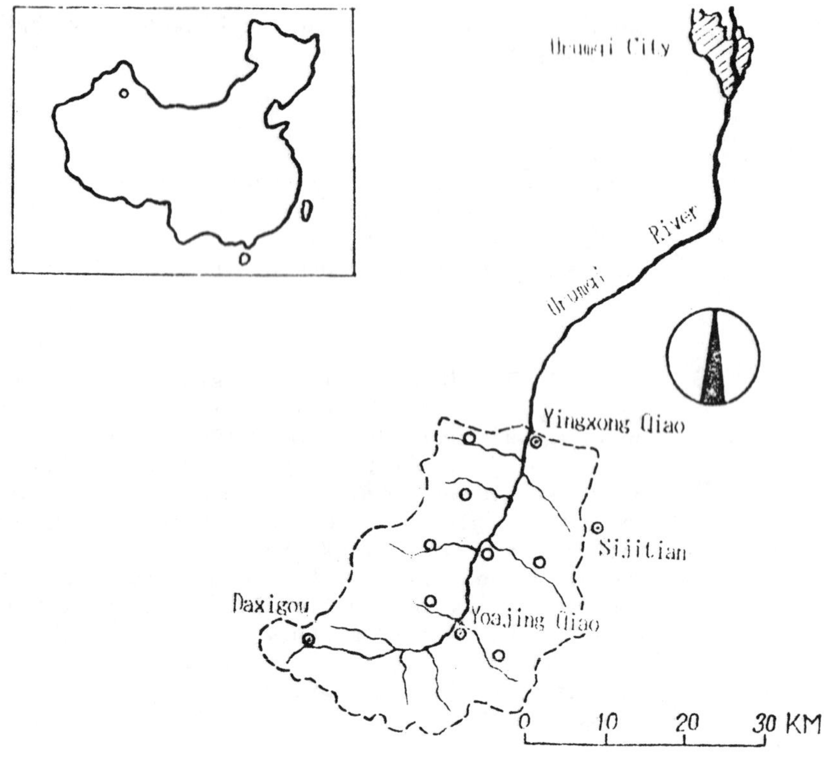

FIG. 1 Location of Urumqi River Basin.

TABLE 1 Hydrological belts for Tank model calculation.

Belt	Altitude (m)	Area (km^2)	Geographic background	representative station
A	3500–4486	272.5	High mountain, glacier, permanent snow	Daxigou meteorological station (3539 m a.s.l.)
B	3000–3500	260.9	High mountain, grassland, ice and snow	Daxigou, YaoJing Qiao (2336 m a.s.l.) stations
C	2500–3000	240.9	Sub-high mountain, grassland, mixture of rain and snow	Sijitian station (2570 m a.s.l.)
D	1920–2500	203.7	Forest belt, rainfall	Yoajing Qiao and Yingxong Qiao hydrometric station (1920 m a.s.l.)

variation of producing runoff characteristics on the surface of the river basin, four belts are divided by the altitude from 1920 to 4486 m a.s.l. for the tank model. The geographic characteristics of each belt are listed in Table 1.

SIMULATING OF HYDROLOGICAL ELEMENTS

The preliminary hydrology elements of the input to the Tank model before output process calculation are as following:
(a) determining the actual amount of the snowfall and rainfall;
(b) determining the melting value of the glacier and snow;
(c) determining the evaporation from the river basin.

Determining the actual amount of snowfall and rainfall

According to the intercomparison measurement of precipitation in the basin (Yang et al, 1988), chinese standard gauge undercatches rainfall and snowfall. Thus correction is neccesary. The corrected amount of rainfall and snowfall is obtained by multipling average correction ratio (SN) 1.15 and 1.30 to the measured rainfall and snowfall respectively.

Snow melt simulation

A simplified formula is used to calculate the daily amount of the snow melt:

$$ME = RA\ \bar{T}day \qquad (1)$$

Where ME represents daily snowmelt (mm); RA is the melting coefficient (mm $day^{-1}\ {}^{o}C^{-1}$) Which is determined as 3.5 (mm $day^{-1}\,{}^{o}C^{-1}$); Tday is the average daily temperature. Due to the large daily amplitude of the temperature in Urumqi river basin and in order to consider the effects of the daily temperature changes to the quantity of melting snow, the daily temperature changes are assumed a sine curve with amplitude A shown as in Fig. 2 based on the observed temperature data. when $\bar{T}day < -A$, ME = 0; If $-A < \bar{T}day < +A$, the quantity of daily melting snow is determined by the area in which the temperature is higher than 0°C. Dr Sugaware et al (1984) consider the area can be represented by $(\bar{T}day + A)^2/4\ A$, thus the amount of daily melting snow can be calculated by the following formula:

$$ME = RA\ (\bar{T}day + A)^2/4\ A \qquad (2)$$

amplitude A can be achieved from temperature measurement, e.g. 5°C at YingXong Qiang hydrometric station, 6.5°C at Sijientian Ststion and 6.0 C and 3.0°C at Yaojing Qiang and Daxigou meteorological station respectively.

The actual snowmelt in each belt is determined by the snow-covered area in the belt. It is can be calculated by the following formula:

$$MT = ME\ KV \qquad (3)$$

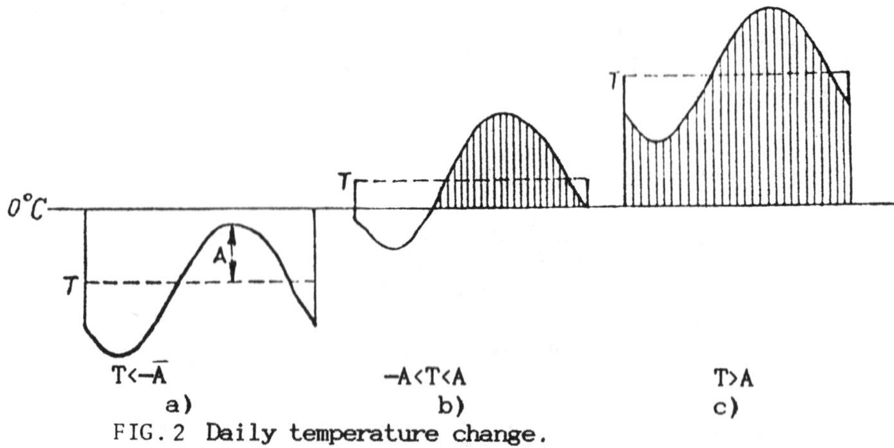

FIG.2 Daily temperature change.

Where MT is the actual amount of daily snowmelt(mm); KV is a factor depending on snowfall, wind speed and geomorphy. The formula is listed bellow:

$$KV = (sc/CM)^{1.5} \qquad (sc<CM) \tag{4}$$

where sc is areal value of water equivalenof the snow(mm); CM is a limit value for the snow water equivalant(mm). When sc>CM, KV=1.0.

It is difficult to determine the value of CM because it is relevant to the factores of meteorology and geomorphy snow will stay long durance in the river basin in the wintertime. Because of wind drafting, snow would concentrate in the leeward slope and lower areas, which could cause inhomogeneous distribution of snow and lower snow covering ratio. In such case, CM should be bigger. Because of the shorter stayment of snow and less effect of wind in summer, CM should be small. The value of CM in each month can be determined with final adjustment and the amount of daily snowmelt can be inputed in the Tank model.

Evaporation calculation

The actual evaporation in the basin is determined by the potential evaporation and soil moisture. Evaporation data from a 20 diameter pan is available only. The observed value multiplied by correction coefficient can be considered as the evaporation capacity. Once the evaporation capacity is decided, the actual evaporation is determined by the variation of the soil moisture in the basin. Thus evaporation capacity is multiplied by the correcting coefficient of soil moisture to calculate the actual evaporation in basin. Obviously, it is hard to get each coefficient respectively. Thus a synthetic evaporation correcting coefficient CE is multiplied by the observed value E of the evaporation pan of 20 cm diameter to calculate the actual evaporation EA in the basin, i.e. EA = CE E .

Coefficient CE is relevant to the soil moisture in the basin, which changes in seasonso. Using the data of 1980–1987 in Urumqi river basin to establish the correlation between the relative precipitation

(Pyear/Pyear) and coefficient CE, the correlation coefficient 0.946 is achieved (Fig.3). This shows larger CE in wet years and small CE in dry years.

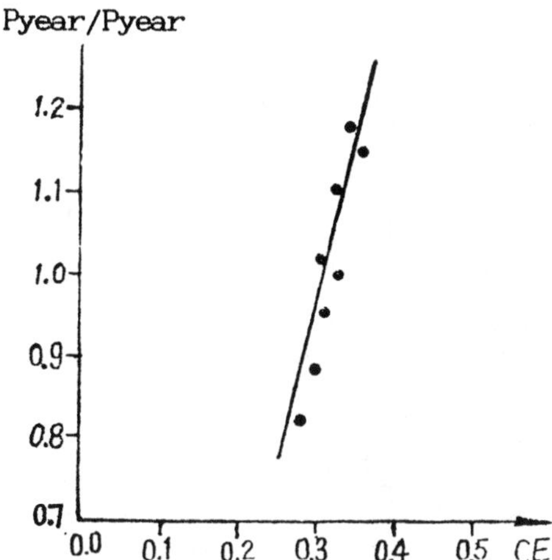

FIG. 3 Correlation between Pyear/Pyear and CE.

TANK MODEL WITH GLACIER AND SNOW MELTING COMPONENT

Dr Sugawara created Tank model, which has achieved fruitly results in many applications all over the world. However, it is the first time to be used in the arid area in the inland of XinJiang. The following sections will discuss the determination of structure and parameters for Tank Model in Urumqi river basin.

Model structure

According to the feature of Urumqi river basin, two types of Tank Model structure are established to make comparison studies(Fig.4).

Tank model 1 The river basin is divided into four zones and each zone can be represented by a tank model (Fig.4a). Zone A above 3500 m a.s.l. consists permanent frozen layer, thus two layer tanks are established in zone A to simulate the effect of frozen layer. In considering the different characteristics of glacier runoff, the glacier in zone A is taken to make simulation of a single waters. The amount of snowmelt will be input into river directly. The next zone consists four layer tanks. Rainfall and snowmelt would be put into the top layer of Tank in each zone and evaperation would be directly subduced from the top layer of Tank. The calculated runoff in each zone is input into river.

Tank model 2 According to the different characteristics of runoff from snowmelt and rainfall, two groups of snowmelt and rainfall Tanks are set in each zone (Fig.4b). Considering the frozen zone below snow surface, snowmelt Tanks are set as two layers to simulate the effect of frozen soil. Rainfall is still in combination by the four layer tanks. Snowmelt and rainfall will go to their own

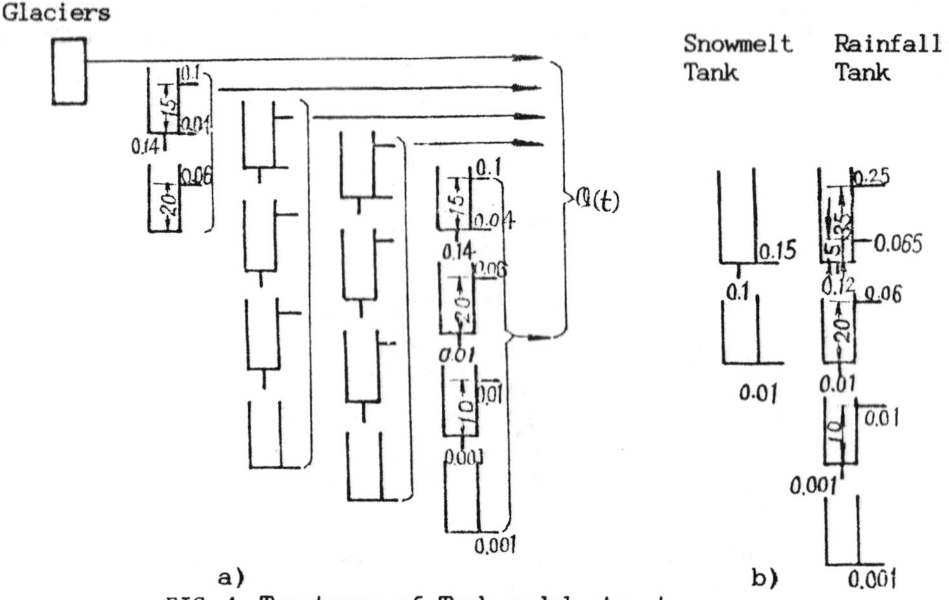

FIG.4 Two types of Tank model structure.

tanks respectively. The output of each colum of tanks will be input to the river.

Determination of model parameters

Determination the model parameters are determined by repeated tests to achieve the optimal fit between calculated and observed hydrographs. Parameters of each tank are list in Fig.4.

TESTING AND ANALYSIS TO THE SIMULATING RESULTS

Criteria of test

The ralative error and passing ratio are used to evaluate the accuracy of annual and monthly runoff simulation respectively and also for daily runoff calculation:

(a) objective function (OB) is given by use the following formula:

$$OB = | Q^{*}day - Qday | / N \bar{Q}day \tag{5}$$

where $Q^{*}day$ is the calculated daily runoff; Qday is observed daily runoff; N is the total days of a year.

(b) evaluation criteria CR of tank model was developed by Sugawara et al, 1984.

Analysis of simulation results

Tank model 1 can be divided into two conditions: Tank model 1(I) selects 0.33 as the average correcting coefficient CE of evaporation. Tank model 1(II) use difference CE by years, which increases the model precise. Tank model 2 tries to simulate various patterns of runoff from rainfall and snowmelt. The simulated results in 1984 show 0.3062 of CR which is the best in the simulation, but not ideal for the 1986 simulation which needs further research. Table 2 shows the simulation results of each model. Due to the paper limitation only the comparison between simulated and observed daily runoff process in 1984 is drawn (Fig. 5).

TABLE 2 The simulation results of models.

Model	Year	Observed runoff (mm)	calculated runoff (mm)	Passing rate of month(%)	OB	CR
Tank1(I)	1984	261.2	263.4	92	0.1823	0.3454
	1985	219.2	191.2	100	0.2178	0.4170
	1986	199.7	220.9	84	0.2987	0.4826
	1987	265.9	283.1	84	0.2416	0.4183
Tank1(II)	1984	261.2	263.4	100	0.1472	0.3454
	1985	219.2	219.2	100	0.1902	0.3221
	1986	199.7	201.2	84	0.2910	0.4535
	1987	265.9	268.1	84	0.2269	0.4411
Tank2	1984	261.2	262.6	100	0.1690	0.3062
	1985	219.2	206.1	100	0.2273	0.3983
	1986	199.7	203.2	84	0.3421	0.4845
	1987	265.9	272.7	84	0.2282	0.4646

DISCUSSION

(a) Tank model has better suitability and resilience. For those rivers with higher proportion of glacier and snow feeds in arid area, Tank model can achieve better results if certain adjustment can be made based on the characteristics of river basin.

(b) It is hard to seperate rain from snow in the rainfall and snowfall replecement period. There is poor precise of simulation. How use tank model to simulate snowmelt runoff needs further research.

(c) Evaporation calculation has an obvious effect on the accuracy of runoff simulation for the rivers in inland arid area. However it is difficult to simulate the effect of soil moisture to the evaporation, which needs further research and improvement.

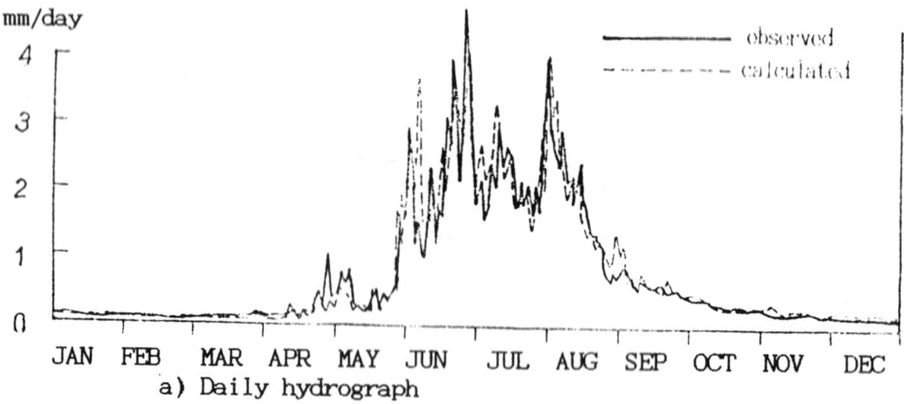

a) Daily hydrograph

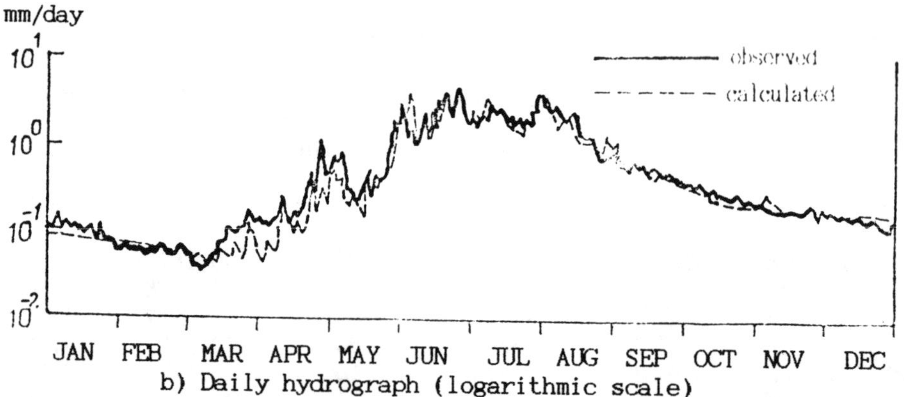

b) Daily hydrograph (logarithmic scale)

FIG.5 The comparison between simulated and observed daily runoff in 1984.

ACKNOWLEDGEMENTS Dr M. Sugawara has provided sincere advices during the preparation for the paper. Mr Zhou yuchao, the senier engineer of XinJiang Hydrological Burean, offered many valuable commenty for the paper. To their kindness, the authors are grateful.

REFERENCES

M.Sugawara, I.Watanabe, E.Ozaki & Y.Katsuyama (1984) Tank model with snow component. Published by the National Research Center for Disaster Prevention, Japan, 1-17.

Yang Daqing, Jiang Tong, Zhang Yinsheng & Kang Ersi (1988) Analysis and correction of error in precipitation measurement at the head of Urumqi River, Tianshan. Journal of glociology and geocryology Vol.10. No.4. 384-399. P.R. of China.

Topic D:

Interaction Between Acid Rain and Pedological and Geological Basin Characteristics

Hydrology in Mountainous Regions. I - Hydrological Measurements; the Water Cycle (Proceedings of two Lausanne Symposia, August 1990). IAHS Publ. no. 193, 1990.

Formalization of proton balances in elementary basins based upon the alkalinity concept and graph properties

G. BOURRIE
Laboratoire de Science du Sol, INRA, 65 rue de Saint Brieuc, F35042 Rennes Cedex, France
F. LELONG
Laboratoire d'Hydrogéologie, Université d'Orléans, BP 6759, F45067 Orléans Cedex, France

ABSTRACT Atmospheric sources of acidity add to the oxidation of organic matter, and to the uptake of cations by biomass, to constitute the global sources of protons. The main sinks of protons are the hydrolysis of soil minerals and the immobilization of anions in soils or their uptake by the biomass. The global balance of these processes is expressed in the balance of protons. Due to gaseous exchange of CO_2, the proton balance cannot be directly deduced from the pH of inputs and of outputs, but must be deduced from the balance of Alkalinity of solutions and from the balances of cations and anions. Graph properties allow to express very conveniently the formalization of input-output balances and the constraints due to the nature of the different compartments and their interrelationships, and to derive the mass balance equations.

INTRODUCTION

Soils play a major role in the acquisition of solutes by waters, and conversely interaction between minerals and waters is a major process of soil formation. Management of waters and soils are thus closely bound. Fossil fuel combustion generates both CO_2 and strong mineral acidity, that add to natural atmospheric acidity - Nitrogen photooxidation and volcanogenic sulfuric acid- and increase the total proton input in ecosystems at a global scale. Monitoring of elementary watersheds (Bourrié & Paces, 1987) is a means of evaluating the effects of such changes. This paper will be focused on the particular aspect of proton balances, that allow to assign sources and sinks of protons in the ecosystems to either internal or external processes. Due to CO_2 exchange with the atmosphere, the computation of the balances implies to use a conservative parameter, namely alkalinity, and not directly H^+ or HCO_3^- concentrations. First will thus be derived from the equation of alkalinity the proper formalism of proton balance in water. Then it will be shown that a given ecosystem can be considered as made of interconnected compartments, linked by paths where matter flows, and that graphs allow very conveniently to describe the global properties of the system and to write the mass balance and proton balance equations. This formalism will be illustrated with the data collected in the experimental watersheds of Mont Lozère (South of Central Massif, France) by Lelong et al. (1988), Durand (1989).

ALKALINITY OF WATER, A CONSERVATIVE ALGEBRAIC PARAMETER

Alkalinity can be defined as the acid neutralizing capacity of water (Stumm & Morgan, 1970). It is equal to the sum of the products of the concentrations of bases by the number of protons neutralized in the reaction, minus the concentration of H^+ in the solution (Bourrié, 1976, 1978). It is zero in pure water or in a neutral salt solution, positive if there is an excess of bases, negative if there is an excess of acids. It is conservative by mixing, evaporation or dilution. Its derivative is the buffer capacity of the solution. During evaporation, pH decreases, remains constant or increases according to alkalinity being respectively negative, zero or positive. Other functions, named residual alkalinities can be derived in the same manner when some elements are affected by precipitation of minerals during the evaporation (Al Droubi, 1976; Al Droubi et al., 1980). It is directly measured by acidimetric titration using Gran transformation.
From the above definition, in a solution where weak bases include carbonate, bicarbonate and ion pairs of these ions with Na, K, Ca and Mg, its expression is given by:

$$[Alk] = [HCO_3^-] + [NaHCO_3^\circ] + [KHCO_3^\circ] + [MgHCO_3^+] + [CaHCO_3^+] + 2\,[CO_3^{2-}] + 2\,[NaCO_3^-] + 2\,[KCO_3^-] + 2\,[MgCO_3^\circ] + 2\,[CaCO_3^\circ] + [OH^-] - [H^+] \qquad (1)$$

Combining this equation with the equations of mass balance for cations and anions and electroneutrality equation, one obtains:

$$[Alk] = [Na^+]_t + [K^+]_t + 2\,[Mg^{2+}]_t + 2\,[Ca^{2+}]_t + [NH_4^+]_t - [Cl^-]_t - [NO_3^-]_t - 2\,[SO_4^{2-}]_t \qquad (2)$$

where the subscript t designates total molalities of the element, i.e. includes all ion pairs or complexes. From pH and [Alk], partial pressure of equilibrating CO_2 can be computed using Eq.1, whereas Eq.2 can be used to check the accurateness or completeness of the analysis, or to calculate Alkalinity if it was not directly measured, but with much less precision than by direct titration of course. When organic bases are present, they must be included in Eq.1. It was demonstrated (Keller et al., 1987) that by direct and reverse titrations, carbonate and non carbonate alkalinities can be analyzed, and that much lower values of pCO_2 are obtained using carbonate alkalinity in Eq.1. It is thus recommended that the analysis of alkalinity be included in routine monitoring of water chemistry.

Non carbonate alkalinity and carbonate alkalinity reflect respectively the effect of partial and total oxidation of organic matter in soils as proton sources. It is thus a means of indirectly assessing the influence on Carbon biogeochemistry of environmental changes, e.g. heavy metals toxical effects on microflora (Keller et al., 1987).

When using carbonate alkalinity instead of total alkalinity, lower values of pCO_2 are obtained, in the range 0.001 to 0.01 atm. In soils developed upon chalk, pCO_2.is relatively constant near 0.02 atm. from 0.3 to 1 m depth (Dever, 1985).

Non carbonate alkalinity is closely correlated with dissolved organic carbon (DOC), with a ratio of 4 meq. g Carbon $^{-1}$ (Keller et al., 1987), but higher values were obtained, such as 13.8 meq.of carboxylic acidity g Carbon $^{-1}$ in free waters issuing from the "sols bruns ocreux" in Aubure watershed (B. Guillet's personal communication).

ACIDITY OF PRECIPITATIONS AS A NEGATIVE ALKALINITY

In acid rain, alkalinity is negative due to a large excess of H^+ over weak bases present, and the sum [Alk] + [H^+] is close to zero, or only slightly positive (Table 1). There appears a clear opposition between Vosges catchments (Aubure is in the Vosges) and Central Massif catchments (Margeride and Mont Lozère), that are not or only slightly submitted to acid rains.The input flux of acidity as mineral acids (nitric or sulfuric acid), is then directly equal to a negative alkalinity input flux. This of course does not include potential acidity due to ammonium input or to gaseous or dry deposit fluxes from atmosphere to soil.

INTERNAL SOURCES AND SINKS OF PROTONS

The sources and sinks of protons can be deduced from the balances of cations and anions. Due to gaseous exchanges, nitrogen balance in catchments cannot be directly made by

TABLE 1 Mean acidity parameters of rain in some experimental catchments.

Site	pH	$[H^+]$	[Alk]	$[Alk]+[H^+]$	Ref.
Vosges (1973-74)	4.19	0.076	-0.052	0.024	(1)
Aubure (1986-87)	4.47	0.034	-0.030	0.004	(2)
Margeride (1973-74)	5.51	0.003	0.025	0.028	(1)
Mt Lozère (1981-85)	4.60	0.025	-0.019	0.006	(3)

Concentrations are in meq l^{-1}. 1. Bourrié, 1978. 2. Probst *et al.*, 1989. 3. Lelong *et al.*, 1988.

input-output balance. However, as was shown by Van Breemen *et al.* (1983), the net contribution of nitrogen species as proton donors or acceptors can be derived from the input-output budget of the difference $[NH_4^+]_t - [NO_3^-]_t$, i.e. $([NH_4^+]_{in} - [NH_4^+]_{out}) - ([NO_3^-]_{in} - [NO_3^-]_{out})$ Thus the contributions of any element to acid-base reactions are directly derived from its stoichiometric coefficient in the equation of alkalinity, changing the sign , as acidity is the opposite of alkalinity.

USE OF GRAPH PROPERTIES TO REPRESENT THE RELATIONSHIPS AND FLUXES BETWEEN THE COMPARTMENTS

The main compartments and fluxes

As limits of the system, we consider the canopy and the outlet of the watershed. Thus, throughfall is considered as an internal flux, as are uptake by biomass, or weathering, and the only external fluxes are supposed to be input by rain or snow from the atmosphere and output in drainage water to the hydrosphere. As previously made by Van Breemen *et al.* (1983) and Lelong *et al.* (1988), roots, living organisms are globally considered as "biomass" and weatherable minerals as "mineral reserve". In addition, are considered the litter and the "exchange complex". Fluxes between the compartments are denoted Q_f, where the subscript f designates the particular flux, (Fig.1).

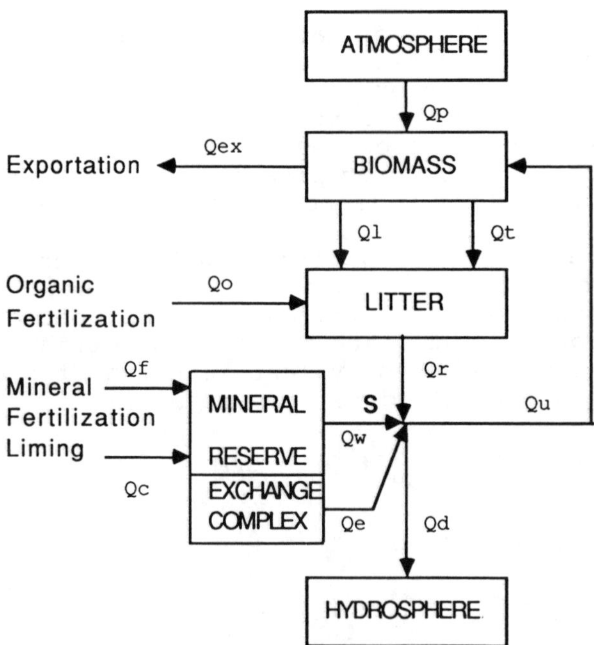

FIG. 1 Graph representation of fluxes in a basin p: precipitations (rain, snow); t: throughfall; l: litter fall; r: flux issuing from the litter; w:weathering of minerals or newformation (reverse weathering); u: uptake by biomass; e: exchange reactions; d: drainage; ex: exportation of biomass; o: organic fertilization; f: mineral fertilization; c: liming S: soil solution.

The soil solution as a node

If we consider a long enough period, one year or more, we can neglect the *variations* of the salt content of soil solution with respect to not only the masses of elements held in the biomass or the minerals, but also with respect to the fluxes of matter that flow in the system. This implies the equality of the sum of fluxes that enter the soil solution and of the sum of fluxes that leave it. There is no accumulation of matter in the soil solution, that can be considered as a node in the system, point S in Fig.1 (Lelong & Bourrié, in preparation).

Graph representation of the system

Fig.1 shows an example of a simplified graph representation of a catchment. The boxes represent the compartments and edges the paths of flows of matter as usual. Arrows indicate the direction in which fluxes are considered positive. Some of the basic properties of the system, or assumptions are directly expressed by the *topology* of the graph, i.e. the way the compartments are connected:

(a) the interception of precipitations by the canopy is total, and thus there is no direct flux from the atmosphere to the litter;

(b) the coverage of soil by litter is total, and thus there is no direct flux of throughfall to the soil.

The mass balance equations for each compartment are then easily derived by application to each box of the mass conservation law, whose equivalent is Kirchoff's current law. With the above notations, one obtains:

$$- Q_{ex} - Q_l - Q_t + Q_u + Q_p = \Delta BM \tag{3}$$

$$- Q_r + Q_l + Q_t + Qo = \Delta L \tag{4}$$

$$Q_r + Q_w + Q_e - Q_u - Q_d = 0 \tag{5}$$

$$Q_f + Q_c - Q_w = \Delta RM \tag{6}$$

$$Q_e = \Delta EC \tag{7}$$

where ΔBM, ΔL, ΔRM and ΔEC stand for the biomass, the litter, the mineral reserve and the exchange complex variations respectively. The solution of this set of 5 equations with 16 unknowns necessitates to measure 11 fluxes or stock variations. Fortunately, a certain number of simplifying assumptions can be made, either a priori or a posteriori. This will be made in the case of Mont Lozère A catchment, a small (0.54 km^2) undisturbed catchment, covered by a beech forest under mountain mediterranean climate (Lelong et al., 1988; Durand, 1989):

(a) in the absence of mineral or organic fertilization and of liming and of exportation of biomass, these fluxes are set to zero;

(b) the litter is supposed to be in steady state, ΔL = 0.

(c) analyses showed that the variations of the exchange complex were negligible, hence ΔEC = 0.

By substituting and rearranging, this leads to the following set of equations:

$$- Q_r + Q_u + Q_p = \Delta BM \tag{8}$$

$$Q_r + Q_w - Q_u - Q_d = 0 \tag{9}$$

$$- Q_w = \Delta RM \tag{10}$$

This set can be further transformed by defining:

$$Q_b = \Delta BM = - Q_r + Q_u + Q_p \qquad (11)$$

and substituting in Eq.9, that becomes:

$$(Q_w - Q_b) + (Q_p - Q_d) = 0 \qquad (12)$$

where the first term inside parentheses is the sum of internal fluxes and the second the sum of external fluxes. From the properties of graphs, one may replace any compartment whose stock variation is zero by a node and suppress any branch whose flux is zero. Fig.1 is then simplified into Fig.2, that represents Eqs.11 and 12.

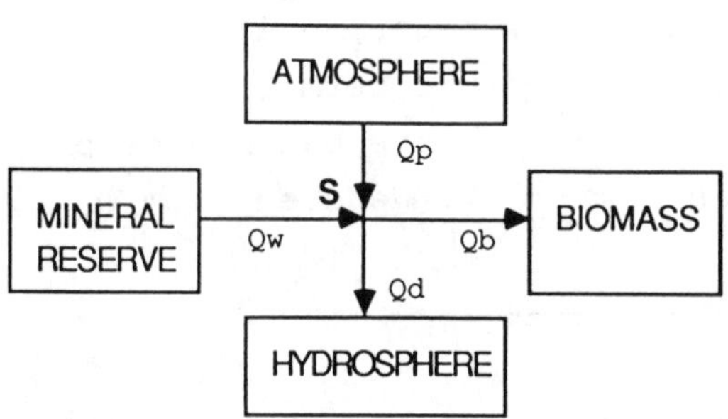

FIG.2 Graph representation of fluxes in a basin Q_p: precipitations; Q_b= net flux to biomass (Eq.11); Q_w: weathering; Q_d: drainage.

The system is then solved if one knows the balance input - output ($Q_p - Q_d$) and the stock variation of the biomass. It must be stressed that the input flux Q_p is the flux over the canopy and that it is not necessary - at this level of integration - to measure the throughfall, or more precisely, the measurement of the throughfall will only give a supplementary insight on the system if simultaneously is measured the stock variation of the litter or the flux of litter fall, according to Eq.4.

The values of Q_b, Q_p, Q_d measured in Mont Lozère allow to compute Q_w from Eq.12 and are given in Table 2 (Lelong _et al_., 1988).

PROTON BALANCE

Proton balance is directly derived by substituting to the concentrations of the elements in Eq.2 the corresponding fluxes, and changing the sign as acidity is a negative

TABLE 2 Terms of mass balance in Mont Lozère experimental catchment A (Lelong <u>et</u> <u>al</u>., 1988; Lelong & Bourrié, in preparation).

Fluxes	Ca^{2+}	Mg^{2+}	K^+	Na^+	Cl^-	SO_4^{2-}	N[(a)]	Alk.[(b)]
Q_p	271	83	54	470	524	615	181	-341
$-Q_d$	-231	-146	-70	-584	-474	-340	12	-242
$-Q_b$	-100	-33	-77	-41	0	-16	-193	-545
Q_w[(c)]	60	96	93	155	-50	-259	-	1128

Fluxes are expressed in mole ha^{-1} $year^{-1}$, and positive if entering the soil solution, negative if leaving it.
a).Values for $NH_4^+ - NO_3^-$, the term Q_b stands here for the sum $Q_b + Q_w$; b) deduced from the balance of protons following Eq.2 (see text); c). deduced from Q_b, Q_p and Q_d using Eq.12.

alkalinity. This allows to identify the main sources and sinks of protons in the system (Table 3).

<u>Sources of protons:</u>

(a) Acidity input by precipitations is given by the negative flux of alkalinity: 341 eq ha^{-1} $year^{-1}$;
(b) Cation net absorption by biomass either by uptake or by interception from the precipitations is obtained by summing the Q_b terms for cations with the coefficients of Eq.2: 384 eq ha^{-1} $year^{-1}$;
(c) The global contribution of nitrogen cycle is obtained from the balance of $NH_4^+ - NO_3^-$: 193 eq ha^{-1} $year^{-1}$.
(d) The contribution of the CO_2 dissociation in soil:
The internal supply of protons by the dissociation of CO_2 or of weak organic acids resulting from the oxidation of soil organic matter is derived from the balance of Alkalinity. Its contribution is then obtained as : 242 eq ha^{-1} $year^{-1}$. This supply of protons appears in the balance as a flux of alkalinity leaving the soil solution towards the hydrosphere.
The sum of the *external and internal sources of protons* is then: 1160 eq ha^{-1} $year^{-1}$.

Sinks of protons:

(e) Anion net absorption by biomass is obtained by summing the Q_b terms for anions: -32 eq ha^{-1} $year^{-1}$;
(f) Hydrolysis of soil minerals is obtained by summing the Q_w fluxes for cations: - 560 eq ha^{-1} $year^{-1}$;
(g) Anion fixation by soil is obtained by summing the Q_w terms for anions : - 568 eq ha^{-1} $year^{-1}$.
The sum of the sinks of protons is then: - 1160 eq ha^{-1} $year^{-1}$.
The equality of the sums of sources and sinks is a mere consequence of the linearity of Eq.2 and of all the calculations. The omission of any fluxes, such as acid atmospheric solid deposits, or the errors in the estimations of the measured fluxes result in an error in the terms that are derived from the balance equation, i.e. the chemical weathering terms Q_w.

TABLE 3 Balances of protons in Mont Lozère A watershed (1981-1985) (Lelong et al., 1988) (eq ha^{-1} $year^{-1}$).

Input	CO_2	N	Biomass		Mineral reserve	
(Rains)		cycle	Cations	Anions	Cations	Anions
341	242	193	384	-32	-560	-568
Total sources: 1160				Total sinks: - 1160		

CONCLUSIONS

Graphs are a convenient tool to express the relationships between the compartments and the fluxes that flow in the system, allowing to clearly translate the structure of the system and the approximations or assumptions made in topological relations, and to derive the mass balance equations for each compartment.
Proton balance is directly derived from the balance of alkalinity whose terms are the alkalinity consumed by the biomass (proton pump) and the alkalinity produced by the hydrolysis of soil minerals. These terms can be derived from the variation of the stock of biomass and input -output balances of cations and anions. The proton balances obtained express very concisely the hierarchy of the external (atmospheric) and internal (soil-plant) processes of production or consumption of acidity, providing thus a valuable tool for soil and water resource management.

REFERENCES

Al Droubi, A.(1976) Géochimie des Sels et des Solutions concentrées par évaporation. Modèle thermodynamique de simulation. Application aux sols salés du Tchad. Sci. Géol. Mém., 46, Strasbourg.

Al Droubi, A., Fritz, B., Gac, J.Y. & Tardy, Y. (1980) Generalized Residual Alkalinity concept; application to prediction of the chemical evolution of natural waters by evaporation. Am. J. Sci.280, 560-572.

Bourrié, G. (1976) Relations entre le pH, l'Alcalinité, le pouvoir tampon et les équilibres de CO2 dans les eaux naturelles. Science du Sol, 141-159.

Bourrié G. (1978) Acquisition de la composition chimique des eaux en climat tempéré. Application aux granites des Vosges et de la Margeride. Sci. Géol. Mém.52, Strasbourg.

Bourrié, G. & Paces, T.(1987) A comparison of the Geochemistry of Runoff from small basins receiving or not receiving Acid Deposition: a trend from Brittany (France) to Bohemia (Czechoslovakia). In Moldan, B. & Paces, T.(Eds) GEOMON, International Workshop on Geochemistry and Monitoring in Representative Basins, Prague, 278-280.

Dever, L. (1985) Approches chimiques et isotopiques des interactions fluides - matrice en zone non saturée carbopnatée. Thèse, Univ. Paris Sud.

Durand, P. (1989) Biogéochimie comparée de trois écosystèmes (Pelouse, Hêtraie, Pessière) de moyenne montagne granitique (Mont Lozère, France). Thèse, Univ. Orléans.

Keller, C., Bourrié, G. & Vedy, J.C. (1987) Formes de l'Alcalinité dans les eaux gravitaires. Influence des Métaux Lourds contenus dans des composts. Science du Sol 25, 17-29.

Lelong, F., Durand, P. & Didon, J.F. (1988) Comparaison des Bilans Hydrochimiques, des taux d'Altération et d'Acidification dans trois petits bassins versants granitiques similaires à végétation contrastée (Mont Lozère, France). Sci. Géol. Bull. 41, 263-278.

Probst, A., Viville, D., Ambroise, B., Fritz, B., Dambrine, E. & Le Goaster, S. (1989) Aubure catchment. Influence of Acid Atmospheric Inputs on Surface Water chemistry and Mineral fluxes in a declining Spruce stand. In IUFRO Symp."Management of nutrition in forests under stress", Field excursion to the Vosges mountains.

Stumm, W. & Morgan, J.J. (1970) Aquatic Chemistry. An Introduction emphasizing Chemical Equilibria in Natural Waters. Wiley Interscience, New York.

Van Breemen, N., Mulder, J. & Driscoll C.T. (1983) Acidification and Alkalinization of soil. Plant and Soil 75, 283-308.

Hydrology in Mountainous Regions. I - Hydrological Measurements; the Water Cycle
(Proceedings of two Lausanne Symposia, August 1990). IAHS Publ. no. 193, 1990.

The influence of forest decline and soil acidification on water yield from forest catchments of the northern Black Forest, FR Germany

H. J. CASPARY
Institute for Hydrology and Water Resources, University of Karlsruhe, Kaiserstr. 12, D-7500 Karlsruhe 1, Federal Republic of Germany

The precipitation/runoff relationship of the declining forests of the Eyach catchment in the Northern Black Forest/ Federal Republic of Germany is analyzed. The uninhabited catchment is totally covered with coniferous forest, mostly Norway spruce. Long-term monitoring from 1973-1986 indicates a significant increase in water yield and the runoff coefficient for the growing season, although there has been no extensive cutting in the catchment. An "Ecohydrological Systems Model" was developed by the incorporation of field data and plant physiological processes to describe the increase in water yield. The model indicates that the observed increase in water yield is likely to be caused by a reduction of forest transpiration. This change in water yield is linked to forest decline and soil acidification caused by anthropogenic sources of air pollution.

INTRODUCTION

The recent inventories of forest damage in the Federal Republic of Germany indicate a rapid increase of forest decline along the ridges of the low mountain ranges (Schöpfer, 1987). The need to quantify the hydrologic implications of forest decline has been discussed by Brechtel & Both (1986), Caspary (1985) and Plate et al. (1986). This paper reports the results of a long-term, whole catchment study of forest decline. The study was conducted on the Eyach catchment in the Northern Black Forest. The catchment is vegetated with coniferous forest that has been partially affected by forest decline. The primary objective of this study is to describe and quantify, when possible, the linkages between forest decline, soil acidification and water yield increases.

STUDY AREA

The Eyach catchment is situated in the Northern Black Forest in the south-west of the Federal Republic of Germany, near the city of Karlsruhe. The uninhabited catchment is totally covered with coniferous forest, mostly Norway spruce [Picea abies (L.) Karst.]. The catchment is subdivided into four subcatchments each with a recording streamflow gauge. Precipitation is measured by five raingauges (Fig. 1). The subcatchment areas for Dürreych, Brotenau, Eyachmühle and Rotenbach

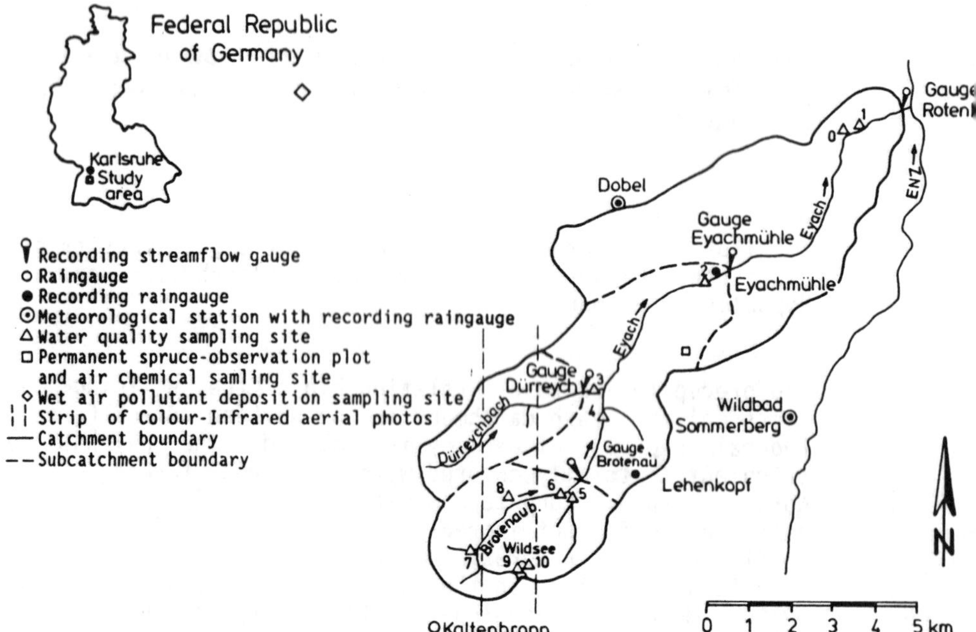

FIG. 1 The Eyach catchment, Northern Black Forest, showing instrumentation and sampling sites.

are 6.88, 9.85, 29.97 and 52.28 km². During autumn 1983 and spring 1984 water quality samples were taken at 11 water quality sampling sites also shown in Fig. 1. The altitude range of the catchment is 350 - 940 m above sea level. Total stream length of the Eyach is about 17 km. Slopes are 600 - 1000 m long and relatively steep (average 30%). The catchment is in the suboceanic, montane climate region. Mean annual gross precipitation is 1460 mm. Mean annual temperature is 7.2°C. The catchment is largely underlain by Middle Bunter sandstone. The dominant soils are podsolized Major Bunter sandstones. These soils are oligotrophic, low-buffered quartz sand soils. Lime is completely missing and magnesium and potassium concentrations are very low. A layer of leaf litter and organic matter is relatively common due to the cool humid climate and the coniferous forest vegetation.

FOREST BIOMASS AND FOREST DECLINE

Except for the narrow meadows of the valleys, the total Eyach catchment is covered with coniferous forest. Forest inventory data of the two subcatchments Dürreych and Brotenau indicate:

1. Forest cover of both subcatchments is similar with 95% of the catchment areas covered with coniferous forest.
2. Norway spruce (Picea abies (L.) Karst.) is the dominant tree species, stocking about 60% of both catchments. Scotch pine (Pinus sylvestris L.) and European silver fir (Abies alba Mill.) cover each about 10-16% of the catchment areas.
3. For the Brotenau catchment 52 % and for the Dürreych catchment 38 % of the trees are older than 60 years. About 15 % of the trees of both catchments are younger than 20 years.

4. The mean annual cutting during 1973-1985 was minimal, under 2 % of the total volume for both catchments. In October 1985 total standing volume was about 250 m^3/ha for Dürreych and 300 m^3/ha for Brotenau.

To get a representative estimate of the degree of forest damage in the headwater catchments colour-infrared (CIR) aerial photographs were taken in the summer of 1983 and 1985 for a 1200 m wide strip crossing the Dürreych and Brotenau catchment from north to south (Fig.1). CIR aerial photo interpretation was performed for a 200 x 200 m regular grid. At each grid point 20 trees were analyzed. CIR photos from the summer of 1983 and 1985 were analyzed in each case for 95 grid points for a total of 1900 trees. Results given in Table 1 indicate that the forest in the headwater catchments Dürreych and Brotenau was already strongly damaged in the summer of 1983 with 30 % belonging to damage class 2 (26-60% needle loss) and about 10 % in damage class 3 (strongly damaged: 61-99% needle loss. The sum of the percentages of the damage classes 2 and 3 increased drastically from 39% in 1983 to 52.2% in 1985.

TABLE 1 Results of the forest damage inventories for the Eyach headwater catchments Dürreych and Brotenau using colour-infrared aerial photos from the summer of 1983 and 1985. Number in parantheses are percentages of needle loss.

Tree Species	Year	Damage Classification					Sum of a tree species [%]
		0 [0 -10%]	1 [11-25%]	2 [26-60%]	3 [61-99%]	2 + 3	
Norway spruce	1983	21.9	40.1	28.7	9.3	38.0	49.1
	1985	10.3	35.2	42.2	12.3	54.5	50.8
European silver fir	1983	15.5	41.4	35.7	7.4	43.1	32.2
	1985	11.7	37.2	44.3	6.8	51.1	31.0
Scotch pine	1983	25.3	32.9	28.9	12.9	41.8	13.1
	1985	15.9	33.5	39.5	11.1	50.6	12.3
Japanese Larch	1983	40.0	45.3	12.0	2.7	14.7	2.7
	1985	26.9	44.3	26.9	3.9	30.8	4.1
Deciduous hardwoods	1983	37.5	21.9	18.7	21.9	40.6	1.7
	1985	7.1	21.4	57.1	14.3	71.4	1.5
All Trees	1983	21.2	39.5	30.2	9.1	39.3	100
	1985	12.1	35.7	42.1	10.1	52.2	100

RESULTS OF WATER YIELD INVESTIGATIONS FOR THE GROWING SEASON

Water yield changes due to forest decline can be expected, especially during the growing season. Therefore rainfall-runoff data were evaluated separately for the growing season (May-Sept.) and dormant season (Oct.-April). Catchment average gross rainfall (N) was determined for each of the four catchments using Thiessen polygons. The corresponding water yield (Q) was taken by integrating the runoff data of the recording streamflow gauges. The runoff coefficient (φ) was calculated as φ

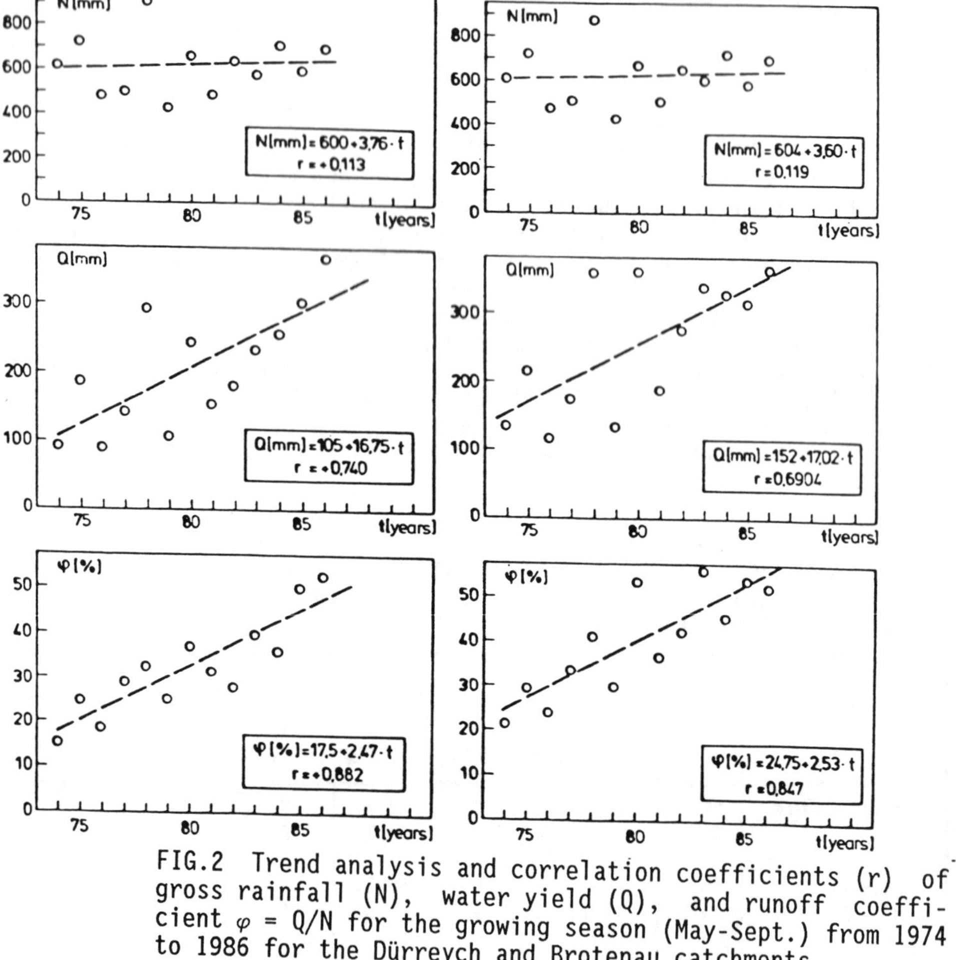

FIG.2 Trend analysis and correlation coefficients (r) of gross rainfall (N), water yield (Q), and runoff coefficient φ = Q/N for the growing season (May-Sept.) from 1974 to 1986 for the Dürreych and Brotenau catchments.

= Q/N. For the three parameters N, Q and φ, a trend analysis was carried out. Fig. 2 shows the results for the subcatchments Dürreych and Brotenau for the growing seasons of the long-term monitoring period from 1974-1986. Fig. 2 indicates that there is no trend and no correlation with time for N. Conversely water yield versus time shows a strongly increasing trend with correlation coefficients (r) significant at the 99% level of 0.74 for Dürreych and 0.69 for Brotenau. The correlation between φ and time is even stronger with r = 0.88 for Dürreych and r = 0.85 for Brotenau. The increasing trend rate $\Delta\varphi/\Delta t$ of 2.5% per year is nearly the same in both catchments. For the dormant seasons no significant change in water yield can be detected. More detailed results of the water yield investigations are given by Caspary (1989).

As known from Bosch & Hewlett (1982) and Hiege (1985) Q and φ should not have changed significantly because of the light cutting of only 1.6% and 1.9% of the standing volume per year in Brotenau and Dürreych and the present age of the trees.

THE ECOHYDROLOGICAL SYSTEMS MODEL

In order to clarify the explanation of the increased water yield for the growing seasons an "Ecohydrological Systems Model" was developed (Fig. 3). The model is based on the integrative evaluation of long-term field measured data of the Eyach catchment and comparable neighbouring regions. Data supporting the hypothesis of the model are pre-

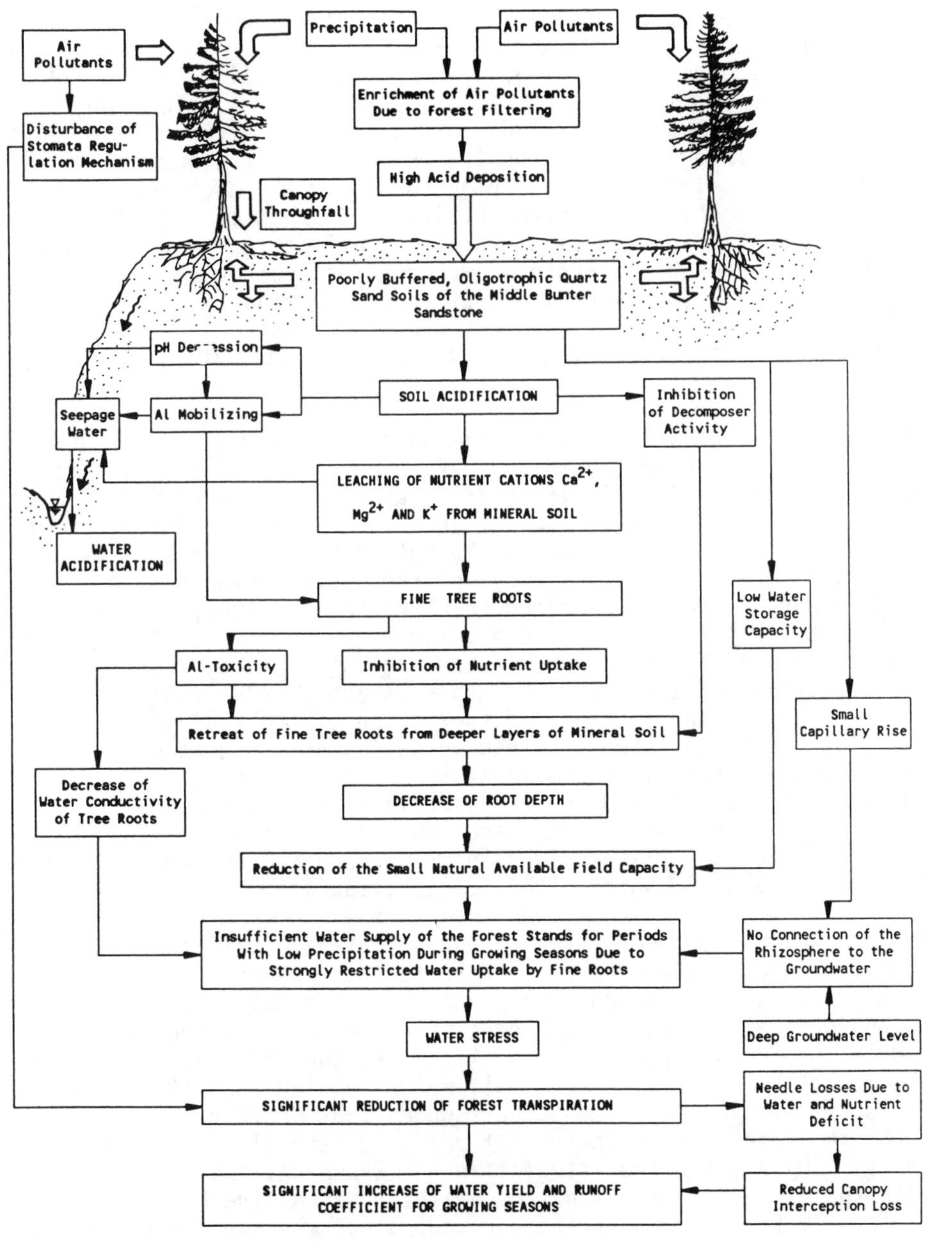

FIG. 3 The ecohydrological systems model.

sented in detail by Caspary (1990). The coniferous forests of the Eyach catchment filter out air pollutants. In combination with the high annual gross rainfall of about 1460 mm this causes pollutant enrichment in the canopy throughfall (Adam et al., 1987). Thus, an elevated acid deposition reaches the soil. The forest soils of the Eyach catchment are poorly buffered, oligotrophic quartz sand soils derived from the Middle Bunter sandstone. As shown by Fölster (1985) the acid deposition exceeds the buffering capacity of the soils and induces soil acidification. Soil acidification causes a depression of pH-values and a reduction of base-saturation of exchangeable cations with subsequent losses of Ca and Mg from the soil by leaching [Ulrich, 1986; Matzner and Ulrich, 1987]. The nutrient cations (Ca^{2+}, Mg^{2+} and K^{+}) percolate in the soil with seepage water, come to the surface at springs, and are transported outside of the catchment by surface streamflow. In addition to the low pH-values of the Bunter sandstone soils, nutrient leaching is also supported by the high annual precipitation and the high soil permeability. A direct consequence of soil acidification is an increasing water acidification. For the headwater catchments Dürreych and Brotenau water acidification has been verified by Kohler et al. (1986) by many water quality measurements. Soil acidification also induces an increased mobility of potentially root toxic ions especially Al^{3+} into the soil solution (Matzner et al., 1985).

The cation leaching and the mobilizing of Al^{3+} ions has induced a significant reduction of the molar Ca/Al and Mg/Al ratios of the soil solution during the last 10-15 years. Laboratory studies with low molar Ca/Al and Mg/Al ratios induced a significant reduction of root growth and an inhibition of the Ca and Mg uptake by fine roots as well as a reduction of water conductivity of the roots (Stienen et al., 1984; Rost-Siebert, 1985; Jorns and Hecht-Buchholz, 1985). Ulrich (1986) called this phenomenon "acid toxicity" and it is documented by studies in many forest stands (Matzner et al., 1985; Matzner et al., 1986; Matzner et al., 1988; Murach & Matzner, 1988). In forest stands on Middle Bunter sandstone in the region of the study area Evers et al. (1986) substantiated a Ca and Mg deficiency in needles. The lack of nutrient cations in the mineral soil and the high Al concentrations in soil solution induce an extensive loss of fine tree roots so that today fine roots of forest stands in this area can be found almost only in the organic layer (Evers et al., 1986; Häußling, 1990; Murach & Matzner, 1988; Schönhar, 1987; Ulrich, 1986).

The changes in soil chemistry by air pollutant deposition induced soil acidity leads to a chemical stress to the fine roots of the trees. This causes the ecological and plant physiological reaction of the reduced root depth. Full hydrologic appreciation of reduced root depth should be considered in conjunction with the physical properties of the forest soils. Due to the small water-holding capacity of the sandy soils of the Eyach catchment the reduced root depth causes a significant reduction in the amount of moisture naturally available to the forest. Hydrogeological studies in the Eyach catchment indicate that, with the exception of the narrow valley regions, the groundwater table is from 20 to 150 m under the surface. Since the capillary rise of the sandy soils is small the rhizosphere of the forest stands has no connection to the groundwater. The reduced root depth of the forest stands in combination with the deep groundwater level and the unchanged precipitation may greatly limit water uptake by tne roots. This induces an insufficient water supply of the forest stands for times with low precipitation during the growing season.

Another consequence of soil acidification is a drastic reduction in root growth and root branching. Eichhorn (1985), Schönhar (1987 and 1989) and Häußling (1990) reported this phenomenon for old Norway spruce stands stocking on acid soils of Middle Bunter sandstone as it is common in the Eyach catchment. How closely root water uptake of coniferous forests is connected to a regular root growth and root branching is shown by Bartsch (1985) and Häußling et al. (1988). A reduced root branching diminishes the number of places for root water uptake. Due to the disturbed root growth and root branching the trees even seem not to be able to use the available moisture of the upper soil layer where a relatively high biomass of fine tree roots is existing and where enough soil moisture is available. This leads to the important conclusion that forest stands suffer from "waterstress" although there is a good water availibility of the soil due to the soil physical properties. Water stress leads to the reduction of forest transpiration which is reflected in the increase of water yield and the runoff coefficient for the growing seasons.

The lack of water in addition to the nutrient limitations gives rise to increased needle losses (Gross & Pham-Nguyen, 1987). The raised needle loss as a symptom of forest decline is especially evident in the ridge areas of the Eyach headwater catchments as documented by the analysis of colour-infrared aerial photos. Through needle loss, canopy interception loss is reduced while litter interception increases. Summarizing both processes this causes also an increase in water yield.

Schweizer & Arndt (1988) showed that transpiration also can be reduced by disturbance of the stomata regulation mechanism induced by the direct influence of air pollutants on needles.

The present data do not allow determination of the portion of reduced transpiration due to the "soil path" and the portion due to the "needle path". Further ecophysiological studies are needed. However it can be concluded that the measured change in water balance of the Eyach catchment is primarily induced by the significant reduction of transpiration and less due to reduction of interception loss.

CONCLUSIONS

1. Water yield and rainfall data of the declining coniferous forest of the Eyach catchment in the Northern Black Forest/West Germany were analyzed. Long-term field measurements from 1973-1986 indicated a significant increase in water yield and runoff coefficient for the growing seasons, although there has been no extensive cutting in the catchment during the measurement period.

2. In order to explain the increased water yield, hydrological, hydrogeological, geological, soil physical and chemical, water and air-chemical and forest inventory data of the Eyach catchment and neighbouring areas were integrated and evaluated in the light of

plant physiological processes. Summarizing all these data, an "Eco-hydrological Systems Model" was developed.

3. The increased water yield for the growing season appears to be caused by a reduction in transpiration induced by forest decline and soil acidification due to air pollutants. The forest stands suffer from air pollutant induced "water stress" although the amount of gross precipitation has not changed compared with mean annual long-term conditions.

4. Significant changes in water yield can be detected before needle loss is very high and obviously visible. Therefore, the water balance of forest catchments may be used as an indicator of forest damage, which may not yet be apparent when considering only needle loss.

5. The results of this study are a contribution to the search for causal explanation of the results of the present forest decline for forested catchments with similar soils, geology and air pollutant deposition. It must be emphasized that the detected "water stress" of the forest stands induced by air pollutants is presumably an important reason for forest decline in such regions. Nevertheless it seems that forest decline research should focus more on the pollutant-induced changes in the water balance of trees.

ACKNOWLEDGMENTS The author is grateful to the Forestry Administration, the Water Resources Administration and the Environmental Protection Agency of the State of Baden-Württemberg and the Federal German Weather Service for the use of forestry data, colour-infrared photos, precipitation and streamflow data as well as for their good cooperation. This work was supported by the National German Science Foundation (DFG).

REFERENCES

Adam, K., Evers, F. H. & Littek, T. (1987) Ergebnisse niederschlagsanalytischer Untersuchungen in südwestdeutschen Wald-Ökosystemen 1981-1986, Forschungsbericht Kernforschungszentrum Karlsruhe, KfK-PEF 24, 1-119.

Bartsch, N. (1985) Ökologische Untersuchungen zur Wurzelentwicklung an Jungpflanzen von Fichte (Picea abies (L.) Karst.) und Kiefer (Pinus Sylvestris L.). Berichte des Forschungszentrums Waldökosysteme/Waldsterben 15.

Bosch, J.M. & Hewlett J. D. (1982) A review of catchment experiments to determine the effect of vegetation changes on water yield and evapotranspiration, J. Hydrol. 55, 3-23.

Brechtel, H.- M. & Both, M. (1986) Wasser und Boden - Wirkungszusammenhänge und Auswirkungen des Waldsterbens in hydrologischer und wasserwirtschaftlicher Sicht. in: Zur monetären Bewertung von Umweltschäden - Methodische Untersuchungen am Beispiel der Waldschäden. ed. Ewers, H.-J., Berichte 4/86 des Umweltbundesamtes, 5.1-5.123, Erich Schmidt Verlag, Berlin.

Caspary, H. J. (1985) Auswirkungen des Waldsterbens und der Gewässerversauerung auf den Wasserhaushalt - Ein Beitrag zur Problemerfassung -. Deutsche Gewässerkundlichen Mitteilungen 29, 145-150.

Caspary, H. J. (1989) Abflußbilanzänderungen von Waldeinzugsgebieten des Buntsandstein - Schwarzwaldes infolge neuartiger Waldschäden. Wasserwirtschaft 79 (12), 602-608.

Caspary, H. J. (1990) An ecohydrological framework for water yield changes of forested catchments due to forest decline and soil acidification. *Wat. Resour. Res.* in press, May 1990.

Eichhorn, J. (1987) Vergleichende Untersuchungen von Feinwurzelsystemen bei unterschiedlich geschädigten Altfichten (Picea abies Karst.). Forschungsberichte Hessische Forstl. Versuchsanstalt 3, Hann. Münden.

Evers, F.H., Hildebrand, E. E., Kenk, G. & Kremer W. L. (1986) Boden-, ernährungs und ertragskundliche Untersuchungen in einem stark geschädigten Fichtenbestand des Buntsandstein-Schwarzwaldes. Mitt. Verein für Forstl. Standortskunde und Forstpflanzenzüchtung 32, 72-80.

Fölster, H. (1985) Proton consumption rates in holocene and present day weathering of acid forest soils. in: The Chemistry of Weathering. ed. Drever, J. I. 197-209, Reidel Publ. Co., Dordrecht.

Gross, R. & Pham-Nguyen, T. (1987) Einfluß von langfristigem konstantem Wassermangelstreß auf die Netto-Photosynthese und das Wachstum junger Fichten (Picea abies [L.] Karst) und Douglasien (Pseudotsuga menziesii [Mirb.] Franco) im Freiland, Forstw. Cbl. 106, 7-26.

Häußling, M., Jorns, C.A., Lehmbecker, G., Hecht-Buchholz, Ch., Marschner, H. (1988) Ion and water uptake in relation to root development in Norway Spruce (Picea abies (L.) Karst.)". J. Plant Physiol., 133, 486-491.

Häußling, M., im Druck (1990) Wurzelwachstum, pH-Gradienten in der Rhizosphäre und Nährstoffaufnahme bei Fichte auf unterschiedlichen Standorten in Baden-Württemberg". Dissertation Universität Hohenheim.

Hiege, W. (1985) Wasserhaushalt von Forsten und Wäldern und der Einfluß des Wassers auf Wachstum und Gesundheit von Forsten und Wäldern: eine Literaturstudie, Studiecommissie Waterbeheer Natur, Bos en Landschap, Utrecht (Holland).

Hildebrand, E.E. (1986) Zustand und Entwicklung der Austauschereigenschaften von Mineralböden aus Standorten mit erkrankten Waldbeständen, Forstw. Cbl. 105, 60-76.

Jorns, A. & Hecht-Buchholz, Ch. (1985) Aluminium-induzierter Magnesium- und Calciummangel im Laborversuch bei Fichtensämlingen". AFZ, no.41, 1248-1252.

Kohler, A., Schoen, R. & Neubauer, D. (1986) Gewässerversauerung in Baden-Württemberg, Bericht für das Ministerium für Ernährung, Landwirtschaft, Umwelt und Forsten B.-W.,

Matzner, E., Ulrich, B., Murach, D. & Rost-Siebert, K. (1985) Zur Beteiligung des Bodens am Waldsterben. Der Forst- u. Holzwirt 40 (11), 303-309.

Matzner, E., Murach, D., Fortmann, H. (1986) Soil acidity and its relationship to root growth in declining forest staands in Germany. Water, Air and Soil Pollution 31, 273-282.

Matzner, E. & Ulrich, B. (1987) Results of studies on forest decline in Northwest Germany. in: Effects of Atmospheric Pollutants on Forests, Wetlands and Agricultural Ecosystems. ed. Hutchinson, T. C. & Meema, K. M. NATO ASI Series, vol. G 16, 25-42, Springer Verlag, Berlin.

Matzner, E., Blanck, K., Hartmann G., Stock R. (1989) Needle chlorosis pattern in relation to soil chemical properties in two Norway spruce (picea abies Karst.) forests of the German Harz mountains. In: IUFRO Conf.: Air Pollution and Forest Decline ed. Bucher J.B. & Bucher-Wallin, I., (Proc. Interlaken Oct. 1988) 195-199, Birmensdorf.

Murach, D. & Matzner, E. (1989) The influence of soil acidification on root growth of Norway Spruce (Picea abies Karst.) and European Beech (Fagus silv. L.)". Int. Union Forest Research Organisations (IUFRO) Workshop "Woody plant growth in a chanching chemical and physical environment, July 1987, University of British Coloumbia, Vancouver (CDN), 171-187.

Plate, E.J., Pfaud, A. & Paschke, G. (1986) Auswirkungen der Waldschäden auf die Wasserwirtschaft aus quantitativer Sicht, Bericht der Landesanstalt f. Umweltschutz Baden-Württemberg 40, Karlsruhe.

Rost-Siebert, K. (1985) Untersuchungen zur H^+ - und Al-Ionentoxizität an Keimpflanzen von Fichte (Picea abies Karst.) und Buche (Fagus silvatica L.) in Lösungskultur, Ber. d. Forschungszentrums Waldökosysteme/Waldsterben 12, Univ. Göttingen.

Schönhar, S. (1987) Untersuchungen über das Vorkommen pilzlicher Parasiten an Feinwurzeln 70- bis 90-jähriger Fichten (Picea abies Karst.). Mitteilungen des Vereins für Forstliche Standortkunde und Forstpflanzenzüchtung, no.33, 77-80.

Schönhar, S. (1989) Untersuchungen über Feinwurzelschäden und Pilzbefall in Fichtenbeständen des Nordschwarzwaldes und der Schwäbischen Alb. Proc. Int. Kongreß Waldschadensforschung, Friedrichshafen 2.-6. 10. 1989, 265-266.

Schöpfer, W., Bösch, B. & Hannak, C. (1987) Waldschadenssituation 1987 in Baden-Württemberg. Der Forst- u. Holzwirt 42, (20), 546-548.

Schweizer, B. & Arndt, U.(1988) Gaswechselmessungen an immissionsbelasteten Tannen und Fichten in den Hohenheimer Open-Top-Kammern, in: Proc. 4. Statuskolloquium des PEF. 1, Kernforschungszentrum Karlsruhe KfK- PEF 35, Karlsruhe.

Stienen, H., Barckhausen, R., Schaub, H. & Bauch, J. (1984) Mikroskopische und röntgenenergiedispersive Untersuchungen an Feinwurzeln gesunder und er krankter Fichten verschiedener Standorte, Forstw. Cbl. 103, 262-274.

Ulrich, B. (1986) Die Rolle der Bodenversauerung beim Waldsterben: Langfristige Konsequenzen und forstliche Möglichkeiten, Forstw. Cbl. 105, 421-435.

Hydrology in Mountainous Regions. I - Hydrological Measurements; the Water Cycle
(Proceedings of two Lausanne Symposia, August 1990). IAHS Publ. no. 193, 1990.

A multivariate model of solute behaviour for an episodic acid stream in the Black Forest, FR Germany

H. MEESENBURG
Institute for Physical Geography, University of Freiburg, Federal Republic of Germany

ABSTRACT A small episodic acid stream in the Black Forest, FRG, was studied for variations in stream water chemistry during 1985 using a stepwise multiple regression technique. 10 independent variables reflecting catchment hydrological, meteorolocical, and biological conditions were examined for being important controls for the response of 16 solutes. Discharge and antecedent precipitation were found to be the most important factors that determine solute behaviour. Seasonally related variables, however, have great impact on solute concentrations in many cases. Up to 98% of the variance can be explained by the regression models and six predictors are included in the most complex equations. Nevertheless, in some cases, the explained variance reaches only 40% and only one predictor is incorporated in the model.

INTRODUCTION

In recent years an increasing interest was noticable concerning the role of atmospheric deposition on stream water chemistry in Central Europe (Wieting et al., 1984, Schoen et al., 1984, UBA, 1987). Whereas the occurence of chronic acid streams in the Federal Republic of Germany is well documented (Einsele et al., 1986, Schoen, 1986, Hamm et al., 1989), less attention has so far been paid to the detection of episodic decreases of streamwater pH and alkalinity (Feger & Brahmer, 1987, Meesenburg, 1987). Several studies have shown that episodic acidification in surface waters is caused by major storm events or snowmelt (Johannessen et al., 1980, Galloway et al., 1987). Acid surges cause an increased leaching of aluminium and subsequent damage to fish and other aquatic fauna (Segner et al., 1988).

In most streams solutes are inversely related to discharge, but in acidified reaches which have generally low ionic content, some solutes show rising concentrations with rising discharge (Johnson et al., 1969, Meesenburg & Schoen, 1989). Although discharge is often a major control for solute concentrations some other factors are important in many cases (Keller, 1970, Foster, 1978, Casey & Clarke,

1979). In order to examine some of these factors that possibly control the variations of solute concentration, multivariate regression models have been developed for examination of solute variation of the R. Haslach in the Black Forest.

MATERIALS AND METHODS

Study area

The study area is located in the southern Black Forest in the Federal Republic of Germany. The catchment (0.34 km^2) is formed by a corrie in the headwaters of the R. Haslach valley. Elevations range from 1100 to 1300 m a.s.l.. The bedrock is an acid granite, extremly poor in bases. The very acid soils, some of which are usually waterlogged, are derived from periglacial solifluction layers and moraines that are derived only from the underlying granite (Stahr et al., 1980). The area is mainly covered with spruce plantations which are damaged by forest decline since the beginning of the seventies. The climate is characterised by 1900 mm a^{-1} precipitation and an annual mean temperature of 4°C. In 1985, however, precipitation was only about 1450 mm. The hydrologic regime is influenced by snow accumulation resulting in low flow conditions during winter followed by large snowmelts in spring. Occasionally melting periods occur in winter. In summer, intensive storms often cause high peak flows. In autumn, dry periods of several weeks are quite common.

Sampling and analytical methods

Grab samples were collected weekly between February and December 1985. During several rain storms samples were taken more frequently. Discharge was measured with a sharp crested 90° v-notch weir and a permanent water level recorder. pH value and water temperature were also recorded continuously.

In all samples specific electric conductivity (SEC), pH, Na, K, Mg, Ca, Cl, NO_3, SO_4, alkalinity, Al, Fe, Mn, Zn, u.v. absorbance at 254 nm and colour at 436 nm were analysed. U.v. absorbance and colour were used as measures for the content of organic substances. Measurement of pH in grab samples, which was problematical because of low ionic content, low buffering capacity, and high organic content of the samples (Meesenburg, 1990), was carried out potentiometrically according to the procedure proposed by Turk (1986). Na, K, Mg, Ca, Fe, Mn and Zn were determined using atomic spectrometry, Al with flameless AAS. Cl, NO_3 and SO_4 were analysed by ion chromatography. Alkalinity was measured by potentiometric titration to pH 4.3 (DEV, 1986). Bicarbonate was calculated from alkalinity.

Statistical analyses have been carried out using the SPSSX package.

CHARACTERIZATION OF SOLUTE BEHAVIOUR

Stream water chemistry of the R. Haslach is characterized by low ionic content and low buffering capacity. The most important cations were Ca and Na with mean values of 73 and 67 $\mu eq\ l^{-1}$, respectively (Fig. 1). Concentration of Na showed considerable variation in time, which was closely related to the hydrologic situation. Bicarbonate showed a similar pattern, with a mean value of 38 $\mu eq\ l^{-1}$. Both solutes were strongly diluted with increasing discharge (Meesenburg & Schoen, 1989). They originate mainly from the baseflow supplied by the groundwater storage.

In general, Ca showed little temporal variation except during some storm events in late summer, when concentrations increased. Mg and K, with mean values of 21 and 10 $\mu eq\ l^{-1}$, respectively, indicated little annual variability but notible high concentration during some peak flows in May and September (Fig. 1). Nevertheless, a seasonal trend with minimum values in summer due to biological uptake seemed to be apparent.

Chloride, with a mean concentration of 22 $\mu eq\ l^{-1}$, showed very little variation over the year. Relatively high correlations between Cl and Na (r=0.51), and Cl and Mg (r=0.66) suggest a slight input of sea spray.

NO_3 concentrations (mean value = 10 $\mu eq\ l^{-1}$) generally increased with rising water stage. Moreover there was an annual cycle showing minimum values in summer because of biological uptake (Meesenburg, 1989).

The recorded pH values ranged from 4.35 to 6.67. During heavy rainfalls pH depressions up to 2 units within a few hours were observed. Episodic acidification caused mobilisation of metals such as Al, Fe, and Zn.

DEVELOPMENT OF A MULTIVARIATE MODEL

In an attempt to explain the variations of the measured chemical variables, multivariate regression models have been developed. Purposes of the models are the identification of dominant processes controlling solute behaviour in the stream and the prediction of stream water chemistry. The predictors, which have been considered for the models (Table 1) could be either recorded continuously or could be computed. They allow the improvement of conventional applied simple concentration-discharge relations. The independent variables were regarded to present controls on solute response. Four of them, Q, Q^2, Q^3, and P_{24} representing measures of catchment hydrological conditions. Discharge (Q) was considered in simple, quadratic and cubic form to explain not only linear concentration-discharge relations, but also curvilinear relations (Casey &

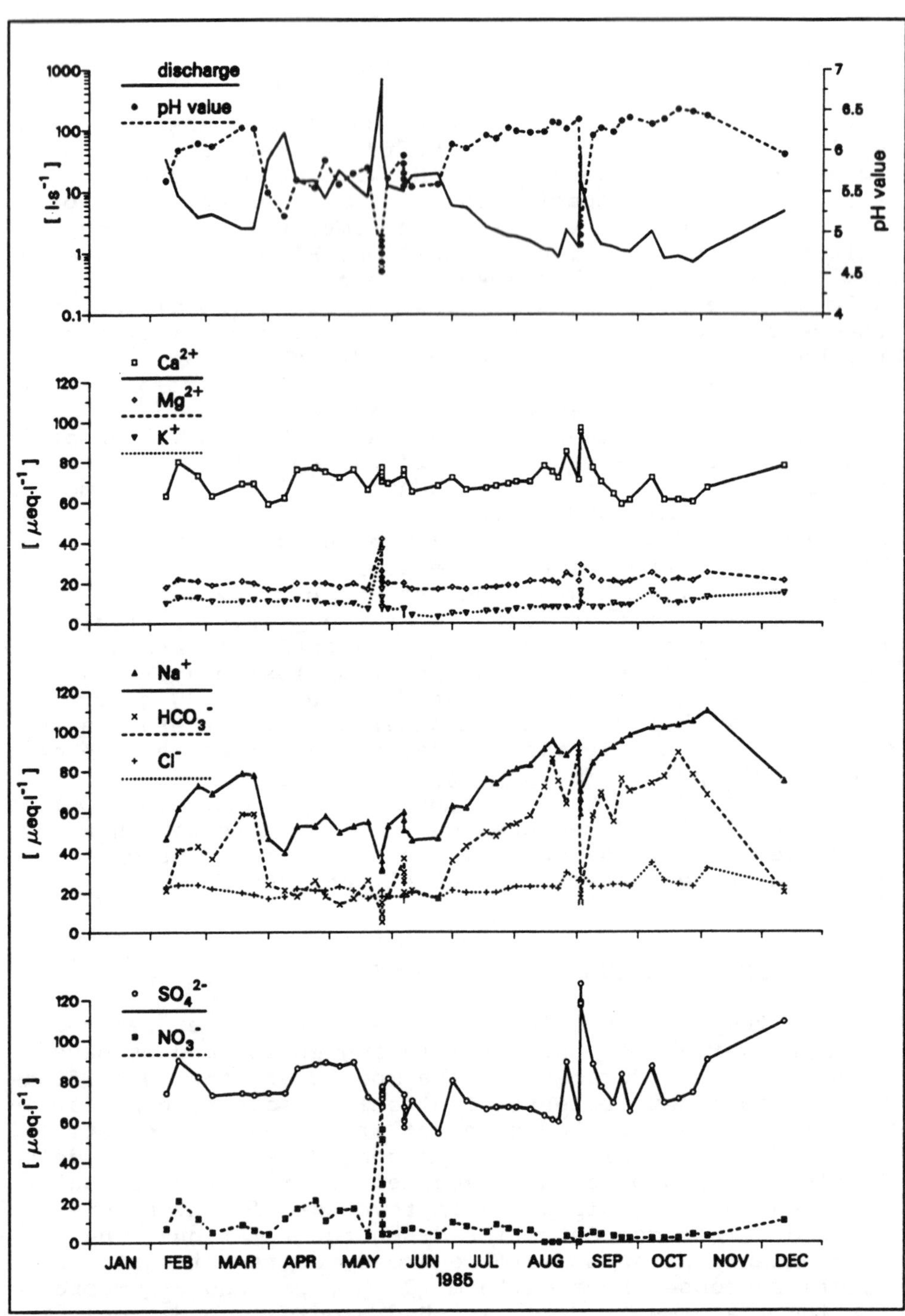

FIG. 1 Time series of discharge, pH, and major ions of R. Haslach at time of sampling.

Clarke, 1979). According to Feher (1983), Q^2 can be used as a variable substituting quickflow. The amount of precipitation 24 hours prior to sampling (P_{24}) has been considered as a further measure for hydrological conditions. Turbidity (TB) as a measure for supended material in the stream was included since adsorption and desorption processes can influence the concentration of metals and other solutes in the stream.

Three independent variables, TA, TW, and a seasonality index (SI) provide measures for biological activity and other processes which vary on a seasonal scale in the catchment. SI has been determined separately for each dependent variable by fitting harmonic functions to the variables (Meesenburg, 1989):

$$y_{(t)} = y_0 + 1/2\ A \sin[(t - t_0)\ 2\pi/T] \quad (1)$$

where $y_{(t)}$ = independent variable at time t, y_0 = mean of time series, A = amplitude, t_0 = starting point of sine function, T = length of periodic function = 365 d. With exception of Ca, SO_4, Mn, and Zn, all dependent variables show significant simple correlations with harmonic functions.

U.v. absorbance (UV) was considered for all metal cations, because organic substances are able to form complexes with metals. pH was only considered for those metals (Al, Fe, Mn, and Zn), which were regarded incapable of influencing pH significantly.

TABLE 1 Independent variables for regression models.

Variable		Unit	Transformation
Q	discharge	$l\ s^{-1}$	log
Q^2	discharge^2	$l\ s^{-1}$	log
Q^3	discharge^3	$l\ s^{-1}$	log
P_{24}	precipitation (last 24 h)	mm	-
TB	turbidity	m^{-1}	$10/x^2$
T_W	temperature of water	°C	-
T_A	temperature of air	°C	x^3
SI	seasonality index	-	-
DT	day time of sampling	-	-
UV	u.v. absorbance	m^{-1}	log
pH	pH value	-	x^3

The models have been established by a stepwise regression technique. All variables were tested for normal frequency distribution with the Kolmogoroff-Smirnow test ($p \leq 0{,}05$). If necessary, dependent as well as independent variables were transformed to produce a normal frequency distribution of the data (Table 1, 3). It should be noted, that logarithmic transformation, which is suggested to be appropriate for hydrological data, only fitted well in few cases. Independent variables were included in the stepwise regression at the 0.05 significance level. The models were examined for autocorrelation of the residual values by Durbin-Watson test. Multicollinearity has been excluded by the computer program by multiple correlation analyses between the predictors. The zero-order correlation matrix of the independent variables (Table 2) indicated high correlations between Q and Q^3, between Q and pH, between pH and P_{24}, and between Q^3 and TB. If these predictors are included together in one regression equation, instability of regression coefficients may arise due to multicollinearity.

TABLE 2 Zero-order correlations of independent variables.

Var.	Q	Q^2	Q^3	TB	T_A	T_W	DT	UV	pH
Q^2	0.36								
Q^3	0.81	0.73							
TB	0.71	0.62	0.74						
T_A	0.10	0.38	0.24	0.41					
T_W	-0.20	0.09	-0.11	0.23	0.69				
DT	0.26	0.09	0.12	0.20	0.33	0.16			
UV	0.61	0.18	0.42	0.68	0.44	0.49	0.42		
pH	-0.95	-0.28	-0.70	-0.66	-0.17	0.11	-0.45	-0.68	
P_{24}	0.63	0.08	0.37	0.41	0.06	0.05	0.51	0.67	-0.77

RESULTS AND DISCUSSION

Results of the multivariate regression analyses are presented in Table 3. Included predictors are tabulated in order of declining beta weights. Beta weights are providing a measure for the variation of the dependent variable which is being produced by a standardized change in the independent variable, while the other predictors are controlled. The signs of the beta weights are given to each predictor to indicate a positive or inverse relation between predictor and dependent variable.

The regression analyses indicated the hydrologic variables precipitation and discharge to be the most important factors that determine solute behaviour. Each of the solutes can be explained by one or more of the independent variables P_{24}, Q, Q^2, and Q^3. In 10 out of 16 regression equations these predictors are the most important variables (on the basis of beta weights). For sulfate, calcium, magnesium, manganese and zink, P_{24} is the most important predictor. During the course of the year these ions are not highly correlated with discharge, but they exhibit rising concentrations during individual storm events. As SO_4, together with H+, is introduced to the catchment partly by atmospheric deposition, Ca probably is mobilisized in the soil by exchange with H^+ and leached together with the mobile anion sulfate to the stream water.

Another important group of variables are the seasonally related predictors SI, T_W, T_A, which occur in 12 out of 16 regression equations. In six cases, two of these variables are included together in one equation.

The predictor TB was included in the regression equations of Al, Fe, Zn, Mn, and SO_4. The direct relation between TB and the metals Al, Fe, Zn, and Mn indicated the desorption of these metals from suspended matter during high flows.

UV was incorporated in the models of colour, Al, Fe, Mg, and K, in the latter case with negative sign. Al, Fe, and Mg are forming strong complexes with humic acids, which are represented by UV.

Of minor importance are the predictors pH value and time of the day of sampling, each of them being included in only one model.

TABLE 3 Transformation for dependent variables, independent variables in order of beta weights, and explained variance (r^2) in regression models.

Variable	Transform.	Predictors	r^2
SEC	$1/x$	SI, Q^2, P_{24}	0.681
H^+	$1/\sqrt{x}$	Q, T_A, P_{24}, $-Q^2$, T_W	0.922
Na^+	-	-Q, SI, Q^2, P_{24}, T_W	0.976
K^+	log	-UV, Q^2, P_{24}, SI, Q, T_A	0.774
Mg^{2+}	$10/x^2$	P_{24}, Q^2, SI, UV	0.624
Ca^{2+}	$10/x^2$	P_{24}	0.391
SO_4^{2-}	$10/x^2$	P_{24}, -TB, T_W	0.452
NO_3^-	$\log(x+1)$	Q^3, SI, $-Q^2$, -Q	0.666
HCO_3^-	$x^{0.3}$	-Q, Q^2, -DT	0.914
Cl^-	$1/x$	SI, P_{24}, T_W, T_A	0.679
Al	$1/\sqrt{x}$	Q, UV, SI, T_W, P_{24}, TB	0.929
Fe	$x^{0.3}$	-pH, Q^2, SI, P_{24}, UV, TB	0.870
Mn	$x^{0.3}$	P_{24}, -Q, $-T_W$, SI, TB	0.396
Zn	$x^{0.1}$	P_{24}, TB	0.514
Cu	$\sqrt{x}$	SI, Q	0.410
colour	$x^{0,3}$	UV, $-P_{24}$	0.960

In the case of Sodium, 98% of the variance is explained by Q, SI, Q^2, P_{24}, and T_W. Although 86% of the variance of Na can be explained by Q, four further predictors have been included in the model. 93% of the variance of aluminium is explained by Q, UV, SI, T_W, P_{24}, and turbidity. The models of K, Al, and Fe are the most complex with six predictors incorporated, but, in the case of K, the explained variance is not extraordinary high (77%). The complexity of the K model is in good agreement with the findings of Foster (1978), who showed the behaviour of K to be influenced by discharge, antecedent precipitation, water temperature, seasonal variations, and soil moisture deficit.

Nevertheless, in some cases (Ca, Mn, Cu) the explained variance reaches only about 40%. Some other factors such as soil moisture conditions may be important for these elements and should be taken into account in further research.

ACKNOWLEDGEMENTS The project was supported by the FEDERAL ENVIRONMENTAL AGENCY (Umweltbundesamt), Berlin, project-no.: 102 04 342. I thank Ms S. Ernst for help with the translation.

REFERENCES

Casey, H. & Clarke, R. T. (1979) Statistical analysis of nitrate concentrations from the River Frome (Dorset) for the period 1965-76. Freshwater Biol. 9, 91-97.

DEV (1986) Deutsche Einheitsverfahren zur Untersuchung von Wasser, Abwasser und Schlamm. VHC, Weinheim.

Einsele, G., Ehmann, M., Irouschek, T. & Seeger, T. (1986) Auswirkungen atmogener Stoffeinträge auf flache und tiefe Grundwässer im Buntsandstein-Schwarzwald. Z. Dt. Geol. Ges. 138, 463-475.

Feger, K.-H. & Brahmer, G. (1987) Biogeochemical and hydrological processes controlling water chemistry in the Black Forest (West Germany). In: Proc. Intern. Symp. on Acidification and Water Pathways, Bolkesjo, Norway, 4.-8.5.1987, Vol. II, 23-32.

Feher, J. (1983) Multivariate analysis of quality parameters to determine the chemical transport of rivers. IAHS publ. no. 141, 91-98.

Foster, I. D. L. (1978) A multivariate model of storm solute behaviour. J. Hydrol. 39, 339-353.

Galloway, J. N., Hendrey, G. R., Schofield, C. L., Peters, N. E. & Johannes, A. H. (1987) Processes and causes of lake acidification during spring snowmelt in west-central Adirondack Mountains. Can. J. Fish. Aquat. Sci. 44, 1595-1602.

Hamm, A., Wieting, J., Schmitt, P. & Lehmann, R. (1989) Documentation of areas potentially inclined to water acidification. Wat. Res. 23, 1-5.

Johannessen, M., Skardveit, A. & Wright, R. F. (1980) Streamwater chemistry before, during and after snowmelt. In: Drablos, D. & Tollan, A. (eds.), Proc., Int. conf. ecol. impact acid precip., Sandefjord, Norway, 224-225.

Johnson, N. M., Liken, G. E., Bormann, F. H., Fisher, D. W. & Pierce, R. S. (1969) A working model for the variation in stream water chemistry at the Hubbard Brook Experimental Forest, New Hampshire. Wat. Resour. Res. 5, 1353-1363.

Keller, H. M. (1970) Factors affecting water quality of small mountain catchments. J. Hydrol. (N.Z.) 9, 133-141.

Meesenburg, H. (1987) Effects of acid deposition on river water quality in the southern Black Forest. Documenta Ist. Ital. Idrobiol. 14, 143-154.

Meesenburg, H. (1989) Jahreszeitlich unterschiedliche Versauerungsmechanismen in einem Fließgewässer im Südschwarzwald. In: Proc. conf. Societas Internationalis Limnologiae and Deutsche Ges. f. Limnologie, Goslar, FRG, 2.-6.10.1988, vol. 2, 112-121.

Meesenburg, H. (1990) Surface water acidification: A comparison of methods for pH determination in weackly buffered waters. Verh. Internat. Verein. Limnol. 24, submitted.

Meesenburg, H. & Schoen, R. (1989) Der Einfluss atmogener Depositionen auf die Hydrochemie eines kleinen Fliessgewässers im Südschwarzwald. DVWK-Mitteilungen 17, 307-312.

Schoen, R. (1986) Water acidification in the Federal Republic of Germany proved by simple chemical models. Water, Air, and Soil Pollut. 31, 187-196.

Schoen, R., Wright, R. F. & Krieter, M. (1984) Gewässerversauerung in der Bundesrepublik Deutschland: Erster regionaler Überblick. Naturwissenschaften 71, 95-97.

Segner, H., Marthaler, R. & Linnenbach, M. (1988) Growth, aluminium uptake and mucous cell morphometrics of early life stages of brown trout, Salmo trutta, in low pH water. J. Environ. Fish Biol. 21, 153-161.

Stahr, K., Zöttl, H. W. & Hädrich, F. (1980) Transport of trace elements in ecosystems of the Bärhalde watershed in the southern Black Forest. Soil Science 130, 217-224.

Turk, J. T. (1986) Precision of a field method for determination of pH in dilute lakes. Water, Air, and Soil Pollut. 27, 237-242.

UBA (ed.) (1987) Gewässerversauerung in der Bundesrepublik Deutschland. UBA-Texte 22/87.

Wieting, J., Lenhart, B., Steinberg, C., Hamm, A. & Schoen, R. (eds.) (1984) Gewässerversauerung in der Bundesrepublik Deutschland. UBA-Materialien 1/84.

Hydrology in Mountainous Regions. I - Hydrological Measurements; the Water Cycle
(Proceedings of two Lausanne Symposia, August 1990). IAHS Publ. no. 193, 1990.

Fate of atmospheric deposition in small forested catchments depending on local factors

H. SAGER, J. BITTERSOHL, T. HAARHOFF, I. HABERGER & K. MORITZ
Bayer. Landesamt für Wasserwirtschaft, Lazarettstraße 67, D-8000 München 19, Germany (FRG)
A. KNORR & H.-H. LECHLER
Bayer. Forstliche Versuchs- und Forschungsanstalt, Schellingstraße 12-14, D-8000 München 40, Germany (FRG)

ABSTRACT In order to estimate the effects of aerial pollutants and their deposition on the groundwater in forested areas, components of the hydrologic cycle have been investigated in a two-week rhythm. Two case study areas are potentially endangered by acidification due to the weak base supply underground (red sandstone, granite) in contrast to the third control area (quaternary limestone gravel). The acidification processes have already progressed down to the groundwater in the *Fichtelgebirge*, resulting in very low pH values and increased aluminum and sulphate concentrations. Buffering by base mobilization from cation exchange and weathering is no longer sufficient. In the *Spessart* there is relatively little mobilization considering the low buffering capacity of the soil and rock. This is most likely due to the lower amount of acid input. However, at the moment this results in a prevention of the fast progress of underground acidification and the influx of displaced cations (Mn, Al) into the groundwater. The calcareous gravel groundwater of the *Ebersberger Forst* is not endangered by acidification but has been exposed to nitrate, sulphate and chloride from the atmosphere and from boundary inflow.

OBJECTS AND DESCRIPTION OF THE CASE STUDY AREAS

Acidification of parts of the hydrologic cycle down towards the groundwater mobilizes hazardous substances, for example:
(a) iron and manganese, which cause corrosion in metal pipe systems,
(b) aluminum, which is regarded to be a health hazard as well as creating corrosion problems.
In order to estimate the effects of deposited aerial pollutants on the groundwater in forested areas and thus on the public water supply, the Bavarian Department of the Interior initiated a research project. This project is being carried out by the Bavarian Agency for Water Resources Management in cooperation with the Bavarian Forest Experiment and Research Station.

The goal is to determine changes in groundwater recharge and quality with respect to the development of forest decline. The changes are to be deduced from estimated water cycle and substance balances for the case study areas (Haarhoff, 1989). Small watersheds or headwaters were chosen in areas where soils and bedrock have low buffering capacities and are thus potentially endangered by acidification:

(a) Metzenbach/Birkwasser in the *Spessart*
size: 4.4 km^2; altitude: 420-590 m a.s.l.; geology: red sandstone (*Volpriehausen Sandstein*), locally weathered to a depth of 10 m, pleistocenic overburden; soils: mostly cambisols (FAO) with mireous humus layer; stands: 81% beech, 19% oak, some spruce.

(b) Lehstenbach in the *Fichtelgebirge*
size: 4.2 km^2; altitude: 770-880 m a.s.l.; geology: porphyric granite, locally slacky and loamy, pleistocenic overburden; soils: podsolic cambisols (FAO) and gleysols with duffy humus layer, locally boggy; stands: 100% spruce.
In addition, one case study area with high buffering capacity and without surface runoff was chosen as a control area and for testing sampling instruments and methods:

(c) Ebersberger Forst in the *Münchner Schotterebene (Munich glacial gravel plain):*
size 15.0 km^2; altitude: 520-560 m a.s.l.; geology: young pleistocenic, fluvioglacial gravel (60% calcareous); soils: cambisols (FAO) with mireous humus layer; stands: 95% spruce, 5% deciduous trees.

In the forest stands the data collection is realized in integrated measurement plots (4 to 7 per area), where canopy throughfall, seepage water (down to a depth of 4 m) and groundwater are sampled. The data from the *bulk deposition collectors* in the stands are compared with similarly collected data from open field stations. The catchment runoff is measured by gauges. Additionally the sources and surface runoff are sampled at various points. All measurements and samples are taken every two weeks with the exception of the groundwater samples (8 weeks). The data collection programs are accompanied by various repeated inventory programs concerning the health condition of the forest stands and chemical investigations of the soil and the bedrock. They are essential for the interpretation of the water sample data.

RESULTS TO DATE

Using the data gained from summer 1987 until summer 1989 the chemical alteration of the precipitation on its way through the canopy and the unsaturated zone towards the groundwater is shown at typical plots of each area and interpreted with regard to the present hydrochemical situation.

Input to the hydrologic cycle by deposition

Among the substances input by anthropogenic deposition in forested areas acids and nitrogen compounds are of special interest for forestry and water management. The open field deposition of those substances (i.e. protons, sulphur, nitrogen) are relatively similar in the three case study areas (Fig. 1a).

In contrast, the deposition in the stands varies due to the changes in the chemical quality of the precipitation during its passage through the canopy. Substances filtered from the air during dry periods, deposited by previous rains or leached from the foliage

(Matzner & Ulrich, 1984) are added to the crown drip water depending on the state of health of the forest stands. By evaluating the results according to tree species and age the effectiveness of the filtering process can be estimated (Fig. 1b):

(a) For the elements shown, the deposition in forest stands is up to four times higher than that in the open areas of the same catchment.
(b) The deposition is smaller in younger stands than in older stands.
(c) Under beech the deposition is smaller than under spruce.

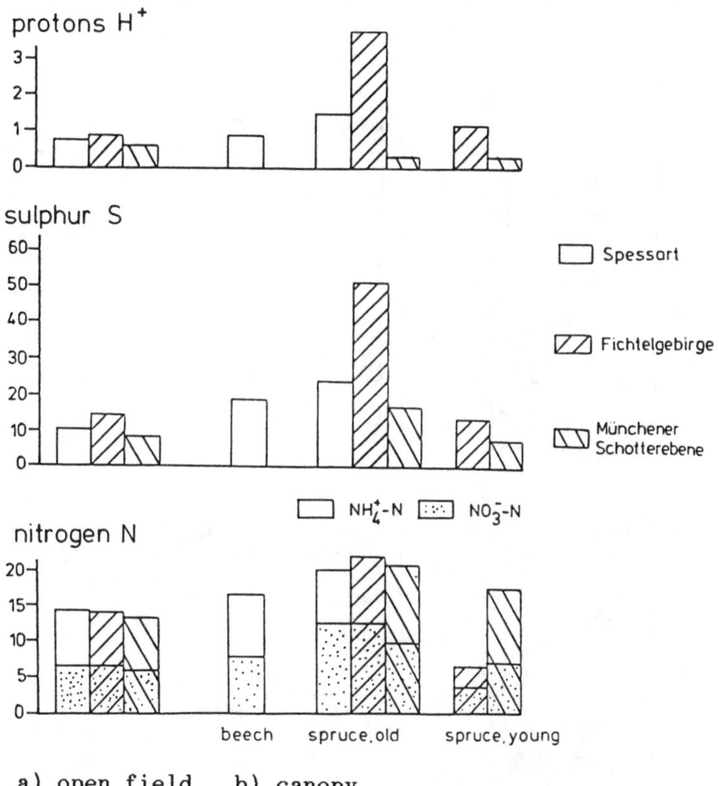

a) open field b) canopy

FIG. 1 Input by precipitation in 1988 (kg ha^{-1} $year^{-1}$).

In a comparison of the case study areas the *Fichtelgebirge* is most affected by gaseous pollutants and had the highest loads in 1988 (site 01: SO_4^{2-} 157 kg ha^{-1} $year^{-1}$, H^+ 3.7 kg ha^{-1} $year^{-1}$). The acid deposition in the *Spessart* (H^+ 1.5 kg ha^{-1} $year^{-1}$) represents a typical situation for a mountainous location far away from pollution sources. In the *Münchner Schotterebene* buffering reactions in the canopy reduce the already small acid loads of the precipitation.

The input of nitrogen is enforced by filtration and deposition during dry periods. The observed amounts reach the critical value of 20 kg ha^{-1} $year^{-1}$, which in soils with high nitrogen content may cause considerable increases of nitrate concentrations in the seepage water (Hüser & Rehfuess, 1988). The total input of nitrogen is influenced by high amounts of ammonium-nitrogen not only in the *Ebersberger Forst* with neighbouring agricultural areas but also in the other catchments (Fig. 1).

Acidification of the seepage and groundwater

Acidific stress on the groundwater occurs when the reserve of acid-buffering base cations is used up or cannot be mobilized in sufficient time and quantity. Below pH 5 the buffering of the imported protons is carried out by aluminum and heavy metal ions. At the same time high loads of sulphate and nitrate accelerate the washout and decrease of cations in the percolated soils and layers (Ulrich, 1981).

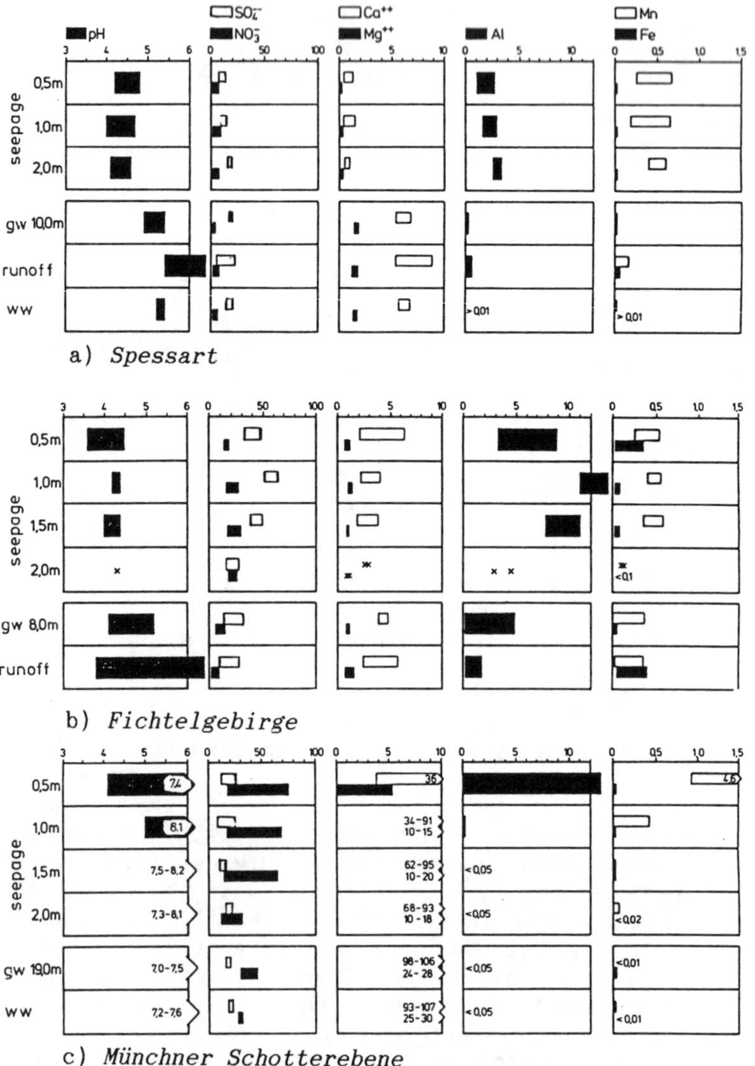

FIG. 2 Range of concentrations (ppm) and pH values in the water cycle of the three case study areas (selected substances).

In the *Spessart* area the aluminum buffering zone has progressed into deeper regions due to the poorness of base cations in the red sandstone (Fig. 2a). Thus the seepage water on plot 01 shows a constant pH value around 4.4 and aluminum concentrations of ca. 3 ppm throughout all depth gradients (Fig. 3a). The concentrations of magnesium and calcium are very low because an intensive washout of base cations has already taken place down to a depth of 2 m. However, first samples from suction cups at 4 m below surface show that the buffering mechanism by weathering of the silcates and by base cation exchange is still working there (Fig. 3a) and continues towards the groundwater (Fig. 3b). Aluminum contents around 0.1 ppm together with pH values of 5 indicate, however, that the neutralisation of the seepage water has reached its limits at least in the more permeable areas upstream.

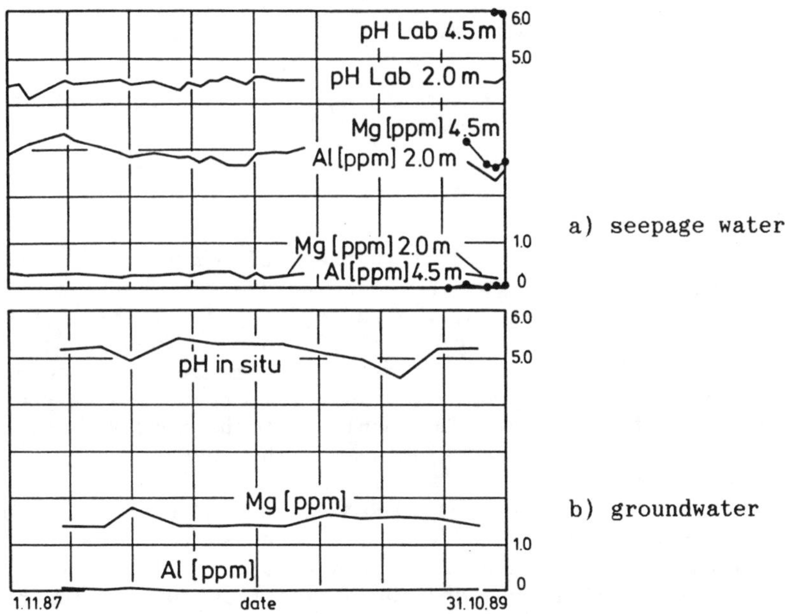

FIG. 3 Concentrations of aluminum and magnesium, pH values at plot 01 in the *Spessart*.

In contrast, the wells of a water supply installation situated downstream show a natural groundwater chemistry not yet affected by acidification (Fig. 2a). The chemistry of the surface runoff is chiefly dominated by the groundwater but also influenced by acidified top layers and by influences from the calcareous gravel of the forest roads (Fig. 2a).

In the *Fichtelgebirge* the base content in the canopy throughfall (from the interception of the tree-tops and leaching of the needles) is higher than in the *Spessart* (Fig. 4). Nevertheless, the higher input of acids here is only partly buffered. Despite the fact that trees take up protons in the canopy by exchange with base cations there is no decrease in acid loads because the roots emit equivalent protons back to the soil solution (Matzner & Ulrich, 1984).

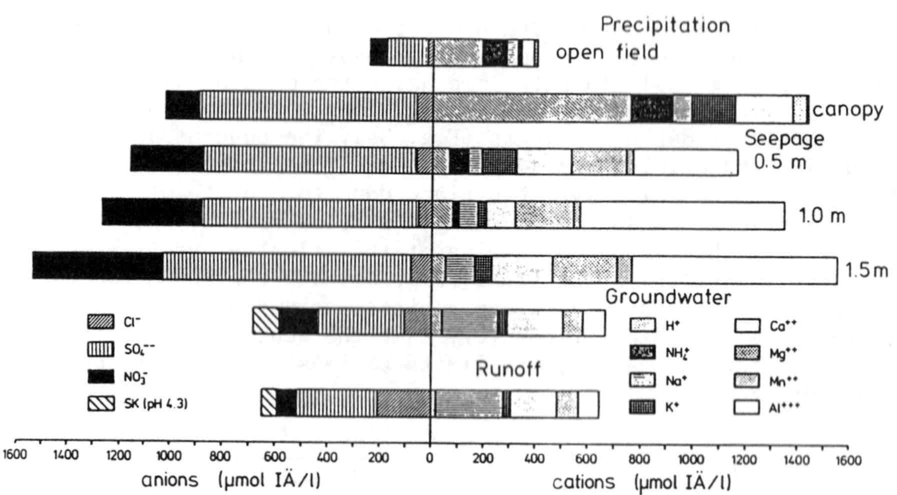

FIG. 4 Mean concentrations in the *Lehstenbach* area in the *Fichtelgebirge*.

The deeply acidified site 01 in the *Fichtelgebirge* catchment shows a high mobility of cations in the seepage water. There is a high wash out rate of base cations, the buffer status, however, is dominated by the high concentrations of aluminum and pH values 3.6-4.4 (Fig. 2b). The results to date also suggest that some of the percolating sulphate is fixed in the upper soil layers but is resoluble at greater depth together with aluminum. The results for the *Spessart* show a similar increase in sulphate and aluminum in the seepage water at a depth of 2 m (Figs 2a and b).

The nitrate which is transported down to a depth of 1.5 m cannot be taken up by the roots and thus may increase the total acidification of the seepage water in the form of nitric acid. That may increase the removal of base cations and the mobilization of metals (Fig. 4).

The degree of groundwater acidification is partly determined by the varying hydrogeological situation. On sites with higher permeability or along preferred routes of percolation, high concentrations of aluminum (up to 4.8 ppm) and sulphate (up to 35 ppm) reach the groundwater. The low total amount of ions in the groundwater is probably caused by the storage of aluminum sulphate in the deeper seepage zone, but these substances are expected to be resoluable depending on changes in the local hydrochemistry (Prenzel, 1982).

The catchment runoff varies depending on its domination by differently acidified groundwater or interflow and overland flow. The high iron concentrations are caused by partly reduced waters with high amounts of organic substances.

The turnover of ions in a soil which is decalcified but rich in bases is demonstrated with the results of the *Ebersberger Forst* (Fig. 2c). The precipitation causes rapid percolation of acid water from the top soil towards the front of decalcification (depth 0.5 m below surface). Concentration increments of aluminum and manganese occur over short periods (Fig. 5). In the deeper calcareous zone (1.0 m b.s.)

some peaks of manganese were observed together with decreases of the pH to 5.0, but the concentrations of aluminum are constantly low around the detection limit (0.01 ppm). The atmospheric input of nitrogen at the same site seems to cause a high rate of nitrification. Another reason may be the effects of the heavy hail storm in 1984, which caused a defoliation of the stands and thus accelerated the decomposition of the humus layer with an increasing release of nitrogen. Therefore a reduction of the anthropogenic load of nitrate which reaches the groundwater upstream is not to be expected.

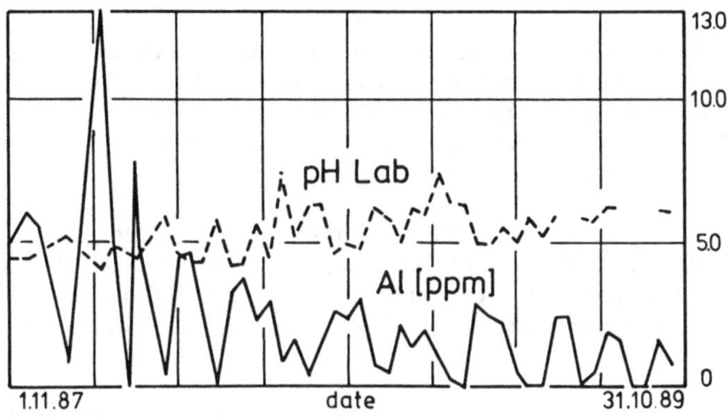

FIG. 5 Aluminum concentrations and pH values of seepage water (depth 0.5 m) in the *Ebersberger Forst*.

CONCLUDING REMARKS AND OUTLOOK

In view of the determined total acidification stress, the groundwater in the *Spessart* seems not to be directly endangered. At present the total input of acid by canopy throughfall is rather low and the buffering capacities of the deeper layers are still sufficient to prevent a breakthrough of acids and dissolved metals into the groundwater. In the *Fichtelgebirge* the acid loads are already so high that the mobilization of base cations in the seepage zone is no longer sufficient to prevent an acidification of the groundwater over wide areas of the observed catchment.

To describe and to quantify functional connections between parts of the hydrologic cycle, the water and substance balances of the case study areas are to be put into relation with the chemical and physical results of the soil and rock sample analyses. Together with the results of the forest decline and soil inventory, the influence of local factors will be described. The goal of this research is a model system which enables forecasts of the groundwater quality in forested areas.

ACKNOWLEDGEMENTS The authors are grateful for permission to publish by the *Oberste Baubehörde* in the Bavarian Department of Interior, which finances and supervises the project.

REFERENCES

Haarhoff, T. (1989) Effects of acid rain and forest die-back on groundwater - Case studies in Bavaria, Germany (FRG). *Atmospheric Deposition (Proc. Baltimore Symp., May 1989)*, IAHS Publ. 178, p. 229-235.

Hüser, R. & Rehfuess, K.-E. (1988) Stoffdeposition durch Niederschläge in ost- und südbayerischen Waldbeständen (Deposition by precipitation in Eastern and Southern Bavarian forests). *Forstl. Forschungsberichte München*, vol. 86, 153 p.

Kreutzer, K. (1989) Änderungen im Stickstoffhaushalt der Wälder und die dadurch verursachten Auswirkungen auf die Qualität des Sickerwassers (Changes in the nitrogen balance of forests and their effects on the quality of the seepage water). *Mitt. Dtsch. Verb. Wasser- u. Kulturbau*, vol. 17. p. 121-130.

Matzner, E. & Ulrich, B. (1984) Raten der Deposition, der internen Produktion und des Umsatzes von Protonen in zwei Waldökosystemen (Rates of depositon, internal production and turnover of protons in two forest ecosystems). *Z. Pflanzenernähr. Bodenkunde.*, 147, p.290-308.

Prenzel, J. (1982) Ein bodenchemisches Gleichgewichtsmodell mit Kationenaustausch und Aluminiumhydroxosulfat (A model for soil-chemical equilibria of cation exchange and aluminum hydroxo-sulphate). *Göttinger Bodenkundl. Ber.*, vol 72, p. 1-113.

Ulrich, B (1981) Ökologische Gruppierung von Böden nach ihrem chemischen Bodenzustand (An ecological classification of soils according to their chemical conditions). *Z. Pflanzenernähr. Bodenkunde*, 144, p. 289-305.

Hydrology in Mountainous Regions. I - Hydrological Measurements; the Water Cycle (Proceedings of two Lausanne Symposia, August 1990). IAHS Publ. no. 193, 1990.

Groundwater contributions to the hydrochemistry of an alpine basin

MARK WILLIAMS, RICHARD KATTELMANN & JOHN MELACK
Center for Remote Sensing and Environmental Optics and
Marine Science Institute
University of California, Santa Barbara, CA 93106 USA

ABSTRACT The overall importance of groundwater contributions to the chemistry of surface waters in the Emerald Lake basin, a small alpine tarn, depended on the timing of inputs to the lake from snowmelt runoff and from groundwater, not from the total volume of these sources of streamflow. Groundwater release during the 7-8 month period of low-flow was four percent of annual discharge in 1986 and 13 percent in 1987. However this groundwater release supplied 20-30 percent of the annual basin production of silica, acid neutralizing capacity and base cations. Replenishment of ion exchange sites by chemical weathering in subsurface reservoirs during periods of low-flow is hypothesized to be important in regulating the pH of surface waters. Release of water from groundwater storage controlled the chemistry of stream water and made a major contribution to the chemistry of lake water for 7-8 months of the year.

INTRODUCTION

Modification of atmospheric inputs to surface waters by biological and chemical processes is known to depend on flow paths within a basin and on the residence time of water in vadose and groundwater reservoirs. Montane watersheds often have thin soils, exposed bedrock, and steep slopes; hence, hydraulic residence time is often short. Therefore groundwater contributions to the hydrochemistry of alpine watersheds are thought to be low, but little information currently exists on this subject. Recent research has shown that groundwater discharge is important in determining the surface water chemistry of forested catchments (Bottomley et al., 1984; Chen et al., 1984; Bottomley et al., 1986). Groundwater discharge in such catchments can control the chemistry of lake water (Anderson & Bowser, 1986).

We hypothesize that groundwater storage and discharge are important to the hydrochemistry of alpine basins in the southern Sierra Nevada, California. To test this hypothesis, release of solutes from subsurface storage were studied by means of water and chemical mass balances, and by measuring the chemistry of surface water and groundwater seepage over a two-year period in 1986 and 1987 in the Emerald Lake basin. We emphasize the hydrochemistry during low-flow conditions. Low-flow period is defined as the time period from when snow-covered area of the basin declined to less than 10 percent to the start of the following snowmelt runoff season. The hydrologic and hydrochemical contributions from vadose and groundwater reservoirs are combined as discharge from subsurface reservoirs.

STUDY AREA

The Emerald Lake basin is a north-facing granitic cirque located on the upper Marble Fork of the Kaweah River drainage, in the southern Sierra Nevada of California, USA (36°35'49"N, 118°40'30"W). Basin area is 120 ha; elevation ranges from 2800 m at the lake outlet to 3416 m at the summit of Alta Peak (Fig. 1). Topography is steep and

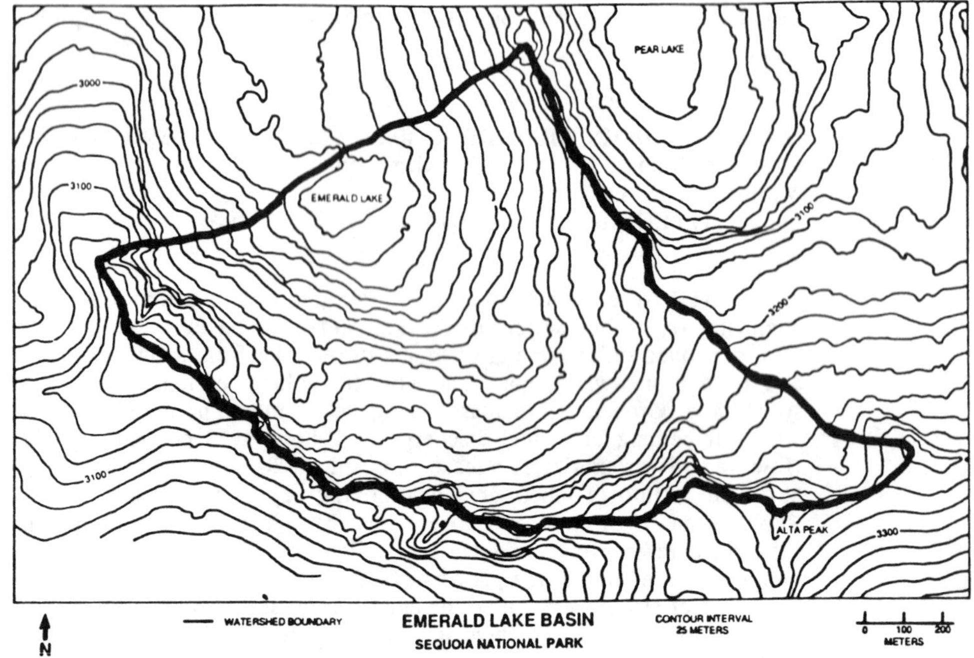

FIG. 1 Topographic map of the Emerald Lake basin.

rugged, with a mean slope of 31°.

Emerald Lake is a 2.72 ha cirque lake at the bottom of the basin, fed by two main inflows and six intermittent streams, and drained by a single outflow. The lake has a mean depth of 5.9 m and a maximum depth of 10.5 m, and is ice-covered from November through May to July. Emerald Lake and the streams in its watershed are weakly buffered, calcium-bicarbonate waters (Melack et al., 1989), which are typical of high-altitude Sierran waterbodies (Melack et al., 1985; Melack & Stoddard, in press).

Exposed rocks comprise 33 percent of the basin area; unconsolidated clays, sand, gravels, and talus cover about 47 percent. Bedrock in the basin is composed mainly of granodiorite, with some mafic intrusions, aplite dikes, and pegmatite veins (Sisson & Moore, 1984; Clow, 1987). Conversion of plagioclase to kaolinite is the predominant weathering reaction in the basin (Clow, 1987). Poorly developed soils cover about 20 percent of the basin, and these are acidic and weakly buffered (Huntington & Akeson, 1986; Lund et al., 1987). Vegetation is sparse, including only scattered coniferous trees, although low woody shrubs are often abundant where soils occur (Rundel et al., 1989).

The rock of the Emerald Lake basin contains numerous joints which range in size from the master joint trending along the northwest boundary of the basin to barely detectable cracks. The joints permit some minor subsurface storage and transmission of water and are important sites of physical and chemical weathering. The only deposits of unconsolidated material that are moderately deep (2-4 m) occur in the master joint delineating the northeast boundary of the basin. The unweathered nature of the bedrock has important implications to the hydrology and hydrochemistry of the basin: groundwater storage, water residence time, and chemical buffering capabilities are all low (Moore & Wahrhaftig, 1984).

METHODS

Hydrologic processes were monitored for two complete water years (October 1985 to September 1987). Stage height in the outflow and two main inflows was measured with a Montedero-Whitney pressure transducer and recorded on an Omnidata data logger. Stage-discharge relationship were developed using the salt dilution technique (Dozier et al., 1987). Snow covered area was evaluated from aerial and oblique photographs of the basin. Mini-piezometers and seepage meters were installed in Emerald Lake to check for the presence of groundwater discharged directly into the lake (Melack et al., 1989). Temperature measurements were also made along lake bottom sediments by divers to check for direct seepage into the lake. Surface water samples of all inflows, Emerald Lake, and the lake outflow were collected in acid-washed polyethylene bottles for chemical analyses approximately weekly beginning in spring and through the summer months, and monthly during the winter period. Groundwater samples from seeps near Emerald Lake were collected for chemical analyses during the snow-free season in 1987. Wet deposition was collected on an event basis in 1986 and 1987, with the exception of snowpack chemistry in 1987, which was sampled at the period of maximum snow accumulation. All water samples were analyzed for major inorganic ions, silica, and acid neutralizing capacity (ANC). Analytical protocols and error analyses are presented in Melack et al. (1989) and Dozier et al. (1989).

RESULTS AND DISCUSSION

Hydrology

Total snowpack water equivalence was about 2000 mm in water year 1986 (about twice the 50-year mean for the region) and 670 mm in water year 1987 (about half the 50-year mean for the region). Snow dominated the water balance during this period, accounting for 95 percent of the precipitation. Direct runoff from snowmelt resulted in 90 percent of basin discharge in 1986 (April through August) and 85 percent of basin discharge in 1987 (April through June) (Fig. 2A). Typical flows during the peak of snowmelt ranged from 10 000 to 30 000 m^3 day^{-1} (8 to 25 mm day^{-1}).

Total groundwater storage for the Emerald Lake basin was estimated independently by several different methods as 120 000 m^3 ± 60 000 m^3 (Kattelmann, 1989). This volume is equivalent to 100 mm storage averaged over the basin area of 1.2 km^2. Analyses of the streamflow recessions in late summer of 1986 and 1987 provided estimates of the total basin storage (S_a) remaining in the basin at time of some arbitrary starting point (Chow, 1964):

$$S_a = -\frac{Q_a}{\ln K_r}$$

where Q_a is discharge at the beginning of the recession calculation and K_r is the recession coefficient (less than 1).

Recession coefficients calculated for the periods 30 August to 30 September, 1986 and 1 July to 30 August, 1987 were 0.930 and 0.939, respectively. Criteria for the selection of these time periods were snow-covered area less than 10 percent and no precipitation input. Storage volumes calculated from streamflow recession were 34 000 m^3 at the end of August 1986, and 35 000 m^3 at the beginning of July 1987. Subsurface storage at the end of the snowmelt runoff period was only one percent of annual basin discharge in 1986, and only five percent of annual basin discharge in 1987. Subsurface storage was partially recharged by precipitation in summer and autumn (140 mm in 1986 and 30 mm in 1987), as well as from small quantities of snowmelt during winter caused by ground heat.

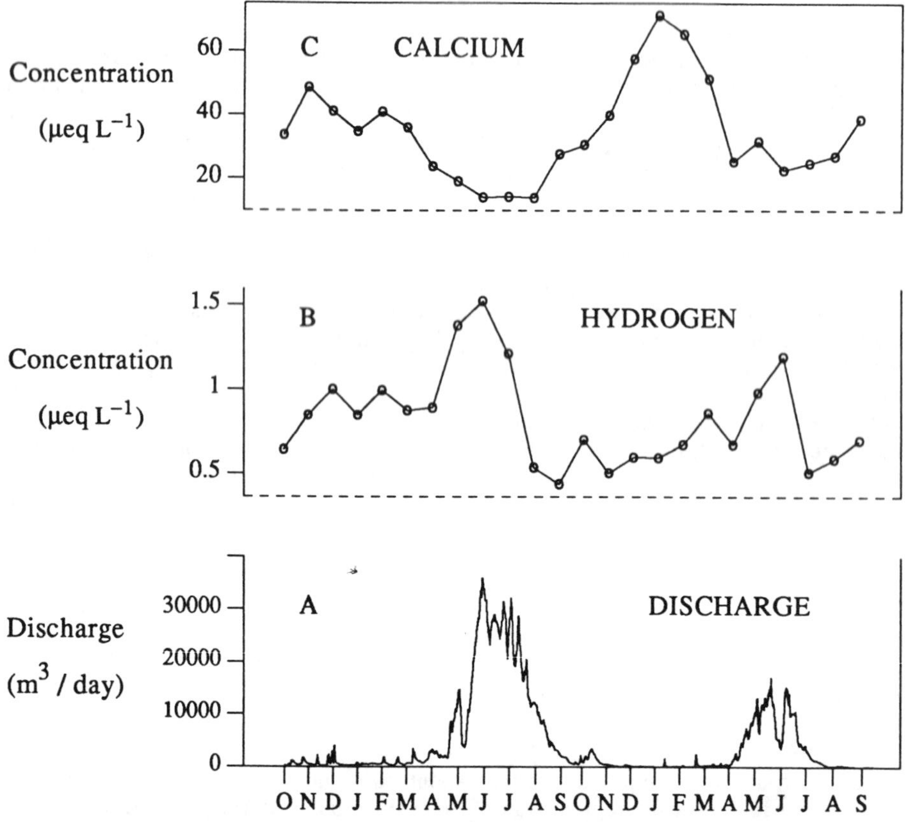

FIG. 2 Discharge and monthly volume-weighted mean ionic concentrations of Ca^{2+} and H^+ in inflowing streams for water years 1986 and 1987.

Water Chemistry

The input of solutes from wet deposition to the basin and the output of solutes from the basin to the lake were measured to evaluate the contribution of biogeochemical processes to the chemistry of surface water. Volume-weighted mean concentrations of the major ions in annual wet deposition for water years 1986 and 1987 were very low. Individual ions had concentrations less than 5 $\mu eq\ L^{-1}$, except for H^+, which was 5.7 $\mu eq\ L^{-1}$ in 1986 (Dozier et al., 1989). Wet deposition was slightly acidic, with a volume-weighted pH of about 5.3. About 90 percent of the annual solute deposition occcured during the period of snowmelt runoff, either from snowpack release or rain-on-snow events (Dozier et al., 1989). About 80 percent of the H^+ in wet deposition in 1986 did not reach Emerald Lake (Table 1). Geochemical processes within the watershed produced about 8-fold more base cations than wet deposition added to the basin. Furthermore, there was no detectable silica or ANC in wet deposition, yet 65 000 moles of silica and 50 000 equivalents (eq) of ANC were delivered to Emerald Lake by its inflowing streams. The input-output of strong acid anions was conservative.

There was a strong seasonal variation to the concentration of solutes in the inflowing streams to Emerald Lake. Base cations, silica and ANC all decreased during the period of snowmelt runoff (Melack et al., 1989), which Fig. 2C demonstrates for Ca^{2+}. During the period of streamflow recession concentrations of these solutes slowly increased to their annual maxima. However H^+ concentration differed (Fig. 2B): during the period of

TABLE 1 Annual Solute Flux in Wet Deposition to the Basin Compared to Annual Streamwater Loading to Emerald Lake for Water Year 1986.

Source	H^+ (10^3 eq)	Σ+ (10^3 eq)	Σ− (10^3 eq)	ANC (10^3 eq)	Si (10^3 moles)
Precipitation (P)	15.4	9.1	27.8	0	0
Streamwater (SW)	2.9	78.4	29.1	50.8	65.4
SW/P (times 100)	19%	860%	105%	----	----

Σ+ is the sum of $Ca^{2+} + Mg^{2+} + Na^+ + K^+$.
Σ− is the sum of $Cl^- + NO_3^- + SO_4^{2-}$.

snowmelt runoff, H^+ concentration in surface waters reached its maximum, about 3-fold higher than at its minimum, which occured during streamflow recession.

Chemical weathering in the basin clearly modifies the atmospheric input of solutes. Weathering reactions neutralize H^+ and produce base cations, silica and ANC, as has been reported in other areas of the Sierra Nevada (Stoddard, 1987; Melack & Stoddard, in press). The observed neutralization of H^+ during snowmelt runoff must be from geochemical processes with rapid kinetics, such as ion exchange and H^+ adsorption. Hydrologic residence time during snowmelt runoff is on the order of hours to days, with a large component (up to 40 percent) of snowmelt runoff occurring as overland flow (Dozier et. al., 1989). The reaction kinetics of chemical weathering are not sufficiently rapid to be the source of the observed neutralization of H^+ (e.g. Schnoor & Stumm, 1986). Furthermore, that the pH of surface waters did not change appreciably until the later stages of snowmelt runoff suggests that ion exchange sites within and on clay particles became saturated with H^+ towards the end of snowmelt runoff. Replenishment of these exchange sites before the next snowmelt runoff season is necessary if the H^+ in snowmelt runoff is to be buffered. Chemical weathering in subsurface reservoirs during periods of low-flow generates new exchange sites.

Mass balance calculations clearly demonstrate that the production of ANC, silica and base cations during the low-flow period are important to the annual yield of these solutes from the basin. Subsurface release of solutes during the period of low-flow was evaluated by calculating the loading of solutes in the inflowing streams annually and during the low-flow period, then subtracting the atmospheric loading from wet deposition. During the period of low-flow in water year 1986, subsurface release to streams accounted for 20 percent of the annual silica, 21 percent of the annual ANC, and 20 percent of the annual sum of base cations (Σ+) discharged into Emerald Lake (Table 2). Discharge during this time period was only four percent of annual discharge. The supply of major solutes to Emerald Lake during the low precipitation year of 1987 by subsurface water during low-flow conditions was slightly higher, as was the percentage of discharge (Table 2). Dry deposition and biogeochemical processes may also contribute to the solute loading in stream water at this time. However chemical weathering in subsurface reservoirs is the source of ANC, silica, and Σ+ (e.g. Schnoor and Stumm, 1986).

Two methods were used to test the hypothesis that subsurface release of solutes controls the chemistry of stream and lake water during the low-flow period. The first method was a mass balance calculation of the contribution of subsurface discharge to surface discharge and water chemistry during the period of low-flow. Release of water from subsurface storage was calculated by subtracting the water in rainfall from that of discharge during the low-flow period. Subtracting the 37 000 m^3 of water from rainfall

TABLE 2 Annual and Low-Flow Discharge (10^4 m^3), Silica (10^3 moles), ANC (10^3 eq) and Sum of Base Cations ($\sum$+) (10^3 eq) Loading in Inflowing Streams for Water Years 1986 and 1987.

	1986			1987		
	Annual	Low-Flow	Ratio	Annual	Low-Flow	Ratio
Discharge	204	7.9	4%	63	8.2	13%
Silica	65.4	12.8	20%	28.4	6.7	24%
ANC	50.9	10.5	21%	23.8	6.1	25%
$\sum$+	76.4	15.4	20%	29.2	8.9	30%

Low-flow is defined as the period after snow-covered area of the basin has declined to less than 10%.
Ratio of low-flow to annual values (x 100).

during the low-flow period of 1987 from the 82 000 m^3 discharged leaves 45 000 m^3 of discharge unaccounted for. Snowmelt during winter caused by ground heat accounted for a small but unknown amount of discharge. Therefore the estimated 35 000 m^3 of water in subsurface storage during low-flow agrees reasonably well with our estimate of subsurface discharge in water year 1987. A similar accounting scheme for water year 1986 shows that subsurface release plus rainfall input equals stream discharge. Some rain input during the period of low-flow recharges subsurface reservoirs. Therefore release from subsurface storage into streams controlled the hydrochemistry of inflowing streams (inflows 1 and 2) to Emerald Lake during the period of low-flow.

The second method employed was to compare the chemistry of stream and lake water with that of a perennial groundwater seep fed by flow from deep deposits and fractures. Concentrations of ANC (about 55 $\mu eq\, L^{-1}$) and $\sum$+ (e.g. about 40 $\mu eq\, L^{-1}$ for Ca^{2+}) in the groundwater seep were similar to those of inflow 2 and higher than in inflow 1 (ANC 25 $\mu eq\, L^{-1}$, Ca^{2+} 20 $\mu eq\, L^{-1}$) (Fig. 3). Discharge was 5-fold greater in inflow 1 than inflow 2 on 10 August, 1987. Subsurface discharge into inflow 2 was from deeper deposits and fractures, and subsurface discharge into inflow 1 was from shallower soils and fractures. Base cation (Ca^{2+} 23 $\mu eq\, L^{-1}$) and ANC (32 $\mu eq\, L^{-1}$) concentrations in the lake's outflow were intermediate in value between those of inflow 1 and inflow 2.

Groundwater discharged during the period of low-flow makes an important contribution to the chemistry of lake water. A simple mixing model shows that the ANC and base cation concentration in the lake's outflow can be explained as a mixture of water from inflow 1 and 2. However NO_3^- and SO_4^{2-} concentrations in the lake's outflow are higher than in the inflows (Fig. 3). Additionally, silica concentrations in the lake's outflow are much lower than the inflows (Melack et al., 1989). In forested catchments subsurface release of solutes can control the chemistry of lake water (Anderson & Bowser, 1986). At Emerald Lake in-lake processes may have been as important or more important than the chemistry of inflowing waters in determining the chemistry of some solutes.

Direct seepage of groundwater into the lake does not appear to be an important source of water or solutes to the lake. During August 1985 and September 1987, periods of minimum streamflow, the volume of water entering the lake could be accounted for by the lake outflow and estimated evaporation from the lake surface. Piezometers, seepage meters, and temperature measurements showed no discernable seepage into lake

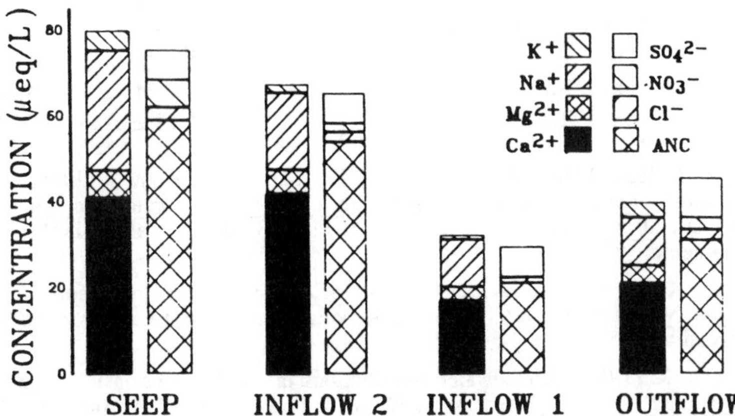

FIG. 3 Major inorganic ions in a groundwater seep, inflows 1 and 2, and the lake outflow, on August 10, 1987.

sediments (Melack et al., 1989).

CONCLUSIONS

The role of groundwater in the hydrochemistry of alpine terrain in the Sierra Nevada is easily overlooked because of the low magnitude of groundwater storage compared to the large volume of direct snowmelt runoff. However, snowmelt runoff occurs over only a three to four month period each spring. During the remainder of the year, streamflow is sustained by slow release of subsurface water. This water has much higher pH, acid neutralizing capacity, and concentrations of silica and base cations than streamflow during the snowmelt period. Subsurface release of water during low-flow periods makes an important contribution to the chemistry of lake water.

ACKNOWLEDGEMENTS

We thank Kelly Elder for his discussions on the possible importance of groundwater on the hydrochemistry of the Emerald Lake basin and his help in compiling the hydrologic balance. We thank Jim Sickman for his help with the hydrochemical mass balance, and thank Steve Hamilton and Susanne Sippel for collecting the groundwater seepage samples. Funding was partially provided by California Air Resources Board contracts A3-103-32, A6-147-32, and A6-184-32, and an NSF Pre-doctoral Fellowship.

REFERENCES

Anderson, M. P. & Bowser, C. P. (1986) The role of groundwater in delaying lake acidification. Water Resources Research 22 (7), 1101-1108.

Bottomley, D. J., Craig, A D. , & Johnston, L. M. (1984/1985) Neutralization of acid runoff by groundwater discharge to streams in Canadian Precambrian Shield watersheds. Journal of Hydrology 75 1-26.

Bottomley, D. J., Craig, A D. , & Johnston, L. M. (1986) Oxygen-18 studies of snowmelt runoff in a small Precambrian Shield watershed: implications for streamwater acidification in acid-sensitive terrain. Journal of Hydrology 75 1-26.

Chen, C. W., Gherini, S., Peters, N. E., Murdoch, P. S., Newton, R. M. & Newton, R. A. (1984) Hydrologic analysis of acidic and alkaline lakes. Water Resources Resources 20, 1875-1882.

Chow, V. T. (1964) Runoff. In: Handbook of Applied Hydrology (V. T. Chow, ed.), McGraw-Hill, New York,

Clow, D. (1987) Geologic controls on the neutralization of acid deposition and on the chemical evolution of surface and ground waters in the Emerald Lake watershed, Sequoia National Park, California. M. S. Thesis, Department of Geology, California State University, Fresno.

Dozier, J., Melack, J. M., Elder, K., Kattelmann, R., Williams, M. & Marks, D. (1989) Snow, snow melt, rain, runoff, and chemistry in a Sierra Nevada watershed. Final Report, Contract A6-147-32, California Air Resources Board, Sacramento.

Dozier, J., Melack, J. M., Marks, D., Elder, K., Kattelmann, R. & Williams, M. (1987) Snow deposition, melt, runoff, and chemistry in a small alpine watershed, Emerald Lake Basin, Sequoia National Park. Final Report, Contract A3-106-32, California Air Resources Board Sacramento.

Huntington, G. L. & M. Akeson (1986) Pedologic investigations in support of acid rain studies, Sequoia National Park, CA. Technical Report, Department of Land, Air and Water Resources, University of California, Davis.

Kattelmann, R. (1989) Groundwater contributions in an alpine basin in the Sierra Nevada. In: Headwaters Hydrology (Woessner, W. W. & Potts, D. F. eds.), American Water Resources Association, Bethesda, MD, 361-369.

Lund, L. J., Brown, A. D., Lueking, M. A., Nodvin, S. C., Page, A. L. & Sposito, G. (1987) Soil processes at Emerald Lake Watershed. Final Report, Contract A3-105-32, California Air Resources Board, Sacramento.

Melack, J. M., Cooper, S. C., Jenkins, T. M. Jr., Barmuta, L., Hamilton, S., Kratz, K., Sickman, C., & Soiseth, C. (1989) Chemical and biological characteristics of Emerald Lake and the streams in its watershed, and the response of the lake and streams to acidic deposition. Final Report, Contract A6-184-32, California Air Resources Board, Sacramento.

Melack, J. M. & Stoddard, J. L. (in press) Acidic deposition and aquatic ecosystems: Sierra Nevada, California Regional Case Studies: Acidic Atmospheric Deposition and Ecological Consequences. (D. F. Charles, ed.), Springer-Verlag, New York.

Melack, J. M., Stoddard, J. L. & Ochs, C. A. (1985) Major ion chemistry and sensitivity to acid precipitation of Sierra Nevada lakes. Water Resources Research 21, (1), 27-32.

Moore, J. G. & Wahrhaftig C. (1984) Geology of Emerald Lake basin in relation to acid precipitation. In: Geomorphology and Glacial Geology, Wolverton and Crescent Meadow Areas and Vicinity, Sequoia National Park, California, Open File Report 84-400, U.S. Geological Survey, Reston, 36-39.

Rundel, P. W., Herman, D., Berry, W. & St. John, T. W. (1989) Integrated Watershed Study: Vegetation Process Studies, 3, Final Report, Contract A6-081-32, California Air Resources Board, Sacramento.

Schnoor, J. L. & Stumm, W. (1986) The role of chemical weathering in the neutralization of acidic deposition. Schwiz. Z. Hydrol 48 171-195.

Sisson, T. W. & Moore, J. G. (1984) Geology of the Giant Forest-Lodgepole area, Sequoia National Park, CA. Open-file Report No. 84-254, U.S. Geological Survey, Reston.

Stoddard, J. L. (1987) Alkalinity dynamics in an unacidified alpine lake, Sierra Nevada, California. Limnology and Oceanography 32 (4), 825-839.

Symposium on Quantitative and Qualitative Water Cycle Aspects in Heterogeneous Basins

Topic E:

Assessment of the Utilization Potential of Surface Water Resources

Hydrology in Mountainous Regions. I - Hydrological Measurements; the Water Cycle (Proceedings of two Lausanne Symposia, August 1990). IAHS Publ. no. 193, 1990.

Surface water potential and its utilisation in India

SUBHRA CHAKRAVARTY (MRS)
Council of Scientific & Industrial Research, Anusandhan Bhavan, Rafi Marg, New Delhi - 110001, INDIA

ABSTRACT India experiences an average rainfall of about 3816 thousand million cubic meters (TMC), fourteen major rivers contributing 1406 TMC average annual water yield, forty four medium rivers providing 112 TMC and a number of minor streams contributing about 127 TMC.

Although the above figures may be impressive, not more than 600 TMC can be put to use till date. Storage facilities for 160 TMC have been constructed and there are programme of constructing additional storage of 180 TMC. Apart from storage, the variability of available water in time and space is so great that almost every year floods and droughts are occuring simultaneously inflicting heavy damages to the country's economy.

Surface water can be effectively integrated with the local water supply through suitable harvesting systems, water evaporation control films and biological treatment. In India, a number of demonstration of these measures have been carried out during recent years, which have been presented.

INTRODUCTION

The systems approach to water resource engineering problems has its main objective, the maximisation of the regional welfare. In doing so, it takes into account all the connected phases from the formulation of a problem to its solution and implementation. This implies an extension of classical scientific methods to determine the best out of numerous alternatives. From the spectrum of alternatives obtained on a preliminary examination, a few are chosen for detailed study, which leads to the final best solution possible under the various restraints.

A great deal of infrastructure has been established to estimate the changes in hydrological characterstics, which includes 5000 rain gauge stations, 1500 river gauge and discharge stations and efforts have been started to measure the glacier inventories in Punjab and Kashmir regions.

The application of remote sensing techniques also help in inventoring the surface water bodies including lakes, snow glaciers, soil moistures as well as flood plain characterstics. Characterstics of river beds such as width, depth, roughness can be obtained from remote sensing surveys which can help in flood mapping and delineating flood hazard areas. In fact remote sensing can contribute a great deal of reduction of field work involved in the reconnaissance level studies for the development of National water plans.The satellite imageries also provide data, hydrological, geological and land use features, required for water resources engineering.

THE WORLD WATER

The Global Water Resources comprise of @ 1.5x10 cu k.m. of which ocean waters are 98%, and the other surface waters including lakes, rivers, soil moistures and biological waters are not more than 1% of the remaining 2%. The evaporation from ocean and other surface waters provide about 110,000 cu k.m. water every year, but most of this amount goes to the ocean leaving only 25% for replenishing the land based water system. The polar ice caps and glaciers form a major source of fresh water. At present glaciers cover 16.2 mil $k.m.^2$ or about 11% of land surface. 99% of the total glacial ice on earth, estimated to be 27 $mil.k.m.^3$ is concentrated in Antarctica and Greenland. The rest can be considered for supplementing the surface water sources through natural and artificial melting processes. Many river discharges are supplemented by seasonal melting of glaciers, however, consolidated man made effort in this direction should be supported by adequate environmental impact studies.

Runoff is major factor affecting the water available on ground. This is often associated with runout of the neighbouring ground water components. The length of total shoreline is about 370000 k.m. and the discharge of 304 major rivers is about 661.960 m^3 per sec.The drainage area of these rivers is about 61930 $k.m.^2 x10^3$. These comprise of about 60% of total world runoff.

Precipitation supplements the land based water systems including runoff as indicated below :

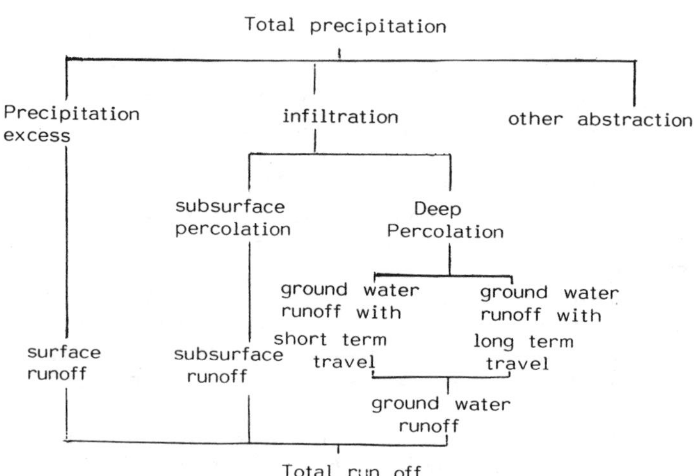

The integrated System as indicated above can be summarised by the equation:

$$P = R+E+\Delta S$$

P is Precipitation

R is run off

E is evaporation

Δs is storage change which can be positive or negative.

There is a sharp asymmetry in the quantitative distribution and dynamical significance among the elements of global water system. The basic features of the surface water systems and those of the streamflow regime are specified by the climatical conditions. Under the given climatical conditions the amount and time variation of baseflow are controlled by geohydrological characterstics. From the hydrological point of view the present decade represents a transient period from natural regime into man controlled or influenced regime. This will be achieved by extending water resources planning and operation activity to more areas.

In particular the surface water reacts sensitively to all man-induced changes within drainage area. The subsurface component of river runoff formed by underground runoff different types from aquifers, drained by hydrographic network provides the genetic and quantitative index of relation between surface runoff and underground runoff. Subsurface flow represents one of the main components of the water cycle during the formation of water regime of river basins. Quantitative estimation of subsurface flow provides a quantitative coordination of precipitation, river runoff and ground water to characterise the relations between the main sources of ground water recharge, and would help in estimating direct underground discharge into seas and oceans. Estimation of basins by hydrologic hydrogeological method for the separation of river runoff hydrographs would also give an indication of the parameters of subsurface inflow in to rivers from the permanent aquifers. This will develop methods for the forecast of seasonal variation of discharge of river basins. Information on hydrology and physics of soils, hydrochemistry, hydrodynamics, geomorphology and other related sciences, are required for reliable estimation of the water resources at a given time and space.

SURFACE WATER IN INDIA

The Indian subcontinent has an unique geographic position. In the north the Himalayas, snow capped ranges feed the great Himalayan rivers, one fifth of their flow being snowmelt. To the South spread the tropical seas between 10°N and 10°S latitudes which is the generation zone of tropical cumulus clouds. The rainfall during June-September from the South-West monsoon and November-February from the North-East monsoon comes to an average of 105 cms.

India has fourteen major rivers, fortyfour medium rivers and a great number of minor streams with a total annual runoff of 1645 thousand million cubic meter (TMC).The annual rainfall is estimated to be contributing about 3816 TMC. There are about 1500 glaciers in the Himalayan region with total volume of ice of the order of 1400 $k.m^3$. There are a few large natural lakes like Dal and Wullar lakes in Jammu and Kashmir, Kolleru in Andhra Pradesh, Chilka in Orissa, Pulikat in Tamil Nadu etc. The potential of these lakes have not yet been scientifically studied. About 2.8 m.k.m. of Indian-territory is reported to be ground water worthy and 30% of the total ground water is generally used for water supply net work.

In India 90% of the water required is used for irrigation, but only 50% of the net sown area may be brought under irrigation till the end of the century, by implementing the ultimate potential of major medium and minor surface water and ground water based irrigation projects. This will cover about 113 m.ha of agriculture area and about 60% of agriculture will continue to be rainfed.

The anticipated need of water for a population of 900 mil is estimated to be about 850 TMC. The surface water sources alone can provide 1440 mil acre feet, which is same as in USA. But in USA, its utilisation is five times 'of that in India. The storage capacity in India will not exceed 200 mil acre feet by 2000 A.D. which will be affected by heavy silting by that time. Already one third of the country is drought prone and about 40 mil ha land is affected by flood annually. An efficient system of water management alone can help in meeting the agriculture target as well as avoid the natural calamities and associated losses.

Some preliminary studies indicate, by making optimum use of water resources through construction of storages in the head reaches of the rivers and by interlinking the river systems as well as by effecting economics in water use on the existing irrigation systems, the ultimate irrigation potential in the country may be increased to 140-145 m.ha.

Presently the efficiency in water usage for irrigation i.e. the ratio of water requirement of crop to the water delivered, is not more than 30-40%. It is hampered by the inappropriate field channels, inadequate preparation of land and lack of consolidation of land holdings. Marginal and small farmers holding less than 2 ha land each have 70% of their lands irrigated by small tanks and stored rain water.

Another major aspect to be considered for efficient water management is development of waste lands. These are caused due to factors such as water logging due to restriction of flow of water by the construction of roads, rail tracks, canals; construction of natural drainage by culverts and bridges; seepage from canal systems including water courses and field channels, deep percolation in canal irrigated areas, often as a result of over irrigation and heavy rainfall and floods. Alkalinity and salinity are caused due to lack of leaching and drainage in particular areas.

It is desired therefore that construction of irrigation projects are not undertaken in isolation without simultaneous command area development and watershed management. These activities along with engineering works should be brought under same authority for Development of surface water resources.

SCIENTIFIC WATER MANAGEMENT

The economic effects of the way runoff moves through the watershed are determined by the state of simultaneous watershed economic development. Flood plain Development, the extent of available uses for fresh water, and the number of participants in agricultural activities translate the sequence of physical flow events into a lime pattern of derived economic value. Structures are used to alter the physical system and thereby the time and space pattern of flows and storage within the watershed. If the resulting increase in derived economic value or system utility exceeds the cost of structure their installation is justified.

The interdependence of surface and ground waters in India

may be represented as follows :

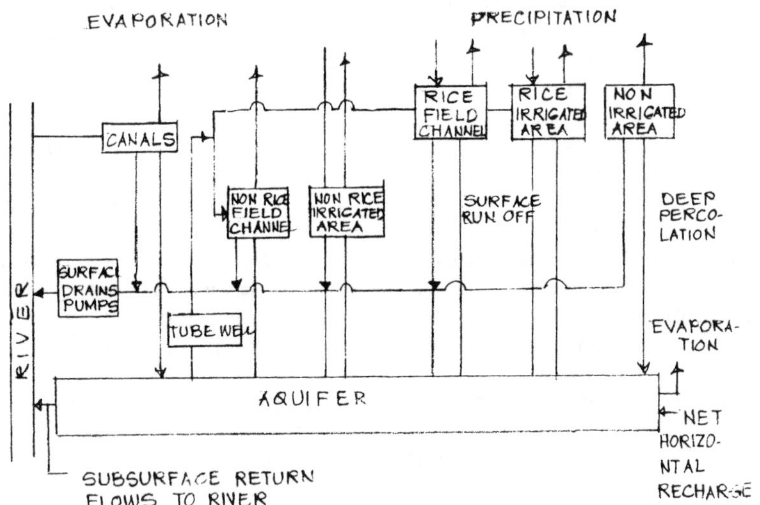

This shows the linkages between the irrigated field contributing to surface run off and river and ground water in relation to distribution of precipitation as well as evaporation.

The river water supply being seasonal, thus need to be stored or supplemented by ground water to meet the multiple cropping demand and other deficit areas.

In designing the systems appropriate cropping pattern and water losses criteria has to be taken into consideration along with the distribution and accessibility to farmers. The cost of irrigation projects may be around Rs.20000 per. ha and the economic return can be improved by improving performance capability and operating characterstics. Existing systems can be modernised by changing the cross section of major canals, building parallel canals, canal lining, increasing control structure changing design of gates, constructing a higher proportion of the distribution system to reach closer to the farmer, conjunctive use of ground water and many other changes Modernisation can yield quite high rates of return by overcoming constraints to reliable and efficient water distribution.

CONCEPTUAL MODEL IN WATER RESOURCES PLANNING

For the conceptual model of water resources planning, the major dimensions to be kept in view are space time, economic value, the three hydraulic dimensions of flow, chemical and biological quality as well as political and public support. The resources geometry operates with four basic interconnected vectors, resources, demand, pollution and upgrading. The effect of unpredictable climatic (stochastic) factors on the resources can be derived from pattern of data available for the past.

The basic operational policy of the resources geometry is to optimise application of intervention vector upon the resources vectors so as to comply with the requirements of the demand vector and the systems target. The probabilistic nature of the resources can be overcome by supplementary provisions, in long term planning, as man made water will prevail upon the natural water sources, at a specified cost. As such, the limitation imposed by natural resources , on the model, will be of economic nature (Richardian). When the proportion of costly man made fresh water to cheaper natural water become substantial, the economic efficiency of prevailing water applications will have to be revaluated and the present uses of water for low value production will have to be reconsidered.

To put it in a more general form, the system space of planning will have to be expanded from the limited contents of new water and demand streams to include both introduction of new water application techniques and reallocation of existing water uses. For achieving such higher level system approach, the area of analysis for long term planning has to include following manipulative patterns :

a) Selection of management patterns for the natural water resources and the over-all water result in optimal water yields and qualities.
b) Technological intervention into natural water cycle that will within economic limits improve the yields and quality of the natural water resources.
c) Shifting of water applications in keeping with anticipated rising water costs.
d) Adjusting and changing water utilisation technology so as to adapt it to anticipated higher cost of man-made water.

The unit of management of water supply system should be a hydrological basin rather than fragmented for individual communities within basin, as this will provide realistic basin data on flow pattern, spell of dry season, maximum flood flow, average flow on a long term basis, as well as the extent of urbanisation, industriali-sation and number of housing units planned for the region. This will also help in integration of available manpower and better distribution of water between upstream and downstream users.

UPGRADING OF RESOURCES

Upgrading of water resources in arid countries like India comprise of six complexes.

a) The water supply function conceived within the framework of the hydrological cycle.
b) Possible modification of the hydrological cycle by human intervention.
c) The composition of the resources base of production complexes and services into which water enters as a substantial input.
d) Man made water
e) Resources pollution
f) Political and institutional implications

Upgrading the quantity of water by applying measures related to complexes a,b and d and improving its quality by applying measures related to complex c will have to complete with measures related to modification of the resources base (complex e), while complexf (politico institutional) will usually be treated as a constraint. The optimum solution will select the lowest cost measures and modifications of the resources base that will make it possible to maintain the desired and economically justifiable scope of production of commodities and services.

Various appropriate technologies have been developed and demonstrated for augmentation of surface water both by quantitative and qualitative measures which should be propagated through socio-political will for benefit of population suffering with scarcity. The important ones which have been accepted in general in India, are described below :

Seasonal water may be channelised from the slopes, especially in hilly terrains with the help of mini chek dams in lined ponds or closed tanks. Thin walled tanks consuming substantially less cement can be constructed locally by laying iron wiremesh within the building material using special moulds and techniques. A capacity range from 600 lit to 20000 lit has been achieved by application of this technique. It is normally recommendable to build the storage facility for individual household or small communities residing in far off places in desert affected areas. When single pipeline supply has been arranged, ferrocement structures for storage can be gainfully utilised. In some cases the rain water falling on the roof top of a house is channelised to a storage tank to supplement the water requirement of the family. The demand of water and number of rainy days including the magnitude of rainfall should be taken into consideration while designing the storage capacity.

Open tanks with shallow bottoms have been extensively used for harvesting rain water in the plains. These are prepared by raising side elevation by eight to ten feet.Use of impervious lining of bricks covered by polyelthy lene/PVC sheets help in longer retention of water. Evaporation control with long chain either based composites layers spread over water surface has been able to control upto 80% loss by evaporation at a nominal cost upto wind velocity of 40 miles per hour. With increasing cost of other opportunities, these techniques are expected to become more widely accepted.

Another area of technical approach is to increase the efficiency of water use by crops. Water retention polymers have been used by cash crops, orchard and other crops with average increase of 30 to 80% in yield. Large scale manufacture of these polymers have been taken up by indegenous industries and widespread consumption practice is expected to follow .

Some of the more traditional methods adopted in rain water harvesting, surface water proofing and runoff farming may not be out of place to be mentioned here. Few tested surface impervious covers are soil bentonite, soil cement, mud plaster (mixture of soil, wheat husk and cow dung) use of oil emulsion with soil and tank silt, mechanical stablisation, sodium carbonate spray and grass (lasirus sindicus) cover at 25 cmsx25 cms spacing. Among these methods, oil emulsion has been found most effective in improving the runoff of the catchment area.

Higher crop yield have been found in farms of arid zones like Rajasthan by recycling the runoff, use of micro catchment with moisture barrier of bentonite clay and 40 cms furrow and 60 cm ridge method of planting. It has been found that furrows are more effective in conserving moisture upto 30 cm depth. Contour-trenching conserve moisture from 28% to 46% contour bunds conserve from 20% to 44% and contour furrowing 51% to 109% under variable rainfall conditions. Many village households in arid North West India have successfully harvested rain water from roof top and collected in ground tanks. This is used for cattle as well as domestic uses other than cooking and drinking.

In use of surface water great deal vigilance is required to be practised with respect to its bacteriological nature. Presence of turbidity and coliforms are essentially found in water flowing or accumulated on the surface. In addition, there is presence of dissolved salts, pesticides etc occuring on account of characterstics of the land and its use. Accordingly the available water may be required to be treated chemically, physically or biologically for making it suitable for the end use.

Biological upgradation is usually carried by application of chlorine or other oxidizing agent in a suitable form, for removal of faecal coliform from drinking water.Chlorine tablet,slow sand filtration, pot chlorination are few among the methods used for village water supply in India.Yet another biological water-borne menace for human health predominent in half a dozen states are guinea worm vector cyclops which are propagated through human contact with water bodies. These are controlled by separation as well as use of pesticides.Superior methods are under advanced stage of demonstration, which incorporate use of plastic dispensors as well as nontoxic chemicals.

The physical upgradation is carried out by removal of suspended impurities and colloidal matters.For this purpose traditional coagulation and filtration techniques are still found most suitable. Mixing of various grades of water may be a futuristic approach in cases where such opportunities are possible to be derived.

Chemical upgradation involves removal of undesirable chemical ingradients with the help of physicochemical actions, Membrane separation processes with the application of high pressure of electromotive forces are widely applicable for water pretreated for removal of biological and physical impurities. Polymeric membranes have been used for reduction of dissolved solids by reverse osmosis and electrodialysis methods. The cost of such treatment is dependent upon the quality of input and output water, the nature of membrane and the rate of power available. A large number of such plants have been installed throughout the world including India. These processes are possible to be used for desalinating sea water and highly brackish water in the coastal region.

CONCLUSION

It is necessary for men to be fully conversant with the nature of water which is going to be consumed for various purposes, in order to take optimised steps for its supply. The quality assessment is an essential step in this direction. There is a tendancy to take the available water for granted and accept it by physical appearance and taste which often create health and other hazards. Many water supply stations distribute their water without minimum basic tests for presence of bacteria or residual chlorine. The toxic ingradients and dissolved impurities are hardly estimated even at state headquarters level. Localised management of total water and integration of the macro and micro systems are expected to enable us to cope up with the ever increasing demand of water for continuance of life on mother earth.

Hydrology in Mountainous Regions. I - Hydrological Measurements; the Water Cycle (Proceedings of two Lausanne Symposia, August 1990). IAHS Publ. no. 193, 1990.

Evaluation des potentialités d'utilisation des eaux de surface en Suisse

A. GOETZ
Division de la protection contre les crues, de la correction des cours d' eau et de l'économie des eaux générale
Office fédéral de l'économie des eaux,
CH-3001 Berne

RESUME Hydrologiquement parlant, les ressources de la Suisse sont assurées par les précipitations dont la hauteur moyenne annuelle sur l'ensemble du territoire est de 1456 mm, ce qui représente un volume annuel de l'ordre de 60,1 milliards de m³ d'eau. 67 % de ces précipitations s'écoulent dans les rivières; le solde, 33 % environ, se résorbant par évapotranspiration et variation des réserves. Si l'on compare les ressources et les besoins en eau, on pourrait croire à première vue qu'il n'y aura jamais un manque d'eau en Suisse. Ce n'est pourtant pas le cas. Ces ressources sont inégalement réparties selon les régions et le temps.

LE PAYS

Superficie

La Suisse, pays montagneux situé au sud de l'Europe centrale est non seulement le château d'eau qui alimente quatre grands fleuves d'Europe - le Rhin, le Rhône, le Danube et le Pô - mais aussi un noeud important de communications et de transit entre le nord et le sud, l'est et l'ouest, qui détermine son destin historique et son rôle international.

TABLEAU 1 Suisse (superficie, frontières).

Superficie	41 293 km²	Frontières	1 882 km
Transversale nord-sud	220 km	Pays limitrophes:	
Transversale est-ouest	348 km	Italie	741 km
Altitude maximale	4 634 m	France	572 km
Altitude minimale	193 m	Allemagne	363 km
Surface productive	30 715 km²	Autriche	165 km
Surface improductive	10 578 km²	Liechtenstein	41 km

Démographie

En 1989, la Suisse comptait environ 6 620 000 habitants, ce qui donne une densité moyenne globale relativement faible de 160 habitants km^{-2}.

Mais il y a lieu de préciser qu'un quart environ de cette superficie est inhabitée et improductive, et qu'un autre quart est conservé en forêts. Si bien qu'en définitive, les 3/5 de la population suisse vivent en communautés urbaines de plus de 10 000 habitants km^{-2}, alors que les 2/5 seulement de la population vit en petites communautés non urbaines, à densité comprise entre 100 et 600 habitants km^{-2}.

Climat

La Suisse est située au nord de la zone tempérée, dans le secteur d'influence du Gulf Stream. Malgré son exiguité, elle présente de grandes variations climatiques.

La chaîne des Alpes, qui s'étend d'ouest en est, forme une véritable frontière climatique: au sud règne le climat méditerranéen; au nord agissent tour à tour le climat maritime de l'Europe occcidentale, régulier, humide et doux et le climat continental de l'Europe orientale, chaud en été, froid en hiver.

Par leur altitude, de nombreuses régions du pays se rattachent à la zone subalpine des forêts et à celle des neiges éternelles. Les conditions locales du climat varient également selon la configuration ou l'orientation des vallées.

Régime juridique des eaux en Suisse

Pays fédéraliste par exellence, où 26 cantons et demi-canto jouissent d'une grande autonomie, la Confédération ne dispo que des compétences qui lui sont attribuées par la Constitution fédérale. En matière des eaux, les compétences découle des articles constitutionnels 24 et surtout 24bis.

Le premier, remontant aux origines de l'adoption de la Constitution fédérale en 1874, consacre le principe selon lequel la Confédération a le droit de haute surveillance sur la police des endiguements et des forêts.

Quant à l'article 24bis du 20 juin 1975, il définit de manière explicite le programme de l'économie hydraulique du pays: assurer l'utilisation rationnelle et la protection des ressources en eau et lutter contre l'action dommageable des eaux, compte tenu de l'ensemble de l'économie des eaux.

D'une manière générale, les cours d'eau et les lacs, dans la mesure où ils sont situés sur le territoire suisse, relèvent du domaine public. Il appartient donc aux pouvoirs publics de les gérer, soit directement (ce qui est généralement le cas en matière de police des eaux et de lutte contr la pollution des eaux), soit indirectement en octroyant de droits d'eau à des tiers (cas le plus fréquent en matière d'utilisation des eaux).

Soulignons encore que la compétence en matière d'économie des eaux appartient, pour l'essentiel, aux cantons. Par ce fait, il est garanti qu'il pourra être tenu compte au mieux des intérêts et circonstances qui varient selon les régions. Cela est important parce que le pays est divisé en régions nettement marquées, souvent très petites, ayant chacune des caractéristiques démographiques et hydrologiques fortement différenciées.

La Confédération ne statue, avec la coopération des cantons, que si les rapports internationaux ou intercantonaux sont en jeu (dans la seconde hypothèse, seulement lorsque les cantons concernés ne parviennent pas à s'entendre entre eux).

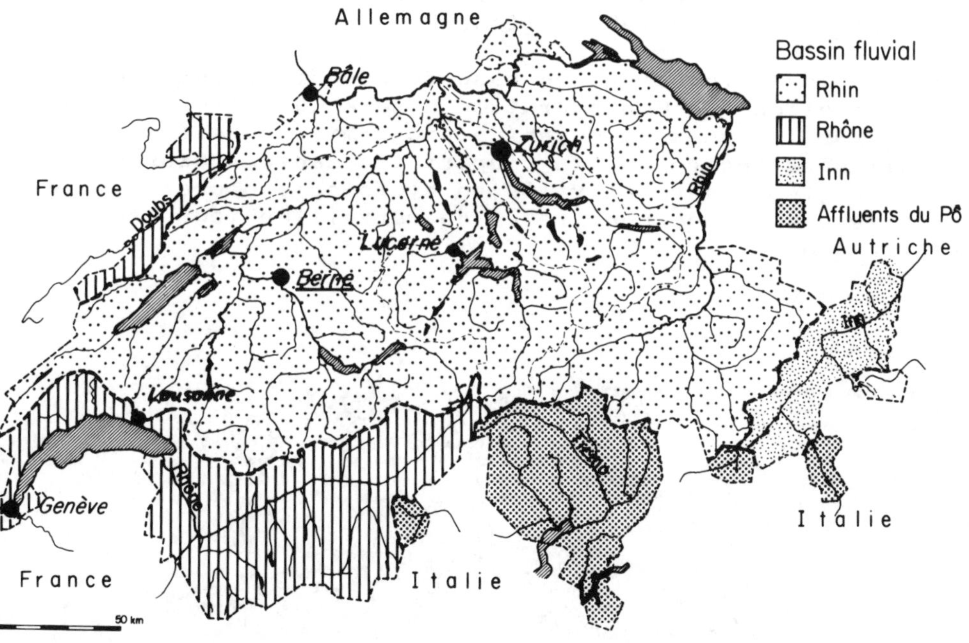

FIG. 1 Les principaux bassins versants de la Suisse.

LES RESSOURCES

Aspects hydrologiques

Par la suite de l'évolution des problèmes de gestion des eaux - lutte contre les inondations, mise en valeur des forces hydrauliques, vision globale du cycle de l'eau en tant qu'élément fondamental de notre vie - l'hydrologie est entrée dans les tâches importantes de l'Etat.

A mesure que le besoin s'en faisait sentir, la Confédération s'est équipée de services spécialisés dans l'étude des diverses phases du cycle hydrologique. C'est d'eux que dépendent, par exemple, les réseaux d'observation suivants:

- réseau météorologique, comptant environ 600 stations d'observation ;
- réseau d'observation du manteau neigeux, comptant environ 100 stations;
- réseau d'observation des glaciers, qui comprend l'observation d'environ 120 langues glaciaires;
- réseau des stations hydrométriques fédérales, comptant environ 340 stations, réparties sur les cours d'eau et les lacs du pays, permettant d'effectuer différents programmes d'observation (niveaux, débits, paramètres physiques et chimiques);
- réseau complémentaire de stations pour mesure des crues, comptant environ 100 stations.

En plus des programmes de base de ces différents réseaux d'observation, la Confédération assure la collecte de données hydrologiques au moyen de programmes spécifiques.
Soulignons encore que la plupart des cantons exercent depuis longtemps des activités en hydrologie opérationelle, dans le but de reconnaître et de surveiller leurs ressources en eau.

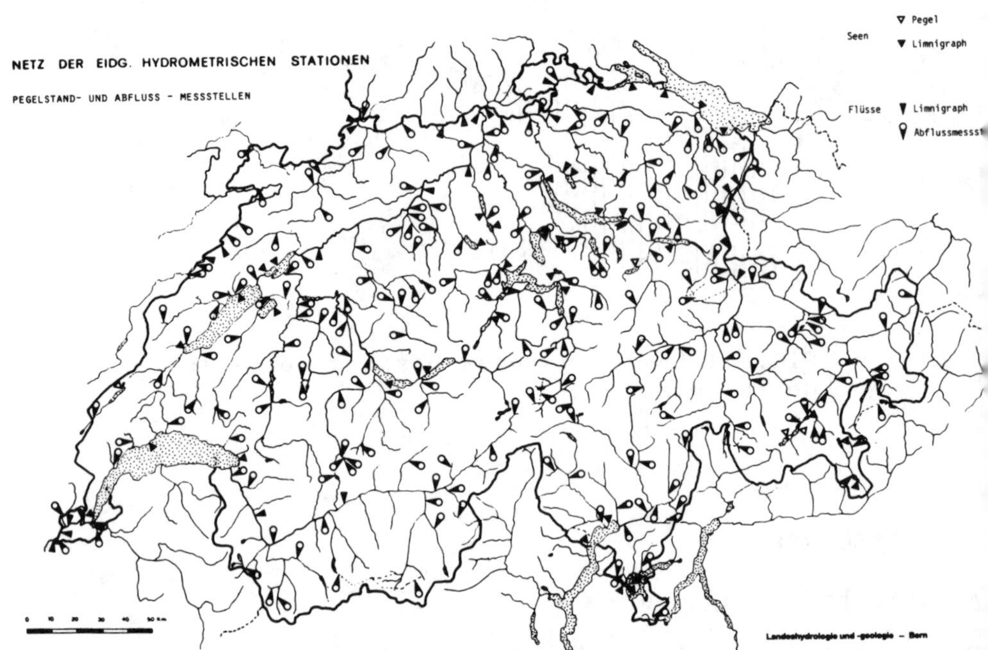

FIG. 2 Réseau des stations hydrométriques fédérales. Mesure des niveaux d'eau et des débits. Etat au 1er janvier 1990.

Quant aux relations entre l'hydrologie et la gestion des eaux, celles-ci sont fixées dans une ordonnance du Département de l'intérieur du 19 mars 1979.

TABLEAU 2 Relations entre l'hydrologie et la gestion de l'eau.

RESSOURCES EN EAU				
Précipitations	Stock neigeux	Glaciers	Eaux de surface	Eaux souterraines

Phase I	Observations hydrologiques	DONNEES
Phase II	Elaboration et analyse classique des données	DE BASE
Phase III	Analyse hydrologique statistique	HYDRO-
Phase IV	Etudes hydrologiques - Etudes générales systématiques - Etudes liées à des projets concrets	LOGIQUES

=> Connaissance des ressources disponibles
=> Connaissance de l'effet des interventions humaines

GESTION DES RESSOURCES EN EAU

=> Mesures et décisions concernant
- la répartition des ressources entre usagers
- la protection quantitative et qualitative
- la lutte contre la surabondance ou le manque d'eau

Bilan hydrique de la Suisse

En 1985, le Service hydrologique national a fait le point des connaissances sur les aspects quantitatifs du cycle de l'eau en Suisse, au moyen d'une analyse des données d'observation de la période 1901 à 1980. Pour cette période de 80 ans, on a calculé les précipitations, l'écoulement, les variations des réserves (lacs et glaciers) et l'évaporation.

Les précipitations annuelles moyennes ont été de 1456 mm, l'écoulement moyen de 978 mm (coefficient d'écoulement de 0,67) et la variation des réserves de -6 mm pour l'ensemble du pays.

En dehors d'une longue période sèche durant les années 40, les valeurs annuelles des précipitations sont restées à peu près les mêmes. Par contre, l'évaporation a augmenté de 13% environ (60 mm) depuis le début du siècle.
Quant aux écoulements, ils n'ont diminué que d'environ 5% (55 mm). Le recul des glaciers a permis de les soutenir.

TABLEAU 3 Bilan hydrique de la Suisse 1901- 1980.

	Lame d'eau $mm\ a^{-1}$	Volume mio m^3	Ecoulement $m^3\ s^{-1}$
Précipitations	1'456	60'100	
Ecoulement	978	40'400	1'280
Var.des réserves	-6	250	
Evaporation	484	19'950	
Apports	318	13'100	415
Ecoulement total	1'296	53'500	1'695

En comparaison avec le reste de l'Europe, les quantités d'eau stockées en Suisse sont élevées. Environ 132 km^3 se trouvent dans les lacs naturels, 74 km^3 (soit environ 23 km^3 de moins qu'en 1901) sont retenus sous forme solide dans les glaciers et les névés, et 4 km^3(contre 0 en 1901) dans les lacs artificiels.

Précipitations

Les précipitations se répartissent de façon très irrégulière dans l'espace et dans le temps. C'est ainsi que l'on note par exemple des valeurs annuelles moyennes de 640 mm à Sion, de 800 mm à Bâle, de 1 415 mm à Zurich, de 900 à 1 200 mm sur le Plateau suisse et de 1 500 à 3 200 mm dans les Alpes (essentiellement sous forme de neige).
L'examen de la répartition saisonnière des précipitations indique que, pour l'ensemble du pays, à l'exception des régions élevées et exposées sur la chaîne des Alpes, le minimum se place en janvier/février; les plus grandes valeurs mensuelles se présentent, elles, sur le versant sud des Alpes, généralement en octobre, mais aussi en mai et en août, et atteignent 2,4 à 3,7 fois les valeurs de janvier/février. Pour les bassins du Rhône, du Rhin et de l'Inn, ce sont les mois de juin, juillet et parfois août qui, avec des précipitations de 1,3 à 2,4 fois plus élevées qu'en hiver, fournissent les plus grandes valeurs de l'année.

Régime d'écoulement

Parmi les principaux facteurs ayant une influence sur le

régime d'écoulement des cours d'eau, quelques considérations seront faites sur l'effet de la neige, des glaciers, des lacs et des interventions humaines.

Au cours des mois de janvier à mars, le nombre de jours durant lesquels plus de la moitié du territoire suisse est recouvert de neige dépasse 50 %. Au nord des Alpes, dans les bassins exempts de glaciers, le plus grand débit moyen mensuel se situe le plus souvent en mars et avril; pour les altitudes supérieures à 1500 m en mai, et pour des altitudes inférieures à 700 m en février. Des afflux d'air chaud accompagnés de pluie peuvent toutefois provoquer au gros de l'hiver une fonte des neiges jusqu'à 1500 m environ.

Dans les régions très élevées, une fonte des neiges en hiver est exclue et la fusion nivale se prolonge jusque tard en été. Celle-ci est renforcée, de juillet à septembre, par la fonte des glaciers. Les glaciers et névés (3,8 % de la surface totale de la Suisse) représentent un facteur stabilisateur de ce régime " alpin pur " caractérisé par de faibles débits d'hiver et de forts débits d'été.

Les nombreux lacs naturels de la Suisse exercent aussi un effet régulateur sur le régime des débits. Par ailleurs, les grands lacs du pied des Alpes stabilisent les variations saisonnières.

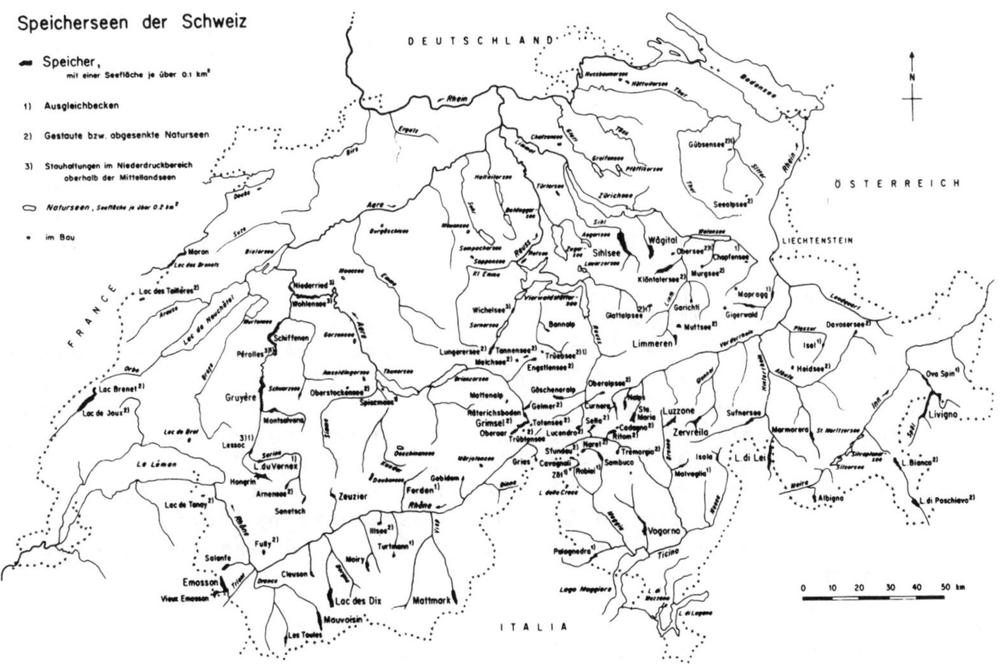

FIG. 3 Lacs d'accumulation en Suisse.
Capacité utile 3,4 milliards de m³

Signalons enfin que le régime naturel des cours d'eau a subi des modifications notables au cours des temps, à la suite de diverses interventions humaines; grandes corrections de cours d'eau, régularisation de tous les grands lacs (à l'exception de ceux de Constance et de Walenstadt), améliorations foncières, aménagements hydro-électriques, imperméabilisation de surfaces de plus en plus grandes par suite de l'urbanisation, etc.

En ce qui concerne les lacs d'accumulation, avec une capacité utile de 3,4 milliards de m³ et une surface de 113 km², il convient de relever que les eaux stockées durant le printemps et l'été sont utilisées principalement en hiver, lorsque la consommation d'énergie est la plus grande, relevant ainsi les débits des cours d'eau relativement faibles durant cette saison.

LES BESOINS

Approvisionnement en eau

Selon les chiffres des services publics de distribution d'eau, ces derniers utilisent 1,13 milliards de m³ par an, soit 2 % de l'écoulement total.

L'eau utilisée pour les besoins de l'industrie, pour le refroidissement des centrales thermiques et pour l'irrigation correspond à 2,1 milliards de m³.

A l'avenir, l'accroissement des besoins en eau devrait rester relativement faible pour tous les genres d'utilisation. Ainsi, à moyen terme, un part d'environ 6 à 7 % seulement de l'eau qui s'écoule de Suisse (sans l'utilisation de la force hydraulique) sera utilisée.

Il en résulte que, pour la Suisse, considérée dans son ensemble, les ressources en eau existantes doivent suffire à assurer à longue échéance la couverture des besoins en eau de la population et de l'économie. Ce n'est donc pas sans raison que la Suisse est appelée le " château d'eau de l'Europe ".

Il ne faut cependant pas se leurrer sur la signification des chiffres indiqués. En effet, si les ressources en eau sont suffisantes dans l'ensemble, leur répartition irrégulière dans le temps et l'espace, la concentration de la population et de l'économie dans certains centres ou axes de développement privilégiés, le danger accru de pollution des ressources dans ces secteurs, sont des facteurs expliquant pourquoi, dans certaines régions et à certaines époques, on ne dispose pas de ressources en quantité et en qualité suffisantes pour satisfaire à des utilisations déterminées.

Utilisation des forces hydrauliques

Les hauteurs de chute sous lesquelles les débits d'eau peuvent être utilisés sont un facteur déterminant pour la production d'énergie hydro-électrique. A ce point de vue, la Suisse se trouve dans une situation particulièrement avantageuse.

L'altitude moyenne des lacs naturels se trouve à environ 420 m s.m. Le lac naturel le plus bas (lac Majeur) a une altitude moyenne de 193,5 m s.m. et le lac naturel le plus élevé (lai da Ravais-ch-Suot aux Grisons) est situé à l'altitude de 2505 m s.m.

L'altitude moyenne des lacs d'accumulation se trouve à environ 1375 m s.m., bien que la différence d'altitude entre le lac le plus bas (Wichelsee, 458,6 m s.m.) et le lac le plus élevé (Muttsee, 2446 m s.m.) soit assez semblable à la différence d'altitude des lacs naturels.

Les forces hydrauliques suisses ont été équipées progressivement. A cet effet, on a, soit équipé le tronçon d'un cours d'eau, soit mis en valeur un bassin versant d'une importance plus ou moins grande. Dans tous les cas, la force hydraulique fut utilisées aussi rationellement que possible, en fonction des possibilités techniques de l'époque. A l'heure actuelle, la puissance maximale disponible des usines hydro-électriques s'élève à 11 582 MW et la productibilité moyenne escomptée à 32,842 TWh.

Il est bien clair, toutefois, que la production hydroéléctrique dépend, dans une large mesure, de la variation des conditions atmosphériques. Les fluctuations par rapport au débit moyen ont été évaluées comme suit:

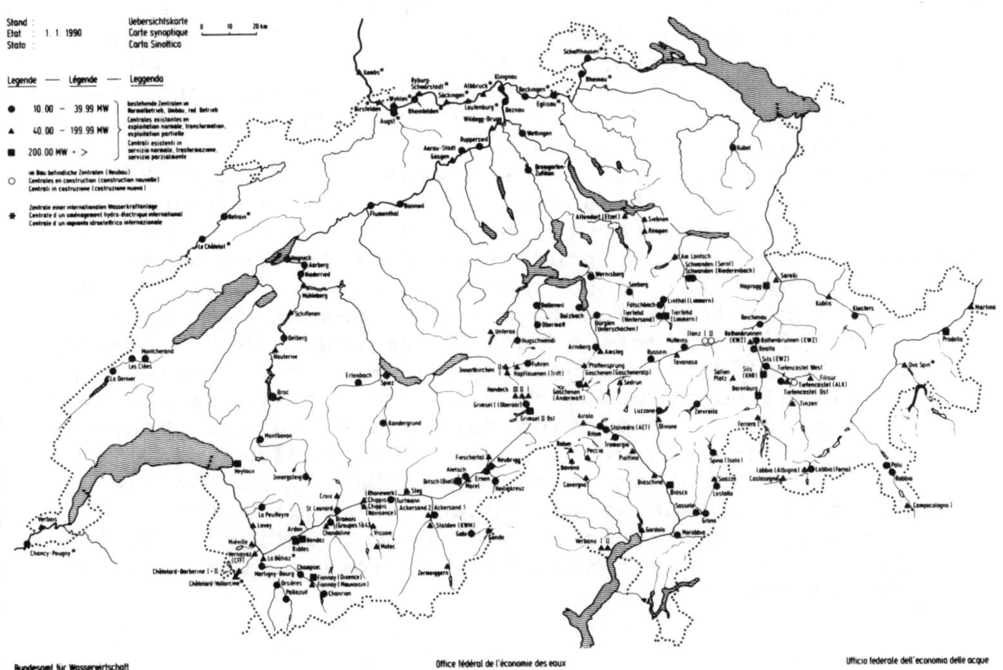

FIG. 4 Centrales d'aménagements hydro-électriques d'une puissance maximale d'au moins 10 MW.

- production inférieure à la moyenne, lors de conditions hydrologiques défavorables: env. 5 TWh, respectivement env. 15 %,
- production supérieure à la moyenne, dans de bonnes conditions hydrologiques: env. 3 TWh, respectivement env. 10 %

Les cours d'eau d'une certaine importance, dont les forces hydrauliques ne sont pas encore exploitées ou ne sont utilisées que partiellement, sont connus.

Des avant-projets ou des études plus ou moins récentes existent pour l'utilisation de la plupart d'entre eux.

De récentes études indiquent que la production escomptée moyenne pourrait être encore augmentée de 5 TWh environ.

Depuis quelques années, les intérêts écologiques rencontrent un écho toujours plus large. Tenir compte de l'environnement ne signifie pas uniquement: protéger le paysage et les cours d'eau, mais respecter l'environnement dans un sens global, c'est-à-dire en tenant compte aussi des ressources.

Afin d'utiliser encore mieux les forces hydrauliques, les usines hydro-électriques existantes sont modernisées et perfectionnées. Vu les exigences de la protection de la nature et de l'environnement, la construction de nouvelles usines hydro-électriques n'est possible que dans certaines limites.

REFERENCES

Schädler, B. (1985) Der Wasserhaushalt der Schweiz. Communication no 6 ; Service hydrologique et géologique national, Office fédéral de l' environnement, des forêts et du paysage, CH-3003 Berne.

Mayer, M. (1980) Aperçu général de l'aménagement des forces hydrauliques en Suisse; Office fédéral de l'économie des eaux, CH-3001 Berne.

Association suisse pour l'aménagement des eaux (1977) Etendue et signification des forces hydrauliques suisses non encore utilisées; WEL, Baden, no 6/7, 1977.

Comité national suisse pour la Conférence des Nations Unies sur l'Eau (1977) La pratique suisse en matière de coopération internationale dans le domaine des eaux, Office fédéral de l'économie des eaux, CH-3001 Berne.

Office fédéral de l'économie des eaux (1973) Examen de la situation actuelle et des perspectives de l'utilisation et de la protection des eaux en Suisse, Monographie nationale pour le Comité des problèmes de l'eau de l'ECE/ONU; "Eau et énergie", Baden, no 10/1973.

Service hydrologique et géologique national (1988) 125 ans d'hydrométrie en Suisse, Communication no 9, Office fédéral de l'environnement, des forêts et du paysage, CH-3003 Berne.

Hydrology in Mountainous Regions. I - Hydrological Measurements; the Water Cycle
(Proceedings of two Lausanne Symposia, August 1990). IAHS Publ. no. 193, 1990.

La régularisation du Lac Léman

P. GRANDJEAN
Département des travaux publics de Genève, Service du lac et des cours d'eau, CH-1211 Genève, Suisse

RESUME Cet article propose un bref tour d'horizon des problèmes liés à la régularisation du lac Léman. Après avoir précisé quelques éléments historiques et hydrologiques, l'article décrit les modèles de prévision des débits qui sont actuellement à l'étude en liaison avec la construction d'un nouveau barrage de régularisation à Genève. Il évoque enfin l'influence des barrages d'accumulation et du mode de gestion du lac Léman sur l'hydrologie du Rhône.

MORPHOLOGIE ET HYDROLOGIE

D'une superficie de 582 km^2 et d'un volume de 89 milliards m^3 le lac Léman est le plus grand lac alpin et subalpin d'Europe occidentale. Son bassin versant total, y compris le lac lui-même, a une superficie de 7975 km^2 dont les 10.6% sont couverts par les glaciers alpins et dont l'altitude moyenne se situe à 1670 m (Burkard, 1984). Le débit moyen de son exutoire, le Rhône à Genève, est de 240 m^{3}s^{-1}, ce qui implique un temps moyen de renouvellement des eaux de 12 ans environ.

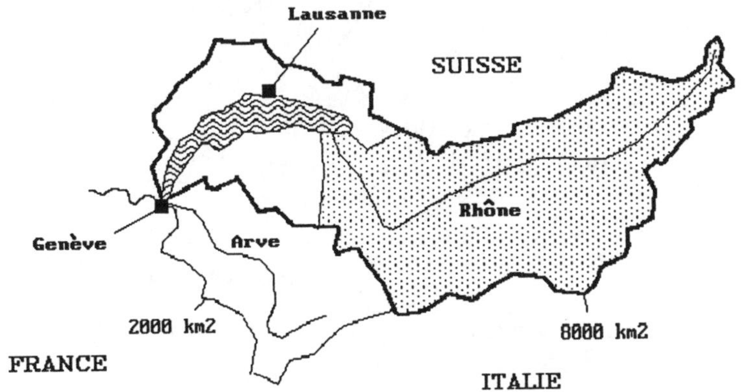

FIG. 1 Représentation schématique des bassins versants du Rhône et de l'Arve.

Son affluent principal, le Rhône, a un bassin de 5220 km^2 dont une grande partie se compose de surfaces glaciaires, rocheuses ou incultes; son débit moyen est de 180 m^{3}s^{-1}, ce qui représente approximativement les trois quarts des apports d'eau au lac. Le régime hydrologique du Rhône, fortement marqué par la présence des glaciers alpins, peut être qualifié de nivo-glaciaire, les apports maximaux se rencontrant en juin, juillet et août ; son débit de crue décennal est évalué à 950 m^{3}s^{-1}.

Parmi les autres affluents du lac, les plus importants sont la Dranse (536 km^2), la Venoge (236 km^2) et l'Aubonne (93 km^2) dont les bassins versants ne présentent pas de surfaces glaciaires. Leurs apports maximaux sont observés pendant la période hivernale ou au printemps. Leurs débits cumulés avec ceux du Rhône constituent plus de 85 % des apports d'eau du Léman.

En ce qui concerne les apports d'eau, citons enfin les précipitations directes sur la surface du lac dont la contribution est évaluée à 8 % des apports annuels. Les précipitations étant épisodiques, elles peuvent prendre ponctuellement une importance beaucoup plus grande ; ainsi la précipitation décennale journalière, estimée en l'état à 60 mm sur l'ensemble du lac, représente un débit d'environ 400 m^3s^{-1} pendant 24 heures qui vient s'ajouter aux apports des affluents.

Ce bref panorama hydrologique ne serait pas complet sans citer l'Arve, affluent qui rejoint le Rhône à Genève en aval du barrage de régularisation. En effet, bien que n'alimentant pas le lac Léman, cette rivière a une influence essentielle sur la régularisation car elle crée à sa jonction avec le Rhône un important barrage hydraulique qui limite, lors des crues, les débits évacuables du lac. Elle est historiquement à l'origine d'inondations catastrophiques en ville de Genève, et nécessite épisodiquement une limitation des débits du Rhône à l'aide du barrage de régularisation. Son bassin versant, d'une surface de 2000 km^2, est recouvert à 6% de glaciers et comprend le massif du Mont-Blanc. Son débit moyen est de 80 m^3s^{-1} et son régime est de type nivo-glaciaire, les apports maximaux apparaissant en mai, juin et juillet. Ses crues, souvent très soudaines, peuvent survenir à n'importe quelle période de l'année et présentent des débits très élevés ; on estime ainsi que le débit de pointe décennal se situe entre 700 et 800 m^3s^{-1}.

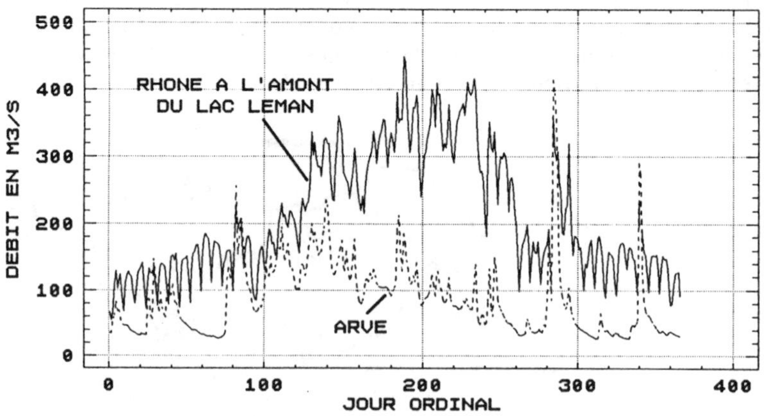

FIG. 2 Débits moyens journaliers de l'année 1988 (année sèche).

HISTORIQUE DE LA REGULARISATION

Les riverains du Léman ont semble-t-il été préoccupés depuis le dix-septième siècle déjà par les exhaussements nuisibles des niveaux du lac ; ils se sont donc tournés très tôt vers Genève, où se trouve l'émissaire, pour réclamer la maîtrise des niveaux. La première génération d'ouvrages, antérieure à 1880, fut une suite de tentatives qui n'eurent que peu d'effet et n'empêchèrent pas les inondations répétées, principalement en raison du contrôle hydraulique (manoeuvres) difficile et de la capacité insuffisante du Rhône à l'aval des ouvrages (Wahl, 1987).

Il fallu attendre 1884 pour qu'une convention intercantonale de régularisation soit ratifiée par les cantons riverains de Genève, Vaud et Valais, sous l'égide de la Confédération suisse. A cette époque furent réalisés à Genève l'usine de la Coulouvrenière, le barrage du pont de la Machine et le dragage des deux bras du Rhône. Cet ensemble d'ouvrages, remarquablement conçus par l'ingénieur Turrettini, est encore en fonction aujourd'hui et a permis d'assurer depuis plus de cent ans la protection contre les inondations sur tout le pourtour du lac Léman, tout en offrant des possibilités accrues d'utilisation de la force hydraulique du Rhône. Néanmoins ces installations, dont l'ouvrage principal est le barrage composé de 39 rideaux en bois, présentent aujourd'hui des signes marqués d'usure ; de plus leur exploitation n'est plus rationelle compte tenu de l'augmentation sans cesse croissante du nombre de manoeuvres requise par l'optimisation de l'utilisation de la force hydraulique.

Pour ces raisons il a été décidé en 1984 de réaliser un nouvel ouvrage de régularisation à Genève. Le "barrage de régularisation et usine hydro-électrique du Seujet" est actuellement en construction et sera mis en service en 1994. Il aura pour fonctions d'assurer :

(a) la régularisation des niveaux du lac Léman
(b) l'évacuation des débits de crue
(c) la maîtrise des débits du Rhône afin de permettre l'écoulement des eaux de l'Arve
(d) la production d'énergie électrique et la modulation des débits pour les usines hydro-électriques au fil de l'eau situées à l'aval

Le but prioritaire de cet ouvrage sera, comme celui du précédent,de garantir la maîtrise des niveaux du lac conformément à la convention intercantonale de 1884 qui restera en vigueur dans les années à venir.

MODE DE REGULARISATION

La convention intercantonale de 1884 et les règlements d'application qui lui sont associés définissent pour chaque mois de l'année les niveaux du lac à respecter (Fig. 3).

Le niveau maximal normal est de 372.30 msm en été et le niveau minimal de 371.70 msm au mois d'avril. Une fois tous les quatre ans le niveau est abaissé à 371.50 msm pour permettre les travaux d'entretien et de réfection des ouvrages situés au bord du lac.

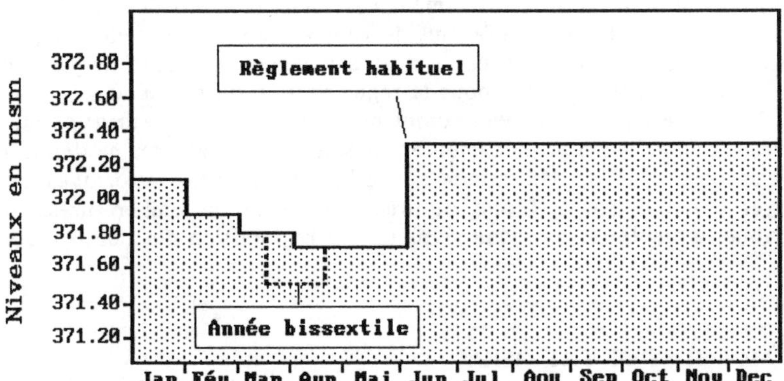

FIG. 3 Niveaux de consigne du lac Léman selon la convention intercantonale de 1884 et ses règlements d'application .

Contrairement à certains règlements en vigueur sur d'autres lacs qui imposent de manière univoque les débits à lâcher selon la période de l'année et le niveau du plan d'eau, le mode de régularisation du lac Léman ne fixe que l'essentiel, soit le niveau du lac à respecter. Cette façon de faire est très souple, mais très exigeante envers l'exploitant du barrage car elle lui laisse l'entière responsabilité du choix des débits à lâcher et des problèmes qui peuvent en découler. Ceci est encore compliqué par les effets épisodiquement limitatifs de l'Arve que nous avons évoqués précédemment.

La régularisation opérationnelle nécessite donc non seulement la connaissance en temps réel des niveaux du lac, mais également celle des débits d'apports et de l'Arve ; elle requiert également des responsables d'excellentes qualités de prévisionniste afin que toutes les variations significatives de débit soient anticipées suffisamment tôt pour que les niveaux puissent être maintenus dans leurs limites admises.

La régularisation du lac Léman est habituellement réalisée au pas de temps journalier, les débits à évacuer étant choisis chaque matin pour la journée qui suit. Néanmoins des options sont parfois prises quelques jours à l'avance, ou, à l'inverse, certaines actions doivent être effectuées très rapidement en cas d'événements hydrologiques exceptionnels tels que les crues du Rhône ou de l'Arve.

Les stations de mesure

En l'état la régularisation du lac Léman ne fait appel qu'à un nombre très restreint de stations de mesure. Il s'agit :

(a) du niveau du lac à St-Prex, station choisie en raison du peu d'influence à cet endroit des effets de vent et de balancement du plan d'eau (seiches...)
(b) du débit du Rhône à la Porte-du-Scex qui fournit les apports de l'affluent principal
(c) du débit du Rhône à Genève à la sortie du barrage de régularisation
(d) du débit de l'Arve à Genève

On dispose en outre depuis peu de temps du système d'information météorologique METEOTEL qui permettra à l'avenir de suivre et de prévoir l'évolution à court terme des situations météorologiques. Cet équipement provoquera probablement à terme des modifications dans la manière d'appréhender la régularisation du lac Léman. Pour la première fois en effet on pourra profiter d'une vision globale des phénomènes touchant l'ensemble du bassin versant, et l'on disposera de la possibilité d'évaluer en temps réel leur évolution à court terme. Il est néanmoins encore impossible à l'heure actuelle d'évaluer quel sera l'apport réel de ce système en terme de prévision de débit , car s'il est aujourd'hui excessivement hasardeux d'établir des prévisions quantitatives de précipitations, il l'est encore plus de vouloir transformer celles-ci en débits dans les émissaires. Seule une expérience de quelques années permettra de juger de l'apport réel du système METEOTEL pour la régularisation du lac Léman.

Pour le reste, l'équipement complémentaire du bassin versant en stations de mesure est actuellement à l'examen en liaison avec l'étude des modèles de prévision. Il s'agit en particulier de déterminer, sur la base de données historiques, si la mesure d'autres affluents que le Rhône, de précipitations ou de températures... peut contribuer à améliorer de façon significative la prévision des débits d'apport.

LES MODELES DE PREVISION

Jusqu'à ce jour la régularisation du lac Léman a été réalisée de manière très intuitive à partir des mesures enregistrées aux stations précitées. Ce mode de faire, basé sur la grande expérience des personnes responsables des manoeuvres du barrage, s'est révélé tout à fait satisfaisant tant que l'unique objectif était le maintien des niveaux du lac aux cotes prévues par la convention de 1884. Depuis les années 70, certaines contraintes supplémentaires sont apparues, en liaison avec la nécessité d'optimiser l'utilisation de nos ressources hydrauliques, et il s'avère actuellement qu'une prévision plus précise des débits d'apport offrirait une sécurité accrue aux riverains du lac tout en autorisant une meilleure gestion énergétique des volumes d'eau disponibles.

Le modèle autorégressif AR(3)

Pour ces raisons, une première étude a été menée entre 1984 et 1986 dans le but d'élaborer un modèle de prévision des apports d'eau au lac Léman. Compte tenu du caractère partiel des données disponibles en temps réel, particulièrement en terme de prévision, le modèle retenu dans un premier temps a été un modèle "historique" de type autorégressif d'ordre 3 (Capitaine, 1986) ; autrement dit, il s'agit d'un modèle qui se base uniquement sur les apports observés pendant les 3 jours précédents pour prévoir ceux du ou des jours suivants. Les limites de ce type de méthodes sont bien connues, et en particulier elles sont incapables d'anticiper une situation de crue. Le calage a été effectué sur la série historique des 20 dernières années et on a calibré les constantes du modèle séparément pour chaque mois de l'année. Testé opérationnellement entre 1987 et 1989 ce modèle n'a pas répondu à tout ce que l'on attendait de lui, si bien qu'on en est revenu à l'heure provisoirement à une estimation intuitive basée sur l'expérience du prévisionniste. Diverses raisons expliquent ce relatif échec :

(a) à l'heure actuelle le calcul des apports d'eau passés, qui "alimentent" le modèle, est basé sur les débits évacués au barrage et la variation de niveau du lac. Ce mode de cacul fournit des résultats souvent douteux, probablement en raison de la relative imprécision de mesure des niveaux du lac (1 cm de lac représente $67m^3s^{-1}$ pendant un jour!)
(b) ce type de modèle n'autorise pas la prise en compte de l'évolution des conditions météorologiques, et en particulier ne permet pas d'anticiper les situations de crue
(c) le calage du modèle n'a pas pris en compte les variations artificielles de débit, parfois importantes, liées à la gestion des ouvrages hydro-électriques situés à l'amont du lac Léman (voir chapitre suivant)

Suite des études

En conséquence une nouvelle étude est actuellement en cours afin d'essayer de corriger les défauts majeurs du modèle AR(3). Il s'agit entre autre :

(a) de trouver un mode de calcul plus fiable des apports d'eau passés, et d'estimer l'éventuelle nécessité d'introduire les débits d'autres affluents que le Rhône dans ce calcul
(b) d'essayer de séparer la part naturelle des débits, de celle artificielle due à la gestion des barrages à accumulation du Valais ; ces deux types de débits devant faire l'objet de prévisions spécifiques et séparées
(c) de juger de l'opportunité de différencier certaines situations caractéristiques telles que période stable, précipitations sans crue, crue pluviale, crue de fonte nivale, fonte glaciaire...et d'établir des lois de prévision propre à chacune de ces situations
(d) d'évaluer si de nouvelles variables, telles que précipitations, températures... devraient être prises en compte pour affiner la prévision
(e) ...

Nous espérons que cette nouvelle étude permettra d'éclaircir une partie des mécanismes hydrologiques participant à la génèse des apports d'eau au Léman, et qu'ainsi de nouveaux éléments décisionnels pourront être mis à disposition des personnes responsables de la régularisation du lac.

INFLUENCE DES AMENAGEMENTS SUR LES DEBITS DU RHONE

Le panorama de la régularisation du lac Léman ne serait pas complet si l'on n'évoquait pas brièvement cette question. qui doit être examinée à l'amont et à l'aval du lac.

Influence des barrages valaisans sur le Rhône à l'amont du lac Léman

Le bassin versant du Rhône à l'amont du lac Léman compte une vingtaine de barrages dont 14 à accumulation saisonnière. Pour la plupart construits vers le milieu de ce siècle, ces 14 aménagements contrôlent une surface de 1400 km², soit approximativement le quart du bassin du Rhône ; ils permettent de stocker un volume de 1150 million m³ qui représente l'équivalent d'une tranche d'eau de 2 m sur le lac Léman (Bezinge, 1985). De manière générale ces barrages, dédiés à la production d'énergie électrique, se remplissent en été et relâchent leurs eaux en hiver pour produire de l'énergie de pointe. L'influence de ces aménagements sur le cycle annuel des débits du Rhône est mise en évidence par la Fig.4 .

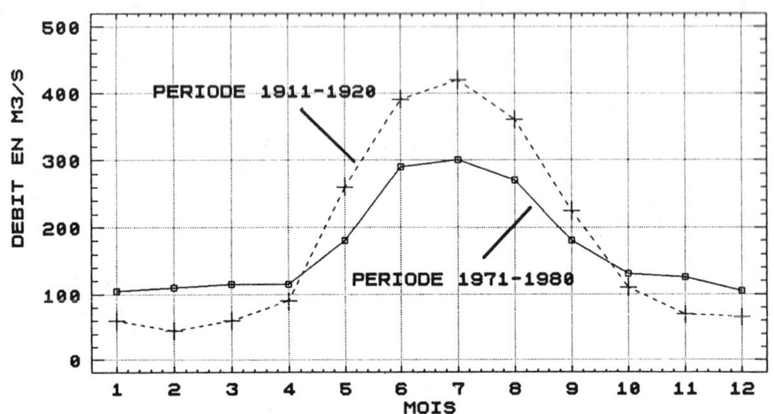

FIG. 4 Débits mensuels moyens du Rhône à la Porte-du-Scex (d'après Emmenegger, 1988).

On constate qu'entre le début du siècle et la période actuelle la mise en service de ces équipements a provoqué une sensible augmentation des débits d'étiage d'hiver alors que les débits d'été ont nettement diminué. Cet état de fait est globalement positif car :

(a) pour la régularisation, il y a diminution des plus forts débits qui ne pouvaient parfois pas être évacués à Genève, faute de capacité hydraulique, et qui provoquaient une surélévation mal venue des niveaux du lac
(b) pour la qualité des eaux du Rhône, l'augmentation des débits hivernaux est favorable en permettant une meilleure dilution des substances polluantes
(c) pour les usines hydro-électriques qui équipent le Rhône jusqu'à Marseille, le gain d'énergie hydraulique hivernale est appréciable

Outre cette modification saisonnière des débits du Rhône on observe également l'effet des modulations hebdomadaires, débits plus forts la semaine que les week-ends, et des modulations journalières, débits plus forts le jour que la nuit. La Fig. 5 qui représente la différence des débits journaliers du Rhône entre le vendredi et le dimanche sur la période 1977-1987 montre l'importance des variations hebdomadaires selon les mois de l'année (Grandjean, 1988).

On constate que les débits du dimanche sont systématiquement plus faibles que ceux du vendredi, en moyenne d'environ 70 m^3s^{-1}, pendant les mois de septembre à avril. En été, de mai à août, les différences sont nettement moins marquées et très variables.L'importance relative de ces différences de débit implique leur prise en compte pour la régularisation du lac Léman si l'on veut éviter des fluctuations indésirables du plan d'eau.

Hormis ces variations périodiques, il existe certainement d'autres fluctuations plus aléatoires liées à la demande d'énergie électrique ; celles-ci sont mal connues et il est peu probable qu'elles pourront un jour être intégrées dans un schéma de prévision.

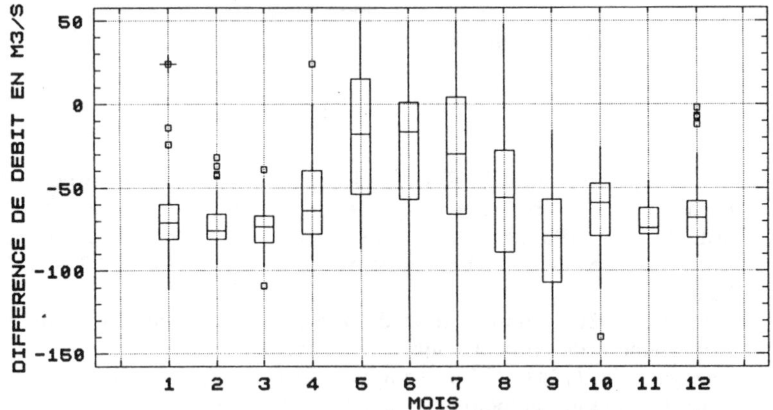

FIG. 5 Différences entre les débits journaliers du dimanche et ceux du vendredi sur la période 1977-1987. Le rectangle représente l'étendue du 50% des valeurs et la barre horizontale situe la valeur médiane.

Influence de la régularisation du lac sur les débits du Rhône

L'influence de la régularisation amène le même type de remarques que celles évoquées pour les barrages valaisans. Le respect des niveaux définis par la convention de 1884 implique un destockage d'eau, donc une augmentation des débits, de décembre à avril, et un stockage, donc une diminution des débits, en mai et juin. Cet effet se cumule avec celui provoqué par les barrages de l'amont et estompe encore un peu plus les différences saisonnières été-hiver par rapport au régime naturel.

Pour le reste, les débits sortant du lac sont également modulés en vue d'optimiser la production hydro-électrique des usines au fil de l'eau situées à l'aval et l'on observe de fortes variations hebdomadaires et journalières. Selon les périodes celles-ci sont particulièrement marquées car, contrairement aux ouvrages valaisans, le barrage de régularisation permet de contrôler les débits provenant de la totalité du bassin versant. Pour cette raison le choix des débits minimaux, ou de dotation, a fait l'objet d'une attention toute particulière lors de l'élaboration du règlement du futur barrage du Seujet ; ceux-ci ont été fixés à 50 m^3s^{-1} en hiver et a 100 m^3s^{-1} pendant la période estivale. Ils sont de ce fait nettement supérieurs aux 10 m^3s^{-1} qu'imposerait la législation fédérale suisse, et, nous l'espérons, mieux adaptés au maintien des fonctions hydrauliques et biologiques du fleuve.

CONCLUSION

La maîtrise des débits de cours d'eau alpins, comme le Rhône ou l'Arve, dont les débits sont souvent capricieux et impétueux, n'est pas chose aisée malgré la capacité de rétention importante qu'offre le lac Léman.

La protection des riverains contre les inondations et le maintien de niveaux propices aux activités lacustres sont les objectifs prioritaires de la régularisation. Ceux-ci doivent néanmoins, dans la mesure du possible, être combinés avec l'optimisation de la gestion de nos ressources hydrauliques.

Dans ce contexte, bien que l'objectif de régularisation n'ait pas changé depuis 1884 et qu'il restera le même dans les années à venir, on constate que le mode d'application de la régularisation du lac Léman est en pleine évolution. On recherche d'une part à satisfaire des contraintes sans cesse plus exigeantes, d'autre part à optimiser le mode de régularisation sur la base d'une prévision hydrologique performante. Cette prévision en est encore à ses débuts, mais elle connaîtra certainement dans les prochaines années d'importants développements.

REFERENCES

Bezinge, A. (1985) Vallée du Rhône - Débits d'étiage d'hiver, production hydro-électrique et environnement. Eau, énergie, air 1/2 1985, Baden, Suisse.

Burkard, P. et al. (1984) Synthèse des travaux de la Commission internationale pour la protection des eaux du Léman contre la polution 1957-1982. CIPEL, Lausanne, Suisse.

Capitaine, G. (1986) Régularisation du niveau du lac Léman. Rapport interne, Département des travaux publics du canton de Genève, Suisse.

Emmenegger, Ch. (1988) 125 ans d'hydrométrie en Suisse - Rétrospective. Service hydrologique et géologique national, publ. no. 9, Berne, Suisse.

Grandjean, P. (1988) Etudes des variations des débits d'apports du Léman sur les périodes de week-end. Rapport interne, Département des travaux publics du canton de Genève, Suisse.

Wahl, J. (1987) Nouvel ouvrage de régularisation à l'émissaire du lac Léman à Genève. Ingénieurs et architectes suisses 21, Suisse.

Hydrology in Mountainous Regions. I - Hydrological Measurements; the Water Cycle (Proceedings of two Lausanne Symposia, August 1990). IAHS Publ. no. 193, 1990.

Hydrology and development of the Arun River, Nepal

RICHARD KATTELMANN
Center for Remote Sensing and Environmental Optics
Computer Systems Lab, 1140 Girvetz Hall
University of California, Santa Barbara, CA 93106,USA

ABSTRACT The Arun River drains a large area of the Tibetan Plateau before crossing the Himalaya into Nepal where its discharge increases dramatically. The steep gradient and relatively high dry-season flow of the Arun have led to plans for major hydroelectric development. Little information about the hydrology of the Arun basin was available to guide the planning efforts. This review of the limited knowledge concerning this river basin illustrates the unique features of Himalayan hydrology that must be considered when assessing the potential for water resources development in this region.

INTRODUCTION

Water resources of the Himalaya are often viewed as the key to successful development of much of the Indian subcontinent. Year-round flow in the mountain rivers provides water for agriculture during the long dry-season and represents enormous hydroelectric potential. Hydroelectric generation in the Himalaya began in 1897 in Darjeeling. Large projects began to be built after Partition of India and Pakistan. In the past decade, much of the hydropower attention has been directed at Nepal, which is seeking rapid economic development, a product for export, and an alternative energy source to fuelwood. The combination of high precipitation and steep terrain provide Nepal with a theoretical potential for hydroelectric production of 83,000 MW, although only a fraction of this amount can be feasibly developed (Shrestha, 1983).

Although many large-scale projects are under consideration in Nepal, hydroelectric development in the Arun Valley in the eastern part of the country appears to be the best prospect for the 1990's. Initially, a cascade of power projects was envisaged for the Arun in a broad plan for the development of the Kosi River basin (Japan International Co-operation Agency [JICA], 1984). Subsequent planning has concentrated on two sites where the river channel has dramatic bends (Figure 1), which minimize the tunnel length for a substantial head loss. These two proposed projects are called Arun-3 and Upper Arun. Pledges of US$550 million in international financing for Arun-3 have already been obtained (Bhattarai, 1989). Planning for these projects has necessarily proceeded with little hydrologic and climatic information. The Arun River example provides a case study of water resource assessment in a mountain region where data is lacking and the hydrology is poorly understood.

GENERAL GEOGRAPHY

The Arun is the largest trans-Himalayan river passing through Nepal and also has the greatest snow- and ice-covered area of any Nepalese river basin. The Arun drains more than half of the area contributing to the Sapt Kosi river system but provides only about a quarter of the total discharge. This apparent contradiction is caused by the location of more than 80 percent of the Arun's drainage area of about 30,000 km^2 in the rain shadow of the Himalaya. Average annual precipitation in Tibet is about 300 mm (Liu, 1989).

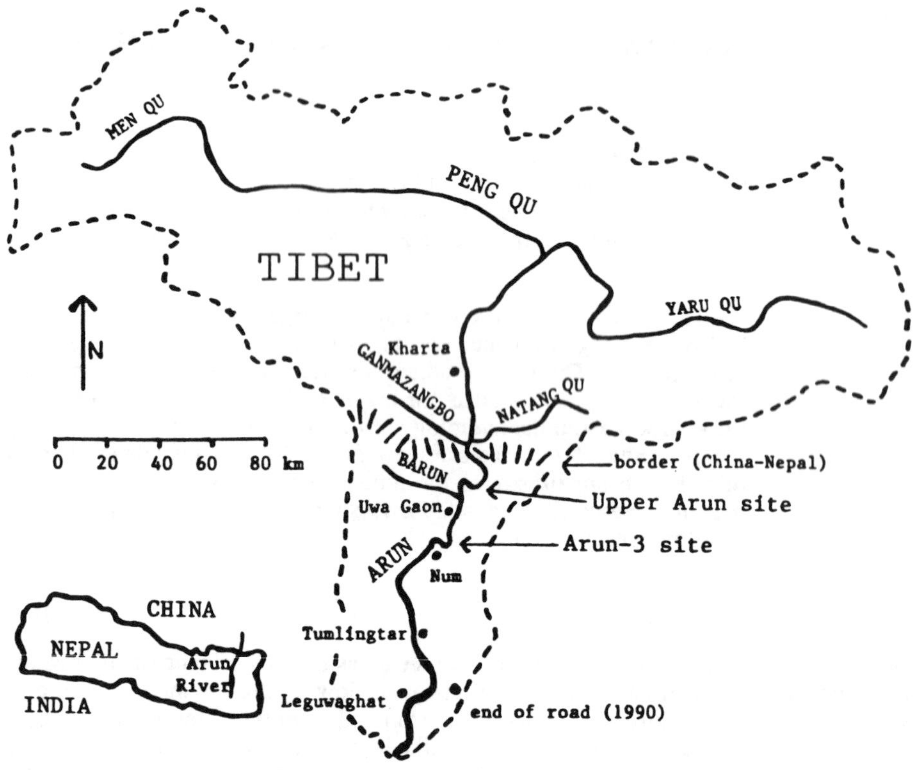

FIG. 1 More than 80 percent of the Arun's drainage area is in Tibet.

In Tibet, the river is known as the Men Qu (Moinqu) in its upper reaches north of Xixabangma and then as the Peng Qu (Pumqu) for most of its course north of the Himalayan crest. After progressing eastward through arid grasslands, the Peng Qu turns south at the 4050 m elevation confluence with the Yaru Qu (Yeyuzangbu). The Peng Qu then flows through the narrow Yo Ri gorge and a broad valley before entering the Longdui gorge at 3500 m at a point below Kharta. The climate changes abruptly in this area from rain-shadow to monsoon-soaked (Howard-Bury, 1922). This portion of the Peng Qu basin may generate much of the streamflow that crosses the border. The Peng Qu crosses the Himalayan crest at an elevation of about 2175 m and becomes known as the Arun in Nepal.

South of the Himalayan crest, the flow of the Arun increases rapidly downstream in the seasonally-humid environment of east Nepal. The 5000 km^2 of land contributing water to the Arun inside Nepal is only 17 percent of the total basin area, but it provides more than 70 percent of the Arun's total flow at its confluence with the Sapt Kosi (JICA, 1984). The landscape south of the border tends to be steep with less than 15 percent of the area having a sustained slope of less than 15° and is strongly dissected by stream channels. Many of the hillslopes are structurally unstable, and the region is seismically active (Kansaker, 1988). An earthquake in August 1988 with an epicenter more than 50 km south of the Arun basin had a magnitude of 6.7 on the Richter scale and resulted in more than 100 deaths in the Arun basin alone (Dunsmore, 1988). Soils tend to be shallow (generally less than 20 cm deep) and stony (Goldsmith, 1981). The alpine zone above 4000 m covers about 5-10 percent of the lower Arun basin (Shrestha, 1988). Several large glaciers are found in the Barun River tributary near the 8000 m peak, Makalu.

The northern third of the Nepalese portion of the Arun basin supports a rich, though human-modified, forest of mixed hardwoods, Chir pine, fir, and rhododendron at elevations of 1000 to 4000 m (Cronin, 1979; Shrestha, 1988). The vegetation in the southern two-thirds of the area has been extensively modified for subsistence agriculture. Most of the half-million people in the Arun basin live in this southern area between 300 and 2200 m in widely scattered villages near the slopes they farm (Dunsmore, 1988). None of the four towns in the basin had more than 14,000 people in 1988. Less than 80 km of motorable road has been built in the low-elevation southeast corner of the basin. The potential for the basin to support either the existing or a growing population under subsistence agriculture is problematic and depends on active conservation of soil and forests (Dunsmore, 1988).

HYDROELECTRIC DEVELOPMENT PLANS

The immense hydropower potential of the Arun River has long been recognized from considerations of the large discharge and steep gradient. The first detailed assessment of the basin estimated that more than 1100 MW of capacity could be developed in a cascade of six generating stations (JICA, 1984). One proposed site, known as Arun-3, was particularly attractive because of a great S-shaped curve in the channel around a ridge of resistant rock. Because a tunnel could cut off the bend and drop more than 200 m in 11 km, this project was judged to be the most efficient development (Nepal Electricity Authority, 1986). Arun-3 would involve diverting up to 150 $m^3\ s^{-1}$ from a dam across the Arun upstream of Num to a powerhouse of 400 MW capacity at Pikuwa. As detailed design work progressed, the estimated construction cost more than doubled from US$240 million (JICA, 1984) to US$550 million (Bhattarai, 1988). An access road of at least 170 km length is necessary to begin construction of the dam, tunnel, powerhouse and transmission line. A minimal road could cost about US$35 million (US$200,000 per km) and take 2 to 3 years to complete (Dunsmore, 1988). However, the planned route of the road has been extended to 193 km to serve as many towns as possible. This alternative alignment has delayed funding and extended construction time to at least 4 years. Consequently, the Arun-3 project is unlikely to be completed before the year 2000.

Another site with characteristics similar to Arun-3 was identified in 1985 near the border with China. This so-called Upper Arun site also takes advantage of a dramatic curve in the channel to minimize the length of the headrace tunnel. This project as currently proposed would divert up to 120 $m^3\ s^{-1}$ from a dam no more than 12 m high through a 7 km tunnel to an underground powerhouse (Nepal Electricity Authority, 1987). The Upper Arun project would have an installed capacity of 350 MW and could generate more than 3000 GWH annually. The total project cost including access road and transmission line is about US$400 million (Nepal Electricity Authority, 1987).

All planning and design work for these potential hydropower developments on the Arun has been conducted with far less information about basic hydrology than is available for projects in North America or Europe. For example, the minimal information that was available at the time of the Kosi Basin Master Plan gave the appearance that streamflow was greater than precipitation in some basins. The critical lack of data and knowledge about the Himalayan hydrologic system has been a persistent difficulty in water resources development throughout the region (Kattelmann, 1987; Gyawali, 1989). The two principal questions that must be asked early in any planning efforts are:

(a) How much water is reliably available for hydroelectric generation?

(b) Is the environment conducive to construction and operation of generating facilities?

Two recent hydroelectric projects elsewhere in Nepal illustrate the risks of constructing projects in the Himalaya with inadequate hydrologic information: (a) in August 1985, a nearly-completed small facility on the upper Dudh Kosi in the Mt.

Everest region was destroyed by flood waters from a glacial lake outburst only 12 km upstream; (b) the reservoir that supplies electricity to the capital city of Kathmandu proved to have insufficient storage to operate continuously following below-average precipitation during the 1988 monsoon. The failure of this project to provide year-round electricity only five years after completion tarnished the promise of hydroelectricity in the minds of many Nepalis. These experiences demonstrate the need for cautious planning and conservative design in Himalayan projects where our understanding of the hydrologic system is limited. The remainder of this paper attempts to synthesize our knowledge of the hydrology of the Arun River.

PRECIPITATION

The climate of the Arun basin obviously reflects the dominating influence of the Indian monsoon. Precipitation is concentrated in the months of June through September, but relatively high precipitation also occurs during the months of April, May, and October. The eastern location of the basin and the topographic trough of the Arun Valley tend to increase the total precipitation and extend the wet season beyond those of most areas of Nepal (Shrestha, 1988). The regional atmospheric circulation during the summer is partially controlled by the creation of a thermal low over much of Tibet, where the ground receives intense solar radiation (Ye, 1981; Liu, 1989). The Arun Valley should enhance the movement of air and water vapor movement from the Bay of Bengal toward the Tibetan Plateau by providing a route through rather than over the Himalaya.

Rainfall in the basin has been measured at six stations for more than 20 years. Lower elevation stations in the southern part of the basin have average annual rainfalls between 1000 and 2000 mm. Average rainfall at a station called Num near the Arun-3 project site is more than 3700 mm per year. Records from Num show a maximum of 350 mm of rainfall in one day and eight days in 26 years with rainfall exceeding 200 mm. The extent of high precipitation up the Arun Valley past the Nepal-China border is unknown. Although no long-term records are available, vegetation distribution documented in photographs and personal accounts of the weather suggest that rainfall is substantial (perhaps 1000-2000 mm) as far north as Kharta (Howard-Bury, 1922; Wager, 1937; Mukhopadhyay, 1982; Webster, 1989). One early explorer noted, "Within a mile [of Kharta] you may pass from the dry climate of Tibet to the moist, steamy air of a Nepalese character, with its luxuriant vegetation" (Wollaston, 1922:298). The area downstream of Kharta and north of the border is about 2600 km^2 (Academia Sinica, 1981).

STREAMFLOW REGIME

Knowledge of the streamflow regime of the Arun is largely based on ten years of record from a single gage at Tumlingtar, about 50 km downstream of the Arun-3 site. Thus, the streamflow data is strongly biased toward the zone of intense rainfall, the area of which more than doubles between the project site and gaging station. The feasibility studies have attempted to compensate for the influence of this downstream region and have generated several estimates of flow at the project sites. Estimates of dependable low flow and probable peak flow at the project site have been developed that provide some basis for engineering design (Nepal Electricity Authority, 1986 and 1987). In addition to the record of streamflow at Tumlingtar since 1975, a gage was operated farther downstream at Leguwaghat from 1979 to 1983, and new gages were installed at Uwa Gaon (between Arun-3 and Upper Arun) in 1986 and just above the Upper Arun dam site in 1989 (Fahlbusch, F., Morrison-Knudsen Engineers, personal communication). Staff gages have also been monitored near the Arun-3 site and on the Barun tributary (Thapa, 1987).

Mean annual streamflow at Tumlingtar from 1975 to 1984 was 420 $m^3 s^{-1}$. At this gage, streamflow is about 1000 $m^3 s^{-1}$ during the peak month of August, on the average, and about 120 $m^3 s^{-1}$ during the minimum flow period in February. Crude annual hydrographs based on monthly flows at Tumlingtar and extrapolations to the two project sites (Nepal Electricity Authority, 1986 and 1987) illustrate the seasonal distribution of streamflow (Figure 2).

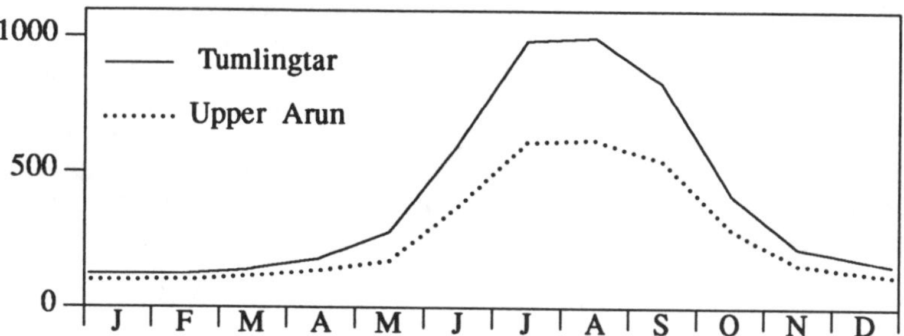

FIG. 2 The difference between streamflow (m^3s^{-1}) measured at Tumlingtar and that estimated at the Upper Arun site (NEA, 1987) increases dramatically during the monsoon period of June to September.

Flow characteristics at the China-Nepal border are less well-known because of the absence of any continuous records. However, measurements were made at the border and at several stations upstream and of tributaries over the course of a year during a multidisciplinary expedition in 1976 (Academia Sinica, 1981). These studies estimated mean annual flow of the Peng Qu at the border to be 156-170 $m^3 s^{-1}$. However, a large fraction of this flow is generated in the two southernmost tributaries, Ganmazangbo and Natang Qu, which together drain only 1,650 km^2 (7 percent of the Peng Qu area), but contribute more than 45 percent of the total flow of the Peng Qu. A recent expedition to the southern part of the Peng Qu estimated the mean annual flow at the border to be about 100 $m^3 s^{-1}$ based on one month of measurements and apparent application of the seasonal distribution of flow in another Tibetan river, Yarlung Zangbo at Nugesha (Guan and Chen, 1981). Concurrent measurements of the tributaries mentioned above suggested that their flow was again about 45 percent of that of the Peng Qu at the border.

The rate of increase of discharge with distance downstream of the border is a critical unknown relating to the basic question of how much runoff is generated in different portions of the basin. We made a series of crude float-velocity—area measurements as a first approximation in November, 1986. This field survey suggested that streamflow in the post-monsoon season increased at least four-fold over a 30 km reach upstream of the Arun-3 site whereas drainage area increased only a few percent. Our estimates of bankfull discharge from channel dimensions also supported this large increase in streamflow with only a small change in drainage area. Given their inherent uncertainty, these estimates of bankfull discharge correspond surprisingly well with independent estimates of mean annual flood at the Upper Arun and Tumlingtar sites.

Dry-Season Flow

Dependable flow during the dry portion of the year is, of course, crucial to the success of run-of-river projects. The Arun is particularly favorable in this regard because its dry-season flow is greater in absolute terms than any other river of east Nepal with comparable elevation or channel gradient near the measurement site. Based on tabulations of average flow in dry and wet seasons (Nepal Electricity Authority, 1987), the ratio of average streamflow in the dry season to that in the wet season is much higher in the Arun (0.23) than in other tributaries of the Sapt Kosi (average about 0.15). Low-season discharge in the Arun also tends to be consistent between years with a coefficient of variation of 0.12 in February over the ten-year record at Tumlingtar. Most of the flow in the Arun at Tumlingtar during the dry season has been assumed to come from Tibet (Nepal Electricity Authority, 1986 and 1987; Liu and Sharma, 1989). However, dry-season contributions from the Nepalese tributaries to the Arun may have been underestimated. For example, the Barun River, which has a small low-elevation drainage area (less than 200 km^2), has a minimum flow of about 7 m^3 s^{-1} (Thapa, 1987). Discharge measured below the glacierized portion of the Barun, about 200 km^2 of alpine terrain, provided about one percent of the flow at the Arun-3 dam site in November, 1986. A simple set of discharge measurements at several sites (every bridge between the stream gages at the Upper Arun site and Tumlingtar and all major tributaries) over a week in January or February in a couple of years would help resolve the question of where low-season flow is generated.

Floods

The Himalayan foothills in the Arun basin are subject to intense and prolonged rainfall during summer that produces locally-high river levels and contributes to downstream flooding. Flood-generating overland flow has even been observed in the cloud forests of the upper Arun (Cronin, 1979). Several regional flood-frequency analyses have been performed in the Kosi basin (i.e., Karmacharya, 1982; JICA, 1984; Nepal Electricity Authority, 1986 and 1987). The mean annual flood of the Arun has been estimated to be about 2250 m^3 s^{-1} at Tumlingtar and about 650 m^3 s^{-1} at the Upper Arun diversion site (Nepal Electricity Authority, 1987). Earlier estimates from the Arun-3 feasibility study were substantially lower (Nepal Electricity Authority, 1986). Such a comparison is not intended as a criticism of the analyses, but it clearly illustrates the problems of working with limited data sets.

The greatest peak flows in the Himalaya tend to result from sudden releases of water following failure of some natural impoundment (Ives, 1986). Such dams include glaciers, glacial moraines, and mass movement deposits. Several million m^3 of water may enter the river in just a few hours. Such floods, where they occur, far exceed peak flows resulting from rainfall or snow- and ice-melt in upstream areas. Even though these flash floods are attenuated downstream, the potential for destruction from these dense debris flows is likely to be far above that caused by rainfall floods. A recently completed study identified more than 200 glacial lakes in the entire Arun basin (Liu and Sharma, 1988). Most of these lakes were thought to be stable and present little flood hazard. Our field survey of the Barun basin led to similar conclusions. Outburst floods in the Barun valley are inevitable but should lose much of their power and sediment passing through two broad flat areas.

A substantial glacial-lake outburst flood is known to have swept through the Arun valley in recent decades. On the afternoon of 21 September, 1964, large amounts of ice from a glacier slid into Gelhaipuco, a 25 million m^3 lake in the Natang Qu basin just north of the China-Nepal border (Academia Sinica, 1979). The wave generated by the falling ice burst the moraine dam impounding the lake. Discharge of the ensuing debris flow was about 6000 m^{3}s^{-1} at the confluence with Natang Qu and about 3200 m^{3}s^{-1} 30 km downstream. The flood and debris flow damaged a road in the Natang Qu basin and carried 12 logging trucks downstream. This event was recalled by Nepalis who reported seeing concrete, logs, and truck bodies in the debris (Nepal Electricity Authority, 1987). The Arun-3 and Upper Arun feasibility studies have recommended designs resistant to glacial lake outburst floods of 7,700 and 10,000 m^{3}s^{-1}, respectively. Planning for such risks is a necessary part of water resources development in the Himalaya.

Sediment

The Arun is generally recognized to transport the least sediment of the major tributaries to the Sapt Kosi (JICA, 1984). Most of the area in Tibet is both of low slope and low drainage density and contributes relatively little sediment to the rivers. However, the estimates of 10 million m^3 per year at the upper Arun site (Nepal Electricity Authority, 1987) and 35 million m^3 per year at the confluence with the Kosi (JICA, 1984) are still enormous by comparison to most other areas of the world. Simply stated, the Himalayan zone produces vast quantities of weathering products for eventual transport by streams. The relative importance of suspended load, bed load, and transport during and after infrequent debris-flows in the Arun is unknown. The occasional destabilization of river channels and deposition of huge quantities of sediment from outburst floods can affect the load of the river for several years (Ives, 1986). Measurements of suspended load at the new Uwa Gaon stream gage and geomorphic studies during the design of the proposed projects should improve understanding of the sediment dynamics of the basin.

PROSPECTS

Although the rerouting of the access road will undoubtedly increase construction costs and delay completion of the hydropower project(s), it also provides the opportunity to improve basic data collection and begin process-oriented studies of the Arun's hydrology. Improved knowledge will reduce levels of uncertainty and assumptions, and it will also provide a better basis for project design and operation. The experience in the Arun demonstrates the need to install a basic streamflow monitoring program as soon as a project with any chance of implementation is proposed. If a gage had been installed near the China-Nepal border in 1985 when flow from Tibet was recognized as critical unknown, we would now have several years of data and an adequate basis for assessing the geographic distribution of runoff-production.

Another factor in the development of the Arun River basin is the planned eastward extension of Sagarmatha National Park to include the Makalu-Barun area (Taylor-Ide and Shrestha, 1985). An international peace park in the Peng Qu / Arun border area was proposed and endorsed at the Mohonk Mountain Conference in April, 1986 (Ives and Ives, 1987). Most of the western part of the Peng Qu basin has now been designated as a large park called the Qomolungma Nature Preserve (Himal, 1989). If the plans for the Makalu-Barun Conservation Area are carried out, then a large fraction of the Peng Qu / Arun catchment will be be under active management conducive to protection and enhancement of the water resource.

ACKNOWLEDGEMENTS Nima Wangchu and Mike Zika provided invaluable assistance with the field measurements. Fred Fahlbusch, Krishana Malla, Nick Mandeville, Ramiro Mayor-Mora, Shi Jiancheng, Bhaskar Thapa, and Xu Daoming were most helpful in providing data and information about the Arun basin.

REFERENCES

Academia Sinica (1979) The debris flow in Xizang. In: Comprehensive Expedition of Academia Sinica in the Qing-Zang Plateau. Chengdu Institute of Geography, Chengdu, 85-90, cited by Liu and Sharma (1988).

Academia Sinica (1981) Irrigation of Xizang In: Comprehensive Expedition of Academia Sinica in the Qing-Zang Plateau. Nat'l. Stat. Bur., Beijing, 185-196, cited by Liu & Sharma (1988).

Bhattarai, B. (1989) Marsyangdi and Arun III. Himal 2 (3), 20.

Cronin, E. W. (1979) The Arun: A Natural History of the World's Deepest Valley. Houghton Milfin Co., Boston.

Dunsmore, J. R. (1988) Mountain environmental management in the Arun River basin of Nepal. Occasional Paper No. 9, International Centre for Integrated Mountain Development (ICIMOD), Kathmandu.

Goldsmith, P. F. (1981) The land and soil resources of the KHARDEP area. Report No. 16, Koshi Hill Area Rural Development Programme, cited by Dunsmore (1988).

Guan, Z. & Chen, C. (1981) Hydrographical features of the Yarlung Zangbo. In: Geological and Ecological Studies of Qinghai-Xizang Plateau (D. Liu, ed) Science Press, Beijing, 1693-1704.

Gyawali, D. (1989) Water in Nepal. Occasional Paper No. 8, East-West Environment and Policy Institute, East-West Center, Honolulu.

Himal (1989) Protecting the roof of the world Himal 2 (5), 12.

Howard-Bury, C. K. (1922) Mount Everest: The Reconnaissance, 1921. Longmans Green, NY.

Ives, J. D. (1986) Glacial lake outburst floods and risk engineering in the Himalaya. Occasional Paper No. 5, International Centre for Integrated Mountain Development, Kathmandu.

Ives, J. D. & Ives, P. [eds.] (1987) The Himalaya-Ganges Problem. Mountain Research and Development 7 (3), 181-344.

Japan International Co-operation Agency (1984) Master Plan Study on Kosi River Water Resources Development—Interim Report. Tokyo.

Kansakar, D. R. (1988) Geology and geomorphology of the Arun River basin. International Centre for Integrated Mountain Development, Kathmandu, cited by Dunsmore (1988).

Karmacharya, J. L. (1982) Hydrological studies of Nepal. Water and Energy Commission, HMG, Kathmandu.

Kattelmann, R. C. (1987) Uncertainty in assessing Himalayan water resources. Mountain Research and Development 7 (3), 279-286.

Liu, C. & Sharma, C. K. [chief editors] (1988) Report on First Expedition to Glaciers and Glacier Lakes in the Pumqu (Arun) and Poiqu (Bhote-Sun Kosi) River Basins, Xizang (Tibet), China. Science Press, Beijing.

Liu, G. (1989) Hydrometeorological characteristics of the Tibet Plateau. In: Atmospheric Deposition, IAHS Pub. 179, 267-280.

Mukhopadhyay, S. C. (1982) The Tista Basin: A Study in Fluvial Geomorphology. K. P. Bagchi and Company, Calcutta.

Nepal Electricity Authority (1986) Final report of feasibility study on Arun-3 hydroelectric power development project. Kathmandu.

Nepal Electricity Authority (1987) Upper Arun hydroelectric project feasibility study.

Shrestha, H. M. (1983) Some thoughts on the planning of hydroelectric development in Nepal. Water Resources Development in Nepal, The Nepal Digest, Kathmandu.

Shrestha, T. B. (1988) Development ecology of the Arun River basin. ICIMOD, Kathmandu.

Taylor-Ide, D. & Shrestha, T. B. (1985) The Makalu National Park, a proposal. In: Proceedings of the International Workshop on the Management of National Parks and Protected Areas in the Hindu Kush-Himalaya. King Mahendra Trust for Nature Conservation, Kathmandu.

Thapa, B. (1987) Barun Hydroelectricity Feasibility Study. unpublished M.S. thesis, Carnegie-Mellon University, Pittsburgh.

Wager, L. R. (1937) The Arun River drainage pattern and the rise of the Himalaya. Geographical Journal 89 (3), 239-250.

Webster, E. (1989) Four against the Kangshung. American Alpine Journal 31 (63), 1-17.

Wollaston, A. F. R. (1922) Natural history notes. In: Mount Everest: The Reconnaissance, 1921 (C. K. Howard-Bury, ed.), Longmans, Green & Co., New York.

Ye, D. (1981) Some characteristics of the summer circulation over the Qinghai-Xizang (Tibet) Plateau and its neighborhood. Bull. Am. Met. Soc. 62 (1), 14-19.

Hydrology in Mountainous Regions. I - Hydrological Measurements; the Water Cycle
(Proceedings of two Lausanne Symposia, August 1990). IAHS Publ. no. 193, 1990.

Water and energy in Austria

S.RADLER
Institut fuer Wasserwirtschaft, Hydrologie und konstruktiven Wasserbau, Universitaet fuer Bodenkultur, Gregor Mendel-Str.33, A-1180 Vienna, Austria

ABSTRACT Austria has optimal climatic and topographic conditions for the development of hydropower. That led already to its industrial and urban application in the last century. Worldwide seen Europe has the highest percentage in the use of the available hydropower. But the highest potential on earth holds Asia, especially China. Beside this country Nepal reaches peak values in the specific hydropower potential.

INTRODUCTION

The hydrological situation of a country or state depends on various parameters such as climate, topography and land management. Austria is characterized by the west-east declension of the Alps as well as the west-east layout of the draining rivers and it has the highest portion of forestry in all of Europe (Fig.1).

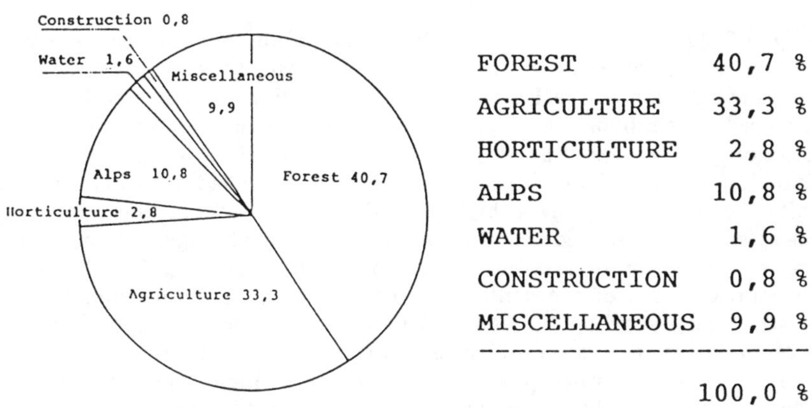

FIG. 1 Land use in Austria (ÖSTZ, 1987).

Worldwide seen, Austria is well provided with regard to precipitation and available water and due to the high portion of grassland, agricultural land and forestry, the austrian water balance is even.

This balance is the basis of an efficient use of the available water energy to supply Austria with electricity, which has been carried out for more than hundred years.

WATER CYCLE

The water cycle can be defined as the perpetual change of the location and the state of the matter of water on the surface of the earth. The most important parameters are precipitation, discharge and evaporation. In the long run, surface and subsurface storage of water are not that important due to its cumulative effect. Therefore it can be neglected. Figure 2 gives a general idea of the austrian water cycle and budget. The mean annual rainfall is 1190 mm and the mean land evaporation was determined with 480 mm per year.

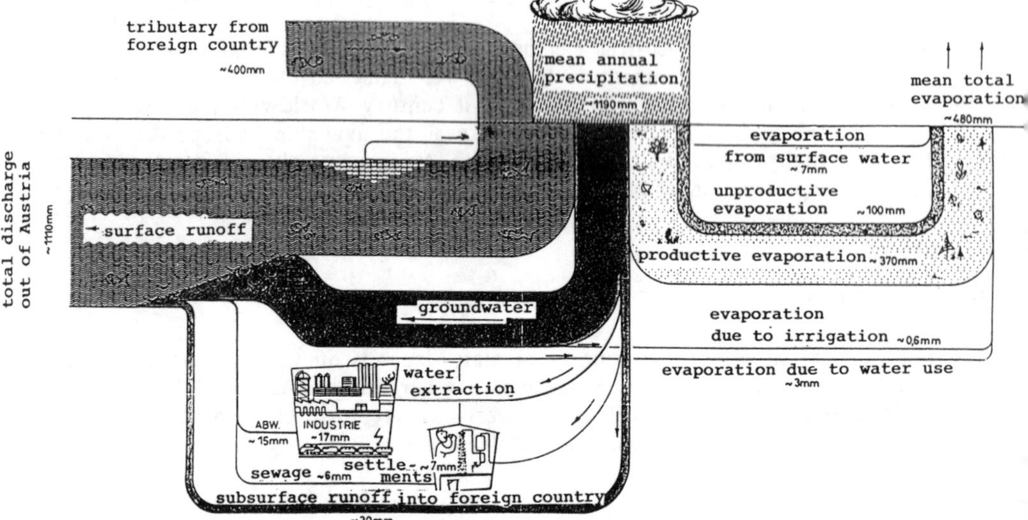

FIG. 2 The Austrian water balance (KRESSER, 1968).

But figure 3 shows clearly the strong fluctuation of the water discharge caused by the decreasing precipitation from the west to the east. In some exposed locations in Eastern Austria such as the Retzer Becken and sections of the Marchfeld, which can be classified as semihumid areas, there is no available discharge at all.

In addition to the west-east decrease of the rainfall, this fact is overlaid by a vertical dependence of the precipitation, which is called pluviometric gradient or oceanity. For Central Europe a high probability in the direct linear relation between the increase of rainfall and the altitude can be assumed. Figure 4 shows a map with the mean distribution of rainfall in Austria for the period 1901 to 1950 and gives a rough approximation of the contours of equal rates of precipitation. Compared with the austrian map showing the contours of equal altitude, it can be pointed out that most of the areas in Austria which are suitable for agricultural purpose beacause of rainfall, have to be ruled out because of their high elevation. These are the unproductive areas of the mountains where all the alpine reservoirs are located.

In the annual average 60 % of the rainfall runs off, the rest evaporates. The amount of evaporation is determined by the available water, climatic factors, the vegetation and by soil parameters. The maximal possible evaporation due to the climate is called potential evaporation and has to be distinguished from the actual evaporation which is determined by the available amount of water.

ENERGY POTENTIAL

Comsidering the great discharge of the rivers and the available head (Grossglockner: 3797 mMSL and Lake Neusiedler See: 112 mMSL), a considerable energy potential is

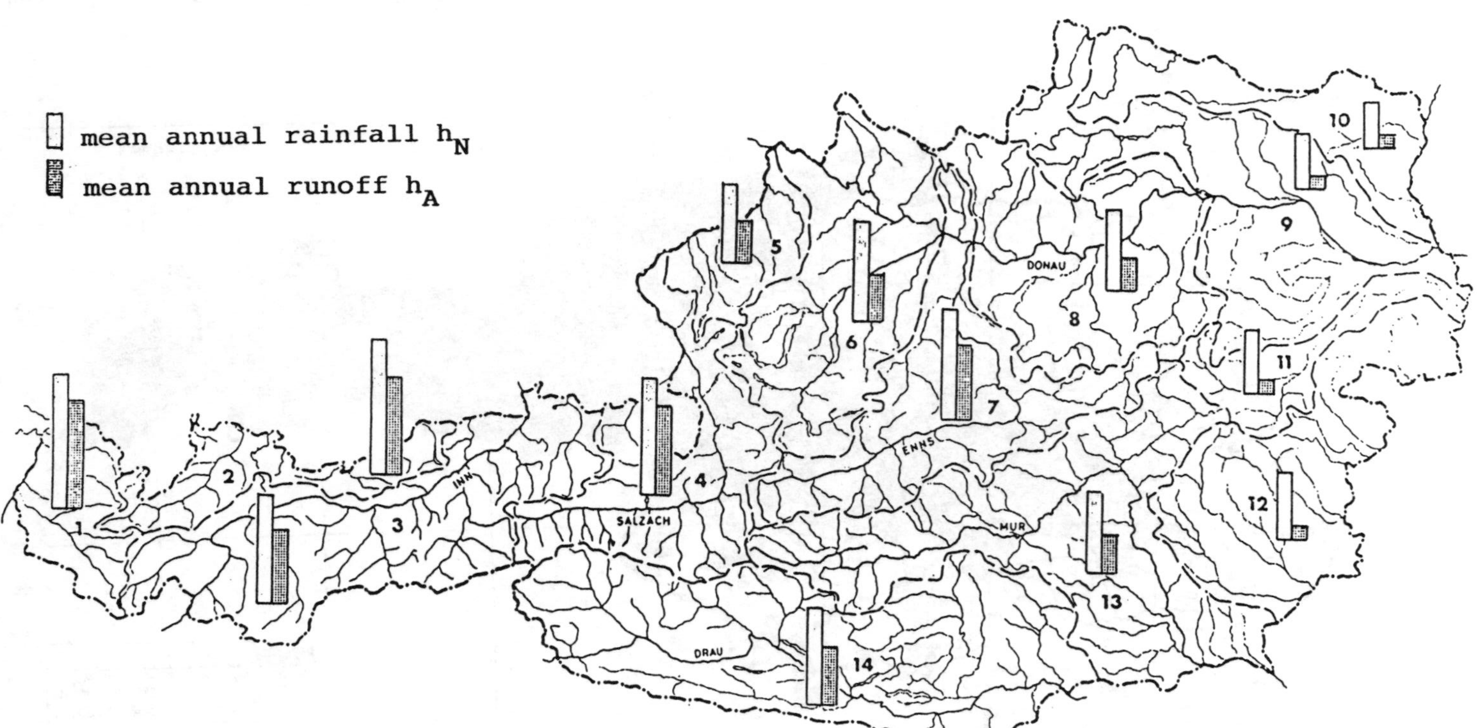

FIG. 3 Rainfall and discharge in the different austrian river catchments.

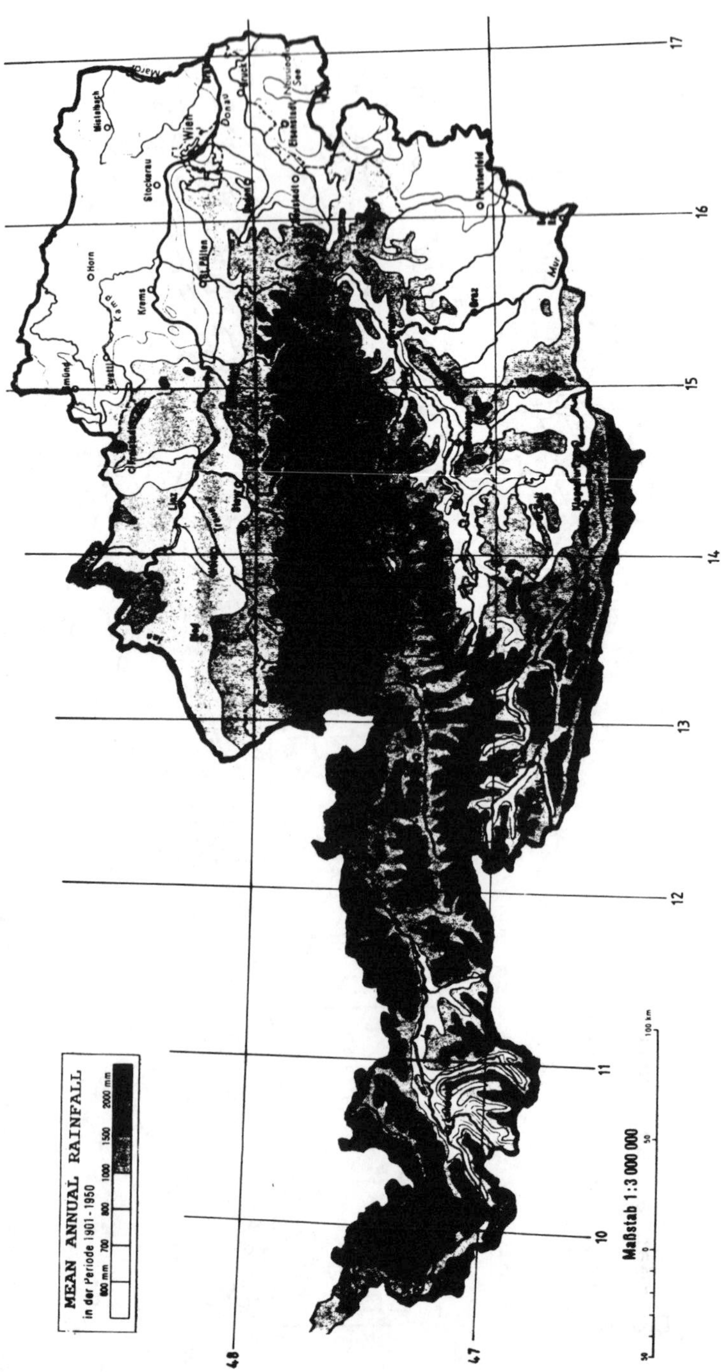

FIG. 4 Mean annual rainfall distribution in Austria in the period from 1901 to 1950.

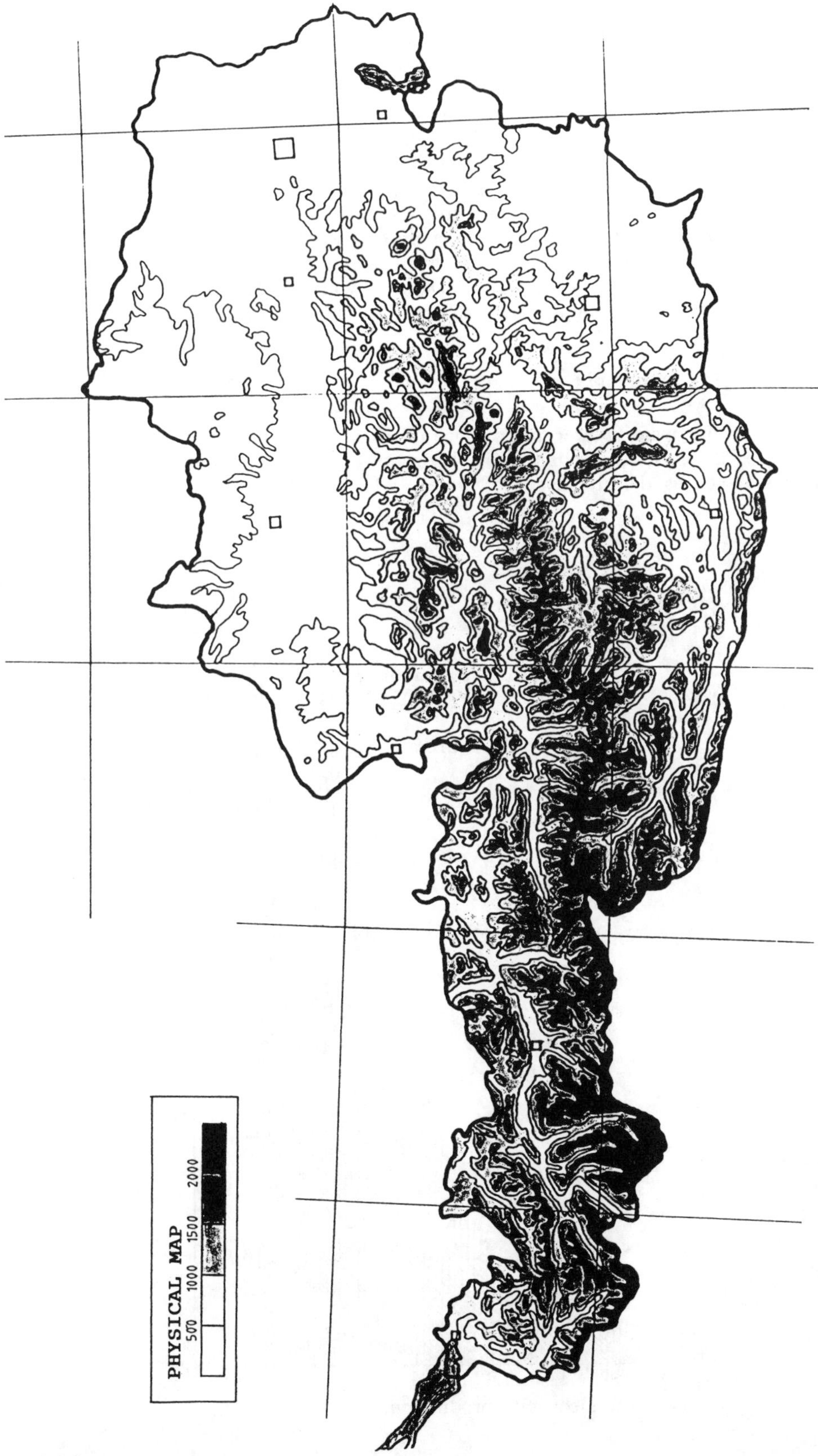

PHYSICAL MAP

500 1000 1500 2000

FIG. 5 Physical map of Austria.

available. Considering all rivers with an annual mean discharge greater than 1 m^3/s, the potential is 74,4 TWh/year. The potential of the rivers with a discharge less than 1 m^3/s can be estimated to be around 3 to 4 TWh/year.

Only a few years ago it was announced that the energy potential could be extended up to 53,7 TWh/year. But due to environmental concerns for these rivers the value will not be reached. The present development reaches 34,2 TWh/year. The portion of energy produced by runoff river stations comes up to approximately 72 % and small hydropower plants with a power up to 5 MW support 7 % of this energy.

For the management of austrian energy it is interesting to know the fact that 35 % of the usable potential energy of the Danube, which is 15,6 TWh/year, is situated in Austria. From this potential 11,7 TWh/year are developed.

HISTORICAL DEVELOPMENT

The use of the water power plays a major role in the electricity supply, because almost 75 % of it is produced by hydropower (Fig. 6). The excellent natural conditions such as the abundance of water and available heads, used already in the

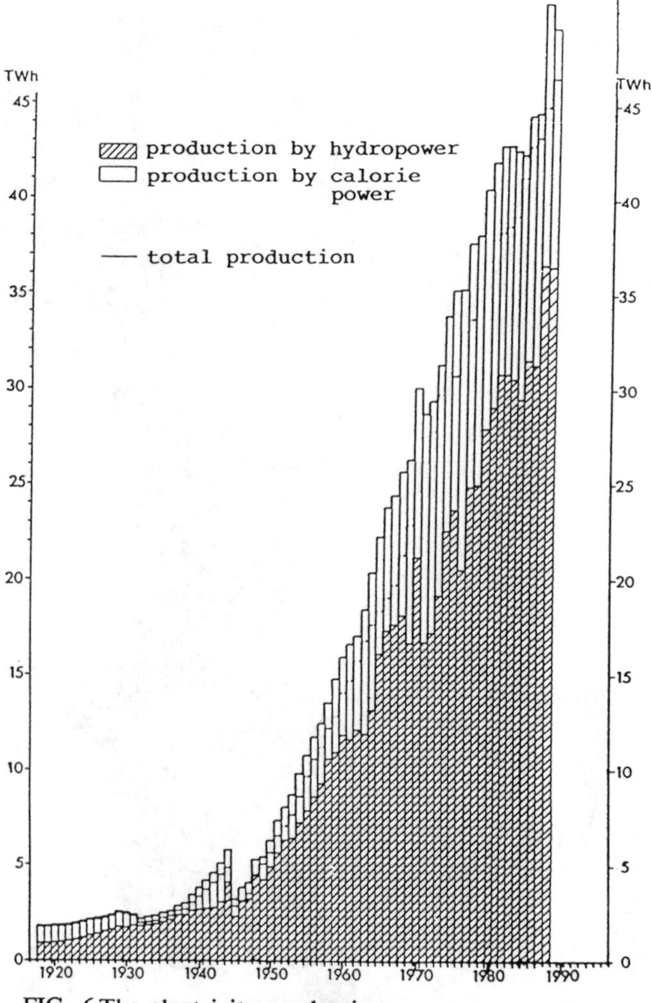

FIG. 6 The electricity production.

Middle Ages as power sources, together with the invention of turbines by Francis & Pelton and the alternator by Siemens in the 19th century, led to the construction of the first hydropower plants. They were either used to support local electric networks or factories and industries with power for electric light, or to run motors. Due to the demand of efficient long distant transmission lines, power plants were only built on little rivers in the lower alpine region to support the nearby industries, such as wood, paper, steel, textil, chemical and the mining industry. The power plants of Scheibbs, Salzburg, Innsbruck and Bregenz which were set up between 1886 and 1891, should be noted as being historical examples for urban electricity supply. At the same time the construction of local electrical trains, such as the Stubaitalbahn, Mittenwaldbahn and Mariazellerbahn began, which were all supplied by hydropower.

While in 1918 the electricity production by hydropower and caloric power of a total of 1800 GWh/year was equally shared, this relation changed under the loss of the coalmine areas of the Austrian Empire in favour of the hydropower. Today 75 % of electric energy is gained by hydropower and only 25 % are produced by caloric power plants.

Following the economical depression between the two world wars, the energy sector developed slowly, stimulated shortly during World War II because of the armament industry, but stagnated completely in 1945. Hydropower plants that were started during the last war, such as on the rivers Enns and Drau, as well as the group of alpine reservoirs of the storage power plant in the central austrian Glockner-Kaprun area, could only be finished under enormous material and financial difficulties, years after they were started. But the economy recovered quickly and already in 1955 the hydropower potential was approximately 8 TWh/year. Double of this amount was reached only ten years later. The hydropower boom continued into the seventies mentioning the hydropower developments in the Danube in connection with the set up of the Rhein-Main-Donaukanal waterway.

The development of different energy carriers, the high costs of the hydropower development and finally the negative environmental impacts of big hydropower plants leaded to a stagnation of its continuing development in Austria, too. In spite of the oil crises, problems in running and disposing caloric and nuclear power plants and a change in the philosophy of constructing hydropower plants, the set up of new power plants is almost completely stopped, due to a highly concerned society. This fact even does not change by the circumstance that the already built nuclear power plant in Zwentendorf did not go into operation and might be broken up after a plebiscite.

GLOBAL EXAMINATION OF THE HYDROPOWER POTENTIAL

The theoretical global hydropower potential is estimated with 36000 TWh/year and the usable potential is announced with approximatley 19000 TWh/year.

Europe shows the highest percentage on already used potential. An increase between 1981 and 2000 of 10 %, up to 43 %, is expected (Fig.7).

Between all continents Asia stands out with the highest hydropower potential, where only China holds a usable potential of more than 1900 TWh/year. This is more than 10 % of the global potential. More than 50 % of it can be gained on the river Yangtzekiang, where also the biggest hydropower plant on earth is planned (Three-Gorge-Project). With its announced annual output of 66,7 TWh and its installed power of 13000 MW it will slightly exceed the biggest known hydropower plant Itaipu on the boarder between Brazil and Uruguay on the river Parana. Today the developed potential is 5,2 %, the electricity consumption is 450 KWh/person, which is roughly 8 % of the austrian consumption.

Also in Asia, Nepal is the country with the highest specific energy potential. Following the enormous difference in the altitude of the state (approximately 8800

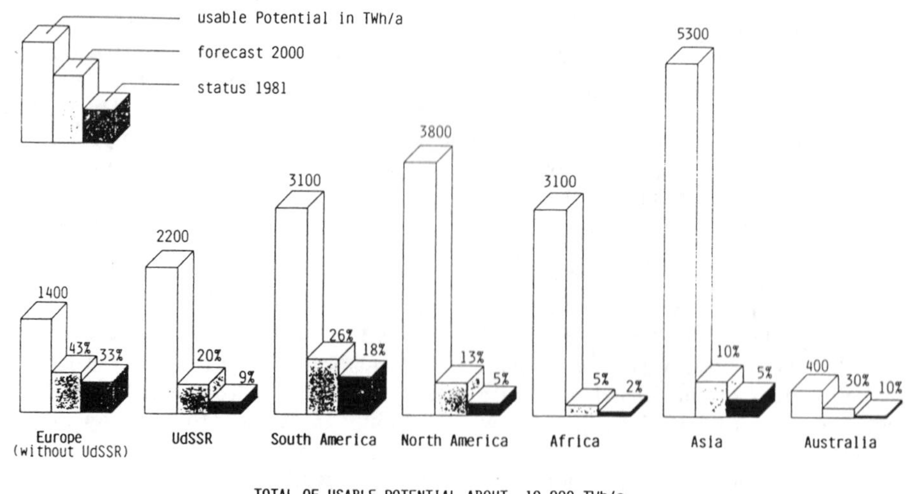

FIG. 7 Utilisation of Hydropower.

m) and its abundance of discharge (assume a mean annual precipitation rate of 1800 mm), the specific annual energy potential results in a value of approximately 6 GWh/km^2, in comparsion to Austria with 0,6 GWh/km^2.

REFERENCES

KRESSER W.: Das Wasser. Wiener Mitteilungen Bd.1, 1968.

ÖSTERREICHISCHES STATISTISCHES ZENTRALAMT: Stat. Handbuch f.d. Republik Österreich, 1987.

WEC: "World Energy Horizons: 2000-2020". 14th Congress-Montreal, 1989.

Hydrology in Mountainous Regions. I - Hydrological Measurements; the Water Cycle (Proceedings of two Lausanne Symposia, August 1990). IAHS Publ. no. 193, 1990.

Methods for evaluating hydro potential

H. W. WEISS & A. O. FAEH
Basler & Hofmann, Consulting Engineers, Forchstrasse 395
8029 Zürich, Switzerland

ABSTRACT Hydro potential constitutes one type of surface water resource on which renewed interest has been focused. Apart from considerations pertaining to the renewal of existing hydro power plants, hitherto undeveloped hydro power resources are being reappraised. Of the various methods in use for determining hydro potential, three are described in short. The proper use and interpretation of hydrologic background information is emphasized. A few case studies are sketched and typical results compared; due consideration is given to the so-called line potential study. The need for an early inclusion of environmental aspects is stressed.

DESCRIPTION OF THREE BASIC METHODS

The area potential is determined solely on the basis of the prevailing topographical and hydrological conditions and as such constitutes a measure for the upper limits of the hydro potential. Normally mean annual precipitation is used to calculate the potential. If net precipitation or area-runoff is used, losses due to evaporation and seepage are considered. The potential corresponds to that which is contained in a system of equivalent reservoirs as illustrated in Fig. 1(a). For evaluation a catchment is subdivided into squares of equal area using a grid. The potential of each square is a function of the precipitation, the surface area of the square and its head difference to some predefined point of reference.

The line potential denotes the theoretical potential of streams and rivers and could be harnessed through a continuous chain of imaginary run-of-river plants. The relevant hydro potential is obtained by subdividing a stream or river into reaches along which discharge and longitudinal slope are approximately uniform as illustrated in Fig. 1(b). It is normally defined on the basis of mean annual discharge and the difference in elevation between beginning and end of each reach. Depending on the size and importance of a tributary, its line potential may be evaluated separately.

In order to determine the utilizable potential, some knowledge must firstly be had of the yearly distribution of runoff. A design discharge is then defined and head losses as well as turbine and generator efficiency are considered. This may be done on the basis of experience or by using available hydro power plant designs (Fig. 1(c)). Once construction and production costs have been estimated, it can be decided whether a scheme promises to be technically as well as economically feasible or not. When all environmental aspects have in addition been dealt with can one determine its acceptance from an environmental point of view.

(a) Area potential = function of precipitation (or net precipitation = area-runoff), surface area of a square and representative difference in head Δh_i

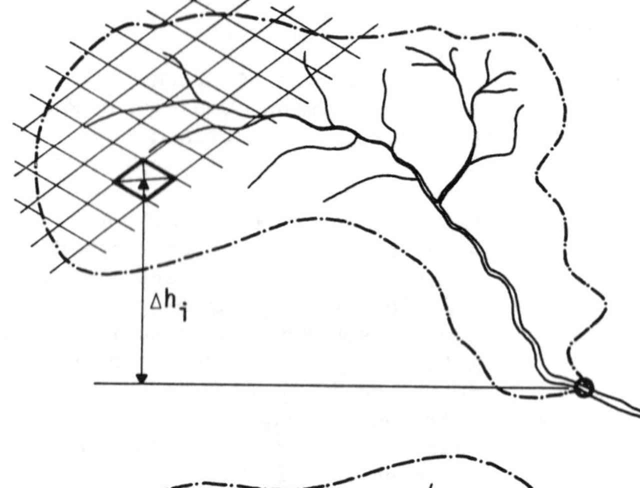

(b) Line potential = function of mean annual discharge and head difference Δh_i of a reach

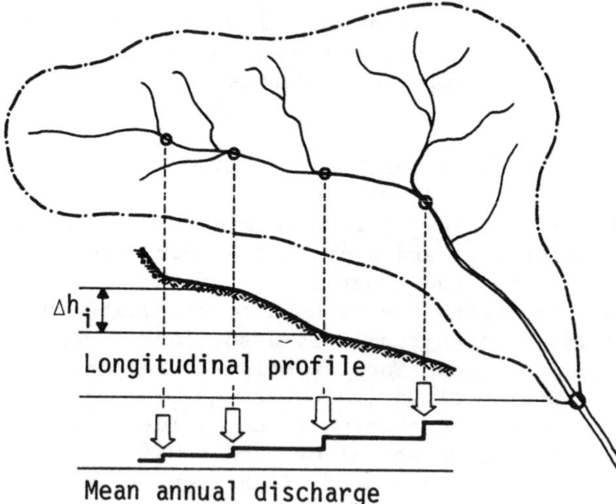

(c) Utilizable potential = function of utilizable volume of water, turbine and generator efficiency etc. and net difference in head Δh_n

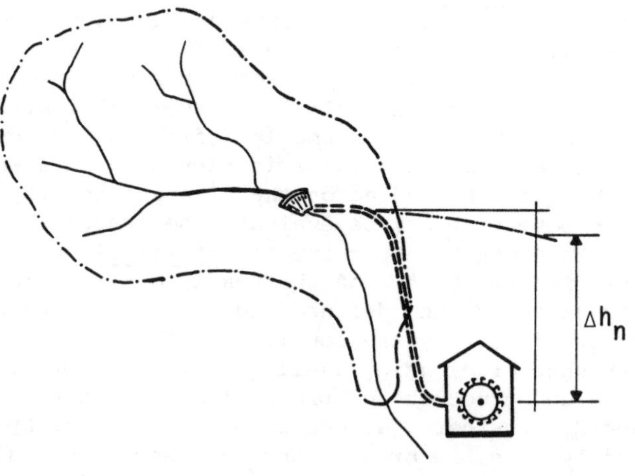

FIG. 1 Illustration of three basic methods for determining hydro potential.

HYDROLOGICAL BACKGROUND

Crude estimates of the potential may be made with mean annual discharge. For better accuracy, however, more labour is involved and more data is needed to derive flow duration curves. If the seasonal distribution of runoff and reliability of supply are considered, long flow records are required. The utilizable volume of water may thereby be obtained and more realistic estimates of the hydro potential made.

Even in areas with gauging stations, standardized hydrological information might help in supplementing flow records. Some interesting work in this direction is described for instance by Aschwanden & Weingartner (1985). With their classification of runoff regimen in Switzerland, it is possible to estimate representative long-term annual hydrographs on a regional basis. An attempt was made to make use of this in the BWW-study (1987) for the Upper Toggenburg (Fig. 2), for which insufficient information on flow records within the catchment especially for the tributaries was available. Unfortunately three different regime types (viz. Np, Nt, Na) straddle the 200 km^2 catchment. As a result, the difference in representative discharges between the regime boundaries turned out to be inordinately large. Records from adjacent gauging stations were thus included in the analysis.

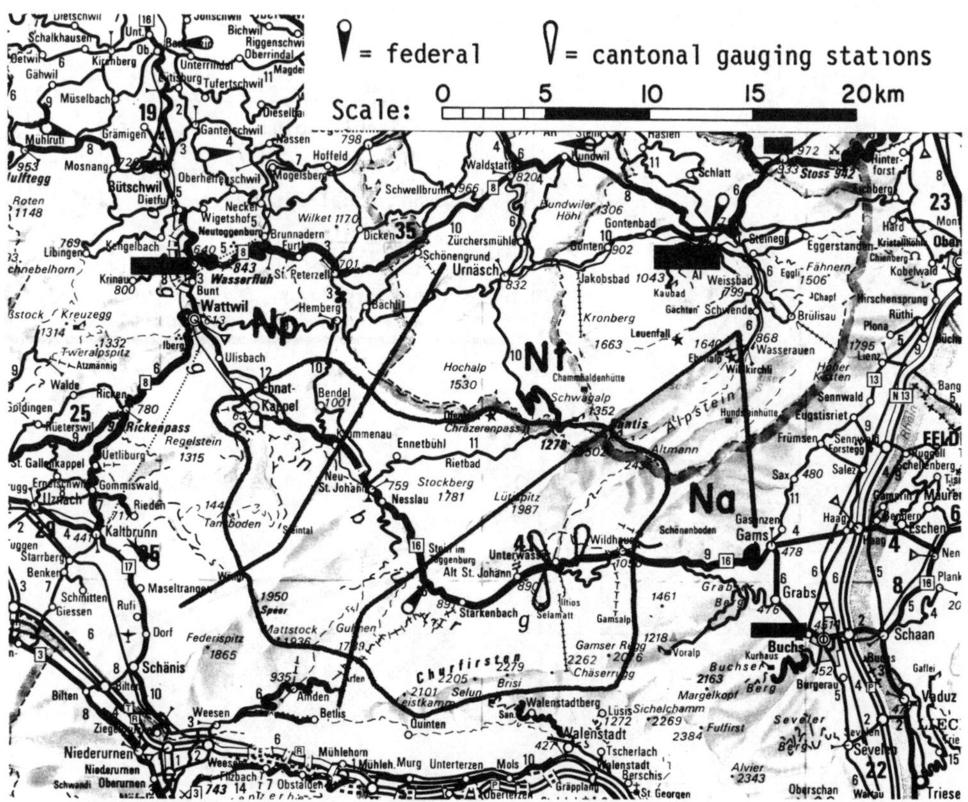

FIG. 2 Test catchment Upper Toggenburg with gauging stations and demarcation of the runoff regimen Np, Nt, Na.

HYDRO POTENTIAL EQUATIONS

For evaluating the line potential, a catchment is firstly divided into subcatchments. River reaches with approximately uniform discharge and longitudinal slope are then demarcated. The hydro potential may be calculated as power and/or energy potential P_m and E respectively as follows:

$P_m = 9.8 \times Q_m \times \Delta h$ = mean (hydro) power potential (kW)

$p_m = P_m / \Delta l$ = specific mean power potential ($kW\ m^{-1}$)

$E = 9.8 \times V_n \times \Delta h/3600$ = (hydro) energy potential (kWh)

where: Q_m = mean annual discharge of river reach ($m^3\ s^{-1}$)

Δh = difference in head along river reach (m)

Δl = horizontal length of river reach (m)

V_n = utilizable volume of water (m^3) (i.e. net volume, after deduction of losses)

With the help of representative flow duration curves (Fig. 3), the utilizable volume of water V_n may be determined.

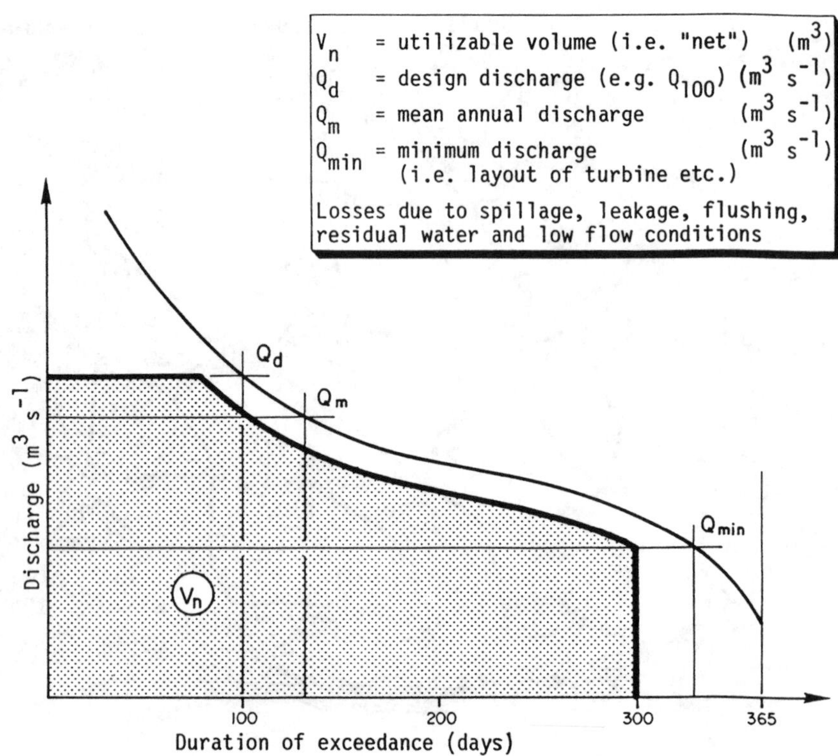

FIG. 3 Representative flow duration curve.

DETERMINATION OF HYDRO POTENTIAL: APPLICATIONS

Radler (1981) states that "many developing countries have ample, as yet untapped hydrological resources, such as scattered streams and rivulets, that often could be profitably exploited by means of mini-hydroelectric generation plants". In Switzerland, a comprehensive report on small-scale hydro was published recently (BWW-study, 1987). A USA-study dealing with small-scale hydro (less than 15 MW potential) attempts to estimate the hydro power potential of Californian watersheds: Poppe & Yeh (1982) present annual yield and hydro potential estimation equations with the help of the stepwise multiple linear regression analysis. Dotan & Willer (1986) developed two new computer software programs with which the optimum size, layout and best potential economics for hydro power projects can be evaluated.

In the past, potential evaluations were of major interest mainly for large-scale hydro. In Switzerland for instance, the utilizable potential was chiefly determined on a project basis (SWV-study, 1987). The generally accepted view is that the bulk of the Swiss hydro potential is today utilized. Regional reappraisals are nevertheless being done, as is illustrated by two recent studies mentioned below.

In 1982 the Swiss Canton Graubünden commissioned a study (Graubünden-study, 1983) for the evaluation of its remaining (i.e. hitherto undeveloped) hydro potential. Within the 7000 km^2 catchment, roughly 550 kilometers of rivers and streams were analysed. The line potential study conducted by the authors was based on river reaches with subcatchments of an average size of 25 km^2. Due to the limited time and funds available, the analysis made use only of the mean annual discharge. The results (e.g. specific mean power potential) were presented on maps to a scale of 1:100 000 thereby pinpointing those areas with remarkable potential. Remarkable in the given context implies that, on the basis of general experience, the relevant potential seems worthy of further investigation.

In the BWW-study (1987) the results of a preliminary design investigation evaluating the utilizable potential on strictly technical and economic terms in the 200 km^2 catchment of the Upper Toggenburg situated in northeastern Switzerland are presented. For the investigation, 23 sites for possible small-scale power plants were proposed and analysed. For comparison, a line potential study using flow duration curves was performed by the authors, subsequent to, but independent of, the preliminary design study. The smallest catchment units covered on average 2.5 km^2. The results were presented on maps to a scale of 1:25 000. The comparison proved to be satisfactory, as is described in the following chapter.

COMPARISON OF METHODS AND RESULTS

Although the same basic principles are applied in determining hydro potential, results of the various investigations differ, in some cases quite considerably. This may be due to the inclusion or exclusion of evaporation and seepage losses, of tributaries, head losses, factors of efficiency, the use of either power or energy potential and the degree to which details are analysed etc. An interesting comparison is given in Table 1 (Wittenberg & Schulte (1987)).

TABLE 1 Comparison of results from studies evaluating hydro potential (potential in TWh = Terawatthours = 10^9 kWh).

Country or region, year of publication	Area	Area potential based on: precipi-tation	run-off	Line poten-tial	Techni-cally & economi-cally utilizable potential	Average annual utili-zation today
	(10^3km^2)	(TWh)	(TWh)	(TWh)	(TWh)	(TWh)
W.Germany 1985	249		95	99	21	17
Austria 1979	84	252	150	74	49	26
Guatemala 1976	109	326	160	95	38	0.25
Hessen 1981	21		3.6		0.815	0.278
Werra-Meiss. 1981	1			0.235	0.067	0.010

Another illustration is given in a very recent publication concerning a study in the West German State of Baden-Württemberg (Hildebrand & Kern, 1989). In the course of the study, 23 river systems with a total catchment area of 36 000 km^2 were investigated. There, the line potential corresponds to approximately 75% of the area potential, with some considerable deviations for various subcatchments. The study concludes that "for economic and environmental reasons, only a fraction of the theoretical potential should, however, be utilized".

Watt et al. (1979) conducted a study on the hydro potential of Peru and Guatemala. In the case of Peru, 80 000 km of rivers in 111 separate basins were analysed. The utilizable potential turned out to be approximately 30% of the theoretical (line) potential.

Although for the previously mentioned Graubünden-study (1983) the remarkable undeveloped potential was deliberately not specified, a rough estimate of the total remaining potential was performed subsequently. It was found that the remaining line potential corresponds roughly to that which is today already utilized. Due to financial and environmental considerations, surely only a fraction thereof will be additionally utilized. The study on the other hand provides the communal authorities with a tool on the basis of which the decision whether or not to reappraise local hydro potential resources in more detail can be made. The cantonal authorities on the other hand expect to review future applications for hydro power concessions in a broader context.

For the Upper Toggenburg (BWW-study, 1987), a comparison between the results of the preliminary design study with the line potential study proved to be satisfactory. It was found that the 23 power plants proposed with the former method lay more or less on those reaches where, with the latter method, remarkable potential was pointed out. The line potential study was done at a fraction of the cost of that for the preliminary design study. Unfortunately an attempt to roughly estimate costs with the line potential study, on the basis of past experience gained, using unit cost for installed capacity or net energy, was not successful. The large scatter found was ascribed to a high dependence on local conditions.

CONCLUDING REMARKS

Several methods and numerous models for determining hydro potential are available. Depending on the location of the area in question as well as the nature and accuracy of the answers sought, some methods may be more suitable than others. The accuracy and reliability of the topographic and hydrologic background information should be consistent with that to which technical and economic feasibility can be determined. For early stage investigations as well as for regional hydro potential resource appraisal, the line potential study serves as an effective tool, helping to point out areas with remarkable, hitherto undeveloped potential.

If hydro potential resources are found to be utilizable, i.e. both technically and economically feasible, some doubt still remains whether or not they should actually be utilized. Stringent requirements regarding environmental aspects are nowadays laid down. These pertain to siting, flushing, safety, minimum flow requirements (i.e. residual water) and so forth. Whereas formerly optimization of hydro potential resources was the main criterium applied, today optimization of surface water resources as a whole is of foremost importance.

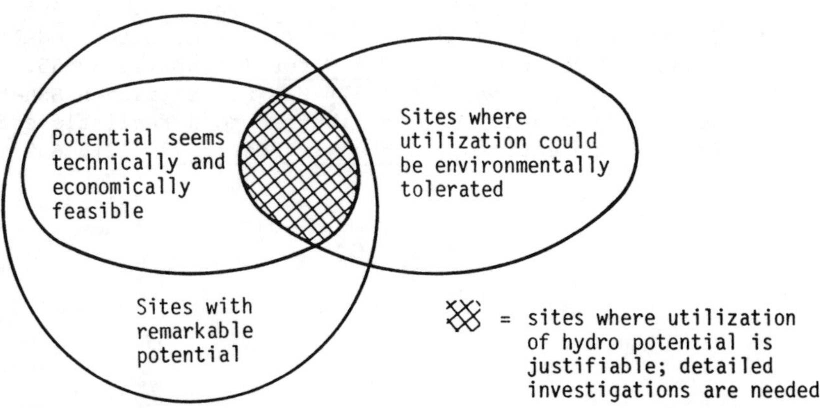

FIG. 4 Hydro potential and environmental aspects can be defined simultaneously before detailed investigations are started.

If the need for investigations on the availability of hydro potential arises, adequate tools must be employed. An approach as outlined in Fig. 4 seems appropriate. Emphasis is thereby placed on procedures which, from the outset, take account of scientific, technical, economical and environmental aspects simultaneously. Decisions for more detailed investigations would thus be taken on a mutual basis. It is hoped that some of the frustration and antagonism involved with recent appraisals of hydro potential resources could thereby be avoided.

REFERENCES

Aschwanden, H. & Weingartner, R. (1985) Die Abflussregimes der Schweiz (Runoff regimen in Switzerland). Geogr. Inst. Univ. Bern, Switzerland, Publik. Gewässerkunde 65.

BWW-study (1987) Kleinwasserkraftwerke in der Schweiz (Petits aménagements hydroélectriques en Suisse), Teil III. Bundesamt für Wasserwirtschaft, Mitt. Nr. 2, CH-3000 Bern.

Dotan, A. & Willer, D. C. (1986) Instant hydro forecasting. Civil Engineering (August), 58-63.

Graubünden-study (1983) Das verbleibende Wasserkraftpotential im Kanton Graubünden. Bau- und Forstdepartement des Kantons Graubünden. Wasser, energie, luft - eau, énergie, air 75 (7/8), 137-138.

Hildebrand, H. & Kern, K. (1989) Ermittlung des Wasserkraftpotentials für grosse Regionen am Beispiel von Baden-Württemberg (Determination of hydropower resources for large regions. A survey in the State of Baden-Württemberg). Wasserwirtschaft 79 (11), 562-567.

Poppe, D. A. & Yeh, W. W-G. (1982) Estimation of small-scale hydropower potential. Proc. Am. Soc. Civ. Engrs., J. Wat. Res. Div. ASCE 108 (WR1), 145-151.

Radler, S. (ed.)(1981) Symposium on project design and installation of small hydro power plants. Inst. für Wasserwirtschaft, Univ. für Bodenkultur, A-1180 Vienna.

SWV-study (1987) Der mögliche Beitrag der Wasserwirtschaft an die Elektrizitätsversorgung der Schweiz - Contribution possible de l'énergie hydraulique à l'approvisionnement en électricité de la Suisse. Wasser, energie, luft - eau, énergie, air 79 (9), 175-184.

Watt, T., Morariu, SG. & Gärtner, M. (1979) Computer models aid national hydro studies. World Water (October), 32-35.

Wittenberg, H. & Schulte, B. (1987) Zur realistischen Schätzung von Wasserkraftpotentialen (Contribution to a realistic estimation of hydropower potentials). Wasserwirtschaft 77 (12), 659-662.

Topic F:

General Paper

Hydrology in Mountainous Regions. I - Hydrological Measurements; the Water Cycle
(Proceedings of two Lausanne Symposia, August 1990). IAHS Publ. no. 193, 1990.

Quantitative and qualitative water cycle aspects in heterogeneous basins

H. J. MOREL-SEYTOUX
Department of Civil Engineering, Colorado State University, Fort Collins, Colorado 80523, United States of America

ABSTRACT Using abstracts submitted for presentation at the Lausanne symposium, a synthesis of current efforts in the area of mountain hydrology is attempted. In the process a definition of mountain hydrology emerges. Mountain hydrology is the branch of hydrology characterized by the facts that: (1) altitude differences introduce an additional source of heterogeneity and (2) site accessibility for ground instrumentation and measurements varies from very difficult to virtually impossible. As a result, progress in mountain hydrology comes from relief-conscious hydrologic modeling and/or use of remote sensing.

INTRODUCTION

This article is primarily a concise review of the extended abstracts of papers to be presented at the 1990 Lausanne IAH-IAHS conference on "Water Resources in Mountainous Regions", more specifically at the symposium on "Quantitative and Qualitative Water Cycle Aspects in Heterogeneous Basins". The theme of the symposium was divided into five topics and their titles are used as Rank 1 headings in this article.

One of the first questions that come to mind is: what is different about water resources in mountainous regions as opposed to other regions? What are the specific features of the mountainous regions water cycle? As is clear from many of the abstracts submitted, mountain regions are often taken as synonymous with cold regions, places where snow and glaciers are abundant. From the abstracts it was not possible to form a coherent view of what might be called mountain hydrology, being for the most part a composite of high slopes watershed hydrology and cold regions hydrology. The bottom line may be that, in mountain hydrology, as opposed to general hydrology, there is one additional source of heterogeneity, that created by significant altitude differences within a basin. The altitude variations within a basin induce, or have induced in geological times, variations in weather, climate and geologic environment. It is thus a trivial corollary that understanding of mountain hydrology requires a more detailed description and distributed representation of the water cycle, certainly in space and, possibly, in time as well.

Having recognized the additional degree of complexity in hydrology brought about by the elevation differences, as an additional source of heterogeneity, one may wonder if that specificity in hydrologic problems of mountain regions leads also to a specificity in approaches and methodology. The general impression from the Abstracts is that it does not. Most abstracts incorporate descriptions and techniques which are not at all specific to a mountainous environment. Maybe mountain hydrology is simply general hydrology applied to a mountainous region. That seems to be the viewpoint implicit in most abstracts. However, whereas a casual knowledge of hydrology may be adequate to solve problems in Plains hydrology, a mountain hydrologist must be well grounded in basic mechanics, physic and chemistry. In other words she must be a well rounded hydrologist.

In the review process the abstracts were divided into two categories; (1) those which tried to address problems specific to mountain hydrology and (2) those that applied general hydrologic knowhow to a mountainous basin or region. Only the articles in the first category are further discussed. Many of the abstracts in the second category included original ideas but they were not specific. Of course there were many border line cases.

QUANTITATIVE SPACE-TIME WATER VARIABILITY

Several abstracts tried to describe the heterogeneous nature of precipitation in various parts of the globe, e.g., in South America (Roche et al.), in the West Indies (Denness) and in Algeria (Cayla and Taibi). Roche et al. attempt to explain the precipitation regime as the interaction between the general atmospheric circulation and the strong orographic influence of the Bolivian Andes. Dennes reports on the use of a deterministic forecasting of rainfall for the Dominica island which rises up to 1200 m. One may wonder, however, about the real potential of a suggested export scheme: "A review of local rainfall data .... exposed a cyclic trend over several years inverse to that in the midwest of the USA, a potential client for Dominica's fresh water as it enters a long-term period of erratic drought that began in the summer of 1988 - as forecast by the deterministic model several years before." Would it be bottled under a Perrier license?

Cayla and Taibi provide a theoretical basis for a regional synthesis of rainfall, maximum daily or annual values. They have verified that some parameters characterizing the statistical distributions of maximum daily and annual values do not depend upon altitude but are rather conditioned by meteorologic perturbations. Of special practical value is their conclusion that "it is possible to use older annual isohyet maps to derive from them the complete probability laws for annual and daily rainfall."

Humbert has found for the High Vosges mountains of France, where "spectacular rainfall gradients obtain, in excess of 200 mm per year per km", that "among various morphometric variables only the density drainage distribution is significant for predictive purposes of flood volume, base flow, etc." Cheng of Taiwan, by "comparison of rainfall intensities with infiltration capacity..." comes to the conclusion that "streamflows of these headwaters forested watersheds are best described as resulting from hydrologic processes and mechanisms associated with mixed surface-subsurface pathways." The elementary and oversimplified concepts of runoff generation must be reconsidered and the processes studied in a more detailed and physical basis. Bolivia is the site again of another investigation (Bourges et al.) but more concerned with stream discharges and sediment concentrations. The hydrology is dominated by the high precipitation variability and the high flood wave celerities.

Finally, energy input considerations are introduced for basins with significant snow and ice covers. Collins and Taylor investigate "the effects of glacierisation on year to year variability of runoff" in the Swiss Alps. "Relationships between energy inputs and precipitation with runoff were assessed using correlation analysis". (In most papers correlation seems to be the major tool of analysis). "Reduction of glacier surface area has had little impact on variability of runoff and in recent warmer years runoff totals of 1950's magnitudes have recurred despite glacier retreat". The aim of the study by Brown and Tranter in the Valais, Switzerland is "to perform unique chemograph and hydrograph separation of the diurnal discharge cycle." They hope to "determine the controls on the composition of the two endmembers, the dilute englacial component and the concentrated subglacial component, which comprise the bulk meltwater".

Ziemer and Rice using "electronic hydrologic data loggers" point out that contrary to generally held concepts, but developed from observations on larger rivers, their data "do not show significant lags or reductions in unit area peak discharges at downstream gauging stations. These preliminary findings suggest that hydrologists concerned about small mountainous drainage basins should avail themselves of the capabilities of modern electronic instrumentation to determine how their basins are <u>actually</u> performing."

The abstract by Dingman et al. is somewhat typical of a number of studied reported in these Proceedings. The essential tool is that of multiple regression, usually on the logarithms of the variables. While the authors report, in this case, the co-called "standard error of estimate" which is hardly an error of estimate being always a very optimistic lower bound, they do not report the mean and standard deviations of the "explaining" variables, such as mean basin elevation. To make a realistic estimation of the error of prediction one must use the "standard error of prediction" which is the larger the more the basin's explaining variables deviate from the mean of the sample from which the regression is developed. It is hoped that in their paper and in other papers the coefficients of variation of the explaining variables are provided. A useful discussion of the "error of prediction" is given e.g. in Mood and Graybill (1963) and an application in hydrology in Siegenthaler and Morel-Seytoux (1985)

QUALITATIVE SPACE-TIME VARIABILITY

In the qualitative realm most investigations are concentrated in the Alps and concerned primarily with snow. Langenegger presents results of chemical precipitation analyses. The rather original and intriguing goal is to "study the changes of the composition of snow

.... in order to assess the potential of snow with regard to storing information on air pollution." Parriaux et al. want to assess the influence of the aquifers on the chemical composition of the transiting water. The analysis requires knowledge of both input and output composition. Priority is currently given to measurement of the composition of recharge water. Results show the major influence of distance from urban centers and of altitude. As in the precious reports, Page's subject is primarily that of instrumentation of watersheds with snow cover for the later evaluation of the role of snow cover as a natural reservoir for suitable water supply from a quantitative and qualitative points of view. The next two abstracts deal with the rapid fluctuations of water quality with time. Keller is concerned with the mixing of surface and subsurface runoff during rain events and snowmelt with base flow originating from deep soil horizons." Such events may, therefore, be critical when the water is used for water supply ..... Occasions which show extreme .... are analyzed with the aim to find typical weather and seasonal patterns during which such extreme conditions of chemical composition occur." According to Gurnell and Warburton, "sediment flushes are brief events, of the order of a few to tens of minutes. Their brevity is of great significance in relation to the derivation of suspended sediment concentration time series .... depending upon the degree to which a sampler intercepts these events." The authors do not discuss the origin of the sediment flushes.

HYDROLOGICAL MODELING IN REGIONS OF RUGGED RELIEF

Kite explains the reasons for the evident infatuation of mountain snow hydrologists with remote sensing. "Because of the difficult terrain and the expense of operating in remote areas, mountainous basins have always been particularly difficult to instrument and satellite data are particularly appropriate." The paper describes the SLURP hydrologic model and results of its application to a basin in the Canadian Rockies. Leavesley and Stannard also discuss a modular watershed-modeling system and particularly its linkage with a digital-terrain-analysis module. "Alogrithms are being developed to combine point and remotely sensed measured of snowpack water equivalent with remotely sensed snow-covered area data to provide improved spatial and temporal estimates of snowpack water equivalent." Rango et al. also discuss the use of remote sensing but with a more practically oriented goal of real time forecasting "Initial forecasting tests have produced positive results on the Rio Grande basin in Rocky Mountains of Colorado."

Three papers discuss in some details the required structure of models suitable to represent the rainfall-runoff process in regions of high relief. Fundamentally the three abstracts emphasize that the model must describe infiltration, Hortonian overland flow, saturation overland flow and channelized flow. Moore and Nieber point out that a proposed "new structure in hydrologic modeling is compatible with Digital Terrain Models and Geographic Information Systems." Using similar models Shu and Jan in Taiwan and Yoshino et al. in Japan report good results for two catchments (of size 254 km^2 in Japan with square grids with side size of 200 m). Both used rainfall patterns defined on an hourly basis. From this author's point of view this is the very upper limit of definition of the time pattern beyond which a detailed watershed model no longer has advantages over cruder models (Morel-Seytoux and Al Hassoun, 1987, 1989; Morel-Seytoux, 1989). It is not clear from the abstracts that the models have been validated on events not used for calibration. Weingartner and Jordan et al. use simpler models but to address the same problem, i.e., the presence of multiple processes in runoff generation. Weingartner is emphatic that "the SCS model is not adaptable to define the runoff coefficient for Swiss catchments, as it estimates an augmentation of the runoff ratio, within an increasing duration of rainfall, whereas, in fact, there is none observed. A model developed on contributing areas is, however, well experienced."

Zhihuai's paper is original, being the only one to consider explicitly the "effects of the frozen soil on the runoff forming". Daily discharge is simulated for the Binggou basin with a "variable source model". One abstract deals with the rainfall-runoff process in arid mountainous catchments. The hydrologic processes are somewhat reversed from those observed in humid temperate climates. "The watersheds consist of highlands with high rainfall intensity, shallow soil, low infiltration and steep slopes and thick alluvials in the wadi channels with low rainfall intensity and high permeability." Several models were used and compared. A modified version of the SCS model to account for the arid zone catchment behavior seems to give the best results (Sorman and Abdulrazzak).

A rather interesting model structuration is proposed by Vinogradov which seems particularly suited to mountain regions. According to this author "the account of dynamics of heat energy and phase transformations in the snow-soil system from the point of view soil "cementation" by ice influence on surface runoff formation is an important peculiarity of the model". The model was applied to a basin with an elevation range of 982 to 4,881 m and a drainage area of 1270 km^2.

Another, apparently similar, model is proposed by Shentzis with, in addition, considerable use of "airborne data of observations, gamma survey and satellite information".

INTERACTION BETWEEN ACID RAIN AND PEDOLOGICAL AND GEOLOGICAL BASIN CHARACTERISTICS

According to Domergue "in almost all the soils formed under climatic conditions where rainfall exceeds evapotranspiration, one observes a gradient of pH, with a progressive acidification toward the surface." A factorial model due to Jenny which accounts for factors defining the state and history of soils is used to explain soil genesis. The factors are climate, organisms, topography, parent material and time. "The originality of this system is that it explains the pedogenetic processes, the actual soil behaviour and the composition of percolation waters and accounts for the action of acid precipitations." Durand et al. propose no theory, simply report results for three small mountain catchments. Even though "bulk precipitations in Mont Lozére, in France, are medium salt-medium acid type, but due to heavy precipitations .... nevertheless the high sulfate retention in the soil and the occurrence of some events of high flows with marked net losses of sulphate indicate trends of intense acidification, mainly in the resinous ecosystem."

Meesenburg addresses the question of impact of atmospheric depositions on stream water chemistry in the Black Forest of Germany. Regression analysis showed that precipitation and discharge are the most important factors to determine solute behaviour. In another part of the Black Forest, in the north, Caspary has found that the "observed increased water yield is caused by a drastic reduction of forest transpiration induced by forest decline and soil acidification due to air pollutants." ...."The changes in soil chemistry by soil acidity leads to a chemical stress to the tree fine roots ... Due to the small water-holding capacity of the sandy soils the reduced root depth causes a significant reduction of the naturally small available moisture of the forest stands. By this a strongly restricted water uptake by the roots and a reduced transpiration is induced for times with low precipitation during the growing season .... Significant changes in water yield can be detected before needle loss of the forest stands is very high and obviously visible .... Therefore the water balance of forest catchments may be used as an ecohydrological indicator of forest damage."

The problem of soil acidification is further documented by Sager et al. "In the Fichtelgebirge, the zone of increased manganese and aluminum mobility has progressed down to 2 m and the iron concentrations in the surface soils have already increased .... The acidification processes have already progressed from the soils down to the groundwater, resulting in very low pH values (4.1-5.5) and increased aluminum and sulfate concentrations ($Al \leq 1.7$; $SO_4 \leq 35.0$ ppm)." Dzhamalov and Zlobina document further the effect of acid precipitation on groundwater composition. "The salinity of rainwater substantially increases under the human impact. Outside urban and industrial areas, the rainwater salinity does not exceed 100 mg/l, while under the human impact it may reach 800 mg/l.... Meltwater is a second type of polluted precipitation entering groundwater .... The analysis and generalization of data obtained reveal the appreciable role of sulphate ion in snowmelt acidification .... In areas of recharge, hydrocarbonate concentrations in groundwater reduce down to 48 mg/l which is indicative of substantial acidification of groundwater." Williams et al. investigated the groundwater contributions to the hydrochemistry of an alpine basin. They report that "subsurface storage and release of water controlled the inputs of solutes to Emerald Lake for 7-8 months of the year, even though the quantity of subsurface water was less than one percent of the total quantity of water that moved through the basin .... Geochemical interactions between atmospheric deposition and surficial deposits were important in neutralizing acidic inputs to this alpine basin."

ASSESSMENT OF THE UTILIZATION POTENTIAL OF SURFACE WATER RESOURCES

Grandjean explores the possibility of a better utilization of the waters of lake Leman for downstream hydro-electric production. Currently a simple autoregressive model is used to predict in a statistical average sense the inflows to the lake in order to maintain the lake elevation at seasonal target levels.

"The Arun river" (Kattelmann) "provides an example of the uncertainty and risks in developing Himalayan rivers .... In August 1985, a nearly-completed small facility on the upper Dudh Kosi in the

Mt. Everest region was destroyed by flood waters from a glacial lake outburst only 12 km upstream .... The latest feasibility study has recommended a design resistant to a flood of 7700 m^3/s from a glacial lake outburst." Kattelman makes a point that in countries such as Nepal water resources planning is carried out with minimal amounts of hydrologic information and understanding. Here again, remote sensing should play an important role.

As in Switzerland and Nepal, the main concern for water utilization in mountain regions of the Soviet Union seems to be hydro electric power. Svanidze reports that for water energy resources "Georgia takes the fourth place among the Soviet republics, while per unit area it takes first place in the USSR and one of the first places in the world". Sergeev deviates from this primary focus with a goal of development of a "mathematical model of water flow formation and its mineralization under the effect of irrigation." The irrigated areas and the main river channels are divided into zones and segments. "The river is considered both as a source and sink of sewage (sic) water from irrigated fields". As mentioned in the very beginning of this article, it is not apparent in many papers in what ways the problem considered is specific to mountain regions. In this abstract the <u>only</u> clue as to the relevance of the article to mountainous regions is that Sergeev's place of work is located in Tashkent!

CONCLUSIONS

The number of contributions to the five themes (topics) of symposium 2 varied greatly, with specially rare contributions to topic 4 and particularly topic 5. Water resources assessment seems of concern only to developing countries (India, Nepal, USSR's Georgia and Uzbek republics). Ecological concerns (topics 2 and 4) seem to be strong among the Germans and the Swiss and to a lesser degree with the French and Russians. Switzerland seems to be the favorite hydrologic playground for the English. The French in large numbers seem intent to compete with the U.S.A. in meddling in Latin American affairs, fortunately more peacefully. Their contagious mathematical prowess has crossed over to the Maghreb (topic 1). Proponents of use of high technology (remote sensing, DTM, GIS) are, not surprisingly, (topic 3) North Americans, Japanese, Taiwanese and Swiss. Everybody loves mathematical hydrologic modeling (topic 3).

Rather clearly a review of mountain hydrology based on abstracts can only be very superficial. It does provide a, hopefully useful, summary of current trends in hydrologic research and of issues of serious concern. Mountain hydrology is intrinsically a more complex branch of hydrology for reasons previously discussed: the additional source of heterogeneity provided by the significant altitude differences and the extreme difficulty of access for instrumentation and measurement. It is an important branch that deserves more attention. The organizers of this symposium and the host, the Ecole Polytechnique Federale of Lausanne, deserve praise for their efforts for the enhancement of this hydrologic discipline. Wouldn't it be wonderful, and quite natural, if the EPFL could become the repository of a specialized library collection on MOUNTAIN HYDROLOGY? With an international newsletter to advertise its stock and new additions, data base, etc.? Enclosed is my subscription!

REFERENCES

NOTE: Practically all references in this article are to papers in these Proceedings and can be found from the names of the authors.

Mood, A.M. & Graybill, F.A. (1963) *Introduction to the Theory of Statistics*, McGraw-Hill Book Co., 2nd edition, New York, 443 pages.

Morel-Seytoux, H. J. (1988) Soil-Aquifer-Stream Interactions: A Reductionist Attempt Toward Physical-Stochastic Integration. *J. Hydrology*, 102, 355-379.

Morel-Seytoux, H. J. & Al Hassoun, S. (1987) SWATCH: A Multi-Process Watershed Model for Simulation of Surface and Subsurface Flows in a Soil-Aquifer-Stream Hydrologic System . HYDROWAR Reports Division, HYDROLOGY DAYS Publications, 1005 Country Club Road, Fort Collins, Colorado 80524, 296 pages.

Morel-Seytoux, H. J. & Al Hassoun, S. (1989) The Unsaturated Components of SWATCH: A Multiprocess Watershed Model for Runoff Generation and Routing . Chapter in: *Unsaturated Flow in Hydrologic Modeling*, H. J. Morel-Seytoux, editor, Kluwer Academic Publishers, Dordrecht, Boston, London, 413-433.

Siegenthaler, M. & Morel-Seytoux, H.J. (1985) Flood Prediction from Gage Records and Regressions . Proc. Fifth annual AGU Hydrology Days, Hydrology Days Publications, 1005 Country Club Road, Fort Collins, Colorado 80524, pp 313-323.